Quantitative Management

Quantitative Management

Guisseppi A. Forgionne
University of Maryland Baltimore County

The Dryden Press
Chicago   Fort Worth   San Francisco   Philadelphia
Montreal   Toronto   London   Sydney   Tokyo

Acquisitions Editor: Robert Gemin
Developmental Editor: Joanne Smith
Project Editor: Cate Rzasa
Design Manager: Alan Wendt
Production Manager: Barb Bahnsen
Director of Editing, Design, and Production: Jane Perkins

Text and Cover Designer: C. J. Petlick, Hunter Graphics
Production Services: Publication Services, Inc.
Compositor: Publication Services, Inc.
Text Type: 10/12 Times Roman

Library of Congress Cataloging-In Publication Data
Forgionne, Guisseppi A., 1945–
    Quantitative management / Guisseppi A. Forgionne.
      p. cm.
    Bibliography: p.
    Includes index.
    ISBN 0-03-026649-1
1. Decision-making—Mathematical models. 2. Management-
-Mathematical models. 3. Management science. I. Title.
HD30.23.F693 1989
658.4'033–dc19   89-1635

Printed in the United States of America
901-040-987654321

Address orders:
The Dryden Press
Orlando, FL 32887

Address editorial correspondence:
The Dryden Press
908 N. Elm Street
Hinsdale, IL 60521

The Dryden Press
Holt, Rinehart and Winston
Saunders College Publishing

Cover Source: Photograph © David Lesh.

The Dryden Press Series in Management

Preface

Modern organizations operate in a world of rapid economic, political, and social changes. The resulting decision problems are complex and challenging. To solve these problems successfully, managers must use systematic, rational approaches based on information and scientific analysis. Quantitative methods provide such approaches.

This book gives an introductory survey of quantitative methods. The text provides complete coverage of today's major quantitative models and shows how they are applied to managerial problems in public and private organizations. Much effort has been spent in making each topic interesting, accessible, and easy to read. The purpose is to provide the user with a sound conceptual understanding of the role of quantitative analysis in the decision-making process.

FOCUS

The focus of *Quantitative Management* is on the practical and applied. The text explains how to formulate decision problems, how to solve them with an appropriate quantitative analysis, and how to apply the recommended solution. There is an emphasis on concepts rather than mechanical manipulation. A significant part of the discussion is devoted to problem formulation, technique assumptions, potential, limitations, and interpretation of the results of an analysis from the decision maker's perspective. In addition, the discussion highlights the connection between management science/operations research and computer information systems. Computer data and models are presented, solutions are discussed, and results are interpreted.

Mathematics is kept at an accessible level for the beginning user of quantitative decision making. The only prerequisite is college algebra. Other relevant mathematics, such as elementary probability and basic statistics, are developed as needed. The orientation should put the material within reach of a junior, senior, or MBA student.

Quantitative tools are presented simply and logically, with extensive use of examples, graphs, tables, and other illustrative devices. Additional pedagogical aids include:

- Clearly defined learning objectives for each chapter.
- "Procedure Recaps," at appropriate points in the text discussion, which concisely summarize the methodology for the student.

- "In Practice" exhibits, which outline a variety of actual management applications of the methodologies, such as Bayesian analysis, PERT/CPM, and Dynamic Programming.
- End-of-Chapter glossaries for a clear review of all new terminology.
- Extensive recommended reading lists arranged by topic area.

A comprehensive package of computer programs, called **Quantitative Management (QM),** is fully integrated within the text discussion. Yet the computer discussion is presented in a generic way, allowing the instructor to easily use the text with other popular computer software that may already be in use at his or her institution. For example, **QM** is very similar in format to the popular mathematical programming package LINDO, while avoiding some of the problems users have encountered with that package. As a result, the computer discussion in the text can apply equally well to both **QM** and LINDO packages.

EXAMPLES

Beginners can facilitate their understanding by using concepts in the types of situations actually encountered by decision makers. Therefore, there are many realistic examples of problems encountered in public and private organizations. Each chapter contains:

- A chapter-opening "Quantitative Analysis in Action" example showing how actual organizations have used quantitative management techniques to solve problems and save money.
- Numerous in-text examples, called "Management Situations," used to illustrate the presentation and development of techniques.
- A case at the end of each chapter requiring students to apply a variety of methodologies.

EXERCISES

Nearly 600 in-text exercises provide students with extensive practice and application opportunities and give professors a wide range of options in making class assignments. End-of-chapter exercises are divided into:

- Thought Exercises (extension of basic concepts).
- Technique Exercises (practice of procedures).
- Computer Exercises (practice with programs), where appropriate.
- Applications Exercises (selection of concepts and techniques, and development of solution).

Cases require integration and extension of text concepts, quantitative analysis, formulation of a decision recommendation, and presentation of results in a form understandable to management.

ORGANIZATION

The book is organized in a logical progression that provides a coherent treatment of the subject. First, major topics are divided into modules or parts for optimal flexibility in structuring your course. Part I provides the foundation. It defines the nature of management science, discusses its role in the decision-making process, and identifies the steps necessary for its successful implementation. There is also a discussion of forecasting and its role in quantitative management. Part II presents a general decision-making framework and shows how systematic strategies can be formed in various decision environments. Under this approach, Part II gives the student a general framework for structuring problems and developing data—not just as a series of solution techniques (Bayesian analysis, game theory, and so on). Part III applies these concepts to linear and other mathematical (integer, goal, and nonlinear) programming problems and methods. Part IV applies these mathematical programming concepts in a comprehensive review of general network flow problems, including transportation, transshipment, assignment, minimal spanning trees, cycles and routes, maximal flows, and PERT/CPM. Part V builds on the preceding concepts and considers some standard analytical models involving sequential decisions, queuing, and inventory problems. In many cases, available analytical models are of little value because of the complex or unstructured nature of the problem; Part VI, on simulation, presents an approach designed for these situations.

Each part is also designed to eliminate the effect of variability in student capabilities and motivation. Starting at the simplest level, there is a gradual development of ideas and applications. Eventually, the student progresses to the state of the art in the field. Similar independent modularity is provided within the chapters. Each chapter starts with elementary concepts, progresses through increasingly complex material, and ends with the most advanced topics. With this arrangement, students can be assigned a continuous sequence of pages within a module. Then, when the level within the module exceeds the course objectives, students can be directed to another part of the book. In this way, the instructor can easily control the level for any particular topic.

MODULARITY AND FLEXIBLE COURSE PLANNING

The text takes a user/practitioner viewpoint by presenting the decision analysis framework and then the techniques, but the parts are essentially independent. Thus, faculty preferring other approaches can order the topics as desired and readily satisfy different course plans. For example, some professors may prefer to present Part III (Mathematical Programming) before Part II (Decision Analysis). In addition, some professors may prefer to limit the coverage in Part II to parts of Chapter 4 and most of Chapter 5. The modular nature of the book segments, chapters, and sections within chapters is designed to provide the instructor the flexibility necessary for matching content with course objectives and student profiles.

TOPIC COVERAGE

The selection of topics reflects the introductory nature of the text. The book emphasizes the most popular quantitative approaches used today by public and private organizations. Some techniques, such as nonlinear programming, require a preparatory background in management science/operations research. In these instances, the topic is merely identified and illustrated, and text notations and a bibliography refer the user to appropriate advanced treatment. However, the book provides the essential, relevant material covered in almost all one-semester/two-quarter introductory survey courses in quantitative management. Topic coverage is summarized in the following table.

Topic	Chapter
Technology of Management	
Classical optimization	Appendix A
MIS/DSS	2
Probability concepts	4, 5, and Appendix B
Probability distributions	13, 14, 15, and Appendix B
Influence diagrams	4
Forecasting	3
Decision Analysis	
Decision theory	4
Decision trees	4 and 5
Bayesian analysis	5
Utility theory	6
Multiple criteria decision making	6 and 10
Game theory	6
Mathematical programming	
Linear programming	7, 8, 9, and 10
Karmarkar's algorithm	8
Integer programming	10
Goal programming	10
Stochastic programming	10
Chance constrained programming	10
Nonlinear programming	10
Dynamic programming	10 and 16

Topic	Chapter
Networks	
Transportation problem	11
Assignment problem	11
Transshipment	11
Minimal spanning tree	12
Shortest route	12
Traveling salesperson	12
Maximal flow	12
PERT/CPM	13
Operations Management	
Inventory	14
Queuing theory	15
Markov models	16
Simulation	
Artificial intelligence	17
Heuristic programming	17
Management games	17
System simulation	17

COMPUTER SOFTWARE

A complete package of computer programs is fully integrated within the text discussion and with complete end-of-chapter computer problems. The programs, which run on IBM-compatible microcomputers, are very user friendly, offering (1) a main menu of procedures, (2) prompted responses, (3) interactive, full screen editing and processing, and (4) detailed output. Instructions are provided as a text file accessed from the main menu and through help facilities with each program module. The following algorithms are included:

- Forecasting
  - Time series analysis
  - Regression
- Decision analysis
  - Decision Theory
  - Bayesian analysis
- Mathematical programming
  - Linear programming
  - Integer programming
  - Goal programming

- Networks
  - Distribution (transportation and assignment)
  - Network models (minimal spanning tree, shortest route, and maximal flow)
  - PERT/CM
- Operations management
  - Inventory
  - Queuing
  - Markov
- Simulation
  - Inventory
  - Queuing

The software is available packaged with the textbook to give your students all the tools they need for the course.

SUPPLEMENTARY MATERIAL

In addition to the software package, we offer a complete set of supplemental teaching and learning materials.

- A *Solutions Manual* provides fully worked-out solutions to all thought, technique, computer, and applications exercises and to each case in the text. There is also a brief description of each problem, an assessment of its level of difficulty, and the relationship between the text concept and the problem.

- A separate *Instructor's Manual* contains sample course outlines, transparency masters, chapter-by-chapter ideas for presenting the material, and hints in selecting problems for student assignments.

- A *Test Bank*, written by Darlene Lanier of Louisiana State University, provides more than 600 examination questions including true/false, multiple choice, and worked-out problems. Complete solutions are also included.

- There is also a *Study Guide* for students written by William Darrow and W. R. Brown of Towson State University. The workbook begins with an introduction that discusses how to use the study guide and offers tips for being successful in the course. Each chapter provides study goals, a concise review of the text concepts and key terms, step-by-step practice problems, and a self-test section.

ACKNOWLEDGMENTS

This textbook has been shaped and developed with the help of many of my colleagues. Each stage has been carefully reviewed and scrutinized to ensure the highest quality textbook available. I would like to express my gratitude to the following professors:

Dr. William M. Bassin
Shippensburg University of Pennsylvania

Asit P. Basu
University of Missouri - Columbia

Fabienna Godlewski
Arizona State University

Michael E. Hanna
University of Houston, Clear Lake

Ron Horswell
Louisiana State University

Ann Hughes
Georgia State University

Harvey J. Iglarsh
Georgetown University

Han J. Kim
South Dakota State University

John A. Lawrence, Jr.
California State University, Fullerton

Barbara J. Mardis
University of Northern Iowa

Edward Minieka
University of Illinois, Chicago

Joseph G. Ormsby
Stephen F. Austin State University

J. Wayne Patterson
Clemson University

John R. Pickett
Georgia Southern College

Gary Reeves
University of South Carolina

Lee Tangedahl
University of Montana

Elizabeth Trybus
California State University, Northridge

I wish to thank the staff of The Dryden Press for their helpful suggestions. In particular, Robert Gemin, my acquisitions editor, and Joanne Smith, my developmental editor, did excellent jobs. I also appreciated the work of the designer, Alan Wendt, and the production editor, Cate Rzasa. I would like to express my appreciation to my colleagues, students, and family, who have contributed greatly to the project. Also, I am indebted to the administration of the University of Maryland, Baltimore County, for their support, especially Shirley Haas and the rest of the staff of the Information Systems Management Department.

Guisseppi A. Forgionne
September 1989

Contents in Brief

Contents

Foundations

PART I will provide you with the necessary foundations to comprehend and use the concepts of quantitative decision making.

Chapter 1 is an introduction. It begins with a historical perspective, then outlines the characteristics of the approach, and concludes with a discussion of the areas of application. After reading this chapter, you should understand the nature, purpose, and relevance of the discipline.

In Chapter 2, you will learn about the management science process and its role in modern decision making. This chapter presents the steps involved in quantitative decision making and model construction and analysis, as well as the role of computer information systems. It concludes with a discussion of implementation problems and strategies.

Quantitative management relies on accurate data, and in many cases the required facts must be forecasted or estimated. Chapter 3 represents systematic methods for developing the necessary estimates. It addresses the issues involved, examines approaches that extrapolate historical patterns, and discusses ways to measure relevant cause-and-effect relationships.

After reading this module, you should be able to

- Recognize situations in which quantitative management would be helpful.
- Identify popular quantitative management methodologies.
- Perform the management science process.
- Make forecasts.

Such background also provides the perspective needed to fully comprehend the text's remaining parts.

Introduction

Chapter Outline

1.1 Evolution of Quantitative Management
Origins

Early Development

Maturity

Current Developments

1.2 Characteristics
Focus on Problems

Systems Approach

Team Approach

Scientific Method

Mathematics and Computers

Technology

1.3 Applications

Case: The Cookbook Conspiracy

Learning Objectives

- Understand the nature of management science/ operations research
- Identify the stages of historical development for the discipline
- Investigate current developments in the field
- Determine the characteristics of management science/operations research
- Examine areas in which the discipline can be, and has been, applied

General Motors Looks to the PLANETS

MULTINATIONAL planning is a complex task for management at General Motors. The task involves the manufacture and distribution of thousands of products that must be supported by hundreds of facilities worldwide. To guarantee timely delivery at competitive prices, these facilities must be designed, tooled, and located properly. Lead times for tooling and facility changes can run three years or more and involve $100 million or more in capital expenditures.

Since bad decisions can be very costly, management decided that the company needed a system to assist strategists in the planning process. A concerted corporate effort led to the development of the Production Location Analysis Network System (PLANETS). The original version helped company planners to define a business environment, perform specified problem analysis, and generate required management reports. It has evolved into a flexible framework for determining what products to produce; when, where, and how to make the products; which markets to pursue; and which resources to use. In addition, PLANETS provides detailed shipping allocations and capital spending schedules.

Several benefits have been realized from using PLANETS. For one thing, worldwide use of the system throughout General Motors has helped managers to better understand and deal with business problems. In addition, by using PLANETS for site selection and tooling allocation, managers have been able to save a projected $1 billion in documented costs. The system also has resulted in an estimated 2% to 3% saving on overall capital expenditures.

Source: R. L. Breitman and J. M. Lucas, "PLANETS: A Modeling System for Business Planning," *Interfaces* (January–February 1987): pp. 94–106.

Contemporary organizations, such as General Motors (GM), exist in a dynamic world of rapid social and political change, increased global competition, and resource shortages. The resulting decision problems (such as GM's product planning tasks) are more challenging, significant, and complex than ever before. In this environment, today's manager can make proper decisions only by using systematic, rational approaches based on information and scientific analysis. These approaches, such as GM's PLANETS, constitute **management science**. Depending on the user's focus, the discipline may also be called operations research, decision science, quatitative decision making, quantitative methods, or quantitative management.

The past three decades have seen a steady—and, at times, spectacular—growth in the development and application of quantitative approaches to decision making. As a result, there has been a continually increasing demand on managers to participate in the design of, provide data for, and use the output from these methods. Of particular

5

significance has been the phenomenal impact of the computer on the traditional tasks of management. Our first section traces this historical development.

Applications. In this chapter, the following applications appear in text, examples, tables, or exercises:

- advertising media selection
- deployment of fire-fighting equipment
- fleet management
- forecasting of military battles
- fuel management

- inventory management
- managing a sales force
- profit planning
- tar sands mining
- vehicle routing

1.1 EVOLUTION OF QUANTITATIVE MANAGEMENT

Prior to the twentieth century, enterprises functioned in a relatively simple, stable, and predictable environment. As a result, managers were able to make effective decisions based on intuition or by repeating procedures successfully used by other executives. Such approaches often did not attack the problem in a systematic manner and did little to improve or advance the managerial decision process.

Nevertheless, we can find some early examples of systematic approaches to decision making. In the fifteenth century, for example, Venetian shipbuilders used an assembly line of sorts in outfitting their vessels. And based on his analysis of straight pin manufacturing, Adam Smith suggested a division of labor in 1776. In 1832, Charles Babbage presented several concepts of industrial engineering, including a skill differential in wages. However, a truly progressive movement did not begin until the late nineteenth century.

Origins

In the late 1800s, and American engineer named Frederick Taylor formally advocated a scientific approach to the problems of manufacturing. According to Taylor, there was one "best," or most efficient, way to accomplish a given task. He used time studies to analyze work methods, establish standards, and evaluate worker performance. A contemporary, Henry L. Gantt, extended these concepts by including human behavioral factors. He also emphasized the importance of the personnel department to the scientific approach to management. Perhaps Gantt's greatest contribution, however, was his scheduling system for loading jobs on machines. Basically a recording device that showed work planned and completed over time, Gantt's chart minimized job completion delays by permitting machine loadings to be scheduled months in advance.

These early scientific approaches were limited mainly to establishing or improving efficiency for specific tasks in the lower levels of organizations. In the early twentieth century, however, several pioneers applied a number of mathematical techniques to a variety of problems at various organizational levels. Table 1.1 gives a summary of these approaches. Still, despite such advances in the scientific approach to management, quantitative decision making did not emerge as a field until World War II.

Table 1.1   **Early Scientific Approaches to Management**

Date	Originator	Method	Application
1914	F. W. Lanchester	Mathematical equation	Forecasting outcomes of military battles
1915	F. W. Harris	Lot size formula	Economic order quantity for inventory control
1917	A. K. Erlang	Queuing theory	Prediction of waiting time for callers using an automatic telephone exchange
1924	W. Shewhart	Theory of probability and statistical inference	Production quality control charts
1927–28	H. Dodge and H. Romig	Theory of probability and statistical inference	Production sampling inspection
1930s	H. C. Levinson	Mathematical expressions	Study of marketing relationships

Early Development

World War II created unprecedented problems in resource allocation, production planning and scheduling, inventory and quality control, transportation and logistics, and other areas. No one was experienced in dealing with these new, unique, and enormously complex problems. Thus, decision makers did not derive much success from repeating tested procedures. Also, the problems were much too important to justify solution by the haphazard approaches of intuition and guesswork. Leaders recognized the need for an innovative approach based on analytical reasoning. Therefore, teams of physical scientists, engineers, mathematicians, and military leaders were formed to study these problems and recommend solutions. They were called operations analysis or operations research groups, and their multidisciplinary, or team, approach became a characteristic of such studies.

Mathematics is the language of the scientific disciplines. Thus, it was natural for operations research groups to formulate the problems mathematically. In addition, the advent of computer technology provided the means to analyze certain mathematical formulations of the operations problems.

After World War II, many of the former participants in military operations research applied the same concepts to related industrial problems. However, few universities had formal academic programs in operations research. The few professionals in the field usually had backgrounds in engineering, mathematics, or the physical sciences. Professional societies were formed in the late 1940s and early 1950s, and their journals communicated the latest developments in the field.

Industrial applications spread in the 1950s, when computer technology was further developed and made commercially available. However, the technology was not sufficient to handle large-scale, sophisticated mathematical models. Hence, operations research focused on the development of techniques to solve practical, well-defined, and well-structured small-scale operations problems.

Formal academic programs in operations research/management science became well established in the 1960s, and trained graduates eventually attained managerial positions. These people made their organizations aware of the innovative methods of the new discipline, and this in turn encouraged further development of the field.

Academic growth encouraged a focus of interest and research on the tools and techniques of operations research/management science. New solution techniques were developed and others refined. Advances in computer technology provided the means to solve the more sophisticated mathematical models. In addition, "canned" computer programs were developed for various standard techniques, and the advent of computer-based management information systems helped supply some of the data required by the procedures.

Unfortunately, some researchers forgot that the original motivation for developing the field was to aid the process of decision making. Application and implementation received little emphasis in the 1960s, and this neglect created certain difficulties. The most serious problems involved behavioral and monetary factors. Many managers with limited technical background and experience did not fully understand the nature of management science and its potential benefits. Yet operations research analysts frequently did not have enough organizational training, patience, or diplomatic skill to effectively explain, interpret, and justify their methods and recommendations. In other cases, managers perceived the new procedures as a threat to their job security and decision-making power. Also, managers were skeptical about the ability of management scientists to deliver timely and profitable results. When attempting to "sell" the quantitative disciplines, most analysts did not consider these political and monetary factors or the personalities of the managers. In addition, decision makers accused management scientists of being more interested in finding a problem that fit the techniques than in starting with a managerial problem and deciding how best to analyze it. Predictably, some organizations had unsuccessful initial experiences with the field. However, professionals gained a more realistic view of the potentials and limitations of operations research/management science.

Maturity

The field matured in the 1970s. Operations research/management science again concentrated on providing assistance to decision makers. New techniques were developed, but there was also an emphasis on solving managerial problems. Implementation problems still persisted in the 1970s, but were less severe than in the 1960s. Furthermore, there was more interest in strategies for implementing decision science concepts within the organizational framework.

Advances in computer-based information systems also enhanced implementation by providing better data for the management science techniques. Concurrently, the development of time-sharing computer systems made it possible for decisions makers to interact directly with the quantitative formulations. In addition, a library of computer programs for management science, called **SHARE**, was developed and made available commercially on a national basis at a nominal cost to users. Such systems made the power of large-scale computers available to small organizations at a reasonable price.

These factors promoted a rapid expansion in the range of quantitative decision-making applications.

Current Developments

During the 1980s, management science/operations research (MS/OR) experienced stagnation. Few entirely new concepts were developed. Many formal MS/OR groups in government and industry were disbanded, and personnel were absorbed into planning staffs. In response, academic institutions offered fewer and less conventional MS/OR programs. Much of the discipline's subject matter was incorporated into other business programs, such as operations management and finance.

The retrenchment has not diminished the need for effective management science/operations research. Instead, it has clarified that MS/OR itself offers only one important set of tools to address management problems. Other valuable tools include practical constructs (such as budgets and income statements) form accounting, methodologies (such as forecasting) from statistics, and insights and judgments provided by technicians and other experts.

The current developments have necessitated changes in management science/operations research practice. Experts have integrated, more fully than before, MS/OR with other decision-making tools. Also, mechanisms have been developed that deliver the integrated tools effectively to managers.

Computer-based technology has facilitated the evolution. Powerful microcomputers and accompanying user-friendly software (such as **What's Best, LINDO/PC,** and **Network II.5**) have allowed even small enterprises to employ management science/operations research. Professional insights and judgments have been organized as sets of formal rules and offered, through **expert systems**, as electronic counselors to managers. Other sophisticated information systems have been developed to support the entire decision-making process.

1.2 CHARACTERISTICS

Management science/operations research has evolved into a unique discipline with the following characteristics:

1. A primary *focus on problems* of management.
2. An integrated, global approach, or *systems approach*, to managerial decision making.
3. The use of methods and knowledge from several disciplines, or a *team approach*.
4. The application of the *scientific method* to decision making.
5. A reliance on *mathematics*.
6. A dependence on high-speed *computers*.
7. The use of an integrated, formal *technology* to assist individuals and groups with the process of management.

Focus On Problems

Frequently, managers are faced with extremely complex problems that do not have obvious solutions. Some situations involve problems for which the decision maker has no past experience. In addition, the problem may have very significant financial and organizational impacts. Consequently, management may want to conduct a thorough analysis before attempting a decision. Also, there are repetitive problems that, once formulated and standardized, do not require the manager's continuous attention.

Under these circumstances, the decision maker may recognize the need for some assistance in formulating and analyzing the problem. A management scientist could be asked to study the problem, develop appropriate quantitative techniques, and recommend a solution. This primary focus on managerial problems is a central theme in MS/OR.

Systems Approach

We should recognize that the organization is a collection of interrelated parts (divisions, departments, machinery, people, and so on) intended to accomplish specific objectives. As such, it constitutes a **system**. Furthermore, a decision made in one part of the organization may significantly affect the operations of other segments. An inventory problem within a firm's production department, for example, may disrupt marketing, finance, accounting, and personnel functions. Therefore, when possible, the problem should be examined from the overall organizational point of view. Such a viewpoint is called the **systems approach**. This systems perspective is a key characteristic of management science/operations research.

It is also important to realize that the organization itself is merely a component of the environment in which it operates. The firm's actions may affect market, social, and political conditions. Similarly, actions by unions, consumers, competing firms, and government can affect the firm's operations. Incorporating these environmental factors into the analysis, where applicable, should be part of the systems approach.

Team Approach

Many managerial problems have behavioral, social, political, economic, statistical, mathematical, physical, biological, engineering, and business aspects. By assembling a group with a variety of backgrounds, managers often can obtain innovative approaches to problems. The scientific minds from each discipline extract the essential elements of the situation and then relate the structure to similar problems encountered in their own fields. After drawing such analogies, the researcher may determine whether or not the problem can be solved with methods traditionally successful in his or her field. When scientists from several disciplines collectively follow this process, the pool of possible approaches is large enough to reinforce the individual disciplines. As a result, management science/operations research is frequently characterized by this **team** or **multidisciplinary, approach**.

However, some problems are simple enough to be handled by a single qualified researcher, especially one with multidisciplinary training. Also, relevant information about other disciplines can often be retrieved quickly, easily, and at nominal cost. In that case, a person with minimal training in several fields may be able to employ (and benefit from) a team approach.

Figure 1.1 **Scientific Method**

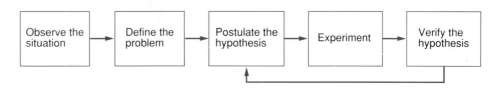

Scientific Method

Another fundamental characteristic of management science/operations research is its scientific approach to decision making. This approach, which involves the process shown in Figure 1.1, is also known as the **scientific method**.

The method begins when the manager observes the decision situation through inspection, review of reports, or some other means. Often, this examination reveals that the enterprise has a problem. For example, a review of recent market data may show that Dial® Soap has significantly declining sales.

When there is an unsettled question, as in the Dial situation, the manager must next define the precise nature of the problem. Usually, further investigation and some analysis will be needed to complete this step. For example, the brand manager's evaluation of sales force and purchaser surveys may indicate that grocery stores are stocking large volumes of competitors' brands and that Dial's soap price is the highest, among the majors, in the market. Such information implies that the problem is to determine a new price policy that will increase Dial sales.

The decision maker must now postulate a hypothesis, or propose a tentative explanation (or even a solution), for the problem. For example, the brand manager's experience may suggest that soap sales will decline as Dial's price rises relative to the competition. As a result, the manager may hypothesize that a price decrease will lead to more sales.

Experiments are designed and performed to test and verify the hypothesis. For example, Dial's brand manager can lower prices in selected markets for a trial period and observe the effect on soap sales. Test results can be used to confirm or disprove the initial price hypothesis.

In addition, the verification process can be used to refine the initial hypothesis or develop alternative explanations. Valid hypotheses then can help the manager to predict future system behavior and to implement appropriate decision recommendations. For example, Dial's brand manager could use the test market results to help identify a precise price reduction policy.

Unfortunately, organizations operate in a constantly changing, complex environment. Furthermore, many of the relevant factors are beyond the firm's control. In the soap illustration, for example, there is no guarantee that competitors' actions will be stable in the test market during the trial period. Also the test markets may not be truly representative of the general consuming public. Consequently, complete verification is not always possible. However, that does not preclude the use of a scientific approach to decision making. It simply means that there is usually some degree of uncertainty about the final results. In general, the manager can be far more confident in a scientific decision than in one based on hunches and guesses.

Mathematics And Computers

Mathematics is the language of science. In addition, it is often the most useful way to express the complex interrelationships involved in many managerial problems. Where applicable, mathematical analysis is usually less expensive, less cumbersome, quicker, and more flexible than other methods. Consequently, most management science/operations research projects rely on at least some formal mathematical techniques.

Many mathematical techniques, however, involve a substantial computational effort. In fact, without computer assistance, the analyst may need days, or even weeks, to complete the required calculations and evaluations manually. Moreover, the manual effort would be tedious, prone to error, and costly. That is why the use of computers has been closely associated with management science/operations research.

As information science has evolved, there has been an even greater dependence of management science/operations research on high-speed computers. Required data have been provided economically and in a timely manner at the user's workstation through information systems. The data have then served as input for MS/OR analyses performed by the user with computer assistance. Indeed, the evolution of management science/operations research closely parallels the advance in computer-based information technology.

Technology

Historically, management practice has been largely an art that involved a set of skills, abilities, insights/judgments, and specific functional knowledge. Management science/operations research has enabled decision makers to blend science with art when addressing business and government problems.

Recently, a technology has evolved to assist individuals and groups with the process of management. This **technology of management** consists of (1) methodologies and models from MS/OR and statistics, (2) theoretical and practical constructs from economics and accounting, (3) hardware, software, and systems from information science, and (4) practical experience embedded in expert knowledge. It uses the methodologies, constructs, and experience in computer-based information systems to provide facts relevant for effective management. The knowledge may sometimes be in the form of summarized information. On other occasions, the information could be a forecast of a required business/economic condition or a recommended action. Typically, the facts are provided at the executive's workstation in readily understandable formats such as tables, graphs, or pictorial images.

The technology of management is expected to have significant effects on the art and science of management. It will provide an effective vehicle to integrate management science/operations research with other scientific decision aids, such as statistics and economics. Also, interactive communications with the technology, especially the expert knowledge component, will enable a manager to incorporate insights and judgments into a systematic evaluation of the decision problem. Moreover, the technology will change the role of the computer from a computational aid to an extension of the executive's mind. By using the technology in a creative and intelligent manner, the decision maker can observe the decision's sensitivity to changes in assumptions and in approach.

Table 1.2   **Major Professional Societies**

Society	Founded	Journal
Operational Research Society of the United Kingdom	1948	*Journal of the Operational Research Society*
Operations Research Society of America (ORSA)	1952	*Operations Research*
The Institute of Management Science (TIMS)	1953	*Management Science*
Decision Sciences Institute (DSI)	1969	*Decision Sciences*

1.3 APPLICATIONS

Currently, management science/operations research is an international discipline with professional societies in North America, Europe, and Asia. Table 1.2 lists the major societies and their principal publications. At least 10 other journals, including *Interfaces,* the *Journal of Operational Research*, and the *European Journal of Operational Research*, publish articles dealing with management science/operations research. Also, there are thousands of teachers, researchers, and practitioners throughout the world.

Most large firms, many smaller companies, and various government agencies practice some form of quantitative decision making or consult management scientists. Table 1.3 gives a partial list of the applications. Furthermore, recent studies report increases in the breadth and depth of management science activities. Most organizations receive substantial benefits from these applications, as Table 1.4 illustrates.

As you can see from Tables 1.3 and 1.4, management science has been applied by a variety of organizations to a wide range of problems. Included are regional, national, and international enterprises of all sizes in both private and public sectors. There have been applications to general management, the functional areas of production, finance, marketing, and logistics, as well as the staff areas of accounting, personnel, and auxiliary services. Benefits typically have been in the magnitude of several million dollars.

Regardless of the organization or position, there is a strong possibility that a decision maker will be involved with management science. For this reason, private and public organizations are more attracted to current or prospective employees with training in quantitative decision making. Universities are responding by offering education in the field.

Future organizations will exist in a world even more complex and dynamic than today's. Decision makers will need to rely further on rational means for developing and justifying various courses of action. Consequently, management science will be more widely practiced in all types of institutions. In particular, we can expect a continuation of the recent trend toward public applications, especially in nonprofit organizations such as museums, theater companies, and private foundations. Experts also will develop new approaches to ill-defined, ill-structured, complex problems. These new approaches will include the psychological aspect of the human decision-making process, a science of data measurement and collection, and interactive computer systems. The purpose of these new tools will be to enhance the intuitive powers of managers.

Table 1.3   **Applications of Quantitative Decisions Making***

Private Institutions	Public Institutions
Finance	***Health***
Capital budgeting	Ambulance depot location
Corporate financial planning	Diet planning
Dividend policy determination	Evaluation of health care delivery systems
Equipment replacement analysis	Hospital staffing
Portfolio management	Inventory control of human blood
Marketing	***Military***
Advertising media selection	Missile allocation for national defense
Analysis of packaging effectiveness	Reliability analysis of military equipment
Assessment of competitive marketing strategies	Search and rescue effort
Assignment of sales personnel	War games simulation
Location of distribution facilities	Weapon systems analysis
Marketing budget mix determination	
Sales forecasting	***Social and Environmental***
	Courtroom scheduling
Production	Deploying fire fighting and police facilities
Allocation of production resources	Educational planning and scheduling
Inventory control	Highway and air traffic control
Maintenance policy formulation	Mass transit systems analysis
Plant layout analysis	Political redistricting analysis
Production planning and scheduling	Public utilities regulation
Product quality control	Refuse collection scheduling and routing
	Urban planning
Others	Water and air pollution control
Airline scheduling and routing	
Agricultural feedmix planning and control	***Others***
Auditing policy formulation	Forecasting general economic conditions
Professional sports draft selection analysis	Queuing analysis of toll facilities
Telephone circuit switching policies	Regional and international economic development
Utilization of banking facilities	Reliability analysis of space vehicles

*Applications are taken mainly from recent issues of *Interfaces*.

Table 1.4   **Benefits from Management Science***

Company	Application	Benefits
Public Sector		
British Airways	Profit planning and analysis	Increased profits by more than $25 million per year.
DuPage County, Illinois	Land use planning	Reduced use of "high-cost" acreage by 50%.
New York City	Deploying fire-fighting companies	Maintained safe level of service with six fewer fire companies for a cost savings of $5 million per year.
U.S. Postal Service	Vehicle routing	Reduced travel time per truck by 2 hours per day and distance traveled by 25%.

Table 1.4   *continuing*

Company	Application	Benefits
Private Sector		
Booth Fisheries	Materials management	Reduced inventories by 55%, transport costs by 9%, and production expenses by 8%; increased order fill rate by 8%.
Cahill May Roberts	Facilities and resource planning	Reduced delivery costs by 23% and transportation expenses by 20%.
Cerro de Pasco	Production planning	Increased profits by several million dollars.
Flying Tiger Line	Flight crew scheduling	Saved $300,000 per year.
Getty Oil Company	Financial planning and analysis	Increased earnings by several million dollars.
Hertz Rent-a-Car	Fleet management	Increased productivity by 10%.
National Airlines	Fuel management	Saved millions of dollars.
RCA	Establishing a satellite communication system	Established least-cost state-of-the-art system.
Scott Paper Company	Resource allocation	Increased productivity by two million cases per year.
Syncrude of Canada Ltd.	Tar sands mining	Established least-cost state-of-the-art mining system.
Union Carbide	Distribution planning	Saved several million dollars.
United Airlines	Sales force management	Increased sales productivity by 8%.
Whirlpool Corporation	Distribution management	Saved several million dollars per year.

*Illustrations are taken primarily from recent issues of *Interfaces*.

SUMMARY

This chapter has been an introduction to quantitative decision making. The subject originated with the scientific approach to management in the late 1800s. It grew into a recognized discipline between 1940 and 1970 and matured into a significant aid to public and private decision makers during the 1970s.

Depending on the focus of the user, the discipline is also called management science, operations research, decision science, quantitative methods, or quantitative management. It is characterized by a focus on managerial problems, a systems and team approach, the application of the scientific method, a reliance on mathematics and the computer, and the use of an integrated, formal technology of management.

Quantitative decision making has become an international discipline with thousands of teachers, researchers, and practitioners. The concepts have been successfully applied by a wide range of private and public sector organizations to a broad scope of problems. As the world becomes even more complex and dynamic, the need for management science will be even greater.

Glossary

expert systems Microcomputer-based channels for transmitting formal rules and professional insights to users.

management science/operations research All systematic and rational approaches to decision making that are based on information and scientific analysis.

scientific method The process of observing the situation, defining the problem, postulating a hypothesis, experimenting, and verifying the hypothesis.

SHARE A library of computer programs for management science, commercially available on a national basis at a nominal cost to users.

system A collection of interrelated parts intended to accomplish specific objectives.

systems approach A method of examining a problem from a systems prospective.

team approach A collective effort in which individuals from several disciplines analyze a problem.

technology of management Management method that utilizes methodologies and models from MS/OR and statistics, theroretical and practical constructs from economics and accounting, information systems, and practical experience embedded in expert knowledge.

Thought Exercises

1. It had been said that quantitative decision making originated in the early systematic and scientific approaches to decision making. What elements of these approaches are characteristic of management science/operations research? How did the early scientific approaches to decision making differ from management science?

2. Do you think that an operations research discipline would have emerged in the 1940s if there had not been a world war? Explain.

3. Why did the early development of management science/operations research take as long as 20 years? What were the crucial factors leading to a maturity in the discipline?

4. For each of the following situations, identify whether management science can be used to assist the manager in formulating and analyzing the problem. Explain.
   a. Marketing a new product
   b. Making a plant location decision
   c. Establishing an inventory control policy
   d. Engaging in nuclear warfare

5. Identify the appropriate system in each of the following decision situations. Explain.
   a. Buying a new house
   b. Installing pollution control equipment
   c. Manufacturing cement
   d. Regulating electricity rates

6. Briefly discuss how the scientific method can be applied to each of the following problems:
   a. Establishing railway schedules
   b. Introducing a new educational program
   c. Establishing a government budget
   d. Growing oranges

7. Identify whether a team approach is desirable in each of the following situations. Explain.
   a. A merger decision
   b. A student project
   c. Writing a sports article
   d. Developing advertising strategy

8. Explain why you agree or disagree with each of the following statements:
   a. Scientific management is the same thing as management science.
   b. Management science will eventually replace the manager.

   c. Some problems can be solved by intuition, hunches, and guesses.

   d. Management science consists of a group of techniques in search of problems.

   e. A computer-based information system, in and of itself, constitutes the technology of management.

Technique Exercises

9. Go to your library and compile a list of sources on management science, operations research, decision science, systems analysis, and quantitative decision making. Using these sources, obtain a definition for each of these terms. How do the definitions differ? How are they similar? Use this information to develop a consensus definition.

10. Compile a list of journals from your library that publish articles on management science/operations research.

11. Most of the applications in Table 1.3 are taken from recent issues of *Interfaces*. Using the volumes of this journal in your library, compile a list of references that deal with these applications.

12. Most of the illustrations in Table 1.4 are taken from recent issues of *Interfaces*. Using the volumes of this journal in your library, compile a list of references that deal with these illustrations.

13. Use the management science/operations research journals to compile a list of the most recent applications in the following areas:
   a. Health care administration
   b. Banking
   c. Government
   d. Education
   e. Retail and wholesale companies
   f. Hotel, travel, and restaurant management

14. Use the management science/operations research journals to compile a list of the most recent applications in your area of interest.

15. Several references in the "For Further Reading" section at the end of this chapter discuss management science/operations research activities in practice. Identify these references. Use these references or any other studies you can find in your library to report the managerial problem areas in which MS/OR has been used most frequently.

Applications Exercises

16. The production manager for Eronoco Enterprises, Inc., is concerned about the quality of the company's plastic containers. Recently, Eronoco has received many consumer complaints about the product's durability. The manager wants to develop a new quality control program to alleviate the problem. Eronoco's general manager, however, first wants a preliminary study that will identify the overall impact of such a program. The study should identify the relevant objective, affected departments, and appropriate market influences. Assume that you are the production manager and prepare the report.

17. The Federal Drug Administration (FDA) has been commissioned to certify whether the latest cold remedy, Cold Gone, is fit for use by the general public. Suppose you were put in charge of this project. Describe how you would scientifically conduct Cold Gone's certification process.

18. Jalestown University's athletic department has been given a grant to develop an Olympic training program for gymnasts. The program will consider nutrition, physical and psychological development, gymnastic exercises, and social behavior. O. M. Swell, the university's athletic director, will administer the program. Whom should Swell include on the training staff? Explain.

19. Howard Humphrey is chief commissioner on the state's Public Utility Board (PUB). Recently, a major natural gas company serving the southeastern portion of the state has petitioned for a rate hike to offset its latest cost increases. The company claims that the hike is necessary to maintain the "fair" return on investment previously granted by the PUB. Describe how Humphrey could employ a scientific, multidisciplinary systems approach to make the rate decision.

For Further Reading

Evolution of Quantitative Management

Aldag, R. J., and D. J. Power. "An Empirical Assessment of Computer-assisted Decision Analysis." *Decision Sciences* (Fall 1986):572.

Duncan, W. J. "The Researcher and the Manager: A Comparative View of the Need for Mutual Understanding." *Management Science* (April 1974):1157.

Gass, S. I. "Presidents' Symposium: A Perspective on the Future of Operations Research." *Operations Research* (March–April 1987):320.

Huysmans, J. H. *The Implementation of Operations Research.* New York: Wiley, 1970.

Kraemer, K. L., and J. L. King. "Computer-Based Models for Policy Making Uses and Impacts in the U.S. Federal Government." *Operations Research.* (July–August 1986):501.

Lilien, G. L. "MS/OR: A Midlife Crisis." *Interfaces* (March–April 1987):35.

Pierskalla, W. P. "Presidents' Symposium: Creating Growth in OR/MS," *Operations Research* (January–February 1987): 153.

Powell, G. N. "Implementation of OR/MS in Government and Industry: A Behavioral Science Perspective." *Interfaces* (August 1976):83.

Radnor, M., and R. Neal. "The Progress of Management Science Activities in Large U.S. Industrial Corporations." *Operations Research* (March–April 1973):427.

Tingley, G. A. "Can MS/OR Sell Itself Well Enough?" *Interfaces* (July–August 1987):41.

Characteristics

Forgionne, G. A., and S. D. Willits. "Effective Delivery of Management Technology." *Information Management Review* (Summer 1987):59.

Kitchener, A. "The Impact of Technology on the Information Systems and Operations Research Professions." *Interfaces* (May–June 1986):20.

Lawrence, J. A. "Business Schools Offer Diverse Approaches to Quantitative/Computer Topics." *OR/MS Today* (April 1988):10.

Simon, H. *The New Science of Management Decisions.* Rev. ed. Englewood Cliffs, N. J. :Prentice-Hall, 1977.

Private Sector Applications

Kivijarvi, H., P. Korhonen, and I. Wallenius. "Operations Research and Its Practice in Finland." *Interfaces* (July–August 1986):53.

Klingman, D., et. al. "The Successful Deployment of Management Science throughout Citgo Petroleum Corporation." *Interfaces* (January–February 1987):4.

Papageorgiou, J. C. "Management Science/Operations Research in Greece." *Interfaces* (July–August 1986):24.

Public Sector Applications

McKenna, C. K. *Quantitative Methods for Public Decision Making.* New York:McGraw-Hill, 1980.

White, C. P. "A Survey of Recent Management Science Applications in Higher Education Administration." *Interfaces* (March–April 1987):97.

Case: The Cookbook Conspiracy

There once was a kingdom called Usalium, a peaceful, contented place. The functioning of Usalium was highly dependent on the efficient operation of its kitchens, because gastric delights were of prime importance to the populace. All was well for many years. The School of Chefs was staffed by a competent group of gastric scientists skilled in the preparation of nutritious meals and pleasurable menus, and in the principles and methodology of basic constructs of gastric delight. The school always produced skilled chefs who were immediately equipped to apply their knowledge in the kitchens of Usalium. Graduate chefs were able to adopt the methodology of the School of Chefs to please the specific tastes of even the most fastidious Usalii.

But alas, even kingdoms change. The Usalii began to multiply. Alien recipes were brought home by Usalium's foreign merchants and armed forces. The Usalii's interest slowly shifted to specific recipes, and the king decreed that the School of Cookery be established to meet this demand.

The School of Cookery began to flourish, and cookery pervaded the entire kingdom. The School of Cookery offered such delightful curricula as the principles of baked beans, the placement of knives and forks, and the preparation of french fries and other gastric delights imported from various foreign Schools of Cookery. Cookbooks soon proliferated throughout Usalium, containing recipes of unimaginable variety and peculiarity. In time, the School of Chefs was phased out, and eventually nearly all the chefs disappeared. Usalii thought that the techniques and specific details of various recipes were more important than the ideas and methodological foundations of these gastric pleasures. It was a gourmet's delight! Soon, the entire curriculum of the School of Cookery was aimed at "how to do it" recipes. The cooks of the kingdom considered themselves too sophisticated to be concerned with the curriculum of the old School of Chefs.

But things were not going well in the kingdom. Stomach irritation became prevalent, the populace developed various peculiar maladies, and, most important, the king frequently had indigestion. The maladies caused a slowing of the operations of the kingdom, and there were enormous inefficiencies in its main activities. Because of bulging midriffs, basking in the sunshine was no longer a favorite occupation, hospital time was interfering with work activities (such as sowing wild oats and basket weaving), and the king's armies were no longer able to function effectively (overweight horses, men, and the like). Even the king's efficiency expert (the queen) was beginning to show the signs of excess.

What's more, young cooks graduating from the School of Cookery were failing to adjust to the real-life kitchens of Usalium. It seems that the recipes that they had learned were not always applicable to the specific gastric pleasures of their various placements. Also, the young cooks were unaware of the whys and wherefores of the recipes, nor did they understand the principles and methodologies of gastric delight. Reference to the many cookbooks in the kingdom did not seem to help, for these books contained more specific recipes.

The queen took action. As efficiency expert, she demanded a formal investigation of the problem. The king responded in the usual way: He had the chief cook of the School of Cookery guillotined. However, nothing seemed to work. New chief cooks were appointed, but all seemed to fail. Meanwhile, the kingdom was on the verge of collapse.

Just when things looked worst, there was some encouraging news from Calpolot, a remote province of Usalium. It seems that Calpolot had none of the maladies of Usalium. The prince (under threat of the guillotine) was commissioned to examine the situation and isolate the source of gastric contentment. And here is what the prince discovered: One of the few remaining graduates from the old School of Chefs had moved to Calpolot. Therefore, the cookery revolution had not materialized there. Instead, the principles of the School of Chefs were still being practiced.

The king immediately summoned the retired chef of Calpolot to save Usalium. The chef was able to restore the curriculum of the old School of Chefs, the School of Cookery was disbanded, the cooks were sent back to school for retraining, cookbooks were outlawed, and the chef was made a wizard in arms. Amazingly, the kingdom gradually returned to its former peaceful contented state.

1. What moral does the fable have for businesses? For business schools? For students?

2. Do you see any analogy between the cookbook approach depicted in the fable and developments in the academic history of decision sciences? Explain.

3. There are other analogies in the fable. Explain those relating to each of the following:
   a. The maturation phase in the history of decision sciences
   b. The implementation problem in decision sciences
   c. The potential applications of decision sciences
   d. The role of quantitative analysis in the decision-making process

Chapter 2

The Management Science Process

Chapter Outline

Learning Objectives

- Understand the nature of decision making
- Identify quantitative methods' role in the decision-making process
- Examine the steps involved in quantitative analysis
- Understand how to construct and analyze a model
- Investigate the relationship between computer information systems and management science/operations research (MS/OR)
- Determine how decision support systems facilitate management science/operations research
- Identify MS/OR implementation problems and strategies to resolve the difficulties

Filling the Army Ranks

M ORE than 600,000 soldiers are enlisted in a variety of skills, grades, and units around the world in the U.S. Army. The Army's mission determines how many of these soldiers will be required in various skill categories, pay grades, and geographic locations. Training, pay, and allowances for the enlistees cost nearly $15 billion a year. In addition, approximately $140 million a year is spent on bonuses to attract enlisted soldiers into critical skills.

Given the magnitude of the expenditures, officials decided that a system was needed to help the Army manage its personnel. Work began in 1979, and the effort ultimately led to the development of the Military Occupational Specialty System (MOSLS). This system contains a variety of management science methodologies that enable the user to project, over a seven-year period, the Army's enlisted strength, broken down by pay grade and skill. MOSLS also generates the promotion, reenlistment, reclassification, and skill training recommendations needed to meet the projected personnel requirements. The methodologies are delivered through computer aids that permit the user to perform the necessary analysis quickly and easily and to generate required reports in a timely fashion.

Since MOSLS was implemented in 1984, the system has been used by an increasing number of army personnel managers. Such utilization has enabled the Army to reduce noncommissioned officer (NCO) force imbalances from 48 percent in 1983 to 30 percent in 1986. This adjustment has saved the Army about $65 million per year from NCO position alignments alone.

Source: A. Eiger et al., "The U.S. Army's Occupational Specialty Manpower Decision Support System," *Interfaces* (January–February 1988): 57–73.

Everyone makes decisions. People choose their friends, entertainment, work, food, clothes, home, car, life-style, and other personal matters. Consumers select brands of merchandise, the stores they will shop, and their method of payment. Political organizations and politicians identify the groups they will represent, funding techniques, and campaign strategies. Doctors, lawyers, teachers, and other professionals choose their area of expertise, clientele, and schedules. Managers formulate plans and strategies, establish an organization, hire employees, allocate resources, and control activities.

Some decisions such as buying toothpaste and choosing a movie are relatively simple and insignificant. Others such as building a factory or engaging in war are complex and very important. The U.S. Army's occupational specialty assignments, which involve national security and million-dollar budget issues, fall into the latter category.

Whether simple or complex, all decisions involve the same basic process. This chapter examines the process and shows what quantitative analysis contributes to effective decision making. First we will explain the proper way to define a decision problem and show how to develop a quantitative formulation. Then we will investigate the methods for gathering, processing, and analyzing relevant data, and we will review the most popular solution techniques. As the Army situation illustrates, computer information systems greatly facilitate such analysis and solution. Our investigation will therefore explore the relationships between these systems and management science. We will conclude with a discussion of implementation problems and strategies.

Applications. In this chapter, the following applications appear in text, examples, and exercises:

- advertising
- beauty products
- career selection
- commuting
- food purchasing
- national income forecasting

- product pricing
- production planning
- sales forecasting
- Sunday newspapers
- typing service
- university bookstores

2.1 QUANTITATIVE FORMULATION

Although most people do not stop to think about it, decision making involves the basic process shown in Figure 2.1. The decision maker observes a real situation and is dissatisfied with its current state. He or she recognizes a problem and identifies alternative courses of action. Qualitative and quantitative information is gathered and used to evaluate the alternatives. Next, the decision maker selects the alternative that is most preferable in terms of his or her evaluation criteria. Then the decision maker implements the choice. Furthermore, the decision-making process is continuous. After the choice is implemented, the decision maker should observe and, where appropriate, follow through with problem recognition, the identification of alternatives, and so on.

Management Situation 2.1 illustrates a routine decision.

Management Situation 2.1

Food Purchasing

Jack Johnson needs salt. Four brands are available: Min at 18 cents, Sed at 15 cents, Tug at 16 cents, and Doe at 17 cents per package (all packages the same size). All brands may be purchased at the store closest to his home.

Jack's home economics education and experience indicate that the four brands are comparable in quality. Thus, he typically buys salt at the lowest price.

Jack's simple problem is to decide which brand of salt to buy. Prices are quantitative information, whereas quality is qualitative. Since the qualitative information provides no

Figure 2.1   **Decision-making Process**

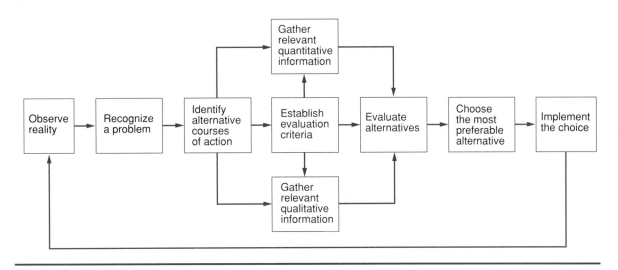

help, the purchase price per package is the sole criterion for evaluating the brands. By using the available information, Jack will find that Sed is the preferred brand. Therefore, he should go to the store and buy this brand.

Managers in public and private organizations go through the same decision-making process. However, their decisions are usually more complex. The problem is more significant in scope and impact, and alternatives are more numerous and often difficult to define. Qualitative knowledge may be available, but it is more difficult to obtain reliable, relevant quantitative information. There are many evaluation criteria, which are often difficult to measure. Evaluation of alternatives is usually more sophisticated than a simple numerical comparison of outcomes. Also, the decision maker must act as an agent of change if he or she hopes to implement the selected alternative in the organization.

Judgment is required at all stages of the decision-making process. Management science/operations research aids such judgment by structuring problems, providing relevant quantitative information, and evaluating alternatives. To obtain this assistance, however, the decision maker must understand the quantitative analysis process. Although professional expertise will not be necessary, managers should be able to recognize situations in which MS/OR would be appropriate. In addition, they should have some skill in formulating problems and selecting relevant techniques. To be confident about implementing the results, managers must also understand the assumptions, limitations, and benefits from the analysis.

In short, quantitative decision making is not a substitute for competent management. Rather, it is a methodology that can significantly improve the executive's ability to make effective decisions. To see how, let us examine the management science process shown in Figure 2.2.

Figure 2.2   **Management Science Process**

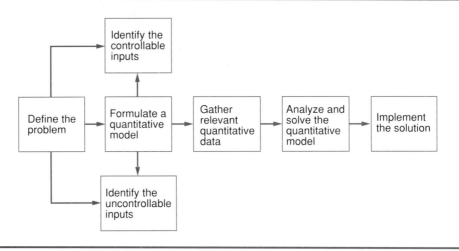

Defining the Problem

Quantitative decision making is problem oriented, so the first step is to define the managerial problem clearly and concisely. The goal should be specified, and relevant restrictions identified. Since this step affects the outcome of the entire process, it is extremely important and deserves careful consideration. Many operations research studies fail simply because the problem is poorly defined.

The problem must be stated precisely to be suitable for analysis. We start with a broad, or general, description and refine to a specific, well-defined statement. For example, an organization may translate the broad problem of declining production into a specific objective of maximizing output subject to an available resource constraint.

Many people should be involved in defining the problem. Top management can provide input on the nature of the problem, overall objectives and constraints, policies, and guidelines. Middle and first-line managers have firsthand knowledge about their operations and the corresponding constraints. Specialists in computer programming, accounting, personnel services, and other areas can offer their own insights. In addition, all these groups or individuals may eventually be affected by the project; by encouraging their active participation, the decision scientist will have a better chance of gaining support and acceptance of the project.

The problem may also have an impact on several parts of the organization and be significantly influenced by the environment in which the firm operates. Consequently, the systems approach should be used to define the problem.

Formulating a Quantitative Model

A **model** is a simplified representation of a real object or situation. The representation includes only essential, relevant features. For example, a scale model railroad is a physical replica of the general appearance and operating characteristics of the real thing.

However, the model excludes some important elements of a real railroad, such as personnel, that are usually irrelevant to most railway modelers.

Building and studying a model facilitate our understanding of the real situation or object. Hobbyists, for instance, can gain insight into railroading by constructing, operating, and maintaining a scale model. Railway officials might use a similar procedure to comprehend more fully the implications of organizational objectives, policies, constraints, and operating assumptions. Much as a physical scientist uses a laboratory, the decision analyst can use the model to perform experiments and test hypotheses. Hence, railway officials may use a model railroad to study various real operating problems and experiment with prospective decisions. Such decisions may involve train length, schedule, route, types of cargo, equipment, and facilities. An analysis of the model enables the decision maker to draw conclusions about the real object or situation.

Experimenting with models is generally less expensive, less time-consuming, and less risky than experimenting with the real thing. Certainly, a model railroad is quicker and less expensive to build and study than a real railroad. In addition, a bad decision that causes the model railroad to operate inefficiently might then be avoided in the real situation.

However, we should realize that a model is not an exact representation. Many assumptions and simplifications are embodied in the model, often without ever being made explicit. Hence, the validity of the conclusions and decisions will depend on how accurately the model represents the real situation. For instance, the more closely the model railroad represents the real railroad, the more accurate will be the predictions and conclusions about railway operations.

Management and operating personnel are the people most closely involved with the decision situation. Thus, they are in the best position to determine whether the assumptions are good approximations of reality. Wise managers will probe for these assumptions and question their validity and reasonableness. Also, management and operating personnel can provide the information necessary for constructing an accurate model. Consequently, they should be encouraged to participate actively in the model-building process.

When formulating a model, we also must consider data and solution requirements. Although it is important to develop an accurate representation of the real situation, implementation should be the primary concern. A model will be of limited practical use unless the decision maker is able to gather relevant data and identify a solution to the problem.

Remember, a model is an abstraction of reality and, as such, cannot capture all aspects of the problem. In fact, if decision makers attempt to incorporate all elements, they may have a model too large and complex to implement. It would be better to formulate a simpler and more easily understood model that *can* be implemented.

Of course, the model's usefulness can be severely limited if the simplifications produce a grossly distorted representation of the problem's important and relevant characteristics. Such distortions can (and should) be avoided by encouraging management and operating personnel to participate in the model-building process.

Types of Models

Models can be presented in various forms. A physical replica, such as the scale model railroad, is called an **iconic model**. Other examples include toys, photographs, aircraft

Figure 2.3   **Structure of a Mathematical Model**

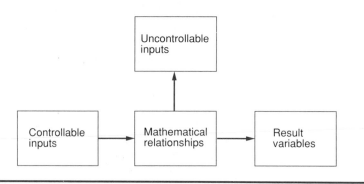

and space vehicle training simulators, mannequins, and scale models of production plant and retail store interior layouts.

Other situations or objects deal with more abstract concepts such as speed, temperature, time, space, processes, and ideas. These concepts are usually represented with **analog models**, which are in a physical form but do not look like the real thing. Figure 2.1 is an analog model of the decision-making process. In this diagram, boxes, lines, and arrows represent a chain of thoughts in reaching a decision. A mercury thermometer is an analog model representing temperature. The position of the mercury in the thermometer represents the degree of heat. Other examples include an automobile speedometer, a watch, an oil dipstick, blueprints, maps, sales charts, organizational charts, and tables and graphs.

Some situations are so complex that they cannot be represented physically. Or a physical representation may be too cumbersome, time-consuming, or expensive to construct and manipulate. **Mathematical models** are typically used for these circumstances. Such models represent the real situation with a system of symbols and mathematical expressions. The approach forces the model builder to explicitly state his or her assumptions about the important elements and cause-and-effect relationships of the real situation. Mathematical models also facilitate scientific experimentation and analysis. Such representations are an essential part of any quantitative approach to decision making. Since this text deals primarily with mathematical models, let us look more closely at the structure of these representations.

Mathematical Models

All mathematical models have the general structure illustrated in Figure 2.3. When initially considering a problem, the analyst specifies one or more measures that will be used to evaluate the performance or effectiveness of the system. Such measures are called **result variables**. Examples include profit, rate of return, cost, market share, and customer satisfaction.

Inputs are the other elements of a mathematical model. **Controllable inputs**, or **decision variables**, are the factors that influence the model's outcome and are controlled or determined by the decision maker. That is, the decision maker can change and manipulate these variables at will. Examples might include the level of output, the number of sales personnel assigned to a territory, and the timing of investment. **Uncontrollable inputs**, or **environmental variables**, are factors that must be considered but are beyond the decision maker's control. Interest rates, building codes, tax regulations, and import prices are possible illustrations. However, it is important to recognize that an uncontrollable input in one circumstance may be a controllable input in another, and vice versa. For example, available capacity may be limited today and hence uncontrollable. Yet, in time, a firm could build additional facilities and effectively make capacity a decision variable.

Result, decision, and environmental variables are tied together by sets of mathematical relationships. The expressions include a statement of the objective and possibly one or more restrictions or limitations. Management Situation 2.2 illustrates.

Management Situation 2.2

A Typing Service

Leslie Jackson is a college student who earns money typing letters and manuscripts in her spare time. She has a given amount of spare time available in a given period, and each page of a project utilizes a specified amount of that time. Leslie earns a given profit per page.

There is practically an unlimited demand for her work. Leslie wants to earn as much money as possible.

Objective Function. Since Leslie wants to earn as much money as possible, her objective is to maximize profit. Total earnings are determined by multiplying the profit per page times the number of pages. By letting

$$P = \text{total profit}$$

$$p = \text{profit per page}$$

$$Q = \text{quantity of pages}$$

Leslie's objective can be stated as follows:

(2.1)   maximize $P = pQ$

This type of mathematical expression, which describes the goal of the problem, is called an **objective function**.

Constraints. Total profit is restricted by Leslie's available time. The demand for her work will equal the time used per page multiplied by the quantity of pages. This demand must not exceed her available time. Letting

$$t = \text{the time utilized per page}$$

and $T = \text{Leslie's available time per period}$

the relationship can be described with the following mathematical expression:

(2.2) $tQ \leq T$

Figure 2.4   **Structure of Leslie's Model**

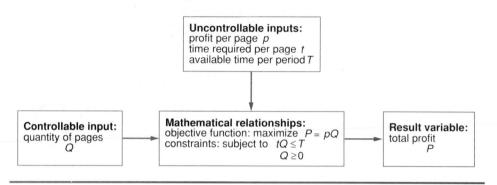

The symbol $\leq$ indicates that the total time required (tQ) must be less than or equal to the available time T. This type of expression is referred to as a **constraint**. Another restriction is that Leslie cannot type a negative number of pages. That is,

(2.3) $Q \geq 0$

which states that the quantity of pages must be greater than or equal to zero.

Complete Model. Leslie's problem is to determine the quantity of pages Q that will maximize her profit P per period from the typing service. Also, the recommended quantity must not require more than her available time. Expressions (2.1)–(2.3), or

$$\text{maximize } P = pQ$$

$$\text{subject to } tQ \leq T$$

$$Q \geq 0$$

provide a complete mathematical model for her problem.

In this model, the quantity of pages Q is Leslie Jackson's only controllable input. Profit p per unit, the time t required per page, and the available time T per period are all uncontrollable inputs. Cost of materials and equipment and the demand for typing might influence profit per page, but Leslie has little, if any, control over these factors. Similarly, academic and social activities are factors that make available time and time required per page uncontrollable. The only result variable or measure of performance is total profit P. Consequently, the structure of Leslie's mathematical model would appear as in Figure 2.4.

Variation. Depending on the information available, the values of the uncontrollable inputs may be exactly known or uncertain and subject to variation. For example, Leslie may know her exact schedule in the coming week and the precise form of the manuscripts to be typed. Based on this information, she may be able to forecast the values of p, t, and T with certainty. In this case, Leslie knows the exact values of the uncontrollable inputs, and her model is said to be **deterministic**. On the other hand, unforeseen examinations,

Figure 2.5   **CIS Process**

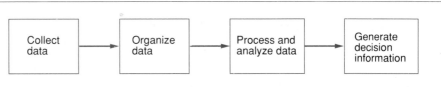

dates, and other activities may create uncertainty about her available time for typing in the coming month. Depending on the nature of these activities, T could be any one of several values in a given range. In this situation, the value of an uncontrollable input is uncertain and subject to variation, and Leslie's model is said to be **stochastic**. In fact, profit p and the time t required per page may also be uncertain. Then there may be several alternative stochastic models.

Gathering Relevant Quantitative Data

Models require data on the values of the uncontrollable inputs. Since we cannot perform a thorough analysis or recommend a solution without this information, data collection is a critical part of the management science process. Leslie Jackson, for example, must know the values of unit profit (p), typing time per page (t), and available time (T) before she can determine the most profitable quantity of work.

In Leslie's case, the necessary information might be available from her experience, records on past jobs, published social and academic schedules, and recorded commitments. Organizations could gather data from past accounting, sales, financial, inventory, production, and engineering records and reports. Published documents, such as research studies and government statistical summaries, are other sources. Managers and operating personnel can provide information about markets, financial conditions, productivity, and other factors that are unavailable elsewhere.

Computer Information Systems. Most organizations have a tremendous volume of data available, and considerable time is required to capture, store, and retrieve these facts. Since the facts are usually not in a form suitable for management purposes, additional effort is necessary to manipulate the data and to interpret and report the results. That is why formal systems, called **computer information systems (CIS)**, have been developed to transform data into relevant, timely, and usable information.

CIS Process. Figure 2.5 illustrates how a CIS generally makes the transformation. First, data are collected from available sources, sometimes manually (as when a clerk registers a grocery purchase) and other times in an automated fashion (as when an assembly-line sensor reads container weight). Next, the facts are arranged into files (such as purchase and production records) and a **data base**, or a collection of organized files. Facts from the data base are then processed and analyzed to generate information useful for decision-making purposes. Since such processing and analysis can take a variety of forms, specific CIS types have been developed to meet various managers' unique needs. Table 2.1 outlines the most popular.

Table 2.1   **Popular Computer Information Systems**

Type	Primary End Users	Key Characteristics	Example
Transaction Processing System (TPS)	First line supervisors Operations managers	Captures and stores detailed transactions, organizes data, and retrieves desired information	Airline reservations Automated bank tellers
Management Information System (MIS)	Control staff Middle managers	Uses statistical methods to analyze transactions and then generates status reports and forecasts	EDP auditing
		Uses MS/OR models to solve very structured management problems	Inventory control
Office Automated System (OAS)	Office staff Middle and top managers	Captures, stores, edits, and retrieves documents	Library microfilm
		Facilitates oral and written communication	Electronic and voice mail
Decision Support System (DSS)	Middle and top managers	Captures, stores, edits, and retrieves focused information and documents	Executive information system
		Utilizes user judgments and insights to formulate and structure problems	Expert system
		Uses statistical, economic, and accounting models to analyze summaries and produce focused status reports and forecasts	Corporate planning
		Uses ad hoc MS/OR models to evaluate decision alternatives and generate recommended strategies	War games

2.2 ANALYSIS AND SOLUTION

As Table 2.1 demonstrates, some computer information systems (such as TPS and OAS) primarily organize and summarize data for interested managers. Such summaries can provide the quantitative, and even qualitative, information needed by the manager for decision making. However, additional computer information systems (such as MIS and DSS) are required to help managers analyze the summaries and solve the corresponding decision problems.

Processing Inquiries

Management frequently must determine the effects of various conditions and decisions on business activities. Here are some typical questions that may be asked:

1. What will be the effect on profits if product prices are changed?
2. How will the production rate be affected by a wage increase?
3. What will be the effect on the corporate debt structure if there is an increase in interest rates?
4. How will the inflation rate affect the state budget?
5. What will be the effect on regional employment patterns if the eastern warehouse is closed?

Table 2.1 suggests that a **management information system (MIS)** is one CIS designed to help managers perform these types of "what if" analyses.

Figure 2.6   **Management Information Systems (MIS)**

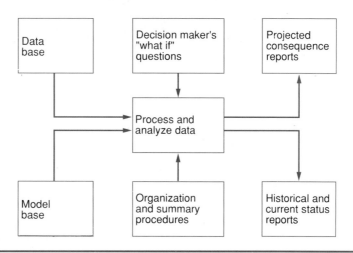

Figure 2.6 illustrates how a typical MIS works. The system has a data base, an organized collection of mathematical expressions known as a **model base**, and usually some appropriate computer hardware and software. Managers use the hardware/software to access the data base and generate status reports similar to, but more focused than, the summaries from a transaction-processing system. When the problem is well defined and well structured, an MIS can also take the decision maker's "what if" questions, perform the necessary analyses, and create reports summarizing the projected results.

To answer the "what if" questions, the MIS model base must contain data analysis procedures. The most common are statistical methods that forecast important uncontrollable inputs (such as interest rates and inflation). In addition, the model base should include mathematical expressions that project the effects of forecasted conditions and specified decisions on relevant measures of performance (such as the corporate debt structure and the state budget). Such a model base provides the crucial ingredient that enables the MIS to progress from a simple report-generating device to an evaluative tool.

Powerful microcomputers and accompanying spreadsheet software (such as **Lotus 1-2-3, VP-Planner**, and **SuperCalc**) have enabled even nontechnical managers in small enterprises to use this MIS concept. Management Situation 2.3 provides an illustration.

Management Situation 2.3

A Small-Scale MIS

Leslie Jackson has the same problem presented in Management Situation 2.2. She wants to determine the quantity of pages Q that will

$$\text{maximize} \quad P = pQ$$
$$\text{subject to} \quad tQ \leq T$$
$$Q \geq 0$$

Leslie knows her schedule and the type of manuscripts she will be typing on her microcomputer during the coming week. Using a spreadsheet computer package, she has developed a database of all past and current typing jobs and a formula to make simple forecasts. Based on her spreadsheet analyses, Leslie estimates that the manuscripts will require exactly 6 minutes (0.1 hour) per page. Leslie also predicts that she will have exactly 20 hours of spare time available in the coming week. Her estimated earnings are 80 cents per page.

Quantitative Model. Leslie has used a simple forecasting routine to generate exact values for the uncontrollable inputs (p, t, and T) from her work file (data base). In this case, $p = \$0.80$, $t = 0.1$ hour, and $T = 20$ hours. Hence, Leslie's problem can be expressed as follows:

$$\text{maximize } P = \$0.80Q$$

$$\text{subject to } 0.1Q \leq 20 \text{ hours}$$

$$Q \geq 0$$

Since all values of the uncontrollable inputs are exactly known, this model is deterministic.

"What If" Analyses. At this stage, Leslie can use the mathematical model to evaluate the effects of various trial quantities on the resource constraint ($0.1Q \leq 20$ hours) and total profit ($P = \$0.80Q$). For instance, what if she typed $Q = 100$ pages during the coming week? Since each page requires $t = 0.1$ hour, this quantity would use

$$t \times Q = 0.1(100) = 10 \text{ hours}$$

which is within her time constraint ($T = 20$ hours). Such a policy would also yield a projected profit of

$$P = p \times Q = \$0.80(100) = \$80$$

Leslie can use this simple MIS in a similar manner to evaluate other potential strategies. Table 2.2 presents a possible projected-consequences report for this system.

In addition, Leslie might want to see how changes in the uncontrollable inputs will affect time utilization and profits. By inputting trial changes for p, t, and T into her MIS, she can obtain revised time utilization and total profit information. In this way, Leslie can evaluate the consequences of future conditions and test prospective strategies before making a final decision.

Solving the Quantitative Model

After formulating the model and collecting, processing, and analyzing the data, the manager is ready to develop a solution to the decision problem. A solution is an output of the model, projecting what would happen if particular values of the controllable and uncontrollable inputs occurred in the real situation.

Table 2.2 **Summary Report from Leslie Jackson's MIS**

Quantity of Pages (Q)	Projected Profit (P = $0.80Q)	Total Time Required (T = 0.1Q)	Is Total Time Required ≤ Available Time? (0.1Q ≤ 20 hours)
0	0	0	Yes
50	40	5	Yes
100	80	10	Yes
150	120	15	Yes
200	160	20	Yes
250	200	25	No
300	240	30	No

Trial and error is one method of obtaining a solution. In this approach, the model is used to test and evaluate alternative values for the controllable inputs. The actual analysis, in practice, may be performed by an MIS. Leslie Jackson used such a system to evaluate the impact of selected trial quantities on her resource constraints ($0.1Q \leq 20$ hours, $Q \geq 0$) and total profit ($P = \$0.80Q$). From the projected results in Table 2.2, you can see that the trial quantity of $Q = 300$ pages leads to the largest profit $P = \$240$. Unfortunately, the 30 hours required to type this quantity is more than Leslie's available time (20 hours) for the week. Hence, this solution is not feasible. Among the feasible alternatives, $Q = 200$ pages is the quantity leading to the largest profit $P = \$160$. According to this trial and error, then, Leslie should type 200 pages during the coming week.

Since Leslie has not tested all possible quantities, however, this trial and error recommendation may not represent the problem's best solution. In fact, trial and error seldom guarantees an optimal solution, and the approach is also cumbersome and time-consuming, especially for large-scale problems. For these and other reasons, experts have developed special methodologies to solve various classes of problems. According to a recent survey, the most popular of these among large U.S. corporations are shown in Table 2.3.

This text includes an introductory coverage of all methodologies listed in Table 2.3. There is an emphasis on frequently used approaches such as computer simulation, linear programming, and PERT/CPM. In addition, the text presents the popular statistical approaches of decision analysis, forecasting, and (in an appendix) probability.

There is also a discussion about some important extensions to the basic MS/OR methodologies. Utility and game theory, for example, are tools for decision making under special types of risky circumstances. Goal programming deals with mathematical (primarily linear and integer) programming problems that involve multiple, and some-times conflicting, objectives. Transportation, assignment, routing, and PERT/CPM are all different forms of network flow problems. Markov analysis is another variety of sequential decision making. In fact, many organizations use these extensions but report them in surveys under more general titles (such as statistics and linear programming).

Some methodologies, such as linear programming and inventory theory, provide an optimal solution. Other approaches, such as simulation, use systematic search procedures

---

Table 2.3   **Popular Quantitative Management Methodologies**

Methodology	Uncontrollable Inputs	Typical Application	Firms Using (%)
Statistics*	Stochastic	Forecasting, risky decisions, and experimentation	98
Simulation	Deterministic and stochastic	Studying ill-structured, complex problems	87
Linear programming	Deterministic	Allocating scarce resources	74
PERT/CPM	Deterministic and stochastic	Planning, scheduling, and controlling projects	74
Queuing theory	Stochastic	Analyzing service systems	60
Inventory theory	Deterministic and stochastic	Maintaining and controlling inventories	52
Nonlinear programming	Deterministic	Interdependent activities	47
Dynamic programming	Deterministic and stochastic	Sequential decisions	38
Game theory	Stochastic	Conflict situations	30

---

*Statistics includes Bayesian decision analysis, forecasting, and probability.
Source: Guisseppi A. Forgionne, "Corporate Management Science Activities: An Update," *Interfaces* (June 1983): 20–23.

that identify good, or approximate, answers. Still other methodologies, such as queuing theory and Markov analysis, merely describe and predict the behavior of the relevant system.

Decision Support Systems

Many of the popular management science techniques will generate a recommended decision. Furthermore, there are computer packages available that will provide a recommendation from data inputted by the decision maker. A few organizations have even incorporated such packages into their management information systems. In such cases, the MIS has the capability of ultimately translating "what if" questions into automated decisions. Often these automated decisions are outputted from the MIS as part of a status or projected consequence report.

On the other hand, many problems are too poorly structured and too complex to be solved completely with a straightforward application of any single methodology. Filling the U.S. Army occupational specialty ranks is one such problem. Corporate planning is another.

In the corporate planning situation, the decision maker must establish overall company objectives and develop corresponding policies that will affect marketing, production, and financial operations in complex, dynamic, and uncertain ways. To adequately address the problem, the planner will need at least some technology of management (such as MS/OR and statistical methodologies and economic/accounting constructs). Table 2.1 suggests that this technology can be delivered effectively to the decision maker with the CIS known as a **decision support system (DSS)**.

Figure 2.7 illustrates how a typical DSS, such as the U.S. Army's MOSLS, works. As in any CIS, a variety of inputs are processed with available technology to generate a range of outputs.

Figure 2.7   **Decision Support System (DSS)**

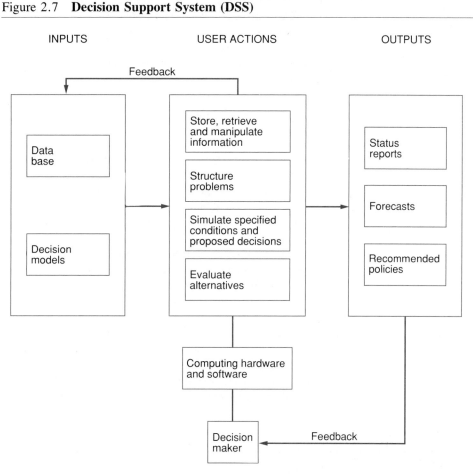

Inputs. On the input side, the DSS must incorporate a fairly sophisticated decision model base and a data base. The model base can include standard MS/OR and statistical methodologies (such as linear programming and decision analysis), accounting/economics constructs (such as cost and production functions), and specific models developed by users for specialized purposes (such as facilities location or plant layout). Many believe that expert and other knowledge-based systems also should be integral components of the model base. To perform DSS-type processing, users will require summarized information that is focused on specific management analyses and evaluations. Consequently, users must develop the data base, often from other CIS (such as OAS and MIS) outputs, for their unique processing needs.

User Actions. The decision maker is the focal point and primary user of the system. He or she uses the DSS to (1) store, retrieve, and manipulate information, (2) structure problems, (3) simulate proposed decisions under specified conditions, and (4) evaluate alternatives. This processing can be accomplished with an existing computer package (such as the **Quantitative Management** software), a modeling language (such as IFPS), or an expert system shell (such as **Personal Consultant**). The packages, languages, or shells can be run on a microcomputer by an individual (such as an Army officer) or on a network of micro, mini, and mainframe computers by a group (such as a corporate planning team). Feedback from user actions can provide additional data base entries (such as estimated Army personnel requirements) and enhanced decision models (such as an updated corporate planning model).

Outputs. The DSS processing generates focused status reports (such as the cash flow and production cost under current corporate policies), forecasts (such as the Army's projected personnel requirements), and recommended decision strategies (such as Army training advice). Such outputs typically are provided quickly in neatly arranged executive reports with accompanying tables and graphs. Feedback from the outputs can then be used to modify or extend the original analysis and evaluation.

Decision-Making Support. A DSS does not predefine the problem, impose solutions, or otherwise automate the decision-making process. Instead, the system delivers specialized tools that support (not replace) the manager's process of exploring and structuring decision situations, evaluating and interpreting solutions, and implementing recommendations. As the Army discovered with MOSLS, an effective DSS can expand the manager's capability for dealing with problems and significantly improve outcomes from the decision-making process. Also, DSS development and operation fosters collaboration between the manager, MS/OR analyst, and information scientist. Such collaboration facilitates the implementation of results, and it takes us one step closer to a true systems approach in management.

2.3 IMPLEMENTATION

The quantitative analysis process is not complete until the model's solution information is reported to the decision maker and the results are implemented. Such data constitute only one of the inputs considered by the manager when a final decision is being made. Therefore, it is essential to present the quantitative information in a managerial report that will be easily understood by the decision maker. The report should include the recommended decision and a concise summary of other pertinent information about the model results that may be helpful to the decision maker. Relevant information might include the model's assumptions, alternative solutions, and qualitative considerations.

The process does not end, however, with the delivery of the running model and report to management. Even the most carefully developed and tested model may not work as planned. Management scientists must get feedback from the decision maker regarding the validity of the model and, if necessary, make appropriate adjustments or modifications. Moreover, there may be other problems in implementing management science concepts within the organizational framework.

Table 2.4   **Barriers to MS/OR Implementations**

Problem	Percentage of Respondents*
1. Lack of adequate data	61
2. Poor communication between MS/OR analyst and management	58
3. Shortage of resources	54
4. Lengthy completion time required for MS/OR projects	37

*Since several respondents had more than one barrier, the total percentage is greater than 100.
Source: Guisseppi A. Forgionne, "Corporate Management Science Activities: An Update," *Interfaces* (June 1983): 20–23.

Barriers to Implementation

According to a recent study, the most serious implementation barriers are those shown in Table 2.4. Some involve particular aspects of the project, such as the time needed for analysis (item 4). Other barriers deal with the implementation climate. For example, there are organizational problems, such as the lack of adequate data (item 1) and the shortage of resources (item 3). There are also behavioral factors, including the communication difficulties between managers and MS/OR analysts (item 2).

Implementation Strategies

Several steps have been suggested for alleviating various problems and promoting more successful implementation. Perhaps the most important action is to obtain management participation in, and support of, the entire quantitative analysis process. Management science projects often affect a variety of departments, groups, and individuals within the enterprise. Top management specifies organizational objectives and constraints, translates them into policies and guidelines, and communicates the information to appropriate personnel. Thus, these managers are in the best position to assess potential program contributions, guide project formulation, provide relevant input, evaluate results, and encourage organizational support. Similarly, middle management has a firsthand comprehensive understanding of operations and the corresponding limitations and constraints. Such input is necessary to any management science project. Moreover, operating management's support may be transmitted to the people directly affected by the proposed changes.

Another important step is to improve communication and cooperation between management scientists and managers. Through education, training, and dialogue with executives, management scientists can gain a better understanding of managers' information needs, schedule needs, and cost constraints. To further facilitate mutual understanding, the initial stages of quantitative projects should begin with small, tentative formulations and be characterized by end user involvement. Later, when the need is clearly justified, the initial statement can evolve into a more comprehensive formulation. At the same time, executive development programs and intensive project involvement will give managers a better understanding of the resource requirements in quantitative analysis.

Advances in the technology of management and in decision support systems also will enhance implementation by providing better data for quantitative decision making, encouraging management participation in the process, and providing relevant results in a timely and cost-effective manner.

SUMMARY

In this chapter we examined decision making and the role of management science in this process. We saw how management scientists provide quantitative information to help the manager reach a final decision.

The first step in the process is to define the managerial problem clearly and concisely. Next, we represent the essential features of the situation with a model. Several types of models were discussed, including physical replicas, analogs, and mathematical representations.

Models require information; therefore, data collection, processing, and analysis are a critical part of the management science process. A computer information system (CIS) can aid this process by providing accurate, relevant, and timely information to decision makers. Several computer information systems were presented, including the MIS.

After formulating a model and collecting and analyzing data, the manager is ready to develop a solution to the problem. Trial and error is one method of obtaining a solution. However, it is too cumbersome and time-consuming for most realistic management problems. For these and other reasons, management scientists have developed special solution techniques for various classes of problems. Table 2.3 summarized the popular approaches.

We also saw how decision support systems integrate CIS and management science concepts. Using a DSS, management is able to store, retrieve, display, and manipulate data; select and build models; and evaluate recommendations. In effect, these systems deliver the technology to support the process of exploring and structuring decision situations, evaluating and interpreting alternative solutions, and implementing recommendations in real time.

Implementation is the final step in the management science process. It begins with the delivery of a formal report and running model to the decision maker. In addition, management scientists must get feedback from the decision maker regarding the validity of the model and, if necessary, make appropriate adjustments and modifications. Even then, there may be barriers to implementing management science concepts within the organizational framework. The most significant barriers were summarized in Table 2.4.

Several steps were suggested for alleviating problems and promoting more successful implementation. Perhaps the most important action is to obtain management participation in, and support of, the entire quantitative analysis process. Another useful step is to improve communication and cooperation between management scientists and managers. Advances in DSS are also expected to enhance implementation by providing better data and directly involving management in the quantitative analysis process.

In spite of the implementation barriers, management science is readily accepted by executives in public and private enterprises because the methodology can significantly improve their ability to make effective decisions. In subsequent chapters we will show you how to use this methodology. We will consider managerial problems, examine the appropriate quantitative approaches, and develop recommended solutions. The objective is not to train you for work as a management scientist, but to show how you can become a more effective decision maker by using quantitative analysis to augment your other managerial skills.

Glossary

analog model Physical object or picture that represents a concept such as time, speed, temperature, or thought processes. Such models include clocks, speedometers, thermometers, and flow charts.

computer information system (CIS) A formal system for processing, analyzing, and reporting data.

constraint An enforced limitation, such as $tQ < T$.

controllable inputs or decision variables Factors that influence a model's outcome and are controlled by the decision maker, such as level of output and timing of investment.

data base An electronic collection of organized files of data.

decision support system (DSS) A CIS that translates "what if" questions into automated decision using MS/OR and statistical methodologies and economic/accounting constructs. One example is the U.S. Army's MOSLS.

deterministic model A model in which the exact values of the uncontrollable inputs are known.

iconic model A physical replica, such as scale model trains, aircraft simulators, and photographs.

management information system (MIS) A CIS used for performing "what if" analyses and making predictions.

mathematical model Representation of a complex situation using symbols and mathematical expressions.

model A simplified representation of a real object or situation.

model base An organized collection of mathematical expressions used in an MIS.

objective function A mathematical function that describes the problem goal, such as maximize $P = pQ$.

result variables Measures used to evaluate the performance or effectiveness of a system, including profit, rate of return, cost, market share, and customer satisfaction.

stochastic model A model in which the value of an uncontrollable input is uncertain and subject to change.

uncontrollable inputs or environmental variables Factors that must be considered in a model but that are beyond the decision maker's control, such as interest rates, building codes, and tax regulations.

Thought Exercises

1. Use Figure 2.1 to outline your decision-making process for the following personal decisions:
   a. Choice of life-style
   b. Choice of an automobile
   c. Selection of a brand of toothpaste
   d. Selection of a holiday vacation
   e. Choice of movie

2. Explain how quantitative analysis can help you to make each of the personal decisions listed in Thought Exercise 1.

3. Illustrate the potential value of management science to each of the following decision makers:
   a. A hospital administrator
   b. The production manager of a large petroleum company

    c. The marketing director of a medium-sized grocery chain

    d. The vice president in charge of loans for a small credit union

    e. Your present or potential position

4. Explain how a computer information system can benefit each of the following decision makers:

    a. A marketing manager who needs a sales history in selected territories for each of the firm's products

    b. A government analyst who needs a forecast for selected components of the economy's gross national product

    c. A financial executive who wants a forecast of interest rates in the next quarter

    d. A production manager who wants to determine which of several specified output levels results in least cost

5. Refer to Figure 2.6. Suppose the MIS was made interactive with the decision maker using projected consequence feedback to refine "what if" questions. Illustrate how you would modify Figure 2.6 to account for this interaction.

6. Observe how customers are served at a checkout facility (for example, a grocery store checkout register, a theater box office, or a restaurant checkout stand). Develop iconic, analog, and mathematical models of the process. Explain how your models would be affected by rush hour traffic.

7. Explain how a decision support system could benefit each of the following managers:

    a. A U.S. president's evaluation of alternative economic policies

    b. A military commander's evaluation of alternative retirement programs

    c. An executive's evaluation of alternative management compensation plans

    d. A public utility commissioner's evaluation of a telephone company's request for a rate increase

8. Do you agree or disagree with the following statements? Explain.

    a. There is no need for managers to study quantitative decision making; if they need that type of information, they can have a quantitative specialist perform the analysis.

    b. Quantitative specialists are the true agents of change in modern organizations.

    c. The best practice for an aspiring quantitative analyst is to search for decision problems that fit available tools and techniques.

    d. Quantitative models are invalid because they do not incorporate all the factors in a decision problem.

    e. Decision makers can eliminate their responsibility to make decisions by employing quantitative models.

    f. Since we cannot unconditionally determine the optimal solution to a stochastic model, this formulation is more difficult to solve than a deterministic representation.

Technique Exercises

9. A company uses the following equation to forecast sales for a particular product:

$$Q = 20,000 - 300P + 5A + 2Y$$

where Q = annual number of units sold, P = price (in dollars), A = advertising expenditures, and Y = average household income. Suppose the price is \$120, advertising expenditures are \$50,000, and household income averages \$20,000 this year. What is the sales forecast?

10. The marketing analyst for a company has determined that revenue for their product is given by the following mathematical expression:

$$R = 30,000P - 60P^2$$

where R = total revenue (in dollars) and P = price (in dollars).
   a. If the price is \$20, what will be the corresponding revenue?
   b. Use trial and error to find the price that maximizes revenue. Restrict the search to prices between \$200 and \$300. Also, search only in increments of \$10 (\$200, \$210, \$220, and so on).

11. A government economist has developed the following simple model to forecast national income:

$$Y_t = C_t + I_t + G_t$$

$$C_t = 0.4Y_{t-1} + 100$$

$$I_t = 2(Y_{t-1} - C_{t-1} - G_{t-1})$$

$$G_t = 0.3(C_t + I_t)$$

where Y = national income (in billions of dollars), C = consumption (in billions of dollars), I = investment (in billions of dollars), G = government expenditures (in billions of dollars), t = current time period, and $t-1$ = immediately preceding period. Suppose preceding income was \$600 billion. Of this amount, \$300 billion was consumption and \$200 billion was government expenditures. What will be the forecast for national income this year?

12. Consider the following mathematical model of production:

$$\text{maximize } Q = 20L$$

$$\text{subject to } L \leq 400 \text{ hours}$$

$$L \geq 0$$

where Q = total output in a given time period and L = total number of labor hours employed in a given time period.
   a. What is the objective? What are the controllable and uncontrollable inputs?
   b. What is the maximum output?
   c. Suppose each hour of labor generates only 10 units of output; what is the maximum output? What is the maximum output if each labor hour generates 30 units of output?
   d. Assume there are 200 labor hours available; what is the maximum output? What is the maximum output if there are 500 available labor hours?

13. Refer to Management Situations 2.2 and 2.3. Leslie Jackson wanted to determine the quantity of pages Q that would

$$\text{maximize } P = \$0.80Q$$

$$\text{subject to } 0.1Q \leq 20 \text{ hours}$$

$$Q \geq 0$$

Trial and error indicated that the optimal solution was to type $Q = 200$ pages per week for a maximum profit of $P = \$160$. Use mathematics to determine the optimal solution. (*Hint:* Start with the available time constraint expression.) Does your answer agree or disagree with the trial and error solution? Explain.

14. Table 2.3 lists popular management science techniques. Make a list of the computer packages available at your institution that deal with these techniques.

15. Use the management science/operations research journals (for example, *Management Science, Operations Research, Decision Sciences,* and *Interfaces*) to compile a list of the most recent applications of decision support systems.

16. Again refer to Management Situations 2.2 and 2.3. Suppose Leslie Jackson is now typing manuscripts that require nine minutes per page and that earn $1.20 per page. However, Leslie is uncertain about how much spare time she will have available in the coming month. Depending on her academic and social activities, it could be 60, 90, or 120 hours.
    a. Formulate the appropriate model for this situation. How does it differ from the model given in Management Situations 2.2 and 2.3? Explain.
    b. Determine the optimal solution for the new problem.
    c. Suppose Leslie could hire an assistant. How would this affect the new situation? Explain.

17. Ace Products, Inc., originally had the following problem:

$$\text{maximize } \pi = \$0.60Q$$

$$\text{subject to } Q \leq 2,000 \text{ hours of productive capacity per month}$$

$$Q \geq 0$$

where $Q =$ number of jars of Ace Cream sold per month and $\pi =$ total dollar profit. Now the company adds another product, Ace Lotion, which sells for 20 cents a bottle. Lotion requires two hours of productive capacity. Capacity has recently been expanded to 10,000 hours per month. All other conditions remain the same.
    a. Assuming that the objective is still to maximize profit, formulate Ace's new problem. Let B represent the number of bottles of Ace Lotion.
    b. What are the controllable and uncontrollable inputs?
    c. How many bottles of lotion and how many jars of cream should Ace produce to maximize total monthly profit?
    d. Solve Ace's original problem. Interpret the difference between the solution to Ace's original problem and the solution to Ace's new problem.

Applications Exercises

18. A commuter is concerned about the energy crisis and wishes to minimize his monthly fuel purchases. He knows that the cost of fuel will depend on the number of miles that he drives. He also knows that he drives at least a given number of miles per month to and from work. Other known facts are the cost per gallon of fuel and his car's number of miles per gallon.

    a. Develop a mathematical model for the commuter's problem using the symbols Q for number of miles, C for total cost, c for cost per gallon of fuel, M for minimum total monthly miles, and m for miles per gallon.

    b. What is the objective? What are the controllable and uncontrollable inputs?

    c. Use your own experience to gather data on the uncontrollable inputs. Is your model deterministic or stochastic? Explain.

    d. Assume that you are the commuter. Use the data you gathered and the model you developed to determine the minimum monthly fuel cost.

19. A small newsstand orders a specific number of Sunday newspapers from a distributing agent. It costs $1 to place an order. The exact number of orders depends on demand, which has been steady at 10 purchases per Sunday. In addition, each newspaper costs the newsstand 10 cents for display and other inventory expenses. The newsstand wants to order the number of Sunday papers that will minimize the total cost of ordering plus display.

    a. Formulate a mathematical model of the newsstand's problem. Use Q to represent the quantity of Sunday newspapers ordered.

    b. Enumerate the costs associated with quantities ranging from 0 to 12.

    c. Which quantity results in minimum total cost? What are the ordering and display costs at this quantity?

20. A local automobile dealership wants to attract more customers to its showroom. Ads are placed in local newspapers and on local radio broadcasts. A radio spot costs a given amount C_r, and is expected to generate a given amount a_r of new shoppers, while a newspaper ad costs C_n and is expected to generate a_n new shoppers. The dealership wants to spend no more than D dollars for a given time period, and it wants to obtain a maximum of A new shoppers.

    a. Formulate a mathematical model of this decision problem, specifying the objective and the controllable and uncontrollable inputs.

    b. Gather data on the uncontrollable inputs from a local automobile dealership and from local newspapers and radio stations. Is your model stochastic or deterministic?

    c. Determine the dealership's maximum number of new shoppers for a given month.

21. Bright University publishes texts written by its faculty for use in courses offered on campus. These texts are sold to the students through the university bookstore. Jonathan Smart has just completed a text for his introductory accounting course. The university is trying to decide whether or not to publish and sell the text. Publishing the text will involve production and marketing costs. These costs can be recovered only if there are sufficient book sales. The relevant financial data are as follows:

Fixed costs	
Printing setup	$1,000
Shelf display and promotion material	500
Total	$1,500
Variable costs	
Material per book	$ 5
Labor per book	5
Total	$10
Selling price per book	$15

a. Formulate a profit model for this problem.

b. What sales volume will the university need to break even (earn zero profit)?

c. How many books must be sold to earn a 20 percent return on fixed costs?

d. Suppose approximately 400 students take the course each year. Should the university publish the text? Explain.

For Further Reading

Quantitative Formulation

Kroeber, D. W., and H. J. Watson. *Computer-Based Information Systems*. Second Ed., New York: Macmillan, 1987.

McAulay, K. "The Changing Role of Management in Information Systems Development." *Interfaces* (May–June 1987):47.

Rivett, P. *Model Building for Decision Analysis*. New York: Wiley, 1980.

Analysis and Solution

Carlsson, C. "Decision Support Systems—Dawn or Twilight for Management Science?" *Human Systems Management* 5(1985):29.

DeSanctis, G., and R. B. Gallupe. "A Foundation for the Study of Group Decision Support Systems." *Management Science* (May 1987):589.

Forgionne, G. A. "Building Effective Decision Support Systems." *Business* (January 1988):19.

Forgionne, G. A. "Corporate Management Science Activities: An Update." *Interfaces* (June 1983):20.

Forgionne, G. A. "Organizing for the Effective Delivery of Management Technology." *Information Processing & Management* 24(1988):57.

Henderson, J. C. "Finding Synergy Between Decision Support Systems and Expert Systems Research." *Decision Sciences* (Summer 1987):333.

Ntuen, C. A. "The Seven R Paradigms: What Managers Should Know About Decision Support Systems." *Information Management* (January–February 1986):19.

Simon, H. A. "Two Heads Are Better than One: The Collaboration between AI and OR." *Interfaces* (July–August 1987):8.

Sprague, R. H., and H. J. Watson, eds. *Decision Support Systems: Putting Theory into Practice*. Englewood Cliffs, NJ: Prentice-Hall, 1986.

Vedder, R., and C. H. Nestman. "Understanding Expert Systems: Companion to DSS and MIS." *Industrial Management* (March–April 1985):1.

Implementation

Doktor, R., R. L. Schultz, and D. P. Slevin, eds. *The Implementation of Management Science*. Providence, RI: TIMS Studies in the Management Sciences, 1979.

Ginzberg, J. J., and R. L. Schultz. "The Practical Side of Implementation Research." *Interfaces* (May–June 1987):1.

Lockett, A. G., and E. Polding. "OR/MS Implementation—A Variety of Processes." *Interfaces* (November 1978):45.

Schultz, R. L., and M. J. Ginzberg, eds. *Management Science Implementation*. Greenwich, CT: JAI Press, 1984.

Case: Jane Allen's Career Choice

Jane Allen has recently graduated from college cum laude with a major in accounting. She is trying to plan a career. There are many choices available. She could become an accountant, but is undecided about the specific field or type of employer. Jane also enjoys the academic atmosphere, so she is considering graduate study and a subsequent career in university teaching. Also, Jane and her boyfriend have talked about marriage. Her boyfriend has a good job, and Jane would have the option of being primarily a housewife and mother. She is attracted to a family environment. In addition, several companies have offered her positions in sales and office management.

Jane has some quantitative facts: graduate aptitude test scores, graduate study expenses, available fellowships and other financial aid, her boyfriend's estimates of his salary and potential earning power, published general salaries in various positions, and general living costs in different geographical areas. Friends, family, professors, and other personal advisors have also provided qualitative information: job duties and responsibilities for different career choices, opinions on her aptitude for various positions, opinions about life-styles, and opinions about the degree of personal satisfaction she can expect in various career choices.

Jane's career goals are to achieve personal happiness and financial security. She defines financial security as a positive net financial worth for the career: earnings plus fringe benefits less employment and living costs for the life of the career. One career has greater financial security than another if it has a higher net financial worth. Jane admits that it is difficult to devise an objective measure of personal happiness. However, she believes that it is possible to use the available qualitative information to subjectively evaluate each identified career choice.

1. What is Jane's problem? What are her alternative courses of action? What are her criteria of evaluation?

2. If you were Jane, how would you outline your decision-making process for this problem?

3. Construct a tabular net financial worth model for each identified alternative.

4. Gather relevant data for your quantitative model and evaluate each alternative's net financial worth.

5. Gather relevant qualitative information on your personal happiness in each career. Use the information to subjectively rank the alternatives.

6. On the basis of your analysis, what career would you advise Jane to choose?

Forecasting

Chapter Outline

Learning Objectives

- Identify the decision maker's forecasting needs and the methodologies available to meet these needs
- Identify patterns in data expressed over time
- Use those patterns to develop a forecast by hand and with the aid of a computer
- Determine the accuracy of a forecast
- Structure the relationships among variables
- Utilize those relationships to develop a forecast by hand and with the aid of a computer
- Interpret the forecasts and use the results for decision making

Quantitative Analysis in Action
Housing the Turks

O VER the last three decades, rapid industrialization promoted a high growth rate in Turkey's population. Unfortunately, there was no parallel development in power, water, transportation, and sanitation facilities. The public facility deficiency led to a decrease in housing investment. By 1983, there was a serious housing shortage in the country.

Social concern, and economic problems resulting from the shortage caused the government to act. The Istanbul Chamber of Industry (ICI) was commissioned to diagnose the reasons for the shortage and suggest remedial actions. Many experts also were recruited for the study.

By using forecasting methodologies, the study group was able to identify the major causes of the housing crisis and to project the impact of proposed remedial policies on the Turkish economy. Specifically, the group estimated how the policies would affect housing supply and demand, interindustry trade, production, inflation, and unemployment. The group's final report, which was sent to interested parties before the beginning of the 1983 legislative year, contained a number of specific recommendations for alleviating the housing problem.

After the November 1983 elections, Turkish housing laws and regulations were altered to accommodate many of the study group's recommendations. As a result, the rate of growth in housing permits increased dramatically, from 8.5 percent in 1983 to 41.8 percent in 1986. Moreover, most housing experts agree that the Turkish housing problem was directed toward a solution.

Source: I. Kavrakoglu et al., "A Systems Approach for the Turkish Housing Problem," *Interfaces* (September–October 1987): 1–10.

Successful decision making often will be based on management's ability to generate accurate predictions for key inputs. Managers using a systematic methodology to generate these predictions are said to be **forecasting**, and the resulting estimates are known as **forecasts**.

As the Turkish situation demonstrates, forecasting can involve substantial benefits. The Istanbul Chamber of Industry (ICI) used forecasting to identify the major causes of Turkey's housing crisis and to project the impact of proposed remedial policies on the economy. This analysis led to laws and regulations that dramatically alleviated the Turkish housing problem.

Other public and private enterprises can obtain similar benefits. An airline can use route demand forecasts to plan a profitable flight schedule. State government can utilize maintenance expense estimates to design a cost-efficient highway construction program. Retailers can use purchase pattern estimates to help establish employee and stock requirements.

This chapter presents popular forecasting methodologies. It begins with a discussion about the forecasting process. Next, the chapter presents some methodologies that have been designed to develop a prediction from the historical data pattern. Then the chapter outlines approaches frequently used to explain, rather than merely identify and extrapolate, the observed pattern.

Applications.   In this chapter, the following applications appear in text, examples, or exercises:

- automobile manufacturing
- corporate investment
- department store sales
- federal litigation
- government planning
- housing construction

- investment banking
- national park tourism
- gas utility operations
- prepaid health care
- taxi service
- toys and hobbies

3.1 FORECASTING PROCESS

During planning, management must establish the organization's objectives, identify alternative ways to meet the aims, and develop an appropriate framework for analyzing the alternatives. To perform the analysis properly, management will need accurate forecasts for key decision inputs. Figure 3.1 shows the steps needed to generate these forecasts.

Basic Steps

As Figure 3.1 indicates, the forecasting process involves eight separate, but essential and related, steps. These steps offer a systematic way to initiate, design, and implement an effective forecasting system.

Forecast Objectives. The first step is to determine the objectives of the forecast. These objectives typically reflect specific management needs within a specified organization. For example, federal officials within the Office of Management and Budget (OMB) may require accurate cost projections to develop a fiscal year budget. In this case, the OMB's forecast objective is to estimate the government's expenses.

Similarly, food companies such as General Mills and Kellogg often must formulate marketing strategies for their cereal brands. To perform this task properly, a brand manager might need an assessment of the industry's pricing practices, especially those of major competitors. Under these circumstances, the forecast objective could be to estimate the competitors' average price.

Forecast Items. Usually, there will be numerous inputs that could be relevant to meeting the forecast objective. For example, each government agency generates a variety of

Figure 3.1   **Basic Forecasting Process**

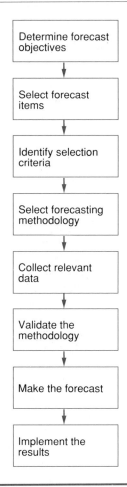

expenses that are candidates for an OMB cost projection. Comparably, cereals are sold by various food companies.

The next step is to select, from among the many potential inputs, the specific items that will be forecasted. For example, federal agencies generally aggregate expenses into major program expenditures. To estimate budget costs, OMB officials must forecast these major expenditures.

In the cereal industry, there are only a few major competitors. Consequently, the food companies' pricing analyses usually concentrate on the practices of these majors. To estimate the industry average, the brand manager must forecast the prices charged by the major competitors.

Criteria and Methodology. At this stage, the manager must select a methodology, or approach, that will be used to develop the required forecasts. Typically, there will be many forecasting methodologies available. As in any decision problem, the manager should identify relevant criteria, use the measures to evaluate the alternatives, and select the best forecasting methodology.

The selection will depend on the circumstances. For example, the federal government maintains a long history of numerical data on major program expenditures, and the OMB wants to project costs for the fiscal year budget accurately and in a timely manner. Data requirements, forecast accuracy, and preparation time are important selection criteria. As a result, OMB officials will seek a methodology that best utilizes the data history to generate an accurate one-year cost forecast.

The cereal illustration involves different circumstances. Here, competitors will react to each other's practices, and pricing will influence every company's industry position. In this situation, explanatory ability and economics are important selection criteria. The brand manager will seek a forecasting methodology that predicts competitors' prices and explains their relationship to industry and organization performance.

Data Collection. The next step in the process is to collect the data needed to implement the selected forecasting methodology. In some cases, the data may be obtained partially or totally from within the organization. For example, the OMB can get the program expenditure data needed to make its cost projections from the affected government agencies (such as the departments of Defense, Health and Human Services, and Commerce).

Other data is obtained from outside the organization through surveys, observations, and field tests. For example, each food company can observe cereal prices in representative test markets over a specified time. Brand managers can then supplement this data by surveying industry executives for company price intentions.

Validation. Inaccurate forecasts lead to poor plans, and inadequate plans result in inefficient and unproductive operations. Consequently, the next step is to confirm the validity of the methodology *before* it is implemented.

In the typical validation step, a portion of the available data is used to develop the relevant forecasting model. For example, OMB officials might use the early data history, and the cereal brand manager might employ data from some test markets. Next, the resulting model is used to predict the remaining levels of the forecast items. For example, OMB officials can use the later data history, and the brand manager can employ data from residual test markets. Then a comparison of actual against predicted item values is used to measure validity. For example, OMB officials will know that the selected methodology is valid if predicted costs are very close to actual costs. Similarly, a valid cereal model will generate forecasted competitors' prices that are very near industry practices.

Forecasting and Implementation. Once the company has a valid approach, management can use the methodology to make the required predictions. When estimates are generated regularly and data collected routinely, the computations used to make the forecast can be done automatically, usually with the aid of a computer. Annual cost projections, such as the OMB program expenditure forecasts, often can be made in such a manner. On the other hand, intermittent estimates made for unique situations will require a high degree of interaction between the user and the system. Environment projections, such as the cereal competitors' price forecasts, typically are made in this way.

The final step in the process is to implement the forecasts. This step can take a variety of forms. Sometimes the projections become measures of the organization's resource requirements. For example, OMB expenditure forecasts identify the estimated costs of providing government programs. In other cases, the forecasts become standards against which managers measure the organization's performance. For example, the projected competitors' average cereal price serves as a benchmark for the brand manager's pricing strategy.

Selecting the Methodology

A crucial aspect of the forecasting process is to match the need with the appropriate methodology. Forecasts are needed for various purposes by a variety of managers in many different organizations. As a result, several important organizational, time, economic, and data factors must be considered when seeking the proper match.

Organizational Factors. Since all managers must plan, each will be required to forecast. Nevertheless, the forecasting needs of top managers (such as chief executive officers, agency directors, and vice presidents of marketing) will differ from those of middle managers (such as project directors and account executives) or first-line supervisors (such as production foremen and administrative assistants).

Management Level. Top managers are responsible primarily for identifying organizational objectives and for establishing strategies or policies that meet these aims. To help identify objectives, these people will need to predict the aggregate level and direction of environmental (competitive, social, economic, and political) conditions. For example, when identifying budget priorities, a governor must project the political mood of constituents, general economic conditions in the coming fiscal year, and business circumstances in neighboring states. To help establish policies, top managers will need forecasting methodologies that explain the relationships among the firm's objectives, its activities, and the relevant environmental conditions. In selecting a future product line, for instance, General Motors' chief executive officer must know the relationship between corporate profits and factors such as current and potential automobile models, designs offered by the domestic and foreign competition, and laws affecting the industry.

Middle managers are responsible mainly for implementing policies and for allocating available resources among and within programs. To help perform such tasks, these managers will need to predict the resource requirements accurately. Moreover, middle managers will benefit from methodologies that explain the relationships among the programs' objectives, activities, and resource constraints. Among other things, the relationships may be used to aid these people in evaluating program resource allocations. For example, to help allocate a budget among available media, a soap company's advertising manager must explain the relationship among audience share from, cost for, and contract restrictions imposed by each medium.

First-line supervisors deal with less complex problems than middle or top managers. Furthermore, the first-line manager is primarily responsible for implementing and controlling a segment of a middle management program. The segment may be a tool shop in the domestic steel plant, an office in a municipal agency, or a clothing section in a department store. To facilitate control, first-line supervisors will need to accurately project segment performance. For example, to determine whether a cookie plant production process needs adjustment, a quality control supervisor must predict moisture content from a sample of baked goods.

Aggregation. Another important organizational consideration is the level of aggregation desired in the forecasted item. Many organizations, such as financial institutions and some federal agencies, will need a forecast of general economic activity, perhaps as measured by the Gross National Product (GNP). Other organizations will be interested in forecasting specific GNP components. For example, an international foodstuffs broker might be interested in the net export segment of GNP, whereas appliance manufacturers might be more interested in the disposable personal income statistics.

At the next levels of aggregation are the industry, individual firm, and intrafirm forecasts. Industry sales (such as aggregate energy demand or cumulative households with television sets) provide an indicator of the total market available to the enterprise and its competition. Individual firm forecasts project the share of the total market that can be captured by the enterprise. Frequently, top management will utilize these market share estimates and the underlying relationships to help establish organizational strategies and policies. A computer vendor, for instance, might use the relationship between projected market share and relative prices (its price relative to the competitors' average price) to formulate a pricing policy on a new line of hardware. Within enterprises, revenue and cost forecasts are made by products, divisions, and strategic business units. These intrafirm forecasts are then used to help plan inventories, people and material requirements, and production schedules.

The prediction at each level of aggregation will depend, to some extent, on the immediately preceding forecast. For example, an industry sales forecast will depend on general economic activity. Similarly, the firm's success will depend on industry conditions. Intrafirm projections, in turn, will depend on the overall company forecast. Consequently, management should use forecasting approaches that are suited to, and that recognize the relevant interrelationships among, the levels of aggregation.

Time Factors. Time is an additional factor that will influence the forecasting approach needed by management. There are at least two dimensions to consider: the time span covered by the forecast and the decision lead time.

Many situations involve short-term problems (within one year) that require quick decisions by managers. Examples include the decisions by a homemaker to purchase next week's grocery supply and by a fast food store's assistant manager to schedule tomorrow's work force. These situations lend themselves to simple forecasting approaches.

Other situations involve long-term (more than three years) or intermediate-term (one to three years) problems that require careful consideration and analysis. A municipal government's decision to build a new waste disposal facility offers an example. Another illustration is a football team owner's decision about a franchise location. In each case, the decision involves a long planning period and requires an extensive evaluation of alternatives. Such cases favor sophisticated forecasting approaches.

Economic Factors. It will cost money to implement a forecasting approach. These costs include the expenses associated with gathering and summarizing data, performing computations and analyses, interpreting the output, and utilizing the results. Moreover, some benefit is expected, either tangible (such as a cost saving) or intangible (such as a reduction in risk). Thus, when selecting an approach, the manager should consider the methodology's cost relative to its benefit.

In some cases, the problem will involve a relatively insignificant decision with few adverse consequences from inaccurate forecasts. Examples include a student's decision to buy notebook filler or a library assistant's decision to order catalog cards. These circumstances favor an inexpensive forecasting approach.

Under other circumstances, the problem will involve a substantial decision with significant adverse consequences from inaccurate forecasts. One example is a federal government's decision to purchase a crucial defensive weapons system. Another illustration is a television network's alterations in its future programming schedule. In each case, an inaccurate forecast could jeopardize the enterprise's future. Such cases lend themselves to expensive forecasting approaches.

Interrelationships. There also are important interrelationships among the organizational, time, and economic factors that help define managements's forecasting needs. Consider, for example, a sales forecast for paper clips in an office steno pool. In this situation, errors from an inaccurate forecast will not be costly, and the decision must be made quickly. Such a short-term, relatively insignificant decision must be implemented quickly, usually by a first-line supervisor, and lends itself to a simple, inexpensive intrafirm forecasting approach.

On the other hand, complex decisions that involve significant expenditures and that are implemented over a longer term, typically by upper-level managers, favor a sophisticated, expensive industry- or firm-level forecasting approach. An example is a major chemical producer's decision about where to locate a new plant. In making this decision, top management must consider a variety of environmental factors that are related in a complex manner. In addition, the decision has long-term finciancial implications, and it involves a long planning period. Moreover, inaccurate forecasts could result in costly decision errors. As a result, such a decision typically will be supported by a forecast that is generated with a sophisticated mathematical model estimated from a large body of quantitative and qualitative data.

Data Factors. Management must acquire data relevant to its organizational, time, and economic needs. The nature of this acquired data will significantly influence the approach that can be used for forecasting.

Qualitative Forecasting. Sometimes, management will be dealing with entirely new circumstances (such as the introduction of a new government program, the opening of a new market in a foreign country, or the imposition of new laws and regulations). Alternatively, the situation could represent a significant change from past circumstances (as would occur with a government-imposed price freeze, extreme climatological conditions, or war). In such cases, large amounts of numerical data will be unavailable, or there will be insufficient time, expertise, or resources to obtain the appropriate measurements. Consequently, managers will have to rely on forecasting approaches that utilize attitudes, judgments, opinions, subjective assessments, and other qualitative measurements. These approaches, which include the Delphi technique, scenario writing, consumer surveys, and executive juries, are known as **qualitative forecasting methods**.

Quantitative Forecasting. Frequently, the organization will be concerned with ongoing operations (such as plant maintenance or services rendered). In these cases, management will have sufficient numerical data to describe a history of past operations (such as maintenance costs over the last 25 months), current performance across sections of the organization (such as claimants served during this quarter by 10 government agencies), or existing outcomes across segments of the environment (such as employment in each state). If the enterprise has sufficient expertise and resouces, the manager can use the numerical data within a mathematical model to generate the required forecast. Such an approach, which can involve a time series analysis or an explanatory methodology, is known as a **quantitative forecasting method**.

In practice, both qualitative and quantitative forecasting methodologies will be needed to put plans into operation. Qualitative approaches can be used in strategy making to help (1) structure the problem; (2) identify the nature and timing of, and the degree of change in, relevant uncontrollable inputs; and (3) forecast the impact of the inputs on policy alternatives. Forecasts from quantitative methodologies, perhaps combined with the projections from additional qualitative methods, could then provide the precise numerical estimates required to set budgets, schedule production, make work assignments, and otherwise convert general strategies and policies into specific operating programs and procedures.

Finding a Match. Table 3.1 relates popular forecasting approaches to some organizational, time, economic, and data factors. It serves as a guide for selecting a forecasting methodology.

Consider, for example, a situation in which a lower-level manager (first-line or low-level middle) has quantitative data for a well-defined problem that requires a short-range projection. Under these circumstances, Table 3.1 shows that the manager could make a low-cost forecast and get moderate benefits with exponential smoothing. Section 3.2 presents this methodology along with other popular forms of time series analysis.

On the other hand, suppose that the upper-level manager (high middle or top) has a theory about the relationship among an item and its determinants. Moreover, quantitative data is available on the determinants, and the information must be used to make a medium-range projection about the item. When management has such a semistructured problem, Table 3.1 shows that a useful forecast can be made at moderate cost and in a reasonably timely manner with regression analysis. Section 3.3 discusses this analysis along with other popular explanatory approaches.

3.2 TIME SERIES ANALYSIS

Good judgment, intuition, and experience give a manager a rough idea of what is likely to happen in the future. To convert the idea into numerical data, such as next quarter's crime figures or next year's budget, management will need a quantitative forecasting analysis. A good place to begin is with a review of the relevant **time series**—a set of observations measured at successive points in time. By analyzing the time series patterns, management can develop a good forecast of the event's future value.

Time Series Patterns

A time series may consist of any, or all, of the following patterns:

1. *Trend* (T)—the long-term general direction of the data.
2. *Cyclical* (C)—the long-term data movements regularly leading to a peak, followed by a recession, succeeded by a trough, and ending with a recovery.
3. *Seasonal* (S)—the short-term fluctuations.
4. *Irregular* (I)—the short-term, random disturbances in the data.

Figure 3.2 shows a time series with all four of these distinct patterns.

Trend. Although data usually involve random fluctuations, a time series still may exhibit a gradual shift, or a movement to relatively higher or lower values, over the long term. For example, a bank may observe substantial month-to-month variability in the number of deposits. A review of yearly deposits, however, could reveal that volume has decreased gradually over time.

The gradual movement, or trend, can be caused by several long-term factors—changes in the size of the population, alterations in the population's demographic characteristics, changes in technology, shifts in consumers' tastes and preferences, and changes in economic conditions. These factors may result in a downward gradual movement (as in the bank deposit example) or in an upward trend (as in Figure 3.2a). In some cases, the long-term factors counterbalance. As a result, there will be no gradual shifting in the time series.

Cyclical. While the data may gradually shift over the long term, management should not expect all future time series values to exactly follow the trend. There will be cycles, or regular runs of observations above and below the trend values. For example, long-term oil prices may follow an upward trend. Yet, within the observed term, there will be times when oil prices decline, reach a relative low point, rise, and reach a relative peak. Moreover, these fluctuations will be repeated on a regular basis over the years.

Most experts believe that the cyclical pattern represents the multiyear business fluctuations that regularly occur in the economy. In particular, there will be regular runs of economic peaks, followed by recessions, succeeded by troughs, and concluded with recoveries. Since enterprises operate within this economic environment, an organization's activities may reflect these business runs. Consequently, a time series of any business activity could include a cyclical pattern, such as the one illustrated in Figure 3.2a.

Seasonal. Many time series also exhibit a regular pattern of variability within the short term. For example, air conditioning distributors anticipate low sales in the fall and winter months but large volume in the spring and summer months. On the other hand, ski shops and topcoat manufacturers expect the opposite yearly sales pattern.

Typically, the regular short-term or seasonal pattern occurs within one year (as in Figure 3.2b). Nevertheless, any regularly recurring movement that is less than one year in

Table 3.1   **Overview of Popular Forecasting Approaches**

Methodology	Description	Organization
Qualitative		
Consumer surveys	Use questionnaire and panel data to anticipate consumer behavior	Upper manager with complex, ill-defined problem
Delphi	Experts anonymously answer questions, receive feedback, and revise estimates	Upper manager with complex, ill-defined problem
Executive juries	Predict events from a consensus of executives	Upper manager with semi-structured problem
Sales force composites	Aggregate estimates from field salespeople	Structured middle manager problem
Scenarios	Experts develop hypothetical view of future events, experiment with conditions, and extrapolate the results	Upper manager with complex, ill-defined problem
Technological forecasting	Predicts the timing of, and degree of change in, future technological attributes and capabilities	Upper manager with complex, ill-defined problem
Quantitative—Time Series Analysis		
Naive	Forecast equals the latest observation	Low level management problem
Moving average	Forecast is an average of a successive group of observations	Lower manager with well-defined problem
Exponential smoothing	Forecast is a weighted average of the most recent actual and estimated values	Lower manager with well-defined problem
Trend analysis	Forecast is an extrapolation of past trend	Well-defined middle manager problem
Decomposition	Forecast the separate components in a time series	Well-defined middle management problem
Box-Jenkins	Identify data patterns, test alternative models, and predict with the best model	Upper manager with semi-structured problem
Quantitative—Explanatory Approaches		
Barometric	Use changes in leading indicators to predict an item's future	Semi-structured middle management problem
Regression	Measure the precise relationship between an item and its determinants	Upper manager with semi-structured problem
Econometric	Use simultaneous equations to estimate a set of unknown variables from a group of predictors	Upper manager with complex, semistructured problem
Input-output analysis	Measure the interdependencies among organizations	Upper manager with complex, well-defined problem

Table 3.1   *continuing*

Time	Economic	Data
Medium-range projection	High cost, medium benefit	Preferences
Long-range estimate and short lead time	Moderate cost, medium benefit	Opinions
Medium-range projection	Low cost, medium benefit	Opinions
Short-range estimate	Low cost, medium benefit	Opinions
Long-range projection and short lead time	Moderate cost, medium benefit	Opinions
Long-range projection and short lead time	Moderate cost, medium benefit	Opinions
Short-range estimate	Low cost, small benefit	Recent past
Short-range estimate	Low cost, small benefit	Long history
Short-range projection	Low cost, moderate benefit	Recent past
Medium-range estimate	Low cost, moderate benefit	Long history
Medium-range estimate	Moderate cost, moderate benefit	Long history
Medium-range estimate and medium lead time	High cost, large benefit	Long history
Short-range estimate	Low cost, small benefit	Recent past
Medium-range estimate, medium lead time	Moderate cost, moderate benefit	Theory, data base
Medium-range estimate and medium lead time	High cost, large benefit	Theory, data base
Medium-range estimate	High cost, moderate benefit	Theory, data base

Figure 3.2 Four Time Series Patterns

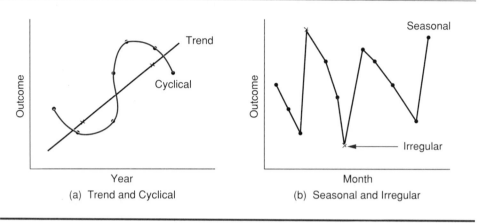

(a) Trend and Cyclical   (b) Seasonal and Irregular

duration can be seasonal in nature. Supermarket customer flow data, for example, show a daily "seasonal" behavior, with peak levels during lunch and after work hours, moderate flow during the evening hours, and light activity in the morning hours. Similarly, amusement park visits exhibit a weekly seasonal pattern, with weekend peaks and lower volume during weekdays.

Irregular. After accounting for trend, cyclical, and seasonal influences, the manager still may observe some random variability in the time series. This random pattern (which is illustrated by the erratic, X-marked movements in Figure 3.2b) occurs because of short-term, unanticipated, and nonrecurring factors that affect the time series. These factors could include employee strikes, weather-related supply delays, and vandalism.

By their nature, random disturbances generally are unpredictable. Consequently, the manager should not try to estimate the level of these disturbances. Instead, he or she should simply account for the irregular pattern when developing a forecast from the time series.

Smoothing Techniques

There are a variety of techniques that attempt to account for the irregular pattern in time series forecasting. Many of these techniques are based on "smoothing out" the random variability through various averaging processes. Some smoothing appraoches are designed for stationary data, or a time series that exhibits no significant trend. Other smoothing techniques adjust the averaging process for trend, and in some cases seasonal, patterns.

Moving Averages. When making a short-term forecast from a time series, the manager will be inclined to weight recent outcomes more heavily than past observations. There is a simple smoothing technique that can be utilized to accommodate this tendency. In the approach, the manager first uses the m most recent observation to compute an average value. The resulting average becomes the forecast for the coming time period. That is,

Table 3.2 **Small Time's Training Staff Hours**

Week	Hours
1	4,100
2	3,600
3	4,200
4	4,000
5	3,500
6	4,300
7	3,900
8	3,800
9	3,700
10	4,000
11	4,400
12	3,800

(3.1)
$$\hat{Y}_t = (Y_{t-1} + Y_{t-2} + \cdots + Y_{t-m})/m$$

where $\hat{Y}_t$ = the forecasted outcome, Y_t = the actual value, t = the time period, and m = the number of periods utilized to compute the average.

As a new value becomes available, it replaces the oldest observation in equation (3.1). In this way, the average will change, or move, as fresh data is obtained. Hence, the model is said to provide a **moving average**.

Management Situation 3.1 illustrates the moving average method.

Management Situation 3.1

Retraining Programs

As part of a social responsibility policy, Small Time Enterprises runs a retraining program for workers displaced from positions in the firm's various businesses. The erratic nature of the displaced employees' training requirements has made it difficult for Enterprise's educational administrator to predict the staff needed for the program. Nevertheless, the administrator has collected the data given in Table 3.2.

Management will use this data to develop a forecast of the hours required to staff the retraining program in week 13 of the current operating period.

Length. To compute a moving average, we first must select the value m that will be utilized in the calculations. This value m cannot exceed the total number of observations in the time series. Also, small m values will generate forecasts that respond quickly to data changes, while large m values will result in predictions that react slowly to movements.

Since Small Time has only 12 weeks of observed staff hours, the moving average must have an $m \leq 12$. In addition, the retraining program is an important aspect of the company's social responsibility policy. Hence, Small Time should respond rapidly to

Table 3.3   Small Time's Three-Week Moving Average Calculations

Week t	Hours Y_t	Moving Average Forecast $\hat{Y}_t = (Y_{t-1} + Y_{t-2} + Y_{t-3})/3$
1	4,100	
2	3,600	
3	4,200	
4	4,000	(4,200 + 3,600 + 4,100)/3 = 3,966.67
5	3,500	(4,000 + 4,200 + 3,600)/3 = 3,933.33
6	4,300	(3,500 + 4,000 + 4,200)/3 = 3,900.00
7	3,900	(4,300 + 3,500 + 4,000)/3 = 3,933.33
8	3,800	(3,900 + 4,300 + 3,500)/3 = 3,900.00
9	3,700	(3,800 + 3,900 + 4,300)/3 = 4,000.00
10	4,000	(3,700 + 3,800 + 3,900)/3 = 3,800.00
11	4,400	(4,000 + 3,700 + 3,800)/3 = 3,833.33
12	3,800	(4,400 + 4,000 + 3,700)/3 = 4,033.33
13		(3,800 + 4,400 + 4,000)/3 = 4,066.67

changes in staff requirements. As a result, the educational administrator will want to use a small number m of recent observations in the moving average calculations.

Of course, there must be at least two outcomes to compute an average. Also, to avoid overly sensitive forecast adjustments, the administrators will want to utilize three or more recent observations in the calculations. If Small Time used an $m = 3$, the forecasts would be as shown in Table 3.3.

According to Table 3.3, Small Time will need 4,066.67 hours to staff the retraining program in week 13 of the current operating period. As Figure 3.3 illustrates, this forecast is obtained by smoothing out the short-term, erratic fluctuations in staff requirements with the three-week moving average. The diagram also shows that the three-week moving average results in significant forecast errors. In some periods (such weeks 6 and 11), the forecasts underestimate actual staff requirements. Other times, such as weeks 5 and 9, the moving averages overestimate actual staff requirements.

Weighted Moving Average. Alternative length (such as four- and five-week) moving averages will lead to different forecast results. Before settling on the precise length of the moving average, the company should experiment with a variety of m values. In addition, management could consider forecasting with the weighted moving average formula:

$$(3.2) \qquad \hat{Y}_t = w_{t-1}(Y_{t-1}) + w_{t-2}(Y_{t-2}) + \cdots + w_{t-m}(Y_{t-m})$$

where $w =$ the observation's weight (between 0 and 1) and the other terms are defined as before. In this formula, the weights must sum to 1. With such a formula, the manager can use judgment and/or past history to emphasize particular observations through the weights.

Measuring Forecast Accuracy. To compare results objectively, management will need some measure of forecast accuracy. In one popular approach, the manager first computes

---

Figure 3.3   **Small Time's Actual Hours and Three-Week
Moving Average Forecasts**

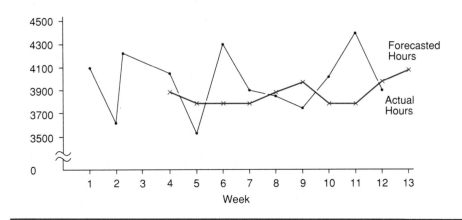

---

the absolute value of the difference between each actual and forecasted outcome. Then, he or she calculates the average, or mean value, of the absolute differences. The resulting measure, known as the **mean absolute deviation (MAD)**, can be expressed mathematically as:

(3.3)
$$\sum_{t=1}^{n} Y_t - \hat{Y}_t \,/n$$

where the symbol | | denotes the absolute value, n = the number of observations, and the other terms are defined as before.

Table 3.4 illustrates how Small Time can use the MAD formula to compare the forecast results from the simple and the weighted three-week moving averages. In the weighted approach, the most recent observation receives three times as much emphasis as the oldest outcome. Also, the next oldest observation is given twice as much weight as the oldest outcome. Put another way, $m = 3$, $w_{t-1} = 3/6$, $w_{t-2} = 2/6$, $w_{t-3} = 1/6$, and the model

$$\hat{Y}_t = (3/6)Y_{t-1} + (2/6)Y_{t-2} + (1/6)Y_{t-3}$$

will be used to compute the weighted three-week moving average.

Some information is lost when computing a moving average. Table 3.4, for example, shows that the three-week moving averages leave only 9, rather than the original 12, observations to compute the mean absolute deviations. The calculations also indicate that Small Time will get a MAD = 255.55 hours with the simple and a MAD = 290.74 hours with the weighted three-week moving average forecasts. This analysis suggests that the simple average yields a more accurate forecast than the weighted alternative.

The mean absolute deviation expresses the forecast error in the same units as the original data. Sometimes, however, a relative number such as a percentage, rather than a magnitude, may be more instructive to management. Other times, managers will need

Table 3.4   **Small Time's MAD Calculations**

Week t	Hours Y_t	Simple 3-Week Moving Average $\hat{Y}_t$	Absolute Error $|Y_t - \hat{Y}_t|$	Weighted 3-Week Moving Average $\hat{Y}_t$	Absolute Error $|Y_t - \hat{Y}_t|$
1	4,100				
2	3,600				
3	4,200				
4	4,000	3,966.67	33.33	3,983.33	16.67
5	3,500	3,933.33	433.33	4,000.00	500.00
6	4,300	3,900.00	400.00	3,783.33	516.67
7	3,900	3,933.33	33.33	3,983.33	83.33
8	3,800	3,900.00	100.00	3,966.67	166.67
9	3,700	4,000.00	300.00	3,916.67	216.67
10	4,000	3,800.00	200.00	3,766.67	233.33
11	4,400	3,833.33	566.67	3,866.67	533.33
12	3,800	4,033.33	233.33	4,150.00	350.00
13		4,066.67		4,033.33	

Sum of absolute error

$$\sum_{t=1}^{n} |Y_t - \hat{Y}_t|$$

    2,299.99   2,616.67

MAD   2,299.99/9 = 255.55   2,616.67/9 = 290.74

$$\sum_{t=1}^{n} |Y_t - \hat{Y}_t|/n$$

alternative measurements to precisely analyze risk and control properly. For these and other reasons, additional approaches have been developed to measure forecast accuracy. Table 3.5 summarizes some of the most popular.

Exponential Smoothing. To implement the moving average approaches successfully, management must acquire and maintain a large volume of historical data. In practice, it will be time-consuming and expensive to do so. Fortunately, experts have developed a smoothing technique that requires only the most recent data.

In the approach, the manager identifies the most recent forecast error. Then he or she adjusts the most recent forecast by a fraction of this error. The resulting adjusted value becomes the forecast for the coming time period. That is,

(3.4) $\hat{Y}_t = \hat{Y}_{t-1} + p(Y_{t-1} - \hat{Y}_{t-1}) = p(Y_{t-1}) + (1 - p)\hat{Y}_{t-1}$

where p = a weight between 0 and 1, called the **smoothing constant**, that identifies the fraction by which to adjust the most recent forecast error, and the other terms are defined as before.

As formula (3.4) demonstrates, the prediction $\hat{Y}_t$ is really a weighted average of the most recent actual (Y_{t-1}) and forecasted ($\hat{Y}_{t-1}$) values. Since earlier forecasts will

Table 3.5 **Additional Measures of Forecast Accuracy**

Measure	Description	Formula
Tracking signal	Measures how well a forecast is predicting actual values. An acceptable forecast has a tracking signal value between 3 and 8.	$\sum\limits_{t=1}^{n}(Y_t - \hat{Y}_t)/MAD$
Mean squared error (MSE)	Gives the average of the squared differences between the actual and predicted outcomes.	$\sum\limits_{t=1}^{n}(Y_t - \hat{Y}_t)^2/n$
Mean absolute percentage error (MAPE)	Gives the average percentage of absolute prediction error.	$\sum\limits_{t=1}^{n}(|Y_t - \hat{Y}_t|/Y_t)/n$
Bias or mean percentage error (MPE)	Gives the average percentage of observed prediction error.	$\sum\limits_{t=1}^{n}(Y_t - \hat{Y}_t)/Y_t]/n$

follow a similar pattern, the prediction $\hat{Y}_t$ eventually will become a weighted moving average of all preceding actual values. Moreover, the weights for successively older observations will decrease exponentially. For this reason, the approach is known as **exponential smoothing**.

Smoothing Constant. To utilize exponential smoothing, we first must specify the smoothing constant. A large p value will generate a prediction that responds quickly to the most recent forecast error, which is desirable when the time series exhibits relatively little random variability. On the other hand, if the time series has substantial random variability, observed changes may be attributed mainly to the irregular disturbances. In these instances, it would be undesirable to overact and adjust the forecasts too quickly, and the user may prefer to use a small p value.

Figure 3.3 indicates that there is significant random variability in Small Time's staff hours. In applying formula (3.4), the educational administrator might want to use a small smoothing constant. With no predicted value available at the beginning of the time series, the administrator also will need a $\hat{Y}_1$ value to initiate the exponential smoothing calculations. If management sets $p = 0.25$ and, as is customary, fixes the initial predicted value ($\hat{Y}_1$), the exponentially smoothed forecasts would be as shown in Table 3.6.

According to Table 3.6, Small Time will need 3,970.62 hours to staff the retraining program in week 13 of the current operating period. The table also illustrates how the exponential smoothing method adjusts the forecasts to compensate for prediction errors. For example, the overestimate in week 2 leads to a substantial downward revision in the week 3 forecast. On the other hand, the underestimate in week 10 results in a significant upward adjustment in the week 11 forecast.

Still, exponential smoothing, with $p = 0.25$, results in significant forecast errors. In some periods (such as weeks 6 and 11), the forecasts underestimate actual staff requirements. Other times, such as weeks 2 and 12, the exponential smoothing forecasts overestimate actual staff requirements.

Table 3.6   **Small Time's Exponential Smoothing Forecasts with** $p = .25$

Week t	Actual Hours Y_t	Exponential Smoothing Forecast $\hat{Y}_t = pY_{t-1} + (1-p)\hat{Y}_{t-1}$
1	4,100	4,100.00
2	3,600	$0.25(4,100) + 0.75(4,100) = 4,100.00$
3	4,200	$0.25(3,600) + 0.75(4,100) = 3,975.00$
4	4,000	$0.25(4,200) + 0.75(3,975) = 4,031.25$
5	3,500	$0.25(4,000) + 0.75(4,031.25) = 4,023.44$
6	4,300	$0.25(3,500) + 0.75(4,023.44) = 3,892.58$
7	3,900	$0.25(4,300) + 0.75(3,892.58) = 3,994.44$
8	3,800	$0.25(3,900) + 0.75(3,994.44) = 3,970.83$
9	3,700	$0.25(3,800) + 0.75(3,970.83) = 3,928.12$
10	4,000	$0.25(3,700) + 0.75(3,928.12) = 3,871.09$
11	4,400	$0.25(4,000) + 0.75(3,871.09) = 3,903.32$
12	3,800	$0.25(4,400) + 0.75(3,903.32) = 4,027.49$
13		$0.25(3,800) + 0.75(4,027.49) = 3,970.62$

Alternative smoothing constants (such as $p = 0.10$ and $p = 0.35$) will lead to different forecast results. Before settling on the precise smoothing constant, Small Time may want to experiment with a variety of p values. A better approach might be to find the p value that results in the smallest forecast error (as computed with MAD or other objective measures of accuracy). From time to time, as new data become available, it is also good practice to verify the validity of the smoothing constant.

Smoothing Technique Extensions

Moving averages and simple exponential smoothing are designed to forecast a time series with a predominantly irregular pattern. Many time series, however, also exhibit significant short-term trend and seasonal movements that are simply too important to overlook. Fortunately, experts have developed smoothing techniques to account for these additional important movements. Some of the most popular are summarized in the following table.

Methodology	Patterns	Formulas*
Adaptive response rate	Irregular	$E_{t-1} = r(Y_{t-1} - \hat{Y}_{t-1}) + (1-r)E_{t-2}$ $M_{t-1} = r\|Y_{t-1} - \hat{Y}_{t-1}\| + (1-r)M_{t-2}$ $p_t = \|E_{t-1}/M_{t-1}\|$ $\hat{Y}_t = p_tY_{t-1} + (1-p_t)\hat{Y}_{t-1}$
Holt's linear exponential smoothing	Linear trend and irregular	$\hat{Y}_{t-1} = pY_{t-1} + (1-p)(\hat{Y}_{t-2} + T_{t-2})$ $T_{t-1} = g(\hat{Y}_{t-1} - \hat{Y}_{t-2}) + (1-g)T_{t-2}$ $\hat{Y}_t = \hat{Y}_{t-1} + T_{t-1}$

Methodology	Patterns	Formulas*
Brown's quadratic exponential smoothing	Quadratic trend and irregular	$Y_{t-1}^1 = pY_{t-1} + (1-p)Y_{t-2}^1$ $Y_{t-1}^2 = pY_{t-1}^1 + (1-p)Y_{t-2}^2$ $Y_{t-1}^3 = pY_{t-1}^2 + (1-p)Y_{t-2}^3$ $a_{t-1} = 3Y_{t-1}^1 - 3Y_{t-1}^2 + Y_{t-2}^3$ $b_{t-1} = [p/2(1-p)^2][(6-5p)Y_{t-1}^1$ $\qquad - (10-8p)Y_{t-1}^2 + (4-3p)Y_{t-1}^3]$ $c_{t-1} = [p^2/(1-p)^2](Y_{t-1}^1 - 2Y_{t-1}^2 + Y_{t-1}^3)$ $Y_t = a_{t-1} + b_{t-1} + (1/2)c_{t-1}$
Winter's method	Linear trend, seasonal, and irregular	$S_{t-1} = q(Y_{t-1}/\hat{Y}_{t-1}) + (1-q)S_{(t-1)-L}$ $\hat{Y}_{t-1} = p[Y_{t-1}/S_{(t-1)-L}] + (1-p)(\hat{Y}_{t-2} + T_{t-2})$ $T_{t-1} = g(\hat{Y}_{t-1} - \hat{Y}_{t-2}) + (1-g)T_{t-2}$ $\hat{Y}_t = (\hat{Y}_{t-1} + T_{t-1})S_{t-1}$

*E = the smoothed actual error, M = the smoothed absolute error, r = the response rate, g = the trend smoothing constant, Y^1 = the single, Y^2 = the double, Y^3 = the triple smoothed value, while a, b, and c are the trend parameters, q = the seasonal constant, L = the length of the seasonal period, and the other terms are defined as before.

Trend Analysis

To plan and control properly, management must be alert to gradual shifts that may occur in factors such as technology, consumer tastes and preferences, and economic conditions. Marketing managers, for example, like to keep track of the general direction of sales. Similarly, various football coaches monitor performance trends for their players and the opposing players.

There is a standard statistical methodology available to measure the trend pattern. Management Situation 3.2 illustrates.

Management Situation 3.2

Accident Prevention

As part of a safety program, the management of Falls Lumber Company monitors accidents on a yearly basis. Table 3.7 reports data for the past 10 years of operation.

The safety manager wants to identify the long-term trend of accidents. She also seeks to forecast the level of accidents that would occur in future years if the historical pattern continued.

Figure 3.4 graphs Falls's yearly time series. The diagram shows that the data have some up and down movement over the 10-year period. Yet accidents appear to exhibit a downward trend. Also, the trend seems to be declining in a linear fashion.

Table 3.7   **Fall's Accident Pattern**

Year	Number of Accidents
1	370
2	330
3	280
4	350
5	300
6	170
7	180
8	150
9	200
10	50

Figure 3.4   **Falls's Yearly Accident Pattern**

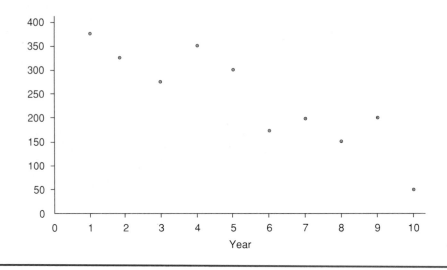

Year

Least Squares Estimation. When the gradual shift follows a linear pattern, the trend can be expressed as follows:

(3.5) $T_t = a + bX_t$

where a = the trend when $X_t = 0$, b = the per-period change in trend, X_t = the index assigned to time t, and the other terms are defined as before. The user will fix the index number X_t sequence, and the process could be as simple as assigning the value 1 to year 1, the number 2 to year 2, and so on. Usually the **least square method** is used to find the trend parameters. In this method, the user seeks the values of a and b that minimize the sum of squared forecast errors, or that

$$\text{minimize} \sum_{t=1}^{n} \left(Y_t - T_t\right)^2 = \sum_{t=1}^{n} \left[Y_t - \left(a + bX_t\right)\right]^2$$

Table 3.8   **Estimating Fall's Least Squares Calculations**

Year X	Number of Accidents Y	XY	X^2
1	370	370	1
2	330	660	4
3	280	840	9
4	350	1,400	16
5	300	1,500	25
6	170	1,020	36
7	180	1,260	49
8	150	1,200	64
9	200	1,800	81
10	50	500	100
$\Sigma X = 55$	$\Sigma Y = 2{,}380$	$\Sigma XY = 10{,}550$	$\Sigma X^2 = 385$

$b = [n \Sigma XY - (\Sigma X)(\Sigma Y)]/[n \Sigma X^2 - (\Sigma X)^2]$

$\quad = 10(10{,}550) - (55)(2{,}380)]/[10(385) - (55)^2] = -30.79$

$a = \Sigma Y/n - b(\Sigma X/n) = (2{,}380/10) - (-30.79)(55/10) = 407.33$

where n again represents the number of observed outcomes, and the other terms are as before. These a and b values are given by the following formulas:

$$(3.6) \qquad b = \frac{n \Sigma XY - (\Sigma X)(\Sigma Y)}{n \Sigma X^2 - (\Sigma X)^2}$$

$$(3.7) \qquad a = \frac{\Sigma Y}{n} - b\frac{\Sigma X}{n}$$

For readability, the t subscript notations have been omitted from the formulas.

By using the data from Table 3.7 in the least squares formulas, Falls's management would get the results shown in Table 3.8.

Trend Projections. Table 3.8 shows that the trend value in year zero (or at the origin of the observed history) is estimated to be $a = 407.33$ incidents. The table also indicates that the number of accidents has changed by $b = -30.79$ incidents per year. That is, over the past 10 years, Falls's accidents have decreased by an average of 31 incidents annually. Therefore, the expression

$$T_t = a + bX_t = 407.33 - 30.79X_t$$

$$(3.8) \qquad (\text{origin} = \text{year } 0, \ X_t = 1 \text{ year})$$

can be used to measure Falls' accident trend pattern.

Notice that the origin (year 0) and the units of measurement ($X_t = 1$ year) of the time series are identified in parentheses below the trend equation. Such identification enables the user to better understand and interpret the trend formula.

If the past is a good indicator of the general direction of accidents, management can use formula (3.8) to project the future trend of accidents. For example, according to this formula, Falls will experience

$$T_{11} = 407.33 - 30.79X_t = 407.33 - 30.79(11) = 68.64$$

accidents in year 11 and

$$T_{12} = 407.33 - 30.79X_t = 407.33 - 30.79(12) = 37.85$$

accidents in year 12 of the time series.

Trend Analysis Extensions

Although Falls's data exhibit a linear trend, other time series follow nonlinear patterns. Management then must utilize nonlinear models to describe trend. Some of the most popular are outlined below.

Trend Pattern	Example Graph	Trend Model	Typical Application
Exponential		$T_t = ab^{X_t}$	Learning curves
Quadratic		$T_t = a + bX_t + cX_t^2$	Revenue behavior
Logit or S-shaped		$T_t = e^{[a + (b/X_t)]}$	Product life cycle
Cubic		$T_t = a + bX_t + cX_t^2 + dX_t^3$	Cost behavior

Typically, management will need specialized procedures rather than linear least squares procedures to estimate the parameters of the nonlinear models. Fortunately, experts have developed the necessary procedures, and their work is reported in the time series readings at the end of the chapter.

Decomposition

In many cases, the relevant data will contain all four time series patterns. Furthermore, various managers in the enterprise will be interested in different patterns. An operations manager, for example, might need seasonal demand movements to schedule production and stock inventory adequately. On the other hand, a marketing manager might seek the trend of competitors' promotional expenditures, while a financial executive might require a cyclical projection to estimate cash requirements properly.

When essential data is captured and stored effectively, management can accommodate diverse needs by retrieving the information and decomposing the time series into distinct patterns. Management Situation 3.3 illustrates.

Management Situation 3.3

Investment Banking

Downtown Bank offers its customers the opportunity to invest in a professionally managed corporate bond fund. Yield data is efficiently and effectively captured, stored, and retrieved through the bank's transaction processing system. This system also regularly generates reports that summarize fund performance over time. Table 3.9 presents a portion of the latest summary, with entries representing actual fund yields (in millions of dollars).

As part of a service program, the bank's investment advisor will forecast for customers on a quarterly basis the yield expected on the fund's portfolio. Since Downtown offers a toll-free telephone connection to the advisor, customers utilize the service frequently to request yield projections. These people also become very upset when the projections are inaccurate. To better provide the service, the advisor needs the seasonal pattern, if any, in the time series. On the other hand, the fund manager must identify the yield trend to help formulate a long-term investment strategy.

Figure 3.5 gives a pictorial representation of Downtown's time series. The diagram shows that yields rise gradually in a linear fashion over the observed four-year period. Figure 3.5 also indicates that the fund experiences lower yields in the second and third quarters and higher earnings in the first and fourth quarters of every year. In short, the time series appear to follow predominantly trend and seasonal patterns.

Seasonal Factors. The seasonal pattern can be determined through a simple averaging process. First, a benchmark is established by computing the average outcome for all

Table 3.9   **Downtown's Portfolio Yields**

Year	First	Second	Third	Fourth	Total
		Quarter			
1	120	99	96	143	458
2	168	135	128	187	618
3	216	171	160	231	778
4	264	207	192	275	938
Total	768	612	576	836	2,792

Figure 3.5   **Downtown's Portfolio Yields**

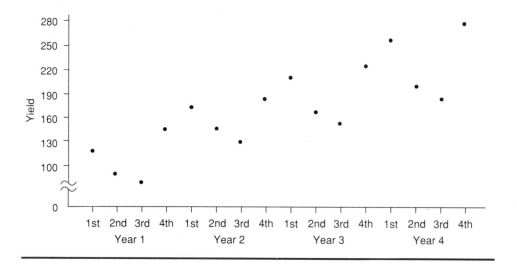

observed periods. Then, the manager calculates the ratio of each seasonal period's average outcome to the benchmark. The resulting ratios, called **seasonal factors**, measure the short-term, regularly recurring movements in the data. That is,

$$(3.9) \qquad S_j = \bar{Y}_j/\bar{Y}_t = \left(\sum_{j=1}^{J} Y_j/J \right) \Big/ \left(\sum_{t=1}^{n} Y_t/n \right)$$

where S_j = the seasonal factor for period j, $\bar{Y}_t$ = the average outcome for all observed time periods, $\bar{Y}_j$ = the average outcome for seasonal period j, J = the number of seasonal (j) periods, and the other terms are defined as before.

In Downtown's case, the fund has cumulative earnings of \$2,792 million over the observed n = 16-quarter (four-year) period. Hence, the portfolio earns an overall average yield of

$$\bar{Y}_t = \sum_{t=1}^{n} Y_t/n = 2,792/16 = 174.5$$

Table 3.10   **Downtown's Seasonal Factors**

Quarter	Quarterly Total	Quarterly Average	Seasonal Factor
j	$\sum_{j=1}^{J} Y_j$	$\overline{Y}_j = \sum_{j=1}^{J} Y_j/J$	$S_j = \overline{Y}_j/\overline{Y}_t$
1st	768	768/4 = 192	192/174.5 = 1.10
2nd	612	612/4 = 153	153/174.5 = .88
3rd	576	576/4 = 144	144/174.5 = .82
4th	836	836/4 = 209	209/174.5 = 1.20
Total			4.00
Average			4.00/4 = 1.00

million dollars per quarter. Moreover, there are $J = 4$ observations for each quarter in the series. By using these facts and Table 3.9's data, management will get the results shown in Table 3.10.

Table 3.10 indicates that Downtown's fund will earn 110 percent of the overall average, or 10 percent above the benchmark, yield in the first quarter. Yields will be 88 percent of the overall average, or 12 percent below the benchmark, in the second quarter and 82 percent of the overall average, or 18 percent below the benchmark, in the third quarter. During the fourth quarter, the yield will be 120 percent of the overall average, or 20 percent above the benchmark. This quarterly seasonal pattern will repeat itself every year in the time series.

Deseasonalizing the Data. When studying long-term movements, management often seeks to remove seasonal effects. For example, government officials remove seasonal labor market fluctuations (such as student summer employment) before interpreting unemployment statistics. Similarly, bank officials may be interested in eliminating seasonal activity (such as early spring tax-related transactions) before examining long-term deposit changes. Removing the seasonal pattern is known as **deseasonalizing** the time series.

The process will be influenced by the relationship between the four distinct time series components. Although the components can be independent, the usual assumption is that the movements combine in an interrelated manner. If so, the actual outcome can be computed with the multiplicative model:

$$(3.10) \qquad\qquad Y_t = T_t \times C_t \times S_t \times I_t.$$

Deseasonalized data then is created with the formula

$$(3.11) \qquad\qquad T_t \times C_t \times I_t = Y_t/S_t$$

or by dividing the seasonal factors into the corresponding actual outcomes.

Deseasonalized Trend. Since Downtown's portfolio yields exhibit a quarterly seasonal pattern, the bank should deseasonalize the data before performing any further analysis.

Table 3.11   Downtown's Deseasonalized Trend Calculations

Period	Period Index X_t	Yield Y_t	Seasonal Factor S_t	Deseasonalized Yield Y_t/S_t	X_t^2	$X_t(Y_t/S_t)$
Q1/Y1	1	120	1.10	109.09	1	109.09
Q2/Y1	2	99	.88	112.50	4	225.00
Q3/Y1	3	96	.82	117.07	9	351.21
Q4/Y1	4	143	1.20	119.17	16	476.68
Q1/Y2	5	168	1.10	152.73	25	763.65
Q2/Y2	6	135	.88	153.41	36	920.46
Q3/Y2	7	128	.82	156.10	49	1,092.70
Q4/Y2	8	187	1.20	155.83	64	1,246.64
Q1/Y3	9	216	1.10	196.36	81	1,767.24
Q2/Y3	10	171	.88	194.32	100	1,943.20
Q3/Y3	11	160	.82	195.12	121	2,146.32
Q4/Y3	12	231	1.20	192.50	144	2,310.00
Q1/Y4	13	264	1.10	240.00	169	3,120.00
Q2/Y4	14	207	.88	235.23	196	3,293.22
Q3/Y4	15	192	.82	234.15	225	3,512.25
Q4/Y4	16	275	1.20	229.17	256	3,666.72
	136			2,792.75	1,496	26,944.38

$$b = [n\sum X(Y/S) - (\sum X)(\sum (Y/S)]/[n\sum X^2 - (\sum X)^2]$$
$$= 16(26,944.38) - (136)(2,792.75)]/[16(1,496) - (136)^2] = 9.429$$
$$a = \sum (Y/S)/n - b(\sum X/n) = (2,792.75/16) - (9.429)(136/16) = 94.4$$

Afterward, the fund manager can use the deseasonalized data with the least squares method to isolate the yield trend. Table 3.11 reports the calculations, with Q1/Y1 representing the first quarter of year 1, Q3/Y4 denoting the third quarter of year 4, and so on.

According to Table 3.11, the deseasonalized yield trend can be expressed with the equation:

(3.12) $T_t = 94.4 + 9.429X_t$

(origin = the fourth quarter of year 0, $X_t = 1$ quarter).

This equation suggests that, in the fourth quarter of year 0, Downtown's fund yielded an estimated $94.4 million. It also indicates that, over the past 16 quarters, the yield has increased by about $9.429 million per quarter.

Decomposition Forecasting. If the past is a good indicator of the time series' general direction, the fund manager can use the trend equation to project the deseasonalized yield trend in future quarters. For example, in the third quarter of year 5, Downtown will be $X_t = 19$ quarters from the origin, and the deseasonalized yield trend will be

$$T_{19} = 94.4 + 9.429X_t = 94.4 + 9.429(19) = 273.551$$

or approximately $273,551,000.

The investment advisor can use knowledge of the trend and other data patterns with the multiplicative model (3.10) to generate a quarterly forecast for a customer. For example, Table 3.10 shows that Downtown's portfolio has a seasonal factor of .82 in the third quarter of every year. Also, since Figure 3.5 does not show any discernible cyclical or irregular yield movements, these patterns can be treated as "normal" (or $C_t = I_t = 1$) for any quarter in the time series. According to model (3.10), the advisor can anticipate an estimated portfolio yield of

$$Y_{19} = T_{19} \times C_{19} \times S_{19} \times I_{19} = 273.551(1)(.82)(1) = 224.312$$

or about \$224,312,000 in the third quarter of year 5.

Decomposition Extensions

Although Downtown's yield data has negligible cyclical and irregular movements, such patterns are important in many time series. In these series, the following classical method can be used to isolate the four components:

1. Identify the length L of the seasonal period: $L = 12$ for monthly data, $L = 4$ for quarterly data, and so on.

2. Compute a moving average of the L most recent observations. The result is the combined trend and cyclical (T_tC_t) pattern.

3. Divide the T_tC_t values into the actual (Y_t) observations. The result is the combined seasonal and irregular (S_tI_t) pattern.

4. Calculate simple averages of the S_tI_t values for each of the L periods in the time series. If the sum of the simple averages equals L, then the results represent the seasonal (S_t) pattern. Otherwise, the seasonal pattern will equal the simple averages divided by an adjustment factor. The adjustment factor will equal the sum of the simple averages divided by L.

5. Divide the S_t values into the actual observations. The result is the deseasonalized $(T_tC_tI_t)$ time series pattern.

6. Use the $T_tC_tI_t$ values with the least squares procedure to find the deseasonalized trend equation.

7. Use the trend equation to compute deseasonalized trend values.

8. Divide the deseasonalized trend values into the $T_tC_tI_t$ values. The result is the combined cyclical and irregular (C_tI_t) pattern.

9. Compute a short-term moving average of the C_tI_t values. The result in the cyclical (C_t) pattern.

10. Use the deseasonalized trend equation to predict time series values.

11. Multiply the deseasonalized trend projections by the seasonal and, if available, cyclical factors. The results represent the predicted $(\hat{Y}_t)$ values for the corresponding future time series periods.

Another elaborate approach, though not necessarily more precise, is the Census II method. The end of chapter readings discuss these methods in detail.

Table 3.12   **Time Series Analysis Summary**

Pattern	Analysis	Model
Trend (T)	Linear trend analysis	$T_t = a + bX_t$ where $b = [n\sum XY - (\sum X)(\sum Y)]/n\sum X^2 - (\sum X)^2]$ $a = \sum Y/n - b(\sum X/n)$
	Nonlinear trend analysis	See trend analysis extensions
Cyclical (C)	Decomposition	See decomposition extensions
Seasonal (S)	Simple averages	$S_j = \overline{Y}_j/\overline{Y}_t = (\sum_{j=1}^{J} Y_j/J)/(\sum_{t=1}^{n} Y_t/n)$
Irregular (I)	Moving average	$\hat{Y}_t = (Y_{t-1} + Y_{t-2} + \ldots + Y_{t-m})/m$
	Weighted moving average	$\hat{Y}_t = w_{t-1}(Y_{t-1}) + w_{t-2}(Y_{t-2}) + \ldots + w_{t-m}(Y_{t-m})$
	Exponential smoothing	$\hat{Y}_t = p(Y_{t-1}) + (1-p)\hat{Y}_{t-1}$
	Other smoothing	See smoothing technique extensions

Computer Analysis

Table 3.12 summarizes the time series analyses presented in the chapter. In practice, it will be cumbersome and time-consuming to execute these methods by hand, especially for large-scale problems. Fortunately, computer packages are available to perform the computations and report the results. One of the most comprehensive, and user friendly, is *Futurcast*.

A similar package is provided with the **Quantitative Management (QM)** computer software. The package is accessed by selecting the Time Series Forecasting module on the main menu. Figure 3.6 then illustrates how the module generates predictions for Small Time's retraining situation.

The user executes this module by selecting the Exponential smoothing command from the Time Series Analysis menu. Data input begins with the Edit selection from the Input menu. Report options also can be chosen from the Output menu. The program than requests information about the problem.

As Figure 3.6 demonstrates, the user first must enter the number of observations. Since Small Time has 12 weeks of staff hours, the manager should respond with the value 12 after the prompt. Next, the user enters the outcomes in the table that appears on the screen. The time series data then can be saved as a file for future use. Another option is to examine the historical data pattern with a plot of the time series.

At this stage, the manager must specify the constant used in the exponential smoothing. A response of 0 will trigger the program to compute and use the smoothing constant that minimizes the forecast error. After receiving the user's response, the program processes the data and generates the requested output.

As Figure 3.6 illustrates, the summarized output consists of the appropriate exponential smoothing equation and next period's prediction. This output indicates that Small Time's best smoothing constant is $p = .095$, rather than the $p = .25$ utilized in Table

---

Figure 3.6   **Small Time's Computer Analysis**

Time Series Analysis:	Input:	Output:
* Moving average	* Edit	* Full
* Weighted moving average	* Load	* Summary
* Exponential smoothing	* Print	* Plot
* Trend analysis	* Save	* Print
* Decomposition		* Save

Problem Formulation:
How many observations (enter a number up to 1000)?   12
Enter the observations in the following table.

Period (t)	Outcome (Y_t)
1	4100
2	3600
3	4200
4	4000
5	3500
6	4300
7	3900
8	3800
9	3700
10	4000
11	4400
12	3800

What is the smoothing constant p (enter 0 if you want the program to find the best value)?   0

Recommend forecasting equation: $\hat{Y}_t = .095Y_{t-1} + .905\hat{Y}_{t-1}$

Next period's forecast: 3994.88

3.6's calculations. Also, according to the recommended forecasting equation, Small Time will need 3,994.88 staff hours in week 13 of the retraining program.

3.3 EXPLANATORY APPROACHES

Time series analysis assumes that the historical data pattern will be the main determinant of an event's future outcome. The analysis, however, does not attempt to explain the underlying reasons for the observed pattern. For example, it is well known that advertising affects Maytag's historical washer sales pattern. Yet, most time series analyses will not use any advertising data to help predict the company's sales.

Unfortunately, changes in underlying causal factors can lead to significant alterations in the historical data pattern. Consequently, time series analysis, which does not fully consider such factors, frequently fails to accurately predict data turning points. Moreover, insufficient knowledge about causal factors will hinder a decision maker's efforts to formulate and evaluate management policies. For these and other reasons, experts have developed **explanatory** or **causal approaches** to explain, as well as predict, relevant organizational outcomes.

Table 3.13   **Federal Appellate Court Data**

District	Annual Appeals (Thousands)	Number of Lawyers (Thousands)
1	12	31
2	21	36
3	16	40
4	28	41
5	20	38
6	24	45
7	26	42
8	30	48
9	25	44
10	34	50

Regression

One popular explanatory approach is **regression** analysis. In this approach, management first uses theory and practice to identify:

1.   The event or criterion, called the **dependent** or **response variable**, that must be estimated or predicted, and

2.   Indicators, known as **independent** or **predictor variables**, that will influence the event/criterion outcome.

Next, the user obtains a representative sample of data on the dependent and independent variables. The data is used to develop a mathematical expression, called a **regression equation**, that measures the relationship between these variables. Management then utilizes data on the independent variable and the regression equation to forecast the dependent variable.

Simple Regression. Sometimes, the outcome of the dependent variable will be influenced primarily by one independent variable. This so-called simple regression can be illustrated with Management Situation 3.4.

Management Situation 3.4

Federal Litigation

Administrators for the federal appellate court system need a case load forecast to better allocate available staff and budget. These people believe that the quantity of appeals is related to the number of lawyers certified by the federal courts. Districts with large certified attorney concentrations are expected to face more appeals than the courts stationed near small masses of certified lawyers. If the hypothesized relationship can be established, staff can use certification data to predict the case load.

To study the relationship, court staff collected data from a representative sample of 10 districts. Table 3.13 summarizes these data.

Figure 3.7   **Federal Appellate Court Scatter Diagram**

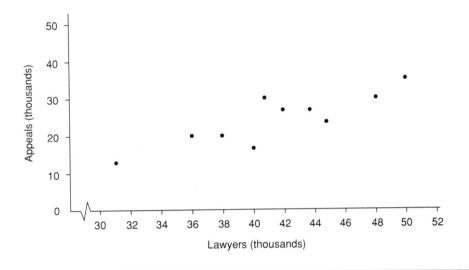

Regression Model. Figure 3.7 graphs the federal appellate court data. This graph, which is called a **scatter diagram**, shows the dependent variable (appeals) on the vertical axis and the independent variable (lawyers) on the horizontal axis. It provides an overview of the data and enables the manager to draw some preliminary conclusions about a possible relationship between the variables.

Figure 3.7 shows that the number of appeals increases with the number of lawyers certified in an appellate court district. Furthermore, the scatter diagram appears to follow a linear pattern. As a result, the precise relationship between the variables can be expressed with the following regression equation:

(3.13) $$\hat{Y}_i = a + bX_i$$

where

$\hat{Y}_i$ = the estimated value of the dependent variable for observation i

X_i = the actual value of the independent variable for observation i

a = the estimated value of the dependent variable when $X_i = 0$

b = the alteration in the estimated value of the dependent variable
     for each one unit change in the independent variable.

Notice that the linear regression equation (3.13) looks very much like the linear trend equation (3.5). That is because equation (3.5) really represents a special case of equation (3.13). Indeed, in the linear trend equation, the dependent variable is trend and the independent variable is time. Court staff can use the least squares method to find the regression (a and b) parameters.

Table 3.14   **Estimating the Court's Regression Equation**

District i	Appeals Y_i	Lawyers X_i	X_i^2	X_iY_i
1	12	31	961	372
2	21	36	1,296	756
3	16	40	1,600	640
4	28	41	1,681	1,148
5	20	38	1,444	760
6	24	45	2,025	1,080
7	26	42	1,764	1,092
8	30	48	2,304	1,440
9	25	44	1,936	1,100
10	34	50	2,500	1,700
	$\sum Y = 236$	$\sum X = 415$	$\sum X^2 = 17,511$	$\sum XY = 10,088$

$$b = [n\sum XY - (\sum X)(\sum Y)]/[n\sum X^2 - (\sum X)^2]$$

$$= 10(10,088) - (415)(236)]/[10(17,511) - (415)^2] = 1.019$$

$$a = \sum Y/n - b(\sum X/n) = (236/10) - (1.019)(415/10) = -18.688$$

By utilizing the sample data from Table 3.13 with the least squares method, the court staff will obtain the results shown in Table 3.14. These results suggest that the regression equation

$$(3.14) \qquad \hat{Y}_i = a + bX_i = -18.688 + 1.019X_i$$

can be used to measure the precise relationship between the court's case load and a district's certified lawyer base. Among other things, this equation indicates that the court can estimate hearing $b = 1.019$ thousand (1,019) extra appeals for each 1,000 additional lawyers certified in a district.

Regression Forecasting. If the regression model adequately describes the situation, the court administrators can use equation (3.14) to forecast the case load in a specific district. For example, a district with $X_i = 35$ thousand lawyers will generate an estimated average case load of

$$\hat{Y}_i = -18.688 + 1.019(35) = 16.977$$

thousand (16,977) appeals. Similarly, a district with $X_i = 43$ thousand lawyers will have an estimated average case load of

$$\hat{Y}_i = -18.688 + 1.019(43) = 25.129$$

thousand (25,129) appeals.

Forecast Error. The regression equation predicts only the dependent variable's average value. Random variation and the influence of unexplained independent variables will cause the actual values to deviate from the predicted outcomes for the dependent variable. Figure 3.8 illustrates. For readability, the horizontal axis in the diagram is broken between the values of 0 and 30. Consequently, it is not possible to accurately depict the point at which the regression line intercepts the vertical axis.

Figure 3.8   **Federal Appellate Court Regression Equation**

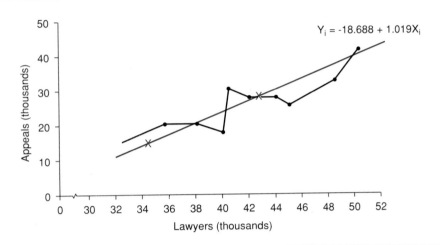

As Figure 3.8 illustrates, some of the sample observations are above, and others are below, the line depicting the court's linear regression equation. Few, if any, of the actual outcomes fall exactly on the line. Hence, the court staff may want to account for the variation when forecasting.

Standard Error.   Random fluctuations within the sample of observations can be measured with the following formula:

$$(3.15) \qquad\qquad s_{YX} = \sqrt{\sum_{i=1}^{n} \left(Y_i - \hat{Y}_i \right)^2 / (n - 2)}$$

This formula provides an estimate of the error s_{YX} called the **standard error of estimate**, that management can anticipate when using the regression equation to make a forecast. In addition, the regression estimate $(\hat{Y}_i)$ and the standard error of estimate (s_{YX}) can be used to develop a range that will include, with a specified probability, the actual outcome (Y_i) for the dependent variable.

The court's standard error of estimate is calculated in Table 3.15.
These calculations suggest that administrators can anticipate with a high likelihood an estimated error of $s_{YX} = 3.331$ thousand appeals when using equation (3.14) to forecast the case load in any of the 10 sampled districts.

Simple Regression Extensions

If there is a relatively high standard error of estimate, predictions from the corresponding regression model will be imprecise. Such a condition indicates that the model may be inappropriate. The measures summarized below also will help the manager evaluate a specified linear regression equation.

Statistic	Formula	Interpretation
Standard error of the regression coefficient b (s_b)	$s_b = s_{YX} / \sqrt{\sum_{i=1}^{n} (X_i - \bar{X})}$	Measures the variation that can be expected in the regression parameter b
Standard score for the regression coefficient b (t_b)	$t_b = b/s_b$	Measures whether of not the independent variable X_i has a significant effect on the dependent variable Y_i
Coefficient of determination (r^2)	$r^2 = 1 - \left[\sum_{i=1}^{n} (Y_i - \hat{Y}_i)^2 / \sum_{i=1}^{n} (Y_i - \bar{Y})^2 \right]$	Measures the percentage of variation in the dependent variable that is accounted for by the variation in the independent variable
Correlation coefficient (r)	$r = \sqrt{r^2}$	Measures the degree of association, or correlation, between the dependent and independent variables

When the statistical measures suggest that the linear model is inappropriate, the manager could consider a nonlinear regression equation. Alternatively, poor statistical performance might be caused by management's failure to include important independent variables in the regression analysis.

Multiple Regression. In most applications, the dependent variable's outcome will be influenced by multiple predictors. Fortunately, simple regression analysis can readily be extended to handle this **multiple regression** case. Management Situation 3.5 illustrates.

Management Situation 3.5

Toys and Hobbies

A toy train manufacturer knows that its annual sales will be determined by the product's price. Market research indicates that sales also will be influenced by the competitors' average price, disposable income, and (as a measure of potential replacement demand) the previous year's sales. Moreover, management believes that the predictors (prices, income, and previous sales) have a linear relationship to the response variable (current sales).

Time series data are available to measure the precise relationship between current sales and its predictors. By using this data with variations of the least squares method, the company developed the following multiple regression equation:

(3.16) $\hat{Y}_i = 4,000 - 2X_{1i} + 1.5X_{2i} + .5X_{3i} + .2X_{4i}$

Table 3.15   **Estimating the Court's Standard Error of Estimate**

District i	Actual Appeals Y_i	Predicted Appeals $\hat{Y}_i = -18.688 + 1.019X_i$	Error $(Y_i - \hat{Y}_i)$	Squared Error $(Y_i - \hat{Y}_i)^2$
1	12	12.90	− .90	.81
2	21	18.00	3.00	9.00
3	16	22.07	−6.07	36.87
4	28	23.09	4.91	24.10
5	20	20.03	− .03	.00
6	24	27.17	−3.17	10.03
7	26	24.11	1.89	3.57
8	30	30.22	− .22	.05
9	25	26.15	−1.15	1.32
10	34	32.26	1.74	3.02

$$\sum_{i=1}^{n}(Y_i - \hat{Y}_i)^2 = 88.77$$

$$s_{YX} = \sqrt{\sum_{i=1}^{n}(Y_i - \hat{Y}_i)/(n-2)} = \sqrt{88.77/(10-2)} = 3.331$$

where

$\hat{Y}_i$ = the estimated value of current sales at time i

X_{1i} = the toy's price at time i

X_{2i} = the competitors' average price at time i

X_{3i} = the consumers' disposable personal income at time i

X_{4i} = previous sales = actual sales at time $i - 1$

The latest market information indicates that the competitors' average price is $X_{2i} = \$20$, and disposable personal income is $X_{3i} = \$22,000$. Last year, the manufacturer sold $X_{4i} = 12,000$ trains, and the toy's current price is $X_{1i} = \$25$. Management will use this knowledge to forecast current sales.

As equation (3.16) illustrates, predictors could include:

1. Decision variables, such as the manufacturer's price (X_{1i}).
2. Market actions, such as the competitors' average price (X_{2i}).
3. Economic or demographic measures, such as income (X_{3i}).
4. Time-related factors, such as the previous year's sales (X_{4i}).

Time-related factors could be of particular importance. Indeed, an **autoregressive model**, or a multiple regression equation in which the independent (or predictor) variables are successively older values of the dependent variable, often is an appropriate description of reality.

By using the available predictor (prices, income, and previous sales) knowledge with equation (3.16), management can estimate that the company will sell

$$\hat{Y}_i = 4,000 - 2(25) + 1.5(20) + .5(22,000) + .2(12,000) = 17,380$$

toy trains during the current period. As in the simple regression case, the manager should evaluate this equation, with measures analogous to the Simple Regression Extensions exhibit's statistics, before implementing the forecast.

Econometrics. While many problems can be described adequately with single equation regression models, other cases may require a system of equations to depict the relevant relationships. Equation (3.16), for example, may provide a reasonable description of toy train demand. To set the price (X_{1i}) properly, however, management also may need an equation that accounts for product costs.

A specialized approach will be needed to analyze the added complexity. To illustrate, suppose an economic study reveals that the toy train's current price is determined by its current average manufacturing cost and by the previous year's price. By using available data with variations of the least squares method, management developed the following simultaneous equations:

(3.17) $$\hat{Y}_i = 4,000 - 1.5X_{1i} + 1.5X_{2i} + .5X_{3i} + .2X_{4i}$$

(3.18) $$X_{1i} = 9 + .7X_{5i} + .2X_{6i}$$

where

X_{5i} = the train's average manufacturing cost at time i

X_{6i} = the previous year's price = the actual price at time $i - 1$

and the other terms are defined as before. Also, current records indicate that $X_{5i} = \$12$ and $X_{6i} = \$23$.

Equations (3.17) and (3.18) form a system of two simultaneous equations with two unknown variables (current sales $\hat{Y}_i$ and the current price X_{1i}). Five variables (the competitors' price X_{2i}, disposable income X_{3i}, the previous year's sales X_{4i}, the average cost X_{5i}, and the previous price X_{6i}) are used to determine the unknowns. Such as a system of equations is known as an **econometric model**. Moreover, the unknowns ($\hat{Y}_i$ and X_{1i}) are called **endogeneous variables**, while the determinants (X_{2i} through X_{6i}) are known as **exogeneous variables**.

Management can use knowledge about the exogeneous variables with the econometric model to estimate the values of the endogeneous variables. For example, by using the available X_{2i} through X_{6i} values with equations (3.17) and (3.18), the company will find that the current price would be estimated as

$$X_{1i} = 9 + .7(12) + .2(23) = \$22$$

with resulting forecasted sales of

$$\hat{Y}_i = 4,000 - 1.5(22) + 1.5(20) + .5(22,000) + .2(12,000) = 17,397$$

trains during the current period.

Figure 3.9   **Explanatory Forecasting Approaches**

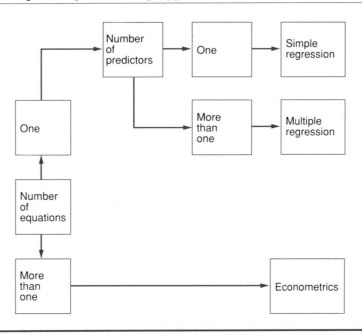

Computer Analysis

Figure 3.9 summarizes the chapter's explanatory forecasting approaches. In practice, it would be very cumbersome and time-consuming to implement these methods by hand, especially for large-scale problems. Fortunately, computer programs are available to perform the necessary computations and report the results. Some of the most comprehensive packages available for regression analysis and econometric modeling are **RATS, SAS,** and **SPSS**.

A similar program for regression analysis is available on the **QM** computer software. The program is accessed by selecting the Regression Forecasting module from the package's main menu. Figure 3.10 then illustrates how the module can be used to develop the federal litigation forecast.

The user executes this module by selecting the Simple command from the Regression Analysis menu. Data input begins with the Edit selection from the Input menu. Report options also can be chosen from the Output menu. The program then requests information about the problem.

As Figure 3.10 demonstrates, the user first must enter the number of observations. Since the court has 10 districts, the administrator should respond with the value 10 after the prompt. Next, the user enters the outcomes in the table that appears on the screen. The data then can be saved as a file for future use. Additional options are to examine the historical data pattern with a scatter diagram and to forecast. If a forecast is requested, the user must specify the value of the independent variable.

Figure 3.10   Federal Appellate Court's Computer Analysis

Regression Analysis:	Input:	Output:
* Simple	* Edit	* Full
* Multiple	* Load	* Summary
	* Print	* Plot
	* Save	* Print
		* Save
		* Forecast

Problem Formulation:
How many observations (enter a number up to 1000)?   10
Enter the observations in the following table.

Observation i	Dependent Variable Y_i	Independent Variable X_i
1	12	31
2	21	36
3	16	40
4	28	41
5	20	38
6	24	45
7	26	42
8	30	48
9	25	44
10	34	50

Recommend forecasting equation: $\hat{Y}_i = -18.688 + 1.019X_i$
Standard error of estimate: $s_{YX} = 3.331$
What is the value of the independent variable?   43
Forecast: 25.129

After receiving the user's input, the program processes the data and generates the requested output. As Figure 3.10 illustrates, the summarized output consists of the recommended forecasting equation, the standard error of estimate, and the requested forecast. This output shows that, in a district with 43,000 lawyers, the court can anticipate an estimated 25,129 appeals.

SUMMARY

Forecasts are needed for various purposes by a variety of managers in many different organizations. To meet these needs, management will acquire data from numerous sources and convert the measurements into predictions with some forecasting methodology. Figure 3.1 shows the steps needed to generate these forecasts.

A crucial aspect of the process will be to match the need with the appropriate methodology. Organizational, time, economic, and data factors should be considered when seeking the proper match. Table 3.1 relates popular forecasting approaches to some organizational, time, economic, and data factors and thereby serves as a guide for selecting a forecasting methodology.

One major quantitative forecasting methodology is time series analysis. This approach recognizes that time series data may consist of a trend, cyclical, seasonal, and irregular pattern. By isolating these movements and measuring their apparent effects, it is possible to forecast future outcomes. Some time series analyses smooth out the random variability in the data through various averaging processes, while other approaches project the long-term general direction of the data. In other cases, the relevant data will contain all four time series patterns. Furthermore, various managers in the enterprise will be interested in different data patterns. When essential data are captured and stored effectively, management may be able to accommodate the diverse needs by retrieving the relevant information and decomposing the time series into the appropriate component movements. Table 3.12 summarizes the time series analyses presented in the chapter.

Time series analysis does not attmept to fully explain the underlying reasons for the observed historical data pattern. Yet, changes in the underlying causal factors can lead to significant alterations in this pattern. Moreover, insufficient knowledge about these factors will hinder a decision maker's efforts to formulate and evaluate management policies. For these and other reasons, experts have developed causal forecasting approaches to explain and predict relevant organizational outcomes.

Popular causal approaches include regression analysis and econometric modeling. In these approaches, management first employs theory and practice to identify relevant dependent and independent variables. The user obtains a representative sample of data on these variables, develops mathematical expressions that measure the variables' relationships, and then uses the expressions to forecast. Figure 3.9 summarizes the chapter's explanatory forecasting approaches.

Glossary

autoregressive model A multiple regression equation in which the independent, or predictor, variables are successively older values of the dependent variable.

cyclical A time series pattern of long-term data movements regularly leading to a peak, followed by a recession, succeeded by a trough, and ending with a recovery.

dependent or response variable In regression analysis, the event or criterion that must be estimated or predicted.

deseasonalizing Removing seasonal fluctuations from time series patterns.

econometric model A system of equations, featuring unknown variables and determinants, used to study economic data.

endogeneous variables The unknown variables used in econometric models.

exogeneous variables Factors used in econometric models to estimate the values of endogeneous, or unknown, variables.

explanatory or casual approaches Forecasting technique that used causal factors, such as marketing approaches or economic trends, to predict an event's outcome.

exponential smoothing A technique in which the manager identifies the most recent forecast error, adjusts the most recent forecast by a fraction of this error, and obtains an adjusted forecast for the coming time period. Weights for successively older observations decrease exponentially.

forecasting Using a systematic methodology to make accurate predictions.

forecast A prediction of a foreseeable event or condition.

independent or predictor variable In regression analysis, the indicators that will influence the event/criterion outcome.

irregular A time series pattern of short-term, random disturbances in the data.

least squares method A technique for finding trend parameters by seeking the values that minimize the sum of squared forecast errors.

mean absolute deviation (MAD) The measure resulting from computing the absolute value of the difference between each actual and forecasted outcome, and then calculating the average, or mean value, of the absolute differences.

moving average A weighted average that changes continuously as new values are obtained and inserted in the model.

multiple regression A case in which the dependent variable's outcome will be influenced by multiple predictors.

qualitative forecasting methods Forecasting approaches used for new or significantly changed circumstances with little available numerical data. Based on attitudes, judgments, opinions, and subjective assessments, these include the Delphi technique, scenario writing, consumer surveys, and executive juries.

quantitative forecasting methods Forecasting approaches for ongoing operations with adequate numerical data to describe past and current operations or existing outcomes across segments of the environment.

regression A function that yields the mean value of a random variable under the condition that one or more independent variables have specified values.

regression equation A mathematical expression that measures the relationship between dependent and independent variables.

seasonal A time series pattern of short-term fluctuations.

seasonal factors Ratios measuring short-term fluctuations. Determined by computing the average outcome of all observed periods to establish a benchmark, then calculating the ratio of each seasonal period's average outcome to the benchmark.

scatter diagram A graph showing the dependent variable on the vertical axis and the independent variable on the horizontal axis, with points indicating intersecting pairs of variables.

smoothing constant A weight between 0 and 1 that identifies the fraction by which to adjust the most recent forecast error. Used in exponential smoothing techniques.

standard error of estimate Error or random fluctuation that management can anticipate when using the regression equation to make predictions.

time series A set of observations measured at successive points in time.

trend A time series pattern exhibiting the long-term general direction of the data.

Thought Exercises

1. Rup Rost, chief economist for the Midland Overseas Bank, claims that he always uses the same forecasting methodology, regardless of management's needs. He looks at the history, if any, for the item to be forecast. When there is no history, Rup asks experts from within and outside the organization to subjectively develop future estimates for the item. Based on the historical, or subjectively provided, pattern in the data, Rost identifies an appropriate forecasting technique. Next, he utilizes the technique to generate an estimate or prediction. Then, Rup presents the estimate to the relevant manager, receives feedback, and uses the feedback to revise, if necessary, the prediction.

    Do you think that Rup's approach is a good one? Explain.

2. What forecasting methodology is most applicable in each of the following situations? Explain.
    a.   A person planning the daily food ration for her or his pet.
    b.   A large city bank planning its annual loan issue.
    c.   A foreign state department's planning an aid request for a U.S. military agency.

   d. An automobile manufacturer planning total output requirements.
   e. A telephone utility planning service and distribution facility expansion.

3. In the chapter's Quantitative Analysis in Action exhibit, the Istanbul Chamber of Industry
   (ICI) used forecasting methodologies to diagnose the causes of Turkey's housing shortage
   and to suggest remedial actions. From the information presented in the exhibit, which
   methodologies did the ICI seem to utilize? Explain.

4. The following diagram plots the total output of the Intercity Municipal Gas Company
   over a recent period.

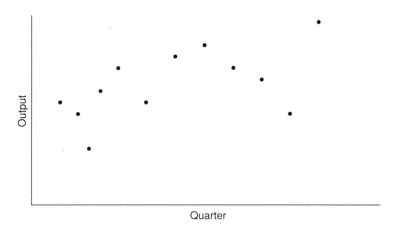

   What does the graph suggest about the nature of Intercity's output movements over time?
   Which form of time series analysis do you think would provide the most accurate forecast
   of Intercity's output requirements? Explain.

5. Show that the forecasted value $\hat{Y}_t$ in the exponential smoothing model

$$\hat{Y}_t = \hat{Y}_{t-1} + p(Y_{t-1} - \hat{Y}_{t-1}) = p(Y_{t-1}) + (1 - p)\hat{Y}_{t-1}$$

   is really an exponentially weighted average of past time series observations.

6. Gembill's Department Store has observed the sales shown on page 90.
        Management wants to forecast sales and use the predictions to help plan labor and
   store operating requirements. Staff are asked to provide the following information from
   a time series analysis:
   a. A trend forecast for year 12.
   b. The seasonal factors for sales.
   c. The expected sales in February of year 12.
   What type of time series analysis is being suggested by management? Explain.
        Management has been using simple exponential smoothing with a $p = .2$ to forecast
   sales. Do you think the approach suggested to the staff is more appropriate than this
   exponential smoothing? Which method will lead to the most accurate forecasts?
   Explain.

Month	Year				
	0	1	2	3	4
January	100,000	100,000	200,000	200,000	100,000
February	100,000	200,000	100,000	100,000	200,000
March	200,000	300,000	200,000	200,000	200,000
April	200,000	300,000	300,000	400,000	300,000
May	200,000	400,000	300,000	400,000	400,000
June	300,000	400,000	400,000	600,000	500,000
July	100,000	200,000	100,000	200,000	300,000
August	100,000	200,000	200,000	300,000	200,000
September	200,000	300,000	300,000	400,000	400,000
October	100,000	500,000	300,000	500,000	400,000
November	100,000	500,000	300,000	700,000	400,000
December	300,000	600,000	300,000	1,000,000	600,000
Total	2,000,000	4,000,000	3,000,000	5,000,000	4,000,000

7. The National Bureau of Parks director wants to predict attendance at the Grand Valley Regional Zoo. She believes that attendance is related to the zoo's advertising. To study the hypothesis, the director asked her assistant to gather and plot data on these variables. The results are shown below.

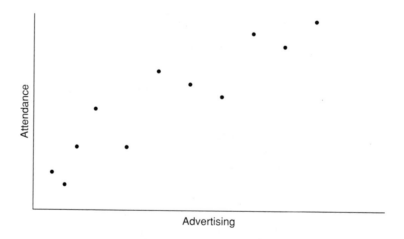

Which factor is the dependent variable? The independent variable? What does the diagram tell the director about her hypothesis? Explain.

8. A university estimates enrollment with the following equation:

$$E = 14.26 + .36J - .01T + .23H + .11Y$$

$$(11.33)\ (.008)\ (.002)\ (.04)\ (.62)$$

where

E = the Fall Term's enrollment (thousands)

J = area junior college graduates in the previous term (hundreds)

T = tuition per term (hundreds of dollars)

H = area high school graduates in the previous term (thousands)

Y = area household income (thousands of dollars)

Numbers in parentheses below the equation give the standard errors of the corresponding regression coefficients. For example, the .008 gives the standard error of the regression coefficient .36, and .04 is the standard error of the regression coefficient for the independent variable H. The computer program that generated the results also indicated that the equation had a standard error of estimate of 2.53 and a coefficient of determination of .83. Data from 60 school terms were used to perform the statistical analysis.

Explain the meaning of the multiple regression equation to university officials. Do you think that the equation is a reasonable description of university enrollment? Explain.

9. Tonkiland, a developing African country, has established a national planning agency. A main responsibility for agency management is to forecast general economic conditions. Zac Celestine, the agency's chief economist, has used surveys and theory to develop the following simplified econometric model:

$$GNP_t = C_t + I_t + G_t$$

$$C_t = 10 + .5GNP_t + .5C_{t-1}$$

$$I_t = 100 - 200r_t$$

$$G_t = 1.2G_{t-1}$$

where

GNP_t = Tonkiland's GNP at time t

C_t = consumption expenditures at time t

I_t = investment expenditures at time t

G_t = government expenditures at time t

r_t = the average interest rate in the economy at time t

C_{t-1} = consumption expenditures at time $t - 1$

G_{t-1} = government expenditures at time $t - 1$

All expenditures are expressed in millions of dollars.

Explain the meaning of each equation in the econometric model in language that would be understandable to the average citizen of Tonkiland. Which variables are exogeneous to the model? Endogeneous? Explain.

Suppose that the previous year's government expenditures were $100 million, the current interest rate averages 8 percent, and the previous year's consumption expenditures were $50 million. What are the forecasts for the current year's GNP, consumption, investment, and government expenditures?

10. Explain why you agree or disagree with each of the following statements?
   a. When utilizing qualitative forecasting approaches, the manager will not require highly accurate numerical forecasts.
   b. When predicting the direction of interest rates or the timing of consumer purchases, the manager will require highly accurate numerical forecasts.
   c. When utilizing a moving average to make a short-term forecast, we must assume that the length m is appropriate for both the past and future data.
   d. The autoregressive model is really a form of time series analysis.
   e. When a manager utilizes an econometric model, the coefficients should have about the same values as the parameters in a corresponding single equation regression model.

Technique Exercises

11. A forecasting model was used to predict Parkview General Hospital's daily patient costs over a recent period. The results are shown below.

Quarter	Actual Cost	Estimated Cost	Quarter	Actual Cost	Estimated Cost
1	154	138	11	260	276
2	151	149	12	279	277
3	167	172	13	311	300
4	165	178	14	319	326
5	190	186	15	309	328
6	211	197	16	345	333
7	220	213	17	341	345
8	209	224	18	323	338
9	237	228	19	315	321
10	279	257	20	317	319

Calculate the MAD, and explain what this measure suggests about the accuracy of the hospital's forecasting model?

12. A ballet company utilizes two models to forecast costs. Recent experience with the models provides the data on page 93.

Compute the MAD from each model. Which model provides the most accurate cost forecast? Explain.

Observation	Actual Cost ($ Thousands)	Forecasted Cost ($ Thousands) Time Series Model	Regression Model
1	24	22.5	25.4
2	28	28.4	28.6
3	34	31.5	38.2
4	27	27.8	26.7
5	32	32.1	30.9
6	38	36.7	38.4
7	35	34.9	35.3
8	41	40.5	41.1
9	44	44.2	43.2
10	39	39.4	38.7
11	37	36.1	37.1
12	48	46.6	47.9

13. Refer to Table 3.4 from Management Situation 3.1 in the text.
   a. Compute a four-week moving average of staff hours.
   b. Calculate the MAD that results from the four-week moving average.
   c. Compute a five-week moving average of staff hours.
   d. Calculate the MAD that results from the five-week moving average.
   e. Which moving average (three-, four-, or five-week) provides the highest degree of forecast accuracy? Explain.

14. Inventory of a liquid detergent at the local supermarket has followed the pattern shown in the following table.

Week	Inventory	Week	Inventory	Week	Inventory
1	1,210	6	1,219	11	1,226
2	1,181	7	1,205	12	1,217
3	1,194	8	1,199	13	1,214
4	1,207	9	1,208	14	1,221
5	1,225	10	1,215	15	1,209

   a. Use a three-week moving average to forecast inventory.
   b. Compute the MAD from the three-week moving average.
   c. Utilize a five-week moving average to forecast inventory.
   d. Calculate the MAD from the five-week moving average.
   e. Which moving average provides the most accurate forecast? Explain.

15. Refer to Table 3.4 from Management Situation 3.1 in the text. Show how management computed the weighted three-week moving average of staff hours.

16. Aircraft mechanics at an air force base replaced ammunition in a jet fighter at the rate shown in the following table:

Day	Rounds of Ammunition	Day	Rounds of Ammunition
1	2,400	8	2,340
2	2,350	9	2,390
3	2,290	10	2,410
4	2,380	11	2,375
5	2,415	12	2,350
6	2,405	13	2,395
7	2,370	14	2,420

a. Using a weight of 5/8 for the most recent observation, 2/8 for the next oldest outcome, and 1/8 for the oldest observation, compute a weighted three-day moving average ammunition forecast.

b. Calculate the MAD from the three-day moving average.

c. Using a weight of 1/4 for the most recent observation, 2/4 for the next oldest outcome, and 1/4 for the oldest observation, compute a weighted three-day moving average ammunition forecast.

d. Calculate the MAD from the forecasts in part c.

e. Which weighted moving average leads to the most accurate forecasts? Explain.

f. Use exponential smoothing with $p = .5$ to develop an ammunition forecast.

g. Compute the MAD from the exponential smoothing forecast?

h. Which method provides the most accurate forecast? Explain.

17. Refer to Table 3.6 from Management Situation 3.1 in the text.

a. Use exponential smoothing with $p = .10$ to develop a staff hour forecast.

b. Compute the MAD from the forecasts in part a.

c. Use exponential smoothing with $p = .35$ to develop a staff hours forecast.

d. Calculate the MAD from the forecasts in part c.

e. Which smoothing constant leads to the smallest MAD?

f. Use exponential smoothing with $p = .095$ to develop a staff hour forecast.

g. Compute the MAD from the forecasts in part f.

h. Which exponential smoothing model would you recommend? Explain.

18. Premiums for the state's Emergency Aid Fund (EAF) have followed the pattern shown in the following table.

Year	Premiums ($ Thousands)	Year	Premiums ($ Thousands)
1	28	6	35
2	31	7	36
3	29	8	40
4	34	9	38
5	39	10	41

a. Plot the historical data.
b. What is the long-term general direction of the EAF premiums? Explain.
c. Develop an equation that can be used to forecast the premium trend.
d. Compute the MAD associated with the trend forecasts.

19. Residential construction permits in a local community over a recent period are reported in the following table:

Year	Number of Permits	Year	Number of Permits
1	205	7	179
2	186	8	181
3	192	9	174
4	178	10	170
5	183	11	177
6	175	12	168

a. Plot the historical data.
b. What is the long-term general direction of the construction permits? Explain.
c. Develop an equation that can be used to forecast the construction trend.
d. Use the trend equation to forecast the number of construction permits that can be expected in years 13 and 15 of the planning period.

20. Refer to Management Situation 3.3 in the text.
a. Use the yield data in Table 3.9 and the least-squares method to determine Downtown's trend equation.
b. Determine the trend values for each quarter in Downtown's time series.
c. Plot the trend and the original yield data on the same graph.
d. Determine the deseasonalized trend values for each quarter in Downtown's time series.
e. Plot the deseasonalized trend and the deseasonalized yield data on the same graph.
f. Compare the plots found in parts c and e. Comment on the results.
g. Forecast sales for each quarter in year 5.

21. Expenses at the Eastview Mountain Resort over a recent period are reported in the table below:

Year	Quarter	Expenses ($ Thousands)	Year	Quarter	Expenses ($ Thousands)
1	1	18	3	1	13
	2	23		2	20
	3	30		3	25
	4	15		4	11
2	1	16	4	1	12
	2	21		2	19
	3	27		3	22
	4	14		4	9

a. Plot the time series.
b. Does the time series have any noticeable patterns? Explain.
c. Find the trend.
d. Determine the seasonal pattern.
e. Deseasonalize the time series.
f. Find the deseasonalized trend.

22. Over the past five years, a minor league hockey team has experienced the revenue pattern shown in the table below.

Year	Quarter	Revenue ($ Thousands)
1	1	120
	2	70
	3	100
	4	150
2	1	130
	2	75
	3	90
	4	160
3	1	145
	2	105
	3	100
	4	175
4	1	160
	2	90
	3	110
	4	140
5	1	150
	2	120
	3	105
	4	180

a. Plot the time series.
b. Identify any apparent time series movements.
c. Determine the seasonal pattern.
d. Deseasonalize the time series.
e. Find the deseasonalized trend pattern.
f. Forecast revenue in quarter 3 of year 6.

23. You are given the observations shown in the following table:

Y	X	Y	X	Y	X
11	29	17	35	23	49
17	27	21	40	24	52
14	22	27	43	27	55
9	23	31	62	30	56
12	31	25	53	34	51

Y	X	Y	X	Y	X
6	30	22	49	29	48
5	25	19	45	24	45
18	20	24	41	23	44
13	18	26	40	20	47
10	16	29	48	12	41

a. Plot the scatter diagram of the data.

b. What does the scatter diagram indicate about the relationship between Y and X? Explain.

c. Develop an equation that can be used to forecast the Y values.

24. You are on the planning staff of a local chemical producer. To help management prepare the firm's annual report, you are asked to determine the relationship between the rate of return and the corresponding capital expenditures. Relevant financial data are shown in the table below.

Division	Rate of Return (%)	Capital Expenditures ($ Millions)
A	5	2
B	7	3
C	10	4
D	15	5
E	17	6
F	18	7
G	19	8
H	19.5	9
I	19	10
J	17	11

a. Plot the scatter diagram relating the rate of return to capital expenditures.

b. What does the scatter diagram suggest about the relationship between the two variables? Explain.

c. Develop an equation that can be used to forecast the rate of return associated with a specified capital investment.

d. If a division plans to spend $20 million on capital, what rate of return should be expected by management?

Computer Exercises

25. Refer to Management Situation 3.1 in the text. Use the **Quantitative Management (QM)** computer software to:

a. Plot Small Time's time series,

b. Develop a full output report of a three-week moving average forecast, and

c. Develop a full output report of a weighted three-week moving average using $w_{i-1} = 3/6$, $w_{i-2} = 2/6$, and $w_{i-3} = 1/6$.

Based on the outputs, which moving average would you recommend? Explain.

26. Interest rates on automobiles issued by the Second Trust and Thrift Association over the last 12 weeks appear in the table below. Use the **QM** software to develop an equation that will accurately predict future interest rates.

Week	Interest Rate (%)	Week	Interest Rate (%)
1	12.9	7	12.4
2	13.6	8	11.9
3	13.2	9	12.6
4	13.8	10	13.0
5	13.5	11	13.2
6	12.9	12	14.3

27. Refer to Management Situation 3.2 in the text. Use the **QM** software to generate a full output report of Falls' trend analysis.

28. A managerial economist employed by a large manufacturer of heavy industrial equipment is responsible for estimating aggregate costs for the company. She has divided costs into four major categories: administrative, selling, fixed production, and variable manufacturing expenses. Data from company records indicate that these expanses have followed the pattern below.

	Expense ($ Thousand)			
Quarter	Administration	Sales	Fixed Production	Variable Manufacturing
1	205	182	385	1,241
2	209	182	388	1,253
3	198	184	396	1,264
4	176	183	409	1,291
5	212	191	412	1,304
6	216	190	453	1,309
7	222	189	467	1,333
8	195	176	505	1,351
9	183	181	511	1,371
10	206	182	519	1,389
11	235	183	533	1,400
12	241	185	550	1,407
13	203	190	571	1,453
14	245	191	574	1,482
15	253	193	576	1,495
16	262	192	577	1,512
17	273	194	580	1,518
18	272	195	582	1,573
19	270	205	584	1,532
20	268	204	587	1,530
21	263	198	607	1,562
22	288	196	608	1,555
23	296	195	670	1,584
24	305	200	653	1,609

Projections for each category will be combined to form the aggregate cost forecast. Use the **QM** software to develop the forecast for quarter 25 in the planning period.

29. Refer to Management Situation 3.3 in the text. Use the **QM** software to perform the decomposition of the time series. In the process, develop a
   a.   Plot of the time series,
   b.   Full output report, and
   c.   Forecast of yields in each quarter of year 5.

30. Gigantic, Ltd. has experienced the production and marketing expenses shown in the following table.

		Expenses ($ Million)	
Year	Quarter	Production	Marketing
1	1	245	12
	2	219	15
	3	286	11
	4	274	16
2	1	291	21
	2	303	25
	3	298	23
	4	301	29
3	1	300	31
	2	305	30
	3	309	34
	4	299	37
4	1	307	42
	2	320	38
	3	325	44
	4	326	41
5	1	329	53
	2	318	57
	3	314	50
	4	322	49
6	1	345	46
	2	333	55
	3	337	61
	4	351	66
7	1	350	72
	2	347	75
	3	342	67
	4	339	64
8	1	336	62
	2	331	58

Use the **QM** software to:
a.   Plot a scatter diagram of the data, and
b.   Develop a full output report of a regression equation that will fit the data.
If the company plans to spend $70 million on marketing during the third quarter of year 8, what should management budget for production?

Applications Exercises

31. The executive board of Prepaid Dental Group (PDG) wants to design a plan that will provide services desired and needed by consumers. To meet the objective, the board has hired a research organization to sample 40 potential customers of the plan in PDG's immediate service area. One of the relevant consumer characteristics is family income. Indeed, the board believes that an accurate estimate of income will enable the group to better set plan premiums and co-payments.

Several models have been proposed to forecast income from survey data. These models' preliminary results are summarized in the table below:

Family	Actual Income ($ Thousands)	Forecasted Income ($ Thousands)		
		Model X	Model Y	Model Z
Jackson	18.9	17.7	16.9	20.4
Brown	16.5	15.6	16.2	18.1
Thomas	24.3	20.8	23.6	25.0
Allen	28.7	27.9	28.2	29.3
Jones	22.2	22.1	23.5	21.9
Smith	35.0	33.0	34.3	35.4
Allison	36.3	35.8	36.1	36.6
Kerr	27.4	25.0	24.9	26.4
Green	23.9	23.7	24.2	23.8
James	19.7	18.8	18.9	19.4
Orr	42.3	37.3	40.0	41.1
Lane	37.6	37.4	37.0	38.0
Ino	51.2	49.7	50.4	51.1
Chen	29.9	31.4	28.6	29.0
Montez	33.4	33.0	31.9	32.5
Gambi	17.8	17.3	17.2	17.7
Twayne	25.5	24.9	25.2	26.0
Slias	23.2	23.0	22.8	24.3
Onri	35.9	35.0	34.7	36.4
Olane	43.6	41.9	42.8	45.2
Fine	30.1	29.7	29.4	31.8
Tomt	28.0	28.4	27.8	28.9
Olzeski	24.4	23.6	24.3	24.9
Black	26.3	26.2	26.1	26.0
Jimaniz	21.1	21.0	20.6	21.9
Lee	39.7	39.3	38.8	40.4
Tizak	30.8	30.4	31.2	29.7
Libby	42.9	40.8	41.7	41.4
Owens	44.4	45.1	45.7	44.3
Dole	48.0	47.4	47.7	51.2
Fonte	55.0	49.0	48.6	57.3
Jatson	47.3	47.1	47.0	47.7
Johnson	39.1	38.7	39.8	40.1
Lange	27.8	26.4	25.3	27.9
Bowen	35.1	34.4	34.7	35.0
Bickel	31.7	32.2	33.6	31.5
Trinz	24.8	24.9	25.0	24.4
Lopez	19.0	18.3	17.9	20.5
Owenby	36.6	36.0	36.4	36.8
Chavez	39.0	38.3	39.5	39.4

What forecasting methodology is being utilized by the group? Which forecasting model should be utilized by PDG management? Explain.

32. General Way Corporation operates a chain of supermarkets in the southeastern United States. Planning for the chain is done at the corporate headquarters in Landale by a staff of top executives. One outcome of the process is a budget for the entire chain that decomposes expenditures into major product categories. To establish such a budget, the staff must forecast product sales in each appropriate category.

   The planning staff has compiled a sales history for the most important product from corporate records, and the data is presented below.

| Quarter | Sales ($ Thousands) | | | |
	Year 1	Year 2	Year 3	Year 4
1	212	173	196	217
2	187	215	188	201
3	205	276	209	179
4	293	234	244	207

Staff members have access to sophisticated computer systems for storing, manipulating, and retrieving large volumes of data. Since these people also have had successful experiences with smoothing approaches, there is a consensus for developing the forecast with a three-quarter moving average. Some would like to weight the middle quarter twice as much as the other periods, while others favor equal weights. None, however, believe that a series of declining weights would be appropriate for this situation.

   Do you think that the moving average approach is appropriate for the sales forecasting problem? If so, which staff faction seems to be suggesting the relevant methodology? Explain. Develop the product's sales forecast with the most appropriate methodology.

33. The Desert Dunes Country Club is concerned about the monthly water bill for its golf course. It seems that the staff did not effectively monitor and manage usage for irrigation, drinking fountains, rest rooms, and golf ball washing machines. To help correct these deficiencies, the directors seek a methodology that will accurately predict water usage. Staff have obtained a history of usage from water company bills, and the data is reported below.

| Day | Water Use (Gallons) | | |
	Week 1	Week 2	Week 3
Monday	200	170	195
Tuesday	225	185	200
Wednesday	170	205	220
Thursday	195	190	210
Friday	150	185	205
Saturday	100	165	190
Sunday	125	175	185

Desert Dunes cannot afford a sophisticated computer system for storing, manipulating, and retrieving data.

What forecasting method should the staff utilize to predict water usage from past utility bills? Explain. If the staff adopted your approach, what forecast error could management anticipate? Be specific.

34. The chief accountant at Eberhand Manufacturing is responsible for managing the firm's cash reserves. In particular, cash flows into the enterprise from product sales, and the money is disbursed throughout the organization for short-term material and supply requirements. Any idle funds are invested in short-term securities.

Since neither inflows no disbursements are known in advance, each must be forecasted on the basis of the historical record. Relevant data gathered by the accountant are shown in the following table. These data are considered to be representative of reality.

| | Cash ($ Thousands) | |
Week	Inflows	Disbursements
1	12	7
2	13	14
3	8	12
4	11	6
5	24	5
6	17	21
7	15	18
8	20	20
9	25	19
10	31	35
11	16	27
12	18	13
13	22	16
14	21	18
15	26	23
16	34	43
17	30	35
18	27	27
19	28	24
20	37	32

The accountant seeks a model that would forecast the net cash reserve (inflows minus disbursements). What model would you suggest? Explain. To illustrate your recommendation, forecast the net cash reserve for the next six weeks. If the firm could earn 12 percent per year on its idle funds, how much would Eberhard accumulate from the forecasted net cash reserve investments? Explain.

35. The Columbia Gas Company provides natural gas for cooking and heating purposes to over 30,000 customers in the York, Pennsylvania area. A major management aim is to improve the accuracy of month-to-month gas consumption estimates. The task is critical for effective production planning and for cost control. Consequently, top management employed a well-known consultant to seek ways off improving the gas consumption forecasts.

To start, the consultant asked for the entire available history of gas consumption. Company's archives provided the data reported in the table below. Entries represent thousands of cubic feet consumed per thousand customers.

Month	Year				
	1	2	3	4	5
January	24	22	25	24	30
February	20	19	21	23	28
March	17	18	19	19	22
April	14	12	14	15	17
May	13	13	15	16	17
June	11	10	9	12	11
July	8	6	7	9	9
August	6	7	9	7	6
September	6	6	8	8	9
October	8	9	10	10	12
November	12	10	11	13	15
December	18	20	17	16	24

After examining a plot of the data, the consultant believes that an accurate forecast can be developed for any future month by utilizing a combination of the trend and seasonal patterns. You are a staff engineer for Columbia who has been assigned to work with the consultant on the forecasting project. Explain to company management how the consultant arrived at her conclusion. Develop a methodology that would implement the consultant's belief. Then, utilize the methodology to forecast gas consumption for each month in the next year of the planning period.

36. Johnsville County Bank is very concerned about the growing number of foreclosures on its outstanding mortgages. Based on a preliminary examination of the original loan applications, officials believe that the default balance is related to the size of the down payment. Management would like to utilize the relationship in the evaluation of new loan applications.

Since the bank staff does not have the necessary expertise, a consultant has been hired to develop a model of the required relationship. The staff provide the consultant with the following data:

Loan	Default Balance ($ Thousands)	Down Payment ($ Thousands)
342	44	22
1,045	25	45
927	33	30
121	152	15
24	81	18
693	63	23
7	200	25
185	109	16
64	41	18
406	57	23

Loan	Default Balance ($ Thousands)	Down Payment ($ Thousands)
333	30	11
74	18	14
1,196	37	20
49	112	23
566	93	21
888	21	17
5	19	19
707	189	28
9	100	24
100	59	16

If you were the consultant, how would you carry out the assignment? Perform your recommended analysis. Based on this analysis, what will be the estimated default balance for a loan with a down payment of $35,000? What will be the expected default balance for another loan with a $12,000 down payment? Explain the results and the mortgage policy implications in language that would be understandable to Johnsville's management.

For Further Reading

Forecasting Process

Ashton, A. H., and R. H. Ashton. "Aggregating Subjective Forecasts: Some Empirical Results." *Management Science* (December 1985):1499.

Bopp, A. E. "On Combining Forecasts: Some Extensions and Results." *Management Science* (December 1985):1492.

Guerard, J. B., and C. R. Biedleman. "Composite Earnings Forecasting Efficiency." *Interfaces* (September–October 1987):103.

Kang, H. "Unstable Weights in the Combination of Forecasts." *Management Science* (June 1986):683.

Kucukemiroglu, O., and K. Ord. "The Impact of Extreme Observations on Simple Forecasting Methods." *Decision Sciences* (Summer 1985):299.

Martino, J. P. *Technological Forecasting for Decision Making*. Second edition. New York: Elsevier, North–Holland, 1983.

Russell, T. D., and E. E. Adam. "An Empirical Evaluation of Alternative Forecasting Combinations." *Management Science* (October 1987):1267.

Time Series Analysis

Bhattacharyya, M. N. *Comparison of Box-Jenkins and Bonn Monetary Model Prediction Performance*. New York: Springer-Verlag, 1980.

Carbone, R., and S. Makridakis. "Forecasting When Pattern Changes Occur beyond the Historical Data." *Management Science* (March 1986):257.

Harvey, A. C. "Analysis and Generalisation Of A Multivariate Exponential Smoothing Model." *Management Science* (March 1986):374.

Koreisha, S. G. "A Time-Series Approach for Constructing Expectations Models." *Decision Sciences* (Spring 1984):177.

Makridakis, S., and R. Carbone. *FUTURCAST*. Pittsburgh: Futurion Associates, 1985.

Makridakis, S., et. al. *The Forecasting Accuracy of Major Time Series Methods*. New York: Wiley, 1984.

McKenzie, E. "Renormalization of Seasonals in 'Winters' Forecasting Systems: Is It Necessary?" *Operations Research* (January–February 1986):174.

Wheelwright, S., and S. Makridakis. *Forecasting Methods for Management*. Third edition. New York: Wiley, 1980.

Wright, D. J. "Forecasting Data Published at Irregular Time Intervals Using an Extension of Holt's Method." *Management Science* (April 1986):499.

Explanatory Approaches

Abraham, B., and J. Ledotter. *Statistical Methods For Forecasting*. New York: Wiley, 1983.

Hanke, J. E., and A. G. Reitsch. *Business Forecasting*. Second edition. Newton MA: Allyn and Bacon, 1986.

Pindyck, R., and D. Rubinfeld. *Econometric Models and Economic Forecasts*. New York: McGraw-Hill, 1976.

Regression Analysis of Time Series. Minneapolis: VAR Econometrics, 1984.

SAS User's Guides. Version 5 editions. Cary, NC: SAS Institute, 1985.

SPSS^X User's Guide. Chicago: SPSS, 1983.

Private Sector Applications

Brandon, C., J. E. Jarrett, and S. B. Khumawala. "Comparing Forecast Accuracy for Exponential Smoothing Models of Earnings-per-share Data for Financial Decision Making." *Decision Sciences* (Spring 1986):186.

Conroy, R., and R. Harris. "Consensus Forecasts of Corporate Earnings: Analysts' Forecasts and Time Series Methods." *Management Science* (June 1987):725.

DeSarbo, W. S., and P. E. Green. "An Alternating Least-Squares Procedure for Estimating Missing Preference Data

in Product-Concept Testing." *Decision Sciences* (Spring 1986):163.

Womer, N. K. "Estimating Learning Curves From Aggregate Monthly Data." *Management Science* (August 1984): 982.

Public Sector Applications

Cohen, R., and F. Dunford. "Forecasting For Inventory Control: An Example of When 'Simple' Means 'Better.'" *Interfaces* (November–December 1986):95.

Eschenbach, T. G., and G. A. Geistauts. "A Delphi Forecast for Alaska." *Interfaces* (November–December 1985):100.

Kettner, G. "Multivariate Analysis of the Navy's Project UPGRADE." *Interfaces* (November–December 1984):44.

Case: Franklin Taxi Service

The Franklin Taxi Service is the only transportation alternative to the automobile in the small town of Arlingame. Taxis operate on a first call, first serve basis year-round. Customers are charged a flat rate per mile while the cab is on the fare. Currently, the charge is 50 cents per mile.

Paul Franklin, the owner and operator of the service, used his business experience and hunches about taxi service to set the customer fare. Since Franklin has been losing money, Paul realizes that a more systematic analysis may be needed to determine the best fare rate. Pamela, Paul's daughter and a recent management science graduate of a major university, has offered to help.

Pamela begins by collecting data on the company's monthly costs for office rent, utilities, dispatcher and secretary salaries, and cab leases, insurance, and maintenance charges. The accumulated monthly expenses are reported in the following table.

Month	Year				
	1	2	3	4	5
January	4,000	4,100	4,300	4,200	4,500
February	4,200	4,500	4,400	4,700	4,700
March	4,100	4,200	4,300	4,200	4,800
April	3,500	4,000	4,200	4,700	5,100
May	3,200	3,500	3,600	3,400	3,800
June	3,000	3,500	4,000	3,800	4,400
July	2,800	3,100	3,200	3,000	3,700
August	2,600	3,000	3,000	3,100	3,300
September	2,700	3,200	3,400	3,600	3,800
October	3,400	3,500	3,900	4,400	4,600
November	4,000	4,300	4,200	4,500	4,500
December	4,400	5,000	4,700	4,900	5,000

Entries in the table are expressed in dollars.

In addition, Pamela has determined that gasoline and oil for each of the company's 10 cabs costs Franklin about 15 cents per mile. Each cab is operated by two drivers, and each driver is paid $500 per month plus 25 cents per mile while the cab is on a fare. Drivers are local college students and other people seeking to supplement their incomes.

Pamela also believes that there is a relationship between the fair miles and the fair rate. Hence, she has used company records and industry reports to develop the data shown below.

Company	Miles Driven	Fare (dollars)
A	3,750	.52
B	2,250	1.11
C	3,000	.83
D	2,500	1.02
E	4,000	.41
F	3,500	.60
G	3,375	.65
H	3,350	.74
I	2,875	.87
J	2,000	1.25
K	2,375	1.08
L	2,750	.91
M	2,625	.95
N	2,125	1.12
O	1,750	1.30

Entries in the table give the monthly miles driven and the fare per mile for an average cab operated by companies of approximately the same size and in service areas similar to

Franklin. Paul and his drivers agree that the data appear to adequately describe the relationship between the two variables in Franklin's service area.

Unfortunately, Mr. Franklin is overwhelmed by the data. Therefore, he asks Pamela to prepare a report that:

a. Gives an accurate prediction of the company's monthly fixed expenses for the next year.

b. Provides a model that accurately measures the relationship between the miles driven and the fare charged.

c. Recommends a fare that will maximize Franklin's monthly profit.

d. Determines the annual profit that will result from implementing the fare.

Prepare the report in language that would be understandable to Franklin. (Hint: The best fare will be given by the following equation:

$$p^* = (D + a)/2b$$

where

p^* = the best fare

D = the total drivers' salaries per cab

a = the miles driven per cab when the fare = 0

b = the change in the miles driven per cab for each one dollar increase in the fare.)

Part II

Decision Analysis

P ART I presented the foundations of quantitative decision making. It defined the nature of management science, discussed its role in the decision-making process, and identified the steps necessary for successful implementation. We showed that management science involves an explicit formulation, systematic analysis, and solution of decision problems. This next part of the text develops a general structure or framework within which managers can conceptualize these problems. It also presents rational ways to perform the systematic analysis and develop a recommended solution.

Chapter 4 introduces the decision theory approach. It shows how to structure a problem, identify the nature of the decision environment, and develop appropriate strategies for various situations. Often, the situation involves a series of interrelated decisions. This fourth chapter also presents a model specifically designed for such problems.

You will see that formulating an appropriate decision strategy depends on adequate information. If little information is available, a strategy may be extremely risky. Chapter 5 explores ways in which managers can reduce the risk involved in decision making. It shows how to incorporate additional information from sampling and experimentation into the analysis, measure its value, and evaluate the effects on the decision.

In Chapter 6, we consider several extensions to the basic decision theory concepts. We see how to develop strategies in terms of the manager's perceived (rather than the actual monetary or physical) value for the decision outcomes. In addition, this chapter covers methods of decision making for problems with multiple (often conflicting) objectives. There is also a discussion of conflict situations.

After reading this part of the text, you should be able to:

- Recognize the various types of decision-making situations.
- Measure the value of decision-making information.
- Develop decision strategies for various types of situations.

This background will also facilitate your understanding of the concepts in subsequent chapters.

Decision Theory

Chapter Outline

Learning Objectives

- Understand how to structure a decision problem
- Identify the nature of the decision-making situation
- Develop appropriate decision strategies by hand and with the aid of a computer
- Determine how to deal with problems that involve a series of interrelated decisions

Zipping the U.S. Mail

Labor accounts for about 85 percent of the total costs for the U.S. Postal Service (USPS). Since much of the labor is used to sort mail, USPS management believes that significant cost savings could be achieved by automating the process. The strategy is to encourage the use of a nine-digit ZIP code (ZIP + 4) by high-volume mailers. Mail can be sorted more precisely with ZIP + 4 than with the older five-digit code. Specialized equipment, rather than high-cost labor, then would read ZIP + 4 and automatically sort the mail.

In March 1984, the Office of Technology Assessment (OTA) was asked to investigate the advisability of the strategy on both technical and economic grounds. An engineering firm, contracted by OTA, quickly determined that the USPS strategy was technically feasible. Furthermore, an alternative technology and several vendors of the needed equipment were identified in the assessment process.

A management consulting firm was contracted by OTA to determine the economic outlook for the USPS strategy. In this regard, the firm discovered that the postal automation options involved capital investments of more than $350 million and annual maintenance and other costs that could escalate to more than $300 million a year. However, by using decision theory concepts, the firm found that the automation strategy could save the USPS up to $1.5 billion annually in reduced clerk and carrier costs. The analysis also helped OTA to recognize other postal automation options.

Source: J.W. Ulvila, "Postal Automation (ZIP + 4) Technology: A Decision Analysis," *Interfaces* (March–April 1987): 1–12.

In Chapter 2, we saw that decision making involves a relatively well defined process. First, the manager precisely states the problem and its objectives. Next, he or she identifies the available alternatives and collects relevant information. This information is then used to evaluate the alternatives, develop a recommended solution, and implement the choice.

In many cases, the manager has only limited information about the decision environment. For example, the U.S. Postal Service (USPS) has incomplete knowledge about the economic and technical impact of its automation strategy. A rational methodology, called **decision analysis** or **decision theory**, has been developed to conceptualize, analyze, and solve such problems. As the USPS discovered, managers can significantly improve the organization's performance by utilizing this methodology effectively.

This chapter begins with a section on how to structure a problem in decision theory format. It identifies the essential components and formulates an appropriate decision model, or framework, for analysis. As you will see, the appropriate decision strategy depends on the nature of the decision environment. We then go on to identify the various types of environments and examine rational methods for making decisions in each of these situations. All these approaches focus on one-time decisions. In many situations, however, the manager must make a series of interrelated decisions. The final section presents a model specifically designed for such problems.

Applications. In this chapter, the following applications appear in text, examples, and exercises:

- buying or renting equipment
- car pools
- food preparation
- health system design
- insurance coverage
- investment analysis
- new product strategy

- pest control
- plant construction
- product pricing
- product testing
- television programming
- university staffing
- vendor selection

4.1 STRUCTURING THE PROBLEM

Every decision problem will have the same basic elements. The manager's initial tasks are to identify these elements and to organize and summarize them into a formal representation of the problem.

Elements

Decision theory, like any management science process, begins with a clear and concise definition of the problem. This definition should identify objectives, available choices, anticipated conditions, and decision outcomes.

Objectives. Every decision problem involves one or more objectives. It may be to select the most fuel-efficient and comfortable automobile, to choose the least expensive transportation route, or to find the most profitable and least risky investment. Some objectives, like cost and profit, can be measured in monetary terms. Other physical measures include quantity, distance, time, and market share. Goals such as comfort and risk, on the other hand, involve the perceptions and attitudes of the decision maker. As a result, these objectives are usually expressed in psychological terms.

Decision Alternatives. Typically, several choices will be available to achieve the problem's objectives. Since the choices are made by the manager, they are equivalent to the controllable inputs of the mathematical model in Chapter 2. In decision theory, these controllable inputs are known as **courses of action** or **decision alternatives**.

In many cases, the problem may involve an unlimited number of decision alternatives. For example, when blending fuel, a petroleum manager could choose among an infinite number of mixes. Often, however, current knowledge, past experience, and the nature of the problem will limit the number of available actions. The "rules of good blending," for instance, may limit the manager's alternatives to a very narrow range of fuel mixtures. Similarly, there may be only four investment alternatives currently available to a particular investor.

Sometimes, the decision alternatives are expressed in qualitative terms. Thus, a car buyer may describe each alternative by the autombile make and model, and an airline may designate route options by origin and destination codings. In other situations, the alternatives are described quantitatively. Each course of action in a manufacturing problem, for example, may be a specific production quantity. In a similar manner, research and development alternatives could be represented by the various dollar amounts spent on a particular project.

States of Nature. The effectiveness of each decision alternative will depend on future circumstances or anticipated conditions. Since such conditions are usually beyond the manager's control, they are equivalent to the uncontrollable inputs of Chapter 2's mathematical model. In decision theory, these uncontrollable inputs are called **events, possible futures,** or **states of nature**.

States of nature may result from many economic, social, political, and physical forces pushing in various directions. In a car purchase decision, for example, future laws and regulations will affect each automobile model's fuel efficiency and comfort and thus influence the buyer's choice. Yet, these laws and regulations are beyond the buyer's control. Frequently, the uncontrollable future conditions result from actions taken by competing decision makers. For example, the effectiveness of a firm's advertising will depend on the competitor's promotional strategy.

In many situations, the number of possible futures is unlimited, particularly when these conditions are expressed in quantitative terms. A firm's profit, for instance, may depend on total industry sales, and theoretically there could be an infinite variety of potential demands. In other cases, experience or the problem form will limit the number of events to a very narrow, finite range of values. Furthermore, the decision maker may prefer to describe the range with a few qualitative categories. For example, potential economic conditions could be classified simply as poor, fair, or good. Similarly, an electric utility's nuclear plant construction decision could face a political climate that might be described as favorable, indifferent, or unfavorable.

It is necessary to define the states of nature in a way that precludes any two (or more) events from occurring simultaneously. The occurrence of one state will then exclude all others. Such events are said to be **mutually exclusive.** Also, in defining the events, the decision maker should include all possible future situations. The group of events is then said to be **collectively exhaustive.**

Payoffs. To evaluate the choices, management must measure the outcome that will result from each possible combination of decision alternative and state of nature. These outcomes are equivalent to the result variables of the mathematical model from Chapter 2. In decision theory, these result variables are referred to as **payoffs** or **decision outcomes**.

The payoffs must be measured in terms relevant to the decision objective. In selecting the least costly transportation route, for instance, a shipping agent will want to express the decision outcomes in terms of appropriate operating and financial expenses. Frequently, it is also important to specify an appropriate time frame. When using present value

---

Figure 4.1   Decision Situations

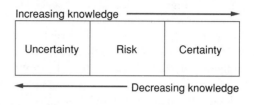

---

to evaluate long-term investments, for example, the decision maker must selectively discount returns and costs over the relevant planning period.

Decision Environment

Each situation will involve different degrees of knowledge about the states of nature. It is customary to divide this knowledge into the three segments, or zones, shown in Figure 4.1.

Uncertainty. At one extreme is the situation in which the decision maker can identify the possible states of nature, but he or she does not have enough information to assess even the likelihood for each event. Such a situation, known as **uncertainty**, is undesirable but occasionally unavoidable. It may arise when there is a completely new phenomenon, such as the 1973 energy crisis or the space shuttle program. Innovative circumstances, such as the introduction of a completely novel product or the development of new technology, can also create uncertainty.

Risk. Usually, the decision maker has enough information available to at least determine the probability for each state of nature. Such a situation, called **risk**, arises in many planning, operating, and control problems.

The probability information can be acquired in a number of ways. Managers are one source. They can use their intuition, wealth of experience, and individual and collective knowledge, beliefs, and judgment to subjectively assign probabilities for each state of nature. Such **subjective probabilities** are most useful for problems like product line expansion, plant relocation, and educational program development. In these cases, the future conditions are familiar to the decision maker, but observed data are unobtainable, insufficient, or unreliable indicators of the future. Subjective input also is one way to incorporate intangible factors into the analysis.

A major difficulty is that each manager may assign a different probability to the same state of nature. Moreover, peer pressure, emotion, and learning can cause the decision maker to change his or her assessment. Consequently, it may be difficult in practice to arrive at a consistent or consensus subjective probability.

Often it is not necessary to rely solely on subjective assessments. In many situations, the underlying process is relatively stable, and future conditions will follow the same pattern as past events. Examples include airline travel, insurance, department store sales, and quality control. Under these circumstances, the decision maker can observe past events or conduct laboratory, statistical, or market experiments. The data can then be processed through a computer information system (CIS) to identify the proportion of times that each event was actually observed in the past or in the experiment. Such a proportion, called an **objective probability**, becomes the likelihood for the corresponding state of nature. Objective probabilities also can be used as additional inputs to update subjective assessments.

Certainty. At the other extreme is the situation where the manager has acquired enough information to know exactly which state of nature will occur. Such a situation is referred to as **certainty**. Although not as prevalent as risk, certainty nevertheless occurs. Standardized and routine operating systems, such as highly automated production lines or a series of mechanized electricity transmission stations, tend to create an environment of certainty. It also may arise in contractual situations (like the commodity and currency "futures" markets), in problems involving budgets or quotas, and when there is a short-term planning horizon.

Importance of Knowledge. Certainty is equivalent to Chapter 2's deterministic model, while risk and uncertainty are stochastic representations. As Figure 4.1 indicates, managers can move from uncertainty toward certainty and thus make more informed decisions by increasing their knowledge of the decision environment. Fields like computer information systems, marketing research, research and development, and statistics provide such knowledge. And that is precisely why they are so important in modern decision making.

One-time versus Sequential Decisions

In some problems, the decision maker at an isolated point in time selects from among several independent alternatives. Furthermore, the resulting outcome is a direct consequence of the single alternative selected. Examples include a developer's site selection for a shopping mall, the advertising copy selected by Wilson for the next issue of *Golf Digest*, and the date for the restart of a nuclear power plant. Such situations are known as *one-time, single-period,* or *single-stage decisions.*

Frequently, however, the problem involves a series of interrelated decisions. Under some of these circumstances, such as production scheduling, actions are required at specific times. For other cases, like product research and development, there is a natural order for the relevant tasks, but the dates might not be so important. In both situations, the manager must progressively select from among several separate but related alternatives. Additionally, the outcome will depend on the entire sequence of actions taken. Such situations are referred to as **sequential decisions**. They are also called **multiperiod decisions** when the required actions are represented by time or **multistage decisions** if there is a natural order of tasks.

Decision Tables

When the problem involves a one-time, single-stage, or single-period decision, a special table can be used to model the problem. Management Situation 4.1 illustrates.

Management Situation 4.1

Plant Construction

Naddol Toy Company is introducing a revolutionary new children's toy, the Star Cruiser. A new plant will be needed to manufacture this product, and four different sizes are under consideration—small, moderate, large, and very large. Experience indicates that the appropriate size will depend on the output volume. A small plant can be operated most economically at low volume, be run most inefficiently at moderate volume, and break even with high volume. A moderate-sized plant can be operated most economically at medium volume and most inefficiently at low volume. Larger plants are most economical at high volume and most inefficient at low volume.

Naddol would like to produce the exact volume desired by consumers. However, the precise annual product demand is uncertain. It also could be low, medium, or high.

Management has used the best information available and forecasting methodologies within a decision support system (DSS) to estimate the profits associated with each plant size. If the company builds a small plant, the DSS analysis forecasts a $250,000 profit with low demand, a $40,000 loss with medium demand, and $0 profit with high demand. A moderate plant is projected to yield a $50,000 loss with low demand, a $350,000 profit with medium demand, and a $60,000 profit with high demand. The large plant gets an estimated $100,000 loss with low demand, an $80,000 profit with medium demand, and a $400,000 profit with high demand. If the company builds a very large plant, the DSS analysis predicts a $120,000 loss with low demand, a $75,000 profit with medium demand, and a $400,000 profit with high demand.

Management wants to determine the most profitable plant size.

Naddol's problem is to determine, at the current time, the most profitable plant size for future operations. The single objective, profit maximization, is expressed in monetary (dollar) terms. There are a finite number of qualitatively-expressed decision alternatives (the small, moderate, large, and very large plant sizes). Similarly, there are a finite number of qualitatively-expressed states of nature (the mutually exclusive and collectively exhaustive events of low, medium, and high demand). The payoffs are the profits associated with each combination of plant size and demand condition. For instance, if the company builds a moderate plant and there is medium demand, it will earn a $350,000 profit. On the other hand, this same alternative will result in only a $60,000 profit with high demand.

By denoting Naddol's decision alternatives as

$$a_1 = \text{build a small plant}$$

$$a_2 = \text{build a moderate plant}$$

$$a_3 = \text{build a large plant}$$

$$a_4 = \text{build a very large plant}$$

and the states of nature as

Table 4.1   **Naddol's Decision Table**

Decision Alternatives	States of Nature		
	s_1 = low demand	s_2 = medium demand	s_3 = high demand
a_1 = build a small plant	$250,000	−$40,000	$0
a_2 = build a moderate plant	−$50,000	$350,000	$60,000
a_3 = build a large plant	−$100,000	$80,000	$400,000
a_4 = build a very large plant	−$120,000	$75,000	$400,000

Loss   Profit

$$s_1 = \text{low demand}$$

$$s_2 = \text{medium demand}$$

$$s_3 = \text{high demand}$$

we can conveniently organize and summarize Naddol's problem elements as Table 4.1. Each row in this table represents a decision alternative, and each column depicts a state of nature. Entries in the squares (cells) give the corresponding payoffs. Such a format, called a **payoff table** or **decision table**, gives an analog model of Naddol's decision problem.

Dominance

At this stage, the decision maker can perform an initial screening to determine if some alternatives can be eliminated from consideration. To illustrate, let us compare alternatives a_3 and a_4 in Table 4.1. When there is low demand (s_1), the large plant (a_3) leads to a smaller loss than the very large plant (a_4). Similarly, in a medium-demand situation (s_2), the $80,000 profit from the large plant is better than the $75,000 gain with a very large plant. If the demand is high (s_3), the profits are identical from both the large and very large plants. Regardless of the demand, a_3 provides outcomes equal to (when s_3 occurs) or better than (for s_1 and s_2) the payoffs for a_4. In such a case, we say that a_3 **dominates** a_4.

Dominated actions are inferior to other alternatives and thus can be disregarded. Since a_4 is a dominated alternative in Naddol's problem, management should eliminate from further consideration the possibility of building a very large plant, obtaining Table 4.2.

The decision maker should continue to screen the alternatives until all dominated actions have been eliminated. Occasionally, a single alternative will dominate all others and thus represent a solution to the problem. A check of Table 4.2, however, will show that there is no additional dominance in Naddol's problem. Consequently, company

Table 4.2   **Naddol's Relevant Decision Table**

Decision Alternatives	States of Nature		
	s_1 = low demand	s_2 = medium demand	s_3 = high demand
a_1 = build a small plant	$250,000	-$40,000	$0
a_2 = build a moderate plant	-$50,000	$350,000	$60,000
a_3 = build a large plant	-$100,000	$80,000	$400,000

Loss   Profit

management still must develop some method for selecting among the three remaining relevant plant sizes.

4.2 DECISION CRITERIA

Once the problem has been properly structured, the manager should select the alternative that best meets the decision objectives. Several logical methods, called **decision criteria**, can be used to make this selection. The choice of a criterion will be based on the manager's knowledge of the decision environment.

Decision Making Under Uncertainty

In its present form, Naddol's plant construction decision involves uncertainty. The company has been able to identify the courses of action, states of nature, and outcomes and then structure the problem with a decision table (Table 4.1 and then Table 4.2). However, the Star Cruiser toy is so revolutionary that management does not have enough information to even assign probabilities for the possible demand conditions. Yet, like most problems involving uncertainty, the decision will substantially affect operations for some time and have a significant financial impact on the firm. Several criteria have been proposed for making decisions in this type of environment.

Optimism. In one approach, the decision maker assumes that each alternative will result in the most favorable possible outcome. Then he or she selects the alternative that leads to the best of these most favorable outcomes. This selection procedure is known as the **optimistic criterion**. When the objective is to select the largest outcome, as with profit or output, such an approach is also labeled the **maximax criterion** (maximum of the maximum). If the objective is to select the smallest outcome, as with cost or time, the optimistic procedure is often called the **minimin criterion** (minimum of the minimum).

In applying this optimistic criterion to Naddol's problem, management first determines the largest profit (most favorable outcome) associated with each plant size (deci-

Table 4.3   **Naddol's Most Favorable Outcomes**

Decision Alternative	Largest Profit
a_1 = build a small plant	$250,000
a_2 = build a moderate plant	$350,000
a_3 = build a large plant	$400,000 ← —— Maximum of the largest profits

sion alternative). From Table 4.2, you can see that the decision to build a small plant (a_1) could result in three possible outcomes. There will be a $250,000 profit if demand is low (s_1), a $40,000 loss with medium demand (s_2), and no net change if there is a high demand (s_3). Clearly, the most favorable outcome for alternative a_1 would be the $250,000 profit. Similarly, $350,000 is the largest profit associated with a_2, and a $400,000 profit is the most favorable outcome for alternative a_3. Table 4.3 summarizes this information.

Naddol's management then selects the decision alternative that results in the maximum of these largest profits. As Table 4.3 indicates, that alternative is a_3. Hence, the recommended decision with the optimistic (in this case, maximax) criterion is to build a large plant.

Although the optimistic criterion provides the opportunity for the largest possible profit ($400,000), it also exposes Naddol to the possibility of the maximum ($100,000) loss. In using this criterion, the decision maker, in effect, is acting like a gambler who disregards the dangers and looks forward only to the rewards. A company should not use such an approach unless it can afford the potential loss and unless this loss is small compared to the possible gain.

Pessimism. Another approach is to assume that each alternative will result in the worst possible outcome. Then the decision maker selects the alternative that leads to the best of these worst outcomes. Such a selection procedure is referred to as the **Wald** or **pessimistic criterion**. When the decision maker seeks the largest outcome, this approach is also called the **maximin criterion** (maximum of the minimum). If the objective is to select the smallest outcome, the pessimistic approach is often labeled the **minimax criterion** (minimum of the maximum).

In applying this pessimistic criterion to Naddol's problem, management first determines the largest loss (or smallest profit) associated with each plant size. Table 4.2 shows that the decision to build a small plant (a_1) could result in a loss of as much as $40,000. This worst possible outcome occurs if there is medium demand (s_2). Similarly, $50,000 is the largest loss associated with a_2, and a $100,000 loss is the worst outcome associated with alternative a_3. The information is summarized in Table 4.4.

Naddol's management then selects the decision alternative that results in the minimum of these largest losses. As Table 4.4 indicates, that alternative is a_1. Thus, the recommended decision with the pessimistic (in this case, maximin) criterion is to build a small plant.

Table 4.4   **Naddol's Worst Possible Outcomes**

Decision Alternative	Largest Loss (Negative Profit)	
a_1 = build a small plant	−$40,000 ←———	Minimum of the
a_2 = build a moderate plant	−$50,000	largest losses
a_3 = build a large plant	−$100,000	

By using this criterion, management avoids the possibility of extremely unfavorable outcomes. Naddol, for instance, can do no worse than a $40,000 loss. However, it also neglects potentially rewarding opportunities. Decision makers are inclined to have such an ultraconservative outlook when potential losses may be unacceptable and even ruinous for the organization. Military or defense decisions often involve this criterion.

Weighted Extremes. In practice, most decision makers are neither perfect optimists nor pure pessimists. Rather, their outlook tends to be somewhere in between. This observation leads to a compromise criterion in which the manager first identifies both the best and worst outcomes associated with each decision alternative. Next, a scale of 0 to 1 is used to measure the decision maker's degree of optimism concerning the attainment of the most favorable outcomes. On such a scale, 0 represents complete pessimism and 1 signifies total optimism. The actual measurement, labeled alpha (α), is known as the **coefficient of optimism**. Each best outcome is weighted by this coefficient α, and the corresponding worst outcome is multiplied by the index of pessimism $(1 - \alpha)$. The resulting value

(4.1) $\alpha(\text{best outcome}) + (1 - \alpha)(\text{worst outcome})$

gives a weighted outcome for each decision alternative. Then the decision maker selects the alternative that provides the best of these weighted outcomes. Such a procedure is referred to as the **Hurwicz** or **coefficient of optimism criterion**.

In applying this criterion to Naddol's problem, let us assume that management is 40 percent confident that the company will always get the best possible outcome. Hence $\alpha = .4$, and Naddol expects the worst to happen $1 - \alpha = 1 - .4 = .6$, or 60 percent, of the time. Using these weights, the best and worst outcome data from Tables 4.3 and 4.4, respectively, and expression (4.1), management would obtain the results shown in Table 4.5. As the table indicates, decision alternative a_2 leads to the largest weighted profit ($110,000). Therefore, the recommended decision with the coefficient of optimism criterion is to build a moderate plant.

This coefficient of optimism procedure is a more general approach than either the optimistic or pessimistic criterion. In fact, the optimistic and pessimistic criteria are merely special cases of the Hurwicz method. When $\alpha = 1$, for instance, all the weight is given to the best outcome. In that case, the coefficient of optimism criterion leads to the same recommendation as the optimistic criterion. Alternatively, if $\alpha = 0$, then all the weight is given to the worst outcome. In this case, the decision with the coefficient of optimism criterion is identical to the decision with the pessimistic criterion.

Table 4.5   **Naddol's Weighted Outcomes with** $\alpha = .4$

Decision Alternative	Largest Profit	Largest Loss (Negative Profit)	Weighted Profit $= \alpha$(Largest Profit)$+$ $(1-\alpha)$(Largest Loss)
a_1 = build a small plant	$250,000	$-$40,000	(.4)($250,000) $+$ (.6)($-$40,000) $=$ $ 76,000
a_2 = build a moderate plant	$350,000	$-$50,000	(.4)($350,000) $+$ (.6)($-$50,000) $=$ $ 110,000 $\leftarrow$
a_3 = build a large plant	$400,000	$-$100,000	(.4)($400,000) $+$ (.6)($-$100,000) $=$ $ 100,000

Largest weighted profit ————————

However, there are difficulties with the coefficient of optimism approach. The main problem is how to measure the value of α. Since α is a personal index of optimism, it should be based on the decision maker's subjective assessments. In practice, however, it is difficult to make such assessments in a consistent manner or arrive at a consensus.

Another concern involves the amount of data utilized in the approach. In computing weighted payoffs, the coefficient of optimism criterion considers only the best and worst outcomes. As a result, this approach ignores other outcomes that may be relevant to the decision. The optimistic and pessimistic criteria have a similar shortcoming.

Lost Opportunity. Other approaches consider more than just the two extreme outcomes. In one of these procedures, the evaluation is based on the remorse that the manager might experience after selecting a decision alternative. To see what is involved, let us again examine Table 4.2.

Suppose that Naddol builds a small plant (a_1) and then learns that there is a high demand (s_3) for Star Cruisers. Table 4.2 indicates that the resulting profit will be $0. But if management knew beforehand that demand was going to be high, then the company would have built a large plant (a_3) and earned $400,000 profit. The difference between the best possible payoff ($400,000) and the outcome actually received ($0) is known as the **regret** or **opportunity loss** from the decision. Hence, when state of nature s_3 occurs, Naddol will incur an opportunity loss of

$$\$400,000 - \$0 = \$400,000$$

if they selected alternative a_1.

Regrets can be calculated in a similar manner for each combination of decision alternative and state of nature. Table 4.2 indicates that $350,000 is the largest profit possible when there is medium demand (s_2). But if Naddol builds a small plant (a_1), then the company will *not* earn the $350,000 under the s_2 condition and in fact will lose $40,000. In other words, Naddol will have a regret of

$$\$350,000 - (-\$40,000) = \$390,000.$$

On the other hand, if the company builds a moderate plant (a_2) and then state of nature s_2 occurs, it will earn the largest possible profit ($350,000). Thus, the company will have a

$$\$350,000 - \$350,000 = \$0$$

Table 4.6   **Naddol's Regret Table**

Decision Alternatives	States of Nature		
	s_1 = low demand	s_2 = medium demand	s_3 = high demand
a_1 = build a small plant	$0	$390,000	$400,000
a_2 = build a moderate plant	$300,000	$0	$340,000
a_3 = build a large plant	$350,000	$270,000	$0

Regret or opportunity loss

Table 4.7   **Naddol's Largest Possible Regrets**

Decision Alternative	Largest Regret
a_1 = build a small plant	$400,000
a_2 = build a moderate plant	$340,000 ← Smallest of the largest regrets
a_3 = build a large plant	$350,000

opportunity loss, or no regret. Table 4.6 summarizes the opportunity loss information for Naddol's problem. Such a representation is called a **regret table** or **opportunity loss table**. Note that by its nature, the value of regret can never be negative.

Poor decisions will result in high opportunity losses. Hence, it has been argued that managers should avoid alternatives associated with large regrets. There are several ways to do so. One suggested approach is to identify the largest possible opportunity loss for each decision alternative, then select the alternative that leads to the smallest of these largest opportunity losses. Such a procedure is known as the **Savage** or **minimax regret criterion**. Since this criterion is equivalent to selecting the best of the worst regrets, like the Wald approach, it is pessimistic in nature.

Naddol's management can apply the Savage criterion by first using the opportunity loss data from Table 4.6 to determine the largest possible regret for each plant size. Table 4.7 reports the results.

Then the decision maker selects the plant size that results in the minimum of these largest opportunity losses. As Table 4.7 indicates, that alternative would be a_2. Therefore, the recommended decision with the minimax regret criterion is to build a moderate plant.

By using this criterion, management will avoid extremely regretful decisions. Naddol, for instance, will limit its opportunity loss to $340,000. On the other hand, it also forgoes the potential benefits from exceptionally good decisions. In this respect, the Savage criterion is similar to hedging, that is, settling for an intermediate outcome rather than engaging in speculative ventures. The practice is prevalent in international and domestic commodity and currency trade.

Table 4.8   **Naddol's Simple Average Outcomes**

Decision Alternative	Simplest Average of Profits
a_1 = build a small plant	($250,000 − $40,000 + $0)/3 = $70,000
a_2 = build a moderate plant	(−$50,000 + $350,000 + $60,000)/3 = $120,000
a_3 = build a large plant	(−$100,000 + $80,000 + $400,000)/3 = $126,666.67

Best of the
average profits

Unfortunately, there is a technical difficulty with the regret criterion. Remember, the opportunity losses from a particular state of nature are determined by comparing the outcomes for all available decision alternatives. Thus, when management adds or drops some alternatives, there are corresponding changes in the opportunity losses. If these added or dropped actions are not the best choices, they should have no effect on the selection of the remaining alternatives. But the opportunity loss changes could alter the ranking of alternatives and result in a revised recommendation. In addition, although all outcomes are considered in computing opportunity losses, the regret criterion utilizes only a portion of this information (the largest losses) to reach a decision.

Average Outcome. It is possible to incorporate all outcome information in the evaluation process. A suggested approach is to find the simple average of the outcomes associated with each decision alternative, then select the alternative that results in the best of these average outcomes. This method is known as the **Laplace** or **rationality criterion**.

Table 4.8, for example, indicates that when Naddol builds a small plant (a_1), the company earns $250,000 profit if demand is low (s_1). On the other hand, it loses $40,000 when there is medium demand (s_2) and breaks even in a high-demand situation (s_3). Consequently, this a_1 alternative will result in an average profit of

$$\frac{\$250,000 - \$40,000 + \$0}{3} = \frac{\$210,000}{3} = \$70,000.$$

The simple average for each decision alternative is reported in Table 4.8. As the table indicates, decision alternative a_3 leads to the largest of the simple average profits ($126,666.67). Therefore, the recommended decision with the rationality criterion is to build a large plant.

By using the rationality criterion, the decision maker implicitly assumes that each state of nature is equally likely. This assumption is based on the **principle of insufficient reason**. According to this principle, if there is no basis for claiming that one event has a higher probability than another, each should be assigned an equal likelihood. In many practical situations, however, it would be difficult to accept the equal likelihood assumption. Why would a government budget analyst, for instance, believe that prosperity and depression are equally likely to follow a period of economic stagnation? Similarly, it seems unreasonable for a maintenance manager to assume that the probability of a breakdown will be the same on old and new equipment.

Table 4.9   Criteria for Decision Making Under Uncertainty

Optimism	Pessimism	Coefficient of Optimism	Minimax Regret	Rationality
1. Identify the most favorable outcome associated with each decision alternative. 2. Select the alternative that leads to the best of the most favorable outcomes.	1. Identify the worst outcome associated with each decision alternative. 2. Select the alternative that leads to the best of the worst outcomes.	1. Identify both the best and worst outcomes associated with each decision alternative. 2. Identify the decision maker's coefficient of optimism (α). The coefficient has a value between 0 and 1. 3. Calculate the following weighted outcome for each decision alternative: α (best outcome) + $(1-\alpha)$ (worst outcome) 4. Select the alternative that leads to the best weighted outcome.	1. Calculate the regret associated with each state of nature. Regret is the difference between the best possible payoff and the outcome actually recieved from selecting a decision alternative. 2. Identify the largest regret associated with each decision alternative. 3. Select the alternative that leads to the smallest of largest regrets.	1. Compute the simple average outcome for each decision alternative. The simple average is the sum of outcomes divided by the number of events. 2. Select the decision alternative that leads to the best of these simple average outcomes.

There is another problem with the rationality criterion. Suppose that a decision problem originally has three states of nature. Management subsequently separates one of them into two distinct events, each with the same outcomes as the original state of nature. Although there are now four events instead of three, the basic structure of the problem remains the same. Consequently, the separation should not affect the selection of a decision alternative. Remember, however, that the simple average is found by summing the outcomes for a particular alternative and dividing the result by the number of events. When management creates the additional states of nature, it implicitly assigns a weight of $1/4 + 1/4 = 1/2$ rather than $1/3$ to the outcomes for the original event. In effect, the separation changes the original simple average. Unfortunately, such changes could alter the ranking of alternatives and lead to a revised decision.

Comparison of Criteria. Table 4.9 summarizes the criteria for decision making under uncertainty. In applying these criteria to Naddol's problem, we have arrived at the following conclusions:

1.   The pessimistic recommendation is to build a small plant (a_1).

2.   The coefficient of optimism (with $\alpha = .4$) and regret decisions are to build a moderate plant (a_2).

3.   The optimistic and rationality choices are to build a large plant (a_3).

Hence, even for this simple situation, there is lack of agreement among the criteria about the selection of a decision alternative. Such a result should not be surprising. Each manager has a unique attitude, outlook, and philosophy. Ultimately, this person will select a decision criterion that, according to his or her judgment, is consistent with these personal characteristics and is most appropriate for the situation. Our five criteria merely reflect what some decision makers might do. You may do something else and thus devise your own personal decision criterion.

Although the criteria provide rational ways to evaluate alternatives for an individual, the ambiguous nature of decision making under uncertainty can cause problems for groups. In practice, many decisions are made by committees. When these committees consist of individuals with conflicting philosophies, it may be difficult to arrive at a consensus. Even if conflicts can be resolved, there could be significant and costly delays in group decisions.

In addition, each of the proposed criteria has a deficiency that can cause the manager to make a disastrous decision. These inadequacies can be traced to the same cause: None of the criteria utilize all the information generally available to the decision maker.

Decision Making Under Risk

Uncertainty about the states of nature limits the manager's ability to analyze the decision situation. Increasing his or her knowledge of the environment will enable the manager to make wiser decisions. That is why most organizations will not make a final decision until enough information is acquired to at least measure the uncertainty with probabilities. Management Situation 4.2 illustrates.

Management Situation 4.2

Toy Demand

This problem is a modified version of Management Situation 4.1. Naddol's board president thinks that the plant construction decision is too important to make under such uncertain conditions. Consequently, she polls a group of company executives, industry officials, and consumer panels about the potential marketability of the Star Cruiser toy. Based on this information, she believes that there is a 30 percent chance of low, 60 percent chance of medium, and 10 percent chance of high demand.

The president wants to use this information for selecting the most profitable plant size.

Naddol's board president has used executive and consumer opinions, as well as her own judgment, to subjectively assign probabilities for the states of nature. Specifically, if

$$P(s_1) = \text{probability of low demand}$$
$$P(s_2) = \text{probability of medium demand}$$
$$P(s_3) = \text{probability of high demand}$$

she believes that

$$P(s_1) = .3$$

$$P(s_2) = .6$$

$$P(s_3) = .1.$$

Each state of nature has some likelihood of occurrence, and since the demand levels are collectively exhaustive and mutually exclusive, the sum of the probabilities is $.3 + .6 + .1 = 1$. As a result, Naddol's situation now involves risk rather than uncertainty.

Most Probable Event. Sometimes, a decision maker assumes that the most likely state of nature is the event that will actually occur. The individual then selects the decision alternative that leads to the best outcome associated with this event. Such a procedure is known as the **maximum likelihood (ML) criterion**.

In applying this criterion to Naddol's problem, recall that the probabilities for the states of nature are .3 for s_1, .6 for s_2, and .1 for s_3. Hence, medium demand (s_2) is most likely event. According to Table 4.2, when s_2 occurs, the company will incur a $40,000 loss if a small plant is built (a_1). On the other hand, there will be a $350,000 profit from a moderate plant (a_2) and an $80,000 gain from a large plant (a_3). As you can see, a_2 is the most profitable alternative associated with the most likely event (s_2). Therefore, the recommended decision with the maximum likelihood criterion is to build a moderate plant.

Some nonrepetitive decisions are based on this criterion. A new venture, for instance, may have a high (.9 or more) likelihood of success. Although there is a chance of failure, the decision often will be based only on what happens when the venture succeeds (the most likely event).

There are some serious shortcomings in the maximum likelihood criterion. The major deficiency is that the approach ignores all but the most likely state of nature and thus uses only a small portion of the available information. In addition, suppose there are numerous events and each has a small, nearly equal probability of occurrence. Under these circumstances, it may be difficult (if not impossible) to make a decision with this criterion.

Expected Value. In a risk situation, any one of the events is possible. Thus, decision criteria should, in some way, consider the outcomes associated with each state of nature. The criteria that best utilize all available information are based on expected outcomes.

One approach is to first compute a weighted average outcome for each alternative. This average, called an **expected value**, is found by multiplying each outcome by its probability of occurrence and then summing the results. The decision maker then selects the alternative that leads to the best expected value. For obvious reasons, such a procedure is referred to as the **expected value (EV) criterion**. When the outcomes are measured in monetary terms, such as dollar profit or cost, this approach is also called the **expected monetary value (EMV) criterion**.

In applying this criterion to Naddol's problem, management must first determine the expected profit from each plant size. To do so, it will need the profit data from Table 4.2 and the chairperson's subjective probability assessments. This information indicates that the decision to build a small plant (a_1) will earn \$250,000 during $P(s_1) = .3$ of the time (when there is low demand). In addition, alternative a_1 will provide a \$40,000 loss during $P(s_2) = .6$ of the time (medium demand) and \$0 during $P(s_3) = .1$ of the time (high demand). Therefore, Naddol's weighted average or expected profit will be

$$\$250,000(.3) - \$40,000(.6) + \$0(.1) = \$51,000$$

if the company builds a small plant.

You can see that the more likely outcomes are given more weight than less probable payoffs. Furthermore, the probability of occurrence for an outcome is equivalent to the likelihood of the corresponding state of nature. In general, the expected monetary value for decision alternative a_i is given by the expression

(4.2)
$$\text{EMV}(a_i) = \sum_{j=1}^{n} [P(s_j)O_{ij}]$$

where O_{ij} = monetary outcome resulting from alternative a_i when state of nature s_j occurs, $P(s_j)$ = probability that state of nature s_j will occur, n = number of states of nature, and $\text{EMV}(a_i)$ = expected monetary value from alternative a_i. By using expression (4.2) to calculate the expected profit for each plant size, Naddol's management will get the results shown in Table 4.10.

Using the expected value criterion, the company would select the plant size that leads to the largest expected profit. According to Table 4.10, that would be alternative a_2. Thus, the recommended decision with the expected monetary value criterion is to build a moderate plant.

It is important to realize that the expected value is not the outcome that the decision maker will get when he or she selects the recommended alternative. If Naddol builds a moderate plant, for instance, the company should not expect to receive a \$201,000 profit. Indeed, as Table 4.2 shows, depending on the level of demand, actual profits will be $-\$50,000$, \$350,000, or \$60,000. Rather, the expected value represents the average outcome that results over the long run from continually repeating the decision alternative. Suppose, for example, that Naddol plans to build a large number of moderate toy plants. Then the expected value of \$201,000 will provide a good estimate of the average profit from such ventures.

An expected value approach can also be appropriate and valuable for one-time, non-repetitive decision situations. A company may have to make several one-time decisions that each involve the same relative magnitude and structure. Such a situation resembles a single decision that will be repeated many times. By consistently using an expected value approach for each one-time decision, management will obtain an average outcome similar to that for the repetitive situation.

Expected Opportunity Loss. A related approach is to base the evaluation on the regret that the manager could expect from selecting each alternative. In this method, the decision maker first redefines the outcomes in terms of opportunity losses. Next, he or she calculates the expected value of the opportunity losses associated with each decision alternative. Then the manager selects the alternative that leads to the smallest of these expected opportunity losses. Such a procedure is referred to as the **expected opportunity loss (EOL) criterion**.

Table 4.10   **Naddol's Expected Profits**

a_1 = **Build a Small Plant**			
State of Nature s_j	Probability $P(s_j)$	Profit O_{ij}	Probability × Profit $P(s_j)O_{ij}$
s_1	.3	$250,000	$75,000
s_2	.6	−40,000	−$24,000
s_3	.1	$0	$0
		Expected Profit EMV(a_1) = $51,000	

a_2 = **Build a Moderate Plant**			
State of Nature s_j	Probability $P(s_j)$	Profit O_{ij}	Probability × Profit $P(s_j)O_{ij}$
s_1	.3	−$50,000	−$15,000
s_2	.6	$350,000	$210,000
s_3	.1	$60,000	$6,000
		Expected Profit EMV(a_2) = $201,000	

a_3 = **Build a Large Plant**			
State of Nature s_j	Probability $P(s_j)$	Profit O_{ij}	Probability × Profit $P(s_j)O_{ij}$
s_1	.3	−$100,000	−$30,000
s_2	.6	$80,000	$48,000
s_3	.1	$400,000	$40,000
		Expected Profit EMV(a_3) = $58,000	

Table 4.6 gives Naddol's opportunity losses. These data and the chairperson's subjective probabilities indicate that alternative a_1 will involve no ($0) regret 30 percent of the time (occasions of low demand). However, this alternative will generate a $390,000 opportunity loss 60 percent of the time (occasions of medium demand) and a $400,000 regret 10 percent of the time (occasions of high demand). Therefore, Naddol's expected opportunity loss from building a small plant will be

$$\text{EOL}(a_1) = \$0(.3) + \$390,000(.6) + \$400,000(.1) = \$274,000.$$

Similarly, if the company builds a moderate plant, there will be an expected opportunity loss of

$$\text{EOL}(a_2) = \$300,000(.3) + \$0(.6) + \$340,000(.1) = \$124,000$$

and if the company constructs a large plant, the expected opportunity loss will be

$$\text{EOL}(a_3) = \$350,000(.3) + \$270,000(.6) + \$0(.1) = \$267,000.$$

Table 4.11   **Decision Making Under Risk**

Expected Value (EV)	Expected Opportunity Loss (EOL)	Maximum Likelihood (ML)
1. Calculate the expected value for each decision alternative. 2. Select the alternative that leads to the best expected value.	1. Calculate the regret associated with each state of nature. 2. Compute the expected opportunity loss for each decision alternative. 3. Select the alternative that leads to the smallest expected opportunity loss.	1. Identify the state of nature that has the largest probability of occurence. 2. Select the decision alternative that leads to the best outcome associated with the most likely state of nature.

These results indicate that alternative a_2 leads to the smallest expected opportunity loss. Consequently, the recommended decision with the EOL criterion is to build a moderate plant.

Recall that the expected monetary value criterion also recommended alternative a_2. This is not a coincidence. *The decision alternative with the best expected monetary value will always be the action that leads to the smallest expected opportunity loss.* Indeed, the EMV and EOL approaches are merely different sides of the same coin. Each offers a different philosophical explanation of why people make particular choices. Chapter 5 will show how this relationship between the EMV and EOL can be used to measure the value of information.

Evaluation of Criteria. Table 4.11 summarizes the criteria for decision making under risk. Note that the expected value (EV) and expected opportunity loss (EOL) criteria always lead to the same decision recommendation and hence are interchangeable. These approaches are best suited for repetitive decisions or a group of one-time, nonrepetitive situations that involve a similar structure and magnitude of outcomes. Since the EV and EOL approaches both utilize all available problem information, they are the preferred criteria for decision making under risk.

An expected value measure, however, may be meaningless or inappropriate for a few rare, nonrepetitive decisions. In such cases, the decision maker can resort to the maximum likelihood criterion.

Decision Making Under Certainty

Suppose Naddol introduces the Star Cruiser in a wide variety of test markets and then measures sales over a period of several months. The company also continues to use the product in its consumer panels. Based on the test performance, panel data, and collective staff opinion, management is certain that there will be a medium demand for the toy. In effect, then, the decision maker can assign a probability of 1 to state of nature s_2. As a result, Naddol is now in a situation of certainty.

When there is certainty, the situation can be mapped as a decision table with a single column. In particular, Naddol's decision table would look like Table 4.12. In this

Table 4.12   **Naddol's Decision Table Under Certainty**

Decision Alternatives	States of Nature
	s_2 = medium demand
a_1 = build a small plant	−$40,000
a_2 = build a moderate plant	$350,000
a_3 = build a large plant	$80,000

environment, the decision maker compares all the outcomes associated with the single state of nature and then selects the alternative that best meets the decision objective.

Table 4.12 supplies the relevant data for Naddol's problem. According to the table, when there is medium demand, the company will lose $40,000 with a small plant (a_1), gain $350,000 with a moderate plant (a_2) and gain $80,000 with a large plant (a_3). Since management wants to maximize profits, the best decision alternative under certainty is to build a moderate plant.

At first glance, it may appear that problems under certainty are quite simple to solve. In reality, decision making under certainty can be surprisingly difficult. The major obstacle arises from the large number of alternatives that the decision maker usually has to consider. In cases involving a finite number of options, it might be possible to examine each alternative with the aid of a computer. Typically, however, the decision maker has neither the time nor the resources to expend such an effort. And when there are an infinite number of alternatives, it is physically impossible to examine each possibility.

To some extent, these same computational difficulties exist for problems involving risk and uncertainty. That is why management scientists have developed mathematical models specifically designed for large-scale decision-making problems. Many of these models, including mathematical programming, network flows, sequential formulations, queuing and inventory theory, and simulation, will be discussed later in the text.

Computer Analysis

Figure 4.2 summarizes the decision theory process. In practice, the calculations involved in this process can be quite cumbersome and time-consuming, especially for large-scale problems. Fortunately, there are computer programs available to perform the necessary computations and report the results in an easily understandable format. One such program is accessible through the **QUANTITATIVE MANAGEMENT (QM)** software.

The program is accessed by selecting Decision Theory from **QM**'s main menu. Figure 4.3 then illustrates how the program solves Naddol's plant construction problem with a decision environment of risk.

The user executes this module by selecting the Decision making under risk command from the Decision Theory menu. Data input begins with the Edit selection from the Input menu. Report options also can be chosen from the Output menu. The program then requests information about the problem.

Figure 4.2   Decision Theory Process

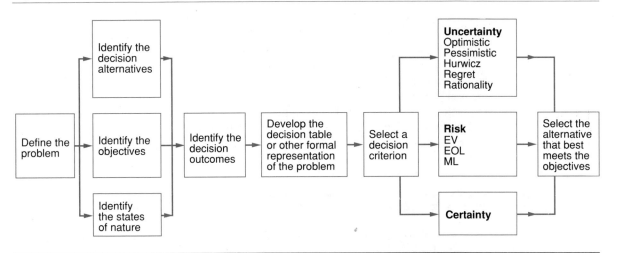

Figure 4.3   Computer Analysis of Naddol's Problem

Decision Theory:
- Decision making under uncertainty
- * Decision making under risk
- Decision making under certainty
- Sequential decisions

Input:
- * Edit
- Load
- Print
- Save

Output:
- Full
- * Summary
- * Print
- Save

Problem Formulation:
How many states of nature? (enter a number up to 40) 3
How many decision alternatives? (enter a number up to 40) 3
Enter the outcomes in the payoff table below.

	s_1	s_2	s_3
a_1	250	−40	0
a_2	−50	350	60
a_3	−100	80	400

Enter the probabilities for the states of nature below.

$$P(s_1) = .3 \qquad P(s_2) = .6 \qquad P(s_3) = .1$$

Do you want to maximize (MAX) or minimize (MIN) the objective? MAX

Criterion	RECOMMENDATIONS Recommended Alternative	Expected Outcome
Expected value	a_2	201
Expected opportunity loss	a_2	124
Maximum likelihood	a_2	350

As Figure 4.3 demonstrates, the user first must enter the number of states and alternatives. Since Naddol has three demand conditions and three nondominated plant sizes, the manager should respond with the value 3 after both the state and alternative prompts. Next, the user enters the outcomes in the payoff table that appears on the screen. To save keystrokes, outcomes are entered in thousands of dollars in Figure 4.3.

At this stage, the decision maker must specify the probability for each state of nature and the decision objective (maximization MAX or minimization MIN). After receiving the user's response, the program processes the data and generates the recommendations for each decision criterion. For example, Figure 4.3 illustrates that probabilities of $P(s_1)$ = .3, $P(s_2)$ = .6, and $P(s_3)$ = .1 with a maximization objective (MAX response) provide outputs that match the text recommendations.

4.3 SEQUENTIAL DECISIONS

A review of the decision theory process is outlined in Figure 4.2. This process can also be applied to sequential problems. In the process, however, these problems typically are structured as graphs rather than decision tables. Management Situation 4.3 illustrates.

Management Situation 4.3

Pest Control

An infestation by the Adriatic fruit fly (adfly) is threatening the state's agricultural economy. In response to this threat, the governor has assembled a panel of pest control specialists and asked them to study the problem and develop some methods for attacking the adfly. After careful deliberations, the panel has identified three possible approaches. One method is to spray the infested areas from the air with an insecticide called malathion. Although such a program is expected to be 100 percent effective, it will cost $10 million and result in "environmental damages" totaling an additional $5 million.

A second proposal calls for a multiple-step eradication program. In the first stage, a special scent will be used to lure male adflies into mechanical traps. It will cost $2 million to place and collect the traps. Next, agriculture personnel will conduct tests on the scent/trap results to determine the number of fertile males remaining in the native population. Previous experience indicates that these traps have a 60 percent chance of reducing the fertile male population to a small number. There is also a 40 percent chance that the remaining number will be large. After studying the test results, the state will choose either one of two actions. One alternative is to sterilize the trapped males in a laboratory and then release them in the native population. Although sterilization has an estimated $3 million cost, it would, if successful, eradicate the adfly in a relatively short time and limit crop damage to $4 million. Otherwise, the damage is expected to reach $12 million. Previous studies indicate that if the traps leave a small number of fertile males, sterilization will succeed 70 percent of the time and fail 30 percent of the time. When the remaining number is large, however, there is only a 20 percent chance of success and an 80 percent likelihood of failure. A second alternative after testing the trap results is to spray the infested areas on the ground with malathion. Ground spraying

---

Figure 4.4   **The Government's Initial Decision Point**

---

will cost $6 million and result in another $4 million worth of "environmental damage," but it will completely eradicate the adfly.

The third proposal is to spray the infested areas from the air with a juvenile hormone that prevents the larvae from maturing into adult adflies. This program will cost $7 million but create no environmental damage. If it works, the adfly will become extinct in a short time, and crop damage will be limited to $3.5 million. Otherwise, the damage is expected to total $20 million. Previous experience indicates that the hormone has worked 50 percent of the time and failed on 50 percent of its applications.

The governor wants to use the least costly pest control program.

The pest control problem is different from our previous examples in two important ways. For one thing, the situation involves two separate but related decisions. The state government first must choose from among aerial malathion spraying, a scent/trap program, and the juvenile hormone approach. If it sets traps, officials must conduct tests, analyze the results, and then either release sterile male flies or ground-spray with malathion. Also, the same events do not apply to each decision alternative. Aerial malathion spraying has a certain known outcome, while the two other alternatives each involve a unique risk.

It would be difficult and cumbersome to depict such a problem with a decision table. That is why management scientists developed a tool designed specifically for these complex sequential decision problems.

Decision Trees

The decision maker can use a graph to conveniently organize and summarize the elements of the state's pest control problem. The decision maker starts by depicting the initial choice that must be made. The choice to be made is usually designated by a square with the alternatives shown as lines branching out to the right. In this graphic approach, such a square is referred to as a **decision point**.

Figure 4.4 portrays the initial decision point in the pest control problem. It shows that the government initially has three decision alternatives: to air-spray malathion, place scent traps, or air-spray the juvenile hormone.

The next step is to identify the immediate consequences of selecting each of the initial alternatives. Aerial spraying, for instance, has only one effect: It will completely

Figure 4.5   The Government's Initial Chance Points

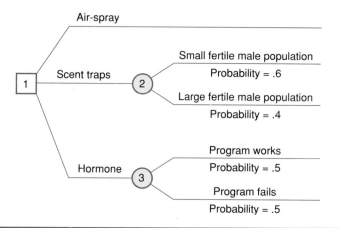

Figure 4.6   The Government's Second Decision Points

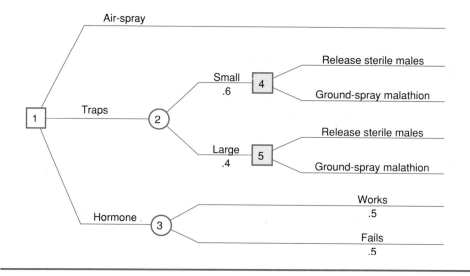

eradicate the adfly. Scent traps, however, are another matter. The immediate result of this program is to leave either a small or a large number of fertile male flies in the native population. There is a 60 percent chance that the remaining number will be small and a 40 percent likelihood of it being large. Similarly, the juvenile hormone will either work (50 percent of the time) or fail (50 percent of the time).

Such stochastic events are typically shown as circles with lines branching to the right. In this graphic approach, these circles are called **event points** or **chance points**. The government's initial chance points are illustrated in Figure 4.5. Notice that on a chance point branch, the state of nature appears above the line and the probability below the line.

Figure 4.7   **The Government's Second Chance Points**

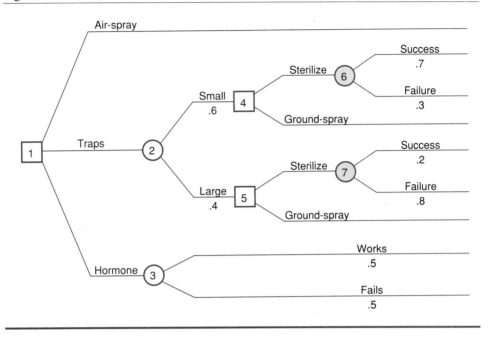

Management must continue this process of branching from left to right until it has identified all possible decision and chance points involved in the problem. At this stage (Figure 4.5), the scent trap program is the only initial alternative that involves further branching. After collecting traps, conducting tests, and studying the results, the government must make another choice. It will either sterilize the trapped male flies in a laboratory and then release them in the native population, or it will spray the infested areas on the ground with malathion. The choice must be made whether the number of remaining fertile males is large or small. The second decision points are shown in Figure 4.6.

The government is certain that ground spraying will eradicate the adfly. Hence, this action will create no further branching. On the other hand, if the traps leave a small number of fertile males, sterilization will succeed 70 percent of the time and fail 30 percent of the time. When the remaining number is large, there is only a 20 percent chance of success with sterilization. As a result, the problem involves the additional chance points shown in Figure 4.7.

After constructing all the branches, the decision maker must then identify the corresponding outcomes. For example, aerial malathion spraying will cost $10 million and result in "environmental damages" totaling an additional $5 million. Thus, there will be a $15 million cost associated with the air-spray branch in Figure 4.7. Similarly, the scent traps cost $2 million and sterilization another $3 million, and when this scent/sterilization program is successful, crop damage for the adfly will be limited to $4 million. Consequently, the traps/small/sterilize/success (or traps/large/sterilize/success) branch in Figure 4.7 results in a cost of $9 million. However, when scent/sterilization

Figure 4.8   The Government's Decision Tree

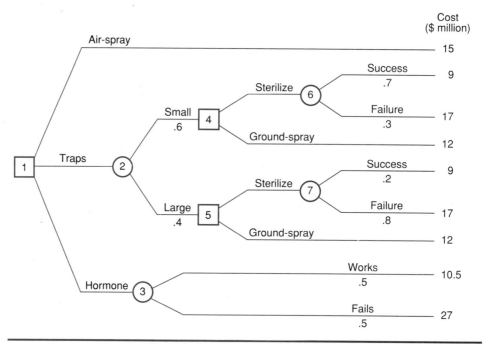

Figure 4.9   Small Portion of the Government's Decision Tree

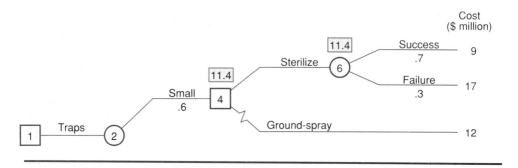

is a failure, crop damage will reach $12 million. Thus, the traps/small/sterilize/failure (or traps/large/sterilize/failure) branch has a cost of $17 million.

The outcomes associated with each branch in the government's pest control problem are shown at the right of Figure 4.8. This type of graphic representation is referred to as a **decision tree**. It shows at a glance the order in which decisions are expected to be made, the consequences of these actions, and the resulting outcomes. As such, the decision tree serves as an excellent management communication device.

Although decision trees are best suited for complex sequential managerial problems, they are also applicable to simpler single-stage situations. In other words, the decision tree can be an effective substitute for a payoff table.

Backward Induction

The government is now in a position to evaluate the three pest control plans. To do so, it first must identify the outcomes that can be expected from each decision alternative. In the case of aerial malathion spraying, the identification process is easy. The government is certain that this spraying will cost $15 million. However, the two other alternatives involve risk, and one of these also requires a sequence of decisions. As a result, it will be more difficult to determine the expected costs of the scent/trap and juvenile hormone programs.

Consider the scent/trap program. As Figure 4.8 indicates, if the traps leave a large number of fertile males and the government subsequently ground-sprays the infested areas, the cost will total $12 million. On the other hand, the government can release sterile males in the native population rather than ground-spraying the infested areas. If successful, sterilization in this situation will result in a cost of only $9 million. Thus, the cost of the scent/trap program will depend on the events that occur and the resulting actions taken after the government sets the traps. Consequently, to determine this cost, the decision maker must start at the right of the decision tree and work backward to the initial decision point.

For example, let us examine the action required if the traps leave a small number of fertile male flies in the native population. Figure 4.9 shows the relevant portion of the government's decision tree. As you can see, the action involves decision point 4.

If the government decides to sterilize, it will be faced with the risk depicted by chance point 6. That is, there will be a .7 probability of incurring a $9 million expense and a .3 chance that the cost will be $17 million. In this situation, sterilization has an expected cost of

$$\$9(.7) + \$17(.3) = \$11.4 \text{ million.}$$

For convenience, this value is placed above the applicable chance point inside a rectangle.

The decision to ground-spray at decision point 4 will lead to a certain cost of $12 million. Since the expected cost ($11.4 million) for sterilization is less than $12 million, the government should disregard ground-spraying at decision point 4. That is, if the traps leave only a small number of fertile males, the decision maker should release sterile flies in the native population. This choice, of course, assumes that expected monetary value is an appropriate decision criterion for the government officials.

For convenience, the branch of the disregarded alternative in Figure 4.9 is marked with a jagged line. Also, the best outcome ($11.4 million) is placed inside a rectangle above the applicable decision point (4).

Government officials can handle decision point 5 in a similar manner, as Figure 4.10 illustrates. In this situation, the $12 million cost of ground-spraying is less than the

$$\$9(.2) + \$17(.8) = \$15.4 \text{ million}$$

expected cost for sterilization. Thus, if the traps leave a large number of fertile males, the government should ground-spray the infested areas with malathion. Also, note that the $12 million cost for decision point 5 becomes the outcome associated with the branch emerging from chance point 2 for a large number of fertile males. Furthermore, there is a 40 percent chance of incurring this cost. Similarly, the $11.4 million expected cost for decision point 4 becomes the outcome associated with the branch emerging from chance

---

Figure 4.10   Large Portion of the Government's Decision Tree

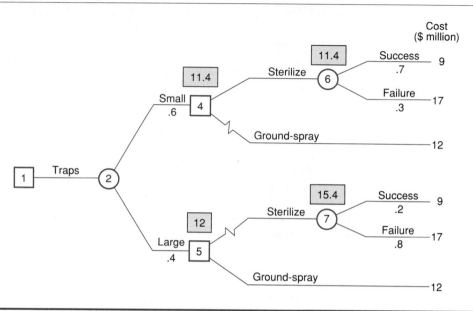

point 2 for a small number of fertile males. There is a 60 percent likelihood of incurring this expense.

Management must continue to "prune" branches in a similar manner by successively working from right to left through the decision tree. The right-to-left movement will end when the decision maker has evaluated each alternative at the initial decision point. Management scientists refer to this process as **backward induction**.

Figure 4.11 completes the process for the government's pest control problem. As the figure indicates, the trap program's expected cost ($11.64 million) is less than the known expense ($15 million) for aerial malathion spraying. The scent/trap approach also has a lower expected cost than the $18.75 million juvenile hormone program. Thus, at decision point 1, the government should select the scent/trap program and disregard the aerial malathion spraying and juvenile hormone program. We indicate this choice in Figure 4.11 by marking the air-spray and hormone branches with a jagged line. Also, the lowest expected cost ($11.64 million) is placed inside a rectangle above decision point 1.

Optimal Strategy. According to the backward induction analysis, the government should institute the scent/trap program. If the traps leave a small number of fertile males, the government should then release sterile flies in the native population. However, if the number of remaining fertile males is large, the government is advised to ground-spray the infested areas with malathion. This decision plan, illustrated by the "unpruned" branches that remain on the decision tree in Figure 4.11, provides the minimum expected cost ($11.64 million) of adfly control.

Figure 4.11   **The Government's Backward Induction Analysis**

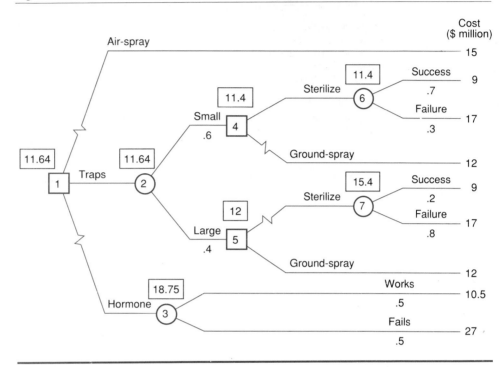

Computer Analysis

Computer programs, such as **ARBORIST** and **SUPERTREE**, are available to solve sequential problems through a backward induction analysis of a decision tree. The **QUANTITATIVE MANAGEMENT (QM)** software contains a program that performs a similiar analysis.

Once more, the program is accessed by selecting Decision Theory from **QM**'s main menu. Figure 4.12 then illustrates how the program solves the government's pest control problem.

Problem Formulation. As Figure 4.12 demonstrates, the user executes this module by selecting the Sequential decisions command from the Decision Theory menu. Data input again begins with the Edit selection from the Input menu, and report options also can be chosen from the Output menu. Then the program requests information about the problem.

The user first must enter the number of branches in the decision tree. Since Figure 4.8 has 15 branches, the manager should respond with the value 15 after the prompt. Next, the user inputs the following data (in the order listed), branch by branch, from the decision tree into the table that appears on the screen:

1. The decision or chance point from which the branch emerges.

2. The destination point for the branch.

Figure 4.12   **Computer Analysis of the Pest Control Problem**

Decision Theory:	Input:	Output:
▪ Decision making under uncertainty	* Edit	▪ Full
▪ Decision making under risk	▪ Load	* Summary
▪ Decision making under certainty	▪ Print	* Print
* Sequential decisions	▪ Save	▪ Save

Problem Formulation:
How many branches in the decision tree? (enter a number up to 80)   15
Enter the branch number, start point number, end point number, probability, and outcome in the table below.

Branch Number	Start Point Number	End Point Number	Probability	Outcome
1	1	8	0.00	15.0
2	1	2	0.00	0.0
3	2	4	.60	0.0
4	4	6	0.00	0.0
5	6	9	.70	9.0
6	6	10	.30	17.0
7	4	11	0.00	12.0
8	2	5	.40	0.0
9	5	7	0.00	0.0
10	7	12	.20	9.0
11	7	13	.80	17.0
12	5	14	0.00	12.0
13	1	3	0.00	0.0
14	3	15	.50	10.5
15	3	16	.50	27.0

Do you want to maximize (MAX) or minimize (MIN) the objective? MIN

OPTIMAL DECISION STRATEGY

Start Point Number	End Point Number	Expected Value
1	2	11.64
4	6	11.40
5	14	12.00

---

3. The probability associated with the branch.

4. The outcome, if any, associated with the branch.

In this program, each branch must have both a starting and ending point. As in the decision tree, Figure 4.12 records outcomes (costs) in millions of dollars.

For example, consider the Air-spray branch in the government's decision tree (Figure 4.8). This branch is recorded as the first entry in the **QM** screen table (Figure 4.12). It emerges from decision point 1, ends at the artificial point 8, involves no probability (shown as 0.00 in the screen table), and results in an outcome of 15. Similarly, the Works branch from Figure 4.8 is presented as the fourteenth entry in Figure 4.12's screen table. This branch emerges from chance point 3, ends at the artificial point 15, has a probability of .50, and results in a 10.5 outcome. Artificial points (such as 8 and 15) are created merely to have distinct ending points for the program's branches.

At this stage, the decision maker must specify the decision objective (maximization MAX or minimization MIN). After receiving the user's response, the program processes the data and generates the optimal decision strategy.

Optimal Decision Strategy. Figure 4.12 illustrates that the government can minimize (MIN) pest control costs at $11.64 million by going first from point 1 to point 2. This action corresponds to the selection of the Traps program at decision point 1 in Figure 4.8. Then, if the government encounters point 4 (follows the Small branch in the decision tree), it should go to point 6. Such an action is equivalent to selecting the Sterilize alternative at decision point 4 in Figure 4.8. Alternatively, if the government encounters point 5 (follows the Large branch in the decision tree), it should go to point 14 (select the Ground-spray alternative emerging from decision point 5 in Figure 4.8).

This optimal strategy

Institute the scent/traps program and	
If	**Then**
the traps leave a small number of fertile males	release sterile flies in the native population
the traps leave a large number of fertile males	ground-spray the infested areas with malathion

matches the recommendation obtained from the backward induction analysis.

Influence Diagrams

Decision trees cannot completely and concisely depict the detail needed to adequately describe some problems. Details that may be missing include loops between events (as when a budget deficit influences borrowings, which in turn affects interest payments and the deficit) and indirect variable relationships (as when advertising influences profit through cost and revenue). If such details are important, the manager can use another graphic device, called an **influence diagram**, to model the situation.

An influence diagram, like a decision tree, is formed from the relationships among the decision alternatives, states of nature, and payoffs. In fact, a decision tree can be converted into an influence diagram by adding some special labeling conventions. Figure 4.13 illustrates for the pest control problem (Management Situation 4.3).

The diagram shows that the government can initially select traps, air-spraying, or the hormone treatment. Each decision alternative is shown inside a rectangle. Air-spraying generates a certain cost, and this relationship is depicted by a straight arrow from the alternative to the payoff. The payoff (cost) is shown inside an oval or ellipse.

Hormones have an uncertain result, and this relationship is depicted in Figure 4.13 with a squiggly arrow from the alternative to the event. The event (result) is shown inside a circle. Moreover, the result is a stochastic variable, and any such variable is noted with a tilde ($\sim$) symbol. Once the result is known, the government can calculate

Figure 4.13   **Influence Diagram of the Pest Control Problem**

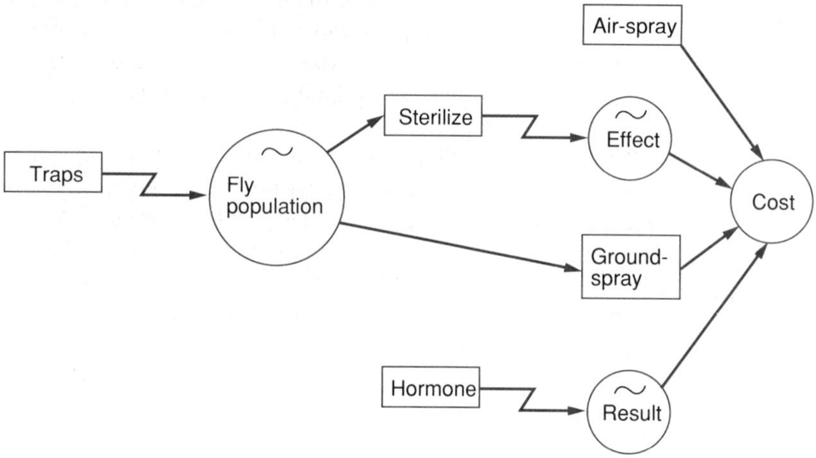

Decision Theory in Practice

Decision theory is applied to a wide variety of management problems. Here are a few areas in which this quantitative analysis is used.

Area	Application
Finance	Determining the plan that best meets an investor's financial objectives Selecting a feasible, low-cost mortgage Identifying a plan that will minimize a multinational company's exposure to currency-exchange risks
Marketing	Establishing a price discount policy Determining the most effective promotional strategy Setting a hotel's reservation policy
Production	Establishing the order of research and development tasks Selecting the sites for drilling exploratory wells Developing the best strategy for a football, baseball, or other athletic contest Identifying the best series of actions to take when expanding a company's plant
Public sector	Selecting the best space flight trajectory Determining the best treatment policy for an infectious illness

the exact cost of the hormone treatment. As indicated by the straight arrow, the result has a certain influence on the cost payoff.

Figure 4.13 shows that the trap alternative also has an indirect relationship to the cost payoff. Traps have an uncertain influence on the stochastically-expressed fly population, which in turn has a certain influence on the decision to sterilize or to ground-spray. Ground-spraying generates a certain cost, while the sterilize alternative has an uncertain effect. The effect, which is a stochastic variable, then has a certain influence on cost.

As the influence diagram highlights, there are some details in the pest control problem that warrant further consideration. Figure 4.13, for example, shows that traps have an uncertain influence on the fly population. Other potentially important and perhaps neglected influences could include weather and the presence of natural predators. Furthermore, weather may influence the presence of predators, which in turn affects the fly population. Since such a loop cannot be accommodated in a decision tree, officials may want to perform an additional analysis before accepting the backward induction (Figure 4.11) recommendation. One possibility is to build a model that describes the officials' understanding of the problem and then use a decision support system to solve the ad hoc model.

SUMMARY

This chapter introduced the subject of decision theory. We begin by identifying the essential elements of a decision problem. These elements consist of one or more objectives, at least two decision alternatives, several states of nature, and various resulting outcomes. The elements are then organized and summarized in a decision table. This formal structure, or model, provides a framework for analyzing simple, single-stage decision problems. It also makes it easier to perform an initial screening and eliminate any dominated strategies from further consideration.

The next step in the decision theory approach is to select the alternative that best meets the objectives. Several criteria can be used to make this selection. The choice of a criterion is based on the manager's degree of knowledge about the states of nature. In this respect, there are situations of uncertainty, risk, and certainty.

In a situation of uncertainty, the decision maker knows the possible states of nature but is unable to assign probabilities to the events. Under these circumstances, the manager can use the optimistic, pessimistic, Hurwicz, regret, or rationality criterion to select a decision alternative. (Table 4.9 summarized these criteria.) Unfortunately, each of the criteria has a deficiency that can cause the manager to make a disastrous decision. These inadequacies exist because none of the criteria utilize all the information generally available to the decision maker.

Since uncertainity severely limits the analysis, most decision makers acquire additional information before making a final decision. If the knowledge enables the manager to assess state of nature probabilities, the situation is called risk. In this situation, management can use the expected value (EV), expected opportunity loss (EOL), or maximum likelihood (ML) criterion to select an alternative. (Table 4.11 summarized these criteria.) The expected monetary value and expected opportunity loss criteria are interchangeable. Each is best suited for repetitive decisions or a group of one-time, nonrepetitive situations that involve similar structures and magnitudes of outcomes. The maximum likelihood approach is appropriate for the few rare nonrepetitive situations in which an expected value measure would be meaningless.

When the decision maker knows exactly which state of nature will occur, the situation is called certainty. In this environment, management compares all outcomes associated with the single event and then selects the alternative that best meets the objectives. The major obstacle is the large number of alternatives that usually must be considered.

Figure 4.2 summarized the decision theory process. Then the analysis was extended to problems involving a series of interrelated decisions. In such cases, the problem is best portrayed as a decision tree consisting of decision points, branches, and event or chance points. Management selects the best sequence of actions with a backward induction analysis of the decision tree.

Glossary

backward induction The process of evaluating alternatives by successively working from right to left through the decision tree.

certainty A situation where the decision maker knows exactly which state of nature will occur.

coefficient of optimism A value between 0 and 1 that measures the decision maker's degree of optimism concerning the attainment of the most favorable outcomes in a decision problem.

collectively exhaustive events A group of events that includes all possible future situations.

courses of action (decision alternatives) The controllable inputs, or the options available to and controlled by the decision maker.

decision analysis (decision theory) A rational way to conceptualize, analyze, and solve problems in situations involving limited information about the decision environment.

decision criteria Logical methods for choosing the alternative that best meets the decision objectives.

decision point In a graph, the square depicting the choice that must be made, with the alternatives shown as lines branching out to the right.

decision tree A graphic representation which shows at a glance the order in which decisions are expected to be made, the consequences of these actions, and the resulting outcomes.

dominance A situation in which one alternative provides an outcome superior to another alternative.

event (chance) point In a graph, a circle depicting stochastic events with lines branching to the right. On each branch, the state of nature appears above the line and the probability below the line.

events, possible futures, or states of nature The uncontrollable inputs facing by the decision maker.

expected monetary value (EMV) criterion Procedure of selecting the alternative that leads to the best expected dollar profit or cost value.

expected opportunity loss (EOL) criterion Procedure of selecting the alternative that leads to the smallest expected regret.

expected value A weighted average outcome determined by multiplying each outcome by its probability of occurrence and then summing the results.

Expected value (EV) criterion Procedure of selecting the alternative that leads to the best expected value.

Hurwicz (coefficient of optimism) criterion Procedure in which the coefficient of optimism is used to determine the best outcome.

influence diagram A graphic device used to depict loops between events and indirect variable relationships. Like a decision tree, it is formed from the relationships among decision alternatives, states of nature, and payoffs.

Laplace (rationality) criterion Incorporating all outcome information by finding the simple average of the outcomes associated with each decision alternative, and then selecting the alternative that results in the best of these average outcomes.

maximax criterion Optimistic procedure in which the goal is to select the largest favorable outcome, as with profits or output.

maximin criterion Pessimistic approach in which the decision maker seeks the largest of the worst possible outcomes.

maximum likelihood (ML) criterion Procedure of selecting the decision alternative that leads to the best outcome associated with the most likely state of nature.

minimax criterion Pessimistic approach in which the decision maker seeks the smallest of the worst potential outcomes.

minimin criterion Optimistic procedure in which the objective is to select the smallest favorable outcome, as with costs or time.

multiperiod decision Sequential decisions in which the required actions are represented by time.

multistage decision Sequential decisions in which there is a natural order of tasks to be completed.

mutually exclusive events Events that cannot occur simultaneously; the occurrence of one state will exclude all others.

objective probability Proportion assigned from past events or experiments.

optimistic criterion Selection process in which the alternative producing the most favorable outcome is chosen.

payoff (decision outcome) The result of a possible combination of decision alternative and state of nature.

payoff table (decision table) A format for summarizing a finite number of decision alternatives and states of nature, with entries in the cells giving the corresponding payoffs.

principle of insufficient reason The assumption that if there is no basis for claiming that one event has a higher probability than another, each should be assigned an equal likelihood.

regret (opportunity loss) The difference between the best possible payoff and the outcome actually received.

regret table (opportunity loss table) Format in which the regret, or opportunity loss, is represented.

risk A situation in which the decision maker has enough information available to determine the probability for each state of nature.

Savage (minimax regret) criterion A pessimistic approach whereby the largest possible opportunity loss for each decision alternative is identified, and then the alternative that leads to the smallest of these largest opportunity losses is chosen.

sequential decision Decision in which the outcome will depend on the entire sequence of interrelated actions taken.

subjective probability Proportion assigned by management judgement.

uncertainty The situation in which the decision maker can identify the possible states of nature but does not have enough information to assess even the likelihood for each event.

Wald (pessimistic) criterion Selection approach in which it is assumed that each alternative will result in the worst possible outcome, and the decision maker selects the alternative that leads to the best of these worst outcomes.

Thought Exercises

1. Identify the courses of action and states of nature in each of the following situations. Explain.
   a. The proprietor of a newspaper stand must decide how many copies of tomorrow's edition to order. He does not know how many copies will be purchased.
   b. Jane Tompkins it trying to decide on the amount of the deductible for the collision insurance on her automobile. Her decision will be influenced by the potential damage that may occur in an accident.
   c. Mammoth Enterprises can invest its excess cash in blue-chip growth stocks. The potential profits depend on stock market trends. There can be continued growth, stability, or a gradual decline.

2. Consider the following statements:
   a. If I buy a T plus account, the savings and loan association will pay me the prevailing Treasury bill rate plus 1/4 percent.
   b. These three gallons of gasoline will allow me to drive 90 miles.
   c. Depending on weather conditions, our boat will sail 10, 20, or 30 miles today.
   d. We can build three homes on each acre of land.
   Identify the decision environment described by each statement. Explain.

3. For each of the following situations, indicate whether the decision maker should use a subjective or objective method to assign probability. Explain.
   a. A real estate agent wants to know the probability that interest rates will rise next month.
   b. A product shipment is known to contain one defective part. The purchasing manager wants to determine the probability that a randomly chosen part will turn out to be defective.
   c. NASA has just launched a unique rocket mission to Venus. Its director is asked to estimate the mission's chance for success.
   d. The manager of a large department store wants to know the probability that a randomly chosen person who enters the store will make a purchase.
   e. A movie producer wants to estimate the chance that her new picture will earn a profit.

4. A television executive is attempting to assign probability values to the possible viewing audience for a new program. Relying on knowledge, experience, and intuitive judgment, the executive subjectively assigns the following probabilities:

$$P(\text{under two million viewers}) = .20$$

$$P(\text{two to five million viewers}) = .45$$

$$P(\text{over five million viewers}) = .25$$

Before the executive uses these estimates to perform further probability calculations, what advice would you offer?

5. To save on gasoline expenses, Janet and Joe agree to form a car pool for traveling to and from school. After limiting the travel routes to two alternatives, the students cannot agree on the best way to get to school. The situation is represented by the following payoff table, in which entries represent travel time.

	States of Nature	
Decision Alternatives	s_1 = light freeway traffic	s_2 = heavy freeway traffic
a_1 = take freeway	10 minutes	40 minutes
a_2 = take Walnut Avenue	20 minutes	20 minutes

The students do not know the condition of the freeway ahead of time. If Janet is an optimist, which route do you think she prefers? Explain. If Joe is a pessimist, which route do you think he prefers? Explain.

6. A marketing manager has the product-pricing problem represented by the following payoff table, in which entries represent the percentage change in demand for the product. Research indicates that $P(s_1) = .1$, $P(s_2) = .7$, and $P(s_3) = .2$.
   This manager always treats the most likely event as if it were certain to occur. Then he selects the course of action that will lead to the best payoff for that state. Can you predict what price policy this manager will select? Explain.

	States of Nature		
Courses of Action	s_1 = low brand loyalty	s_2 = moderate brand loyalty	s_3 = high brand loyalty
a_1 = no change in price	0%	2%	10%
a_2 = lower the price	1%	3%	5%

7. Two university presidents have the same staffing problem. It is represented by the following payoff table, where entries represent the change in the net revenue for the university. At these universities, each enrollment state is equally likely.

	States of Nature		
Courses of Action	s_1 = increase in enrollment	s_2 = no change in enrollment	s_3 = decrease in enrollment
a_1 = hire more faculty	$200,000	$0	-$100,000
a_2 = keep the same number of faculty	$150,000	$50,000	-$20,000
a_3 = fire some faculty	$10,000	$30,000	$50,000

One university president selects the course of action that leads to the most preferred total payoff. The other simply adds the payoffs for each action (row) and selects the alternative with the most preferred total payoff. Yet each arrives at the same decision. Can you explain this result?

8. U. N. Able has the investment problem represented by the following payoff table, in which entries represent return on investment. Historical data indicate that the probabilities of the economic conditions are $P(s_1)$ = .3, $P(s_2)$ = .5, and $P(s_3)$ = .2.

	States of Nature		
Courses of Action	s_1 = recession	s_2 = stability	s_3 = expansion
a_1 = invest in savings	$10,000	$10,000	$10,000
a_2 = invest in bonds	$5,000	$20,000	$25,000
a_3 = invest in stocks	-$10,000	$15,000	$50,000

According to Able's investment counselor, the bond investment will lead to the smallest possible regret. On that basis, the counselor recommends a_2. How did the counselor reach this conclusion? What would you recommend? Explain.

9. Refer back to Management Situations 4.1 and 4.2 in the text. Suppose Naddol's board chairperson has continued the consultation process with marketing and sales personnel, industry officials, and consumer groups. Through this additional consultation, she learns that toys like the Star Cruiser have life spans of approximately two years. The information also reveals that her subjective probabilities of $P(s_1)$ = .3, $P(s_2)$ = .6, and $P(s_3)$ = .1 are appropriate for market conditions mainly during the first half of the product life cycle. Industry experience reveals that sales could rise, remain the same, or fall during the second year. According to available data, there is a 20 percent chance for a sales increase and a 30 percent likelihood that they will remain stable.

Based on this information, the chairperson instructs company management to adopt a wait-and-see approach. At the beginning of the two-year cycle, Naddol will build a small, moderate, or large plant. One year later, management will compare plant output to market demand. At that time, they must decide whether or not to expand capacity. Expansion will be considered only if the first-year demand is sufficient to warrant additional capacity. Hence, Naddol might want to expand when the original plant is small and first-year sales are medium or large. Similarly, there could be expansion if sales are high but the plant is moderate in size.

The experts believe that Table 4.2 represents only the first-year profits and losses. If Naddol expands, they could obtain an additional $50,000 profit when the initial plant is small, first-year demand is medium, capacity expands, and second-year sales increase. Other possibilities are summarized in the following table.

Initial Plant Size	First-Year Demand	Second Action	Second-Year Sales	Additional Profit ($ thousand)
Small	Medium	Expand	Rise	50
Small	Medium	Expand	Same	−10
Small	Medium	Expand	Fall	−30
Small	Medium	Do not expand	Rise	0
Small	Medium	Do not expand	Same	0
Small	Medium	Do not expand	Fall	−5
Small	High	Expand	Rise	85
Small	High	Expand	Same	−10
Small	High	Expand	Fall	−30
Small	High	Do not expand	Rise	0
Small	High	Do not expand	Same	0
Small	High	Do not expand	Fall	−5
Moderate	High	Expand	Rise	125
Moderate	High	Expand	Same	110
Moderate	High	Expand	Fall	75
Moderate	High	Do not expand	Rise	0
Moderate	High	Do not expand	Same	0
Moderate	High	Do not expand	Fall	0

a. How does this problem differ from Management Situations 4.1 and 4.2?

b. How would you structure this decision problem? Develop such a structure.

c. What decision plan should Naddol's management follow in this new situation? Explain.

d. How does your recommendation compare with the solution for Management Situation 4.2? Explain.

e. Develop an influence diagram for this extended situation. Does the diagram suggest any problem detail that warrants further consideration? Explain.

10. Explain why you agree or disagree with each of the following statements:

a. Courses of action are independent of the states of nature.

b. States of nature are mutually exclusive and collectively exhaustive events.

c. Decision trees are most useful when the problem involves a sequence of decisions.

d. In one sense, management science can be thought of as an attempt to move the decision maker from a state of uncertainty toward a state of certainty.

e.   Since the criteria for decision making under uncertainty can lead to different recommendations, these approaches are too ambiguous to use in practice.

f.   The best decision is always the one that leads to the minimum expected opportunity loss.

g.   The criteria for decision making under uncertainty are also appropriate for risk situations.

h.   In the coefficient of optimism criterion, the α weight is given to the state of the nature.

i.   In the coefficient of optimism criterion, the real decision is the choice of α.

j.   When the decision maker utilizes the maximum likelihood criterion, he/she is, in effect, changing the situation from risk to certainty.

Technique Exercises

11. You are given the following decision table. Develop the corresponding decision tree.

Courses of Action	States of Nature	
	s_1	s_2
a_1	20	50
a_2	30	10
a_3	80	60

12. Develop the decision table that corresponds to the following decision tree.

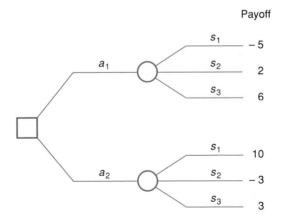

13. You are given the following decision table, where entries represent profits in millions of dollars.

Decision Alternatives	States of Nature		
	s_1	s_2	s_3
a_1	−2	2	6
a_2	−1	0	5
a_3	2	3	1

What is the recommended decision under each of the following criteria?
a.   Optimistic
b.   Pessimistic
c.   Hurwicz with $\alpha = .3$, then $\alpha = .8$
d.   Regret
e.   Rationality

14. Consider the following decision tree. What is the recommended decision under each of the following criteria?
    a.   Optimistic
    b.   Pessimistic
    c.   Hurwicz with $\alpha = .5$
    d.   Regret
    e.   Rationality

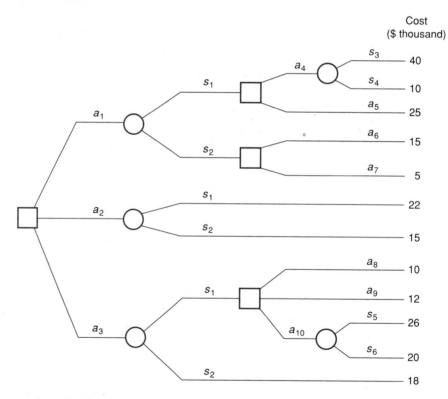

15. Consider the following decision table for a particular investment problem. The payoffs represent profits in millions of dollars.
    a.   Develop the corresponding decision tree.
    b.   What is the recommended optimistic decision?
    c.   What is the recommended pessimistic decision?
    d.   If the investor knows that prices will remain stable, what is the recommended decision?

Courses of Action	States of Nature		
	s_1 = prices go up	s_2 = prices remain stable	s_3 = prices go down
a_1 = invest in project A	2	1	−.5
a_2 = invest in project B	4.5	.2	−.3
a_3 = do not invest	0	0	0

16. Icetown Ski Resort is considering the addition of equipment that would create artificial snow. The situation is represented by the following decision table, in which the entries in the cells are weekly profits or losses.

Decision Alternatives	States of Nature		
	s_1 = light snowfall	s_2 = moderate snowfall	s_3 = heavy snowfall
a_1 = buy a machine	$15,000	$10,000	−$5,000
a_2 = modify equipment	$12,000	$8,000	−$1,000
a_3 = do not invest	−$6,000	$0	$4,000

    a. What is the recommended regret decision?

    b. Assume that the resort manager has a coefficient of optimism of α = .6. Using the Hurwicz criterion, what is the recommended decision?

17. You are given the following decision table, in which entries represent monetary returns. Also $P(s_1)$ = .3, $P(s_2)$ = .5, and $P(s_3)$ = .2.

Courses of Action	States of Nature		
	s_1	s_2	s_3
a_1	$50,000	$100,000	$150,000
a_2	$100,000	$20,000	$0
a_3	−$30,000	$0	$200,000

    a. What is the recommended EMV decision?

    b. What is the recommended EOL decision?

    c. Compare the results from parts (a) and (b).

    d. What is the recommended ML decision?

18. Consider the following payoff table, in which entries represent costs in millions of dollars. Also, $P(s_1)$ = .2, $P(s_2)$ = .4, $P(s_3)$ = .3, and $P(s_4)$ = .1.

    a. What is the recommended EMV decision?

    b. What is the recommended EOL decision?

    c. Compare the results from parts (a) and (b).

    d. What is the recommended ML decision?

Decision	States of Nature			
Alternatives	s_1	s_2	s_3	s_4
a_1	5	2	1	-4
a_2	-3	0	2	4

19. Refer to exercise 15. Assume that $P(s_1) = .2, P(s_2) = .5$, and $P(s_3) = .3$.
  a. What is the recommended EOL decision?
  b. What is the expected profit from the EOL decision in part (a)?
  c. Determine the expected profit for each of the recommended decisions in exercise 15.
  d. Compare the results of parts (b) and (c).

20. Refer to Icetown's equipment decision (exercise 16). Assume that $P(s_1) = .3, P(s_2) = .4$, and $P(s_3) = .3$.
  a. What is the recommended EOL decision?
  b. What is the expected profit from the EOL decision in part (a)?
  c. Determine the expected profit for each of the recommended decisions in exercise 16.
  d. Compare the results of parts (b) and (c). What does the comparison indicate?

21. Consider Naddol's plant construction problem (Management Situation 4.1). It is represented by the following decision table.

Courses of Action	States of Nature		
	s_1 = low demand	s_2 = medium demand	s_3 = high demand
a_1 = build a small plant	$250,000	-$40,000	$0
a_2 = build a moderate plant	-$50,000	$350,000	$60,000 ← Profit
a_3 = build a large plant	$100,000	$80,000	$400,000

Loss

Assume that $P(s_1) = .2, P(s_2) = .6$, and $P(s_3) = .2$. What is the recommended EMV decision? Compare this decision to those recommended by the criteria for decision making under certainty and uncertainty. Comment.

22. A local government agency is planning its paper supply needs for the coming month. The situation is represented by the following payoff table, where the entries in the cells give the annual purchase costs.

Decision Alternatives	States of Nature		
	s_1 = low usage	s_2 = moderate usage	s_3 = high usage
a_1 = order from supplier A	$100,000	$200,000	$400,000
a_2 = order from supplier B	$50,000	$150,000	$500,000

a. Assume that the agency's director has a coefficient of optimism of $\alpha = .9$. Using the Hurwicz criterion, what is the recommended decision?

b. Develop the opportunity loss table.

c. Develop the corresponding decision tree (in terms of opportunity losses).

d. Use the decision tree to determine the recommended regret decision.

e. Assume that $P(s_1) = .1$, $P(s_2) = .4$, and $P(s_3) = .5$. What is the recommended EOL decision? Show the backward induction involved in the decision tree.

f. Compare the EOL for the results in parts (d) and (e). Comment.

23. You are given the following decision tree. What decision plan do you recommend? What will the expected revenue be from your plan?

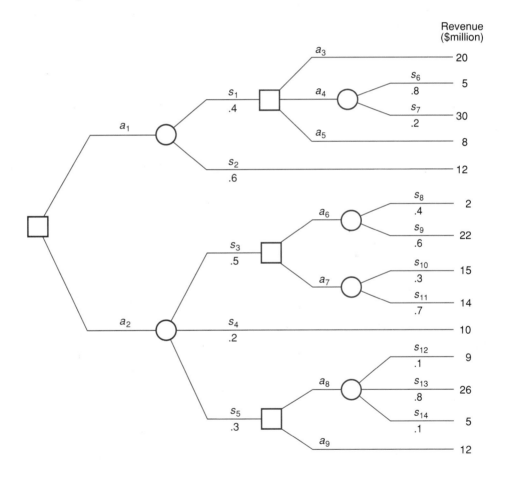

24. A personnel manager has the following decision tree. The numbers to the right of the decision tree represent the change in an employee's monthly output. What testing/promotion policy would you recommend? What will be the expected change in monthly output from your plan?

Convert the decision tree into an influence diagram. Does the diagram suggest any problem detail that warrants further consideration? Explain.

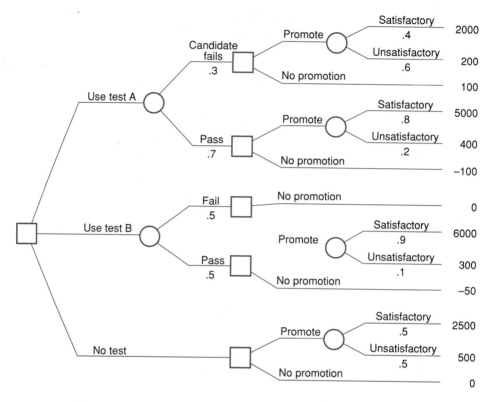

Computer Exercises

25. A large government agency has a variety of projects that could be performed in the coming fiscal year. Each project's cost/benefit ratio will depend on a variety of factors, including the available budget, staff capabilities, general economic conditions, and the political environment. Agency management has developed a coding scheme to identify the appropriate combinations of factors, and the following table summarizes the relevant data.

	Condition Code									
Project	**A**	**B**	**C**	**D**	**E**	**F**	**G**	**H**	**I**	**J**
1	3.5	2.9	1.8	5.0	.7	2.0	.6	1.4	2.4	3.8
2	1.8	4.0	1.7	2.0	1.2	.5	3.0	2.9	2.3	6.0
3	1.1	8.0	.9	1.0	3.0	.1	1.8	1.7	1.2	.7
4	.4	.8	2.6	4.0	2.0	1.0	1.6	3.0	3.0	4.0
5	2.7	1.4	4.2	.8	2.9	3.0	1.0	1.9	1.0	4.0
6	4.1	2.0	3.4	1.7	4.0	3.0	1.5	4.0	2.0	3.8
7	.1	2.1	2.6	2.5	3.1	3.0	4.0	4.2	4.0	3.7
8	1.5	2.6	5.0	2.3	.3	2.4	3.6	2.0	2.1	3.9
9	1.2	.7	3.0	.4	2.2	1.7	2.5	2.4	.5	5.0

Cell entries represent cost-benefit ratios.

Agency management would like to select the project that has the lowest cost/benefit ratio. However, the relevant decision makers are uncertain about the conditions in the coming fiscal year. Use the **QUANTITATIVE MANAGEMENT (QM)** software to identify appropriate project alternatives.

26. Educational Planning Associates specializes in investment services for university professors. Currently, the firm has $6 million of stockholders' pension funds to invest, and management is considering money market instruments, corporate bonds, government bonds, stocks, and real estate trusts. Management believes that the returns on the investments will depend on the value of an economic index constructed by the firm's planning staff. Relevant data are summarized in the following table.

| | Value of Economic Index | | | | | |
Investment	1400	1500	1600	1700	1800	1900
Money market	390	420	450	480	510	540
Corporate bonds	375	410	445	480	515	550
Government bonds	420	415	400	385	450	560
Stocks	360	395	420	510	530	575
Real estate trusts	400	405	425	445	480	510

Entries in the table represent annual returns, in thousands of dollars.

Associate's management wants to select only one of the investment options. However, the decision group does not know which economic scenario will occur. Utilize the **QM** software to identify appropriate investment alternatives.

27. Easysoftware Development Corporation has been commissioned to develop an information system for Harden Enterprises. Several types of systems are being considered, and the costs will depend on the processing needs of Harden's users. A feasibility study provides the data shown below.

| | Processing Needs | | | | |
Information System	Detailed	Summarized	Focused	Analytical	Graphic
Transaction processing	250	325	380	400	425
Management information	275	410	320	380	460
Decision support	405	380	350	260	240
Office automated	500	400	250	480	225

Entries represent system design, development, and implementation costs in thousands of dollars.

Harden's management wants to select the system that will lead to the lowest cost. After consulting with Harden's users, Easysoftware's management believes that there is a 20 percent likelihood of detailed, a 15 percent chance of summarized, a 25 percent probability of focused, and a 30 percent likelihood of analytical processing needs. Use the **QM** software to develop an information system recommendation.

28. Happy Valley Cheese Company (HVCC) sells fresh cheese, which is purchased in Denmark for $7 per pound (including the transportation costs) and sold for $11 per pound. Any cheese not sold by the end of the week can be processed into a fancy sandwich spread and sold for a net price of $2 per pound. According to the past 100-week experience, weekly demand for the fresh cheese has been as follows.

Pounds Per Week	Number of Weeks
10	10
15	20
20	50
25	10
30	10
	100

Use the **QM** software to determine the quantity that maximizes expected profit.

29. Electronic Games, Ltd. of Italy has been engaged in the business of manufacturing and distributing highly advanced toys to North American markets. Recently, the company sold 280,000 Canadian dollars worth of products to a Toronto department store chain. Payment is due in 60 days.

Electronic's management has four alternative ways to reduce the transaction exposure that may result from fluctuating foreign exchange rates between the Canadian dollar and the Italian lira. First, the Italian firm may decide to take the transaction risk. Currently, each Canadian dollar can be exchanged for approximately 1,000 Italian lira in most major markets. Some investment analysts believe that 800 or 1,500 lira will be needed to buy a Canadian dollar in 60 days.

If Electronic's management wants to hedge its transaction exposure in one of the three forward markets, then the company would have a covered transaction with no foreign exchange risk. Under these circumstances, the amount of money to be received in 60 days is fixed, regardless of future foreign exchange rates between the Canadian dollar and the Italian lira. Currently, spot exchange and 60-day forward rates in the relevant money markets are as follows.

Market	Lira Per Canadian Dollar	
	Spot	Forward
New York	1000	1250
London	1000	900
Hong Kong	1000	950

Electronic's management believes that they can identify the exact direction of future foreign exchange rates. Assume you are part of the company's management, and use the **QM** software to develop a recommended foreign exchange policy.

30. An organization has a problem represented by the following decision tree. Use the **QM** software to determine the optimal strategy.

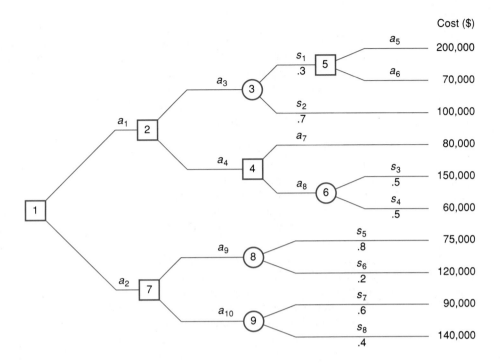

Cost ($)

a_5 — 200,000
a_6 — 70,000
s_2 .7 — 100,000
a_7 — 80,000
s_3 .5 — 150,000
s_4 .5 — 60,000
s_5 .8 — 75,000
s_6 .2 — 120,000
s_7 .6 — 90,000
s_8 .4 — 140,000

31. Refer to Thought Exercise 9. Use the **QM** software to develop the optimal strategy.

Applications Exercises

32. The public service television network has been receiving low ratings for its 5–7 PM time slot. Currently, management is considering three alternatives for this slot: a sports show, travel films, or a political discussion program. The percent of viewing audience estimates depend on the demographic characteristics of the viewers. Audiences are demographically classified as "family-oriented" or "sensation-oriented." Market research indicates that the network can expect 10 percent of a "family-oriented" audience to view the sports show telecast. Five percent of a "family-oriented" audience can be expected to view travel films, and 40 percent of this audience will watch the political discussion program. Among the "sensation-oriented" viewers, the network can expect 20 percent to watch the sports show, 25 percent to view travel films, and 5 percent to watch the political discussion program.

a. The network public relations executive is completely optimistic and wants to select the program that leads to the best possible percentage of the viewing audience. Which program should this executive select?

b. The program manager points out the risk involved and believes that the network should try to minimize the largest possible regrets. Which program should this executive select?

c. Which program would you select? Explain.

33. The state treasurer is considering the purchase of a fire insurance policy for the new governor's mansion. A nondeductible policy provides complete coverage for an annual cost of $5000. The deductible plan only costs $2000 a year, but the state must absorb the first $28,000 of damage. If minor fire damage occurs to the mansion, the state anticipates a refurbishing cost of $20,000. It would cost $200,000 to replace the structure if there were major damage or total destruction.

The treasurer wants to make the most realistic decision. She is reasonably optimistic and believes there is a 5 percent chance that the worst will happen. Which policy, if any, should she buy? Explain.

34. A consumer products testing agency is currently experiencing an increased demand for its services. It is considering hiring more testing personnel to meet the additional demand. The agency could hire a small, moderate, or large number of testers. The staffing decision depends on whether the uncertain additional demand will be low, medium, or high.

Preliminary research indicates the following profit possibilities. If the company hires a small number of additional testers, the incremental profit will be $100,000 for any additional demand. If they hire a moderate number, the incremental profit will be $200,000 if the additional demand is either medium or high. However, profit increases by only $50,000 if they hire a moderate number and additional demand is low. If the company hires a large number of additional testers, profit will decrease by $100,000 when additional demand is low. Profit will not change if they hire a large number and additional demand is moderate. Yet a large additional staff will increase profit by $300,000 when there is a high additional demand.

The staffing decision will be made by an executive committee consisting of J. Lemon, T. Grape, and O. Right. Lemon is a pessimist, while Grape is an optimist. Right always selects the action that results in the smallest of the largest possible regrets. What will be Lemon's, Grape's, and Right's recommended decisions? What decision do you recommend? Why?

35. An investment analyst believes that there is a 40 percent chance of an upturn in the steel industry during the third quarter of the year. Also, there is about an equal likelihood of no change and a downturn. A client is considering the investment of $50,000 either in a mutual fund specializing in steel industry common stocks or in corporate AAA bonds yielding 10 percent per year. If the steel industry experiences an upturn during the third quarter, the value of the mutual fund shares will increase a net 20 percent during the next twelve months. The value will increase by a net 6 percent when there is no change. If there is a downturn, the value will decrease by 15 percent. What investment should the client make? What is the resulting dollar return?

36. Samson Enterprises manufactures athletic equipment. The company is considering the introduction of a new universal exerciser, the Body Builder. Profit potential depends on whether demand is low, moderate, or high. If the company markets the Body Builder, profit will be $-$100,000 with low sales, $20,000 with moderate sales, and $200,000 with high sales. Market research indicates that there is a 30 percent chance of high sales. Low and moderate sales are equally likely. Should Samson introduce the Body Builder? If so, what is the expected profit?

37. The federal government is considering two national health plans. One would provide complete funding from general tax revenues. The alternative would make it mandatory for every citizen to purchase some form of health insurance from privately owned companies.

Mandatory health insurance would be subsidized by the federal government, so that the cost would be within everyone's reach. The cost of the various plans depends on the social and economic conditions that give rise to various diseases. These conditions are classified as low, moderate, or high illness states.

In a low illness state, it would cost $2 billion to finance the general revenue plan and $1 billion for the mandatory insurance program. In a moderate illness state, it would cost $5 billion for the general revenue program and $7 billion for the mandatory plan. A high illness state would cost the federal government $15 billion under the general revenue program and $8 billion under the mandatory plan.

The third alternative is to continue with existing health care systems. Currently, these systems cost the federal government $3 billion in indirect expenses (Medicare, Medicaid, and other related welfare) in a low or moderate illness state. The cost is $5 billion in a high illness state.

Government health officials estimate that there is a 60 percent chance of a moderate illness state. Also, they believe that low and high illness states are equally likely. The government wants to select the system that leads to the smallest expected cost. Which system should the government select?

38. Mammoth Enterprises (ME) is a major producer and distributor of natural gas. Currently, they must decide whether to develop a particular exploration site or sell the rights to independent companies. Development will be desirable, of course, if there are substantial deposits of natural gas beneath the surface. Before making the decision, ME has the option of taking seismographic readings. These readings will provide geological and geophysical information that will enable them to determine if the subsurface structures are conducive to natural gas formation. However, natural gas has sometimes been found where no suitable subsurface structure was detected, and vice versa. Thus, there will still be some uncertainty remaining after the seismic testing.

It will cost Mammoth $3 million to develop the site, but it will yield an expected $8 million in revenues. Each seismic test costs $150,000. On the other hand, ME could sell the rights, before development or testing, for $500,000. If Mammoth takes seismographic readings and no subsurface structure is detected, the site will be considered almost worthless by other companies. In this case, ME will barely be able to sell the rights for $50,000. When a substructure is indicated, however, Mammoth can sell the rights for $2 million. If no natural gas is found, there will be no value attached to the exploration site.

There is a .25 probability of finding natural gas without any test. Previous experience indicates that 35 percent of all seismographic tests detect a suitable subsurface structure. If there is a suitable substructure, Mammoth will have a 75 percent chance of finding natural gas. If the substructure is unsuitable, there will be an 80 percent likelihood of finding no deposits.

What should Mammoth do? Explain.

For Further Reading

Structuring the Problem

Holloway, C. A. *Decision Making Under Uncertainty.* Englewood Cliffs, NJ: Prentice-Hall, 1979.

Jones, J. M. *Introduction to Decision Theory.* Homewood, IL: Irwin, 1977.

White, D. J. *Decision Methodology.* New York: Wiley, 1975.

Decision Criteria

Barron, F. H. "Behavioral Decision Theory: A Topical Bibliography for Management Scientists." *Interfaces* (November 1974):56.

Bell, D. E. "Disappointment in Decision Making under Uncertainty." *Operations Research* (January–February 1985):1.

Conrath, D. W. "From Statistical Decision Theory to Practice: Some Problems with the Transition." *Management Science* (April 1973):873.

Harrison, E. F. *The Managerial Decision Making Process.* Boston: Houghton Mifflin, 1975.

Huber, G. P. *Managerial Decision Making.* Dallas: Scott, Foresman, 1980.

Sarin, R. K. "Elicitation of Subjective Probabilities in the Context of Decision Making." *Decision Sciences* (January 1978):37.

Sequential Decisions

Bodily, S. E. *Modern Decision Making: A Guide to Modeling with Decision Support Systems.* New York: McGraw-Hill, 1985.

Brown, R. V., et al. *Decision Analysis for the Manager.* New York: Holt, Rinehart & Winston, 1974.

Howard, R. A. "Decision Analysis: Practice and Promise." *Management Science* (June 1988):679.

Oxenfelt, A. R. *A Basic Approach to Executive Decision Making.* New York: AMACOM, 1978.

Financial Applications

Cooper, D. O., et al. "A Tool for More Effective Financial Analysis." *Interfaces* (February 1975):91.

Luna, R. E., and R. A. Reid. "Mortage Selection Using a Decision Tree Approach." *Interfaces* (May–June 1986):73.

Sesit, M. R. "Avoiding Losses." *The Wall Street Journal*, March 5, 1985.

Wheelwright, S. C. "Applying Decision Theory to Improve Corporate Management of Currency-Exchange Risks." *California Management Review* (Summer 1975):48.

Zanakis, S. H., L. P. Mavrides, and E. N. Roussakis. "Applications of Management Science in Banking." *Decision Sciences* (Winter 1986):114.

Marketing Applications

Braverman, J. D. "A Decision Theoretic Approach to Pricing." *Decision Sciences* (January 1971):1.

Digman, L. A. "A Decision Analysis of the Airline Coupon Strategy." *Interfaces* (April 1980):97.

Turban, E., and N. P. Loomba. *Readings in Management Science.* Dallas: Business Publications, 1976.

Williams, F. E. "Decision Theory and the Innkeeper: An Approach for Setting Hotel Reservation Policy." *Interfaces* (August 1977):18.

Production/Operations

Flinn, R. A., and E. Turban. "Decision Tree Analysis for Industrial Research." *Research Management* (January 1970):27.

Stoughton, N. M. "A Decision Theory Example in Football: A Comment." *Decision Sciences* (Summer 1986):424.

Sullivan, W. G., and W. W. Claycombe. "The Use of Decision Trees in Planning Plant Expansion." *Advanced Management Journal* (Winter 1975):29.

Public Sector Applications

Dyer, J. S., and R. F. Miles. "An Actual Application of Collective Choice Theory to the Selection of Trajectories for the Mariner Jupiter Saturn 1977 Project." *Operations Research* (March–April 1976):220.

Fries, B. E. "Bibliography of Operations Research in Health-Care Systems." *Operations Research* (September–October 1976):801.

Case: The Healthy Food Store

The Healthy Food Store sells health foods in a beach community. Oliver Healthy, the manager, is filling out the orders for the next supply of fortified yeast. He has a contract with a major supplier that calls for orders of either one, two, or three batches every six days. Each batch contains 100 pounds.

It costs Oliver $2 to prepare a pound of yeast for sale, and the product sells for $4 per pound. Since it takes two days to prepare the product, Healthy must order in advance. The exact demand is unknown, but Oliver can list the possible demands as 100, 200, or 300 pounds. If the customers order more than Healthy has prepared, Oliver must purchase a higher quality substitute yeast. The substitute is already prepared, but it costs $6 per pound.

Since the new yeast cannot be stored more than four days without spoilage, Healthy cannot inventory excess production until the next six-day order. Therefore, if the customers order less than Oliver has prepared, the excess production must be reprocessed. The reprocessed yeast has a value of only $1 per pound.

1. Oliver wants to prepare the quantity that will lead to the smallest of the largest possible regrets. How many batches will he want to order?

2. Oliver's wife, Marissa, is concerned about the risk involved in this ordering decision. She wants to order the most realistic quantity. Marissa is only 30 percent

confident that the best outcome will always occur. How many batches will she want to order?

3. Compare the recommended decisions in parts (1) and (2). What does this comparison indicate?

4. The supplier's research indicates that there is a 50 percent likelihood of a two-batch demand and a 30 percent chance of a three-batch demand. Based on this information, how many batches do you think Oliver should order?

5. Compare your recommendation to Marissa's and Oliver's. What does this comparison indicate?

6. Suppose that Oliver could purchase the original yeast from another health food store in the next town for $3.50 rather than ordering the prepared higher quality substitute for $6. Furthermore, there is a 60 percent chance that the other store would have up to 100 pounds already in stock and available to Healthy Food Store. In addition, there is a 20 percent chance that the other store would have up to 200 pounds available and a .2 probability for a maximum availability of 300 pounds. How would this situation affect Oliver's decision?

Bayesian Analysis

Chapter Outline

Learning Objectives

- Identify the nature of risk in a decision problem
- Measure the value of perfect information
- Incorporate additional information into the decision analysis
- Measure the value of the additional information
- Use the additional information to develop a decision strategy

Quantitative Analysis in Action

Physician Help Thyself

PATIENTS are admitted daily to the Medical College of Pennsylvania's hospital for surgical diagnosis and treatment. Although doctors rarely can be certain about the diagnosis of a medical condition, surgeons still must make the difficult decision of operating or not operating on the patient. Since an incorrect choice could lead to an unnecessary operation or to a more serious illness, this decision involves much risk.

Physician and patient concern about the risk led scientists at the college to study the surgical decision-making process. During the study, the scientists found that the process could be represented by a decision tree. In addition, they discovered that decision analysis could be used to improve the doctor's ability to make a sound surgical decision. For example, the percentage of correct surgical decisions increased from 59 to 69 percent when just a limited form of decision analysis was used to assist the surgeons.

Additional benefits are anticipated from the complete application of decision analysis to the clinical practice of medicine. In particular, the decision analysis will generate good data bases that can be used by health care providers to improve the estimates of treatment probabilities and outcomes. Moreover, clinical judgment is the ability of a doctor to arrive at a conclusion in the face of uncertainty. Therefore, the improved probability and outcome estimates should lead to better patient care.

Source: J. R. Clarke, "The Application of Decision Analysis to Clinical Medicine," *Interfaces* (March–April 1987):27–34.

As Chapter 4 demonstrated, the manager's degree of knowledge about the states of nature is a key element in decision analysis. Information about the patient's condition, for example, is crucial to a doctor's surgical diagnosis and treatment prescription. As with the Medical College of Pennsylvania, most organizations have enough existing data to develop an initial assessment of the probabilities for uncertain events. Consequently, these decisions will be made under risk, usually with the expected value criterion.

The expected value calculations are affected by the probabilities assigned to the states of nature. Indeed, the recommended decision often may be altered by slight changes in these probabilities. Hence, the probability assessments play a crucial role in the decision analysis. As a result, management may be willing to expend additional effort in refining these probability assessments before making a final decision.

One approach is to gather additional information about the states of nature. Potential sources include experiments, such as raw material sampling, product testing, and test marketing; surveys, such as attitude and opinion polls; and statistical reports. Then the additional information can be used to revise or update the initial assessment of the event probabilities. Such an approach is referred to as **Bayesian analysis**.

As in the Medical College of Pennsylvania situation, the additional information should at least reduce the risk involved in decision making. Occasionally, this knowledge may even remove the risk completely and provide an environment of certainty. Such information, however, is usually costly to obtain. Thus, an important aspect of Bayesian analysis is to compare these costs with the resulting benefits.

This chapter examines the Bayesian approach to decision analysis. In the opening section, we discuss the relevance of and potential benefits from knowledge about event probabilities. We begin by considering a methodology for determining the sensitivity of the recommended decision to changes in these probabilities. Then we see how to identify and measure the resulting risk. Such an analysis may indicate that the decision maker should seek additional information about the states of nature. The second section shows how this additional information can be used to revise or update the initial assessment of the event probabilities.

The availability of additional information, however, creates a sequential decision problem. First, management must decide whether or not to obtain the extra knowledge. Depending on the results of this first action, it will then select the decision alternative that best meets the original objectives. The final section shows how the revised probabilities can be used to develop an optimal decision plan under these circumstances.

Applications.   In this chapter, the following applications appear in text, examples, and exercises:

- advertising efficiency
- Christmas toys
- college admissions
- computer purchasing
- flight routing
- hardware products
- industrial engineering
- international competition
- lease or buy
- marketing research

- new product marketing
- office operations
- peacekeeping
- postal delivery
- professional journals
- public transportation
- recreation planning
- research and development
- quality control
- sanitation

5.1 VALUE OF INFORMATION

Decisions are often made with only preliminary information about the states of nature. Such an approach, however, can lead to regretful decisions. Management Situation 5.1 illustrates.

Management Situation 5.1

New Product Marketing

Pucter and Simple (PS) is a consumer household goods manufacturer that wants to consider the introduction of a new toothpaste. The new product, which will be labeled

Table 5.1   Pucter and Simple's Decision Table

	States of Nature	
Decision Alternatives	s_1 = low sales	s_2 = high sales
a_1 = market Brite	−$500,000	$1,000,000
a_2 = modify Kist	$100,000	$400,000

Brite, could replace a relatively low-profit existing brand called Kist. Product profits would depend on sales volume, which could be low or high. The situation is depicted by Table 5.1, where entries represent potential profits. Based on available current data and experience with similar products, management believes there is a 45 percent chance of low sales. The company wants to select the alternative that results in the maximum expected profit.

In this marketing situation, the probability of low sales is $P(s_1) = .45$. Assuming that the states of nature are mutually exclusive and collectively exhaustive, the probability of high sales must therefore be

$$P(s_2) = 1 - P(s_1) = 1 - .45 = .55$$

Since these likelihoods are based on prior experience and existing information, they could be thought of as preliminary assessments of the state of nature probabilities. Such initial assignments are referred to as **prior probabilities**.

By using these prior probabilities and the profit data from Table 5.1, PS management will find that alternative a_1 has an expected profit of

$$-\$500,000(.45) + \$1,000,000(.55) = \$325,000$$

while the expected profit from a_2 is

$$\$100,000(.45) + \$400,000(.55) = \$265,000.$$

The available current information indicates that PS can maximize expected profit at $325,000 by marketing Brite (a_1). Since the selection is based on the initial probability assessments, this action may be referred to as the **prior decision**.

Sensitivity of the Decision

From Table 5.1, you can see that the prior decision (a_1) may potentially lead to severe consequences (a $500,000 loss) if there are low sales (s_1). Furthermore, PS management may not be completely confident in the prior probability assessments. Consequently, the company might be unwilling to accept the risk of marketing Brite without further reassurance.

As a first step, management could measure the sensitivity of the prior decision to changes in the probabilities for the states of nature. Such an approach is referred to as

sensitivity analysis. If the sensitivity analysis reveals that very large errors are necessary to change the prior decision, then management can be reasonably confident with the prior decision. On the other hand, when small changes in the event probabilities alter the decision recommendation, then management will have little confidence in the prior action.

Expected Value Expressions. In Pucter and Simple's case, management knows that marketing Brite (a_1) will yield an expected profit of

(5.1) $-\$500,000 \ P(s_1) + \$1,000,000 \ P(s_2)$

This expected profit will be \$1,000,000 when $P(s_1) = 0$ (so that $P(s_2) = 1$) and $-\$500,000$ when $P(s_1) = 1$ (so that $P(s_2) = 0$). Since expression (5.1) involves a linear relationship, PS can find other expected profit combinations by plotting the two extreme points (\$1,000,000 at $P(s_1) = 0$ and $-\$500,000$ at $P(s_1) = 0$) on a graph and connecting these two points with a straight line. If management does so, it will get the solid line shown in Figure 5.1.

Similarly, the expected profit from modifying Kist (a_2) is given by the following expression:

(5.2) $\$100,000 \ P(s_1) + \$400,000 \ P(s_2)$

This expected profit will be \$400,000 when $P(s_1) = 0$ and \$100,000 when $P(s_1) = 1$. By plotting these two extreme points on a graph and connecting them with a straight line, PS management will get the dotted line shown in Figure 5.1.

Indifference Probability. Figure 5.1 also shows the expected profits from marketing Brite and from modifying Kist on the same graph. As the figure indicates, when the probability of low sales $P(s_1)$ is relatively small, the expected profit from marketing Brite (a_1) exceeds the corresponding return from modifying Kist (a_2). Hence, in these circumstances, PS management would prefer alternative a_1 rather than a_2. As $P(s_1)$ increases, however, marketing Brite becomes a less attractive alternative. In fact, at some probability value, each alternative will have an identical expected outcome. At this point, the decision maker will be indifferent between (equally attracted to) marketing Brite and modifying Kist.

From expressions (5.1) and (5.2), you can see that the expected profits from a_1 and a_2 are equal when

$$-\$500,000 \ P(s_1) + \$1,000,000 \ P(s_2) = \$100,000 \ P(s_1) + \$400,000 \ P(s_2)$$

or

$$\$600,000 \ P(s_2) = \$600,000 \ P(s_1)$$

Since $P(s_2) = 1 - P(s_1)$, PS management will be indifferent between marketing Brite (a_1) and modifying Kist (a_2) if there is a

$$\$600,000[1 - P(s_1)] = \$600,000 \ P(s_1)$$

or

$$P(s_1) = .5$$

probability of low sales. Such a likelihood is known as an **indifference probability**.

Figure 5.1   **Pucter and Simple's Expected Profits**

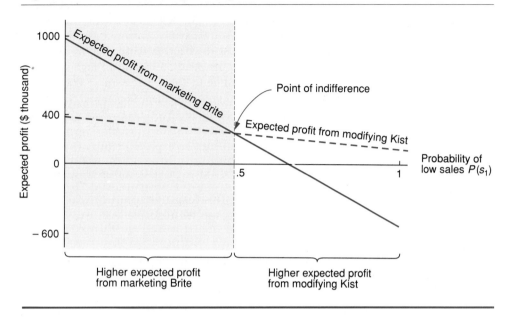

Evaluation. As Figure 5.1 illustrates, when $P(s_1)$ exceeds the indifference probability (.5), Pucter and Simple can get a larger expected profit from modifying Kist than from marketing Brite. Furthermore, the indifference probability (.5) is very close to management's initial assessment of the low sales likelihood (.45). Hence, if management has slightly underestimated the likelihood (say, $P(s_1)$ should have been .51 instead of .45), then the prior decision recommendation (to market Brite) would be wrong. Given the relatively high degree of sensitivity in this situation, the company may want to collect additional information before making a final decision.

Procedure Recap. The following procedure is used to evaluate the sensitivity of the prior decision to changes in the event probabilities:

1. Develop equations that measure the expected values for each decision alternative.

2. Use the equations to find the indifference probabilities that equate the expected values.

3. Compare the indifference probabilities to the corresponding prior probabilities.

Perfect Information

Since it will cost money to acquire additional information, management must ensure that the knowledge has sufficient value to the organization. A maximum value can be measured by comparing the expected outcome with exact knowledge against the expected outcome from the prior decision.

Expected Value Under Certainty. Pucter and Simple has a $P(s_1) = .45$ likelihood of experiencing low sales and a $P(s_2) = .55$ chance of having high sales. In other words, over the course of, say, 100 months, sales will be low 45 percent and high 55 percent of the time. If management knew exactly which 45 months would have low sales (s_1), it could offer a modified Kist (a_2) during those months and, according to Table 5.1, earn \$100,000 profit. During the other 55 months of high sales (s_2), the company could market Brite (a_1) and, according to Table 5.1, earn \$1,000,000 profit.

Over the course of the 100 months, then, Pucter and Simple will be mixing decision alternatives, selecting a_2 (and earning \$100,000) when s_1 occurs and selecting a_1 (and earning \$1,000,000) when s_2 occurs. Since s_1 occurs 45 percent and s_2 occurs 55 percent of the time, the company will earn an expected profit of

$$\$100,000(.45) + \$1,000,000(.55) = \$595,000$$

over the 100-month period. This long run average, called the **expected value under certainty (EVC)**, gives the expected outcome with exact knowledge about the risky states of nature.

Procedure Recap. When the number of decision alternatives and states of nature is finite, the following procedure can be used to compute the expected value under certainty (EVC):

1. List each state of nature.
2. Identify the probability for each state of nature.
3. Identify the best decision alternative associated with each state of nature.
4. Identify the outcome that is associated with each best decision alternative.
5. Multiply each best outcome by the corresponding probability and total the results.

Expected Value of Perfect Information. Mixing decision alternatives is possible if the decision maker has exact knowledge (knows exactly when each state of nature will occur in a risk situation). Initially, however, PS knows only the probability (rather than the exact timing) of each market condition. The imprecise nature of this information leads management to select the single alternative of marketing Brite (a_1), regardless of the environment. As a result, the company does not obtain EVC = \$595,000, but instead must settle for the \$325,000 maximum expected profit from the prior decision.

In effect, then, the lack of precise information results in a regret, or opportunity loss, of

$$\$595,000 - \$325,000 = \$270,000.$$

Such a penalty is referred to as the **expected value of perfect information (EVPI)**. Symbolically,

(5.3) $$\text{EVPI} = |\text{EVC} - \text{EV}^*|$$

where EV^* stands for the best expected value from the prior decision and the symbol $|\ |$ represents the absolute value. Since a negative expected outcome would not be meaningful to management, the absolute value is used to avoid having a minus EVPI in a minimization problem (where $\text{EVC} \leq \text{EV}^*$).

Table 5.2 **Pucter and Simple's Opportunity Loss Table**

Decision Alternatives	States of Nature	
	s_1 = low sales	s_2 = high sales
a_1 = market Brite a_2 = modify Kist	$600,000 $0	$0 $600,000

Expected Opportunity Loss

There is another way to look at the problem. Let us again consider Pucter and Simple's decision table (Table 5.1). Suppose that management decides to market Brite (a_1) and afterwards learns that there are low sales (s_1). According to Table 5.1, the resulting outcome is a negative profit (financial loss) of $500,000. On the other hand, in this s_1 situation, if the company modifies Kist (a_2) it could net a $100,000 profit. Hence, under these circumstances, there is a

$$\$100,000 - (-\$500,000) = \$600,000$$

opportunity loss, associated with alternative a_1 when s_1 occurs. Similarly, Pucter and Simple will incur a

$$\$1,000,000 - \$400,000 = \$600,000$$

opportunity loss if the company selects alternative a_2 when s_2 occurs.

Table 5.2 presents the opportunity losses associated with each decision alternative and state of nature combination in Pucter and Simple's problem. Notice that there is no opportunity loss when management selects the best alternative for a particular state of nature. We have just noted, for instance, that when there are low sales (s_1), the best alternative is to modify Kist (a_2). Thus, as Table 5.2 indicates, if PS selects a_2 when s_1 occurs, there will be a $0 regret.

By using the opportunity loss data from Table 5.2 and prior probabilities $P(s_1) = .45$ and $P(s_2) = .55$, PS management will find that marketing Brite (a_1) involves an expected opportunity loss of

$$\$600,000(.45) + \$0(.55) = \$270,000.$$

Similarly, if the company modifies Kist (a_2), there will be a

$$\$0(.45) + \$600,000(.55) = \$330,000$$

expected opportunity loss.

Recall that alternative a_1 has an expected profit of $325,000 and a_2 an expected profit of $265,000. Also, in this problem, the expected value under certainty (EVC) is $595,000. Table 5.3 compares these expected profits with the corresponding opportunity losses and relates them to EVC.

Table 5.3   **Pucter and Simple's Expected Profits and Opportunity Losses**

Decision Alternative	Expected Profit	Expected Opportunity Loss	Expected Profit + Expected Opportunity Loss = EVC
a_1	$325,000	$270,000	$595,000
a_2	$265,000	$330,000	$595,000

As Table 5.3 demonstrates, the expected profit plus expected opportunity loss from each decision alternative will always equal the expected value under certainty. In a maximization problem, we can express this relationship as

(5.4) $$EVC = EV(a_i) + EOL(a_i)$$

where $EV(a_i)$ = the expected value from decision alternative a_i and $EOL(a_i)$ = the expected opportunity loss from decision alternative a_i. Since EVC will be no larger than the $EV(a_i)$ when the criterion is cost, time, or distance,

(5.5) $$EVC = EV(a_i) - EOL(a_i)$$

in a minimization problem.

Expression (5.4) suggests that the alternative (a_1) with the largest expected profit ($325,000) must necessarily have the smallest expected opportunity loss ($270,000). If Pucter and Simple had perfect information, then, they could earn the

$$EVC = EV(a_1) + EOL(a_1) = \$325,000 + \$270,000 = \$595,000.$$

The lack of such precise knowledge, however, limits profit to $EV(a_1) = \$325,000$ and results in an

$$EVPI = EVC - EV(a_1) = EV(a_1) + EOL(a_1) - EV(a_1)$$

or

$$EVPI = EOL(a_1) = \$270,000$$

from the prior decision to market Brite.

In effect, then, the minimum expected opportunity loss from the prior decision also represents the expected value of perfect information. That is,

(5.6) $$EVPI - EOL^*$$

where EOL^* is the smallest expected opportunity loss from the prior decision. Table 5.4 summarizes this opportunity loss procedure for finding the EVPI and compares it with the EVC approach. These procedures assume that the number of decision alternatives and states of nature is finite.

Pricing the Information

The imprecise nature of Pucter and Simple's initial knowledge about market conditions leads management to select a single alternative (a_1) regardless of the decision

Table 5.4   **Finding the Expected Value of Perfect Information (EVPI)**

Outcome Approach [Equation (5.3)]	Opportunity Loss Approach [Equation (5.6)]
1. Develop the decision table.	1. Develop the opportunity loss table.
2. Identify the prior probabilites for the states of nature.	2. Identify the prior probabilites for the states of nature.
3. Calculate the expected values for each decision alternative.	3. Calculate the expected opportunity losses for each decision alternative.
4. Identify the decision alternative that leads to the best expected value. This action is the prior decision.	4. Identify the decision alternative that leads to the smallest expected opportunity loss.
5. Determine the expected value under certainty (EVC).	5. The expected value of perfect information (EVPI) is equal to the smallest expected opportunity loss.
6. Take the difference between the EVC and the expected value of the prior decision. The result is the expected value of perfect information (EVPI).	

environment. Such an action limits the expected profit to $325,000 and results in a regret (lost expected profit) equal to the EVPI of $270,000. If the company had more accurate market condition information, it could increase the initial $325,000 expected profit by as much as $270,000.

In effect, then, the EVPI measures the maximum potential value that can be obtained by collecting additional information about the states of nature. As a result, it also identifies the upper limit on the price that management should be willing to pay for such knowledge.

By collecting more accurate market condition information, for example, Pucter and Simple could expect a maximum additional profit of EVPI = $270,000. If the cost of obtaining the additional knowledge is less than this EVPI, then the company may benefit from a further market study. But management should not pay more than $270,000 for such a study.

Computer Analysis

Computer programs are available to perform a prior decision analysis and report the results in an easily understandable format. One such program is accessible through the **Quantitative Management (QM)** software.

The program is accessed by selecting Bayesian Analysis from **QM**'s main menu. Figure 5.2 then illustrates how the program generates information about Pucter and Simple's prior decision.

The user executes this module by selecting the Prior decision command from the Bayesian Analysis menu. Data input begins with the Edit selection from the Input menu. Report options also can be chosen from the Output menu. The program then requests information about the problem.

As Figure 5.2 demonstrates, the user first must enter the number of states and alternatives. Since Pucter and Simple has two sales conditions and two marketing choices, the manager should respond with the value 2 after both the state and alternative prompts. Next, the user enters the outcomes in the payoff table that appears on the screen.

Figure 5.2   **Computer Analysis of Pucter and Simple's Prior Decision Problem**

Bayesian Analysis:	Input:	Output:
* Prior decision	* Edit	▪ Full
▪ Updating probabilities	▪ Load	* Summary
▪ Decision making with	▪ Print	* Print
additional information	▪ Save	▪ Save

Problem Formulation:
How many states of nature? (enter a number up to 40) 2
How many decision alternatives? (enter a number up to 40) 2
Enter the outcomes in the payoff table below.

	s_1	s_2
a_1	-500000	1000000
a_2	100000	400000

Enter the prior probabilities for the states of nature below.

$$P(s_1) = .45 \qquad P(s_2) = .55$$

Do you want to maximize (MAX) or minimize (MIN) the objective? MAX

PRIOR DECISION RECOMMENDATION

Recommended decision alternative: a_1
Best expected value (EV*): 325000
Indifference probabilities: $P(s_1) = .50 \qquad P(s_2) = .50$
Expected value of perfect information (EVPI): 270000

At this stage, the decision maker must specify the prior probability for each state of nature and the decision objective (maximization MAX or minimization MIN). After receiving the user's responses, the program processes the data and generates the prior decision recommendation with its implications. For example, Figure 5.2 illustrates that prior probabilities of $P(s_1) = .45$ and $P(s_2) = .55$ with a maximization objective (MAX response) provide outputs that match the text recommendations.

5.2 UPDATING PROBABILITIES

In a risk situation, the state-of-nature probabilities have a significant influence on the decision recommendation. When the decision is based only on the initial probability assessments, there may be considerable opportunity loss. For that reason surveys, experiments, and simulations are used to gather additional information about the states of nature. Such knowledge enables management to sharpen and refine the initial probability assessments. It may even identify precisely which event will actually occur. Then the decision maker can select the best alternative for each potential event and avoid any opportunity loss.

This section shows how the additional information is used to revise the initial probability assessments. In the next section, we will consider a method for evaluating the potential benefits from such knowledge and discuss the effects of this information on the decision-making process. Management Situation 5.2 will illustrate the analysis.

Management Situation 5.2

Marketing Research

This problem is an extension of Management Situation 5.1. Pucter and Simple's management is concerned about the relatively high expected opportunity loss associated with the prior decision to market Brite. Consequently, the company will consider hiring Research Corporation (RC) for a fee of $20,000 to do a test market study of the potential market demand. Such a study is expected to indicate either a favorable or an unfavorable market for the new product Brite.

Pucter and Simple subscribes to an external information service that regularly rates the performance of Research Corporation and similar organizations. In addition, PS has employed RC in the past for comparable studies on related products. By using a decision support system to analyze the external ratings and the past experience, PS management has developed the following calibration statistics on RC's market indicators:

1. When actual sales have been low, the test study beforehand has forecasted a favorable market 14 percent of the time.

2. When actual sales have been high, the test study beforehand has predicted an unfavorable market 6 percent of the time.

Pucter and Simple will use these statistics to evaluate the potential benefits from Research Corporation's test study before making a commitment.

Sample Data

Recall that Pucter and Simple initially assigns a probability of $P(s_1) = .45$ to low sales and $P(s_2) = .55$ to high sales. The RC test market study will provide additional knowledge about these demand conditions. Specifically, the test will indicate whether there is a favorable or unfavorable market for Brite. Let us denote these test outcomes as follows:

I_1 = favorable market for Brite

I_2 = unfavorable market for Brite

Such additional knowledge is usually referred to as **sample** or **indicator information**.

There are several important probability relationships between Research Corporation's indicator information and Pucter and Simple's states of nature. Some are specified in the problem, while others must be derived from the available data.

According to the data in Management Situation 5.2, there is a 14 percent chance that the test will indicate a favorable market (I_1) when there actually have been low sales (s_1). Using shorthand notation, this likelihood of I_1 given the condition that s_1 has occurred is written as

$$P(I_1|s_1) = .14$$

where the vertical bar stands for "given the condition that." Such a likelihood is referred to as a **conditional probability**.

There are two mutually exclusive and collectively exhaustive indicators (I_1 and I_2). Hence, given a specific state of nature, the sum of the conditional probabilities for the indicators must equal 1. In the case of low sales (s_1), for instance,

$$P(I_1|s_1) + P(I_2|s_1) = 1.$$

Consequently,

$$P(I_2|s_1) = 1 - P(I_1|s_1) = 1 - .14 = .86.$$

In other words, there is an 86 percent chance that the test will indicate an unfavorable demand condition (I_2) when actually there have been low sales (s_1).

Also, according to the data in Management Situation 5.2, there is a 6 percent likelihood that the test will indicate an unfavorable market (I_2) when sales actually have been high (s_2). That is,

$$P(I_2|s_2) = .06.$$

Since

$$P(I_1|s_2) + P(I_2|s_2) = 1$$

there is a probability of

$$P(I_1|s_2) = 1 - P(I_2|s_2) = 1 - .06 = .94$$

that the test will indicate a favorable market (I_1) when sales actually have been high (s_2).

Joint Probabilities. Figure 5.3 organizes the prior and conditional indicator probabilities in a convenient format. This type of diagram is called a **probability tree**. As chance point 1 at the left of the figure indicates, Pucter and Simple's sales can be either low (s_1) or high (s_2). The initial probability assessments, $P(s_1) = .45$ and $P(s_2) = .55$, are written below the corresponding sales branches emerging from this point. These initial assessments will be revised by Research Corporation's study results. However, the test is not infallible. Favorable or unfavorable test results can be obtained regardless of the true market conditions. For example, as chance point 2 in Figure 5.3 demonstrates, when sales are actually low (s_1), the test result could either be favorable ($I_1|s_1$) or unfavorable ($I_2|s_1$). The corresponding probabilities $P(I_1|s_1) = .14$ and $P(I_2|s_1) = .86$ appear below the appropriate branches emerging from this point. Similarly, chance point 3 identifies the relevant test results when sales are high (s_2). Branches emerging from this point show that when s_2 occurs, the test has a $P(I_1|s_2) = .94$ chance of reporting favorable conditions and a $P(I_2|s_2) = .06$ likelihood of suggesting an unfavorable market.

Figure 5.3   **Pucter and Simple's Probability Data**

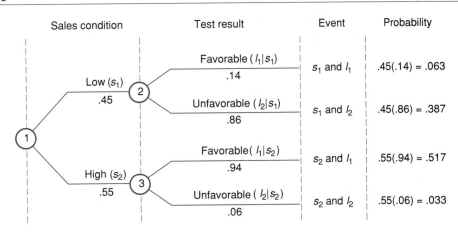

Notice that there are now four distinct events:

1. Low sales and a favorable test (s_1 and I_1).
2. Low sales and an unfavorable test (s_1 and I_2).
3. High sales and a favorable test (s_2 and I_1).
4. High sales and an unfavorable test (s_2 and I_2).

As Figure 5.3 illustrates, each of these events is depicted as a separate path through the probability tree. For instance, the path along the s_1 and $I_1|s_1$ branches identifies the s_1 and I_1 event. In a similar manner, the s_1 and I_2 event corresponds to the path along the s_1 and $I_2|s_1$ branches of the tree.

The likelihood of such an event is given by the product of the probabilities along the branches of the corresponding path through the tree. Consider, for example, the s_1 and I_1 event. Figure 5.3 shows that there is a $P(s_1) = .45$ chance of low sales and, given this market condition, a $P(I_1|s_1) = .14$ likelihood of a favorable test. Thus, the probability of both low sales and a favorable test is

$$P(s_1 \text{ and } I_1) = P(s_1) \times P(I_1|s_1) = .45(.14) = .063$$

Also, since $P(I_2|s_1) = .86$, there is a

$$P(s_1 \text{ and } I_2) = P(s_1) \times P(I_2|s_1) = .45(.86) = .387$$

chance of both low sales and an unfavorable test. These likelihoods are referred to as **joint probabilities**.

In general, the joint probability for state of nature j and indicator i can be found with the following expression:

(5.7) $$P(s_j \text{ and } I_i) = P(s_j) \times P(I_i|s_j)$$

where $P(s_j)$ = prior probability for state of nature j and $P(I_i|s_j)$ = conditional probability of indicator i given the condition that state j has occurred. By using this expression for each state and indicator combination, PS management will obtain the joint probabilities presented at the right of the corresponding sales/test paths (events) in Figure 5.3. Since the events are mutually exclusive and collectively exhaustive, these joint probabilities must (and do) add up to 1.

Marginal Probabilities. The event information is also useful in computing the probability of each indicator. Consider, for example, the favorable market situation (I_1). As Figure 5.3 demonstrates, there are exactly two events that involve a favorable indicator:

1. Low sales and a favorable test (s_1 and I_1).
2. High sales and a favorable test (s_2 and I_1).

Since

$$P(s_1 \text{ and } I_1) = .063$$

and

$$P(s_2 \text{ and } I_1) = .517$$

there must be a

$$P(I_1) = P(s_1 \text{ and } I_1) + P(s_2 \text{ and } I_1) = .063 + .517 = .58$$

likelihood of obtaining a favorable indicator.

Similarly, Figure 5.3 shows that there are only two events that lead to an unfavorable (I_2) condition:

1. Low sales and an unfavorable test (s_1 and I_2).
2. High sales and an unfavorable test (s_2 and I_2).

Furthermore,

$$P(s_1 \text{ and } I_2) = .387$$

and

$$P(s_2 \text{ and } I_2) = .033.$$

Hence, there is a

$$P(I_2) = P(s_1 \text{ and } I_2) + P(s_2 \text{ and } I_2) = .387 + .033 = .42$$

chance that the test study will indicate an unfavorable market condition. Cumulative likelihoods—such as $P(I_1)$ and $P(I_2)$—are called **marginal probabilities**.

In effect, the marginal probability of a particular indicator is simply the sum of the corresponding joint probabilities. By letting $P(I_i)$ = marginal probability of indicator i and n = number of mutually exclusive and collectively exhaustive states of nature, we can express the relationship as follows:

$$P(I_i) = P(s_1 \text{ and } I_i) + P(s_2 \text{ and } I_i) + \cdots + P(s_n \text{ and } I_i)$$

or

(5.8)
$$P(I_i) = \sum_{j=1}^{n} P(s_j \text{ and } I_i)$$

In addition, since the indicators are mutually exclusive and collectively exhaustive, their probabilites also must (and do) sum to 1. Put another way, for the case of Pucter and Simple, there is a probability of

$$P(I_1) + P(I_2) = .58 + .42 = 1$$

or a 100 percent chance that the test will indicate either a favorable or an unfavorable market.

Revised Probabilities

Pucter and Simple's management can use the test market (indicator) information to update the initial (prior) probability assessments for potential sales. In particular, the company can now determine the likelihood of each sales level, given the results of the test market study.

Suppose, for instance, that the test study indicates a favorable market condition (I_1). Management knows that this condition will occur $P(I_1) = .58$, or 58 percent of the time. On these occasions, there is a

$$P(s_1 \text{ and } I_1) = .063$$

likelihood that there will also be low sales (s_1). Consequently, there is only a

$$P(s_1|I_1) = \frac{P(s_1 \text{ and } I_1)}{P(I_1)} = \frac{.063}{.580} = .11$$

probability of obtaining low sales if the test study indicates a favorable market. Similarly, since $P(s_2 \text{ and } I_1) = .517$, Pucter and Simple has a

$$P(s_2|I_1) = \frac{P(s_2 \text{ and } I_1)}{P(I_1)} = \frac{.517}{.580} = .89$$

chance of achieving high sales when the test study indicates a favorable market. These revised or updated likelihoods, $P(s_1|I_1)$ and $P(s_2|I_1)$, are called **posterior probabilities.**

Generally, the posterior probability for state of nature j, given indicator i, can be found with the following equation:

$$\textbf{(5.9)} \qquad P(s_j|I_i) = \frac{P(s_j \text{ and } I_i)}{P(I_i)}$$

In other words, a posterior probability is the ratio of a joint probability to a marginal probability. This relationship is also known as **Bayes's formula** or **Bayes's theorem.** A schematic representation of the Bayesian revision process is presented in Figure 5.4.

According to Bayes's formula (5.9), if the test study indicates an unfavorable market (I_2), Pucter and Simple has a

$$P(s_1|I_2) = \frac{P(s_1 \text{ and } I_2)}{P(I_2)} = \frac{.387}{.420} = .92$$

chance of obtaining low sales (s_1). Also, under these circumstances, there will be a

$$P(s_2|I_2) = \frac{P(s_2 \text{ and } I_2)}{P(I_2)} = \frac{.033}{.420} = .08$$

probability of achieving high sales (s_2).

Figure 5.4   **Updating Probabilities with Bayes's Formula**

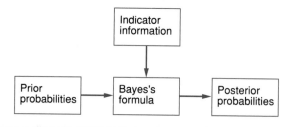

Figure 5.5   **Tabular Approach to Bayesian Analysis**

a. Favorable Market (I_1)

Event (s_j)	Prior Probability $P(s_j)$	Conditional Indicator Probability $P(I_1|s_j)$	Joint Probability $P(s_j \text{ and } I_1)$	Posterior Probability $P(s_j|I_1)$
s_1	.45	.14	.45(.14) = .063	.063/.58 = .11
s_2	.55	.94	.55(.94) = .517	.517/.58 = .89
			Marginal Probability $P(I_1) = .580$	

b. Unfavorable Market (I_2)

Event (s_j)	Prior Probability $P(s_j)$	Conditional Indicator Probability $P(I_2|s_j)$	Joint Probability $P(s_j \text{ and } I_2)$	Posterior Probability $P(s_j|I_2)$
s_1	.45	.86	.45(.86) = .387	.387/.42 = .92
s_2	.55	.06	.55(.06) = .033	.033/.42 = .08
			Marginal Probability $P(I_2) = .420$	

Procedure Recap. When the number of indicators and states of nature is finite, the following procedure can be used to update probabilities with Bayes's formula:

1. List the events, prior probabilities, and conditional indicator probabilities associated with a specific indicator.

2. Multiply each prior probability by the corresponding indicator probability. The results give the joint probabilities.

3. Sum the joint probabilities. The result is the marginal probability of the indicator.

4. Divide each joint probability by the marginal probability. The results are the updated, or posterior, probabilities.

5. Repeat steps 1 through 4 for each indicator.

Figure 5.5 illustrates how this procedure can be applied in a tabular fashion to Pucter and Simple's situation.

Figure 5.6   **Computer Analysis of Market Indicator Information**

Bayesian Analysis:	Input:	Output:
▪ Prior decision	* Edit	▪ Full
* Updating probabilities	▪ Load	* Summary
▪ Decision making with	▪ Print	* Print
additional information	▪ Save	▪ Save

Problem Formulation:
How many states of nature? (enter a number up to 40) 2
Enter the prior probabilities for the states of nature below.

$P(s_1) = .45$ $P(s_2) = .55$

How many indicators? (enter a number up to 40) 2
Enter the conditional indicator probabilities in the table below.

$I_i\|s_j$	s_1	s_2
I_1	.14	.94
I_2	.86	.06

BAYES'S FORMULA RESULTS

For I_1	Joint Probabilities $P(s_j \text{ and } I_i)$	Posterior Probabilities $P(s_j\|I_i)$
	.063	.11
	.517	.89
Marginal Probability $P(I_i) = .580$		

For I_2	Joint Probabilities $P(s_j \text{ and } I_i)$	Posterior Probabilities $P(s_j\|I_i)$
	.387	.92
	.033	.08
Marginal Probability $P(I_i) = .420$		

Computer Analysis

It can be cumbersome and time-consuming to update probabilities in practice, especially for large-scale problems. Fortunately, computer programs, including one on the **QM** software, are available to perform the necessary calculations and report the results in an easily understandable format.

The **QM** program again is accessed by selecting Bayesian Analysis from the main menu. Figure 5.6 then illustrates how the program generates Pucter and Simple's posterior probability information.

The user executes this module by selecting the Updating probabilities command from the Bayesian Analysis menu. Once more, data input begins with the Edit selection from the Input menu, and report options are chosen from the Output menu. The program then requests information about the problem.

As Figure 5.6 demonstrates, the user first must enter the number of states. Since Pucter and Simple has two sales conditions, the manager should respond with the value 2 after the prompt. Next, the user must specify the prior probability for each state of nature and then enter the conditional indicator probabilities into the table that appears on the screen.

After receiving the user's responses, the program processes the data and generates the Bayes's formula results. Figure 5.6 shows that these results include the joint, marginal, and posterior probabilities associated with each indicator. Moreover, the outputs match the text computations.

5.3 DECISION MAKING WITH ADDITIONAL INFORMATION

Research Corporation's indicator information is not perfect. After all, there is only a $P(I_2|s_1) = .86$ probability that the test will indicate an unfavorable market when sales actually have been low. Furthermore, if sales have been high, there is just a $P(I_1|s_2) = .94$ likelihood that the test will indicate a favorable market. Yet these sample data have enabled PS management to refine (update) its initial (prior) probability assessments.

Initially, Pucter and Simple's management felt that there was a $P(s_1) = .45$ chance of low product sales and a $P(s_2) = .55$ likelihood of high sales. Now the company knows that if the test indicates a favorable market (I_1), there is only a $P(s_1|I_1) = .11$ probability of low sales but a $P(s_2|I_1) = .89$ chance of high sales. On the other hand, when the test indicates an unfavorable market (I_2), there is a $P(s_1|I_2) = .92$ likelihood of low sales and a $P(s_2|I_2) = .08$ probability of high sales.

Observe that the prior probability of low sales, $P(s_1)$, is different from each of the corresponding posterior probabilities, $P(s_1|I_1)$ and $P(s_1|I_2)$. In addition, the prior probability of high sales, $P(s_2)$, differs from each corresponding posterior probability, $P(s_2|I_1)$ and $P(s_2|I_2)$. Consequently, the expected profits from actions taken with the prior knowledge will be different from the corresponding returns with the additional indicator information.

The test results are also important. Notice that $P(s_1|I_1)$ is different from $P(s_1|I_2)$, and $P(s_2|I_1)$ does not have the same value as $P(s_2|I_2)$. Hence, the expected profit from marketing Brite (a_1) under favorable test circumstances (I_1) will be different from the corresponding earnings for unfavorable test conditions (I_2). Similarly, the expected profit from modifying Kist (a_2) will differ in the I_1 and I_2 indicator situations.

Pucter and Simple still wants to maximize expected profits, and these earnings again depend on the company's actions (a_1 and a_2). However, such actions will now be influenced by the availability and nature of the RC test market information. As a result, PS management must consider a series of interrelated decisions.

Sequence of Decisions

By letting a_3 denote the alternative of buying RC's indicator service and a_4 the action of not purchasing the service, Pucter and Simple's problem can be depicted by Figure 5.7. Again, decision points are portrayed by squares and chance points by circles.

Figure 5.7   **Pucter and Simple's Decision Tree**

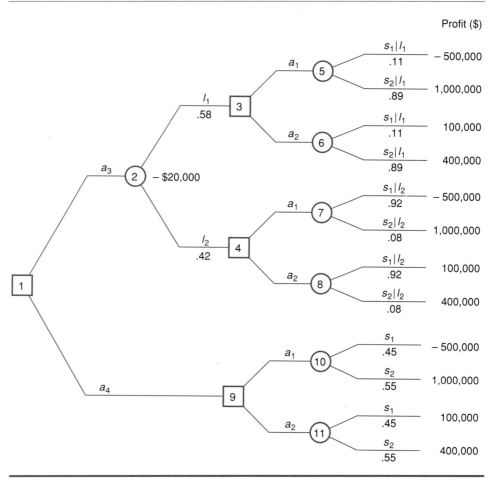

Profit ($)

Management first must decide whether to buy (a_3) or not buy (a_4) the RC indicator service. This initial choice is shown as decision point 1 in Figure 5.7. If PS buys the service (follows the a_3 branch emerging from decision point 1), it must pay a $20,000 fee to Research Corporation. Although this fee can be subtracted from all subsequent profits (or losses), such an approach will make it awkward to compute (and interpret) an important statistic needed by management later in the analysis. Hence, the fee is shown as a negative $20,000 profit when it actually occurs at chance point 2.

Next, PS must identify the test study outcome. Branches emerging from chance point 2 show that the test could indicate either a favorable market (I_1) or unfavorable market (I_2). Decision points 3 and 4 illustrate that in each of these situations, PS management then has the choice of either marketing Brite (a_1) or modifying Kist (a_2). The resulting profits will depend on product sales.

Let us consider the case when there is a favorable indicator (I_1). If PS markets Brite (follows the a_1 branch emerging from decision point 3), chance point 5 shows that the company could obtain either low ($s_1|I_1$) or high ($s_2|I_1$) sales. Low demand (the $s_1|I_1$ branch emerging from point 5) results in a \$500,000 loss, while high demand (the $s_2|I_1$ branch) leads to a \$1 million profit. When PS modifies Kist (follows the a_2 branch emerging from decision point 3), chance point 6 illustrates that the company also could obtain either low ($s_1|I_1$) or high ($s_2|I_1$) sales. In this case, however, low sales (the $s_1|I_1$ branch emerging from point 6) lead to a \$100,000 profit; high demand (the $s_2|I_1$ branch) results in a \$400,000 profit.

There is a similar sequence when the indicator is unfavorable (I_2). If PS markets Brite (follows the a_1 branch emerging from decision point 4), chance point 7 demonstrates that the company could get either low ($s_1|I_2$) or high ($s_2|I_2$) sales. Low sales again result in a \$500,000 loss, and high demand results in a \$1 million profit. If PS modifies Kist (follows the a_2 branch emerging from decision point 4), chance point 8 shows that the company could obtain either low ($s_1|I_2$) or high ($s_2|I_2$) sales. In this situation, low demand leads to a \$100,000 profit. High sales result in a \$400,000 profit.

Finally, suppose that PS does not purchase the RC indicator service and hence follows the a_4 branch emerging from decision point 1. In this case, PS will make its new product decision (shown as decision point 9) with only the initial information. If the company markets Brite, chance point 10 illustrates that it could obtain either low (s_1) or high (s_2) sales. Low sales result in a \$500,000 loss, while high sales lead to a \$1 million profit. If the company modifies Kist, chance point 11 shows that it also could get either low or high sales. Under these circumstances, however, low sales lead to a \$100,000 profit; high demand (the s_2 branch) results in a \$400,000 profit.

Evaluating the Information

As Figure 5.7 demonstrates, Pucter and Simple's test market decision (a_3 versus a_4) will depend on the profits achievable from the resulting product actions. To compute these profits, management must start at the right of the tree and progressively work backward through the appropriate chance and decision points. Figure 5.8 illustrates the calculations from the a_4 segment of the decision tree.

Backward Induction. As Figure 5.8 shows, marketing Brite (a_1) under these circumstances leads to an expected profit of

$$-\$500,000(.45) + \$1,000,000(.55) = \$325,000.$$

This value is recorded in a rectangle above chance point 10. On the other hand, by modifying Kist (a_2), PS can obtain an expected profit of only

$$\$100,000(.45) + \$400,000(.55) = \$265,000$$

Thus, if Pucter and Simple does not purchase the indicator service (selects the a_4 alternative), the best product action is to market Brite (a_1). By doing so, the company will maximize expected profit at \$325,000. This recommendation is depicted in Figure 5.8 by "pruning" the a_2 branch and placing the \$325,000 in a rectangle above decision point 9.

By working backward through the a_3 segment of the decision tree in a similar manner, management will obtain the results presented in Figure 5.9. Let us first consider

Figure 5.8   **Evaluating the a_4 Segment of the PS Decision Tree**

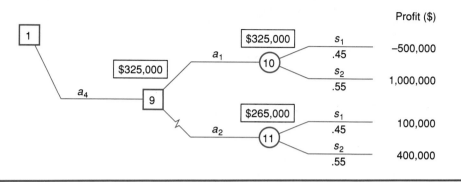

Figure 5.9   **Evaluating the a_3 Segment of the PS Decision Tree**

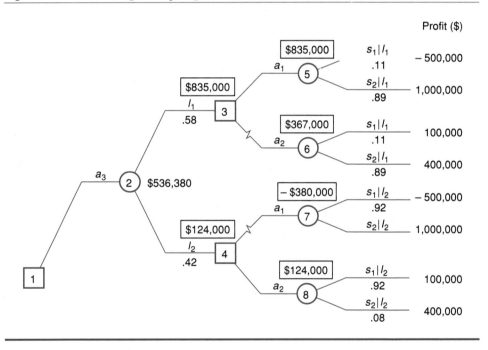

the I_1 segment of Figure 5.9. According to the computations in this diagram, Pucter and Simple can obtain an expected profit of

$$-\$500,000(.11) + \$1,000,000(.89) = \$835,000$$

by marketing Brite (a_1) under these I_1 conditions. This expected value appears in a rectangle above chance point 5. Alternatively, if the company modifies Kist (a_2), the expected profit will be only

$$\$100,000(.11) + \$400,000(.89) = \$367,000.$$

Hence, if the test study indicates a favorable (I_1) situation, Pucter and Simple should market Brite (a_1) and obtain a maximum expected profit of $835,000. The recommendation is depicted in Figure 5.9 by "pruning" the a_2 branch emerging from decision point 3 and placing the $835,000 in a rectangle above that point.

A similar analysis of the I_2 segment of Figure 5.9 shows that the a_1 alternative leads to an expected profit of

$$-\$500,000(.92) + \$1,000,000(.08) = -\$380,000.$$

Under these circumstances, action a_2 results in an expected profit of

$$\$100,000(.92) + \$400,000(.08) = \$124,000.$$

These values are placed in rectangles above chance points 7 and 8, respectively. According to these results, if the test indicates an unfavorable (I_2) market, Pucter and Simple can maximize expected profit at $124,000 by modifying Kist (a_2).

Figure 5.9 also shows that there is a $P(I_1) = .58$ probability of a favorable indicator and a $P(I_2) = .42$ likelihood of an unfavorable indicator. Consequently, if Pucter and Simple buys the indicator service (selects alternative a_3), the company will earn a gross expected profit of

$$\$835,000(.58) + \$214,000(.42) + \$536,380.$$

This value is reported next to chance point 2 in the diagram.

Expected Value of Sample Information. When Pucter and Simple uses only the prior knowledge (selects alternative a_4), the company earns an expected profit of no more than $325,000. Thus, the additional RC indicator information could increase Pucter and Simple's gross expected profit (in the long run, on average) by a potential

$$\$536,380 - \$325,000 = \$211,380.$$

This potential long run, average outcome is referred to as the **expected value of sample information (EVSI)**.

Note that the expected value of sample information is simply the difference between the best expected value with indicator information and the best expected value with prior knowledge. By letting EVS^* = the best expected value with sample, or indicator, information and by defining other terms as before, we can express the relationship with the equation

(5.10) $$EVSI = |EVS^* - EV^*|$$

Once again, the absolute value is used to avoid having a minus EVSI in a minimization problem (where $EVS^* \leq EV^*$).

The EVSI, in effect, measures the maximum potential benefit that can be obtained from the indicator information. However, such knowledge usually involves some costs. Thus, to properly evaluate the information, management must compare these benefits and costs.

Expected Net Gain from Sampling. Pucter and Simple can gross an $EVSI = \$211,380$ (in the long run, on average) by using the indicator information. Therefore, management should never pay more than this amount for such knowledge. Since Research Corporation charges a fee of only $20,000, PS can net an expected profit of

$$\$211,380 - \$20,000 = \$191,380$$

in the long run, on average from the test market service. This difference is called the **expected net gain from sampling (ENGS)**. That is,

(5.11)   ENGS = EVSI − CS

where CS denotes the cost of the indicator information.

It will be worth gathering the indicator information as long as there is a positive expected net gain from sampling (ENGS > 0). Since the RC indicator information has ENGS = $191,380 (greater than zero), Pucter and Simple should purchase the test market service.

Efficiency Rating. Another useful measure of evaluation can be derived from the EVSI. Recall that perfect knowledge enables the decision maker to identify exactly which state of nature will occur. The economic value of this knowledge is measured by the EVPI. Indicator information usually will not be as accurate as perfect knowledge. However, it will provide a gross economic benefit equal to the EVSI. Thus, management can use the equation

(5.12) $$E = \frac{EVSI}{EVPI} \times 100$$

to rate indicator information. The value E is known as the **efficiency rating**.

Sample information will have an efficiency rating somewhere between 0 and 100 percent. A high (close to 100 percent) rating indicates that the sample data are almost as good as perfect information. Low (close to 0 percent) ratings suggest that the indicator information is a poor substitute for perfect knowledge.

In effect, E measures the ability of the indicator information to accurately predict the states of nature. As a result, when there is a low efficiency rating, the decision maker may want to consider better and/or additional data sources.

Recall that Pucter and Simple has an EVPI equal to $270,000 and an EVSI equal to $211,380. Hence, besides being worthwhile (having an ENGS > 0), Research Corporation's test market service is

$$E = \frac{EVSI}{EVPI} \times 100 = \frac{\$211,380}{\$270,000} \times 100 = .783$$

or 78.3 percent as efficient as perfect information. Consequently, PS management should feel relatively confident about using the RC sample data to help make the product decision.

Procedure Recap. The process of evaluating the indicator information (computing and analyzing ENGS and E), known as **preposterior analysis**, can be summarized as follows:

1. Develop a decision tree that accurately describes the sequential nature of the problem.

2. Assign the prior, indicator, and posterior probabilities to the appropriate branches of the decision tree.

3. Work backward through the decision tree to determine the expected values of each decision alternative.

4. Find the expected value of sample information (EVSI) by taking the absolute difference between the best expected value with indicator information (EVS*) and the best expected value with prior knowledge (EV*).

5. Find the expected net gain from sampling (ENGS) by subtracting the cost of the indicator information (CS) from the EVSI.

6. If the ENGS > 0, obtain the indicator information.

Developing a Strategy

Pucter and Simple can use the preposterior results to develop a complete decision strategy. Figure 5.10 illustrates.

If Pucter and Simple does not purchase the indicator service (selects alternative a_4), then the company must use only the prior knowledge to make the product decision. As Figure 5.10 demonstrates, under these circumstances the company can maximize expected profit at $325,000 by marketing Brite (selecting the a_1 branch emerging from decision point 9).

On the other hand, if PS buys the service (selects a_3), it can use both prior and test information to make the product decision. Figure 5.10 shows that the following strategy is appropriate in this case:

Wait for the test results before making the product decision, and	
If	**Then**
the test indicates a favorable market (l_1)	market Brite (a_1)
the test indicates an unfavorable market (l_2)	modify Kist (a_2)

By adjusting the decision strategy as shown in the box, Pucter and Simple can earn a gross expected profit of $536,380 in the long run, on average. Since Research Corporation charges a $20,000 fee for the test service, however, PS can net an expected profit of only

$$\$536,380 - \$20,000 = \$516,380$$

from alternative a_3. This long run, average value is recorded in a rectangle above chance point 2.

Since a_3 provides more earnings than a_4, Pucter and Simple should buy the service and use the test results to help make the product decision. This recommendation is depicted in Figure 5.10 by "pruning" the a_4 branch and placing the $516,380 expected profit from the selected alternative (a_3) in a rectangle next to decision point 1.

Procedure Recap. The process of using sample, or indicator, information to develop a decision strategy, referred to as **posterior analysis**, can be summarized as follows:

1. Use the preposterior results to work backward through the entire decision tree.

2. Select the decision strategy (sequence of actions) that results in the best expected value at each decision point in the tree.

Figure 5.10   **Working Backward through the Entire PS Decision Tree**

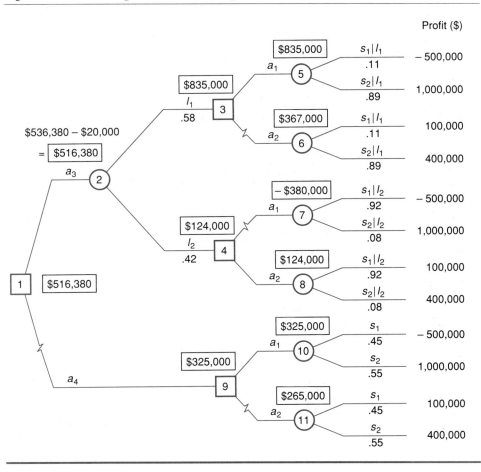

Computer Analysis

Computer programs, such as **Arborist** and **SuperTree**, are available to complete a preposterior and posterior decision analysis. The **Quantitative Management (QM)** software contains a program that performs a similar analysis.

Once more, the program is accessed by selecting Bayesian Analysis from **QM**'s main menu. Figure 5.11 then illustrates how the program solves Pucter and Simple's sequential decision problem.

As Figure 5.11 demonstrates, the user executes this module by selecting the Decision making with additional information command from the Bayesian Analysis menu. Data input again begins with the Edit selection from the Input menu, and report options are chosen from the Output menu. Then the program requests information about the problem.

Problem Formulation. The user first must enter the number of branches in the decision tree. Since Figure 5.10 has 22 branches, the manager should respond with the value 22

Figure 5.11   Computer Analysis of Pucter and Simple's Sequential Problem

---

Bayesian Analysis:	Input:	Output:
▪ Prior decision	* Edit	▪ Full
▪ Updating probabilities	▪ Load	* Summary
* Decision making with	▪ Print	* Print
additional information	▪ Save	▪ Save

Problem Formulation:
How many branches in the decision tree? (enter a number up to 80) 22
Enter the branch number, start point number, end point number, probability, and outcome in the table below.

Branch Number	Start Point Number	End Point Number	Probability	Outcome
1	1	2	0.00	−20000
2	2	3	.58	0
3	3	5	0.00	0
4	5	12	.11	−500000
5	5	13	.89	1000000
6	3	6	0.00	0
7	6	14	.11	100000
8	6	15	.89	400000
9	2	4	.42	0
10	4	7	0.00	0
11	7	16	.92	−500000
12	7	17	.08	1000000
13	4	8	0.00	0
14	8	18	.92	100000
15	8	19	.08	400000
16	1	9	0.00	0
17	9	10	0.00	0
18	10	20	.45	−500000
19	10	21	.55	1000000
20	9	11	0.00	0
21	11	22	.45	100000
22	11	23	.55	400000

Do you want to maximize (MAX) or minimize (MIN) the objective? MAX

POSTERIOR ANALYSIS RESULTS

Expected Value of Sample Information (EVSI)	=	211380
Cost of the Sample/Indicator Information (CS)	=	20000
Expected Net Gain from Sampling (ENGS)	=	191380
Efficiency Rating (E)	=	.783

OPTIMAL DECISION STRATEGY

Start Point Number	End Point Number	Expected Value
1	2	516380
3	5	835000
4	8	124000

Bayesian Analysis in Practice

Bayesian Analysis is applied to a wide variety of management problems. Here are a few areas in which this quantitative analysis is used.

Area	Application
Finance	Determining a strategy for speculating in commodities markets
	Establishing a fee schedule for automobile insurance
	Selecting the best financial auditing plan
Marketing	Establishing a pricing policy for new products
	Determining the best way to distribute durable products and services
	Selecting the best product design and packaging
Production	Identifying the best location for a new plant
	Selecting the most reliable manufacturing process
	Identifying the best testing policy in a quality control shop
	Establishing the best starting height for pole-vaulting
Public sector	Assessing the success of enterprise zones
	Identifying the best way to avoid excess damage from forest fires
	Determining the best strategy to equitably distribute public risks

after the prompt. Next, the user inputs the following data (in the order listed), branch by branch, from the decision tree into the table that appears on the screen:

1. The decision or chance point from which the branch emerges.

2. The destination point for the branch.

3. The probability associated with the branch.

4. The outcome, if any, associated with the branch.

In this program, each branch must have starting and ending points.

For example, consider the buy RC indicator service (a_3) branch in the Pucter and Simple's decision tree (Figure 5.7). This branch is recorded as the first entry in the **QM** screen table (Figure 5.11). It emerges from decision point 1, ends at chance point 2, involves no probability (shown as 0.00 in the screen table), and results in a $-$20,000 profit. Similarly, the $S_1|I_1$ branch at the top of Figure 5.7 is presented as the fourth entry in Figure 5.11's screen table. This branch emerges from chance point 5, ends at an artificial point 12, has a probability of .11, and results in a $-$500,000 profit. Artificial points (such as 12) are created merely to have distinct ending points for the branches in the program.

At this stage, the decision maker must specify the decision objective (maximization MAX or minimization MIN). After receiving the user's response, the program processes the data and first generates the results of the preposterior analysis (the EVSI, CS, ENGS, and E). Then, the **QM** program reports the optimal decision strategy.

Optimal Decision Strategy. Figure 5.11 illustrates that Pucter and Simple can maximize (MAX) expected profit at $516,380 by first going from point 1 to point 2. This action corresponds to the selection of alternative a_3 at decision point 1 in Figure 5.10. Then, if the company encounters point 3 (follows the I_1 branch in the decision tree), it should go to point 5. Such an action is equivalent to selecting alternative a_1 at decision point 3 in Figure 5.10. Alternatively, if PS encounters point 4 (follows the I_2 branch in the decision tree), it should to to point 8 (select alternative a_2 emerging from decision point 4 in Figure 5.10). This optimal strategy matches the recommendation obtained from the backward induction analysis shown in Figure 5.10.

SUMMARY

The manager's degree of knowledge about the states of nature is a key element in any decision analysis. Usually, the decision maker has enough information to make an initial assessment of the probabilities of the uncertain events. Consequently, these decisions will be made under risk, typically with the expected value criterion.

Often, however, the expected value calculations are very sensitive to changes in the probability values. In such cases, the decision maker may want to gather additional information and perform a Bayesian analysis before making the final decision. This chapter examined this Bayesian approach.

The first section discussed the relevance and potential benefit from accurate knowledge about the event probabilities. We considered a methodology for determining the sensitivity of the recommended decisions to changes in these probabilities. Then we saw how to identify and measure the resulting risk. We saw that if management knew exactly when each event would occur in a risk situation, it could expect to earn as much as the expected value under certainty (EVC). However, since decision makers usually do not have such precise knowledge, they incur a penalty equal to the expected value of perfect information (EVPI). Table 5.4 summarized the procedures for calculating the EVPI.

A relatively large EVPI indicates that there is a substantial opportunity loss associated with the prior decision. In such cases, it is wise for the decision maker to consider collecting additional information before making a final decision. The second section showed how this additional information can be used to update the initial probability assessments. Figure 5.4 illustrated the process. The last section presented a method for evaluating the potential benefits from such knowledge and discussed the effects of this information on the decision-making process.

Glossary

Arborist and SuperTree Computer programs designed to solve sequential decision problems.

Bayesian analysis The process of using additional information to revise and update the initial assessments of the event probabilities.

Bayes's formula (Bayes's theorem) The relationship that states that a conditional probability is the ratio of a joint probability to a marginal probability. In decision analysis, it is used primarily to find the updated, or posterior, probabilities for the states of nature.

conditional probability The probability of one event, given the condition that some other event has occurred.

efficiency rating The ratio of EVSI to EVPI multiplied by 100. It measures the ability of the sample, or indicator, information to accurately predict the states of nature.

expected net gain from sampling (ENGS) The difference between the EVSI and the cost of the sample or indicator information.

expected value of perfect information (EVPI) The difference between the expected value under certainty (EVC) and the best expected value with only prior knowledge. It measures the expected value of information that would tell the decision maker exactly which state of nature will occur.

expected value of sample information (EVSI) The difference between the best expected value with the indicator information and the best expected value with only prior knowledge. It is a measure of the economic benefit that can be obtained from the specified sample, or indicator, information.

expected value under certainty (EVC) The best possible expected value of the objective if the decision maker knows exactly when each state of nature will occur.

indifference probability The event probability that equates the expected outcomes of the decision alternatives.

joint probability The probability that two or more events will jointly occur.

marginal probability The cumulative probability that an event will occur.

posterior analysis The process of using sample, or indicator, information to develop a decision strategy.

posterior probability The revised or updated probability of a state of nature, given the condition that a particular indicator has occurred.

preposterior analysis The process of evaluating sample, or indicator, information.

prior decision A decision based on the prior probabilities.

prior probabilities Preliminary, or initial, assessments of the probabilities for the states of nature.

probability tree A diagram that organizes the prior and conditional indicator probabilities in a convenient format.

sample (indicator) information The new or additional knowledge provided through surveys, experiments, or simulations.

sensitivity analysis Measuring the sensitivity of an optimal decision to changes in the uncontrollable inputs.

Thought Exercises

1. Col. Jolley Ender is the logistics officer at Flywell AFB. Currently, she is trying to minimize the expected round-trip flight time for a particular cargo shipment. There are several possible routes. Flight time over these routes depend on uncertain weather conditions. Based on current available data on weather probabilities, the best expected flight time is 2 hours and 20 minutes. If Col. Ender knew when each weather condition was going to occur, she could reduce the time to 1 hour and 50 minutes by rescheduling flights. Each hour of "wasted" time involves a $20,000 opportunity loss to the base.

   How much should Col. Ender be willing to pay for more accurate weather information? Explain.

2. East Western University offers a course in business policy. It is typical for the professor to invite executives as guest lecturers. Recently, the manager of a large financial institution closed his presentation with the following statements: "All decision makers know that time involves money. We in the financial world also know that uncertainty has its price. That's why we constantly seek updated information about market conditions. Few financial analysts would pay for such information if they knew exactly what was going to happen."

   During the next class meeting, the business policy professor noted that the financial manager's comments really were a practical interpretation of the EVPI. As an assignment, the professor asked the class to give an EVPI interpretation of the manager's closing statements. Pretend you are a member of the class and do the assignment.

3. The mayor of Smithfield must decide whether or not to approve a sanitation department project that would expand the city's sewer system. Her action will depend on the projected demand for the facilities. Based on the best current available forecast, the mayor would approve the project. Such an action would maximize expected cash flow. However, the decision involves a $500,000 opportunity loss when there is a low demand and a $2 million penalty if demand is moderate. The best initial estimates indicate a 10 percent chance of low demand and a 20 percent likelihood of moderate demand.

   The regional planning commission estimates that it would cost $525,000 to obtain additional information about demand conditions. There is no other way of obtaining the knowledge at a lower cost within the time frame required for decision making. What should the mayor do? Explain.

4. Adam Full, advertising manager of T. J. Mentals Tobacco Company, is considering a media proposal from his assistant, Cynthia Lorelly. Ms. Lorelly suggested spending $300,000 in advertising on a new filter cigar. Full returned the proposal to Cynthia with the following comment: "If you can convince me that there is at least a 75 percent chance that the product will earn $150,000 more than the media cost, I'll authorize your proposal." After several days of research, Cynthia projected sales as follows:

Sales (Millions)	Probability
1	.05
2	.15
3	.30
4	.40
5	.10

   The company would make 15 cents per cigar. Can Ms. Lorelly convince her boss? Explain.

5. *Management Researcher* is a professional publication that supports itself mainly by subscription fees. The managing editor has calculated that variable costs are $10 per subscription. Fixed costs are $100,000 annually. A subscription is $30 per year. The journal's planning board estimates that total subscriptions will show the following distribution:

Subscriptions (Thousands/Year)	Probability
5	.10
10	.40
15	.30
20	.20

   Based on this information, the editor decides to continue publishing *Management Researcher*. However, he is worried about the probability of a financial loss. The editor is considering a poll of past subscribers, professors, business people, and other interested parties in order to get a more accurate estimate of subscriptions. Such a poll would cost $100.

Explain why the editor decided to continue publishing the journal. What is the probability of loss associated with the decision? Should the poll be taken? Explain.

6. Do you think that a Bayesian decision analysis is appropriate in each of the following situations? Explain.
   a. A company is trying to decide whether or not to introduce a new cooking appliance. Each unit would contribute a constant amount to cost and would sell for a fixed price. Total profit would depend on the sales volume, and demand would follow a normal distribution.
   b. A laundry is trying to decide whether to lease or buy a line of automatic washing machines. The decision will depend on work volume. This volume is normally distributed with a known mean and standard deviation. The lease involves a fixed charge plus a constant variable expense per unit of volume. If the machines are owned, the variable cost is expected to decrease as volume increases.
   c. A city's department of education wants to install electronic games in its high school recreation rooms. The department is considering three brands. Each brand has a constant operating cost per hour of use. Profit will depend on the total hours of use. There is a normal distribution of use.
   d. The government's printing office is trying to decide whether or not to publish the final statistics of a terminated agency. There is a constant profit per volume. The publication can be sold only in whole unit quantities. However, sales volume can be approximated by a normal distribution.

7. Hamilton Tang is the general manager of Universal Hardware, Inc. He must decide whether his firm should produce a new line of power tools. In his judgment, there is a 70 percent likelihood that the line will be successful. Based on this assessment and available profit data, the best decision is to introduce the tools. The expected profit from this decision is $300,000. If Universal knew that the product would ultimately be successful, it could expect to make $500,000.

   A market survey firm has submitted a bid for doing the fieldwork of interviewing hardware store owners. The company wants $20,000 for a report containing the following data:

   ▪ If there is a favorable market condition, Universal should introduce the line. The maximum expected profit would then be $400,000. There is a 60 percent chance of a favorable condition.

   ▪ If there is an unfavorable market condition, Universal should not introduce the power tools. Then the maximum expected profit would be $350,000.

   Should Universal buy the survey? Explain.

8. Do you agree or disagree with each of the following statements? Explain.
   a. In a deterministic model, the expected value of perfect information is zero.
   b. The prior decision and EVC both involve the selection of a single course of action, regardless of the decision environment.
   c. Bayes's formula is not appropriate when there are an infinite number of states of nature.

d.   In Bayes's formula, the sum of all (conditional, indicator, and posterior) probabilities must equal 1.

e.   We should obtain sample information as long as the EVPI is greater than the cost of the additional knowledge.

f.   The EVSI can never be negative.

Technique Exercises

9.   You are given the situation represented by the following decision table, where entries in the cells represent millions of dollars of profit. The prior probabilities are $P(s_1) = .6$ and $P(s_2) = .4$.

	States of Nature	
Decision Alternatives	s_1	s_2
a_1	2	−1
a_2	−3	6

a.   Use the prior probabilities to find the optimal decision.

b.   Find the expected value under certainty.

c.   Use the expected value under certainty to find the expected value of perfect information.

10.   Consider the cost minimization problem represented by the following decision table, where entries in the cells represent cost. The prior probability of s_1 is .3.

	States of Nature	
Decision Alternatives	s_1	s_2
a_1	$150,000	$85,000
a_2	$90,000	$125,000
a_3	$115,000	$105,000

a.   Use the prior probabilities to find the optimal decision.

b.   Find the expected value under certainty (EVC).

c.   Use the EVC to find the EVPI.

d.   Determine the opportunity loss table.

e.   Find the course of action that minimizes expected opportunity loss (EOL).

f.   Compare the minimum EOL with the EVPI. What do you find?

11.   A company is considering the introduction of a new product. The planned selling price is $410 per unit. There is a fixed cost of $200,000 for developing and manufacturing the product, while the variable cost would be $210 per unit. Demand for the product is described by the following distribution:

Demand	Probability
1000	.05
1500	.10
2000	.15
2500	.50
3000	.20

   a. Based on the current available data, should the company introduce the product?
   b. What is the probability of a loss?
   c. What is the EVPI?

12. JM Enterprises, Inc., is going to buy a new machine that could generate significant labor cost savings on a certain operation. The company is considering two brands, X and Y. Brand X involves a fixed charge of $500,000 and a variable operating cost of $250 per hour of operation. Brand Y has a fixed expense of $600,000 and a variable operating cost of $200 per hour. Annual operating hours are distributed as follows:

Operating Hours	Probability
100	.1
200	.2
300	.3
400	.2
500	.2

   a. Based on the current available data, which brand should JM Enterprises buy?
   b. What is the EVPI?

13. You are given $P(s_1) = .3$ and $P(s_3) = .3$. Also, indicator information shows that $P(I_1|s_1) = .4, P(I_2|s_2) = .8$, and $P(I_1|s_3) = .2$
   a. Use Bayes's formula to develop an equation that will give $P(s_2|I_2)$.
   b. Use the equation you developed in part (a) to find $P(s_2|I_2)$.

14. A decision maker has a problem with four states of nature. The prior probabilities are $P(s_1) = .2$, $P(s_2) = .3$, $P(s_3) = .4$, and $P(s_4) = .1$. Additional research is conducted. Indicator probabilities are given as follows:

$P(I_1|s_1) = .1$ $P(I_1|s_2) = .6$ $P(I_1|s_3) = .7$ $P(I_1|s_4) = .9$

$P(I_2|s_1) = .4$ $P(I_2|s_2) = .3$ $P(I_2|s_3) = .2$ $P(I_2|s_4) = .1$

$P(I_3|s_1) = .5$ $P(I_3|s_2) = .1$ $P(I_3|s_3) = .1$ $P(I_3|s_4) = 0$

   a. Show the probability tree for this problem.
   b. Use the tabular method to find the desired posterior probability calculations.

15. Consider the following decision table, where the entries in the cells represent returns. The prior probabilities are $P(s_1) = .8$ and $P(s_2) = .2$.

Decision Alternatives	States of Nature	
	s_1	s_2
a_1	18	13
a_2	11	15
a_3	7	32

   a. Using the prior probabilities, find the course of action that maximizes expected return.

   b. Find the EVPI.

   c. Suppose some indicator information I_1 and I_2 is obtained. It shows that $P(I_1|s_1) = .6$ and $P(I_2|s_2) = .7$. Construct the appropriate decision tree.

   d. Work backward through the tree to develop the optimal decision strategy. Show your work on the tree.

16. Refer back to Pucter and Simple's evaluated decision tree (Figure 5.10). Use the data in this tree to compute the expected value of perfect information (EVPI). Show your work on the decision tree.

17. Consider the following segment of a decision tree representation of a problem with two indicators, two decision alternatives, and two states of nature.

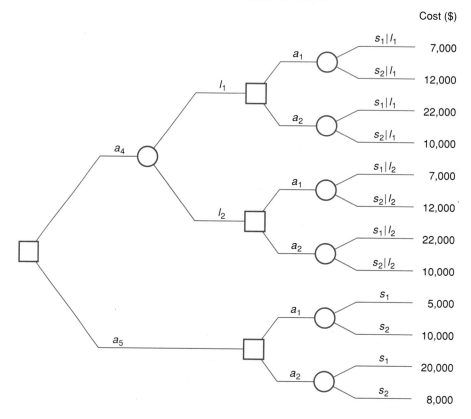

The values at the end of the tree include the cost of the indicator information. Assume the following conditional probability information: $P(s_1) = .3$, $P(I_2|s_1) = .4$, and $P(I_1|s_2) = .8$.

a. What are the values for $P(I_1)$ and $P(I_2)$?

b. What are the values of $P(s_1|I_1)$, $P(s_2|I_1)$, $P(s_1|I_2)$, and $P(s_2|I_2)$?

c. Work backward through the decision tree to determine the optimal decision strategy.

d. What is the expected value of the optimal decision without the indicator information?

e. What is the expected value of the optimal decision with the indicator information?

f. Find the EVSI, CS, and ENGS.

18. A company's decision situation is represented by the following decision table, where entries represent returns. The prior probabilities are $P(s_1) = .2$, $P(s_2) = .6$, $P(s_3) = .2$.

Decision Alternatives	States of Nature		
	s_1	s_2	s_3
a_1	$-\$500,000$	$\$100,000$	$\$1,000,000$
a_2	$\$10,000$	$\$200,000$	$\$400,000$

a. Which alternative maximizes expected returns? Show your work.

b. Find the EVC and EVPI.

c. Suppose a market research firm can provide the following indicator information: $P(I_1|s_1) = .1$, $P(I_1|s_2) = .5$, and $P(I_1|s_3) = .8$. The firm charges a $10,000 fee for its service. Find the indicator and posterior probabilities.

d. Construct a decision tree that describes the sequential nature of the problem.

e. Find the EVSI and ENGS.

f. Use the decision tree to develop an appropriate decision strategy.

Computer Exercises

19. Wisconsin Electronics, Inc. has five plants that manufacture read only memory (ROM) boards for microcomputers. The Green Bay plant manufactures 35 percent of the total output, the Milwaukee plant produces 25 percent, the Sturgeon Bay facility manufactures 20 percent, the Madison plant produces 15 percent, and the Wausau facility manufactures the remaining 5 percent of the output. Manufacturing management has been very concerned about product quality. After evaluating quality control records, staff assistants have calculated the following percentages of defective boards.

Plant	Defective Boards (%)
Green Bay	4
Milwaukee	1
Sturgeon Bay	3
Madison	5
Wausau	2

Use the **Quantitative Management (QM)** software to determine the chances of getting a defective board from each plant.

20. The management of a Brazilian-based multinational, multiproduct company is seriously considering the expansion of its distribution facilities in Central America. Competition,

however, is severe in that region of the world. As a reaction to aggressive marketing practices by the competition, company management has decided to install a service-oriented system (SOS) in one of its four Central American distribution centers.

The award will be made to the center with the best service performance in the past year. Staff assistants have compiled the following data on the percentage of customers "satisfied" by the relevant centers.

Center	Percentage of Total Volume	Percentage of Satisfied Customers
Costa Rica	20	85
Guatemala	40	86
Honduras	25	90
Panama	15	88

Use the **QM** software to determine the chances of finding satisfied customers at each center. Based on the results, which center should receive the SOS? Explain.

21. The decision tree corresponding to the government's pest control problem (Management Situation 4.3) is shown below.

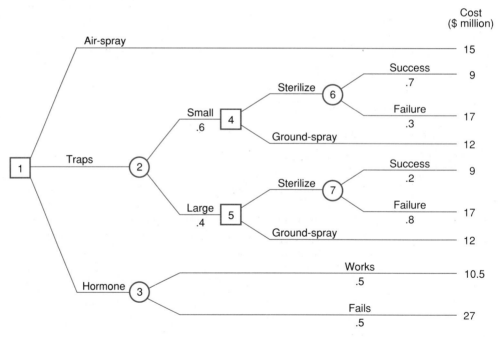

Use the **QM** software to determine the optimal pest control policy. What are the EVSI and ENGS? Explain.

22. Marylin Dohl needed a new computer. The model that appealed to her had a retail price of $1,200 at local computer vendors. In an attempt to save money, Marylin visited a discount merchant who comes to the area twice a year. Sure enough, the merchant had the computer that Marylin wanted at a sales price of $1,000. After inspecting the

equipment, Marylin thought that the basic computer was fine, but the monitor seemed questionable. From experience, she felt there was a 20 percent chance that the monitor would be unacceptable. A new monitor would cost $300.

Fortunately, local computer vendors would allow Marylin to test the monitor on the same model computer for a fee of $50. The test is accurate about 95 percent of the time. However, the discount merchant would allow Marylin to test the monitor only if she made a nonrefundable $50 deposit.

Use the **QM** software to evaluate Marylin's alternatives. What is the optimal strategy? What are the EVPI, EVSI, and ENGS? Explain.

23. France is seriously considering participating with other member nations in a United Nations peacekeeping force in Northern Ireland. The French government believes that at least a moderate number of peacekeeping troops should be sent to support the fragile local government. However, the hostile IRA has formally announced that any UN forces will be countered by increased insurgency. French officials believe there is an 80 percent likelihood that the IRA will carry out its threats.

If the threats are not carried out, the expected likelihoods of a stable local government are as follows:

UN Forces	Stability Rating
Small	50
Moderate	75
Large	85

Many experts also believe that the IRA will wait to see the size of the UN force before taking any actions. Stability ratings for the local government than are expected to follow the pattern outlined below.

UN Forces	IRA Reaction	Probability	Stability Rating
Small	Limited Insurgency	.6	80
	Massive Insurgency	.4	45
Moderate	Limited Insurgency	.5	75
	Massive Insurgency	.5	55
Large	Limited Insurgency	.2	95
	Massive Insurgency	.8	50

UN member nations want to determine the political strategy that would provide the most stable local government. Use the **QM** software to develop the recommended strategy. What are the EVSI and ENGS? Explain.

Applications Exercises

24. The administration of South Southern College feels that four characteristics should be considered when selecting students for admission to its MBA program. These factors are the undergraduate grade point average, the entrance test score, recommendations, and professional experience. Each of the factors is given a standardized score on a 100-point scale. At this time, there are four candidates for the one available position. Student factor scores are given in the following table.

Student	Factor			
	Grade Point Average	Test Score	Recommendations	Professional Experience
Adamson	85	90	95	70
Caine	90	90	85	80
Dante	95	70	95	85
Mueller	90	80	90	95

Based on their knowledge and experience, the admissions board believes that recommendations are twice as important as the undergraduate grade point average. Also, professional experience is three and one half times more important than the undergraduate grade point average. The entrance test score and professional experience are considered of equal importance.

The admissions committee wants to select the student with the highest expected total score. Using the current available data, which student should be admitted to the program?

Suppose that admissions standards are an important determinant of college accreditation. In an attempt to increase the total expected score of accepted students, South Southern will collect additional admission factor information. Such knowledge will enable the admissions committee to more accurately forecast the relative importance of each criterion. What is the maximum number of points that the new information can add to the total expected score for accepted MBA students?

25. Cyanide Chemical Company has a new processing machine on trial and must either return it or buy it this week. The machine costs $150,000, but it saves about $100 per hour in operating expenses. H. T. Oh, the equipment manager, estimates there will be 2,000 operating hours annually. However, Oh is only 50 percent confident in this estimate. She also feels that there is a 30 percent chance for the actual operation to involve 1,500 hours. The other possibility is that the machine will be needed for 3,000 hours of annual operation.

a. Based on current available data, should Cyanide invest in the machine? Explain.

b. Suppose that Cyanide's industrial engineering department can do a production study that would forecast operating hours almost exactly. What price should Oh be willing to pay for such a study?

26. An office manager will lease a photocopy machine from one of two manufacturers. The Fastpace leases for $10 per week plus a duplication charge of 5 cents per page. Alternatively, the Quietone leases for $25 per week plus a duplication charge of 4 cents per page. Each manufacturer requires a five-year lease. During its useful life, the photocopy machine's volume of work is not expected to change. Based on current available information, the manager believes there is a 40 percent chance that volume will be 1,000 copies per week. He also feels that the actual volume could differ from this estimate by plus or minus 200 copies. Each of these differences is thought to be equally likely.

The manager wants to lease the machine that will minimize expected total lease cost. Which brand should he lease? Suppose that one of the photocopy machine manufacturers offers to conduct a work study that would forecast the duplication volume more accurately. What is the maximum premium that the office manager should be willing to pay for the study results? Explain.

27. The research and development manager for Slippery Oil Corporation is considering whether the company should commercialize a new lubricant. It is assumed that the product will be a major success, a minor product line expansion, or a failure. If the product is a major success, it will contribute $2 million annually to corporate profit. Since the product will help sell other products in Slippery's line, even a minor commercial expansion will contribute $100,000 profit per year. However, a product failure will cost the company $1.5 million. Based on the opinion of the research team and the manager's own belief, there is a 20 percent likelihood of a major success and a 10 percent chance of failure. The manager feels that the decision is too important to base it on this preliminary information. Therefore, the company will delay the decision pending the outcome of a series of experiments by an independent research institute. Do you agree with this assessment? Explain.

   The research institute wants a fee to develop a report that would contain scientific data on the technical aspects of the lubricant. Past records show that on 90 percent of the occasions when a product has been a major commercial success, its technical report has been sound. When a product has been a minor product line expansion, its technical report has been sound 40 percent of the time. Also, 80 percent of the time that a product has been a failure, it had an unsound technical report. What would be Slippery's optimal decision strategy with the additional information? How much should the company be willing to pay for the new knowledge?

28. United Post Services delivers a particular package weekly from Millard to Fillmore. There are three possible routes: northern, central, or southern, and delivery time depends on uncertain weather conditions. It could rain, be overcast, or be clear. Over the northern route, it takes 30 minutes to deliver the package when it rains, 25 minutes when it is overcast, and 15 minutes in clear weather. Delivery over the central route takes 40 minutes in rain, 15 minutes when overcast, and 10 minutes when it is clear. It takes 20 minutes to deliver the package over the southern route no matter what weather conditions prevail.

   Preliminary weather information indicates that there is a 20 percent chance of rain and a 30 percent likelihood of clear conditions. Based on this preliminary information, what route would result in the minimum expected delivery time? If United has more accurate weather information, how many minutes could they reduce the expected delivery time?

   Suppose that the company could subscribe to a satellite-based weather-forecasting service. This service will indicate whether the conditions will be fair or inclement. Past records show that the service has forecasted fair conditions when it has rained 30 percent of the time. They have forecasted inclement conditions when it has been overcast 40 percent of the time. Also, on 80 percent of the clear occasions, the service has predicted fair weather. What would be United's optimal decision strategy with the additional information? How much do you think the company would benefit from the new knowledge? Explain.

29. Management at Bittell Toys, Inc. must decide whether the company should produce a new Christmas toy, the Computerized Chocolate Bar. The executive administrator

feels that there is a 60 percent chance that the toy will be successful. If the product is successful, the firm will earn $600,000. On the other hand, an unsuccessful Chocolate Bar will cost Bittell $400,000.

Two market survey firms have submitted bids for doing the fieldwork of interviewing toy store owners. Delta Research, Inc. is known to conduct highly accurate surveys at rather high cost. Its fee is $40,000 for a report containing data on owners' product impressions. Past studies show the following results:

- When a product has been successful, 90 percent of the interviewed owners have been favorably impressed.

- When a product has been unsuccessful, 75 percent of the interviewees have been unfavorably impressed.

Iota Surveys Corporation has a lower fee, but tends to provide less accurate information. This corporation wants $20,000 for the same basic report as Delta's. Iota's past studies show the following results:

- When a product has been a success, 80 percent of the interviewees have been favorably impressed.

- When a product has been a failure, 60 percent of the interviewees have been unfavorably impressed.

Should Bittell's management buy no survey, buy Delta's survey, or buy Iota's survey?

For Further Reading

Value of Information

Howard, R. A., and J. E. Matheson, eds. *Readings on the Principles and Applications of Decision Analysis*. Mead Park, CA: Strategic Decision Group, 1984.

McNamee, P., and J. Celona. *Decision Analysis for the Professional*. Redwood City, CA: The Scientific Press, 1987.

Updating Probabilities

Winkler, R. L. *An Introduction to Bayesian Inference and Decision*. New York: Holt, Rinehart & Winston, 1972.

Winkler, R. L. "Expert Resolution." *Management Science* (March 1986):298.

Decision Making with Additional Information

LaValle, I. H. "Response to 'Use of Sample Information in Stochastic Recourse and Chance-Constrained Programming Models': On the Bayesability of CCP's." *Management Science* (October 1987):1224.

Wiginton, J. C. "A Bayesian Approach to Discrimination among Economic Models." *Decision Sciences* (April 1974):182.

Accounting/Financial applications

Bradford, D. F., and H. H. Kalejian. "The Value of Information for Crop Forecasting with Bayesian Speculators: Theory and Empirical Results." *Bell Journal of Economics* (Spring 1978):123.

Ferreira, J. "The Long-Term Effects of Merit-Rating Plans on Individual Motorists." *Operations Research* (September–October 1974):954.

Reinmuth, J. E. "On the Application of Bayesian Statistics in Auditing." *Decision Sciences* (July 1972):139.

Marketing Applications

Lilian, G. L., et al. "Bayesian Estimation and Control of Detailing Effort in a Repeat Purchase Diffusion Environment." *Management Science* (May 1981):493.

Thomas, J., and P. Chhabra. "Bayesian Models for New Product Pricing." *Decision Sciences* (January 1975):51.

Ulvila, J. W., et al. "A Case in On-Line Decision Analysis for Product Planning." *Decision Sciences* (July 1977):598.

Production/Operations Applications

Carroll, T. M., and R. D. Dean. "A Bayesian Approach to Plant-Location Decisions." *Decision Sciences* (January 1980):81.

Grossman, S. J., et al. "A Bayesian Approach to the Production of Information and Learning by Doing." *Review of Economic Studies* (October 1977):553.

Ladany, S. P. "Optimal Starting Height for Pole-Vaulting." *Operations Research* (September–October 1975):968.

Ronen, B., and J. S. Pliskin. "Decision Analysis in Microelectronic Reliability: Optimal Design and Packaging of a Diode Array." *Operations Research* (March–April 1981):229.

Public Sector Applications

Cohan, D., et al. "Using Fire in Forest Management: Decision Making Under Uncertainty." *Interfaces* (September–October 1984):8.

Keeney, R. L., and R. L. Winkler. "Evaluating Decision Strategies for Equity of Public Risks." *Operations Research* (September–October 1985):955.

Miesing, P., and T. C. Dandridge. "Judgement Policies Used in Assessing Enterprise-Zone Economic Success Criteria." *Decision Sciences* (Winter 1986):50.

Wangt, M., et al. "A Bayesian Data Analysis System for the Evaluation of Social Programs." *Journal of the American Statistical Association* (December 1977):711.

Case: Municipal Transit Authority

Municipal Transit Authority provides public transportation for the growing city of Metroville. The Authority must expand facilities to meet the ever-increasing demand for services. Some plan must be developed to finance the expansion. The Authority is considering three possibilities: a fare increase, a subsidy from city general revenues, or an issue of municipal bonds. Net revenues from the expanded facilities will depend on demand for public transportation in the next ten years. The demand may grow at or above the current rate, or it may grow rapidly in the next three years and then stabilize. Also, it may actually decline after the initial growth period. Continued growth would create a demand of more than 2 million passenger-miles in the next ten years. Rapid growth followed by stability would involve between 1 and 2 million passenger-miles. Decline after initial growth means a demand for less than 1 million passenger-miles.

Wade Trinkle, Municipal's rate engineer, believes that the most likely demand is 1.5 million passenger-miles. He also feels that there is a 95% likelihood that demand will be between 520,000 and 2.48 million passenger-miles.

A fare increase would be the best method of finance if there is natural continued growth. The subsidy would be most economical under conditions of rapid growth followed by stability. Bonds would work best if there is a decline after initial growth. Sada Tontor, Municipal's chief economist, has done a financial analysis of the situation. The results can be summarized as follows:

- A fare increase would involve a net loss of $1 million if there is decline after initial growth. On the other hand, this policy would generate a net revenue of $200,000 under rapid growth/stable conditions and $3 million with continued growth.

- The subsidy would earn a net revenue of $400,000 under growth/decline conditions and $1.5 million for a rapid growth/stable state. Such a policy would involve a $600,000 loss if there is continued growth.

- The bond strategy would earn a net revenue of $1.6 million for a growth/decline state and $100,000 under rapid growth/stable conditions. However, this policy would create a $1.2 million loss if there is continued growth.

Agnes Peron, Municipal's general manager, realizes the economic importance of the decision. Thus, she wants to consider additional demand information before making a final decision. Two state agencies can provide some new knowledge for the cost of their reports. For $100,000, the Office of Planning (OP) can project economic growth in Metroville. From similar studies of public services, OP has been able to relate economic growth to demand. Its report will include the following data:

- On those occasions involving a growth/decline demand state, there has been economic decline 70 percent of the time and stable economic growth 20 percent of the time.

- When there has been a rapid growth/stable demand condition, there has been a 40 percent chance of economic decline and a 50 percent likelihood of economic stability.

- If there has been continued demand growth, there has been a 20 percent chance of economic stability and a 60 percent likelihood of economic growth.

For $200,000, the state Budget Department (BD) can project price trends in the Metroville area. From similar studies of public services, BD has been able to relate prices to demand. Its report will include the following data:

- In a growth/decline demand state, there have been stable prices 80 percent of the time.

- There has been a 90 percent likelihood of stable prices when there has been a growth/stable demand condition.

- On the occasions involving continued demand growth, there has been a 70 percent chance of rising prices.

Ms. Peron forms an executive analysis committee made up of you, Wade Trinkle, and Sada Tontor. The committee is given the assignment of evaluating the financial policy alternatives and recommending an action. Peron wants the evaluation presented in a concise managerial brief. It should contain the following information:

1. The decision table for the problem.

2. The preliminary probabilities for the demand conditions.

3. The recommended decision based on the preliminary probabilities.

4. The price that Municipal should be willing to pay for more accurate demand information.

5. Decision trees for the problem with OP's and BD's additional information.

6. Updated demand probabilities from OP's and BD's additional information.

7. The optimal decision strategies with OP's and BD's additional information.

8. A recommendation on whether Municipal should obtain no additional demand information, buy OP's report, or purchase BD's study.

Prepare the assigned management report. (*Hint:* You will have to use normal distribution concepts in developing the prior probabilities. The end-of-book probability appendix is available for those who need a review on this distribution.)

Advanced Decision Analysis

Chapter Outline

Learning Objectives

- Develop nonmonetary measures of performance
- Use the nonmonetary measures for decision making
- Deal with problems involving multiple criteria
- Develop approaches to decision making in conflict situations

Quantitative Analysis in Action
Going for the Black Gold

TOMCO Oil Corporation is a small, independent producer with no pipeline system. The company secures its own financing and drills its own wells. In choosing between drill sites, the company president has used an informal decision process that relies on minimal information about relevant geological, engineering, economic, and political factors.

To improve the company's chances for a successful site selection in Kansas, Tomco's president employed an oil industry consultant. The consultant found that the problem could be represented as a decision tree. In the tree, outcomes were expressed in terms of a composite measure that accounted for return and risk. Decision analysis then was used to determine the preferred exploratory drilling strategy.

By using the decision analysis, Tomco selected a site that successfully produced oil at an initial rate of 10 barrels per day and water at an initial rate of 90 barrels a day. These output rates generated an expected net profit, in present value terms, of approximately $38,000 during the projected seven-year life of the site. Furthermore, the decision analysis provided the company with a systematic way of planning site selection and a clearer understanding of the financial consequences of the decision.

Source: J. Hosseini, "Decision Analysis and Its Application in the Choice between Two Wildcat Oil Ventures," *Interfaces* (March–April 1986):75–85.

Chapters 4 and 5 have presented the fundamental concepts of decision analysis. As these chapters have demonstrated, management should always select the alternative that best meets its criteria, or measures of performance. Hence, it is important to develop appropriate and accurate outcome measures.

The decision problems considered in the earlier chapters have used monetary values or other absolute numerical values as outcomes. In many cases, however, such values are inappropriate or incomplete performance measures. Tomco, for example, needs a composite measure that accounts for both return (a monetary value) and risk (an intangible factor) to determine the preferred exploratory drilling strategy. This chapter's first section examines situations like Tomco's, and then shows how to develop and use a comprehensive criterion (such as Tomco's composite measure) in decision making.

Our previous decision analysis has also assumed that there is a single objective. Frequently, however, managerial problems involve several (sometimes conflicting) criteria. The second section presents methods designed to deal with these multiple criteria problems and shows how these concepts can be used in decision making.

Finally, many decision problems involve a conflict between competing parties. In such cases, each party's actions will be influenced by the reaction pattern of the competitors. The last section presents a framework for analyzing these situations and shows how the model can be used to develop a decision strategy.

Applications. In this chapter, the following applications appear in text, examples, and exercises:

- automobile marketing
- business expansion
- equipment purchasing
- fire insurance
- franchise location
- land-use planning

- management training
- real estate investment
- state lottery
- technical staffing
- television programming
- treaty negotiation

6.1 UTILITY THEORY

It may seem natural to express decision outcomes in terms of monetary values (like costs, revenues, and profits) or some other absolute numerical measure (such as quantity, time, and distance). However, many practical real-life situations involve intangible factors that are difficult to express on an absolute numerical scale.

Risk and the decision maker's attitude toward this factor are among the most important intangibles. Investments provide a good illustration. Many savers cannot afford substantial financial losses or have an aversion toward risk. As a result, these people frequently invest in guaranteed rate, federally insured bank time deposits (such as T bills), even though these accounts usually yield lower returns than more risky alternatives. On the other hand, others will gamble on a highly speculative venture (like mineral exploration) in the hope of obtaining very large profits. Such investors may also be attracted to the risk or have significant discretionary funds.

A related intangible deals with the perspective of the decision maker. Consider, for example, an identical lump sum $1,200 annual pay raise granted to both a low-paid clerical worker and a high-salaried executive. In all likelihood, the raise will have a more substantial impact on the clerk's spending and savings plans than on the executive's. Hence, the $1,200 will be more valuable to the clerk than to the executive.

Enjoyment and satisfaction are other very important intangible factors. For instance, an interstate highway may be the most rapid and shortest route between two cities. However, it could also bypass many beautiful places and gratifying entertainment centers along the way. Consequently, a family on vacation may prefer to travel along a scenic route that includes these attractions rather than take the interstate.

In these situations, an absolute numerical measure (like monetary value, time, or distance) may be inadequate or inappropriate, and management will need a more comprehensive criterion that incorporates relevant intangibles as well as these absolute numerical values. In addition, the criterion must measure the true worth of the outcomes to the decision maker. This type of composite measure is known as **utility**.

Measuring Utility

Mathematicians and economists have been trying to develop a precise measure of utility since the eighteenth century, but their efforts have not produced a universal or absolute

Table 6.1   **Medfern's Decision Table**

Decision Alternatives	States of Nature		
	s_1 = prices go up	s_2 = prices remain stable	s_3 = prices go down
a_1 = invest in condominiums	$2,000,000	$1,000,000	−$300,000
a_2 = invest in houses	$4,500,000	$200,000	−$500,000
a_3 = do not invest	$0	$0	$0
	Profit		Loss

scale of measurement. Nevertheless, it is possible to infer a specific set of utility values from the observed decision behavior of an individual. The concepts can be illustrated with Management Situation 6.1.

Management Situation 6.1

Real Estate Investments

Medfern Associates is a real estate investment firm operating in the southwestern part of the state. A large developer recently offered Medfern the opportunity to invest in two building projects. One involves a condominium development in an attractive area of Oceanside, and the other deals with a housing tract under construction in Springdale. Profits from the investments would depend on uncertain real estate market conditions.

By processing all available data through Medfern's computer information system, management has developed the problem representation shown in Table 6.1. The computer analysis also suggests that real estate prices have a $P(s_1) = .1$ chance of rising, a $P(s_2) = .3$ likelihood of remaining stable, and a $P(s_3) = .6$ probability of falling. At present, the company can afford only one investment.

Initially, Medfern was interested in the most profitable investment. However, the company's current financial position is weak. In fact, management feels that a substantial loss on the next investment could force the company out of business. To properly evaluate the development opportunity, Medfern must consider the risk of financial loss as well as profit.

By using the data from Table 6.1 and the event probabilities, Medfern will find that the expected profit is

$$.1(\$2,000,000) + .3(\$1,000,000) + .6(-\$300,000) = \$320,000$$

from the condominium investment (a_1),

$$.1(\$4,500,000) + .3(\$200,000) + .6(-\$500,000) = \$210,000$$

from the housing tract alternative (a_2). and \$0 if the company does not make an investment (a_3). Since alternative a_1 leads to the largest expected profit (\$320,000), the company initially may be inclined to invest in condominiums.

As Table 6.1 demonstrates, however, the condominium investment (a_1) exposes Medfern to a potential \$300,000 financial loss (if real estate prices go down). Since such a loss is unacceptable, management should determine the true worth, or utility, of each profit before attempting a decision.

Management can begin by arbitrarily assigning utility values to both the best and worst outcomes in the problem. Any values will work as long as the best outcome is given a higher utility than the worst payoff.

As the data from Table 6.1 indicate, Medfern's best possible profit is the \$4,500,000 associated with alternative a_2 and event s_1. Suppose that management assigns a utility U of 100 to this profit. That is,

$$U(\$4,500,000) = 100.$$

Also, Table 6.1 shows that the worst outcome is the \$500,000 loss (negative profit) associated with alternative a_2 and event s_3. If Medfern's management assigns a utility of 0 to this outcome, then we have

$$U(-\$500,000) = 0.$$

All other payoffs in Table 6.1 are better than the worst ($-\$500,000$) but not as good as the best (\$4,500,000) outcome. Hence, these other outcomes should have utility values somewhere between 0 and 100. The proper utility values can be inferred from the decision maker's answers to a series of questions dealing with his or her preferences for various outcomes.

Lottery Indifference Probability. Let us consider the \$2,000,000 profit associated with alternative a_1 and event s_1. First, Medfern's management is asked to visualize a hypothetical situation in which it would have the option of investing in either (1) a project that is sure to yield the \$2,000,000 profit or (2) a lottery ticket that has a p chance of earning the \$4,500,000 best possible profit but a $(1 - p)$ likelihood of obtaining the $-\$500,000$ worst outcome. This option is similar to the proposition offered to contestants on some popular television game shows.

Clearly, the decision maker's preference will depend on the value of p. Since p is a probability, it will have a value between 0 and 1. If p is very close to 0, the lottery ticket virtually ensures a \$500,000 loss. Under these circumstances, most managers would select the project yielding the sure \$2,000,000 profit. However, as p increases, the lottery ticket will grow in value and hence become increasingly more attractive. Eventually, at some p value, the executive will have no greater preference for the sure \$2,000,000 profit than for the lottery ticket. This p value is called the **lottery indifference probability**. Beyond this point, the preference for the sure project will change into a preference for the lottery. In particular, if p is very close to 1, the lottery ticket practically assures a \$4,500,000 profit and thus should be preferable to a project yielding \$2,000,000.

Each decision maker, of course, will have his or her own personal lottery indifference probability. Some trial and error questioning may be required to identify the precise value. It begins with the arbitrary assignment of a probability, say $p = .85$, to the

$4,500,000 best outcome from the lottery. Next, the decision maker is asked if he or she prefers the sure $2,000,000 profit to the lottery ticket with this $p = .85$ probability. If the decision maker answers yes, then the lottery is made progressively more attractive by slowly increasing p to $p = .86$, $p = .87$, and so on. The adjustment process continues until the executive is indifferent between the sure return and the ticket. If, on the other hand, there is a preference for the lottery, then the value of p should be adjusted downward to the indifference point by a similar trial and error process.

Certainty Equivalent. Suppose these queries indicate that Medfern's management would be indifferent between the sure $2,000,000 and the lottery if there is a 90 percent chance of obtaining the $4,500,000 best outcome. In this case, the lottery indifference probability is $p = .9$. The sure $2,000,000 profit is known as the **certainty equivalent** of this particular lottery.

If Medfern is indifferent between the sure $2,000,000 and the lottery ticket at a specified p value, then these two alternatives must have the same utility to management. That is,

$$U(\$2,000,000) = pU(\$4,500,000) + (1 - p)U(-\$500,000)$$

$$\underbrace{}_{\substack{\text{Utility of} \\ \text{the certainty} \\ \text{equivalent}}} \qquad \underbrace{}_{\substack{\text{Expected utility of the} \\ \text{lottery ticket}}}$$

Since $p = .9$, $U(\$4,500,000) = 100$, and $U(-\$500,000) = 0$, the utility of the $2,000,000 profit is

$$U(\$2,000,000) = .9(100) + (1 - .9)(0) = 90.$$

In other words, Medfern's management gets 90 units of utility from a $2,000,000 profit.

Similar hypothetical lotteries can be used to find the utilities for Table 6.1's other outcomes. For instance, suppose a series of trial and error questions reveals that, when $p = .8$, management is indifferent between a sure $1,000,000 profit and the lottery ticket. In this case, management gets

$$U(\$1,000,000) = pU(\$4,500,000) + (1 - p)U(-\$500,000)$$

or

$$U(1,000,000) = .8(100) + .2(0) = 80$$

units of utility from the $1,000,000 profit. Furthermore, assume that the $200,000 profit involves a lottery indifference probability of $p = .6$, while $0 is associated with $p = .5$, and the $300,000 loss entails a $p = .2$. Then the corresponding utilities would be the values presented in Table 6.2.

Procedure Recap. When the number of decision alternatives and events is finite, the following lottery ticket approach can be used to measure utility:

1. Identify the best and worst outcomes in the problem.
2. Arbitrarily assign different utility values to the best and worst outcomes. Any values will work as long as the best outcome is given a higher utility than the worst payoff.

Table 6.2   **Medfern's Utility Calculations**

Profit	Lottery Indifference Probability (p)	Utility
$4,500,000	Does not apply	100
2,000,000	.9	$.9(100) + (.1)(0) = 90$
1,000,000	.8	$.8(100) + (.2)(0) = 80$
200,000	.6	$.6(100) + (.4)(0) = 60$
0	.5	$.5(100) + (.5)(0) = 50$
−300,000	.2	$.2(100) + (.8)(0) = 20$
−500,000	Does not apply	0

Table 6.3   **Medfern's Utility Table**

Decision Alternatives	States of Nature		
	s_1 = prices go up	s_2 = prices remain stable	s_3 = prices go down
a_1 = invest in condominiums	90	80	20
a_2 = invest in houses	100	60	0
a_3 = do not invest	50	50	50

Units of utility to management

3. Define a hypothetical situation in which the decision maker has the option of investing in either:
   a. a project that is sure to yield a particular outcome between the best and worst payoffs, or
   b. a lottery ticket that has a p chance of earning the best outcome but a $(1 − p)$ likelihood of obtaining the worst payoff.
4. Use a series of trial and error questions to determine the value of p that makes the decision maker indifferent between the sure outcome and the lottery ticket. This value of p is called the lottery indifference probability for the sure outcome.
5. Use the formula

$$U(\text{sure outcome}) = pU(\text{best outcome}) + (1 − p)U(\text{worst outcome})$$

to calculate the utility of the sure outcome.

Decision Making with Utility

By substituting the utility values from Table 6.2 for the corresponding outcomes in Table 6.1, Medfern will obtain the results presented in Table 6.3. Since Table 6.3 identifies the utility of each decision outcome to management, it is called a **utility table**.

Remember, there is a $P(s_1) = .1$ chance that prices will go up, a $P(s_2) = .3$ likelihood that they will remain stable, and a $P(s_3) = .6$ probability that they will fall. Using these probabilities and the data in Table 6.3, Medfern will find that the condominium investment (a_1) leads to an expected utility of

$$90(.1) + 80(.3) + 20(.6) = 45.$$

On the other hand, there is an expected utility of

$$100(.1) + 60(.3) + 0(.6) = 28$$

from the housing project (a_2) and

$$50(.1) + 50(.3) + 50(.6) = 50$$

from the no investment alternative (a_3).

Management wants to obtain as much total worth, or utility, as possible. Since decision alternative a_3 leads to the largest expected utility (50), Medfern should not invest in either real estate venture.

Attitudes Toward Risk

Notice that the expected monetary value (profit) recommendation (a_1) is different from the recommended decision (a_3) from the expected utility analysis. The difference results from the attitude of Medfern's management toward risk.

Risk Premium. According to Table 6.2, Medfern's maximum expected utility of 50 corresponds to a $0 profit. The table also suggests that, at this utility value, management is indifferent between the sure $0 profit and a lottery ticket in which the company has a $p = .5$ chance of earning $4,500,000 and a $1 - p = .5$ likelihood for a $500,000 loss. Even though the lottery has an expected profit of

$$.5(\$4,500,000) + .5(-\$500,000) = \$2,000,000$$

then, Medfern would just as soon take the sure $0 profit as this ticket.

The $2,000,000 difference between the expected monetary value of the lottery ($2,000,000) and the corresponding certainty equivalent ($0) is known as the **risk premium**. In the maximization problem, we can express this premium as

(6.1) $RP = EV(\text{Lottery}) - CE$

where RP = the risk premium, $EV(\text{Lottery})$ = the expected value from the lottery and CE = the corresponding certainty equivalent. Since $EV(\text{Lottery})$ will be no larger than CE when the criterion is cost, time, or distance

(6.2) $RP = CE - EV(\text{Lottery})$

in a minimization problem. Such a premium, which measures the price (in terms of opportunity loss or regret) that will be incurred to avoid risk, can identify the decision maker's attitude toward risk.

Risk Averse. By not investing (selecting a_3), Medfern will sacrifice the opportunity for profit to avoid the risk of any potential financial loss. In the process, the company will absorb a risk premium of

$$RP = EV(\text{Lottery}) - CE = \$2,000,000 - 0 = \$2,000,000.$$

Figure 6.1   **Medfern's Utility Curve**

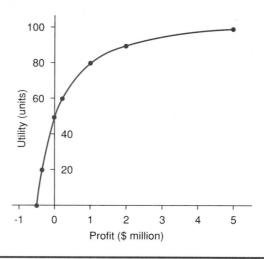

As in Medfern's case, when there is a positive risk premium, the decision maker has a **risk-averse** attitude.

Utility Curve. Medfern's attitude can be examined from another perspective. Using the data in Table 6.2, we can develop a graph that shows the relationship between monetary value and utility. The result is called a **utility curve**.

As Figure 6.1 demonstrates, a growth in monetary value leads to an increase in utility. This property is characteristic of all utility curves. In Medfern's case, however, the increase is not proportional. For example, a $300,000 loss involves 20 units of utility, while a $0 profit has a 50-unit utility to company management. Hence, within this range of monetary values, utility increases at the rate of

$$\frac{\text{increase in utility}}{\text{increase in profit}} = \frac{50 - 20}{\$0 - (-\$300,000)} = \frac{30}{\$300,000} = 0.0001$$

unit per $1 growth in profit. On the other hand, between profit levels of $0 and $200,000, utility increases at the rate of

$$\frac{\text{increase in utility}}{\text{increase in profit}} = \frac{60 - 50}{\$200,000 - \$0} = \frac{10}{\$200,000} = 0.00005$$

unit per $1 growth in monetary value.

A value of 0.00005 is smaller than 0.0001. Thus, the rate of increase in utility declines with the growth in monetary value. In other words, Medfern's utility does not grow as fast as profit. This characteristic, known as a **diminishing marginal utility** for monetary gain, reflects management's desire to avoid the higher risks associated with the larger profits. Namely, it is a consequence of the company's risk aversion.

In effect, then, a risk-averse decision maker will have a diminishing marginal utility for monetary gain. Furthermore, such a manager's utility curve will have the shape shown in Figure 6.1.

Table 6.4   **Speculative's and Conglomerate's Utility Values**

Profit ($)	Speculative		Conglomerate	
	Lottery Indifference Probability (p)	Utility	Lottery Indifference Probability (p)	Utility
4,500,000	Does not apply	100	Does not apply	100
2,000,000	.25	25	.50	50
1,000,000	.10	10	.30	30
200,000	.03	3	.14	14
0	.02	2	.10	10
−300,000	.01	1	.04	4
−500,000	Does not apply	0	Does not apply	0

Risk Seeking. Decision makers may have other attitudes, besides risk aversion, as Management Situation 6.2 illustrates.

Business Expansion

This problem is an extension of Management Situation 6.1. Suppose that Medfern is now trying to expand by selling stock. Each of the two prospective buyers wants enough stock to take over effective control of the company. One of the potential owners, Speculative Enterprises, has a surplus of cash and a very stable future. The company is looking for investments that may be risky but have a potential for substantial profit. The other prospective purchaser, Conglomerate Incorporated, is a very large international petroleum company. This firm would neither suffer greatly from a $500,000 loss nor increase its wealth significantly with a $4.5 million profit.

Before offering the stock, Medfern wants to determine both Conglomerate's and Speculative's attitudes toward risk. In this respect, the lottery ticket approach is used to poll the executives of each prospective firm concerning their attitudes about Medfern's outcomes (Table 6.1). For comparison purposes, the pollster again arbitrarily assigns 100 utility units to the best ($4.5 million) and 0 units to the worst (−$500,000) outcome. Table 6.4 presents the results.

By substituting the utility values from Table 6.4 for the corresponding dollar outcomes in Table 6.1, Speculative will obtain its own unique utility table. Multiplying the probabilities from Management Situation 6.1 by the corresponding utilities then would show that Speculative gets an expected utility of

$$.1(25) + .3(10) + .6(1) = 6.1$$

from the condominium alternative (a_1),

$$.1(100) + .3(3) + .6(0) = 10.9$$

from housing (a_2), and

$$.1(2) + .3(2) + .5(2) = 2$$

if it does not invest (a_3). This company's management can therefore maximize its expected utility at 10.9 units by investing in houses.

According to Table 6.4, Speculative's maximum expected utility of 10.9 corresponds to a profit somewhere between \$1 million and \$2 million. The table also suggests that, at the lower limit, management is indifferent between a sure \$1 million profit and a lottery ticket in which the company has a $p = .10$ chance of earning \$4.5 million and a $1 - p = .90$ likelihood for a \$500,000 loss. Even though the lottery has an expected profit of only

$$.10(\$4,500,000) + .90(-\$500,000) = \$0,$$

Speculative would just as soon take this ticket as the sure \$1 million profit.

At the upper limit, management is indifferent between a sure \$2 million profit and a lottery ticket in which the company has a $p = .25$ likelihood of earning \$4.5 million and a $1 - p = .75$ chance for a \$500,000 loss. Even though this lottery has an expected profit of only

$$.25(\$4,500,000) + .75(-\$500,000) = \$750,000,$$

Speculative is indifferent between the ticket and the sure \$2 million.

Either way, Speculative will take a high risk of absorbing a \$500,000 loss to have an opportunity for a \$4.5 million gain. In the process, the company will absorb a risk premium somewhere between

$$RP = EV(\text{Lottery}) - CE = \$0 - \$1,000,000 = -\$1,000,000$$

and

$$RP = EV(\text{Lottery}) - CE = \$750,000 - \$2,000,000 = -\$1,250,000$$

As in Speculative's case, when there is a negative risk premium, the decision maker has a **risk-seeking** attitude.

Risk Neutral. Conglomerate exhibits a third type of attitude. By using the utility values from Table 6.4, the corresponding dollar outcomes in Table 6.1, and the probabilities from Management Situation 6.1, Conglomerate will find that there is an expected utility of

$$.1(50) + .3(30) + .6(4) = 16.4$$

from the condominium alternative (a_1),

$$.1(100) + .3(14) + .6(0) = 14.2$$

from housing (a_2), and

$$.1(10) + .3(10) + .6(10) = 10$$

Figure 6.2   **Utility Curves for Medfern, Conglomerate, and Speculative**

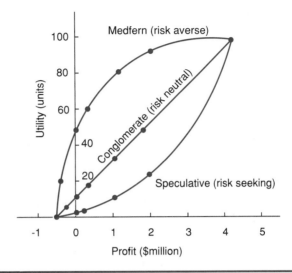

if it does not invest (a_3). This company's management then can maximize its expected utility at 16.4 units by investing in condominiums.

Table 6.4 indicates that Conglomerate's maximum expected utility of 16.4 corresponds to a profit somewhere between $200,000 and $1 million. The table also suggests that, at the lower limit, management is indifferent between a sure $200,000 profit and a lottery ticket in which the company has a $p = .14$ chance of earning $4.5 million and a $1 - p = .86$ likelihood for a $500,000 loss. Notice that the expected profit from this lottery

$$.14(\$4,500,000) + .86(-\$500,000) = \$200,000$$

is the same as the sure $200,000 profit.

The same thing will happen at the upper limit: the expected profit from the lottery will equal the sure $1 million profit. In effect, Conglomerate is neither seeking nor avoiding risk. Monetary value, rather than risk, is the main consideration. As a result, the company will absorb a risk premium of

$$RP = EV\,(\text{Lottery}) - CE = \$200,000 - \$200,000 = \$0.$$

When there is a risk premium of zero (as in Conglomerate's case), the decision maker has a **risk-neutral** attitude.

Attitude Comparison.   The prospective buyers' utility curves provide another perspective. By using the data from Table 6.4 to develop these curves and then superimposing the results on Figure 6.1, we get the graph shown in Figure 6.2.

As Figure 6.2 illustrates, Speculative's utility grows at a faster rate than profit. Such a property is known as an **increasing marginal utility** for monetary gain. On the other hand, Conglomerate's rate of increase in utility remains the same as profit increases. A curve with this characteristic is said to have a **constant marginal utility** for monetary gain.

Figure 6.3   **Risk-Complex Attitude toward Risk**

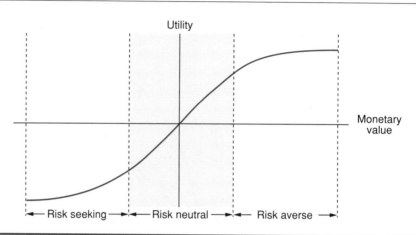

In effect, risk-seeking decision makers like Speculative will show an increasing marginal utility for monetary gain. Their utility curve will be shaped like Speculative's curve in Figure 6.2. Also, risk-neutral managements like Conglomerate will have a constant marginal utility for monetary gain and a linear utility curve.

Risk-Complex. Most people have both a speculative side and a conservative side. Thus, it is possible for a decision maker to display all three risk attitudes toward the range of monetary values in a particular situation. Such a pattern, referred to as a **risk-complex** attitude, might generate the utility curve shown in Figure 6.3.

Large monetary losses usually create a great deal of anxiety and typically motivate a change from the status quo. Many decision makers try to eliminate these losses by engaging in very risky ventures. Such a risk-seeking attitude is depicted as the portion of the utility curve to the left of the shaded region in Figure 6.3. As the losses diminish, management may become indifferent toward risk. This risk-neutral attitude, shown as the straight line in the shaded portion, may prevail as long as the monetary gains are modest. Continual growth in monetary value, however, generally involves an increase in risk. Eventually, the decision maker may sacrifice some gains to avoid this risk. This risk aversion is represented by the portion of the utility curve to the right of the shaded region.

Small business owners (such as local building contractors or new dentists) often display a risk-complex attitude. When the business is first started, the owner may incur significant expenditures to set up an office, buy equipment, and stock materials. These expenditures encourage the owner to finance the investment with loans and to aggressively seek customers or clients. Such actions represent a risk-seeking attitude by the owner.

As the business generates revenues and as payments are made on the loans, the owner begins to focus on profits or some similar performance measure. This focus corresponds to a risk-neutral perspective. Continued growth in the business, however, will consume more of the owner's time and will require additional staff and facilities. Eventually, the owner may sacrifice some profits to preserve his/her health and to avoid new financial commitments. If so, the owner will be exhibiting a risk-averse attitude.

Limitations

Utility analysis may be troublesome to implement in practice. It is a highly subjective approach that can be time-consuming, costly, and frustrating to apply. In addition, the decision maker may not fully understand, appreciate, or relate to the trial-and-error questioning involved in the process. As a result, it may be difficult to develop an accurate and reliable assessment of utility.

The concept itself creates additional difficulties. Utility is a reflection of management expectations, attitudes, and perceptions regarding a particular decision situation at a specific point in time. Perspectives, however, can change over time. Hence, a decision maker's previous utility assessment may not be appropriate for current or future conditions. Consequently, management must continually update the assessment prior to each decision.

Another difficulty arises when a manager's personal attitude toward risk conflicts with the organization's needs. Since the organization can absorb a larger loss than an individual, the manager often should be less risk-averse with the company's funds than with personal money. Otherwise, profitable projects that have acceptable risks may be lost to the competition. Yet it may be hard for a manager to put aside personal attitudes when making decisions for the organization. Indeed, some experts blame the trade problems faced by some U.S. companies on their managers' overly risk-averse decision making.

There is a related limitation. Each person has a unique perspective. Thus, several managers may each describe the same situation with a different utility curve. Then, using these individual curves, each decision maker could arrive at a different solution to the same problem.

In fact, that is exactly what happens in Management Situations 6.1 and 6.2. Medfern exhibits risk aversion toward the real estate venture, which leads management to select the noninvestment (a_3) alternative. On the other hand, Speculative's risk-seeking attitude causes it to choose the housing investment (a_2), while Conglomerate's risk-neutral behavior causes it to select the condominium (a_1) alternative.

Many decisions, in practice, are made by committees. When these groups consist of several people with divergent viewpoints, it may be difficult to arrive at a consensus expected utility recommendation.

The limitations often discourage organizations from using utility as an outcome measure. Instead, managers are inclined to use the more familiar monetary value analysis. If risk is the only other relevant factor and the decision maker has a risk-neutral attitude, this practice will involve little danger. To see why, let us compare Medfern's expected monetary value analysis and Conglomerate's expected utility analysis of the real estate venture. Notice that risk-neutral Conglomerate makes the investment (a_1) recommended by the expected monetary value analysis. This result is not a coincidence. In fact, *when management is risk neutral (has a straight-line utility curve), an expected utility analysis and an expected monetary value analysis always lead to the same decision.*

However, when management (such as Medfern's) has substantial risk aversion or (like Speculative's) seeks risk, an expected utility analysis and an expected monetary value analysis generally result in different decisions. Under these circumstances, it would be wise for the decision maker to consider an expected utility analysis. Such an analysis would identify (1) inconsistencies in the use of probability information, (2) overly conservative risk aversion, and (3) risk treatment by managers in various parts of the organization. At the very least, the utility analysis would facilitate intrafirm communication of corporate policies toward risk. A utility analysis also may be advisable if the problem involves many goals or several intangible factors.

6.2 MULTIPLE CRITERIA DECISION MAKING

So far, our discussion has focused on situations that involve a single objective, such as profit maximization or cost minimization. In many situations, however, the decision maker must consider many, often conflicting criteria. Consider, for example, a college graduate just entering the job market. He or she wants a position with the largest possible salary and fringe benefits, most pleasant work environment, and favorable advancement opportunities. Unfortunately, high-paying jobs frequently involve unpleasant working conditions or unfavorable promotional prospects. In selecting a position, the graduate must analyze each alternative in terms of its potential impact on these criteria.

There are several ways to deal with multiple-criteria decision situations. Many of the concepts can be illustrated with Management Situation 6.3.

Management Situation 6.3

Book Publishing

A local university publishes texts written by its faculty for use in courses on campus. Then the texts are sold through the bookstore to students.

Jonathan Smart has just completed a manuscript for an introductory accounting course, and the bookstore must now decide how many copies to publish. The production alternatives will be influenced by the estimated demand. Although this demand can be any whole unit value (such as 1,099 or 1,351 books), economically it is most efficient for the bookstore to produce the manuscript in batches of 100 and store any excess for future use.

Previous experience with similar projects has provided the bookstore with data on potential demand, sales probabilities, economical production volumes, cash requirements (for materials, staff, and facilities), and profits (revenues less production costs less display and overhead expenses). The bookstore also has available forecasting methodologies and spreadsheet models that can be delivered to management through a microcomputer-based decision support system (DSS). By using the DSS, management has found that

1. The bookstore will sell an estimated 1,000 to 1,400 copies of Smart's text per academic year.

2. The most economical production quantities within the forecasted sales range will be 1,000, 1,200, or 1,400 copies.

3. There is a 30 percent chance of selling 1,000 copies, a 50 percent likelihood for a 1,200-unit demand, and a 20 percent probability of selling 1,400 copies.

Table 6.5   **University Bookstore's Decision Table**

Decision Alternatives	States of Nature		
	s_1 = sell 1,000	s_2 = sell 1,200	s_3 = sell 1,400
a_1 = publish 1,000	profit = $3,500 cash requirement = $11,500	profit = $3,100 cash requirement = $14,900	profit = $3,700 cash requirement = $17,300
a_2 = publish 1,200	profit = $2,800 cash requirement = $14,200	profit = $4,500 cash requirement = $13,500	profit = $2,900 cash requirement = $16,900
a_3 = publish 1,400	profit = $2,600 cash requirement = $16,400	profit = $3,800 cash requirement = $16,200	profit = $4,950 cash requirement = $15,500

The DSS analysis also has projected the anticipated cash requirements and estimated profits from each production/sales combination. Table 6.5 summarizes the information. This information will be used to evaluate each production alternative.

Bookstore management will consider both profit and cash requirements before making its publication decision. That is why each cell in the decision table (Table 6.5) has an entry (outcome) for both of these attributes.

Separate criteria can be developed for each decision attribute. For instance, the bookstore may want to publish the quantity of texts that maximizes profit or minimizes cash requirements. However, by separately applying each criterion, the decision maker could arrive at two or more different conclusions. To generate a single recommendation, management must evaluate each alternative's simultaneous impact on all criteria.

Priority Systems

Criteria may not all be equally important to management. If not, the decision maker could identify priorities for the criteria and then use the ordering scheme to help select an alternative.

Goal Constraints. In one approach, management first identifies the most important decision criterion. This primary criterion is treated as the single objective of the problem. Next, acceptable or target levels are established for the other criteria and additional relevant attributes. These targets, or goals, become restrictions on the primary criterion. Then the decision maker selects the alternative, among those satisfying all constraints, that best meets the primary objective.

Suppose, for example, that the highest priority of the university bookstore is to maximize expected profit. However, management does not want the expected cash requirements for Smart's manuscript to exceed $15,000. Also, although the bookstore has no explicit sales objective, management feels that there must be at least a 60 percent chance of selling the published quantity of texts.

Under these circumstances, the objective of the bookstore is to select the publication quantity that maximizes expected profit. This objective is constrained by the expected cash requirements and demand goals.

We can begin the analysis with the target on the probability of demand. According to Management Situation 6.3, there is a $P(s_1) = .3$ chance of selling 1,000 copies of Smart's book. The bookstore also has a $P(s_2) = .5$ likelihood of making 1,200 sales and a $P(s_3) = .2$ probability for 1,400 sales. Thus, there is a

$$P(s_1) + P(s_2) + P(s_3) = .3 + .5 + .2 = 1$$

or 100 percent chance of at least 1,000, a

$$P(s_2) + P(s_3) = .5 + .2 = .7$$

or 70 percent likelihood for at least 1,200, and a

$$P(s_3) = .2$$

or 20 percent probability for at least 1,400 sales. Since management wants at least a 60 percent chance of selling the selected production quantity, the university should publish no more than 1,200 copies of Smart's text.

Now consider cash requirements. By using the data from Table 6.5 and the probability information, the bookstore will find that the expected cash requirement for publishing 1,000 texts (a_1) is

$$\$11,500(.3) + \$14,900(.5) + \$17,300(.2) = \$14,360.$$

Similarly, there is an expected cash requirement of

$$\$14,200(.3) + \$13,500(.5) + \$16,900(.2) = \$14,390$$

for publishing 1,200 texts (a_2) and

$$\$16,400(.3) + \$16,200(.5) + \$15,500(.2) = \$16,120$$

for publishing 1,400 copies (a_3). Since management does not want this requirement to exceed $15,000, the bookstore should publish no more than 1,200 copies.

The university can therefore satisfy both the cash requirements and the demand constraints by publishing either 1,000 or 1,200 texts. Data from Table 6.5 and the probability information indicate that there is an expected profit of

$$\$3,500(.3) + \$3,100(.5) + \$3,700(.2) = \$3,340$$

from publishing 1,000 copies (a_1) and

$$\$2,800(.3) + \$4,500(.5) + \$2,900(.2) = \$3,670$$

from producing 1,200 copies (a_2). Therefore, management can achieve its primary objective of maximizing expected profit at $3,670 per academic year by publishing 1,200 texts. This quantity will also meet the cash requirements and demand goals.

The decision maker could encounter some difficulties in applying this goal constraint approach. For one thing, it may not be possible to find a decision alternative that satisfies all the constraints. In such cases, management will have to add alternatives, relax the constraints, or alter the objectives. Also, goals are viewed differently by various individuals and groups within the organization. Furthermore, changes in the decision situation, organization, or environment could alter the original goal structure. As a result, the decision maker may be unable to identify a stable preeminent criterion or establish a consensus on the acceptable levels of the other objectives.

Ranked Priorities. There are situations in which management cannot specify, will not identify, or has no goal constraints. Under these circumstances, the organization can use a second kind of priority system. In this second approach, the decision maker first establishes a priority ranking for the objectives. Next, each decision alternative is rated in terms of the objective with the highest priority. If two or more alternatives receive the same rating, management then uses the second-ranked objective to evaluate these options. The evaluation process continues, in sequence, through lower-priority objectives until management identifies a single best alternative or exhausts the list of objectives.

Suppose, for instance, that the most important objectives of the university bookstore are to maximize expected profit and minimize expected cash requirements. Previous calculations have already indicated that the store can earn an expected profit of \$3,340 from alternative a_1 and \$3,670 from alternative a_2. Also, by using the data from Table 6.5 and the probability information in Management Situation 6.3, management will find that there is an expected profit of

$$\$2,600(.3) + \$3,800(.5) + \$4,950(.2) = \$3,670$$

from producing 1,400 texts (a_3). Thus, the bookstore can maximize expected profit at \$3,670 by publishing either 1,200 or 1,400 copies of Smart's text.

The highest-priority criterion, expected profit maximization, eliminates a_1 but does not provide an unequivocal recommendation regarding the other alternatives (a_2 and a_3). Consequently, management must now evaluate the survivors in terms of the second-ranked objective (minimizing expected cash requirements).

Previous computations have shown that there is an expected cash requirement of \$14,390 associated with a_2 and \$16,120 associated with a_3. Hence, among these two highest-profit alternatives, a_2 has the smallest expected cash requirement. According to this ranked priority approach, then, the bookstore should publish 1,200 copies of Smart's manuscript.

The ranked priority approach, however, has its own unique limitations. One of the difficulties is that the approach may identify a single best alternative without considering all relevant objectives. Under some circumstances, a recommendation could be obtained after evaluating the alternatives in terms of only the highest-priority objective. In such cases, the ranked priority approach effectively becomes a single criterion system. Also, several participants in the formulation process could develop different assessments of the priorities for the objectives. Furthermore, these assessments can change over time and in different decision situations. Consequently, the decision maker may be unable to establish a stable consensus hierarchy of objectives.

Table 6.6   **University Bookstore's Decision Table in Terms of ROI**

Decision Alternatives	States of Nature		
	s_1	s_2	s_3
a_1	\$3,500/\$11,500 = .3043	\$3,100/\$14,900 = .2081	\$3,700/\$17,300 = .2139
a_2	\$2,800/\$14,200 = .1972	\$4,500/\$13,500 = .3333	\$2,900/\$16,900 = .1716
a_3	\$2,600/\$16,400 = .1585	\$3,800/\$16,200 = .2346	\$4,950/\$15,500 = .3194

ROI = profit/cash requirement

Single Composite Transformation

Neither the goal constraint nor ranked priority system is designed to deal with problems involving several essentially equal criteria. This fact and the theoretical and practical limitations of priority systems have led to the development of other approaches to multiple-criteria decision making. In one approach, the decision maker begins by transforming all attributes into a single composite measure. This measure should, in some way, reflect the impact of each alternative on the original attributes. Management next develops a decision criterion from the single composite measure and then selects the alternative that best meets this criterion.

Composite Measure. High profits and small cash requirements, for example, are each desirable attributes for the university bookstore. Management also may be happy with the following combinations: (1) high profits and stable cash requirements, (2) stable profits and small cash requirements, or (3) stable profits and stable cash requirements. However, the bookstore would not want small profits and large cash requirements.

The ratio of profit to cash requirements, which could be called the *return on investment (ROI)*, reflects each of these consequences. Hence, it may be useful for management to transform the original two attributes into this composite ROI measure, in which case the bookstore's decision situation would be represented by Table 6.6. An appropriate objective for this situation, then, is to select the alternative that maximizes the ROI.

Decision Making. By using the data from Table 6.6 and the probability information from Management Situation 6.3, management will find that the expected ROI from alternative a_1 is

$$.3043(.3) + .2081(.5) + .2139(.2) = .2381.$$

Similarly, there is an expected return on investment of

$$.1972(.3) + .3333(.5) + .1716(.2) = .2601$$

from a_2 and

$$.1585(.3) + .2346(.5) + .3194(.2) = .2287$$

from a_3. Hence, a_2 yields the largest expected ROI at 26.01 percent. According to this composite criterion, the bookstore should publish 1,200 copies of Smart's text.

Limitations. Many problems involve intangibles or noncomparable attributes. In these cases, the decision maker may be unable to define a single composite measure. Even when such a measure is available, management usually must make some subjective trade-offs between the component attributes. For instance, falling profit is an undesirable attribute for the university bookstore. Yet its ROI could increase under these circumstances if the corresponding cash requirements fall more rapidly than profit. Thus, by using the composite ROI criterion, bookstore management implicitly is willing to trade off the reduced profit for the more substantial decrease in cash requirements.

Multiattribute Utility Theory

To describe trade-offs more explicitly, experts have developed a multiattribute utility system for decision making. In this approach, the decision maker first assigns utility values to each multiattribute outcome in the problem. The purpose of this step is to transform the original attributes into the single composite measure of utility. Management then selects the alternative that maximizes expected utility.

The multiattribute nature of the outcomes, however, complicates the task of assigning utilities. Still, there are several methods available for this purpose. In the traditional method, a separate utility curve is developed for each relevant attribute in the problem. The lottery ticket approach typically is used to construct these curves. Individual curves are then amalgamated into a multiattribute utility assessment.

Separate Utility Assessments. If the university bookstore uses this methodology, it must develop separate utility curves, through the lottery ticket approach, for the profit and cash requirement attributes. Management begins by assigning arbitrary utility values to the best and worst profits in the problem.

According to Table 6.5, the largest profit of $4,950 is obtained when the bookstore publishes and sells 1,400 copies of Smart's manuscript. The smallest profit of $2,600 occurs when the bookstore publishes 1,400 copies but sells only 1,000. If management assigns a utility of 100 to the $4,950 and 0 to the $2,600, then

$$U(\$4,950) = 100$$

denotes the utility of the best profit and

$$U(\$2,600) = 0$$

denotes the utility of the worst profit.

These values can then be used in various hypothetical lottery situations to derive the utilities for the other profit levels in Table 6.5. In one of these situations, for example, bookstore management could be given the option of investing in either (1) a project that is sure to yield the \$3,500 profit associated with the a_1 and s_1 combination in Table 6.5 or (2) a lottery ticket that has a p chance of earning the best (\$4,950) profit but a $(1 - p)$ likelihood of yielding the worst (\$2,600) profit. Next, a series of trial-and-error questions is employed to determine the value of p that makes management indifferent between the sure \$3,500 and the lottery. Then the bookstore can use this lottery indifference probability (p) in the formula

$$U(\$3,500) = pU(\$4,950) + (1 - p)U(\$2,600)$$

to find the utility of the \$3,500 profit.

If the indifference probability for this lottery is $p = .65$, then

$$U(\$3,500) = .65U(\$4,950) + (1 - .65)U(\$2,600)$$

or, since $U(\$4,950) = 100$ and $U(\$2,600) = 0$,

$$U(\$3,500) = .65(100) + .35(0) = 65.$$

This lottery ticket process is then repeated for each bookstore profit. Let us assume that such a process provides the results shown in Table 6.7.

A similar process can be used to find the utility values for the cash requirement attribute. Table 6.5 indicates that the smallest (best) cash requirement of \$11,500 is obtained when the bookstore publishes and sells 1,000 copies of Smart's book. The largest (worst) cash requirement of \$17,300 occurs when the bookstore publishes 1,000 copies but sells 1,400. Hence, if management assigns a utility of 100 to \$11,500 and a utility of 0 to \$17,300, then

$$U(\$11,500) = 100$$

and

$$U(\$17,300) = 0.$$

These values are then used in various hypothetical lottery situations to derive the utilities of the other cash requirement levels in Table 6.5.

In the situation involving the a_1 and s_2 combination, for instance, bookstore management could be given the option of receiving either (1) an order that is sure to require \$14,900 cash or (2) a lottery ticket that has a p chance of generating the best (\$11,500) cash requirement but a $(1 - p)$ likelihood for the worst (\$17,300) cash requirement. If a series of trial-and-error questions reveals that $p = .50$ for this lottery, then

$$U(\$14,900) = pU(\$11,500) + (1 - p)U(\$17,300)$$

or

$$U(\$14,900) = .5(100) + .5(0) = 50.$$

Again, this lottery ticket approach is then repeated for each cash requirement. Let us assume that such a process provides the results shown in Table 6.8.

Amalgamation Process. Management must amalgamate the separate utility assessments for the individual profit and cash requirement attributes into a composite multiattribute

Table 6.7   **The Utility of Profit to Bookstore Management**

Profit ($)	Lottery Indifference Probability (p)	Utility
4950	Does not apply	100
4500	.90	90
3800	.75	75
3700	.70	70
3500	.65	65
3100	.55	55
2900	.40	40
2800	.15	15
2600	Does not apply	0

Table 6.8   **The Utility of Cash Requirements to Bookstore Management**

Cash Requirement ($)	Lottery Indifference Probability (p)	Utility
11,500	Does not apply	100
13,500	.80	80
14,200	.60	60
14,900	.50	50
15,500	.35	35
16,200	.25	25
16,400	.20	20
16,900	.10	10
17,300	Does not apply	0

utility measure. If we assume that profits are independent of, and equally important as, cash requirements, the bookstore can obtain this composite measure with a simple additive approach. First, the decision maker identifies the attribute levels for each outcome and then sums the corresponding utility values. The results create a new scale that is comparable to, and preserves the essential relationships involved in, each attribute's separate utility curve.

Table 6.5 shows that the bookstore obtains a profit of $3,500 and needs $11,500 in cash when it publishes and sells 1,000 texts. As Tables 6.7 and 6.8 indicate, management separately assigns 65 units of utility to the $3,500 profit and 100 units to the $11,500 cash requirement. Under the additive amalgamation approach, this a_1 and s_1 combination receives a multiattribute utility assessment of $65 + 100 = 165$.

If the bookstore repeats this additive approach for each multiattribute outcome, it will obtain the results presented in Table 6.9. By substituting the utility values from Table 6.9 for the corresponding multiattribute outcomes in Table 6.5, the bookstore will obtain Table 6.10.

Remember, there is a $P(s_1) = .3$ chance that the store will sell 1,000 texts, a $P(s_2) = .5$ likelihood of 1,200 sales, and a $P(s_3) = .2$ probability of selling 1,400 copies.

Table 6.9   **The University Bookstore's Multiattribute Utility Values**

Alternative/Event Combination	Outcomes		Utilities		Multi-attribute Utility Values
	Profit ($)	Cash Requirement ($)	Profit ($)	Cash Requirement ($)	
a_2 and s_2	4,500	13,500	90	80	170
a_1 and s_1	3,500	11,500	65	100	165
a_3 and s_3	4,950	15,500	100	35	135
a_1 and s_2	3,100	14,900	55	50	105
a_3 and s_2	3,800	16,200	75	25	100
a_2 and s_1	2,800	14,200	15	60	75
a_1 and s_3	3,700	17,300	70	0	70
a_2 and s_3	2,900	16,900	40	10	50
a_3 and s_1	2,600	16,400	0	20	20

Table 6.10   **The Bookstore's Multiattribute Utility Table**

Decision Alternatives	States of Nature		
	s_1	s_2	s_3
a_1	165	105	70
a_2	75	170	50
a_3	20	100	135

Units of multiattribute utility to management

Using these probabilities and the data from Table 6.10, management will find that there is an expected utility of

$$165(.3) + 105(.5) + 70(.2) = 116$$

from a_1,

$$75(.3) + 170(.5) + 50(.2) = 117.50$$

from a_2, and

$$20(.3) + 100(.5) + 135(.2) = 83$$

from a_3. Therefore, the bookstore can maximize expected multiattribute utility at 117.50 units by publishing 1,200 copies of Smart's book (a_2).

Extensions. Although the simple additive model assumes that each attribute has an independent and equally important influence on the decision, these assumptions are not crucial in multiattribute utility theory. There are models that allow for interactions between the attributes and formulations in which each attribute has a different weight.

When accurate and consistent weights are available, the composite multiattribute utility measure is found in the additive model by computing the weighted sum of the attributes' separate utilities. For example, if profits are twice as important as cash requirements, the bookstore would assign a weight of 2/3 to each profit utility and a weight of 1/3 to each cash requirement utility. The multiattribute utility value from the a_2 and s_2 combination then would be

$$(2/3)90 + (1/3)(80) = 86.66$$

rather than the 170 units shown in the first row of Table 6.9. Similarly, the composite measure for the a_2 and s_1 combination would be

$$(2/3)15 + (1/3)60 = 30$$

rather than the 75 units shown in the sixth row of Table 6.9. The rest of the analysis would be completed as before.

In practice, accurate and consistent weights may not be readily available. Instead, it may be necessary to derive them with a systematic procedure, such as the approach presented in the next section.

Interactions between the attributes add further complexity to the multiattribute utility formulations. Though a discussion of such interactions is well beyond the text's scope, the interested reader can find the details in the chapter's references.

Analytic Hierarchy Process

The bookstore's attributes (profits and cash requirements) are measured in absolute numerical terms. Many problems, however, involve primarily vague and fuzzy attributes (such as quality and ability/talent). Although multiattribute utility theory can accommodate these "fuzzy" situations, many experts prefer alternative multiple-criteria approaches better suited to such problems. One of the most popular alternatives is the analytic hierarchy process (AHP).

In AHP, the manager first breaks down the problem into a hierarchy of interrelated decision elements. The overall decision criterion is placed at the top, attributes in the middle, and alternatives at the bottom of the hierarchy. Next, elements (alternatives or attributes) at one level are compared pairwise for their relative importance in attaining the elements (attributes or overall criterion) at the next higher level. This data is used to estimate the relative weights of the attributes. Then, the weights are aggregated into a set of ratings for the decision alternatives. Management Situation 6.4 illustrates.

Management Situation 6.4

Medical Promotions

Two nurses at General Hospital, James Dean and Rose Carter, are being considered for a promotion to the position of Emergency Room Supervisor (EMS). The hospital administrator will base her decision on the candidates' technical abilities and supervisory skills. In the evaluation, the supervision attribute will receive twice as much weight as the technical attribute.

Figure 6.4   **General Hospital's Decision Hierarchy**

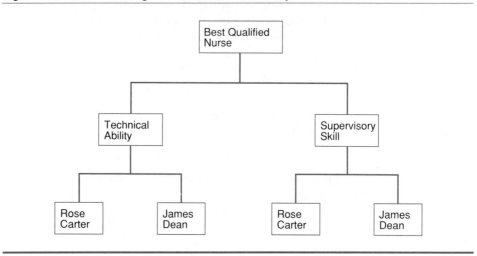

After reviewing the candidates' personnel files, her interview notes, and standardized personnel test results, the hospital administrator rates James four times as high as Rose on technical ability. On the other hand, Rose is rated three times as high as James on supervisory skill.

Decision Hierarchy. General Hospital's decision problem is to select the best qualified nurse for the EMS position. The overall criterion, best qualified nurse, is determined by the candidates' technical ability and supervisory skill attributes. To fill the position, the hospital administrator can choose either the James Dean or Rose Carter alternative. In this situation, the decision hierarchy is as shown in Figure 6.4.

Relative Weights. Supervisory skill is twice as important as technical ability in selecting the best qualified nurse. Hence, the supervision attribute should receive a weight of 2/3 and the technical attribute should get a weight of 1/3 in the overall evaluation.

The hospital administrator's review also indicates that James Dean has four times as much technical ability as Rose Carter. Consequently, James should receive a weight of 4/5 and Rose should get a weight of 1/5 in the technical evaluation. Similarly, since Rose is rated three times as high as James on supervisory skill, Ms. Carter should receive a weight of 3/4 and Mr. Dean should get a weight of 1/4 in the supervision evaluation.

Decision Alternative Ratings. By aggregating the relative weights through the hierarchy, the hospital administrator will obtain an overall rating for each EMS candidate. Figure 6.5 illustrates the calculations.

Figure 6.5, for example, shows that James Dean receives a weight of 1/4 for the supervision, and a weight of 4/5 for the technical attribute. Furthermore, the supervision

Figure 6.5   **EMS Ratings**

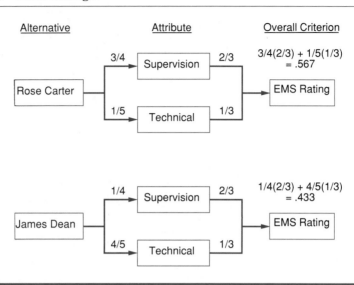

attribute contributes a weight of 2/3, while the technical attribute contributes a weight of 1/3 toward the overall criterion. As a result, James Dean has a

$$1/4(2/3) + 4/5(1/3) = .433$$

EMS rating.

The overall criterion ratings provide a basis for selecting among the decision alternatives. In the medical situation, for example, the EMS rating is .567 for Rose Carter and only .433 for James Dean. These ratings suggest that Rose Carter should be promoted to the EMS position.

Extensions. Although General Hospital's situation involves a small hierarchy, other situations could involve several levels with many attributes and alternatives. In these larger-scale problems, the decision maker will need mathematical approaches based on matrix algebra rather than a simple arithmetic analysis to generate relative weights (and eventually overall ratings) from the pairwise comparisons. Computer programs, such as **Expert Choice**, have been developed to perform the necessary computations and report the results in an easily understood format. While a discussion of such analyses is far beyond the text's scope, the interested reader can find the details in the chapter's references.

Sensitivity Analysis

Table 6.11 summarizes the approaches to multiple-criteria decision making that have been discussed in this section.

All the approaches, in effect, attempt to create a single objective from the multiple criteria in the problem. Individual criteria are either integrated into a composite measure (as in the traditional multiattribute utility theory) or treated as secondary considerations

Table 6.11 Multiple-Criteria Decision Making Approaches

Priority Systems		Transformations		
Goal Constraints	Ranked Priorities	Single Composite Measure	Traditional Multiattribute Utility Theory	Analytic Hierarchy Process (AHP)
1. Identify the most important decision criterion. 2. Establish target levels or goals for the other criteria and/or additional relevant attributes. 3. Select the decision alternative, among those satisfying all goals, that optimizes the primary criterion.	1. Establish a priority ranking for the objectives. 2. Rate each alternative in terms of the highest-priority objective. 3. Continued the evaluation process, in sequence, through lower-priority objectives until you identify a single best alternative or exhaust the list of criteria.	1. Transform all attributes into a single composite measure that in some way reflects the impact of each alternative on the original attributes. 2. Develop a decision criterion from the composite measure. 3. Select the alternative the best meets the single composite criterion.	1. Develop a separate utility curve for each relevant attribute. 2. Amalgamate the individual curves into a multiattribute utility assessment of each decision alternative. 3. Select the alternative that maximizes expected multiattribute utility.	1. Break down the problem into a hierarchy of inter-related decision elements. 2. Compare pairs of elements at one level for their relative importance in attaining the elements at the next higher level in the hierarchy. 3. Use this comparison of pairs to estimate the relative weights of the attributes. 4. Aggregate the weights into a set of ratings for the decision alternatives.

Multiple-Criteria Decision Making in Practice

Multiple-criteria decision making is applied to a wide variety of management problems. Here are a few areas in which this quantitative analysis is used.

Area	Application
Finance	Selecting the best portfolio of investments Allocating financial resources among the divisions of a firm Evaluating financial auditing strategies
Marketing	Establishing the best mix of new products Determining the best advertising design Selecting the best department store layout
Production	Planning computerized office systems Rating suppliers and product quality Identifying the best strategy for expanding production capacity Selecting solar energy research and development projects
Public sector	Assessing the public health risks from infections Identifying a country's best long-range economic plan Determining the best arms control policy

---

(as in the ranked priority system). Also, some of these approaches require the decision maker to supply the essential information. In the acquisition process, it may be necessary to create artificial situations (like lottery tickets) that could seem unrealistic or irrelevant to management. Consequently, management may be unable to accurately and completely furnish the relevant information.

Since multiple-criteria decision making is far from a precise process, management should test the sensitivity of the recommendation to changes in assumptions and in inputs before making a final choice. Relevant questions could include the following:

1. Are the evaluator's attribute weights consistent?

2. What were the most important attributes in making the decision?

3. Would the recommendation change if one attribute were weighted a little more or a little less?

Some multiple-criteria approaches even incorporate the sensitivity analysis within the methodology. For example, in large-scale problems, the AHP includes a formal procedure for checking the consistency of the evaluator's weights. In the other approaches, management must perform the sensitivity analysis outside the methodology.

6.3 GAME THEORY

Until now, we have discussed situations in which the states of nature result from the independent actions taken by many people (as when the interplay between investors sets future gold prices) or from natural phenomena (such as weather conditions). Under these circumstances, when management selects an alternative, it can anticipate a passive reaction from the environment.

In many situations, however, the states of nature (the s_j values in our decision analysis framework) depict the actions taken by the organization's key competitors. Examples include athletic competition, collective bargaining, military operations, and television programming. Since such cases involve conflict between competing parties, the decision maker can anticipate an active (rather than passive) reaction from the environment. Moreover, outcomes will be determined by the collective actions of all competitors, rather than by a choice from a single competitor.

To make effective decisions in conflict situations, management must consider the opponents' alternatives, anticipate the competitors' actions, and then develop an appropriate strategy. Within the past 40 years, a special decision analysis methodology has been developed to help managers perform such an evaluation. Because the evaluation resembles parlor and casino games, this methodology has been labeled **game theory**. Its concepts can be illustrated with Management Situation 6.5.

Management Situation 6.5

Collective Bargaining

Under a new law, state employees will be represented in pay and benefit negotiations by the union federation CSPT. The personnel board (PB), a committee of government officials, will be the sole state representative in the collective bargaining.

Although budget realities often require frugal state pay/benefit policies, other economic factors (such as living costs and private sector salaries) may force the PB to make moderate concessions during the negotiations. In addition, the personnel board knows that state employees are a very powerful constituency that can significantly affect future elections. Moreover, windfalls (such as unforeseen tax revenues and expense cuts) occasionally provide additional discretionary funds. For these reasons, the personnel board sometimes will adopt a generous bargaining stance.

Since most employees desire better living standards, the CSPT usually will make robust pay/benefit demands. However, such demands can alienate taxpayers, especially when the government appears to be making concessions, and may ultimately work against the union's interests in the bargaining. Also, time pressures and dissension in the ranks often force CSPT to make only modest requests during the negotiations. Even then, any lingering public resentment may encourage a concession-oriented PB to overly restrict pay/benefits.

Once the negotiations start, the outcomes will be determined by the collective actions taken by both PB and CSPT. Each party has used judgment and the experience in neighboring states to estimate these outcomes. The consensus can be summarized as follows (outcomes are expressed in real terms after adjusting for inflation):

1. If CSPT makes robust demands, there will be no change in the package when PB is frugal. Also, this policy will result in an average pay/benefit decrease of $300 per year per worker when PB makes moderate concessions and a $1,500 increase when PB is generous.

2. When CSPT makes modest requests, each worker will get an average pay/benefit increase of $1,250 per year if PB is frugal. Such a policy also will result in a $1,200 increase when PB makes moderate concessions and a $2,000 increase when PB is generous.

The union federation seeks the largest possible pay/benefit increase, while the personnel board wants to limit the package as much as possible.

Characteristics

Problems such as the CSPT/PB collective bargaining are known as **games**. They will have several important characteristics.

Conflict. *First, there will be two or more competing parties striving for a common attribute.* In Management Situation 6.5, these parties are the union federation (CSPT) and the state personnel board (PB), and they have a common interest in the pay/benefit package. The CSPT will negotiate with PB to increase pay/benefits as much as possible. On the other hand, PB will attempt to limit the increase as much as possible and perhaps even negotiate for no increase or even a decrease.

Decision Alternatives. *Second, each competitor can select various decision alternatives.* Although the collective bargaining problem can be examined from the perspective of either party, it seems more realistic to describe the outcomes (pay/benefit changes) from a labor perspective. Hence, we will treat the union federation (CSPT) as the decision maker, and it can select from the following two alternative bargaining positions:

$$a_1 = \text{make robust demands}$$

$$a_2 = \text{make modest requests}$$

The choice will be influenced by the negotiation stance of the state personnel board (PB). The three possibilities for PB, which represent the states of nature facing CSPT, can be denoted as follows:

$$s_1 = \text{be frugal}$$

$$s_2 = \text{make moderate concessions}$$

$$s_3 = \text{be generous}$$

Nevertheless, CSPT does not know PB's strategy in advance.

Game Table. *Third, all parties know the outcomes associated with each alternative/competitors' action combination.* For example, CSPT and PB both know that the potential outcomes of the bargaining process will be as summarized in Table 6.12.

In this representation, which is referred to as a **game table**, each row gives a CSPT decision alternative and each column lists an action by PB (a state of nature facing CSPT). Entries in the cells give the outcomes (real annual average pay/benefit increases per worker) obtained by CSPT.

Table 6.12   **Game Table for the Collective Bargaining Problem**

Union Federation Alternatives	Personnel Board Actions		
	s_1 = be frugal	s_2 = make moderate concessions	s_3 = be generous
a_1 = make robust demands	$0	−$300	$1,500
a_2 = make modest demands	$1,250	$1,200	$2,000

Action/Reaction. *Fourth, each party will react to the competitors' actions.* For example, when PB is generous (s_3), CSPT can maximize the annual pay/benefit increase at $2,000 per worker by making modest requests (a_2). But if PB knows that CSPT will make these requests, the board can react by making moderate concessions (s_2) rather than being generous. In this way, the government can limit pay/benefits to an average of $1,200 per year per employee. Similarly, when the union federation makes robust demands (a_1), PB can force an average $300 decrease in pay/benefits by making moderate concessions (s_2). On the other hand, if CSPT knows that PB will make moderate concessions, instead of making robust demands, the union can make modest requests (a_2) and obtain an average $1,200 annual increase in each employee's pay/benefits.

Uncertainty. *Fifth, each party is uncertain about the competitors' actions and reactions.* CSPT and PB, for instance, would each like to wait until the other acts before reacting. Unfortunately, each opponent is uncertain about the other's bargaining position. The union federation, for instance, does not know when the personnel board will be frugal (s_1), make moderate concessions (s_2), or be generous (s_3). In fact, CSPT does not even know the probabilities of PB's actions. Also, PB does not know when CSPT will make robust demands (a_1) or modest requests (a_2) or even the probabilities of these actions. Yet both parties simultaneously must develop negotiation positions before the bargaining begins.

Game Strategy. *Finally, each party must develop a game plan.* Since pay/benefit increases must be negotiated from time to time, the collective bargaining process will be repeated often. Hence, each opponent must develop a complete, predetermined plan for selecting a decision alternative under every possible circumstance. Furthermore, this plan, called a **game strategy**, should lead to the best expected outcome for each competitor, regardless of the opponents' actions.

Dominance

Each competitor can apply Chapter 4's dominance concept and thereby reduce the scope of the problem or even identify a game solution. For example, in Table 6.12, compare the union federation's outcomes from the robust demands (a_1) and modest requests

(a_2) alternatives. When the personnel board is frugal (s_1), the union would prefer the $1,250 associated with a_2 rather than the $0 from a_1. The modest requests alternative (a_2) also yields a preferable outcome ($1,200 instead of −$300) for the union when PB makes moderate concessions (s_2). Indeed, a_2 always leads to better outcomes for the union than a_1, regardless of the board's bargaining position. That is, a_2 dominates a_1. Consequently, the union federation should never make robust demands (a_1) in the negotiations.

Pure Strategy. In effect, then, the union federation (CSPT) will always make modest requests (a_2), regardless of the personnel board (PB) strategy. Now, PB has the same information and thus knows that the union will adopt its dominant (a_2) bargaining position. The board can react by being frugal (s_1), by making moderate concessions (s_2), or by being generous (s_3). According to Table 6.12, s_1 would provide a $1,250, s_2 a $1,200, and s_3 a $2,000 pay/benefit increase for state employees. Since the personnel board wants to limit the package as much as possible, it should always make moderate concessions (s_2) in the negotiations.

Note that each party in the collective bargaining situation repeatedly selects only one alternative, regardless of the opponent's actions. The union federation will make modest requests all of the time, while the personnel board will always make moderate concessions. In such cases, each competitor is said to have a **pure strategy**.

Value of the Game. According to Table 6.12, when each party adopts its pure strategy (CSPT always making modest requests and PB always making moderate concessions), the outcome is an annual average $1,200 pay/benefit increase for each state employee. This payoff, which represents the expected outcome of the conflict when each party repeatedly selects the optimal strategy, is called the **value of the game**.

Pessimistic Criterion

There is another way to look at the collective bargaining situation. In this game, the personnel board (PB) wants to limit expenditures. Consequently, the board should react to each union federation (CSPT) action by adopting the strategy that would provide employees with the worst pay/benefit package possible.

Maximin Strategy. Table 6.12 shows that when the union makes robust demands (a_1), public employees will get a $0 pay/benefit increase if the personnel board reacts by being frugal (s_1). There will be a $300 decrease if PB makes moderate concessions (s_2) and a $1,500 increase if the board reacts by being generous. Under these circumstances, the board's rational reaction is to make moderate concessions (s_2) and thus force a $300 pay/benefit decrease. Similarly, when the union makes modest requests (a_2), the board's rational reaction is to make moderate concessions (s_2) and grant a $1,200 pay/benefit increase.

By anticipating these rational personnel board reactions, the union federation can get an expected pay/benefit increase of

- −$300 if it makes robust demands (a_1), and

- $1,200 when it makes modest requests (a_2)

Notice that each expected outcome represents the minimum value (worst union payoff) in the corresponding row of Table 6.12.

In light of the anticipated PB reactions, the public employees' objective (getting the largest possible pay/benefit package) is best achieved when CSPT makes modest requests (a_2) during the negotiations. Then each employee can be guaranteed an average $1,200 pay/benefit increase, regardless of the personnel board's actions. Since this $1,200 increase is the maximum of the employees' minimum expected outcomes, alternative a_2 represents the union's maximin strategy.

Minimax Strategy. The government knows that the union wants to enlarge the pay/benefit package. Hence, when the personnel board is frugal (s_1), the rational CSPT reaction is to make modest requests (a_2) and strive for a $1,250 pay/benefit increase. Also, if PB makes moderate concessions (s_2), the union's rational reaction is to push for a $1,200 increase by making modest requests (a_2). When PB is generous (s_3), the union's rational reaction will be to press for a $2,000 increase by again making modest requests (a_2).

By anticipating these rational union federation reactions, the personnel board can grant an expected pay/benefit increase of

- $1,250 if it is frugal ($s_1$)

- $1,200 when it makes moderate concessions (s_2), and

- $2,000 if it is generous (s_3).

Notice that each expected outcome represents the maximum value (worst personnel board payoff) in the corresponding column of Table 6.12.

In light of the anticipated CSPT reactions, the government's objective (limiting the pay/benefit package as much as possible) is best achieved when PB makes moderate concessions (s_2) during the negotiations. Then the government will never have to give each employee more than an average $1,200 pay/benefit increase, regardless of the union's actions. Since this $1,200 increase is the minimum of the maximum expected losses (costs) for the government, alternative s_2 represents the board's minimax strategy.

Saddle Point. As long as the personnel board sticks with this minimax (s_2) strategy, the union federation should adhere to its maximin (a_2) strategy. Otherwise, as Table 6.12 shows, state employees will receive a decrease in pay/benefits rather than the average $1,200 per worker per year guaranteed by the maximin strategy. Similarly, as long as the union adheres to its maximin (a_2) strategy, the board should stick with its minimax (s_2) strategy. Under these circumstances, Table 6.12 indicates that any deviation by the board from this minimax strategy will force the government to grant more than the planned maximum $1,200 increase in pay/benefits.

In effect, when CSPT clings to its maximin strategy and PB to its minimax strategy, the opponents create an equilibrium from which neither can advantageously deviate. At the equilibrium, also known as a **saddle point**, each negotiator adopts a pure strategy and each state employee receives an average $1,200 increase in pay/benefits. This payoff, which represents the value of the game, is simultaneously the best of the worst expected outcomes for each participant in the game. Put another way, the game strategy is derived from an application of Chapter 4's pessimistic criterion.

Procedure Recap. The following procedure can be used to solve pure strategy games:

1. Develop the game table.

2. Use the dominance concept to reduce the size of the game and, if possible, to identify the pure strategy for each competitor.

3. Find the maximin strategy for the row competitor. The maximin is the pure strategy for this competitor.

4. Find the minimax strategy for the column competitor. The minimax is the best pure strategy for this competitor.

5. Identify the outcome from the saddle point created by the maximin and minimax strategies. This outcome is the value of the game.

Mixed Strategy

A game may involve no dominance and yet have a pure strategy or saddle point solution. If such a solution exists, it can always be found with the pessimistic (maximin/minimax) criterion. A variation of the same criterion can be used to develop recommendations for the many conflict situations that do not involve a pure strategy solution. Management Situation 6.6 illustrates.

Management Situation 6.6

Athletic Competition

Prudence Tech and Swami U have advanced to the final game of the Division 6 National Collegiate Rugby Championship. Lew Cross, Tech's coach, must decide whether to use his "quick" or "strong" team. Amy Allweather, Swami's coach, must make the same decision. In each case, the quick team is composed of different athletes than the strong unit.

Using ratings of the athletes' relative abilities and comparative scores against common opponents, the "experts" have estimated the chances that each team will win the championship. The consensus is summarized in Table 6.13. Since this table views the game from Lew's perspective, the entries in the cells represent Tech's chances of winning the championship. Swami's chances would be 100 percent minus the percentages given in Table 6.13.

Each coach wants to select the strategy that will give his or her team the best chance of winning the game.

Action/Reaction. An examination of Table 6.13 shows that neither opponent has a dominant alternative. Hence, each coach must consider both available actions/alternatives when developing an optimal game strategy. Cross can guarantee that Tech will have at least a 40 percent chance of capturing the championship. Amy Allweather, on the other hand, can increase her team's likelihood of winning by adopting a strategy that limits Tech's chances as much as possible. In this respect, Table 6.13 shows that her quick team (s_1) will provide Tech with a maximum 70 percent chance of capturing the

---

Table 6.13   **The Rugby Championship Game Table**

Tech's Alternatives	Swami's Actions	
	s_1 = use the quick team	s_2 = use the strong team
a_1 = use the quick team	40%	80%
a_2 = use the strong team	70%	10%

---

championship. When Swami uses the strong team (s_2), Tech has as much as an 80 percent likelihood of winning the game. Therefore, by adopting a minimax strategy and always selecting alternative s_1, Amy can guarantee that Tech would have no more than a 70 percent chance of capturing the championship.

Suppose that Amy starts the game with her minimax strategy (s_1) and Lew with his maximin strategy (a_1). As soon as Lew notices that Amy is always using her quick team (s_1), he will switch to a strong team (a_2). Table 6.13 shows that in this way Tech's chances of capturing the championship will increase from 40 to 70 percent. However, when Amy notices that Lew is always using his strong team (a_2), she will switch to a strong unit (s_2). As Table 6.13 indicates, Amy will thereby reduce Tech's chances from 70 to 10 percent. Yet when Lew notices that Swami always has its strong team (s_2) in the game, he will switch back to a quick unit (a_1). Then Tech's chances of capturing the championship will increase from 10 to 80 percent. To reduce these chances from 80 to 40 percent, Amy again will counter with her quick team (s_1). At this point in the game, Amy has reverted to her minimax strategy (s_1) and Lew to his maximin strategy (a_1). Consequently, the second guessing will begin all over again.

In effect, neither coach has a pure strategy that simultaneously guarantees each team the best of its worst possible outcomes. Put another way, there is no saddle point in the rugby championship. Under these circumstances, each coach must keep the other guessing by randomly changing teams during the game. Such random shifting from one decision alternative to another is known as a **mixed strategy**. Therefore, each coach's problem is to find the mixed strategy that gives his or her team the greatest expected chance of capturing the championship, regardless of the opponent's actions.

Maximin Mixed Strategy. Suppose that Lew Cross randomly uses his quick team (a_1) in the proportion $P(a_1)$ and the strong unit (a_2) on $P(a_2)$ occasions during the championship game. As Table 6.13 indicates, this mixture of strategies will give Tech an expected outcome of

$$40\% P(a_1) + 70\% P(a_2)$$

if Swami uses its quick team (s_1) and

$$80\% P(a_1) + 10\% P(a2)$$

when Swami employs its strong unit (s_2).

Figure 6.6   **Tech's Expected Outcomes**

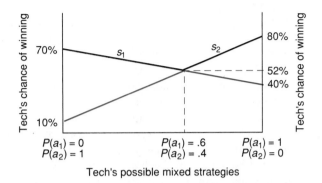

Figure 6.6 shows how these expected outcomes will vary with each possible combination of $P(a_1)$ and $P(a_2)$. The straight line labeled s_1 represents Tech's expected outcome

$$40\%P(a_1) + 70\%P(a_2)$$

if Swami uses its quick team (s_1). At one extreme, Lew Cross can adopt the pure strategy of always using his strong team (a_2). In this case, $P(a_1) = 0$ and $P(a_2) = 1$, and Tech's expected outcome will be

$$40\%(0) + 70\%(1) = 70\%.$$

Lew's other extreme is to adopt the pure strategy of always using his quick team (a_1). Then $P(a_1) = 1$ and $P(a_2) = 0$, and Tech's expected outcome will be

$$40\%(1) + 70\%(0) = .4.$$

Points on the line connecting these extremes give Tech's expected outcomes from every possible combination of $P(a_1)$ and $P(a_2)$ when Swami selects s_1. Such combinations, in effect, provide various mixed strategies.

Similarly, the straight line labeled s_2 represents Tech's expected outcome

$$80\%P(a_1) + 10\%P(a_2)$$

if Swami uses its strong team (s_2). Under these circumstances, the $P(a_1) = 0$ and $P(a_2) = 1$ combination gives Tech a

$$80\%(0) + 10\%(1) = 10\%$$

chance, while the $P(a_1) = 1$ and $P(a_2) = 0$ combination provides a

$$80\%(1) + 10\%(0) = 80\%$$

likelihood of winning the game. Points on the line connecting these extremes present Tech's expected outcomes from each possible combination of $P(a_1)$ and $P(a_2)$ when Swami selects s_2.

Observe what happens in Figure 6.6 when Lew uses his quick team (a_1) between $P(a_1) = 0$ and $P(a_1) = .6$. In this situation, Tech will have a larger expected chance of winning the game if Swami counters with its quick (s_1) rather than its strong (s_2) team. Since Amy wants to limit Tech's chances as much as possible, Swami's rational reaction will be to select s_2. But if Lew uses his quick team (a_1) more often than $P(a_1) = .6$, Tech will have a smaller expected outcome when Swami counters with s_1 instead of s_2. Hence under these circumstances, Swami's rational reaction will be to use its quick team (s_1). By anticipating these rational Swami reactions, Lew Cross can plan on Tech achieving the expected outcomes indicated by the colored lines in Figure 6.6.

In light of Swami's anticipated reactions, Lew can best achieve Tech's objective (giving the team the best possible chance of capturing the championship) by adopting the maximin mixed strategy. That is, Lew should use the mixed strategy that leads to the maximum of Tech's minimum expected outcomes. Figure 6.6 shows that such a maximum occurs at the intersection of the s_1 and s_2 lines. At this point

$$\underbrace{40\% \ P(a_1) + 70\% \ P(a_2)}_{\substack{\text{Expected outcome if} \\ \text{Swami selects } s_1}} = \underbrace{80\% \ P(a_1) + 10\% \ P(a_2)}_{\substack{\text{Expected outcome if} \\ \text{Swami selects } s_2}}$$

or

$$60\% P(a_2) = 40\% P(a_1).$$

And since $P(a_2) = 1 - P(a_1)$, we have

$$P(a_1) = .6$$

with

$$P(a_2) = .4.$$

Furthermore, by randomly using his quick team (a_1) with a frequency of $P(a_1) = .6$ and the strong unit (a_2) with a frequency of $P(a_2) = .4$, Lew will guarantee Tech the same

$$40\% P(a_1) + 70\% P(a_2) = 80\% P(a_1) + 10\% P(a_2)$$

or

$$40\%(.6) + 70\%(.4) = 80\%(.6) + 10\%(.4) = 52\%$$

expected chance of capturing the championship, regardless of Swami's actions.

To achieve this expectation, however, Lew must be sure to use the a_1 and a_2 actions in a random fashion. There must be no apparent pattern. For example, he should not always use his quick team for a duration of three minutes and then bring in the strong squad for the next four minutes. Otherwise, Amy will detect this pattern, and Swami will no longer be uncertain about Tech's strategy. In other words, there would no longer be a game.

Minimax Mixed Strategy. Amy Allweather can determine her optimal mixed strategy in a similar manner. For example, suppose Amy randomly uses her quick team (s_1) on $P(s_1)$ occasions and the strong unit (s_2) in the proportion $P(s_2)$ during the game. Table 6.13 indicates that this mixture of strategies will give Swami an expected outcome of

$$40\% P(s_1) + 80\% P(s_2)$$

Figure 6.7   **Swami's Expected Outcomes**

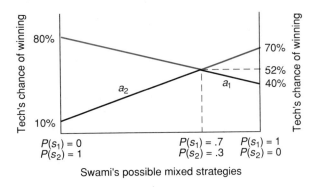

if Tech uses its quick team (a_1) and

$$70\%P(s_1) + 10\%P(s_2)$$

when Tech employs its strong team (a_2).

By plotting these expected outcomes as before, Amy will get Figure 6.7. In this diagram, the straight line labeled a_1 represents Swami's expected outcomes if Tech uses its quick team, and the line labeled a_2 gives Swami's expected outcomes when Tech uses its strong unit.

Observe what happens in Figure 6.7 when Amy uses her quick team (s_1) between $P(s_1) = 0$ and $P(s_1) = .7$. In this situation, Tech will have a larger expected chance of winning the game if Lew counters with his quick (a_1) rather than his strong (a_2) unit. Since Lew wants Tech's chances to be as great as possible, his rational reaction will be to select a_1. But if Amy uses her quick team (s_1) with a frequency greater than $P(s_1) = .7$, Tech will have a smaller expected outcome when Lew counters with a_1 instead of a_2. Hence, under these circumstances, Tech's rational reaction will be to use its strong team (a_2). By anticipating these rational Tech reactions, Amy Allweather can plan on Swami achieving the expected outcomes indicated by the colored lines in Figure 6.7.

In light of Tech's anticipated reactions, Amy can best achieve Swami's objective (limiting Tech's chances of capturing the championship as much as possible) by adopting the minimax mixed strategy. That is, Amy should use the mixed strategy that leads to the minimum of Tech's maximum expected outcomes. Figure 6.7 shows that such a minimum occurs at the intersection of the a_1 and a_2 lines. At this point

$$\underbrace{40\%\ P(s_1) + 80\%\ P(s_2)}_{\substack{\text{Expected outcome if} \\ \text{Tech selects } a_1}} = \underbrace{70\%\ P(s_1) + 10\%\ P(s_2)}_{\substack{\text{Expected outcome if} \\ \text{Tech selects } a_2}}$$

or

$$70\%P(s_2) = 30\%P(s_1)$$

Table 6.14   **Rugby Championship Solution**

Tech's Best Strategy	Outcome of the Game	Swami's Best Strategy
Randomly use the quick team (a_1) 60% of the time. Randomly use the strong team (a_2) 40% of the time.	Tech can expect to have a 52% chance of capturing the championship.	Randomly use the quick team (s_1) 70% of the time. Randomly use the strong team (s_2) 30% of the time.

And since $P(s_2) = 1 - P(s_1)$, we have

$$P(s_1) = .7$$

with

$$P(s_2) = .3.$$

Furthermore, by randomly using her quick team (s_1) with a frequency of $P(s_1) = .7$ and the strong unit (s_2) with a frequency of $P(s_2) = .3$, Amy will limit Tech to the same

$$40\% \, P(s_1) + 80\% \, P(s_2) = 70\% \, P(s_1) + 10\% \, P(s_2)$$

or

$$40\%(.7) + 80\%(.3) = 70\%(.7) + 10\%(.3) = 52\%$$

expected chance of capturing the championship, regardless of Lew's actions.

To achieve this expectation, however, Amy also must be sure to use the s_1 and s_2 actions in a random fashion. Otherwise, she will take away Tech's uncertainty and, in effect, eliminate the game.

Mixed Strategy Solution. Table 6.14 summarizes the mixed strategy solution to the rugby championship game. There are some important characteristics to note about this solution. Recall that when Lew adopts the pure maximin strategy of always using his quick team (a_1), Tech is willing to settle for a 40 percent likelihood of winning the game. As Table 6.14 demonstrates, however, by using his best mixed strategy to confuse the opponent, he increases Tech's chances from 40 percent to an expected 52 percent. There is a similar result for Swami. Remember, when Amy adopts the pure minimax strategy of always using her quick team (s_1), she is willing to concede Tech a 70 percent likelihood of capturing the championship. But by using her best mixed strategy and thereby keeping the opponent guessing, Amy reduces Tech's chances from 70 percent to an expected 52 percent. In this game, then, each coach can obtain a better expected outcome for his or her team from a mixed rather than a pure strategy.

In addition, Tech's and Swami's best mixed strategies both lead to the same expected outcome, regardless of the opponent's actions. Hence, each coach should feel very secure with his or her strategy. Furthermore, as Figures 6.6 and 6.7 demonstrate, the resulting outcome is the best that each team can expect in light of the opponent's anticipated reactions. Consequently, neither coach has any incentive to change his or her strategy. In other words, the solution in Table 6.14 creates an equilibrium from which neither Lew nor Amy can advantageously deviate.

Procedure Recap. When there are only two participants and each has two decision alternatives, the following procedure can be used to solve mixed strategy games:

1. Develop the game table.

2. Eliminate all dominated decision alternatives for each competitor.

3. Formulate expected value expressions for each column in the table.

4. Use the expressions to find the optimal mixed strategy for the row competitor and the resulting value of the game.

5. Formulate expected value expressions for each row in the table.

6. Use the expressions to find the optimal mixed strategy for the column competitor.

Extensions

There are only two opponents in the rugby game. Hence, Tech's likelihood plus Swami's likelihood of capturing the championship must sum to a constant 100 percent. Put another way, Swami's outcome will equal the difference between Tech's chances and this constant sum. For example, if each coach adopts his or her best mixed strategy, Tech will have an expected outcome of 52 percent (Table 6.14). As a result, Swami can expect to have a $100 - 52 = 48$ percent probability of winning the game. Such a situation is referred to as a **constant sum game**.

The collective bargaining situation is a special type of constant sum game. In this situation, the employee union federation is negotiating with the government personnel board for a change in the pay/benefit package. Under these circumstances, a gain (more pay/benefits) for public employees is necessarily an equivalent loss (more expense) for the government. Similarly, a loss (less pay/benefits) for public employees must necessarily be an equivalent gain (less expense) for the government. In each case, the sum of the union's outcome plus the board's payoff is zero. Therefore, such a situation is called a **zero sum game**.

Variable Sum Games. In practice, however, taxes, special expenses, and other factors create differences between the gain of one participant and the loss of the opponent. Income taxes, for instance, would reduce the pay/benefit package received by public employees from the personnel board. Also, each opponent may attach a different total worth, or utility, to the outcomes in a game. For example, instead of striving for maximum security, Tech and Swami both may prefer to gamble on winning the rugby championship. Assuming that Amy and Lew have separate risk-taking attitudes, each coach would then make a different utility assessment of the outcomes in Table 6.13. In addition, each opponent could have complementary as well as competing interests. The only two banks in a small rural town, for instance, both may want to encourage

Table 6.15   **Prisoner's Possible Sentences**

Azon's Alternatives	Bungle's Actions	
	s_1 = confess	s_2 = remain silent
a_1 = confess	Azon's prison term = 3 years Bungle's prison term = 3 years	Azon's prison term = 1 year Bungle's prison term = 8 years
a_2 = remain silent	Azon's prison term = 8 years Bungle's prison term = 1 year	Azon's prison term = 2 years Bungle's prison term = 2 years

community development, even though one might gain more than the other. Finally, each game participant could have a different set of multiple criteria that vary in both form and number over time. One of the rural banks may want to increase deposits and reduce mortgages, while the other may prefer an increase in profits and additional facilities.

In these instances, each combination of the opponents' decision alternatives typically will yield a different outcome sum to the participants. Put another way, the sum of the outcomes will be variable. Hence, such situations are known as **variable sum games**. Behavioral factors play an important role in the solution of these variable sum games, as Management Situation 6.7 illustrates.

Management Situation 6.7

Prisoners' Dilemma

Two men suspected of committing a crime together are awaiting trial in separate cells. Each suspect may either confess (and plea bargain for a shorter sentence) or remain silent (and risk a long jail term). The possible consequences of their actions are described in Table 6.15.

Azon and Bungle both want to receive the smallest possible prison term.

An examination of Table 6.15 will show that Azon can always get a smaller prison term by confessing (a_1) rather than remaining silent (a_2), regardless of Bungle's action. Also, Bungle can always receive a shorter sentence by confessing (s_1) instead of remaining silent (s_2), regardless of Azon's actions. Thus, if each prisoner acts independently and rationally selects his dominant strategy, both will confess and receive three-year prison terms.

Such a strategy, however, assumes that the prisoners have diametrically opposed interests. In reality, both Azon and Bungle can gain by cooperating and forming an agreement to remain silent. As Table 6.15 demonstrates, in this way, each will receive a two-year, rather than a three-year, sentence.

Management Situation 6.7 illustrates the importance of communication and cooperation in a variable sum game. Yet these features create additional complications. Now

Game Theory in Practice

Game theory is applied to a wide variety of management problems. Here are a few areas in which this quantitative analysis is used.

Area	Application
Finance	Competitive bidding for offshore petroleum leases Playing the stock market Speculating in foreign currencies
Marketing	Establishing the best advertising strategy Determining the best peak-load electricity prices Selecting the best product distribution policy
Production	Training executives Establishing the best schedule of television programs Identifying the best agenda for executive meetings Selecting the best strategy for contract negotiations with material and equipment suppliers
Public sector	Evaluating military officers Determining the best airport landing fees Waging war

each participant must consider the personality, psychological status, needs, and relative bargaining strength of the opponent. Moreover, each participant must also evaluate threats, bluffs, and the impact of various collusive agreements.

Multiple Players. Another important consideration is the number of participants. Although our discussion has focused on two-party situations, practical games typically involve several opponents. When there are three or more participants, the competitors may attempt to form collusive agreements or coalitions for their mutual benefit.

The draft of college athletes by professional football teams is an illustration of a collusive agreement. In the absence of the draft, there would be competitive bidding among the teams for the services of the best athletes. By forming a binding agreement to select players in a predetermined order, each team obtains its share of quality athletes. The draft also reduces the athletes' options and, in effect, limits the overall salary scale.

World War II provides an example of a coalition. Germany, Japan, Italy, France, the Soviet Union, the United States, and the United Kingdom were all participants in this military conflict. France, the United Kingdom, the United States, and later the Soviet Union had similar political interests or economic resources that complemented one another's needs. Consequently, these countries became allies and formed a coalition against their common enemies, Germany, Japan, and Italy. Meanwhile, Germany, Japan, and Italy formed a coalition against the Allies.

Unfortunately, a game with several participants can involve a very large number of possible collusive arrangements and coalitions. Furthermore, opponents often can alter existing coalitions or form new ones by making payments to selected participants. In addition, each coalition may form a variety of collusive agreements. Since the formation and alteration processes can go on indefinitely, there may never be a stable group of competing parties or outcomes in the game.

SUMMARY

Chapters 4 and 5 focused on decision problems that involve a single, absolute measure of performance. The previous discussion also assumed that there was a passive decision environment. This chapter has extended the decision analysis to situations that involve intangibles, multiple criteria, and conflict between parties.

In the first section, we saw that many real-life problems involve intangibles such as risk, the decision maker's attitude, and enjoyment. Since these factors are difficult to express on an absolute numerical scale, the more comprehensive measure of utility was proposed as the appropriate criterion for such circumstances. As the analysis demonstrated, separate decision makers can assign different utility values to the same outcome. Often, the assignment depends on whether management has a risk-averse, risk-neutral, risk-seeking, or risk-complex attitude. The first section, in addition, showed how to use utility for decision making and presented the limitations of such an analysis.

In the second section, we saw that the decision maker also must frequently consider problems with several often conflicting criteria. Several methods were presented to deal with these situations. Some, like the goal constraint and ranked priority approaches, attempt to focus on the most important objectives. Others, such as the transformation and multiattribute utility concepts, integrate the multiple criteria into a single overall objective. Table 6.11 summarized these various methods but each approach has its limitations.

The final section presented a framework for dealing with problems that involve a conflict situation between competing parties. Such situations, called games, include war, athletic competition, collective bargaining, and television programming. In some games, each decision maker has a single dominant alternative, or pure strategy, that provides the best outcome, regardless of the opponent's actions. For other games, each participant's best approach is to keep the opponent guessing, with a mixed strategy, by randomly switching from one decision alternative to another.

These pure and mixed strategy solution procedures assume that the decision maker is faced with a two-party, constant sum game. As we saw, however, practical games typically involve multiple parties and variable sums. We saw how such games include the possibility of communication, cooperation, collusive agreements, and coalitions. Such features add considerable complexity to the analysis.

Glossary

analytic hierarchy process Multiple-criteria approach whereby manager breaks down problem into hierarchy of interrelated criteria, attributes, and alternatives, then compares and weights pairs of elements before assigning ratings for decision alternatives.

certainty equivalent The sure outcome that the decision maker considers equivalent to a lottery providing a p chance for the best and a $(1 - p)$ likelihood of the worst outcome in a decision problem.

constant marginal utility Property whereby the rate of increase in utility remains the same as monetary value increases.

constant sum game A game in which the outcomes to each participant sum to a constant value.

diminishing marginal return A consequence of risk aversion whereby the rate of increase in utility declines with growth in monetary value.

games Problems that involve a conflict situation between two or more competing parties, each of whom knows the decision outcomes but is uncertain about the opponent's actions and reactions.

game strategy A complete, predetermined plan for selecting a decision alternative for every possible circumstance. This plan should lead to the best expected outcome for the decision maker, regardless of the opponent's actions.

game table A table showing the outcomes associated with each combination of decision alternatives in a conflict situation.

game theory A framework for analyzing conflict situations.

increasing marginal utility Property whereby utility grows at a faster rate than monetary gain.

lottery indifference probability The probability that will make the decision maker indifferent to receiving a specified sure outcome or a risky lottery ticket. The lottery provides a p chance of earning the best possible outcome but a $(1 - p)$ likelihood of obtaining the worst payoff in a decision problem.

mixed strategy The strategy whereby a participant in a game randomly shifts from one decision alternative to another.

pure strategy The strategy whereby each party repeatedly selects only one decision alternative, regardless of the competitor's strategy.

return on investment The ratio of profit to cash requirements.

risk averse Willing to sacrifice some monetary value in order to avoid risk.

risk complex Displaying a combination of risk-averse, risk-neutral, and risk-seeking attitudes toward a range of monetary values.

risk neutral Neither seeking nor avoiding risk, but instead prizing money at its face value.

risk seeking Willing to take a high risk of a large loss in order to have an opportunity for a substantial gain.

saddle point The equilibrium solution formed when each participant in a game adopts a pure strategy.

utility A comprehensive criterion that incorporates absolute numerical measures (like monetary value) and intangible factors (such as attitudes and perceptions). It measures the true worth of the outcomes to the decision maker.

utility curve A graph that shows the relationship between monetary value and utility.

utility table A table that identifies the utility to management of each decision outcome.

value of the game The expected outcome of the conflict when each opponent repeatedly selects its optimal strategy.

variable sum game A game in which each combination of the opponents' decision alternatives typically will yield a different outcome sum to the participants.

zero sum game A game in which the gains of one participant are necessarily the equivalent losses to the opponent. It represents a special type of constant sum game in which the sum of the outcomes is always zero.

Thought Exercises

1. What is the most appropriate payoff measure in each of the following situations? Explain.

   a. A company is considering a transfer of its headquarters to a different geographical region. The move will be based on a combination of economic, political, and personal preference considerations.

   b. A large department store is considering the introduction of its own brand of men's shirts. The profitability of this new product will depend on the level of demand.

   c. A young couple used all their savings to purchase a new home. They are trying to decide how much (if any) fire insurance to take on the house.

2. Describe each of the following decision makers' attitudes toward risk. Explain.
   a. Ann Arturin is approached by an associate with an investment proposition. She is given the option of getting a guaranteed return of 10 percent or a lottery ticket. The lottery involves a 20 percent chance of getting a 5 percent return. Ann would be equally happy with either option.
   b. Robert Sane is a great baseball fan with a moderate amount of wealth. He is thinking of buying a baseball team. The selling price is $500,000. Robert will be happy if the expected profit equals the sales price. There is a 50 percent chance that the team will have a $3 million profit and a 50 percent chance of a $2 million loss.
   c. A struggling student has just enough money to get through the school term. A friend offers an 80 percent chance at winning $5,000. The bet will cost $1,000, which happens to be the total value of the student's assets. The student does not take the bet.

3. Amy Carter owns a house worth $60,000. Insurance statistics indicate that there is a probability of only .002 that the house will burn down this year. Hence, her expected loss from a fire that totally destroys the house is $60,000 × .002 = $120.

   A Global Insurance Company representative wants to sell Amy a fire insurance policy with a $300 premium this year. Amy buys the policy even though its expected cost ($300) is larger than the expected loss from a major fire ($120). Can you explain her action?

4. Ken Care is interested in his state's lottery. A ticket costs $2. If Ken wins, he will get $1 million. However, the probability of winning is only .000001. Thus, the expected monetary value (EMV) of the lottery ticket is

$$\text{EMV (ticket)} = \$1,000,000(.000001) + (-\$2)(.999999)$$

or $$\text{EMV (ticket)} = -\$0.999998.$$

   Ken buys the lottery ticket even though he can expect to lose about $1. That is, the expected monetary value of the lottery is negative ($-\$0.999998$). Can you explain his action?

5. A municipal library is considering the expansion of its reference section. The objectives are to attract federal grant money, provide increased community service, and enhance the library's reputation. A composite utility measure, ranging in value between 0 and 100, will be used to evaluate the program. Ultimately, the program's success depends on whether there will be favorable or unfavorable community acceptance. The situation is represented by the following utility table.

Decision Alternatives	States of Nature	
	s_1 = favorable community acceptance	s_2 = unfavorable community acceptance
a_1 = expand the reference section	90	10
a_2 = take	30	70

Utility value

Dianne Bookworth, the director of the library, is 80 percent confident that community acceptance will be favorable. On this basis, she decides to expand the reference section. Explain how Dianne arrived at her decision.

6. For each of the following, explain whether game theory is appropriate:
   a. A local gasoline station that wants to maximize its yearly profit
   b. Efforts of the postal service to maximize the "efficiency" of its delivery system
   c. The Vietnam War
   d. College football

7. What types of collusive arrangements or coalitions may exist in the following situations?
   a. Three major automobile manufacturers competing for a share of the market
   b. A running competition involving four teams each with three athletes
   c. The major petroleum companies competing for offshore drilling rights
   d. An auction

8. Explain whether each of the following games involves a zero sum:
   a. Two consumer products firms competing for a share of the laundry detergent market
   b. Two movie houses showing their major attractions at the same time
   c. Two men playing poker
   d. Two boxers' agents competing for a share of the purse

9. Adam McPhadom is known as the antibusiness congressman. In a recent senate committee meeting, McPhadom presented the following game situation. Two firms must decide whether or not to advertise. If neither company advertises, each makes $3,000 per month. When both advertise, each loses $10,000 per month. If company A advertises and company B does not, A gets $5,000 profit per month and B loses $15,000. When B advertises and A does not, A loses $20,000 and B makes $8,000 per month.

   According to McPhadom, this game shows that advertising leads to economically undesirable consequences. How did he arrive at this conclusion? Do you see anything wrong with his reasoning?

10. Two executives were participating in a seminar in game theory at a professional management conference. One said, "Game theory does attempt to show the actual competitive reactions we find in practice. However, it is inapplicable in all but exceptional circumstances." Can you explain this paradox? Use the tobacco, oil, and airline industries as guidelines in developing your answer.

11. Each year, a given number of new professional engineers join either Omicron or Phloton. The presidents of these societies want to select the recruitment policy that will maximize their new memberships. The situation is summarized in the following table, where entries represent the percentage of new engineers that join Phloton.

Phloton's Strategies	Omicron's Strategies	
	s_1 = a "hard sell" policy	s_2 = a "soft sell" policy
a_1 = use a "hard sell" recruitment policy	50	60
a_2 = use a "soft sell" recruitment policy	60	50

Phloton's president uses game theory to develop the society's optimal mixed strategy. Based on the analysis, the society decides to use a "hard sell" policy for the first six months of the recruiting year and then shift to a "soft sell" policy for the last six months. Phloton expected 55 percent of the new engineers to join their society. In actual practice, only 50 percent became members.

Show how Phloton arrived at its optimal mixed strategy and the expected payoff. Can you explain why actual membership did not meet expectations?

12. Do you agree or disagree with each of the following statements? Explain.
  a. There is a unique utility curve for every decision situation.
  b. We can select any initial utility values and still come up with relatively the same utility scale.
  c. A risk avoider's utility curve will have the same shape in a cost problem or a return problem.
  d. For a risk taker, the expected monetary value of the lottery is always greater than the guaranteed payoff.
  e. For a risk-neutral decision maker, the expected monetary value of the lottery is always equal to the guaranteed payoff.
  f. Game theory can be viewed as the special case of decision theory that involves active states of nature.
  g. A game exists when one competitor knows the probabilities of the other's strategies.
  h. Games may involve any number of players and any number of strategies for each competitor.
  i. A pure strategy solution is really a special case of dominance.
  j. Each of the game theory solution methods results in a saddle point.

Technique Exercises

13. A decision maker expresses the following indifference probabilities for a lottery having a payoff of $1,000 with probability p and a payoff of $0 with probability $(1 - p)$.

Outcome	Lottery Indifference Probability (p)
$800	.95
$600	.80
$400	.50
$200	.25

Assign a utility of 100 to the $1,000 payoff and a utility of 0 to the $0 outcome. Then find the utility value for each of the other outcomes.

14. Three decision makers express the following indifference probabilities for a lottery having a profit of $200,000 with probability p and a profit of $0 with probability $(1 - p)$.

Profit	Lottery Indifference Probability (p)		
	Person A	Person B	Person C
$150,000	.80	.60	.75
$100,000	.60	.40	.50
$50,000	.30	.10	.25

   a. Find the utility value of the payoffs for each decision maker. Use a utility of 100 for the best payoff and 0 for the worst payoff.

   b. Plot each decision maker's utility curve on the same graph.

   c. Describe each decision maker's attitude toward risk.

15. A manager has the following decision table.

Decision Alternatives	States of Nature			
	s_1	s_2	s_3	s_4
a_1	$2,000	−$1,000	−2,000	−$4,000
a_2	$6,000	$2,000	$0	−$1,000
a_3	$10,000	$6,000	$2,000	−$5,000

The manager has the following lottery indifference probabilities for the profits in the decision table.

Profit	Lottery Indifference Probability (p)
$6,000	.60
$2,000	.20
$0	.10
−$1,000	.05
−$2,000	.02
−$4,000	.01

   a. Find a utility value for each profit in the decision table. Assign a utility of 100 to the best payoff and 0 to the worst payoff.

   b. Develop the utility table.

   c. Graph the decision maker's utility curve.

   d. Describe the decision maker's attitude toward risk.

16. A manager has the following decision table.

Decision Alternatives	States of Nature		
	s_1	s_2	s_3
a_1	$200	$400	$500
a_2	$500	$100	$100 ← Cost
a_3	$400	$200	$100

The manager also has the following lottery indifference probabilities: $p = .6$ for $200 and $p = .2$ for $400.

   a. Find the utility value for each profit in the decision table, assigning a utility of 100 to the best payoff and 0 to the worst payoff. Develop the utility table.

   b. Find the utility value for each profit in the decision table, assigning a utility of 200 to the best payoff and −100 to the worst payoff. Develop the utility table.

   c. Assume that $P(s_1) = .3, P(s_2) = .4$, and $P(s_3) = .3$. What is the recommended expected monetary value decision?

d. Using the probabilities in part (c), what is the expected utility recommendation when we use the values in part (a)?

e. What is the expected utility recommendation when we use the values in part (b)?

f. Compare the results in parts (d) and (e). What do you find?

17. You are given the following decision data.

Decision Alternative	State of Nature	Value of Attribute (units)	
		A	B
a_1	s_1	100	50
a_1	s_2	250	25
a_1	s_3	400	10
a_2	s_1	300	60
a_2	s_2	200	80
a_2	s_3	150	150

a. Develop the decision table.

b. If $P(s_1) = .4$ and $P(s_2) = .5$, which decision alternative maximizes the value of attribute A? Which alternative minimizes the value of attribute B? Explain.

c. Suppose attribute A has the highest priority, but the expected value of B must not exceed 75. If it is desirable to have high values of A but low values of B, which alternative do you recommend?

d. Assume that a composite measure can be formed by dividing the value of attribute B into the value of attribute A. Develop an appropriate decision table and then select the alternative that maximizes the expected value of this composite measure. Which alternative minimizes the expected value of this measure?

e. Suppose the appropriate composite measure is found by dividing the value of attribute A into the value of attribute B. Show how this new composite measure changes the analysis in part (d).

f. What is the main decision-making implication of all these results?

18. A tire manufacturer is considering various locations in a particular geographical area for a franchise retail store. After careful consideration, the company represents the problem with the following decision table. Note that there is a $P(s_1) = .6$ probability of economic growth.

Decision Alternatives	States of Nature	
	s_1 = economic growth	s_2 = economic stagnation
a_1 = locate in Beachtown	annual sales = $400,000 market share = 10% annual profit = $30,000	annual sales = $250,000 market share = 25% annual profit = $20,000
a_2 = locate in Sun City	annual sales = $200,000 market share = 20% annual profit = $31,000	annual sales = $150,000 market share = 8% annual profit = $18,500
a_1 = locate in Oldville	annual sales = $100,000 market share = 15% annual profit = $22,000	annual sales = $175,000 market share = 17.5% annual profit = $32,000

a. Suppose that the company's objectives, in rank order, are to maximize expected profit, attain the largest expected market share, and achieve the highest expected sales. Which decision alternative do you recommend? Explain.

b. Assume that management has the following lottery indifference probabilities.

Annual Profit		Market Share		Annual Sales	
Outcome ($)	Lottery Indifference Probability (p)	Outcome (%)	Lottery Indifference Probability (p)	Outcome ($)	Lottery Indifference Probability (p)
32,000	Does not apply	25	Does not apply	400,000	Does not apply
31,000	.95	20	.70	250,000	.50
30,000	.90	17.5	.50	200,000	1/3
22,000	.40	15	.35	175,000	.25
20,000	.25	10	.10	150,000	1/6
18,500	Does not apply	8	Does not apply	100,000	Does not apply

For each attribute, assign a utility value of 100 to the best outcome and a value of 0 to the worst payoff. Next, find the utility values for the other outcomes. Then describe the decision maker's attitude toward risk.

c. Suppose the company could sum the individual values for each attribute to form a multiattribute utility assessment. Develop the resulting multiattribute utility table. Which decision alternative leads to the maximum expected utility?

19. The production manager in an assembly plant has a problem that can be described by the following decision table. There is a $P(s_1) = .7$ chance that operations will be normal.

Decision Alternatives	States of Nature	
	$s_1 = $ normal operations	$s_2 = $ extended operations
$a_1 = $ use process X	production cost = $50,000 output = 450	production cost = $80,000 output = 550
$a_2 = $ use process Y	production cost = $90,000 output = 500	production cost = $70,000 output = 700
$a_3 = $ use process Z	production cost = $40,000 output = 400	production cost = $100,000 output = 200

a. Calculate the expected production cost and the expected output for each decision alternative. Which alternative minimizes the expected production cost? Which alternative maximizes the expected output?

b. Assume that output has the highest priority. However, management does not want the expected cost to exceed $60,000. Which alternative should management select? Explain.

c. Suppose management wanted to express the problem in terms of cost per unit of output. Develop the decision table that corresponds to this single composite measure. Which alternative minimizes the cost per unit of output? Explain.

d. The production manager has expressed the following lottery indifference probabilities.

Production Cost		Output	
Outcome ($)	Lottery Indiffernce Probability (p)	Outcome (units)	Lottery Indifference Probability (p)
40,000	Does not apply	700	Does not apply
50,000	.90	550	.65
70,000	.75	500	.50
80,000	.55	450	.35
90,000	.20	400	.10
100,000	Does not apply	200	Does not apply

For each attribute, assign a utility value of 100 to the best outcome and a value of 0 to the worst payoff. Next, find the utility values for the other outcomes. Then describe the manager's attitude toward risk. What do you find?

e. Suppose the manager assigns equal weight to each attribute. Develop a multiattribute utility assessment for each decision outcome. Express each multiattribute utility assessment in terms of a value beten 0 and 100. Use these results to transform the decision table into a multiattribute utility table. Which alternative leads to the maximum expected utility?

f. If the manager thought that output was three times as important as production cost, would you change the recommendation in part (e)? Explain.

20. A multiple-criteria problem involves the decision hierarchy shown below. In addition, attribute 1 is one and one half times as important as attribute 2 in achieving the overall decision criterion. Alternative A generates three times as much of attribute 1 as alternative B. On the other hand, alternative B has five times as much of attribute 2 as alternative A. What alternative should the decision maker select? Why?

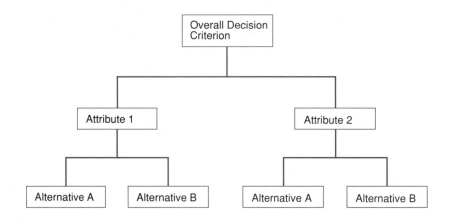

21. In each of the following games, the entries represent payoffs to player A, and the constant sum is either 0 or 10. Determine whether any of the games involves a pure strategy solution. Identify the pure strategy solution if it exists.

A's Alternatives	B's Alternatives	
	s_1	s_2
a_1	2	−3
a_2	−4	1

Game 1

A's Alternatives	B's Alternatives	
	s_1	s_2
a_1	4	7
a_2	3	8

Game 2

A's Alternatives	B's Alternatives	
	s_1	s_2
a_1	3	−5
a_2	4	−10

Game 3

22. You are given the following zero sum game.

A's Alternatives	B's Alternatives	
	s_1	s_2
a_1	−18	25
a_2	30	−15

  a. Find the $P(s_1)$ and $P(s_2)$ that equate the expected value of a_1 to the expected payoff of a_2. Show your results graphically.
  b. Find the $P(a_1)$ and $P(a_2)$ that make the expected outcomes from s_1 and s_2 the same value. Show your results graphically.
  c. Use the resulting probabilities to determine the value of the game. Show your results graphically.

23. You are given the following constant sum game. The constant sum is 25.

A's Alternatives	B's Alternatives		
	s_1	s_2	s_3
a_1	10	15	20
a_2	15	10	5
a_3	8	6	5

  a. Use the dominance concept to find the relevant game.
  b. Determine each participant's optimal mixed strategies and the value of the game. Show the results graphically.

24. You are given the following zero sum game.

A's Alternatives	B's Alternatives			
	s_1	s_2	s_3	s_4
a_1	5	−3	2	4
a_2	0	−4	1	4
a_3	6	2	2	1

  a. Use the dominance concept to find the relevant game.
  b. Determine each participant's optimal mixed strategies and the value of the game. Show your results graphically.

25. Consider the following situation faced by two neighborhood gas stations, each of which wants weekly sales to be as large as possible.

Union Stop's Alternatives	Mobiline's Alternatives	
	s_1 = keep prices the same	s_2 = reduce prices
a_1 = keep prices the same	Union's weekly sales = 1,300 gallons Mobilines's weekly sales = 1,200 gallons	Union's weekly sales = 900 gallons Mobilines's weekly sales = 1,400 gallons
a_2 = reduce prices	Union's weekly sales = 1,500 gallons Mobilines's weekly sales = 800 gallons	Union's weekly sales = 1,100 gallons Mobilines's weekly sales = 1,050 gallons

a. Develop a separate game table for each participant.
b. Use game theory to determine the optimal strategies and the value of the game for each participant.
c. Is there a better solution? Explain.

Applications Exercises

26. Two management trainees for a department store chain are being evaluated for promotion. An important part of the evaluation process deals with the trainee's attitude toward risk. Each person is presented with the following situation. The chain has recently purchased land for a shopping center development in a suburban town. Various sizes of development are possible, but uncertain economic conditions make it difficult to ascertain the demand for the store's facilities. An oversized facility could be very costly to the chain. Yet an undersized store will unnecessarily limit the chain's profits. The possible profits are $2 million, $1 million, $500,000, $0, −$500,000, and −$1 million.

The trainees are asked to state a preference between a guaranteed profit and the following lottery:

Lottery: The trainee gets a $2 million profit with probability p and −$1 million with probability $(1 - p)$.

Trainee Al is indifferent between a guaranteed profit of $1 million and this lottery when $p = .8$. His other indifference probabilities are $p = .6$ when the guaranteed profit is $500,000, $p = .4$ when it is $0, and $p = .2$ when it is −$500,000. On the other hand, trainee Alice is indifferent between a guaranteed profit of $1 million and the lottery when $p = .6$. Her other indifference probabilities are $p = .45$ when the guaranteed profit is $500,000, $p = .3$ when it is $0, and $p = .1$ when it is −$500,000.

If the company prefers risk-avoiding managers, which trainee has the best chance for promotion?

27. The public-service television network has been receiving low ratings for its 5–7 P.M. time slot. Currently, management is considering three alternatives for this slot: a sports show, travel films, or a political discussion program. The percent of viewing audience estimates depends on the demographic characteristics of the viewers. Audiences are demographically classified as "family-oriented" or "sensation-oriented." Market research indicates that the network can expect 10 percent of a family-oriented audience to view the sports show telecast; 5 percent of a family-oriented audience can be expected to view travel films; and 40 percent of this audience will watch the political discussion program. Among the sensation-oriented viewers, the network can expect 20 percent to watch the sports show, 25 percent to view travel films, and 5 percent to watch the political program.

The network public relations executive is completely optimistic and wants to select the program that leads to the best percentage of the viewing audience. Which program should this executive select?

The program manager points out the risk involved and believes that the network should incorporate this factor into the analysis. This manager suggests using utility as the appropriate payoff measure. He assigns a utility of 100 to the best payoff and a utility of 0 to the worst payoff. Then the manager assigns the following lottery indifference probabilities to the other payoffs:

Percent of Audience	Lottery Indifference Probability (p)
25	.7
20	.5
10	.2

The program manager wants the network to select the format that leads to the maximum expected utility. He believes that there is a 70 percent likelihood that audiences will be "sensation oriented." Which program should this executive select?

28. Storage Inc. is considering purchasing a theft insurance policy for its warehouse in New York. The policy has an annual cost of $20,000. If there is a minor theft, the company anticipates a cost of $200,000. A major theft would cost $1 million. Insurance records indicate that there is a 95 percent chance of no theft and a 4 percent chance of a minor theft.

After considering the risk and other related factors, company executives believe that utility is the appropriate payoff measure. The company president assigns a utility value of 100 to the best payoff and a utility value of 0 to the worst payoff. His indifference probabilities are $p = .01$ for the $20,000 cost and $p = .1$ for the $200,000 cost. the company president wants to maximize expected utility.

Should the company buy the policy? What is the price that the company president is apparently willing to pay to avoid the risk of theft?

29. An investor can buy stock in company A, company B, or both A and B. The return on investment depends on general economic conditions. Historically, there has been prosperity 10 percent of the time, stagnation 55 percent of the time, and recession 35 percent of the time. If she buys stock in A, the return will be $10,000 no matter what economic conditions occur. Stock in B has an expected return of $20,000 in prosperity, $2,000 with stagnation, and a loss of $10,000 in recession.

However, the investor is also concerned with risk and other intangible factors. Consequently, the investments will be evaluated in terms of their utility to the decision maker. The investor's utility values are given as follows:

Return ($ thousand)	Utility
30	100
20	90
12	80
10	70
2	55
0	50
−10	0

a. Which investment leads to maximum expected utility?

b. Which investment leads to the maximum expected dollar return?

c. What is the difference in expected monetary value between the two recommendations? Can you rationalize this difference?

30. Sally Tally, a recent college graduate, is considering three job offers. The possibilities are a position in personnel management with the telephone company, a job as a financial analyst with a bank, and a job as a salesperson in real estate. Several factors are important to Sally. She is concerned with salary, fringe benefits, and advancement possibilities. Fringe benefits are expressed as a percentage of salary, while advancement opportunites are measured by the anticipated salary increments.

The attribute values for each position depend on economic conditions. After considering all relevant data, Sally has compiled the following information about the attributes: In this table, base salaries, fringe benefits, and salary increments are expressed as annual averages adjusted for inflation and discounted to present values over Sally's three-year planning horizon. Furthermore, government statistics indicate that there is a 50 percent likelihood of a growing economy.

| Position | Growing Economy | | | Declining Economy | | |
	Annual Base Salary ($)	Annual Fringe Benefits ($)	Annual Salary Increments ($)	Annual Base Salary ($)	Annual Fringe Benefits ($)	Annual Salary Increments ($)
Telephone company personnel manager	20,000	6,000	1,000	18,000	5,500	500
Bank financial analyst	24,000	4,500	1,500	16,000	3,500	500
Real estate sales	25,000	4,000	2,000	15,000	3,000	0

If Sally wants to maximize the expected total dollar worth of the job attributes, which offer should she accept? Suppose that expected base salary has the highest priority and that the second most important attribute is the possibility of advancement. Also, Sally wants the positon to provide at least $4,000 in annual fringe benefits. Under these circumstances, which job offer should she accept?

31. A tornado has recently swept through a southwestern state, leaving vast areas utterly destroyed. Among such areas is one rural county with a long history of low income and

high unemployment. The state planning commission is asked to recommend a general land-use program for the region. Public hearings are held to identify the priorities of such a program. The consensus is that the plan should provide for recreation, encourage employment opportunities, and conserve the natural beauty of the area. After careful deliberation, the commission proposes the following alternatives:

- Fully exploit the recreational potential of the area with parks, beaches, campsites, etc.

- Set aside the tillable land for agriculture only and use the rest for a community of vacation homes.

- Use the land only as a state forest preserve with hiking trails but very limited service factilities.

Each alternative is expected to provide some land for recreation, jobs and wilderness areas. The specific amounts of these attributes will depend on future regional socioeconomic conditions. In this respect, it is possible to have either a growth in population density and per capita income or a stable population with declining per capita income. The commission feels that there is a 65 percent chance of population and income growth.

A preliminary study provides the following data:

	Population/Income Growth			Stable Population/Declining Income		
Land Use Alternatives	Recreational Land (Thousand Acres)	Jobs (Thousands)	Wilderness Area (Thousand Acres)	Recreational Land (Thousand Acres)	Jobs (Thousands)	Wilderness Area (Thousand Acres)
Parks/Beaches	20	150	10	15	125	12
Agriculture	12	275	14	11	200	17
State forest	16	100	20	13	75	22

Recreational Land		Jobs		Wilderness Area	
Outcome (Thousand Acres)	Lottery Indifference Probability (p)	Outcome (Thousand Jobs)	Lottery Indifference Probability (p)	Outcome (Thousand Acres)	Lottery Indifference Probability (p)
20	Does not apply	275	Does not apply	22	Does not apply
16	.50	200	.625	20	.95
15	.40	150	.375	17	.70
13	.20	125	.250	14	.50
12	.10	100	.125	12	.25
11	Does not apply	75	Does not apply	10	Does not apply

Alternatives will be evaluated by a utility measure that consolidates aspects of the consensus priorities. To facilitiate such an analysis, the commission develops the following lottery indifference probabilities regarding the attribute outcomes. Each attribute is equally important to the commission.

If the commissioners want to select the program that maximizes expected utility, which alternative should they recommend?

32. A consumer wants to select the best television satellite dish, but the decision is difficult because each of the two available products is both powerful and stylish. Power is twice as important to the consumer as style. The latest independent reports suggest that the Clear Channel brand is three times as powerful as the Hideaway brand. However, these reports also rate the Hideaway as six times more stylish than the Clear channel.

    Based on this information, what satellite dish should the consumer purchase? Explain the recommendation (complete with illustrations) in language that would be understandable to the consumer.

33. Southwest and Heartland railroads will each purchase a computerized dispatching system. Dynamo, Inc. and Electron Corp. are trying to get the railroads to adopt their systems. Research indicates that the probability of a sale is directly related to the relative number of sales calls. For example, if Dynamo sends two salespeople and Electron sends one, then Dynamo has a two-thirds, or a 67 percent, chance of making a sale. When neither sends any salespeople, each has a 50 percent chance of obtaining the business. Currently, Dynamo has three salespeople available, while Electron has only two. Geography and time considerations make it necessary for the manufacturers to have different salespeople call on each railroad. For instance, one of Dynamo's alternatives would be to have all three people call on Southwest. Or the company could send two people to Southwest and one to Heartland. And so on. Similarly, Electron could send both salespeople to Southwest, one to each railroad or both to Heartland.

    Each manufacturer wants to get the largest expected number of sales. How many salespeople should each firm send to each railroad? What is the expected number of sales for each manufacturer?

34. Quesar is a developing oil sheikdom in the Middle East. Zambisee Motors and Stophagle, Inc. are the only two manufacturers granted permits to sell automobiles to the goverment staff. Zambisee calls its car the Executive, while Stophagle calls its car the Luxurus. Each company's profits depend on the marketing mix actions of the two firms. Past experience has enabled each to know the mixes that the others intends to adopt and the resulting market shares. However, each is still uncertain about the proportions of the mixes.

    Zambisee's possible marketing policies are as follows:

    ▪   A price of $10,000 with annual marketing expenditures of $500,000
    ▪   A price of $15,000 with annual marketing expenditures of $600,000

    Stophagle could adopt the following policies:

    ▪   A price of $12,000 with annual marketing expenditures of $1,200,000
    ▪   A price of $15,000 with annual marketing expenditures of $1,300,000

    In similar markets in the past, when Zambisee has adopted the first policy, the company has obtained a 70 percent share if Stophagle has used its first policy. Zambisee has received a 60 percent share when Stophagle has employed its second action. When Zambisee has used its second policy, the company has obtained a 20 percent share if Stophagle has gone with its first policy. Zambisee's market share has been 70 percent when Stophagle has played its second action.

    What strategy should each employ? What market share can each firm expect?

35. Two lawyers are trying a civil suit involving substantial financial damages. The attorneys have faced each other under similar circumstances in the past. Sally Fine typically adopts one of three alternatives: aggression, a reconciling attitude, or a legally technical approach. On the other hand, Mort Tort usually uses either trickery or deceit.

   The lawyers are representing the insurers of the litigants. The loser will have to pay financial damages to the winner of the trial. If Sally uses aggression, her client will win $50,000 when Mort tries trickery and $100,000 when Mort tries deceit. Furthermore, when Mort is deceitful, his client will win $30,000 if Sally takes a reconciling attitude and $50,000 if she takes a legally technical approach. Also, if Mort uses trickery, Sally's client will win $10,000 when she adopts a reconciling attitude and $60,000 when she uses the legally technical alternative.

   What strategy should each lawyer adopt? What is each insurer's expected financial gain or loss?

36. The United States and the Soviet Union are negotiating a space territorial treaty. Samuel Spade, the American delegate, and Igor Ivanov, the Russian representative, have bargained many times in past similar circumtstances. Igor knows that Samuel will be defiant or compromising, and Samuel knows that Igor has the same two alternatives.

   In this particular session, the parties are negotiating the number of military craft each will allow in a given sector of outer space. Through previous similar bargaining, Samuel and Igor each have some idea of the possible outcomes for the various alternatives.

   When Samuel is defiant, the United States will be allowed 10 craft if Igor is defiant and 26 if the Russian is compromising. But if Samuel is compromising, his country will obtain only 8 vehicles when Igor is defiant but 20 vehicles if the Russian compromises. On the other hand, when Igor is defiant, the Soviet Union will be allowed 10 craft if Samuel is defiant and 28 when the American compromises. However, if Igor is compromising, his country will obtain only 7 vehicles when Samuel is defiant but 20 if the American compromises.

   Communication and cooperation are encouraged by the leaders of the two governments, but each country wants to obtain the best possible treaty. Which strategy should each negotiator adopt? What is the outcome that each country can expect from the resulting treaty?

For Further Reading

Utility Theory

Bell, D. E., and P. H. Farquhar. "Perspectives on Utility Theory." *Operations Research* (January–February 1986):179.

Fishburn, P. C. *Utility Theory for Decision Making.* New York: Wiley, 1970.

Laskey, K. B., and G. W. Fischer. "Estimating Utility Functions in the Presence of Response Error." *Management Science* (August 1987):965.

Multiple Criteria Decision Making

Brans, J. P., and P. H. Vincke. "A Preference Ranking Organisation Method." *Management Science* (June 1985):647.

Jensen, R. E. "Comparison of Consensus Methods for Priority Ranking Problems." *Decision Sciences* (Spring 1986):195.

Klein, G., et al. "Assessment of Multiattributed Measurable Value and Utility Functions via Mathematical Programming." *Decision Sciences* (Summer 1985):309.

Minch, R. P., and G. L. Sanders. "Computerized Information Systems Supporting Multicriteria Decision Making." *Decision Sciences* (Summer 1986):395.

Rosenthal, R. E. "Principles of Multiobjective Optimization." *Decision Sciences* (Spring 1985):133.

Zahedi, F. "The Analytic Hierarchy Process—A Survey of the Method and Its Applications." *Interfaces* (July–August 1986):96.

Zeleny, M. *Multiple Criteria Decision Making.* New York: McGraw-Hill, 1982.

Game Theory

Shubik, M. *The Uses and Methods of Game Theory*. New York: Elsevier-North Holland, 1975.

Spinetto, R. D. "Fairness in Cost Allocations and Cooperative Games." *Decision Sciences* (July 1975):482.

Wilson, J. G. "Subjective Probability and the Prisoner's Dilemma." *Management Science* (January 1986):45.

Finance Applications

Bell, R., and T. M. Cover, "Game-Theoretic Optimal Portfolios." *Management Science* (June 1988): 724–733.

Golabi, K., et al. "Selecting a Portfolio of Solar Energy Projects Using Multiattribute Preference Theory." *Management Science* (February 1981):174.

Haung, C. L., et al. *Multiple Objective Decision Making, Methods, and Applications: A State of the Art Survey*. New York: Springer-Verlag, 1979.

Levy, H., and M. Sarnat. *Financial Decision Making under Uncertainty*. New York: Academic Press, 1977.

Reece, D. K. "Competitive Bidding for Offshore Petroleum Leases." *Bell Journal of Economics* (Autumn 1978):369.

Marketing Applications

Shane, H. D. "Mathematical Models for Economic and Political Advertising Campaigns." *Operations Research* (January–February 1977):1.

Sorenson, J. R., et al. "A Game Theoretic Approach to Peak Load Pricing." *Bell Journal of Economics* (Autumn 1976):497.

Wolf, G., and M. Shubik. "Market Structure, Opponent Behavior, and Information in the Market Game." *Decision Sciences* (July 1978):421.

Zusman, P., and M. Etgar. "The Marketing Channel as an Equilibrium Set of Contracts." *Management Science* (March 1981):284.

Production/Operations Applications

Bowen, K. C. *Research Games: An Approach to the Study of Decision Processes*. New York: Halsted Press, 1978.

Brams, S. J. "The Network Television Game: There May Be No Best Schedule." *Interfaces* (August 1977):102.

Harsanyi, J. C. *Rational Behavior and Bargaining Equilibrium in Games and Social Situations*. New York: Cambridge University Press, 1977.

Keeney, R. L. et al., "An Analysis of Baltimore Gas and Electric Company's Technology Choice," *Operations Research* (January–February 1986): 18–39.

McKelvey, R. D. "A Theory of Optimal Agenda Design." *Management Science* (March 1981):303.

Public Sector/Nonprofit Applications

Cox, L. A. "A New Measure of Attributable Risk for Public Health Applications." *Management Science* (July 1985):800.

Friedman, Y. "Optimal Strategy for the One-against-many Battle." *Operations Research* (September–October 1977):884.

Littechild, S. C., and G. F. Thompson. "Aircraft Landing Fees: A Game Theory Approach." *Bell Journal of Economics* (Spring 1977):186.

Washburn, A. R. "Search-Evasion Game in a Fixed Region." *Operations Research* (October–November 1980):1290.

Case: Rural Vehicles, Inc.

Rural Vehicles, Inc., is a small rural distributor of agricultural vehicles in central Iowa. There are no competitors in the vicinity. Combines are the most popular vehicle, and the company places one order for this equipment each March. Although past experience indicated that Rural will sell no more than four combines during the season, the exact demand is known. However, historical records provide the following data:

Combines Sold	Probability
0	.0625
1	.2500
2	.3750
3	.2500
4	.0625

Rural will have the following expenses this year:

Mortgage	$20,000
Office supplies	500
Electricity, gas and telephone	1,500
Salaries	30,000
Promotion	8,000
Total	$60,000

This year, a combine wholesales for $40,000. rural will sell it for $50,000. There is also a rebate deal with the manufacturer. At the end of the season, all unsold combines are returned to the supplier. Rural then receives cost plus 5 percent. However, it costs Rural approximately 10 percent of its total expenses to hold a combine for the entire season. In addition, if a combine is not available at Rural, a customer will buy elsewhere. A lost sale, including loss of potential service revenue, will cost Rural an estimated $12,000 per combine.

Rural's owner, U. R. Wright, wants to order the number of combines that will maximize the expected return on the economic investment. Wright defines this return as the ratio of profit to total costs, where costs are equal to expenses plus the combine holding cost plus lost service revenue. Wright's wife, Unifer, thinks that such a measure does not fully account for the risk and other intangibles involved in the problem. In her opinion, they first should separately establish the total worth of the profit and total cost attributes to the company. This total worth would reflect the monetary value of these attributes and U. R. and Unifer's personal assessment of the inherent risk and other intangibles. In this respect, Unifer wants to avoid risk. The individual total worths next could be consolidated into an overall assessment of total worth. Then the company would order the number of combines that maximizes the expected overall total worth.

Suppose that you are brought in as a consultant.

1. Develop the decision table in terms of U. R.'s return measure.

2. Set up the lotteries that would be involved in a utility analysis of this problem.

3. There are many sets of lottery indifference probabilities that a risk avoider might have for the monetary values in this problem. Assume that you and Unifer have exactly the same risk-avoiding viewpoint. Identify your lottery indifference probabilities (and Unifer's) for each attribute in this problem.

4. How many combines would the company order if it used U. R.'s return on economic investment measure? What is the probability that Rural will not satisfy demand with this policy?

5. How many combines would the company order if it used Unifer's overall total worth measure with U. R.'s view toward risk? Explain.

6. How many combines would you (and Unifer) order? What is the probability that Rural will not meet demand with this policy?

7. Demand for combines will depend on the age of existing machines, the amount farmers plant, and many other factors. Assume that the crop size is the only variable factor in this particular season. In this respect, there are many farmers from other areas competing with Rural's customers for shares of the same relatively fixed crop market. Consequently, the demand for the crops of Rural's customers, and thus its combine sales, could be determined by a game process between the two competing farmer groups. How would this possibility affect the analysis? Explain.

Prepare a report outlining this information in a form that would be understandable to U. R. and Unifer Wright.

Part III

Mathematical Programming

THE previous chapters have dealt with the general topic of quantitative decision making. We showed how to identify and classify decision situations, develop a framework for analyzing each of these general situations, and generate a recommended solution. In the remainder of the text, our focus will shift from these general situations to specific types of decision problems.

Many of these problems are centered around the best way to achieve the objectives of the enterprise in the face of environmental constraints. These constraints can take the form of limited resources (such as time, labor, energy, material, and money) or restrictive guidelines (such as nutritional recipes and engineering specifications). Management scientists have developed a body of knowledge, known as mathematical programming, designed to solve such problems.

The most widely used mathematical programming approach, linear programming, is introduced in Chapter 7. Typical linear programming models are formulated, characteristics are discussed, and the graphic solution method is developed. Chapter 8 discusses the simplex method, an efficient procedure for solving the large-scale problems encountered in practice. Other relevant solution topics and special situations are also considered.

Important products of a linear programming analysis are the economic values of the scarce resources. Chapter 9 shows how to determine and interpret these values. In addition, this chapter shows how to analyze the decision impact of potential changes in the values of the uncontrollable inputs. It also presents an appropriate computer analysis.

Linear programming is based on a set of rather restrictive assumptions. The final chapter of this part, Chapter 10, discusses these assumptions and presents the limitations of a linear programming analysis. Other relevant methodologies, including integer, goal, and nonlinear programming, are then identified and developed.

After reading this part of the text, you should be able to:

- Identify situations that can be effectively analyzed with mathematical programming approaches.
- Identify the relevant mathematical programming methodology.
- Formulate various types of mathematical programming problems.
- Solve these problems graphically, algebraically, and with the aid of available computer packages.
- Interpret the results.
- Develop other appropriate decision information from the results.

This background will facilitate your understanding of later parts of the text.

Linear Programming

Chapter Outline

Learning Objectives

- Identify the nature and characteristics of a linear programming problem
- Understand how to formulate linear programs
- Examine various linear programming applications
- Solve simple linear programs with a graphic approach
- Interpret the solution and utilize the results in decision making

Stemming the Flood

THE Investment Fund Services (IFS), an organization within Canada Systems Group Incorporated, provides a variety of processing activities for its clients. From the beginning, IFS was the only firm in the transaction processing business large enough to handle the high seasonal registered retirement savings plans (RRSP) contributions.

During the spring of 1984, there was an unanticipated 100 percent growth in transaction volume. A series of ad hoc measures were implemented to deal with the crisis. Unfortunately, the measures resulted in processing errors, unnecessary paperwork, lengthy delays, significant overtime, under-utilization of staff, and high personnel turnover. These conditions increased IFS's labor-related costs by $500,000 for the short six-week RRSP season. The situation also damaged the organization's reputation.

A new operations manager and two staff members, all with some management science background, were hired to plan for a successful 1985 RRSP season. After studying the problem, these people realized that linear programming could be used to help management systematically plan the RRSP season's staffing requirements. Indeed, by using such an approach, IFS was able to save, despite higher wage rates and 25 percent greater volume, about $320,000 in labor-related costs during the six weeks of the 1985 season. The savings represented a 188 percent productivity gain over 1984. IFS's restored reputation helped the company to receive contract renewals from nearly all major clients and to successfully bid for new related business.

Source: C. H. von Lanzenauer et al., "RRSP Flood: LP to the Rescue," *Interfaces* (July–August 1987):27–33.

The Investment Fund Services (IFS) must systematically plan staffing requirements to meet transaction demand during the six-week RRSP season. Everyone, at one time or another, will face similar situations. As a student, for example, you must plan the time needed for studying, sleeping, eating, and recreation during the academic year. Since financial resources are usually limited, you also must make difficult decisions regarding the utilization of funds.

Managers in all types of organizations also have the problem of allocating scarce resources among competing activities. Limited resources (including machinery, labor, materials, physical space, time, and money) are available to produce various products (such as furniture, food, and automobiles) or services (such as advertising strategies, investment plans, and shipping schedules). Typically, there are many competing ways to produce these products and services. Furthermore, the environment may impose guidelines (such as contract terms and engineering specifications) that restrict the ways in which the resources can be transformed into products or services. Management must decide which activities most effectively use the firm's resources and meet the restrictive guidelines.

A methodology, called **linear programming**, has been developed to help managers (such as IFS's operations manager) make such decisions in the best interests of the organizational unit. This unit may be the overall enterprise (as in the IFS case) or some department within the firm. In fact, the methodology has been used successfully at many organizational levels in all types of industries, including manufacturing, financial services, transportation, energy, education, and government.

This chapter introduces linear programming. It describes the characteristics of the methodology, shows how to formulate various linear programs, develops a graphic solution procedure, and examines how the results can be used in decision making. Such material also serves as a foundation for the large-scale solution procedures and management extensions that will be discussed in later chapters.

Applications. In this chapter, the following applications appear in text, examples, and exercises:

- Air Force operations
- audit staffing
- cargo loading
- capital budgeting
- computer systems design
- dental insurance
- diet selection
- equipment leasing
- fertilizer composition
- flight scheduling

- government appropriations
- information center operations
- machine shop management
- media selection
- political campaigning
- production scheduling
- purchasing
- sales force deployment
- school busing
- waste management

7.1 CHARACTERISTICS

Every linear programming problem will have the same essential characteristics. The manager will need a firm understanding of these characteristics and the underlying assumptions that create the properties. Otherwise, he or she could misuse the methodology and make bad decisions.

Problem Form

All linear programming problems will have the same general form. There will be an objective and a finite number of restrictions on the objective. Management Situation 7.1 illustrates.

Machine Shop Management

Saferly, Inc., manufactures two types of kitchen utensils: knives and forks. Both must be pressed and polished. The shop manager estimates that there will be a maximum of 70 hours available next week in the pressing machine center and 100 hours in the polishing center. Each case of knives requires an estimated 12 minutes (0.2 hour) of pressing and 30 minutes (0.5 hour) of polishing, while each case of forks requires 24 minutes (0.4 hour) of pressing and 15 minutes (0.25 hour) of polishing. The company can sell as many knives as it produces at the prevailing market price of $12 per case. Forks can be sold for $9 per case. It costs $4 to produce a case of knives and $3 to produce a case of forks. Saferly wants to determine how many cases of knives and forks the company should produce to maximize total dollar profit.

Objective. Saferly's total dollar profit will equal the contribution from knives plus the contribution from forks. Since it costs $4 to produce each case of knives, and since each case can be sold for $12, there is a contribution to profit of $12 − $4 = $8 per case of knives. The $8-per-case contribution multiplied by the number of cases will then give the total dollar profit from knives. Similarly, each case of forks can be produced for $3 and sold for $9. Hence, forks have a profit contribution of $9 − $3 = $6 per case. This $6-per-case contribution multiplied by the number of cases gives the total profit from forks.

By letting

X_1 = the number of cases of knives Saferly produces next week

X_2 = the number of cases of forks Saferly produces next week

Z = Saferly's total dollar profit

we can represent Saferly's total dollar profit by

$$Z = \$8X_1 + \$6X_2$$

Company management has the discretion of setting the output levels (number of knives and forks produced). Thus X_1 and X_2 represent the controllable inputs in this problem. In linear programming, these controllable inputs are referred to as **decision variables**.

   The company wants to choose the levels of the decision variables (X_1 and X_2) that maximize total dollar profit (Z). This objective can be expressed as

$$\text{maximize } Z = \$8X_1 + \$6X_2$$

Such an expression, which gives the precise mathematical relationship between the decision variables and the criterion value, is called the **objective function**.

Restrictions. Available pressing and polishing capacity will limit the number of knives and forks that Saferly can produce. Since each case of knives uses 0.2 hour of pressing time, $0.2 \times X_1$ is the total time required to press X_1 knives. In addition, each case of forks uses 0.4 hour of pressing time. Hence, $0.4 \times X_2$ is the total time required to press X_2 forks. Consequently,

$$0.2X_1 + 0.4X_2$$

gives the total time required to press X_1 knives and X_2 forks.

Saferly can select any product combination that does not require more total pressing time than the 70 hours available. In other words, management must satisfy the following condition:

(7.3)　　　　　　　　$\underbrace{0.2X_1 + 0.4X_2}_{\substack{\text{Total pressing} \\ \text{time required}}} \leq \underbrace{70 \text{ hours}}_{\substack{\text{Total pressing} \\ \text{time available}}}$

where the symbol $\leq$ means "less than or equal to." Such an expression, which gives a restriction on the decision variables that limits the criterion value, is known as a **system**, **technological**, or **structural constraint**.

Another system constraint deals with polishing operations. In particular, management knows that each case of knives uses 0.5 hour and each case of forks uses 0.25 hour of polishing time. Since there are only 100 hours of polishing time available,

$$\underbrace{0.5X_1 + 0.25X_2}_{\substack{\text{Total polishing} \\ \text{time required}}} \leq \underbrace{100 \text{ hours}}_{\substack{\text{Total polishing} \\ \text{time available}}}$$

That is, the demand for polishing time cannot exceed the available supply.

Also, it is physically impossible for Saferly to produce a negative number of knives and forks. Therefore, management must ensure that decision variables X_1 and X_2 have values greater than or equal to zero. Symbolically,

$$X_1 \geq 0 \text{ and } X_2 \geq 0$$

or, in abbreviated form,

$$X_1, X_2 \geq 0$$

where the symbol $\geq$ means "greater than or equal to." Such expressions, which require each decision variable to have a positive or zero value, are called **nonnegativity conditions**.

Linear Program. By collecting the objective function, system constraints, and nonnegativity conditions, Saferly's management can represent the machine shop problem with the following mathematical model:

maximize　　　　　　　　$Z = \$8X_1 + \$6X_2$　　　　　　　Objective function

subject to　　$0.2X_1 + 0.4X_2 \leq 70 \text{ hours}$　　(Pressing)

$0.5X_1 + 0.25X_2 \leq 100 \text{ hours}$　　(Polishing)　　$\Bigg\}$　System constraints

$X_1, X_2 \geq 0$　　　　Nonnegativity conditions

This type of model is called a **linear program**.

Saferly's linear program states that the company wants to produce the quantity of knives (X_1) and forks (X_2) that will maximize total dollar profit (Z). The output levels, however, are subject to some restrictions. For one thing, the demand for pressing and polishing time cannot exceed the available supply of these resources. Also, the output levels must be positive or zero.

Assumptions

Linear programming assumes the existence of a single measurable objective, divisible decision variables, linear relationships, deterministic information, and a one-time decision.

Single Measurable Criterion. As we saw in Chapter 6, a decision problem can involve multiple objectives, which may be expressed in terms of different and sometimes conflicting criteria. Moreover, any or all of the criteria could be difficult to measure on a precise numerical basis. To use linear programming methodology, however, the decision maker must have a problem with a single objective, and the objective must be measured in precise numerical terms (such as quantity, time, or monetary value).

Depending on the circumstances, the single measurable objective may be to maximize a performance measure or to minimize a criterion value. For example, Saferly's objective is to produce the quantities of knives (X_1) and forks (X_2) that will maximize total dollar profit (Z).

Divisible Decision Variables. Each decision variable must be divisible into a fractional value. For example, Saferly's knife and fork quantities are measured by the case. Since there can be a fraction of a case produced in a week, the company can have $X_1 = 76.5$ cases of knives and $X_2 = 127.33$ cases of forks.

Linear Relationships. In linear programming, each decision variable will have an independent effect on the objective and will contribute a constant, proportional amount to it. For example, Saferly's objective is to maximize

$$Z = \$8X_1 + \$6X_2$$

According to this function, each case of knives (X_1) contributes a constant $8 to profit, regardless of the fork output (X_2). Hence, $8X_1 gives the total profit from knives. Under these conditions, a 36 percent decrease in knife output will reduce the utensil's profit by 36 percent, a quadrupling of knife output will quadruple the utensil's profit, and so on. Similarly, each case of forks contributes a constant $6 to profit, and this utensil's total profit contribution is $6X_2, regardless of knife output.

When the problem involves such proportional and independent contributions, the decision variables are said to have a **linear relationship** to the criterion value. Saferly's objective function shows that, in a linear relationship, each decision variable (X_1 and X_2) appears in a separate term and is raised to the first power (has an exponent of 1).

As with the objective function, each system constraint will involve a linear relationship. For example, Saferly's pressing constraint is

$$0.2X_1 + 0.4X_2 \leq 70 \text{ hours}$$

Since each decision variable appears in a separate term of the constraint, knives (X_1) and forks (X_2) can be pressed independently. The fixed coefficients (0.2 for X_1 and 0.4 for X_2) mean that each product uses a constant and proportional number of pressing hours.

Deterministic Information. In linear programming, each decision variable's contribution to the objective will be fixed and known with perfect certainty. For example, we assume that Saferly knows the exact profit contribution from each utensil ($8 per knife and $6 per fork). Put another way, this firm is assumed to have a deterministic (rather than stochastic) objective function.

There will also be deterministic system constraints. Any limits or requirements and the rates at which the limits or requirements are converted into each decision variable will be fixed and known with perfect certainty. For example, we assume that Saferly will have exactly 70 pressing hours and exactly 100 polishing hours available next week. In addition, we assume that each case of knives will use exactly 0.2 pressing hours and 0.5 polishing hours, and each case of forks is presumed to require exactly 0.4 pressing hours and 0.25 polishing hours.

All uncontrollable inputs (contributions to the objective, system constraint limits or requirements, and so on) in a linear program are assumed to be fixed and known with perfect certainty. Thus, a linear program is a deterministic model.

One-Time Decision. In linear programming the decision maker, at an isolated point in time, selects from among several independent alternatives. Furthermore, the resulting outcome is a direct consequence of the single alternative selected. For example, Saferly's total profit (Z) next week will be a direct result of the knife and fork output (X_1 and X_2 values) actually produced during the week. Put another way, this firm is assumed to be making a one-time (rather than sequential) decision.

Applicability. Linear programming's underlying assumptions (a single measurable objective, divisible decision variables, deterministic information, linear relationships, and a one-time decision) may seem quite restrictive. Yet these assumptions are met, or closely approximated, in many applications, as the Investment Fund Services (IFS) case and the Linear Programming in Practice exhibit demonstrate.

Linear Program Structures

In Management Situation 7.1, the decision variables are product (knife and fork) outputs, and there is a maximization objective. The system constraints involve limited resource supplies (maximum times available next week in the machine centers). Other linear programs can involve a variety of additional structures.

Objective Function. As noted previously, depending on the circumstances, the single measurable objective may be to maximize a performance measure or to minimize a criterion value. For example, the Social Security Administration (SSA) may want to minimize the cost of processing monthly retirement checks. On the other hand, Montgomery Ward may seek to maximize catalog profits. Similarly, Metropolitan Edison Company

Linear Programming in Practice

Linear programming is applied to a wide variety of management problems. Here are a few areas in which this quantitative analysis is used.

Area	Application
Finance and Accounting	Selecting the minimum time assignment of senior accountants to audit supervisions
	Determining the investments that maximize total expected yield
	Allocating a capital budget among investment projects
	Identifying the clerk schedule that minimizes a bank's float (uncollected outstanding checks)
Marketing	Assigning representatives to the districts that maximize total sales
	Allocating an advertising budget among media in a way that maximizes audience exposure to the message
	Selecting the most profitable marketing mix
Production	Planning the least-cost menu or fertilizer mix
	Establishing the least-cost production schedule
	Identifying the best mix and quantity of equipment to repair, build, or purchase
	Minimizing the cost of obtaining supplies from vendors
	Determining the cargo loads that maximize revenues
Public sector	Assigning police patrol cars to areas in a city
	Achieving an air force's largest total target "kills"
	Minimizing the time to bus high school students
	Maximizing the quality of mental health care

may want to maximize total electricity output, whereas TRW may seek to minimize the completion time on a computer system contract.

Decision Variables. The decision variables for maximization and minimization problems can depict processes employed, products manufactured and distributed, services provided, or other management and organizational efforts. For example, Metropolitan Edison may be able to achieve its objective of maximizing electricity output by using the right combination of power (coal, hydrothermal, and nuclear) plants. Similarly, the Social Security Administration can accomplish its cost minimization objective by processing retirement checks with the right combination of staff, equipment, and administrative effort.

System Constraints. System constraints for maximization and minimization problems can take several forms, including any or all of the following types:

1. A limited resource supply (as when a budget limits the hours of operation at Metropolitan Edison's power plants or when the available labor pool restricts Montgomery Ward's catalog sales).

2. A minimum requirement (as when beneficiary demand requires the Social Security Administration to process a minimum number of retirement checks per month or when a contract requires TRW's computer system to meet minimum specifications and operating standards).

3. A balance condition (as when regulations require Metropolitan Edison to supply exactly as much electricity as consumers demand).

4. A specified decision variable relationship (as when the work involved requires the Social Security Administration to use equipment for at least a specified portion of the check-processing effort).

Nonnegativity Conditions. In most management problems (including Saferly's machine shop situation), it would not make any sense to have negative values for the decision variables. For example, what would a negative number of staff hours mean to the Social Security Administration, and how would Metropolitan Edison interpret negative hours of operation at a coal plant? Moreover, the nonnegativity conditions are necessary because negative decision variables cause problems in linear programming's standard solution procedures.

Nevertheless, there are situations in which negative decision variables do make sense. In these situations, the linear program can be modified to accommodate such a situation, as the Special Formulation Issues exhibit at the end of Section 7.2 will illustrate.

The rest of this chapter (and others in the text) will provide illustrations of these other types of linear program structures.

Recap. A linear programming problem is one which seeks to maximize or minimize a linear objective function subject to linear constraints. Its general characteristics are as follows:

1. There is a single, measurable objective.

2. Several divisible decision variables can be used to achieve the objective.

3. There is an objective function that relates the decision variables to the objective's criterion value in a linear (proportional and independent) and deterministic manner.

4. There are a finite number of system constraints and nonnegativity conditions that restrict the objective.

5. There are linear and deterministic relationships in each system constraint.

6. There is a linear program that seeks the combination of decision variables that optimizes the objective function's criterion value, subject to the restrictions imposed by the system constraints and nonnegativity conditions.

7. The linear program is a deterministic model, and it involves a one-time decision.

7.2 FORMULATING LINEAR PROGRAMS

If the decision maker is satisfied that the problem has linear programming characteristics, he or she next must formulate the appropriate linear program. The formulation process will be as shown in Figure 7.1.

Process

As Figure 7.1 emphasizes, the objective, the decision variables, and the restrictions (system constraints and nonnegativity conditions) should be identified and clearly stated

Figure 7.1   **Formulating a Linear Program**

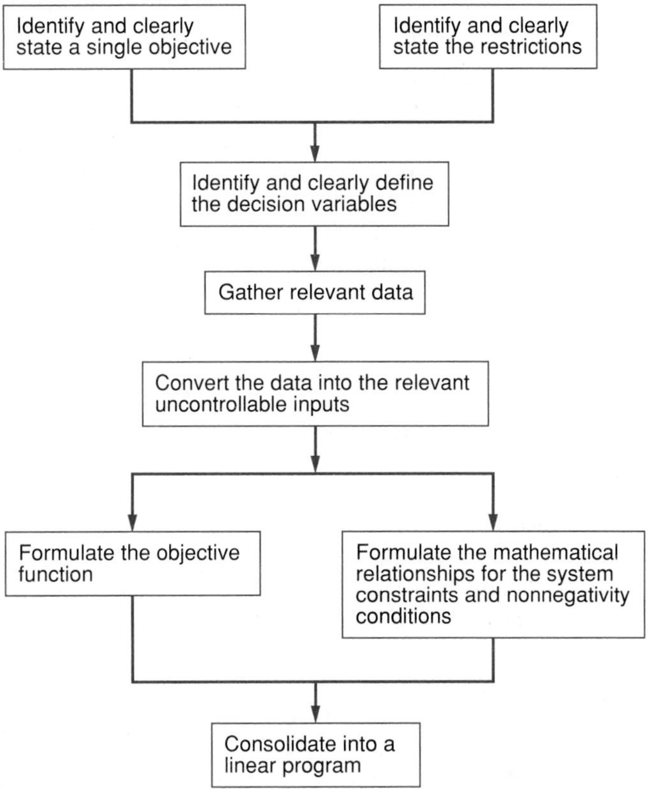

in words before any attempt is made to develop corresponding mathematical expressions. Such a practice also will help identify the data needed to measure the relevant uncontrollable inputs, which include

1. Decision variables' rates of contribution to the objective.

2. System constraint limits/requirements.

3. Rates at which these limits/requirements are converted into decision variables.

4. Specification in any balance condition or decision variable relationship.

Inputs. The data can be gathered internally from a variety of sources, including sales invoices, production records, and accounting and financial statements. Additional data can be assembled from external sources such as government records, trade studies, and commercial market research reports. Executive polls and surveys of employees and customers are also useful sources of information. Management then can use a systematic methodology (such as forecasting), perhaps delivered through a computer information system (such as a DSS), to transform the collected data into the uncontrollable inputs required for the linear program.

Problem Classes. As indicated in Section 7.1, linear programming can be used to solve many different kinds of management problems. The most frequent applications have been in five general decision problem classes: resource allocation, planning and scheduling, blending, transportation, and assignment.

Resource Allocation

Often, there are situations in which decision activities compete for various scarce resources. Each activity contributes a given amount to an objective and utilizes some of the resources. In these circumstances, a manager wants to allocate available resources among activities in a way that optimizes his or her decision objective. Management Situation 7.2 illustrates.

Management Situation 7.2

Dairy Financing

The Lincoln Dairy Cooperative has a large milk processing plant outside Nebraska's capital city. During the next quarter, the cooperative will begin the processing of three new skim milk brands—Green Pastures (GP), Savemuch (SM), and Health Stores (HS). Since these new brands require an expansion of current facilities, management will need operating funds to cover material and labor expenses during the initial processing period. Revenue from the new brands will be unavailable until next quarter, when Lincoln starts selling the products. Thus, the cooperative must arrange financing for the operating expenses before processing begins.

Management has set aside $50,000 from the cooperative's cash reserve to cover initial processing expenses. Any other necessary funds must be borrowed from the cooperative's main external financier, the Midland Bank and Trust Company. Midland has offered a short-term line of credit of up to $300,000 at 3 percent interest per quarter, providing that Lincoln's *acid (quick) test ratio* is at least 4:1 while the loan is outstanding. This financial ratio is defined as

$$\frac{\text{Cash on hand after production } + \text{ Accounts receivable}}{\text{Accounts payable}}$$

Lincoln will draw credit, as needed, during the processing, but interest will not start accruing until the beginning of the next period. Shipments will be made, on credit, at the end of the processing period, while sales revenues will be received and outstanding liabilities will be liquidated at the end of the next period.

There are other factors to consider. Distributor agreements require the cooperative to offer at least as much Health Stores as the other two brands combined. For promotional purposes, Lincoln also wants Green Pastures to constitute at least 20 percent of all brand offerings. In addition, the brands have different formulas and thereby must be processed independently through the cooperative's milking, inspection, and packaging operations. Milking includes the operations of drawing the milk from the cows, deleting unwanted ingredients (such as fat), and adding some nutrients (such as vitamins A and D). During

Table 7.1   Dairy Price, Cost, and Capacity Information

Brand	Selling Price ($ per gallon)	Processing Cost ($ per gallon)	Required Hours (per gallon)		
			Milking	Inspection	Packaging
GP	0.88	0.65	0.16	0.030	0.08
SM	0.82	0.54	0.12	0.045	0.06
HS	1.02	0.87	0.18	0.040	0.05

inspection, the processed milk passes through tubes with sensoring devices that record any deviations from predetermined ingredient and nutrient standards. Then, automated equipment is used to prepare cartons, fill them with the inspected milk, and move the packaged brand to a shipping area.

During the initial processing period, the cooperative can devote only 400,000 hours of milking, 80,000 hours of inspection, and 150,000 hours of packaging capacity to the new brands. By analyzing time and motion study results, historical production records, and market data with the cooperative's milk-flow information system (MFIS), management also has developed the price, cost, and processing requirements reported in Table 7.1. Management wants to maximize total profits from the new brands.

Objective. Lincoln's single measurable objective is to maximize the total profit from the three new skim milk brands. This profit will equal the total revenue obtained from selling the brands minus the total cost incurred in processing the brands.

Cost is incurred by using capacity and borrowed fund resources to process milk, while revenue is generated by selling the resulting brands. Management influences these costs and revenues (and, therefore, profits) by setting the quantity of each brand and by fixing the amount borrowed. These decision variables can be depicted as follows:

GP = gallons of Green Pastures processed during the production period

SM = gallons of Savemuch processed during the production period

HS = gallons of Health Stores processed during the production period

B = dollars borrowed from Midland during the production period

Each brand will contribute to profit its quantity multiplied by the corresponding unit profit (selling price minus unit processing cost). For example, since Savemuch can be sold for a constant 82 cents and processed for a constant 54 cents per gallon, this brand's contribution to profit will be

$$(\$0.82 - \$0.54)SM = \$.28SM$$

Total profit will equal the sum of the brands' independent contributions, or

$$($0.88 - $0.65)GP + ($0.82 - $0.54)SM + ($1.02 - $0.87)HS$$

less the cost associated with any borrowed funds.

Since Midland charges 3 percent interest, it will cost Lincoln

$$0.03B$$

to borrow B dollars during the production period. The cooperative's total profit (profit from the brands less the cost of borrowing) can then be expressed as the following objective function:

$$DP = $0.23GP + $0.28SM + $0.15HS - 0.03B$$

where DP = total profit and the other terms are defined as before. Management seeks the decision variable (GP, SM, HS, and B) values that will maximize the objective function's criterion value (DP).

Restrictions. One set of system constraints on the objective must ensure that the cooperative processes no more milk than capacity allows. For example, Table 7.1 shows that it takes a constant 0.16 hour (about 10 minutes) to milk a gallon of Green Pastures, a constant 0.12 hour (about 7 minutes) to milk a gallon of Savemuch, and a constant 0.18 (about 11 minutes) to milk a gallon of Health Stores. The total demand for milking capacity will be the sum of the independent brand requirements or

$$0.16GP + 0.12SM + 0.18HS.$$

Since this total demand cannot exceed the 400,000 hours available, the milking operation resource limit can be written as:

$$0.16GP + 0.12SM + 0.18HS \leq 400,000 \text{ hours.}$$

Similar resource limits are

$$0.03GP + 0.045SM + 0.04HS \leq 80,000 \text{ hours} \qquad \text{for inspection}$$

$$0.08GP + 0.06SM + 0.05HS \leq 150,000 \text{ hours} \qquad \text{for packaging}$$

Another set of system constraints must guarantee that the cooperative satisfies its financial obligations. First, the dollars borrowed from Midland during the processing period must not exceed the $300,000 line of credit or

$$B \leq $300,000.$$

Also, the cooperative must not use more funds than will be available to process the brands. The use of funds will equal the sum of the brands' independent processing costs or

$$$0.65GP + $0.54SM + $0.87HS$$

while the source of funds will be the $50,000 cash reserve plus the amount borrowed. Consequently, this funds resource limit can be written as follows:

$$$0.65GP + $0.54SM + $0.87HS \leq $50,000 + B$$

or as $\qquad$ $\$0.65GP + \$0.54SM + \$0.87HS - B \le \$50,000.$

Another financial system constraint requires Lincoln to maintain an acid-test ratio of

$$\frac{\text{Cash on hand after production} \; + \; \text{Accounts receivable}}{\text{Accounts payable}} \ge 4$$

while the loan is outstanding. Cash on hand after production will equal the funds available less the processing costs or

$$(\$50,000 + B) - (\$0.65GP + \$0.54SM + \$0.87HS).$$

Accounts receivable are the sales revenues to be collected at the end of next quarter or

$$\$0.88GP + \$0.82SM + \$1.02HS.$$

Accounts payable will equal the bank loan to be liquidated at the end of next quarter plus interest for one quarter or

$$B + 0.03B = 1.03B.$$

Therefore, the minimum acid-test requirement can be written as follows:

$$\frac{[(\$50,000 + B) - (\$0.65GP + \$0.54SM + \$0.87HS)]}{1.03B}$$

$$+ \frac{\$0.88GP + \$0.82SM + \$1.02HS}{1.03B} \ge 4$$

or as $\qquad$ $\$0.23GP + \$0.28SM + \$0.15HS - 3.12B \ge -\$50,000$

or, if we multiply both sides of the expression by -1, as

$$-\$0.23GP - \$0.28SM - \$0.15HS + 3.12B \le \$50,000.$$

A final set of system constraints must ensure that the brand combinations satisfy the distributor agreements and promotional considerations. The distributor agreements require Lincoln to offer as much Health Stores as the other two brands combined. This required decision variable relationship can be written as

$$HS \ge (GP + SM)$$

or as $\qquad$ $HS - GP - SM \ge 0$

For promotional purposes, Green Pastures must constitute at least 20 percent of the offerings, which means that

$$GP \ge 0.20(GP + SM + HS)$$

or $\qquad$ $0.80GP - 0.20SM - 0.20HS \ge 0.$

The nonnegativity conditions of

$$GP, \; SM, \; HS, \; B \ge 0$$

guarantee that the cooperative will process zero or positive quantities of milk and borrow a zero or positive amount of money.

Linear Program. Lincoln wants to process the gallons of milk and borrow the amount of money that, within the problem's (capacity, financial, and distributor) restrictions, will maximize the total profit from the new brands. That is, management seeks to:

Maximize $\quad\quad DP = \$0.23GP + \$0.28SM + \$0.15HS - 0.03B$

Subject to

$$0.16GP + 0.12SM + 0.18HS \leq 400,000 \text{ hours} \quad \text{(Milking)}$$

$$0.03GP + 0.045SM + 0.04HS \leq 80,000 \text{ hours} \quad \text{(Inspection)}$$

$$0.08GP + 0.06SM + 0.05HS \leq 150,000 \text{ hours} \quad \text{(Packaging)}$$

$$B \leq \$300,000 \quad \text{(Credit)}$$

$$\$0.65GP + \$0.54SM + \$0.87HS - B \leq \$50,000 \quad \text{(Funds)}$$

$$-\$0.23GP - \$0.28SM - \$0.15HS + 3.12B \leq \$50,000 \quad \text{(Acid-test)}$$

$$HS - GP - SM \geq 0 \quad \text{(Distributor)}$$

$$0.80GP - 0.20SM - 0.20HS \geq 0 \quad \text{(Promotion)}$$

$$GP, SM, HS, B \geq 0$$

This consolidated statement of the objective function, system constraints, and nonnegativity conditions gives the linear program for Lincoln's one-time (capacity and borrowed fund) resource allocation problem.

Planning and Scheduling

Many problems involve planning or scheduling. That is, the decision maker must plan or schedule present and future actions to achieve a future goal. In these cases, the problem is to identify the combination of decision variables that maximizes return or minimizes costs subject to various time period constraints. Management Situation 7.3 illustrates.

Management Situation 7.3
_____

Steel Exporting

Honsha Enterprises of Seoul exports steel to customers in Western Europe, Canada, and the United States. Although demand varies from quarter to quarter, contracts specify in advance the exact quarterly requirements. By processing these contracts through the company's management information system (MIS), sales staff have determined that Honsha must deliver 2.5, 4, 3, and 4.5 million tons of steel in the next four quarters.

There are several ways to meet the requirements. One possibility is to "track" demand with production. Although this option enables Honsha to carry no inventory, it creates employee turnover and training problems and leaves substantial unused capacity at times. Another approach is to produce steel at a constant rate and allow inventory to absorb the fluctuations in demand. Such an approach offers manufacturing efficiency, but it typically involves a large inventory investment. Between these two extremes is the moderate option of carrying some inventory while varying the production level somewhat.

Past experience indicates that the moderate option works best in Honsha's operations. Management now must determine the production and inventory levels that will minimize the costs of fulfilling the company's steel contracts.

Currently, Honsha has 500,000 tons of steel in stock, and the company is manufacturing steel at the rate of 3 million tons per quarter. By processing historical manufacturing data through the MIS, the operations manager has forecasted that production costs will be $100, $120, $90, and $110 per ton over the next four quarters. A similar MIS analysis of historical changeover (labor and facility adjustment) data has indicated that it will cost $12 per ton to increase and $3 per ton to decrease production from one quarter to the next.

By processing historical purchasing, bookkeeping, and storage transactions through the MIS, the operations manager also has estimated that it will cost 5 percent of the product's value to inventory steel for one quarter. Company accounting policy requires the operations manager to assess this cost on the end-of-quarter inventory. At the end of four quarters, Honsha wants no more than 400,000 tons of steel in inventory.

Objective. Honsha's single measurable objective is to minimize the total cost of fulfilling the company's steel contracts. This total cost will equal the production plus changeover plus inventory expenses that are incurred from manufacturing steel during the next four quarters of operation.

Management affects these expenses by setting the production schedule—the quantity of steel that will be manufactured in each of the next four quarters. These decision variables can be depicted as follows:

Q_j = the tons of steel manufactured in quarter j

where the subscript j = a code with a value of 1 for quarter 1, 2 for quarter 2, etc. Such selections, in turn, determine the changes (up or down) in production and the inventory needed to meet demand. These additional decision variables can be defined as follows:

U_j = the increase (change up) in the tons of steel manufactured during quarter j

D_j = the decrease (change down) in the tons of steel manufactured during quarter j

I_j = the tons of steel in inventory at the end of quarter j

where the subscript j is defined as before.

Each quarter's output will contribute to expense its quantity multiplied by the corresponding unit cost. For example, since steel can be manufactured in the first quarter for a constant $100 per ton, the quarter 1 contribution to production expenses will be

$$\$100Q_1.$$

Similarly, it costs a constant 5 percent of the product's value to inventory steel for one quarter. Hence, the inventory expense for the first quarter will be

$$.05(\$100)I_1 = \$5I_1.$$

Each category's total expense will equal the sum of the four quarters' independent contributions. For example, the total changeover expense will be

$$\$12(U_1 + U_2 + U_3 + U_4) + \$3(D_1 + D_2 + D_3 + D_4).$$

Honsha's total cost (production plus changeover plus inventory expenses) can be expressed as the following objective function:

$$
\begin{aligned}
SC = {}& \$100Q_1 + \$120Q_2 + \$90Q_3 + \$110Q_4 \\
& + \$12(U_1 + U_2 + U_3 + U_4) + \$3(D_1 + D_2 + D_3 + D_4) \\
& + \$5I_1 + \$6I_2 + \$4.50I_3 + \$5.50I_4
\end{aligned}
$$

where SC = the total cost of fulfilling Honsha's steel contracts and the other terms are defined as before. Management seeks the decision variable (Q_j, U_j, D_j, and I_j) values that will minimize the objective function's criterion value (SC).

Restrictions. One set of system constraints on the objective must guarantee that the production schedule meets the contract requirements. Since the required steel can come from production or from inventory, these constraints will take the form of the following balance (sources = uses) conditions:

$$\text{beginning inventory} \; + \; \text{production} \; - \; \text{ending inventory} \; = \; \text{demand.}$$

For example, customers will demand 2.5 million tons of steel in quarter 1, and Honsha will begin that quarter with 500,000 tons in inventory. As a result, quarter 1's balance condition will be

$$500{,}000 + Q_1 - I_1 = 2{,}500{,}000 \text{ tons}$$

or

$$Q_1 - I_1 = 2{,}000{,}000 \text{ tons.}$$

Similarly, the balance conditions will be

$$I_1 + Q_2 - I_2 = 4{,}000{,}000 \text{ tons} \qquad \text{for quarter 2}$$

$$I_2 + Q_3 - I_3 = 3{,}000{,}000 \text{ tons} \qquad \text{for quarter 3}$$

$$I_3 + Q_4 - I_4 = 4{,}500{,}000 \text{ tons} \qquad \text{for quarter 4}$$

Another set of system constraints must ensure that the production schedule reflects increases or decreases in the quarters' manufacturing levels. For example, Honsha will start quarter 1 with a production rate of 3 million tons per quarter. During quarter 1, the change in output must equal the tons manufactured during the quarter (Q_1) less 3 million. Since this change will be either an increase (U_1) or a decrease (D_1) in output, the decision variable relationship can be expressed as follows:

$$Q_1 - 3{,}000{,}000 = U_1 - D_1$$

or

$$Q_1 - U_1 + D_1 = 3{,}000{,}000 \text{ tons.}$$

In a similar manner,

$$Q_2 - Q_1 = U_2 - D_2$$

or $Q_2 - Q_1 - U_2 + D_2 = 0$ for quarter 2

and

$$Q_3 - Q_2 = U_3 - D_3$$

or $Q_3 - Q_2 - U_3 + D_3 = 0$ for quarter 3

and

$$Q_4 - Q_3 = U_4 - D_4$$

or $Q_4 - Q_3 - U_4 + D_4 = 0$ for quarter 4

For each such relationship, one or both of the changes (either U_j or D_j) will be zero and thereby drop out of the equation.

A final system constraint must ensure that quarter 4's ending inventory is no more than 400,000 tons, or that

$$I_4 \leq 400,000 \text{ tons.}$$

The nonnegativity conditions of

$$Q_j, \ U_j, \ D_j, \ I_j \geq 0 \qquad \text{for all } j$$

guarantee that Honsha will manufacture and inventory zero or positive quantities of steel.

Linear Program. Honsha wants to manufacture the tons of steel in each quarter that, within the problem's restrictions, will minimize the total cost of fulfilling the customer contracts. That is, management seeks to:

Minimize

$$SC = \$100Q_1 + \$120Q_2 + \$90Q_3 + \$110Q_4$$
$$+\$12(U_1 + U_2 + U_3 + U_4) + \$3(D_1 + D_2 + D_3 + D_4)$$
$$+\$5I_1 + \$6I_2 + \$4.50I_3 + \$5.50I_4$$

Subject to		
$Q_1 - I_1 = 2,000,000$ tons	(Quarter 1 balance)
$I_1 + Q_2 - I_2 = 4,000,000$ tons	(Quarter 2 balance)
$I_2 + Q_3 - I_3 = 3,000,000$ tons	(Quarter 3 balance)
$I_3 + Q_4 - I_4 = 4,500,000$ tons	(Quarter 4 balance)
$Q_1 - U_1 + D_1 = 3,000,000$ tons	(Quarter 1 change)
$Q_2 - Q_1 - U_2 + D_2 = 0$	(Quarter 2 change)
$Q_3 - Q_2 - U_3 + D_3 = 0$	(Quarter 3 change)
$Q_4 - Q_3 - U_4 + D_4 = 0$	(Quarter 4 change)
$I_4 \leq 400,000$ tons	(Inventory)
$Q_j, \ U_j, \ D_j, \ I_j \geq 0$	for all j

This consolidated statement of the objective function, system constraints, and nonnegativity conditions gives the linear program for Honsha's one-time (scheduling current production) problem. It also provides the framework for dealing with the current as well as future production scheduling problems.

Blending

In blending problems, several raw ingredients are mixed into a finished product that meets various specifications. Each ingredient contributes various properties to the finished product at a given cost. The objective is to determine the blend of ingredients that minimizes cost or maximizes contribution subject to technical specifications and supply requirements. Management Situation 7.4 illustrates.

Management Situation 7.4

Waste Management

A major eastern city has a plant that takes collected organic and inorganic solid wastes, treats the wastes with a cleansing agent, and incinerates the treated refuse. By using a decision support system to analyze test data from simulated operations, plant engineers have found that it costs a constant $2 to process each pound of organic waste. They also discovered that inorganic waste can be processed independently at a constant cost of $3 per pound. The plant has the capacity to process 9 million pounds of treated refuse per week.

Incineration of treated refuse creates a high-grade ash and a mineral compound as by-products of the process. Each by-product will contain both processed organic and inorganic wastes. By altering plant operations, management can set the blend of these wastes in the by-products.

Fertilizer producers will purchase, at a fixed price of $4 per pound, up to 7 million pounds of the ash per week. To meet these purchasers' needs, processed organic waste must constitute no more than 60 percent of the ash's blend by weight. Also, the city must supply at least 4 million pounds of ash per week.

Chemical companies will buy up to 6 million pounds of the mineral compound per week at a fixed price of $5 per pound. To meet their needs, processed inorganic waste must constitute at least 50 percent but no more than 75 percent of the compound's blend by weight.

The city wants to earn as much profit from the by-products as possible.

Objective. The city's single measurable objective is to maximize the profit from generating waste by-products. This profit will equal the total revenue obtained from selling the processed wastes minus the total cost incurred in processing the wastes.

Revenue is earned, and cost is incurred, by blending treated refuse into the desired by-products. Management sets the blend by selecting the quantity of each ingredient (processed organic and processed inorganic waste) in each by-product. These decision variables can be depicted as follows:

OA = the pounds of processed organic waste in high-grade ash

IA = the pounds of processed inorganic waste in high-grade ash

OM = the pounds of processed organic waste in the mineral compound

IM = the pounds of processed inorganic waste in the mineral compound

The city then will create $OA + IA$ total pounds of ash and $OM + IM$ total pounds of the mineral compound from a blend. Also, it will use $OA + OM$ total pounds of processed organic waste and $IA + IM$ total pounds of processed inorganic waste in a blend.

Each by-product will contribute to revenue its quantity multiplied by the corresponding price. For example, since high-grade ash can be sold for a constant $4 per pound, this by-product's contribution to revenue will be

$$\$4(OA + IA)$$

Total revenue will equal the sum of the by-products' independent contributions or

$$\$4(OA + IA) + \$5(OM + IM).$$

Each ingredient will contribute to cost its quantity multiplied by the corresponding unit processing expense. For example, since organic waste can be processed for a constant $2 per pound, this ingredient's contribution to cost will be

$$\$2(OA + OM).$$

Total cost will equal the sum of the ingredients' independent contributions or

$$\$2(OA + OM) + \$3(IA + IM).$$

The city's total profit (total revenue − total cost) can be expressed as the following objective function:

$$TP = [\$4(OA + IA) + \$5(OM + IM)] - [\$2(OA + OM) + \$3(IA + IM)]$$

or $TP = \$2OA + \$1IA + \$3OM + \$2IM$

where TP = total profit and the other terms are defined as before. Management seeks the decision variable (OA, IA, OM, and IM) values that will maximize the objective function's criterion value (TP).

Restrictions. One system constraint on the objective must ensure that the city processes no more waste than the plant can handle (9 million pounds per week). This capacity limit can be expressed as follows:

$$OA + IA + OM + IM \leq 9,000,000 \text{ pounds}$$

where the symbol $\leq$ means "less than or equal to."

Another set of system constraints must ensure that the city supplies no more by-products than its customers demand (7 million pounds of ash and 6 million pounds of the mineral compound per week). These demand limits can be written as follows:

$$OA + IA \leq 7,000,000 \text{ pounds} \qquad \text{for high-grade ash}$$

$$OM + IM \leq 6,000,000 \text{ pounds} \qquad \text{for the mineral compound}$$

To satisfy fertilizer producers, the city also must supply at least 4 million pounds of ash per week. This minimum requirement can be expressed as follows:

$$OA + IA \geq 4,000,000 \text{ pounds}$$

where the symbol $\geq$ means "greater than or equal to."

A final set of system constraints must ensure that the city blends the ingredient combinations desired by its customers. Fertilizer producers want processed organic waste to constitute no more than 60 percent of the ash's total weight. This specified decision variable relationship can be written as

$$OA \leq .60(OA + IA)$$

or in the alternative form of

$$.40OA - .60IA \leq 0.$$

Similarly, chemical companies want inorganic waste to constitute at least 50 percent but no more than 75 percent of the mineral compound's blend by weight. These specified decision variable relationships can be expressed as

$$IM \geq .50(OM + IM)$$

or $\qquad\qquad .50IM - .50OM \geq 0 \qquad\qquad$ for the lower limit

and as

$$IM \leq .75(OM + IM)$$

or $\qquad\qquad .25IM - .75OM \leq 0 \qquad\qquad$ for the upper limit

The nonnegativity conditions of

$$OA \geq 0 \qquad IA \geq 0 \qquad OM \geq 0 \qquad IM \geq 0$$

or, in abbreviated form,

$$OA, IA, OM, IM \geq 0$$

guarantee that the city will blend zero or positive quantities of each ingredient into each by-product.

Linear Program. The city wants to blend the treated refuse into the desired by-products in a way that, within the problem's (capacity, demand, and supply) restrictions, will maximize the total profit from the processing. That is, plant management seeks to

Maximize $\qquad\qquad TP = \$2OA + \$1IA + \$3OM + \$2IM$

Subject to

$$OA + IA + OM + IM \leq 9,000,000 \text{ pounds} \qquad \text{(Plant capacity)}$$

$$OA + IA \leq 7,000,000 \text{ pounds} \qquad \text{(Maximum ash demand)}$$

$$OM + IM \leq 6,000,000 \text{ pounds} \qquad \text{(Maximum mineral demand)}$$

$$OA + IA \geq 4,000,000 \text{ pounds} \qquad \text{(Minimum ash supply)}$$

$$.40OA - .60IA \leq 0 \qquad \text{(Ash blend)}$$

$$.50IM - .50OM \geq 0 \qquad \text{(Mineral blend lower limit)}$$

$$.25IM - .75OM \leq 0 \qquad \text{(Mineral blend upper limit)}$$

$$OA, \ IA, \ OM, \ IM \geq 0$$

This consolidated statement of the objective function, system constraints, and nonnegativity conditions gives the linear program for the city's one-time blending problem.

Transportation

In distribution problems, it is necessary to transport goods and services from supply sources to demand destinations. Each source has an available supply, and each destination requires a given demand. In addition, there are various costs or returns to transport a unit from each source to each destination. The problem is to determine the transportation pattern that minimizes total cost or maximizes total return, while meeting all demand and supply conditions. Management Situation 7.5 illustrates.

Management Situation 7.5

Building Materials Franchises

Dealerships in the panelized housing business are expensive and difficult to obtain. They are allocated to wholesalers by location, and if a particular area has a dealership, the owner can claim territorial rights. Then no other person or firm will be allowed to offer the product in the area.

Raphael Enterprises has just run into the dealership problem. Its most profitable line of panelized homes, Weather Protector Structures, are distributed to wholesalers in such a way that Raphael can maintain wholesale dealerships in only three locations: Davendale, Swinson, and Oldtown. From these locations, shipments are made to Raphael's retail outlets in Springfield and Manchester. In addition, Raphael has a reciprocity agreement that enables it to supply panels for another firm's retail outlets in Yorkville and Jessup.

According to the franchise agreement, 64,000 linear feet of panels will be available annually for shipment from the Davendale dealer, 48,000 linear feet will be available from the Swinson dealer, and 55,000 linear feet will be available from the Oldtown dealer. By processing historical data through Raphael's MIS, management has forecasted that annual panel orders will be 50,000 linear feet from Springfield, 47,000 linear feet from Manchester, 30,000 linear feet from Yorkville, and 40,000 linear feet from Jessup. An MIS analysis of motor and rail carrier tariffs also has provided the shipping cost information shown in Table 7.2.

Raphael wants to minimize the cost of shipping the panels from its wholesale dealerships to the retail outlets.

Objective. Raphael's single measurable objective is to minimize the cost of shipping the Weather Protector panels. This cost will be determined by the manner in which management makes the shipments from the wholesale dealerships to the retail outlets.

Table 7.2   **Raphael's Shipping Costs**

From	Shipping Cost ($ per linear foot) To			
	Springfield	**Manchester**	**Yorkville**	**Jessup**
Davendale	2.50	4	3	1.75
Swinson	4.25	2	4	2.25
Oldtown	2.75	3	2	4.50

Since three different dealers can supply four separate outlets, there will be a total of $3 \times 4 = 12$ possible shipments. One possibility, for example, is to ship panels from Swinson to Manchester, and another is to transport panels from Davendale to Jessup. In each case, management influences the shipping cost by setting the quantity of panels in the shipment. Such a decision variable can be depicted as follows:

X_{ij} = the linear feet of panels shipped from dealer i to outlet j

where i = a code with a value of 1 for Davendale, 2 for Swinson, and 3 for Oldtown

     j = a code with a value of 1 for Springfield, 2 for Manchester, 3 for Yorkville, and 4 for Jessup

For this problem, the double-subscripted X_{ij} notation will be more descriptive (and perhaps more compact) than using different symbols for each variable.

Since each route involves a constant tariff, the cost of a shipment will be the unit shipping expense multiplied by the quantity transported. For example, Table 7.2 shows that it will cost $4 to ship a linear foot of the panel from the Davendale dealer to the Manchester store. Therefore, Raphael will pay

$$\$4X_{12}$$

to transport a quantity of X_{12} linear feet of panels over this route.

Also, since the shipments are made independently (from different dealers to separate outlets), the total cost of shipping all panels will equal the sum of the individual transportation expenses. That is, Raphael's objective function will be

$$TC = \$2.50X_{11} + \$4X_{12} + \$3X_{13} + \$1.75X_{14}$$
$$+ \$4.25X_{21} + \$2X_{22} + \$4X_{23} + \$2.25X_{24}$$
$$+ \$2.75X_{31} + \$3X_{32} + \$2X_{33} + \$4.50X_{34}$$

where TC = the total cost of shipping the panels (the criterion value) and the decision variables (X_{ij} values) are defined as before. Management seeks the shipments (X_{ij} values) that will minimize the total transportation cost (TC).

Restrictions. One set of system constraints on the objective must assure that the shipments from each dealer are exactly equal to the available supply. For example, since the Davendale dealer has 64,000 linear feet of panels available, this wholesaler's total shipments (to Springfield, Manchester, Yorkville, and Jessup) must constitute the entire available supply, or

$$X_{11} + X_{12} + X_{13} + X_{14} = 64,000 \text{ linear feet.}$$

Similar balance conditions are

$$X_{21} + X_{22} + X_{23} + X_{24} = 48,000 \text{ linear feet} \qquad \text{for Swinson}$$

$$X_{31} + X_{32} + X_{33} + X_{34} = 55,000 \text{ linear feet} \qquad \text{for Oldtown}$$

Another set of system constraints is needed to assure that each outlet receives exactly the quantity it demands. For example, since the Springfield store needs 50,000 linear feet of panels, the shipments to this store (from the Davendale, Swinson, and Oldtown sources) must equal demand, or

$$X_{11} + X_{21} + X_{31} = 50,000 \text{ linear feet.}$$

In a similar manner,

$$X_{12} + X_{22} + X_{32} = 47,000 \text{ linear feet} \qquad \text{for Manchester}$$

$$X_{13} + X_{23} + X_{33} = 30,000 \text{ linear feet} \qquad \text{for Yorkville}$$

$$X_{14} + X_{24} + X_{34} = 40,000 \text{ linear feet} \qquad \text{for Jessup}$$

The nonnegativity conditions of

$$X_{ij} \geq 0 \qquad \text{for all } i \text{ and } j$$

guarantee that Raphael will ship a zero or positive number of linear feet over each transportation route.

Linear Program. Raphael wants to ship the quantities (linear feet of panels) over each available route that, within the transportation (supply and demand) restrictions, will minimize the total shipping cost. That is, management seeks to

Minimize
$$TC = \$2.50X_{11} + \$4X_{12} + \$3X_{13} + \$1.75X_{14}$$
$$+ \$4.25X_{21} + \$2X_{22} + \$4X_{23} + \$2.25X_{24}$$
$$+ \$2.75X_{31} + \$3X_{32} + \$2X_{33} + \$4.50X_{34}$$

Subject to

$$X_{11} + X_{12} + X_{13} + X_{14} = 64,000 \text{ linear feet} \qquad \text{(Davendale)}$$

$$X_{21} + X_{22} + X_{23} + X_{24} = 48,000 \text{ linear feet} \qquad \text{(Swinson)}$$

$$X_{31} + X_{32} + X_{33} + X_{34} = 55,000 \text{ linear feet} \qquad \text{(Oldtown)}$$

$$X_{11} + X_{21} + X_{31} = 50,000 \text{ linear feet} \qquad \text{(Springfield)}$$

$$X_{12} + X_{22} + X_{32} = 47,000 \text{ linear feet} \qquad \text{(Manchester)}$$

$$X_{13} + X_{23} + X_{33} = 30,000 \text{ linear feet} \qquad \text{(Yorkville)}$$

$$X_{14} + X_{24} + X_{34} = 40,000 \text{ linear feet} \qquad \text{(Jessup)}$$

$$X_{ij} \geq 0 \qquad \text{for all } i \text{ and } j$$

This consolidated statement of the objective function, system (supply and demand) constraints, and nonnegativity conditions gives the linear program for Raphael's one-time transportation problem.

Assignment

In assignment problems, there are various facilities (such as people and machines) available to complete several required tasks (such as jobs and processes). Each facility can be assigned to only one task. The objective is to assign facilities to tasks in a way that will maximize performance or minimize costs. Management Situation 7.6 illustrates.

Management Situation 7.6

Information Center Operations

Raycot Pharmaceuticals has an information center (IC) that helps managers and other professionals with their individual computer applications. The center employs six "end-user specialists" who have varying degrees of experience, computer abilities, functional (finance, marketing, and production) and technical (accounting, economic, and engineering) knowledge, and communication skills. Janet Jones, the IC Director, wants to keep all specialists busy.

There are six information center jobs that require different levels of expertise. The jobs are described as follows:

1. Help a brand manager set up a data base (DB) on her microcomputer.
2. Show a financial executive how to use the company's mainframe-based executive information system (EIS).
3. Provide word processing (WP) training for a secretary in the company's legal division.
4. Evaluate a group of electronic mail (E-MAIL) packages for the Director of Computer Services.
5. Assist a production manager in developing a mainframe-based inventory simulation and analysis (ISA) model.
6. Train a group of new accountants in the use of the company's minicomputer-based accounting (ACC) software.

Each specialist was asked to estimate how many hours it would take to complete the jobs. Since some were unfamiliar with particular computer systems, a few estimates were high, indicating a necessary learning period. Specialists' wages and past performances on similar jobs were available from the company's personnel data base. By processing these data through Raycot's time and cost estimation models within Raycot's management information system (MIS), Janet was able to derive the information summarized in Table 7.3. Entries in the table's cells give the hours it will take for each specialist to complete each job. The numbers in parentheses below the specialists' names identify the person's constant hourly wage.

Ms. Jones wants to get the current jobs done in the least costly manner.

Table 7.3   **Raycot's Personnel Information**

Specialist	Job					
	DB	**EIS**	**WP**	**E-MAIL**	**ISA**	**ACC**
Davis ($22/hour)	10	8	12	4	18	32
Florino ($24/hour)	7	6	16	3	13	25
Lippincott ($25/hour)	14	9	9	5	20	28
Thomas ($18/hour)	6	7	10	2	35	42
Torrez ($30/hour)	11	10	12	6	15	24
Webber ($20/hour)	9	11	12	4	16	38

Objective. Janet Jones's single measurable objective is to minimize the cost of completing the six current information center jobs. This cost will be determined by the manner in which she assigns the "end-user specialists" to the jobs.

Since six different specialists are available to perform six separate jobs, there will be a total of $6 \times 6 = 36$ possible assignments. One possibility is to assign Lippincott to the word processing (WP) job; another is to assign Davis to the executive information system (EIS) job. In each case, the choice is either to assign or not to assign the specialist to each job. Under such (assign/don't assign) circumstances, the decision variables can be represented with the following one-zero format:

$$X_{ij} = \begin{cases} 1 \text{ if specialist } i \text{ is assigned to job } j \\ 0 \text{ if specialist } i \text{ is not assigned to job } j \end{cases}$$

where i = a code with a value of 1 for Davis, 2 for Florino, 3 for Lippincott, 4 for Thomas, 5 for Torrez, and 6 for Webber.

j = a code with a value of 1 for DB, 2 for EIS, 3 for WP, 4 for E-Mail, 5 for ISA, and 6 for ACC.

For this problem, the double-subscripted X_{ij} notation will be more descriptive (and perhaps more compact) than using different symbols for each variable.

With a one-zero decision variable format, cost will be incurred only when a specialist is assigned to an information center job. Since each specialist is paid a constant hourly wage, the cost of an assignment will be the pay rate multiplied by the value of the decision variable. For example, Table 7.3 shows that Torrez earns $30 per hour, and it will take the person 15 hours to complete the ISA job. Therefore, it will cost the information center $30(15)X_{55} = \$450X_{55}$ to assign Torrez to the ISA job.

Also, since each specialist works independently, the total cost of completing all current jobs will equal the sum of the individual assignment expenses. That is, the information center's objective function will be

$$JC = \$220X_{11} + \$176X_{12} + \$264X_{13} + \$88X_{14} + \$396X_{15} + \$704X_{16}$$
$$+ \$168X_{21} + \$144X_{22} + \$384X_{23} + \$72X_{24} + \$312X_{25} + \$600X_{26}$$
$$+ \$350X_{31} + \$225X_{32} + \$225X_{33} + \$125X_{34} + \$500X_{35} + \$700X_{36}$$
$$+ \$108X_{41} + \$126X_{42} + \$180X_{43} + \$36X_{44} + \$630X_{45} + \$756X_{46}$$
$$+ \$330X_{51} + \$300X_{52} + \$360X_{53} + \$180X_{54} + \$450X_{55} + \$720X_{56}$$
$$+ \$180X_{61} + \$220X_{62} + \$240X_{63} + \$80X_{64} + \$320X_{65} + \$760X_{66}$$

where $JC =$ the total cost of completing all current jobs (the criterion value) and the decision variables (X_{ij} values) are defined as before. Janet Cook seeks the assignments (X_{ij} values) that will minimize the total cost of completing all current jobs (JC).

Restrictions. There will be restrictions on the objective. One set of system constraints must assure that each specialist is assigned to exactly one job. For example, since Davis can do only one job (among the DB, EIS, WP, E-Mail, ISA, or ACC alternatives) at a time, this person's total assignments must sum to 1, or

$$X_{11} + X_{12} + X_{13} + X_{14} + X_{15} + X_{16} = 1$$

Similar balance conditions are

$$X_{21} + X_{22} + X_{23} + X_{24} + X_{25} + X_{26} = 1 \qquad \text{for Florino}$$
$$X_{31} + X_{32} + X_{33} + X_{34} + X_{35} + X_{36} = 1 \qquad \text{for Lippincott}$$
$$X_{41} + X_{42} + X_{43} + X_{44} + X_{45} + X_{46} = 1 \qquad \text{for Thomas}$$
$$X_{51} + X_{52} + X_{53} + X_{54} + X_{55} + X_{56} = 1 \qquad \text{for Torrez}$$
$$X_{61} + X_{62} + X_{63} + X_{64} + X_{65} + X_{66} = 1 \qquad \text{for Webber}$$

Another set of system constraints is needed to assure that each job is assigned to exactly one specialist. For example, since the data base (DB) job can only be done by one specialist (among the Davis, Florino, Lippincott, Thomas, Torrez, or Webber alternatives) at a time, this job's total assignments must sum to 1, or

$$X_{11} + X_{21} + X_{31} + X_{41} + X_{51} + X_{61} = 1$$

In a similar manner,

$$X_{12} + X_{22} + X_{32} + X_{42} + X_{52} + X_{62} = 1 \qquad \text{for the EIS job}$$
$$X_{13} + X_{23} + X_{33} + X_{43} + X_{53} + X_{63} = 1 \qquad \text{for the WP job}$$
$$X_{14} + X_{24} + X_{34} + X_{44} + X_{54} + X_{64} = 1 \qquad \text{for the E-Mail job}$$
$$X_{15} + X_{25} + X_{35} + X_{45} + X_{55} + X_{65} = 1 \qquad \text{for the ISA job}$$
$$X_{16} + X_{26} + X_{36} + X_{46} + X_{56} + X_{66} = 1 \qquad \text{for the ACC job}$$

Finally, Janet must ensure that each decision variable has a value of 1 (if the specialist is assigned to the job) or 0 (if the specialist is not assigned to the job). That is, she will need the following set of restrictions:

$$X_{ij} = 1 \text{ or } 0 \qquad \text{for all } i \text{ and } j$$

These restrictions (which can be viewed as special types of nonnegativity conditions) together with the set of 12 (specialist and job) system constraints also will eliminate any fractional (and thereby impractical) assignments.

Linear Program. Janet Jones wants to assign each available specialist to a current information center job in a way that, within the assignment restrictions, will minimize the total cost of completing the jobs. That is, she seeks to

Minimize

$$JC = \$220X_{11} + \$176X_{12} + \$264X_{13} + \$88X_{14} + \$396X_{15} + \$704X_{16}$$

$$+ \$168X_{21} + \$144X_{22} + \$384X_{23} + \$72X_{24} + \$312X_{25} + \$600X_{26}$$

$$+ \$350X_{31} + \$225X_{32} + \$225X_{33} + \$125X_{34} + \$500X_{35} + \$700X_{36}$$

$$+ \$108X_{41} + \$126X_{42} + \$180X_{43} + \$36X_{44} + \$630X_{45} + \$756X_{46}$$

$$+ \$330X_{51} + \$300X_{52} + \$360X_{53} + \$180X_{54} + \$450X_{55} + \$720X_{56}$$

$$+ \$180X_{61} + \$220X_{62} + \$240X_{63} + \$80X_{64} + \$320X_{65} + \$760X_{66}$$

Subject to

$X_{11} + X_{12} + X_{13} + X_{14} + X_{15} + X_{16} = 1$	for Davis
$X_{21} + X_{22} + X_{23} + X_{24} + X_{25} + X_{26} = 1$	for Florino
$X_{31} + X_{32} + X_{33} + X_{34} + X_{35} + X_{36} = 1$	for Lippincott
$X_{41} + X_{42} + X_{43} + X_{44} + X_{45} + X_{46} = 1$	for Thomas
$X_{51} + X_{52} + X_{53} + X_{54} + X_{55} + X_{56} = 1$	for Torrez
$X_{61} + X_{62} + X_{63} + X_{64} + X_{65} + X_{66} = 1$	for Webber
$X_{11} + X_{21} + X_{31} + X_{41} + X_{51} + X_{61} = 1$	for the DB job
$X_{12} + X_{22} + X_{32} + X_{42} + X_{52} + X_{62} = 1$	for the EIS job
$X_{13} + X_{23} + X_{33} + X_{43} + X_{53} + X_{63} = 1$	for the WP job
$X_{14} + X_{24} + X_{34} + X_{44} + X_{54} + X_{64} = 1$	for the E-Mail job
$X_{15} + X_{25} + X_{35} + X_{45} + X_{55} + X_{65} = 1$	for the ISA job
$X_{16} + X_{26} + X_{36} + X_{46} + X_{56} + X_{66} = 1$	for the ACC job

$$X_{ij} = 1 \text{ or } 0 \qquad \text{for all } i \text{ and } j$$

This consolidated statement of the objective function, system (specialist and job) constraints, and one-zero (special types of nonnegativity) conditions gives the mathematical model for Janet's one-time (current job assignment) problem.

Since such a model involves integer (0 or 1) decision variables, it is not a linear program. Strictly speaking, it is an **integer program**. However, because of its special structure, which will be exploited in a later chapter, the model can be treated as a linear program.

Special Formulation Issues

Although the five problem classes account for a large percentage of applications, managers may encounter an actual linear program that fits none of the five categories or that is actually a combination of two or more classes. Indeed, you will run into several additional linear program types throughout this module's text, examples, and exercises. The formulation process for these additional programs will be as shown in Figure 7.1.

In formulating some of these problems, managers may encounter special characteristics that are inconsistent with linear programming formulations. Fortunately, these inconsistencies frequently can be overcome in a way that allows the manager to formulate the problem as a linear program. The following table outlines important special characteristics, the resulting difficulties, and appropriate remedies.

Special Characteristic	Example	Linear Program Difficulty	Linear Program Remedy
Nonpositive variable (sign condition of $X_j \leq 0$)	X_3 = the trade balance for a firm that will not export more than it imports	Violates the nonnegativity condition	Replace X_3 with the negative of a nonnegative variable, such as $-T_3$, where T_3 = the firm's trade deficit
Unrestricted variable (sign condition that X_j can be positive, zero, or negative)	X_2 = the change in a firm's assets	Violates the nonnegativity condition when there is a decrease in assets	Replace X_2 with the difference between two nonnegative variables, such as $(IA_2 - DA_2)$, where IA_2 = the increase in assets and DA_2 = the decrease in assets
Strict inequality	$ST + BD <\$180,000$ where ST = dollars invested in stocks, BD = dollars invested in bonds, and the \$200,000 is a budget	Solution methodology requires weak inequalities ($\leq$ or $\geq$) or equalities ($=$)	Replace \$180,000 with a value that is within an acceptable tolerance, such as \$179,999.99

Also, linear programming's solution methodology requires us to place all decision variables on the left side and a nonnegative constant on the right side of each system constraint. That is why such a format was created when formulating the linear programs for Management Situations 7.1 through 7.6.

7.3 GRAPHICAL SOLUTION PROCEDURE

After the decision maker properly formulates the linear program, he or she next must develop a recommended problem solution. It will take special mathematical methodologies, such as the one presented in the next chapter, to solve problems like those encountered in Management Situations 7.2 through 7.6 (and their even larger-scale counterparts). These methodologies first identify **feasible solutions**, or decision variable combinations that simultaneously satisfy all restrictions in the linear program. A systematic procedure then is used to find the most preferred solution among the feasible combinations.

The concepts can be illustrated graphically through a simple linear programming problem with only two decision variables, such as the one presented in Management Situation 7.7.

Management Situation 7.7

Media Selection

The advertising agency promoting the new Rapido sports car wants to get the best possible exposure for the product within the available $200,000 budget. To do so, the agency must decide how much to spend on its two most effective media: evening television spots and large magazine ads. Each television spot costs $20,000 and a magazine ad involves a $5,000 expenditure. Fractional spots and ads can be purchased from the media. By processing industry ratings data through the company's media evaluation information system (MEIS), research staff have estimated that 400,000 people will be reached with each television spot and 150,000 people will be reached with a magazine ad.

Dawn Shaw, the agency director, knows from experience that it is important to use both media. In this way, the advertising will reach the broadest spectrum of potential Rapido customers. As a result, she decides to contract for at least 4, but no more than 12, television spots and a minimum of 6 magazine ads.

Formulating the Linear Program

The advertising agency's problem is to determine the media combination that will maximize total audience exposure. This combination must satisfy Dawn Shaw's spot/ad specifications and must involve an expenditure that is within the advertising budget.

Objective. The agency's single measurable objective is to maximize the total audience exposure from the media placements. Dawn Shaw can influence this exposure by setting the quantity of each spot/ad. These decision variables can be depicted as follows:

$$TV = \text{the number of evening television spots}$$

$$MG = \text{the number of large magazine ads}$$

Each spot/ad will contribute its quantity multiplied by the corresponding reach. For example, since each television spot reaches a constant 400,000 people, this instrument's contribution to audience exposure will be

$$400,000TV.$$

Total audience exposure will equal the sum of the spot/ad independent contributions, so that the agency's objective function will be

$$A = 400,000TV + 150,000MG$$

where A = the total audience exposure (the criterion value) and the decision variables (TV and MG) are defined as before. Dawn Shaw seeks the placements (TV and MG values) that will maximize the total audience exposure (A).

Restrictions. One system constraint on the objective must ensure that the agency spends no more money on advertising than is available in the budget. Each television spot costs a constant $20,000, while a magazine ad costs $5,000. The total demand for budget dollars will be the sum of the independent spot/ad requirements or

$$\$20,000TV + \$5,000MG.$$

Since this total demand cannot exceed the $200,000 available, the budget resource limit can be written as:

$$\$20,000TV + \$5,000MG \leq \$200,000.$$

Another set of system constraints must ensure that the placements satisfy Dawn Shaw's minimum television spot and magazine ad requirements and her maximum television spot specification. For example, Dawn wants to contract for no more than 12 television spots, or have

$$TV \leq 12.$$

In addition, the agency must contract for at least four television spots, or have

$$TV \geq 4$$

and contract for at least six magazine ads, or have

$$MG \geq 6.$$

The nonnegativity conditions of

$$TV, \ MG \geq 0$$

guarantee that the agency will place a zero or positive number of television spots and magazine ads.

Linear Program. Dawn Shaw wants to place the number of television spots and magazine ads that, within the budget and spot/ad specification restrictions, will maximize the total audience exposure to the Rapido sports car. That is, the agency seeks to

Maximize $A = 400,000TV + 150,000MG$

Subject to

$\$20,000TV + \$5,000MG \leq \$200,000$ (Budget)

$TV \leq 12$ (Maximum television)

$TV \geq 4$ (Minimum television)

$$MG \geq 6 \qquad\qquad\qquad \text{(Minimum magazine)}$$

$$TV, \ MG \geq 0$$

This consolidated statement of the objective function, system constraints, and nonnegativity conditions gives the linear program for the agency's one-time media selection problem.

Feasible Solutions

The nonnegativity conditions

$$TV, \ MG \geq 0$$

require the decision variables to have values greater than or equal to zero. These conditions are displayed graphically as Figure 7.2.

In Figure 7.2, TV's values are shown along the horizontal axis, while MG's values are shown along the vertical axis. A point on the graph indicates the values of TV and MG by its position relative to the respective axes. For example, the origin point (0, 0) signifies a combination of $TV = 0$ spots and $MG = 0$ ads. Since each point on the graph identifies a potential solution to the problem, it is referred to as a **solution point**.

As Figure 7.2 demonstrates, the nonnegativity conditions are satisfied by the solution points (combinations of TV and MG values) that are on or to the right of the vertical axis and on or above the horizontal axis. Many of these points, however, will not satisfy the system constraints.

Budget Constraint. The inequality

$$\$20,000TV + \$5,000MG \leq \$200,000$$

gives the budget constraint. Media combinations that use all of the available budget will satisfy the equality part of the constraint, or have

$$\$20,000TV + \$5,000MG = \$200,000.$$

Since this equality involves a linear relationship, we can graph the budget first by finding two solution points that satisfy the equation and then by using these points to plot a straight line.

We can readily find the two solution points (combinations of TV and MG values) that satisfy the budget equation (use all of the available budget). One such point is $TV = 0$ spots and

$$\$20,000(0) + \$5,000MG = \$200,000$$

or $\qquad\qquad\qquad MG = \$200,000/\$5,000 = 40$

ads. Another solution point is $MG = 0$ ads and

$$\$20,000TV + \$5,000(0) = \$200,000$$

or $\qquad\qquad\qquad TV = \$200,000/\$20,000 = 10$

spots. Figure 7.3 then shows the line connecting the first ($TV = 0$, $MG = 40$) and second ($TV = 10$, $MG = 0$) points superimposed on the nonnegative solution area of Figure 7.2.

Figure 7.2   **The Agency's Nonnegativity Conditions**

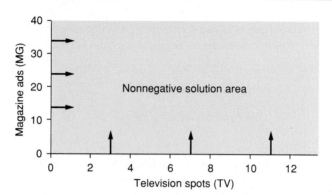

Any solution point below the budget ($\$20,000TV + \$5,000MG = \$200,000$) line in Figure 7.3 will spend fewer dollars than are available. That is, such points will satisfy the strict inequality

$$\$20,000TV + \$5,000MG < \$200,000.$$

For example, the solution point (3, 10) spends only

$$\$20,000TV + \$5,000MG = \$20,000(3) + \$5,000(10) = \$110,000$$

which is $\$200,000 - \$110,000 = \$90,000$ less than the available budget. Points above the line spend more than the available budget and are thereby unacceptable media combinations. An example is the combination of $TV = 12$ spots and $MG = 30$ ads. This solution point (12, 30) spends

$$\$20,000TV + \$5,000MG = \$20,000(12) + \$5,000(30) = \$390,000$$

which is $\$390,000 - \$200,000 = \$190,000$ more than the available budget.

Only solution points on or below the budget line in Figure 7.3 satisfy the budget constraint and the nonnegativity conditions. Such nonnegative budget-feasible points will be on the boundary lines and within the shaded region in Figure 7.3.

Spot/Ad Specifications. Placements that exactly meet the maximum television spot specification ($TV \leq 12$) will have

$$TV = 12$$

(regardless of MG's value) and appear as the vertical line in Figure 7.4, which again is superimposed on the nonnegative solution area of Figure 7.2.

Only solution points on or to the left of the maximum television ($TV = 12$) line in Figure 7.4 satisfy the maximum television spot specification and the nonnegativity conditions. For example, the solution point (6, 15) has fewer than the maximum allowable television spots and thereby is an acceptable combination. Such nonnegative maximum television-feasible points will be on the boundary lines of and within the shaded region in Figure 7.4.

Figure 7.3   **The Agency's Budget Constraint**

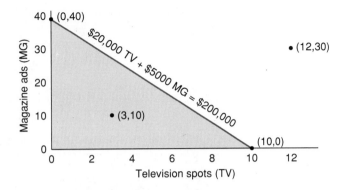

Figure 7.4   **The Agency's Maximum Television Constraint**

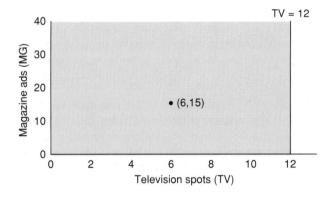

The inequality

$$TV \geq 4$$

depicts the minimum television spot requirement. Placements that exactly meet the requirement will satisfy the equality part of this constraint, or have

$$TV = 4$$

(regardless of MG's value) and appear as the vertical line in Figure 7.5, which again is superimposed on the nonnegative solution area of Figure 7.2.

Any solution point to the right of the minimum television ($TV = 4$) line in Figure 7.5 will have more spots than the minimum requirement. That is, such points will satisfy the strict inequality

$$TV > 4$$

For example, the solution point (8, 25) has

$$TV = 8$$

Figure 7.5   **The Agency's Minimum Television Constraint**

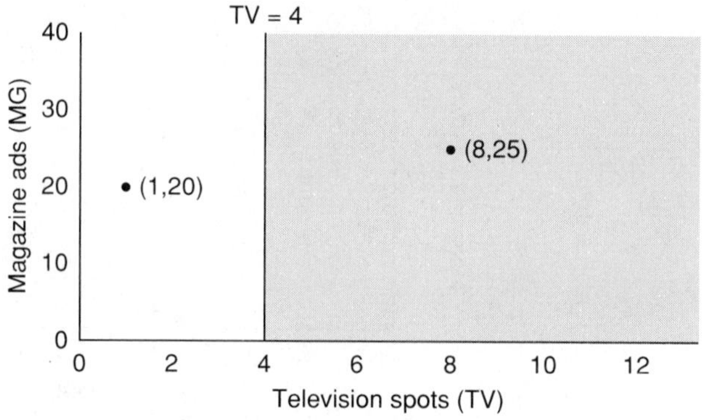

or $8 - 4 = 4$ spots more than the minimum requirement. Points to the left of the line involve fewer than the minimum required spots and are thereby unacceptable media combinations. An example is the solution point (1, 20), which has

$$TV = 1$$

or $4 - 1 = 3$ spots less than the minimum requirement.

Only solution points on or to the right of the minimum television line in Figure 7.5 satisfy the minimum television spot requirement and the nonnegativity conditions. Such nonnegative minimum television-feasible points will be on the boundary lines and within the shaded region in Figure 7.5.

The graph of the minimum magazine

$$MG \geq 6$$

can be constructed in a similar manner. Placements that exactly meet the requirement will satisfy the equality part of this constraint or have

$$MG = 6$$

(regardless of TV's value) and appear as the horizontal line in Figure 7.6, which again is superimposed on the nonnegative solution area of Figure 7.2.

Only solution points on or above the minimum magazine ($MG = 6$) line in Figure 7.6 satisfy the minimum magazine ad requirement and the nonnegativity conditions. For example, the solution point (9, 35) has more than the minimum required magazine ads and thus is acceptable. However, the solution point below the line (4, 3) has fewer than the minimum required ads and thus is unacceptable. Nonnegative minimum magazine-feasible points will be on the boundary lines and within the shaded region in Figure 7.6.

Feasible Solution Area. By plotting the nonnegativity conditions (Figure 7.2) and the system constraints (Figures 7.3 through 7.6) on the same diagram, Dawn Shaw will obtain

Figure 7.6   **The Agency's Minimum Magazine Constraint**

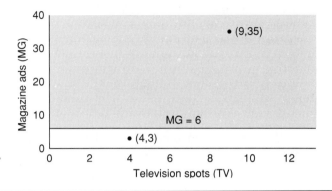

Figure 7.7   **The Agency's Feasible Solution Area**

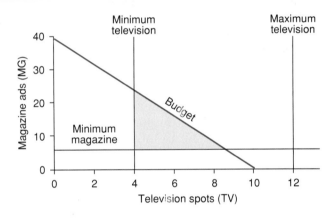

a graph, Figure 7.7, that simultaneously displays all the restrictions in the advertising agency's problem. The solution points on the boundary lines of and within the shaded region of Figure 7.7 are the only ones that simultaneously satisfy all restrictions. Since such points identify feasible solutions to the problem, this shaded region (including its boundary lines) is known as the **feasible solution area**.

Notice that the agency's feasible solution area is defined completely by the minimum television, minimum magazine, and budget constraint lines. The maximum television restriction line has no effect on this area. In fact, Dawn Shaw could satisfy the maximum television specification automatically by spending no more than the available budget on television and magazine advertising. The maximum television restriction then is unnecessary in solving the problem. Such a system constraint, which does not affect the feasible solution area, is called a **redundant restriction**.

Optimal Solution

There are an infinite number of points in the agency's feasible solution area. Unlimited media combinations can be selected to generate audience exposure with the available budget and within the spot/ad specifications. Since it would be physically impossible as well as impractical to evaluate each possibility, Dawn Shaw will need a systematic procedure to find the combination that maximizes total audience exposure.

In one popular approach, a plot of the objective function first is superimposed on the graph of the feasible solution area. Then, the function is shifted in a direction that improves the criterion value. Such shifting continues until an optimal solution is found.

Objective Function Line. Total audience exposure (A) is measured with the agency's objective function of

$$A = 400,000TV + 150,000MG.$$

Since this relationship is linear, we can graph the objective function by (1) selecting an arbitrary positive value for the criterion value A, (2) finding two solution points that satisfy the resulting equation, and (3) using these points to plot a straight line.

For example, when audience exposure is $A = 2,500,000$ people, the objective function becomes

$$2,500,000 = 400,000TV + 150,000MG.$$

One solution point that satisfies this equation is $TV = 0$ spots and

$$2,500,000 = 400,000(0) + 150,000MG$$

or $$MG = 2,500,000/150,000 = 16.67$$

ads. Another solution point is $MG = 0$ ads and

$$2,500,000 = 400,000TV + 150,000(0)$$

or $$TV = 2,500,000/400,000 = 6.25$$

spots. Figure 7.8 then shows the line connecting the first $(TV = 0, MG = 16.67)$ and second $(TV = 6.25, MG = 0)$ points superimposed on the feasible solution area of Figure 7.7.

Shifting the Line. Any solution point (media combination) on the $A = 2,500,000$ objective function line in Figure 7.8 will generate the same audience exposure of 2,500,000 people. One such combination is at the intersection of two restriction lines (minimum television and minimum magazine) that bound, or form a so-called **corner point** or **extreme point** of, the agency's feasible solution area. Therefore, this combination enables the agency to generate an audience exposure of 2,500,000 people with its available budget, while meeting Dawn's spot/ads specifications.

Nevertheless, there are feasible solution points (TV and MG values) above and to the right of the 2,500,000 objective function line. These points involve more spot/ad placements and thereby larger audience exposures than the feasible media combination on the 2,500,000 line. To attain such preferable points, the agency must shift the objective function line out to the right and upward. Since the media make constant unit and

Figure 7.8   **The Agency's 2,500,000 Objective Function Line**

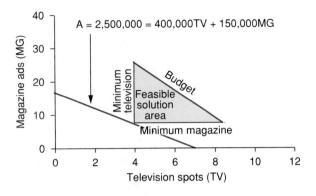

Figure 7.9   **Shifting the Agency's Objective Function Lines**

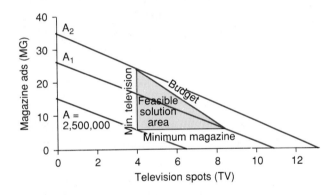

independent contributions, such shifting will create a series of parallel objective function lines, such as A_1 and A_2 in Figure 7.9.

Optimal Solution Point. As Figure 7.9 demonstrates, the agency cannot shift the objective function beyond the A_2 line without moving outside the feasible solution area. Put another way, A_2 is the largest feasible, or optimal, audience exposure.

Figure 7.9 also shows that only one solution point (media combination) on the A_2 objective function line is feasible. This single optimal combination is at a corner (or extreme) point of the agency's feasible solution area. Such a result is not a coincidence. *An optimal solution to every linear program (if it exists) occurs at a corner point or extreme point of the feasible solution area (if it exists).*

In the agency's case, Figure 7.9 shows that the relevant corner point is formed by the intersection of the budget constraint line

$$\$20,000TV + \$5,000MG = \$200,000$$

and the minimum television constraint line

$$TV = 4.$$

As a result, the optimal media combination is $TV = 4$ spots and

$$\$20,000(4) + \$5,000MG = \$200,000$$

or $$MG = (\$200,000 - \$80,000)/\$5,000 = 24$$

ads. Since the objective function is

$$A = 400,000TV + 150,000MG$$

this optimal media combination will maximize total audience exposure at

$$A = 400,000(4) + 150,000(24) = 5,200,000.$$

The graphic analysis then indicates that the agency can maximize total audience exposure at 5,200,000 people, within the budget and spot/ad specification restrictions, by placing 4 evening television spots and 24 large magazine ads. Notice that this optimal media combination involves $24/4 = 6$ times as many magazine ads as television spots, although each spot generates $400,000/150,000 = 2.67$ times as much audience exposure as each ad. Such a result seems more logical, however, when we realize that each television spot costs $20,000/\$5,000 = 4$ times as much as each magazine ad.

Procedure Recap. When there are only two decision variables, the following graphic procedure can be used to solve a linear programming problem:

1. Use the restrictions to graph the feasible solution area.
2. Superimpose an arbitrary objective function line on the graph of the feasible solution area.
3. Shift the objective function line in a parallel fashion toward more preferred criterion values until further shifting becomes infeasible.
4. Use the results to locate an optimal solution point.
5. Simultaneously solve the constraint equations that form the optimal solution point for the best values of the decision variables.
6. Substitute the optimal decision variable combination into the objective function to find the best criterion value.

Slack and Surplus Variables

The examination of the optimal media combination reiterates an important principle: when developing a solution, the decision maker must focus on the whole (the objective and its restrictions) rather than on a specific part of the linear program. It also suggests that additional insight can be gained by studying the managerial ramifications of the optimal solution. An investigation of any unused limit or surplus requirement will provide some of the insight.

Slack. According to the budget constraint ($\$20,000TV + \$5,000MG \leq \$200,000$), the agency can select a media combination that spends less than the available \$200,000.

Put another way, there can be some unused budget dollars. Since the actual expenditure ($20,000TV + $5,000MG) can be any amount up to $200,000, this unused budget will be a variable.

To account for any potential difference between the actual expenditure and the budget limit, the agency must define a new variable (with a subscript of 1 because this budget restriction is the first system constraint in the linear program):

$$S_1 = \text{the unused budget dollars.}$$

Such a variable, which accounts for any unused system constraint limit, is known as a **slack variable**. By adding this variable to the left side of the original restriction, we can write the budget constraint as

$$\$20,000TV + \$5,000MG + S_1 = \$200,000.$$

That is, the action transforms the original less-than-or-equal-to restriction into an equality relationship.

The agency's maximum television constraint ($TV \leq 12$) can be transformed into an equality by a similar process. First, Ms. Shaw defines another slack variable (with a subscript of 2 because this maximum television restriction is the second system constraint in the linear program)

$$S_2 = \text{spots less than the maximum television limit}$$

to account for any difference between the actual placement (TV) and the limit (12). By adding S_2 to the left side of the original restriction, she can write the maximum television constraint as

$$TV + S_2 = 12.$$

At the agency's optimal solution point, $TV = 4$ and $MG = 24$. Consequently, this solution will involve

$$\$20,000(4) + \$5,000(24) + S_1 = \$200,000$$

or $$S_1 = \$200,000 - \$200,000 = \$0$$

of unused budget, which means that the optimal solution point will be on the budget line in Figure 7.9. Also, the solution will involve

$$S_2 = 12 - TV = 12 - 4 = 8$$

spots less than the maximum television limit, which means that the optimal point will be eight spots to the left of the maximum television line in Figure 7.7.

Since unused budget dollars (S_1) and underspecified television spots (S_2) do not generate audience exposure, neither of these slack variables will have any effect on the objective function. Nevertheless, the S_1 and S_2 values can provide valuable decision information.

The no-slack budget ($S_1 = \$0$) finding indicates that the agency is fully utilizing its current available funds. Thus, Dawn will be unable to place more spots/ads (and thereby increase audience exposure) until she finds additional budget resources. On the other hand, the S_2 value suggests that the maximum television specification is eight spots above the level needed to achieve the current optimal media combination. Conditions must change then before this specification becomes an important decision consideration.

Surplus. According to the minimum television constraint ($TV \geq 4$), the agency can select a television placement that has more spots than the minimum requirement. In other words, there can be some excess television spots above the minimum requirement. Since the actual number of spots can be any amount over four, this excess placement will be a variable.

To account for any potential difference between the actual placement and the minimum requirement, the agency must define a new variable (with a subscript of 3 because the minimum television restriction is the third system constraint in the linear program):

$S_3 = $ spots in excess of the minimum television requirement.

Such a variable, which accounts for any excess amount beyond a specified minimum requirement, is known as a **surplus variable.** By subtracting this variable from the left side of the original restriction, we can write the minimum television requirement as

$$TV - S_3 = 4.$$

That is, the action transforms the original greater-than-or-equal-to restriction into an equality relationship.

The agency's minimum magazine constraint ($MG \geq 6$) can be transformed into an equality by the same process. First, Ms. Shaw defines another surplus variable

$S_4 = $ spots in excess of the minimum magazine requirement

to account for any difference between the actual placement (MG) and the minimum requirement (6). By subtracting S_4 from the left side of the original restriction, she can write the minimum magazine constraint as

$$MG - S_4 = 6.$$

At the agency's optimal solution point, $TV = 4$ and $MG = 24$. Consequently, this solution will involve

$$S_3 = TV - 4 = 4 - 4 = 0$$

spots in excess of the minimum requirement, which means that the optimal solution point will be on the minimum television line in Figure 7.9. Also, the solution will involve

$$S_4 = MG - 6 = 24 - 6 = 18$$

ads in excess of the minimum requirement, which means that the optimal point will be 18 spots above the minimum magazine line in Figure 7.9.

Since excess television spots (S_3) and excess magazine ads (S_4) do not generate new audience exposure, neither of these surplus variables will have an effect on the objective function. Still, the S_3 and S_4 values can offer valuable decision information.

The S_3 value indicates that the agency is placing the exact minimum required number of television spots, while the S_4 value shows that the minimum magazine specification is 18 spots below the level in the current optimal media combination. These findings suggest that the minimum television requirement is needed to achieve the "balance" desired by Ms. Shaw. If Dawn feels strongly that additional television spots are required to reach a broader spectrum of potential Rapido customers, then she should consider increasing the minimum television requirement.

Binding Constraints. Since there is no slack in the budget constraint and no surplus in the minimum television constraint at the optimal solution, these restrictions effectively prohibit the agency from further increasing audience exposure. Such restrictions, which prevent further improvement in the objective function, are known as **binding constraints**. On the other hand, there is slack in the maximum television constraint and surplus in the minimum magazine constraint at the optimal solution. These restrictions do not prevent further improvement in the objective function and thus are called **nonbinding constraints**.

Minimization Problems

The same graphic solution procedure can be applied to linear programs that involve two decision variables and a minimization objective, as Management Situation 7.8 illustrates.

Management Situation 7.8

Herb Farming

Sunnybrook Farms must determine the least-cost mixture of fertilizer ingredients to use on its experimental herb acreage. Zaleum, which costs 50 cents per ounce, and oritung, which costs 60 cents per ounce, can be used in the blend. By processing government data through its computer information system (CIS), staff have found that each ounce of zaleum is 24 percent potassium, 12 percent calcium, and 22 percent potash. A similar CIS analysis shows that an ounce of oritung is 20 percent potassium, 18 percent calcium, and 15 percent potash. Also, computer projections indicate that the experimental herb will require at least 10 pounds of potassium, 8 pounds of calcium, and 10 pounds of potash per tract.

   As part of the experiment, scientists want the mixture to contain no more oritung than triple the amount of zaleum. The scientific team also has a $1,000 budget to conduct the experiment.

Linear Program. Sunnybrook wants to select the zaleum and oritung quantities that will minimize the total cost of blending the herb subject to nutrient (potassium, calcium, and potash), budget, and mixture restrictions. This problem can be expressed as the following linear program:

Minimize $BC = \$8ZA + \$9.60OR$

Subject to $0.24ZA + 0.20OR \geq 10$ pounds   (Potassium)

                  $0.12ZA + 0.18OR \geq 8$ pounds   (Calcium)

                  $0.22ZA + 0.15OR \geq 10$ pounds   (Potash)

                  $\$8ZA + \$9.60OR \leq \$1,000$ (Budget)

Figure 7.10   Sunnybrook's Feasible Solution Area

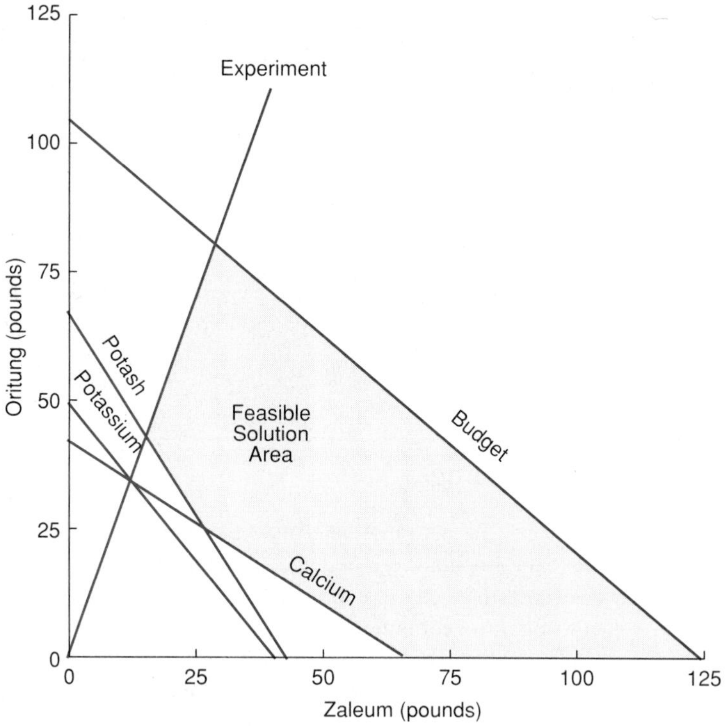

$$-3ZA + OR \leq 0 \qquad \text{(Experiment)}$$

$$ZA,\ OR \geq 0$$

where BC = the total cost of blending the experimental herb, ZA = the pounds of zaleum in the blend, and OR = the pounds of oritung in the blend.

Feasible Solution Area. By plotting the nonnegativity conditions and the system (potassium, calcium, potash, budget, and experiment) constraints on the same diagram, the scientific team will obtain Figure 7.10, which simultaneously displays all the restrictions in Sunnybrook's blending problem. The solution points on the boundary lines and within the shaded region of Figure 7.10 identify the farm's feasible solution area. In this figure, notice that the potassium constraint does not affect Sunnybrook's feasible solution area and is therefore a redundant restriction.

Optimal Solution. Total blending cost (BC) is measured with the farm's objective function of

$$BC = \$8ZA + \$9.60OR.$$

Figure 7.11   Sunnybrook's Optimal Solution

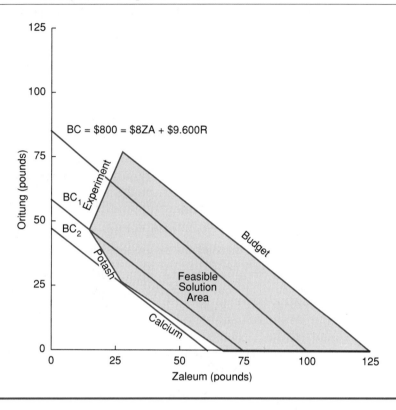

When this cost is set at an arbitrary value of $BC = \$800$, the objective function becomes

$$\$800 = \$8ZA + \$9.60OR.$$

Figure 7.11 then shows a plot of this objective function line superimposed on the feasible solution area of Figure 7.10.

By shifting the $BC = \$800$ objective function line down and to the left, the scientific team will reduce the pounds of zaleum and oritung in the blend and thereby lower costs. Since these ingredients make constant unit and independent contributions, such shifting will create a series of parallel objective function lines, such as BC_1 and BC_2 in Figure 7.11. As this figure indicates, Sunnybrook cannot shift the objective function beyond the BC_2 line without moving below the feasible solution area. Thus, BC_2 is the lowest cost feasible, or optimal, experimental herb blend.

Figure 7.11 also shows that only one solution point (herb blend) on the BC_2 objective function line is feasible. This single optimal blend is formed at a corner point by the intersection of the calcium constraint line

$$0.12ZA + 0.18OR = 8 \text{ pounds}$$

and the potash constraint line

$$0.22ZA + 0.15OR = 10 \text{ pounds.}$$

As a result, the optimal blend will have

$$OR = (10 - 0.22ZA)/0.15 = 66.6667 - 1.4667ZA$$

and by substitution

$$0.12ZA + 0.18(66.6667 - 1.4667ZA) = 8$$

or $\qquad ZA = (12 - 8)/(0.264 - 0.120) = 27.7778$

pounds of zaleum and

$$OR = 66.6667 - 1.4667(27.7778) = 25.925$$

pounds of oritung. Such a solution will minimize at

$$BC = \$8ZA + \$9.60OR = \$8(27.7778) + \$9.60(25.925) = \$471.10,$$

the total cost of blending the experimental herb.

Slack and Surplus Variables. To account for any potential difference between the actual potassium content in the blend $(.24ZA + .20OR)$ and the minimum requirement (10 pounds), the scientific team must subtract the surplus variable

$$S_1 = \text{excess pounds of potassium}$$

from the left side of the original restriction. The potassium constraint then can be written as the following equality:

$$0.24ZA + 0.20OR - S_1 = 10 \text{ pounds.}$$

Similarly, the calcium constraint can be written as

$$0.12ZA + 0.18OR - S_2 = 8 \text{ pounds}$$

and the potash constraint can be expressed as

$$0.22ZA + 0.15OR - S_3 = 10 \text{ pounds}$$

where $S_2 = $ the excess pounds of calcium and $S_3 = $ the excess pounds of potash in the experimental blend.

At Sunnybrook's optimal solution $(ZA = 27.7778$ and $OR = 25.925)$, there will be

$$0.24(27.7778) + 0.20(25.925) - S_1 = 10 \text{ pounds}$$

or $\qquad S_1 = 11.852 - 10 = 1.852$

excess pounds of potassium,

$$0.12(27.7778) + 0.18(25.925) - S_2 = 8 \text{ pounds}$$

or $\qquad S_2 = 8 - 8 = 0$

excess pounds of calcium, and

$$0.22(27.7778) + 0.15(25.925) - S_3 = 10 \text{ pounds}$$

or $\qquad\qquad\qquad\qquad\qquad S_3 = 10 - 10 = 0$

excess pounds of potash. Put another way, the optimal herb blend will need exactly the minimum required potash and calcium but 1.852 pounds more than the minimum required potassium.

To account for any potential difference between the actual expenditure ($\$8ZA + \$9.60OR$) and the budget ($\$1,000$) limit, the scientific team must add the slack variable

$$S_4 = \text{ unused budget dollars}$$

to the left side of the original restriction. The budget constraint then can be written as

$$\$8ZA + \$9.60OR + S_4 = \$1,000.$$

In a similar manner, the experiment constraint can be expressed as

$$-3ZA + OR + S_5 = 0$$

where S_5 = the pounds of oritung below the triple zaleum limit.

Sunnybrook's optimal solution ($ZA = 27.7778$ and $OR = 25.925$) will involve

$$\$8(27.7778) + \$9.60(25.925) + S_4 = \$1,000$$

or $\qquad\qquad\qquad S_4 = \$1,000 - \$471.10 = \$528.90$

unused budget dollars and

$$-3(27.7778) + (25.925) + S_5 = 0$$

or $\qquad\qquad\qquad S_5 = 83.3334 - 25.925 = 57.4084$

pounds of oritung below the triple zaleum limit. In other words, the optimal herb blend can be mixed for $528.90 less than budgeted, and it will contain an almost equal amount of zaleum and oritung.

Special Solution Issues

As Management Situations 7.6 and 7.7 illustrate, the feasible solution area can take a variety of forms. Among other things, it can be bounded by an axis of the graph (as in Figure 7.10), be in the middle of the nonnegative solution area (as in Figure 7.7), or be a line segment (as when the linear program has an equality constraint). Indeed, you will run into several feasible solution area forms throughout the exercises.

Since an optimal solution to every linear program (if it exists) occurs at a corner point of the feasible solution area (if it exists), the decision maker can find this best solution with the following procedure:

1. Use the restrictions to graph the feasible solution area.

2. Identify the extreme points of the feasible solution area.

3. Substitute each extreme point into the objective function.

4. The optimal solution is the extreme point that leads to the most preferred value of the objective.

This corner point method can be used as an alternative to the objective function line approach presented earlier.

In attempting to solve the problem with either alternative, the manager may encounter the special situations outlined in the following table.

Special Situation	Description	Example	Typical Interpretation
Infeasible problem	No combination of decision variables simultaneously satisfies all problem restrictions	In the example, the plot of the constraints does not form a feasible solution area	The problem has no feasible solution, or it has been improperly formulated (maybe because important constraints have been overlooked or expressed incorrectly or because the constraints' uncontrollable inputs are inaccurate)
Unbounded problem	The restrictions do not put an effective limit on the values of the decision variables	In the example, shifting the objective function line out toward better criterion values never becomes infeasible	The problem has been improperly formulated (usually because important constraints have been overlooked)
Multiple optimal solutions	The linear program has more than one optimal solution	In the example, the best objective function line (closest to the origin) is tangent to a line segment of the feasible solution area	The manager can consider additional (perhaps qualitative) criteria and then implement the most advantageous optimal solution

Since such situations can affect the development of a problem solution, they warrant the manager's attention. In attending to these special situations, the decision maker should focus on the typical interpretations suggested in the table. Thought Exercises 10, 11, and 12 will provide illustrations.

SUMMARY

This chapter introduced a methodology, called linear programming, that can help decision makers solve a variety of management problems. The initial section presented the characteristics of the methodology. It showed that a linear program consists of an objective function, system constraints, and nonnegativity conditions. To use this methodology properly, the manager must assume that the problem involves divisible decision variables, additive and proportional relationships, a single objective, deterministic information, and a one-time decision. We explained that these assumptions are met or closely approximated in many applications.

Once the decision maker is satisfied that the problem has linear programming characteristics, he or she next must use the process shown in Figure 7.1 to formulate the appropriate linear program. The second section demonstrated this process with illustrations drawn from five major classes of linear programming applications: assignment, blending, planning and scheduling, resource allocation, and transportation. This second section also presented special formulation issues.

After the decision maker properly formulates the linear program, he or she must develop a recommended problem solution. The chapter's third section graphically explained how the manager can generate such a solution. It showed that the decision maker first must identify feasible solutions, or decision variable combinations that simultaneously satisfy all restrictions in the linear program. A systematic procedure is then used to find the most preferred solution among the feasible combinations. We also studied the ramifications of this decision and special solution issues.

Glossary

binding constraint A restriction that prevents further improvement in the objective function.

corner (extreme) point A point at the intersection of two restriction lines that form the boundary of the feasible solution area.

decision variables Controllable inputs representing processes employed, products manufactured, services provided, etc.

feasible solution A decision variable combination that simultaneously satisfies all restrictions in a linear program.

feasible solution area The shaded region on a graph that identifies feasible solutions to a problem.

linear program A deterministic model that collects the mathematical expressions for the objective function, system constraints, and nonnegativity conditions of a problem.

linear programming A methodology for solving linear programs.

linear relationship A relationship in which each variable appears in a separate term and is raised to the first power (has an exponent of one).

nonbinding constraint A restriction that does not prevent further improvement in the objective function.

nonnegativity condition Restriction that requires each decision variable to have a positive or zero value.

objective function Precise mathematical relationship between the decision variables and the criterion value.

redundant restriction A system constraint that does not affect the feasible solution area.

slack variable A variable that accounts for any unused system constraint limit.

solution point A point on a graph identifying a potential solution.

surplus variable A variable that accounts for any excess amount beyond a specified minimum requirement.

system (structural or technological) constraint A restriction on the decision variable that limits the criterion value.

Thought Exercises

1. Determine if linear programming is appropriate in each of the following situations. Speculate on the nature of the objective function and constraints and how these factors influence your answer.

   a. A national steel manufacturer wants to know the number of units that should be produced each day in a sequential schedule so as to maximize total steel production while meeting certain contractual, budget, and order constraints.

   b. A student wants to know the combinations of goods to purchase in the university cafeteria so as to minimize the cost of his diet while meeting certain minimum nutritional constraints.

   c. A homeowner wants to place a second mortgage on her dwelling to obtain cash for investment in the stock market. She wants to know what combination of stocks in related industries to buy for her portfolio while meeting certain minimum investment requirements and her budget constraint.

   d. A regional electric utility wants to maximize its revenue from two customer groups while meeting certain service, budget, and capacity requirements.

2. Advertising Associates, Inc. handles radio and television promotional jobs and placements for a wide range of clients. The agency's objective is to maximize the total audience exposure for its clients' products. Research indicates that each radio spot results in 1,000 exposures, while each television spot contributes an independent 3,000 exposures. A radio spot costs $4,000 and a television spot costs $20,000. Clients provide Associates with a maximum monthly budget of $1 million. Contracts with radio networks require a minimum of 100 spots per month. The agency employs account executives to place the spots. Past experience indicates that each radio spot takes 20 hours of executive effort and each television spot uses 50 hours. The agency's account executives are available for 4,000 hours per month.

   a. Define the appropriate criterion and decision variables for this problem.

   b. Develop the relevant linear program.

3. A financial counselor wants to develop an investment portfolio that will maximize a customer's total dollar return. Two types of independent investments are available: stocks, whose average return is 10 percent, and bonds, which return an average 6 percent over cost. The customer has $1,000 available and prefers to invest exactly twice as much in bonds as in stocks. As a result of other commitments, the counselor can devote no more than 90 hours to research and placement of the customer's portfolio. Past experience Indicates that stocks require 6 minutes (0.1 hour) of effort per dollar invested and bonds require 12 minutes (0.2 hour).

   a. Define the appropriate criterion and decision variables for this problem.

   b. Develop the relevant linear program.

4. A bank operations manager has four different tellers who are available to perform separate customer service duties on checking, loan note, and savings accounts. Each teller has different qualifications, and work sampling studies have shown that they can handle the customer loads shown in the following table.

	Customers Served Per Hour		
Teller	Checking	Loan Note	Savings
Samuels	45	65	30
Jacobson	55	40	50
Santini	40	80	45
Martinez	70	25	60

The extra teller will be assigned to a task (transaction processing) that will not directly serve any customers. The manager wants to serve as many customers as possible.

a. Define the appropriate criterion and decision variables for this problem.

b. Formulate the relevant linear program.

5. Rippon Enterprises wants to prototype a new voice-driven microcomputer that will be used by business executives for decision support activities. The company's electrical engineering department has developed the necessary electronic technology, and its mechanical engineering will make the plastic case.

Rippon's mechanical engineers prefer to use the polymer ABS for the case, because this material has superior heat deflecting properties and it is strong and stable. However, ABS is expensive, and heavy competition is forcing top management to become very cost-conscious. Consequently, the mechanical engineering department head, Amos Tone, has been asked to investigate the possibility of reducing the case's cost with a blend of several compatible but separate materials. Potential materials and their per-pound costs are reported in the following table:

Material	Cost ($/pound)
ABS	1.10
Glass beads	2.05
Polypropylene	0.60
Polystyrene	0.85
Talc	0.20

By processing engineering specifications through the department's computer information system (CIS), Amos has projected several important relationships between the materials. Strength losses will limit the blend to no more than 18 percent talc. Moreover, since polypropylene is very unstable, this material should constitute no more than 45 percent of the total for the other base plastics (polystyrene and ABS). For cosmetic purposes, glass beads and talc should total no more than 22 percent of the material blend. To assure sufficient mold life, glass beads should be limited to 16 percent of the blend.

The CIS analysis also suggests that the three base plastics (ABS, polypropylene, and polystyrene) in total account for at least 75 percent of the blend. Furthermore, too much polypropylene or polystyrene can cause problems in the extrusion mold. Therefore, at least 65 percent of the total fraction of base plastics should be ABS.

Management wants to select the fractions of each compatible material that will generate the least-cost blend for the plastic microcomputer case.

a. Define the appropriate criterion and decision variables for this problem.

b. Formulate the relevant linear program.

6. Janis Page, Director of Streets in Owentown, must decide how much gasoline and salt to purchase for the approaching winter season. These supplies will be used by the town's fleet of trucks to remove snow from the town's streets, either by plowing or salting.

Although salting is generally less expensive, any excess must be inventoried until next winter. The resulting storage cost will reduce salt's end-of-winter salvage value. On the other hand, excess gasoline can readily be used in other town vehicles. Consequently, it has a higher salvage value than salt.

Ms. Page classifies a winter as either mild or severe, and town records indicate that there is a .5 probability of a mild season. Supplies can be purchased now or later. Experience indicates that vendors will charge a premium to fill salt and gasoline orders quickly during or after winter.

By processing past and current transactions through the town's computer information system (CIS), Janis has estimated that (exclusive of fuel and salt) it will cost $130 to operate a truck during a mild winter day and $150 during a severe winter day. A similar CIS analysis has generated the additional costs presented below (where a truck-day is the amount of the supply consumed by one truck in a day):

| When Purchased | Winter Condition | Cost Per Truck-Day | |
		Gasoline	Salt
Now	—	$85	$30
Later	Mild winter	$90	$45
	Severe winter	$90	$50

The analysis also has indicated that gasoline has an end-of-season salvage value of $80 per truck-day, while salt has a salvage value of only $17 per truck-day.

During the approaching winter season, the existing fleet will have a capacity of 7,200 truck-days. If the town plows but does not salt, a mild winter will require a computer-projected 3,800 truck-days of snow removal, whereas a severe winter will require an estimated 7,300 truck-days.

Trucks are more effectively used for salting than for plowing. In a mild winter, 1 truck salting is equivalent to 1.4 trucks plowing, while the equivalency drops to 1.05 in a severe winter. Due to the limited fleet capacity, the town will need some salting in a severe winter.

Janis Page seeks the supply purchase plan that will minimize the total cost of snow removal.

a. Define the appropriate criterion and decision variables for this problem.

b. Formulate the relevant linear program.

7. James Ingram, Vice President of Marketing at General Foods, has a $600,000 budget, 20 account managers, and 40 salespeople available to launch a new breakfast cereal in the next three months. The workweek is 50 hours for an average account manager and 40 hours for an average salesperson. An account manager can develop promotions, work on packaging, help price the cereal, or work on distribution. General Foods' broad-based and comprehensive training programs have qualified each account manager to perform each of these jobs. Salespeople, however, are trained only to distribute the cereal.

By processing historical data on similar ventures through the company's MIS, James has developed the following report:

Staff	Hours of Effort per Dollar Spent on			
	Promotion	Packaging	Pricing	Distribution
Account manager	0.02	0.025	0.015	0.03
Salesperson	—	—	—	0.04

A similar CIS analysis forecasts that General Foods will realize 30 sales per hundred dollars spent on promotion, 10 sales for each hundred dollars spent on pricing and packaging combined, and 20 sales for every hundred dollars spent on distribution.

Experience indicates that distribution expenditures should account for between 30 and 60 percent of the total budget. Otherwise, merchants tend to avoid stocking the product. James also believes that a successful marketing mix must satisfy the following conditions:

1. Packaging plus pricing expenditures should be at least 25 percent of the total for promotion and distribution.

2. Pricing and packaging expenditures each should constitute at least 10 percent of the total budget.

He seeks the mix that will maximize the new cereal's sales.

a. Define the appropriate criterion and decision variables for this problem.

b. Formulate the relevant linear program.

8. Federal regulations require Guendon to bus students between the township's main residential areas and its schools in a way that will achieve an appropriate ethnic balance. Currently, the township consists of four areas with the following characteristics:

Area	Fraction of Minorities	Number of Students
East	0.15	800
North	0.45	600
South	0.20	400
West	0.65	900

The latest government statistics indicate that students have the same ethnic mix as the area in which they live.

By studying the existing balance, at the request of a civil rights group, federal officials have found that the township must increase minority enrollment by 350 students at Jefferson, 405 students at Washington, and 300 students at Lincoln High School. These officials have informed the township about the discrepancies, and the city supervisor has directed the school superintendent to take relevant corrective action. The superintendent is developing a busing plan to meet this directive.

By processing map data through the township's computer information system, the superintendent's assistant has found that the distances in miles between each area's center and the schools are as shown on the next page.

School	Area			
	East	North	South	West
Jefferson	0.8	0.7	1.3	2.1
Lincoln	1.4	1.6	0.5	0.9
Washington	0.6	0.4	0.3	0.5

Parental pressure has forced the superintendent to implement a rule that no student be bused more than 1.7 miles from the center of an area. In fact, she wants to minimize the distance traveled by the students.

a. Define the appropriate criterion and decision variables for this problem.

b. Formulate the relevant linear program.

9. Intuitively explain why the optimal solution to a linear programming problem must occur at an extreme point. Illustrate your explanation graphically.

10. A government agency wants to maximize the total number of cases it handles. Ordinarily, the agency deals with projects that are labeled type A and type B. This agency has been provided with a $10,000 budget, 100 staff hours, and 200 administrative hours. It usually takes 5 staff hours to complete each type A case and 50 staff hours for a type B case. Also, each type A and type B case costs the same $100 to complete. A type A case uses 50 administrative hours, while a type B case takes 40 administrative hours.

a. Define the appropriate criterion and decision variables for this agency.

b. Formulate the relevant linear program.

c. After reviewing this linear program, a budget analyst in the government's accounting office advises the chair of the Congressional Appropriations Committee that this agency's budget can be reduced considerably. How did the analyst arrive at this conclusion? How much can the budget be reduced?

11. An airline executive seeks the combination of domestic and foreign flights that will maximize total quarterly profit. Each domestic flight contributes $2,500 to profit, and a foreign flight contributions $5,000 to profit. Airline regulations require the company to schedule exactly 1,000 flights per quarter. A second regulation requires the number of foreign flights to be no more than 1/4 of the number of domestic flights. This airline can staff as many as 10,000 hours per quarter. Past experience indicates that a domestic flight takes 20 staff hours and each foreign flight takes 40 staff hours per quarter.

a. Define the appropriate criterion and decision variables for the airline.

b. Develop the relevant linear program.

c. Determine the solution to this problem. How would this solution influence the company's case in future regulatory hearings?

12. A product mix problem is represented by the following linear program:

maximize $Z = \$10X_1 + \$25X_2$

subject to $X_1 + X_2 \geq 2,000$ boxes   (Demand)

$5X_1 + 20X_2 \geq 20,000$ hours   (Sales staff)

$X_1, X_2 \geq 0$

where X_1 = the number of boxes of standard pads, X_2 = the number of boxes of legal pads, and Z = the total monthly profit. The office supply company finds that this problem is unbounded. After a careful reevaluation, the company concludes that the following constraint should have been included in the linear program:

$$20X_1 + 40X_2 \le 80,000 \text{ units} \qquad \text{(Production capacity)}$$

How does this new constraint affect the problem? Explain and illustrate graphically.

13. If a linear program has multiple best solutions, does the optimal solution point still occur at an extreme point? Explain and illustrate graphically.

14. How can the existence of alternative optima aid the following decision makers?
    a. A plumbing contractor seeks the minimum cost combination of two types of fixtures while meeting legal requirements, budget constraints, and customer preferences.
    b. A plant manager seeks the maximum profit combination of two types of products while meeting capacity limitations and union contractual requirements.
    c. An amusement park director seeks the combination of hours of operation for two types of attractions that will maximize profit, subject to budget and capacity limitations and a union contractual requirement on minimum staff size.

15. Do you agree or disagree with each of the following statements? Explain.
    a. Linear programming is a useless technique since its assumptions are so restrictive.
    b. Minimization and maximization problems in linear programming do not differ in any way in terms of the graphic solution procedure.
    c. A linear programming problem cannot be solved by the graphic solution method if there are three or more constraints.
    d. The prime purpose of the linear programming analysis is to overload the decision maker with unnecessary information.
    e. Points between corners on the boundary of the feasible solution area are never as desirable as points at the corners.
    f. In a minimization problem, the graphic objective is to find the feasible activity combination as close to the origin as possible.
    g. To find the optimal solution to a linear program, the decision maker must evaluate each extreme point.
    h. A minimization problem cannot be unbounded.

Technique Exercises

16. Consider the following product mix problem:

    maximize $Z = \$7X_1 + \$5X_2$

    subject to $.2X_1 + .5X_2 \le 60 \text{ hours} \qquad \text{(Labor)}$

    $.4X_1 + .2X_2 \le 40 \text{ hours} \qquad \text{(Capital)}$

    $X_1, X_2 \ge 0$

    where Z = the total dollar profit per period, X_1 = the number of units of product A, and X_2 = the number of units of product B.

   a. Determine the feasible solution area.

   b. Show that any point lying within that area leads to lower profit contribution than any point on the boundary. Use a maximum of three such point comparisons in your demonstration.

   c. Solve the problem.

17. Refer to Management Situation 7.1. Determine the optimal solution to Saferly's machine shop problem. Does the solution involve any slack pressing or polishing hours?

18. Determine the optimal solution to the following problem for an investment counselor:

maximize $Z = .15X_1 + .1X_2$

subject to $X_1 + X_2 \leq \$1,000$ (Investment)

                 $.1X_1 + .2X_2 \leq 90$ hours   (Counselor's time)

                 $X_1 = .5X_2$ (Customer preference)

                 $X_1, X_2 \geq 0$

where Z = the total dollar return, X_1 = the dollar amount invested in stocks, and X_2 = the dollar amount invested in bonds. Explain the solution to the counselor's customer.

19. Determine the optimal solution to the following linear programming problem facing a small machine shop:

maximize $Z = \$10X_1 + \$30X_2$

subject to $6X_1 + 12X_2 \leq 120$ hours   (Center 1)

                 $12X_1 + 3X_2 \leq 120$ hours   (Center 2)

                 $X_1, X_2 \geq 0$

where Z = the total profit per period, X_1 = the number of units of product A, and X_2 = the number of units of product B.

20. Solve the following linear programming problem:

minimize $Z = \$100X_1 + \$50X_2$

subject to $10X_1 + 40X_2 \geq 10,000$ units   (Ingredient 1)

                 $80X_1 + 20X_2 \geq 20,000$ units   (Ingredient 2)

                 $X_1, X_2 \geq 0$

where Z = the total cost of a diet per period, X_1 = the number of units of food A, and X_2 = the number of units of food B.

21. Determine the optimal solution to the following linear programming problem:

maximize $Z = \$1,000X_1 + \$250X_2$

subject to $\$1X_1 + \$2X_2 \geq \$100$ (Contract)

                 $\$3X_1 + \$2X_2 \leq \$600$ (Budget)

$$\$1X_2 \leq \$200 \qquad \text{(Legal)}$$

$$\$1X_1 + \$10X_2 \geq \$300 \qquad \text{(Request)}$$

$$X_1, X_2 \geq 0$$

where Z = the total dollar return per period, X_1 = the number of units of product A, and X_2 = the number of units of product B.

22. Solve the following production technique problem:

minimize $Z = \$1X_1 + \$20X_2$

subject to $100X_1 + 200X_2 \geq 1,000$ hours   (Contract)

$X_1 + X_2 = 20$ units   (Order)

$X_1 \geq 5$ units   (Policy)

$X_1, X_2 \geq 0$

where Z = the total production cost per period, X_1 = the number of units produced by technique 1, and X_2 = the number of units produced by technique 2.

23. Solve the following linear programming problem facing the fire chief of a small rural community:

minimize $Z = X_1 + X_2$

subject to $X_1 \geq \$10,000$ (Contract)

$X_1 + X_2 = \$30,000$ (Budget)

$X_2 \leq \$20,000$ (Chief's preference)

$X_1, X_2 \geq 0$

where Z = the total dollar cost of fire equipment, X_1 = additional dollars spent on labor, and X_2 = additional dollars spent on fire equipment. Explain the solution.

24. Refer back to Thought Exercises 2 and 3.
    a. Determine the optimal values of the decision variables and criteria for each of these problems.
    b. Determine whether the optimal solutions for each of these problems meet the system constraints exactly.

25. Determine the optimal solution to the following problem faced by a school district's finance director:

maximize $Z = .5X_1 + 2X_2$

subject to $X_1 + X_2 \leq \$400,000$ (Available funds)

$X_1 \geq 2X_2$ (Customer preference)

$X_1, X_2 \geq 0$

where $Z =$ the total dollar return, $X_1 =$ dollars invested in "conservative" ventures, and $X_2 =$ dollars invested in "speculative" ventures. Also, determine whether the optimal solution involves a combination of decision variables that meets each system constraint exactly. Explain your results to the school board.

Application Exercises

26. A computer systems manufacturer has just introduced two time-sharing programs for the generation of a wide range of statistical output useful to decision makers. Preliminary market research indicates that each hour of usage of STAT will result in $4 of profit, and each hour of REG will result in $10 of profit for the company. The company is capable of producing a combined total of 1,000 hours per month for both programs. In addition, production requires processing in two divisions, programming and storage. There is a maximum monthly budget of $40,000 for programming and $60,000 for storage. Each hour of STAT uses $20 of the programming budget and $50 of the storage budget, while each hour of REG uses $80 of the programming budget and $100 of the storage budget.

   a. What combination of STAT and REG should the manufacturer produce to maximize profit?

   b. What is the resulting profit level?

   c. Are there any idle resources at the optimum? If so, how would you interpret them?

27. A rancher raises milking cows and goats, which he feeds with two types of mixes, Boreto and Calfa. Each bag of Boreto costs $10 and contains 100 units of calcium and 400 units of protein; each bag of Calfa costs $15 and contains 200 units of calcium and 200 units of protein. The livestock need a minimum of 6,000 units of calcium and 12,000 units of protein per day. Also, a contract with the feed producer requires the rancher to purchase at least two bags of Boreto for every bag of Calfa.

   a. What combination of mixes should the rancher buy to minimize daily feed cost?

   b. What is the daily feed cost?

   c. Are there any excess requirements? If so, how would you interpret them?

28. A politician running for a state senate seat in an upcoming election can spend his campaign contributions in two ways: on media promotions and on public appearances. Each media promotion costs an average of $10,000 per spot and is expected to "return" 1,000 voters, while each public appearance costs $5,000 and is expected to "return" 500 voters. The candidate has a maximum campaign budget of $1 million. In addition, the promotional messages require staff time for preparation. Each media spot requires 100 hours of preparation, and each personal appearance requires 20 hours of preparation. The size of the candidate's staff limits the number of total hours available to a maximum of 5,000 hours.

   a. How many media spots and public appearances should the candidate make in order to maximize the total "return" of voters?

   b. If the candidate has a personal dislike for public appearances, how will this secondary goal influence his decision?

29. Union membership in the United Brotherhood of Brothers and Sisters entitles the card-holder to the fringe benefit of prepaid dental insurance. There are two separate plans: a fee plan and a deductible fully paid plan. Each member covered by the fee plan costs the union $200, while the other plan costs $100 per member. Total membership in the union is a minimum of 1,000 people per month. Contracts between the union and the insurance carrier also require a minimum of 500 covered members per month under the fee plan and a maximum of 800 members per month under the deductible plan. An additional constraint faced by the union is staff time required to administer the plans. The union estimates a minimum requirement of 2,000 staff hours per month, with each member under the fee plan requiring 10 hours per month and each deductible member requiring 5 hours per month.

   a. How many members under each plan should the union encourage in order to minimize its monthly dental insurance cost?

   b. What is that monthly cost?

   c. What does the optimal solution imply about the staff constraint? Explain.

30. County Purchasing Agency is responsible for procuring additional special-document copying machines to meet an anticipated increase in demand. There is not enough demand to justify an outright purchase, so the equipment is rented. Two brands are available: ABM and Texox. It is possible to rent each machine for any part of a month. An ABM rents for $120 per month and occupies 24 square feet of floor space. The Texox rents for $150 per month and requires 18 square feet. The total budget available for the expansion program is $1,200 per month, and there is a maximum of 192 square feet of floor space available for the new machines. An ABM usually produces 150 copies of the special documents per day, while the Texox usually produces 185 copies per day.

   a. How many machines of each type should the agency rent per month? Assume a 20-day work month.

   b. Does it seem reasonable to use a fraction of a machine per month? Explain.

31. Channel Island Construction Company is developing a tract of new homes called Harbor Shores. Two models will be available: the luxury and the standard. Each luxury home is expected to contribute $5,000 to the company's profits. It will be constructed on a 2/3-acre lot. The standard model will be constructed on a 1/4-acre lot and is expected to contribute $2,000 to the builder's profit. Local ordinances restrict Harbor Shores to a six-acre plot. There must also be twice as many luxury homes as standard types. Labor contracts require the company to use exactly 100 workers on the project. Each worker is expected to be available for 20 days next month. A luxury home requires 200 people-days to complete, while a standard home requires only 100 people-days.

   a. How many homes can the company complete in the next month?

   b. How would you interpret a solution with a fractional number of homes?

For Further Reading

Characteristics

Anderson, D. R., et al. *Linear Programming for Decision Making*. St. Paul: West, 1974.

Daellenbach, H. G., and E. G. Bell. *User's Guide to Linear Programming*. Englewood Cliffs, NJ: Prentice-Hall, 1970.

Levin, R. I., and R. P. Lamorne. *Linear Programming for Management Decisions*. Homewood, IL: Irwin, 1969.

Formulating Linear Programs

Gass, S. I. *An Illustrated Guide to Linear Programming*. New York: McGraw-Hill, 1970.

Kolman, B., and R. E. Beck. *Elementary Linear Programming with Applications*. New York: Academic Press, 1980.

Loomba, N. P. *Linear Programming: A Managerial Perspective*. Second ed. New York: Macmillan, 1976.

Finance/Accounting Applications

Anderson, D. "Models for Determining Least-Cost Investments in Electricity Supply." *Bell Journal of Economics* (Spring 1972):267.

Balbirer, S. D., and D. Shaw. "An Application of Linear Programming to Bank Financial Planning." *Interfaces* (October 1981):77.

Rosenblatt, M. J., and J. V. Jucker. "Capital Expenditures Decision Making: Some Tools and Trends." *Interfaces* (February 1979):63.

Schleef, H. J. "Using Linear Programming for Planning Life Insurance Purchases." *Decision Sciences* (July 1980):522.

Summers, E. L. "The Audit Staff Assignment Problem: A Linear Programming Analysis." *The Accounting Review* (July 1972):443.

Marketing Applications

Byrd, J., and L. T. Moore. "The Application of a Product Mix Linear Programming Model in Corporate Policy Making." *Management Science* (September 1978):1342.

Freed, N., and F. Glover. "A Linear Programming Approach to the Discriminant Problem." *Decision Sciences* (January 1981):68.

Thomas, J. "Linear Programming Models for Production-Advertising Decisions." *Management Science* (April 1971):474.

Production/Personnel/Operations Applications

Avani, S. "A Linear Programming Approach to Air-Cleaner Design." *Operations Research* (March–April 1974):295.

Brosch, L. C., et al., "Boxcars, Linear Programming, and the Sleeping Kitten," *Interfaces* (December 1980):53–61.

Bandyopadhyay, J. K., et al. "A Resource Allocation Model for an Employability Planning System." *Interfaces* (October 1980):90.

Chappell, A. E. "Linear Programming Cuts Costs in Production of Animal Feeds." *Operational Research Quarterly* (March 1974):19.

Dyckhoff, H. "A Linear Programming Approach to the Cutting Stock Problem." *Operations Research* (November–December 1981):1092.

Hilal, S. S., and W. Erikson. "Matching Supplies to Save Lives: Linear Programming the Production of Heart Valves." *Interfaces* (December 1981):48.

Nash, B. "A Simplified Alternative to Current Airline Fuel Allocation Models." *Interfaces* (February 1981):1.

Thie, H. J., and R. C. Lorbeer. "Better Personnel Management through Applied Management Science." *Interfaces* (May 1976):68.

Public Sector/Nonprofit Applications

Feldstein, M., and H. Luft. "Distribution Constraints in Public Expenditure Planning." *Management Science* (August 1973):1414.

Heroux, R. L., and W. A. Wallace. "Linear Programming and Financial Analysis of the New Community Development Process." *Management Science* (April 1973):857.

Kohn, R. E. "Application of Linear Programming to a Controversy on Air Pollution Control." *Management Science* (June 1971):609.

Laidlaw, C. D. *Linear Programming for Urban Development and Plan Evaluation*. New York: Praeger, 1972.

Leff, H. S., et al. "An LP Planning Model for a Mental Health Community Support System." *Management Science* (February 1986):139.

McKeown, P., and B. Workman. "A Study in Using Linear Programming to Assign Students to Schools." *Interfaces* (August 1976):96.

Might, R. J. "Decision Support for Aircraft and Munitions Procurement." *Interfaces* (September–October 1987):55.

Case: Aviation Unlimited

Aviation Unlimited is an air freight carrier servicing the western region of the United States. It has 100 airplanes, 200 pilots, 20 ground crews of 10 workers per crew, and 150 administrators and other office personnel. T. T. Greedy, Aviation's chief accountant, has prepared a summary report of estimated expenses for the next quarter of operations, as shown in Table 7.4.

Aviation classifies its flights in either of two routes: long haul or short haul. Al Transport, Aviation's transportation engineer, has provided data on estimated tonnage and revenues for each of the route types. These data appear in Table 7.5.

You are asked to provide a management report to Hy Flyer, Aviation's president, containing the following information:

Table 7.4   **Estimated Expenses for Aviation**

Item	Amount
Total fixed costs	$18,000,000
Administrative	1,500,000
Airplane maintenance	15,000,000
Pilot salaries	1,500,000
Total variable costs per average flight	$6,000
Fuel	4,000
Ground personnel	2,000

Table 7.5   **Estimated Tonnage and Revenues for Aviation**

Route	Revenue Per Average Flight	Tonnage	Gallons of Fuel	Ground Crew Hours
Long haul	$9,500	10	5,000	6
Short haul	$8,500	30	3,000	4
Maximum available per quarter		450,000	75,000,000	96,000

1. The number of each type of flight per quarter that will enable Aviation to maximize its total contribution to profit (revenue less variable cost)

2. The resulting profit contribution

3. The influence of fixed costs on the recommendation

In your report, it is important that you outline the procedure used in formulating your recommendation in a way that Flyer can understand. President Flyer is not interested in linear programming jargon, only in an intuitively appealing explanation of your recommendation.

Simplex Method

Chapter Outline

Learning Objectives

- Understand the nature of a popular method designed to solve large-scale linear programming problems

- Learn how to formulate problems in a format suitable for analysis by this method

- Examine the step-by-step procedure involved in applying the method

- Solve simple linear programs with the methodology

- Interpret the solution and utilize the results in decision making

- Determine how to deal with special situations that can arise when implementing the methodology

- Survey alternative linear programming algorithms

Just When You Thought the Forest Was Safe

The budworm is the most destructive defoliator of spruce-fir forests in North America. Since 1972, the Maine Forest Service has conducted annual aerial spray programs to control the damage and to mitigate an anticipated shortage of wood. Several types of aircraft, flying from six airfields, are used to spray 250 to 300 infested areas. The contracting costs for the aircraft and crews represent at least one-third of the program's annual costs.

In 1983, the Forest Service began investigating ways to reduce aircraft needs and contracting costs and to increase the efficiency of aircraft assignments under the program. By 1985, the investigators had developed a linear program that modeled the situation quite realistically. Given a set of airfields and the aircraft characteristics, the model determines the lowest cost set of flight plans that will accomplish the required spraying.

The linear programming analysis has helped the Forest Service to save considerable time in preparing specifications for the spray contractors. These time savings enable the project staff to respond more quickly to changes in political conditions (such as the closing of an airfield by demonstrators) and in analytical factors (such as the availability of a new spray aircraft). The analysis also helps the program staff to develop a more efficient spray plan. In 1984, for example, the Forest Service met its spraying requirements with fewer aircraft covering one-third less acreage than previously specified. Such efficiency resulted in substantially lower bid costs for the spray contracts.

Source: D. L. Rumpf et al., "Improving the Efficiency in a Pest Control Spray Program," *Interfaces* (September–October 1985): pp. 1–11.

Practical linear programming problems, such as the pest control question faced by the Maine Forest Service, involve many decision variables and a large number of restrictions. Managers, like the Maine Forest Service's pest control specialists, need systematic methodologies to solve these large-scale problems. One of the most popular methodologies is called the **simplex method**.

In this chapter we will examine the simplex method. The first section illustrates the fundamental methodology. It shows how to formulate a linear program in simplex format, identify an initial feasible solution, and then develop an optimal solution. The second section presents a tabular format that conveniently organizes and helps perform the calculations involved in the simplex method. This section also demonstrates how the format can be used to develop an optimal solution of a linear program. The final section discusses some important extensions to the fundamental methodology.

Typical managers will use computer programs rather than manual calculations to solve large-scale linear programming problems in practice. Nevertheless, most of these programs are based on the simplex method. Consequently, a fundamental knowledge about this method will help you understand what is going on inside the programs, and it will enhance your ability to accurately interpret and completely utilize the computer output. For the sake of clarity, we also will illustrate the concepts with simple small-scale problems. Such an approach will be less cumbersome, and it will offer a better understanding of the graphic properties of linear programs and their simplex solutions.

Applications. In this chapter, the following applications appear in text, examples, and exercises:

- advertising strategy
- athletics
- bakery operations
- baseball manufacturing
- budget allocation
- cafeteria operations
- energy management
- fire fighting
- highway construction

- house painting
- mining
- nursery schools
- project planning
- producing office supplies
- production/inventory scheduling
- production planning
- solar housing
- work force planning

8.1 FUNDAMENTAL METHODOLOGY

The simplex method is essentially a search procedure. It starts from a convenient initial solution, progressively moves to better solutions (if possible), and ends when the criterion value can no longer be improved. Since this search is performed algebraically, the decision maker must convert any inequalities in the linear program into equality relationships before he or she starts the process. Once more, slack and surplus variables are used to make the conversions.

We can illustrate the fundamental simplex methodology with Management Situation 8.1.

Management Situation 8.1

Baseball Manufacturing

Daspling Incorporated manufactures two sizes of baseballs: Little League and Major League. By processing historical production and sales data through the company's computer information system, its chief accountant has projected that Daspling will earn a profit of $2 per box of Little League baseballs and $3 per box of Major League baseballs.

Each product must be assembled and packaged (boxed, labeled, and affixed with promotional material). There will be a maximum of 1,800 hours available in the assembly department and 1,800 hours available in the packaging department during the next three months. By processing historical manufacturing data through the company's management information system, the production manager has estimated that it will take 9 minutes to assemble a box of Little League baseballs and 15 minutes to assemble a box of Major League baseballs. A box of Little League baseballs will require 11 minutes of packaging, and it will take 5 minutes to package a box of Major League baseballs.

Management seeks the combination of Little League and Major League baseballs that will maximize total profit within the available assembly and packaging time.

Daspling wants to manufacture the boxes of Little League and Major League baseballs that will maximize total dollar profit. In the process, management must ensure that the output levels do not use more than the available assembly and packaging time. By using the fomulation techniques developed in Chapter 7, the mathematical model for this problem can be expressed as the following linear program:

maximize $\qquad Z = \$2X_1 + \$3X_2$

subject to $\qquad 9X_1 + 15X_2 \leq 108{,}000$ minutes $\qquad$ (Assembly)

$\qquad\qquad\quad 11X_1 + 5X_2 \leq 108{,}000$ minutes $\qquad$ (Packaging)

$\qquad\qquad\quad X_1, X_2 \geq 0$

where Z = the total dollar profit, X_1 = the boxes of Little League baseballs, and X_2 = the boxes of Major League baseballs.

In the simplex method, the decision variables (X_1 and X_2 in Daspling's case) are also know as **real variables**. Throughout this chapter, we will adopt the convention of depicting these variables with the subscripted X symbols, and we will use the symbol Z to denote the criterion value. Such notation will provide a consistent (and perhaps descriptive) point of reference for later simplex analysis.

Standard Form

To account for any potential difference between the assembly time actually used ($9X_1 + 15X_2$) and the amount available (1,800 hours or 108,000 minutes), management must define a slack variable (with a subscript of 1 because this assembly restriction is the first system constraint in Daspling's linear program)

$$S_1 = \text{unused assembly minutes}$$

By adding this variable to the left side of the original restriction, the decision maker can write the assembly constraint as the following equality:

$$9X_1 + 15X_2 + S_1 = 108{,}000 \text{ minutes}$$

Similarly, the packaging constraint can be expressed as

$$11X_1 + 5X_2 + S_2 = 108{,}000 \text{ minutes}$$

where S_2 = unused packaging minutes.

Variables such as S_1 and S_2, which are included to convert the linear program's system constraints into an equivalent set of simultaneous equations, are known as **supplemental variables** in the simplex method. Since unused assembly time (S_1) and unused packaging time (S_2) do not generate any output, neither of these supplemental variables will make any contribution to profit. That is, S_1 and S_2 each will have \$0 coefficients in Daspling's objective function. On the other hand, supplemental (like decision) variables must have values greater than or equal to zero. Therefore, the nonnegativity conditions must be expanded to include the supplemental variables.

By including slack variables, Daspling will create the following augmented linear program:

maximize $Z = \$2X_1 + \$3X_2 + \$0S_1 + \$0S_2$

subject to $9X_1 + 15X_2 + S_1 + 0S_2 = 108{,}000$ minutes   (Assembly)

$11X_1 + 5X_2 + 0S_1 + S_2 = 108{,}000$ minutes   (Packaging)

$X_1, X_2, S_1, S_2 \geq 0$

This format clearly shows that the decision maker must determine the values of the slack variables (S_1 and S_2) as well as the decision variables (X_1 and X_2) to obtain the optimal solution to the linear program.

Notice that in the linear program's augmented form

1. each system constraint is expressed as an equality relationship,
2. all real and supplemental variables appear on the left side and a nonnegative constant appears on the right side of each system constraint, and
3. all the variables are nonnegative.

A linear program with this format is said to be in its **standard form**.

Basic Feasible Solutions

In Daspling's standard form linear program, the assembly and packaging constraints create a system of $m = 2$ linear equations with $n = 4$ unknowns (X_1, X_2, S_1, and S_2). Since the unknowns outnumber the equations ($n > m$), there are an infinite number of solutions (combinations of X_1, X_2, S_1, S_2 values) that will satisfy the system constraints.

Management can limit the solutions to a finite number first by arbitrarily setting any $(n - m) = 4 - 2 = 2$ of the original four variables equal to zero. These $(n - m)$ variables, which have been set equal to zero, are termed **nonbasic variables**. Then, the two system constraint (assembly and packaging) equations can be used to solve for the values of the remaining $m = 2$ variables. These m variables are called **basic variables** and are said to constitute a **basis**. In the simplex method, the combination of basic and nonbasic variable values is called a **basic solution**.

This finite number of basic solutions can be reduced further by considering only **basic feasible solutions**, or the basic solutions that satisfy the nonnegativity conditions. Still, it will be impractical in most actual applications to search for the optimal solution by enumerating and evaluating every basic feasible solution.

Iteration Process

The simplex method avoids the need for complete enumeration by developing the optimal solution in stages. It starts with a convenient basic feasible solution, which is found by

Figure 8.1 Daspling's First Iteration

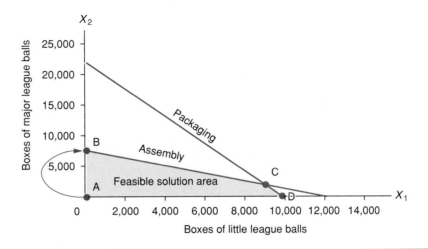

setting the decision (and, where appropriate, surplus) variables equal to zero and by reading the values of the remaining variables from the right sides of the corresponding standard form system constraint equations. Then, the method iteratively searches for the basic feasible solution (if it exists) that best meets the objective.

Figure 8.1 illustrates the beginning of the simplex search for Daspling's problem. The solution points on the boundary lines and within the shaded region of this figure identify the company's feasible solution area, and the coordinates labeled A through D represent the extreme points of the area.

Initial Basic Feasible Solution. If the decision maker sets $X_1 = 0$ and $X_2 = 0$, he or she can read the values of S_1 and S_2 from the right sides of the standard form assembly and packaging constraint equations. The resulting initial basic feasible solution of

$$X_1 = 0 \qquad S_1 = 108,000$$

$$X_2 = 0 \qquad S_2 = 108,000$$

corresponds to corner point A in Figure 8.1. Such a result is not a coincidence. *In linear programming, a corner point is the same thing as a basic feasible solution.*

First Iteration. According to Daspling's standard form objective function, the company's initial basic feasible solution earns

$$Z = \$2X_1 + \$3X_2 + \$0S_1 + \$0S_2$$

$$= \$2(0) + \$3(0) + \$0(108,000) + \$0(108,000) = \$0$$

total profit. This function also indicates that the initial criterion value ($Z = \$0$) can be increased a net $2 per box by producing Little League baseballs (X_1) or a net $3 per box by manufacturing Major League baseballs (X_2).

Although both X_1 and X_2 can increase Daspling's initial profit, management can obtain a larger per-box contribution by manufacturing Major League baseballs. Since the simplex method seeks improvement by one variable at a time, Daspling most likely will want to bring X_2 into the basis. A variable such as X_2, which will be brought into the basis, is referred to as an **entering variable**.

The process of bringing the X_2 variable into the basis is equivalent to the movement indicated by the arrow in Figure 8.1 along the X_2 axis to corner point B. At this point, Daspling is producing $X_1 = 0$ boxes of Little League baseballs, and (since B is on the assembly constraint line) there are $S_1 = 0$ unused assembly minutes. Hence, the X_1 variable remains nonbasic, but the S_1 variable goes from a basic to a nonbasic variable and thereby leaves the basis. A variable such as S_1, which will be removed from the basis, is known as a departing or **leaving variable**.

By substituting the $X_1 = 0$ and $S_1 = 0$ values into the standard form assembly and packaging constraint equations, Daspling also will find that

$$9X_1 + 15X_2 + S_1 + 0S_2 = 108,000 \text{ minutes}$$

or $$X_2 = [108,000 - 9(0) - 0 - 0S_2]/15 = 7200$$

boxes of Major League baseballs

and

$$11X_1 + 5X_2 + 0S_1 + S_2 = 108,000 \text{ minutes}$$

or $$S_2 = [108,000 - 11(0) - 5(7200) - 0(0)] = 72,000$$

unused packaging minutes at corner point B.

Second Iteration. Figure 8.2 superimposes two objective function lines on Daspling's feasible solution area. This figure shows that the company's second basic feasible solution of

$$X_1 = 0 \qquad S_1 = 0$$
$$X_2 = 7,200 \qquad S_2 = 72,000$$

earns a total profit of

$$Z = \$2(0) + \$3(7,200) + \$0(0) + \$0(72,000) = \$21,600$$

or it enables Daspling to reach the $Z = \$21,600$ objective function line.

However, the movement indicated by the arrow in Figure 8.2, from corner point B along the assembly constraint line to corner point C, will enable the company to reach a preferable ($Z = \$23,400$) objective function line. Since C is on both the assembly and packaging constraint lines, this corner point involves $S_1 = 0$ unused assembly and $S_2 = 0$ unused packaging minutes. By utilizing these values with the standard form assembly and packaging constraint equations, Daspling also will find that

$$9X_1 + 15X_2 + S_1 + 0S_2 = 108,000 \text{ minutes}$$

or $$X_2 = [108,000 - 9X_1 - 0 - 0S_2]/15 = 7,200 - .6X_1$$

and by substitution

$$11X_1 + 5X_2 + 0S_1 + S_2 = 108,000 \text{ minutes}$$

Figure 8.2   **Daspling's Second Iteration**

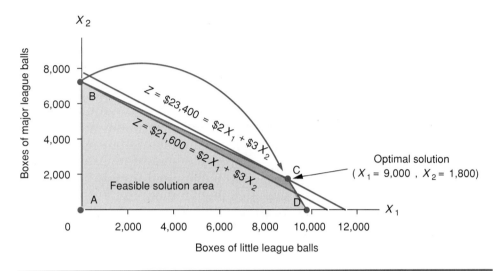

or $\qquad X_1 = [108,000 - 5(7,200) - .6X_1) - 0(0) + 0]/11 = 9,000$

boxes of Little League baseballs with

$$X_2 = 7,200 - .6X_1 = 7,200 - .6(9,000) = 1,800$$

boxes of Major League baseballs at corner point C.

Optimal Solution. As Figure 8.2 demonstrates, Daspling cannot shift the objective function beyond the $Z = \$23,400$ line without moving outside the feasible solution area. Thus, the third basic feasible (corner point C) solution of

$$X_1 = 9000 \qquad S_1 = 0$$
$$X_2 = 1800 \qquad S_2 = 0$$

represents the optimal solution to the company's baseball manufacturing problem. That is, Daspling can maximize total profit at $Z = \$23,400$ by producing 9,000 boxes of Little League and 1,800 boxes of Major League baseballs. In the process, the company will use all available assembly and packaging time.

Pivoting. Notice that the simplex method searches for the optimal solution by moving from one basic feasible solution (corner point) to another. In the process, it determines whether or not the objective function can be improved by exchanging a basic variable for a nonbasic variable. For example, in moving from corner point B (the second basic feasible solution) to corner point C (the third basic feasible solution), the previous nonbasic variable X_1 replaces the previous basic variable S_2 in the basis. This process of moving from one basis to another, called **pivoting**, continues until we can no longer improve the criterion value.

Procedure Recap. The fundamental simplex methodology can be summarized as follows:

1. Set up the standard form of the linear program.
2. Find the initial basic feasible solution.
3. Search for the optimal solution by pivoting among the basic feasible solutions of the linear program.

8.2 SIMPLEX TABLES

Simplex calculations can be very complicated and confusing, especially in large-scale linear programs. Fortunately, there is a tabular format that conveniently organizes and helps perform the calculations necessary to obtain successive basic feasible solutions. Figure 8.3 presents the model for this type of format, which is known as a **simplex tableau** or **simplex table**.

Initial Simplex Table

The first simplex table always presents the decision information involved in the initial basic feasible solution of the standard form linear program. Table 8.1, for example, gives the simplex information corresponding to Daspling's initial basic feasible solution (extreme point A in Figures 8.1 and 8.2).

Objective. In Table 8.1, the top two rows outline the information contained in Daspling's standard form total profit equation

$$Z = \$2X_1 + \$3X_2 + \$0S_1 + \$0S_2$$

Each variable is listed in a separate column of the Variables row, and the per-box contributions are given in the corresponding columns of the C_j row.

Exchange. Entries in the main body (middle two rows under the X_1 through S_2 columns) of Table 8.1 give the coefficients of the corresponding real and supplemental variables in the standard form system constraints

$$9X_1 + 15X_2 + 1S_1 + 0S_2 = 108,000$$
$$11X_1 + 5X_2 + 0S_1 + 1S_2 = 108,000$$

Amounts column entries in these middle two rows identify the matching nonnegative constants on the right sides of the constraints.

The coefficients also tell us the amount of a basic variable that must be given up to get *one* unit of any real or supplemental variable in the standard form linear program. For example, the entry in the S_2 row and X_2 column indicates that five minutes of unused packaging minutes (S_2) must be given up to produce one box of Major League baseballs. A zero entry (such as the 0 in the S_1 row and S_2 column) simply means that no exchange occurs, while an entry of one (such as the 1 in the S_2 row and S_2 column) signifies that there is an even (one-for-one) exchange between the variables.

Figure 8.3   **Simplex Table (Tableau)**

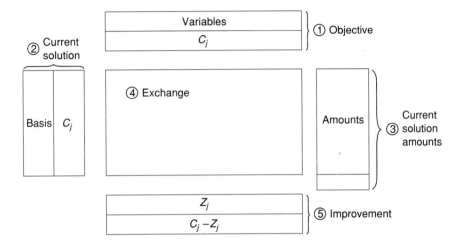

① *Objective*
    Variables: a list of all the variables (real and supplemental) in the linear program
    C_j: the per-unit contribution of each variable (real and supplemental) to the objective

② *Current solution*
    Basis: a list of the basic variables in the current solution
    C_j: the per-unit contribution of each basic variable to the objective

③ *Current solution amounts*
    Amounts: a list of the amounts of each basic variable and the total contribution of the current
                solution

④ *Exchange:*   the amounts of each basic variable in the current solution that must be given up to
                get one unit of each variable (real and supplemental) in the linear program

⑤ *Improvement*
    Z_j: in the Variables columns, entries that give the contribution lost by bringing one unit
                of each variable (real and supplemental) into the basis; in the Amounts column, the
                Z_j entry that gives the total value of the objective for the current basic feasible solution
    $C_j - Z_j$:   the net effect on the objective of bringing one unit of each variable (real and
                supplemental) into the basis

Current Solution and Amounts. Information about the current (initial) basic feasible solution is presented in the Basis, C_j, and Amounts columns. Each row of the Basis column lists a basic variable (S_1 and S_2), while the C_j column gives the matching per-box profit contributions ($\$0$ for S_1 and $\$0$ for S_2). All decision or supplemental variables that do not appear in the Basis column (such as X_1 and X_2) are nonbasic and therefore will have zero quantities in the current solution. Quantities for the basic variables (108,000 for S_1 and 108,000 for S_2) are reported in the corresponding rows of the Amounts column.

Table 8.1   Daspling's First Simplex Table

Variables		X_1	X_2	S_1	S_2		
Basis	C_j	$2	$3	$0	$0	Amounts	Trade Ratios
S_1	$0	9	(15)	1	0	108,000	$\dfrac{108{,}000}{15} = 7{,}200 \leftarrow$ Take out (pivot row)
S_2	$0	11	5	0	1	108,000	$\dfrac{108{,}000}{5} = 21{,}600$
	Z_j	$0	$0	$0	$0	$0	
	$C_j - Z_j$	$2	$3	$0	$0		

↑
Bring in
(pivot column)

Improvement. Entries in the Z_j row of Table 8.1 measure the economic value of the current basis. The Amounts column entry gives Daspling's total profit from the initial basic feasible solution. It is found by multiplying the basic variables' Amounts column entries (108,000 for S_1 and 108,000 for S_2) by the corresponding C_j column entries ($0 for S_1 and $0 for S_2) and then summing the results. The resulting $0 total tells management that the company will not earn any profit by holding all available capacity idle (and thereby producing no baseballs).

Other Z_j row entries (in the X_1 through S_2 columns) measure the *decrease* in this initial total profit that will occur if one unit of each matching decision/supplemental variable is brought into the basis (exchanged for a current basic variable). These entries are obtained by multiplying the basic variables' per-box profit contributions (given in the C_j column) by the corresponding decision/supplemental variables' exchange rates (given in the X_1 through S_2 columns). For example, the X_1 column in Table 8.1 shows that 9 unused assembly minutes (S_1) and 11 idle packaging minutes (S_2) must be surrendered to produce one box of Little League baseballs. As the C_j column entries indicate, however, an unused assembly minute and an idle packaging minute each contribute $0 to profit. Therefore, the company will lose (have a Z_j row entry in the X_1 column of)

$$\$0(9) + \$0(11) = \$0$$

by putting this idle time (S_1 and S_2) to productive use in making Little League baseballs (X_1).

By subtracting each Z_j row entry (per-box profit decrease) from the corresponding C_j row entry (per-box profit increase), Daspling will determine the net effect of bringing one unit of any decision/supplemental variable into the basis. These net effects, which tell management whether or not it can improve the current solution, are reported in the $C_j - Z_j$ row of Table 8.1.

The $C_j - Z_j$ row entries indicate that Daspling can increase the initial $Z = \$0$ total profit a net $2 per box by producing Little League baseballs (X_1) and a net $3 per box by manufacturing Major League baseballs (X_2). These entries also illustrate the following important property: *In a maximization problem, a basic feasible solution can be improved as long as there are positive entries in the $C_j - Z_j$ row of the simplex table.*

Optimality Criterion. Since Major League baseballs make the largest per-box contribution (\$3) to the profit objective, X_2 will be the entering variable in the pivoting process. This selection demonstrates the following optimality criterion: *In a maximization problem, always bring into the basis the variable with the largest positive entry in the $C_j - Z_j$ row of the simplex table.* If there is a tie, arbitrarily designate one of the tied variables as the entering variable.

In the simplex table, the entering variable's column is known as the **pivot column**. Daspling's initial pivot column (X_2) in Table 8.1 is shaded, denoted with the vertical arrow (↑), and labeled with the "Bring in" notation.

Feasibility Criterion. Since Major League baseballs (X_2) make a \$3 per-box profit contribution, Daspling will want this entering variable's quantity to be as large as possible. It can identify the possibilities by dividing Table 8.1's pivot column entries into the corresponding Amounts column entries. The resulting ratios (computed alongside Table 8.1) show that the company has enough idle assembly minutes (S_1) to produce $108,000/15 = 7,200$ boxes and sufficient packaging slack (S_2) for $108,000/5 = 21,600$ boxes of Major League baseballs. Such values, which identify the maximum amounts of the entering variable that can be exchanged or traded for the entire quantities of the basic variables, are known as **exchange** or **trade ratios**.

Although management would prefer to produce 21,600 boxes of Major League baseballs, there is enough assembly slack (S_1) for only 7,200 boxes. By manufacturing this $X_2 = 7,200$ box maximum feasible quantity of the entering variable, the company will utilize all the available assembly slack and thereby force S_1 out of the basis (make S_1 the leaving variable). This result illustrates the following feasibility criterion: *Always take out of the basis the variable with the smallest nonnegative exchange or trade ratio.*

In the simplex table, the leaving variable's row is referred to as the **pivot row**. Daspling's initial pivot row (S_1) in Table 8.1 is shaded, denoted with the horizontal arrow (←), and labeled with the "Take out" notation.

Pivot Element. The circled entry at the intersection of the pivot row and pivot column in Table 8.1 is also important. This value, which gives the amount of the departing variable that must be given up to obtain one unit of the entering variable, is called the **pivot element**. It will be used to find the exchange and amounts entries in the next simplex table.

Second Simplex Table

Pivoting (replacing the leaving variable with the entering variable) will not affect the list of decision/supplemental variables or their unit contributions to the objective. As a result, the simplex table's Variables and C_j row entries (Objective portion) always will remain constant from one tableau to another.

Table 8.2   Daspling's Second Simplex Table

Variables		X_1	X_2	S_1	S_2		
Basis	C_j	$2	$3	$0	$0	Amounts	Trade Ratios
X_2	$3	$\frac{3}{5}$	1	$\frac{1}{15}$	0	7,200	$\frac{7{,}200}{3/5} = 12{,}000$
S_2	$0	(8)	0	$-\frac{1}{3}$	1	72,000	$\frac{72{,}000}{8} = 9{,}600 \leftarrow$ Take out (pivot row)
	Z_j	$\$\frac{9}{5}$	$3	$\$\frac{1}{5}$	$0	$21,600	
	$C_j - Z_j$	$\$\frac{1}{5}$	$0	$-\$\frac{1}{5}$	$0		

$\uparrow$
Bring in
(pivot column)

The process, however, creates a new basic feasible solution. Hence, the rest of the simplex table (current solution, exchange and amounts, and improvement portions) entries must be modified to reflect this new solution. Daspling's initial pivoting will result in Table 8.2.

New Current Solution. In Table 8.2, the entering variable X_2 replaces the leaving variable S_1, while packaging slack (S_2) remains, as Basis column entries. The C_j column entries give the corresponding per-box profit contributions ($3 for X_2 and $0 for S_2).

Exchange and Amounts—New Basic Variable. Table 8.1's 7200-box smallest non-negative trade ratio identifies the quantity of the new basic variable (the Amounts column entry in the X_2 row of Table 8.2). We determine how much of this amount must be given up to get one unit of each decision and supplemental variable (the X_1 through S_2 columns' entries in the X_2 row of Table 8.2) with the following formula:

(8.1)
$$\frac{\text{Old pivot row's exchange entries}}{\text{Old circled pivot element}}$$

or in Daspling's case

$$\frac{X_1 \text{ through } S_2 \text{ column entries in the } S_1 \text{ row of Table 8.1}}{\text{Circled pivot element in Table 8.1}}$$

Exchange and Amounts—Remaining Basic Variable. The remaining basic variable's old quantity and exchange rates (the Amounts and X_1 through S_2 column entries in the S_2 row of Table 8.1) must be adjusted to account for the new basic variable's impact on the solution. These adjustments are made with the following formula:

$$(8.2) \quad \begin{pmatrix} \text{Remaining basic} \\ \text{variable's old} \\ \text{exchange and} \\ \text{Amounts column} \\ \text{entries} \end{pmatrix} - \left[\begin{pmatrix} \text{Remaining basic} \\ \text{variable's old} \\ \text{pivot column} \\ \text{entry} \end{pmatrix} \begin{pmatrix} \text{New basic} \\ \text{variable's} \\ \text{exchange} \\ \text{and Amounts} \\ \text{column} \\ \text{entries} \end{pmatrix} \right]$$

or in Daspling's case

$$\begin{pmatrix} X_1 \text{ through Amounts} \\ \text{column entries in} \\ \text{the } S_2 \text{ row of} \\ \text{Table 8.1} \end{pmatrix} - \left[\begin{pmatrix} X_2 \text{ column entry} \\ \text{in the } S_2 \text{ row} \\ \text{of Table 8.1} \end{pmatrix} \begin{pmatrix} X_1 \text{ through} \\ \text{Amounts} \\ \text{column entries} \\ \text{in the } X_2 \text{ row} \\ \text{of Table 8.2} \end{pmatrix} \right]$$

The results give the remaining basic variable's new, or adjusted, exchange rates and quantity (the X_1 through Amounts columns' entries in the S_2 row of Table 8.2).

For example, such computations show that Daspling has

$$\begin{pmatrix} \text{Amounts column} \\ \text{entry in the } S_2 \\ \text{row of Table 8.1} \end{pmatrix} - \left[\begin{pmatrix} X_2 \text{ column} \\ \text{entry in} \\ \text{the } S_2 \text{ row} \\ \text{of Table 8.1} \end{pmatrix} \begin{pmatrix} \text{Amounts column} \\ \text{entry in the} \\ X_2 \text{ row of Table} \\ 8.2 \end{pmatrix} \right] = \begin{pmatrix} \text{Amounts} \\ \text{column} \\ \text{entry in} \\ \text{the } S_2 \text{ row} \\ \text{of Table 8.2} \end{pmatrix}$$

or $108,000 - (5 \times 7,200) = 72,000$

unused packaging minutes remaining after accounting for Major League output. The calculations also indicate that the company must give up

$$\begin{pmatrix} X_1 \text{ column entry} \\ \text{in the } S_2 \text{ row} \\ \text{of Table 8.1} \end{pmatrix} - \left[\begin{pmatrix} X_2 \text{ column} \\ \text{entry in the } S_2 \text{ row} \\ \text{of Table 8.1} \end{pmatrix} \begin{pmatrix} X_1 \text{ column} \\ \text{entry in} \\ \text{the } X_2 \text{ row} \\ \text{of Table 8.2} \end{pmatrix} \right] = \begin{pmatrix} X_1 \text{ column} \\ \text{entry in the} \\ S_2 \text{ row of} \\ \text{Table 8.2} \end{pmatrix}$$

or $11 - (5 \times 3/5) = 8$

of these remaining unused packaging minutes to get one box of Little League baseballs.

Improvement. Table 8.2's Basis and corresponding Amounts columns' entries show that Daspling's second basic feasible solution (corner point B in Figures 8.1 and 8.2) has

$$X_2 = 7,200 \text{ boxes of Major League baseballs}$$

$$S_2 = 72,000 \text{ unused packaging minutes}$$

and, since X_1 and S_1 are not in the basis, no Little League output and no unused assembly minutes.

The Z_j row entries in Table 8.2 again are found by multiplying the C_j column entries by the corresponding X_1 through Amounts column entries and then summing the results. These computations, for example, show that Daspling earns

$$(\$3 \times 7,200) + (\$0 \times 72,000) = \$21,600$$

total profit from the second basic feasible solution and that the company will lose

$$(\$3 \times 3/5) + (\$0 \times 8) = \$9/5$$

of this total profit per box of Little League baseballs (X_1) brought into the basis.

Once more, Table 8.2's $C_j - Z_j$ row entries are obtained by subtracting the Z_j row entries from the corresponding C_j row entries. Such computations, for example, show that Daspling can increase the $Z = \$21,600$ total profit a net $\$2 - \$9/5 = \$1/5$ per box of Little League baseballs brought into the basis.

Entering Variable. Since Little League baseballs make the largest per-box profit contribution (have the largest positive $C_j - Z_j$ row entry), X_1 will be the entering, or pivot column, variable. In Table 8.2, this pivot column (X_1) again is shaded, denoted with the vertical arrow, and labeled with the "Bring in" notation.

Leaving variable. By dividing the pivot (X_1) column entries into the corresponding Amounts column entries, management once more will get the trade ratios. These ratios, which are computed alongside Table 8.2, indicate that Daspling can exchange all Major League output (X_2) for $7,200/(3/5) = 12,000$ boxes and all remaining packaging slack (S_2) for $72,000/8 = 9,000$ boxes of Little League baseballs.

Since packaging slack has the smallest nonnegative trade ratio (9,000), S_2 will be the leaving, or pivot row, variable. In Table 8.2, this pivot row (S_2) again is shaded, denoted with the horizontal arrow, and labeled with the "Take out" notation. The circled entry at the intersection of this pivot row and the pivot column becomes the pivot element for the second simplex table.

Optimal Simplex Table

Daspling's second pivoting (replacing S_2 with X_1) results in Table 8.3.

New Current Solution. In Table 8.3, the entering variable X_1 replaces the leaving variable S_2, while Major League baseballs (X_2) remain, as Basis column entries. The C_j column entries again give the corresponding per-box profit contributions (\$3 for X_2 and \$2 for X_1).

Exchange and Amounts—New Basic Variable. Table 8.2's 9000-box smallest nonnegative trade ratio represents the quantity of the new basic variable (the Amounts column entry in the X_1 row of Table 8.3). The new basic variable's exchange rates (X_1 through S_2 column entries in the X_1 row of Table 8.3) again are found with formula (8.1), or in this case

$$\frac{X_1 \text{ through } S_2 \text{ column entries in the } S_2 \text{ row of Table 8.2}}{\text{Circled pivot element in Table 8.2}}$$

Table 8.3   Daspling's Third (Optimal) Simplex Table

Variables		X_1	X_2	S_1	S_2	
Basis	C_j	$2	$3	$0	$0	Amounts
X_2	$3	0	1	$\frac{11}{120}$	$-\frac{3}{40}$	1,800
X_1	$2	1	0	$-\frac{1}{24}$	$\frac{1}{8}$	9,000
	Z_j	$2	$3	$\$\frac{23}{120}$	$\$\frac{1}{40}$	$23,400
	$C_j - Z_j$	$0	$0	$-\$\frac{23}{120}$	$-\$\frac{1}{40}$	

These computations, for example, indicate that Daspling must give up one-eighth of a box of Little League baseballs (X_1) to get one unused packaging minute (S_2).

Exchange and Amounts—Remaining Basic Variable. Once more, the remaining basic variable's exchange rates and quantity must be adjusted with formula (8.2), or in this case

$$\begin{pmatrix} X_1 \text{ through Amounts} \\ \text{columns' entries} \\ \text{in the } X_2 \text{ row of} \\ \text{Table 8.2} \end{pmatrix} - \left[\begin{pmatrix} X_1 \text{ column entry} \\ \text{in the } X_2 \text{ row} \\ \text{of Table 8.2} \end{pmatrix} \begin{pmatrix} X_1 \text{ through Amounts} \\ \text{columns' entries} \\ \text{in the } X_1 \text{ row of} \\ \text{Table 8.3} \end{pmatrix} \right]$$

The results give the remaining basic variable's (the X_2 row's) X_1 through Amounts column entries in Table 8.3.

For example, such calculations show that Daspling has

$$\begin{pmatrix} \text{Amounts column} \\ \text{entry in the} \\ X_2 \text{ row of Table} \\ 8.2 \end{pmatrix} - \left[\begin{pmatrix} X_1 \text{ column} \\ \text{entry in} \\ \text{the } X_2 \text{ row} \\ \text{of Table} \\ 8.2 \end{pmatrix} \begin{pmatrix} \text{Amounts column} \\ \text{entry in the} \\ X_1 \text{ row of} \\ \text{Table 8.3} \end{pmatrix} \right] = \begin{pmatrix} \text{Amounts} \\ \text{column} \\ \text{entry in} \\ \text{the } X_2 \\ \text{row of} \\ \text{Table 8.3} \end{pmatrix}$$

or
$$7,200 - (3/5 \times 9,000) = 1,800$$

boxes of Major League baseballs remaining after accounting for Little League output. The computations also indicate that the company must give up

$$\begin{pmatrix} S_1 \text{ column} \\ \text{entry in} \\ \text{the } X_2 \text{ row} \\ \text{of Table 8.2} \end{pmatrix} - \left[\begin{pmatrix} X_1 \text{ column} \\ \text{entry in} \\ \text{the } X_2 \text{ row} \\ \text{of Table} \\ 8.2 \end{pmatrix} \begin{pmatrix} S_1 \text{ column entry} \\ \text{in the } X_1 \text{ row} \\ \text{of Table 8.3} \end{pmatrix} \right] = \begin{pmatrix} S_1 \text{ column} \\ \text{entry in} \\ \text{the } X_2 \text{ row} \\ \text{of Table} \\ 8.3 \end{pmatrix}$$

or

$$1/15 - (3/5 \times -1/24) = 11/120$$

of these remaining boxes to get one unused assembly minute.

Improvement. Multiplying Table 8.3's C_j column entries by the corresponding X_1 through Amounts column entries and summing the results gives the Z_j row entries. These calculations, for example, show that Daspling earns

$$(\$3 \times 1800) + (\$2 \times 9000) = \$23,400$$

total profit from the third basic feasible solution.

By subtracting Table 8.3's Z_j row entries from the corresponding C_j row entries, management gets the $C_j - Z_j$ row entries. Since these $C_j - Z_j$ row entries are either zero or negative, Daspling cannot increase the $Z = \$23,400$ profit by bringing any variable into the basis. Thus, Table 8.3 gives the optimal solution to the company's linear program. This result also illustrates the following important property: *In a maximization problem, the optimal solution is found when there are no positive entries in the $C_j - Z_j$ row of the simplex table.*

Optimal Solution. Table 8.3's Basis and Amounts column entries indicate that Daspling can maximize total profit at $23,400 by producing

$$X_2 = 1,800 \text{ boxes of Major League baseballs}$$

$$X_1 = 9,000 \text{ boxes of Little League baseballs}$$

Since S_1 and S_2 do not appear in the Basis column, this third basic feasible solution (corner point C in Figures 8.1 and 8.2) will involve no unused assembly and no idle packaging minutes.

Procedure Recap. The following procedure can be used to find the optimal linear programming solution with simplex tableaus or tables:

1. Set up the standard form of the linear program.
2. Establish a convenient initial basic feasible solution and record the information in a simplex table.
3. Select as the entering variable the nonbasic variable with the best per-unit contribution to the objective. Ties may be broken arbitrarily.
4. Select as the leaving variable the basic variable with the smallest nonnegative trade ratio.
5. Modify the simplex tableau to reflect the new solution.
6. Continue pivoting until the optimal solution is found.

8.3 EXTENSIONS

So far, the discussion has focused on a maximization problem that involves only less-than-or-equal-to restrictions. Practical linear programs, however, may have a variety of constraint formats and may involve a minimization objective. This next section shows how the simplex method deals with these additional formulations and other special situations that may be encountered in practice. It also overviews some common extensions to the simplex algorithm and briefly discusses an alternative to simplex-based procedures.

Big M Method

When a linear program involves restrictions with greater-than-or-equal-to ($\geq$) or equality ($=$) relationships, a special process is required to transform the program into its standard form. Management Situation 8.2 illustrates.

Management Situation 8.2

Work Force Planning

Shock, Inc. is a contractor that employs electricians for wiring commercial and residential structures. Including fringe benefits, master electricians earn \$20 per hour and journeymen earn \$10 per hour. Since business is expanding, the manager plans to hire additional electricians. There is a \$300,000 budget available for hiring purposes, and management plans to spend the entire amount.

Union contracts require Shock to satisfy the following condition:

$$\left(\begin{matrix} \text{journeyman} \\ \text{hours} \end{matrix} \right) \geq \left[\left(\begin{matrix} \text{twice the} \\ \text{master hours} \end{matrix} \right) - \left(\begin{matrix} 5,000 \\ \text{hours} \end{matrix} \right) \right]$$

The 5,000 hours are set aside for company orientation and journeyman training. Also, the contractor wants to employ additional journeymen for at least 10,000 hours during the proposed hiring period.

By processing past revenue and cost data through the contractor's computer information system, management has found that a master contributes \$6 and a journeyman contributes \$2.50 per hour to profit. Shock wants to hire the additional master and journeyman combination that will maximize total profit.

Shock's problem can be expressed as the following linear program:

maximize $Z = \$6X_1 + \$2.50X_2$

subject to $\$20X_1 + \$10X_2 = \$300,000$ (Budget)

$X_2 \geq 10,000$ hours   (Journeymen)

$X_2 \geq 2X_1 - 5,000$ hours or $2X_1 - X_2 \leq 5,000$ hours   (Union)

$X_1, X_2 \geq 0$

where Z = the total dollar profit, X_1 = additional master hours employed, and X_2 = additional journeyman hours employed.

Since we want all variables on the left side and a nonnegative constant on the right side, the union constraint is restated in its alternative form ($2X_1 - X_2 \leq 5,000$ hours). This alternative form is obtained by first multiplying the original expression by -1 and then adding $2X_1$ to both sides of the result.

Slack and Surplus Variables. Once restated, the union constraint can be written in its standard form of

$$2X_1 - X_2 + S_3 = 5,000 \text{ hours}$$

by adding the slack S_3 (with a subscript of 3 because this restriction is the third constraint in the program) to the left side of the expression. The union slack S_3, which accounts for any potential difference between the hours actually employed ($2X_1 - X_2$) and the 5,000-hour training reserve, represents the unused training reserve hours.

Shock can define the surplus variable

$$S_2 = \text{excess journeyman hours}$$

to account for any potential difference between actual journeyman hours (X_2) and the 10,000-hour minimum. By subtracting this surplus variable S_2 from the left side of the original expression, management will get a constraint

$$X_2 - S_2 = 10,000 \text{ hours}$$

that is an equality but not yet in a suitable standard form.

Artificial Variables. The simplex starting solution will have zero values for all decision variables or, in Shock's case, $X_1 = 0$ and $X_2 = 0$. According to the journeymen constraint equation, however, this starting solution will involve

$$S_2 = X_2 - 10,000 = 0 - 10,000 = -10,000$$

excess journeyman hours and thereby be infeasible.

To avoid this problem, management can restate the journeymen constraint equation as

$$X_2 - S_2 + A_2 = 10,000 \text{ hours}$$

by adding the new fictitious variable A_2 (with a subscript of 2 because this restriction is the second constraint in the program) to the left side of the expression. When $X_2 = 0$, there will be no excess journeyman hours ($S_2 = 0$) and

$$A_2 = 10,000 - X_2 + S_2 = 10,000 - 0 + 0 = 10,000$$

hours. The A_2 variable accounts for the difference between the starting simplex solution's 0 hours and the 10,000-hour minimum specification.

Similarly, management can restate the budget constraint as

$$\$20X_1 + \$10X_2 + A_1 = \$300,000$$

by adding another fictitious variable A_1 (with the subscript of 1 again identifying the constraint number) to the left side of the original expression. Then, when $X_1 = 0$ and $X_2 = 0$

$$A_1 = \$300,000 - \$20X_1 - \$10X_2 = \$300,000 - \$20(0) - \$10(0) = \$300,000$$

or the A_1 variable accounts for the difference between the starting simplex solution's $0 and the $300,000 budget.

Fictitious variables, such as A_1 and A_2, are known as **artificial variables**. Although these variables have no real meaning in the original problem, they enable us to develop standard form system constraints that provide a convenient starting basis for the simplex method.

Standard Form. Since artificial variables are meaningless, they should be excluded from the optimal solution (if it exists). This result can be guaranteed by giving each artificial variable a very heavy penalty (customarily denoted by the symbol M) in the objective function. The penalty takes the form of a $+M$ unit contribution in minimization problems and a $-M$ unit contribution in maximization problems. Such an approach, which makes each artificial variable an unattractive decision alternative, is called the **method of penalties** or the **big M method**. (A very high value, such as 10 billion, is substituted for M when implementing the method with a computer program.) Shock, for example, can assign a $-\$M$ (very large negative) unit profit contribution to each artificial variable (A_1 and A_2). Then, its standard form linear program will be

maximize $\quad Z = \$6X_1 + \$2.50X_2 + \$0S_3 + \$0S_2 - \$MA_1 - \$MA_2$

subject to $\quad \$20X_1 + \$10X_2 + \$0S_3 + \$0S_2 + A_1 + \$0A_2 = \$300,000 \quad$ (Budget)

$$0X_1 + X_2 + 0S_3 - S_2 + 0A_1 + A_2 = 10,000 \text{ hours} \quad \text{(Journeymen)}$$

$$2X_1 - X_2 + S_3 + 0S_2 + 0A_1 + 0A_2 = 5,000 \text{ hours} \quad \text{(Union)}$$

$$X_1, X_2, S_3, S_2, A_1, A_2 \geq 0$$

Procedure Recap. The procedure for establishing the standard form of a linear program can be summarized as follows:

1. Put all the decision variables on the left side and a nonnegative constant on the right side of each system constraint in the original linear program.

2. Convert each less-than-or-equal-to ($\leq$) system constraint into a equality by adding a slack variable to the left side.

3. Convert each greater-than-or-equal-to ($\geq$) system constraint into an equality by adding an artificial variable and subtracting a surplus variable from the left side.

4. Add an artificial variable to the left side of each equal-to ($=$) system constraint.

5. Assign a very large penalty (a $+M$ coefficient in minimization problems and a $-M$ coefficient in maximization problems) to each artificial variable in the objective function.

6. Include the supplemental (slack, surplus, and artificial) variables in the nonnegativity conditions.

Initial Basic Feasible Solution. Shock's standard form linear program has $n = 6$ variables (X_1, X_2, A_1, A_2, S_2, and S_3) and $m = 3$ system constraint (budget, journeymen, and union) equations. Management obtains the initial basic feasible solution by first

Table 8.4   Shock's First Simplex Table

Variables		X_1	X_2	S_1	S_2	A_1	A_2		
Basis	C_j	$6	$2.5	$0	$0	$-$M$	$-$M$	Amounts	Trade Ratios
A_1	$-$M$	20	10	0	0	1	0	300,000	$\frac{300,000}{20} = 15,000$
A_2	$-$M$	0	1	0	-1	0	1	10,000	$\frac{10,000}{0} = $ undefined
S_3	$0	(2)	-1	1	0	0	0	5,000	$\frac{5,000}{2} = 2,500 \leftarrow$ Take out (pivot row)
	Z_j	$-$20M$	$-$11M$	$0	M	$-$M$	$-$M$	$-$310,000M$	
	$C_j - Z_j$	$6 + $20M$	$2.5 + $11M$	$0	$-$M$	$0	$0		

↑
Bring in
(pivot column)

setting the decision variables (X_1 and X_2) and the surplus variable (S_2) equal to zero and then reading the values of the remaining variables

$$A_1 = \$300,000 \qquad A_2 = 10,000 \text{ hours} \qquad S_3 = 5,000 \text{ hours}$$

from the right sides of the standard form system constraint equations. This initial solution (and the acompanying simplex information) is recorded in Table 8.4.

Pivoting. Since there are positive entries in the X_1 and X_2 columns of the $C_j - Z_j$ row, Table 8.4 does not provide the optimal simplex solution. Among these entries, $6 + $20M$ is a larger positive number than $2.50 + $11M$. Therefore, X_1 will be the entering, or pivot column, variable. Also, the resulting trade ratios indicate that S_3 (with the smallest nonnegative trade ratio of 2,500) will be the leaving, or pivot row, variable. The pivot element is the circled entry of 2 at the intersection of the pivot row and pivot column.

Optimal Solution. By continuing with the pivoting process, Shock will eventually obtain Table 8.5. Since all $C_j - Z_j$ row entries are either negative or zero, this table provides the optimal simplex solution. According to the Basis and Amounts column entries, Shock can maximize total profit at $83,750 by employing

$$X_2 = 12,500 \text{ additional journeyman hours}$$

$$X_1 = 8,750 \text{ additional master hours}$$

which creates

$$S_2 = 2,500 \text{ excess journeyman hours}$$

and, since A_1, A_2, and S_3 do not appear in the basis, creates no fictitious activity and no unused training reserve hours.

Figure 8.4   Shock's Feasible Solution Area and Extreme Points

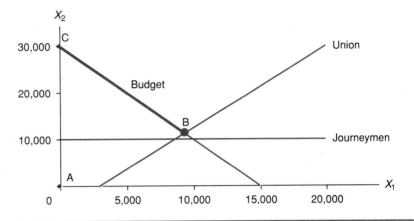

Table 8.5   Shock's Optimal Simplex Table

Variables		X_1	X_2	S_1	S_2	A_1	A_2	
Basis	c_j	$6	$2.5	$0	$0	−$M	−$M	Amounts
S_2	$0	0	0	$-\frac{1}{2}$	1	$\frac{1}{20}$	−1	2,500
X_2	$2.5	0	1	$-\frac{1}{2}$	0	$\frac{1}{20}$	0	12,500
X_1	$6	1	0	$\frac{1}{4}$	0	$\frac{1}{40}$	0	8,750
z_j		$6	$2.5	$.25	$0	$.275	$0	$83,750
$c_j − z_j$		$0	$0	−$.25	−$0	−$M−$.275	−$M	

Original versus Simplex Solution. Figure 8.4 graphs the restrictions to Shock's original linear program. The darkened line segment on the budget constraint line indentifies the company's feasible solution area, and the corner points are labeled B and C. Point A depicts the origin of the graph (where $X_1 = 0$ and $X_2 = 0$).

Shock's initial basic feasible solution (Table 8.4) corresponds to point A in Figure 8.4. As the figure demonstrates, this solution does not provide a feasible solution to the company's original linear program. Such a result illustrates the following important property: *If an artificial variable appears in the Basis column of a simplex table with a positive Amounts column entry, the corresponding solution will be infeasible for the original linear program.*

By pivoting, the company moves toward and eventually reaches point B in Figure 8.4. This point gives the optimal solution to Shock's original linear program. Since point B corresponds to Table 8.5, the simplex method with penalties (the big M method) then generates an optimal basis that represents the best solution to the original linear program.

Minimization Problems

Although the basic pivoting process remains the same, the simplex method's optimality criterion is applied differently in a minimization than in a maximization problem. Management Situation 8.3 illustrates.

Management Situation 8.3

A Mine Planning Problem

The Northeastern Company operates two separate coal mines. It costs \$5,000 a day to operate the Alpha shaft and \$3,000 a day to operate the Beta mine. After crushing, coal ore is processed into premium and standard grades. Dealer contracts call for at least 300 tons of premium and 600 tons of standard in a given time period. The Alpha shaft averages 30 tons of premium grade and 90 tons of standard grade per day. The Beta mine averages 50 tons of premium and 25 tons of standard per day. Management wants to determine the least costly mine-operating plan.

After careful deliberation, management has been able to formulate the problem as the following linear program:

minimize $\qquad$ $Z = \$5,000X_1 + \$3,000X_2$

subject to $\qquad$ $30X_1 + 50X_2 \geq 300$ tons $\qquad$ (Premium)

$\qquad\qquad\quad$ $90X_1 + 25X_2 \geq 600$ tons $\qquad$ (Standard)

$\qquad\qquad\quad$ $X_1, X_2 \geq 0$

where Z = Northeastern's total operating cost, X_1 = the number of days of operation for the Alpha shaft, and X_2 = the number of days of operation for the Beta mine.

Standard Form. By using supplemental variables (subtracting surplus variables and adding artificial variables to both constraints), management can write Northeastern's linear program in the following standard form:

minimize $\quad$ $Z = \$5,000X_1 + \$3,000X_2 + \$0S_1$

$\qquad\qquad\quad$ $+ \$0S_2 + \$MA_1 + \$MA_2$

subject to $\quad$ $30X_1 + 50X_2 - S_1 + 0S_2 + A_1 + 0A_2 = 300$ tons $\qquad$ (Premium)

$\qquad\qquad$ $90X_1 + 25X_2 + 0S_1 - S_2 + 0A_1 + A_2 = 600$ tons $\qquad$ (Standard)

$\qquad\qquad$ $X_1, X_2, S_1, S_2, A_1, A_2 \geq 0$

where S_1 = excess tons of premium coal, S_2 = excess tons of standard coal, A_1 = artificial tons of premium coal, and A_2 = artificial tons of standard coal. Note that to make the fictitious activities unattractive, management gives A_1 and A_2 very large (\$$M$) per-unit costs in the objective function.

Table 8.6   **Northeastern's First Simplex Table**

Variables		X_1	X_2	S_1	S_2	A_1	A_2		
Basis	C_j	$5,000	$3,000	$0	$0	$M	$M	Amounts	Trade Ratios
A_1	$M	30	50	−1	0	1	0	300	$\frac{300}{30} = 10$
A_2	$M	(90)	25	0	−1	0	1	600	$\frac{600}{90} = \frac{20}{3}$ ← Take out (pivot row)
	Z_j	$120M	$75M	−$M	−$M	$M	$M	$900M	
C_j	−Z_j	$5,000−$120M	$3,000−$75M	$M	$M	$0	$0		

↑
Bring in
(pivot column)

Initial Basic Feasible Solution. Northeastern's standard form consists of $n = 6$ variables $(X_1, X_2, S_1, S_2, A_1,$ and $A_2)$ and $m = 2$ system constraint (premium and standard coal) equations. By setting the decision $(X_1$ and $X_2)$ and surplus $(S_1$ and $S_2)$ variables equal to zero, management will get the initial basic feasible solution and accompanying simplex information recorded in Table 8.6.

Improvement. The entries in the $C_j - Z_j$ row of Table 8.6 indicate that Northeastern can change the initial total cost a net $5,000 − $120M$ by mining for a day in Alpha (X_1) and a net $3,000 − $75M$ by mining a day in Beta (X_2). Since both of these net changes are negative numbers, management can improve the objective function value (reduce cost) by bringing either X_1 or X_2 into the basis. This result illustrates the following important property: *In a minimization problem, a basic feasible solution can be improved as long as there are negative entries in the $C_j - Z_j$ row of the corresponding simplex table.*

Entering Variable. Since mining in the Alpha shaft contributes the largest daily expense reduction (has the largest negative $C_j - Z_j$ row entry in Table 8.6), X_1 will be the entering, or pivot column, variable. This selection demonstrates the following optimality criterion: *In a minimization problem, always bring into the basis the variable with the largest negative entry in the $C_j - Z_j$ row of the simplex table.*

Leaving Variable. The feasibility criterion is the same in minimization as in maximization problems. Since the smallest nonnegative trade ratio is the 20/3 associated with the artificial tons of standard coal, A_2 will be the leaving, or pivot row, variable. The circled entry of 90 in Table 8.6 at the intersection of this pivot row and the pivot column becomes the pivot element.

Optimal Solution. By continuing with the pivoting process, Northeastern will eventually obtain Table 8.7. Since all entries in the $C_j - Z_j$ row are either positive or zero, this

Table 8.7   **Northeastern's Optimal Simplex Table**

Variables		X_1	X_2	S_1	S_2	A_1	A_2	
Basis	C_j	$5,000	$3,000	$0	$0	$M	$M	Amounts
X_2	$3,000	0	1	$-\frac{3}{125}$	$\frac{1}{125}$	$\frac{3}{125}$	$-\frac{1}{125}$	$\frac{12}{5}$
X_1	$5,000	1	0	$\frac{1}{150}$	$-\frac{6}{450}$	$-\frac{1}{150}$	$\frac{6}{450}$	6
	Z_j	$5,000	$3,000	$-\$\frac{116}{3}$	$-\$\frac{128}{3}$	$\$\frac{116}{3}$	$\$\frac{128}{3}$	$37,200
	$C_j - Z_j$	$0	$0	$\$\frac{116}{3}$	$\$\frac{128}{3}$	$M-\$\frac{116}{3}$	$M-\$\frac{128}{3}$	

table provides the optimal basic feasible solution to the company's linear program. This result illustrates the following important property: *In a minimization problem, the optimal solution is found when there are no negative entries in the $C_j - Z_j$ row of the simplex table.*

According to the Basis and Amounts column entries in Table 8.7, Northeastern can minimize total cost at $37,200 by scheduling

$$X_2 = 12/5 = 2.4 \text{ days of operation in the Beta mine}$$

$$X_1 = 6 \text{ days of operation in the Alpha mine}$$

Since A_1, A_2, S_1, and S_2 do not appear in the Basis column, this solution involves no fictitious activity and no excess tons of premium or standard coal.

Special Situations

When attempting to solve a linear program, the decision maker may encounter special situations. This section identifies these situations and discusses their effects on the simplex method.

Degeneracy. In the situations presented so far, the number of positive-valued variables in the solution was exactly equal to the number of system constraints. Sometimes, however, the solution will be **degenerate**, or have fewer positive-valued variables than system constraints. Management Situation 8.4 illustrates.

Management Situation 8.4

Production Planning

A small firm has the problem represented by the following linear program:

maximize $\qquad\qquad Z = \$30X_1 + \$20X_2$

Figure 8.5   **Small Firm's Degeneracy**

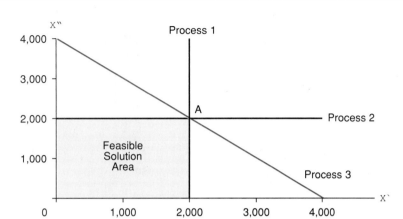

subject to $\qquad X_1 \le 2{,}000$ units $\qquad$ (Process 1)

$\qquad\qquad\qquad X_2 \le 2{,}000$ units $\qquad$ (Process 2)

$\qquad\qquad\qquad X_1 + X_2 \le 4{,}000$ units $\qquad$ (Process 3)

$\qquad\qquad\qquad X_1, X_2 \ge 0$

where Z = the total dollar profit, X_1 = the number of units of product A, and X_2 = the number of units of product B.

Management wants to evaluate the problem with the simplex method.

Figure 8.5 presents the graphic solution to the small firm's linear program. In this figure, the shaded region depicts the firm's feasible solution area and point A identifies the optimal solution.

At point A, both decision variables (X_1 and X_2) have positive values, but there is no slack for processes 1, 2, or 3. Since this solution has fewer positive-valued variables (2) than system constraints (3), it is degenerate. Geometrically, degeneracy occurs when the number of system constraint lines passing through a corner point is greater than the number of real (decision) variables.

In the simplex method, degeneracy occurs when one or more basic variables has a value of zero. For example, by using the simplex method, the small firm will eventually get Table 8.8. The $C_j - Z_j$ row entries in this table indicate that X_2 will be the entering, or pivot column, variable. However, there is a tie between process 2 slack (S_2) and process 3 slack (S_3) for the smallest nonnegative trade ratio. Consequently, it is unclear whether S_2 or S_3 will be the leaving, or pivot row, variable.

If S_3 is arbitrarily treated as the leaving variable, the pivoting process will lead to Table 8.9. While the entering variable X_2 replaces S_3 in this table's Basis column, the tied variable S_2 (which remains in the basis) also ends up with a zero value. Therefore,

Table 8.8   Second Simplex Table for the Production-Planning Problem

Variables		X_1	X_2	S_1	S_2	S_3		
Basis	C_j	$30	$20	$0	$0	$0	Amounts	Trade Ratios
X_1	$30	1	0	1	0	0	2,000	$\frac{2000}{0}$ = undefined
S_2	$0	0	1	0	1	0	2,000	$\frac{2000}{1}$ = 2,000
S_3	$0	0	1	−1	0	1	2,000	$\frac{2000}{1}$ = 2,000
	Z_j	$30	$0	$30	$0	$0	$60,000	
	$C_j - Z_j$	$0	$20	−$30	$0	$0		

↑
Bring in
(pivot column)

Table 8.9   Third Simplex Table for the Production-Planning Problem

Variables		X_1	X_2	S_1	S_2	S_3	
Basis	C_j	$30	$20	$0	$0	$0	Amounts
X_1	$30	1	0	1	0	0	2,000
S_2	$0	0	0	1	1	−1	0
X_2	$20	0	1	−1	0	1	2,000
	Z_j	$30	$20	$10	$0	$20	$100,000
	$C_j - Z_j$	$0	$0	−$10	$0	−$20	

Table 8.9's basic feasible solution (which corresponds to corner point A in Figure 8.5) is degenerate.

A degenerate optimal solution (such as Table 8.9 or Figure 8.5's corner point A) in itself is not a problem. When degeneracy occurs during the pivoting process, however, there is a theoretical possibility that the algorithm will cycle or loop repetitively through intermediate (and nonoptimal) basic feasible solutions. Such cycling often can be resolved by returning to the tied trade ratios and simply selecting an alternative leaving variable. Other times, advanced procedures (not treated here) will be needed to overcome the difficulty.

In practice, the theoretical cycling has seldom occurred. Hence, in all but the most sophisticated computer codes, this situation is ignored.

Unbounded Problems. In some linear programs, the restrictions do not put an effective limit on the values of the decision variables. Management Situation 8.5 provides an illustration.

Figure 8.6 **The Office Supply Problem**

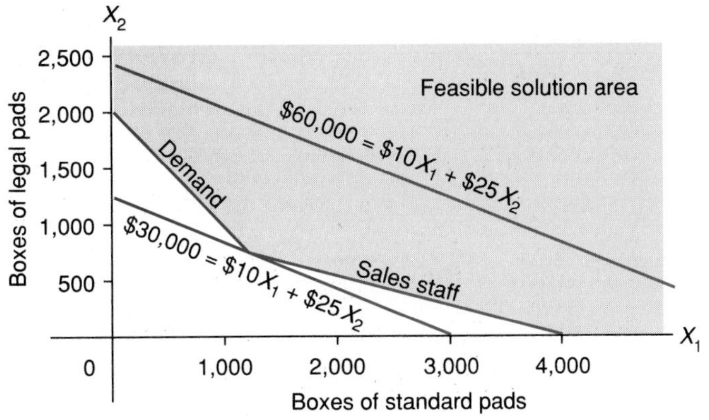

Management Situation 8.5

A Product Mix Problem

An office supply company manufactures two types of paper pads. The standard pad earns \$10 profit per box, and the legal pad yields \$25 profit per box. Customers require a combined total of at least 2,000 boxes per month. The company's sales staff will have to work at least 20,000 hours per month to meet this demand. Past experience indicates that salespeople need 5 hours to sell a box of standard pads and 20 hours to sell a box of legal pads. Sales effort includes travel time, presentations, order taking, and follow-up. The company seeks the combination of pads that maximizes total monthly profit.

By letting

X_1 = the number of boxes of standard pads

X_2 = the number of boxes of legal pads

Z = the total monthly profit

we can express the company's problem by the following linear program:

maximize $Z = \$10X_1 + \$25X_2$

subject to $X_1 + X_2 \geq 2{,}000$ boxes (Demand)

$5X_1 + 20X_2 \geq 20{,}000$ hours (Sales staff)

$X_1, X_2 \geq 0$

Table 8.10　Fourth Simplex Table for the Office Supply Problem

Variables		X_1	X_2	S_1	S_2	A_1	A_2		
Basis	C_j	$10	$25	$0	$0	$-\$M$	$-\$M$	Amounts	Trade Ratios
X_1	$10	1	4	0	$-\frac{1}{5}$	0	$\frac{1}{5}$	4,000	$4{,}000/-\frac{1}{5} = -20{,}000$
S_1	$0	0	3	1	$-\frac{1}{5}$	-1	$\frac{1}{5}$	2,000	$2{,}000/-\frac{1}{5} = -10{,}000$
	Z_j	$10	$40	$0	$-\$2$	$0	$2	$40,000	
	$C_j - Z_j$	$0	$-\$15$	$0	$2	$-\$M$	$-\$M-\$2$		

↑
Bring in
(pivot column)

A graphic representation of this linear program is presented in Figure 8.6. As the figure demonstrates, the system constraints in the office supply company's linear program do not place an upper boundary on the feasible solution area. This region extends outward indefinitely from the demand and sales staff constraint lines. Hence, it is feasible for the company to produce an unlimited quantity of standard and legal pads. Also, look at the profit lines in this graph. It is always possible to move toward a higher-valued profit line and still have a feasible solution point. As a result, the company can obtain any monthly profit it wants, even one that is unlimited or infinitely large. Such a linear program is known as an **unbounded problem**.

In the simplex method, the unbounded condition will make it impossible to determine the leaving variable during some phase of the pivoting process. For example, by using the simplex method, the office supply company will eventually get Table 8.10. The $C_j - Z_j$ row entries in this table indicate that S_2 will be the entering, or pivot column, variable. Since there are no nonnegative trade ratios, however, neither X_1 nor S_1 will be driven out of the basis (forced to a zero value) no matter how large S_2 becomes. Total profit will increase by $2 per unit indefinitely and thereby be unbounded.

Few, if any, problems in practice are really unbounded. Experience tells us that it is impossible to increase profits indefinitely. Thus, when a linear program is unbounded, it typically means that the problem has been improperly formulated or the model is inappropriate.

Infeasible Problems. In some linear programs, there is no combination of decision variables that simultaneously satisfies all the restrictions in the problem. Management Situation 8.6 illustrates.

Management Situation 8.6

A Space Allocation Problem

I. M. Warm, an environmental design professor, has been given a federal grant to develop a prototype solar-powered home. Preliminary research indicates that the living

Figure 8.7   Warm's Space Allocation Restrictions

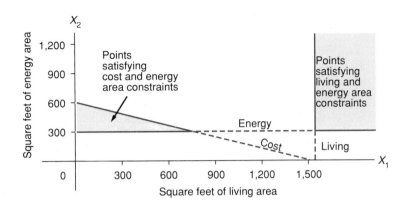

area of such a home can be constructed for $40 per square foot. The house also requires a separate area for the installation and operation of solar energy equipment. This energy area can be constructed for $100 per square foot. The solar house must be competitive in the new housing market. To do so, it must have at least 1,600 square feet of living area and cost no more than $60,000. Under current solar technology, at least 300 square feet of energy area are needed to power such a home. The government wants Warm to determine the maximum feasible size of such a house.

By letting

$$X_1 = \text{the number of square feet of living area}$$

$$X_2 = \text{the number of square feet of solar energy area}$$

$$Z = \text{the total number of square feet of the solar home}$$

Warm can represent the problem with the following linear program:

maximize $Z = X_1 + X_2$

subject to $\$40X_1 + \$100X_2 \leq \$60,000$ (Cost)

$X_1 \geq 1,600$ square feet   (Living area)

$X_2 \geq 300$ square feet   (Energy area)

$X_1, X_2 \geq 0$

Figure 8.7 offers a graphic representation of the restrictions in Warm's linear program. You can see that there is no feasible solution area. That is, there are no solution points that simultaneously satisfy all the restrictions. The shaded area in the left-hand portion of the graph depicts the points satisfying the cost and energy area constraints, while the shaded region in the right-hand portion identifies the points that satisfy the

Table 8.11 **Warm's Second Simplex Table**

Variables Basis	C_j	X_1 1	X_2 1	S_1 0	S_2 0	S_3 0	A_1 $-M$	A_2 $-M$	Amounts
X_1	1	1	$\frac{5}{2}$	$\frac{1}{40}$	0	0	0	0	1,500
A_1	$-M$	0	$-\frac{5}{2}$	$-\frac{1}{40}$	-1	0	1	0	100
A_2	$-M$	0	1	0	0	-1	0	1	300
Z_j		1	$\frac{5}{2}+\frac{5}{2}M$	$\frac{1}{40}+\frac{1}{40}M$	M	M	$-M$	$-M$	$1,500-400M$
$C_j - Z_j$		0	$-\frac{3}{2}-\frac{5}{2}M$	$-\frac{1}{40}-\frac{1}{40}M$	$-M$	$-M$	0	0	

living area and energy area restrictions. However, there are no points that satisfy all three constraints (cost, living area, and energy area). Therefore, there is no feasible solution to the linear program. Such a program is known as an **infeasible problem**.

The simplex method uses artificial variables to identify any infeasible conditions. For example, by using the simplex method, Warm will eventually obtain Table 8.11. The negative and zero $C_j - Z_j$ row entries indicate that the professor cannot improve the objective function value by changing this table's basis. Since such a basis includes artificial variables (A_1 and A_2) with positive Amounts column entries, Warm must conclude that there is no feasible solution to the original space allocation problem.

Infeasibility ordinarily indicates that the constraints have been formulated improperly or that the conditions are too restrictive. Linear programming concepts can be used to identify the causes of infeasibility and to suggest appropriate remedies.

Figure 8.7, for example, shows that the solar home's cost constraint line is to the left of (below) the living area restriction line. Feasible solution points for the living area restriction, however, are to the right of (above) or on the living area constraint line. Thus, it is not possible to construct a solar house with the minimum desirable living area (1600 square feet) at the maximum acceptable cost ($60,000).

However, a solar house could be feasible if consumers would be satisfied with a smaller living area. The decision maker can find the feasible size by shifting the living area constraint line to the left. This shift should continue until a point of tangency is reached between the living area constraint line and the boundary of the shaded region in the left-hand portion of Figure 8.7. The appropriate movement is illustrated in Figure 8.8. As you can see, tangency would occur at the intersection of the cost and energy constraint lines. At this point,

$$\$40X_1 + \$100X_2 = \$60,000 \qquad \text{(Cost)}$$

$$X_2 = 300 \qquad \text{(Energy area)}$$

Thus, the feasible size would be

$$X_2 = 300 \text{ square feet of energy area}$$

Figure 8.8   **Feasible Living Area for Warm's House**

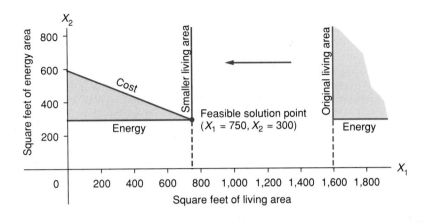

and

$$\$40X_1 + \$100(300) = \$60,000$$

or

$$X_1 = 750 \text{ square feet of living area}$$

for a total of

$$Z = X_1 + X_2 = 300 + 750 = 1,050 \text{ square feet}$$

Alternatively, a solar home could be feasible if consumers would be willing to pay more for the house. Warm can find the higher cost by shifting the cost constraint line to the right. This shift should continue until a point of tangency is reached between the cost constraint line and the boundary of the shaded region in the right-hand portion of Figure 8.7. The appropriate movement is illustrated in Figure 8.9. You can see that the tangency would occur at the intersection of the living area and energy area constraint lines. At this point,

$$X_1 = 1,600 \text{ square feet of living area}$$

and

$$X_2 = 300 \text{ square feet of energy area}$$

for a total of

$$Z = X_1 + X_2 = 1,600 + 300 = 1,900 \text{ square feet.}$$

The feasible cost would then be

$$\$40X_1 + \$100X_2 = \$40(1600) + \$100(300) = \$94,000.$$

Multiple Optimal Solutions. A linear program can have more than one optimal solution, or **multiple optimal solutions**. In fact, if a linear program has more than one optimal

Figure 8.9   Feasible Cost for Warm's House

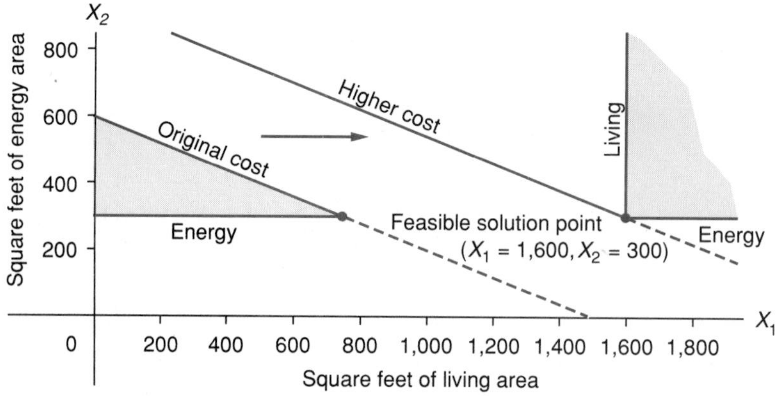

solution, it has an infinite number of optimal solutions. Management Situation 8.7 illustrates.

Management Situation 8.7

A Blending Problem

A homeowner wants to paint the interior of his dwelling with flat and enamel finishes. Flat paint costs $6 per gallon, while each gallon of enamel costs $12. An average of two hours is needed to apply a gallon of flat, and four hours are needed for each gallon of enamel paint. The job will take at least 80 hours to complete. There are at least 2,200 square feet of living area to paint. Each gallon of flat paint covers an average of 100 square feet, while a gallon of enamel covers 20 square feet. The homeowner wants to use the combination of paints that minimizes the cost of the job.

The homeowner's paint-blending problem can be represented by the following linear program:

minimize $Z = \$6X_1 + \$12X_2$

subject to $100X_1 + 20X_2 \geq 2,200$ square feet   (Size)

                 $2X_1 + 4X_2 \geq 80$ hours   (Time)

                 $X_1, X_2 \geq 0$

where Z = the total cost of the job, X_1 = the number of gallons of flat paint, and X_2 = the number of gallons of enamel paint.

Figure 8.10   Optimal Solutions to the Homeowner's Blending Problem

---

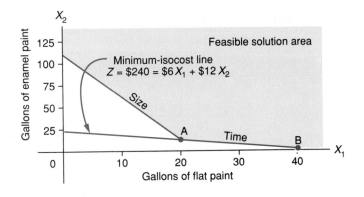

Table 8.12   Homeowner's Final Simplex Table

Variables		X_1	X_2	S_1	S_2	A_1	A_2		
Basis	C_j	$6	$12	$0	$0	$M	$M	**Amounts**	**Trade Ratios**
X_1	$6	1	0	$-\frac{1}{90}$	$\frac{1}{18}$	$-\frac{1}{90}$	$-\frac{1}{18}$	20	$20/-\frac{1}{90} = -1{,}800$
X_2	$12	0	1	$\frac{1}{180}$	$-\frac{5}{18}$	$-\frac{1}{180}$	$\frac{5}{18}$	10	$10/\frac{1}{180} = 1{,}800$ ← Take out (pivot row)
	Z_j	$6	$12	$0	$-$3	$0	$3	$240	
	$C_j - Z_j$	$0	$0	$0	$3	$M	$M-$3		

↑
Bring in
(pivot column)

Figure 8.10 provides a graphic solution to the homeowner's linear program. This figure shows that the minimum-cost objective function line

$$Z = \$240 = \$6X_1 + \$12X_2$$

is parallel to, and hence coincides with, the binding time constraint line. As a result, all points on the line segment AB represent optimal solutions to the linear program. Since there are an infinite number of these points, or multiple optimal solutions, the homeowner has an unlimited number of paint blends (combinations of X_1 and X_2 values) that will minimize total cost at $240.

In the simplex method, there are multiple optimal solutions when a *nonbasic* variable has a $C_j - Z_j$ row entry of zero in the final table. For example, by using the simplex method, the homeowner will eventually get Table 8.12 (which corresponds to corner point A in Figure 8.10). Since all $C_j - Z_j$ row entries are either positive or zero, this table gives an optimal solution to the problem.

Table 8.13　Homeowner's Alternative Optimal Simplex Table

Variables		X_1	X_2	S_1	S_2	A_1	A_2	
Basis	C_j	$6	$12	$0	$0	$M	$M	Amounts
X_1	$6	1	2	0	$-\frac{1}{2}$	0	$\frac{1}{2}$	40
S_1	$0	0	180	1	-50	-1	50	1,800
Z_j		$6	$12	$0	$-$3	$0	$3	$240
$C_j - Z_j$		$0	$0	$0	$3	$M	$M-$3	

Also, the $C_j - Z_j$ row entry of $0 for the nonbasic variable S_1 indicates that cost will not change if this variable is brought into the basis. Thus, another optimal solution can be found by treating S_1 as the entering, or pivot column, variable. The resulting trade ratios, which are computed alongside Table 8.12, tell us that X_1 will be the leaving, or pivot row, variable.

By continuing with the pivoting process, the homeowner will obtain Table 8.13 (which corresponds to corner point B in Figure 8.10). Since all $C_j - Z_j$ row entries are positive or zero, this table gives another optimal solution to the homeowner's blending problem.

Additional optimal solutions can be found by calculating weighted averages of the basic variables from Tables 8.12 and 8.13. For example, if each table's basis is weighted equally, one of the additional solutions will be

$$X_1 = 0.5(20) + 0.5(40) = 30$$

$$X_2 = 0.5(10) + 0.5(0) = 5$$

$$S_1 = 0.5(0) + 0.5(1,800) = 900$$

When Table 8.12's basis receives a 0.2 weight, another optimal solution will be

$$X_1 = 0.2(20) + 0.8(40) = 36$$

$$X_2 = 0.2(10) + 0.8(0) = 2$$

$$S_1 = 0.2(0) + 0.8(1,800) = 1,440$$

Since S_2 does not appear in the Basis column of Tables 8.12 and 8.13, there will be no excess painting hours in any of the multiple optimal solutions.

Multiple optimal solutions enable management to consider other (perhaps qualitative) criteria and then implement the most expedient solution. For example, if the homeowner does not like to work with enamel paint (wants $X_2 = 0$), he could select the optimal blend given in Table 8.13 (corner point B in Figure 8.10). On the other hand, if the homeowner prefers to paint the minimum space (wants $S_1 = 0$), he could select the optimal blend given in Table 8.12 (corner point A in Figure 8.10).

Figure 8.11   **Karmarkar's Algorithm**

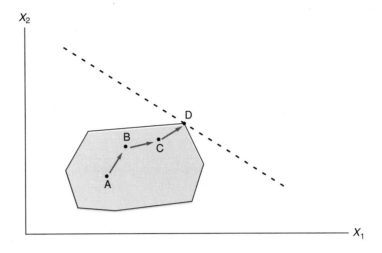

Karmarkar's Algorithm

The widespread use of linear programming has promoted the development of simplex extensions that solve either large-scale problems or special structures more efficiently than the original algorithm. These extensions include the:

1. *Revised simplex method*—uses matrix algebra and only nonbasic variable tableau information to solve problems with thousands of constraints and thousands of variables.

2. *Dual simplex method*—solves an alternative form of the problem and uses the results to infer the optimal solution for the original problem.

3. *Decomposition method*—decomposes the original problem into subproblems, optimizes the subproblems, and then synthesizes the separate solutions into an overall optimal solution.

Competing Algorithms. There are classes of problems that, in theory, would take years to solve with the simplex method and its extensions. This theoretical possibility has encouraged work on algorithms that avoid the potential worst case behavior. Such work has produced two simplex competitors, Khachian's algorithm and Karmarkar's algorithm, each named after its developer.

While Khachian's algorithm has demonstrated some efficiency for worst case problems, it has not performed as well as the simplex method on average or typical problems. Karmarkar's algorithm has shown more promise.

Karmarkar versus Simplex. The simplex method solves a linear programming problem by examining corner points on the boundary of the feasible solution area. On the other hand, **Karmarkar's algorithm** searches the interior of the feasible solution area until it reaches an optimal solution on the area's boundary. Figure 8.11 illustrates Karmarkar's approach for a simple linear program with a maximization objective and two decision variables. In the diagram, the shaded region gives the feasible solution area and the dashed line identifies the highest attainable value line.

Karmarkar's algorithm first finds a solution, at point A, near the center of the feasible solution area. Next, the method moves in the direction of the steepest ascent toward, but not all the way to, the boundary of the feasible solution area. This movement ends at the new interior point B. Then, the method moves the new point B to another place, at point C, near the center of the feasible solution area. The search continues until the optimal solution is found at point D on the boundary of the feasible solution area.

Performance. As of this writing, there is no straightforward implementation of Karmarkar's approach that is widely available and consistently beats the performance of the simplex method. The few available implementations also require some form of simplex postprocessing to generate the postoptimality analysis usually desired by management.

SUMMARY

This chapter has presented the simplex method for solving large-scale linear programs. This method is essentially a search procedure that starts with a convenient solution. It seeks improvement by successively moving from one basic feasible solution to another. Such pivoting continues until it is no longer possible to improve the objective function value.

A convenient starting solution is obtained by first converting the linear program into its standard form. Once in this form, the linear program consists of n variables and m constraint equations. The initial basic feasible solution is found by assigning zero values to $n - m$ variables and then reading the remaining m variables' values from the right-hand portions of the system constraint equations.

Simplex tableaus or tables (with the format described in Figure 8.3) are usually used to organize, monitor, and help perform the calculations involved in the pivoting process. This process indicates that the criterion value can be improved for a maximization problem as long as there are positive $C_j - Z_j$ row entries in the simplex table. In a minimization problem, improvement is possible as long as this $C_j - Z_j$ row contains negative elements. The solution is improved by bringing into the basis the variable that leads to the largest net improvement in the criterion value. In a maximization problem, such a variable has the largest positive $C_j - Z_j$ row entry. In a minimization problem, the decision maker brings into the basis the variable with the largest negative $C_j - Z_j$ row element. Management knows that it has found the maximum criterion value when there are no positive $C_j - Z_j$ row entries. Alternatively, the minimum criterion value involves an absence of negative entries in the $C_j - Z_j$ rows.

We also examined how degeneracy, unbounded problems, infeasibility, and multiple optimal solutions affect the simplex method. When there is degeneracy, a basic variable has a value of zero in a simplex solution. As long as there is no cycling, this condition does not create any difficulties.

In an unbounded problem, none of the basic variables has a nonnegative trade ratio for the entering variable. As a result, it is impossible to determine the leaving variable during some phase of the pivoting process. A problem is infeasible if the final simplex table has artificial variables in the Basis column with positive Amounts column entries. Unbounded and infeasible problems typically mean that the linear program is formulated improperly.

When a nonbasic variable has a $C_j - Z_j$ row entry of zero in the last simplex table, the linear program has multiple optimal solutions. One of the other optimal solutions can be found by treating the zero $C_j - Z_j$ valued nonbasic variable as the entering variable in the pivoting process.

Finally, we outlined some simplex-based procedures for solving large-scale problems or specially structured problems. Also, we examined a new methodology, known as Karmarkar's algorithm, that eventually may perform better than the simplex method in solving some classes of large-scale linear programming problems.

Glossary

artificial variables Fictitious variables inserted to facilitate developing standard form system constraints that provide a starting basis for the simplex method.

basic feasible solution The basic solutions that satisfy the nonnegativity conditions in a standard form linear program.

basic solution The combination of decision and supplemental variables that simultaneously satisfies all system constraints in the standard form linear program.

basic variable In a standard form linear program, the variables not set to equal zero.

basis The values of the basic variables in a standard form linear program.

big M method (method of penalties) An approach that assigns a very heavy penalty (denoted by the symbol M) in the objective function to artificial variables.

degeneracy A special situation having fewer positive-valued variables than system contraints.

entering variable The pivot column variable, which will be brought into the basis in a minimization problem.

exchange (trade) ratio Ratio values that identify the maximum amounts of the entering variable that can be exchanged or traded for the entire quantities of the basic variables.

infeasible problem A linear program with no feasible solution.

Karmarkar's algorithm A simplex competitor that searches the interior of the feasible solution area until it reaches an optimal solution on the area's boundary.

leaving variable The pivot row variable, which will be removed from the basis in a minimization problem.

multiple optimal solutions A linear program with more than one optimal solution.

nonbasic variable In a standard form linear program, the variables that are set equal to zero.

pivot column The entering variable's column in the simplex table.

pivot element The intersection of the pivot row and pivot column, which gives the amount of the leaving variable that must be given up to obtain one unit of the entering variable.

pivot row The leaving variable's row in a simplex table.

pivoting The process of moving from one basis to another until the criterion value cannot be improved.

real variable Decision variables in the simplex method.

simplex method A popular systematic methodology used to solve large-scale linear programming problems.

simplex table (tableau) A tabular format that organizes and helps perform calculations to obtain successive basic feasible solutions.

standard form A linear program in which each system constraint is expressed as an equality relationship, all real and supplemental variables appear on the left and a nonnegative constant appears on the right side of each system constraint, and all variables are nonnegative.

supplemental variables Variables used in the simplex method to convert a linear program's system constraints into an equivalent set of simultaneous equations.

unbounded problem A linear program with unlimited dimensions.

Thought Exercises

1. A marketing executive seeks the brand combination that maximizes total profit contribution. The combination must also satisfy a production cost constraint imposed by top management, a minimum contractual requirement, and a maximum staff availability. A marketing analyst is able to formulate the problem as the following linear program:

$$\text{maximize} \quad Z = \$100X_1 + \$200X_2 + \$300X_3$$

$$\text{subject to} \quad \$50X_1 + \$100X_2 + \$40X_3 = \$40,000 \qquad \text{(Production cost)}$$

$$X_1 + X_2 + X_3 \geq 500 \text{ units} \qquad \text{(Contract)}$$

$$X_1 + 4X_2 + 2X_3 \leq 1,000 \text{ hours} \qquad \text{(Staff availability)}$$

$$X_1, X_2, X_3 \geq 0$$

where Z = the total profit contribution per time period, X_1 = the number of units of brand A, X_2 = the number of units of brand B, and X_3 = the number of units of brand C. Explain the nature of the objective and constraints in this linear program in a way that is understandable to a nonquantitatively-oriented decision maker.

2. Explain whether slack, surplus, and/or artificial activities are appropriate in the following situations, and give their decision-making interpretations. Assume that the problems have feasible solutions. (To answer this question properly, trace out a rough sketch of your conception of the objective function and constraints.)
   a. A fire department seeks the combination of trucks, fire fighters, and equipment that minimizes the cost of fire protection in a community, subject to constraints on the minimum number of calls per month, a maximum budget, and a maximum number of personhours available per month.
   b. An advertising agency seeks the combination of different types of industry accounts that maximizes its sales revenue, subject to constraints on a maximum annual operating budget, maximum staff capacity, and minimum account coverage requests from each industry classification.
   c. A major national soap manufacturer seeks the combination of soap types that will maximize profit, subject to constraints of maximum production capacity, distribution contracts requiring minimum production levels for each type of soap, and a maximum operating budget.
   d. A retail sporting goods store seeks the combination of wearing apparel and equipment that maximizes profit per period while still meeting budget, hours of operation, and size of staff constraints.
   e. A nursery school seeks the combination of elementary and intermediate classes that minimizes operating cost per period while meeting minimum schedule and staff requirements.

3. Towilly, Inc. is a manufacturer of pollution control equipment. The company offers three products: a converter, a synthesizer, and an evaporator. Each product is produced and marketed by separate divisions. Monthly production, marketing, and administrative information is summarized in the following report:

Budget	Budget Required to Produce One Unit			Available Budget
	Converter	Synthesizer	Evaporator	
Production	$10	$5	$20	$30,000
Marketing	$5	$10	$40	$40,000
Administration	$20	$10	$5	$10,000
Per-unit profit contribution	$100	$40	$50	

Management wants the combined quantity of converters and synthesizers to be at least as large as the quantity of evaporators. The company also is going to save ten crates of evaporators for promotional purposes. In light of the restrictions, the company seeks the combination of equipment that will maximize total profit.

a. Formulate the company's problem as a linear program.
b. Develop the appropriate standard form.

4. Use Management Situations 8.1 and 8.2 to explain, in language understandable to management, why slack, surplus, and artificial variables must have nonnegative values.

5. Refer back to Management Situation 8.1. In Daspling's second basic feasible solution, there is an entry of $-1/3$ in the S_1 column of the S_2 row of the corresponding simplex table (Table 8.2). Give an intuitive explanation of the derivation and meaning of this entry.

6. State Senator J. M. McConnell has been investigating highway construction from three independent projects, coded A, B, and C. Project A costs $200 per hour to complete, project B costs $100 per hour to complete, and project C costs $500 per hour to complete. There must be a total of at least 2,500 hours spent on the projects in order to satisfy contractual requirements of the construction bidders. In addition, the total expenditures on the projects cannot exceed the maximum politically determined budget of $200,000 for the given time period. Each hour devoted to project A adds 0.2 mile to highway development, each hour devoted to project B adds 0.1 mile, and each hour devoted to project C adds 0.6 mile. The governor's stated objective is to maximize the number of additional miles of highway development for the given time period.

   Senator McConnell's staff includes an operations research analyst. After a linear programming analysis of the problem, the analyst advises the senator that the governor's objective is not attainable. How did he arrive at this conclusion? Do you see any way of overcoming this difficulty?

7. Custom Costumes manufactures and distributes tuxedos, theatrical costumes, and seasonal costumes at a profit of $100, $50, and $30 per carton, respectively. The company has a minimum total demand of 5,000 cartons of tuxedos per month and a minimum total demand of 8,000 cartons of each type of costume per month. Also, the company must operate its facilities at a minimum of 20,000 hours to meet these demands. Each carton of tuxedos requires two hours of facility operation, each carton of theatrical costumes requires five hours, and each carton of seasonal costumes requires two hours.

I. M. Bewilder, the company's general manager, has been unable to determine the combination of products that leads to maximum monthly profit. It appears to him that the company should produce an unlimited number of cartons of each type of product, but this conclusion is contrary to his experience in these circumstances. Can you see how he arrived at his conclusion? Can you think of any other factors that may account for his experience to the contrary? Use linear programming analysis to answer these questions.

8. There is a close analogy between the simplex procedure and the movement between the extreme points of the graphic feasible solution area. The simplex method, in effect, starts at the origin of the graph and proceeds toward the optimal solution by searching extreme points of the feasible solution area. Use Management Situations 8.2 and 8.3 to illustrate this analogy.

9. Brightstar, Inc., is a manufacturer of three types of television picture tubes: black-and-white, solid-state color, and tube color. Each type is produced and marketed independently. Each tube also goes through the same three processes: it is produced in the manufacturing center, packaged in a distribution center, and sold through a wholesale center.

The company wants to produce and market the combination of tubes that maximizes total profit and satisfies the available capacity constraints in each center. Brightstar's general manager, with assistance from the corporate operation's research analyst, has formulated the problem as a linear program. An optimal solution is reported in the following simplex table:

Variables		X_1	X_2	X_3	S_1	S_2	S_3	
Basis	C_j	$50	$100	$75	$0	$0	$0	Amounts
X_1	$50	1	0	0	$-\frac{3}{10}$	$\frac{1}{10}$	$\frac{1}{5}$	700
X_2	$100	0	1	0	$\frac{1}{5}$	$\frac{2}{5}$	$-\frac{2}{5}$	1,500
X_3	$75	0	0	1	$\frac{1}{5}$	$-\frac{1}{3}$	$\frac{2}{5}$	1,000
	Z_j	$50	$100	$75	$20	$20	$0	$260,000
	$C_j - Z_j$	$0	$0	$0	-$20	-$20	$0	

In this problem, Z = the total dollar profit, X_1 = the number of crates of black-and-white picture tubes, X_2 = the number of crates of solid-state color tubes, X_3 = the number of crates of tube color types, S_1 = unused manufacturing hours, S_2 = unused distribution hours, and S_3 = unused wholesaling hours.

a. Explain why the solution presented in this table is optimal.

b. How many black-and-white, solid-state color, and tube color picture tubes should the company produce and sell?

c. What is the maximum total profit the company can expect? Are there any alternative ways to achieve this maximum profit? Explain.

d. How can such knowledge benefit the marketing executive?

10. A company wants to determine the optimal production and inventory schedule for the coming year. The general manager has formulated the problem as the following linear program:

minimize $Z = \$10X_1 + \$15X_2 + \$5X_3$

subject to $X_1 + X_2 + X_3 \geq 2{,}000$ units   (Demand)

   $3X_1 + 2X_2 + 6X_3 \leq 3{,}000$ hours   (Production capacity)

   $X_1, X_2, X_3 \geq 0$

The final solution is given in the following simplex table:

Variables		X_1	X_2	X_3	S_1	S_2	A_1	
Basis	C_j	$\$10$	$\$15$	$\$5$	$\$0$	$\$0$	$\$M$	Amounts
A_1	$\$M$	$-\frac{1}{2}$	0	-2	-1	$-\frac{1}{2}$	1	500
X_2	$\$15$	$\frac{3}{2}$	1	3	0	$\frac{1}{2}$	0	1,500
	Z_j	$-\$\frac{1}{2}M+\$\frac{45}{2}$	$\$15$	$-\$2M+\$45$	$-\$M$	$-\$\frac{1}{2}M+\$\frac{15}{2}$	$\$M$	$\$500M+22{,}500$
	$C_j - Z_j$	$\$\frac{1}{2}M-\$\frac{25}{2}$	$\$0$	$\$2M-\$40$	$\$M$	$\$\frac{1}{2}M-\$\frac{15}{2}$	$\$0$	

In this problem, Z = the total manufacturing cost, X_1 = the number of units produced in the first half of the year, X_2 = the number of units produced in the second half of the year, X_3 = the number of units held in inventory at the end of the year, S_1 = the number of units produced in excess of yearly demand, S_2 = unused hours of production capacity, and A_1 represents the artificial variable for the demand constraint.
   What does this table tell the general manager? Explain.

11. Century Products, Inc. produces citizens band (CB) radios. There are three models: deluxe, standard, and economy. The products are sold to commercial enterprises (governments and companies), as well as to private citizens. Commercial demand is at least 2,000 units in a given time period. Private citizen demand is at least 1,000 units in that same time period.
   The company wants to produce and market the combination of CB radios that maximizes total profit and satisfies consumer demand. Century's manager has formulated the problem as a linear program. The last solution is reported in the following table:

Variables		X_1	X_2	X_3	S_1	S_2	A_1	A_2	
Basis	C_j	$\$20$	$\$30$	$\$10$	$\$0$	$\$0$	$-\$M$	$-\$M$	Amounts
S_2	$\$0$	0	0	0	-1	1	1	-1	2,000
X_2	$\$30$	1	1	1	-1	0	1	0	3,000
	Z_j	$\$30$	$\$30$	$\$30$	$-\$30$	$\$0$	$\$30$	$\$0$	$\$90{,}000$
	$C_j - Z_j$	$-\$10$	$\$0$	$-\$20$	$\$30$	$\$0$	$-\$M-\$30$	$-\$M$	

In this problem, Z = the total profit, X_1 = the number of deluxe units, X_2 = the number of standard units, X_3 = the number of economy units, S_1 = unmet commercial demand, S_2 = unmet citizen demand, and A_1 and A_2 represent the artificial variables for the commercial and citizen demand constraints, respectively.

What can Century conclude from this last table? Explain.

12. Figure 8.11 illustrates how Karmarkar's algorithm would solve a simple linear programming problem with a maximization objective and two decision variables. Use the same diagram to illustrate how the same problem would be solved by the simplex method. Which approach performs better in this situation? Explain.

13. Explain why you agree or disagree with each of the following statements:
    a. There can be an infinite number of basic and/or basic feasible solutions.
    b. The Basis and C_j columns in a simplex table are segments of the Variables and C_j rows.
    c. In a simplex table, there must always be an even (one-for-one) exchange between a basic variable and itself.
    d. In the first simplex table, the exchange segment corresponds to the left-hand side and the Amounts column to the right-hand side of the appropriate standard form system constraint equations.
    e. All Z_j elements in a simplex table will be zero when there are only slack variables in the basis.
    f. Basic variables always have zero entries in the $C_j - Z_j$ row of a simplex table.
    g. In a simplex table, each basic variable column will have an entry of 1 in one row and zeros elsewhere.
    h. When a surplus variable and an artificial variable appear in the same constraint, these variables will have exchange segment entries in the simplex tables that are the same value but opposite in sign.
    i. Redundant restrictions always lead to degeneracy.
    j. In the simplex method, there can only be a finite number of alternative optima.

Technique Exercises

14. Consider this brand mix problem given in Thought Exercise 1:

    maximize $Z = \$100X_1 + \$200X_2 + \$300X_3$

    subject to $\$50X_1 + \$100X_2 + \$40X_3 = \$40,000$ (Production cost)

    $X_1 + X_2 + X_3 \geq 500$ units   (Contract)

    $X_1 + 4X_2 + 2X_3 \leq 1,000$ hours   (Staff availability)

    $X_1, X_2, X_3 \geq 0$

    Convert this problem into its standard form. Then solve by the simplex method.

15. Consider the following maximization problem:

    maximize $Z = 2X_1 + .1X_2$

subject to
$$X_1 + X_2 \leq 100$$
$$X_1 \leq 1.5X_2$$
$$X_1, X_2 \geq 0$$

Solve the linear program by the graphic solution procedure. Then convert the program into its standard form and solve by the simplex procedure. Compare the two solutions. What observations can you make?

16. Consider the following minimization problem:

minimize
$$Z = 2X_1 + 1.5X_2$$

subject to
$$400X_1 + 200X_2 \geq 2,000$$
$$300X_1 + 600X_2 \geq 2,400$$
$$X_1, X_2 \geq 0$$

Solve the linear program by the graphic and simplex solution procedures. Compare the results. Are they identical? Explain. Do you see any advantage for the simplex procedure?

17. Solve the following linear programming problem by the simplex method:

maximize
$$Z = 12X_1 + 8X_2 + 9X_3$$

subject to
$$2X_1 + 4X_2 + 4X_3 \leq 260$$
$$3X_1 + 2X_2 + X_3 \geq 300$$
$$X_1 + X_2 \leq 200$$
$$X_1, X_2, X_3 \geq 0$$

18. Solve the following linear programming problem by the simplex method:

minimize
$$Z = X_1 + 2X_2 + 3X_3$$

subject to
$$20X_1 + 10X_2 + 5X_3 \geq 3,500$$
$$X_1 + X_3 \geq 600$$
$$100X_1 + 200X_2 \geq 50,000$$
$$X_1, X_2, X_3 \geq 0$$

19. Ivy College must purchase footballs, baseballs, and basketballs for its athletic department for the coming academic year. The athletic director wants the combination of balls that minimizes total purchase cost and meets the department's educational and team competition requirements. Ivy's problem is formulated as the following linear program:

minimize $\quad Z = \$20X_1 + \$15X_2 + \$30X_3$

subject to $\quad 10X_1 + 30X_2 + 20X_3 \geq 200$ trips $\quad$ (Competition)

$\quad 20X_1 + 10X_2 + 40X_3 \geq 200$ classes $\quad$ (Education)

$\quad X_1, X_2, X_3 \geq 0$

where $Z =$ the total purchase cost, $X_1 =$ the number of packages of footballs, $X_2 =$ the number of packages of baseballs, and $X_3 =$ the number of packages of basketballs.

Solve this problem by the simplex method. Explain your findings in language that the athletic director will understand.

20. You are given the following linear program:

maximize $Z = X_1 + X_2$

subject to $50X_1 + 100X_2 \leq 55,000$

$$X_1 + X_2 \geq 1,200$$

$$X_2 \leq 300$$

$$X_1, X_2 \geq 0$$

a. Graph this problem. Do you notice anything unusual? Explain.
b. Set up the standard form of the linear program and attempt to solve the problem by the simplex method.
c. Compare the graph and the resulting simplex tables. What observations can you make?

21. Demonstrate how the linear program or standard form of the following problems was derived:
a. Management Situation 8.2
b. Management Situation 8.3
c. Management Situation 8.4
Then show how the following tables were derived:
a. Tables 8.4 and 8.5 for Management Situation 8.2
b. Tables 8.6 and 8.7 for Management Situation 8.3
c. Tables 8.8 and 8.9 for Management Situation 8.4
What is the optimal solution for Management Situation 8.4?

22. You are given the following linear program:

maximize $Z = \$300X_1 + \$200X_2 + \$1,000X_3$

subject to $X_1 + 2X_2 + 8X_3 \leq 8,000$ hours   (Plant 1)

$$5X_1 + 6X_2 + 45X_3 \leq 45,000 \text{ hours} \qquad \text{(Plant 2)}$$

$$16X_1 + 8X_2 + X_3 \leq 80,000 \text{ hours} \qquad \text{(Plant 3)}$$

$$X_1, X_2, X_3 > 0$$

where $Z =$ the total profit, $X_1 =$ the number of units of product A, $X_2 =$ the number of units of product B, and $X_3 =$ the number of units of product C.
a. Develop the appropriate standard form of the linear program.
b. Determine the first and second simplex tables. Do you notice anything unusual in the second simplex table? Explain.
c. Determine the optimal solution.

23. Consider the office supply problem given in Management Situation 8.5:

maximize $\qquad Z = \$10X_1 + \$25X_2$

subject to $\qquad X_1 + X_2 \geq 2{,}000$ boxes $\qquad$ (Demand)

$\qquad\qquad\quad 5X_1 + 20X_2 \geq 20{,}000$ hours $\qquad$ (Sales staff)

$\qquad\qquad\quad X_1, X_2 \geq 0$

where $X_1 =$ the number of boxes of standard pads, $X_2 =$ the number of boxes of legal pads, and $Z =$ the total monthly profit. Note that this problem is unbounded.

a. Develop the standard form for this problem.

b. You are given the fourth simplex solution for this problem in Table 8.10. Determine the first, second, and third simplex tables.

24. Consider the space allocation problem given in Management Situation 8.6:

maximize $\qquad Z = X_1 + X_2$

subject to $\qquad \$40X_1 + \$100X_2 \leq \$60{,}000 \qquad$ (Cost)

$\qquad\qquad\quad X_1 \geq 1{,}600$ square feet $\qquad$ (Living area)

$\qquad\qquad\quad X_2 \geq 300$ square feet $\qquad$ (Energy area)

$\qquad\qquad\quad X_1, X_2 \geq 0$

Note that this problem is infeasible.

a. Develop the standard form for this problem.

b. You are given the second simplex solution in Table 8.11. Determine the first simplex table.

25. The blending problem given in Management Situation 8.7 is represented in the following linear program:

minimize $\qquad Z = \$6X_1 + \$12X_2$

subject to $\qquad 100X_1 + 20X_2 \geq 2{,}200$ square feet $\qquad$ (Size)

$\qquad\qquad\quad 2X_1 + 4X_2 \geq 80$ hours $\qquad$ (Time)

$\qquad\qquad\quad X_1, X_2 \geq 0$

You are given two optimal solutions to this problem in Tables 8.12 and 8.13 in the text. Set up the standard form for the problem and then show how these tables were derived. Are there any other optimal solutions to this problem? Explain.

26. Refer back to Thought Exercise 3. Solve this problem with the simplex method. Show all your work.

27. The first basic feasible solution to a linear program is given in the following simplex table. You want to minimize the value of the objective. Determine the optimal solution. Show all the simplex tables.

Variables		X_1	X_2	X_3	X_4	S_1	S_2	S_3	A_1	A_2	A_3	
Basis	C_j	1.5	.15	.5	.1	0	0	0	*M*	*M*	*M*	**Amounts**
A_1	*M*	.1	.25	.1	.05	−1	0	0	1	0	0	1,000
A_2	*M*	.25	.2	.02	.3	0	−1	0	0	1	0	2,000
A_3	*M*	.05	.05	.15	1.5	0	0	−1	0	0	1	3,000
	Z_j	.4*M*	.5*M*	.27*M*	1.85*M*	−*M*	−*M*	−*M*	*M*	*M*	*M*	6,000*M*
	$C_j - Z_j$	1.5−.4*M*	.15−.5*M*	.5−.27*M*	.1−1.85*M*	*M*	*M*	*M*	0	0	0	

Applications Exercises

28. Tough Crack Concrete Packagers must decide how many packages of each type of concrete mix to distribute. There are three types of packages—large, medium, and small—and there are two types of mixes—regular and premium. Each large package holds 100 pounds of regular mix or 90 pounds of premium; a medium package holds 50 pounds of regular or 40 pounds of premium; and a small package holds 30 pounds of regular or 20 pounds of premium. Production and inventory capacity in the given time period limits the available regular mix to 600,000 pounds and the premium mix to 500,000 pounds. Also, the company must mix a minimum of 3,000 small packages to meet consumer demand. In addition, the number of large packages must equal the total quantity of medium and small packages.

   The company can obtain $6 of profit for each large package, $4 for each medium package, and $2 for each small package.

   a. What quantity of each size package should Tough Crack distribute to maximize its profit?

   b. What is that profit level?

   c. Does that combination involve any idle regular or premium mix capacity? Does it involve any surplus packages above the minimum demand?

29. A hospital uses three major types of fuel in its normal activities: electricity, natural gas, and uranium (for X-ray and other related medical equipment). Each kilowatt of electricity costs 3 cents, each cubic foot of natural gas 2 cents, and each gram of uranium $100. The fuels are used for three basic functions: medical, administrative, and patient environmental (room heating, air conditioning, and the like). The hospital administrator forecasts a minimum requirement of 2,000 hours for the medical function, 1,000 hours for the administrative function, and 3,000 hours for environmental functions in a given time period. Each kilowatt of electricity provides $\frac{1}{4}$ hour of medical function, $\frac{1}{3}$ hour of administrative function, and $\frac{4}{5}$ hour of environmental function. A cubic foot of natural gas gives $\frac{1}{2}$ hour of medical, $\frac{2}{5}$ hour of administrative, and $\frac{1}{2}$ hour of environmental function. Each gram of uranium supports 5 hours of medical, $\frac{1}{10}$ hour of administrative, and $\frac{1}{5}$ hour of environmental function. Research and patient care typically generate a demand for at least 10 grams of uranium during the given time period.

   What combination of fuels should the administrator use to minimize the total cost of meeting the three hospital needs? Is there any surplus of medical, administrative, or environmental hours associated with the minimum cost? Explain, giving your interpretation of the results and a recommendation for future activities.

30. TRT Association is a private research organization specializing in the development of new chemical and physical processes. In the coming quarter, the association can work on three independent projects dealing with the development of commercial uses of solar energy. Project Alpha involves the development of a home-heating device and is expected to generate $10 of profit to the association for every hour of research effort. Project Beta deals with the conversion of office-lighting equipment and is expected to yield $30 of profit per hour of research effort. Project Centurion, which involves the development of a military weapon, is expected to give the association a profit of $5 per research hour.

The association does have research capacity, budget, and administrative report-writing restrictions, however. They are specified in the following table, along with the utilization rates of these resources by each research activity:

Project	Quantity of Resource Used Per Hour of Research		
	Capacity	Budget	Administration
Alpha	1	$50	2
Beta	1	$30	4
Centurion	1	$100	40
Maximum available	8,000 hours	$300,000	20,000 hours

Internal corporate commitments also require the Alpha project to be at least as large as the Beta research effort, while Beta's should not exceed Centurion's endeavors.

a. How many hours of research should be used on each project to maximize quarterly profit?

b. What is that total profit level?

c. Does the maximum profit project combination involve any idle research capacity, unspent budget dollars, or unused administrative hours? Explain.

31. A university cafeteria hires student employees to assist in three shifts of operation: breakfast, lunch, and dinner. Scheduling of classes and other considerations necessitate hiring different students for each shift. Employee costs are also different for each shift, because the work quantity and quality differ. It costs the cafeteria $2 per hour for student assistance at the breakfast shift, $3 per hour at lunch, and $4 per hour at dinner.

Past experience and recent cafeteria forecasts indicate that a minimum of 500 meals will be served per day. The breakfast shift is capable of serving 10 meals per student hour employed, the lunch shift 20 meals per hour, and the dinner shift 5 meals per hour. Policy of the university limits the total hours employed to a maximum of 75 per day.

To ensure that all meals are properly covered, the cafeteria has a policy that the number of student hours employed during the dinner shift must equal the combined effort at the other two meals. Also, management wants to use at least 6 student hours during the breakfast shift.

How many hours of student assistance should the cafeteria employ during each shift to minimize its total daily cost of assistance? Are there any surplus meals prepared or idle student hours employed under this policy?

32. Garbat Baby Foods, Inc. is in the midst of an advertising campaign and must decide its television promotional schedule. Management must decide on the number of advertising spots to place in the Saturday morning lineup, weekday afternoon period, weekday prime-time period, and weekend prime-time period. Spots are defined as one-minute messages, but it is also possible to use fractional spots at proportionately lower rates and with proportionately less audience exposure.

Audience exposure is measured by a proportional index of audience points. Each Saturday morning spot has an estimated 1,500 audience points, each weekday afternoon spot 2,000 points, a weekday prime-time spot 1,200 points, and a weekend prime-time spot 2,100 points. Garbat is restricted in its placements by an advertising budget of $6 million and by a network contract requiring a minimum of 250 total spots. There is also a network limitation that requires the number of prime-time spots in a given time period to be at least as large as the sum of all other spots less 180. Also, the network requires a commitment for a minimum of 10 spots in each time slot. Each Saturday morning spot costs $20,000, each weekday afternoon spot $12,000, each weekday prime-time spot $30,000, and each weekend prime-time spot $40,000.

a. How many spots of each type should the company place to maximize total audience points?

b. Does this combination use the entire advertising budget?

c. Are there any surplus spots?

33. Delicious Pastries is a local bakery shop that makes its products on the premises and sells them to the public. The shop uses four basic ingredients: milk, sugar, eggs, and flour. Milk costs $1.50 per gallon, sugar 25 cents a pound, eggs 75 cents a dozen, and flour 15 cents a pound. The bakery sells three basic types of product: cakes, pies, and breads. Each week the shop has a minimum demand for 150 packages of cakes, 150 packages of pies, and 300 packages of bread. It takes 6.4 fluid ounces (0.05 gallon) of milk, 8 ounces (0.5 pound) of sugar, 3 (0.25 dozen) eggs, and 9.6 ounces (0.6 pound) of flour to make a package of cakes. Each package of pies requires 19.2 fluid ounces (0.15 gallon) of milk, 6.4 ounces (0.4 pound) of sugar, 2 (1/6 dozen) eggs, and 8 ounces (0.5 pound) of flour. It takes 7.68 fluid ounces (0.06 gallon) of milk, 1.6 ounces (0.1 pound) of sugar, 1 (1/12 dozen) egg, and 1.5 pounds of flour to make a package of bread.

Also, according to the bakery's recipe policy, the total ingredients of any product must contain no more than 10 percent sugar, at least 5 percent milk, no more than 60 percent flour, and a minimum 15 percent eggs.

a. How many gallons of milk, pounds of sugar, dozens of eggs, and pounds of flour should Delicious buy to minimize its total purchase cost?

b. What is that total purchase cost?

c. Are there any surplus packages of cakes, pies, or breads at this minimum cost?

For Further Reading

Simplex Methodology

Bradley, S. P., et al. *Applied Mathematical Programming.* Reading, MA: Addison-Wesley, 1977.

Gribik, P. R., and K. O. Kortanek. *Extremal Methods of Operations Research.* New York: Marcel Dekker, 1985.

Jeter, M. W. *Mathematical Programming: An Introduction.* New York: Marcel Dekker, 1986.

Lee, S. M. *Linear Optimization for Management.* New York: Petrocelli/Charter, 1976.

Lev, B., and H. J. Weiss. *Introduction to Mathematical Programming.* New York: Elsevier North-Holland, 1982.

Rottenberg, R. *Linear Programming.* New York: Elsevier North-Holland, 1980.

Special Issues

Hooker, J. N. "Karmarkar's Linear Programming Algorithm." *Interfaces* (July–August 1986):75.

Sharmer, R. "The Efficiency of the Simplex Method: A Survey." *Management Science* (March 1987):301.

Tardoes, E. "A Strongly Polynomial Algorithm to Solve Combinatorial Linear Programs." *Operations Research* (March–April 1986):250.

Table 8.14   **Data Report**

Accounting Classification	Plastic	Product Aircraft	Ground
Fixed costs	$100,000	$600,000	$200,000
R & D	$ 60,000	$500,000	$170,000
Administrative	$ 40,000	$100,000	$ 30,000
Per-unit variable costs	$ 6,000	$ 50,000	$ 35,000
Labor	$ 3,000	$ 10,000	$ 5,000
Materials	$ 2,000	$ 30,000	$ 20,000
Testing	$ 500	$ 6,000	$ 9,000
Other	$ 500	$ 4,000	$ 1,000
Per-unit selling price	$ 36,000	$120,000	$ 85,000
Monthly Per-Unit Usage Rate of Resource			
Product	Production Capacity	Labor Availability	Marketing Budget
Plastic	20 hours	500 hours	$100
Aircraft	100 hours	200 hours	$200
Ground	40 hours	100 hours	$280
Maxmium resource available	10,000 hours	50,000 hours	$60,000

Case: Lowe Chemical, Inc.

Lowe Chemical, Inc. is a large international manufacturer of chemical products. A subsidiary division produces military bombs and explosives for the armed services, foreign governments, and other parties. Products are classified into three independent categories: plastic explosives, aircraft-delivered bombs, and ground-vehicle-delivered bombs.

An executive planning committee has assembled data on estimated revenues, costs, and technical production rates for the three units, which may include several complete bombs or spare bomb parts (fractions of a purchase unit). Costs and selling prices are presented in the Data Report (Table 8.14). Units are manufactured with the company's limited production facilities and labor and then marketed within the constraints of the available promotional budget. The per-unit usage rate of each of these resources by each product and the levels of the available resources are also given in the Data Report.

The company wants to produce and market the combination of products that will maximize its profit for the planning period. As a secondary goal, it would like a product mix that involves some idle productive, labor, or marketing capacity to use as a reserve for unforeseen contingencies.

You are employed as a management consultant by the company's executive committee, and you are asked to prepare a decision report that includes the following information:

1. A formulation of the company's problem as a linear programming model

2. An explanation of the applicability of that model to the problem

3. An explanation of the role of the company's fixed costs in the problem

4. A recommendation concerning the optimal product mix

5. A recommendation concerning any potential alternative product mix that would incorporate management's secondary goal

6. The role that fixed costs play in this choice between alternatives

Remember that your report is directed to an executive committee, so be careful to define all terms. Also, make sure that you present your report in language understandable to that committee.

Chapter 9

Postoptimality Analysis

Chapter Outline

9.1 Shadow Prices

Graphic Analysis

Simplex Analysis

Managerial Applications

The Dual

Minimization Problems

9.2 Sensitivity Analysis

Objective Function

System Constraint Amount

Exchange Coefficients

Other Postoptimality Analysis

9.3 Computer Analysis

Optimal Solution

Sensitivity Analysis

Other Postoptimality Analysis

Case: The Tennis Shop

Learning Objectives

- Measure the economic value of scarce resources and restrictive guidelines

- Interpret and utilize these economic values in decision making

- Measure the sensitivity of the optimal solution and the economic values to changes in the parameters of the original linear program

- Interpret and utilize the sensitivity information for decision making

- Use a computer program to generate the linear programming information

Getting the Wood Out

WELLBORN Cabinet, Inc. is a manufacturer in central Alabama that employs 375 people and generates about $16 million in annual sales. The company's market is concentrated on the east coast and in the southeastern United States. There is constant pressure on Wellborn to manufacture quality kitchen cabinets at competitive prices. Since wood comprises about 45 percent of the company's total material costs, management needs a rational procurement policy to control the quality and expense of this item.

In 1986, Wellborn sought technical assistance in developing the needed policy through Auburn University's Technical Assistance Center. Faculty assigned to the project discovered that the problem could be represented realistically with a linear programming model. Given the sawmill and dry kiln capacities, required manufacturing output, and available raw material supplies, the model determines the least-cost wood procurement policy. An information system was developed to capture, store, and retrieve the data and model, perform the necessary linear programming analysis, and report the recommended policy in a timely fashion.

By following the guidelines recommended by the system, Wellborn can anticipate a 32 percent, or approximately $412,000, saving per year in wood raw material costs. Postoptimality analysis also can assess the impact of changes in market/economic factors (such as new log and lumber prices) and in operating conditions (such as altered capacity) on the recommended procurement policy.

Source: H.F. Carino and C.H. LeNoir, "Optimizing Wood Procurement in Cabinet Manufacturing," *Interfaces* (March–April 1988): 10–19.

Frequently, management is concerned primarily with the optimal solution to a linear program. Yet such a solution provides input for additional analyses that can generate information useful for management planning and control.

Some of the further knowledge is obtained by examining the original linear program from an alternative perspective. In a typical product mix problem, for example, the decision maker seeks the product or service combination that maximizes profit from available resources. Under these circumstances, management usually concentrates on the products or services that generate the maximum profit. Nevertheless, the firm cannot produce any products or services unless it acquires the necessary resources at a reasonable cost. Furthermore, the appropriate cost will depend on the economic value of these resources to the firm. Consequently, the resource values are important additional aspects of the product mix problem. To obtain these values, however, management must focus on the resources rather than on the products or services. In the first section of this chapter, we discuss the two ways of looking at a linear program and show how such an analysis can benefit the decision maker.

Decisions are made in a dynamic environment. Prices and costs change over time, new machines and processes are developed, people change jobs, and so on. These variations can change the variables' unit contributions, restriction amounts, and constraint utilization rates in the original linear program. Hence, management must determine how such changes might affect the optimal solution and identify any revisions that are needed to accommodate the variations. The chapter's second section demonstrates how to obtain this important additional information without reworking the entire problem.

The alternative viewpoint and variation knowledge are gained from an examination of the optimal solution to the original linear program. As a result, these further evaluations can be referred to as **postoptimality analysis**. Wellborn, for example, used such postoptimality analysis to assess the impact of changes in market/economic factors (such as new log and lumber prices) and in operating conditions (such as altered capacity) on the recommended procurement policy.

A complete linear programming analysis, including the postoptimality evaluation, can be very time-consuming and cumbersome if done by hand. That is why firms such as Wellborn Cabinet use computer-based information systems to capture, store, and retrieve the data and model, perform the necessary linear programming analysis, and report the recommended policy in a timely fashion. The third section of this chapter demonstrates how such systems can be used to solve linear programming problems and perform the postoptimality analysis.

Applications. In this chapter, the following applications appear in text, examples, and exercises:

- antiques refurbishing
- bike manufacturing
- dog racing
- hamburger sales
- making or buying batteries
- meal planning

- mutual fund investments
- oil refining
- production scheduling
- staff scheduling
- thrift shop operations
- tobacco farming

9.1 SHADOW PRICES

A linear program's system constraints limit the objective function value. Changes in these constraints thus could alter this value. For planning and control purposes, it would be useful to know each restriction's **shadow price**, or the change in the criterion value that results from a one-unit change in the amount of the constraint. Management Situation 9.1 illustrates.

Management Situation 9.1

A Product Mix Problem

Ancient Enterprises specializes in the refurbishing and sale of antique clocks and stoves. Each refurbished clock can be sold for an estimated average profit of $20 and each stove for \$40. A clock requires three labor hours and one hour of machine time for restoration, while a stove needs five labor hours and five hours of machine time for restoration. In addition, 25 pounds of a particular cast iron are needed to refurbish a typical antique stove. There are an estimated 1,000 machine hours and 1,800 labor hours available per month with current facilities. Also, management will provide funds sufficient to purchase a maximum 3,750 pounds of cast iron per month. It is possible to start the restoration in one month and complete the project in a subsequent time period. The company wants to refurbish the number of clocks and stoves that will maximize total monthly profit.

By letting

Z = the total monthly profit

X_1 = the number of clocks refurbished

X_2 = the number of stoves refurbished

Ancient's problem can be expressed as the following linear program:

maximize $Z = \$20X_1 + \$40X_2$

subject to $3X_1 + 5X_2 \leq 1,800$ hours   (Labor)

$1X_1 + 5X_2 \leq 1,000$ hours   (Machine)

$25X_2 \leq 3,750$ pounds   (Cast iron)

$X_1, X_2 \geq 0$

That is, the company seeks the antique mix (combination of X_1 and X_2 values) that will maximize total monthly profit (Z). However, management must ensure that the optimal mix does not utilize more than the available labor, machine, and cast iron capacities.

The graph in Figure 9.1 depicts the company's linear programming problem. As you can see, Ancient can maximize total monthly profit at $Z = \$12,800$ by refurbishing

$$X_1 = 400 \text{ clocks}$$

and

$$X_2 = 120 \text{ stoves.}$$

Furthermore, the optimal solution point ($X_1 = 400$, $X_2 = 120$) is at the intersection of the labor and machine constraint lines. As a result, such a combination of decision variables utilizes all available labor and machine hours. In other words, Ancient's optimal product mix involves no idle labor or machine resources.

Figure 9.1 also shows that the optimal solution point lies below the iron constraint line. Consequently, this combination of decision variables involves some idle or unused pounds of cast iron. That is, Ancient has more than enough cast iron to generate the optimal product mix.

Figure 9.1   Ancient's Optimal Solution

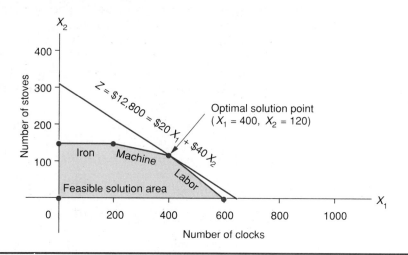

Graphic Analysis

Current resource capacity limits Ancient's profit to a total of $12,800 per month. On the other hand, if management procures additional resources, the company can refurbish more clocks and/or stoves and possibly increase profits. In other words, it may be worthwhile for the firm to expand capacity. To evaluate this properly, however, the decision maker must determine the economic value of an additional unit of each resource.

Consider Ancient's labor resource. If management acquires one additional labor hour, the labor constraint expression becomes

$$3X_1 + 5X_2 \leq 1,801 \text{ hours.}$$

When other conditions (available machine hours, unit profits, and so on) remain the same, such a change produces the effects shown in Figure 9.2. The square in the upper right-hand portion of the figure shows that the additional capacity shifts the labor constraint line to the right. This shift makes the feasible solution area wider than before. Nevertheless, as the graph demonstrates, the optimal solution point of

$$X_1 = 405.5$$

and $$X_2 = 119.9$$

is still at the intersection of the labor and machine constraint lines.

Figure 9.2 also indicates that the shift in the labor constraint line enables Ancient to reach the $Z = \$12,806$ profit line. Before the shift, the company was able to earn only a $Z = \$12,800$ total profit. Ancient will therefore obtain a

$$\$12,806 - \$12,800 = \$6$$

increase in monthly profit if it can procure one additional labor hour.

Figure 9.2   **Ancient's Optimal Solution with One Additional Labor Hour**

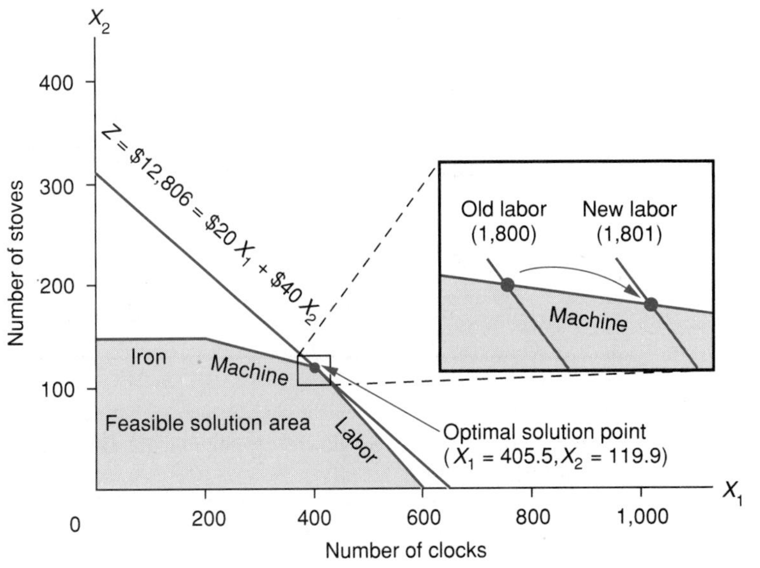

This $6 increase in profit, in effect, represents the incremental economic value of the labor resource. It also identifies the maximum incremental price that management should pay to acquire one additional labor hour. This incremental, or shadow, price is actually a premium over and above the wages and fringe benefits already accounted for in the clock and stove per-unit profit contributions.

Each system constraint in a linear program will have its own shadow price. If Ancient performs graphic analyses similar to Figure 9.2, it will find that the shadow price is $2 per hour of machine time and $0 per pound of cast iron.

Simplex Analysis

The decision maker can also obtain the relevant shadow prices from the information contained in the optimal simplex table. Table 9.1, for instance, presents the simplex data corresponding to Ancient's optimal basic feasible solution (the $X_1 = 400$ and $X_2 = 120$ point in Figure 9.1). In this table S_1 denotes unused labor hours and S_2 idle machine hours, while S_3 represents the slack pounds of cast iron. As the Basis and Amounts columns demonstrate, Ancient can maximize total profit at $Z = \$12,800$ by restoring

$$X_1 = 400 \text{ clocks}$$

and

$$X_2 = 120 \text{ stoves}$$

while leaving

$$S_3 = 750 \text{ unused pounds of cast iron.}$$

Table 9.1 Ancient's Optimal Simplex Table

Variables		X_1	X_2	S_1	S_2	S_3	
Basis	C_j	$20	$40	$0	$0	$0	Amounts
S_3	$0	0	0	$\frac{5}{2}$	$-\frac{15}{2}$	1	750
X_1	$20	1	0	$\frac{1}{2}$	$-\frac{1}{2}$	0	400
X_2	$40	0	1	$-\frac{1}{10}$	$\frac{3}{10}$	0	120
Z_j		$20	$40	$6	$2	$0	$12,800
$C_j - Z_j$		$0	$0	-$6	-$2	$0	

However, since S_1 and S_2 do not appear in the Basis column of the table, the optimal solution will involve

$$S_1 = 0 \text{ unused labor hours}$$

and $\qquad\qquad S_2 = 0$ unused machine hours.

That is, Ancient's optimal product mix utilizes all currently available labor and machine capacity.

Now, suppose the company wants to use 1,799 rather than the available 1,800 labor hours. In that case, $S_1 = 1$ unused labor hour must be brought into the optimal basis. According to the $C_j - Z_j$ row entry in the S_1 column of Table 9.1, this smaller labor capacity would decrease the company's total profit by $6. On the other hand, assume that the decision maker can increase labor capacity from 1,800 to 1,801 hours. Under these circumstances, the $6 represents the increase in Ancient's total profit that can be obtained from an additional labor hour. In other words, the $C_j - Z_j$ row entry in the S_1 column of Table 9.1 indicates that labor has a shadow price of $6 per hour.

Such a result illustrates the following important property: *Each system constraint's shadow price is given by the absolute value of the $C_j - Z_j$ row entry in the corresponding supplemental variable column in the optimal simplex table.* In this regard, there is a $-$2 entry in the unused machine time (S_2) column in the $C_j - Z_j$ row of Table 9.1. Hence, Ancient's machine time has a shadow price equal to the absolute value of the $-$2 entry, or

$$|-\$2| = \$2$$

per hour. Similarly, the $C_j - Z_j$ row entry in the S_3 column indicates that unused cast iron has a shadow price of $0 per pound.

Managerial Applications

Shadow price information is useful for management planning and control. This information can be used to establish constraint priorities, evaluate proposed changes in constraint amounts, and evaluate new decision variables.

Constraint Priorities. Shadow prices can establish the relative importance to the organization of various scarce resources or restrictive guidelines. In Ancient's case, cast iron has a shadow price of $0 per pound. This price indicates that an extra pound would increase the resource's idle capacity but generate no further product output or profit. In other words, the company currently has more than enough cast iron to refurbish the optimal mix of clocks and stoves. As a result, additional cast iron capacity will have no immediate economic value to the firm.

On the other hand, labor has a $6 shadow price and capital a $2 shadow price. Hence, both of these resources are more valuable to Ancient than cast iron. Furthermore, these prices indicate that an additional hour of labor will increase monthly profit by $6 − $2 = $4 more than an equivalent amount of machine time. Consequently, management knows that additional labor capacity is $6/$2 = 3 times more valuable to the company than extra machine time.

Changes in Constraint Amounts. Shadow prices also can be used to evaluate proposed changes in resource capacities or in restrictive guidelines. For example, suppose Ancient is considering the use of overtime as a means of increasing capacity. Each overtime hour will cost an additional $5 over and above the wages and fringe benefits already accounted for in the product per-unit profit contributions. Another option is to increase machine capacity by renting extra machinery for $3 per hour, which again would be in addition to the equipment expenses already accounted for in the product per-unit profit contributions.

Let us first consider the overtime option. When management utilizes overtime, Ancient's labor cost will increase by $5 per hour. Yet the shadow price of labor indicates that an additional hour of this resource will increase profit by $6 per hour. Overtime will result in a net $6 − $5 = $1 per-hour increase in monthly profit. Thus, such an option represents a worthwhile endeavor for the company.

The machinery option is a different matter. If the company rents extra machinery, machine cost will increase by $3 per hour. However, the shadow price of machine time indicates that an additional hour of this resource will increase profit by only $2 per hour. The extra machinery will generate

$$\$2 - \$3 = -\$1$$

or a $1 per hour decrease in Ancient's monthly profit. Therefore, such an option is not advisable for the firm.

New Variables. Shadow prices are also useful in evaluating new decision variables. For example, suppose Ancient is thinking about adding table refurbishing to its antiques business. Each table is expected to contribute a $30 profit. Yet experience indicates that it will take an average of four labor hours and two machine hours, but no cast iron, to restore a typical table. All other conditions in the problem remain the same.

Ancient's available labor and machine hours currently are being used to refurbish the optimal mix of $X_1 = 400$ clocks and $X_2 = 120$ stoves. To obtain the capacity necessary for table restoration, management must divert its resources from the other projects. In the process, however, the company will reduce clock and/or stove output and thus lose some profit.

Now, remember that Ancient's shadow prices measure the changes in monthly profit that result from unit changes in the resource amounts. In particular, the shadow price of labor indicates that the company will lose $6 in profit for each one-hour reduction in labor availability. Since each table diverts four labor hours for restoration, the new product will result in a

$$4 \text{ labor hours @ } \$6 \text{ per hour } = \$24$$

loss in profit from the other projects. Similarly, the shadow price of machine time suggests that the firm will lose $2 in profit for each hour reduction in machine availability. In addition, management knows that each table diverts two machine hours from clock and/or stove refurbishing. Therefore, when the company restores one table, it will lose

$$2 \text{ machine hours @ } \$2 \text{ per hour } = \$4$$

in profit from the other projects.

In refurbishing each table, Ancient must divert enough resources to reduce the monthly profit from the other projects by a total of $28. Nevertheless, the company can earn $30 gross profit each month for each table it refurbishes, leaving a net profit of

$$\$30 - \$28 = \$2$$

per table. Thus, the proposed product expansion is a worthwhile endeavor for Ancient Enterprises.

Table 9.2 summarizes the various managerial applications procedures.

The Dual

Further insights can be gained by examining the product mix problem (Management Situation 9.1) from a resource perspective. In the original problem, management focuses on the products (clocks and stoves) that generate the maximum profit from the available resources (labor, machine time, and cast iron). Yet Ancient would be unable to refurbish any products if it could not acquire the necessary resources at a reasonable cost. A related problem then is to determine how much the company should pay for its resources.

Objective Function. Ancient should pay each resource at the rate of its marginal (incremental) economic value or at its shadow price. Multiplying the shadow prices by the corresponding resource capacities (1,800 hours for labor, 1,000 hours for machine time, and 3,750 pounds for cast iron) and summing the results then will give the total payments. That is, the company's objective function in the resource valuation phase will be

$$C = 1,800U_1 + 1,000U_2 + 3,750U_3$$

where C = total resource payments, U_1 = labor's shadow price, U_2 = machine time's shadow price, and U_3 = cast iron's shadow price.

Restrictions. It takes three labor hours, one machine hour, and no cast iron to refurbish one clock. The corresponding shadow prices indicate that these resources will increase Ancient's profit by a total of

$$3U_1 + 1U_2 + 0U_3.$$

Table 9.2   **Shadow Price Applications Procedures**

Establishing Constraint Priorities	Evaluating Changes in the Constraint Amounts	Evaluating a New Decision Variable
1. Identify the shadow price for each constraint. 2. Establish from these shadow prices the relative importance of each constraint to the decision criterion.	1. Identify the tasks necessary to implement a proposed change in a constraint amount. 2. Determine the per-unit value (cost or benefit) of these tasks. 3. Identify the constraint's shadow price. 4. Compute the difference between the shadow price and the tasks' per-unit value. 5. Adopt the proposed change only if this difference represents a desirable change in the criterion value.	1. Identify the constraints affected by the new decision table. 2. Identify the shadow prices corresponding to the affected constraints. 3. Identify the quantity of each constraint needed for (or contributed by) one unit of the new decision variable. These quantities represent exchange coefficients. 4. Multiply each shadow price by the corresponding exchange coefficient and sum the results. This sum represents the decrease in the criterion value that results from the addition of one unit of the new decision table. 5. Identify the new decision variable's per-unit contribution to the criterion table. 6. Take the difference between the value identified in step 5 and the sum found in step 4. This difference represents the net effect on the criterion value of adding one unit of the new decision variable. 7. Add the new decision variable only if this net effect is desirable.

If this total is at least as much as the clock's \$20 per-unit profit contribution, it will be worthwhile to refurbish a clock. Otherwise, the company will be better off using the resources on more attractive antique restoration projects. Such a minimum profit requirement can be written as the following system constraint:

$$3U_1 + 1U_2 + 0U_3 \geq \$20.$$

There is a similar system constraint for stove restoration. It takes five labor hours, five machine hours, and 25 pounds of cast iron to restore one stove. When these resources increase Ancient's profit by at least as much as the stove's \$40 per-unit profit contribution, or when

$$5U_1 + 5U_2 + 25U_3 \geq \$40$$

it will be worthwhile to refurbish a stove.

Also, shadow prices (like most monetary measures) must have values greater than or equal to zero. Hence, these prices must satisfy the nonnegativity conditions

$$U_1, U_2, U_3 \geq 0.$$

Dual Linear Program.   Ancient seeks the shadow prices (U_1, U_2, and U_3) that minimize the total resource payments (C) while satisfying the system constraints (clock and

---

Table 9.3   **Ancient's Primal and Dual Linear Programs**

Primal	Dual
maximize $Z = \$20X_1 + \$40X_2$ subject to $3X_1 + 5X_2 \leq 1{,}800$ hours (Labor) $1X_1 + 5X_2 \leq 1{,}000$ hours (Machine) $0X_1 + 25X_2 \leq 3{,}750$ hours (Cast Iron) $X_1, X_2 \geq 0$ where $Z =$ the total monthly profit $X_1 =$ the number of refurbished clocks $X_2 =$ the number of refurbished stoves	minimize $C = 1{,}800U_1 + 1{,}000U_2 + 3{,}750U_3$ subject to $3U_1 + 1U_2 + 0U_3 \geq \$20$ (Clocks) $5U_1 + 5U_2 + 25U_3 \geq \$40$ (Stoves) $U_1, U_2, U_3 \geq 0$ where $C =$ the total resource payments $U_1 =$ shadow price per labor hour $U_2 =$ shadow price per machine hour $U_3 =$ shadow price per pound of cast iron

---

stove minimum profit requirements) and nonnegativity conditions. This problem can be expressed as the following linear program:

minimize $C = 1,800U_1 + 1,000U_2 + 3,750U_3$

subject to $3U_1 + 1U_2 + 0U_3 \geq \$20$ (Clocks)

                 $5U_1 + 5U_2 + 25U_3 \geq \$40$ (Stoves)

                 $U_1, U_2, U_3 \geq 0$

Such a linear program is known as the **dual** of the original product mix problem, while the original linear program is referred to as the **primal**.

Primal and Dual Relationships. Table 9.3 presents Ancient's primal and dual linear programs side by side. This table illustrates the following important primal/dual relationships:

1. *The sense of optimization is opposite in the primal and dual problems.* For example, Ancient's primal is a maximization problem, while the dual is a minimization problem.

2. *Primal system constraints correspond to dual variables and vice versa.* For example, Ancient's two primal variables (refurbished clocks X_1 and refurbished stoves X_2) correspond to the dual's two system constraints (clocks and stoves).

3. *Primal system constraint amounts become dual objective function coefficients and vice versa.* For example, Ancient's primal profit coefficients (\$20 for X_1 and \$40 for X_2) become the dual's system constraint amounts.

4. *The row coefficients in the primal's system constraints become the column coefficients in the dual's system constraints and vice versa.* For example, the product coefficients (3 for X_1 and 5 for X_2) in the primal's labor constraint become labor's shadow price (U_1) coefficients in the dual's system constraints. Similarly, the shadow price coefficients (5 for U_1, 5 for U_2, and 25 for U_3) in the dual's stoves constraint become refurbished stove (X_2) coefficients in the primal's system (labor, machine, and cast iron) constraints.

Table 9.4   Simplex Table for Ancient's Optimal Dual Solution

Variables		U_1	U_2	U_3	R_1	R_2	A_1	A_2	
Basis	C_j	1,800	1,000	3,750	0	0	M	M	Amounts
U_1	1,800	1	0	$-\frac{5}{2}$	$-\frac{1}{2}$	$\frac{1}{10}$	$\frac{1}{2}$	$-\frac{1}{10}$	$6
U_2	1,000	0	1	$\frac{15}{2}$	$\frac{1}{2}$	$-\frac{3}{10}$	$-\frac{1}{2}$	$\frac{3}{10}$	$2
	Z_j	1,800	1,000	3,000	-400	-120	400	120	$12,800
	$C_j - Z_j$	0	0	750	400	120	$M-400$	$M-120$	

Also, ancient's primal linear program is in its **canonical form**, or is a maximization problem that has all $\leq$ system constraints and all variables nonnegative. As a result, the dual is in its canonical form, or is a minimization problem that has all $\geq$ system constraints and all variables nonnegative. The decision maker can use these primal/dual relationships to readily transform any primal into its dual linear program and vice versa.

Shadow Prices and Reduced Costs. Besides providing a useful economic perspective, the dual generates information that is valuable for management planning and control. The optimal values of the dual variables give the appropriate shadow prices for the corresponding primal system constraints. For example, Table 9.4 presents the simplex information corresponding to Ancient's optimal dual solution. According to the Basis and Amounts column entries, the company's shadow prices should be

$$U_1 = \$6 \text{ per labor hour}$$

$$U_2 = \$2 \text{ per machine hour}$$

and, since U_3 does not appear in the Basis column, $U_3 = \$0$ per pound of cast iron.

In addition, the dual solution identifies the **reduced costs**, or the improvements that must be made in the per-unit contributions before the corresponding variables will enter the optimal basis. These reduced costs are the dual's analogies to the primal's surplus (and, where appropriate, slack) variables. For example, clock's reduced cost is depicted as R_1, while stove's reduced cost is denoted as R_2 in Table 9.4. Since R_1 and R_2 do not appear in this table's Basis column, no improvement in clock and stove profit contributions are needed to make these products attractive decision alternatives. Indeed, that is why both clocks (X_1) and stoves (X_2) are in the optimal primal basis (Table 9.1).

Optimal Objective Function Value. The optimal shadow prices generate a dual criterion value that will equal the primal's optimal objective function value. For example, the Amounts column entry in the Z_j row of Table 9.4 indicates that Ancient's shadow prices minimize total resource payments at $C = \$12,800$. This sum equals the maximum total profit (Table 9.1's $Z = \$12,800$) earned from using the resources to refurbish clocks and stoves. In fact, that is why the company does not shift these resources to alternative antique restoration projects.

Table 9.5   **Complementary Slackness Rules**

Dual Variable's Solution	Rule	Primal Variable's Solution
optimal shadow price is zero ($U_i = 0$)	corresponding primal supplemental (surplus or slack) variable has an optimal value that is positive ($S_i > 0$)	$C_j - Z_j$ row entry in the shadow price (U_i) column of the dual's optimal simplex table
optimal shadow price is positive ($U_i > 0$)	corresponding primal supplemental (surplus or slack) variable has an optimal value of zero ($S_i = 0$)	$C_j - Z_j$ row entry in the shadow price (U_i) column of the dual's optimal simplex table
optimal reduced cost is zero ($R_j = 0$)	corresponding primal real variable has an optimal value that is positive ($X_j > 0$)	$C_j - Z_j$ row entry in the reduced cost (R_j) column of the dual's optimal simplex table
optimal reduced cost is positive ($R_j > 0$)	corresponding primal real variable has an optimal value of zero ($X_j = 0$)	$C_j - Z_j$ row entry in the reduced cost (R_j) column of the dual's optimal simplex table

Complementary Slackness. There are important relationships, collectively known as **complementary slackness**, between the optimal values of the primal and dual variables. When the linear program is in its canonical form and when the problem has neither degenerate nor multiple optimal solutions, these relationships will follow the rules summarized in Table 9.5.

Complementary slackness rules can be used to solve the primal from the dual. For example, the $C_j - Z_j$ row entries in the U_1 through U_3 columns of Table 9.4 indicate that Ancient's optimal primal solution will involve

$$S_1 = 0 \text{ unused labor hours}$$

$$S_2 = 0 \text{ unused machine hours}$$

$$S_3 = 750 \text{ unused pounds of cast iron}$$

Moreover, the $C_j - Z_j$ row entries in the R_1 and R_2 columns tell us that the company's optimal primal solution has

$$X_1 = 400 \text{ clocks}$$

$$X_2 = 120 \text{ stoves}$$

Converse complementary slackness rules can be used to solve the dual from the $C_j - Z_j$ row entries in the primal's optimal simplex table. We have already used such rules to find Ancient's shadow prices from the $C_j - Z_j$ row entries in the S_1 through S_3 columns of Table 9.1. Also, the $C_j - Z_j$ row entries in the X_1 and X_2 columns of this table show that the reduced costs are $R_1 = \$0$ for clocks and $R_2 = \$0$ for stoves.

Minimization Problems

In the case of Ancient Enterprises, shadow price and dual concepts are used to examine the impact of scarce resources on a maximization objective. The same concepts can also be applied to minimization problems involving restrictive guidelines. Management Situation 9.2 illustrates.

Management Situation 9.2

A Blending Problem

Millips Oil Company plans to develop a new engine additive called Wear Prevention. The additive will be a blend of what the company calls types A and B crude oil. Both types of oil contain the same two secret compounds, coded JT and WY, that are required to produce the additive. However, the percentage of the compounds in each type of crude oil differs. Each gallon of type A crude has 30 percent of compound JT and 10 percent of WY. A gallon of type B contains 20 percent of JT and 40 percent of WY. Millips will need at least 2,000 gallons of JT and at least 3,000 gallons of WY daily to produce the new additive. Each gallon of type A costs 15 cents, while a gallon of type B costs 20 cents. The company wants to purchase the quantity of each type of crude that will satisfy production requirements at least cost.

After careful consideration, management has been able to express the problem as the following linear program:

minimize $Z = \$0.15X_1 + \$0.20X_2$

subject to $0.3X_1 + 0.2X_2 \geq 2,000$ gallons (JT)

$0.1X_1 + 0.4X_2 \geq 3,000$ gallons (WY)

$X_1, X_2 \geq 0$

where Z = the total daily purchase cost, X_1 = the number of gallons of type A crude oil, and X_2 = the number of gallons of type B crude oil.

Optimal Primal Solution. Table 9.6 is the optimal simplex table for Millips's primal linear program. In this table, S_1 denotes the surplus (excess gallons) of the JT compound, S_2 depicts the surplus for the WY compound, and A_1 and A_2 are artificial variables. According to the Basis and Amounts column entries, the company can minimize the total daily purchase cost at $Z = \$1,700$ by blending

$X_1 = 2,000$ gallons of type A

$X_2 = 7,000$ gallons of type B

crude oil. Also, since S_1 and S_2 do not appear in the Basis column, the optimal blend has no surplus of either compound.

Dual Linear Program. Current production requirements prohibit Millips from reducing the total daily purchase cost below $1,700. If the company can lower these requirements

Table 9.6   **Optimal Simplex Table for the Millips Primal Linear Problem**

Variables		X_1	X_2	S_1	S_2	A_1	A_2	
Basis	C_j	$0.15	$0.20	$0	$0	$M	$M	**Amounts**
X_1	$0.15	1	0	-4	2	4	-2	2,000
X_2	$0.20	0	1	1	-3	-1	3	7,000
Z_j		$0.15	$0.20	-$0.40	-$0.30	$0.40	$0.30	$1,700
$C_j - Z_j$		$0	$0	$0.40	$0.30	$M - $0.40	$M - $0.30	

(perhaps through improved technology), it will use less oil and thereby save on purchase costs. The shadow prices

$$U_1 = \text{cost savings obtained by using one less gallon of JT}$$

and

$$U_2 = \text{cost savings obtained by using one less gallon of WY}$$

give the decreases in purchase costs that result from unit changes in Millips's production requirements.

Millips's dual problem is to determine the shadow prices (U_1 and U_2) that maximize the total cost savings. Moreover, these shadow prices must ensure that the cost savings from the compounds are no more than each oil's unit purchase cost. Otherwise, Millips would be better off using the compounds on more attractive blending alternatives. This dual problem can be expressed as the following linear program:

maximize $\qquad C = 2000U_1 + 3000U_2$

subject to $\qquad 0.3U_1 + 0.1U_2 \leq \$0.15 \qquad$ (Type A oil)

$\qquad\qquad 0.2U_1 + 0.4U_2 \leq \$0.20 \qquad$ (Type B oil)

$\qquad\qquad U_1, U_2 \geq 0$

where C denotes the total cost savings obtained by using the compounds for oil blending.

Optimal Dual Solution. Management again can use complementary slackness and the information in the primal's optimal simplex table to find the optimal dual solution. For example, the $C_j - Z_j$ row entries in the S_1 and S_2 columns of Table 9.6 tell us that Millips optimal shadow prices (marginal potential purchase cost savings) are

$$U_1 = \$0.40 \text{ per gallon for the JT compound}$$

$$U_2 = \$0.30 \text{ per gallon for the WY compound}$$

According to the Z_j row entry in the Amounts column of this table, these shadow prices maximize the company's total cost savings at $C = \$1,700$ per day. Also, the $C_j - Z_j$ row entries in the X_1 and X_2 columns indicate that the reduced costs (unit purchase cost decreases needed to make the oils attractive decision alternatives) are $R_1 = \$0$ for type A and $R_2 = \$0$ for type B crude oil.

Dual Extensions

Unlike Management Situations 9.1 and 9.2, primal linear programs are not usually in their canonical forms. In such cases, the original primal can be converted into its canonical form with the transformations below.

Primal Condition	Transformation
nonpositive variable ($X_j \leq 0$)	replace the nonpositive variable (X_j) with the negative of a nonnegative variable ($-X'_j$)
unrestricted variable (X_j can be positive, zero, or negative)	replace the unrestricted variable (X_j) with the difference between two nonnegative variables ($X'_j - X''_j$)
minimize the objective function value (minimize Z)	maximize the negative of the objective value (maximize $-Z$)
equality ($=$) system constraint	write the restriction as two equivalent inequalities, one of which is a $\leq$ and the other a $\geq$ system constraint
$\geq$ system constraint	multiply both sides of the restriction by -1 to obtain a $\leq$ system constraint

For example, such transformations convert the primal linear program

minimize $Z = 10X_1 + 8X_2 + 16X_3$

subject to $4X_1 + 6X_2 + 2X_3 \leq 500$

$$8X_1 - 4X_2 + 4X_3 \geq 250$$

$$2X_1 + 2X_2 - X_3 = 100$$

$$X_1 \leq 0,\ X_2 \geq 0,\ X_3 \text{ unrestricted}$$

into its canonical form

maximize $-Z = 10X'_1 - 8X_2 - 16(X'_3 - X''_3)$

subject to $-4X'_1 + 6X_2 + 2(X'_3 - X''_3) \leq 500$

$$8X'_1 + 4X_2 - 4(X'_3 - X''_3) \leq -250$$

$$-2X'_1 + 2X_2 - (X'_3 - X''_3) \leq 100$$

$$2X'_1 - 2X_2 + (X'_3 - X''_3) \leq -100$$

$$X'_1,\ X_2,\ X'_3,\ X''_3 \geq 0$$

The primal/dual relationships then can be used to transform this canonical primal into the canonical dual.

In the canonical dual, there will be two variables associated with the original equality $(2X_1 + 2X_2 - X_3 = 100)$ constraint. As a result, the corresponding shadow price will be given by the difference (which could be negative) between the optimal values of the two dual variables.

Aside from its theoretical and managerial usefulness, the dual offers some computational advantages. Often, the dual is easier to solve than the primal, especially when the primal has a significantly larger number of system constraints than variables. In addition, models with special structure (such as the transportation problem) can be solved efficiently with dual concepts. Also, the dual is useful in performing additional forms of postoptimality analyses (such as studying the effects of adding a new variable or a new system constraint).

9.2 SENSITIVITY ANALYSIS

To properly formulate a linear program, the decision maker must know the values of the following key parameters:

1.   Each variable's unit contribution to the criterion value.

2.   The system constraint amounts.

3.   Each variable's constraint exchange coefficient.

In Management Situation 9.2, for example, Millips needs each crude oil's per-gallon purchase cost, each compound's production requirement, and the amount of the compounds in each oil. Yet these values rarely are known with complete certainty. Instead, they often represent estimates made at a selected point in time. Oil purchase costs, for example, may be the average quotation of several suppliers on a specific date. Similarly, production requirements and oil content data might come from experiments with current technology.

Unfortunately, conditions change, and the changes can make the original estimates inaccurate. If some oil suppliers go out of business and others alter their price quotations, Millips's purchase cost approximations may be seriously in error. And changes in technology might substantially alter the company's production requirement and oil content estimates.

In spite of the uncertainties, the decision maker will need the original estimates to develop an initial solution to the linear programming problem. After identifying the solution, management should also determine how changes in the parameters could affect the optimal primal and dual solutions. Otherwise, the company may be unprepared for changes in the problem conditions that could invalidate the decision variable and shadow price recommendations.

Linear programming sensitivity analysis can be used to investigate the impact of parameter changes on the optimal primal and dual solutions without completely reworking the problem. Management Situation 9.3 illustrates.

Management Situation 9.3

A Resource Allocation Problem

Country Farms in North Carolina grows tobacco and cotton on its 200 acres of land. An acre of tobacco brings a $100 profit, and an acre of cotton earns a $50 profit. Government regulations limit tobacco farming to a maximum of 40 acres. During the planting season, there are 500 people-hours of time available. Each acre of tobacco requires six people-hours, while each acre of cotton requires two people-hours for cultivation. Country wants to plant the number of tobacco and cotton acres that will maximize total profits.

After careful consideration, management has been able to express Country's problem as the following linear program:

maximize $Z = \$100X_1 + \$50X_2$

subject to $X_1 + X_2 \leq 200$ acres   (Land)

                $X_1 \leq 40$ acres   (Tobacco regulation)

                $6X_1 + 2X_2 \leq 500$ people-hours   (Planting)

                $X_1, X_2 \geq 0$

where Z = the total profit, X_1 = the number of acres of tobacco, and X_2 = the number of acres of cotton.

Figure 9.3 gives the solution to Country's primal linear program. This figure shows that Country can maximize total profit at $Z = \$11,250$ by planting $X_1 = 25$ acres of tobacco and $X_2 = 175$ acres of cotton. Since this optimal solution point is on the land and planting constraint lines, there will be $S_1 = 0$ unused acres of farmland and $S_3 = 0$ unused people-hours. It will leave $S_2 = 40 - X_1 = 40 - 25 = 15$ unused acres of tobacco.

Objective Function

In one form of sensitivity analysis, management examines the potential impact of changes in each decision variable's unit contribution to the objective. Figure 9.4 illustrates such an analysis for tobacco's per-acre profit. In this figure, A through C identify corner points of the feasible solution area, and B is the original optimal solution point.

Range of Optimality. When tobacco's per-acre profit changes and other parameters remain constant, X_1's objective function coefficient will equal the original $100 plus the change Δc_1. If the change is an increase (if $\Delta c_1 > 0$), the original objective function line rotates in a clockwise direction toward the $Z_1 = (\$100 + \Delta c_1)X_1 + \$50X_2$ line in Figure 9.4. This rotation (per-acre profit increase) eventually results in alternative optimal solutions along the BC line segment. Further increases then exclude B as the optimal solution point.

Figure 9.3   Country's Optimal Solution

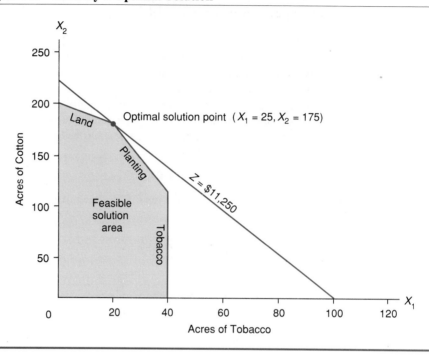

Along the line segment BC, the objective function line $Z_1 = (\$100 + \Delta c_1)X_1 + \$50X_2$ is tangent to the planting constraint line $6X_1 + 2X_2 = 500$. As a result, the two lines have the same slope or

$$-(\$100 + \Delta c_1)/\$50 = -6/2$$

so that

$$\Delta c_1 = (\$300 - \$200)/2 = \$50.$$

This Δc_1 value tells us that tobacco's per-acre profit can increase by as much as $50 without altering Country's original optimal solution.

Similarly, when tobacco's per-acre profit decreases (when $\Delta c_1 < 0$), the original objective function line rotates in a counterclockwise direction toward the $Z_2 = (\$100 + \Delta c_1)X_1 + \$50X_2$ line in Figure 9.4. This rotation (per-acre profit decrease) eventually results in alternative optimal solutions along the AB line segment. Further decreases then exclude B as the optimal solution point.

Along the line segment AB, the objective function line $Z_2 = (\$100 + \Delta c_1)X_1 + \$50X_2$ has the same slope as the land constraint line $X_1 + X_2 = 200$ or

$$-(\$100 + \Delta c_1)/\$50 = -1/1$$

so that

$$\Delta c_1 = \$50 - \$100 = -\$50$$

This Δc_1 value indicates that tobacco's per-acre profit can decrease by as much as $50 without altering Country's original optimal solution. Coincidentally, this allowable decrease happens to be the same $50 as the permitted increase.

Figure 9.4   **Sensitivity Analysis for Country's Per-Acre Tobacco Profit**

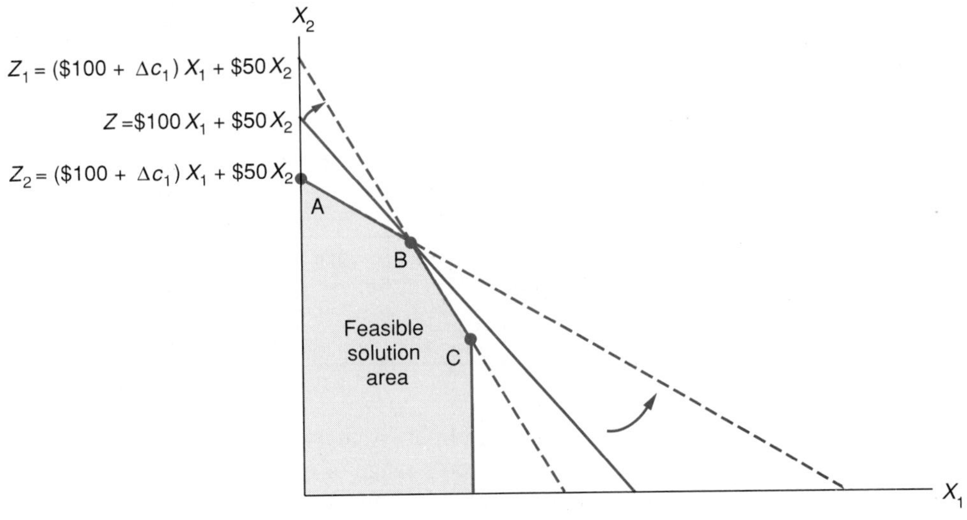

In effect, then, point B in Figure 9.4 will remain optimal as long as

$$-\$50 \le \Delta c_1 \le \$50$$

or tobacco's per-acre profit equals the original $100 estimate plus or minus $50. Hence, Country's actual per-acre profit can fluctuate in the range between $50 and $150 without affecting the optimal crop mix. Such a range, identifying the limits between which an objective function coefficient can fluctuate without altering the optimal solution point, is known as a **range of optimality**.

A graphic analysis similar to Figure 9.4 will show that cotton's range of optimality is $33.33 to $100 per acre. Since slack variables do not contribute anything to profit, it would be meaningless to develop ranges of optimality for unused acres of farmland (S_1), unused acres of tobacco (S_2), and unused people-hours (S_3).

Evaluating Parameter Changes. The optimal solution point will not change as long as the decision variables' objective function coefficients remain within their ranges of optimality. Parameter movements within these ranges, however, will alter the optimal objective function value when the corresponding decision variables have positive values in the solution.

For example, Country's original recommended crop mix ($X_1 = 25$ and $X_2 = 175$ or point B in Figure 9.4) remains optimal as long as tobacco's actual per-acre profit (X_1's objective function coefficient) is within its $50 to $150 range of optimality. The farm will earn a maximum total profit of

$$Z = \$50X_1 + \$50X_2 = \$50(25) + \$50(175) = \$10,000$$

at the range's $50 lower limit and a maximum total profit of

$$Z = \$150X_1 + \$50X_2 = \$150(25) + \$50(175) = \$12,500$$

Table 9.7   Optimal Simplex Table for Country Farms' Primal Linear Program

Variables Basis	C_j	X_1 $100	X_2 $50	S_1 $0	S_2 $0	S_3 $0	Amounts
S_2	$0	0	0	$\frac{1}{2}$	1	$-\frac{1}{4}$	15
X_1	$100	1	0	$-\frac{1}{2}$	0	$\frac{1}{4}$	25
X_2	$50	0	1	$\frac{3}{2}$	0	$-\frac{1}{4}$	175
	Z_j	$100	$50	$25	$0	$\frac{25}{2}$	$11,250
	$C_j - Z_j$	$0	$0	$-$25	$0	$-$\frac{25}{2}$	

at the range's $150 upper limit. Actual total profit then will fluctuate between $10,000 and $12,500 within tobacco's range of optimality.

When a variable's objective function coefficient is outside its range of optimality, there will be a change in the optimal solution point (as well as a change in the objective function value). For example, if favorable market conditions increase Country's tobacco profit from $100 to $180 per acre, the original objective function line will rotate in a clockwise direction beyond the Z_1 line in Figure 9.4. As a result, C will become the optimal solution point.

Since point C is at the intersection of the tobacco ($X_1 = 40$) and planting ($6X_1 + 2X_2 = 500$) constraint lines, the new optimal solution will have

$$S_2 = 0 \qquad \text{unused acres of tobacco}$$
$$S_3 = 0 \qquad \text{idle people-hours}$$
$$X_1 = 40 \qquad \text{acres of tobacco}$$

and
$$6(40) + 2X_2 = 500$$

or
$$X_2 = (500 - 240)/2 = 130 \qquad \text{acres of cotton.}$$

Moreover, this point C solution will maximize total profit at

$$Z = \$180X_1 + \$50X_2 = \$180(40) + \$50(130) = \$13,700$$

while leaving

$$S_1 = 200 - X_1 - X_2 = 200 - 40 - 130 = 30$$

unused acres of farmland.

Simplex Analysis. The simplex method also can be used to perform a sensitivity analysis on the objective function's coefficients. Table 9.7, for example, presents the simplex data corresponding to Country's optimal basic feasible solution (corner point B in Figure 9.4). In this table, S_1 denotes the unused acres of farmland, S_2 depicts the idle acres of tobacco, and S_3 gives the slack people-hours.

Table 9.8   **The Effects of Changes in Tobacco Profit on Country's Optimal Simplex Table**

Variables Basis	C_j	X_1 $\$100+\Delta c_1$	X_2 $\$50$	S_1 $\$0$	S_2 $\$0$	S_3 $\$0$	Amounts
S_2	$\$0$	0	0	$\frac{1}{2}$	1	$-\frac{1}{4}$	15
X_1	$\$100+\Delta c_1$	1	0	$-\frac{1}{2}$	0	$\frac{1}{4}$	25
X_2	$\$50$	0	1	$\frac{3}{2}$	0	$-\frac{1}{4}$	175
	Z_j	$\$100+\Delta c_1$	$\$50$	$\$25-\$\frac{1}{2}\Delta c_1$	$\$0$	$\$\frac{25}{2}+\$\frac{1}{4}\Delta c_1$	$\$11,250+\$25\Delta c_1$
	C_j-Z_j	$\$0$	$\$0$	$-\$25+\$\frac{1}{2}\Delta c_1$	$\$0$	$-\$\frac{25}{2}-\$\frac{1}{4}\Delta c_1$	

When tobacco's per acre profit changes, the new unit contribution ($100 + \Delta c_1$) replaces the old coefficient ($\$100$) in the C_j row of the X_1 column and alongside X_1 in the C_j column of Table 9.7. These substitutions will in turn change the Z_j and $C_j - Z_j$ row entries. By making the pertinent substitutions and resulting computations, management will obtain the revised optimal simplex data presented in Table 9.8.

Since Country's linear program involves a maximization objective, the farm's basis (and basic variable amounts) will remain optimal as long as all

$$C_j - Z_j \leq 0$$

or as long as there are no positive entries in the $C_j - Z_j$ row of Table 9.8. These conditions will occur when the $C_j - Z_j$ row entry for the nonbasic variable S_1 has

$$-\$25 + \$1/2\Delta c_1 \leq 0$$

so that

$$\Delta c_1 \leq \$50$$

and if the $C_j - Z_j$ row entry for the nonbasic variable S_3 has

$$-\$25/2 - \$1/4\Delta c_1 \leq 0$$

so that

$$\Delta c_1 \geq -\$50.$$

Table 9.8's Basis and Amounts column entries will not change as long as

$$-\$50 \leq \Delta c_1 \leq \$50.$$

As a result, tobacco's per-acre profit has a range of optimality of $\$100 + \Delta c_1 = \$100 \pm \$50$, or $50 to $150.

Parameter changes within tobacco's range of optimality will alter Country's maximum total profit. The Z_j row entry in the Amounts column of Table 9.8 suggests that this total profit will fluctuate between

$$\$11,250 + \$25\Delta c_1 = \$11,250 + \$25(-50) = \$10,000$$

and

$$\$11,250 + \$25\Delta c_1 = \$11,250 + \$25(50) = \$12,500$$

within the crop's $50 to $150 range of optimality.

If an activity's objective function coefficient is outside its range of optimality, there will be changes in the optimal basis, in the basic variable amounts, and in the optimal criterion value. As an illustration, suppose that favorable market conditions increase Country's tobacco profit from $100 to $180 per acre. This new $180 contribution is beyond the relevant range of optimality's $150 upper limit and represents a

$$\Delta c_1 = \$180 - \$100 = \$80$$

increase from the original $100 estimate. According to the $C_j - Z_j$ row entry in the S_3 column of Table 9.8, such a change will alter Country's optimal total profit by

$$-\$25/2 - \$1/4\Delta c_1 = -\$25/2 - \$1/4(80) = -\$32.50$$

for each unused people-hour brought into the basis. That is, if tobacco earns $180 per acre, the farm will decrease profit a net $32.50 by keeping a people-hour idle. Consequently, management still should not bring S_3 into the basis.

On the other hand, observe, the $C_j - Z_j$ row entry in the S_1 column of Table 9.8. This entry indicates that $\Delta c_1 = \$80$ will alter the optimal criterion value by

$$-\$25 + \$1/2\Delta c_1 = -\$25 + \$1/2(80) = \$15$$

for each unused acre of farmland brought into the basis. That is, when tobacco earns $180 per acre, Country can increase total profit a net $15 by keeping an acre of farmland idle. Therefore, the decision maker should now bring S_1 into the basis.

To find the revised optimal solution, Country must treat S_1 as the entering variable and then complete the simplex iteration process. If management does this, it will obtain the results presented in Table 9.9. The entries in the Basis and Amounts columns identify the revised optimal solution. These entries indicate that if tobacco earns $180 per acre, Country can maximize total profit at $Z = \$13,700$ by planting

$$X_1 = 40 \text{ acres of tobacco}$$

and

$$X_2 = 130 \text{ acres of cotton}$$

while leaving

$$S_1 = 30 \text{ unused acres of farmland.}$$

Also, since S_2 and S_3 do not appear in the Basis column of the table, such a crop mix will involve no unused acres of tobacco or idle people-hours.

Nonbasic Variables. Country's primal linear program has two decision variables (X_1 and X_2), and both are included in the farm's optimal crop mixes (Tables 9.7 and 9.9). For other cases, one or more decision variables may not be in the optimal basis (may be nonbasic).

In a maximization problem, a decision variable will be nonbasic because it makes an insufficient contribution to the objective. Any decrease in this contribution will make the nonbasic variable an even less desirable decision alternative. Consequently, the lower limit on the range of optimality for such a nonbasic variable will be an infinitely large negative value or negative infinity $(-\infty)$.

The corresponding upper limit can be found from the nonbasic variable's $C_j - Z_j$ row entry in the optimal simplex table. This entry's absolute value effectively measures the smallest amount by which the unit contribution must increase before the nonbasic variable becomes attractive enough to be included in the optimal basis. The upper limit

Table 9.9   Country's Optimal Solution When Profit Per Acre of Tobacco Is $180

Variables		X_1	X_2	S_1	S_2	S_3	
Basis	C_j	$180	$50	$0	$0	$0	Amounts
S_1	$0	0	0	1	2	$-\frac{1}{2}$	30
X_1	$180	1	0	0	1	0	40
X_2	$50	0	1	0	-3	$\frac{1}{2}$	130
	Z_j	$180	$50	$0	$30	$25	$13,700
	$C_j - Z_j$	$0	$0	$0	$-30	$-25	

on the range of optimality for such a nonbasic variable will equal the original objective function coefficient plus this smallest required increase.

In a minimization problem, a decision variable will be nonbasic because it makes an excessive contribution to the objective. Under these circumstances, the lower limit on the range of optimality will equal the original objective function coefficient minus the nonbasic variable's $C_j - Z_j$ row entry in the optimal simplex table. The corresponding upper limit will be an infinitely large value or positive infinity (∞).

As long as a nonbasic variable's objective function coefficient remains within its range of optimality, there will be no change in the optimal basis or in the corresponding basic variable amounts and criterion value. This optimal solution will change if the coefficient is outside its range's relevant limit (upper limit in a maximization problem or lower limit in a minimization problem). To find the revised optimal solution, management again would treat such a nonbasic variable as the entering (pivot column) variable and then complete the simplex pivoting process.

Procedure Recap. The following procedure can be used to perform sensitivity analysis on a decision variable's objective function coefficient:

1. Denote the change in the coefficient c_j as delta-c_j (Δc_j), and add this change to the original coefficient.
2. Find the values of Δc_j that keep the solution optimal.
3. Establish the range of optimality as follows:
   a. Set the upper limit equal to the original objective function coefficient plus the smallest positive Δc_j value. If there is no positive Δc_j, set the upper limit equal to positive infinity (∞).
   b. Set the lower limit equal to the original objective function coefficient minus the smallest absolute value of the negative Δc_j changes. If there is no negative Δc_j, set the lower limit equal to negative infinity ($-\infty$).
4. Evaluate the effects on the optimal solution of changes in the objective function coefficient.

Such a procedure is applicable for basic and nonbasic variables in maximization or minimization problems.

System Constraint Amount

In another form of sensitivity analysis, the decision maker examines the impact of changes in each system constraint amount. Figure 9.5 illustrates such a sensitivity analysis for Country's available farmland. To make the graph easier to read, the farm's objective function lines are omitted. If these lines did appear, they would indicate that M, B, and N are optimal solution points, with B identifying the original optimal solution point ($X_1 = 25$, $X_2 = 175$).

Range of Feasibility. When the available farmland changes and other parameters remain constant, the first system constraint's right-hand amount will equal the original 200 acres plus the change Δb_1. If the change is an increase (if $\Delta b_1 > 0$), the original land constraint line ($X_1 + X_2 = 200$) shifts upward parallel to itself toward the Maximum land (250 acres) line in Figure 9.5. This shift (farmland increase) expands the feasible solution area and eventually results in a new optimal solution at point M.

Since there are 250 acres of farmland at point M

$$\Delta b_1 = 250 - 200 = 50$$

acres. Larger increases ($\Delta b_1 > 50$) will shift the land constraint line above point M and exclude this restriction from the feasible solution area (make it redundant). As a result, there will be unused acres of farmland ($S_1 > 0$) as well as unused tobacco acres ($S_2 > 0$) and cotton planting ($X_2 > 0$) in any new optimal solution, but tobacco planting ($X_1 > 0$) will become infeasible (violate the Planting constraint). The $\Delta b_1 = 50$ value tells us that Country's farm can increase by as much as 50 acres before a variable in the original optimal solution (X_1) becomes infeasible.

When the size of the farm decreases (when $\Delta b_1 < 0$), the original land constraint line shifts downward parallel to itself toward the Minimum land (170 acres) line in Figure 9.5. This shift (farmland decrease) shrinks the feasible solution area and eventually results in a new optimal solution at point N.

Since there are 170 acres of available farmland at point N

$$\Delta b_1 = 170 - 200 = -30.$$

Larger decreases will shift the land constraint line below point N and exclude the planting restriction from the feasible solution area (make the Planting constraint redundant). Consequently, there will be idle people-hours ($S_3 > 0$) as well as tobacco planting ($X_1 > 0$) and cotton planting ($X_2 > 0$) in any new optimal solution, but idle tobacco acreage ($S_2 > 0$) will become infeasible (violate the Tobacco constraint). The $\Delta b_1 = -30$ value indicates that Country's farm can decrease by as much as 30 acres before a variable in the original optimal solution (S_2) becomes infeasible.

In effect, Country should continue to plant tobacco (have $X_1 > 0$), plant cotton (have $X_2 > 0$), and have idle tobacco acreage (have $S_2 > 0$) as long as

$$-30 \le \Delta b_1 \le 50$$

Figure 9.5   Sensitivity Analysis for Country's Available Farmland

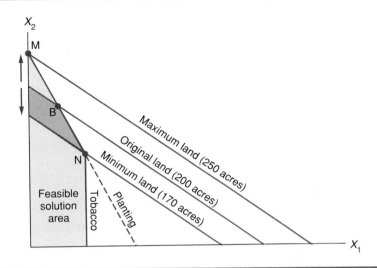

---

or there is no more than a 30-acre reduction or no more than a 50-acre increase in the original 200-acre land estimate. Thus, Country's actual farm can fluctuate in the range between 170 acres and 250 acres without altering the original planting recommendation. Such a range, identifying the limits between which a system constraint amount can fluctuate before the variables in the optimal solution (the optimal basis) become infeasible, is known as a **range of feasibility**.

Graphic analyses similar to Figure 9.5 will show that the range of feasibility is

$$25 \text{ acres to an infinitely large number of acres}$$

for the tobacco regulation and

$$400 \text{ to } 560 \text{ people-hours}$$

for the planting restriction.

Evaluating Parameter Changes. Although the optimal basis does not change as long as the system constraint amounts remain within their ranges of feasibility, parameter movements within these ranges will alter the solution values of the variables. When the constraint has no corresponding supplemental variable amount in the optimal solution, such parameter movements also will change the optimal objective function value.

For example, Country's original planting recommendation ($X_1 = 25$ and $X_2 = 175$) will remain feasible ($X_1, X_2, S_2 \geq 0$) as long as available farmland stays within its 170 to 250 acre range of feasibility. At the 170-acre lower limit, the optimal solution is at point N in Figure 9.5. Since this point is at the intersection of the planting ($6X_1 + 2X_2 = 500$) and tobacco ($X_1 = 40$) constraint lines, such a solution has $S_2 = 0$ unused acres of tobacco and $S_3 = 0$ idle people-hours. It also involves $X_1 = 40$ acres of tobacco

$$6(40) + 2X_2 = 500$$

or
$$X_2 = (500 - 240)/2 = 130$$

acres of cotton, while leaving

$$S_1 = 170 - X_1 - X_2 = 170 - 40 - 130 = 0$$

unused acres of farmland, and generating a

$$Z = \$100X_1 + \$50X_2 = \$100(40) + \$50(130) = \$10,500$$

maximum total profit.

At the 250-acre upper limit, the optimal solution is at point M (where the planting constraint line intersects the X_2 axis) in Figure 9.5. Such a solution leaves $S_3 = 0$ idle people-hours, and it involves $X_1 = 0$ acres of tobacco,

$$6(0) + 2X_2 = 500$$

or
$$X_2 = 500/2 = 250$$

acres of cotton,

$$S_1 = 250 - X_1 - X_2 = 250 - 0 - 250 = 0$$

unused acres of farmland,

$$S_2 = 40 - X_1 = 40 - 0 = 40$$

idle tobacco acres, with a

$$Z = \$100X_1 + \$50X_2 = \$100(0) + \$50(250) = \$12,500$$

maximum total profit.

Within farmland's range of feasibility, idle tobacco acreage (S_2) will fluctuate between 0 and 40 acres, tobacco planting (X_1) between 40 and 0 acres, cotton planting (X_2) between 130 and 250 acres, and maximum total profit will fluctuate between $10,500 and $12,500. When the system constraint amounts are outside their ranges of feasibility, there will be changes in the optimal basis as well as alterations in the basic variable amounts and in the optimal objective function value.

Simplex Analysis. The sensitivity analysis on the system constraint amounts also can be performed with the simplex method. For example, the Basis and Amounts columns in Table 9.7 identify Country's original optimal solution. A Δb_1 change in the farm's size will alter this table's Amounts column entries.

To find the new entries, Δb_1 is viewed as a change in idle farmland (S_1). Multiplying the S_1 column entries (idle farmland's exchange coefficients) in Table 9.7 by Δb_1 effectively measures the changes in the basic variable amounts that will result from this farmland alteration. By adding these changes to the original amounts, management then will obtain the revised optimal simplex table shown as Table 9.10.

Country's original optimal solution will remain feasible as long as the basic variable amounts are nonnegative (or if S_2, X_1, $X_2 \geq 0$). For such conditions to occur, the Amounts column entries in Table 9.10 must have

Table 9.10   **The Effect of Changes in Acres of Land on Country's Optimal Simplex Table**

Variables		X_1	X_2	S_1	S_2	S_3	
Basis	C_j	$100	$50	$0	$0	$0	**Amounts**
S_2	$0	0	0	$\frac{1}{2}$	1	$-\frac{1}{4}$	$15 + \frac{1}{2}\Delta b_1$
X_1	$100	1	0	$-\frac{1}{2}$	0	$\frac{1}{4}$	$25 - \frac{1}{2}\Delta b_1$
X_2	$50	0	1	$\frac{3}{2}$	0	$-\frac{1}{4}$	$175 + \frac{3}{2}\Delta b_1$
Z_j		$100	$50	$25	$0	$\frac{25}{2}$	$11,250 + \$25\Delta b_1$
$C_j - Z_j$		$0	$0	$-$25	$0	$-\$\frac{25}{2}$	

$$15 + 1/2\Delta b_1 \geq 0 \qquad \text{so that} \qquad \Delta b_1 \geq -30$$

$$25 - 1/2\Delta b_1 \geq 0 \qquad \text{so that} \qquad \Delta b_1 \leq 50$$

$$175 + 3/2\Delta b_1 \geq 0 \qquad \text{so that} \qquad \Delta b_1 \geq -350/3$$

This table's Basis column entries remain feasible then as long as

$$-30 \leq \Delta b_1 \leq 50.$$

As a result, the range of feasibility for available farmland is $200 + \Delta b_1 = 200 - 30 = 170$ acres to $200 + \Delta b_1 = 200 + 50 = 250$ acres.

Parameter changes within farmland's range of feasibility will alter Country's basic variable amounts and its maximum total profit. The Amounts column entries in Table 9.10 suggest that

$$S_2 = 15 + 1/2\Delta b_1 = 15 + 1/2(-30) = 0$$

$$X_1 = 25 - 1/2\Delta b_1 = 25 - 1/2(-30) = 40$$

$$X_2 = 175 + 3/2\Delta b_1 = 175 + 3/2(-30) = 130$$

with a maximum total profit of

$$\$11,250 + \$25\Delta b_1 = \$11,250 + \$25(-30) = \$10,500$$

at this range's 170-acre lower limit (where $\Delta b_1 = -30$). These entries also indicate that

$$S_2 = 15 + 1/2\Delta b_1 = 15 + 1/2(50) = 40$$

$$X_1 = 25 - 1/2\Delta b_1 = 25 - 1/2(50) = 0$$

$$X_2 = 175 + 3/2\Delta b_1 = 175 + 3/2(50) = 250$$

with a maximum total profit of

$$\$11,250 + \$25\Delta b_1 = \$11,250 + \$25(50) = \$12,500$$

at the range's 250-acre upper limit (where $\Delta b_1 = 50$). Thus, idle tobacco acreage (S_2) will fluctuate between 0 and 40 acres, tobacco planting (X_1) between 40 and 0 acres, cotton planting (X_2) between 130 and 250 acres, and maximum total profit will fluctuate between \$10,500 and \$12,500 within the range of feasibility for Country's available farmland.

Basic Variables. Unlike unused farmland (S_1) and idle people-hours (S_3), unused tobacco acreage (S_2) is a basic variable in Country's original optimal solution (Table 9.7 or point B in Figure 9.5). When a supplemental variable is in the optimal basis, the range of feasibility for the corresponding system constraint amount can be found in a relatively straightforward manner.

The Amounts column entry in the S_2 row of Table 9.7 indicates that the optimal crop mix leaves $S_2 = 15$ idle tobacco acres. Management could reduce the original 40-acre tobacco allowance by as much as 15 acres before S_2 is driven out of the optimal basis. As a result, the lower limit on the tobacco regulation's range of feasibility is the original system constraint amount minus the corresponding basic variable's optimal value or

$$40 - 15 = 25 \text{ acres.}$$

Since Country does not plant 15 of the 40 acres allowed by current government regulations, the allowance can be increased to an infinitely larger amount without altering the farm's optimal basis. Consequently, the upper limit on tobacco regulation's range of feasibility is positive infinity (∞).

In effect, the range of feasibility for the tobacco regulation is 25 acres to ∞ acres. Within this range, there will be no changes in the optimal basis or in the optimal objective function value, but parameter movements will alter the basic variables' amounts. When the system constraint amount is outside its range of feasibility, there will be changes in the optimal basis as well as alterations in the basic variable amounts and in the optimal objective function value.

Shadow Prices. There is an important relationship between the optimal shadow prices and the ranges of feasibility for the corresponding system constraint amounts. For example, the $C_j - Z_j$ row entry in the S_1 column of Table 9.7 suggests that Country's farmland has a shadow price of $|-\$25| = \$25$ per acre. According to this shadow price, total profit increases a net \$25 for each acre added to the original farm size. Such a profit increase cannot continue indefinitely, however. As the farm grows, the available acreage will reach the 250-acre upper limit on the farmland's range of feasibility. Further acreage increases then will lead to a change in the optimal basis.

The shadow price also indicates that total profit decreases a net \$25 for each acre subtracted from the original farm size. This profit decrease can continue only until the available acreage reaches the 170-acre lower limit on farmland's range of feasibility. Further acreage decreases then will lead to a change in the optimal basis.

Any change in the optimal basis will alter the $-\$25$ entry in the S_1 column of the $C_j - Z_j$ row of Table 9.7. In effect, Country's land has a shadow price of \$25 only if the farm does not shrink below 170 acres or expand above 250 acres. This result illustrates the following important principle: *An optimal shadow price is valid only within the range of feasibility for the corresponding system constraint amount.* When a system constraint amount is outside its range of feasibility, there will be a change in the corresponding shadow price.

Procedure Recap. The following procedure can be used to perform sensitivity analysis on a system constraint's right-hand amount:

1. Denote the change in the amount b_i as delta-b_i (Δb_i).

2. Find the values of Δb_i that keep the optimal basis feasible.

3. Establish the range of feasibility with the following formulas:

Type of System Constraint	Lower Limit	Upper Limit
Less than or equal to ($\leq$) or equality ($=$)	$\begin{bmatrix} \text{original} \\ \text{constraint} \\ \text{amount} \end{bmatrix} - \begin{bmatrix} \text{smallest absolute} \\ \text{value of the} \\ \text{negative } \Delta b_i \text{ amounts} \end{bmatrix}$ or $-\infty$ if there is no negative Δb_i	$\begin{bmatrix} \text{original} \\ \text{constraint} \\ \text{amount} \end{bmatrix} + \begin{bmatrix} \text{smallest} \\ \text{positive} \\ \Delta b_i \text{ value} \end{bmatrix}$ or ∞ if there is no positive Δb_i
Greater than or equal to ($\geq$)	$\begin{bmatrix} \text{original} \\ \text{constraint} \\ \text{amount} \end{bmatrix} - \begin{bmatrix} \text{smallest} \\ \Delta b_i \\ \text{value} \end{bmatrix}$ or $-\infty$ if there is no positive Δb_i	$\begin{bmatrix} \text{original} \\ \text{constraint} \\ \text{amount} \end{bmatrix} + \begin{bmatrix} \text{smallest absolute} \\ \text{value of the} \\ \text{negative } \Delta b_i \text{ amounts} \end{bmatrix}$ or ∞ if there is no negative Δb_i

4. Evaluate the effects on the optimal solution of changes in the system constraint amount.

Such a procedure is applicable to system constraints that involve basic and nonbasic supplemental (slack, surplus, and artificial) variables in maximization or minimization problems.

Exchange Coefficients

In a third form of sensitivity analysis, the decision maker examines the potential impact of changes in each decision variable's system constraint utilization rate. Consider, for instance, Country's planting restriction. According to Management Situation 9.3, it originally takes six people-hours to plant one acre of tobacco. Now, suppose a technological innovation reduces this time by one hour. In that case, the expression

$$5X_1 + 2X_2 \leq 500 \text{ people-hours}$$

would represent the new planting restriction. That is, the X_1 decision variable will have an exchange coefficient of 5 rather than 6.

Figure 9.6 illustrates the effects of the increase in tobacco-planting efficiency. To make the graph easier to read, the farm's profit lines are omitted. If these lines did appear, they would indicate that the optimal solution points are as shown in the graph.

In Figure 9.6, you can see that the reduction in the X_1 variable's exchange coefficient makes the planting constraint line steeper. Such a shift enables Country to plant more

**Figure 9.6   The Effect of a Decrease in the People Hours Needed
to Plant One Acre of Country's Tobacco**

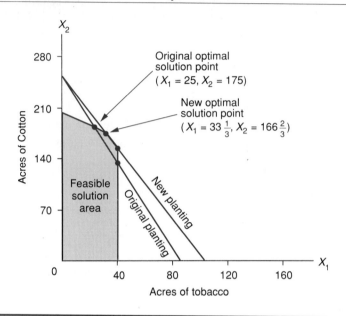

acres of tobacco than before with the same work force capacity. For example, the farm originally could plant a maximum of

$$\frac{500 \text{ available people-hours}}{6 \text{ people-hours per acre of tobacco}}$$

or 83.33 acres of tobacco with 500 people-hours. After the technological innovation, however, management can produce 500/5 = 100 acres of this crop with the same work force. Figure 9.6 also demonstrates that the increased efficiency alters the shape of the feasible solution area. As a result, Country's optimal solution point changes from $(X_1 = 25, X_2 = 175)$ to $(X_1 = 33\frac{1}{3}, X_2 = 166\frac{2}{3})$.

Management Situation 9.3 shows that total profit is given by the expression

$$Z = \$100X_1 + \$50X_2.$$

Hence, the farm obtains a total profit of

$$Z = \$100(33\tfrac{1}{3}) + \$50(166\tfrac{2}{3}) = \$11,666.67$$

after the technological innovation, rather than the original

$$Z = \$100(25) + \$50(175) = \$11,250.$$

In other words, the innovation increases profit by encouraging Country to plant more tobacco but less cotton than before the change.

A similar approach can be used to determine the effects of an increase in the time needed for planting an acre of tobacco. Although not treated here, it is possible to find the range over which this exchange coefficient could fluctuate without altering Country's optimal basis.

Other Postoptimality Analysis

Our sensitivity analyses have been confined to the consideration of a discrete change in a single parameter for the original linear program. All other parameters are assumed to remain at their original values during the sensitivity analysis. In some cases, however, the decision maker may want to examine the effects of

1. Continuous, rather than discrete, variations in a program parameter.
2. A change in the form of the linear program (such as the addition of a new constraint or a new decision variable).
3. Simultaneous changes in several program parameters.

New Variables and Constraints. As discussed in Section 9.1, shadow prices can be used to determine the effects of adding a new variable to the original linear program. When such an evaluation indicates that the new variable is desirable, management should add this variable to the original linear program and then solve the restated problem for the optimal solution.

New policies, revised regulations, and innovations often create additional or altered system constraints. If the original optimal solution satisfies these new or revised constraints, this solution will still remain feasible. When the original optimal solution violates the new system constraints (is infeasible), management should add these restrictions to the original linear program and then solve the restated problem for the new optimal solution.

Deleting Variables or Constraints. Changing conditions may encourage the decision maker to delete a variable or a system constraint from the linear program. When the variable is excluded from the optimal solution, or when the system constraint is nonbinding, such deletions will not alter the original recommendation. If the original solution includes the deleted variable, or if the deleted system constraint is binding, the linear program should be reformulated and resolved for the new recommendation.

Parametric Programming. Another methodology, called **parametric programming**, examines how continuous variations in selected parameters (such as c_j values) influence the optimal linear programming solution. For example,

$$Z(\Delta) = (50 + k_1\Delta)X_1 + (25 + k_2\Delta)$$

is a parametric programming objective function. It shows that the objective function value (Z) depends on the relative rates of simultaneous change ($k_1\Delta$ and $k_2\Delta$) in the decision variables' contributions (50 for X_1 and 25 for X_2).

The decision maker would specify the relative rates (k_1 and k_2) and a range of values for the change (Δ). A simplex-based procedure then would be used to provide the optimal objective function value (Z) and the optimal values of the decision variables (X_1 and X_2) each as a function of the change (Δ).

9.3 COMPUTER ANALYSIS

Most practical linear programming problems are too complex for solution with the graphic or manual simplex procedures. As a result, management scientists have developed computer programs especially designed to solve large-scale linear programs. These prewritten (canned) programs are widely available for mainframe, minicomputer, and microcomputer applications. Some popular mainframe/minicomputer programs include *LINPRO, MPSX, OPTIMA, ALPS, LP, LINPROG, SIMPLEX,* and *LINDO.* Popular programs for microcomputers include *LINDO/PC, LPS, LP88,* and *MAX.*

Although each computerized linear programming package is slightly different, the basic features are essentially the same. In each package, the user must access the program, supply the pertinent data, and request the appropriate analysis. To provide this information, of course, the user must fully understand the nature and purpose of a linear program. The computer will then perform the necessary linear programming computations, typically with some version of the simplex method, and generate the requested output. Such output may include

1. The simplex tables.
2. The optimal level of each variable.
3. The criterion value.
4. The optimal shadow prices.
5. A complete sensitivity analysis.

Naturally, a fundamental knowledge about simplex and sensitivity analysis concepts would enhance the user's ability to accurately interpret and completely utilize the computer output.

The **Quantitative Management (QM)** software has a linear programming module that is similar to *LINDO* (and *LINDO/PC*). This module is accessed by selecting the Linear Programming command from **QM**'s main menu. Figure 9.7 then shows how the module can be used to solve Country's linear program (Management Situation 9.3).

As Figure 9.7 demonstrates, the user executes the module by choosing the Optimal solution or Sensitivity analysis option from the Linear Programming menu. Next, the linear program is formulated (or revised) through the Edit command from the Input menu. Figure 9.7, for example, shows that Country wants to maximize (MAX) its objective function value ($100X_1 + 50X_2$), subject to (ST) the three specified system constraints. When formulating the linear program for **QM**, all decision variables must be on the left and a nonnegative constant must be on the right of each system constraint.

The Input menu also enables the user to Print and Save the formulated problem or to Load a previously saved linear program. For example, Figure 9.7 shows that Country's

---

Figure 9.7   Computer Solution of Country's Linear Problem

Linear Progamming:	Input:	Output:
* Optimal solution	* Edit	▪ Full
▪ Sensitivity analysis	▪ Load	* Summary
	▪ Print	* Print
	* Save	▪ Save

Filename: FARM

Problem Formulation:

$$\text{MAX } 100X_1 + 50\ X_2$$
$$\text{ST} \quad 1X_1 + \quad 1X_2 <\ = 200$$
$$1X_1 \qquad\qquad <\ = 40$$
$$6X_1 + \quad 2X_2 <\ = 500$$

RECOMMENDATION

Decision Variable	Optimal Value	Reduced Cost
X_1	25.00	0.00
X_2	175.00	0.00

Supplemental Variable	Optimal Value	Shadow Prices
S_1	0.00	25.00
S_2	15.00	0.00
S_3	0.00	12.50

Optimal Objective Function Value: 11250.00

---

linear program will be saved under the Filename "FARM." Report options then are specified through the Output menu.

Optimal Solution

If the user selects the Optimal solution option from the Linear Programming menu, **QM** will convert the linear program into its standard form, solve the problem with a version of the simplex method, and display:

1. The optimal value of each decision (real) variable and the corresponding reduced cost.

2. The optimal value of each supplemental (slack or surplus) variable and the corresponding shadow price.

3. The optimal objective function value.

Original Recommendation. Figure 9.7 shows that Country can maximize total profit at \$11,250 by planting $X_1 = 25$ acres of tobacco and $X_2 = 175$ acres of cotton. This optimal solution leaves $S_1 = 0$ unused acres of farmland, $S_2 = 15$ idle tobacco acres, and $S_3 = 0$ unused people-hours.

Figure 9.8   Computer Sensitivity Analysis of Country's Linear Problem

---

Linear Progamming:	Input:	Output:
▪ Optimal solution	▪ Edit	▪ Full
* Sensitivity analysis	* Load	* Summary
	* Print	* Print
	▪ Save	▪ Save

Filename: FARM

Problem Formulation:

$$\text{MAX } 100X_1 + 50X_2$$
$$\text{ST} \quad 1X_1 + 1X_2 <\, = 200$$
$$1X_1 \qquad\quad <\, = 40$$
$$6X_1 + 2X_2 <\, = 500$$

RANGES OF OPTIMALITY

Decision Variable	Lower Limit	Allowable Decrease	Original Coefficient	Allowable Increase	Upper Limit
X_1	50.00	50.00	100.00	50.00	150.00
X_2	33.33	16.67	50.00	50.00	100.00

RANGES OF FEASIBILITY

System Constraint	Lower Limit	Allowable Decrease	Original Coefficient	Allowable Increase	Upper Limit
1	170.00	30.00	200.00	50.00	250.00
2	25.00	15.00	40.00	∞	∞
3	400.00	100.00	500.00	60.00	560.00

Shadow Prices and Reduced Costs. The $0 reduced costs for the decision variables suggest that no per-acre profit improvements are needed to justify the planting of tobacco (X_1) and cotton (X_2). Figure 9.7's shadow prices also indicate that Country can increase total profit a net $25 per acre of additional farmland (S_1), $0 for each acre added to the tobacco regulation (S_2), and $12.50 per additional people-hour of planting (S_3).

Sensitivity Analysis

When the user selects the Sensitivity analysis option from the Linear Programming menu, **QM** will determine the ranges of optimality and the ranges of feasibility. It then displays:

1. Each decision variable's original objective function coefficient and the corresponding range of optimality information.

2. Each system constraint's original amount and the corresponding range of feasibility information.

Such sensitivity analyses can be performed on a newly formulated problem or on a previously saved linear program. For example, Figure 9.8 shows how the module performs sensitivity analysis on Country's linear program (stored under the Filename "FARM").

Ranges of Optimality. Figure 9.8 indicates that tobacco's (X_1's) original $100 per-acre profit contribution can decrease by as much as $50 (to a lower limit of $50) or increase by as much as $50 (to an upper limit of $150) without altering Country's optimal crop mix. Such a mix will also remain optimal if cotton's (X_2's) original $50 per-acre profit contribution does not decrease by more than $16.67 (to a lower limit of $33.33) or increase by more than $50 (to an upper limit of $100).

Ranges of Feasibility. The computer output shows that Country's original 200-acre farm can decrease by as much as 30 acres (to a lower limit of 170 acres) or increase by as much as 50 acres (to an upper limit of 250 acres) without making the optimal basis infeasible. Such a basis will also remain feasible if the tobacco regulation is within the range of 25 to ∞ acres or if the planting effort is within the range of 400 to 560 people-hours.

Other Postoptimality Analysis

The **QM** software can be used to perform other forms of postoptimality analysis. For example, suppose the government replaces the original tobacco regulation with a new constraint that requires farms to use no more than 20 percent of available people-hours on tobacco planting. Under these circumstances, Country will delete the second system constraint

$$X_1 \leq 40 \text{ acres}$$

and add the new restriction

$$6X_1 \leq 0.2(500)$$

or

$$6X_1 \leq 100 \text{ people-hours}$$

to its original linear program.

Since the farmland's original optimal solution ($X_1 = 25$ and $X_2 = 175$) violates the new restriction, there will be a change in the crop mix recommendation. Figure 9.9 shows how **QM** finds the new optimal solution.

Editing. In Figure 9.9, the Optimal solution selection from the Linear Programming menu instructs **QM** to solve the linear program specified by the user. Country's original linear program next is retrieved from the file named "FARM" through the Input menu's Load command. By choosing the Edit command from this Input menu, the user can delete the original tobacco regulation ($1X_1 < = 40$) and insert the new restriction ($6X_1 < = 100$) in a full-screen editing mode. Report option selection then completes the computer processing.

Optimal Solution. Figure 9.9 shows that Country now can maximize total profit at $10,833.33 by planting $X_1 = 16.67$ acres of tobacco and $X_2 = 183.33$ acres of cotton, while leaving $S_1 = 0$ unused acres of farmland, $S_2 = 0$ idle tobacco planting hours, and $S_3 = 33.33$ unused people-hours. In effect, the new government restriction reduces tobacco planting by $25 - 16.67 = 8.33$ acres, increases cotton planting by $183.33 - 175 = 8.33$ acres, and decreases the farm's total profit by $11,250 - \$10,833.33 = \$416.67$.

Figure 9.9   **Computer Solution of Country's Revised Linear Problem**

Linear Progamming:
* Optimal solution
▪ Sensitivity analysis

Input:
* Edit
▪ Load
▪ Print
* Save

Output:
▪ Full
* Summary
* Print
▪ Save

Filename: FARM

Problem Formulation:

$$\text{MAX } 100X_1 + 50X_2$$

ST	$1X_1$	+	$1X_2$	$\leq = 200$	
	$1X_1$			$\leq = 40$	\<Deleted\>
	$6X_1$			$\leq = 100$	\<Inserted\>
	$6X_1$	+	$2X_2$	$\leq = 500$	

RECOMMENDATION

Decision Variable	Optimal Value	Reduced Cost
X_1	16.67	0.00
X_2	183.33	0.00

Supplemental Variable	Optimal Value	Shadow Prices
S_1	0.00	50.00
S_2	0.00	8.33
S_3	33.33	0.00

Optimal Objective Function Value: 10833.33

Shadow Prices and Reduced Costs. Tobacco and cotton planting (X_1 and X_2) again have $0 reduced costs. The new shadow prices are $50 for each additional acre of farmland (S_1), $8.33 for each additional tobacco planting hour (S_2), and $0 per added people-hour (S_3). In effect, the new government regulation has made additional farmland more valuable and additional people-hours less valuable than before.

SUMMARY

In this chapter we saw how postoptimality analysis generates information useful for management planning and control. Some of the knowledge is obtained by examining the original or primal linear program from its dual perspective.

By studying the dual, the decision maker obtains valuable insights into the economic nature and management implications of the primal linear program. In addition, the dual solution generates the optimal shadow prices for the primal system constraints. These prices, which measure the variations in the optimal criterion value that result from unit changes in the constraint amounts, can be applied to decision making, as summarized in Table 9.2. Also, the primal and dual relationships offer practical procedural benefits. In fact, sometimes it is easier to solve the dual rather than the primal linear program.

Under such circumstances, management should solve the dual and then derive the optimal primal solution from the results.

The optimal primal and dual solutions are based on the original estimates of the linear program parameters. Yet variations in decision conditions often change these original estimates. As a result, the decision maker must determine the effects of such changes on the optimal primal and dual results. The second section of the chapter demonstrated how sensitivity analysis can provide this information without the decision maker having to completely rework the problem.

In one form of sensitivity analysis, management examines the potential impact of changes in each decision variable's unit contribution to the objective. Such an analysis establishes the variable's range of optimality, or the scope over which its objective function coefficient could change without altering the optimal basis in the linear program.

In another form of sensitivity analysis, the decision maker examines the impact of changes in each system constraint amount. Such an analysis establishes the range of feasibility, or the scope over which a constraint amount can fluctuate without altering the optimal basis in the linear program. Also, we saw that the optimal basis and the restriction's shadow price do not change as long as the relevant system constraint amount remains within its range of feasibility. Parameter movements within the range, however, alter the optimal quantities of the basic variables.

It is also possible to investigate the potential impact of changes in each decision variable's system constraint utilization rate. By performing this and the other forms of sensitivity analysis, management is able to determine how sensitive the optimal solution is to variations in the linear program parameters. Consequently, management is in a better position to evaluate the efficiency of obtaining better parameter estimates.

Most practical linear programming problems are too complex for solution with the graphic or manual simplex procedures. As a result, management scientists have developed computer programs especially designed to solve large-scale linear programs. These canned (prewritten) programs are available through computer manufacturers, distributors, and service companies to academic, business, and government organizations. The final section of the chapter showed how a typical computerized package is used to solve a linear program and perform the corresponding sensitivity analysis.

Glossary

canonical form A primal/dual relationship in which a primal maximization program has all $\leq$ system constraints and all variables nonnegative, and a dual minimization problem has all $\geq$ system constraints and all variables nonnegative.

complementary slackness The relationships between the optimal values of the primal and dual variables.

dual A linear programming problem that provides an alternative and complementary way of looking at the original (primal) program.

linear programming sensitivity analysis A methodology for investigating the impact of parameter changes

on the optimal primal and dual solutions to a linear program.

parametric programming A form of postoptimality analysis in which the decision maker examines how specified continuous variations in the uncontrollable inputs influence the optimal linear programming solution.

postoptimality analysis The examination of the optimal solution to an original linear program to identify the economic values of scarce resources and restrictive guidelines and to determine the effect of parameter changes on the problem.

primal The original linear programming problem.

range of feasibility The range of values over which a constraint amount can fluctuate without altering the optimal basis in a linear program.

range of optimality The range of values over which an objective function coefficient can fluctuate without altering the optimal basis and basic variable amounts in a linear program.

reduced costs Improvements that must be made in the per-unit contributions before corresponding variables will enter the optimal basis. Dual's analogies to the primal's surplus and slack variables.

shadow price The change in the criterion value that results from a one-unit change in the amount of a constraint.

Thought Exercises

1. An opportunity cost is defined as the difference between the outcomes of the best and next best alternatives. Why are the optimal values of the dual variables or shadow prices considered opportunity costs?

2. Interpret the dual for each of the following primal linear programs. (Give a verbal interpretation of the dual objective function and system constraints.)
   a. A winery wants to determine the product mix of wines that will maximize profit. Labor, grapes, and sugar are used to make the wines, and each of these resources is in limited supply.
   b. A dog kennel wants to determine the minimum cost mix of various dog food products. A dog food mix must contain minimum amounts of various nutrients to provide a balanced dog diet.
   c. An armed forces public relations agency wants to determine how many "spots" to place in various media so as to maximize audience exposure. Total dollars spent cannot exceed the available budget. Also, the total number of spots placed in each medium cannot exceed the quantity offered for armed forces public service messages.

3. Interpret the shadow price for the specified system constraint in each of the following decision situations:
   a. A company wants to determine how many machines of each type it should purchase so as to maximize the machines' daily output (in units). One constraint specifies that the total floor space used by the machines must be less than or equal to the available square footage.
   b. A market research company wants to determine a plan that will minimize interview costs. A contractual constraint specifies that the company must contact a minimum number of households with a given set of characteristics.
   c. A university credit union wants to determine how much of its budget to allocate to various investments so as to maximize dollar return. The company cannot invest more than the available funds.
   d. A government agency wants to determine how many professionals of various types to hire to fill the agency's positions at minimum recruiting cost. One constraint specifies that the total recruitment of two of the professional groups must meet a minimum agency quota.

4. The primal of a linear program has six decision variables but only two constraints. You are interested only in the optimal criterion value. Your instructor suggests that it may be easier to solve the dual rather than the primal of this problem. Why do you think your instructor made such a recommendation?

5. A missile system requires a minimum number of hours for research and development (R&D), a minimum budget, and a minimum quantity of plutonium. The least-cost system creates shadow prices of $1,000 per added R&D hour, $666 per added budget dollar, and $1,280 per added gram of plutonium. Interpret these shadow prices and use them to establish priorities for the constraints.

6. Software Engineers, Inc. can hire two new application programmers to complete a "rush" job for an important client. Each programmer will be paid $3,000 per month in salary and fringe benefits. Applications programming has a shadow price of $4,800 (which accounts for additional profit and the opportunity cost associated with client ill will). Should Software hire the new programmers? Explain.

7. Hanton Shoes is thinking about adding a new jogger model to its product line. The jogger will earn a $5 profit per pair. Each shoe in the pair will use four ounces of materials, take five minutes to assemble, and require three minutes to package. Hanton's product line generates shadow prices of $2.50 per ounce of materials, $4 per hour of assembly, and $6 per hour of packaging. Should Hanton introduce the new jogger model? Explain.

8. The Dual Extensions exhibit in the text presents the following canonical form of a primal linear program:

maximize

$$-Z = 10X_1' - 8X_2 - 16(X_3' - X_3'')$$

subject to

$$-4X_1' + 6X_2 + 2(X_3' - X_3'') \leq 500$$
$$8X_1' + 4X_2 - 4(X_3' - X_3'') \leq -250$$
$$-2X_1' + 2X_2 - (X_3' - X_3'') \leq 100$$
$$2X_1' - 2X_2 + (X_3' - X_3'') \leq -100$$
$$X_1', X_2, X_3', X_3'' \geq 0$$

  a. Formulate the dual of this canonical primal.
  b. Solve the resulting canonical dual.
  c. Interpret the canonical dual's solution in terms of the original primal linear program.

9. Smooth Cycles, Inc., manufactures three types of bicycles: the Lady Ride, the Neutral, and the Macho Man. The bikes must be manufactured and assembled. There is limited available capacity for each of these operations. The company's planning department formulates the problem as the following linear program:

maximize $Z = \$20X_1 + \$30X_2 + \$40X_3$

subject to $0.2X_1 + 0.2X_2 + 0.1X_3 \leq 120$ hours   (Manufacturing)

$0.4X_1 + 0.1X_2 + 0.3X_3 \leq 120$ hours   (Assembly)

$X_1, X_2, X_3 \geq 0$

where Z = the total profit, X_1 = the number of cartons of Lady Ride, X_2 = the number of cartons of Neutral, and X_3 = the number of cartons of Macho Man. Smooth's planning director provides the following optimal dual solution information:

$$C = \text{total resource payments} = \$24,000$$

$$U_1 = \text{shadow price of a manufacturing hour} = \$100$$

$$U_2 = \text{shadow price of an assembly hour} = \$100$$

$$R_1 = \text{excess cost of a Lady Ride} = \$40$$

The director also indicates that neither the Neutral nor the Macho Man model involves any reduced cost. You are called in as a consultant and asked the following questions:

a. How many bikes of each type should Smooth produce to maximize profit?

b. What is the maximum profit?

c. Is there any unused capacity?

d. Smooth is considering a new product: Kiddy Cycles. A Kiddy would earn $25 profit and take six minutes to manufacture and three minutes to assemble. Should Smooth manufacture the Kiddy Cycle?

Prepare a report that provides this information.

10. Pioneer Hamburger House specializes in three types of burgers: regular, whopper, and double whopper. Labor, meat, and seasoning ingredients are used to make each type of burger. Pioneer's management has not been satisfied with recent profits and has therefore employed a local management consulting firm. The consultant has formulated an appropriate linear program and has arrived at the following optimal simplex table. In this table,

$$X_1 = \text{regulars sold per quarter (in thousands)}$$

$$X_2 = \text{whoppers sold per quarter (in thousands)}$$

$$X_3 = \text{double whoppers sold per quarter (in thousands)}$$

$$Z = \text{profit (in thousands of dollars)}$$

$$S_1 = \text{idle labor hours}$$

$$S_2 = \text{unused pounds of meat}$$

$$S_3 = \text{idle packages of seasoning ingredients}$$

Variables		X_1	X_2	X_3	S_1	S_2	S_3	
Basis	C_j	$0.10	$0.12	$0.20	$0	$0	$0	**Amounts**
X_2	$0.12	2	1	0	−3	6	0	200
S_3	$0	−4	0	0	1	−3	1	1,000
X_3	$0.20	1	0	1	2	4	0	150
	Z_j	$0.44	$0.12	$0.20	$0.04	$1.52	$0	$54
	$C_j - Z_j$	−$0.34	$0	$0	−$0.04	−$1.52	$0	

On the basis of these results, the consultant advises Pioneer to stop selling regular hamburgers unless the profit per regular can be increased by at least 34 cents. The consultant also advises Pioneer to use more meat and labor. Meat is said to be a much more profitable source of expansion than labor.

How did the consultant arrive at these recommendations?

11. Hamilton Bender, Inc., manufactures three main health care products: packaged brewer's yeast, multiple vitamins, and protein powder. Plants in Springfield and McAllister manufacture sufficient quantities of these products to meet forecasted monthly demand at least cost. However, management has not been satisfied with recent cost experience. As a result, management has referred the problem to its planning staff for consideration and analysis. The staff has formulated an appropriate linear program and has arrived at the optimal simplex table below:

Variables		X_1	X_2	S_1	S_2	S_3	A_1	A_2	A_3	
Basis	c_j	$6,000	$4,500	$0	$0	$0	$M	$M	$M	Amounts
X_2	$4,500	0	1	0	$\frac{1}{5}$	$\frac{3}{5}$	0	$-\frac{1}{5}$	$-\frac{3}{5}$	25
S_1	$0	0	0	1	$\frac{2}{3}$	-4	1	$-\frac{2}{3}$	4	3,000
X_1	$6,000	1	0	0	$-\frac{1}{6}$	$-\frac{1}{2}$	0	$\frac{1}{6}$	$\frac{1}{2}$	20
	z_j	$6,000	$4,500	$0	$-$100	$-$300	$0	$100	$300	$232,500
	$c_j - z_j$	$0	$0	$0	$100	$300	$M	$M + $100	$M + $300	

In this table, A_1, A_2, and A_3 are artificial variables, while

$$X_1 = \text{days worked per month at the Springfield plant}$$

$$X_2 = \text{days worked per month at the McAllister plant}$$

$$Z = \text{total monthly production cost}$$

$$S_1 = \text{excess cases of brewer's yeast}$$

$$S_2 = \text{excess cases of multiple vitamins}$$

$$S_3 = \text{excess cases of protein powder}$$

On the basis of these results, the planning director advises management to reduce yeast output by 3,000 cans per month. In addition, the director offers the following suggestions:

- A decrease in protein powder demand will be more cost-effective than an equivalent reduction in multiple vitamin sales.

- The company should operate the Springfield plant 20 days per month and the McAllister facility 25 days per month as long as protein powder demand is between 160 and 241.67 cases per month. Sales were originally forecasted to be 200 cases per month.

- The same production schedule will be appropriate as long as the actual demand for brewer's yeast does not exceed the original 8,000-case forecast by more than 3,000 cases.

How did the planning director arrive at these recommendations?

12. Refer back to Ancient Enterprise's product mix problem (Management Situation 9.1). By using the *LINDO* computer package to solve the linear program for this problem, the decision maker will get the following output:

```
                    LP OPTIMUM FOUND AT STEP      3
                       OBJECTIVE FUNCTION VALUE
          1)     12800.0000
     VARIABLE          VALUE              REDUCED COST
        X1          400.000000                0.000000
        X2          120.000000                0.000000

        ROW     SLACK OR SURPLUS          DUAL PRICES
         2)         0.000000                 6.000000
         3)         0.000000                 2.000000
         4)       750.000000                 0.000000

     NO. ITERATIONS =      3
     DO RANGE(SENSITIVITY) ANALYSIS?
     > YES

     RANGES IN WHICH THE BASIS IS UNCHANGED
                    OBJ COEFFICIENT RANGES
     VARIABLE     CURRENT      ALLOWABLE     ALLOWABLE
                   COEF        INCREASE      DECREASE
        X1       20.000000     4.000000      12.000000
        X2       40.000000    60.000000       6.666667

                  RIGHTHAND SIDE RANGES
        ROW      CURRENT      ALLOWABLE     ALLOWABLE
                   RHS        INCREASE      DECREASE
         2     1800.000000   1200.000000    300.000000
         3     1000.000000    100.000000    400.000000
         4     3750.000000     INFINITY     750.000000
```

Interpret the computer output in language that would be understandable to Ancient's management.

Suppose that plastic is now used to refurbish clocks and stoves. Each clock needs 12 ounces of this material, while a stove requires 8 ounces. Ancient can buy no more than 400 pounds of plastic per month with the current budget. All other conditions will remain the same. Will this change alter Ancient's optimal product mix? Explain.

13. Refer back to Millips Oil Company's blending problem (Management Situation 9.2). By using the *LINDO* computer package to solve the linear program for this problem, the decision maker will obtain the output on page 421.

Interpret the computer output in language that would be understandable to Millips's management.

Suppose that the company can purchase a new crude oil (type C) to include in the blend of the Wear Prevention additive. A gallon of type C crude oil costs 18 cents and has 15 percent of compound JT and 30 percent of WY. All other conditions are the same as in the original problem. Should Millips purchase the new type of oil? Explain.

```
                        LP OPTIMUM FOUND AT STEP
                        OBJECTIVE FUNCTION VALUE
          1)     1700.00000
       VARIABLE          VALUE            REDUCED COST
          X1         2000.000000            0.000000
          X2         7000.000000            0.000000

       ROW      SLACK OR SURPLUS        DUAL PRICES
          2)         0.000000            -.400000
          3)         0.000000            -.300000

       NO. ITERATIONS =      2
       DO RANGE(SENSITIVITY) ANALYSIS?
       > YES

       RANGES IN WHICH THE BASIS IS UNCHANGED
                        OBJ COEFFICIENT RANGES
       VARIABLE     CURRENT     ALLOWABLE     ALLOWABLE
                     COEF       INCREASE      DECREASE
          X1        .150000      .150000       .100000
          X2        .200000      .400000       .100000

                       RIGHTHAND SIDE RANGES
       ROW        CURRENT      ALLOWABLE     ALLOWABLE
                    RHS        INCREASE      DECREASE
        2       2000.000000   7000.000000    500.000000
        3       3000.000000   1000.000000   2333.333333
```

14. Do you agree or disagree with each of the following statements? Explain.
    a. A shadow price is the same as an accounting, or nominal, cost, such as a wage or interest payment.
    b. The dual of the dual is the primal.
    c. If the primal is an unbounded problem, then the dual will have no feasible solution.
    d. The dual plays no role in postoptimality analysis.
    e. The dual is a form of sensitivity analysis.
    f. The optimal values of the dual variables remain the same for changes that are within the various ranges of optimality.
    g. The range of feasibility's upper and lower limits each result in degeneracy.

Technique Exercises

15. You are given the following product mix problem:

    maximize $Z = \$13X_1 + \$8X_2$

    subject to $4X_1 + X_2 \le 48$ units   (Resource A)

                            $3X_1 + 2X_2 \le 72$ units   (Resource B)

                            $X_1, X_2 \ge 0$

    where $Z =$ the total profit, $X_1 =$ the number of units of product 1, and $X_2 =$ the number of units of product 2. Find the optimal shadow prices graphically.

16. Management Situation 7.7 involves a problem that can be represented with the following linear program:

maximize $A = 400,000TV + 150,000MG$

subject to $\$20,000TV + \$5,000MG \leq \$200,000$ (Budget)

$TV \leq 12$ (Maximum television)

$TV \geq 4$ (Minimum television)

$MG \geq 6$ (Minimum magazine)

$TV, MG \geq 0$

where $A =$ the total audience exposure, $TV =$ the number of evening television spots, and $MG =$ the number of large magazine ads.
   Find the optimal shadow prices graphically.

17. Management Situation 7.8 involves a problem that can be described with the following linear program:

minimize $BC = \$8ZA + \$9.60OR$

subject to $0.24ZA + 0.20OR \geq 10$ pounds   (Potassium)

$0.12ZA + 0.18OR \geq 8$ pounds   (Calcium)

$0.22ZA + 0.15OR \geq 10$ pounds   (Potash)

$\$8ZA + \$9.60OR \leq \$1,000$ (Budget)

$-3ZA + OR \leq 0$ (Experiment)

$ZA, OR \geq 0$

where $BC =$ total cost of blending the experimental herb, $ZA =$ the pounds of zaleum in the blend, and $OR =$ the pounds of oritung in the blend.
   Find the optimal shadow prices graphically.

18. You are given the following production technique problem:

minimize $Z = \$10X_1 + \$200X_2$

subject to $200X_1 + 400X_2 \geq 2,000$ hours   (Contract)

$X_1 + X_2 = 20$ units   (Order)

$X_1 \geq 5$ units   (Policy)

$X_1, X_2 \geq 0$

where $Z =$ the total production cost, $X_1 =$ the units produced by the Anderson method, and $X_2 =$ the units produced by the Johnson method.
   Find the optimal shadow prices graphically.

19. You are given the following blending problem:

minimize $Z = \$60X_1 + \$20X_2 + \$75X_3$

subject to

$$20X_1 + 8X_2 + 10X_3 \geq 275 \text{ units} \qquad \text{(Compound A)}$$

$$5X_1 + 2X_2 + 10X_3 \geq 250 \text{ units} \qquad \text{(Compound B)}$$

$$X_1, X_2, X_3 \geq 0$$

where Z = the total cost, X_1 = the number of units of ingredient 1, X_2 = the number of units of ingredient 2, and X_3 = the number of units of ingredient 3.

Formulate the dual and solve it graphically. Interpret the optimal values of the dual variables.

20. Consider the following resource allocation problem:

maximize

$$Z = \$10X_1 + \$20X_2 + \$30X_3$$

subject to

$$X_1 + 4X_2 + 5X_3 \leq 70 \text{ hours} \qquad \text{(Labor)}$$

$$2X_1 + 4X_2 + 10X_3 \leq 100 \text{ hours} \qquad \text{(Capital)}$$

$$X_1, X_2, X_3 \geq 0$$

where Z = the revenue from gizmos, X_1 = the number of units produced by the economy method, X_2 = the number of units produced by the regular method, and X_3 = the number of units produced by the quality method. You are given the following optimal simplex table for this problem:

Variables		X_1	X_2	X_3	S_1	S_2	
Basis	C_j	$\$10$	$\$20$	$\$30$	$\$0$	$\$0$	Amounts
X_2	$\$20$	0	1	0	$\frac{1}{2}$	$-\frac{1}{4}$	10
X_1	$\$10$	1	0	5	-1	1	30
	Z_j	$\$10$	$\$20$	$\$50$	$\$0$	$\$5$	$\$500$
	$C_j - Z_j$	$\$0$	$\$0$	$-\$10$	$\$0$	$-\$5$	

In this table, S_1 represents unused labor hours and S_2 gives unused capital hours.

Formulate the dual linear program, and determine the optimal dual solution from this optimal simplex table. Do you notice anything unusual? Explain. Interpret the optimal values of the dual variables.

21. Refer back to Ancient Enterprises' product mix problem (Management Situation 9.1).
a. Show how Figure 9.1 was developed.
b. Develop graphs similar to Figure 9.2 for the company's iron and machine constraints.
c. Show how Tables 9.1 and 9.4 were derived.

22. Refer back to Millips Oil Company's blending problem (Management Situation 9.2).
a. Show how Table 9.6 was derived.
b. Develop a graphic interpretation of the shadow price concept for each system constraint in this problem. Use Figure 9.2 as a guide in the development.

23. Consider the sales problem of a local ice cream parlor:

maximize $Z = \$.20X_1 + \$.30X_2 + \$.40X_3$

subject to $4X_1 + 2X_2 + 2X_3 \leq 800$ units   (Ingredient A)

$8X_2 + 4X_3 \leq 400$ units   (Ingredient B)

$X_1, X_2, X_3 \geq 0$

where Z = profit, X_1 = the number of containers of vanilla ice cream sold, X_2 = the number of containers of chocolate ice cream sold, and X_3 = the number of containers of butterscotch ice cream sold.

a. Formulate the standard form of this primal program.
b. Formulate the dual linear program and its standard form.
c. Solve the dual graphically.
d. Use the primal-dual relationships and the principles of complementary slackness to find the optimal primal solution.

24. You are given the following staff-scheduling problem:

minimize $Z = \$30X_1 + \$45X_2 + \$70X_3$

subject to $X_1 + 2X_2 + 3X_3 \geq 3000$ hours   (Project A)

$2X_1 + X_2 + 6X_3 \geq 3000$ hours   (Project B)

$X_1, X_2, X_3 \geq 0$

where Z = cost, X_1 = the number of units of output by group 1, X_2 = the number of units of output by group 2, and X_3 = the number of units of output by group 3.

a. Formulate the standard form of this primal linear program.
b. Formulate the dual linear program and its standard form.
c. Solve the dual graphically.
d. Use the primal-dual relationships and the principles of complementary slackness to find the optimal primal solution.

25. Refer back to Country Farm's resource allocation problem (Management Situation 9.3).

a. Show how Table 9.7 was derived.
b. Show how Figure 9.4 was developed.
c. Show how Tables 9.9 and 9.10 were developed.
d. Show how Figures 9.5 and 9.6 were derived.
e. Set up the dual linear program for this problem.
f. Use the results from Table 9.7, the primal-dual relationships, and the principles of complementary slackness to find the optimal dual solution.

26. Again refer to Management Situation 9.3.

a. Show how the range of optimality for cotton's unit profit contribution was determined.
b. Suppose unfavorable market conditions decrease cotton's unit profit contribution from $50 to $20. How will this change affect Country's plans? Explain.

c. Show how the range of feasibility for available people-hours was determined.
d. Suppose that Country is thinking about adding a soybean crop. It would take two people-hours to plant one acre of soybeans. Yet each acre of the crop would provide a $60 profit. All other conditions are the same as in the original problem. Should management plant soybeans? Explain.

27. Management Situation 8.1's problem is represented by the following linear program:

maximize $\qquad$ $Z = \$2X_1 + \$3X_2$

subject to $\qquad$ $9X_1 + 15X_2 \leq 108,000$ minutes $\qquad$ (Assembly)

$\qquad\qquad\quad$ $11X_1 + 5X_2 \leq 108,000$ minutes $\qquad$ (Packaging)

$\qquad\qquad\quad$ $X_1, X_2 \geq 0$

where $Z =$ Daspling's total dollar profit, $X_1 =$ boxes of Little League baseballs, and $X_2 =$ boxes of Major League baseballs.
a. Graphically find the range of optimality for the Major League baseball profit contribution.
b. Suppose that favorable market conditions increase the Major League baseball profit to $4.50 per box. What will be the effect on the optimal solution?
c. Graphically find the range of feasibility for assembly time.
d. Suppose that a fire reduces Daspling's assembly capacity to 97,000 minutes. What will be the effect on the optimal product mix?
e. Suppose that it takes 9 (instead of 11) minutes to package a box of Little League baseballs. Graphically illustrate the effect of this change on the optimal solution.

28. Management Situation 8.2's problem is represented with the following linear program:

maximize $\qquad$ $Z = \$6X_1 + \$2.50X_2$

subject to $\qquad$ $\$20X_1 + \$10X_2 \leq \$300,000$ $\qquad$ (Budget)

$\qquad\qquad\quad$ $X_2 \geq 10,000$ hours $\qquad$ (Journeymen)

$\qquad\qquad\quad$ $2X_1 - X_2 \leq 5,000$ hours $\qquad$ (Union)

$\qquad\qquad\quad$ $X_1, X_2 \geq 0$

where $Z =$ Shock's total dollar profit, $X_1 =$ additional master hours employed, and $X_2 =$ additional journeyman hours employed.
a. Graphically find the range of optimality for additional master hours employed.
b. Suppose that declining worker abilities reduce the master profit to $5.75 per hour. What will be the effect on the optimal solution?
c. Graphically find the range of feasibility for the budget.
d. Suppose that a windfall increases Shock's budget to $350,000. What will be the effect on the work force plan?
e. Suppose journeymen's earnings become $12 (rather than $10) per hour. Graphically illustrate the effect of this change on the optimal solution.

29. Management Situation 8.3's problem is represented by the following linear program:

minimize $\qquad\qquad\qquad$ $Z = \$5,000X_1 + \$3,000X_2$

subject to
$$30X_1 + 50X_2 \geq 300 \text{ tons} \quad \text{(Premium)}$$
$$90X_1 + 25X_2 \geq 600 \text{ tons} \quad \text{(Standard)}$$
$$X_1, X_2 \geq 0$$

where Z = Northeastern's total operating cost, X_1 = days of operation for the Alpha shaft, and X_2 = days of operation for the Beta mine.

a. Graphically find the range of optimality for the Alpha shaft's daily operating cost.
b. Suppose that improved technology reduces the operating cost in the Alpha shaft to $4,700 per day. What will be the effect on the optimal solution?
c. Graphically find the range of feasibility for standard grade coal's requirement.
d. Suppose that a new contract decreases the minimum standard grade requirement to 540 tons. What will be the effect on the optimal mining plan?
e. Suppose that an accident causes the Beta mine to average 42 (rather than 50) tons of premium coal per day. Graphically illustrate the effect of this change on the optimal solution.

30. Management Situation 8.4's problem can be represented with the following linear program:

maximize
$$Z = \$30X_1 + \$20X_2$$

subject to
$$X_1 \leq 2,000 \text{ units} \quad \text{(Process 1)}$$
$$X_2 \leq 2,000 \text{ units} \quad \text{(Process 2)}$$
$$X_1 + X_2 \leq 4,000 \text{ units} \quad \text{(Process 3)}$$
$$X_1, X_2 \geq 0$$

where Z = the total dollar profit, X_1 = units of product A, and X_2 = units of product B.

a. Graphically find the range of optimality for product B's unit profit.
b. Suppose that product B's profit decreases to $12 per unit. What will be the effect on the optimal solution?
c. Graphically find the range of feasibility for Process 3's amount.
d. Suppose that Process 3's maximum amount increases to 4,500 units. What will be the effect on the optimal production plan?

31. Quality Products, Inc., has the product mix problem represented by the following linear program:

maximize
$$Z = \$20X_1 + \$40X_2$$

subject to
$$3X_1 + 5X_2 \leq 1,800 \text{ hours} \quad \text{(Labor)}$$
$$X_1 + 5X_2 \leq 1,000 \text{ hours} \quad \text{(Capital)}$$
$$X_1, X_2 \geq 0$$

where Z = the total monthly profit, X_1 = the quantity of product A, and X_2 = the quantity of product B. The optimal simplex table for this program is as follows, where S_1 represents unused labor hours and S_2 gives unused capital hours.

Variables		X_1	X_2	S_1	S_2	
Basis	C_j	$20	$40	$0	$0	Amounts
X_1	$20	1	0	$\frac{1}{2}$	$-\frac{1}{2}$	400
X_2	$40	0	1	$-\frac{1}{10}$	$\frac{3}{10}$	120
	Z_j	$20	$40	$6	$2	$12,800
	$C_j - Z_j$	$0	$0	$-$6	$-$2	

a. Find the range of optimality for the profit per unit of product A.
b. Suppose that the profit per unit of product A decreases to $10. What will be the effect on the optimal solution? Suppose that the profit per unit of product A decreases to $6. What will be the effect on the optimal solution?
c. Find the range of optimality for the profit per unit of product B.
d. Suppose that the profit per unit of product B increases to $80. What will be the effect on the optimal solution? Suppose that the profit per unit of product B increases to $120. What will be the effect on the optimal solution?
e. Find the ranges of feasibility for labor and capital hours.
f. Suppose that it takes five (instead of three) labor hours to produce a unit of product A. Graphically illustrate the effect of this change on the optimal solution.

32. Mertz Components, Inc., will soon begin making and selling a new stereo model at its Archadelphia plant. The product-marketing plan calls for distribution through department stores, a national chain of stereo shops, and discount retail stores. Mertz gets $25 profit from a sale in department stores, $30 from a sale in the chain, and $15 from a sale in the discount stores. The product is promoted with advertising and sales force effort. It takes an estimated $5 of advertising to get a department store sale, $10 of advertising for a sale in the chain shop, and $4 of advertising for the discount store sale. The sales force spends an estimated two hours of effort on this product in department stores, one hour in chain shops, and four hours in the discount stores. Advertising and sales force figures are based on past experience with similar products. Mertz expects to have an advertising budget of $20,000 per month for the new stereo. The sales manager will also allocate 10,000 hours of sales force time per month for the new product. Mertz wants to know how many stereos should be distributed through each outlet in order to maximize monthly profits.

The optimal simplex table for this problem is presented as follows, where S_1 denotes the unused advertising dollars and S_2 the idle hours of sales effort.

Variables		X_1	X_2	X_3	S_1	S_2	
Basis	C_j	$25	$30	$15	$0	$0	Amounts
X_1	$25	1	2	$\frac{4}{5}$	$\frac{1}{5}$	0	4,000
S_2	$0	0	-3	$\frac{12}{5}$	$-\frac{2}{5}$	1	2,000
	Z_j	$25	$50	$20	$5	$0	$100,000
	$C_j - Z_j$	$0	$-$20	$-$5	$-$5	$0	

a. Show how the optimal simplex table was derived.

b. Find the range of optimality for the profit per stereo sold through department stores.

c. Suppose that the profit per department store sale increases to $50. What will be the effect on the optimal solution? Suppose that the profit per department store sale decreases to $15. What will be the effect on the optimal solution?

d. Find the range of optimality for the profit per stereo sold through chain shops.

e. Suppose that the profit per chain shop sale increases to $45. What will be the effect on the optimal solution?

f. Find the range of optimality for the profit per stereo sold through discount stores.

g. Suppose that the profit per discount store sale increases to $30. What will be the effect on the optimal solution?

h. Find the ranges of feasibility for advertising dollars and hours of sales force effort.

33. Millips Oil Company's blending problem is given in Management Situation 9.2 as

$$\text{minimize} \qquad Z = \$0.15X_1 + \$0.20X_2$$

$$\text{subject to} \qquad 0.3X_1 + 0.2X_2 \geq 2,000 \text{ gallons} \qquad (JT)$$

$$0.1X_1 + 0.4X_2 \geq 3,000 \text{ gallons} \qquad (WY)$$

$$X_1, X_2 \geq 0$$

where $Z =$ the total daily purchase cost, $X_1 =$ the number of gallons of type A crude oil, and $X_2 =$ the number of gallons of type B crude oil. The optimal simplex table (Table 9.6) for the problem is reproduced as follows, where S_1 measures the surplus gallons of JT, S_2 gives the surplus gallons of WY, and A_1 and A_2 are artificial variables.

Variables		X_1	X_2	S_1	S_2	A_1	A_2	
Basis	C_j	$0.15	$0.20	$0	$0	$M	$M	**Amounts**
X_1	$0.15	1	0	−4	2	4	−2	2,000
X_2	$0.20	0	1	1	−3	−1	3	7,000
	Z_j	$0.15	$0.20	−$0.40	−$0.30	$0.40	$0.30	$1,700
	$C_j - Z_j$	$0	$0	$0.40	$0.30	$M−$0.40	$M−$0.30	

a. Find the range of optimality for the cost per gallon of type A crude oil.

b. Suppose that the cost per gallon of type A crude oil increases to 20 cents. What will be the effect on the optimal solution? Suppose that the cost per gallon of type A crude oil increases to 30 cents. What will be the effect on the optimal solution?

c. Find the range of optimality for the cost per gallon of type B crude oil.

d. Suppose that the cost per gallon of type B crude oil decreases to 5 cents. What will be the effect on the optimal solution?

e. Find the ranges of feasibility for gallons of compounds JT and WY.

f. Suppose that each gallon of type B crude oil has 20 percent (instead of 40 percent) of compound WY. Graphically illustrate the effect of this change on the optimal solution.

Computer Exercises

34. Management Situation 7.6's problem is represented with the following linear program:

minimize

$$JC = \$220X_{11} + \$176X_{12} + \$264X_{13} + \$88X_{14} + \$396X_{15} + \$704X_{16}$$

$$+ \$168X_{21} + \$144X_{22} + \$384X_{23} + \$72X_{24} + \$312X_{25} + \$600X_{26}$$

$$+ \$350X_{31} + \$225X_{32} + \$225X_{33} + \$125X_{34} + \$500X_{35} + \$700X_{36}$$

$$+ \$108X_{41} + \$126X_{42} + \$180X_{43} + \$36X_{44} + \$630X_{45} + \$756X_{46}$$

$$+ \$330X_{51} + \$300X_{52} + \$360X_{53} + \$180X_{54} + \$450X_{55} + \$720X_{56}$$

$$+ \$180X_{61} + \$220X_{62} + \$240X_{63} + \$80X_{64} + \$320X_{65} + \$760X_{66}$$

subject to $X_{11} + X_{12} + X_{13} + X_{14} + X_{15} + X_{16} = 1$ for Davis

$\qquad\quad X_{21} + X_{22} + X_{23} + X_{24} + X_{25} + X_{26} = 1$ for Florino

$\qquad\quad X_{31} + X_{32} + X_{33} + X_{34} + X_{35} + X_{36} = 1$ for Lippincott

$\qquad\quad X_{41} + X_{42} + X_{43} + X_{44} + X_{45} + X_{46} = 1$ for Thomas

$\qquad\quad X_{51} + X_{52} + X_{53} + X_{54} + X_{55} + X_{56} = 1$ for Torrez

$\qquad\quad X_{61} + X_{62} + X_{63} + X_{64} + X_{65} + X_{66} = 1$ for Webber

$\qquad\quad X_{11} + X_{21} + X_{31} + X_{41} + X_{51} + X_{61} = 1$ for the DB job

$\qquad\quad X_{12} + X_{22} + X_{32} + X_{42} + X_{52} + X_{62} = 1$ for the EIS job

$\qquad\quad X_{13} + X_{23} + X_{33} + X_{43} + X_{53} + X_{63} = 1$ for the WP job

$\qquad\quad X_{14} + X_{24} + X_{34} + X_{44} + X_{54} + X_{64} = 1$ for the E-Mail job

$\qquad\quad X_{15} + X_{25} + X_{35} + X_{45} + X_{55} + X_{65} = 1$ for the ISA job

$\qquad\quad X_{16} + X_{26} + X_{36} + X_{46} + X_{56} + X_{66} = 1$ for the ACC job

$\qquad\quad X_{ij} = 1$ or 0 for all i and j

where JC = Raycot's total cost of completing all current jobs and X_{ij} = the assignment of specialist i to job j. Also $X_{ij} = 1$ if the specialist is assigned and 0 otherwise; i = a code with a value of 1 for Davis, 2 for Florino, 3 for Lippincott, 4 for Thomas, 5 for Torrez, and 6 for Webber; and j = a code with a value of 1 for the DB, 2 for EIS, 3 for WP, 4 for E-Mail, 5 for ISA, and 6 for the ACC job.

a. Solve this problem with the **QUANTITATIVE MANAGEMENT (QM)** software.
b. Find the range of optimality for the X_{42} cost coefficient (for the cost of assigning Thomas to the EIS job).
c. Suppose that a training program reduces the cost of assigning Thomas to the EIS job by $24. What will be the effect on the optimal solution?
d. Find the range of feasibility for Torrez.
e. Suppose that a new employee can be assigned to the WP job at a cost of $123, to the E-Mail job at a cost of $480, or to the ACC job at a cost of $235. This person cannot do any other job. How would this change alter the original optimal solution?

35. Management Situation 7.4's problem is represented with the following linear program:

maximize

$$TP = \$20A + \$11A + \$30M + \$21M$$

subject to

$OA + IA + OM + IM \le 9,000,000$ pounds	(Plant capacity)
$OA + IA \le 7,000,000$ pounds	(Maximum ash demand)
$OM + IM \le 6,000,000$ pounds	(Maximum mineral demand)
$OA + IA \ge 4,000,000$ pounds	(Minimum ash supply)
$.40OA - .60IA \le 0$	(Ash blend)
$.50IM - .50OM \ge 0$	(Mineral blend lower limit)
$.25IM - .75OM \le 0$	(Mineral blend upper limit)
$OA, IA, OM, IM \ge 0$	

where TP = the city's total profit, OA = the pounds of processed organic waste in high-grade ash, IA = the pounds of processed inorganic waste in high-grade ash, OM = the pounds of processed organic waste in the mineral compound, and IM = the pounds of processed inorganic waste in the mineral compound.

a. Solve this problem with the **QM** software.

b. Find the range of optimality for the per-pound profit of processed organic waste in the mineral compound.

c. Suppose that favorable economic and political conditions increase the per-pound profit of processed inorganic waste in high-grade ash by 25 cents. What will be the effect on the optimal solution?

d. Find the range of feasibility for the maximum mineral demand.

e. Suppose that fertilizer purchasers' ash demand drops to 6.4 million pounds. What will be the effect on the optimal solution?

f. Suppose that, to meet chemical companies' new needs, processed inorganic waste must constitute at least 55 percent (instead of 50 percent) but no more than 68 percent (rather than 75 percent) of the compound's blend by weight. How will this change affect the optimal solution?

g. Suppose that new federally imposed environmental standards require the city to process an exact balance between organic and inorganic waste.

36. Management Situation 7.3's problem is represented with the following linear program:

minimize $SC = \$100Q_1 + \$120Q_2 + \$90Q_3 + \$110Q_4$

$$+ \$12(U_1 + U_2 + U_3 + U_4) + \$3(D_1 + D_2 + D_3 + D_4)$$

$$+ \$5I_1 + \$6I_2 + \$4.50I_3 + \$5.50I_4$$

subject to	$Q_1 - I_1 = 2,000,000$ tons	(Quarter 1 balance)
	$I_1 + Q_2 - I_2 = 4,000,000$ tons	(Quarter 2 balance)

$$I_2 + Q_3 - I_3 = 3,000,000 \text{ tons} \qquad \text{(Quarter 3 balance)}$$

$$I_3 + Q_4 - I_4 = 4,500,000 \text{ tons} \qquad \text{(Quarter 4 balance)}$$

$$Q_1 - U_1 + D_1 = 3,000,000 \text{ tons} \qquad \text{(Quarter 1 change)}$$

$$Q_2 - Q_1 - U_2 + D_2 = 0 \qquad \text{(Quarter 2 change)}$$

$$Q_3 - Q_2 - U_3 + D_3 = 0 \qquad \text{(Quarter 3 change)}$$

$$Q_4 - Q_3 - U_4 + D_4 = 0 \qquad \text{(Quarter 4 change)}$$

$$I_4 \leq 4,000 \text{ tons} \qquad \text{(Inventory)}$$

$$Q_j, U_j, D_j, I_j \geq 0 \qquad \text{for all } j$$

where SC = the total cost of fulfilling Honsha's steel contracts, Q_j = the tons of steel manufactured in quarter j, U_j = the increase (change up) in the tons of steel manufactured during quarter j, D_j = the decrease (change down) in the tons of steel manufactured during quarter j, I_j = the tons of steel in inventory at the end of quarter j, and the subscript j = a code with a value of 1 for quarter 1, 2 for quarter 2, 3 for quarter 3, and 4 for quarter 4.

a.   Solve this problem with the **QM** software.
b.   Find the range of optimality for the per-ton cost of manufacturing steel in quarter 3.
c.   Suppose that poor employee-management relations increase the per-ton cost of manufacturing steel in quarter 2 by $11.50. What will be the effect on the optimal solution?
d.   Find the range of feasibility for the quarter 4 inventory limit.
e.   Suppose that quarter 3 steel demand drops by 250,000 tons. What will be the effect on the optimal solution?

37. Management Situation 7.2's problem is represented with the following linear program:

maximize $DP = \$.23GP + \$.28SM + \$.15HS - .03B$

subject to $.16GP + .12SM + .18HS \leq 400,000 \text{ hours}$ (Milking)

$.03GP + .045SM + .04HS \leq 80,000 \text{ hours}$ (Inspection)

$.08GP + .06SM + .05HS \leq 150,000 \text{ hours}$ (Packaging)

$B \leq \$300,000$ (Credit)

$\$.65GP + \$.54SM + \$.87HS - B \leq \$50,000$ (Funds)

$-\$.23GP - \$.28SM - \$.15HS + 3.12B \leq \$50,000$ (Acid-test)

$HS - GP - SM \geq 0$ (Distributor)

$.80GP - .20SM - .20HS \geq 0$ (Promotion)

$GP, SM, HS, B \geq 0$

where DP = the cooperative's total profit, GP = gallons of Green Pastures processed during the production period, SM = gallons of Savemuch processed during the production period, HS = gallons of Health Stores processed during the production period, and B = dollars borrowed from Midland during the production period.

a. Solve this problem with the **QM** software.

b. Find the range of optimality for the per-gallon profit from Health Stores.

c. Suppose that unfavorable economic conditions decrease the per-gallon profit from Savemuch by 6 cents. What will be the effect on the optimal solution?

d. Find the range of feasibility for packaging capacity.

e. Suppose that improved technology increases inspection capacity to 100,000 hours. What will be the effect on the optimal solution?

f. Suppose that, for a new promotion, Lincoln wants Green Pastures to constitute at least 24 (rather than 20) percent of all brand offerings. How will this change affect the optimal solution?

g. Suppose that a new branch will have a processing cost of 61 cents and sell for 82 cents per gallon. Each gallon will require 0.175 hours of milking, 0.029 hours of inspection, and 0.064 hours of packaging capacity. Should the cooperative introduce the new brand?

38. Management Situation 7.5's problem is represented with the following linear program:

minimize $TC = \$2.50X_{11} + \$4X_{12} + \$X_{13} + \$1.75X_{14}$

$$+ \$4.25X_{21} + \$2X_{22} + \$4X_{23} + \$2.25X_{24}$$

$$+ \$2.75X_{31} + \$3X_{32} + \$2X_{33} + \$4.50X_{34}$$

subject to $X_{11} + X_{12} + X_{13} + X_{14} = 64,000$ linear feet   (Davendale)

$X_{21} + X_{22} + X_{23} + X_{24} = 48,000$ linear feet   (Swinson)

$X_{31} + X_{32} + X_{33} + X_{34} = 55,000$ linear feet   (Oldtown)

$X_{11} + X_{21} + X_{31} = 50,000$ linear feet   (Springfield)

$X_{12} + X_{22} + X_{32} = 47,000$ linear feet   (Manchester)

$X_{13} + X_{23} + X_{33} = 30,000$ linear feet   (Yorkville)

$X_{14} + X_{24} + X_{34} = 40,000$ linear feet   (Jessup)

$X_{ij} \geq 0$ for all i and j

where TC = the total cost of shipping the panels and X_{ij} = the linear feet of panels shipped from dealer i to store/outlet j. Also, i = a code with a value of 1 for the Davendale dealer, 2 for the Swinson dealer, and 3 for the Oldtown dealer, while j = a code with a value of 1 for the Springfield store, 2 for the Manchester store, 3 for the Yorkville outlet, and 4 for the Jessup outlet.

a. Solve this problem with the **QM** software.

b. Find the range of optimality for the X_{21} cost coefficient (for the cost of shipping a panel from the Swinson dealer to the Springfield store).

c. Suppose that deregulation reduces the cost of shipping a panel from the Davendale dealer to the Yorkville outlet by 37 cents. What will be the effect on the optimal solution?

d. Find the range of feasibility for the Oldtown dealer's supply.

e. Suppose that the Springfield store increases its orders by 13,000 linear feet. How would this change alter the original optimal solution?

f. Suppose that a new franchise agreement requires only the Swinson and Oldtown dealers to supply the orders from the Yorkville and Jessup outlets. How would this change alter the original optimal solution?

39. Ansco Enterprises manufactures two basic product groups: transformers and towers. There are five basic machines and/or stages of production for the entire range of products manufactured at the company. The equipment/stages consist of a milling machine, a lathe, a painting station, an assembly stage, and the final inspection of the product.

Currently, management is interested in planning production for the company's basic transformer line. The line consists of models A, B, and C transformers. Relevant production data for these lines are summarized below.

Equipment/Stage	Production Time Per Batch (Minutes)			Time Available (Minutes)
	A	B	C	
Mill	70	76	46	2,400
Lathe	60	56	36	3,000
Painting	60	70	50	3,200
Assembly	42	48	30	2,600
Inspection	70	70	50	2,200
Profit Per Batch	$500	$480	$650	

Moreover, Ansco has standing orders for 10 model As, 20 model Bs, and 1 model C every month. Research also indicates that there is a potential demand for 40 model As, 60 model Bs, and 50 model Cs per month.

Management wants to determine the transformer combination that would maximize total profit. In addition, it seeks the value of the resources (machines and stages) used to generate the best profit. Furthermore, management would like to know how sensitive the solution may be to changes in the production and demand data. Use the **QM** software to obtain the required information.

40. J. J. Brown and P. George are the owners and operators of Bluegrass Stables, where they breed racing horses. Four ingredients are mixed into a feed formula that provides the essential nutrients for the animals' health. Various formulas will meet the animals' nutritional needs. The relevant data is summarized below.

Nutrient	Feed Formula (Ounces)					Nutritional Requirement (Ounces)
	1	2	3	4	5	
Potassium	3.5	3.3	3.1	3.7	3.9	1,000
Calcium	4.4	4.1	5.0	5.3	4.6	1,400
Iron	5.2	5.8	6.1	6.0	5.8	2,000
Cost per Ounce	$0.037	$0.034	$0.036	$0.038	$0.033	

Currently, Bluegrass has 200 pounds each of feed formulas 1, 2, and 3 and 100 pounds each of formula 4 and 5 available.

The owners seek the formula mix that will provide the least costly horse diet. They also seek the cost savings possible from a plan that would lower nutriental requirements while maintaining the animals' health. Moreover, the owners would like to know how sensitive the solution may be to changes in nutrient and feed availability data. Use the **QM** software to generate the required information.

41. A local merchant is planning a marketing strategy for a new brand of lawn tractor. The merchant knows that sales will depend on advertising, store displays, inventory, and the product's markup. The merchant expects two sales for every $1000 invested in inventory, and she has budgeted $25,000 for these purposes. On the other hand, each 10 percent increase in the tractor markup is expected to lower sales by three units. The tractor distributor allows a markup of between 25 and 50 percent.

There are other restrictions to consider. Local media will not place ads unless the merchant contracts for a minimum of $5,000 in advertising. In addition, the merchant wants the combined store display and advertising expenditure to be at least 60 percent of the inventory investment.

The merchant seeks the strategy that will maximize total profit. She also wants to determine the relative importance of each restriction. Furthermore, the merchant would like to know how sensitive the solution may be to changes in her parameter estimates. Use the **QM** software to develop the required information.

42. The Department of Defense is faced with a decision on purchasing more planes for the armed services. These planes will be required to provide at least 800 sorties per day over a period of two years. The aircraft, their capabilities, and costs are summarized below.

Plane	Capabilities (Sorties Per Day)	Purchase Cost ($ Million)	Operating Cost ($ Per Flying Hour)
F-16	2.4	15	3,200
F-14	2.0	20	4,500
A-92	3.4	10	2,400
A-57	2.8	12	3,000

Defense Department officials estimate that each type of plane will fly about five hours per day. Based on this estimate, these officials have budgeted no more than $7.5 million for daily flying expenses.

Each branch of the service favors one type of plane. However, Defense Department officials are looking for the mix of planes that would keep everyone relatively happy at a reasonable expenditure. The officials want the number of A planes to equal the quantity of F aircraft. Furthermore, these people feel that the number of A aircraft should be at least 40 percent of the total quantity.

The objective is to select the plane mix that would minimize the total purchase cost during the two-year planning period. Defense officials also seek the cost implications of the political restrictions placed on this objective. Moreover, the officials would like to test the sensitivity of the recommended solution. Use the **QM** software to obtain the desired information.

43. Overseas Shipping, Ltd. transports cargo on the H.M.S. Crimson for various exporters and importers. The Crimson has four main cargo holds: the lower forward (LF) and upper forward (UF) chambers and the lower stern (LS) and upper stern (US) chambers. Volume and weight capacities are summarized below.

	Capacity	
Hold	Volume (Thousands of Cubic Feet)	Weight (Tons)
Lower forward	50	1,800
Upper forward	60	1,200
Lower stern	30	600
Upper stern	40	800

To keep the Crimson trim while sailing, the sum of the tonnage in the forward holds must account for exactly half of the total tonnage in all cargo holds.

Currently, the Crimson is taking on fruit and vegetables destined for a foreign market. Relevant shipping data are summarized below.

	Volume (Cubic Foot per Ton)				Maximum Load (Tons)	Profit Per Ton ($)
Cargo	LF	UF	LS	US		
Bananas	100	100	100	100	1,200	325
Potatoes	75	75	75	75	1,600	190
Apples	50	50	50	50	1,000	410

Management seeks the cargo-loading plan that will maximize profit from the fruit and vegetable shipment. These people also want to know the profit potential from expanding hold capacities and from encouraging larger shipments. In addition, management would like to test the sensitivity of the recommended solution. Use the **QM** software to generate the desired information.

44. Refer back to Thought Exercise 4 in Chapter 7.
    a. Solve this problem with the **QM** software.
    b. Find the range of optimality for Jacobson's per-hour savings account load.
    c. Suppose that a training program enables Santini to increase his checking account load by 15 customers per hour. What will be the effect on the optimal solution?
    d. Find the range of feasibility for loan notes.
    e. Suppose the bank introduces a new account that Samuels can process at the rate of 50 customers per hour and that Martinez can process at the rate of 40 customers per hour. No other person can handle this account. How would this change alter the original optimal solution?

45. Refer back to Thought Exercise 5 in Chapter 7.
    a. Solve this problem with the **QM** software.
    b. Find the range of optimality for polystyrene's per-pound cost.
    c. Suppose that a new contract enables Rippon to purchase ABS for $1 per pound. What will be the effect on the optimal solution?
    d. Suppose that new tests indicate that strength losses will limit the blend to no more than 20 percent talc. How will this change affect the optimal solution?

46. Refer back to Thought Exercise 6 in Chapter 7.
  a. Solve this problem with the **QM** software.
  b. Find the range of optimality for operating cost per truck-day during a mild winter.
  c. Suppose that an unfavorable contract increases salt cost per truck-day $12 in a severe winter. What will be the effect on the optimal solution?
  d. Find the range of feasibility for the fleet's truck-day capacity.
  e. Suppose that a new computer-projection decreases the estimated truck-days required in a severe winter by 500. What will be the effect on the optimal solution?
  f. Suppose that, in a mild winter, 1 truck salting is equivalent to 1.25 (rather than 1.4) trucks plowing. How will this change affect the optimal solution?

47. Refer back to Thought Exercise 7 in Chapter 7.
  a. Solve this problem with the **QM** software.
  b. Find the range of optimality for sales per hundred dollars spent on promotion.
  c. Suppose that favorable market conditions enable General Foods to increase sales by five units for every hundred dollars spent on distribution. What will be the effect on the optimal solution?
  d. Find the range of feasibility for the total sales force.
  e. Suppose that the vice president gets an additional $50,000 budget. What will be the effect on the optimal solution?
  f. Suppose that new experiences with merchants indicate that distribution expenditures should account for between 28 (instead of 30) percent and 63 (rather than 60) percent of the total budget. How will this change affect the optimal solution?
  g. Suppose that James now believes that a successful marketing mix also has a pricing to promotion ratio of at least 5 percent. How will this new condition affect the optimal solution?

48. Refer back to Thought Exercise 8 in chapter 7.
  a. Solve this problem with the **QM** software.
  b. Find the range of optimality for the distance traveled from the Jefferson school to the South area.
  c. Suppose that a new road decreases the distance traveled between the Lincoln school and the East area by one-half mile. What will be the effect on the optimal solution?
  d. Find the range of feasibility for minority enrollment at the Washington school.
  e. Suppose that a new study indicates that Lincoln's minority enrollment must increase by 25 students. What will be the effect on the optimal solution?

Applications Exercises

49. Equity Security Corporation is a mutual fund. The corporation has just obtained $200,000 by converting industrial bonds to cash and is now looking for other investment opportunities for these funds. Equity's financial analysis department has identified three investment opportunities and has projected their annual rates of return. The information is summarized as follows:

Investment	Projected Annual Return (% of Investment)
Eastern Oil's preferred stock	9
Mammoth Steel's common stock	7
City of Los Angeles municipal bonds	6

Equity's management has imposed the following investment guidelines:

- Both types of stock should receive no more than 60 percent of the total new investment.

- Municipal bonds should receive no more than 20 percent of the stock investment plus $50,000.

- It is not necessary to invest the entire $200,000.

The company wants to know how much to invest in each type of opportunity so as to maximize total dollar return. Equity management is also interested in the planning aspects of this problem. Specifically, management would like to know

a. The additional dollar return that can be expected from an additional dollar of available funds.

b. The additional dollar return that can be expected from an additional dollar invested in stocks.

c. The additional dollar return that can be expected from an additional dollar invested in bonds.

Prepare a proposal that provides all the desired information.

50. Caliente Kennels, Inc., raises greyhound dogs for the dog races in Miami, Florida. This company is experimenting with a special diet for its race dogs. The feed components available for the diet are a standard dog feed product, a vitamin-enriched biscuit, and a new vitamin and mineral additive. Nutritional values and cost of each component are summarized as follows:

Diet Requirement	Units of Diet Ingredient per Pound of Feed Component		
	Standard	Enriched Biscuit	Additive
Ingredient A	0.3	0.4	0.6
Ingredient B	0.2	0.6	0.3
Ingredient C	0.2	0.1	0.1
Cost per pound	$0.30	$0.60	$1

The dog trainer sets the minimum daily diet requirement at 1.2 units of ingredient A, 1.2 units of ingredient B, and 0.4 unit of ingredient C.

Caliente Kennels's management wants to mix the feed components in a way that will produce the desired product at least cost. The company is also interested in the cost savings that can be realized from one-unit reductions in each of the three diet ingredients (A, B, and C).

Prepare a diet analysis that provides all the desired information.

51. Goodhope Army operates a specialty thrift shop that sells used carpeting, seconds (rejects from large mills), and damaged-freight carpeting. Each square yard of used carpeting yields a $2 profit, while seconds net $3 per square yard, and the damaged-freight merchandise earns $1 per square yard. This service organization has a policy of earning 50 percent markups on the wholesale costs of seconds and damaged-freight carpeting and 100 percent on used carpeting. The thrift shop can spend no more than its $36,000 projected purchase budget this year.

The thrift shop's operations are also limited by its available work force. It takes an estimated 0.4 peoplehour of work force effort to prepare and sell one square yard of used carpeting. Preparation includes collection, processing, and packaging. Selling includes sales force effort and invoicing. It takes 0.3 peoplehour for a square yard of seconds, and 0.6 hour per square yard of damaged-freight carpeting. The thrift shop will have a maximum of 6,000 people-hours available this year.

Goodhope Army is currently evaluating the thrift shop's operations. As part of the evaluation, Goodhope Army wants the following information:
   a.   The number of square yards of each type of carpeting that the shop should buy and the resulting maximum profit.
   b.   The effect of a proposed deal with an insurance company that would increase the profit from damaged-freight carpeting by $2 per square yard.
   c.   The effect of a proposed deal with a mill that would increase the profit from seconds by $3 per square yard.
   d.   The effect of unfavorable market conditions that would decrease the profit from used carpeting by $2.50 per square yard.
   e.   The range of the purchase budget over which the optimal purchase plan remains valid.
   f.   The range of the available work force over which the optimal purchase plan remains valid.

The manager of the thrift shop is asked to provide the desired information. What responses should be in her report?

52. The Silent Alarm Company is experiencing a tremendous growth in demand for its household burglar alarms. Silent produces both an AC-operated model and a battery-operated model. It has an opportunity to be the exclusive supplier for a major department store chain, the M. W. Panny Company. Panny wants at least 800 cartons of the AC model and 400 cartons of the battery model each week.

Previously, Silent manufactured all of its own products. However, the unanticipated opportunity has left the company with insufficient capacity to satisfy the Panny contract. There is a local subcontractor who can make the same type of alarms for Silent. The subcontractor will charge Silent $150 per carton of the AC model and $90 per carton of the battery model. Also, the subcontractor can supply any combination of AC and battery models up to 600 cartons total per week.

When Silent does its own work, it costs $120 to manufacture a carton of the AC model and $80 per carton of the battery model. Other manufacturing data are summarized in the following table:

Department	Hours Required per Carton of Each Model		Hours Available per Week
	AC	Battery	
Production	4	2	1,800
Packaging	2	4	2,400

Silent's management wants to determine the make-or-buy decision that will meet the contract demands at a minimum total cost. How many cartons of each model should be made and how many purchased?

Management is also interested in the sensitivity of the optimal solution to potential changes in the data. Specifically, the company wants to consider the following possibilities:

a. Suppose that labor negotiations increase the cost of making a battery model to $86. What is the effect on the optimal solution?

b. Suppose that increased efficiency allows the subcontractor to supply the battery model at $84 a carton. What is the effect on the optimal solution?

c. What department is limiting manufacturing volume?

d. Suppose that a plant accident decreases available production time to 1,650 hours. What is the effect on the optimal solution?

e. Suppose that increased efficiency allows the subcontractor to supply 700 cartons per week. What is the effect on the optimal solution?

f. How much would available packaging time have to decrease before there is an effect on the optimal solution?

Suppose that you are hired by Silent as a management consultant. How would you answer each of the company's questions?

53. Golden Age Senior Citizens Center advertises itself as a fun place to gather and have a healthy meal. In keeping with this policy, the director of the center wants the meals to have the highest nutritional value possible. Consequently, the director orders the cook to use as much as possible of the ingredients on hand. Currently, there are 80 pounds of ingredient A, 60 pounds of ingredient B, and 120 pounds of ingredient C available.

The cook knows how to cook just two different recipes: the Chef's Special and the Center's Standard. Each serving of the Special calls for two pounds of A, one pound of B, and four pounds of C. Each serving of the Standard required two pounds of A, four pounds of B, and two pounds of C. One serving of the Special contains 30 nutritional units, while a service of the Standard has 60 nutritional units.

Answer the following questions for the director:

a. How many servings of each recipe should the cook make to maximize the nutritional value of the meals made?

b. Suppose that the nutritional value of a Chef's Special is decreased to 10 units. What is the effect on the optimal solution?

c. Suppose that the nutritional value of a Center's Standard is increased by 20 units. What is the effect on the optimal solution?

d. How many pounds of ingredient A would have to be taken away before there would be a change in the optimal solution?

e. Suppose that each serving of the Standard meal calls for four (instead of two) pounds of ingredient C. What is the effect on the optimal solution?

f. A new recipe is being planned. It will contain 40 nutritional units and require seven pounds of ingredients B and C. Should the Center introduce the new recipe? Explain.

54. Swain Products, Inc., plans to develop a new hair shampoo called Form of Essence. The new product is a blend of the company's regular shampoo base and a new conditioning agent. Three raw materials are used in the blending process: sudsing, conditioning, and perfume ingredients. The final product must have at least 60 grams of the sudsing agent, exactly 40 grams of the conditioning ingredient, and no more than 15 grams of perfume. There are 100 grams of the sudsing agent, 5 grams of the conditioning ingredient, and 10 grams of the perfume in each gallon of the regular shampoo base. Each gallon of the conditioning agent has 200 grams of the conditioning ingredient but none of the sudsing or perfume ingredients. It costs $2 to blend a gallon of the regular shampoo base and $5 for a gallon of the conditioning agent. Swain wants to know how much of each raw material there should be in each gallon of the new shampoo to meet product requirements at minimum cost.

Management is also interested in the sensitivity of the optimal solution to potential changes in the data. In particular, the company wants to consider the following possibilities:

a. Suppose that materials inflation increases the cost of blending the regular shampoo by 30 cents per gallon. What is the effect on the optimal solution?

b. Suppose that a technological innovation reduces the cost of blending the conditioning agent by $1.50. What is the effect on the optimal solution?

c. Which ingredient offers the largest potential cost savings? Explain.

d. Suppose that a new formula reduces the amount of suds in Form of Essence by 40 grams. What is the effect on the optimal solution?

e. How much would the available perfume content of Form of Essence have to increase before there is an effect on the optimal solution?

f. How much would the conditioning agent content in Form of Essence have to change before there is an effect on the optimal solution?

Answer these questions for Swain's management.

For Further Reading

Postoptimality Methodology

Gal, T. *Postoptimality Analyses, Parametric Programming and Related Topics.* New York: McGraw-Hill, 1979.

Knolmayer, G. "The Effects of Degeneracy on Cost-Coefficient Ranges and an Algorithm to Resolve Interpretation Problems." *Decision Sciences* (Winter 1984):14.

Luenberger, D. G. *Linear and Nonlinear Programming.* Second ed. Reading, MA: Addison-Wesley, 1984.

Wendell, R. E. "The Tolerance Approach to Sensitivity Analysis in Linear Programming." *Management Science* (May 1985):564.

Computer Analysis

Avramovich, D., et al. "A Decision Support System for Fleet Management: A Linear Programming Approach." *Interfaces* (June 1982):1.

Schrage, L. *Linear, Integer, and Quadratic Programming with LINDO*. Third ed. Palo Alto, CA: Scientific Press, 1986.

Sharda, R. "The State of the Art of Linear Programming on Personal Computers." *Interfaces* (July–August 1988):49.

Accounting/Finance Applications

Abdel-Khalik, A. R. "Using Sensitivity Analysis to Evaluate Materiality—An Exploratory Approach." *Decision Sciences* (July 1977):616.

Crane, D. B., et al. "An Application of Management Science to Bank Borrowing Strategies." Part 2. *Interfaces* (November 1977): 70.

Sharp, J. F. "The Effects of Income Taxes on Linear Programming Models." *Decision Sciences (July 1975):462*.

Operations/Production Applications

Bhatnagar, S. C. "Implementing Linear Programming in a Textile Unit: Some Problems and a Solution." *Interfaces* (April 1981):87.

Cabraal, R. A. "Production Planning in a Sri Lanka Coconut Mill Using Parametric Linear Programming." *Interfaces* (June 1981):16.

Case: The Tennis Shop

The Tennis Shop is a specialty sporting goods store that makes and sells tennis rackets. There are three models: the Junior, the Intermediate, and the Advanced. The shop operates on a made-to-order basis. Since there is a heavy backlog of orders for the Juniors and Intermediates, the store can sell all these models that are produced.

The Tennis Shop is planning the production schedule for next month. Each racket must be molded, painted, and finished. Next month, the manager expects to have 240 hours available for molding, 70 hours for painting, and 40 hours for finishing. Production of a batch of 120 Juniors requires two hours of molding, four hours of painting, and one hour of finishing. It takes four hours to mold 120 Intermediates, two hours for painting, and two hours for finishing. A batch of 120 Advanced models uses eight hours of molding, one hour of painting and one hour of finishing.

The shop expects to make $350 per batch (120) of the Juniors, $600 per batch of the Intermediates, and $1,000 per batch of the Advanced model. Since there are a limited number of outstanding players, the shop expects to sell no more than 4,800 (40 batches of 120 each) Advanced rackets.

Tennis Shop's manager consults with you and asks you to answer the following questions:

1. How many rackets of each type should be produced next month to maximize profit?

2. Suppose that the unexpected popularity of Juniors increases profit per batch to $400. What is the effect on the optimal solution?

3. Suppose that a decline in demand decreases Intermediate's profit per batch to $480. What is the effect on the optimal product mix?

4. Suppose that unexpected popularity increases the Advanced model's profit per batch to $1600. What is the effect on the optimal solution?

5. How much can the anticipated demand for Advanced rackets decrease before there is an effect on the optimal product mix?

6. Suppose that a machine failure reduces molding capacity to 100 hours. What is the effect on the optimal product mix?

7. Suppose that an increase in employee efficiency increases painting capacity to 75 hours. What is the effect on the optimal solution?

8. Suppose that a new process creates 20 additional finishing hours. What is the effect on the optimal product mix?

9. A new model is being considered. It will earn $800 per batch and require six hours of molding and three hours each for painting and finishing. Should the new model be introduced?

Prepare a management report that gives your recommendations on these issues.

Chapter 10

Advanced Mathematical Programming

Chapter Outline

Learning Objectives

- Understand the assumptions and limitations of a linear programming analysis

- Examine the nature and purpose of alternative mathematical programming methodologies

- Deal with situations in which all or some of the decision variables must have whole-unit values

- Incorporate multiple criteria into a mathematical programming analysis

- Perform advanced mathematical programming analysis with the aid of a computer

Sears Fills the Shopping Malls

HOMART Development Company, a subsidiary of Sears, currently owns or is developing 31 regional shopping centers and 18 major office buildings. The shopping center development business involves identifying opportunities, performing feasibility analysis, obtaining government approvals, supervising design and construction, leasing, and managing the properties. These centers contain about 1 million square feet of selling area, represent $60 million in investments, and contribute substantially to Homart's profits.

Early in the development process, the developer negotiates and arranges accomodations for large department stores. Once Homart situates these major tenants and specifies a general floor plan, management must select the types, sizes, and locations of smaller stores within the mall. In 1984, Homart asked University of Michigan faculty to assist management with this tenant mix problem. The faculty found that the problem could be formulated realistically as a mathematical programming model. Given the mall spaces available in various location classes, allowed tenant types, and interior finish budgets, the model determines the store mix that maximizes the center's present worth.

Validation tests showed that the method yields a potential 10 percent to 26 percent improvement in a center's present worth, approximately $22 to $46 per square foot. In addition, the model has become a tool for generating and updating merchandising plans throughout the leasing process. Also, Homart uses the model for establishing financial standards against which management can measure a center's performance.

Source: J. C. Bean et al., "Selecting Tenants in a Shopping Mall," *Interfaces* (March–April 1988): 1–9.

Linear programming is based on a set of rather restrictive assumptions. Although these assumptions will be valid for many practical problems, there are numerous other situations in which one or more of the suppositions may not be factual. Homart Development Company's tenant mix problem is one such situation. The first section of this chapter presents the fundamental linear programming assumptions, identifies circumstances that could invalidate each supposition, and outlines appropriate alternative methodologies. As the Homart Development case illustrates, these alternative methodologies can dramatically improve decision making.

In one potential circumstance, some or all of the decision variables in the linear program must have whole-unit values only (no fractional values). For example, when an airline decides how many Boeing 767s or DC-10s to purchase, management cannot order 6.29 Boeings and 5.93 DC-10s. Instead the airline must buy 5, 6, 7, 8, or some other whole-unit amount of each aircraft. The second section of this chapter shows how to formulate and solve such whole-unit problems.

Also, the decision maker may have several objectives, not just one. For example, management may want to minimize costs and maintain product quality as well as maximize profit. Furthermore, some of the criteria (such as product quality) may be difficult to quantify, and some of the objectives (such as maintaining product quality and minimizing costs) may conflict. The third section of this chapter demonstrates how multiple criteria can be incorporated into a mathematical programming analysis. Specifically, it shows how to formulate, solve, and interpret such multiple-objective programs.

Applications. In this chapter, the following applications appear in text, examples, and exercises:

- affirmative action recruiting
- ambulance dispatching
- bank management
- building renovation
- cable television programming
- carnival safety
- corporate bond investment
- cutting stock
- department store advertising
- distribution strategy
- farming cooperatives
- fiscal policy

- health resort planning
- household product marketing
- military housing
- missile deployment
- overnight delivery
- political campaigns
- production/labor planning
- production scheduling
- public health
- regional work force planning
- store location
- women's softball

10.1 DECISION CONSIDERATIONS

As Chapters 7 through 9 demonstrated, linear programming is a powerful and readily available methodology for solving a wide variety of decision problems. Moreover, it provides a great deal of information that is very useful for management planning and control. However, the methodology is based on a set of rather restrictive assumptions that limit its application. To avoid the misuse of linear programming, the decision maker must thoroughly understand these suppositions and resulting limitations of the analysis. Management Situation 10.1 will illustrate the concepts.

Management Situation 10.1

Production Scheduling

Quantum Enterprises is thinking of manufacturing and selling video games on an experimental basis over the next three months. Management projects the schedule of manufacturing data and selling prices shown in Table 10.1.

Table 10.1   **Manufacturing Data and Selling Prices for Quantum Enterprises**

Month	Manufacturing Cost ($)	Production Time per Game (Hours)	Capacity (Hours)	Selling Price ($)
December	50	10	20,000	—
January	45	8	24,000	150
February	—	—	—	125

There are no video games on hand at the beginning of December. Furthermore, the quantity manufactured during any month will be accumulated and shipped out in one large load at the end of the month. As a result, it takes one month to gear up and ship out the first batch. Thus, Quantum cannot sell any games during December. Also, the company does not want any video games on hand at the end of February. Consequently, management decides to manufacture no games during February.

Although Quantum can sell as many games as it produces, operations are limited by the size of the company warehouse. Currently, this facility can hold no more than 1,500 video games. Management wants to manufacture and sell the monthly quantities that will maximize total profit for the three-month test period.

After a careful study of the situation, the management staff has been able to formulate the problem as the following linear program:

maximize $Z = \$150X_2 + \$125X_3 - \$50Y_1 - \$45Y_2$

subject to $10Y_1 \leq 20,000$ hours   (December capacity)

$8Y_2 \leq 24,000$ hours   (January capacity)

$Y_1 \leq 1500$ (December inventory)

$Y_1 + Y_2 - X_2 \leq 1,500$ (January inventory)

$Y_1 + Y_2 - X_2 - X_3 = 0$ (February inventory)

$X_2, X_3, Y_1, Y_2 \geq 0$

where Y_1 = the number of video games manufactured during December, Y_2 = the number of video games manufactured during January, X_2 = the number of video games sold during January, X_3 = the number of video games sold during February, and Z = the total dollar profit.

Indivisibility

The linear programming model assumes that each decision variable is divisible into a fractional value. Such an assumption generally will be valid when these variables represent a physical measure (weight, capacity, length, area, or volume), time, monetary values, or percentages.

Under some circumstances, quantity also is divisible into fractions. Consider the linear program in Management Situation 10.1. By using this program to schedule production, managment assumes that X_2, X_3, Y_1, and Y_2 each can have a fractional value such as 944.06 or 1,298.98. Such an assumption may be valid if Quantum can (1) manufacture a portion of the video game during one month and complete the process later and (2) initiate a sale during one month and terminate the transaction in the future. For example, an $X_2 = 42.54$ might indicate that the company has sold 42 games and completed .54, or 54 percent of the transaction work for another game during January. The remaining 46 percent of January's incomplete sales transaction, which may involve delivery and installation, can then be terminated during February. Similarly, a $Y_1 = 956.23$ would mean that 956 complete games and .23, or 23 percent of another game are manufactured during December. The remaining 77 percent of the production work for December's unfinished game could be completed in January.

On the other hand, Quantum's video game experiment is scheduled to last for only three months. As a result, all sales transactions must be terminated by the end of the test in February. Salespeople will be unable to initiate a transaction during February and complete the sale later. In addition, management does not want to manufacture any games during February. Therefore, manufacturing personnel should not have any unfinished games on hand at the end of January.

These test conditions may force the company to manufacture complete, rather than portions of, video games during January. The same circumstances could also compel management to fully, instead of partially, terminate sales transactions during February. In other words, at least two (X_3 and Y_2) of Quantum's four (X_2, X_3, Y_1, and Y_2) decision variables might have to be whole-unit rather than fractional values.

Moreover, Quantum's circumstances are not unusual. Indeed, practical problems often involve situations in which some or all of the decision variables must have whole-unit rather than fractional values. For example, it is impossible for an automobile dealer to stock 11.33 station wagons and 35.89 sedans, because only whole cars will be kept in inventory. Hence, management must stock 10, 11, 12, or some other whole-unit, or integer, number of automobiles. Similarly, when a company decides how many people should be assigned to various projects, the supervisor cannot place 1.8 or 2.55 people in each job. Rather, the supervisor must assign 1, 2, 3, or some other integer number of people to a task.

Linear programming, however, may not provide such whole-unit, or integer, solutions. Fortunately, management scientists have developed a methodology that is designed specifically for situations in which some or all of the decision variables must have integer values. This methodology, which is referred to as **integer programming,** will be presented in the second section of this chapter.

Multiple Objectives

The linear programming model also assumes that there is only a single objective in the problem. Furthermore, it presumes that the objective can be expressed in terms of a numerical criterion such as quantity, time, or revenue. In the linear program of Management Situation 10.1, for instance, Quantum's single objective is to maximize the numerical criterion of total dollar profit (Z).

Frequently, however, practical problems involve several objectives. In addition, each objective may be expressed in terms of a different criterion. A textile company, for example, may want to select the manufacturing process that generates the most output in the shortest possible time frame. Moreover, some criteria can be difficult, if not impossible, to quantify. For instance, it is hard to measure social benefit, customer satisfaction, quality, and similar criteria in numerical terms. Also, there might be a conflict between the objectives, as in the case of a city that is faced with the problem of providing the maximum community safety with the smallest possible police budget.

As demonstrated in Chapter 6, management scientists have developed methodologies for dealing with these multiple-criteria decision problems. One of the approaches, called **goal programming,** is designed to accommodate multiple criteria within the mathematical programming framework. This approach will be presented in the third section of this chapter.

Uncertainty

Linear programming further assumes that the value of each uncontrollable input is known with perfect certainty. That is, the decision maker must have the exact per-unit contribution of each variable to the objective, the exact amount of each system constraint, and the exact rate at which each system constraint amount is transformed into each variable. Put another way, the linear program should be a deterministic model.

Consider the linear program in Management Situation 10.1. Quantum knows the exact per-game profit contribution of each decision variable: $150 for X_2, $125 for X_3, $-\$50$ for Y_1, and $-\$45$ for Y_2. Also, the company knows the precise capacity limitations (20,000 hours for December and 24,000 for January) and inventory limitations (1500 games each in December and January and 0 in February). In addition, management knows the exact rates (10 hours for December and 8 for January) at which each month's manufacturing capacity is transformed into a video game. Hence, Quantum's linear program is a deterministic model.

In practice, such uncontrollable input information typically comes from managerial estimates and formal forecasts. But estimates and forecasts are, by their very nature, imprecise. Quantum's selling prices, for example, will be influenced by uncertain future demand conditions in the video game market. Unforeseen changes in these conditions, such as a shift in consumer recreational habits, may result in prices that are considerably different from the estimates. Simlarly, unanticipated supply circumstances, such as a strike at a raw-material supplier, may invalidate the forecasted manufacturing costs.

There are other sources of uncertainty that can affect the accuracy of Quantum's system constraint amount and utilization rate estimates. A plant accident, for example, might reduce the company's forecasted production capacity during December or January. Moreover, the industrial engineering department could erroneously estimate the times needed to manufacture a video game during December and January. And an unplanned business deal may provide more warehouse space for inventory than the forecasts for December and January indicate.

Postoptimality Analysis. One way of dealing with parameter uncertainty is to perform postoptimality analyses on the original linear program. As demonstrated in Chapter 9, sensitivity analysis can be used to evaluate the effects of discrete changes in the uncontrollable inputs on the optimal linear programming solution. In addition, parametric programming can be used to investigate how specified continuous variations in the parameters influence the optimal solution to the original linear program.

Postoptimality analysis, however, does not utilize any probability information that may be available concerning the uncontrollable inputs. As a result, this analysis can only partially account for the potential impact of parameter uncertainty on the linear programming problem. The difficulty is especially apparent when the uncontrollable inputs depend on the values of the decision variables. Such a situation might arise, for instance, in a model where future profit levels depend on earlier output decisions.

Stochastic Programming. To fully overcome the difficulty, the decision maker must formulate a mathematical programming model that explicitly includes the parameter uncertainty and then use the resulting stochastic model to develop the optimal solution. **Stochastic programming** offers one methodology for doing this. In this approach, the objective function and system constraint segments of the original linear program are expanded to incorporate the impact of the parameter uncertainty on the problem. Such an approach converts the stochastic elements of the problem into an equivalent deterministic form. By solving the enlarged linear program, management obtains an optimal solution that fully considers and directly accounts for the parameter uncertainty.

Although several models (not treated here) have been developed to handle specific problems, there are some difficulties in applying the stochastic programming approach. For one thing, the decision maker must enlarge the original mathematical program to include each possible consequence of the parameter uncertainty. In practice, managers may not be willing or able to identify and precisely define these consequences. Also, the enlarged mathematical program may have an extremely large number of variables and constraints. In fact, the size of the stochastic program might make it difficult, if not practically impossible, to find the optimal solution to the problem.

Chance-Constrained Programming. As a result of these difficulties, an alternative methodology, known as **chance-constrained programming**, has been developed to deal with parameter uncertainty. In this approach, each original system constraint is reformulated in a way that ensures that the optimal solution provides a high probability of meeting the restriction. Typically, such a probability is specified by management judgment or some other relevant analysis.

The chance-constrained reformulation usually has the same size and structure as the original mathematical program. Hence, such a methodology avoids the computational burden associated with the alternative stochastic programming approach. Nevertheless, chance-constrained programming involves some serious practical and conceptual difficulties. First, it only indirectly evaluates the economic consequences of violating each system constraint. More important, there may be virtually no way to ensure that a chance-constrained formulation will give an optimal solution to the original mathematical programming problem.

Nonlinear Relationships

The linear programming model assumes that each decision variable makes a constant, proportional, and independent (a linear) contribution to the objective. It also presumes that there are linear relationships in each system constraint expression.

In Management Situation 10.1, each decision variable (X_2, X_3, Y_1, and Y_2) has an exponent of 1 and appears in a separate term of Quantum's profit function. That is how this function mathematically accounts for the constant, proportional, and independent (the linear) contribution of each month's sales/output to profit. Quantum's system (capacity and inventory) constraints have similar linear relationships between the decision variables (monthly sales/output) and the right-hand amounts (capacity hours and game inventories).

System Constraints. In practice, decision variables do not always utilize a cónstant and independent amount of capacity. Expansion frequently enables work groups to specialize in particular tasks. This specialization, in turn, creates productive efficiencies that can reduce resource utilization rates as the level of activity increases. Under these circumstances, a growth in resource usage will result in a greater-than-proportional increase in output. Tripling production, for example, might require only a doubling rather than a tripling of resource utilization.

In other situations, expansion creates coordination problems for management. Such problems, in turn, can lead to inefficiencies that increase resource usage as the level of activity expands. Under these circumstances, an increase in resource usage will result in a less-than-proportional increase in output. Doubling production, for instance, may require a tripling rather than a doubling of resource utilization.

Thus, as a result of factors such as expansion, a decision variable's constraint utilization rate may fluctuate rather than remain constant as the level of activity changes. Moreover, decision variables often have interrelated, instead of independent, effects on the system constraint relationships. For instance, an electric utility typically uses the same personnel to service residential and commercial customers. That is, each customer group utilizes joint rather than separate resources and facilities. For this reason, an increase in commercial calls could divert available service personnel from residential customer requests. If such a diversion delays service, the completion time per residential request would depend on the number of commercial calls. Put another way, residential and commercial calls have an interrelated effect on the usage of service capacity.

Objective Function. In addition, each decision variable does not always make a constant and independent contribution to the objective. A company, for example, can usually sell a larger quantity by lowering its price. That is, revenue per unit will decrease as the sales quantity increases. Also, *learning by doing* and other related factors often enable work groups to produce larger quantities at a lower unit cost. In other words, manufacturing cost per unit may decline as the output level increases. Thus, a product's or service's per-unit contribution to a profit criterion will fluctuate rather than remain constant as the level of activity changes.

Furthermore, decision variables frequently have interrelated, rather than indepen- dent, effects on the criterion value. For example, suppose that a shaving equipment firm sells razors and blades. Since these products complement each other in the market, management may find that a growth in razor sales increases the demand for blades. Consequently, the profit from blades may depend on the number of razor sales. In other words, razor and blade sales make interrelated contributions to a profit criterion.

Nonlinear Programming When any decision activity makes a variable unit contribution or interrelated contribution to the criterion value, the mathematical program's objective

Table 10.2   **Examples of Nonlinear Programs**

Nonlinear Program	Characteristics	Category
minimize $Z = 5X_1 + 5X_2 - X_1X_2$ subject to $X_1 + 2X_2 = 10$	Nonlinear objective function (X_1 and X_2 both appear in the third term of the expression) Linear system constraint equality	Calculus
Maximize $Z = 10X_1 - 10X_1^2$ $+ 20X_1 - 2X_2^2 + 10X_1X_2$ subject to $2X_1 + 2X_2 \le 12$ $4X_1 + X_2 \le 24$ $X_1, X_2 \ge 0$	Nonlinear objective function (X_1 has an exponent of 2 in the second term, X_2 has an exponent of 2 in the fourth term, and X_1 and X_2 both appear in the last term) Highest exponent of any decision variable is 2 Linear system constraint inequalities Nonnegativity conditions	Quadratic programming
maximize $Z = 3X_1 + 2X_2$ subject to $X_1^4 + 4X_2 \le 200$ $X_1 + 2X_2^3 \le 40$ $X_1, X_2 \ge 0$	Linear objective function Nonlinear system constraint inequalities (X_1 has an exponent of 4 in the first restriction, and X_2 has an exponent of 3 in the second constraint) Nonlinear terms can be approximated by linear expressions Nonnegativity conditions	Separable programming
minimize $Z = \dfrac{1200}{X_1X_2} + 40X_1^2X_2^3$ subject to $6X_1X_2 + X_1X_2 \le 5400$ $X_1, X_2 \ge 0$	Nonlinear objective function (X_1 has an exponent of -1 in the first term and 2 in the second term, X_2 has an exponent of -1 in the first term and 3 in the second term, and X_1 and X_2 both appear in each term of the expression) Nonlinear system constraint inequality (X_1 and X_2 both appear in each term of the expression) Nonlinear terms generally involve the product of some decision variable combination Nonnegativity conditions	Geometric programming
maximize $Z = 5X_1 - X_2^2 - 2X_1X_2$ $X_1^2 + X_1X_2 + X_2^2 \le 50$ $X_1 + X_2 \le 75$ $X_1, X_2 \ge 0$	Nonlinear objective function (X_2 has an exponent of 2 in the second term, while X_1 and X_2 both appear in the third term of the expression) Nonlinear system constraint inequality (X_1 has an exponent of 2 in the first term, X_2 has an exponent of 2 in the third term, and X_1 and X_2 both appear in the second term of the expression) Linear system constraint inequality Nonnegativity conditions	Convex programming

function will not involve a linear relationship. That is, a decision variable will have an exponent different than 1 and/or more than one activity will appear in a single term of the function. In such cases, the expression is said to exhibit a **nonlinear relationship.**

A variable utilization rate or interactions among the decision activities also create a nonlinear relationship in the corresponding system constraint expression. As a result, a company can have a mathematical program that consists of a nonlinear objective function and/or at least one nonlinear system constraint expression. Such a problem, which is referred to as a **nonlinear program,** can take several different forms. Table 10.2 presents some of the possibilities.

Sometimes, the interactions between the decision variables and nonproportional effects are minor. In such cases, it may be possible to reformulate these nonlinearities as linear relationships. Linear programming, then, could still provide a reasonable approximation of the optimal solution to the problem.

When the nonproportionalities and interrelationships are significant, the decision maker must formulate and solve the corresponding nonlinear program. Unlike the simplex method for linear programming problems, however, there is no efficient general-purpose algorithm that can be used to solve all nonlinear programs. In fact, some of these problems cannot be solved in a satisfactory manner by any method. Nevertheless, various computational techniques have been developed to solve some important categories of nonlinear programs. Such methodologies are known collectively as **nonlinear programming.**

Each nonlinear programming category has its own special name. Indeed, many of the important categories are indentified in Table 10.2. One of the methodologies (calculus) is reviewed in the classical optimization appendix of this text.

Sequential Problems

The linear programming model assumes that the problem involves a single one-time decision. In Management Situation 10.1, for instance, Quantum wants to develop a video game production/sales schedule for only the three-month experiment. Moreover, the optimal experimental plan will be unaffected by previous management actions, nor should it have a direct impact on other concurrent or future company activities. Instead, the selected schedule will be the result of an independent decision made at the beginning of the three-month planning period.

Yet, as Chapter 4 demonstrated, many problems involve a series of interrelated decisions. Consider, for example, a military training program. In such programs, all recruits are expected to complete various training phases, such as military indoctrination and physical development. Also, each phase usually contains a specified number of tasks. Physical development, for instance, might consist of 2,000 push-ups, 4,000 knee bends, and so on. Hence, each trainee can be assigned a wide variety of tasks at each stage of the program. Since all training phases are necessary, however, each assignment is influenced by the pattern of previously completed and future required tasks. Put another way, the recruit task assignments entail a series of interrelated, rather than independent, decisions. As a result, camp management must determine the sequence of assignments that minimizes recruits' total time in the training program.

As illustrated in Chapter 4, management scientists have developed methodologies for dealing with these sequential decision problems. One of the approaches, called

Table 10.3   **Alternative Solution Methodologies**

Linear Programming Assumption	Actual Situation	Alternative Approach
Divisible decision variables	Indivisibility	Integer programming
Single objective	Multiple objectives	Goal programming
Deterministic information	Uncertainty	Postoptimality analyses, stochastic programming, chance-constrained programming
Proportional relationships, independent decision variables	Nonproportional relationships, interactions among decision variables	Nonlinear programming
Single one-time decision	Sequential problems	Dynamic programming

dynamic programming, decomposes the original problem into smaller multiple stages. Each smaller part is then solved in sequence through the use of information from each preceding stage.

Unlike the other models presented in this chapter, however, dynamic programming is not a special type of mathematical program. Instead, the methodology represents a general type of approach to problem solving. It would be useful, then, to present the methodology in conjunction with the problem situations for which the technique is best suited. Consequently, the discussion on dynamic programming is deferred until Chapter 16.

Selecting A Methodology

In effect, linear programming is best suited for problems in which

1.   Each decision variable is divisible into a fractional value

2.   There is a single objective that can be expressed in terms of a numerical criterion

3.   The value of each uncontrollable input is known with perfect certainty

4.   There are linear relationships in the objective function and each system constraint

5.   Management must make a single one-time decision

When the actual decision situation does not have each of these characteristics, management should consider an alternative solution methodology. Table 10.3 summarizes the alternatives.

10.2 INTEGER PROGRAMMING

Often, a mathematical programming problem may deal with a one-time decision, have a single objective, involve linear relationships, and contain deterministic information. Yet some or all of the decision variables may be required to have integer values.

Problem Types

In some cases, all decision variables have whole-unit values. For example, judicial administrators will schedule an integer number of hearings (such as 12, 17, or 26) per day in each district court within a city. Such problems, in which all of the decision variables have whole-unit solutions, are called **pure integer programming.**

When the whole-unit solutions are binary (0 or 1) values, the problem is referred to as **zero/one (binary) integer programming.** Consider, for example, the problem of determining police station locations within a new community. Typically, management must select from among a set of potential locations the sites that provide the necessary coverage (service) at least cost. Under these circumstances, each decision variable (police station location) could be depicted as a yes or no choice. The variable can be assigned a value of 1 if the site is selected and 0 when the city bypasses the location.

Other situations involve **mixed integer programming,** or situations in which selected decision variables have integer (binary or pure integer) values while the remaining decision variables have continuous values. For example, a company might use a portion of a work period to manufacture a product, but management must either use or not use each alternative from among a set of potential manufacturing processes. Moreover, only an integer number of people can be employed on any project team. In this case, the work period variable can be fractional, but each manufacturing process must have a binary integer value, while the project team sizes are restricted to whole-unit solutions.

Zero/One Programming

In many management problems, including capital budgeting, resource assignment, vehicle loading, and service area (set) coverage, all decision variables can be depicted with zero/one values. Other situations have special characteristics that can be modeled accurately with binary variables. Some of these characteristics include fixed charges, piecewise linear functions, interdependent variables, and mutually exclusive constraints.

Fixed Charges. Economies often can be achieved by increasing the scale of activity through enhanced technologies, improved processes, or other favorable arrangements. Typically, fixed charges will be incurred to achieve these economies of scale. Such charges then must be accounted for in any model of the situation.

Consider, for example, a manufacturer that must decide whether or not to include a new garden tool in its product line. By including the tool, the company will incur a fixed cost of $800,000 to set up its facilities and will earn a profit of $75 per tool from distributing the item. There is sufficient capacity to manufacture 160,000 new tools per quarter.

The company's new product choice can be depicted with the binary variable

$$G = \begin{cases} 1 \text{ if the tool is introduced} \\ 0 \text{ otherwise} \end{cases}$$

while output can be represented with the pure integer variable Q. Net earnings from the tool then will be profit minus fixed cost or

$$\$75Q - \$800,000G$$

and these earnings will be added to the company's objective function. To ensure that the $800,000 fixed cost is netted out of the tool's earnings, the constraints

$$Q \le 160,000G$$

and
$$G = 0 \text{ or } 1$$

will be included among the problem restrictions.

The fixed charges create a programming problem with binary and pure integer variables. If the optimizing algorithm finds that the new tool should be introduced, it will set $G = 1$. This value will pick up the fixed charge ($800,000) in the objective function and allow tool output up to the capacity limitation (have $Q \le 160,000$). When the optimal $G = 0$, there will be no fixed charge, no output ($Q = 0$), and thereby no net earnings.

Piecewise Linear Functions. Frequently, a decision variable must take on a value that will be in a small set of specified intervals. There is a linear relationship within each interval, and the set of intervals can be pieced together as a single function.

Consider, for example, a gasoline station that must determine the volume to order from a supplier offering a quantity discount. The first 12,000 gallons can be purchased for 80 cents per gallon, while the price drops to 76 cents per gallon for volumes in excess of 12,000 gallons. No more than 23,000 gallons will be purchased.

Total volume can be represented by the continuous variable V, with

$$V = V_1 + V_2$$

where V_1 = purchases of no more than 12,000 gallons and V_2 = purchases in excess of 12,000 but not more than 23,000 gallons. Supply cost will equal these volumes multiplied by the corresponding per-gallon purchase expenses, or it will equal

$$\$0.80V_1 + \$0.76V_2.$$

This piecewise linear cost function will become part of the station's objective function.

To model the quantity discount structure, management first can define the binary variable

$$P = \begin{cases} 1 \text{ if } V_1 \text{ is at its upper bound of 12,000 gallons} \\ 0 \text{ otherwise} \end{cases}$$

Then, the constraints

$$12,000P \le V_1 \le 12,000$$

$$P = 0 \text{ or } 1$$

ensure that V_1 does not exceed its upper bound and that V_1 is at this bound whenever the station receives the quantity discount (that $V_1 = 12,000$ when $V_2 > 0$). Two additional restrictions

$$V_2 \ge 0 \quad \text{and} \quad V_2 \le 11,000P$$

guarantee that V_2 does not exceed its volume limit ($23,000 - 12,000 = 11,000$ gallons) and that the station buys no more than the planned 23,000-gallon total volume.

The piecewise linear cost function creates a mixed integer programming problem. If the optimizing algorithm finds that the quantity discount should be used, it will set

$P = 1$ and fix the purchase volumes V_1 and V_2. When the optimal $P = 0$, there will be no V_2 and no quantity discount.

Interdependent Variables. In some problems, there will be a mutual dependence between the decision variables. To reach an accurate conclusion, then, management must incorporate any such interdependence into the evaluation process.

As an illustration, suppose that a large drugstore chain will not add a new outlet in Sun City unless capacity is expanded at the Newberry warehouse. By depicting the expansion choices with the binary variables

$$NO = \begin{cases} 1 \text{ if the outlet is added} \\ 0 \text{ otherwise} \end{cases}$$

and

$$WE = \begin{cases} 1 \text{ if the warehouse is expanded} \\ 0 \text{ otherwise} \end{cases}$$

management can account for the interdependency with the constraint

$$NO \le WE$$

Then, the new outlet will be added ($NO = 1$) only when the warehouse is expanded (when $WE = 1$). The constraint also gives the option of not adding the outlet (having $NO = 0$) even if there is a warehouse expansion.

Mutually Exclusive Constraints. Sometimes, there will be conditions that are associated only with a particular decision alternative. Other alternatives will involve different and mutually exclusive conditions. Such mutually exclusive conditions then must be accounted for in the problem formulation.

For example, consider a waste management company that must select a site for its new landfill. Lowtown, with an 8,000-ton monthly capacity, Tinersville, with a 7,500-ton monthly capacity, and Zanestown, with an 8,200-ton monthly capacity, are the leading candidates. Only one of the three sites will be selected.

Collections will come from Adams, Johnson, and Jefferson counties. A county's supply can be represented by the continuous variable

$$X_j = \text{tons of waste collected from county } j$$

where the subscript $j = 1$ for Adams, 2 for Johnson, and 3 for Jefferson county. Since supplies cannot exceed landfill capacity

$$X_1 + X_2 + X_3 \le 8,000 \text{ tons}$$

for the Lowtown site,

$$X_1 + X_2 + X_3 \le 7,500 \text{ tons}$$

for the Tinersville site, and

$$X_1 + X_2 + X_3 \le 8,200 \text{ tons}$$

for the Zanestown site.

Management will select the Lowtown, Tinersville, or Zanestown site, but not all three. These choices can be depicted with the binary variables

$$L = 1 \text{ if Lowtown is selected; 0 otherwise}$$

$$T = 1 \text{ if Tinersville is selected; 0 otherwise}$$

$$Z = 1 \text{ if Zanestown is selected; 0 otherwise}$$

To ensure that waste goes only to the selected site, the original capacity restrictions are replaced with the constraints

$$X_1 + X_2 + X_3 \leq 8000L$$

$$X_1 + X_2 + X_3 \leq 7500T$$

$$X_1 + X_2 + X_3 \leq 8200Z$$

$$L + T + Z \leq 1$$

with all $X_j \geq 0$ and L, T, and Z each with a value of 0 or 1.

The mutually exclusive constraints create a mixed integer programming problem. If the optimizing algorithm selects the Lowtown site (sets $L = 1$, $T = 0$, $Z = 0$), capacity at the Tinersville and Zanestown sites each become zero and the company can collect up to 8,000 tons of waste. When Tinersville is the optimal site (when $L = 0$, $T = 1$ and $Z = 0$), capacity at the Lowtown and Zanestown sites each become zero and collections will be limited to 7,500 tons per month. If the algoritm sets $Z = 1$, the landfill will be located at Zanestown and the company can collect as much as 8,200 tons.

Solution Methods

Several methods have been developed to solve integer programming problems. Some of the methods can be applied to all types of integer programming (binary, mixed, and pure) structures. Others are tailored to the special structure of a particular situation, such as a problem with binary decision variables.

Brute Force. When the problem involves zero/one or pure integer programming, the solution can be found from the *total enumeration* of all feasible decision variable combinations. Such an approach will be effective with small-scale problems having relatively few decision variables. However, it could take many years on a fast computer to solve large-scale problems with brute force.

Cutting Algorithms. These approaches begin with the optimal linear programming solution. If the solution violates any integer restrictions on the decision variables, a new system constraint is formulated and added to the linear program. This constraint is designed to "cut away" a portion of the linear program's feasible solution space without eliminating any feasible integer combination. Then the revised linear program is solved by one of the simplex-based procedures. Such a process (adding new "cutting" constraints, one at a time, and solving each successive linear program) continues until a solution satisfies the integer requirements.

Although cutting algorithms find the optimal integer solution (if it exists) in a finite number of iterations, this number can be extremely large. So it might be impractical, even with a computer, to complete cutting algorithms. Moreover, such algorithms leave the user with no "near optimal" or "good" feasible solutions, should there be a need to halt execution because of excessive computer processing times.

Search Algorithms. The feasible region can be viewed as a finite set of integer solutions (in binary and pure integer programming problems) or as partitionable into distinct subregions (in mixed integer programming problems). Search algorithms then can be used to explore promising subregions/sets and to ignore clearly nonoptimal or nonpromising subregions/sets. Such a "divide and conquer" strategy eventually will find the optimal integer solution (if it exists) through a partial enumeration of the feasible integer combinations.

Branch and bound methods and *implicit enumeration* are examples of search algorithms. Implicit enumeration is specifically designed to solve zero/one problems. Branch and bound methods are effective in optimally solving general (binary, mixed, and pure) integer programming problems with a relatively small number (100 or less) of integer variables.

Like cutting algorithms, search algorithms can severely tax computer resources. Unlike cutting algorithms, however, search algorithms will leave the user with a good solution even when the search fails to find the optimal integer answer within a specified time or within a specified budget. Search algorithms also tend to perform better in practice than cutting algorithms.

Heuristics. Frequently, management settles for good feasible (instead of optimal) integer recommendations because of the prohibitive cost and time required to get or verify the optimal solution. At other times, a good initial solution is needed to feed an optimizing algorithm. These good solutions can be obtained with computationally efficient, custom-tailored *heuristic algorithms* that run the gamut from simple common sense to mathematically sophisticated logic. A simple example of such an approach is to round an optimal fractional solution.

Specialized and Hybrid Algorithms. Algorithms have been developed to efficiently solve integer programming problems that exhibit special structures. Some of the techniques discussed in the Network module (Chapters 11 through 13) are examples of these algorithms.

Also, organizations often can combine heuristic, search, cutting, and other methods into *hybrid algorithms* that can efficiently solve large-scale generalized and specialized integer programming models. One example is the calculus-based approach of *Lagrangian relaxation*. In recent years, this tool has increasingly been used to identify the bounds in branch and bound searches for the optimal solutions of large-scale integer programming problems.

Case. Several solution methods can be illustrated with Management Situation 10.2.

Management Situation 10.2

Distribution Strategy

Quality Foods Corporation operates a regional chain of supermarkets in the Midwest. Recently, its board of directors approved a $15.5 million budget to be used for the construction of additional stores and/or warehouses. Each store will cost $1 million to construct and contribute an estimated monthly profit of $30,000. On the other hand, every warehouse will contribute an expected $72,000 monthly profit but cost $3 million to construct. Nevertheless, the board wants to build at least one additional warehouse and no more than five new stores. Quality's objective is to construct the number of additional stores and warehouses that maximizes total profit.

Management realizes that Quality cannot build a fraction of a warehouse or store. After a thorough deliberation, however, the staff has been able to formulate the problem as the following mathematical program:

maximize $Z = \$30,000X_1 + \$72,000X_2$

subject to $\$1,000,000X_1 + \$3,000,000X_2 \leq \$15,500,000$ (Budget)

$\qquad\qquad X_1 \leq 5$ (New Stores)

$\qquad\qquad X_2 \geq 1$ (Additional warehouses)

$\qquad\qquad X_1, X_2 \geq 0$ and are integers

where Z = the total monthly profit, X_1 = the number of new stores, and X_2 = the number of additional warehouses.

In Management Situation 10.2, Quality's problem deals with the isolated action of developing an optimal distribution strategy. Moreover, the single objective of this strategy is to maximize total profit. Also, there are linear relationships in the objective function and system constraints of the corresponding mathematical program, and management knows the exact values of the uncontrollable inputs (unit profit, budget, new store, and additional warehouse guidelines).

The mathematical program in Management Situation 10.2 has nearly all the characteristics of a linear programming problem. The only exception is that Quality must build an integer rather than fractional number of new stores and/or additional warehouses. That is, each decision variable is required to have a whole-unit value. As a result, the company's situation represents a pure integer, instead of linear, programming problem.

Rounding Fractional Solutions

If management temporarily ignores the integer restrictions on the X_1 and X_2 values, Quality's problem can be expressed as follows:

maximize $Z = \$30,000X_1 + \$72,000X_2$

subject to $\$1,000,000X_1 + \$3,000,000X_2 \leq \$15,500,000$ (Budget)

$\qquad\qquad X_1 \leq 5$ (New Stores)

$\qquad\qquad X_2 \geq 1$ (Additional warehouses)

$\qquad\qquad X_1, X_2 \geq 0$

Figure 10.1   **Quality's Optimal Linear Programming Solution**

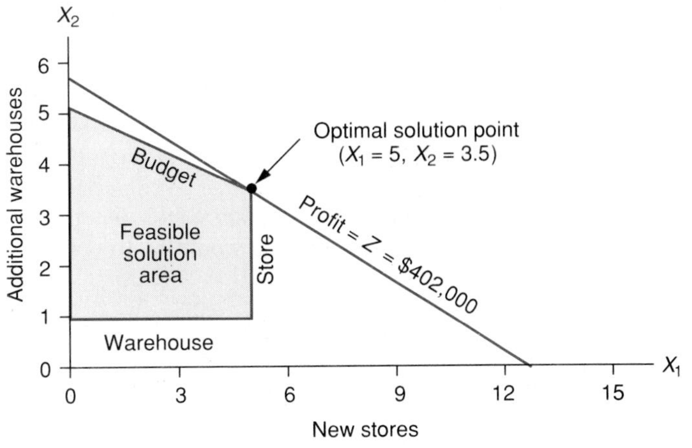

That is, the mathematical program becomes an ordinary linear programming problem. As such, it can be solved with the simplex method or graphic linear programming procedure. By using the graphic procedure, the company will obtain the results shown in Figure 10.1. The shaded region of the diagram identifies the feasible solution area for the linear programming formulation of Quality's mathematical program.

Optimal Linear Programming Solution. Sometimes, the optimal solution to the temporary linear programming formulation will provide whole-unit values for each decision variable. If so, this solution also represents the optimal answer for the original integer programming problem. Usually, however, the linear programming answer contains one or more fractional values, as in Quality's case. As Figure 10.1 demonstrates, the company's optimal linear programming solution involves

$$X_1 = 5 \text{ new stores}$$

and

$$X_2 = 3.5 \text{ additional warehouses}$$

for a total monthly profit of $Z = \$402,000$. But the firm must build a complete structure, not a partial structure. Hence, the recommendation of $X_2 = 3.5$ additional warehouses is an impractical answer for Quality's original integer programming problem.

Feasible Integer Combinations. Often, the fractional portion of a noninteger decision variable has little effect on the optimal recommendation. Consider the following situation encountered by a pencil manufacturer. Each pencil earns 2 cents profit, and the optimal output is 42,196.38 pencils. But it is impossible to sell an unfinished pencil. Under these circumstances, the company will not lose much money by manufacturing 42,196 rather than 42,196.38 pencils. In making its production decision, management will simply round the fractional value to the nearest feasible integer and hence recommend an output of 42,196 pencils.

Quality, on the other hand, is faced with a different situation. Each additional warehouse will cost $3 million and contribute $72,000 to monthly profit. Even a fraction of these amounts would have a substantial financial impact on the company. Still, management might be tempted to find an integer solution by rounding the fractional values in the optimal linear programming answer of $X_1 = 5$ new stores and $X_2 = 3.5$ additional warehouses.

In particular, the decision maker could round $X_2 = 3.5$ to either $X_2 = 3$ or $X_2 = 4$. The alternative recommendations would be to build

$$X_1 = 5 \text{ new stores}$$

$$X_2 = 4 \text{ additional warehouses}$$

or

$$X_1 = 5 \text{ new stores}$$

$$X_2 = 3 \text{ additional warehouses}$$

In fact, there generally will be two possible integer combinations for each fractional decision variable in the solution. Unfortunately, this characteristic can lead to a large number of rounded combinations. For instance, a problem with just three fractional solution values would involve $2^3 = 2 \times 2 \times 2 = 8$ rounded combinations.

However, some of the rounded combinations may not satisfy all the system constraints in the mathematical program. For example, the alternative integer combinations of

$$X_1 = 5, X_2 = 4$$

and

$$X_1 = 5, X_2 = 3$$

each satisfy both the new store restriction

$$X_1 \leq 5$$

and the additional warehouse restriction

$$X_2 \geq 1.$$

The $X_1 = 5$ and $X_2 = 3$ combination also meets the

$$\$1,000,000X_1 + \$3,000,000X_2 \leq \$15,500,000$$

budget restriction. On the other hand, a recommendation of $X_1 = 5$ and $X_2 = 4$ involves an expenditure of

$$\$1,000,000(5) + \$3,000,000(4) = \$17,000,000.$$

Since the company has only a $15.5 million budget, this $X_1 = 5$ and $X_2 = 4$ combination is infeasible.

Optimal Rounded Solution. Any infeasible rounded solutions, such as the $X_1 = 5$ and $X_2 = 4$ combination in Management Situation 10.2, should be eliminated from further consideration. The decision maker can then choose from among the remaining feasible alternatives the rounded solution that best meets the objective. In Quality's case, the elimination of the $X_1 = 5$ and $X_2 = 4$ mixture leaves the $X_1 = 5$ and $X_2 = 3$ combination as the only feasible rounded solution. Thus, the company knows that a distribution strategy of $X_1 = 5$ new stores and $X_2 = 3$ additional warehouses is the feasible rounded solution that provides the largest total profit. In fact, the objective function relationship

$$Z = \$30,000X_1 + \$72,000X_2$$

from the mathematical program indicates that this $X_1 = 5$ and $X_2 = 3$ combination leads to a

$$Z = \$30,000(5) + \$72,000(3) = \$366,000$$

total monthly profit.

Limitations. Unfortunately, the rounding approach has some serious shortcomings. Where there are many fractional values, it is very time-consuming to develop the rounded combinations, check each for feasibility, and identify the best feasible rounded solution. Furthermore, this best rounded solution is only one among many feasible integer combinations. Consequently, the best rounded combination may not represent the optimal solution to the original integer programming problem. To see why, let us examine the graphic approach to pure integer programming.

Graphic Approach

Quality knows that the feasible solution area of Figure 10.1 contains all the decision variable combinations (X_1 and X_2) satisfying the system constraints in its mathematical program. Although there are an infinite number of points in this area, management is interested only in the integer combinations. Each of these feasible integer combinations is identified with a heavy dot (.) in Figure 10.2. The shaded region of the diagram again shows the feasible solution area for the linear programming formulation of Quality's mathematical program.

One of the feasible integer combinations (heavy dots) in Figure 10.2 represents the optimal solution to Quality's mathematical program. To find this solution, management uses a variation of the graphic method presented in Chapter 7. The company's objective function relationship

$$Z = \$30,000X_1 + \$72,000X_2$$

can be used to construct a series of profit lines. Recall that each of these lines gives the decision variable combinations (X_1 and X_2) that generate a specified profit level (Z). Moreover, every line in the series will move progressively away from the origin toward a higher profit level. The decision maker then identifies the largest-valued profit line that passes through an integer combination in the feasible solution area. This combination is the optimal solution to the pure integer programming problem.

Figure 10.2   Quality's Feasible Integer Combinations

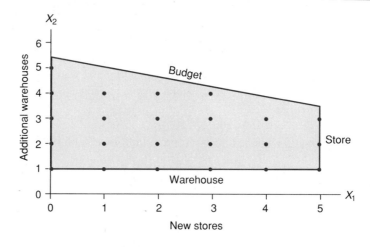

New stores

Optimal Integer Programming Solution. Figure 10.3 illustrates the graphic approach for Quality's mathematical program. As the figure shows, the company's best rounded solution of

$$X_1 = 5 \text{ new stores}$$

and

$$X_2 = 3 \text{ additional warehouses}$$

is on the objective function line that corresponds to a $Z = \$366,000$ total monthly profit. Yet management can move to the $Z = \$378,000$ profit line by constructing

$$X_1 = 3 \text{ new stores}$$

and

$$X_2 = 4 \text{ additional warehouses.}$$

Furthermore, there is no other feasible integer combination that provides a profit larger than \$378,000. Thus, this integer combination ($X_1 = 3$, $X_2 = 4$), rather than the best rounded recommendation ($X_1 = 5$, $X_2 = 3$), provides the optimal solution to the integer programming problem. Indeed, by using the best rounded instead of the optimal integer solution, Quality will get

$$\$378,000 - \$366,000 = \$12,000$$

less per month in profits.

Opportunity Costs. Nonetheless, Figure 10.3 shows that the optimal linear programming solution ($X_1 = 5$, $X_2 = 3.5$) generates a larger criterion value (lies on a higher-valued profit line) than the optimal integer combination ($X_1 = 3$, $X_2 = 4$). This result

Figure 10.3   Quality's Optimal Integer Programming Solution

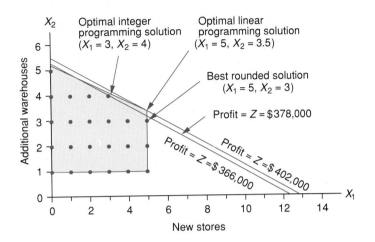

is not a coincidence. In fact, *the optimal integer combination will never provide a criterion value that is better than the best linear programming solution,* because the integer restrictions add additional constraints to the problem and thereby effectively reduce the decison maker's feasible alternatives. Such lost opportunities, in turn, usually lead to lower efficiency, higher costs, and diminished profits.

In Quality's case, the optimal linear programming solution ($X_1 = 5$, $X_2 = 3.5$) is on the objective function line that corresponds to a $Z = \$402,000$ total monthly profit. The integer restrictions on the X_1 and X_2 values, however, prevent the company from reaching this $402,000 profit line. Instead, the optimal integer combination ($X_1 = 3$, $X_2 = 4$) allows the company to achieve a $Z = \$378,000$ total monthly profit. Consequently, the integer restrictions create a monthly opportunity cost of

$$\$402,000 - \$378,000 = \$24,000.$$

Limitations. This graphic approach can be used to solve only those integer programming problems that have two decision variables. Most practical situations, however, involve many decision activities. Consequently, the decision maker will need an alternative solution procedure for these larger integer programming problems.

Enumeration

Remember that each decision variable in a pure integer programming problem must have a whole-unit solution. As a result, there will be a finite number of feasible integer combinations. Thus, the decision maker can list, or enumerate, each combination, calculate the corresponding criterion value, and then identify the feasible integer combination that leads to the best criterion value.

Figure 10.2, for example, demonstrates that there are 23 feasible integer combinations (heavy dots) in Quality's mathematical program. Hence, the company can easily

Table 10.4   **Quality's Feasible Integer Solutions**

| Feasible Integer Combinations | | Total Monthly Profit ($ thousand) $Z = \$30{,}000X_1 + \$72{,}000X_2$ |
New Stores X_1	Additional Warehouses X_2	
0	1	72
0	2	144
0	3	216
0	4	288
0	5	360
1	1	102
1	2	174
1	3	246
1	4	318
2	1	132
2	2	204
2	3	276
2	4	348
3	1	162
3	2	234
3	3	306
3	4	378 ← integer solution (Optimal)
4	1	192
4	2	264
4	3	336
5	1	222
5	2	294
5	3	366

list each combination and calculate the corresponding total monthly profit. Indeed, if management does this, it will obtain the results presented in Table 10.4.

As the enumeration in Table 10.4 demonstrates, $X_1 = 3$ and $X_2 = 4$ is the feasible integer combination that leads to the best criterion value. Specifically, it shows that Quality can maximize total monthly profit at $Z = \$378{,}000$ by constructing

$$X_1 = 3 \text{ new stores}$$

and

$$X_2 = 4 \text{ additional warehouses.}$$

This optimal integer solution, of course, is the same as the recommendation obtained from the graphic approach.

Although the enumeration method will provide the optimal solution to any pure integer programming problem, it is best suited for small-scale situations, since large problems may involve thousands, even millions, of feasible integer combinations. It would be impractical, even with a computer, to list and evaluate each of the these combinations. Consequently, the decison maker needs some systematic way to solve large-scale integer programming problems.

Branch and Bound Method

One popular systematic approach is the **branch and bound method.** It begins by temporarily treating the integer programming problem as a linear program. If the best linear programming recommendation provides whole-unit values for each decision variable, such an answer represents the optimal integer solution. Otherwise, the linear program's feasible solution region is searched in an intelligent manner for the optimal integer combination.

In the first stage of the search, the solution space is partitioned into subspaces by adding constraints to the original linear program. This procedure eliminates portions of the solution space that fail to satisfy integer requirements, without omitting any feasible integer solutions. Since a diagram of the procedure resembles a tree with branches, such a partitioning process is known as *branching*.

Branching creates additional linear programs that can be solved for revised optimal solutions. Each revised solution provides a bound on the objective function value for any optimal integer solution within the corresponding subspace. These bounds are used to eliminate clearly nonoptimal subspaces and to focus the search on promising subspaces.

Promising subspaces are further partitioned into additional subspaces, and bounds again are used to eliminate inferior branches. This branching and bounding continues until we find the optimal integer solution (if it exists).

Initial Branching. In Quality's distribution problem, Figure 10.3 indicates that the optimal linear programming solution involves a fractional number of $X_2 = 3.5$ additional warehouses. Since the company needs integer rather than fractional recommendations, management must exclude this answer from further consideration. Nevertheless, the $X_2 = 3.5$ recommendation suggests that the optimal integer solution should have a value of either $X_2 \leq 3$ or $X_2 \geq 4$.

The decision maker can move toward the optimal integer solution by partitioning the original linear programming formulation into two complementary subproblems. One of these subproblems is created by adding the constraint $X_2 \leq 3$ to the original linear program, while the other is generated by adding the restriction $X_2 \geq 4$ to the original linear program. By performing this initial partitioning, or branching, action, Quality will form the *descendant problems* or subproblems presented in Figure 10.4.

If the company uses the graphic linear programming solution procedure to solve these two subproblems, it will obtain the results shown in Figure 10.5. The unshaded region in this diagram gives the portion of the original feasible solution area that is eliminated by the initial partitioning, or branching, action. On the other hand, the upper shaded region represents the feasible solution area for subproblem 2. Similarly, the lower shaded region identifies the feasible solution area for subproblem 1.

As Figure 10.5 demonstrates, the initial partitioning process, excludes the original optimal linear programming answer ($X_1 = 5$, $X_2 = 3.5$) from the feasible solution area (shaded region) of each subproblem. Yet all attainable integer combinations (heavy dots) still remain within these areas. Consequently, the feasible solution areas (shaded regions) for the subproblems must contain the optimal integer solutions.

Initial Bounding. The partitioning process creates additional restrictions that effectively reduce the decision maker's feasible alternatives. Thus, each subproblem has a solution

Figure 10.4   **Quality's Initial Partitioning Process**

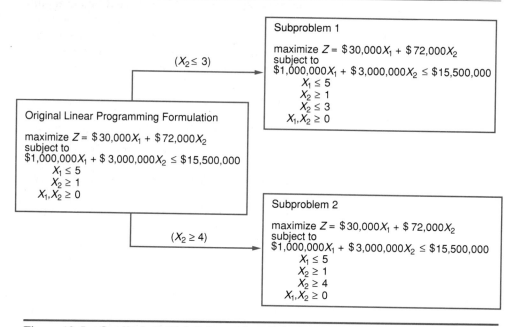

Figure 10.5   **Quality's Initial Subproblem Solutions**

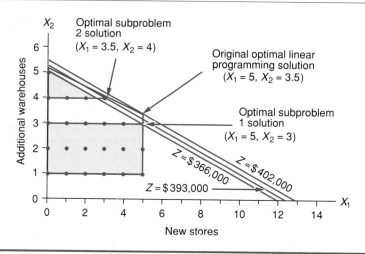

that involves a smaller criterion value than the original optimal linear programming answer. Figure 10.5, for instance, shows that the optimal subproblem 1 and 2 solutions both lead to smaller earnings (lie on lower-valued profit lines) than the optimal linear programming solution.

Descendant problems within the subspaces will be formed by adding constraints to subproblem 1's and subproblem 2's linear programs. Since these linear programs exclude no feasible integer combinations, $Z = \$366,000$ is an upper bound for integer solutions descendant from subproblem 1. Similarly, $Z = \$393,000$ is an upper bound for integer solutions descendant from subproblem 2.

Second Branching. Figure 10.5 shows that subproblem 1 has an optimal solution ($X_1 = 5$, $X_2 = 3$) that involves integer values for each decision variable. The optimal subproblem 2 solution, on the other hand, involves a fractional answer ($X_1 = 3.5$, $X_2 = 4$). Yet the best profit ($Z = \$393,000$) from subproblem 2 is larger than the optimal criterion value ($Z = \$366,000$) for subproblem 1. Hence, the whole-unit recommendation of subproblem 1 does not necessarily represent the optimal solution to Quality's original integer programming problem. Instead, there may be an integer combination within subproblem 2's feasible solution area (the upper shaded region in Figure 10.5) that provides a profit greater than $366,000. To find out, the company must partition subproblem 2 into its two complementary subproblems.

The $X_1 = 3.5$ recommendation suggests that subproblem 2's optimal integer solution should have a value of either $X_1 \leq 3$ or $X_1 \geq 4$. So, one branch is created by adding the constraint $X_1 \leq 3$ to the linear program in subproblem 2, and the other branch is generated by adding the restriction $X_1 \geq 4$ to this linear program. Figure 10.6 reports the results.

Revised Bounding. As Figure 10.6 illustrates, the second partitioning process creates subproblems 3 and 4 from subproblem 2. Since subproblem 4 has an infeasible solution, it can be eliminated from further consideration. In the diagram, this exclusion is indicated by drawing a jagged line (pruning the branch) leading to subproblem 4.

Subproblem 3 has an optimal solution ($X_1 = 3$, $X_2 = 4$) that contains integer values for each decision variable. Hence, this combination represents the best integer answer within subproblem 2's feasible solution area. Figure 10.6 also shows that such an answer provides a profit ($Z = \$378,000$) that is greater than the earnings ($Z = \$366,000$) from the best previous integer recommendation (subproblem 1). As a result, the decision maker can now eliminate subproblem 1 from consideration. In the diagram, the exclusion again is indicated by drawing a jagged line leading to subproblem 1.

Optimal Integer Solution. By following the unpruned branches in Figure 10.6, you can also see that there are no further subproblems that could provide an integer solution with a profit greater than $378,000. Therefore, the best subproblem 3 solution ($X_1 = 3$, $X_2 = 4$) must represent the optimal answer for Quality's integer programming problem.

Procedure Recap. The following branch and bound method can be used to solve general (binary, mixed, and pure) integer programming problems:

1. Solve the integer program as a linear programming problem.

2. If the recommendation violates any integer restriction, partition the solution space into subspaces by adding constraints to the original linear program.

3. Use the bounds provided by the descendant problem solutions to eliminate inferior subspaces.

4. Continue to branch and bound until the process locates the optimal integer solution.

Figure 10.6   **Branch and Bound Solution of Quality's Integer Program**

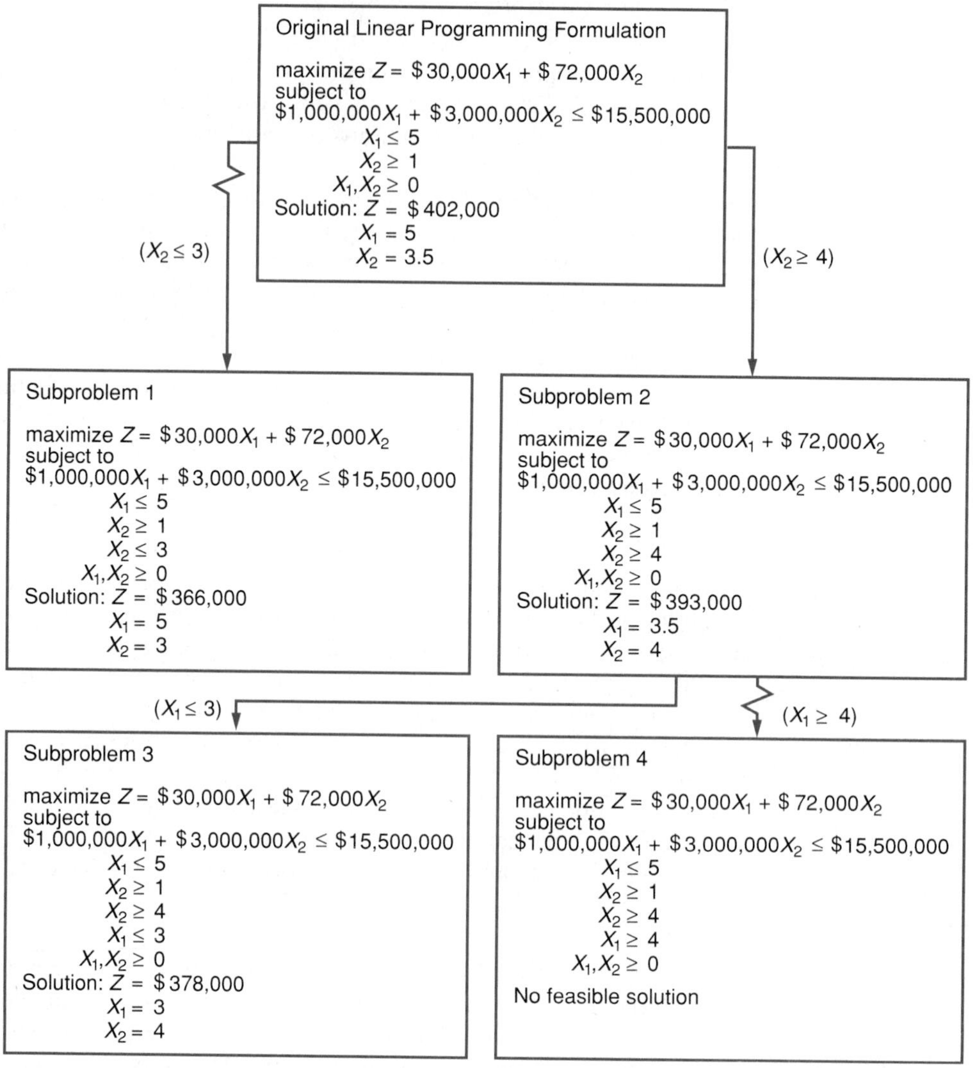

Original Linear Programming Formulation

maximize $Z = \$30,000X_1 + \$72,000X_2$
subject to
$\$1,000,000X_1 + \$3,000,000X_2 \leq \$15,500,000$
$X_1 \leq 5$
$X_2 \geq 1$
$X_1, X_2 \geq 0$
Solution: $Z = \$402,000$
$X_1 = 5$
$X_2 = 3.5$

$(X_2 \leq 3)$

$(X_2 \geq 4)$

Subproblem 1

maximize $Z = \$30,000X_1 + \$72,000X_2$
subject to
$\$1,000,000X_1 + \$3,000,000X_2 \leq \$15,500,000$
$X_1 \leq 5$
$X_2 \geq 1$
$X_2 \leq 3$
$X_1, X_2 \geq 0$
Solution: $Z = \$366,000$
$X_1 = 5$
$X_2 = 3$

Subproblem 2

maximize $Z = \$30,000X_1 + \$72,000X_2$
subject to
$\$1,000,000X_1 + \$3,000,000X_2 \leq \$15,500,000$
$X_1 \leq 5$
$X_2 \geq 1$
$X_2 \geq 4$
$X_1, X_2 \geq 0$
Solution: $Z = \$393,000$
$X_1 = 3.5$
$X_2 = 4$

$(X_1 \leq 3)$

$(X_1 \geq 4)$

Subproblem 3

maximize $Z = \$30,000X_1 + \$72,000X_2$
subject to
$\$1,000,000X_1 + \$3,000,000X_2 \leq \$15,500,000$
$X_1 \leq 5$
$X_2 \geq 1$
$X_2 \geq 4$
$X_1 \leq 3$
$X_1, X_2 \geq 0$
Solution: $Z = \$378,000$
$X_1 = 3$
$X_2 = 4$

Subproblem 4

maximize $Z = \$30,000X_1 + \$72,000X_2$
subject to
$\$1,000,000X_1 + \$3,000,000X_2 \leq \$15,500,000$
$X_1 \leq 5$
$X_2 \geq 1$
$X_2 \geq 4$
$X_1 \geq 4$
$X_1, X_2 \geq 0$

No feasible solution

Computer Analysis

Management Situation 10.2 is a small-scale problem with a fractional answer close to the optimal integer programming recommendation. As a result, relatively few computations are needed to complete the search for the optimal integer solution. In practice, however, computer assistance will be needed to solve typical large-scale integer programming problems.

Figure 10.7   Computer Solution of Quality's Integer Program

Integer Programming:	Input:	Output:
▪ Binary	* Edit	▪ Full
▪ Mixed	▪ Load	* Summary
* Pure	▪ Print	* Print
	▪ Save	▪ Save

Problem Formulation:

$$\text{MAX} \quad 30000\,X_1 + 72000\,X_2$$
$$\text{ST} \quad 1000000\,X_1 + 30000000\,X_2 <\,=\, 15500000$$
$$X_1 \qquad\qquad <\,=\, 5$$
$$X_2 >\,=\, 1$$

RECOMMENDATION

Decision Variable	Optimal Value
X_1	3.00
X_2	4.00

Supplemental Variable	Optimal Value
S_1	500000.00
S_2	2.00
S_3	3.00

Optimal Objective Function Value: 378000.00

A variety of computer software is available to provide the necessary help. Some software, such as *LINDO* and *LINDO/PC,* are designed to efficiently solve selected problem structures (such as a zero/one integer program). Others, such as *MPOS* and *XA*, can solve general integer programming problems.

The **Quantitative Management (QM)** software contains a general integer programming module. It is invoked by selecting Integer Programming from **QM's** main menu. Figure 10.7 then shows how the module is used to solve Quality's (Management Situation 10.2's) distribution problem.

Problem Formulation. As Figure 10.7 illustrates, the user executes the module by selecting the type of problem (pure in Quality's case) from the Integer Programming menu. The problem is formulated through the Edit command from the Input menu. As in **QM's** Linear Programming module, the user enters the objective function of maximizing (MAX) total monthly profit ($30000X_1 + 72000X_2$) subject to (*ST*) the three system constraints (budget, new stores, and additional warehouses). Report options then are chosen through the Output menu.

Optimal Integer Solution. The Recommendation section of the computer output (Figure 10.7) shows that Quality can maximize total monthly profit at \$378,000 by building

$$X_1 = 3 \text{ new stores}$$

and
$$X_2 = 4 \text{ additional warehouses.}$$

Integer Programming in Practice

Integer programming is applied to a wide variety of management problems. Here are a few areas in which this quantitative analysis is used.

Area	Application
Finance	Selecting the projects that minimize the net interest cost for a required investment
	Planning the shopping center development that maximizes annual cash flows to the owners
	Choosing the minimum number of branch sites for a bank
Marketing	Dispatching service equipment to best meet customer needs
	Determining the most efficient distribution of direct mail advertising
Production and Operations	Fixing the order in which a set of jobs is to be processed through a work center
	Sourcing raw materials, distributing raw materials and finished goods, and configuring facilities
	Improving the productivity of a company's purchasing function
Public and Service Sector	Planning hospital services
	Testing for vision loss in patients
	Determining faculty teaching assignments
	Scheduling meetings between students and teachers
	Assigning radio frequencies to different nets in a communications network so that interference is limited

---

Such a solution leaves a \$500,000 unused budget (S_1), 2 less than the maximum allowed new stores (S_2), and 3 more than the minimum required additional warehouses (S_3).

Postoptimality Analysis. Unlike linear programming, integer programming does not generate shadow prices (and reduced costs) as ordinary by-products of the solution process. Hence, such prices (and costs) do not appear as part of Figure 10.7's optimal integer solution. The absence of shadow prices also makes it difficult to perform a systematic sensitivity analysis of the integer recommendation. Instead, the decision maker typically must resort to the ad hoc procedures of resolving the problem several times with slight variations in the coefficients and then checking the effects on the recommended integer solution.

10.3 GOAL PROGRAMMING

Traditional mathematical programming models assume that the decision maker has a single, measurable objective such as maximizing profit or minimizing cost. Instead of posing a single objective, however, managers frequently use multiple criteria in decision making. Moreover, they typically set concrete goals, targets, or aspiration levels as a tactic in the pursuit of objectives. Such goals establish a clear point of reference, provide a keen sense of direction, and measure the progress toward the company's objectives.

When there are multiple goals, it is difficult to exactly achieve all targets. Instead, management may seek the solution that best satisfies the set of aspiration levels in the problem. Goal programming can be used to find such a "satisficing" solution.

In goal programming, the decision maker first identifies the relevant targets and established priorities for these goals. Usually, the goals are rank-ordered and **preemptive weights** are assigned to the targets at each priority level. These preemptive weights, which are generally codes rather than numerical values, require higher-priority goals to be satisfied as well as possible before lower-priority targets are considered. Goal programming then minimizes the deviations from the prioritized goals, subject to the problem constraints. Management Situation 10.3 illustrates.

Management Situation 10.3

Regional Work Force Planning

The State Department of Transportation (SDOT) plans on launching a vast construction project to complete various urban freeway systems. Department engineers estimate that the project will require at least one million skilled labor hours. This work force is to be drawn from unemployed skilled industrial and/or residential construction personnel.

Unemployed industrial personnel can be put to work on local phases of the project immediately at an average wage of $6 per hour. On the other hand, residential construction workers must be retrained for the project at government expense. The retrained labor would then be available locally at an average hourly wage of $10. This amount includes the government training expense. State legislators have allocated a budget of no more than $12 million for project labor costs.

The primary goal of the SDOT project is to alleviate unemployment among construction workers in the state's urban areas. Union and political pressures will also force the department to pursue two additional but less important targets. Specifically, the governor has directed the SDOT to:

1.   Employ skilled residential workers for at least as many hours as construction workers

2.   Supply no more than 400,000 labor hours for the project from the retraining program

Moreover, the employment ratio target is considered more important than the retraining aspiration level.

Department officials want to identify the employment levels that best satisfy the project goals.

Nature of the Problem

The SDOT wants to identify the employment levels that best satisfy the freeway construction goals. These employment levels can be depicted with the decision variables

X_1 = skilled labor hours allocated to unemployed industrial construction workers

and

X_2 = skilled labor hours allocated to unemployed residential construction personnel.

Figure 10.8   **The SDOT Budget and Goal Constraints**

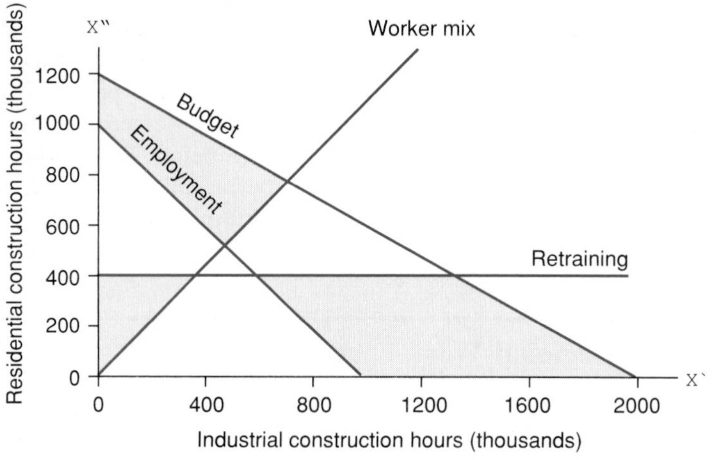

When selecting the employment levels, department officials must consider three criteria: total employment, the industrial/residential construction worker mix, and the retraining program supply. Each criterion is stated in terms of a concrete goal.

The primary goal is to alleviate unemployment in the state's urban areas by using at least one million idle skilled labor hours for the freeway project. This employment goal can be expressed with the constraint

$$X_1 + X_2 \geq 1,000,000 \text{ hours.}$$

After satisfying the first goal, the next target is to employ skilled residential workers for at least as many hours as industrial construction personnel. This worker mix can be written as

$$X_2 \geq X_1.$$

The lowest-priority goal is to supply no more than 400,000 labor hours from the retraining program, or

$$X_2 \leq 400,000 \text{ hours.}$$

In addition to these three goal constraints, the SDOT must ensure that

$$\$6X_1 + \$10X_2 \leq \$12,000,000.$$

That is, the department cannot spend more than the $12 million budget on project labor costs. Such an expression, which deals with a nongoal-oriented limitation, is known as a **technological, structural** or **system constraint.**

The goal and budget constraints are depicted graphically in Figure 10.8. In this figure, the upper shaded region identifies the decision variable combinations (X_1 and X_2) that satisfy the budget restriction and the employment and worker mix aspirations. Similarly, the lower right shaded region gives the work force mix that meets the budget constraint and the employment and retraining targets. The lower left shaded region represents the employment levels that fulfill the budget restriction and the worker mix and retraining goals.

Note that there is no decision variable combination in Figure 10.8 that meets the budget restriction and simultaneously satisfies all three goal constraints. Instead, the retraining target conflicts with either the worker mix or employment aspiration level. To find a feasible project plan, SDOT officials must concentrate on the deviations from the specified goals.

Problem Formulation

The SDOT employment goal is to use at least one million idle skilled labor hours for the freeway project, or have

$$X_1 + X_2 \geq 1{,}000{,}000 \text{ hours.}$$

In practice, however, officials may need more skilled labor or be required to settle for less skilled labor than the one-million-hour target.

Deviational Variables. To account for employment levels above and below the target, the department can define the variables

$$d_1^+ = \text{employment above the one-million-hour aspiration level}$$

and

$$d_1^- = \text{employment below the one-million-hour aspiration level.}$$

Such activities, which measure the amounts by which the goal will be overachieved (d^+) or underachieved (d^-), are known as **deviational variables**.

By subtracting d_1^+ from, and adding d_1^- to, the left-hand side of the employment target expression, the SDOT will obtain the goal equation

$$X_1 + X_2 - d_1^+ + d_1^- = 1{,}000{,}000 \text{ hours.}$$

This relationship accounts for all possible goal circumstances. For instance, if the department meets the one-million-hour target exactly, then

$$X_1 + X_2 = 1{,}000{,}000 \text{ hours}$$

and d_1^+ and d_1^- equal zero. On the other hand, when project employment exceeds the aspiration level, then

$$X_1 + X_2 > 1{,}000{,}000 \text{ hours}$$

with d_1^- equal to zero and d_1^+ equal to the excess of the actual $(X_1 + X_2)$ work force over the one-million-hour goal. Alternatively, if employment falls below the target, then d_1^+ will equal zero, but d_1^- will equal the difference between the one-million-hour goal and the actual work force.

The SDOT must reformulate the other two (worker mix and retraining) goal constraints in a similar manner. Hence, officials should define

$$d_2^+ = \text{residential construction personnel employment}$$
$$\text{above the worker mix aspiration level}$$

and d_2^- = residential construction personnel employment
below the worker mix aspiration level.

By subtracting d_2^+ from, and adding d_2^- to, the left-hand side of the worker mix target expression ($X_2 \geq X_1$), the department will obtain an equation

$$X_2 - d_2^+ + d_2^- = X_1$$

or

$$-X_1 + X_2 - d_2^+ + d_2^- = 0 \text{ hours}$$

that accounts for all possible goal circumstances. Also, the SDOT can define

$$d_3^+ = \text{retraining above the 400,000-hour aspiration level}$$

and

$$d_3^- = \text{retraining below the 400,000-hour aspiration level.}$$

Then, by subtracting d_3^+ from, and adding d_3^- to, the left-hand side of the retraining program target expression ($X_2 \leq 400,000$ hours), the department will get an equation

$$X_2 - d_3^+ + d_3^- = 400,000 \text{ hours}$$

that accounts for all potential retraining goal conditions.

Technological Constraints. Department officials must also spend no more than $12 million on freeway construction labor costs. Unlike the three other constraints (employment, worker mix, and retraining), this budget restriction does not involve a project goal. Consequently, the restriction can be left in its original form ($\$6X_1 + \$10X_2 \leq \$12,000,000$) and treated as a linear programming system constraint that must be satisfied to ensure a feasible problem solution.

Preemptive Weights. Since the department's primary goal is to alleviate unemployment, employment below the one-million-hour target (any positive d_1^- value) would be a very undesirable deviation. The officials' first priority, which can be denoted with the preemptive weight P_1, is to make d_1^- as small as possible, or to

$$\text{minimize} \quad P_1 d_1^-.$$

In this expression, the preemptive weight P_1 is merely a code that tells officials to satisfy the employment target as well as possible before considering any lower-ranked goal.

After satisfying the highest-priority goal, officials next consider the second most important target: to employ skilled residential workers for at least as many hours as industrial construction personnel. Since residential employment below the worker mix target (any positive d_2^- value) would be undesirable, the department's second priority P_2 is to

$$\text{minimize} \quad P_2 d_2^-.$$

Once more, the preemptive weight P_2 is a code that tells officials to satisfy the worker mix target as well as possible before considering any lower-ranked goal.

After fulfilling, in order, the higher-priority goals, the SDOT can then consider the least important target: to supply no more than 400,000 labor hours from the retraining program. Since retraining above the 400,000-hour aspiration level (any positive d_3^+ value) would be undesirable, the department seeks to

$$\text{minimize} \quad P_3 d_3^+$$

where the preemptive weight P_3 indicates that the retraining target is the third-ranking priority.

Objective Function. In pursuing each lower-ranked goal, however, the SDOT must not select employment levels that jeopardize the attainment of any higher-priority targets. Hence, officials should first find the minimum value of the most important (P_1) deviational variable d_1^-. While maintaining d_1^- at its minimum value, they should next minimize the quantity of the second most important (P_2) deviational variable d_2^-. Finally, while sustaining the P_1 and P_2 goal achievements, the department should seek the minimum value of the least important (P_3) deviational variable d_3^+. This hierarchy of objectives can be written as follows:

$$\text{minimize} \quad P_3 d_3^+ \mid \text{minimum } P_2 d_2^- \mid \text{minimum } P_1 d_1^-.$$

The statement after each vertical bar identifies the condition regarding a higher-priority goal that must be satisfied while pursuing the lower-ranked target listed before the bar. Such an expression clearly shows that the decision maker must minimize each goal deviation (d_1^-, d_2^-, and d_3^+) individually in its order of priority (P_1, P_2, and P_3).

Traditionally, however, the hierarchy of objectives has been treated in a different manner. In the conventional approach, the decision maker is assumed to minimize the sum of the preemptively-weighed goal deviations, or, in the SDOT case, to

$$\text{minimize} \quad Z = P_1 d_1^- + P_2 d_2^- + P_3 d_3^+.$$

Unfortunately, this objective function suggests that management has a single criterion (Z) rather than a series of individual goals ($P_1 d_1^-$, $P_2 d_2^-$, and $P_3 d_3^+$). Thus, it is misleading. Moreover, the deviational variables in many applications are expressed in different units of measurement. As a result, the sum Z is often meaningless. Nevertheless, such notation is prevalent in the literature and cannot be ignored.

Goal Program. By collecting the traditional objective function and constraint equations and adding the appropriate nonnegativity conditions, SDOT officials can express the work force problem as follows:

minimize $Z = P_1 d_1^- + P_2 d_2^- + P_3 d_3^+$

subject to $X_1 + X_2 - d_1^+ + d_1^- = 1,000,000$ hours   (Employment)

$-X_1 + X_2 - d_2^+ + d_2^- = 0$ hours   (Worker mix)

$X_2 - d_3^+ + d_3^- = 400,000$ hours   (Retraining)

$\$6X_1 + \$10X_2 \le \$12,000,000$ (Budget)

$X_1, X_2, d_1^+, d_1^-, d_2^+, d_2^-, d_3^+, d_3^- \ge 0$

Such a statement is referred to as a **goal program**.

Recap. The following procedure is used to formulate a goal program:

1. Express each goal and technological (system) constraint in mathematical programming format.

2. Convert each goal constraint into its goal programming format by subtracting a d^+ deviational variable from, and by adding a d^- deviational variable to, the left-hand side of the original expression.

3. Form nonnegativity conditions for all decision and deviational variables.

4. Identify all undesirable goal deviations and assign a preemptive weight to each deviation.

5. Minimize each deviation individually in the order of its priority (preemptive weight).

Graphic Solution

The SDOT can use the employment, worker mix, retraining, and budget equations to identify all feasible work force alternatives. Officials first should set

$$d_1^+ = d_1^- = d_2^+ = d_2^- = d_3^+ = d_3^- = 0$$

and then graph the resulting constraint equations. By so doing, they will get the results presented in Figure 10.9. In this graph, decision variable combinations (X_1 and X_2) on the constraint lines provide zero values for the corresponding deviational (d^+ or d^-) activities. Each point above a line represents a positive d^+ quantity, and any combination below a line corresponds to a positive d^- value.

Feasible Solutions. According to the budget equation in the goal programming formulation, the SDOT cannot choose decision variable combinations that require an expenditure in excess of the $12 million budget. Consequently, officials must select points that are on or below the budget constraint line in Figure 10.9. Although there are an infinite number of such points, many will not satisfy the hierarchy of goals specified in the problem's objective function.

Goal Hierarchy. SDOTs highest priority (P_1) is to minimize employment below the one-million-hour target (d_1^-). To fully achieve this objective, the department must set $d_1^- = 0$ or select points that are on or above the employment constraint line in Figure 10.9. Yet some of these points will not meet the next-highest priority (P_2) of minimizing residential construction employment below the worker mix aspiration level (d_2^-). In fact, points on or above the worker mix line in Figure 10.9 represent the only decision variable combinations that can completely attain the second-ranked objective.

In effect, the shaded region of Figure 10.9 identifies the employment levels that satisfy the budget restriction and fully achieve the project's top two (P_1 and P_2) goals. Management still must consider, however, the third priority (P_3) of minimizing retraining time above the 400,000-hour aspiration level (d_3^+). This time will be minimized if $d_3^+ = 0$ or when the department chooses points on or below the retraining constraint line in Figure 10.9.

Unfortunately, none of the points on or below the retraining line are in the shaded region of Figure 10.9. In other words, there is no work force plan that will satisfy the budget restriction, fully achieve SDOT's top two (P_1 and P_2) goals, and still completely

Figure 10.9   The SDOT Goal Programming Solution

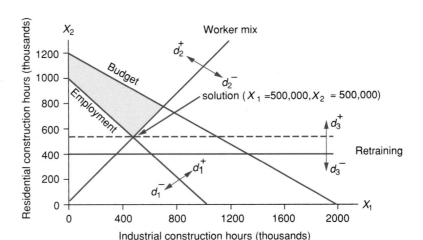

attain the lowest priority (P_3) target. To operate within the budget and fully accomplish the two highest priorities, the department must have some excess retraining hours.

The SDOT should still seek the work force plan that keeps the excess retraining hours (d_3^+) at a minimum. To find such a plan, officials can shift the retraining constraint line upward in parallel fashion until it touches the boundary of the shaded region in Figure 10.9. The parallel shift, which is indicated with the dashed line in the diagram, identifies the point that minimizes d_3^+ without violating the budget restriction and two highest priority goals. In short, this graphical analysis determines the solution to the department's goal programming problem.

Optimal Solution. By examining Figure 10.9, you can see that the solution point involves

$$X_1 = 500,000 \text{ skilled labor hours allocated to}$$
$$\text{unemployed industrial construction workers}$$

and

$$X_2 = 500,000 \text{ skilled labor hours allocated to}$$
$$\text{unemployed residential construction personnel.}$$

Moreover, this point is on both the unemployment and worker mix constraint lines. Hence, the work force plan will have

$$d_1^+ = d_1^- = d_2^+ = d_2^- = 0.$$

That is, the SDOT can fully achieve both the employment and worker mix targets with the freeway project.

Figure 10.9 also shows that the solution point $(X_1 = 500,000, X_2 = 500,000)$ is above the retraining constraint line. As a result, $d_3^- = 0$, but there will be some excess retraining hours. Indeed, according to the retraining constraint equation, the goal programming plan will involve

$$X_2 - d_3^+ + d_3^- = 400,000 \text{ hours}$$

or

$$d_3^+ = X_2 + d_3^- - 400,000 = 500,000 + 0 - 400,000 = 100,000$$

retraining hours above the 400,000-hour target.

Slack. Figure 10.9 demonstrates that the goal programming solution point ($X_1 = 500,000$ and $X_2 = 500,000$) is below the budget constraint line. As a result, the SDOT project will come in under budget. To determine the savings, officials can define the slack variable (with a subscript of 4 because the original restriction is the fourth constraint in the problem)

$$S_4 = \text{ unused budget dollars}$$

and add this slack to the left-hand side of the original constraint. The resulting expression

$$\$6X_1 + \$10X_2 + S_4 = \$12,000,000$$

then indicates that the freeway project will cost

$$S_4 = \$12,000,000 - \$6(500,000) - \$10(500,000) = \$4,000,000$$

less than the $12 million budgeted for labor expenditures.

Procedure Recap. The following graphic procedure can be used to solve a goal programming with two decision variables:

1. Graph all technological (system) constraints superimposed on the nonnegativity conditions (on the graph's northeast quadrant) and identify the corresponding area of feasible solutions. If there is no such area, the problem does not have a feasible solution.

2. Graph the goal constraints and label the corresponding deviational variables.

3. Find the point (or points) within the technologically-feasible solution area that best satisfies the hierarchy of goals.

4. Substitute the solution point (decision variable combination) into each constraint and solve the resulting equations for the corresponding values of the deviational and supplemental (slack and surplus) variables.

Simplex Analysis

Most practical situations have many more than two decision variables. In such cases, nongraphical approaches must be used to solve the goal programming problem.

Reformulation. One approach is to formulate and solve the goal programming problem as a linear program. In this approach, deviational variables are treated just like decision variables, and preemptive weights are given numerical values that will reflect goal priorities.

For example, the SDOT can arbitrarily set $P_1 = 2,000,000$, $P_2 = 1,500$, and $P_3 = 2$ and reformulate its objective function as

$$\text{minimize} \quad Z = 2,000,000 \; d_1^- + 1,500 \; d_2^- + 2 \; d_3^+ .$$

This reformulation will preserve the officials' goal priority structure and, along with the original goal and technological (system) constraints, create a linear program that can be solved with the simplex method for the optimal values of the decision, deviational, and supplemental varibles.

Modified Simplex Method. Assigning realistic numerical values to the preemptive weights can become difficult (and possibly infeasible) as the number of priority levels increases. Therefore, other approaches have been developed to solve large-scale goal programming problems. In one of these other approaches, the simplex method is modified to account for the hierarchy of goals.

An initial basic feasible solution is found by first setting all decision and positive deviational variables equal to zero. The values of the remaining variables then can be read from the right-hand sides of the goal constraints and from the standard form system constraints. For example, SDOT's initial basic feasible solution is

$X_1 = 0$ $d_1^- = 1,000,000$ hours

$X_2 = 0$ $d_2^- = 0$ hours

$d_1^+ = 0$ $d_3^- = 400,000$ hours

$d_3^+ = 0$ $S_4 = \$12,000,000$

Next, the initial solution is recorded in a modified form of the simplex table. A row is established for each goal and system constraint, and a column is created for each decision, deviational, and supplemental (slack, surplus, and artificial) variable. Variable coefficients and right-hand amounts from the constraints are placed in the corresponding cells of the table. In the Z_j and $C_j - Z_j$ segments, there will be one row for each preemptive weight, and these rows will be arranged in rank order from the lowest to highest priority.

Table 10.5 gives the modified simplex table for SDOT's initial basic feasible solution. This table's entries are determined in exactly the same way as in the ordinary simplex method. For example, the C_j and X_1 column entries indicate that the Z_j value for the X_1 column will be

$$(P_1 \times 1) + (P_2 \times -1) + (P_3 \times 0) + (0 \times 6) = 1P_1 - 1P_2 + 0P_3$$

while $0 - (1P_1 - 1P_2 + 0P_3) = -1P_1 + 1P_2 + 0P_3$

gives the corresponding $C_j - Z_j$ value.

Unlike the ordinary procedure, however, the modified table's Z_j and $C_j - Z_j$ segments have separate rows for SDOT's three preemptive weights. In these segments, the weights are recorded in rank order from the lowest (P_3) to highest (P_1). Calculated coefficients are reported in the corresponding cells of the table. For example, the $C_j - Z_j$ value for X_1 is

$$-1P_1 + 1P_2 + 0P_3.$$

Table 10.5   SDOT's Initial Basic Feasible Solution

Variables		X_1	X_2	d_1^+	d_1^-	d_2^+	d_2^-	d_3^+	d_3^-	S_4	Amounts	Trade Ratio
Basis	C_j	0	0	0	P_1	0	P_2	P_3	0	0		
d_1^-	P_1	1	1	-1	1	0	0	0	0	0	1,000,000	1,000,000
d_2^-	P_2	-1	(1)	0	0	-1	1	0	0	0	0	0 ← Pivot Row
d_3^-	P_0	0	1	0	0	0	0	-1	1	0	400,000	400,000
S_4	0	6	10	0	0	0	0	0	0	1	12,000,000	1,200,000
	P_3	0	0	0	0	0	0	0	0	0	400,000	
Z_j	P_2	-1	1	0	0	-1	1	0	0	0	0	
	P_1	1	1	-1	1	0	0	0	0	0	1,000,000	
	P_3	0	-1	0	0	0	0	1	0	0		
$C_j - Z_j$	P_2	1	-1	0	0	1	0	0	0	0		
	P_1	-1	0	1	0	0	0	0	0	0		

↑
Pivot
Column

Consequently, the X_1 column has entries of 0 in the P_3 row, 1 in the P_2 row, and -1 in the P_1 row of Table 10.5's $C_j - Z_j$ segment.

Since SDOT wants to minimize goal deviations in rank order of priority, the entering variable will be in the column having the largest negative entry in the P_1 of Table 10.5's $C_j - Z_j$ segment. As in the SDOT case, ties can be broken at the next lowest (P_2) priority level. The pivot row, pivot element, and the next modified simplex table then can be found with the same procedures as used in the ordinary simplex method.

When all P_1 row coefficients in the $C_j - Z_j$ segment have been driven to nonnegative values, SDOT has achieved the highest priority goal. Attention then can be directed to the second highest priority goal (the P_2 row in the $C_j - Z_j$ segment). Eventually, the modified simplex method will generate a table that meets one of the following conditions:

1. All Amounts column entries in the Z_j segment are 0.

2. For every negative entry, there is at least one positive entry at higher priority levels in the same column of the $C_j - Z_j$ segment.

This table will identify the optimal goal programming solution (if it exists).

Computer Analysis

Usually, a prewritten computer package, such as *GOAL,* is used to implement the goal programming simplex analysis. A program similar to these commercial packages is available on the **Quantitative Management (QM)** software. It is invoked by selecting

---

Figure 10.10   **Computer Solution of SDOT's Goal Program**

Goal Programming: Input: Output:
▪ Reformulated linear programming   * Edit   ▪ Full
* Modified simplex method   ▪ Load   *Summary
                                                         ▪ Print   * Print
                                                         ▪ Save   ▪ Save

Problem Formulation:

MIN $P_1 d_1^- + P_2 d_2^- + P_3 d_3^+$
ST $1X_1 + 1X_2 - 1d_1^+ + 1d_1^- = 1000000$
      $-1X_1 + 1X_2 - 1d_2^+ + 1d_2^- = 0$
      $0X_1 + 1X_2 - 1d_3^+ + 1d_3^- = 400000$
      $6X_1 + 10X_2 \leq 12000000$

RECOMMENDATION

Decision Variable	Optimal Value
X_1	500000.00
X_2	500000.00

Supplemental Variable	Optimal Value
S_4	4000000.00

Deviational Variable	Optimal Value
d_1^+	0.00
d_1^-	0.00
d_2^+	0.00
d_2^-	0.00
d_3^+	100000.00
d_3^-	0.00

Goal Priority	Nonachievement
P_1	0.00
P_2	0.00
P_3	100000.00

Goal Programming from **QM**'s main menu. Figure 10.10 then shows how the program is used to solve SDOT's (Management Situation 10.3's) work force planning problem.

Problem Formulation. As Figure 10.10 illustrates, the user executes the module by selecting the type of analysis (modified simplex method in SDOT's case) from the Goal Programming menu. The problem is formulated through the Edit command from the Input menu. In this case, officials want to minimize (*MIN*) the hierarchy of goal deviations $(P_1 d_1^- + P_2 d_2^- + P_3 d_3^+)$ subject to (*ST*) the three goal constraints and the technological (system) constraint. Report options then are chosen through the Output menu.

Optimal Integer Solution. The Recommendation section of Figure 10.10 shows that SDOT can best achieve its hierarchy of goals by allocating

$X_1 = 500,000$ hours to unemployed industrial construction workers

and $X_2 = 500,000$ hours to unemployed residential construction workers.

Such a solution leaves an unused budget of $S_4 = \$4,000,000$ and involves $d_3^+ = 100,000$ hours more than the desired retraining (third-ranked) goal. The two highest priority (P_1 and P_2) goals will be fully achieved with this solution.

Postoptimality Analysis. Unlike linear programming, goal programming does not generate shadow prices (and reduced costs) as ordinary by-products of the solution process. Hence, such prices (and costs) do not appear in the computer output (Figure 10.10). The absence of shadow prices also makes it difficult to perform a systematic sensitivity analysis of the goal programming recommendation. Nevertheless, there are methods available (not treated here) to perform limited sensitivity analyses on the technological coefficients and on the right-hand sides of the goal and system constraints.

Interactive Goal Programming. Decision maker preferences are seldom clearly defined or fixed. Instead, these preferences depend on specific situations and on the knowledge the decision maker has about the situations. An emerging computer analysis, known as **interactive goal programming,** allows the user to progressively define preferences as the problem is evaluated and solved. With such an analysis, the decision maker can quickly and easily examine the impacts on the recommendation of changes in the priority structure and in the problem setting.

Extensions

There are a number of important extensions to the basic goal programming analysis. These extensions include priority structures, integer and nonlinear goal programming, and other multicriteria models.

Priority Structures. In Management Situation 10.3, each undesirable deviational variable has a different priority to the SDOT. However, two or more deviational variables are frequently given the same priority in the problem. Thought Exercise 10 offers an illustration of such a problem. Furthermore, management might want to give some of the equally-ranked deviational variables more importance or weight than others. Technique Exercises 23 and 24 provide examples. As these exercises will demonstrate, the decision maker can solve the more complex cases with the same principles used in the basic goal programming situation.

Integer and Nonlinear Goal Programming. Many goal programming problems involve decision variables that must have integer (pure integer or zero/one) values. In other goal programming problems, there are nonlinear goal and system constraints. Research is currently under way that will allow decision makers to effectively address these integer and nonlinear goal programming problems.

Other Multicriteria Models. Generally, goal programming minimizes undesirable deviational variables one by one in the order of their priority. As discussed in Chapter 6, management can form a composite measure of divergence. Such a measure will simultaneously consider the set of undesirable deviational variables, but weight each according to its relative importance in the problem. The decision maker can then minimize the composite measure.

In another approach, called **multiobjective programming,** management first establishes a separate objective for each relevant combination of decision variables. Next it finds all feasible solutions that will not improve the value of one criterion without diminishing the quantity of at least one other criterion. The decision maker then can analyze these solutions to identify the most preferable variable combination.

SUMMARY

In this chapter, we examined certain mathematical programming topics that are important to practical decision making. We learned to identify the fundamental assumptions of linear programming and discussed circumstances that could invalidate each supposition, outlining appropriate alternative methodologies. The concepts were summarized in Table 10.3.

One of the most common situations involves a mathematical programming problem in which some or all of the decision variables are required to have integer values. One approach to such problems is to treat the situation as an ordinary linear problem and then round any fractional solution to whole-unit values. As the second section of the chapter demonstrated, however, this rounding procedure is sometimes very time-consuming and often does not provide the optimal solution to the original problem. Consequently, management scientists have developed alternative methodologies to solve these integer programming problems. We reviewed the most popular of these procedures, including the graphic approach, enumeration, the cutting plane method, and the branch and bound procedure. In addition, we saw how a prewritten computer package can be used to solve integer programming problems. We concluded with some important practical extensions to the fundamental methodology.

In the third section of the chapter, we discussed mathematical programming problems in which management has multiple decision criteria expressed in terms of concrete targets, or goals. First we saw how to formulate these goal programming problems. Next we examined a graphic solution methodology designed for small-scale situations. Then we saw how a prewritten computer package can be used to solve large-scale goal programming problems. Finally, the last section outlined some important practical extensions to the fundamental methodology and presented some typical applications of goal programming.

Glossary

branch and bound method An approach that develops an optimal solution by successively partitioning a problem into progressively smaller segments.

chance-constrained programming A methodology that accounts for parameter uncertainty by reformulating each original system constraint in a way that ensures that a mathematical programming solution provides a high probability of meeting the restriction.

cutting algorithm A procedure that obtains an optimal integer solution by successively adding constraints that eliminate fractional answers from a linear programming formulation of the problem.

deviational variables Variables that measure the amounts by which the target in a goal constraint will be exceeded or underachieved.

goal program A mathematical programming problem that involves a hierarchy of specified, concrete targets or aspiration levels.

goal programming A methodology designed to incorporate multiple criteria within the mathematical programming framework.

integer programming A methodology designed to deal with mathematical programming problems in which some or all of the decision variables must have whole-unit values.

interactive goal programming A computer analysis that allows the decision maker to progressively define preferences as the problem is evaluated and solved.

linear relationship A relationship in which each decision variable has an exponent of 1 and appears in a separate term of the relevant mathematical expression.

mixed integer programming problem An integer programming problem in which some, but not all, decision variables must have integer solution values.

multiobjective programming A methodology designed to solve mathematical programming problems that involve separate objective functions for each relevant combination of decision variables.

nonlinear program A mathematical program that consists of a nonlinear objective function and/or at least one nonlinear system constraint.

nonlinear programming Any methodology designed to solve a nonlinear program.

nonlinear relationship A relationship in which a decision variable has an exponent different than 1 and/or more than one activity appears in a single term of the relevant mathematical expression.

preemptive weight A symbol indicating the priority assigned by the decision maker to the corresponding deviational variable.

pure integer programming A situation in which all the decision variables in the mathematical program must have integer solutions.

stochastic programming A methodology that accounts for parameter uncertainty by incorporating stochastic elements into an expanded version of the original mathematical program.

technological, structural or system constraint A restriction that deals with a resource capacity or other non-goal-oriented limitation.

zero/one (binary integer) programming problem An integer programming problem in which each decision variable must have a solution value of one or zero.

Thought Exercises

1. Which mathematical programming methodology seems most appropriate in each of the following situations? Explain.

   a. The Air Force is considering five types of attack missiles to equip its fighter aircraft. Missile effectiveness is determined by the military value of the target destroyed during a specified operation. The effectiveness ratings, personnel requirements, and maintenance costs for each missile are constant and exactly known. Fighter capacity and support requirements are also readily available from design specifications. The problem is to find the quantity of each missile that will maximize the "attack value" of the fighter.

   b. Eastern Regional Savings and Loan Association is preparing to invest no more than 10 percent of its cash reserves. Several alternatives are available, each with its own probability distribution of returns. Association policy, however, places some clear restrictions on any investment portfolio. Management wants to determine the portfolio that maximizes the expected return on the investment while satisfying these policy restrictions.

   c. An overnight delivery service utilizes a fleet of vans in its operations. The company knows the exact purchase price, annual operating cost, and yearly resale value of each van. Management wants to determine the replacement policy (age for replacing a van) that will minimize total fleet cost.

d. A large cooperative in the western part of the state operates a group of farms. Each farm utilizes available acreage, current personnel, and existing equipment to plant and harvest several distinct crops. The cooperative wants to find the crop mix on each farm that will maximize total profit.

e. Government officials currently are considering alternative fiscal (spending and/or tax) and monetary policies to improve national economic conditions. The policies will be evaluated in terms of their effect on gross national product, inflation, unemployment, the international trade balance, and interest rates. All selected policies must also meet prescribed political, social, and economic constraints.

f. A large department store chain plans to allocate some or all of its monthly advertising budget in your town. It can purchase local radio messages, television spots, or newspaper insertions. Although these placements should provide some audience exposure to the advertising message, it is unlikely that the effects will be uniform or independent. Specifically, the company believes that larger placements will lead to increased exposure. Moreover, it thinks that the exposure from radio spots will depend on the number of television and newspaper placements. Management wants to find the media mix that provides the largest audience exposure.

2. Examine each of the nonlinear programming problems listed in the following table:

Problem	Definitions
maximize $Z = 40X_1 + 60X_2 - 10X_1^3 - 20X_2^2$ subject to $5X_1 + 15X_1 \le 40$ hours (Plant 1) $30X_1 + 12X_2 \le 84$ hours (Plant 2) $X_1, X_2 \ge 0$	$Z =$ total profit $X_1 =$ quantity of product A $X_2 =$ quantity of product B
minimize $Z = \$5\left(\dfrac{1000}{X_1 X_2 X_3}\right) + \$30\left(\dfrac{1000}{X_1}\right) + \$25\left(\dfrac{1000}{X_3}\right)$ subject to $X_1 X_3 + 2X_1 X_2 \le 26$ square feet	$Z =$ total shipping cost $X_1 =$ container length $X_2 =$ container width $X_3 =$ container height
maximize $Z = 12X_1 - 2X_1^2 + 15X_2 - X_1 X_2$ subject to $2X_1 + 4X_2 \ge 160$ hours (Labor) $X_1, X_2 \ge 0$	$Z =$ total profit $X_1 =$ yards of high-quality fabric $X_2 =$ yards of low-quality fabric
minimize $Z = 20X_1^2 + 10X_2^2 + 20X_1 X_2 - 40X_1 - 30X_2$ subject to $5X_1 + 4X_2 = 500$ gloves (Output)	$Z =$ total production cost $X_1 =$ shift 1 labor hours $X_2 =$ shift 2 labor hours

a. Identify the category of nonlinear programming that best describes each problem. (Table 10.2 may be useful in the identification process.)

b. Explain the nonlinear relationships in the objective function and/or constraints of each problem in language that would be understandable to management.

3. In the drugstore chain situation discussed in the text, the company will not add a new outlet in Sun City unless capacity is expanded at the Newberry warehouse. This interdependency is accounted for with the constraint

$$NO \le WE$$

where *NO* and *WE* are each binary variables representing the new outlet and warehouse, respectively.

Suppose that the new outlet will be added and capacity will be expanded. How will this co-requisite constraint be represented in the problem?

4. In the waste management situation discussed in the text, the constraints

$$X_1 + X_2 + X_3 \leq 8,000L$$

$$X_1 + X_2 + X_3 \leq 7,500T$$

$$X_1 + X_2 + X_3 \leq 8,200Z$$

$$L + T + Z \leq 1$$

(where X_j = waste collected from county j and L, T, and Z are each binary variables identifying the Lowtown, Tinersville, and Zanestown sites) depicted the fact that the decision maker must select only one site.

How would each of the following conditions affect the formulation?
a. Management must select either the Lowtown or Zanestown site.
b. Amortized fixed costs are $6,000 per month at the Lowtown site, $5,500 at Tinersville, and $7,000 at Zanestown.
c. Amortized fixed costs are the same as in part b, and management must select exactly one site.
d. Amortized fixed costs are the same as in part b, and management can select two sites.

5. Grandy Prancer, the administrator of the South Hills Sanatorium, is interested in enhancing the organization's cash flow situation by expanding its profitable health resort facilities. Unfortunately, her proposal was not completely endorsed by the board of directors. Instead, it authorized only $120,000 in funds to be used for not more than nine additional health resort rooms. Although Grandy was disappointed with the authorization, she decided to try and make the most of this additional budget.

After examining sanatorium operations for a couple of days, Grandy concluded that the additional rooms could be best utilized in the "Blue" and/or "Green" wings of the resort. Since each additional "Green" room would generate $60 and every "Blue" chamber only $30 profit per day, she was tempted to expand only the "Green" wing. However, Grandy remembered that the board insisted on at least three additional "Blue" rooms. Also, expansion will cost $19,000 per "Green" room and only $10,000 for each additional "Blue" chamber. Thus, she can build more "Blue" rooms than "Green" rooms for the same expenditure. The problem is to determine the room mixture that maximizes total additional daily profit.

Dolph Mojon, the administrative assistant at South Hills, had recently completed an executive education seminar in management science methodologies. Hence, Grandy thought that he could offer some useful advice on the problem. Consequently, she provided Dolph with the available information and instructed him to work on the problem while Grandy conducted her weekly staff meeting.

Dolph realized that he was dealing with an allocation problem that could be formulated as a linear program. Yet the optimal solution did not provide an integer number of additional "Green" rooms. As a result, Dolph decided to reexamine the problem from an integer programming perspective. Before he could do so, however, Grandy returned from the meeting and became very upset with Dolph. In particular, she felt that Dolph's management science "background" should have enabled him to develop a recommendation during the hour Grandy spent in the staff meeting.

Grandy then began to examine the problem in her own way. She rationalized that the only alternatives were the following room mixes:

Room Mix		Room Mix	
Blue	Green	Blue	Green
0	9	5	4
1	8	6	3
2	7	7	2
3	6	8	1
4	5	9	0

According to Grandy's analysis of these alternatives, the most profitable plan would consist of six additional "Blue" rooms and three more "Green" rooms. Furthermore, she claimed that "common sense" is the only approach needed to find this plan.

Although disheartened by Grandy's criticism, Dolph continued with his integer programming analysis, which revealed that an alternative room mix provided the same maximum profit as Grandy's "common sense" solution. More important, Dolph's recommendation required a $1,000 lower capital outlay than Grandy's plan. When confronted with these new data, Grandy admitted that the management science seminar "perhaps was worth the investment."

a.   What was the linear programming solution?
b.   How did Grandy obtain her "common sense" solution?
c.   Explain how Dolph was able to save $1,000 in capital outlay.
d.   What is your recommendation? Explain and show all your work.

6. Karen Scatlis, manager of the local college women's softball team, will soon take the varsity on an interconference road trip. There are 20 players on the team, but the school can afford to send only 15 women on the trip.

The coaching staff feels that the team will need at least two catchers, three pitchers, five outfielders, and five infielders to be "competitive" on the trip. Karen also believes that her team must hit well to beat the opposition on the schedule. As a result, she would prefer to select the players who have the highest composite batting average. In this regard, the coaching staff has compiled the following statistics on the team roster:

Player	Position	Batting Average	At Bats	Player	Position	Batting Average	At Bats
Jones	Pitcher	.210	50	White	Catcher	.150	30
Thomas	Infielder	.280	100	Green	Outfielder	.360	110
Adams	Catcher	.320	100	Smith	Outfielder	.310	100
Simmons	Outfielder	.400	120	Kajowski	Catcher	.200	50
Rupp	Outfielder	.350	70	Olivera	Pitcher	.500	10

Player	Position	Batting Average	At Bats	Player	Position	Batting Average	At Bats
Tolliver	Infielder	.220	50	Tonti	Infielder	.270	90
Abraham	Infielder	.250	80	Queen	Infielder	.300	80
Flint	Pitcher	.100	20	King	Pitcher	.180	60
Black	Infielder	.450	100	Howley	Outfielder	.290	120
Brown	Infielder	.260	150	Scott	Outfielder	.340	80

The composite measure is defined as the sum of each player's weighted batting average. In addition, the appropriate weight equals the player's at bats divided by total team at bats.

Formulate the coach's team selection problem.

7. Refer back to Management Situation 10.1. As noted in the text discussion, test conditions will likely force at least two (X_3 and Y_2) of Quantum's four (X_2, X_3, Y_1, and Y_2) decision variables to have integer rather than fractional values. Under these circumstances, management should add the restriction

$$X_3, Y_2 \geq 0 \text{ and are integers}$$

to the original linear program.

Suppose that management did this, then solved the resulting program with the **Quantitative Management (QM)** software and obtained the results displayed in the following figure. According to this printout, what is the recommended solution for Quantum's integer programming problem? Express your answer in language that would be understandable to management.

RECOMMENDATION

Decision Variable	Optimal Value
X_2	4500.00
Y_1	1500.00
Y_2	3000.00
X_3	0.00

Supplemental Variable	Optimal Value
S_1	5000.00
S_2	0.00
S_3	0.00
S_4	1500.00

Optimal Objective Function Value: 465000.00

8. A southwestern university's business school must fill at least 20 faculty positions for the next academic year. The highest priority is to remain within the $1 million budget provided for faculty additions. In this regard, it will cost an average of $30,000 to recruit and pay the first-year salary and benefits of each new faculty member.

Also, the business school faculty currently does not meet Equal Employment Opportunity Commission (EEOC) affirmative action requirements. Thus, the second most important goal is that at least 30 percent of the new employees be minorities. Latins, blacks, women, and native Americans qualify as minorities under EEOC guidelines.

Experience indicates that specialized recruiting procedures and salary inducements for such faculty typically add $16\frac{2}{3}$ percent to the school's recruitment and first-year employment costs.

The administration's lowest priority is to limit total faculty positions as much as possible. Fractional (part-time) faculty appointments are acceptable. Formulate this affirmative action problem. Define each variable and label all expressions.

9. Refer back to Management Situation 10.3. Suppose that the problem is reformulated as the following linear program:

minimize $\qquad Z = d_3^+$

subject to $\qquad X_1 + X_2 \geq 1,000,000$ hours $\qquad$ (Employment)

$\qquad\qquad\quad X_2 \geq X_1 \qquad\qquad\qquad\qquad\qquad$ (Worker Mix)

$\qquad\qquad\quad \$6X_1 + \$10X_2 \leq \$12,000,000 \qquad$ (Budget)

$\qquad\qquad\quad X_1, X_2 \geq 0$

where $d_3^+ = X_2 - 400,000$ and Z represents retraining above the 400,000-hour aspiration level.

What is the optimal solution to the reformulated problem? How does this recommendation compare to the goal programming solution? Explain. What is the implication of your finding?

10. Alright Corporation of Zonton is considering four new household products to replace recently discontinued brands. The problem is to determine the product mix that will best achieve a range of corporate goals. After consulting with the firm's management staff, the firm's Systems Analysis Group has expressed the new product problem as follows:

minimize $\quad Z = P_1 d_1^- + P_2(d_2^+ + d_2^-) + P_3 d_3^+ + P_4 d_4^-$

subject to $\quad \$.2X_1 + \$.5X_2 + \$.4X_3 + \$1X_4 +$

$\qquad d_1^- - d_1^+ = \$8$ million $\qquad\qquad\qquad\qquad$ (Profit goal)

$\qquad .4X_1 + 1X_2 + .2X_3 + .7X_4 + d_2^- - d_2^+ = 10,000 \qquad$ (Employment goal)

$\qquad X_1 + X_2 - X_3 - X_4 + d_3^- - d_3^+ = 0 \qquad\qquad$ (Brand mix goal)

$\qquad \$.3X_1 + \$.2X_2 + \$.6X_3 + \$.4X_4$

$\qquad + d_4^- - d_4^+ = \$20$ million $\qquad\qquad\qquad\qquad$ (Investment goal)

$\qquad 2X_1 + 10X_2 + 5X_3 + 4X_4 \leq 70,000$ hours $\qquad$ (Machinery)

$\qquad X_1, X_2, X_3, X_4, d_1^-, d_1^+, d_2^-, d_2^+, d_3^-, d_3^+, d_4^-, d_4^+ \geq 0$

where X_1 = the number of bars of soap (in millions), X_2 = the number of cans of deodorant spray (in millions), X_3 = the number of tubes of toothpaste (in millions), and X_4 = number of bottles of mouthwash (in millions). In addition, the d_1^- through d_4^+ deviational variables represent the degree of achievement for the corresponding corporate goals.

The Systems Analysis Group has also provided the following **QM** solution for the company's new product problem:

RECOMMENDATION	
Decision Variable	**Optimal Value**
X_1	10.97562
X_2	0.00000
X_3	4.14634
X_4	6.82926
Supplemental Variable	**Optimal Value**
S_5	0.00000
Supplemental Variable	**Optimal Value**
d_1^+	2.68292
d_1^-	0.00000
d_2^+	0.00000
d_2^-	0.00000
d_3^+	0.00000
d_3^-	0.00000
d_4^+	0.00000
d_4^-	11.48780
Goal Priority	**Nonachievement**
P_1	0.00000
P_2	0.00000
P_3	0.00000
P_4	11.48780

Interpret the group's mathematical programming formulation and this resulting computer printout for the management staff. Use language that would be understandable to these executives.

11. Explain why you agree or disagree with each of the following statements:
    a. In a linear program, the same change in all decision variables will result in a proportional change in the criterion value and each system constraint amount.
    b. Integer programming problems generally have fewer feasible solutions than simliar linear programs.
    c. An integer programming problem is easier to solve than a similar linear program.
    d. The optimal integer programming solution will not be as good as the best linear programming solution for the same problem.
    e. The deviational variables in goal programming serve the same purpose as the slack and surplus activities in linear programming.
    f. Whenever a goal programming solution has zero values for all deviational variables, all postulated goals have been met.
    g. Goal programming attempts to optimize the multiple objectives of management.
    h. At least one of the deviational variables in a goal constraint must equal zero.
    i. Goal programming problems are always stated as minimization models.

Technique Exercises

12. Consider the following integer programming problem faced by an airplane manufacturer:

maximize $Z = \$30X_1 + \$60X_2$

subject to $12X_1 + $20X_2 \leq 120 million   (Budget)

$X_1 + X_2 \leq 7$ (Total Output)

$X_1 \leq X_2$ (Product mix)

$X_1 \geq 1$ (Product requirement)

$X_1, X_2 \geq 0$ and are integers

where Z = the profit in millions of dollars, X_1 = the number of T-757s, and X_2 = the number of T-767s.

a. Use the graphic method to find the optimal linear programming solution. Does this recommendation provide an integer solution? If not, round the linear programming solution.
b. Next, determine the optimal integer programming solution first by enumeration and then with the graphic approach. Show all your work.
c. How does the optimal integer programming solution compare to the rounded linear programming recommendation?

13. Refer back to Management Situation 10.2.
   a. Show how the optimal linear programming solution in Figure 10.1 was developed.
   b. Show how the branch and bound subproblem 3 and 4 solutions in Figure 10.6 were developed.
       Show all your work.

14. You are given the following integer programming problem:

maximize $Z = 20X_1 + 50X_2$

subject to $1X_1 + 3X_2 \leq 12$

$X_1 + X_2 \leq 7$

$X_1, X_2 \geq 0$ and are integers

a. Use the graphic method to find the optimal linear programming solution.
b. Determine the optimal integer programming solution by enumeration. Show all your work.
c. How does the optimal integer programming solution compare to the best linear programming recommendation?

15. Consider the following integer programming problem:

maximize $Z = 75X_1 + 50X_2$

subject to $10X_1 + 20X_2 \leq 100$

$12X_1 + 6X_2 \leq 80$

$X_1, X_2 \geq 0$ and are integers

Use the branch and bound method to find the optimal integer programming solution. Show all your work.

16. Use the branch and bound method to solve the following integer programming problem. Show all your work.

minimize $\qquad\qquad Z = 110X_1 + 4X_2 + 2X_3$

subject to $\qquad\qquad 6X_1 - 4X_2 + 8X_3 \geq 16$

$\qquad\qquad\qquad\quad 6X_1 + 8X_2 - 4X_3 \geq 12$

$\qquad\qquad\qquad\quad X_1, X_2, X_3 \geq 0$ and are integers

17. A small town must determine the location of three additional ambulance dispatch stations within the community. The administration wants to select from among a set of potential locations the sites that provide the necessary service at least cost. In this regard, the staff has formulated the problem as follows:

minimize $\qquad Z = \$300{,}000X_1 + \$260{,}000X_2 + \$340{,}000X_3$

subject to $\qquad X_1 + X_2 \geq 1 \qquad\qquad\qquad\qquad$ (Neighborhood A)

$\qquad\qquad\quad X_2 + X_3 \geq 1 \qquad\qquad\qquad\qquad$ (Neighborhood B)

$\qquad\qquad\quad X_1 + X_2 + X_3 \geq 1 \qquad\qquad\quad$ (Neighborhood C)

$\qquad\qquad\quad X_1 + X_3 \geq 1 \qquad\qquad\qquad\qquad$ (Neighborhood D)

$\qquad\qquad\quad X_1, X_2, X_3 = 0$ or 1

where $Z =$ the total costs for the ambulance sites, $X_1 = 1$ if the Omega site is selected and 0 otherwise, $X_2 = 1$ if the Delta site is selected and 0 otherwise, and $X_3 = 1$ if the Epsilon site is selected and 0 otherwise.

Find the optimal set of ambulance sites.

18. Wallington Company, Inc., manufactures two industrial chemicals. Management wants to determine the product mix that will maximize total revenue. Its staff has formulated the problem as follows:

maximize $\qquad Z = \$170X_1 + \$3X_2$

subject to $\qquad 60X_1 + 1X_2 \leq 4{,}000$ pounds $\qquad\qquad$ (Ingredient 1)

$\qquad\qquad\quad 36X_1 + .8X_2 \leq 1{,}600$ pounds $\qquad\qquad$ (Ingredient 2)

$\qquad\qquad\quad 4X_1 + .2X_2 \leq 400$ pounds $\qquad\qquad\quad$ (Ingredient 3)

$\qquad\qquad\quad X_1, X_2 \geq 0$

$\qquad\qquad\quad X_1 \quad$ must be an integer

where $Z =$ the total revenue, $X_1 =$ the number of 100-pound bags of leadoline, and $X_2 =$ the number of dry mixed pounds of philon.

Find the optimal product mix.

19. Consider the following goal programming problem:

minimize $\qquad\qquad Z = P_1 d_3^- + P_2 d_1^+$

subject to $X_1 + X_2 + d_1^- - d_1^+ = 1,800$

$X_1 \leq 1,000$

$2000X_1 + 1500X_2 + d_3^- - d_3^+ = 3,000,000$

$X_1, X_2, d_1^-, d_1^+, d_3^-, d_3^+ \geq 0$

Find the optimal goal programming solution.

20. Refer back to thought exercise 8. Determine the faculty mixture that best satisfies the business school's multiple goals. Suppose that the administration changes its priorities to the following order:

- Have at least 30 percent of the new employees be minorities.

- Limit total faculty positions as much as possible.

- Remain within the $1 million budget.

How will this change affect your recommendation? Explain.

21. A discount department store is considering several locations for a new outlet. Since management wants to draw as many customers as possible, it will select the most centrally located site. The staff has formulated the problem as follows:

minimize $Z = d_1^- + d_1^+ + d_2^- + d_2^+ + d_3^- + d_3^+$

$+ d_4^- + d_4^+ + d_5^- + d_5^+ + d_6^- + d_6^+$

subject to $X_1 + d_1^- - d_1^+ = 5$ miles   (Population center A)

$X_2 + d_2^- - d_2^+ = 3$ miles   (Population center A)

$X_1 + d_3^- - d_3^+ = 7$ miles   (Population center B)

$X_2 + d_4^- - d_4^+ = 8$ miles   (Population center B)

$X_1 + d_5^- - d_5^+ = 2$ miles   (Population center C)

$X_2 + d_6^- - d_6^+ = 10$ miles   (Population center C)

$X_1, X_2, d_1^-, d_1^+, d_2^-, d_2^+, d_3^-, d_3^+, d_4^-, d_4^+, d_5^-, d_5^+, d_6^-, d_6^+ \geq 0$

where Z = the total miles from all population centers, X_1 = the north/south coordinate of the outlet (miles from the map reference point), and X_2 = east/west coordinate of the outlet (miles from the map reference point). Also, the d^- and d^+ deviational variables represent the distances in miles of the outlet from the corresponding population centers.

Find the linear programming solution to this store location problem. Next, use the goal programming approach to develop a recommended outlet site. How does the goal programming solution compare to the best linear programming recommendation? Explain.

Suppose that management feels that the size of the population center should determine the priority of site selection. In this respect, population center B has more people than A, which in turn contains a larger potential market than C. Under these circumstances, the highest priority is to minimize the total distance from population center B.

Similarly, the second most important objective is to minimize the total distance from population center A. How would such considerations affect the analysis and your recommendation? Explain. Interpret all solutions in language that would be understandable to management.

22. Refer back to Table 10.5 in the text. This table gives SDOT's initial basic feasible solution with the modified simplex method. Complete the modified simplex iterations needed to find the optimal goal programming solution. Compare the recommendation to the text solution.

23. You are given the following goal programming problem.

minimize $Z = 2P_1d_4^- + P_1d_5^- + P_2(d_3^- + d_3^+)$

subject to $5X_1 + 3X_2 \leq 30$

$4X_1 + 5X_2 \leq 40$

$10X_1 + 10X_2 + d_3^- - d_3^+ = 120$

$X_1 + d_4^- - d_4^+ = 1$

$X_2 + d_5^- - d_5^+ = 3$

$X_1, X_2, d_3^-, d_3^+, d_4^-, d_4^+, d_5^-, d_5^+ \geq 0$

In the formulation, notice that the d_4^- and d_5^- deviational variables are on the same P_1 priority level. However, d_4^- is given twice as much weight (considered twice as important) within the priority level as the d_5^- variable.
Find the solution to this goal programming problem.

24. Jentron, Inc. manufactures two brands of a particular medical product. Management wants to determine the brand mix that best satisfies the hierarchy of goals expressed in the following problem:

minimize $Z = P_1d_1^- + 10P_2d_2^- + 4P_2d_3^- + P_3d_4^+$

subject to $4X_1 + 3X_2 + d_1^- - d_1^+ = 480$ hours   (Production capacity)

$X_1 + d_2^- - d_2^+ = 80,000$ (Brand A demand)

$X_2 + d_3^- - d_3^+ = 100,000$ (Brand B demand)

$d_1^+ + d_4^- - d_4^+ = 40$ hours   (Overtime)

$X_1, X_2, d_1^-, d_1^+, d_2^-, d_2^+, d_3^-, d_3^+, d_4^-, d_4^+ \geq 0$

where

X_1 = output of brand A (in thousands)

X_2 = output of brand B (in thousands)

d_1^- = unused capacity hours

d_1^+ = overtime hours

d_2^- = output below brand A's 80,000 demand target

$$d_2^+ = \text{output above brand A's 80,000 demand target}$$

$$d_3^- = \text{output below brand B's 100,000 demand target}$$

$$d_3^+ = \text{output above brand B's 100,000 demand target}$$

Also, the d_4^- and d_4^+ deviational variables represent the degree of achievement for the company's 40-hour overtime goal.

Find the solution to this goal programming problem.

Computer Exercises

25. As explained in the text, SDOT's goal programming problem can be reformulated as the following linear program:

minimize $Z = 2,000,000d_1^- + 1,500d_2^- + 2d_3^+$

subject to $X_1 + X_2 - d_1^+ + d_1^- = 1,000,000 \text{ hours}$

$-X_1 + X_2 - d_2^+ + d_2^- = 0 \text{ hours}$

$X_2 - d_3^+ + d_3^- = 400,000 \text{ hours}$

$\$6X_1 + \$10X_2 \leq \$12,000,000$

$X_1, X_2, d_1^+, d_1^-, d_2^+, d_2^-, d_3^+, d_3^- \geq 0$

Solve this linear program with **Quantitative Management (QM)** software. How does the recommendation compare with the text solution?

26. Refer back to Thought Exercise 6. Use the **QM** software to solve the team selection problem you formulated.

27. A local investment counselor has a wealthy client with $100,000 to invest among five available bonds. Three of the instruments are municipal issues, while the remaining bonds are offered by corporations. After-tax yields are reported below.

Bond	After Tax Yield (Annual %)
Corporate A	8.4
Corporate B	7.4
Municipal A	7.9
Municipal B	7.7
Municipal C	8.3

The client wants to invest no more than $30,000 in any one bond. Also, municipals should comprise at least 50 percent of the portfolio. All the municipal bonds can be purchased only in $10,000 units, but it is possible to buy fractional shares of the corporate bonds.

The counselor seeks the portfolio that will generate the largest total return for the client. Use the **QM** software to develop a recommendation.

28. The Army Corps of Engineers must complete the specification phases of an officer housing project within six months. To do so, the project manager will need 100 engineers. Unfortunately, only 40 are currently available. These people would draw $40 per hour against the project budget.

Consultants are another source of help. Such engineering expertise can be obtained on a temporary basis for an hourly fee of $50 per hour. These people, however, typically need time to adjust to Corps and project procedures. In addition, it usually requires extra effort to coordinate the consultants' activities. Consequently, project management has decreed that there shall be at least five engineers on direct charge for every three consultants. Moreover, due to parking and facility limitations, the number of consultants plus direct charge personnel cannot exceed 70.

The third alternative to the work force problem is to subcontract various parts of the project among bidding engineering firms. Varion Enterprises has 30 engineers who could be assigned to the project, with each engineer costing the Corps about $45 per hour. Olton Industries has 15 engineers who could work for $42 per hour. Project managers, however, prefer to use no more subcontractors than the number of direct charge engineers.

Project management seeks the mix of direct charge engineers, consultants, and subcontractors who will get the job done for the least cost. Use the **QM** software to generate a recommendation.

29. Each day, Peptco Power and Light Company (PPLC) must decide which of the two reactors to start up at its Apple Bottom nuclear facility. By processing past operations data through the company's computer information system (CIS), staff have developed the reactor summary reported in Table 10.6.

Table 10.6   **PPLC's Reactor Characteristics**

Reactor	Startup Cost	Fixed Cost Per Operating Period	Variable Cost Per Megawatt Generated	Maximum Period Capacity
Unit 1	$4,500	$1,200	$5.30	2,400
Unit 2	$4,200	$1,650	$4.90	2,100

The startup cost includes the expenses of preparing the reactor and initiating operations, while the fixed cost consists of operator salaries, amortized reactor payments, and administrative expenses. Variable cost is mainly the fuel expense incurred in generating a megawatt of power.

Power is distributed from Apple Bottom during two periods each day—from 4 AM to 1 PM and from 1 PM to 2 AM. A reactor started in the first (4 AM to 1 PM) period may continue operating through the second (1 PM to 2 AM) shift without an additional startup cost. All reactors are shut down for maintenance between 2 AM and 4 AM each day. During this maintenance period, any demand is satisfied with a nearby auxiliary facility.

According to PPLC's Reactor Demand Forecasting Model (RDFM), Apple Bottom must supply at least 2,000 megawatts in the first period and 2,200 megawatts in the second period. Management seeks the least costly reactor utilization plan. Use the **QM** software to determine this plan.

30. The campaign headquarters of Janine Robbins, a candidate for the Board of Administrators, has 100 volunteer workers. One week before election day, there are major strategies available: media advertising, telephone campaigning, door-to-door canvassing, and transporting voters to the polls. It is estimated that each phone call will take about 5 minutes, while every door-to-door personal contact is expected to take 10 minutes. Transporting a voter to the polls will take about 15 minutes. Volunteers who work on advertising will be unable to handle any other duties, and each ad will use the talents of three workers.

Volunteers are committed to work 12 hours per day during the last week of the campaign. Ms. Robbins believes that a minimum of 15,000 phone calls, 10,000 personal contacts, 12,000 voter transports, and three advertisements will be needed during the final week. Nevertheless, she would prefer to see 20,000 calls, 25,000 contacts, 25,000 transports, and five advertisements developed during the final week. Furthermore, Janine feels that advertising is twice as important as either phone calls or personal contacts. Voter transportation is considered to be as important as advertising.

Use the **QM** software to determine the distribution of work that would best achieve Ms. Robbins' goals.

31. Doktor's Investments specializes in converting unique older buildings into offices, speciality shopping malls, and exclusive residences. The firm has just purchased the old 500,000-square-foot railroad station in the downtown area. Management plans to convert the structure into a state-of-the-art health center with a number of medical offices, fitness spas, nutrition shops, clothing stores, and administrative units.

Because of the center's theme and attractive location, many businesses have requested space in the building. Currently, Doktor's is trying to determine the best use of the available space. Preliminary studies indicate that the potential use, with projected space requirements and revenues, would be as follows:

Use	Needed Floor Space (Square Feet)	Annual revenue ($ thousands)
Medical Office	2,000	24
Fitness Spa	4,000	72
Nutrition Shop	1,000	14
Clothing Store	1,200	28
Administrative Center (including open space)	40,000	—

After considerable deliberation and consultation with architectural consultants, management has set the following goals, arranged in priority order:

1. Utilize the entire 500,000 square feet of floor space.

2. Generate at least $500,000 in annual revenue.

3. Dedicate at least 40,000 square feet of space to the administrative center (management offices, service shops, and the employee cafeteria) and to open space.

4. Allocate at least 40 percent of the space to medical offices.

5. Use nor more than 70 percent of the space for shops and stores.

6. Allow at least two spas in the building.

Use the **QM** software to develop a recommendation that best meets these goals.

Applications Exercises

32. Downtown Memorial clinic has recently added the latest medical care equipment to its public health service facility. The facility is available for only two types of patients: indigents and welfare referrals. To enhance health care opportunities for the community, the clinic will process as many patients as possible through the new facility. In this regard, the staff can handle up to 72 indigents and at least 20 welfare referrals per day.

The clinic is the only health care facility readily available to the indigent, while welfare referrals have alternative sources of medical treatment. Hence, the staff believes that indigent care is far more important to the community than the treatment of welfare referrals. In fact, it considers each indigent as the equivalent of three welfare referrals. For similar reasons, the staff wants the clinic to treat at least 42 indigents but no more than 120 welfare referrals per day.

Another important consideration is the available supply of medication. In particular, the clinic receives no more than 1,800 fluid ounces per day of the most popular medication. Moreover, experience indicates that each indigent requires 24 ounces of this medication, and each welfare referral requires 33 ounces.

What is the patient mixture that will provide the maximum benefit to the community? Benefit is defined as the total number of people in the community to be treated in the clinic per day, as per staff guidelines.

33. The Bethel Company manufactures rolls of paper for use in computer printers. These rolls, which are 80 feet long, can be produced only in a 50-inch width. Yet customers demand widths of varying sizes. In fact, the company has committed orders for the following roll sizes in the coming month:

Roll Width (Inches)	Rolls Ordered
10	760
15	590
20	880

Since additional orders may be received during the month, these commitments represent minimum demand levels. Nevertheless, any additional demand will be for one of the three roll sizes listed. In other words, there is no demand for any other width. So Bethel must cut the rolls to the desired final product sizes.

What is the minimum number of 50-inch rolls that will be required to satisfy customer demand? Suppose that management decides to minimize the waste (unused paper). How would this objective affect the recommendation? Explain.

34. Cable Television Network (CTN) is preparing its schedule of programs for the new season. These programs can be classified as news, sports, movies, and variety. Potential earnings from each category differ because of production cost and commercial rate differentials. Typical revenue and cost data are given in the following table:

Program Category	Commercial Revenue ($ million)	Production Costs ($ million)			
		Operations	Equipment	Talent	Technical Support
News	18	3	4	4	3
Sports	25	2	5	6	3
Movies	9	1	0.5	0.5	1.5
Variety	12	2.5	1.5	1	2

Administrative activities, such as accounting, financial analysis, and marketing, make up the operations function. Equipment expenses include camera, videotape, microphone, and other sound/video instrument costs. Talent costs consist of the salaries and benefits for performers, broadcasters, and commentators. Technical support involves activities such as engineering, film processing, and electrical work.

The network has budgeted $5 million for operations, $7 million for equipment, $8 million for talent, and $6 million for technical support activities. Which program categories should management select to maximize total commercial revenue for the new season?

35. The Spilding Company, a major sporting goods manufacturer, is bringing out a new line of aluminum baseball bats. This product will be launched with a national advertising campaign consisting of inserts in the *Baseball News* magazine and commercials during the television game of the week. Each magazine insert costs $15,000 and is expected to reach an estimated 500,000 potential customers. On the other hand, each television slot costs $25,000 but reaches an expected one million possible consumers. These fees are for full-message placements. Nevertheless, it also is possible to buy a fraction (partial) magazine insert and/or television slot.

Spilding has budgeted $600,000 for the advertising campaign. Management has also agreed that this campaign should achieve several goals in the following order of priority:

- Stay within the budget.
- Run at least nine television commercials.
- Place at least five magazine insertions.
- Reach at least 12 million potential customers.

How many ads must Spilding place in each medium to attain these goals? What advertising strategy do you recommend? Explain.

36. Bungling Brothers Carnival provides a portable amusement park for church fairs, shopping center promotions, and social clubs. Recently, the carnival's facilities were inspected by government agents enforcing the Occupational Safety and Health Act (OSHA). The inspectors found violations in two major categories: equipment maintenance and fire protection. Moreover, these agents have proposed safety guidelines designed to reduce the carnival's frequency of accidents and mishap cost per person.
Of course, it will cost Bungling money to achieve the relevant compliance levels. Indeed, the following table presents the cost of achieving a percentage increase in compliance as well as the resulting accident frequency and per-person mishap cost reductions:

Violation Category	Accident Frequency Reduction (Accidents per 10,000 Hours of Exposure)	Reduction in Mishap Cost (per Person)	Compliance Cost (per Percentage Point Increase in Compliance Level)
Equipment Maintenance	.25	$100	$300
Fire Protection	.40	$500	$450

To fully achieve the OSHA guidelines in both categories, the carnival must increase the equipment maintenance compliance level by 25 percentage points and reduce violations in the fire protection category by 50 percentage points. Yet Bungling can afford to spend only $15,000 on safety. The government agents recognize this dilemma. Hence, they are willing to delay punitive action as long as Bungling makes progress toward full compliance. In particular, the agents have established the following goals in the order of their priority:

- Decrease total accident frequency by at least ten mishaps per 10,000 hours of exposure.
- Reduce the total mishap cost per worker by at least $6,000.
- Achieve at least 95 percent compliance in each violation category.

How many percentage points of compliance in each violation category are needed to achieve these OSHA goals? Suppose the government considers equipment maintenance to be twice as desirable for the carnival as fire protection. How would this preference change the recommendation? Explain.

37. Outlands East, one store of a chain in a major metropolitan area, specializes in the sale of hobby supplies. It operates with a staff of nine people: a manager who is compensated by a fixed salary plus bonuses and eight full-time salespeople who are paid an hourly wage. Each salesperson typically works 180 hours per month, while the manager has a regular working schedule of 192 hours per month.

Store operations are based on sale quotas set by top management. Outlands East, for instance, has a sales quota of $35,000 in the current month. The store manager receives a 5 percent bonus on all sales above the monthly quota. To motivate the individuals, the manager sets a sales quota for the entire full-time staff and also pays a 6 percent commission on all sales above the group quota. Moreover, commissions are split equally among the sales staff. In this regard, the manager has established a $28,800 sales quota in the current month for the full-time staff. Past experience indicates that each salesperson can sell, on average, $30 worth of merchandise per hour. On the other hand, the manager has been able to average $40 in sales per hour.

Here are the manager's priorities, in their order of importance:

- Achieve the store sales quotas.
- Have the staff attain the group sales quota.
- Provide a commission of $50 for each salesperson and a $150 bonus for the manager.

For motivation reasons, the commissions are considered to be three times as important as the bonus. How many hours should the manager and sales staff work to achieve the hierarchy of goals?

The salespeople, on the other hand, believe that the commissions and bonuses would provide the motivation necessary to attain the store and staff quotas. Consequently, they propose the following reordering of priorities:

- Provide a commission of $50 for each salesperson.
- Give the manager a $150 bonus.
- Achieve the store sales quota.
- Have the staff attain the group sales quota.

How would such a priority reordering affect the work plan? Which goal structure do you recommend? Explain.

For Further Reading

Integer Programming Methodology

Cooper, M. W. "A Survey of Methods for Pure Nonlinear Integer Programming." *Management Science* (March 1981):353.

Dash, G. H. *Operations Research Software*. Homewood, IL: Irwin, 1988.

Kwak, N. K., and M. J. Schiederjans. *Introduction to Mathematical Programming*. Malabar, FL: Krieger, 1987.

Taha, H. A. *Integer Programming: Theory, Applications, and Computations*. New York: Academic Press, 1975.

Van Roy, T. J. "A Cross Decomposition Algorithm for Capacitated Facility Location." *Operations Research* (January–February 1986):145.

Integer Programming Applications

Bender, P. S. et al. "Improving Purchasing Productivity at IBM with a Normative Decision Support System," *Interfaces* (May–June 1985):106–115.

Bitran, G. R., et al. "Production Planning of Style Goods with High Setup Costs and Forecast Revisions." *Operations Research* (March–April 1986):226.

Dwyer, F. R., and J. R. Evans. "A Branch and Bound Algorithm for the List Selection Problem in Direct Mail Advertising." *Management Science* (June 1981):658.

Kolesar, P. "Testing for Vision Loss in Glaucoma Suspects." *Management Science* (May 1980):439.

Martin, C. H., and S. L. Lubin. "Optimalization Modeling for Business Planning at Trumbull Asphalt." *Interfaces* (November–December 1985):66.

Mathur, K., et al. "Applications of Integer Programming in Radio Frequency Management." *Management Science* (July 1985):829.

McClure, R. H., and C. E. Wells. "A Mathematical Programming Model for Faculty Course Assignments." *Decision Sciences* (Summer 1984):409.

Nauss, R. M., and B. R. Keeler. "Minimizing Net Interest Cost in Management Bond Bidding." *Management Science* (April 1981):365.

Ruth, R. J. "A Mixed Integer Programming Model for Regional Planning of a Hospital Inpatient Service." *Management Science* (May 1981):521.

Tripathy, A. "School Timetabling—A Case in Large Binary Integer Linear Programming." *Management Science* (December 1984):1473.

Goal Programming Methodology

Gass, S. I. "A Process for Determining Priorities and Weights for Large-Scale Linear Goal Programs." *Journal of the Operational Research Society* (August 1986):779.

Hwang, C. L., and A. Masud. *Multiple Objective Decision Making—Methods and Applications*. New York: Springer-Verlag, 1979.

Ignizio, J. P. *Goal Programming and Extensions*. Lexington, MA: Heath, 1976.

Ignizio, J. P. *Linear Programming in Single- and Multiple-Objective Systems*. Englewood Cliffs, NJ: Prentice-Hall, 1982.

Lee, S. M. *Goal Programming for Decision Analysis*. Philadelphia: Auerbach, 1972.

Lee, S. M. *Management By Multiple Objectives*. Princeton, NJ: Petrocelli Books, 1981.

Markland, R. E. and S. K. Vickery. "The Efficient Computer Implementation of a Large-Scale Integer Goal Programming Model." *European Journal of Operations Research* (September 1986):341.

Goal Programming Applications

Jones, L., and N. K. Kwak. "A Goal Programming Model for Allocating Human Resources for the Good Laboratory Practice Regulations." *Decision Sciences* (January 1982):156.

Kendall, K. E. , and R. L. Leubbe. "Management of College Student Recruiting Activities Using Goal Programming." *Decision Sciences* (April 1981):193.

Lee, S. M., and M. J. Schniederjans, "A Multicriteria Assignment Problem: A Goal Programming Approach," *Interfaces* (August 1983):75–81.

Lin, W. T. "A Survey of Goal Programming Applications." *OMEGA* (January 1980):115.

Mellichamp, J. M., et al. "Ballistic Missile Defense Technology Management with Goal Programming." *Interfaces* (October 1980):68.

Morey, R. C. "Managing the Armed Services' Delayed Entry Pools to Improve Productivity in Recruiting." *Interfaces* (September–October 1985):81.

Schiederjans, M. J. et al. "An Application of Goal Programming to Resolve a Site Location Problem." *Interfaces* (June 1982):65.

Taylor, B. W., et al.. "An Integer Nonlinear Goal Programming Model for the Deployment of State Highway Patrol Units." *Management Science* (November 1985):1335.

Triverdi, V. M. "A Mixed-Integer Goal Programming Model for Nursing Service Budgeting." *Operations Research* (September–October 1981):1019.

Nonlinear Programming

Bazaraa, M. S., and C. M. Shetty. *Nonlinear Programming: Theory and Algorithms*. New York: Wiley, 1979.

Jeter, M. W. *Mathematical Programming: An Introduction to Optimization*. New York: Marcel Dekker, 1986.

Jogannathan, R. "An Algorithm for a Class of Nonconvex Programming Problems with Nonlinear Fractional Objectives." *Management Science* (July 1985):847.

Rijckaert, M. J., and E. J. C. Walraven. "Geometric Programming: Estimation of Lagrange Multipliers," *Operations Research* (January–February 1985):85.

Shapiro, J. F. *Mathematical Programming: Structures and Algorithms*. New York: Wiley, 1979.

Zhang, J., et al. "An Improved Successive Linear Programming Algorithm." *Management Science* (October 1985): 1312.

Nonlinear Programming Applications

Corstjens, M., and P. Doyle. "A Model for Optimizing Retail Space Allocations." *Management Science* (July 1981):822.

Fabozzi, F. J., and J. Valente. "Mathematical Programming in American Companies: A Sample Survey." Part 1. *Interfaces* (November 1976):93.

Grotte, J. H. "An Optimizing Nuclear Exchange Model for the Analysis of Nuclear War and Deterrence." *Operations Research* (May–June 1982):428.

Lasdon, L., et al. "Optimal Hydrocarbon Reservoir Production Policies." *Operations Research* (January–February 1986):40.

Stochastic and Chance-Constrained Programming

Hansotia, B. J. "Stochastic Linear Programming with Recourse: A Tutorial." *Decision Sciences* (January 1980):151.

Hogan, A. J., et al. "Decision Problems under Risk and Chance-Constrained Programming: Dilemmas in the Transition." *Management Science* (June 1981):698.

Stancu-Minasian, I. M., and M. J. Wets. "A Research Bibliography in Stochastic Programaming, 1955–75." *Operations Research* (November–December 1976):1078.

Case:　Federated Motors, Inc.

Federated Motors, Inc. is a major automobile manufacturer. One of its major subsidiaries has a labor-planning problem. A decision must be made involving departmental staffing requirements for the next month's production. Since some employees have been cross-trained on two or more jobs, the subsidiary has some labor flexibility. At least some labor can be assigned to more than one department or work center.

The subsidiary is planning to produce truck and automobile batteries during the next month. Batteries are processed in two departments. It takes 0.2 labor hours to process a truck battery and 0.1 labor hour for an automobile battery in department 1. It takes 0.1 labor hour to process a truck battery and 0.2 labor hour for an automobile battery in department 2.

Excess equipment capacity is available and will not be a restriction. However, the subsidiary's labor is limited. After careful consideration of the training and experience qualifications of the workers, the subsidiary's management devises the possible labor assignments presented in Table 10.7. Hence, 2,500 of the 15,000 people-hours available for the month's production can be allocated with some management discretion. That is, the labor assignments to departments are variables. The company makes a profit of $10 per truck battery and $8 per automobile battery. Labor assignment variables do not directly affect profit.

The subsidiary submits the problem to the company's planning department. The subsidiary asks this department to provide recommendations on the following questions:

a. How many batteries of each type should be produced next month to maximize profit?

b. How many people-hours should be allocated to each department as part of the optimal product mix?

Table 10.7 Possible Labor Assignments for Federated Motors

Labor Assignment	People-hours Available
Department 1 only	5,000
Department 2 only	7,500
Department 1 or 2	2,500
Total	15,000

What would you recommend?

Suppose management establishes the following hierarchy of goals:

- Earn at least $300,000 profit.

- Produce an equal number of truck and automobile batteries.

- Utilize at least 5,000 people-hours in department 2.

How would these considerations affect your recommendation? Explain.

Part IV

Networks

M ANY decision problems can be depicted as a set of junction points interconnected by a series of lines. The junction points may represent geographic locations (such as cities), physical facilities (like warehouses), or activities. Connecting lines may portray routes, layout designs, or job relationships. Usually, management wants to find the series of connections that best achieves some specified objective.

Such problems have been solved successfully with network analysis. This part of the text presents some of the most widely used network techniques. Chapter 11 introduces approaches designed to optimally distribute products and services from sources of supply to demand destinations. The chapter shows how to formulate typical distribution problems and develop the recommended solutions. It also outlines the assumptions and limitations of the analysis.

Chapter 12 presents network approaches directed at the flow of items, objects, or people through a system. In this chapter, we see how to design an optimal layout, identify the preferred route, and establish the best flow through the system. The final chapter, Chapter 13, develops the network approaches to project management. In particular, it examines the methods to plan and schedule large-scale projects, control the time and cost aspects of the plan, and analyze the effects of uncertainty.

After reading this part of the text, you should be able to:

- Identify problems suitable for network analysis.

- Formulate the appropriate decision model.

- Develop a recommended solution mathematically and with the aid of a computer.

- Recognize the assumptions and limitations of the network analysis.

This background will also facilitate your understanding of subsequent chapters of the text.

Distribution

Chapter Outline

Learning Objectives

- Examine the nature of transportation and assignment problems
- Formulate models for transportation and assignment problems
- Develop recommended problem solutions by hand and with the aid of a computer
- Deal with important decision considerations

Booking Them at United

IN 1982, United Airlines anticipated a significant expansion in operations. Upper management realized that expanded flight schedules and increased passenger volume would require substantial planning to control labor costs and still maintain desired customer service levels. A manpower planning group was established, directly under United's senior vice president of corporate services. The group was to determine labor needs, identify excess manpower for reallocation, reduce the time required for preparing schedules, make manpower allocation more day and time sensitive, and quantify scheduling costs at busy airport and reservation offices.

Beginning with a few computer programs that automated manual scheduling techniques, the group developed a Station Manpower Planning System (SMPS) by adding enhancements to attain the specified objectives. The SMPS has become a collection of assignment, and other, methodologies delivered through a computer information system. It uses forecasted requirements for 30-minute intervals over a seven-day period to produce monthly shift schedules. These schedules then are combined into posted work assignments based on month-to-month operating rules and employee preferences.

Since SMPS was implemented in 1983, the system has been used to regularly develop work schedules for 4,000 employees. Eventually, SMPS is expected to schedule 10,000 employees, or 20 percent of United's total work force. The system has generated direct labor savings of more than $6 million per year, and it has drawn rave reviews from United's management and affected employees.

Source: T. J. Holloran and J. E. Byrn, "United Airlines Station Manpower Planning System," *Interfaces* (January–February 1986): 39–50.

As in United Airlines' manpower planning, many decision problems involve the allocation of supplies from their origins to their centers of demand. Because supplies are scarce resources and distribution is expensive, it is important to move the supplies from source to destination as efficiently and as effectively as possible. Constraints on demand and supply further complicate the allocation problem. Quantitative models, like the methodologies within United's Station Manpower Planning System (SMPS), have been developed to help managers analyze these situations. As the United vignette illustrates, such models can be of significant benefit to organizations.

This chapter presents these distribution models. We begin with the more general situation—the transportation problem—and discuss its nature, the most efficient solution procedures, and extensions to the basic model. Then we will contrast the assignment problem with the transportation model, and develop its appropriate solution procedures and extensions.

Applications. In this chapter, the following applications appear in text, examples, and exercises:

- bus scheduling
- consumer protection
- dairy operations
- foreign trade
- job ordering
- logistics
- police patrols
- politics
- product shipment

- production scheduling and inventory control
- project scheduling
- purchase decisions
- radio programming
- sports
- waste management
- warehousing

11.1 TRANSPORTATION

In modern economies, firms are often physically separated from their customers. Production facilities typically are located at the source of raw materials, within inexpensive labor markets, in low tax areas, and near transportation facilities. On the other hand, purchase centers may be situated within large population centers that are convenient to customers and close to competition. Seldom are the manufacturing facilities close to the purchase centers. As a result, firms develop distribution systems to overcome these physical separations.

In such systems, items are transported from the supply sources (plants, storage areas, and so on) to the demand destinations (wholesalers, retail outlets, and so forth). Furthermore, each source has an available supply of items, while every destination has a particular demand. Management must therefore select the plan that most effectively distributes available supplies to the requesting destinations. Management Situation 11.1 presents a typical illustration of this resource allocation problem.

Management Situation 11.1

Product Shipment

Tyler Incorporated makes men's suits for a midwestern chain of department stores. The company has production facilities at the sources of its raw materials and labor suppliers in the cities of Milwaukee, Gary, and Flint. It has warehouses in the Chicago, Minneapolis, and Detroit metropolitan areas, where there are concentrations of the department store chain's retail outlets. Milwaukee's plant can supply 1,000 suits per month, Gary's 800, and Flint's 1,200. The Chicago warehouse has a demand for 1,500 suits per month, Minneapolis 500, and Detroit 1,000. Transportation costs per suit, including freight, handling, and insurance, are presented in Table 11.1. Tyler's management seeks the distribution plan that will satisfy all plant capabilities and warehouse demands at least cost.

Table 11.1   **Cost of Transporting One Suit to Each Tyler Warehouse**

	Warehouse Location		
Plant Location	Chicago	Minneapolis	Detroit
Milwaukee	$2	$4	$5
Gary	$1	$6	$2
Flint	$4	$7	$1

Nature of the Problem

As Management Situation 11.1 demonstrates, Tyler has a specified demand for suits at each of its three metropolitan area warehouses. The company can satisfy these demands by transporting the available supplies from its three manufacturing plants to the warehouses. Several alternative routes, each with a specific per-suit transportation cost, can be used to make these shipments. These alternatives are depicted in Figure 11.1 as a set of labeled circles (plant and warehouse locations) interconnected by a series of lines (shipping routes). Also, the lines reflect the flow (movement of Tyler suits) that will occur through the distribution system. Such a map, or diagram, is known as a **network**. In network terminology, the circles are called **nodes**, while the lines are referred to as **arcs, branches, links,** or **edges**. Moreover, when the flows can occur in only one direction, as in Tyler's case, the diagram is known as a **directed network**.

In Figure 11.1, each number next to a node represents a supply available at a plant or a demand emanating from a warehouse. Every value on an arc identifies the cost of transporting one suit along the corresponding shipping route. Management, then, must determine the least costly way of shipping the required quantities of suits over these arcs.

According to Figure 11.1, Tyler can transport a suit over each specified route for a known and constant cost. For example, it costs $2 to ship a suit from Gary to Detroit, regardless of the shipment size. Consequently, the total transportation cost between each plant and warehouse will be directly proportional to the quantity in the shipment. By letting

i = the plant index (1 = Milwaukee, 2 = Gary, 3 = Flint)

j = the warehouse index (1 = Chicago, 2 = Minneapolis, and 3 = Detroit)

X_{ij} = the number of suits transported from plant i to warehouse j each month

Z = total transportation cost

management can use the expression

minimize $\qquad Z = \$2X_{11} + \$4X_{12} + \$5X_{13} + \$1X_{21} + \$6X_{22}$

$\qquad\qquad + \$2X_{23} + \$4X_{31} + \$7X_{32} + \$1X_{33}$

to denote the company's cost minimization objective.

There will be supply and demand constraints on the objective. Since the total monthly supply of suits from the three plants (1,000 + 800 + 1,200 = 3,000) equals the total

Figure 11.1   **Tyler's Shipping Alternatives**

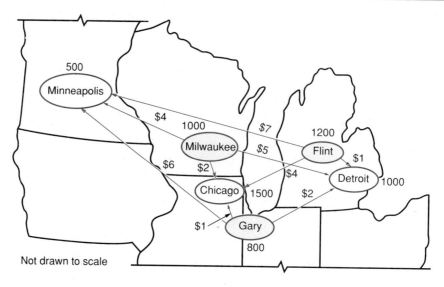

Not drawn to scale

Plant

---

monthly demand at the three warehouses (1,500 + 500 + 1,000 = 3,000), there will be no unused (slack) supplies. Shipments from each plant will exactly equal the available supplies, or

$$X_{11} + X_{12} + X_{13} = 1,000 \text{ suits per month (Milwaukee)}$$
$$X_{21} + X_{22} + X_{23} = 800 \text{ suits per month (Gary)}$$
$$X_{31} + X_{32} + X_{33} = 1,200 \text{ suits per month (Flint)}$$

Another set of restrictions must ensure that each warehouse receives exactly the quantity it demands, or that

$$X_{11} + X_{21} + X_{31} = 1,500 \text{ suits per month (Chicago)}$$
$$X_{12} + X_{22} + X_{32} = 500 \text{ suits per month (Minneapolis)}$$
$$X_{13} + X_{23} + X_{33} = 1,000 \text{ suits per month (Detroit)}$$

The nonnegativity conditions

$$X_{11}, X_{12}, X_{13}, X_{21}, X_{22}, X_{23}, X_{31}, X_{32}, X_{33} \geq 0$$

are the final restrictions on the problem.

  If management collects the objective function, supply and demand constraints, and nonnegativity conditions, it will formulate the following model:

minimize
$$Z = \$2X_{11} + \$4X_{12} + \$5X_{13} + \$1X_{21} + \$6X_{22}$$
$$+ \$2X_{23} + \$4X_{31} + \$7X_{32} + \$1X_{33}$$

subject to
$$X_{11} + X_{12} + X_{13} = 1{,}000 \text{ suits per month (Milwaukee)}$$

$$X_{21} + X_{22} + X_{23} = 800 \text{ suits per month (Gary)}$$

$$X_{31} + X_{32} + X_{33} = 1{,}200 \text{ suits per month (Flint)}$$

$$X_{11} + X_{21} + X_{31} = 1{,}500 \text{ suits per month (Chicago)}$$

$$X_{12} + X_{22} + X_{32} = 500 \text{ suits per month (Minneapolis)}$$

$$X_{13} + X_{23} + X_{33} = 1{,}000 \text{ suits per month (Detroit)}$$

$$X_{11}, X_{12}, X_{13}, X_{21}, X_{22}, X_{23}, X_{31}, X_{32}, X_{33} \geq 0$$

This model, with the objective of finding the most effective way of distributing a commodity from a group of supply sources to a set of demand destinations, is known as a **transportation problem**.

Recap. The transportation problem is to find the best way of distributing items from supply sources to demand destinations. It has the following fundamental characteristics:

1. There are a finite number of supply sources and demand destinations.
2. Each source has a known supply and each destination has a known demand.
3. A decision variable represents the quantity transported from a source to a destination.
4. Each decision variable makes a constant and independent contribution to the objective.
5. The total quantity transported from all sources to a particular destination will be at least as large as the demand required at the destination.
6. The total quantity transported to all destinations from a particular source will not exceed the supply available at the source.

Simplex Analysis

As Tyler's situation demonstrates (and as was discussed in Chapter 7), the transportation problem forms a linear program. There is an objective function that relates a single numerical criterion (total transportation cost) to a group of decision variables (amounts shipped over each arc in the transportation network). This objective is subject to a finite number of constraints, with one restriction for each supply source and demand destination (node) in the transportation network. Moreover, these constraints and the objective function each involve linear relationships. Finally, the decision variables are restricted to nonnegative values. The decision maker, then, can use the simplex method to solve the transportation problem.

Optimal Simplex Solution. If Tyler solves the product shipment problem with the simplex method, it will find that total transportation cost can be minimized at $Z = \$5{,}600$ per month by shipping

$X_{11} = 500$ suits from the Milwaukee plant to the Chicago warehouse

$X_{12} = 500$ suits from the Milwaukee plant to the Minneapolis warehouse

$X_{13} = 0$ suits from the Milwaukee plant to the Detroit warehouse

$X_{21} = 800$ suits from the Gary plant to the Chicago warehouse

$X_{22} = 0$ suits from the Gary plant to the Minneapolis warehouse

$X_{23} = 0$ suits from the Gary plant to the Detroit warehouse

$X_{31} = 200$ suits from the Flint plant to the Chicago warehouse

$X_{32} = 0$ suits from the Flint plant to the Minneapolis warehouse

and $X_{33} = 1,000$ suits from the Flint plant to the Detroit warehouse

As by-products of the simplex analysis, Tyler also would get the shadow prices for the system (plant supply and warehouse demand) constraints and reduced costs for all decision variables (shipping alternatives).

Postoptimality Analysis. Management must know the exact source supplies, destination demands, and per-unit shipping costs to properly implement the transportation model. Yet these cost, demand, and supply parameters typically are based on estimates or forecasts. Changes in consumer tastes, shipping difficulties, and other unforeseen circumstances can create substantial inaccuracies in these estimates/forecasts. Postoptimality analyses, including sensitivity analyses on the per-suit shipping costs (objective function coefficients) and on the plant supplies and warehouse demands (constraint right-hand-side amounts), should be performed to examine the impacts on the recommendation of any changes in the parameter forecasts/estimates.

Special Solution Methods

Since transportation problems tend to have a large number of decision variables and constraints, it can be tedious and time-consuming to input the model's parameters in linear programming format. Moreover, even relatively simple transportation problems, such as Tyler's, may involve considerable computational effort with the simplex method. As a result, additional procedures have been developed to solve a transportation problem more efficiently than the simplex method (or at least to generate an initial basic feasible solution that will considerably reduce the number of simplex iterations).

Network Algorithms. As Figure 11.1 illustrates, a transportation problem can be viewed as a network. Specialized procedures, such as the *out-of-kilter* and *minimal cost flow* algorithms, then can be used to solve the resulting network formulation. Typically, this approach is reserved for problems that are too large or too complex for efficient solution by more traditional methods.

Heuristic Methods. Once the transportation table has been formulated, "rule of thumb" approaches such as the **northwest corner method, Vogel approximation method (VAM)**, and the **minimum cost cell method** can be used to solve the problem. These methods, however, cannot guarantee an optimal transportation solution. Instead, heuristics are primarily used to examine solution characteristics, to obtain a "good" problem recommendation, and to generate initial solutions for transportation algorithms.

Table 11.2   **Tyler's Transportation Table**

From Plant Location	To Warehouse Location			Plant Supply (Suits per Month)
	Chicago	Minneapolis	Detroit	
Milwaukee	$2 X_{11}	$4 X_{12}	$5 X_{13}	1,000
Gary	$1 X_{21}	$6 X_{22}	$2 X_{23}	800
Flint	$4 X_{31}	$7 X_{32}	$1 X_{33}	1,200
Warehouse Demand (Suits per Month)	1,500	500	1,000	3,000

Cell corresponding to shipments from Flint to Chicago

Total supply and total demand

Transportation Algorithms. An examination of the linear programming formulation of Tyler's transportation problem will show that each column of coefficients in the system (demand and supply) constraints has exactly two ones and the rest zeros. In addition, each system constraint's right-hand-side constant is a nonnegative integer. Transportation algorithms, such as the **stepping stone method** and the **modified distribution (MODI) method**, exploit this special structure both to reduce computer processing time and to increase precision.

Transportation Methodology

Transportation algorithms start with a "good" initial solution (usually obtained with a heuristic approach) and then use simplex-based search procedures to find the optimal transportation solution. Although the computations differ in each procedure, these algorithms all utilize a standard format, called the **transportation table**, to conveniently record the data and keep track of the calculations. Table 11.2 illustrates this table with Tyler's product shipment information.

Transportation Table. Each row in the transportation table (Table 11.2) corresponds to a supply source (node) and every column corresponds to a demand destination (node) in the transportation network (Figure 11.1). For example, the first row portrays the Milwaukee plant, and the third column depicts the Detroit warehouse. Also, each cell corresponds to one of the decision variables (X_{ij}) in the problem. The cell at the intersection of the third row and first column, for instance, gives the number of suits (X_{31}) transported from the Flint plant to the Chicago warehouse. Since the company has three plants and three warehouses, there are $3 \times 3 = 9$ cells (decision variables) in the table.

Table 11.3   **Tyler's Minimum Cost Cell Solution**

From Plant Location	To Warehouse Location			Plant Supply (Suits per Month)
	Chicago	Minneapolis	Detroit	
Milwaukee	$2 \\ 700	$4 \\ 300	$5	$1,000 - 700 = 300 - 300 = 0$
Gary	$1 \\ 800	$6	$2	$800 - 800 = 0$
Flint	$4	$7 \\ 200	$1 \\ 1,000	$1,200 - 1,000 = 200 - 200 = 0$
Warehouse Demand (Suits per Month)	1,500 \\ - 800 \\ = 700 \\ - 700 \\ = 0	500 \\ -300 \\ =200 \\ -200 \\ = 0	1,000 \\ -1,000 \\ = 0	

The entry in the upper right-hand corner of each cell represents the cost of transporting one suit over the corresponding arc of the network. Observe, for example, the cell at the intersection of the second row and second column in Table 11.2. The entry in the upper right-hand corner indicates that Tyler must pay $6 to ship one suit from the Gary plant to the Minneapolis warehouse.

In addition, the quantities in the right-hand border give the supply available at each source, while the numbers in the bottom margin identify the demand at every destination. For instance, the entry in the right margin of the first row of Table 11.2 shows that the Milwaukee plant can supply 1,000 suits per month. Similarly, the border value under the first column indicates that the Chicago warehouse demands 1,500 suits per month. Furthermore, the table is set up in a way that ensures that total supply exactly equals total demand. In Tyler's case, the three plants can supply a total of 3,000 suits per month, while the three warehouses demand the same monthly total. Hence, the required balance between total demand and total supply is a characteristic of the company's problem. Cases that contain imbalances between these totals will be dealt with in a later section of the chapter.

Starting Solution. The minimum cost cell method is one popular way to find a good starting solution for transportation algorithms. This method first identifies the lowest cost cell within the transportation table and assigns as many units as feasible to this route. Next, the supply and demand requirements are adjusted to reflect the allocation. Then the procedure is repeated for the next lowest cost cells (routes), in turn, until all supply and demand requirements are satisfied.

In Tyler's case, the minimum cost cell method will generate the solution shown in Table 11.3. The lowest cost in this table is the $1 associated with either the Gary/Chicago or Flint/Detroit cells. Warehouse demands and plant supplies restrict shipments to 800 suits over the Gary/Chicago route or 1,000 suits over the Flint/Detroit route. Therefore, the feasible initial allocation is the 1,000 written in the Flint/Detroit cell.

The initial allocation reduces the supply at the Flint plant from 1,200 to 200 suits per month. It also fully satisfies the Detroit warehouse demand (reduces the demand from 1,000 to 0 suits per month). In the process, the Detroit warehouse (column) is eliminated from further consideration, and the Gary/Chicago route becomes the lowest cost cell.

There are 1,500 suits demanded monthly at the Chicago warehouse, but the Gary plant can meet only 800 suits of this demand. Consequently, the feasible second allocation is the 800 written in the Gary/Chicago cell of Table 11.3. Such an allocation reduces the Chicago demand from 1,500 to 700 suits per month, eliminates the Gary plant (reduces its supply from 800 to 0), and makes the Milwaukee/Chicago route the lowest cost cell.

The Milwaukee plant can supply 1,000 suits, but the Chicago warehouse has a remaining demand of only 700 suits per month. Thus, the feasible third allocation is the 700 written in the Milwaukee/Chicago cell of Table 11.3. This allocation reduces the Milwaukee supply from 1,000 to 300 suits per month, eliminates the Chicago warehouse (reduces its demand from 700 to 0), and makes the Milwaukee/Minneapolis route the lowest cost cell. It also means that management must ship 300 suits over the Milwaukee/Minneapolis route and 200 suits over the Flint/Minneapolis route to satisfy the remaining demand and supply requirements.

Evaluating the Solution. Table 11.3's solution fills five cells of the transportation table, or one less than the sum of the supply sources and demand destinations. *A problem with m supply sources and n demand destinations usually will have a solution that fills $m + n - 1$ cells in the transportation table.* This condition is equivalent to having a basic feasible solution in the simplex method. The filled cells, which are equivalent to the basic variables in a simplex solution, represent the shipping routes utilized in the distribution pattern. Empty cells, which correspond to the nonbasic variables in a simplex solution, identify the unused routes.

Unused routes (empty cells) may be more economical than the currently selected channels (filled cells). To find out, management must evaluate the effects of reallocating shipments from the filled cells (basic variables) to the empty cells (nonbasic variables) in the transportation table. The stepping stone method is one popular way of performing this evaluation.

In the stepping stone method, the decision maker begins with an initial solution consisting of $m + n - 1$ filled cells in the transportation table (a basic feasible solution). Incremental analysis next is used to determine the economic consequences of pairwise exchanges between filled cells (basic variables) and unfilled cells (nonbasic variables). If any exchange is desirable, the most attractive unused route (nonbasic variable) replaces a currently utilized route (basic variable) in the solution. This procedure is continued until management obtains an optimal transportation solution.

Improvement Indexes. All empty cells in the transportation solution (Table 11.3) must be checked for improvement. If Tyler ships one suit over the currently unused route from Flint to Chicago, it will necessitate the series of adjustments shown in Table 11.4. These adjustments trace a **closed path** or **loop** of directed horizontal and vertical lines from the empty cell pivoting only on filled cells back to the empty cell and identify the actions needed to preserve all demand and supply requirements in the problem.

Table 11.4   Flint-to-Chicago Reallocation of the Minimum Cost Cell Solution

From Plant Location	To Warehouse Location			Plant Supply (Suits per Month)
	Chicago	Minneapolis	Detroit	
Milwaukee	$2 700 − 1 =699	$4 300 + 1 =301	$5	1,000
Gary	$1 800	$6	$2	800
Flint	$4 + 1	$7 200 − 1 =199	$1 1,000	1,200
Warehouse Demand (Suits per Month)	1,500	500	1,000	3,000

By examining the costs in the cells along the closed path of Table 11.4, Tyler will find that the shipment will generate the following incremental economic changes:

Route	Change	Effect on Cost
Flint to Chicago	Add 1 suit	+ $4
Milwaukee to Chicago	Subtract 1 suit	− $2
Milwaukee to Minneapolis	Add 1 suit	+ $4
Flint to Minneapolis	Subtract 1 suit	− $7
Net Effect on Transportation Cost		− $1

Namely, transportation cost will decrease by a net $1 for every suit shipped from the Flint plant to the Chicago warehouse. Such an incremental change, which measures the net effect on the objective of shipping one unit over a currently unused route in the transportation network, is known as an **improvement index**. It is equivalent to a $C_j - Z_j$ value in a simplex solution.

Since there will be only one closed path associated with each unused route (empty cell) in the transportation solution (Table 11.3), Tyler can compute the other improvement indexes in a similar manner. By doing so, the decision maker will obtain the results shown in Table 11.5. The circled numbers in this table represent the improvement indexes associated with the corresponding empty cells.

Improving the Solution. Table 11.5's solution generates a total transportation cost of

$$(700 \times \$2) + (300 \times \$4) + (800 \times \$1) + (200 \times \$7) + (1,000 \times \$1) = \$5,800.$$

The positive improvement indexes (circled numbers) in the Milwaukee/Detroit, Gary/Minneapolis, and Gary/Detroit cells indicate that Tyler will increase this total cost by transporting suits over these routes. Conversely, the negative improvement index in

Table 11.5   **Tyler's Improvement Indexes**

From Plant Location	To Warehouse Location			Plant Supply (Suits per Month)
	Chicago	Minneapolis	Detroit	
Milwaukee	$2 700	$4 300	$5 ($7)	1,000
Gary	$1 800	$6 ($3)	$2 ($5)	800
Flint	$4 (−$1)	$7 200	$1 1,000	1,200
Warehouse Demand (Suits per Month)	1,500	500	1,000	3,000

the Flint/Chicago cell tells us that the $5,800 total cost can be reduced a net $1 for each suit shipped over the currently unused Flint-to-Chicago route. Such results illustrate the following important property: *In a minimization problem, the current solution can be improved as long as at least one unused transportation route has a negative improvement index.*

Since Flint-to-Chicago is the only cell with a negative improvement index, a shipment over this route will lead to the largest possible reduction in Table 11.5's (the starting solution's) total transportation cost. This fact illustrates the following important property: *In a minimization problem, the current solution can be improved the most by utilizing the unused transportation route with the largest negative improvement index.* Any tie can be broken arbitrarily. Utilizing the unused transportation route with the best improvement index is equivalent to the simplex process of bringing into the basis the nonbasic variable with the most desirable $C_j - Z_j$ value (the entering variable).

Revised Solution. Every suit shipped over the Flint-to-Chicago route will reduce Tyler's transportation cost by $1. It will also create the changes depicted by the closed path in Table 11.4. Since Tyler wants to minimize total cost, management should ship as many suits as feasible over this route.

According to the closed path in Table 11.4, each suit shipped along the Flint-to-Chicago route takes away a suit from the Milwaukee-to-Chicago and Flint-to-Minneapolis channels. Tyler currently is transporting 700 suits from Milwaukee to Chicago but only 200 from Flint to Minneapolis. Management should reallocate no more than 200 suits from these currently utilized channels to the Flint-to-Chicago route. Otherwise, it will have to take away more suits than are available along the Flint-to-Minneapolis channel. Such a reallocation of the smallest quantity in a minus position along the closed path is analogous to the simplex process of removing from the basis the basic variable with the smallest nonnegative trade ratio (the leaving variable).

To preserve all demand and supply requirements, Tyler must follow the prescriptions of the closed path: add 200 suits on the Flint-to-Chicago route, subtract 200 suits from

Table 11.6   **Tyler's Optimal Transportation Solution**

From Plant Location	To Warehouse Location			Plant Supply (Suits per Month)
	Chicago	Minneapolis	Detroit	
Milwaukee	$2 500	$4 500	$5 ($6)	1,000
Gary	$1 800	$6 ($3)	$2 ($4)	800
Flint	$4 200	$7 ($1)	$1 1,000	1,200
Warehouse Demand (Suits per Month)	1,500	500	1,000	3,000

the Milwaukee-to-Chicago shipment, add 200 suits to the Milwaukee-to-Minneapolis route, and subtract 200 suits along the Flint-to-Minneapolis route. By making the prescribed reallocations, management will obtain the revised solution shown in Table 11.6.

Optimal Solution. As Table 11.6 demonstrates, the company now ships 200 suits over the previously unused Flint-to-Chicago route. Since this route had an improvement index of −$1 in Table 11.5, the total cost of the revised solution (Table 11.6) will be

$$\$5,800 + (200 \times -\$1) = \$5,600$$

or $200 less than before.

By calculating the revised solution's improvement indexes, management will get the circled numbers shown in the empty cells of Table 11.6. All of these indexes are positive, indicating that Tyler will only increase costs by shipping suits over any of the currently unused (Milwaukee/Detroit, Gary/Minneapolis, Gary/Detroit, or Flint/Minneapolis) routes. Therefore, the distribution pattern given in Table 11.6 must represent the company's minimum cost solution. Indeed, it is the same recommendation as the optimal simplex solution presented earlier. This result demonstrates the following important principle: *In a minimization problem, a solution is optimal when the improvement index for each unused transportation route is greater than or equal to zero.*

Procedure Recap. The following procedure can be used to solve a transportation problem with a minimization objective:

1. Set up the transportation table, and use a heuristic method to develop a starting solution.

2. Calculate the improvement indexes. If all indexes are positive, the current table gives the optimal solution. Otherwise, go to step 3.

3. Bring into the solution the variable (unused route) with the best improvement index. Ties can be broken arbitrarily.

4. Trace the best unused route's closed path, and identify the smallest amount for the filled cells in a minus position along this path.

5. Allocate this smallest amount according to the prescriptions of the closed path, and return to step 2.

Transportation Methodology Extensions

As an alternative heuristic to the minimum cost cell method, the decision maker can use the northwest corner method or Vogel's approximation method (VAM) to find a problem solution or to develop a starting solution for a transportation algorithm. These alternative heuristics are outlined below.

Minimum Cost Cell Method	Northwest Corner Method	Vogel Approximation Method (VAM)
1. Identify the lowest cost cell in the transportation table. 2. Allocate as many units as feasible to this route. 3. Adjust the supply and demand requirements to reflect the allocation. 4. Repeat the procedure for the next lowest cost cells, in turn, until all supply and demand requirements are satisfied.	1. Allocate as many units as possible to the cell in the left-hand (northwest) corner of the transportation table. The maximum amount that can be allocated is the smaller of the source supply or destination demand. 2. Reduce the source supply and destination demand by the amount allocated to the cell. 3. If the source supply is now zero, move down the destination column to the next cell. If the destination demand is now zero, move to the right on the source row to the next cell. If both the source supply and destination demand are zero, move down and right one cell to the next cell. 4. Assign as many units as possible to the next cell identified by step 3. 5. Repeat steps 2 to 4 until a first feasible solution is obtained.	1. Compute a penalty cost for each source (row) and destination (column) in the transportation table. The penalty is the difference between the unit cost on the second-best and the best route in the row or column. 2. Identify the source or destination with the largest overall penalty. 3. Identify the most desirable cell in the identified row or column. 4. Allocate as many units as possible to the identified cell. The maximum amount that can be allocated is the smaller of the source supply or destination demand. 5. Reduce the source supply and destination demand by the amount allocated to the cell. 6. If the source supply is now zero, eliminate the source. If the destination demand is now zero, eliminate the destination. If both the source supply and demand are zero, eliminate both the source and destination. 7. Compute the new penalties for each source and destination in the revised transportation table formed by step 6. 8. Repeat steps 2 to 7 until a first feasible solution is obtained.

Although the northwest corner method is relatively quick and easy to use, it ignores the contributions to the objective function (costs in Tyler's case). Consequently, such a method is likely to require more iterations than the objective function-oriented minimum cost cell method and VAM.

When implementing the transportation methodology, the user can use modified distribution (MODI) rather than the stepping stone method to calculate improvement indexes. These alternative methods are outlined below.

Stepping Stone Method	Modified Distribution (MODI) Method
1. Identify the closed path for each unused route in the transportation network. This path begins with the corresponding empty cell in the transportation table and moves in horizontal and vertical directions from one filled cell to another until it returns to the starting point.	1. Set up the equation $U_i + V_j = C_{ij}$ for each *filled* cell in the transportation table. In this equation, $U_i =$ the cost savings associated with source i, $V_j =$ the cost savings for the destination j, and $C_{ij} =$ the cost of allocating one unit to the filled cell. The result is a simultaneous system of equations.
2. For each closed path, put a plus sign ($+$) in the empty cell and a minus sign ($-$) in the first filled cell on a corner of the path.	2. Identify the U_i or V_j that appears in the most equations of the system formed in step 1.
3. Alternate plus and minus signs in sequence for the remainder of the filled cells on the corners of the path in step 2.	3. Set the most frequent U_i or V_j variable equal to zero.
4. Sum the unit transportation costs for the plus ($+$) cells of the path in step 2.	4. Use the system of equations formed in step 1 to solve for the other U_i and V_j variables.
5. Sum the unit transportation costs for the minus ($-$) cells of the path in step 2.	5. Calculate the improvement index $C_{ij} - U_i - V_j$ for each *empty* cell in the transportation table.
6. Calculate the improvement index for each closed path by subtracting the sum in step 5 from the sum in step 4.	6. In a minimization problem, the current solution can be improved as long as at least one unused transportation route has a negative improvement index.
7. In a minimization problem, the current solution can be improved as long as at least one unused transportation route has a negative improvement index.	

The MODI method avoids the need to trace closed paths for each unused route and, in the process, provides a more efficient way than the stepping stone method to compute improvement indexes.

As in a simplex analysis, the transportation methodology can be used to generate shadow prices (and reduced costs) and to perform postoptimality analyses. The chapter's For Further Reading section provides references for the interested reader.

11.2 DECISION CONSIDERATIONS

In recent years, transportation models have been applied to the "distribution" of people, services, money, and information, as well as to the classical problem of shipping merchandise between sources and destinations. This model is also applicable to problems, such as purchasing and inventory control, that have nothing to do with distribution systems. Some of these nonclassical applications are presented in the Management Situations of this section, several are identified in the Transportation in Practice Exhibit, and others appear in the end-of-chapter exercises.

When dealing with a transportation situation (classical or nonclassical), the decision maker may encounter special conditions, including unbalanced supply and demand, prohibited routes, a maximization objective, degenerate solutions, multiple optima, and transfer shipping. In this section, we will see how to identify and deal with such conditions. We will also examine how transportation problems can be solved with the aid of a computer.

Transportation in Practice

Transportation methodology is applied to many management problems. Here are a few areas in which this quantitative analysis is used.

Area	Application
Finance	Determining transmission fees in an electrical power network
	Designing and implementing a check clearing system for a federal reserve bank
	Finding the best investment strategy for a planning period
Marketing	Developing the most cost-effective advertising strategy
	Distributing automobile tires in a national outlet system
	Delivering dairy products along rural routes
Production and Operations	Allocating raw materials among production tasks
	Selecting facility locations
	Controlling inventory costs
Public and Service Sector	Determining optimal ship routing and personnel assignment for naval recruitment in Thailand
	Allocating a city's salt and sand supplies during a winter snow storm
	Processing welfare applications
	Constructing an airport

Unbalanced Supply and Demand

In Management Situation 11.1, Tyler's total plant supply of 3,000 suits per month is exactly equal to the total warehouse demand. But such balance is unlikely in practice. Companies often maintain an excess supply to prepare for potential raw material shortages, strikes, or unforeseen demand. On the other hand, favorable economic conditions, changes in customer preferences, and decreased competition can lead to an excess in total demand over total supply.

The transportation solution methodology, however, requires the total source supply to exactly equal the total destination demand. To use this methodology, the decision maker first must eliminate any imbalance between total supply and total demand. Fortunately, there is an easy way to do this without changing the basic structure of the problem.

Excess Supply. Management Situation 11.2 involves a problem in which the total supply from all sources exceeds the total demand at all destinations.

Management Situation 11.2

Automobile Distribution

Gem Enterprises has created a new automobile: the Jetstream. The car is produced in three plants and sold through three major franchise dealerships throughout the United States. Annual plant supplies and franchise demands are given in Table 11.7, while the costs of transporting a car from each plant to each dealership are given in Table 11.8.

Table 11.7   Annual Plant Supplies and Franchise Demands for Gem Enterprises

Cars Supplied		Cars Demanded	
Plant	Cars per Year	Franchise	Cars per Year
P_1	3,000	F_1	10,000
P_2	7,000	F_2	1,000
P_3	5,000	F_3	2,000
Total supply	15,000	Total demand	13,000

Table 11.8   Gem's Transportation Costs

From Plant	To Franchise		
	F_1	F_2	F_3
P_1	$250	$300	$200
P_2	$100	$200	$350
P_3	$300	$100	$50

Gem wants to minimize the total cost of transporting the Jetstream. How many cars should be shipped from each plant to each franchise dealership?

In Management Situation 11.2, Gem's total plant supply is $15,000 - 13,000 = 2,000$ cars more than the total franchise demand. To account for this superfluity, the decision maker can create a fictitious franchise destination that demands the exact excess supply of 2,000 automobiles. Such a destination is known as a **dummy demand point**.

Since the dummy is imaginary, there actually will be no shipments to this point. Thus, it really costs nothing to transport a car to the fictitious franchise. If there are no other expenses that must be accounted for at the plants, the decision maker then can assign a transportation cost of $0 per car to each dummy route.

By incorporating these considerations into the problem formulation process, Gem will obtain Table 11.9. You can see that the dummy demand point is depicted as a franchise column in Gem's transportation table. Each cell in this column will give the number of cars that will be transported from the corresponding plant to the dummy franchise. In other words, each of these cells represents an unused plant supply. Hence, the cells are equivalent to the slack variables in the simplex method. As with a slack variable, each dummy route is assigned a shipment cost of $0 per car in the upper right-hand corner of the matching cell in Table 11.9.

After balancing total demand and total supply in this manner, management can use the standard transportation methodology to determine the best transportation solution. In the process, the dummy franchise will be treated like any other demand destination.

Table 11.9 **Gem's Transportation Table**

| From Plant | To Franchise Dealership | | | | Plant Supply (Cars per Year) |
	F_1	F_2	F_3	Dummy	
P_1	$250	$300	$200	$0	3,000
P_2	$100	$200	$350	$0	7,000
P_3	$300	$100	$50	$0	5,000
Franchise Demand (Cars per Year)	10,000	1,000	2,000	2,000	15,000

Moreover, the quantity shipped to a dummy destination is interpreted as the corresponding source's supply which cannot be economically utilized under current conditions.

Excess Demand. Management Situation 11.3 gives a problem in which the total demand at all destinations exceeds the total supply from all sources.

Management Situation 11.3

A Purchase Decision

Omnibus Hardware sells two main groups of products: interior and exterior items. The items are supplied by three manufacturers, and each sells both types of products. Omnibus has a monthly demand of 4,000 units for interior equipment and 3,000 units for exterior items. Recent union practices and economic conditions have limited the manufacturers' supplies to the amounts given in Table 11.10. The average per-unit purchase costs are given in Table 11.11. Omnibus wants to determine how many of each product it should purchase from each manufacturer. The objective is to minimize the total purchase cost.

In this problem, there again is a physical movement of merchandise (hardware items) from various supply sources (manufacturers). However, the demand destinations are now product (exterior and interior) categories rather than geographic locations. Moreover, the focus is on purchase costs instead of transportation costs. Still, the situation can be treated as a transportation problem.

There is only one complication. In Management Situation 11.3, the 4,000 + 3,000 = 7,000 unit total demand is 1,000 units greater than the manufacturers' total 6,000-unit supply. To account for this superfluity, management can create a fictitious manufacturing

Table 11.10   Manufacturers' Supplies

Manufacturer	Units Supplied This Month
Olex	2,200
Tilet	2,500
Zanc	1,300
Total supply	6,000

Table 11.11   Purchase Costs for Interior and Exterior Items

	Manufacturer		
Product	Olex	Tilet	Zanc
Interior	$2	$3	$1
Exterior	$4	$3	$6

source that will supply the exact excess demand for 1,000 hardware items. Such a source is referred to as a **dummy supply point**.

Since the dummy is imaginary, there actually will be no shipments from this point. Therefore, it really will cost nothing to purchase a hardware item from the fictitious manufacturer. If there is no preference (and associated penalty) for which product will have unsatisfied demand, the decision maker then can assign a purchase cost of $0 per unit to all allocations from the dummy manufacturer.

By incorporating these considerations into the problem formulation process, Omnibus will obtain Table 11.12. You can see that the dummy supply point is portrayed as a manufacturer row in Omnibus' transportation table. Each cell in this row will give the number of corresponding hardware items that will be purchased from the dummy manufacturer. Such cells (the dummy routes) are each assigned a purchase cost of $0 per unit.

After balancing total demand and total supply in this manner, management can use the conventional transportation methodologies to find the minimum cost solution. In the process, the dummy manufacturer will be treated like any other supply source. Furthermore, the amount purchased from the dummy source is interpreted as the corresponding product's demand which cannot be economically satisfied with the currently available resources.

Prohibited Routes

In practice, it may not be possible or desirable to transport merchandise over one or more routes. This situation may result from consumer or management preferences, carrier strikes, poor weather conditions, road restrictions, or government regulations. Such prohibitions can also arise in transportation-type problems that do not involve the physical shipment of merchandise from one geographic location to another. Management Situation 11.4 illustrates.

Table 11.12   **Omnibus's Transportation Table**

From Manufacturer	To Product		Manufacturer's Supply (Units per Month)
	Interior	Exterior	
Olex	$2	$4	2,200
Tilet	$3	$3	2,500
Zanc	$1	$6	1,300
Dummy	$0	$0	1,000
Product Demand (Units per Month)	4,000	3,000	7,000

Table 11.13   **Pamphlet's Costs per Thousand Leaflets**

Press	Order		
	A	B	C
1	$4	—	$8
2	$6	$3	—

Management Situation 11.4

A Job Order Problem

The Pamphlet Printing Company has three orders for single-page advertising leaflets. Order A calls for 30,000 copies, order B for 20,000, and order C for 30,000. The company has two presses available. Each press can produce 40,000 copies per day. The variable costs (per thousand) in running the orders on the various presses are given in Table 11.13. Management's preventive maintenance policy prohibits the use of press 1 on the jobs required by order B or the use of press 2 on the jobs required by order C. Pamphlet wants to know how many leaflets of each type it should print on each press. The objective is to minimize cost.

Management Situation 11.4 involves an allocation of job requests to printing presses rather than a physical movement of merchandise over shipping routes. As a result, the supply sources and demand destinations are no longer geographic locations. Instead, the job requests are completed by the presses to satisfy the demands from the advertising orders. Also, the focus is on printing costs rather than transportation costs. Nevertheless, the situation can be treated as a transportation problem.

Table 11.14   **Pamphlet's Transportation Table**

| From Press | To Order | | | Supply of Leaflets (Thousands per Day) |
	A	B	C	
1	$4	$M	$8	40
2	$6	$3	$M	40
Demand for Leaflets (Thousands per Day)	30	20	30	80

There is only one complication. As Management Situation 11.4 indicates, the preventive maintenance policy prohibits the use of press 1 on any B order or the use of press 2 for a C request. Hence, Pamphlet must devise a method that will exclude such unacceptable allocations from the recommended job order solution. Management can do this by allocating a very large per-unit cost to each prohibited allocation in the problem. Although any mammoth number would work, it is customary to use the symbol M for this purpose.

By incorporating these considerations into the problem formulation process, Pamphlet will obtain Table 11.14, where the prohibited allocations (press 1/order B and press 2/order C) are portrayed as cells. Such an approach is equivalent to the use of artificial variables in linear programming. Moreover, as with an artificial variable, each prohibited allocation is assigned an M per thousand-copy printing cost.

At this point, Pamphlet can use the conventional transportation methodologies to find the minimum cost printing plan. In the process, the symbol M must be interpreted as a number so large that M less any cost still is approximately equal to M. Thus, an empty cell with an M per-unit printing cost will always be the largest expense and result in undesirable improvement indexes. As a result, such a cell (prohibited allocation) can never be part of the optimal solution to the problem.

Maximization

The objective in Management Situations 11.1 through 11.4 was to minimize cost. Nevertheless, there are many situations in which the decision maker wants to maximize profit, output, or some other measure of return. Management Situation 11.5 illustrates.

Management Situation 11.5

Consumer Protection

Nardi's Sardis is a nonprofit organization that specializes in consumer protection issues. Recently, concerned citizens have brought four cases (labeled 1, 2, 3, and 4) to the attention of the agency. Nardi estimates that case 1 will require 2,000 hours per month, case 2 will require 4,000 hours per month, case 3 will require 1,000 hours per month, and case 4 will require 3,000 hours per month.

Table 11.15   Ratings for Nardi's Sardis by Group and Case

Research Group	Case			
	1	2	3	4
A	90	70	60	80
B	70	60	80	40
C	20	80	70	60

Currently, Sardis has three research groups, (coded A, B, and C) available to work on these cases. Group A can expend 4,000 hours per month, group B can expend 5,000 hours per month, and group C can expend 1,000 hours per month. Moreover, there are many similarities between the cases. Hence, it will be possible for each group to work on several cases simultaneously.

Assignments are based on an index of job performance. The index is a composite of the following criteria: thoroughness and accuracy of research, selection of appropriate remedial recommendations, and success of implementation. After reviewing personnel records, Nardi and his executive committee assign a rating to each group for each potential case. The rating scale goes from a low of zero to a high of 100 points per hour of effort. Nardi believes that the groups will achieve the ratings depicted in Table 11.15. Nardi wants to determine the staff allocation pattern that will maximize the total job performance index.

In Management Situation 11.5, there is an allocation of work effort rather than a physical distribution of merchandise. Also, the supply sources and demand destinations are no longer geographic locations. Instead, the work effort is supplied by the three research groups in response to the demand from the four consumer cases. Moreover, the focus is on a return measure (employee job performance) rather than a cost measure. Still, the situation can be treated as a transportation problem. Indeed, by using the conventional formulation process, Nardi will obtain Table 11.16, where the number in the upper right-hand corner of each cell represents a job performance score.

On the other hand, most of the conventional solution methodologies are designed for transportation problems involving a minimization objective, whereas Nardi wants to maximize the job performance index. Management must therefore adapt the conventional solution methodology to accommodate this maximization objective.

Several methods are available. In general, these approaches either transform the problem from a maximization objective to a minimization objective or modify the procedure for evaluating and improving a transportation solution. Although either approach will work, it is usually easier to convert the objective. Furthermore, the opportunity loss concept offers a convenient vehicle for making this transformation. To see why, we will continue with Nardi's transportation table.

According to the data in the upper right-hand corners of Table 11.16, 90 points is the highest overall rating attainable by any of the research groups. Consequently, such

Table 11.16   **Nardi's Transportation Table**

From Research Group	To Case 1	To Case 2	To Case 3	To Case 4	Supply of Research (Hours per Month)
A	90	70	60	80	4,000
B	70	60	80	40	5,000
C	20	80	70	60	1,000
Demand for Research (Hours per Month)	2,000	4,000	1,000	3,000	10,000

Table 11.17   **Opportunity Costs for Nardi's Sardis**

Research Group	Case 1	Case 2	Case 3	Case 4
A	90−90= 0	90−70=20	90−60=30	90−80=10
B	90−70=20	90−60=30	90−80=10	90−40=50
C	90−20=70	90−80=10	90−70=20	90−60=30

a score gives a standard that Nardi can use to judge job performance. In particular, if management computes the difference between each actual index and the highest overall rating, it will measure the degree to which the corresponding allotments deviate from this standard. These differences, which represent the opportunity costs associated with the matching staff allocations, are calculated in Table 11.17.

Management should then substitute these differences for the corresponding numbers in the upper right-hand corners of the cells in Table 11.16. That is, 0 should replace 90 in the A/1 cell, 10 should replace 80 in the B/3 cell, and so on. In this way, the problem will be expressed in terms of opportunity costs rather than job performance indexes. Since the decision maker must seek the smallest opportunity costs, such a process also transforms the situation from a maximization objective to a minimization objective. Nardi can then use the conventional transportation methodologies to find the optimal staff allocation.

In Nardi's situation, the total demand exactly equals the total supply of research effort. However, the opportunity cost approach is also applicable to maximization problems that involve an imbalance between total supply and demand. In such problems, however, the dummy source or destination must be added *before* the decision maker computes the opportunity costs. Otherwise, the dummy erroneously will appear to have the smallest opportunity costs, and the conventional methodologies may not generate the optimal transportation solution.

Also, Nardi's situation does not involve any prohibited allocations. Nevertheless, such allocations can arise in transportation problems with maximization objectives. In

Table 11.18   **Costs of Tennis Classes in Leaftown**

Instructor	Hourly Cost of Offering Each Class		
	Beginning	Intermediate	Advanced
Ace Serve	$5	$4	$2
Julie Baseline	$3	$6	$1
Chris King	$2	$3	$10

these cases, the decision maker must denote a prohibited allocation by allotting a very large negative $(-M)$ per-unit return to the corresponding cell in the transportation table. Furthermore, the $-M$ allotments must be made *before* the decision maker computes the opportunity costs. Otherwise, the prohibited route erroneously will appear to have a negative opportunity loss, and the conventional methodologies may not generate the optimal transportation solution.

Degeneracy

In many cases, the conventional methodologies will generate a solution that fills fewer than $m + n - 1$ cells in the transportation table. Furthermore, this condition, which is equivalent to degeneracy in linear programming, can arise either in the initial transportation solution or during the reallocation process. Management Situation 11.6 illustrates.

Management Situation 11.6

Tennis Instruction

Leaftown's recreation department hires local amateur and professional players on a part-time basis to conduct its tennis education program. Ace Serve is available for 20 hours per week, Julie Baseline for 40 hours, and Chris King for 40 hours. Three classes are offered at municipal courts: beginning, intermediate, and advanced. Leaftown plans to offer 50 hours of beginning classes per week, 20 hours of intermediate classes, and 30 hours of advanced instruction. The cost of offering each class depends on the instructor's relative teaching skill, class size, and other related factors. These costs are summarized in Table 11.18. Leaftown wants to allocate instructors to classes in the way that minimizes the total cost of offering the tennis education program.

Management Situation 11.6 involves an allocation of instruction rather than a physical distribution of merchandise. Also, the supply sources and demand destinations are not geographic locations. Instead, the education is supplied by the three instructors in response to the demand from the three classes. In addition, the focus is on instruction costs rather than transportation costs. Nevertheless, the situation can be treated as a

Table 11.19   Leaftown's Second Transportation Solution

From Instructor	To Class			Supply of Instruction (Hours per Week)
	Beginning	Intermediate	Advanced	
Ace Serve	$5	$4	$2	20
		20		
Julie Baseline	$3	$6	$1	40
	10		30	
Chris King	$2	$3	$10	40
	40			
Demand for Instruction (Hours per Week)	50	20	30	100

transportation problem. Indeed, by using the transportation methodology, Leaftown will eventually obtain the transportation solution presented in Table 11.19.

Leaftown's problem involves $m = 3$ supply sources (instructors) and $n = 3$ demand destinations (classes). Thus, each solution should fill $m + n - 1 = 3 + 3 - 1 = 5$ cells in the corresponding transportation table. As Table 11.19 demonstrates, however, the city's second transportation solution has only four filled cells. Consequently, this second solution is degenerate.

Even though a degenerate solution will usually be feasible (satisfy all demand and supply requirements), it does not provide the number of filled cells (basic variables) necessary to calculate improvement indexes for all empty cells (nonbasic variables). To handle this difficulty, the decision maker can adjust the degenerate solution by allotting an artificial and very small allocation, denoted by ϵ (epsilon), to additional empty cells in the transportation table. These ϵ allotments should not be placed in just any empty cells. Instead, they should be placed in the empty cells that will provide the relevant improvement index data—either in cells that were filled in the previous solution or in the columns and rows associated with the cells that simultaneously fulfill the supply and demand requirements.

In Table 11.19, for example, the solution is degenerate because the allocation of 20 hours to the Ace/intermediate cell simultaneously satisfies Ace Serve's supply and the intermediate class demand. As a result, the city will not have enough data to calculate the improvement indexes for the Ace/beginning, Ace/advanced, Julie/intermediate, and Chris/intermediate empty cells. Leaftown can thus avoid degeneracy by allotting ϵ hours to any one of these empty cells. Since the Ace/advanced cell has the smallest per-unit cost ($2), the decision maker may prefer to utilize this cell and obtain the nondegenerate transportation solution shown in Table 11.20.

After resolving the degeneracy in this manner, management can use the conventional transportation methodologies to find the minimum cost tennis education program. In the process, ϵ is interpreted as a quantity large enough to be considered an allocation but sufficiently minuscule to be treated as a zero in any computation. When improving a

Table 11.20   **Leaftown's Nondegenerate Second Transportation Solution**

From Instructor	To Class			Supply of Instruction (Hours per Week)
	Beginning	Intermediate	Advanced	
Ace Serve	$5	$4 \\ 20	$2 \\ ϵ	20
Julie Baseline	$3 \\ 10	$6	$1 \\ 30	40
Chris King	$2 \\ 40	$3	$10	40
Demand for Instruction (Hours per Week)	50	20	30	100

transportation solution, the decision maker must regard ϵ as the smallest of the amounts in a minus position along the pertinent closed path. On the other hand, an ϵ allocation is equivalent to adding or subtracting zero units from the corresponding transportation table. Furthermore, there will be no cost for allocating ϵ units.

Multiple Optima

As with any ordinary linear programming situation, a transportation problem may involve more than one optimal solution. Management Situation 11.7 illustrates.

Management Situation 11.7

Bus Scheduling

A small town municipally operated bus line services three main areas designated as zones A, B, and C. There are two main service facilities: the downtown and uptown terminals. Each route involves a particular operating cost, and there are a different number of buses available from each terminal and demanded at each zone. The bus line's prime goal is to minimize the cost of providing the necessary service. However, there are also political and social considerations. Hence, if several alternatives have the same minimum total cost, the bus line would prefer a scheduling pattern that provides the maximum number of uptown buses for zone B.

After much deliberation, the management staff realizes that the situation can be treated as a transportation problem. Moreover, by using the conventional transportation methodologies, management develops the solution shown in Table 11.21. Each number in the upper right-hand corner of every cell represents the cost of operating a bus along the corresponding route. Also, the circled numbers give the improvement indexes associated with each empty cell in the solution.

Table 11.21   **Optimal Bus-Scheduling Solution**

From Terminal	To Zone			Supply of Service (Buses)
	A	B	C	
Downtown	$200	$300	$200	60
	10	30	20	
Uptown	$200	$300	$300	40
	40	($0)	($100)	
Demand for Service (Buses)	50	30	20	100

Table 11.22   **Alternative Optimal Bus-Scheduling Solution**

From Terminal	To Zone			Supply of Service (Buses)
	A	B	C	
Downtown	$200	$300	$200	60
	40	($0)	20	
Uptown	$200	$300	$300	40
	10	30	($100)	
Demand for Service (Buses)	50	30	20	100

In Table 11.21, every empty cell has a nonnegative improvement index (circled number). These indexes indicate that the town cannot decrease operating costs by sending buses over any of the currently unused routes. Therefore, the distribution pattern given in this figure portrays a minimum cost bus schedule.

Nevertheless, the currently unused bus route between the uptown terminal and zone B has a $0 improvement index. The situation is equivalent to having a $C_j - Z_j = 0$ for a nonbasic variable in the simplex method. It means that the town will not change total costs by allocating buses to such a route. Furthermore, the distribution pattern given in Table 11.21 is an optimal solution. As a result, the $0 improvement index implies that there must be alternative ways to minimize the total operating cost of the bus service.

To find one of the alternative optimal solutions, management should treat the empty uptown/zone B cell as the unused transportation route with the best improvement index. Management then can use the standard transportation methodology to develop the revised solution shown in Table 11.22. Since every empty cell in this revised table has a nonnegative improvement index (circled number), Table 11.22 gives an alternative minimum cost bus schedule.

Multiple optima (such as Tables 11.21 and 11.22) give management flexibility in selecting and using resources. The municipal bus line, for example, has political and

Table 11.23   Estimated Cannery Supply and Warehouse Demand

Output		Demand	
Cannery	Truckloads	Warehouse	Truckloads
Seattle	2,500	Portland	1,200
San Francisco	1,500	Los Angeles	2,800

social considerations that are not directly incorporated into operating costs, terminal supply requirements, or zone demand requirements. However, if several alternatives have identical optimal total costs, management will prefer the scheduling pattern that provides the maximum number of uptown buses for zone B. The distribution pattern given in Table 11.22 provides better service (more buses) over the uptown-to-zone B route than the solution portrayed in Table 11.21. Thus, management will prefer the bus schedule in Table 11.22 to the schedule in Table 11.21.

Transfer Shipping

Frequently, distribution systems will have intermediate locations, known as **transshipment points**, that can receive merchandise from one shipping source and then reship it to another destination. Examples of these points include warehouses between plants and retailers, connecting or "hub" airports between a trip's origin and destination, and satellite stations that relay cable television signals from the studio to subscribers. In these systems, the problem is to find the most effective way of distributing the "merchandise" from the supply sources, through the transshipment points, and on to the demand destinations. Such a problem, which is called the **transshipment problem**, can be viewed as an extension of the transportation model. Management Situation 11.8 illustrates.

Management Situation 11.8

Truck Routing

The JBT Company processes and distributes a variety of canned vegetables throughout the Pacific Coast states. One of its main products, corn, is prepared at two canneries (near Seattle and San Francisco) and then shipped by truck to two distributing warehouses (in Portland and Los Angeles). Common carriers are used to truck the canned corn. Cannery supplies and warehouse demands for the upcoming season are estimated as in Table 11.23.

Unfortunately, there is no single trucking company that serves the entire area containing all the canneries and warehouses. Therefore, many of the shipments will have to be transferred to another carrier at least once along the way. Moreover, the carriers are willing to make transfer only at the Portland warehouse, San Francisco cannery, and/or trucking depots in Redding and Fresno.

Table 11.24   **Transportation Costs per Truckload**

From	To					
	Seattle Cannery	San Francisco Cannery	Redding Depot	Fresno Depot	Portland Warehouse	Los Angeles Warehouse
Seattle Cannery	$0	NA	$500	NA	$350	NA
San Francisco Cannery	IA	$0	$250	$300	$700	$550
Redding Depot	IA	$260	$0	$480	$450	NA
Fresno Depot	IA	$310	$480	$0	NA	$280
Portland Warehouse	IA	$700	$430	NA	$0	NA
Los Angeles Warehouse	IA	IA	IA	IA	IA	$0

The costs of transporting a truckload of canned corn between the various shipping points are given in Table 11.24. As the cost data indicate, some shipments are either inappropriate (IA), not available from the carriers (NA), or involve a $0 actual expenditure. Management wants to determine the distribution pattern that will minimize total transportation cost.

Nature of the Problem. JBT's truck-routing situation has several characteristics in common with the transportation problem. The situation can be portrayed as a set of nodes (canneries, trucking depots, and warehouses) linked by a series of branches (shipping routes), and there will be a flow (movement of corn) in only one direction along these branches. Unlike the transportation problem, however, some nodes (the Redding and Fresno depots, the Portland warehouse, and the San Francisco cannery) are transshipment points that act as both supply sources and demand destinations. These points receive canned corn from some source and then reship it to another destination. Management then must find the least costly way of shipping the required quantities of corn from the sources, through the transshipment points, to the destinations.

Problem Formulation. By modifying the standard transportation table to account for transfer shipping, JBT can solve its transshipment problem with the standard transportation methodology. In this approach, each transshipment point (Redding, Fresno, Portland, and San Francisco) will have both a row and a column in the transportation table. Source supplies, destination demands, and transportation costs are found from the problem data.

Consider, for example, the San Francisco cannery. Although this cannery is not a warehouse, it can serve as a transfer point for shipments from the Portland warehouse and the Redding and Fresno depots. Unfortunately, management does not know in advance how much demand there will be for such a service. Nevertheless, the data in Table 11.23 indicate that the total corn demand for the upcoming season is 4,000 truckloads. Since it would be inefficient to send merchandise through the same transshipment point more than once, a quantity of 4,000 truckloads is a safe upper bound on San Francisco's demand.

The San Francisco cannery supply is another matter. According to Table 11.23, this cannery can produce 1,500 truckloads of corn for the upcoming season. Yet it also can transship the truckloads received from the Portland warehouse and the Redding and Fresno depots. Therefore, the San Francisco cannery may have a supply equal to its own output plus the potential transshipments, or 1,500 + 4,000 = 5,500 truckloads.

In effect, then, the supply at each transshipment point can be set equal to the original output plus the total demand at all final destinations. Now, the Portland warehouse and the Redding and Fresno depots are not canneries and therefore have no original outputs. Hence, JBT should plan for a 0 + 4,000 = 4,000 truckload supply at each of these transfer locations.

Similarly, the demand at each transshipment point can be set equal to the original requirement plus the total demand at all final destinations. In this regard, the Redding and Fresno depots are not warehouses and therefore have no original requirements. Thus, the company should plan for a 0 + 4,000 = 4,000 truckload demand at each of these transfer locations.

On the other hand, Table 11.23 indicates that the Portland warehouse has an original demand for 1,200 truckloads of corn during the upcoming season. However, this warehouse can also transship as many as 4,000 truckloads received from other locations. Therefore, the total demand may be equal to the original requirement plus the transshipments, or 1,200 + 4,000 = 5,200 truckloads.

The demand and supply at the locations that are not transshipment points will remain at their original levels. Table 11.23 shows that the Seattle cannery can supply 2,500 truckloads of corn for the upcoming season and the Los Angeles warehouse has a demand for 2,800 truckloads. The costs of transporting a truckload of canned corn between the various shipping and receiving points are given in Table 11.24.

If management utilizes this information to formulate the problem, it will obtain Table 11.25. Inappropriate (IA) and nonavailable (NA) shipments should be treated as prohibited routes in such a formulation. As a result, these shipments are assigned very large positive (M) per-unit costs in Table 11.25.

At this point, JBT can use the standard transportation methodology to find the optimal distribution pattern. Such a pattern can require some locations to receive shipments from themselves. Since the merchandise actually never leaves the premises, these intrasite allocations should be interpreted as unused transshipment capacity.

Other Variations

There are other important extensions and variations to the transportation model. Some of the most important are discussed below.

Conditional Transportation Model. Another aspect of the analysis is to determine the best locations for facilities (such as factories, warehouses, outlets) in the distribution system. Typically, there are several alternative locations, each with a different route setup cost, and management can select only some of the locations. As noted in Chapter 10, such mutually exclusive alternatives can be modeled with zero/one variables, and the resulting problem can be solved with integer programming.

Table 11.25   JBT's Transportation Table

From	To Portland	To Los Angeles	To Redding	To Fresno	To San Francisco	Supply (Truckloads)
Seattle	$350	$M	$500	$M	$M	2,500
San Francisco	$700	$550	$250	$300	$0	5,500
Redding	$450	$M	$0	$480	$260	4,000
Fresno	$M	$280	$480	$0	$310	4,000
Portland	$0	$M	$430	$M	$700	4,000
Demand (Truckloads)	5,200	2,800	4,000	4,000	4,000	20,000

Nonhomogeneous Goods. Sometimes, there are qualitative differences in the merchandise available from the sources. Management then will not regard all suppliers as acceptable sources. To deal with this case, the decision maker can use various ad hoc procedures, including the prohibition of routes and the weighting of shipping costs from unacceptable sources.

Route Restrictions. The classic transportation model assumes that each source is capable of supplying each destination. For many problems, restrictions, such as exclusions or lower bounds, are imposed on routes. As noted in the text, penalties (M values) can be used to deal with exclusions (prohibited routes). When there is a lower bound on a shipment, the decision maker can adjust the transportation table to reflect the requirement and then solve the modified problem.

Variable Transportation Cost. In practice, carriers may offer a quantity discount for shipping large volumes of merchandise or special premiums for utilizing various route combinations. Per-unit transportation costs then will be variable rather than fixed and constant as in the classic transportation model. These variable transportation cost cases can be modeled and solved with nonlinear programming or with dynamic programming.

Computer Analysis

Practical transportation problems often involve hundreds of supply sources and demand destinations. Usually, prewritten computer packages, such as *TRANLP*, are used to implement the transportation methodology in these situations. A program similar to the commercial packages is available on the **Quantitative Management (QM)** software. It is invoked by selecting Distribution from **QM**'s main menu. Figure 11.2 then shows how the program is used to solve JBT's transshipment problem (Management Situation 11.8).

Figure 11.2   Computer Solution of JBT's Transshipment Problem

---

Distribution:	Input:	Output:
* Transportation	* Edit	▪ Full
▪ Assignment	▪ Load	* Summary
	▪ Print	* Print
	▪ Save	▪ Save

Problem Description:
  Minimization (MIN) or Maximization (MAX) Objective: MIN
  Number of Sources: 5
  Number of Destinations: 5

Enter the problem data in the following transportation table.

	PO	LA	RE	FR	SF	Supply
SE	350	9999	500	9999	9999	2500
SF	700	550	250	300	0	5500
RE	450	9999	0	480	260	4000
FR	9999	280	480	0	310	4000
PO	0	9999	430	9999	700	4000
Demand	5200	2800	4000	4000	4000	

RECOMMENDATION

Source	Destination	Shipment	Unit Cost	Shipping Cost
SE	PO	1200	350	420000
SE	RE	1300	500	650000
SF	LA	1500	550	825000
SF	SF	4000	0	0
RE	RE	2700	0	0
RE	FR	1300	480	624000
FR	LA	1300	280	364000
FR	FR	2700	0	0
PO	PO	4000	0	0
Total Transportation Cost				2883000

Problem Formulation. As Figure 11.2 illustrates, the user executes the module by selecting the Transportation option from the Distribution menu. The problem is formulated through the Edit command from the Input menu. In this case, the user provides a description of the problem, including the nature of the objective, the number of sources, and the number of destinations. Figure 11.2, for example, shows that the transshipment problem is a minimization (MIN) problem with five sources and five destinations. Then the program provides a transportation table with blank spaces for the user's entry of source supplies, destination demands, and unit transportation costs.

When entering the unit transportation costs for the transshipment problem, the number 9999 (or any other very large positive value) must be substituted for each *M* symbol. That is because the program cannot interpret an alphabetic entry (*M*) where a numeric value is expected. As Figure 11.2 demonstrates, the input format enables the user to essentially recreate a transportation table for the problem. Report options then are chosen through the Output menu.

Optimal Transportation Solution. The RECOMMENDATION section of Figure 11.2 shows that JBT can minimize its total transportation cost at $2,883,000 by directly shipping

1,200 truckloads from the Seattle (SE) cannery to the Portland (PE) warehouse

1,500 truckloads from the San Francisco (SF) cannery to the Los Angeles (LA) warehouse

and by transshipping

1,300 truckloads from the Seattle cannery to the Redding (RE) depot

1,300 truckloads from the Redding depot to the Fresno (FR) depot

1,300 truckloads from the Fresno depot to the Los Angeles warehouse

In other words, management should transship 1,300 truckloads of corn from the Seattle cannery, through the Redding and Fresno depots, and on to the Los Angeles warehouse. Figure 11.2 also suggests that JBT's optimal distribution pattern will leave 4,000 truckloads of unused transshipment capacity at the San Francisco cannery, 2,700 truckloads each at the Redding and Fresno depots, and 4,000 truckloads of unused transshipment capacity at the Portland warehouse.

Postoptimality Analysis. If the user selects the Full option (not shown here) from the Output menu, **QM** will perform postoptimality analyses and report the results as part of the RECOMMENDATION. These results will include the reduced costs associated with each shipping route and sensitivity analyses on the per-suit shipping costs (objective function coefficients) and on the source supplies and destination demands (constraint right-hand side amounts).

11.3 ASSIGNMENT

In many distribution situations, the resources available from each supply source and the tasks required at each demand destination are indivisible. That is, each resource can be assigned to one and only one task, while each job must be completed by one and only one resource. Management Situation 11.9 illustrates.

Management Situation 11.9

Maintenance Dispatching

The maintenance department of a small manufacturing firm has three available repairpersons: Tom, Alice, and Sam. There are three jobs that must be done in a given time period. Owing to the nature and location of the jobs, only one person can be assigned to one job at any given time. Since each repairperson has different skills and each job requires different tasks, there is a different per-hour cost of assigning each person to

---

Table 11.26   Job Costs in Maintenance-Dispatching Problem

Repairperson	Job Cost per Hour		
	A	B	C
Tom	$3	$6	$10
Alice	$5	$12	$7
Sam	$8	$4	$2

---

each job. The relevant costs are presented in Table 11.26. The maintenance manager wants to establish the maintenance plan that will minimize total repair cost.

Nature of the Problem

In Management Situation 11.9, the manufacturing firm has a demand for one and only one repairperson at each of the three unique jobs. Management can satisfy these demands by assigning one and only one repairperson to each job. Several alternative personnel assignments, each with a specific per-hour cost, can be used to perform the necessary maintenance. These alternatives are depicted in Figure 11.3, where each node (circle) represents a supply source (repairperson) or demand destination (job). The arcs (lines) reflect the flow (movement of repairpersons to jobs) that will occur through the maintenance system. The number above each node depicts the supply available at that source or the demand emanating from that destination. As you can see, there is exactly one repairperson available at each source and precisely one job required at each destination. Every value on an arc identifies the cost of assigning the repairperson to the corresponding job. Because management must determine the least costly way of making the assignments, such a situation is known as an **assignment problem**.

Solution Methods

A variety of procedures can be used to solve assignment problems. Some of the most popular are discussed below.

Total Enumeration. One solution method is to list all possible assignment combinations, compare the outcomes, and then select the best combination. While such an approach might work well for small-scale assignment problems (like Management Situation 11.9), it will be too costly to implement on problems of meaningful size. For example, a problem with 25 resources and tasks will require the decision maker to evaluate 25! (about 1.55×10^{25}) assignment combinations. At a processing time of 0.01 second per solution, it would take about 4.92×10^{15} years to solve this problem on today's typical computer!

Mathematical Programming. As was discussed in Chapter 7, the assignment problem forms an integer linear program. (You will be asked to demonstrate this fact in Thought

Figure 11.3   **Maintenance Assignment Alternatives**

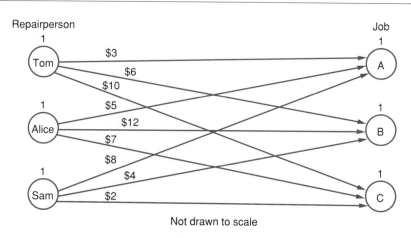

Not drawn to scale

Exercise 6.) Hence, the decision maker can utilize zero/one (binary integer) programming to develop an optimal assignment. If such an approach proves too costly to implement, the assignment problem can be treated as an ordinary linear program and solved with the simplex method. Due to the assignment problem's special structure, the simplex solution will automatically satisfy the integer restrictions. (You will be asked to demonstrate this fact in Thought Exercises 7 and 8).

Transportation Methodology. The assignment problem is a special case of the transportation problem in which only one unit is supplied from each source and only one unit is demanded at each destination. Therefore, the decision maker can use the standard transportation methodology to solve the assignment problem. Although more efficient than the simplex method, the transportation methodology (like the simplex method) will generate a large number of degenerate solutions when applied to the assignment problem.

Network Models. As Figure 11.3 illustrates, an assignment problem can be viewed as a network. Specialized procedures then can be used to solve the resulting network formulation. Using network formulations, enormous and complex assignment problems can be solved with relative ease. As in the transportation situation, network models usually are reserved for these difficult problems.

Assignment Algorithms. In the assignment problem, there is exactly one unit supplied from each source and exactly one unit demanded at each destination. Assignment algorithms, such as the **Hungarian method**, exploit this special structure both to reduce computer processing time and to increase precision.

Hungarian Method

The Hungarian method (also known as **Flood's technique** and **matrix reduction**) is among the most popular assignment algorithms. Based on Chapter 4's opportunity cost

Table 11.27   **Maintenance-Dispatching Assignment Table**

From Repairperson	To Job		
	A	B	C
Tom	$3	$6	$10
Alice	$5	$12	$7
Sam	$8	$4	$2

Job cost per hour

Table 11.28   **Repairperson (Row) Penalty Table**

From Repairperson	To Job		
	A	B	C
Tom	$3−$3 = $0	$6−$3 = $3	$10−$3 = $7
Alice	$5−$5 = $0	$12−$5 = $7	$7−$5 = $2
Sam	$8−$2 = $6	$4−$2 = $2	$2−$2 = $0

concept, it first identifies the penalties associated with each potential assignment. The method then selects the assignments that have zero penalties or no opportunity losses. A standard format, called the **assignment table**, is utilized to conveniently record the data and keep track of the calculations. Table 11.27 illustrates this table with Management Situation 11.9's maintenance dispatching information.

Assignment Table. Each row in the table represents a supply source (node) and every column a demand destination (node) in the manufacturing firm's assignment network. For example, the second row portrays repairperson Alice, and the third column depicts job C. The cells correspond to the potential assignments (arcs) in the maintenance network. The cell at the intersection of the second row and first column, for instance, corresponds to the possible assignment of Alice to job A. Since the firm has three repairpersons and three jobs, there are 3 × 3 = 9 cells (possible assignments) in the table.

Entries in the cells of Table 11.27 give the costs of the corresponding assignments. The entry at the intersection of the second row and first column, for instance, indicates that it costs $5 to assign Alice to job A. Similarly, the entry at the intersection of the third row and second column shows that it costs $4 for Sam to do job B.

In addition, Table 11.27 shows that the number of rows (repairpersons) is exactly equal to the number of columns (jobs). This required balance is a characteristic of the manufacturing firm's maintenance dispatching problem. Nevertheless, there are cases that involve imbalances between the number of resources (rows) and tasks (columns) in the assignment table. Such cases will be discussed later in the chapter.

Penalties. There will be opportunity losses associated with each repairperson and job in the maintenance dispatching problem. In a minimization problem, resource (repairperson)

Table 11.29   **Job (Column) Penalty Table**

From Repairperson	To Job		
	A	B	C
Tom	$0−$0 = $0	$3−$2 = $1	$7−$0 = $7
Alice	$0−$0 = $0	$7−$2 = $5	$2−$0 = $2
Sam	$6−$0 = $6	$2−$2 = $0	$0−$0 = $0

Table 11.30   **Maintenance Assignments with $0 Penalties**

Repairperson	Job		
	A	B	C
Tom	$0	$1	$7
Alice	$0	$5	$2
Sam	$6	$0	$0

penalties are found by subtracting the smallest entry in each row (which represents the least expensive assignment for the resource) from all costs in that row of the assignment table. Table 11.28 shows these repairperson (row) penalty calculations. Having made such an accounting, task (job) penalties then are found by subtracting the smallest entry in each column (which represents the least expensive assignment for the task) from all costs in that column of the resource (repairperson) penalty table. Table 11.29 shows these job (column) penalty calculations.

Optimality Test. To have an optimal assignment, management must avoid any opportunity losses. In the maintenance dispatching situation, this means that each of the three repairpersons must be assigned to a job that he or she can perform without penalty. The potential number of such assignments are found by covering all zero entries in Table 11.29 (which accounts for both repairperson and job penalties) with as few horizontal and vertical lines as possible. Table 11.30 shows the results.

As the lines in Table 11.30 demonstrate, only two $0 penalty assignments are initially possible in the maintenance dispatching situation. Hence, Table 11.29 (or the equivalent Table 11.30) does not give the optimal maintenance plan. This result illustrates the following important principle: *Management will not have an optimal assignment unless the minimum number of lines required to cover all zeros equals the number of rows in the current penalty table.*

Revision Process. Management can improve a nonoptimal pattern by revising the current penalty table to create additional zero penalty assignments. The revision is completed by

Table 11.31   **Tom to Job B**

Repairperson	Job		
	A	B	C
Tom	$0	$0	$6
Alice	$0	$4	$1
Sam	$7	$0	$0

1. Subtracting the smallest penalty not covered by a line ($1 in Table 11.30) from all unlined penalties.
2. Adding this smallest unlined penalty to all numbers lying at the intersection of any two lines (to the $6 in the Sam/job A cell in Table 11.30).
3. Leaving the remaining covered entries unchanged.

This process introduces the least expensive remaining assignment from the current penalty table (Tom to job B from Table 11.30), adjusts other assignment penalties to reflect the change, and results in Table 11.31.

Optimal Assignment. Since no fewer than three lines are needed to cover all the $0 penalties in Table 11.31, each of the three repairpersons now can be assigned to a job that he or she can perform with a $0 penalty. Consequently, the maintenance plan suggested by the line pattern in this table represents the optimal assignment.

Although the optimal assignment may not be apparent from the table, it can be found by: (1) identifying a row or column with only one zero, (2) selecting that assignment, and (3) repeating the process until all assignments are made. Such a process generates the assignment pattern shown with the enclosed $0 penalties in Table 11.31, which indicates that the manufacturing firm can minimize total repair cost by assigning

- Tom to job B.
- Alice to job A.
- Sam to Job C.

According to the data from the original assignment table (Table 11.27), the resulting minimum cost will be $6 + $5 + $2 = $13 per hour.

Procedure Recap. The following procedure can be used to solve an assignment problem with a minimization objective:

1. Set up the assignment table.
2. Calculate the resource (row) and then task (column) penalties.

Assignment in Practice

The assignment model is applied to a wide variety of management problems. Here are a few areas in which this quantitative analysis is used.

Area	Application
Finance and Accounting	Assigning accountants to auditing jobs Matching estate plans to potential clients Allocating cash-on-hand to reserve accounts Matching real estate loan options to potential home buyers
Marketing	Assigning salespeople to territories Scheduling product deliveries to industrial customers Competitive bidding for product and service contracts Assigning delivery vehicles to routes
Production and Operations	Assigning computer personnel to programming jobs Assigning manufacturing personnel to machines Assigning secretaries to office tasks
Public and Service Sector	Assigning university faculty to courses Assigning hospital nurses to duty shifts Automatically rotating Navy personnel between sea and shore duty

Table 11.32   Sales Force Data

Salesperson	Monthly Sales Volume		
	Suits	Shoes	Accessories
Nancy	$300	$300	$200
Joe	$600	$600	—
Barbara	$400	$400	$100
Jim	$200	—	$500

3. Run the optimality test by covering all zero penalties with as few horizontal and vertical lines as possible. If the number of lines equals the number of rows (columns), the optimal assignment can be made. Otherwise, go to step 4.

4. Revise the current table by: (a) subtracting the smallest penalty not covered by a line from all unlined penalties and (b) adding this smallest unlined penalty to all numbers lying at the intersection of any two lines. Return to step 3.

Special Situations

Assignment models have been applied to the situations, such as court scheduling and Navy operations, that have nothing to do with distribution systems, as well as to the classical problem of assigning resources to tasks. Some of these nonclassical applications are presented in the Assignment in Practice Exhibit, and others appear in the end-of-chapter exercises.

When dealing with an assignment situation (classical or nonclassical), the decision maker can encounter special conditions, including an unequal number of resources and tasks, prohibited assignments, a maximization objective, and multiple optimal solutions. In this section, we will show how to identify and deal with such conditions. We also will examine how to solve assignment problems with the aid of a computer. The concepts will be illustrated with Management Situation 11.10.

Management Situation 11.10

Sales Force Allocation

A small clothing store has four salespeople and three departments. Since each person has a different level of experience and ability, each will generate different sales in each department. The store's manager has estimated the sales volume that can be expected from each person in each department. The data are given in Table 11.32.

Joe does not have the interest, knowledge, or ability to sell accessories. Jim has always had trouble selling shoes. Therefore, the store manager does not want to assign Joe to accessories or Jim to shoes. The manager wants to know which salesperson to assign to which department to maximize sales.

Resource-Task Imbalances. In Management Situation 11.9, the manufacturing firm had three repairpersons available to perform three maintenance jobs. That is, the number of resources (repairpersons) was exactly equal to the number of tasks (maintenance jobs). Yet such balance does not always occur in practice. Instead, there may be more resources than tasks, or vice versa. The sales force allocation problem in Management Situation 11.10 offers just such a situation. The store manager has four salespeople but only three departments. Thus, there are more resources (salespeople) than tasks (departments).

The assignment methodology, however, requires the resources and tasks to be in balance. To utilize this methodology, then, the decision maker first must eliminate any imbalances between the number of resources and tasks. As with the transportation problem, the use of fictitious sources or destinations provides an easy way to correct the imbalance without changing the basic structure of the problem.

The store manager, for instance, has $4 - 3 = 1$ more salesperson (resource) than department (task). To account for this excess resource, the manager can create a fictitious department that would demand the extra salesperson. Such a department, which is similar to a fictitious demand point in the transportation problem, can be called a **dummy task**.

Since the dummy is imaginary, there actually will be no assignment to this task. Thus, the store really gets nothing by assigning a salesperson to the fictitous department. Consequently, the manager should list a $0 sales volume for each dummy task assignment.

On the other hand, suppose that the manager of a different store has five salespeople and eight departments. In this case, there are $8 - 5 = 3$ more tasks (departments) than resources (salespeople). Hence, the store executive must create a separate fictitious salesperson to handle each extra department. That is, there would be a need for three imaginary resources. In assignment terminology, each of these fictitious salespeople is

Table 11.33   **Sales Force Assignment Table**

From Salesperson	To Department			
	Suits	Shoes	Accessories	Dummy
Nancy	$300	$300	$200	$0
Joe	$600	$600	−$M	$0
Barbara	$400	$400	$100	$0
Jim	$200	−$M	$500	$0

referred to as a **dummy resource**. Since each dummy is imaginary, there actually will be no assignment of this resource. Therefore, the store really gets nothing by assigning a fictitious salesperson to a department. As a result, the manager would list a $0 sales volume for each dummy resource assignment.

Prohibited Assignments. It may not always be possible or desirable to assign a particular resource to a selected task. This situation can happen because of resource capabilities, task requirements, or management preferences. Management Situation 11.10 is a case in point.

Joe does not have the interest, knowledge, or ability to sell accessories, while Jim has trouble selling shoes. Therefore, the store manager wants to avoid assigning Joe to the accessory department and Jim to the shoe department. As in the transportation situation, such unacceptable allocations can be denoted by allotting a very large negative (−$M) sales volume to each prohibited assignment in the problem.

By incorporating the prohibited assignment and dummy task considerations into the problem formulation process, the clothing store manager will obtain Table 11.33. Note that the dummy task (department) is portrayed as a column in the sales force assignment table. Each entry in this column gives the cost ($0) of assigning a salesperson to such a task. Also, the prohibited assignments (Joe to accessories and Jim to shoes) are depicted as cells with −$M sales volumes.

Maximization. In Management Situation 11.10, the clothing store manager wants to select the salesperson assignments that will maximize sales volume. The conventional solution procedure, however, is designed for assignment problems involving minimization. Management must therefore adapt the customary methodology to accommodate the sales volume objective. As in the transportation situation, management can either transform the objective or modify the analysis. Once more, it is usually easier to transform the objective. Furthermore, the opportunity loss concept still offers a convenient vehicle for making the transformation.

Table 11.33 indicates that $600 is the largest overall volume attainable by any of the salespeople. Such a score, then, establishes a standard that the store manager can use to measure job performance. In particular, if management computes each difference between the actual and highest volume, it will measure the degree to which the corresponding allotment deviates from the standard. These differences, which represent the opportunity losses associated with the matching staff allocations, are calculated in Table 11.34.

Table 11.34   **Revised Sales Force Assignment Table**

From Salesperson	To Department			
	Suits	Shoes	Accessories	Dummy
Nancy	$600−$300 = $300	$600−$300 = $300	$600−$200 = $400	$600−$0 = $600
Joe	$600−$600 = $0	$600−$600 = $0	$600−(−$M) = $600 + $M	$600−$0 = $600
Barbara	$600−$400 = $200	$600−$400 = $200	$600−$100 = $500	$600−$0 = $600
Jim	$600−$200 = $400	$600−(−$M) = $600 + $M	$600−$500 = $100	$600−$0 = $600

As Table 11.34 shows, these differences become substitutes for the corresponding sales volume entries in Table 11.33. That is, $600 + $M replaces the −$M entry in the Jim/shoes cell, $500 supplants the $100 entry in the Barbara/accessories cell, and so on. In this way, the problem will be expressed in terms of opportunity losses rather than sales volumes. Since the decision maker must seek the smallest opportunity losses, such a process also transforms the situation from a maximization objective to a minimization objective.

Management can then use the conventional solution procedure to find the optimal sales force assignment. In the process, the dummy department will be treated like any other task. Moreover, the salesperson sent to the dummy department is interpreted as the resource that cannot be economically assigned under current conditions.

In addition, the symbol M should be construed as a number so large that $M less any opportunity loss is still approximately equal to $M. Thus, a cell with an entry of $M will always generate the largest remaining opportunity loss in the assignment table. As a result, such a cell (prohibited assignment) can never be part of the optimal solution to the problem.

Although the sales force situation deals with a maximization objective, prohibited assignments can also arise in minimization problems. In these problems, we denote a prohibited assignment by allotting a very large positive (M) entry to the corresponding cell in the assignment table. Furthermore, the M allotment again must be made *before* the decision maker computes the opportunity losses.

Multiple Optima. As in the transportation situation, an assignment problem may have more than one optimal solution. Management Situation 11.10 is such a problem. To see why, we will need the opportunity losses associated with the revised sales force assignment table (Table 11.34).

By using the data from Table 11.34 and the conventional assignment procedure, the store manager will eventually obtain the opportunity losses given in Table 11.35. Note that Jim is the only salesperson who can sell accessories with a $0 penalty. Therefore, the store manager should assign Jim to the accessory department. Of course, such a policy will exclude Jim from any other assignment. We depict this fact by enclosing

Table 11.35   **Optimal Sales Force Assignment**

From Salesperson	To Department			
	Suits	Shoes	Accessories	Dummy
Nancy	$0	$0	$100	☐ $0
Joe	$0	☐ $0	$600 + $*M*	$300
Barbara	☐ $0	$0	$300	$100
Jim	$300	$500 + $*M*	☐ $0	$200

the $0 opportunity loss in a square and drawing a line through Jim's row in the table. Also, Nancy is the only salesperson who can perform the dummy task with a $0 penalty. Hence, the store manager should assign her to the dummy department. In effect, this policy means that Nancy will remain idle. Yet it excludes her from any other assignment. We indicate this fact by enclosing the $0 opportunity loss in a square and drawing a line through Nancy's row in the table.

These two assignments (Jim to accessories and Nancy to the dummy department) leave Barbara and Joe for the remaining shoe and suit departments. Moreover, Table 11.35 indicates that Barbara can sell suits and Joe can sell shoes with $0 penalties. Thus, the store manager can assign Joe to shoes and Barbara to suits. We denote such assignments by enclosing the $0 opportunity losses in squares and drawing lines through the suit and shoe columns.

As Table 11.35 demonstrates, the assignments create four lines that cover all the $0 penalties. That is, each of the salespeople is assigned to a separate sales task that he or she can perform with no opportunity loss. Consequently, the following sales force assignment plan suggested by the line pattern in Table 11.35 represents an optimal assignment:

- Nancy to the dummy department.
- Joe to shoes.
- Barbara to suits.
- Jim to accessores.

On the other hand, there are also $0 entries in the Barbara/shoes and Joe/suits cells of Table 11.35. These entries indicate that Barbara can sell shoes and Joe can sell suits with no opportunity loss. As a result, the following assignment is an alternative that will provide the clothing store with the same optimal sales volume as the plan suggested by the enclosed $0 penalties in Table 11.35:

- Nancy to the dummy department.
- Joe to suits.

Figure 11.4   **Computer Solution of the Sales Force Assignment Problem**

Distribution:	Input:	Output:
▪ Transportation	* Edit	▪ Full
* Assignment	▪ Load	* Summary
	▪ Print	* Print
	▪ Save	▪ Save

Problem Description:
  Minimization (MIN) or Maximization (MAX) Objective: MAX
  Number of Resources: 4
  Number of Tasks: 3

Enter the problem data in the following assignment table.

	Suits	Shoes	Access	Dummy
Nancy	300	300	200	0
Joe	600	600	−9999	0
Barb	400	400	100	0
Jim	200	−9999	500	0

RECOMMENDATION

Resource	Task	Return
Nancy	Dummy	0
Joe	Shoes	600
Barb	Suits	400
Jim	Access	500
Total Assignment Return		1500

▪   Barbara to shoes.

▪   Jim to accessories.

Such alternative optima are important because they provide the decision maker with greater flexibility in selecting and utilizing resources. For example, suppose that clothing store experience indicates that suit customers are more likely to harass male salespeople than female salespeople. To promote employee morale, the manager may prefer the optimal assignment that has Barbara rather than Joe at the suit department.

Computer Analysis

Practical assignment problems may involve hundreds, even thousands, of resources and tasks. Prewritten computer packages, such as *ALP*, typically are used to implement the assignment algorithms in these situations. A program similar to the commercial packages is available on the **Quantitative Management (QM)** software. It is invoked by selecting Distribution from **QM**'s main menu. Figure 11.4 then shows how the program is used to solve the clothing store's sales force assignment problem (Management Situation 11.10).

Problem Formulation. As Figure 11.4 illustrates, the user executes the module by selecting the Assignment option from the Distribution menu. The problem is formulated through the Edit command from the Input menu. In this case, the user provides a description of the problem, including the nature of the objective, the number of resources, and the number of tasks. Figure 11.4, for example, shows that the sales force assignment problem is a maximization (MAX) problem with four resources and three tasks. Then the program automatically creates any dummies needed to balance the problem and provides an assignment table with blank spaces for the user's entry of assignment costs or returns.

When entering the returns for the sales force assignment problem, the number -9999 (or any other very large negative value) must be substituted for each $-M$ symbol. That is because the program cannot interpret an alphabetic entry $(-M)$ where a numeric value is expected. As Figure 11.4 demonstrates, the input format enables the user to essentially recreate an assignment table for the problem. Report options then are chosen through the Output menu.

Optimal Assignment. The RECOMMENDATION section of Figure 11.4 shows that the clothing store can maximize total sales volume at $1,500 by assigning

- Nancy to the dummy task.
- Joe to shoes.
- Barbara to suits.
- Jim to accessories.

If the user selects the Full option (not shown here) from the Output menu, **QM** will display all assignment table calculations, including the final penalty table. Management can use the zero-penalty entries in this final table to identify alternative optimal assignments.

SUMMARY

This chapter presented the transportation and assignment problems. It began with a discussion of the nature and relevance of the transportation situation and proceeded to show how to solve these problems. Many solution approaches are available, including linear programming, network algorithms, heuristic methods, and transportation algorithms. Transportation algorithms all utilize the same standard methodology. First, the decision maker obtains a start with a "good" initial solution (usually with a heuristic approach) and then uses simplex-based search procedures to find the optimal transportation solution. Although the computations differ in each procedure, the standard methodology utilizes a transportation table to conveniently record the data and keep track of the calculations.

In the second section of the chapter, we saw how to deal with some special conditions that can arise in transportation situations. These include problems with unbalanced supply and demand (which are handled with dummy demand and supply points), prohibited routes (handled with the M allotments), maximization objectives (which are handled by transforming the objective), degenerate solutions (which are handled with the epsilon (ϵ) allocations), and multiple optima. This section also illustrated how transportation problems can be solved with the aid of a computer, examined the assumptions of the solution methodology, and presented some important managerial applications.

In the final section, we discussed the assignment situation. We began with a discussion of the nature and relevance of the problem and then proceeded to the method used to solve these problems. This section also demonstrated how to recognize and handle the special conditions that can arise in assignment situations. These include problems with resource/task imbalances, prohibited assignments, maximization objectives, and multiple optimal solutions. Finally, we saw how assignment problems can be solved with the aid of a computer and considered some reported management applications of the model.

Glossary

arcs (branches, links, edges) The lines connecting the nodes in a network.

assignment problem A problem whose objective is to find the most effective way of assigning a group of indivisible resources to a set of indivisible tasks.

assignment table A standard tabular format used to conveniently record the data and keep track of the calculations in an assignment problem analysis.

closed path (loop) The series of horizontal and vertical lines that traces the pattern of changes required by a reallocation in the transportation problem.

directed network A network in which flows can occur in only one direction.

dummy demand point A fictitious destination created to account for any excess supply in a transportation problem.

dummy resource A fictitious resource created to account for an excess task in an assignment problem.

dummy supply point A fictitious source created to account for any excess demand in a transportation problem.

dummy task A fictitious task created to account for an excess resource in an assignment problem.

Hungarian method (Flood's technique, matrix reduction) The standard procedure used to find an optimal solution to an assignment problem.

improvement index A value that measures the net effect on the objective of shipping one unit over a currently unused route in the transportation network.

minimum cost cell method A procedure that finds a transportation solution by allocating as many units as feasible to the lowest cost cells in the transportation table.

modified distribution (MODI) method A procedure that evaluates a transportation solution by comparing direct expenses to the cost savings associated with each unused route in the network.

network A diagram consisting of junction points interconnected by a series of lines that carry a flow through the system.

nodes The junction points (circles) of a network.

northwest corner method A procedure that finds an initial feasible solution to a transportation problem through making allocations by moving down and to the right through the transportation table.

stepping stone method A procedure that evaluates a transportation solution by tracing the pattern of changes required with each reallocation.

transportation problem A problem whose objective is to find the most effective way of distributing a commodity from a group of supply sources to a set of demand destinations.

transportation table A standard tabular format used to conveniently record the data and keep track of the calculations in a transportation problem analysis.

transshipment point A location in a distribution network that can receive merchandise from one shipping point and then reship it to another destination.

transshipment problem A problem in which the objective is to find the most effective way of distributing merchandise from a group of supply sources, through transshipment points, and on to a set of demand destinations.

Vogel approximation method (VAM) A procedure that utilizes the opportunity loss concept to find an initial feasible solution to a transportation problem.

Thought Exercises

1. Explain the specific similarities and differences between the transportation and assignment problems. Why do these decisions arise in modern enterprises?

2. Specify whether each of the following circumstances is a transportation situation or an assignment situation. Explain.

    a. A nonprofit research organization's geographic allocation of project engineers to independent projects

    b. A municipal sanitation department's weekly geographic allocation of trucks to streets

    c. A toy manufacturer's allocation of its supply of a given toy from a group of its warehouses to a group of wholesalers

    d. A cigar importer's allocation of its supply of various types of cigars from a given country to a group of distribution outlets

3. Let

    m = the number of sources

    i = the source index ($i = 1, 2, \ldots, m$)

    n = the number of destinations

    j = the destination index ($j = 1, 2, \ldots, n$)

    X_{ij} = the number of units transported from source i to destination j

    c_{ij} = the contribution to the objective of transporting one unit from source i to destination j

    Z = the transportation pattern's total contribution to the objective

    S_i = the supply in units at source i

    D_j = the demand in units at destination j

Use these symbols to develop a general linear programming formulation for the transportation problem. If you utilized the simplex method to solve this problem, what would be the initial basic feasible solution? Explain.

4. Consider the following transportation situation, where entries in the upper right-hand corner of the cells are per-unit allocation costs. What are the penalty costs for the source? Explain.

	Farm	Supermarket	Milk Stand	Health Store
Milk Truck	$3	$10	$4	$3

5. Pamphlet Printing's (Management Situation 11.4) optimal job order plan is given by the following transportation table. Interpret this solution for the company's management. That is, how many leaflets for each job should be printed on each press? What is the resulting minimum total cost?

    Suppose that management wants to print a minimum of 20,000 copies of order A's daily demand on press 1. How would this condition affect the recommendation? Suppose that management wanted to print exactly 15,000 copies of order A's demand on press 2. How would this condition affect the recommendation?

From Press	To Order			Supply of Leaflets (Thousands per Day)
	A	B	C	
1	$4 10	$M	$8 30	40
2	$6 20	$3 20	$M	40
Demand for Leaflets (Thousands per Day)	30	20	30	80

6. Let

m = the number of resources

i = the resource index ($i = 1, 2, \ldots, m$)

n = the number of tasks

j = the task index ($j = 1, 2, \ldots, n$)

$$X_{ij} = \begin{cases} 1 \text{ if resource } i \text{ is assigned to task } j \\ 0 \text{ otherwise} \end{cases}$$

c_{ij} = the contribution to the objective from assigning resource i to task j

Z = the assignment pattern's total contribution to the objective

Use these symbols to develop a general linear programming formulation for the assignment problem. If you utilized the simplex method to solve this problem, what would be the initial basic feasible solution? Explain.

7. Refer back to Management Situation 11.9 in the text. Formulate and solve the linear program for this maintenance dispatching assignment problem. How does the solution compare to the recommendation obtained by the Hungarian method? Explain.

8. Refer back to Management Situation 11.10 in the text. Formulate and solve the linear program for this sales force assignment problem. How does the solution compare to the recommendation obtained by the Hungarian method? Explain.

9. What is the interpretation of the dummy source (resource) or dummy destination (task) in the following circumstances?
   a. An excess number of test pilots for new test aircraft
   b. Excess demand for a group of consumer products in given geographic areas
   c. Excess supply of sugar in international trading markets from particular supplying countries
   d. An inadequate number of football positions for potential high school football players

10. How would the existence of alternative optima help the following decision makers? Speculate on the nature of appropriate secondary goals and their influence on the selection of alternative optima.

    a. A police captain whose prime goal is to assign various officers over particular patrol zones in a way that maximizes some index of performance

    b. A travel agent whose prime goal is to allocate a group of tourists over a group of travel areas in a way that minimizes their travel costs

    c. A manufacturer who seeks the minimum transportation cost for various raw materials from particular suppliers

11. General Commando, chief operations officer for the Third Airlift Command, must deliver three types of new aircraft to three air bases. Only one plane can be delivered to one base at a time. Delivery costs differ because of distance, fuel efficiency, crew size, and so on. Captain Britton, the general's aid, has formulated the problem as an assignment situation and developed the following final opportunity loss table:

From Plane	To Air Base		
	Alton AFB	Bart NAS	Clove AFB
Fighter	$0	$0	$5,000
Bomber	$0	$2,000	$1,000
Transport	$2,000	$0	$0

According to this table, which plane should be assigned on each air base? Explain. Suppose the total delivery costs of each distribution are given as follows:

From Plane	To Air Base		
	Alton AFB	Bart NAS	Clove AFB
Fighter	$3,000	$4,000	$9,000
Bomber	$2,000	$5,000	$4,000
Transport	$2,000	$1,000	$1,000

What is the total delivery cost for the optimal assignment?

12. Refer back to Management Situation 11.8 in the text. Draw the transshipment network that corresponds to JBT's transportation table (Table 11.25). Interpret the nodes, branches, and flows in this network. Explain how the diagram differs from the transportation network.

13. In Management Situation 11.8, suppose that the demand for corn at the Portland warehouse during the upcoming season becomes 2,200 rather than 1,200 truckloads. How will this change affect JBT's optimal distribution pattern?

14. Do you agree or disagree with each of the following statements? Explain.

    a. An assignment problem may need both dummy resources (rows) and dummy tasks (columns).

    b. VAM instead of the northwest corner method should always be used to find the first feasible solution for a transportation problem.

    c. We cannot find the optimal solution to a transportation problem with VAM or the northwest corner method.

   d. Degeneracy cannot exist in an assignment problem.

   e. Row and column reductions leave the amounts in the same relative positions of the opportunity loss table.

   f. In a transportation problem with a minimization objective, penalties are found by taking the difference between the lowest and next lowest costs for each source and destination.

   g. In the Hungarian method, you will never need more lines to cover all zero entries than the number of rows in the assignment table.

   h. The number of decision variables in a transportation problem will equal the number of supply sources multiplied by the number of demand destinations.

Technique Exercises

15. You are given the following transportation table, where entries in the upper right-hand corner of the cells are per-unit costs.

From Origin	To Destination D_1	To Destination D_2	Supply
O_1	5	9	100
O_2	7	4	200
Demand	200	100	300

   a. Find a first feasible solution.

   b. Find the optimal solution.

16. Consider the following transportation problem, where entries in the upper right-hand corner of the cells are per-unit costs.

From Origin	To Destination D_1	To Destination D_2	Supply
O_1	4	2	30
O_2	1	3	10
O_3	5	6	30
Demand	30	40	70

   a. Find a first feasible solution.

   b. Find the optimal solution.

17. Refer back to Management Situation 11.1.

   a. Solve the corresponding linear problem with the simplex method.

   b. Interpret the resulting linear programming solution.

   c. Show how Tables 11.5 and 11.6 were developed.

18. You are given the following transportation problem, where entries in the upper right-hand corner of the cells are per-unit revenues.

From Plant	To Retail Outlet			Production Capacity (Units)
	Springfield	Lincoln	Montclair	
La Cross	$20	$80	$100	5,000
Columbia	$60	$110	$60	4,000
Colton	$120	$70	$90	3,000
Forecasted Demand (Units)	4,500	1,500	3,000	12,000 / 9,000

   a.   Find a first feasible solution.
   b.   Identify any degenerate solutions.
   c.   Find the optimal solution.

19. Refer back to Management Situations 11.2 and 11.3.
   a.   Determine the optimal solution to each problem.
   b.   Interpret the solution in language that would be understandable to management.

20. Refer back to Management Situations 11.4 and 11.5.
   a.   Use the conventional transportation methodologies to determine the optimal solution to each problem.
   b.   Interpret the solution for Management Situation 11.5 in language that would be understandable to management.

21. Refer back to Management Situations 11.6 and 11.7.
   a.   Determine the optimal solution for Management Situation 11.6.
   b.   Show how Tables 11.21 and 11.22 were derived.

22. Consider the following transshipment network:

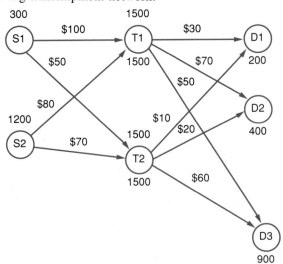

The S1 and S2 nodes identify supply sources, T1 and T2 are transshipment points, and D1 through D3 denote demand destinations. The branches represent the available routes between the nodes, and link values give the unit costs of transporting merchandise over these routes. Supply capacities are listed above the nodes, and the demand requirements appear below the nodes.

What is the optimal distribution pattern for the merchandise? How much will it cost to follow this plan? Show all your work.

23. Refer back to Management Situation 11.8. Find the optimal distribution pattern with the transportation methodology. How does your solution compare with the **QM** recommendation given in Figure 11.2?

24. Refer back to Management Situation 11.10.
   a. List each alternative assignment.
   b. Select the alternative that maximizes sales.
   c. Show how Table 11.35 was developed.
   d. How does the recommendation from 11.35 compare with the answer from part (b)? Explain.

25. Consider the assignment problem given in the following table, where entries in the cells give the times needed by each resource to complete each task.

From Resource	To Task			
	T_1	T_2	T_3	T_4
R_1	6	5	5	2
R_2	3	4	5	7
R_3	4	3	6	1
R_4	5	4	2	6

Find the optimal assignment by the Hungarian method. What is the total time for this optimal assignment?

26. You are given the following assignment table, where entries in the cells give the rankings (from 1 to 3) associated with each assignment. A lower-valued rank is preferred to a higher-valued rank.

From Resource	To Task		
	T_1	T_2	T_3
R_1	3	M	2
R_2	2	3	1
R_3	1	1	M

Use the Hungarian method to find the resource/task assignments that minimize the sum of the rankings. Are there any alternative optima? Explain.

Computer Exercises

27. The city of Pleasureville has 100 contracts up for bids equally divided between five departments: sanitation, police services, parks and recreation, fire services, and administration. Eight different consulting firms are bidding on the contracts: Excello, Safetic, Wyandot, Smothers, Janton, Freet, ATB, and Small and Associates. Excello has personnel for 25 contracts, Safetic for 10, Wyandot for 15, Smothers for 20, Janton for 10, Freet for 5, ATB for 5, and Small for 10 contracts. Bid prices (in thousands of dollars per contract) are summarized below.

	Sanitation	Police	Parks	Fire	Administration
Excello	12	15	18	14	20
Safetic	16	20	10	8	15
Wyandot	9	12	16	10	12
Smothers	11	17	14	13	13
Janton	7	21	17	15	12
Freet	14	11	13	9	22
ATB	21	15	7	11	16
Small	13	14	15	21	17

Management seeks the least costly spending plan. Use the **Quantitative Management (QM)** software to develop a recommendation.

28. Delicious Products produces candy at plants in five cities: Tulsa, Nashville, Houston, Louisville, and Cheyenne. Monthly capacities at the plants are listed below.

Plant	Production Capacity (Thousands of Boxes)
Tulsa	150
Nashville	200
Houston	125
Louisville	325
Cheyene	450

These plants supply candy to wholesale outlets in four cities with the following monthly demands.

Outlet	Demand (Thousands of Boxes)
Phoenix	125
Los Angeles	275
Miami	300
Seattle	200

Revenues, production, and shipping costs vary among the distribution channels. Pertinent net profits per box are reported below.

	Phoenix	LA	Miami	Seattle
Tulsa	6	7	9	4
Nashville	7	11	5	8
Houston	5	7	7	12
Louisville	3	2	6	4
Cheyene	8	6	3	2

Management seeks the most profitable distribution plan. Use the **QM** software to develop a recommendation. What are the reduced costs of the unused routes, and what do these costs tell management?

29. A company has a ten-month demand for its product, broken down as follows: 1,908, 2,160, 1,572, 1,891, 1,668, 2,240, 2,050, 2,360, 2,111, and 1,945 units. The demand can be met through regular and overtime manufacturing. It costs $100 to produce the item during regular hours and $120 during overtime. Enough resources are available to manufacture 1,500 items per month on regular time and 1,000 items per month during overtime. Also, unmet orders in one month can be filled, up to two months later, with subsequent output. Customers receiving late orders get a $10/unit/month discount. Extra output will be carried to the next month at a cost of $30/unit/month.

Management seeks the production and inventory plan that will minimize the cost. Use the **QM** software to develop a recommendation and to test the sensitivity of the recommendation.

30. Local Commuter Airlines has just added six new routes that require additional pilots. In making the schedule assignments, the airline would like to account for the preference intensity of its pilots. For example, one pilot may prefer one route over another with only a slight preference. On the other hand, a second pilot might desperately want the first route and have very little interest in the other.

To incorporate the preference intensities into the selection process, management gives each pilot a card listing the routes and asks the person to distribute 100 points among the choices. The results are shown below.

Pilot	Route					
	1	2	3	4	5	6
A	0	5	15	15	15	50
B	20	10	5	5	0	60
C	0	0	0	0	50	50
D	20	20	5	15	10	20
E	45	5	30	0	0	20
F	100	0	0	0	0	0
G	30	0	30	0	30	10

Higher points indicate stronger preference intensities.

Use the **QM** software to determine the route schedule that best meets pilot preferences.

31. A defense contractor produces components and supplies the elements to other contractors for assembly. Historical quality control records indicate that the number of defective items differed among the work centers. Data on the average number of defects produced by each center per week for the various components are reported below.

Work Center	Component						
	1	2	3	4	5	6	7
A	18	13	16	16	13	19	15
B	17	12	16	12	15	19	11
C	12	12	11	14	15	18	13
D	13	15	13	14	15	11	14
E	11	16	17	14	16	15	18
F	17	13	15	18	17	16	11
G	18	14	19	14	14	17	18

Management would like to assign components among the centers in a way that will minimize the total average weekly defects. Use the **QM** software to develop a recommendation.

32. On Monday morning, Montgomery Sears Automotive Shop has nine cars coming in for service. Seven mechanics will be available to service cars. However, some mechanics do not have the ability to work on specific types of automobiles. Relevant data are summarized below.

	Mechanic						
Car	Alice	Bob	Carl	Dave	Jane	Tom	June
Buick	5.5	6	4.5	6	6	5	1.5
Chevy	4.5	3	5	3	4	3.5	3
Ford	4	UA	3.5	3	2	3.5	4.5
Caddy	4	3	3.5	5	5	4.5	UA
Toyota	UA	5	5.5	6	4	6	3
Mazda	4	6	2	UA	4	2	2
Honda	4.5	UA	3	UA	6	2.5	2
Jeep	5	4.5	2.5	4	3.5	4	4
Jaguar	UA	5	6	5	4	UA	7

Entries in the table represent the hours needed for each mechanic to repair a car. The UA symbol indicates that the mechanic is unable to repair the car.

Management seeks the repair plan that will minimize the total time needed to work on the cars. Use the **QM** software to generate a recommendation.

Applications Exercises

33. Smooth Ride Tire Company stores its radial tires in three centrally located warehouses for distribution to its prime markets. Supply availabilities and demand requirements are as follows:

Warehouse	Supply Available (Thousands of Tires per Week)
Wilmington, Delaware	20
Gary, Indiana	50
Norwalk, California	30

Market	Demand (Thousands of Tires per Week)
New York	30
Chicago	30
Los Angeles	40

Physical handling and freight rates make up most of the following distribution costs between each warehouse and market (costs are in dollars per tire):

	To		
From	New York	Chicago	Los Angeles
Wilmington	3	4	6
Gary	4	2	4
Norwalk	8	5	1

Assuming that Smooth Ride wants to minimize its total distribution costs, how many tires should be allocated from each warehouse to each market? Can you give some possible reasons why Smooth Ride might have located its markets and warehouses in the given locations? List some reasons why the cost, supply, and demand structures for warehouses and markets might be as shown.

34. Fresh Milk Dairy is a small, rural dairy with only three delivery trucks and three geographically separated routes. It is impossible for one truck to handle more than one route per day, but each truck is capable of completing each route in a given day. The dairy pays its drivers on a straight-time basis, with "working time" including driving time from the driver's house (where he or she keeps the truck overnight) to the route and back again. Each driver is paid $5 per hour, but it is estimated that other operating costs for each truck differ (because of the truck's age, make, and so on). Specifically, truck A costs $2 an hour to operate, truck B costs $3 an hour, and truck C costs $4 an hour (a prorated cost per hour based on the total miles driven over the useful life of the truck). .

Each truck is mechanically more efficient in different topographical conditions and can therefore complete each route in a different amount of time per day. Company records indicate that the hours per day that each truck requires to complete each route are as follows:

	Route		
Truck	**1**	**2**	**3**
A	8	6	8
B	4	10	3
C	5	6	8

Which truck should be assigned to each route to minimize total delivery cost? What is that cost?

35. Crimetown's police chief wants to allocate three tactical patrol units to three precincts that have recently been experiencing large increases in crime. The three teams have different numbers of officers, years of experience, and modes of operation. Crime analysts have determined an index of crime deterrence for each team. This index represents the portion of crimes that is expected to be deterred as a result of the tactical unit's effort. The index is from a low of zero to a high of 100. The following table gives the index of crime deterrence for the patrol units and precincts:

	To Precinct		
From Tactical Unit	**1**	**2**	**3**
A	90	80	40
B	20	60	80
C	50	70	20

Team A will be available for 50 hours next month, team B for 40 hours, and team C for 60 hours. Based on the projected number of serious crimes, the chief expects to need 30 hours of effort in precinct 1, 70 hours in precinct 2, and 50 hours in precinct

3. The chief wants to allocate the three teams in such a way as to maximize the index of crime deterrence. How many hours should each team be assigned to each precinct in order to accomplish this goal?

36. A major European city has four incinerator sites for processing solid waste. There are four garbage collection areas within the city. The city wants to determine the least-cost method of disposing of its trash. Each incinerator is characterized by an operating cost for processing each ton of waste. There is also a cost of transporting each ton of waste from each collection area to each incinerator. The total (operating plus transportation) cost per ton is summarized in the following table:

From Collection Area	To Incineration Site			
	1	2	3	4
A	$75	$80	$60	$40
B	$70	$70	$100	$60
C	$90	$40	$50	$100
D	$60	$50	$40	$30

Incinerator site 1 has a monthly capacity of 6,000 tons, site 2 has a capacity of 5,000 tons, and site 3 has a capacity of 8,000 tons. There are 2,000 tons of waste generated at area A, 8,000 tons at area B, and 9,000 tons at area C per month. A total of 20,000 tons of waste per month are generated from all four areas. How many tons of waste from each collection area should be processed at each site in order to minimize the total cost?

37. A major household appliance company manufactures refrigerators at its two main production plants in Industry and Irving. The Industry plant is capable of producing 4,000 refrigerators per month at an average cost of $300 per unit. Irving can manufacture 6,000 refrigerators per month at an average cost of $320 per unit.

The finished products are then distributed through transfer points in Tulsa, Little Rock, Denver, Cheyenne, Columbus, and Grand Rapids on to final distribution centers at Milwaukee and Newark. Milwaukee's facility has a demand for at least 3,000 refrigrators per month and the Newark center for another 7,000 refrigerators per month. The costs associated with transporting a refrigerator between the various shipping points are given in the following table:

From	To							
	Tulsa	Little Rock	Denver	Cheyenne	Columbus	Grand Rapids	Milwaukee	Newark
Industry	NA	NA	$50	$75	NA	NA	NA	NA
Irving	$80	$30	NA	NA	NA	NA	NA	NA
Tulsa	$0	NA	NA	NA	$60	$70	NA	NA
Little Rock	NA	$0	NA	NA	$40	$50	NA	NA
Denver	NA	NA	$0	NA	$80	NA	NA	NA
Cheyenne	NA	NA	NA	$0	$75	$60	NA	NA
Columbus	NA	NA	NA	NA	$0	NA	NA	$20
Grand Rapids	NA	NA	NA	NA	NA	$0	$10	NA

As the cost data indicate, some routes are not available (NA) or involve a $0 actual expenditure.

Management wants to determine the production and distribution plan that will minimize total costs. What plan do you recommend? How much will it cost?

38. Adam Hoop is a professional basketball coach who knows that he must play a different combination of his players for each opposing team if he is to maximize his probability of winning any given game. Only one combination can be employed against any given team at any given time in the game. After careful consideration of his scouting reports and evaluation of his personnel, Adam formulates the following matrix of probabilities of winning:

Player Combination	Opposing Team		
	Dunkers	Burners	Musclemen
Tall	.90	.30	.60
Quick	.40	.50	.80
Strong	.70	.20	.90

Which combination should Hoop employ against each team?

39. A local radio station is considering its new daily programming schedule. The station plans to have three separate formats: 5 hours of news, 10 hours of sports, and 9 hours of music in each 24-hour period. Research indicates that there are four reasonably distinct audiences: 12 midnight to 6 A.M., 6 A.M. to 2 P.M., 2 P.M. to 8 P.M., and 8 P.M. to midnight. Per-hour audience point ratings for each format in each time segment are estimated to be as follows:

Format	Hour			
	12–6	6–2	2–8	8–12
News	100	400	600	200
Sports	600	200	400	300
Music	800	600	300	700

How many hours of each format should the station schedule in each time segment so as to maximize total audience points?

40. Jackson Roykirk, a project director in a NASA program, has three engineers available for assignment to two projects. Only one engineer can be assigned to a project at any given time. Each engineer has special skills and thus does not have the same degree of efficiency on each project. Roykirk has used past experience to set the following project costs:

Engineer	Costs of Project	
	Spacecraft	Computer
Atomon	$10,000	$10,000
Electrot	$20,000	$10,000
Wafe	$5,000	$30,000

The director wants to assign each engineer to a project in a way that minimizes the total cost of the projects. What assignments do you suggest?

Atomon has a recent medical problem. Hence, if possible, Roykirk would prefer not to use this engineer. How does this situation influence your recommendation?

41. A political candidate can make three different speeches: conservative, moderate, or liberal. There are three audiences: a professional society of business people, a university group, and a construction union conference. Her aides know that each speech will have a different impact on each audience. The potential percent of favorable responses from each audience for each speech is estimated as follows:

Speech	Audience		
	Business	College	Union
Conservative	70%	20%	40%
Moderate	60%	40%	50%
Liberal	30%	80%	60%

Which speech should be given to each audience to maximize the percent of favorable responses?

For Further Reading

Distribution Methodology

Beilby, M. H. *Economics and Operations Research.* New York: Academic Press, 1976. Chapters 6–8.

Chandrasekaran, R., and S. S. Rao. "A Special Case of the Transportation Problem." *Operations Research* (May–June 1977):525.

Chvatal, V. *Linear Programming.* New York: W. H. Freeman, 1983.

Shore, H. H. "The Transportation Problem and Vogel Approximation Method." *Decision Sciences* (July–October 1970):441.

Transportation Applications

Aarvik, O., and P. Randolph. "The Application of Linear Programming to the Determination of Transmission Fees in an Electrical Power Network." Part 1. *Interfaces* (November 1975):47.

Burns, L. D., et al. "Distribution Strategies That Minimize Transportation and Inventory Costs." *Operations Research* (May–June 1985):469.

Choypend, P., et al. "Optimal Ship Routing and Personnel Assignment for Naval Recruitment in Thailand." *Interfaces* (July–August 1986):47.

Dutta, A., et al. "On Optimal Allocation in a Distributed Processing Environment." *Management Science* (August 1982):839.

Glover, F., et al. "An Integrated Production, Distribution, and Inventory Planning System." *Interfaces* (November 1979):21.

Gray, P. "The Shirt Allocation Problem." *Operations Research* (July–August 1976):788.

Hansen, P., and L. Kaufman. "Public Facilities Location under an Investment Constraint." *Operational Research.* Amsterdam: North-Holland, 1975.

Hess, S. W. "Design and Implementation of a New Check Clearing System for the Philadelphia Federal Reserve District." Part 2. *Interfaces* (February 1975):22.

Love, R. F., and L. Yerex. "An Application of a Facilities Location Model in the Prestressed Concrete Industry." *Interfaces* (August 1976):45.

Perry, C., and M. Iliff, "From the Shadows: Earthmoving on Construction Projects," *Interfaces* (February 1983):79–84.

Segal, M., and D. B. Weinberger. "Turfing." *Operations Research* (May–June 1977):367.

Zierer, T. K., et al. "Practical Applications of Linear Programming to Shell's Distribution Problems." *Interfaces* (August 1976):13.

Assignment Applications

Balachandran, V. "An Integer Generalized Transportation Model for Optimal Assignment in Computer Networks." *Operations Research* (July–August 1976):742.

Balinski, M. L. "Signature Methods for the Assignment Problem." *Operations Research* (May–June 1985):527.

Bloomfield, S. D., and M. M. McSharry. "Preferential Course Scheduling." *Interfaces* (August 1979):24.

Fisher, M. L., "A Computerized Vehicle Routing Application." *Interfaces* (August 1982):42–52.

Geoffrion, A. M., and G. W. Graves. "Scheduling Parallel Production Lines with Changeover Costs: Practical Application of a Quadratic Assignment/LP Approach." *Operations Research* (July–August 1976):595.

Harwood, G. B., and R. W. Lawless. "Optimizing Organizational Goals in Assigning Faculty Teaching Schedules." *Decision Sciences* (July 1975):513.

Lansdowne, Z. F., and D. W. Robinson. "Geographic Decomposition of the Shortest Path Problem, with an Application to the Traffic Assignment Problem." *Management Science* (December 1982):1380.

Liang, T. T. and T. J. Thompson. "A Large-Scale Personnel Assignment Model for the Navy." *Decision Sciences* (Spring 1987):234.

Miller, H. E., et al. "Nurse Scheduling Using Mathematical Programming." *Operations Research* (September–October 1976):857.

Miller, J. G., and W. L. Berry. "The Assignment of Men to Machines: An Application of Branch and Bound." *Decision Sciences* (January 1977):56.

Tamaki, M. "The Secretary Problem with Optimal Assignment." *Operations Research* (July–August 1984):847.

Case: Oriental Carpets, Inc.

Oriental Carpets is a large multinational manufacturer and distributor of custom carpets. It locates its production facilities at the source of the raw materials and labor supply in five cities: Tokyo, Seoul, Hong Kong, Taipei, and Bangkok. Distribution is carried out by four large import-export merchants located in four major market centers: New York, London, Buenos Aires, and Cairo.

Transportation costs, including freight rates and handling, are constant on a monthly basis between each facility and merchant center. Currently, they are as follows:

Production Facility	Per-Carpet Transportation Cost			
	New York	London	Buenos Aires	Cairo
Tokyo	$50	$30	$60	$20
Seoul	$60	$40	$40	$10
Hong Kong	$30	$40	$70	$40
Taipei	$20	$30	$40	$20
Bangkok	$40	$30	$60	$10

The Tokyo plant is capable of supplying 30,000 rugs per month, Seoul 10,000, Hong Kong 30,000, Taipei 20,000, and Bangkok 10,000. The New York merchant center requires 40,000 rugs per month, London 30,000, Buenos Aires 10,000, and Cairo 20,000.

There are three loading cranes available in each supplying city to accommodate production in three locations. Each of the three locations requires only one loading crane at a time. Cranes are dispatched from a central staging area, and the per-crane allocation cost to each production site varies by its geographic location, the demand for the crane at the site, and maintenance required after use at a

site. Oriental management has found that allocation costs do not differ by city and are given on a weekly basis as follows:

Crane	Per-Crane Allocation Cost to Site		
	1	2	3
A	$5,000	$2,000	$6,000
B	$3,000	$5,000	$2,000
C	$4,000	$4,000	$1,000

1. How many carpets per month should be shipped from each production facility to each merchant center to minimize the total transportation cost under current conditions?

2. What are some of the uncertainties involved in this allocation pattern? How might they affect the decision?

3. Which crane should be assigned to each site in each supplying city to minimize the total loading cost per week?

4. Does the assumption about constant crane allocation cost for each city seem realistic? What other factors seem to be ignored, and how might they affect the decision?

Prepare answers to these questions in a report suitable for a management audience.

Layouts, Routes, and Flows

Learning Objectives

- Determine how to allocate routes between origins and destinations in a network

- Minimize the total length of connections in a network by hand and with the aid of a computer

- Find the shortest route through a network by hand and with the aid of a computer

- Find the shortest round trip from a specified origin to a given destination

- Find the largest possible flow through a system by hand and with the aid of a computer

Improving the Flow at Mobil

IN the spring of 1985, Mobil Oil Corporation implemented a nationwide system that dispatches and processes customer orders for gasoline, diesel fuel, heating oil, and other distillates. This system is used to help manage all aspects of marketing and distribution, from order entry via an audio response computer through credit checking, delivery, and billing. These operations annually generate $4 billion in sales on 600,000 customer orders and use 120 bulk terminals and a fleet of more than 430 vehicles.

The heart of the system is computer-assisted dispatch (CAD), a collection of network methodologies delivered within a real-time, transaction-driven management information system. Dispatchers utilize CAD and their experience and judgment to: (1) select the terminal that will supply each order, (2) assign orders to delivery trucks, (3) fit loads on the trucks, and (4) route the trucks and sequence deliveries. Typically, CAD processing is completed within 5 or 10 minutes.

Since CAD's implementation, Mobil has realized several benefits. For one thing, the system has saved the company about $3 million per year in operating expenses. In addition, Mobil has been able to reduce the number of product control centers from three decentralized to one centralized facility. Also, CAD has enabled the company to improve process control and fleet productivity and to offer better customer service.

Source: G. G. Brown et al., "Real-Time, Wide Area Dispatch of Mobil Tank Trucks," *Interfaces* (January–February 1987): 107–120.

Mobil has the typical distribution problems of locating supply facilities (terminals), of identifying and selecting routes between these facilities and customers, and of transporting goods (distillates) over the routes. Although these problems can be addressed with mathematical programming, Mobil's CAD system utilizes specialized network methodologies to support the transportation and routing decisions.

There are good reasons for using network models rather than mathematical programming. These network models usually are easier to formulate and to understand (particularly by nontechnical decision makers such as Mobil's dispatchers) than the equivalent mathematical programs. Moreover, specialized network algorithms often have been much more efficient than mathematical programming in solving large-scale transportation and routing problems. Some of these specialized algorithms were presented in Chapter 11, and others are discussed in this chapter.

In many situations, there are several geographic junction points (such as the terminals and customer locations in Mobil's distribution system) that can be connected in a variety of ways. Management wants to find the series of connections (such as the set of Mobil's delivery routes) that most efficiently utilizes scarce resources. The chapter's second section shows how to design such a network layout.

Another network problem is to find the shortest route from a specified origin to a particular destination (such as from a terminal to a customer in Mobil's distribution system). At other times, the decision maker seeks the minimum cost, time, or distance involved in making a round trip through the network (such as a delivery sequence in Mobil's distribution system). The chapter's second section focuses on these routing problems.

In another situation, there will be a resource flow from a specified origin through various junction points to a given destination. Further, the flow has restricted capacities in both directions (as when distillates are sent on limited capacity trucks through Mobil's distribution system). The final section of the chapter explains how to find the largest possible flow through the network.

Applications. In this chapter, the following applications appear in text, examples, and exercises:

- amusement park design
- business meetings
- computer system design
- container manufacturing
- defense contracting
- designing equestrian trails
- distributing energy
- flood control
- forklift routing
- golf course design
- household moving
- industrial development

- irrigation
- job interviewing
- job scheduling
- parcel delivery
- plant layout
- replacement scheduling
- scouting
- telecommunications
- theater wiring
- traffic control
- tram routing
- warfare

12.1 MINIMAL SPANNING TREE

All networks have nodes (locations or activities) that can be joined (linked with branches) in many potential ways. The problem is to design the layout that most effectively connects the nodes in the network or to find the best series of links between all nodes. As Table 12.1 illustrates, this layout problem can take on a variety of forms in practice.

Nature of the Problem

When designing the layout, the decision maker needs to connect all nodes with a sequence of branches, a process known as **spanning** the network. For example, terminals in Table 12.1's computer network must all be joined by wires, and communities in the rapid transit system must all be connected by subway lines. Although each link must lead from one node to another, spanning can be accomplished without using every branch in

Table 12.1 **Layout Problems**

Network	Nodes	Branches	Problem
Cable television	Transmitting and receiving stations	Wire cables	Use the minimum amount of wire to link all stations.
Computer	Terminals	Wires	Use the minimum amount of wire to link all terminals.
Circuit board	Circuits	Copper strips	Use the minimum quantity of strips to connect all circuits on the board.
Rapid transit	Communities	Subway lines	Utilize the least costly subway layout that will join all communities.
Electric power	Neighborhoods	Power lines	Utilize the least costly distribution layout that will join all neighborhoods.
Air conditioning	Rooms	Air ducts	Use the air duct layout that will connect all rooms at least cost.

the network. For example, the rapid transit system does not need a subway line between each pair of communities to link all communities. Since the flow usually can move in any direction through the branches between nodes, there also is no need for a **cycle** (a sequence of branches that leads from a node back to itself through other nodes) or a **loop** (a branch from a node back to itself). For example, text and data can be sent through the computer network without a cycle or loop between terminals.

The objective is to find the **minimal spanning tree**, or the series of links that will connect (without a cycle or loop) all nodes in the network with the minimum total branch length (cost, time, distance, or quantity). In Table 12.1, for example, the minimal spanning in the computer network will be the minimum amount of wire to link all terminals, and the least costly subway layout that joins all communities will be the minimal spanning tree in the rapid transit network.

Recap. The minimal spanning tree is a design problem with the following characteristics:

1. It can be portrayed as a network in which a series of nodes (junction points or locations) is interconnected by a series of branches (potential links).

2. Flow (movement of objects or people) can move in any direction over the branches, and branch values measure the distance, time, cost, or capacity associated with the flow.

3. All nodes must be connected by branches, but it is not necessary to utilize every potential link or to have any cycle/loop in the network.

4. The objective is to find the series of links that will minimize the total branch length.

Figure 12.1   **Sunrise's Equestrian Trail System**

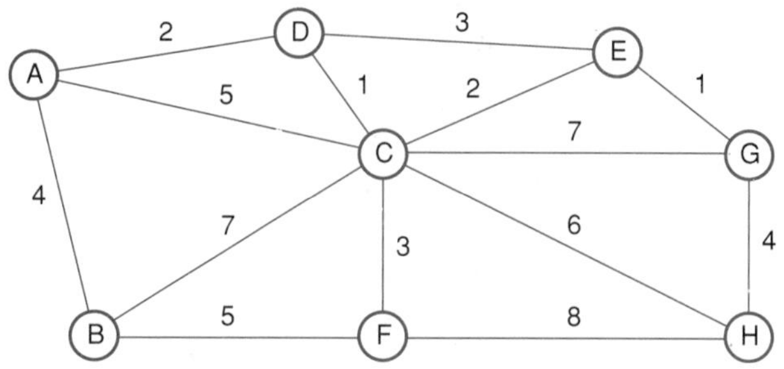

Solution Procedure

The minimal spanning tree can be found with the **greedy algorithm**. In this approach, the decision maker always seeks the least distant unconnected node until he/she spans the network. Management Situation 12.1 illustrates.

Management Situation 12.1

Designing an Equestrian Layout

Prestige Builders, Inc. has set aside a portion of its exclusive housing development, Sunrise, for an equestrian/jogging park. This park will have a system of trails between the controlled entrance and various sites, with each trail consisting of an equestrian path and a separate jogging track. Figure 12.1 shows the proposed trail system.

In this diagram, location A is the entrance into the park. Sites B through H are various rest stations located at scenic points in the park. There is also a scenic overlook at the park entrance and a popular swimming and skating pond at site H. The numbers give the distances of the winding trails in miles.

Water and sewer pipes must be installed under the trails so as to connect all locations (including the park entrance). Since installation is both expensive and disturbing to the natural environment, Prestige wants to connect all sites with the minimum number of miles of pipe.

Problem Formulation. Figure 12.1 depicts a network in which a set of park sites (nodes) is interconnected by a series of trails (branches). The flow over these trails represents the movement of people between the sites. Each branch value (number on the line) measures the distance in miles between the corresponding park sites. Management wants to find the minimal spanning tree, or the series of trails that will connect all sites in the park system with the minimum total miles of water and sewer pipe.

Figure 12.2   **Prestige's First Connection (A to D)**

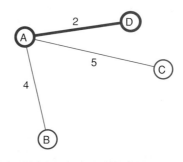

Figure 12.3   **Prestige's Second Connection (D to C)**

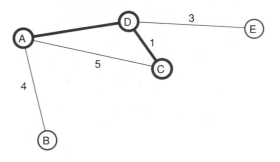

First Connection. The analysis can begin at any site (node) in the network. For ease of reference, we will start at the park entrance (site A in Figure 12.1). Prestige can install a line under the trail from site A to station B (which is 4 miles from A), site C (which is 5 miles from A), or node D (which is 2 miles from A). Since management wants to minimize the total miles of pipe, the first connection should join site D (the nearest node to A) with station A. Figure 12.2 illustrates this first connection.

Second Connection. The next phase of construction may begin from either of the connected sites (A or D). Although A has already been connected to D, Figure 12.1 shows that Prestige can still install pipes from A to B, from A to C, from D to C, or from D to E. Also, site C is 1 mile from D and site E is 3 miles from D. Sites B and C are 4 and 5 miles, respectively, from A. Among these unconnected sites (B, C, and E), C is the closest in miles to a connected node (D). Thus, as indicated in Figure 12.3, management next should connect site C to site D.

Third Connection. At this stage, Prestige has connected A to D and D to C. Since A to D is 2 miles and D to C is another mile, the system currently has 2 + 1 = 3 miles of pipe. In the third phase, management can start a pipeline from any of the three connected

Table 12.2   Potential Connections Following Prestige's Second Connection

From Site	To Station	Distance (Miles)
A	B	4
D	E	3
C	E	2
C	G	7
C	H	6
C	F	3
C	B	7

Figure 12.4   Prestige's Third Connection (C to E)

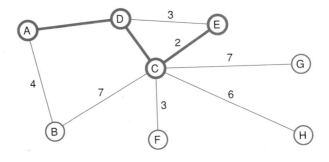

sites (A, C, or D). Potential connections are listed in Table 12.2. (Notice that A to C is not being considered, because nodes A and C already have been connected by other branches or lines.) Among the possibilities, E is the closest site to a connected site (C). As shown in Figure 12.4, then, the third connection is between sites C and E.

Optimal Layout. By continuing in this "greedy" manner until all nodes in the network are connected with branches, management will obtain the minimal spanning tree presented in Figure 12.5. This figure indicates that Prestige can minimize the total miles of pipe required in the park system by installing lines under the following trails:

- 2 miles from A to D
- 1 mile from D to C
- 2 miles from C to E
- 1 mile from E to G
- 3 miles from C to F
- 4 miles from A to B
- 4 miles from G to H

Such a series of connections involves a total of 17 miles of water and sewer pipes.

Figure 12.5   **Prestige's Minimal Spanning Tree**

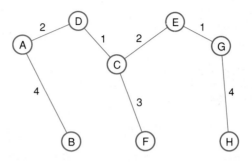

Procedure Recap. The following greedy algorithm can be used to find the minimal spanning tree:

1. Select *any* node and join it to the least distant unconnected node. Ties may be broken arbitrarily.

2. Identify the *unconnected* node that is least distant from any *connected* node. Join this unconnected node to the nearest connected node. Ties may be broken arbitrarily.

3. Repeat step 2 until all nodes in the network have been connected.

Computer Analysis

In large-scale problems, it can be tedious and time-consuming to find the minimal spanning tree by hand. Moreover, the process may be prone to error. Consequently, a prewritten computer program typically is used to perform the necessary computations. One such program is available on the **Quantitative Management (QM)** software. It is invoked by selecting the Network Models option from **QM**'s main menu. Figure 12.6 then shows how the program is used to solve Prestige's equestrian park layout problem.

Problem Formulation. As Figure 12.6 illustrates, the user executes the module by selecting the Minimal spanning tree option from the Network Problem menu. The problem is formulated through the Edit command from the Input menu. In this case, the user first enters the number of nodes (8) and branches (14) in Prestige's network (Figure 12.1). Then, the program provides a table with blank spaces for the user's entry of the name, starting node, ending node, and distance for each branch in the network.

When entering the information, each branch can be given an eight-digit name. This name can be written with letters or numbers (or with a combination of letters and numbers), but spaces are not permitted in the label. Starting and ending nodes must be identified by integers (rather than letters) and numbered sequentially beginning with a value of 1. For example, Figure 12.6's branch 1 (named A-B) depicts the trail between the park entrance (node A) and station B in Sunrise's equestrian network (Figure 12.1). Similarly, branch 7 (named C-E) represents the trail between stations C and E in the network.

Figure 12.6   Computer Solution of Prestige's Layout Problem

Network Problem:	Input:	Output:
* Minimal spanning tree	* Edit	▪ Full
▪ Shortest route	▪ Load	* Summary
▪ Maximal flow	▪ Print	* Print
	▪ Save	▪ Save

Problem Description:
  Number of Nodes: 8
  Number of Branches: 14

Enter the problem data in the following table.

Branch	Name	Starting Node	Ending Node	Distance
1	A-B	1	2	4
2	A-C	1	3	5
3	A-D	1	4	2
4	B-C	2	3	7
5	B-F	2	6	5
6	D-C	4	3	1
7	C-E	3	5	2
8	C-F	3	6	3
9	C-G	3	7	7
10	C-H	3	8	6
11	D-E	4	5	3
12	E-G	4	7	1
13	F-H	6	8	8
14	G-H	7	8	4

RECOMMENDATION			
Branch Name	Starting Node	Ending Node	Distance
A-D	1	4	2
D-C	4	3	1
C-E	3	5	2
E-G	5	7	1
C-F	3	6	3
A-B	1	2	4
G-H	7	8	4
		Total distance =	17

As Figure 12.6 demonstrates, the input format enables the user to essentially recreate the problem's network in tabular form. Report options then are chosen through the Output menu.

Minimal Spanning Tree. After receiving all the network information, **QM** processes the data and generates the minimal spanning tree. The RECOMMENDATION section of Figure 12.6 shows that this minimal spanning tree will have a total distance of 17 and utilize the branches named as follows:

▪   A–D

▪   D–C

- C–E
- E–G
- C–F
- A–B
- G–H

In other words, Prestige can minimize the total pipe required for the project at 17 miles by joining

- the park entrance (node A) with both station B and site D,
- station D with site C,
- site C with both station E and site F,
- station E with site G, and
- site G with the swimming/skating pond (site H).

Such a recommendation is the same minimal spanning tree as the answer derived by the more cumbersome hand calculation.

12.2 ROUTING

Frequently, management is concerned with routing the flow over already existing links in a network. Sometimes, the objective is to find the shortest route from a specified origin to a particular destination. Other times, the flow must start from a given location, visit each site only once, and then return to the origin. This section explains how to formulate and solve such routing problems.

Shortest Route Problem

The minimal spanning tree joins all network nodes with the minimum length sequence of branches, but there is no need for the layout design to start or end at a designated location. In many situations, however, there will be both a specified origin, known as the **source node**, and a designated destination, called the **sink node**, for the network flow. The problem is to find the shortest route from the source node, over already existing links, to the sink node in the network. As Table 12.3 illustrates, this *shortest route problem* can take on a variety of forms in practice.

Solution Procedure

The shortest route can be found with the **labeling and backtracking procedure**. In this approach, the decision maker uses a labeling technique to determine the shortest distance from one specified source to each of the other nodes in the network. Then, he/she backtracks through the network to define the shortest route to each node. Management Situation 12.2 illustrates.

Table 12.3   **Shortest Route Problems**

Network	Nodes	Branches	Problem
Highway	Cities and towns	Roads	Find the shortest route between specified cities.
Parts	Work stations	Pneumatic tube system	Specify the shortest route between a central parts depository and various work stations.
Natural gas	Distribution stations	Pipelines	Determine the shortest route from the main distributor to specified regional stations.
Air travel	Airports	Air lanes	Find the shortest routes between specified airports.
Equipment replacement	Time periods	Replacement options	Determine the times during which the equipment can be replaced at least cost.

Management Situation 12.2

Tram Routing

This example deals with the equestrian trail system portrayed in Figure 12.1. Suppose that the scenery is so beautiful that some Sunrise residents would like to use the park without horseback riding or jogging. Consequently, Prestige has agreed to provide tram service from the park entrance to each site.

In operation, the line will send a different tram from the park entrance to each station. Expenses will be paid from revenues generated by a distance-related fare charged to the users. Therefore, the residents want each tram to follow a route that extends the least total number of miles from the park entrance.

Problem Formulation. Prestige's tram-routing situation again can be portrayed as a network in which a set of park sites (nodes) is interconnected by a series of trails (branches). The flow over these trails represents the movement of trams between park sites, and each branch value (number on the line) measures the distance in miles between the corresponding stations. Since a different tram will be sent from the Sunrise entrance to each station, there is no need for each vehicle to join every node of the network. Residents want every tram to follow the shortest route, or the sequence of trails (branches) that is the fewest total miles from the park entrance.

First Labeling. Since Prestige's tram service originates at the park entrance, site A is the source node for every tram line in the residents' shortest route problem. As Figure 12.7 illustrates, the tram can travel over the trails from site A to station B (which is 4 miles from A), site C (which is 5 miles from A), or node D (which is 2 miles from

Figure 12.7   **First Tram Line Route (A to D)**

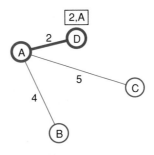

Table 12.4   **Possibilities for Second Tram Route**

Route	Distance (Miles)
A to B	4
A to C	5
A through D to C	2 + 1 = 3
A through D to E	2 + 3 = 5

Figure 12.8   **Second Tram Line Route (A through D to C)**

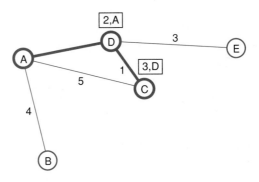

A). Among these possibilities, the shortest route (2 miles) for the first tram line is from the park entrance at site A directly to station D. This first route is highlighted in Figure 12.7, and the connected node is labeled with an enclosed box containing the shortest distance to the source along with the immediately preceding station on the route.

Second Labeling. Table 12.4 lists the possibilities for the second tram line route. For example, a tram still can go the 4 direct miles from the park entrance at node A to site B. Also, since station D has already been connected to A (with the first tram line), the tram can travel from the park entrance through D to site E. This alternative will involve the 2 miles from A to D plus the 3 miles from D to E, or a total of 2 + 3 = 5 miles.

Table 12.5   **Possibilities for Third Tram Route**

Route	Distance (Miles)
A to B	4
A through D to E	2 + 3 = 5
A through D through C to E	2 + 1 + 2 = 5
A through D through C to B	2 + 1 + 7 = 10
A through D through C to G	2 + 1 + 7 = 10
A through D through C to H	2 + 1 + 6 = 9
A through D through C to F	2 + 1 + 3 = 6

Figure 12.9   **Third Tram Line Route (A to B)**

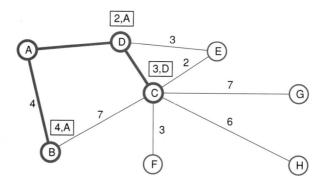

Among Table 12.4's possibilities, the shortest route (3 miles) for the second tram line is from the park entrance at site A through station D on to site C. This second route is highlighted in Figure 12.8, and the connected node is again labeled with an enclosed box containing the shortest distance to the source along with the immediately preceding station on the route. Since the shortest route to site C is through D, management also can eliminate the A to C trail from further consideration.

Third Labeling. The second labeling leaves the possibilities given in Table 12.5 for the third tram line route. For example, a tram still can go the 5 miles from the park entrance at node A through station D and on to site E. Also, since station C has already been connected to D (with the second tram line), the tram can travel from the park entrance through D, through C and on to site G. This alternative will involve the 2 miles from A to D plus the 1 mile from D to C plus the 7 miles from C to G, or a total of 2 + 1 + 7 = 10 miles.

Among Table 12.5's possibilities, the shortest route (4 miles) for the third tram line is from the park entrance at site A direct to station B. This third route is highlighted in Figure 12.9, and the connected node is again labeled with an enclosed box containing

---

Figure 12.10 **Shortest Tram Routes**

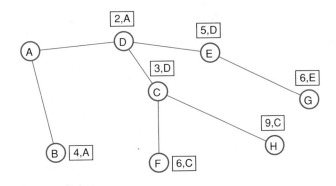

---

the shortest distance to the source along with the immediately preceding station on the route. Since the shortest route to site B is from A, management also can eliminate the C to B trail from further consideration.

Shortest Routes. By continuing with the labeling procedure until the shortest route is found from the origin (park entrance) to each node (site) in the network, management will obtain Figure 12.10. Each boxed node label in this figure gives the shortest distance from the Sunrise park entrance (site A) to the labeled station along with the immediately preceding site on the recommended route. Backtracking through these labels identifies the corresponding shortest route.

For example, the boxed label above node H in Figure 12.10 shows that 9 miles is the shortest distance from the park entrance (site A) to the swimming/skating pond (site H). It also shows that station C is the immediately preceding node to site H on the shortest route from the origin (park entrance). The boxed label above node C lists site D as the preceding node, and station A precedes D. Therefore, the shortest tram line route to the swimming/skating pond (site H) is the 9 miles from the park entrance (node A), through station D and site C.

By backtracking in a similar manner through all boxed node labels in Figure 12.10, management will find that the shortest tram line routes from the park entrance (site A) are as follows:

- 4 miles from A directly to station B
- 2 miles from A directly to site D
- 3 miles from A through site D on to station C
- 5 miles from A through station D on to site E
- 6 miles from A through site D through station C on to station F
- 6 miles from A through station D through site E on to station G
- 9 miles from A through site D through station C on to site H

Procedure Recap. The following labeling and backtracking procedure can be used to find the shortest routes from a source node to every other node in a network:

1. Join the source node to the least distant unconnected node. (Ties may be broken arbitrarily.) Label the connected node with an enclosed box containing the shortest distance to the source along with the immediately preceding node on the route.

2. Identify the unconnected node that is the smallest total distance (either directly or through connected nodes) from the source node. Join this unconnected node to the immediately preceding node on the shortest route from the source node. (Ties may be broken arbitrarily.) Label the connected node with an enclosed box containing the shortest distance to the source along with the immediately preceding node on the route.

3. Repeat step 2 until all nodes in the network have been connected.

4. Backtrack through the labels to identify the shortest route from the source node to all other nodes in the network.

Computer Analysis

In large-scale problems, it can be tedious and time-consuming to find the shortest route by hand. Moreover, the process may be prone to error. As a result, decision makers typically use a prewritten computer program to perform the necessary computations. One such program is available on the **Quantitative Management (QM)** software. It is again invoked by selecting the Network Models option from **QM**'s main menu. Figure 12.11 then shows how the program is used to solve Prestige's tram-routing problem.

Problem Formulation. As Figure 12.11 illustrates, the user executes the module by selecting the Shortest route option from the Network Problem menu. The problem is formulated through the Edit command from the Input menu. As in the Minimal spanning tree option (Figure 12.6), the user essentially recreates the problem's network (Figure 12.1) in tabular form. In this recreation, the user should designate the origin (source) as the starting node for the first branch in the network.

When entering shortest route data, the user also must specify whether the network is **asymmetric** (having at least one pair of nodes with a different length in each flow direction and/or with one-way traffic) or **symmetric** (having nodes with identical length in either flow direction). An asymmetric (ASM) response causes the program to include a Reverse Distance column in the input table. If, as in Prestige's case, the network is symmetric, the user can exclude this unnecessary input column by typing SYM at the prompt. Report options then are chosen through the Output menu.

Shortest Routes. After receiving all the problem information, **QM** processes the data and generates the shortest routes from the source node to each other node in the network. The RECOMMENDATION section of Figure 12.11 shows that the shortest tram line routes from the park entrance (site A) are as follows:

- 4 miles from A directly to station B
- 2 miles from A directly to site D

Figure 12.11   Computer Solution of Prestige's Tram-Routing Problem

Network Problem: Input: Output:
  ▪ Minimal spanning tree   * Edit   ▪ Full
  * Shortest route   ▪ Load   * Summary
  ▪ Maximal flow   ▪ Print   * Print
                      ▪ Save   ▪ Save

Problem Description:
  Number of Nodes: 8
  Number of Branches: 14
  Asymmetric (ASM) or Symmetric (SYM) Network: SYM

Enter the problem data in the following table.

Branch	Name	Starting Node	Ending Node	Distance
1	A-B	1	2	4
2	A-C	1	3	5
3	A-D	1	4	2
4	B-C	2	3	7
5	B-F	2	6	5
6	D-C	4	3	1
7	C-E	3	5	2
8	C-F	3	6	3
9	C-G	3	7	7
10	C-H	3	8	6
11	D-E	4	5	3
12	E-G	4	7	1
13	F-H	6	8	8
14	G-H	7	8	4

RECOMMENDATION

Shortest Route from Source Node	Branch Names	Total Distance
1 - 2	A-B	4
1 - 4	A-D	2
1 - 4 - 3	A-D, D-C	3
1 - 4 - 5	A-D, D-E	5
1 - 4 - 3 - 6	A-D, D-C, C-F	6
1 - 4 - 5 - 7	A-D, D-E, E-G	6
1 - 4 - 3 - 8	A-D, D-C, C-H	9

-   3 miles from A through site D on to station C
-   5 miles from A through station D on to site E
-   6 miles from A through site D through station C on to station F
-   6 miles from A through station D through site E on to station G
-   9 miles from A through site D through station C on to site H

Such recommendations are the same shortest routes as the answers derived by the more cumbersome hand calculations.

Table 12.6	**Traveling Salesman Problems**

Area	Problem
Airline operations	Developing passenger mix flight plans
Engineering	Designing a drilling optimization device
Maintenance	Scheduling vehicle maintenance
Municipal sanitation	Routing and scheduling street sweepers
Sales	Visiting customers within time limits
Security	Routing a guard through his/her rounds
Training	Scheduling crew personnel for recurrent training
Trucking	Planning truck fleet size

Traveling Salesman Problem

There usually is a distinct shortest route from the source to each other node, and it is unnecessary for each of these different routes to follow a cycle through the network. In many situations, however, the flow must follow a **tour**—a single sequence of links that starts at the source, visits each node in the network only once, and then returns to the origin. The problem, which is known as the **traveling salesman** problem, is to find the minimum length tour through the network. Besides the classic problem (for which it is named), this traveling salesman problem can take on a variety of forms in practice, as Table 12.6 illustrates.

Finding the Best Tour

The traveling salesman problem can be solved with the branch and bound method known as the **Eastman/Shapiro algorithm**. It begins by temporarily treating the traveling salesman problem as an assignment problem. If the best assignment provides a complete tour, this recommendation represents the optimal traveling salesman solution. Otherwise, the assignment problem's feasible solution region is searched in an intelligent manner for the optimal tour.

In the first stage of the search, the solution space is partitioned into subspaces by adding constraints to the original assignment problem. This procedure eliminates portions of the solution space that generate a **subtour**—a sequence of links that starts at the source, visits some (but not all) nodes in the network only once, and then returns to the origin—without omitting any complete tour. Such a partitioning process again is known as *branching*.

Branching creates additional assignment problems that can be solved for revised optimal solutions. Each revised solution provides a bound on the objective function value for any optimal traveling salesperson solution within the corresponding subspace. These bounds are used to eliminate clearly nonoptimal subspaces and to focus the search on promising subspaces.

Promising subspaces are further partitioned into additional subspaces, and bounds again are used to eliminate inferior branches. This branching and bounding continues until we find the optimal traveling salesperson solution (if it exists). Management Situation 12.3 illustrates.

Table 12.7   **Jenny Float's Travel Times (in Minutes)**

From	To					
	Townson	**Roystertown**	**Annadel**	**Colutia**	**Ophan**	**Hunter Valley**
Townson	—	11	23	19	13	25
Roystertown	11	—	49	7	46	39
Annadel	20	49	—	12	55	70
Colutia	19	7	12	—	55	57
Ophan	13	46	59	55	—	12
Hunter Valley	28	39	82	57	13	—

Management Situation 12.3

Traveling Salesperson

Jenny Float is a salesperson for Dynamite Exercise Equipment Company. As part of her customer service responsibilities, she must travel each month from the regional sales office in Townson to consumer seminars in Roystertown, Annadel, Colutia, Ophan, and Hunter Valley.

Table 12.7 lists the driving times in minutes required to travel over the existing routes between the towns. As the table indicates, the intercity travel times are not all symmetrical. For example, it takes 23 minutes to travel from Townson to Annadel, but only 20 minutes from Annadel to Townson. Such a situation arises because of traffic patterns, construction detours, and other diversions.

Sales management considers travel time to be costly and unproductive effort. Therefore, it wants Jenny to minimize her travel time. In particular, the sales manager requests that she start at Townson, visit each seminar site only once, and then return to the regional office in the smallest number of minutes possible.

Problem Formulation. Dynamite's traveling salesperson situation again can be portrayed as a network in which a set of cities (nodes) is linked by a series of roads (branches). The flow over these roads represents Jenny's movement between cities, and each branch value measures her travel time in minutes to the corresponding cities. To complete her customer service responsibilities and fulfill her manager's request, Jenny must follow a tour that starts at Townson, visits each seminar site only once, and then returns to the regional sales office. The sales manager wants to find the tour that will minimize her total travel time.

If the group of seminar towns is viewed as a distribution system, Dynamite's situation can be treated as the assignment problem depicted in Table 12.8. In this table, each town represents both an origin and a destination. Table entries identify the driving time in minutes between towns. Pointless intratown travel (such as from Townson to Townson and Annadel to Annadel) is made unattractive by giving these routes very large (*M*-

Table 12.8   **Jenny's Assignment Table**

From	To					
	Townson	Roystertown	Annadel	Colutia	Ophan	Hunter Valley
Townson	*M*	11	23	19	13	25
Roystertown	11	*M*	49	7	46	39
Annadel	20	49	*M*	12	55	70
Colutia	19	7	12	*M*	55	57
Ophan	13	46	59	55	*M*	12
Hunter Valley	28	39	82	57	13	*M*

Driving time in minutes

Table 12.9   **Jenny's Optimal Assignment Table**

From	To					
	Townson	Roystertown	Annadel	Colutia	Ophan	Hunter Valley
Townson	*M*	0̲	4	8	2	11
Roystertown	0̲	*M*	34	0	39	29
Annadel	4	37	*M*	0̲	43	55
Colutia	11	3	0̲	*M*	51	50
Ophan	0	37	42	46	*M*	0̲
Hunter Valley	11	26	61	44	0̲	*M*

Opportunity losses in minutes

minute) driving times. The problem is to determine the town assignments that minimize Jenny's total driving time.

Initial Bounding. By applying Chapter 11's Hungarian method, management will obtain the optimal assignment (identified by the boxed zero values) shown in Table 12.9. This table indicates that Dynamite will minimize Jenny's total travel time by assigning her the following tour:

- From Townson to Roystertown
- From Roystertown to Townson
- From Annadel to Colutia
- From Colutia to Annadel
- From Ophan to Hunter Valley
- From Hunter Valley to Ophan

According to Table 12.8, these optimal assignments will involve 11 + 11 + 12 + 12 + 12 + 13 = 71 minutes of driving time.

Figure 12.12 gives a pictorial representation of Jenny's optimal assignment. As this figure demonstrates, such an assignment creates three separate subtours—Townson to

Figure 12.12 **Jenny's Optimal Assignments**

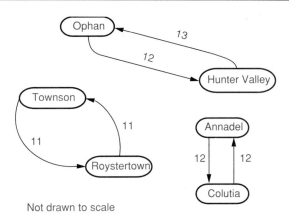

Not drawn to scale

Roystertown to Townson, Ophan to Hunter Valley to Ophan, and Annadel to Colutia to Annadel—rather than a complete tour of the towns on Jenny's itinerary. Table 12.9, then, does not provide a feasible solution to Dynamite's traveling salesperson problem. The optimal assignment's 71-minute value, however, gives an initial lower bound on Jenny's optimal total travel time.

Initial Branching. To move toward a feasible solution, management must add constraints to the assignment problem that will generate more complete sequences of links from the subtours. It is convenient to begin this process with the subtour that has the fewest nodes—either the Townson/Roystertown, Ophan/Hunter Valley, or Annadel/Colutia subtour. Among these possibilities, the Townson/Roystertown subtour is the one that starts at the source node.

Management can break up the Townson/Roystertown subtour (and thereby move toward a complete tour) by making each link on the subtour unattractive. Movement along the Townson-to-Roystertown link of this subtour can be prohibited by replacing the 0 with an *M* entry in the Townson/Roystertown cell of Table 12.9. Similarly, the decision maker can prevent any movement along the Roystertown-to-Townson link of the subtour by replacing the 0 with an *M* entry in the Roystertown/Townson cell of Table 12.9.

The additional restrictions partition the original assignment formulation into two complementary descendant problems. If Dynamite solves each of these descendant problems (not from scratch but by revising Table 12.9), it will obtain the results shown in Figure 12.13.

As Figure 12.13 demonstrates, both descendant problem solutions expand the sequence of towns on Jenny's itinerary. For example, subproblem 1's optimal assignment includes visits to Townson and Roystertown within a larger Townson-to-Annadel-to-Colutia-to-Roystertown-to-Townson subtour. The descendant problems then come closer than the original assignment to forming a complete tour (feasible solution) for Dynamite's traveling salesperson problem.

Figure 12.13   **Dynamite's Initial Partitioning Process**

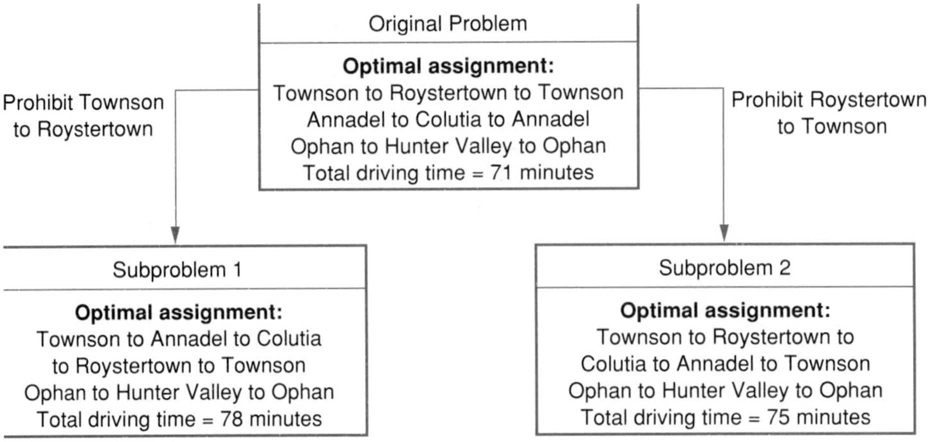

Second Bounding. The initial partitioning process adds constraints that effectively reduce the decision maker's available assignments. As a result, both descendant problems have solutions that involve longer total driving times than the answer to the original assignment problem. Figure 12.13, for example, shows that subproblem 1's subtours require Jenny to drive $78 - 71 = 7$ minutes longer than the original optimal total travel time.

Although the optimal travel time (75 minutes) from subproblem 2 is shorter than the corresponding answer (78 minutes) from subproblem 1, neither of these descendant problems forms a complete tour of the towns on Jenny's itinerary. This result suggests that there are no complete tours with a total travel time of less than 75 minutes. Consequently, 75 replaces 71 minutes as the lower bound on Jenny's optimal total travel time.

Second Branching. Since subproblem 2 generates the current lower bound (75 minutes), it offers the most promising area for search. Among this subproblem's two recommended subtours, Ophan to Hunter Valley to Ophan is the subtour with the fewest nodes. By adding prohibitions (*M*-minute times) that make each link (Ophan to Hunter Valley and Hunter Valley to Ophan) on the subtour unattractive, management will partition subproblem 2 into two complementary descendant problems. If Dynamite solves each of these descendant problems (not from scratch but by revising subproblem 2's optimal assignment table), it will obtain the results shown in Figure 12.14 (where the first letter identifies the town and the arrow depicts the flow direction).

As Figure 12.14 demonstrates, Dynamite creates subproblem 3 when it prohibits the visit from Ophan to Hunter Valley ($O \rightarrow H$), and it creates subproblem 4 by preventing the visit from Hunter Valley to Ophan ($H \rightarrow O$). Subproblems 3's solution forms two subtours ($T \rightarrow R \rightarrow H \rightarrow O \rightarrow T$ and $A \rightarrow C \rightarrow A$). On the other hand, subproblem 4 involves an optimal assignment that forms the Townson-to-Ophan-to-Hunter Valley-to-Roystertown-to-Colutia-to-Annadel-to-Townson ($T \rightarrow O \rightarrow H \rightarrow R \rightarrow C \rightarrow A \rightarrow T$) complete tour of towns on Jenny's itinerary.

Figure 12.14   **Dynamite's Second Partitioning Process**

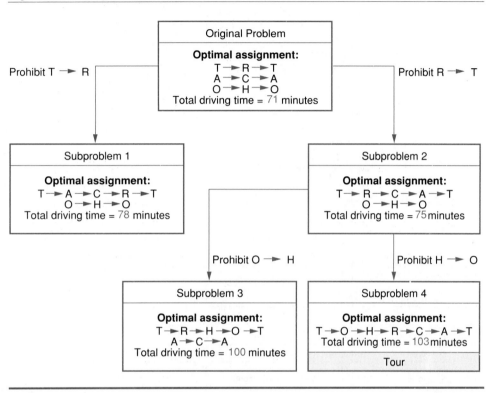

Third Bounding. The Townson-to-Ophan-to-Hunter Valley-to-Roystertown-to-Colutia-to-Annadel-to-Townson sequence is the only complete tour formed by any of the assignment problems shown in Figure 12.14. The 103-minute value resulting from this complete tour then represents an upper bound on Jenny's optimal total travel time.

Figure 12.14 shows that there are two subproblems with shorter travel times than this 103-minute bound. Subproblem 1's optimal assignment requires Jenny to drive $103 - 78 = 25$ minutes less than the complete tour's (subproblem 4) total time, and the optimal travel time from subproblem 3 is $103 - 100 = 3$ minutes less than the upper bound. Although neither subproblem 1 nor subproblem 3 provides a complete-tour solution, these results suggest that 78 should replace 75 minutes as the lower bound on the optimal total travel time. They also indicate that the optimal tour will require Jenny to drive at least 78 minutes (the lower bound) but no more than 103 minutes (the upper bound).

Branch and Bound Solution. By continuing with the branching and bounding process, Dynamite will obtain the results depicted in Figure 12.15. Since subproblem 1 generates the lower bound (78 minutes) after the second branching (Figure 12.14), it is the subproblem next partitioned into complementary descendants—subproblems 5 and 6. Although subproblem 5's solution forms a complete tour (T → A → C → R → H → O → T), it requires Jenny to drive $107 - 103 = 4$ minutes longer than the upper

Figure 12.15   **Dynamite's Branch and Bound Solution**

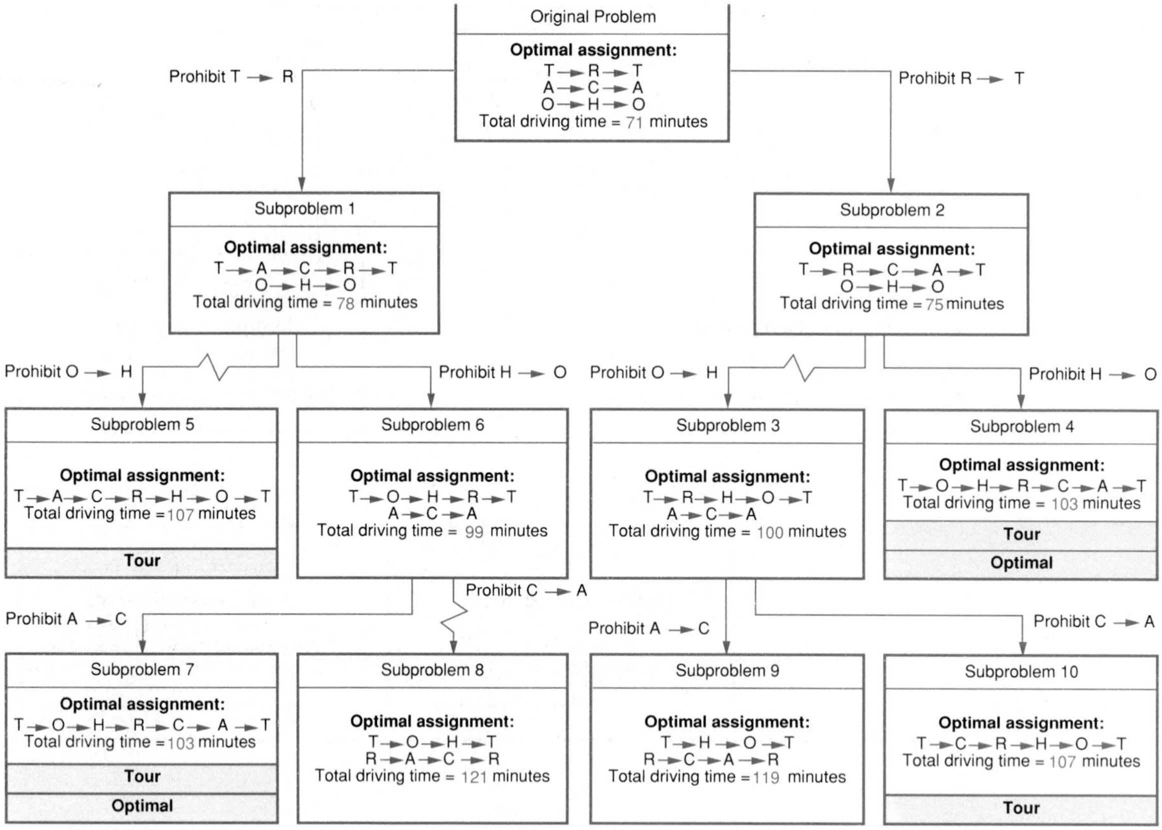

bound (subproblem 4) recommendation. As a result subproblem 5 can be eliminated from further consideration (denoted in Figure 12.15 by drawing a jagged line, or pruning the branch, leading to subproblem 5).

Figure 12.15 also shows that subproblem 6's solution requires Jenny to drive $103 - 99 = 4$ minutes less than the upper bound tour time and $100 - 99 = 1$ minute less than subproblem 3's answer. While neither subproblem 6 nor subproblem 3 provides a complete-tour solution, these results suggest that 99 should replace 78 minutes as the lower bound on the optimal total travel time. They also indicate that subproblem 6 offers the most promising area for search.

By partitioning subproblem 6 into its complementary descendant problems, Dynamite creates subproblems 7 and 8 in Figure 12.15. Since the optimal assignment from subproblem 8 requires Jenny to drive $121 - 103 = 18$ minutes longer than the upper bound tour time, Dynamite can eliminate this descendant from further consideration (again depicted with the jagged line in Figure 12.15). Subproblem 7's optimal assignment generates exactly the same solution as the complete tour formed by the upper bound

Figure 12.16   **Dynamite's Optimal Traveling Salesperson Solution**

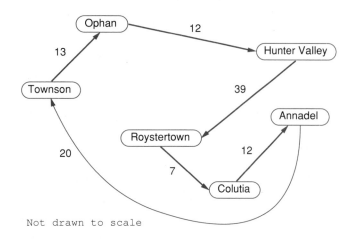

Not drawn to scale

(subproblem 4) recommendation. Such a result confirms that 103 minutes represents the upper bound on Jenny's optimal total travel time.

At this stage of the search, only subproblem 3 in Figure 12.15 has an assignment that requires Jenny to drive fewer minutes (100) than the upper bound time (103 minutes). While this subproblem's solution consists of two subtours (T → R → H → O → T and A → C → A), a descendant problem may form a complete tour with a travel time between 100 and 103 minutes. To find out, Dynamite partitions subproblem 3 into the complementary subproblems 9 and 10. In the process, subproblem 3's 100-minute recommendation replaces subproblem 6's 99-minute answer as the lower bound on the optimal travel time.

Figure 12.15 shows that the optimal assignments for subproblems 9 and 10 both require Jenny to drive longer than the upper bound tour time. Both of these subproblems therefore can be eliminated (pruned) from further consideration. Since such pruning leaves no other subproblems that can form a tour with a driving time shorter than the upper bound, 103 minutes represents Jenny's optimal tour time.

Optimal Tour. By following the unpruned branches in Figure 12.15, Dynamite's sales manager will find that the 103-minute recommendation is obtained from the solution to subproblems 4 and 7. According to these solutions, Jenny's optimal tour is as follows:

- From Townson to Ophan
- From Ophan to Hunter Valley
- From Hunter Valley to Roystertown
- From Roystertown to Colutia
- From Colutia to Annadel
- From Annadel to Townson

This optimal tour is depicted in Figure 12.16.

Procedure Recap. The following branch and bound method can be used to solve a traveling salesman problem:

1. Solve the traveling salesman problem as an assignment problem.
2. If the recommendation does not form a complete tour, partition the solution space into subspaces by adding constraints to the original assignment problem.
3. Use the bounds provided by the descendant problem solutions to eliminate inferior subspaces.
4. Continue to branch and bound until the process locates the optimal traveling salesman solution.

12.3 MAXIMAL FLOW

In the previous layout and route problems, there were no limits placed on the quantity that could flow over the network branches. Many network situations, however, involve links that do have limited flow capacities or flow restrictions. The decison maker often must determine the **maximal flow** — the maximum quantity of items that can move from a specified origin to a particular destination in the network. As Table 12.10 illustrates, this maximal flow problem can take on a variety of forms in practice.

Nature of the Problem

In the maximal flow problem, the flow will follow a **path** through the network — a series of links that leads from the source to the sink node. For example, barges in Table 12.10's waterway network will follow a path over canals from one lock to another, and messages in the communication system will follow a path over lines from a sender to a receiver. The amount of flow between nodes is limited by the capacity of each link in the network. For example, the road types limit automobile flow in Table 12.10's traffic network, and cable/line sizes restrict job flows in the computer system. Except for the source and sink, whatever flows into a node is assumed to flow out of the node. In Table 12.10's production network, for example, we assume that each manufacturing process does not destroy any units flowing through the process.

The objective is to find the path that gives the maximal amount of flow through the network during a specified time period. In Table 12.10, for example, the decision maker seeks the maximal flow of sewage through the sewage network, the total number of units that can flow through the production system, and the maximal flow of messages through the communications network.

Solution Procedure

The maximal flow can be found with a relatively intuitive approach. First, a path is found that has positive flow capacities on all branches from the source to the sink node in the network. As much flow as possible is sent along this path. The process then is repeated until there are no more paths with positive flows on all branches from the source to the sink. Management Situation 12.4 illustrates.

Table 12.10 **Maximal Flow Problems**

Network	Nodes	Branches	Problem
Sewage	Pumping stations	Pipes	Find the maximal flow of sewage through the system.
Waterway	Locks	Canals	Determine the maximal flow of barges through the waterway.
Automobile traffic	Lights and intersections	Roads	Specify the maximal flow of automobiles through the system.
Production	Manufacturing processes	Work flow links	Determine the total number of units that can flow through the system.
Communication	Message receivers and senders	Communication lines	Find the maximal flow of messages through the system.
Computer	Terminals	Cable/lines	Determine the total quantity of jobs that can flow through the network.

Management Situation 12.4

Transmitting Natural Gas

The Atlantic Pacific Company owns a pipeline network that is used to transmit natural gas between its main exploration site and several storage facilities. A portion of the network is depicted in Figure 12.17. In this diagram, the numbers on the branches give the flow capacities in each direction. These numbers are expressed in thousands of cubic feet per hour. Consider, for example, the two numbers on the branch from the exploration site to facility 1. The 10 indicates that the company can transmit 10,000 cubic feet of natural gas from the source to facility 1, while the 0 means that it can send nothing in the opposite direction. Similarly, the two numbers on the branch between facilities 2 and 3 show that 4000 cubic feet of natural gas can be transmitted in either direction between these sites.

Flow capacities differ because of varying pipe sizes. By selectively opening and closing sections of the pipeline network, Atlantic can supply any of the storage locations. Currently, management seeks the maximum quantity of natural gas that can be transmitted from the exploration site to storage facility 6.

Problem Formulation. Atlantic's gas transmission situation again can be portrayed as a network in which a set of nodes (the exploration and storage sites) is interconnected by a series of branches (pipelines). The flow over these pipelines represents the movement of natural gas from the source (the exploration site) to the sink (storage facility 6), and the branch values (numbers on the links) give the flow capacities of the pipelines. Since some nodes (such as facilities 3 and 6) permit only a one-way transmission of gas, these capacities are dependent upon the direction of flow. Atlantic's problem is to determine the maximal flow of natural gas from the exploration site (the source node) to storage facility 6 (the sink node) in the pipeline network.

Figure 12.17   Atlantic Pacific's Pipeline Network

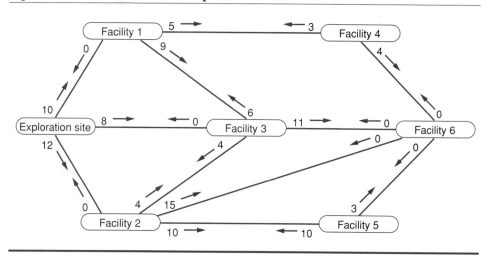

First Path. There are many ways for the company to transmit natural gas from the source (exploration site) to the sink (storage facility 6) node. One possibility is to send the gas from the exploration site through storage facility 3 and on to storage facility 6.

According to Figure 12.17, Atlantic can transmit 11,000 cubic feet of natural gas per hour along the facility 3/facility 6 branch of the exploration site/facility 3/facility 6 path. The exploration site/facility 3 pipeline, however, is big enough to handle only 8,000 cubic feet per hour. To meet this branch flow constraint, therefore, management must send no more than 8,000 cubic feet over each link in the exploration site/facility 3/facility 6 path. In other words, the maximal flow along a path will equal the smallest of all current branch capacities associated with the path.

If the company transmits the maximal flow over the exploration site/facility 3/facility 6 path, it will obtain the results shown in Figure 12.18. The colored links identify the exploration site/facility 3/facility 6 path. The maximal flows over these links are enclosed in boxes above the corresponding path branches. Also, the number entering the source (exploration site) and exiting the sink (facility 6) represents the total quantity of natural gas currently flowing through Atlantic's pipeline network. Once more, the flows are measured in thousands of cubic feet per hour.

Compensating for the Flow Assignment. As Figure 12.18 demonstrates, the maximal flow over the exploration site/facility 3/facility 6 path is 8,000 cubic feet of natural gas per hour. If Atlantic sends this quantity over the denoted path, it will reduce the exploration site/facility 3 pipeline capacity from 8,000 cubic feet to 8,000 − 8,000 = 0 cubic feet per hour. Moreover, the facility 3/facility 6 branch capacity will drop from 11,000 cubic feet to 11,000 − 8,000 = 3,000 cubic feet per hour.

On the other hand, such an action might adversely affect the flow along other potential paths in the system. Furthermore, these alternative paths could enable Atlantic to increase the total flow of natural gas between the source and sink of its pipeline

Figure 12.18   **Maximal Flow Over Atlantic's Exploration
Site/Facility 3/Facility 6 Path**

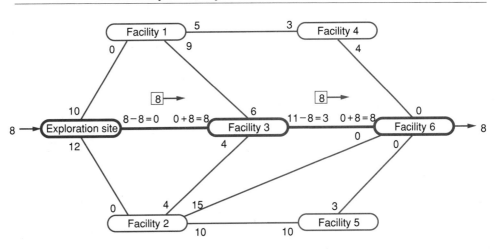

network. As a result, management eventually may want to divert some or all of the exploration site/facility 3/facility 6 flow to the alternative paths.

To allow for desirable revisions, a fictitious flow is added to the branch capacities in the reverse direction (from the sink to the source node) along the selected network path. This fictitious flow, which identifies the capacity available for potential diversion to more desirable network branches, is set equal to the selected path's maximal flow.

In Figure 12.18, for example, Atlantic adds the 8,000 cubic feet maximal flow to the original 0 cubic feet capacities on the facility 6/facility 3 and facility 3/exploration site links of the first path.

Second Path. Figure 12.18 shows that a second possible path is from the exploration site through facility 1, then 4, and on to facility 6. Since this path's smallest branch capacity is 4, it has a maximal flow of 4,000 cubic feet per hour. If management transmits the maximal flow, it will obtain the results shown in Figure 12.19. Once more, the colored links identify the path, the maximal flows over the links are enclosed in boxes above the path branches, and the number entering the source and exiting the sink represents the total flow through the network.

By transmitting the maximal flow over the exploration site/facility 1/facility 4/facility 6 path, Atlantic also changes the branch flow capacities as indicated in Table 12.11. In the process, the total flow through the pipeline network will increase from 8,000 cubic feet per hour (the exploration site/facility 3/facility 6 maximal flow) to 8,000 + 4,000 = 12,000 cubic feet per hour.

Maximal Flow Pattern. By continuing the search in a similar manner, management will obtain the maximal flow pattern depicted in Figure 12.20. According to this figure, Atlantic can transmit a maximal total flow of 30,000 cubic feet per hour by sending natural gas through the existing pipeline network in the following way:

Figure 12.19   Maximal Flow Over Atlantic's Exploration Site/Facility 1/Facility 4/Facility 6 Path

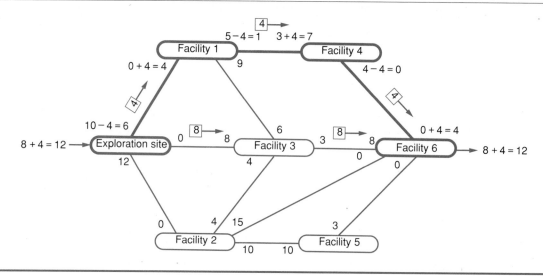

Pipeline	Natural Gas Transmitted (Cubic Feet per Hour)
Exploration site to facility 1	10,000
Exploration site to facility 2	12,000
Exploration site to facility 3	8,000
Facility 1 to facility 3	6,000
Facility 1 to facility 4	4,000
Facility 2 to facility 5	0
Facility 2 to facility 6	15,000
Facility 3 to facility 2	3,000
Facility 3 to facility 6	11,000
Facility 4 to facility 6	4,000
Facility 5 to facility 6	0

Procedure Recap. The following procedure can be used to find the maximal flow through a network:

1. Select any path that has positive flow capacities along all branches from the source to the sink node in the network.

2. Determine the minimum positive flow capacity between any two nodes on the path, and increase the flow along the path by this minimum capacity.

3. Subtract the flow from the capacities leading to the sink and add the flow to the capacities leading back to the source along the path.

4. Repeat steps 1 through 3 until there are no more paths with positive flows on all branches from the source to the sink of the network.

Table 12.11   Branch Flow Capacities

Branch	Original Capacity (Cubic Feet per Hour)	Flow Change (Cubic Feet per Hour)	Revised Capacity (Cubic Feet per Hour)
Exploration site to facility 1	10,000	−4,000	6,000
Facility 1 to facility 4	5,000	−4,000	1,000
Facility 4 to facility 6	4,000	−4,000	0
Facility 6 to facility 4	0	4,000	4,000
Facility 4 to facility 1	3,000	4,000	7,000
Facility 1 to exploration site	0	4,000	4,000

Figure 12.20   Atlantic's Maximal Flow Pattern

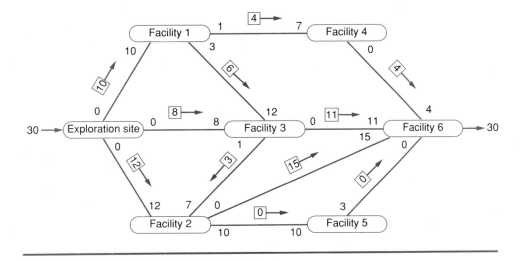

Minimal Cut

There is another way to look at Atlantic's natural gas transmission problem. Suppose, for example, that the company partitions this network into the complementary parts divided by the wavy line in Figure 12.21. If management separates the part on the left from the part on the right, it will completely disconnect the network source (exploration site) from the sink (facility 6). Such a break, which is known as a **cut**, eliminates any flow through the network.

By making the cut indicated by the wavy line in Figure 12.21, Atlantic prevents the flow of 30,000 cubic feet of natural gas away from the exploration site. Since any other cut will stop more than this quantity from flowing to the sink, the 30,000 cubic feet represents the minimum total capacity that can be cut from the company's pipeline network. This network cut with the smallest capacity (the wavy line in Figure 12.21) is referred to as the **minimal cut**.

Figure 12.21   Atlantic's Maximal Cut

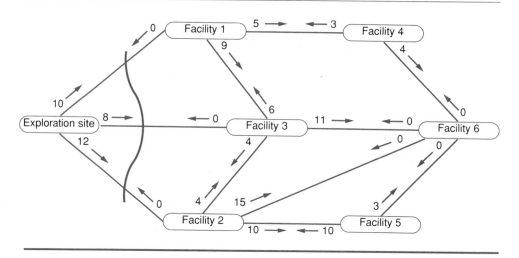

Notice that the 30,000 cubic feet capacity of the minimal cut is exactly equal to Atlantic's maximal total flow through the pipeline network. This result is not a coincidence. It illustrates the following important principle: *For any network with a single source and sink, the maximal total flow will equal the total capacity of the minimal cut.* In linear programming terms, the minimal cut problem is the dual of the maximal flow problem. As a result, minimal cut problems can be formulated and solved as maximal flow problems.

Computer Analysis

Because the maximal flow calculations are tedious, time-consuming, and prone to error, prewritten computer programs have been developed to perform the necessary analysis. One such program is available on the **Quantitative Management (QM)** software and is invoked by selecting the Network Models option from **QM**'s main menu. Figure 12.22 shows how the program is used to solve Atlantic's gas transmission problem.

Problem Formulation. As Figure 12.22 illustrates, the user executes the module by selecting the Maximal flow option from the Network Problem menu. The problem is formulated through the Edit command from the Input menu. As with the other options, the user essentially re-creates the 7 nodes (sites) and 11 branches (pipelines) of Atlantic's network (Figure 12.17) in tabular form. In this recreation, the user should designate the source (exploration site) as node 1, label the intermediate nodes (facilities 1 through 5) with consecutive integers, and assign the highest identification number (7) to the sink (facility 6) node in the network.

When entering the data, the user also must give the flow capacities from both the starting and ending node of each branch in the network. In Figure 12.22, for example, branch 2 (named E-F2) represents the pipeline from Atlantic's exploration site (labeled

---

Figure 12.22   Computer Solution of Atlantic's Gas Transmission Problem

Network Problem:
- Minimal spanning tree
- Shortest route
* Maximal flow

Input:
* Edit
- Load
- Print
- Save

Output:
- Full
* Summary
* Print
- Save

Problem Description:
Number of Nodes: 7
Number of Branches: 11

Enter the problem data in the following table.

Branch	Name	Starting Node	Ending Node	Flow Capacity From Starting Node	Flow Capacity From Ending Node
1	E-F1	1	2	10	0
2	E-F2	1	3	12	0
3	E-F3	1	4	8	0
4	F1-F3	2	4	9	6
5	F1-F4	2	5	5	3
6	F2-F3	3	4	4	4
7	F2-F5	3	6	10	10
8	F2-F6	3	7	15	0
9	F3-F6	4	7	11	0
10	F4-F6	5	7	4	0
11	F5-F6	6	7	3	0

RECOMMENDATION

Branch Name	Starting Node	Ending Node	Net Flow
E-F1	1	2	10
E-F2	1	3	12
E-F3	1	4	8
F1-F3	2	4	6
F1-F4	2	5	4
F2-F6	3	7	15
F3-F2	4	3	3
F3-F6	4	7	11
F4-F6	5	7	4

Maximal total flow: 30

---

node 1), with a flow capacity of 12 thousand cubic feet, to facility 2 (called node 3), with a flow capacity of 0 cubic feet. Similarly, branch 5 (named F1-F4) depicts the pipeline from facility 1 (labeled node 2), with a flow capacity of 5 thousand cubic feet, to facility 4 (called node 5), with a flow capacity of 3 thousand cubic feet. Report options then are chosen through the Output menu.

Maximal Flow. After receiving all the problem information, **QM** processes the data and generates the maximal flow pattern. The RECOMMENDATION section of Figure 12.22 shows that Atlantic can transmit a maximal natural gas flow of 30,000 cubic feet per hour over the pipeline network by sending

- 10,000 from the exploration site (E) to facility 1 (F1)
- 12,000 from the exploration site (E) to facility 2 (F2)
- 8,000 from the exploration site (E) to facility 3 (F3)
- 6,000 from facility 1 (F1) to facility 3 (F3)
- 4,000 from facility 1 (F1) to facility 4 (F4)
- 15,000 from facility 2 (F2) to facility 6 (F6)
- 3,000 from facility 3 (F3) to facility 2 (F2)
- 11,000 from facility 3 (F3) to facility 6 (F6)
- 4,000 from facility 4 (F4) to facility 6 (F6)

Branches not listed in the RECOMMENDATION section should receive no flow. Hence, Atlantic should transmit 0 cubic feet of natural gas over branch 7 (named F2-F5) from facility 2 to facility 5 and 0 cubic feet over branch 11 (named F5-F6) from facility 5 to facility 6.

Network Model Extension

Many problems, such as production planning and equipment replacement, can be depicted as a *capacitated flow network model*. In the generalized model, flows generate costs, and there are upper and possibly lower limits on the flow along specified branches in the network. The problem is to

minimize $\sum_i \sum_j c_{ij} F_{ij}$

subject to $\sum_j F_{ij} - \sum_j F_{ji} = b_i$ $(i = 1, \ldots, n)$

$L_{ij} \leq F_{ij} \leq U_{ij}$ (for all i, j)

where

F_{ij} = the flow along the branch from node i to node j

c_{ij} = unit cost of the flow along the branch from i to j

b_i = new flow for node i ($b_i > 0$ for source nodes, $b_i < 0$ for sink nodes, and $b_i = 0$ for transshipment nodes)

L_{ij} = minimum flow capacity along the branch from i to j

U_{ij} = maximum flow capacity along the branch from i to j

n = the number of nodes in the network

The maximal flow problem (which does not consider cost) and Chapter 11's transshipment model (which is uncapacitated) can be treated as special cases of this generalized formulation.

Like other network models, the generalized problem can be addressed with mathematical programming. (Thought Exercises 7 and 10 will ask you to demonstrate that the shortest route and maximal flow problems are also linear programs). However, the capacitated network flow (and other *combinatorial problems*) often can be solved more efficiently with specialized network algorithms than with mathematical programming.

Network Models in Practice

Network models are applied to a wide variety of management problems. Here are a few areas in which this quantitative analysis is used.

Area	Application
Finance and Accounting	Finding the best layout for a bank's automated teller machine network
	Determining the minimum cost tours for a finance company's delinquent account collection agents
	Routing financial transactions through a computerized accounting system
Marketing	Finding the shortest pizza delivery routes in a city
	Developing product, pricing, and distribution strategies
	Determining the maximal flow of potential buyers through a collection of open houses
Production and Operations	Determining the minimum cost production/purchase plan
	Finding the least-cost agricultural irrigation layout
	Scheduling shifts for airline personnel
Public and Service Sector	Routing mail in the postal system
	Designing a community college's sewer system
	Developing the road layout through an Olympic village

SUMMARY

In this chapter we have considered some of the most widely used network techniques. We began with a discussion of the nature of the minimal spanning tree problem. Then we saw how to select the layout that minimized the total length of connections in a network. The first section of the chapter also illustrated how minimal spanning tree problems can be solved with the aid of a computer. In addition, we reviewed the typical situations in which the methodology has been applied.

In the second section, the discussion focused on network problems in which the flow begins at a particular origin and proceeds to a specified destination. Two such routing situations were examined. In one case, the objective was to find the shortest route from a source to a sink of the network. We also considered typical managerial uses of the methodology and saw how shortest routes can be found with the aid of a computer. The other routing problem dealt with the situation in which a resource could start from a particular location, visit each facility only once, and then return to the origin. In this case, the objective was to find the route that minimized the cost, time, or distance involved in completing such a tour.

The final section of the chapter showed how to formulate and solve a maximal flow problem. In this problem, the decision maker had to determine the maximum quantity that could flow from a specified origin to a particular destination in the network. We also examined some typical applications of the methodology and reviewed the procedure for finding the maximal flow with the aid of a computer.

As the Network Models in Practice exhibit demonstrates, the methodologies discussed in this chapter are applied to a variety of business and economic problems. These methodologies also provide important concepts that will be utilized in later chapters of this text.

Glossary

asymmetric network A network in which the link between at least one pair of nodes is restricted to one-way traffic and/or has a different length in each flow direction.

cut A break that separates the source from the sink and thereby eliminates any flow through a network.

cycle A sequence of branches that leads from a node back to itself through other nodes.

Eastman/Shapiro algorithm A branch and bound methodology designed to solve traveling salesperson problems.

greedy algorithm A procedure that can be used to find the minimal spanning tree.

labeling and backtracking procedure A procedure that can be used to find the shortest route through a network.

loop A branch that leads from a node back to itself.

maximal flow The largest quantity that can be sent through a network with branch flow capacities.

minimal cut The network cut with the smallest total capacity.

minimal spanning tree A series of links that will minimize the total length of the branches required to connect all the nodes in a network.

path The series of links that leads from the source to the sink of a network.

shortest route A series of links that will minimize the total length of the branches required to connect a specified origin with a particular destination in a network.

sink node The specified destination node for the flow over the branches in a network.

source node The specified origin node of the flow over the branches in a network.

spanning The process of connecting all nodes in a network.

subtour A sequence of links that starts at the source, visits some (but not all) nodes in the network only once, and then returns to the origin.

symmetric network A network in which the link between any pair of nodes has an identical length in either flow direction.

tour A sequence of links that starts at the source, visits each node in the network only once, and then returns to the origin.

traveling salesman problem A problem whose objective is to find the minimum length tour through a network.

Thought Exercises

1. Identify the nodes, branches, and flows in each of the following networks:
   a. A highway system
   b. A telephone network
   c. A forest
   d. A pipeline
   e. A factory

2. Identify the nature of the arc values in each of the following situations:
   a. A logging company must use a limited budget to construct a series of roads between various logging centers.
   b. A research and development center must develop a new vaccine within a certain schedule.

    c. A defense contractor with a certain budget must plan and schedule work activity on a new air force bomber.

    d. An international household goods manufacturer must develop a distribution plan for its new bath soap.

3. Indicate whether each of the following situations is a minimal spanning tree or shortest route problem. Explain.

    a. A parcel delivery service wants to find the minimum cost of delivering packages to various cities in the state.

    b. A municipal golf course wants to find the minimum number of water lines to the sprinkler heads.

    c. A troop master wants to find the shortest distance between the boy scout center and the summer camp.

    d. A trucking company wants to use the minimum number of roads between its dispatching center and various delivery points.

4. The minimal spanning tree is often referred to as the "greedy algorithm" because you can try to find the shortest connection each time and still get the optimal solution. How does this fact help you to break ties in using the procedure? Demonstrate with Management Situation 12.1.

5. A local high school principal has asked a planning committee to design the layout of the institution's fire sprinkler system. Potential links between the main water supply and sprinkler fixtures are shown in the following network:

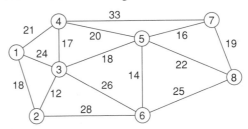

In this diagram, the branches denote the potential pipelines between the fixtures. The numbers on the branches give the distances in feet between the nodes. Site 5 is the location of the institution's main water supply.

    In view of the school's limited budget, the principal wants the design to include the least possible total feet of pipeline. Hence, she has asked the institution's chief financial officer to serve on the committee with the head of the science and mathematics department. After a careful review and evaluation of the problem, they have developed the following computer solution:

Network Problem:	Input:	Output:
* Minimal spanning tree	* Edit	▪ Full
▪ Shortest route	▪ Load	* Summary
▪ Maximal flow	▪ Print	* Print
	▪ Save	▪ Save

Problem Description:
  Number of Nodes: 8
  Number of Branches: 15

Enter the problem data in the following table.

Branch	Name	Starting Node	Ending Node	Distance
1	1-2	1	2	18
2	1-3	1	3	24
3	1-4	1	4	21
4	2-3	2	3	12
5	2-6	2	6	28
6	3-4	3	4	17
7	3-5	3	5	18
8	3-6	3	6	26
9	4-5	4	5	20
10	4-7	4	7	33
11	5-6	5	6	14
12	5-7	5	7	16
13	5-8	5	8	22
14	6-8	6	8	25
15	7-8	7	8	19

RECOMMENDATION

Branch Name	Starting Node	Ending Node	Distance
1-2	1	2	18
2-3	2	3	12
3-4	3	4	17
3-5	3	5	18
5-6	5	6	14
5-7	5	7	16
7-8	7	8	19

Total distance = 114

Interpret this solution for the planning committee. What design should the committee recommend to the principal? How many total feet of pipeline will be used in their recommended design?

6. Although ties may be broken arbitrarily in the shortest route procedure, they may indicate the presence of alternative optimal solutions. The tram-routing situation for Sunrise residents (Management Situation 12.2) is a case in point. Can you identify the alternative optimal solution? Show your work. Can you think of any reasons why the residents might prefer one solution over another? Explain.

7. Refer again to Management Situation 12.2. Suppose that Prestige lets X_{ij} represent the flow (movement of a tram) over the trail (branch) connecting site i with site j. For example, X_{12} would denote the movement of a tram from the park entrance at A (node 1) to site B (node 2). Similarly, X_{68} would give the flow between site F (node 6) and the swimming and skating pond at H (node 8). Also, assume

$$X_{ij} = \begin{cases} 1 & \text{if the link is used} \\ 0 & \text{otherwise} \end{cases}$$

and that the flow can go only from a lower- to a higher-numbered node. Use the symbols and assumptions to develop a linear program for Sunrise's shortest route problem.

8. A company is interested in employing a recent college graduate for an operations management opening at its headquarters. As part of the evaluation process, the firm will fly the graduate to the headquarters for a series of interviews. The available flight routes are shown in the following network:

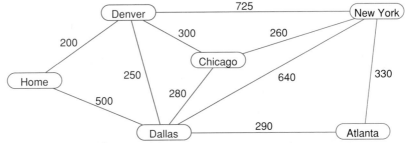

In the diagram, the branches denote the potential links, and the nodes identify the connecting cities in the flight network. The numbers alongside the branches give the first-class air fare in dollars between the nodes. Company headquarters are located in New York.

As the flight network indicates, there is no direct flight from the graduate's home to the company headquarters. Nevertheless, management wants its travel staff to determine the least costly round-trip first-class flight route for the candidate. After a careful review and evaluation of the problem, the staff has developed the following computer solution:

Network Problem:
- Minimal spanning tree
* Shortest route
- Maximal flow

Input:
* Edit
- Load
- Print
- Save

Output:
- Full
* Summary
* Print
- Save

Problem Description:
  Number of Nodes: 6
  Number of Branches: 10
  Asymmetric (ASM) of Symmetric (SYM) Network: SYM

Enter the problem data in the following table.

Branch	Name	Starting Node	Ending Node	Distance
1	H-DE	1	2	200
2	H-DA	1	3	500
3	DE-DA	2	3	250
4	DE-C	2	4	300
5	DE-N	2	6	725
6	DA-C	3	4	280
7	DA-A	3	5	290
8	DA-N	3	6	640
9	C-N	4	6	260
10	A-N	5	6	330

	RECOMMENDATION	
Shortest Route from Source Node	Branch	Total Distance
1-2	H-DE	200
1-2-3	H-DE, DE-DA	450
1-2-4	H-DE, DE-C	500
1-2-3-5	H-DE, DE-DA, DA-A	740
1-2-4-6	H-DE, DE-C, C-N	760

Interpret this solution for management. What flight route should the travel staff recommend to management? How much will it cost to fly the candidate in for interviews?

9. In Management Situation 12.2, Prestige provides tram service from the park entrance to each site in the Sunrise equestrian and jogging park. Moreover, a different tram is sent from the entrance to each station. Suppose that management labels this original service as the blue line.

   Now the company wants to offer an additional green line to the residents. This line will start at the park entrance, visit each site only once, and then return to the origin. Since tram expenses still will be paid by a distance-related fare, the residents want such a line to follow a route that runs the fewest total miles from the park entrance. What route do you recommend for the green line? Explain.

10. Refer back to Management Situation 12.4. Let X_{ij} represent the flow of natural gas over the pipeline joining facility i with facility j. For instance, X_{12} would denote the quantity of natural gas flowing from the exploration site (node 1) to facility 1 (node 2). Similarly, X_{67} would give the flow between facility 5 (node 6) and facility 6 (node 7). Also, suppose that F identifies the total flow through Atlantic's pipeline network. Develop the linear program that corresponds to the company's maximal flow problem. Then formulate and interpret its dual.

11. The Serpentine Corridor is represented by the following network of trails in the mountainous western region separating the warring nations of Northern and Southern Yetmite:

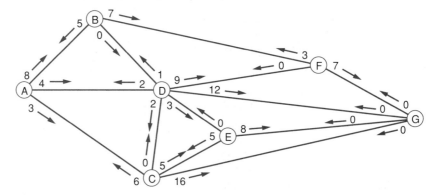

In the diagram, the nodes represent junction points (villages, cities, and towns), while the branches denote trails joining the nodes. Branch values give the number of troops (in thousands) that can be infiltrated each week along the trails. The corresponding arrows identify the infiltration direction.

General Swaggert, the commanding officer of the Northern Yetmite forces, wants to determine the maximal flow of troops that can be infiltrated between Serpentine Corridor points D and G. In this regard, his staff has provided the following computer solution of the maximal flow problem:

Network Problem:
- Minimal spanning tree
- Shortest route
* Maximal flow

Input:
* Edit
- Load
- Print
- Save

Output:
- Full
* Summary
* Print
- Save

Problem Description:
  Number of Nodes: 7
  Number of Branches: 13

Enter the problem data in the following table.

Branch	Name	Starting Node	Ending Node	Flow Capacity From Starting Node	Flow Capacity From Ending Node
1	D-A	1	2	2	4
2	D-B	1	3	1	0
3	D-C	1	4	2	0
4	D-E	1	5	3	0
5	D-F	1	6	9	0
6	D-G	1	7	12	0
7	A-B	2	3	8	5
8	A-C	2	4	3	6
9	B-F	3	6	7	3
10	C-E	4	5	5	5
11	C-G	4	7	16	0
12	E-G	5	7	8	0
13	F-G	6	7	7	0

RECOMMENDATION

Branch Name	Starting Node	Ending Node	Net Flow
D-A	1	2	2
D-B	1	3	1
D-C	1	4	2
D-E	1	5	3
D-F	1	6	7
D-G	1	7	12
A-C	2	4	3
B-A	3	2	1
C-E	4	5	5
E-G	5	7	8
F-G	6	7	7
Maximal total flow: 27			

Interpret this solution for General Swaggert. What is the maximal total flow of troops through the Serpentine Corridor? How should troops be infiltrated every week along each trail in the Corridor?

12. Do you agree or disagree with each of the following statements? Explain.

    a. A minimal spanning tree will form a single series of connections between nodes.

    b. We are not always interested in the shortest route when using the shortest route procedure.

    c. If the decision maker wants to reduce travel or operating (instead of construction or setup) costs, he or she is better off using the shortest route (instead of the minimal spanning tree) procedure.

    d. Most network solution procedures assume that there is a conservation of flow, namely, that the flow in must equal the flow out of a node.

    e. The optimal tour in a traveling salesman problem gives the minimal cost of achieving the required network flow.

    f. If the decision maker wants to reduce flow costs, he or she may be better off using the maximal flow solution procedure.

    g. Assignment and transportation problems can be viewed as special cases of a network flow problem.

    h. The transshipment problem is to find the least-cost path from each source to every sink in a network.

Technique Exercises

13. In Management Situation 12.1, start with node C and show that the greedy algorithm results in the minimal spanning tree shown in Figure 12.5.

14. Figure 12.4 gives Prestige's third connection. Use the greedy algorithm to complete the remaining connections required for the minimal spanning tree (Figure 12.5).

15. The following diagram shows the physical layout and distances (in hundreds of feet) for forklift routes between work centers in a large manufacturing plant. Determine the minimal spanning tree for the network.

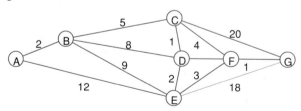

16. Consider the computer system design situation depicted in the following network:

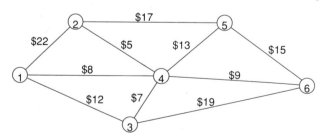

Each node represents the location of a computer terminal, while each branch identifies a potential hookup line between the terminals. Branch values give the costs (in thousands of dollars) for connecting each pair of terminals. The main computer facility is located at site 4.

What is the least costly way to join the main computer with every other terminal in the network? How much will this optimal design cost?

17. Refer back to Management Situation 12.2. Figure 12.9 gives Prestige's third tram line route. Use the labeling and backtracking procedure to complete the remainder of the connections required for the shortest tram route network (Figure 12.10).

18. The following network shows the costs (in hundreds of thousands of dollars) of distributing electricity from the production facility A through various transmission points to a large industrial customer H. Find the least costly routes from A to every other node.

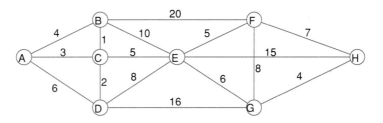

19. Refer back to Thought Exercise 7. Solve the linear program that corresponds to Prestige's shortest route problem. How does the recommended linear programming solution compare with the answer given in the text for Management Situation 12.2? Explain.

20. In the following network, node A is the base center for a delivery service. Arc values represent driving time in hours to various cities within its service area. Find the shortest route from E to every other node.

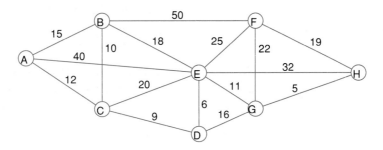

21. Refer back to Management Situation 12.3. Show how Table 12.9 and Figures 12.13, 12.14, and 12.15 were developed.

22. An independent salesperson has customers in six locations throughout the county. The distance in miles between the locations is summarized in the following table:

From	To					
	A	**B**	**C**	**D**	**E**	**F**
A	—	11	23	19	13	25
B	13	—	49	7	46	39
C	11	44	—	12	55	70
D	15	5	13	—	55	57
E	16	51	59	60	—	12
F	28	42	82	62	13	—

The salesperson must start at location A, visit each customer only once, and then return to the origin. Which tour will minimize the total distance traveled? Show all your work.

23. A postal delivery person starts at the main office, delivers mail, makes pickups at various mail boxes around the city, and then returns to the origin. Her delivery system is depicted in the following network:

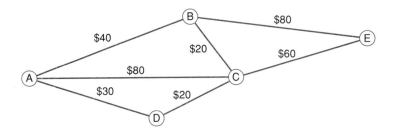

The nodes denote delivery and pickup points, while the branches identify the existing links between these points. The main office is located at node A. Branch values give the daily delivery cost over each link. Find the postal person's least costly delivery tour. What is the corresponding total delivery cost?

24. Figure 12.19 gives the maximal flow over Atlantic's exploration site/facility 1/facility 4/facility 6 path. Use the algorithm presented in the text to find the maximal total flow through the pipeline network (Figure 12.20). Show all your work.

25. Refer back to Thought Exercise 10. Solve the linear program that corresponds to Atlantic's maximal flow problem. How does the recommended linear programming solution compare with the answer given in the text for Management Situation 12.4? Explain.

26. The following network depicts the flow of messages in a telecommunications system.

Nodes identify major switching stations, and the branches represent the available links between these stations. Branch values give the number of simultaneous messages each station can handle per hour. The arrows denote the flow directions.

What is the maximum number of simultaneous messages that this system can handle each hour between the San Francisco (SF) and Philadelphia (PH) locations? How many messages will flow over each link in the network? Show all your work.

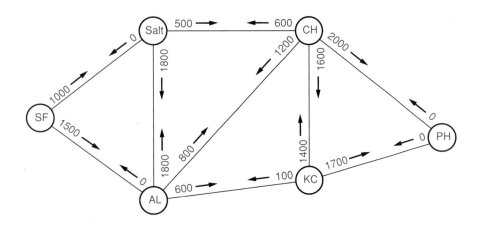

Computer Exercises

27. A developer is completing a new industrial park. The distances in thousands of yards between each facility are summarized below.

From	To										
	A	**B**	**C**	**D**	**E**	**F**	**G**	**H**	**I**	**J**	**K**
A	—	3	2.8	7	6.4	5	7.4	4.8	5.9	6.2	10.4
B	3	—	9	3.4	4.4	4.6	5.8	4.2	3.7	6.1	4.4
C	2.8	9	—	6.2	5.6	3.8	3	3.4	4.3	3.5	5
D	7	3.4	6.2	—	3.8	5	4.6	5.2	3.7	4	5.1
E	6.4	4.4	5.6	3.8	—	7	3.2	6.5	6	7.4	8
F	5	4.6	3.8	5	7	—	11.2	8.4	7	6	5.5
G	7.4	5.8	3	4.6	3.2	11.2	—	5.8	6.3	7.1	8
H	4.8	4.2	3.4	5.2	6.5	8.4	5.8	—	6.2	6.1	3.8
I	5.9	3.7	4.3	3.7	6	7	6.3	6.2	—	4.6	5.3
J	6.2	6.1	3.5	4	7.4	6	7.1	6.1	4.6	—	10
K	10.4	4.4	5	5.1	8	5.5	8	3.8	5.3	10	—

A local telephone company is trying to develop a communications network for the park. The objective is to determine the cable requirements that will minimize the total length of the connections.

Use the **Quantitative Management (QM)** software to determine best cable connections.

28. Twenty Flags Enterprises has recently purchased a large tract of land for a new amusement park. The park will have a single entrance and a single exit. There are 12 major amusement zones within the park, and there are several roadways available to connect the zones. The possibilities are shown below.

In the diagram, the nodes identify the amusement zones, while the branches give the potential roadways between zones. Branch values denote the road lengths in miles.

Park designers seek the road pattern that has the fewest total miles. Use the **QM** software to develop the best design.

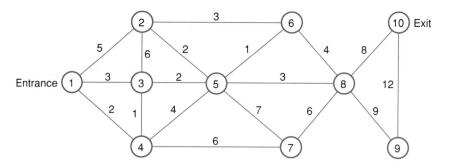

29. Yellow Van Lines is a professional moving company that has just received a contract from a government agency to move several truckloads of computer equipment from Miami to Baltimore. Looking over the map, the dispatching manager has tentatively selected the cities shown on the following network as connecting points for various transportation routes.

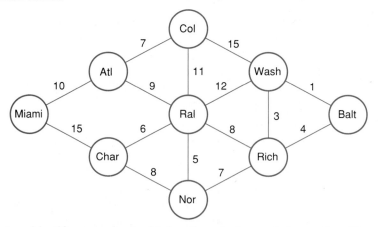

Branch values identify approximate driving time, in hours, between the cities.

Management seeks the shortest routes between Miami and each city in the network. Use the **QM** software to develop the recommended routes.

30. Abby Bind has an important business meeting in Jamestown tomorrow night. There are a number of alternate routes by which she can travel from company headquarters in Washington to the meeting site. The network below summarizes the alternate routes.

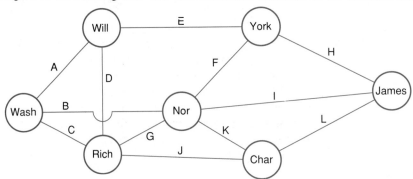

Travel methods, times, and costs for each route are summarized below.

Route	Method	Time (Hours)	Cost ($)
A	Train	2	35
B	Plane	1.5	105
C	Plane	1	80
D	Bus	2.5	40
E	Bus	0.75	15
F	Bus	0.5	8
G	Train	1	25
H	Bus	0.5	5
I	Bus	1.25	20
J	Train	1.25	30
K	Bus	1.75	45
L	Bus	3	55

Abby earns a salary of about $20 per hour.

Abby's boss seeks the least costly route from company headquarters to the business meeting site. Use **QM** software to determine the best travel plan.

31. Cumberland County Conservation District is responsible for operating the irrigation system in the county. Water flows from the source at Lake Williams through several canals to a reservoir at Jackson Run. The reservoir then supplies water to various farms in the county. A graphic model of the irrigation system is shown below.

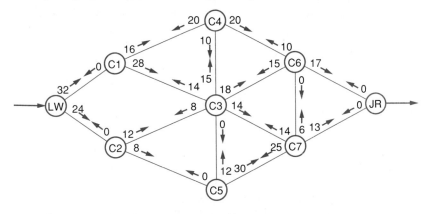

Canal water flow capacities, in thousands of gallons per minute, are listed on the branches of the network.

District officials seek the irrigation plan that will maximize the total water flow through the irrigation system. Use the **QM** software to develop a recommended plan.

32. Solid Elements, Inc. manufactures containers for fast food vendors. Container manufacturing consists of several distinct operations, and the factory is arranged in a way that will accommodate the layout. Pneumatic tubes move the containers through the various manufacturing processes. The process can be represented by the following network.

Values alongside the branches represent production capacities, expressed as hundreds of containers manufactured per minute.

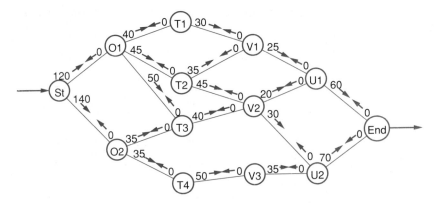

Operations managers seek the production plan that will generate the maximum total output. Use the **QM** software to find a recommended production plan.

Applications Exercises

33. The Universal Outdoor Theater, Inc., holds concerts and plays in the spring, summer, and fall of each year. A renovation program was started last winter and is now complete except for rewiring the facility for sound. Distances between various loudspeakers and other sound equipment are shown in the following table:

		To								
From	Stage	Speaker 1	Speaker 2	Speaker 3	Speaker 4	Speaker 5	Speaker 6	Speaker 7	Speaker 8	Control Center
Stage	—	10	15	20	M	M	M	M	M	50
Speaker 1	10	—	15	5	25	M	M	M	30	M
Speaker 2	15	15	—	10	15	20	M	M	M	M
Speaker 3	20	5	10	—	M	M	15	30	M	M
Speaker 4	M	25	15	M	—	25	10	5	M	M
Speaker 5	M	M	20	M	25	—	15	20	30	35
Speaker 6	M	M	M	15	10	15	—	5	25	40
Speaker 7	M	M	M	30	5	20	5	—	10	15
Speaker 8	M	30	M	M	M	30	25	10	—	10
Control Center	50	M	M	M	M	35	40	15	10	—

The symbol M indicates that the corresponding connection cannot be made because of the theater layout. All other distances are measured in feet.

It costs $2 per foot to wire the layout. Management wants to determine the least cost of wiring the theater. What series of connections do you recommend? What is the corresponding minimum cost?

34. A small Savannah-based transportation company must purchase a special machine for transferring cargo from ships to its dockyard facilities. The machine can be purchased now for $50,000. After two years, the purchase price is expected to be $60,000. The machine can be resold, but the resale price will decrease with age. On the other hand, older machines need more repairs, and thus operating costs will increase with age. The following table shows the effects of age on the resale price and operating costs of the machine for the next six years. Company financial procedures calculate a machine's total net cost as the purchase price minus the resale value plus operating costs.

Machine Age (Years)	Resale Price at Year's End (% of Purchase Price)	Annual Operating Costs ($)
1	90	1,000
2	80	1,800
3	60	2,600
4	40	3,500
5	30	4,500
6	20	5,000

Management wants to determine the machine replacement policy that will minimize total net cost over the next six years. During which years (if any) should the machine be replaced?

35. Quality Products processes six types of operations on the same packaging equipment. In the process, the work crew must change some attachments on the equipment. As a result, there is a changeover, or setup, time required between operations. Moreover, the changeover times depend on the sequence in which the operations are assigned to the equipment. For example, the changeover time from operation A to operation B is 10 hours. Yet it takes only five hours to change over from job E to job B. In fact, production records indicate that the changeover times in hours for all operation sequences are as shown in the following table:

| From | To | | | | | |
	A	B	C	D	E	F
A	—	10	8	3	4	11
B	12	—	5	6	9	2
C	6	13	—	4	2	1
D	15	6	8	—	5	12
E	2	5	6	9	—	3
F	7	12	10	10	14	—

Policy dictates that the work crew set up the original operation after completing the other five activities in a sequence.

Management wants to determine the sequence of operations that will minimize the total changeover time. What sequence do you recommend? How much changeover time will the recommended sequence involve?

36. A new civic center is being planned for Allendale. As part of the planning process, the municipal engineer wants to determine if the streets between the center and a city expressway can accommodate the expected flow of 18,000 cars. Various entries are available, but the flow capacities differ because of variations in available lanes, street lights, and so on. Studies indicate that these capacities are as shown in the following table:

From	To						
	Civic Center	Junction Point 1	Junction Point 2	Junction Point 3	Junction Point 4	Junction Point 5	Expressway
Civic Center	—	8	6	9	NA	NA	NA
Junction Point 1	0	—	6	NA	5	NA	NA
Junction Point 2	0	7	—	NA	4	9	NA
Junction Point 3	0	NA	NA	—	NA	2	7
Junction Point 4	NA	2	5	NA	—	NA	6
Junction Point 5	NA	NA	3	8	NA	—	4
Expressway	NA	NA	NA	0	0	0	—

In this table, the capacities are measured in thousands of cars. Also, NA indicates that the corresponding link is not available.

What is the maximum traffic flow that the streets can accommodate? How many cars will move along each street? Will the streets be able to handle the expected flow after a civic center event?

37. The Ecological Protection Agency wants to build a series of dams on the Postigula River system for flood control purposes. As part of the evaluation process, the agency has developed the following map of the system:

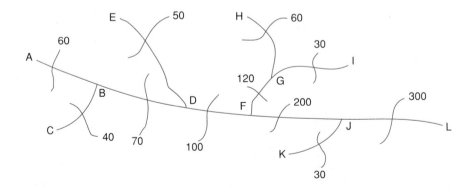

Possible dam locations are indicated on the map with wavy lines. The diagram also identifies the estimated costs (in millions of dollars) for building the dam, relocating displaced residents, and correcting any ecological damage to the environment. Water flows downstream from the highlands above site A to Clean Lake at location L.

Where should the dams be built to minimize the total costs of providing the flood control system? How much must the agency budget for this project?

For Further Reading

Network Models

Aneja, Y. P., and K. P. K. Nair. "Multicommodity Network Flows with Probabilistic Losses." *Management Science* (September 1982):1080.

Bazaraa, M. S., and J. J. Jarvis. *Linear Programming and Network Flows*. New York: Wiley, 1977.

Carpaneto, G., et al. "An Algorithm For the Bottleneck Traveling Salesman Problem." *Operations Research* (March–April 1984):380.

Crowder, H., and M. W. Padberg. "Solving Large-Scale Symmetric Traveling Salesman Problems to Optimality." *Management Science* (May 1980):495.

Glover, F., et al. "Improved Computer-Based Planning Techniques." *Interfaces* (August 1979):12.

Glover, R., and P. Talmey. "Modeling and Solution of Practical Management Problems through Netforms." *OMEGA* 6(1978):305.

Jarvis, J. J., and H. D. Ratliff. "Some Equivalent Objectives for Dynamic Network Flow Problems." *Management Science* (January 1982):106.

Kennington, J. L., and R. V. Helgason. *Algorithms for Network Programming*. New York: Wiley, 1980.

Klingman, D. "Finding Equivalent Network Formulations for Constrained Network Problems." *Management Science* (March 1977):737.

Phillips, D. T., and A. Garcia-Diaz. *Fundamentals of Network Analysis*. Englewood Cliffs, NJ: Prentice-Hall, 1981.

Accounting and Finance Applications

Fitzsimmons, J. A., and L. A. Allen. "A Warehouse Location Model Helps Texas Comptroller Select Out-of-State Audit Offices." *Interfaces* (October 1983):40.

Kennington, J. L. "A Survey of Linear Cost Multicommodity Network Flows." *Operations Research* (March–April 1978):209.

Srinivasan, V., and Y. H. Kim. "Payments in International Cash Management: A Network Optimization Approach." *Journal of International Business Studies* (Summer 1986):1.

Marketing Applications

Ball, M. O., et al. "Planning for Truck Fleet Size in the Presence of a Common-Carrier Option." *Decision Sciences* (January 1983):103.

DaGanzo, C. F. "The Break-Bulk Role of Terminals In Many-to-Many Logistic Networks." *Operations Research* (July–August 1987):543.

Glover, F., et al. "The Passenger-Mix Problem in the Scheduled Airlines." *Interfaces* (June 1982):73.

Klingman, D. et al., "The Challenges and Success Factors in Implementing an Integrated Products Planning System for Citgo." *Interfaces* (May–June 1986): 1–19.

Kolen, A. W. J. "Vehicle Routing With Time Windows." *Operations Research* (March–April 1987):266.

Schultz, H. K. "A Practical Method for Vehicle Scheduling." *Interfaces* (May 1979):13.

Slater, P. J. "On Locating a Facility to Service Areas Within a Network." *Operations Research* (May–June 1981):523.

Production and Operations Applications

Fishman, G. S. "The Distribution of Maximum Flow With Applications to Multistate Reliability Systems." *Operations Research* (July–August 1987):607.

Glover, F., et al. "An Integrated Production, Distribution, and Inventory Planning System." *Interfaces* (November 1979):21.

Magirou, V. F. "The Efficient Drilling of Printed Circuit Boards." *Interfaces* (July–August 1986):13.

Paul, R. J. "A Production Scheduling Problem in the Glass-Container Industry." *Operations Research* (March–April 1979):290.

Schilling, D. A. "Strategic Facility Planning: The Analysis of Options." *Decision Sciences* (January 1982):1.

Shapiro, M. "Scheduling Crewmen for Recurrent Training." *Interfaces* (June 1981):1.

Public and Service Sector Applications

Brodin, I. D., and S. J. Kursh. "A Computer-Assisted System for Routing and Scheduling of Street Sweepers." *Operations Research* (July–August 1978):525.

Fisher, M. L., and R. Jaikumar. "An Algorithm for the Space-Shuttle Scheduling Problem." *Operations Research* (January–February 1978):166.

Rosenthal, R. E. "A Nonlinear Network Flow Algorithm for Maximization of Benefits in a Hydroelectric Power System." *Operations Research* (July–August 1981):763.

Case: General Parcel Service

General Parcel Service (GPS) has been incorporated as a firm specializing in the national delivery of small packages. The service will link major cities with a variety of air and truck routes. Initially, the company will have to design appropriate delivery linkages and identify preferable routes within the design.

Table 12.12   **GPS Fact Sheet**

From	To				
	Boston	**New York**	**Philadelphia**	**Washington**	**Atlanta**
Boston	—	10	15	20	25
New York	10	—	5	3	18
Philadelphia	15	5	—	6	12
Washington	20	3	6	—	10
Atlanta	25	18	12	10	—
Chicago	27	12	14	20	17
Denver	30	25	32	28	34
Dallas	24	20	27	18	12
Seattle	32	30	40	35	50
San Francisco	28	21	24	20	30
Los Angeles	26	21	24	22	20

From	To				
	Chicago	**Denver**	**Dallas**	**Seattle**	**San Francisco**	**Los Angeles**
Boston	27	30	24	32	28	26
New York	12	25	20	30	21	21
Philadelphia	14	32	27	40	24	24
Washington	20	28	18	35	20	22
Atlanta	17	34	12	50	30	20
Chicago	—	16	14	21	18	15
Denver	16	—	18	13	9	11
Dallas	14	18	—	25	14	10
Seattle	21	13	25	—	10	13
San Francisco	18	9	14	10	—	5
Los Angeles	15	11	10	13	5	—

In this respect, management has identified the major cities GPS intends to service and the potential linkages that can be utilized between these locations. The results of the examination are summarized in Table 12.12. The table entries represent delivery time in hours between locations. The delivery cost is $10 plus $12 per hour.

The company intends to have two kinds of service. One service will start a courier from the headquarters in Atlanta, have the courier visit each GPS city only once, and then return the courier to the origin. The other service will send couriers between various sets of cities in GPS's delivery network.

To properly formulate corporate strategy, however, management needs the following information:

1. The delivery system layout that will minimize total travel time

2. The delivery system layout that will minimize total delivery cost

3. The least time-consuming routes from Atlanta to every other city in the selected layout

4. The least costly routes from Atlanta, New York, Chicago, and Los Angeles to every other city in the selected layout

5. The courier tour that minimizes total delivery time from Atlanta

6. The courier tour that minimizes total delivery cost from Atlanta

Prepare a report that provides the needed information in language that would be understandable to management.

Suppose that there are flow capacities in the selected layout. Explain how these constraints would affect the strategy.

Assume that some cities could serve as transfer points for the deliveries. Explain how such a possibility would affect the strategy.

PERT/CPM

Chapter Outline

Learning Objectives

- Understand the nature of CPM, PERT/TIME, and PERT/COST.
- Depict a project management problem with networks.
- Use PERT/CPM to plan and schedule projects by hand and with the aid of a computer.
- Control the time and cost aspects of projects by hand and with the aid of a computer.
- Measure and analyze uncertainty in project management.

Cultivating China's Sweet Tooth

BEFORE 1980, the annual production was not large at a government-run sugar factory in northwest China. Under these conditions, the factory was capable of crushing all supplied sugar beets and still having abundant time to carry out necessary plant maintenance and service. After 1980, however, favorable pricing policies led to a doubling of beet production. As a result, management found it difficult to finish maintenance and service work on schedule.

The maintenance and service work delay was costing the plant about $25,000 per day in lost sugar production. Consequently, the government sent a team of experts to study the problem and recommend a solution. The team recognized that the maintenance and service work could be represented as a CPM network. Moreover, by using CPM techniques, the team determined a work plan, including a redeployment of labor, that would enable the plant to complete the service work in nearly half of the time anticipated by factory management.

Several benefits were derived from the effort. First, the CPM-generated work plan helped the factory to avoid most of the $25,000 per day penalty from lost production. In addition, the success of the project encouraged management to form a permanent study group. The work of this group resulted in a "blueprint" network diagram that was used to plan the factory's annual maintenance and service work.

Source: C. Dequan et al., "Popularization of Management Science in China," *Interfaces* (March–April 1986):2–9.

Large-scale projects consist of numerous specific jobs that must be completed, some in parallel and others in sequence, by various individuals and groups. The projects may be recurring programs, such as maintenance, or large, one-time efforts, like highway construction. In either case, the manager must plan, schedule, and control the jobs so that the entire project is completed on time. When there is a large number of interrelated tasks, timing and coordination become very complex. In these circumstances, network analysis can aid the decision maker in carrying out his or her project management responsibilities. China's sugar factory vignette offers a case in point.

This chapter presents widely used project management tools. The first section introduces the Critical Path Method (CPM). We develop a CPM network, estimate the project duration, and establish a complete activity schedule. Next, we see how the information can be used to manage the time aspects of the project. Then, we discuss the time/cost trade-off and develop a plan for expediting the project.

The last two sections examine the Program Evaluation and Review Technique (PERT). Section 13.2 presents the PERT/TIME methodology. We develop a PERT network, derive time estimates for the project tasks, and show how to incorporate uncertainty into the time-management process. Section 13.3 introduces the PERT/COST extension to the original analysis. We discuss PERT/COST budgeting and then show how the information is used to control project costs.

Although CPM and PERT were developed concurrently and independently, the original methodologies had the same general purpose and used surprisingly similar terminology, notation, and structures. The original version of CPM and PERT, however, had two major differences. First, CPM treated each task's duration as a known (deterministic) value, while PERT used probabilistic time estimates. Second, PERT restricted its attention to time management, whereas CPM was designed to help manage both project time and project cost (especially the time/cost trade-offs).

Contemporary project directors recognize the importance of both time and cost management. As a result, the recent trend has been to merge the two original methodologies into a comprehensive PERT/CPM analysis. In today's usage, then, a complete project analysis combines the essential features of both CPM and PERT.

Applications. In this chapter, the following applications appear in text, examples, and exercises:

- bank expansion
- book publishing
- building a space shuttle
- community theater
- county elections
- defense contracting
- furniture upholstery
- mail order sales
- management training
- marketing research
- monitoring student progress

- office construction
- personnel selections
- planning a convention
- planning an advertising campaign
- plant location
- preparing for exams
- producing a motion picture
- producing minicomputers
- research and development
- selecting a university
- subway maintenance

13.1 CPM

Prior to the 1950s, organizations often used a **Gantt chart** (named after its inventor) to help schedule projects. This chart shows planned and actual progress for the project's tasks displayed with bars against a horizontal time scale. Such a chart shows, at a glance, when a task will be (has been or is being) worked on, but it does not adequately illustrate the interrelationships between the activities.

Unable to manage projects effectively with Gantt charts, J. E. Kelly of Remington Rand and M. R. Walker of DuPont developed in 1957 a network approach called the **Critical Path Method (CPM)** to assist in the building and maintenance of chemical plants. This method helped management to determine the detailed activities involved in a project, plan start and completion times for each activity, schedule resources over the project's life, and monitor and control time and cost performance for the project. Its essential features are illustrated in Management Situation 13.1.

Mail Order Sales

The Mail Order Advertising Company is preparing its new catalog. Based on past experience, management knows that several jobs must be completed in the process. By processing historical data through its computer information system (CIS), management has determined the times needed to complete each job.

First, the company must make a list of criteria for identifying qualified buyers. Such a task, which is expected to take one week, must be completed before Mail Order can select the items for the catalog (an estimated four-week task) and select qualified buyers from a grand list (an estimated five-week process). The item and buyer selection activities can be performed concurrently, but each of these tasks must be completed before the company can design a layout for the catalog (an expected seven-week activity). Buyers also must be selected before mailing labels can be made (an expected two-week process). While the labels are being made, the layout goes to the printer, and three weeks later, the unlabeled catalog is complete. Afterwards, address labels must be affixed to the catalogs. This final task is expected to take one week.

Management wants to know how far in advance it must prepare for the mailing. It also seeks the schedule that must be followed to meet the planned deadline and the critical tasks in this schedule.

Project Network

The Critical Path Method uses a network to graphically portray the project. In developing this network, management first must determine all project **activities**, or the specific tasks that use financial and/or physical resources and require time to complete. These activities are usually depicted as nodes in a CPM network. Next, the decision maker must estimate the time needed to complete each activity and identify the order in which the activities must be performed. Typically, the activity times are shown inside the corresponding nodes, and the activity relationships are denoted with the network branches. Since incorrect activity relationships and inaccurate time estimates will lead to unsuccessful project management, this network development process is a key step in the analysis.

Activities. In Mail Order's case, the project is to prepare a new catalog. This project will require only seven activities, which can be denoted as

A = listing criteria

B = selecting catalog items

C = selecting buyers

D = designing the layout

E = making address labels

F = printing the layout

and G = affixing labels.

Activity Times. Mail Order's management experience and CIS processing provide the information needed to make an accurate single (deterministic) estimate for each activity. According to this information, it will take

- 1 week to list the criteria (A)
- 4 weeks to select catalog items (B)
- 5 weeks to select buyers (C)
- 7 weeks to design the layout (D)
- 2 weeks to make address labels (E)
- 3 weeks to print the unlabeled catalog (F)
- and 1 week to affix the labels (G).

Precedence Relationships. In the Mail Order project, activity A (listing criteria) must immediately precede both activity B (selecting catalog items) and activity C (selecting buyers). Moreover, activity B and activity C (selecting buyers) both must immediately precede activity D (designing the layout). Activity C also must immediately precede activity E (making address labels), while D is an immediate predecessor of activity F (printing the unlabeled catalog). Finally, activities E and F both must immediately precede activity G (affixing labels).

Management can show these activity interrelationships by drawing directed branches from predecessor to successor nodes, as in Figure 13.1. For example, this figure shows directed branches leading from node A to both nodes B and C because activity A immediately precedes both activities B and C in Mail Order's project network. Similarly, there are directed branches from both nodes B and C to node D because activities B and C are immediate predecessors of activity D.

AON Format. In Figure 13.1, activities are shown inside the nodes, and the activity times are shown below the corresponding tasks. Such a diagram, which shows the project activities on the nodes and the precedence relationships with directed branches, is known as an **activity-on-node (AON) network**. It provides a clear, concise, detailed definition (model) of the mail order sales project.

Activity Schedule

Two primary project management objectives are to determine: (1) the time needed to complete the entire project and (2) the schedule that must be followed to meet the planned deadline. The CPM provides some of this information by successively moving forward from the start (source node) through other activities to the end (sink node) of the project network. Then the remaining schedule is obtained by successively moving backward from the sink to the source node of the project network.

Forward Pass. Mail Order's first activity (A = listing criteria) cannot begin earlier than the start of the project, which we will arbitrarily label as week zero. The earliest date a project activity may begin is called an **earliest start time**. Since the listing of criteria will take one week, activity A cannot be finished earlier than

$$0 + 1 = 1 \text{ week}$$

Figure 13.1   **Mail Order's Project Network**

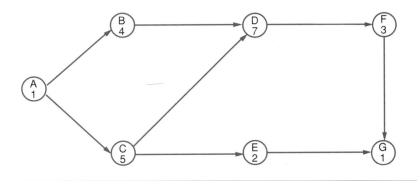

into the project. The earliest date a project activity may be completed is known as an **earliest finish time**.

Notice that the earliest finish time equals the earliest start time plus the expected activity duration, or

(13.1) $EF = ES + t$

where EF = the earliest finish time, ES = the earliest start time, and t = the expected time for an activity. If management knows each earliest start time and each activity time, this formula can be used to find the earliest finish time for all activities in the network.

Although an activity's ES value is not always evident, it can be found in a relatively straightforward manner. When there is a single predecessor, the earliest start time for an activity equals the earliest finish time of the immediately preceding task. Activities B (selecting catalog items) and C (selecting buyers) offer examples. Figure 13.1 shows that activity A is the single immediate predecessor of both activities B and C, and Mail Order already knows that activity A has an earliest finish time of $EF = 1$ week. Activities B and C, then, each have an earliest start time of one week.

When there are two or more immediate predecessors, an activity cannot start until all immediately preceding tasks are complete. For example, Figure 13.1 shows that both activities B and C are the immediate predecessors of activity D (the layout design). Activity B has an earliest start time of $ES = 1$ week and an expected duration of $t = 4$ weeks, while activity C has an $ES = 1$ week and a $t = 5$ weeks. According to formula 13.1, then, the earliest finish time is

$$EF = ES + t = 1 + 4 = 5 \text{ weeks}$$

for activity B and

$$EF = ES + t = 1 + 5 = 6 \text{ weeks}$$

for activity C. Since layout design (activity D) cannot start until both immediate predecessors (activities B and C) have been completed, the earliest start time for activity D is six weeks into the project.

Such an analysis suggests that the following general rule can be used to find the earliest start time for any activity in the project network:

> An activity's earliest start time (ES) equals the largest value of the earliest finish times for the immediately preceding activities.

By using this rule and formula 13.1 to make a **forward pass** (successively move forward from the source to the sink node) through Figure 13.1, management will get the ES and EF for each activity in Mail Order's project network. Figure 13.2 presents the results, with the ES shown as the first number and the EF as the second number in a parenthesis above the corresponding activity (node) in the network.

In Figure 13.2, the earliest finish time for the final project activity G (affixing labels) represents the expected project completion date. It shows that Mail Order can prepare its new catalog in as little as 17 weeks if each activity begins at its earliest start time (ES) and consumes only the expected activity duration (t). Circumstances, however, can delay the start or finish of any activity. As a result, it is also important to know the latest time that each activity could begin and end without extending the projection completion date.

Backward Pass. Mail Order cannot prepare its new catalog on schedule unless activity G (affixing labels) is completed within 17 weeks. The latest date an activity may be completed without delaying the entire project is called a **latest finish time**. Since affixing labels will take one week, activity G cannot be started later than

$$17 - 1 = 16 \text{ weeks}$$

into the project. Such a starting date, which gives the latest time when an activity may begin without delaying the entire project, is known as a **latest start time**.

Notice that the latest start time equals the latest finish time minus the expected activity duration, or

(13.2) $LS = LF - t.$

where LF = the latest finish time, LS = the latest start time, and t = the expected time for an activity. If management knows each latest finish time and each activity time, this formula can be used to find the latest start time (LS) for all activities in the network.

Although an activity's LF value is not always evident, it can be found in a relatively straightforward manner. When there is a single immediate successor, the LF for an activity equals the LS of the immediately following task. Activities E (making address labels) and F (the printing of the layout) offer examples. Figure 13.2 shows that activity G is the single immediate successor of both activities E and F, and Mail Order already knows that activity G has a latest start time of $LS = 16$ weeks. As a result, activities E and F each have a latest finish time of 16 weeks.

When there are two or more immediate successors, an activity must finish before the next tasks begin. For example, Figure 13.1 shows that both activities D and E are the immediate successors of activity C. Moreover, activity D has a single immediate successor (activity F). Activity E has an earliest finish time of $EF = 16$ weeks and an expected duration of $t = 2$ weeks, while activity F has an $EF = 16$ weeks and a $t = 3$ weeks. According to formula 13.2, then, the latest start time is

---

Figure 13.2   Mail Order's Earliest Start and Finish Times

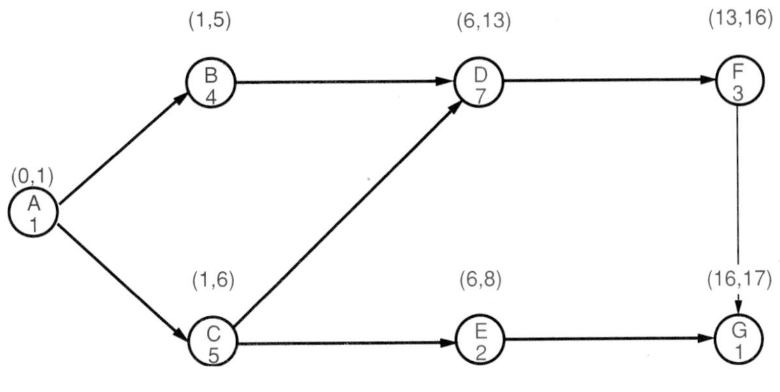

$$LS = LF - t = 16 - 2 = 14 \text{ weeks}$$

for activity E and

$$LS = LF - t = 16 - 3 = 13 \text{ weeks}$$

for activity F. Activity D has a latest finish time of $LF = 13$ weeks (the latest start time for its single immediate successor activity F) and an expected duration of $t = 7$ weeks. Consequently, the latest start time is

$$LS = LF - t = 13 - 7 = 6 \text{ weeks}$$

for activity D. Since the selection of buyers (activity C) must finish before both immediate successors (activities D and E) can begin, the latest finish time for activity C is six weeks into the project.

Such an analysis suggests that the following general rule can be used to find the latest finish time for any activity in the project network:

> An activity's latest finish time (*LF*) equals the smallest value of the latest start times for the immediately following activities.

By using this rule and formula 13.2 to make a **backward pass** (successively move backward from the sink to the source node) through Figure 13.2, management will get the *LS* and *LF* for each activity in Mail Order's project network. Figure 13.3 presents the results (superimposed on Figure 13.2), with the *LS* shown as the first number and the *LF* as the second number in a bracket below the corresponding activity (node) in the network. The latest time estimates assume that each activity begins at its latest start time and consumes only the expected activity duration.

Complete Schedule. Figure 13.3 indicates that Mail Order can prepare its new catalog in 17 weeks by following the detailed schedule given in Table 13.1 (which also displays other pertinent project information). This table, for example, indicates that Mail Order

---

Figure 13.3   Mail Order's Complete Activity Schedule

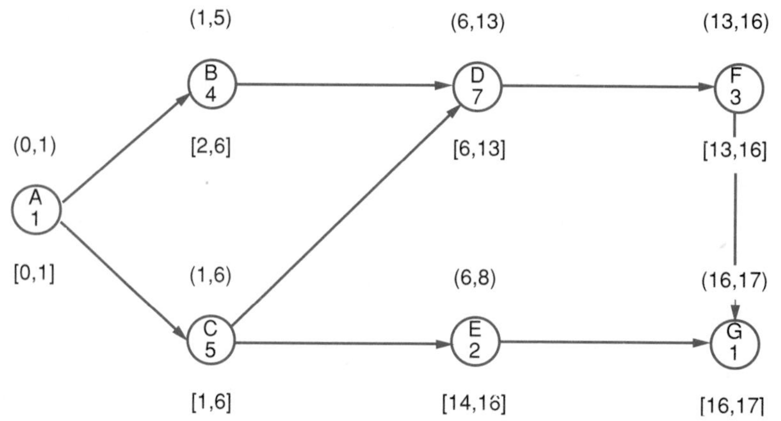

may start making address labels (activity E) as early as $ES = 6$ weeks but no later than $LS = 14$ weeks into the project. Such an activity may be finished as early as $EF = 8$ weeks but no later than $LF = 16$ weeks into the project.

Critical Path

To properly manage the project, the decision maker must determine the critical tasks in the activity schedule. These tasks can be identified by computing the slack associated with each project activity.

Slack. A project will not be completed on schedule unless each activity begins no later than its latest start time, but an activity may begin as soon as its earliest start time. The difference between LS and ES, then, tells management how long an activity may be delayed without extending the project completion date. This difference (or the equivalent difference between LF and EF) is referred to as **activity slack**, and it can be represented by the following formula:

(13.3) $$ASL = LS - ES = LF - EF$$

where ASL = activity slack and the other terms are defined as before.

Table 13.1 computes the slack associated with each activity in Mail Order's project. These calculations, for example, show that activity B has a slack of

$$ASL = LS - ES = 2 - 1 = 1$$

week. This slack tells management that Mail Order can delay the selection of catalog items (activity B) for up to one week (start anytime between weeks 1 and 2) without extending the project beyond 17 weeks.

Table 13.1   **Activity Schedule in Weeks for Mail Order's Project**

Activity	Earliest Start ES	Latest Start LS	Earliest Finish EF	Latest Finish LF	Slack $(LS-ES)$ or $(LF-EF)$	Critical Activity
A	0	0	1	1	0	Yes
B	1	2	5	6	1	No
C	1	1	6	6	0	Yes
D	6	6	13	13	0	Yes
E	6	14	8	16	8	No
F	13	13	16	16	0	Yes
G	16	16	17	17	0	Yes

Critical Activities. When an activity has a positive slack $(ASL > 0)$, it is not critical for the task to begin by its earliest start time or to end by its earliest finish time. Instead, such an activity can be delayed by an amount of time up to the slack without extending the entire project. Table 13.1 shows that activities B and E each have some slack and are thereby noncritical tasks for Mail Order's project.

According to Table 13.1, there is no slack associated with activities A, C, D, F, and G. If the entire project is to be completed within 17 weeks, then, each of these activities must begin by its latest start time $(LS = ES)$ and end by its latest finish time $(LF = EF)$. Such tasks, which must be started and finished without delay (having zero activity slack), are called **critical activities**.

Critical Sequence. The sequence of critical activities that leads from the source to the sink node in the project network is referred to as the **critical path**. In Mail Order's case, the critical path is

$$A \rightarrow C \rightarrow D \rightarrow F \rightarrow G$$

The time it takes to traverse (the sum of Figure 13.3's activity times on) this path,

$$1 + 5 + 7 + 3 + 1 = 17$$

weeks, represents the expected project duration. A delay in any of these tasks will extend the project completion date. Consequently, tasks on the critical path (critical activities) deserve careful monitoring and control.

Procedure Recap. The project schedule and critical path may be found using the following procedure:

1. Develop a network that describes the project activities and their interrelationships.
2. Establish the earliest start (ES) and earliest finish (EF) times for each activity by making a forward pass through the project network. The earliest finish time for the final activity (sink node) in the network is the expected project completion date.

Figure 13.4   **CPM Time/Cost Relationship**

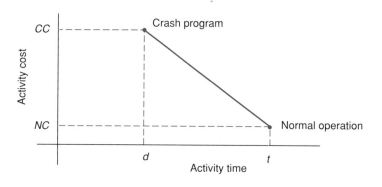

3. Establish the latest start (*LS*) and latest finish (*LF*) times for each activity by making a backward pass through the network.
4. Compute the slack ($ASL = LS - ES = LF - EF$) associated with each activity. Critical activities are tasks with zero slack, and the critical path is the sequence of critical activities that leads from the source to the sink node in the network.

Crashing

Contract penalties and bonuses, emergencies, and organizational requirements (such as the need to free resources for other projects or the desire to reduce facility and personnel costs on the project) may force the decision maker to move up the project completion date. **Crashing**, or adding resources (such as employing more efficient equipment or using overtime) to reduce activity times, is the method typically used to speed up the project. Since additional resources increase expenses, project management then must consider the trade-off between the reduced activity time and the extra cost.

The CPM customarily assumes that the increase in cost is proportional (has a linear relationship) to the reduction in task duration. By letting

NC = the normal activity cost

CC = the cost when the activity is crashed as much as possible

t = the normal or expected activity time

d = the duration when the activity is crashed as much as possible

the time/cost relationship will be as shown in Figure 13.4. If the decision maker knows the exact values for each activity's normal and crash times and costs (as CPM assumes), the unit crash cost can be computed with the following formula:

(13.4) $c = (CC - NC)/(t - d)$

where c = an activity's crash cost per time period. This cost information and the project schedule then can be used to establish a crashing plan, as Management Situation 13.2 illustrates.

Table 13.2   **Mail Order's Normal and Crash Activity Report**

Activity	Time (Weeks)			Cost ($)		
	Normal t	Crash d	Maximum Crash $t-d$	Crash CC	Normal NC	Crash per Week $c=(CC-NC)/(t-d)$
A	1	1	0	400	400	Cannot crash
B	4	2	2	2,850	1,770	540
C	5	4	1	2,500	2,150	350
D	7	5.5	1.5	9,800	7,700	1,400
E	2	2	0	650	650	Cannot crash
F	3	1.6	1.4	8,200	6,800	1,000
G	1	1	0	330	330	Cannot crash
				24,730	19,800	

Management Situation 13.2

Expediting the Catalog

To take advantage of the upcoming shopping season, Mail Order must have its new catalog within 15 weeks (rather than the 17 weeks projected in Figure 13.3). Management has prepared for such a contingency by identifying resources within and outside the organization that could be used to expedite the project. By processing the resource data through an accounting model within the company's computer information system (CIS), it has developed the report shown in Table 13.2. Management seeks the plan that will minimize the cost of crashing the catalog project by the two weeks needed to take advantage of the shopping season.

According to Table 13.2, it will cost $19,800 to prepare Mail Order's new catalog by the expected 17-week project completion date. This table also suggests that Mail Order can reduce the project's normal duration by crashing every task except activities A, E, and G, which simply cannot be crashed. Table 13.2, however, does not identify which activities to crash or how much they should be crashed.

An extreme plan is to crash all activities and (as Table 13.2 shows) incur a project cost of $24,730. This all-crashing plan will enable Mail Order to reduce the catalog preparation time as much as possible, but it will also generate the most costly schedule. There are less expensive approaches to crashing, including a heuristic search method that compresses the project duration by incrementally expediting uncrashed critical activities.

Heuristic Search. Mail Order seeks the least costly plan for crashing the catalog project by two weeks (from the normal 17 weeks to 15 weeks). Since reductions in noncritical activities will not shorten the project duration, the critical activites (A, C, D, F, and G) are the only potential candidates for crashing.

As Table 13.2 shows, the weekly crash costs for all critical activities that can be compressed are

Critical Activity	Crash Cost Per Week (c)
C	$350
D	$1,400
F	$1,000

Since critical activity C is the least expensive ($350 per week) alternative, management should crash this task by the maximum time of one week (the $t - d$ value in Table 13.2). Such an action will reduce Mail Order's project completion date by one week (from 17 to 16 weeks), increase the total project cost by $350 (from $19,800 to $20,150), and create an additional critical path of A → B → D → F → G.

Now that there are two critical paths (A → B → D → F → G and A → C → D → F → G), subsequent reductions in the project duration will require management to simultaneously shorten both paths. Table 13.2 shows that the weekly crash costs for all critical activities that still can be compressed on these two paths are

Critical Path	Critical Activity	Weekly Crash Cost (c)
A-B-D-F-G	B	$540
	D	$1,400
	F	$1,000
A-C-D-F-G	D	$1,400
	F	$1,000

At first glance, Mail Order may be tempted to shorten activity B, which has the smallest remaining weekly crash cost. Since this activity is only on the first critical path, however, compressing B will force management to shorten either D or F on the second path. Otherwise, there will be no reduction in the project duration. As a result, weekly cost will increase by either $540 + $1,400 = $1,940$ (if Mail Order compresses activity D on the second path) or $540 + $1,000 = $1,540$ (if management compresses F on the second path).

The least costly option is to compress only critical activity F by a week (out of the 1.4 week maximum crash value in Table 13.2). Since this activity is on *both* the first and second critical paths, such an action will shorten both paths (and thereby the project duration) from 16 weeks to the desired 15 weeks. It will also restrict the cost increment to a minimum of $1,000 (raising the total project cost from $20,150 to $21,150).

Optimal Crashing Plan. Since management has achieved its objective of shortening the project by two weeks, no further search is necessary. The analysis indicates that Mail Order can prepare its new catalog within the 15 weeks at a minimum total (normal plus crashing) cost of $21,150 by shortening

activity C by one week

and   activity F by one week.

Procedure Recap. The following heuristic search method can be used to find the optimal crashing plan:

1. Estimate regular and crash times and costs for each activity, and identify the desired project completion date.

2. Identify critical activities.

3. Compress critical activities incrementally, in order of increasing costs, until the project duration has been reduced to the desired date. When the crashing process creates multiple critical paths, simultaneously shorten all these paths.

CPM Extensions

For large projects, the manager often can determine the optimal crashing plan more efficiently with mathematical programming than with a heuristic search procedure. In the mathematical programming model, the objective is to minimize total crashing cost, subject to constraints on crash times and restrictions that define the precedence relationships between activities and that define the project deadline.

For example, Mail Order can crash activity B at a weekly cost of $540, C at a weekly cost of $350, D at a weekly cost of $1,400, and F at a weekly cost of $1,000. Since these activities have a linear relationship to expense, the company's total crashing cost will be

$$TC = \$540\, Y_B + \$350\, Y_C + \$1400\, Y_D + \$1000\, Y_F$$

where TC = total crashing cost and Y_B, Y_C, Y_D, and Y_F represent the number of weeks that Mail Order crashes activities B, C, D, and F, respectively. Management seeks the Y values that will minimize total crashing cost (TC).

Each activity cannot be crashed by more than its maximum crash time (given in Table 13.2 as 2 weeks for activity B, 1 week for C, 1.5 weeks for D, and 1.4 weeks for F). Hence, the inequalities

$$Y_B \leq 2 \qquad Y_C \leq 1 \qquad Y_D \leq 1.5 \qquad Y_F \leq 1.4$$

give one set of constraints on the objective. An additional constraint is that the final activity G must be completed no later than the project's crash deadline of 15 weeks, or

$$X_G \leq 15$$

where X_G = activity G's time of completion.

Another series of constraints describes the impact of the crash plan on the precedence relationships in the network. These constraints state that an activity's completion time must be greater than or equal to the activity's duration plus the completion times for all its immediate predecessors. Figure 13.3, for example, shows that activity D has a normal duration of seven weeks and is immediately preceded by activities B and C. After subtracting the crash time Y_D from the normal duration, these precedence relationships can be represented by the constraints

$$X_D \geq X_B + (7 - Y_D) \qquad \text{or} \qquad -X_B + X_D + Y_D \geq 7$$

and $\qquad X_D \geq X_C + (7 - Y_D) \qquad \text{or} \qquad -X_C + X_D + Y_D \geq 7$

where X_B, X_C, and X_D are the completion times for activities B, C, and D, respectively. Similarly,

$$X_A \geq 1 \qquad\qquad\qquad\qquad\qquad\qquad \text{for activity A}$$

$$X_B \geq X_A + (4 - Y_B) \quad \text{or} \quad -X_A + X_B + Y_B \geq 4 \qquad \text{for activity B}$$

$$X_C \geq X_A + (5 - Y_C) \quad \text{or} \quad -X_A + X_C + Y_C \geq 5 \qquad \text{for activity C}$$

$$X_E \geq X_C + 2 \qquad\quad \text{or} \qquad\quad -X_C + X_E \geq 2 \qquad\qquad \text{for activity E}$$

$$X_F \geq X_D + (3 - Y_F) \quad \text{or} \quad -X_D + X_F + Y_F \geq 3 \qquad \text{for activity F}$$

$$X_G \geq X_E + 1 \qquad\quad \text{or} \qquad\quad -X_E + X_G \geq 1 \qquad\qquad \text{for activity G}$$

$$X_G \geq X_F + 1 \qquad\quad \text{or} \qquad\quad -X_F + X_G \geq 1 \qquad\qquad \text{for activity G}$$

The variables X_A, X_E, and X_F denote the completion times for activities A, E, and F, respectively, while the other terms are defined as before.

Nonnegativity conditions for the activity completion times (X values) and crash variables (Y values) complete the linear program. If management solves this linear program, it will obtain the least-cost crashing plan (optimal Y values), the minimum total crashing cost (smallest TC value), and the activity schedule (X values) needed to achieve these results. Thought Exercise 8 will ask you to restate the complete linear program and develop the solution.

Postoptimality analysis will generate additional useful project information. For example, parametric programming will provide a function that relates the minimum crashing cost to the project length. Management then can use this function to help identify the project duration that will give the best trade-off between completion time and all costs, including contracted penalties, interest, and supervisor salaries.

Computer Analysis

There are numerous calculations involved in a CPM analysis, and these computations are cumbersome, time-consuming, and prone to error when done by hand. That is why more than 100 prewritten computer programs have been developed to perform the CPM calculations and report the results. One such program is available on the **Quantitative Management (QM)** software. It is accessed by selecting PERT/CPM from the software's main menu. Figure 13.5 then shows how the program is used for Mail Order's project management.

Problem Formulation. As Figure 13.5 demonstrates, the user executes the program by selecting the CPM option from the Project Management Analysis menu. The problem is formulated through the Edit command from the Input menu. This formulation requires the user to specify the number of activities (seven in Mail Order's case), the desired project length (15 weeks in Mail Order's crashing situation), and a complete project description. The description includes each activity's name, immediate predecessors, times, and costs and is entered in the table provided by the program. Report options then are selected through the Output menu.

Project Information. After receiving the project data, the program analyzes the information for illogical loops and other errors. If there are no errors, it performs the necessary CPM computations and reports the results. As the RECOMMENDATION section of

---

Figure 13.5   **Mail Order's CPM Computer Analysis**

Project Management Analysis:	Input:	Output:
* CPM	* Edit	▪ Full
▪ PERT/TIME	▪ Load	* Summary
▪ PERT/COST	▪ Print	* Print
	▪ Save	▪ Save

Problem Formulation:
  Number of Activities: 7
  Desired Project Length: 15

Enter the project data in the following table.

Activity	Name	Immediate Predecessors	Normal Time	Crash Time	Crash Cost	Normal Cost
1	A		1	1	400	400
2	B	A	4	2	2850	1770
3	C	A	5	4	2500	2150
4	D	B, C	7	5.5	9800	7700
5	E	C	2	2	650	650
6	F	D	3	1.6	8200	6800
7	G	E, F	1	1	330	330

RECOMMENDATION

Activity	Earliest Start ES	Latest Start LS	Earliest Finish EF	Latest Finish LF	Slack (LS−ES) or (LF−EF)	Critical Activity
A	0	0	1	1	0	Yes
B	1	1	5	5	0	Yes
C	1	1	5	5	0	Yes
D	5	5	12	12	0	Yes
E	5	12	7	14	7	No
F	12	12	14	14	0	Yes
G	14	14	15	15	0	Yes

Project Completion Date: 15
Total Project Cost: 21150

Figure 13.5 demonstrates, these results include a complete activity schedule (including slack times and critical activities), the project completion date, and the total project cost. This output indicates that Mail Order can prepare its new catalog in 15 weeks for a total cost of $21,150 by following the listed activity schedule. Every activity except E (making address labels) is critical in such a schedule.

13.2 PERT/TIME

In the late 1950s, the U.S. government was very concerned that the Soviet Union might gain nuclear superiority over the United States. The threat led the Department of Defense to accelerate the development of the Polaris missile. This project was huge, involving thousands of activities and resources. To better plan and control the project, the Navy's Special Projects Office, working with Lockheed Aircraft and the consulting firm of Booz, Allen, and Hamilton, developed a network approach in 1958 known as the **Program Evaluation and Review Technique (PERT)**. The technique was credited with cutting 18 months off the Polaris missile project length. Partly for that reason, PERT is now required on many large government programs.

Like CPM, PERT helps management to plan start and finish times and to monitor and control the project's time performance. Unlike CPM, PERT incorporates the role of uncertainty in the time management process. Management Situation 13.3 illustrates PERT.

Management Situation 13.3

Office Construction

Olan Builders, Inc. will construct a new and unique office building in Springtown for the State Travelers Insurance Company. The project will involve several activities; some can be done concurrently and others must be done in sequence. Based on previous knowledge and experience, Olan's management has identified the activities and the order in which they must be completed. Table 13.3 gives the relevant information.

Since the new office building will be unique, Olan's project manager, T. K. Trueblood, is uncertain about the activity durations. T. K. can make a best guess of the most likely time for each activity, and she also can estimate the times needed to complete each activity under ideal (optimistic) conditions and under the worst possible (pessimistic) circumstances. All three estimates are reported in Table 13.3.

State Travelers wants to know how long it will take to construct the office building. Olan's subcontractors must also know when to schedule each activity. In addition, Olan would like to know how long each activity can be put off without delaying the entire project.

Project Network

As in CPM, PERT uses a network to graphically portray the project. While the same notation can be used in both approaches, PERT usually employs a slightly different convention than CPM to construct the network. Figure 13.6 gives the PERT-type network for Olan's office construction project (Management Situation 13.3).

AOA Format. In PERT, each activity is depicted as a separate directed branch (arc with an arrowhead) in the network. The direction of the arrowheads identifies the precedence relationships among the activities. Nodes identify project milestones or **events**—points in time that mark the beginning and completion of project activities. These nodes are numbered in sequence to follow the order in which events must be achieved during the project.

Table 13.3   **Olan's Construction Data**

Activity	Description	Immediately Preceding Tasks	Optimistic a	Most Likely m	Pessimistic b
			Time Estimates (Days)		
A	Order structural materials	—	1	2	9
B	Obtain structural labor	—	2.5	4.5	9.5
C	Excavate	—	2	5	14
D	Pour foundation	C	4	6.5	18
E	Receive structural materials	A	2	4	18
F	Frame structure	B, D, E	22	30	50
G	Install plumbing	F	15	20	37
H	Install electrical facilites	F	4.5	10	21.5
I	Do interior finishing	G, H	12	15	24
J	Do exterior finishing	G	14	14.5	48
K	Do cleanup	I, J	5	5	5

In Figure 13.6, for example, node 1 represents the event that the project has started, while node 2 designates the event that Olan has completed ordering materials. Similarly, node 4 marks the event that activities E (receipt of materials), B (acquisition of labor), and D (pouring the foundation) have all been completed. It also depicts the fact that these activities (E, B, and D) must occur before Olan can start framing (activity F). Such a diagram, which shows the project activities as the directed branches and the events on the nodes, is referred to as an **activity-on-arrow** or **activity-on-arc (AOA) network**.

Dummy Activities. Since events (project milestones) are not explicitly identified in the activity-on-node (AON) format, an AOA network will be more descriptive than the corresponding AON network. Unlike the AON format, however, fictitious tasks, called **dummy activities**, often are needed to show the proper precedence relationships in an AOA network. Figure 13.6 offers an illustration.

Table 13.3 shows that Olan must install plumbing (complete activity G) before starting exterior finishing (activity J). Also, interior finishing (activity I) cannot be started until the subcontractors install plumbing (activity G) and electrical facilities (activity H). Activities I and J then have an immediate predecessor in common, activity G. Without a dummy activity, this situation would be shown incorrectly as Figure 13.7.

Figure 13.7 shows both activities G and H as immediately preceding J when, in fact, activity G is the only immediate predecessor of J. In this figure, the problem arises because activities G and H both have the same starting (node 5) and ending (node 6) events. The correct AOA network (Figure 13.6) avoids the difficulty by drawing a dummy activity (shown as the dashed directed branch) from node 6 to node 7. Such an action creates separate ending nodes for activities G and H, and the resulting branches and nodes properly show that only G must be completed before J can start and that activity I cannot begin until G and H are completed.

Figure 13.6   Olan's Office Project Network

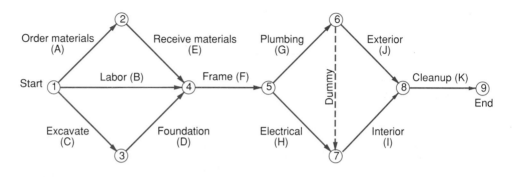

Figure 13.7   Incorrect PERT Network Segment

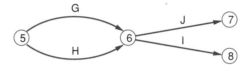

Activity Times

New or unique projects, by their nature, consist largely of novel component tasks. Under these circumstances, it is difficult to precisely estimate the duration of each task. Instead, an activity time is uncertain and perhaps best described with a range of values rather than with a single estimate.

The developers of PERT recognized the activity time uncertainty, and they studied methods for incorporating it into the analysis. In the process, they found that an activity's duration could be reasonably described by a form of the *beta probability distribution*. While the practice has been criticized on theoretical and empirical grounds, this probability distribution still is commonly used to depict the variability in activity time estimates.

Beta Distribution. Figure 13.8 presents a beta probability distribution of the activity times for a particular task. Project management defines the distribution by providing three time estimates. The **optimistic time** (denoted by a) is the time required to complete an activity when the work progresses exceptionally well. Since a is intended to be the shortest possible activity duration, it essentially sets the lower limit on the distribution. The maximum possible duration, or intended upper limit, is called the **pessimistic time** (denoted by b). It gives the time required to complete an activity when the work encounters significant delays or other adverse conditions. Both a and b are considered unlikely but possible times. In fact, the probability of completing the task in less than the optimistic time should not exceed 1 percent. Also, the project planner should be at least 99 percent confident of completing the activity within the pessimistic time. Hence, in about 98 percent of the cases, the activity's duration will be somewhere between the extremes (a and b). The **most likely time** (denoted by m) is intended to be the most

Figure 13.8 **A Beta Distribution for an Activity's Duration**

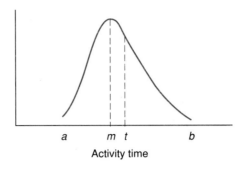

realistic estimate. It represents the time most frequently required to complete an activity under normal conditions.

The beta distribution has several features that make it attractive in practice. Finite limits are set by the optimistic (a) and pessimistic (b) time estimates. The distribution has a single mode with a high concentration of probability surrounding the most likely estimate (m). Its mean and variance can be readily obtained from the three time estimates (a, m, and b). Depending on the nature of the particular activity, the distribution can be symmetrical or skewed to either the right or the left.

Summary Statistics. Of special interest in project management are the mean and variance of each activity time. The mean or **expected activity time** (denoted by the t in Figure 13.8) is computed as a weighted average of the three time estimates with the following formula:

(13.5) $t = (a + 4m + b)/6$

This formula weights the most likely time (m) four times as much as either extreme (a or b). It generates an average (t) that can be equal to the most likely time m (when the distribution is symmetrical), above m (if the distribution is skewed right), or below m (when the distribution is skewed left).

Since the beta distribution has finite limits, all times for an activity must lie within the range ($b - a$). By assuming that this range encompasses six standard deviations of the distribution (which by analogy would include virtually all the area under a normal probability distribution), we find that the *variance (VAR)* of an activity's time is

$$(b - a) = 6\sqrt{VAR}$$

or

(13.6) $VAR = [(b - a)/6]^2$

This formula measures the variation or dispersion between the pessimistic (b) and optimistic (a) activity time estimates. It creates a value that reflects the degree of uncertainty associated with an activity's time. The larger the variance, the greater the uncertainty.

Table 13.4   Olan's Expected Activity Times and Variances

Activity	Expected Time (Days) t	Variances VAR
A	3	1.78
B	5	1.36
C	6	4
D	8	5.44
E	6	7.11
F	32	21.78
G	22	13.44
H	11	8.03
I	16	4
J	20	32.11
K	5	0
Total	134	

By substituting the data from Table 13.3 into equations 13.5 and 13.6, Olan will get the expected activity times and variances shown in Table 13.4. For example, this table shows that the expected time to frame the structure (activity F) is

$$t = (a + 4m + b)/6 = [22 + 4(30) + 50]/6 = 32$$

days. The corresponding variance is

$$VAR = [(b - a)/6]^2 = [(50 - 22)/6]^2 = 21.78$$

Since a dummy activity is fictitious (existing solely to establish proper precedence), it will have a zero completion time and thereby a $t = 0$ and a $VAR = 0$.

Project Management Uses. In PERT, the expected times (t values) are used to plan and schedule activities. Management estimates the probability of completing the project within specified schedules on the basis of the expected time and variance information.

Activity Schedule

Figure 13.9 shows Olan's activity-on-arc (AOA) network with the expected activity times written under the corresponding arcs. As in CPM, PERT establishes earliest start and earliest finish times by making a forward pass through the network (using the earliest start time rule and equation 13.1). Latest start and latest finish times again are found by making a backward pass (using equation 13.2 and the latest finish time rule).

Forward Pass. If Olan begins construction (event 1 in Figure 13.9) at day zero, ordering materials (activity A) will have an earliest start time of $ES = 0$. Since activity A has an expected duration of $t = 3$ days, its earliest finish time (according to equation 13.1) is

$$EF = ES + t = 0 + 3 = 3 \text{ days.}$$

Figure 13.9 **Olan's PERT Network with Expected Activity Times**

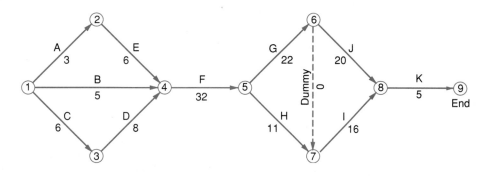

Figure 13.10 **Olan's Earliest Time Analyses**

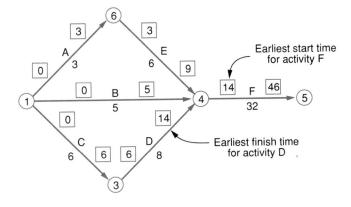

Similarly, the earliest finish time is

$$EF = ES + t = 0 + 6 = 6 \text{ days}$$

for obtaining labor (activity B) and

$$EF = ES + t = 0 + 6 = 6 \text{ days}$$

for excavating (activity C). Figure 13.10 illustrates these analyses, with each *ES* recorded in a box to the left and every *EF* given in a box to the right of the corresponding activity label.

As Figure 13.10 demonstrates, the completion of activity A (at an earliest finish time of three days) brings Olan to event 2 in the project. According to the earliest start time rule, this date (activity A's *EF* = 3) also marks the earliest start time for the immediate successor activity E (receiving materials). Since activity E has an expected duration of *t* = 6 days, its earliest finish time is

$$EF = ES + t = 3 + 6 = 9 \text{ days.}$$

Figure 13.11   Olan's Project Network with Earliest Start and Finish Times

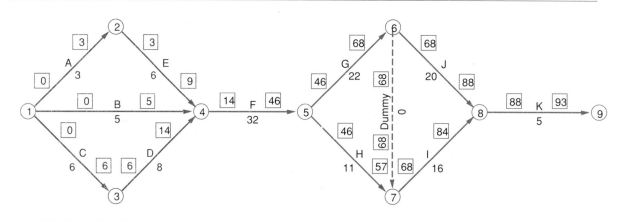

A similar analysis shows that finishing the foundation (activity D) has an $ES = 6$ days (the EF of its only immediate predecessor, C) and an

$$EF = ES + t = 6 + 8 = 14 \text{ days}$$

while framing (activity F) has an $ES = 14$ days (the largest EF of immediate predecessors E, B, and D) and an

$$EF = ES + t = 14 + 32 = 46 \text{ days.}$$

By completing the forward pass through the network (Figure 13.9), Olan will obtain the earliest start (ES) and earliest finish (EF) times for all project activities (including the dummy). Figure 13.11 presents the results, with each ES again recorded in a box to the left and every EF given in a box to the right of the corresponding activity label. The 93-day earliest finish time for the final activity K (cleanup) represents the expected project completion date.

Backward Pass. If Olan wants to complete the office building on schedule, activity K must have a latest finish time of $LF = 93$ days. Since this activity has an expected duration of $t = 5$ days, its latest start time (according to equation 13.2) is

$$LS = LF - t = 93 - 5 = 88 \text{ days.}$$

Figure 13.12 illustrates this analysis, with each LS recorded in a triangle to the left and every LF given in a triangle to the right of the corresponding expected activity time.

As Figure 13.12 demonstrates, the beginning of activity K (at a latest start time of 88 days) marks event 8 in the project. According to the latest finish time rule, this date (activity K's $LS = 88$) also represents the latest finish time for the immediate predecessor activities I (interior finishing) and J (exterior finishing). Since the expected duration is $t = 16$ days for I and $t = 20$ days for J, the latest start time is

$$LS = LF - t = 88 - 16 = 72 \text{ days}$$

Figure 13.12   **Olan's Project Network with Latest Start and Finish Times**

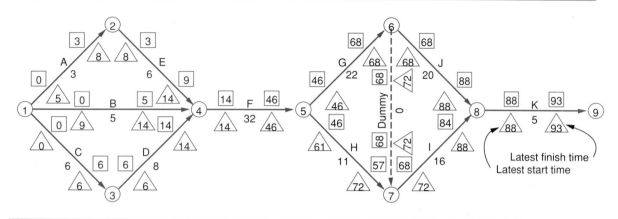

for activity I and

$$LS = LF - t = 88 - 20 = 68 \text{ days}$$

for activity J. Similarly, activity G (install plumbing) has a latest finish time of $LF =$ 68 days (the smallest LS for the immediate successors J and the dummy) and a

$$LS = LF - t = 68 - 22 = 46 \text{ days.}$$

By completing the backward pass through the network, Olan will get the rest of the LF and LS times shown in Figure 13.12 (which is superimposed on Figure 13.11). Once more, each LS is recorded in a triangle to the left and every LF is given in a triangle to the right of the corresponding expected activity time.

Complete Schedule. Figure 13.12 indicates that Olan can construct the office building within 93 days by following the detailed schedule presented in Table 13.5, which also displays other pertinent project information. This table, for example, shows that Olan may start receiving materials (activity E) as early as $ES = 3$ days but no later than $LS = 8$ days into the project. Such an activity may be finished as early as $EF = 9$ days but no later than $LF = 14$ days into the project.

Critical Path

PERT can use the same approach as CPM to determine the critical path through the project network. First, formula 13.3 is used to compute each activity's slack (ASL). The decision maker then identifies the sequence of critical activities (tasks with zero slack) that leads from the source to the sink node.

In Olan's case, formula 13.3 generates the slack information presented in Table 13.5. These calculations, for example, show that receiving materials (activity E) has a slack of

$$ASL = LS - ES = 8 - 3 = 5$$

Table 13.5   **Activity Schedule in Days for Olan's Project**

Activity	Earliest Start ES	Latest Start LS	Earliest Finish EF	Latest Finish LF	Slack (LS−ES or LF−EF)	Critical Activity
A	0	5	3	8	5	No
B	0	9	5	14	9	No
C	0	0	6	6	0	Yes
D	6	6	14	14	0	Yes
E	3	8	9	14	5	No
F	14	14	46	46	0	Yes
G	46	46	68	68	0	Yes
H	46	61	57	72	15	No
I	68	72	84	88	4	No
J	68	68	88	88	0	Yes
K	88	88	93	93	0	Yes

and thereby can be delayed for up to 5 days without extending the project completion date beyond 93 days.

Table 13.5 also shows that A, B, E, H, and I are noncritical activities (have positive slack), while C, D, F, G, J, and K are critical activities (have zero slack). The critical path then is

$$C \to D \to F \to G \to J \to K.$$

If office construction is to be completed within 93 days, Olan must ensure that activities on this path are initiated by their latest start times and completed by their latest finish times.

Project Duration Uncertainty

The preceding analysis presumes that it will take the expected (average) time t to complete each activity. Yet, as each activity's variance indicates, the actual time will vary from this expected value. As a result, Olan cannot be certain about the critical path or about the expected project duration. Indeed, there is a chance that the identified path may not be critical at all or that the project will still be unfinished by the expected project completion date.

Traditional PERT analysis assumes that variations in activity times will not invalidate the identified critical path. It then provides a methodology for measuring the project duration uncertainty.

Summary Statistics. Conventional PERT assumes that the activity times are independent. Under these circumstances, the expected (average) project duration will equal the sum of the critical activities' expected times, or

(13.7)
$$\mu = \sum_{j=1}^{k} t_j$$

Figure 13.13   **Normal Distribution for Olan's Project Duration**

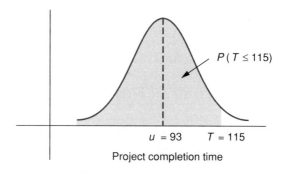

$$P(T \leq 115)$$

$$u = 93 \qquad T = 115$$

Project completion time

where μ = the expected project duration, t_j = the expected time for critical activity j, and k = the number of critical activities. Also, the variance of the project will equal the sum of the critical activities' variances, or

(13.8)
$$\sigma^2 = \sum_{j=1}^{k} VAR_j$$

where σ^2 = the variance of the project duration, VAR_j = the variance for critical activity j, and the other terms are defined as before. The corresponding standard deviation is the square root of the project duration variance or

$$\sigma = \sqrt{\sigma^2}$$

(which is *not* the same as the sum of the critical activities' standard deviations).

Olan's critical activities are C, D, F, G, J, and K. By substituting these activities' expected times and variances from Table 13.4 into equations 13.7 and 13.8, management will find that

$$\mu = t_C + t_D + t_F + t_G + t_J + t_K = 6 + 8 + 32 + 22 + 20 + 5 = 93$$

with a
$$\sigma^2 = VAR_C + VAR_D + VAR_F + VAR_G + VAR_J + VAR_K$$

$$= 4 + 5.44 + 21.78 + 13.44 + 32.11 + 0 = 76.77$$

and a
$$\sigma = \sqrt{\sigma^2} = \sqrt{76.77} = 8.76.$$

These summary statistics indicate that office construction will take an average of 93 days with a standard deviation of 8.76 days.

Normal Distribution. A sum of independent random variables will have an approximately **normal probability distribution** when the number of terms in the sum is large. Conventional PERT uses this statistical concept (known as the **central limit theorem**) to rationalize that a project's duration will follow a normal distribution with a mean (average) of μ and a standard deviation of σ.

Figure 13.13 presents a normal probability distribution for Olan's office project duration. Management defines the distribution by identifying the average duration μ and

Table 13.6 **Cumulative Probabilities for the Normal Distribution**

Z	−.09	−.08	−.07	−.06	−.05	−.04	−.03	−.02	−.01	.00
−3.80	.0001	.0001	.0001	.0001	.0001	.0001	.0001	.0001	.0001	.0001
−3.70	.0001	.0001	.0001	.0001	.0001	.0001	.0001	.0001	.0001	.0001
−3.60	.0001	.0001	.0001	.0001	.0001	.0001	.0001	.0001	.0002	.0002
−3.50	.0002	.0002	.0002	.0002	.0002	.0002	.0002	.0002	.0002	.0002
−3.40	.0002	.0003	.0003	.0003	.0003	.0003	.0003	.0003	.0003	.0003
−3.30	.0003	.0004	.0004	.0004	.0004	.0004	.0004	.0005	.0005	.0005
−3.20	.0005	.0005	.0005	.0006	.0006	.0006	.0006	.0006	.0007	.0007
−3.10	.0007	.0007	.0008	.0008	.0008	.0008	.0009	.0009	.0009	.0010
−3.00	.0010	.0010	.0011	.0011	.0011	.0012	.0012	.0013	.0013	.0013
−2.90	.0014	.0014	.0015	.0015	.0016	.0016	.0017	.0018	.0018	.0019
−2.80	.0019	.0020	.0021	.0021	.0022	.0023	.0023	.0024	.0025	.0026
−2.70	.0026	.0027	.0028	.0029	.0030	.0031	.0032	.0033	.0034	.0035
−2.60	.0036	.0037	.0038	.0039	.0040	.0041	.0043	.0044	.0045	.0047
−2.50	.0048	.0049	.0051	.0052	.0054	.0055	.0057	.0059	.0060	.0062
−2.40	.0064	.0066	.0068	.0069	.0071	.0073	.0075	.0078	.0080	.0082
−2.30	.0084	.0087	.0089	.0091	.0094	.0096	.0099	.0102	.0104	.0107
−2.20	.0110	.0113	.0116	.0119	.0122	.0125	.0129	.0132	.0136	.0139
−2.10	.0143	.0146	.0150	.0154	.0158	.0162	.0166	.0170	.0174	.0179
−2.00	.0183	.0188	.0192	.0197	.0202	.0207	.0212	.0217	.0222	.0228
−1.90	.0233	.0239	.0244	.0250	.0256	.0262	.0268	.0274	.0281	.0287
−1.80	.0294	.0301	.0307	.0314	.0322	.0329	.0336	.0344	.0351	.0359
−1.70	.0367	.0375	.0384	.0392	.0401	.0409	.0418	.0427	.0436	.0446
−1.60	.0455	.0465	.0475	.0485	.0495	.0505	.0516	.0526	.0537	.0548
−1.50	.0559	.0571	.0582	.0594	.0606	.0618	.0630	.0643	.0655	.0668
−1.40	.0681	.0694	.0708	.0721	.0735	.0749	.0764	.0778	.0793	.0808
−1.30	.0823	.0838	.0853	.0869	.0885	.0901	.0918	.0934	.0951	.0968
−1.20	.0985	.1003	.1020	.1038	.1056	.1075	.1093	.1112	.1131	.1151
−1.10	.1170	.1190	.1210	.1230	.1251	.1271	.1292	.1314	.1335	.1357
−1.00	.1379	.1401	.1423	.1446	.1469	.1492	.1515	.1539	.1562	.1587
−.80	.1611	.1635	.1660	.1685	.1711	.1736	.1762	.1788	.1814	.1841
−.80	.1867	.1894	.1922	.1949	.1977	.2005	.2033	.2061	.2090	.2119
−.70	.2148	.2177	.2206	.2236	.2266	.2296	.2327	.2358	.2389	.2420
−.60	.2451	.2483	.2514	.2546	.2578	.2611	.2643	.2676	.2709	.2743
−.50	.2776	.2810	.2843	.2877	.2912	.2946	.2981	.3015	.3050	.3085
−.40	.3121	.3156	.3192	.3228	.3264	.3300	.3336	.3372	.3409	.3446
−.30	.3483	.3520	.3557	.3594	.3632	.3669	.3707	.3745	.3783	.3821
−.20	.3859	.3897	.3936	.3974	.4013	.4052	.4090	.4129	.4168	.4207
−.10	.4247	.4286	.4325	.4364	.4404	.4443	.4483	.4522	.4562	.4602
−.00	.4641	.4681	.4721	.4761	.4801	.4840	.4880	.4920	.4960	.5000

Z	.00	.01	.02	.03	.04	.05	.06	.07	.08	.09
.00	.5000	.5040	.5080	.5120	.5160	.5199	.5239	.5279	.5319	.5359
.10	.5398	.5438	.5478	.5517	.5557	.5596	.5636	.5675	.5714	.5753
.20	.5793	.5832	.5871	.5910	.5948	.5987	.6026	.6064	.6103	.6141
.30	.6179	.6217	.6255	.6293	.6331	.6368	.6406	.6443	.6480	.6517
.40	.6554	.6591	.6628	.6664	.6700	.6736	.6772	.6808	.6844	.6879
.50	.6915	.6950	.6985	.7019	.7054	.7088	.7123	.7157	.7190	.7224
.60	.7257	.7291	.7324	.7357	.7389	.7422	.7454	.7486	.7517	.7549
.70	.7580	.7611	.7642	.7673	.7704	.7734	.7764	.7794	.7823	.7852
.80	.7881	.7910	.7939	.7967	.7995	.8023	.8051	.8078	.8106	.8133
.90	.8159	.8186	.8212	.8238	.8264	.8289	.8315	.8340	.8365	.8399
1.00	.8413	.8438	.8461	.8485	.8508	.8531	.8554	.8577	.8599	.8621
1.10	.8643	.8665	.8686	.8708	.8729	.8749	.8770	.8790	.8810	.8830
1.20	.8849	.8869	.8888	.8907	.8925	.8944	.8962	.8980	.8997	.9015
1.30	.9032	.9049	.9066	.9082	.9099	.9115	.9131	.9147	.9162	.9177
1.40	.9192	.9207	.9222	.9236	.9251	.9265	.9279	.9292	.9306	.9319
1.50	.9332	.9345	.9357	.9370	.9382	.9394	.9406	.9418	.9429	.9441
1.60	.9452	.9463	.9474	.9484	.9495	.9505	.9515	.9525	.9535	.9545
1.70	.9554	.9564	.9573	.9582	.9591	.9599	.9608	.9616	.9625	.9633
1.80	.9641	.9649	.9656	.9664	.9671	.9678	.9686	.9693	.9699	.9706
1.90	.9713	.9719	.9726	.9732	.9738	.9744	.9750	.9758	.9761	.9767
2.00	.9772	.9778	.9783	.9788	.9793	.9798	.9803	.9808	.9812	.9817
2.10	.9821	.9826	.9830	.9834	.9838	.9842	.9846	.9850	.9854	.9857
2.20	.9861	.9864	.9868	.9871	.9875	.9878	.9881	.9884	.9887	.9890
2.30	.9893	.9896	.9898	.9901	.9904	.9906	.9909	.9911	.9913	.9916
2.40	.9918	.9920	.9922	.9925	.9927	.9929	.9931	.9932	.9934	.9936
2.50	.9938	.9940	.9941	.9943	.9945	.9946	.9948	.9949	.9951	.9952
2.60	.9953	.9955	.9956	.9957	.9959	.9960	.9961	.9962	.9963	.9964
2.70	.9965	.9966	.9967	.9968	.9969	.9970	.9971	.9972	.9973	.9974
2.80	.9974	.9975	.9976	.9977	.9977	.9978	.9979	.9979	.9980	.9981
2.90	.9981	.9982	.9982	.9983	.9984	.9984	.9985	.9985	.9986	.9986
3.00	.9987	.9987	.9987	.9988	.9988	.9989	.9989	.9989	.9990	.9990
3.10	.9990	.9991	.9991	.9991	.9992	.9992	.9992	.9992	.9993	.9993
3.20	.9993	.9993	.9994	.9994	.9994	.9994	.9994	.9995	.9995	.9995
3.30	.9995	.9995	.9995	.9996	.9996	.9996	.9996	.9996	.9996	.9997
3.40	.9997	.9997	.9997	.9997	.9997	.9997	.9997	.9997	.9997	.9998
3.50	.9998	.9998	.9998	.9998	.9998	.9998	.9998	.9998	.9998	.9998
3.60	.9998	.9998	.9999	.9999	.9999	.9999	.9999	.9999	.9999	.9999
3.70	.9999	.9999	.9999	.9999	.9999	.9999	.9999	.9999	.9999	.9999
3.80	.9999	.9999	.9999	.9999	.9999	.9999	.9999	.9999	.9999	.9999

the standard deviation σ of the project completion time. The average duration ($\mu = 93$ days) is at the center of the distribution, and the variation (dispersion of the actual project duration) about this average is measured with the standard deviation of $\sigma = 8.76$ days.

Probability of Desired Completion Date. The standard score

$$(13.9) \qquad\qquad Z = (T - \mu)/\sigma$$

is employed to measure how many standard deviations (how many Z scores) a desired completion date T is from the expected (average) project duration. A cumulative standard normal distribution, such as Table 13.6, then is used to convert the Z score into the probability of meeting the desired completion date T.

For example, suppose that State Travelers allots 115 days for the construction project. This allotted time is

$$T - \mu = 115 - 93 = 22 \text{ days}$$

or $\qquad\qquad Z = (T - \mu)/\sigma = (115 - 93)/8.76 = 22/8.76 = 2.51$

standard deviations above the expected project completion date ($\mu = 93$ days). According to Table 13.6, a Z score of 2.51 converts into a cumulative probability of .9940 (which corresponds to the shaded region in Figure 13.13). Even with the project duration uncertainty, then, Olan has an excellent

$$P(T \le 115) = .9940$$

chance of meeting the 115-day deadline.

Procedure Recap. PERT/TIME analysis can be summarized as follows:

1. Develop the project network.
2. Estimate the optimistic (a), most likely (m), and pessimistic (b) task times, and use these estimates to calculate the expected time (t) and variance (VAR) for each activity.
3. Use the expected times to determine the activity schedule and the critical path through the network.
4. Find the expected project duration (μ) by summing the expected times for the critical activities, and determine the corresponding variance (σ^2) by summing the variances of the critical activities.
5. Compute the standard score (Z) associated with a desired project completion date (T), and find the corresponding probability from a cumulative standard normal distribution.

PERT/TIME Extensions

PERT/TIME analysis can identify other kinds of slack besides activity slack (ASL). One type involves events, and another deals with activities.

Each event in a project will have an earliest date (identified as the largest EF for all activities entering the node) and a latest date (identified as the smallest LS for all activities leaving the node). The difference between these earliest and latest dates is called **event slack**, and it can be calculated with the following formula:

$$ESL = LD - ED$$

where ESL = the slack, LD = the latest date, and ED = the earliest date for an event. Event slack tells management how long the event can be delayed without extending the project completion date.

Another type of slack measures **free slack**, or the amount of time an activity can be delayed without delaying the earliest start time of a succeeding activity in the network. It can be found with the following formula:

$$FSL = ASL - NESL$$

where FSL = an activity's free slack, $NESL$ = the event slack associated with the activity's ending node, and ASL is defined as before.

The PERT/TIME analysis assumes that the project paths are independent (that the same activities are not on more than one path). When the paths are very dependent (have many activities on multiple paths), management can use simulation (discussed in Chapter 17) to prepare a probability distribution of the project duration times. This distribution can be used to determine the probabilities of meeting desired project completion dates.

Computer Analysis

PERT/TIME requires many cumbersome and time-consuming computations that are prone to error when done by hand. More than 100 prewritten computer programs are available to perform these computations and report the results. One such program is available on the **Quantitative Management (QM)** software. It is accessed by selecting PERT/CPM from the software's main menu. Figure 13.14 then shows how the program is used for Olan's project management.

Problem Formulation. As Figure 13.14 demonstrates, the user executes the program by selecting the PERT/TIME option from the Project Management Analysis menu. The problem is formulated through the Edit option from the Input menu. This formulation requires the user to specify the number of activities (in Olan's case, 11 actual tasks plus 1 dummy for a total of 12), the number of events (9 in Olan's situation), the desired project completion date (115 days in Figure 13.14), and a complete project description. The description, which includes each activity's name, starting and ending nodes, and three time estimates, is entered in the table provided by the program. Report options then are selected through the Output menu.

Project Information. After receiving the project data, the program analyzes the information for illogical loops and other errors. If there are no errors, it computes the expected times and variances of each activity (which are shown in Full, but not Summary, Output mode) and performs the necessary PERT/TIME analysis. As the RECOMMENDATION section of Figure 13.14 shows, the report includes a complete activity schedule (includ-

---

Figure 13.14   Olan's PERT/TIME Computer Analysis

Project Management Analysis:	Input:	Output:
▪ CPM	* Edit	▪ Full
* PERT/TIME	▪ Load	* Summary
▪ PERT/COST	▪ Print	* Print
	▪ Save	* Save

PERT/TIME Output Filename: OLAN

Problem Formulation:
Number of Activities: 12
Number of Events: 9
Desired Project Length: 115

Enter the project data in the following table.

Activity	Name	Starting Node (Event)	Ending Node (Event)	Optimistic Time	Most Likely Time	Pessimistic Time
1	A	1	2	1	2	9
2	B	1	4	2.5	4.5	9.5
3	C	1	3	2	5	14
4	D	3	4	4	6.5	18
5	E	2	4	2	4	18
6	F	4	5	22	30	50
7	G	5	6	15	20	37
8	H	5	7	4.5	10	21.5
9	Dummy	6	7	0	0	0
10	I	7	8	12	15	24
11	J	6	8	14	14.5	48
12	K	8	9	5	5	5

RECOMMENDATION

Activity	Earliest Start ES	Latest Start LS	Earliest Finish EF	Latest Finish LF	Slack (LS−ES) or (LF−EF)	Critical Activity
A	0	5	3	8	5	No
B	0	9	5	14	9	No
C	0	0	6	6	0	Yes
D	6	6	14	14	0	Yes
E	3	8	9	14	5	No
F	14	14	46	46	0	Yes
G	46	46	68	68	0	Yes
H	46	61	57	72	15	No
I	68	72	84	88	4	No
J	68	68	88	88	0	Yes
K	88	88	93	93	0	Yes

Expected Project Completion Date: 93
Probability of Meeting Desired Project Completion Date: .9940

Table 13.7   **Olan's Activity Time and Cost Data**

Activity	Expected Time (Days)	Budgeted Cost ($)	Budgeted Cost per Day ($)
A	3	300	100
B	5	400	80
C	6	3,000	500
D	8	6,400	800
E	6	900	150
F	32	208,000	6,500
G	22	26,400	1,200
H	11	7,700	700
I	16	25,600	1,600
J	20	35,000	1,750
K	5	300	60
	Total project cost = 314,000		

ing slack times and critical activities), the expected project completion date, and the probability of meeting the desired completion date. This output indicates that the office construction has an expected duration of 93 days, and there is a 99.4 percent chance that the project will be completed within 115 days.

13.3 PERT/COST

Although CPM introduces some expenses into project analysis, the primary emphasis is still on time (rather than cost) management. Often, however, the program director wants to plan, schedule, and control project costs as well. Management usually establishes an initial budget that identifies all project costs and forecasts when expenses are expected to occur. At various stages of the project, the actual expenses can then be compared with the scheduled, or budgeted, costs. If there are discrepancies, corrective action may be taken to keep costs within the budget. PERT/COST is a system designed to assist project directors in this cost management process.

Budgeting

To help management plan and schedule expenses, PERT/COST develops a budget that will show when costs should occur during the project. This budget will be based on project components that are convenient for cost measurement and control. Sometimes, such components are **work packages**, or clusters of related activities under the control of one individual or group. At other times, activities are the basis for budgeting. Management Situation 13.4 illustrates.

Table 13.8   **Olan's Budgeted Costs ($) for an Earliest Start Schedule**

Activity	\multicolumn{13}{c}{Day}

Activity	1	2	3	4	5	6	7	8	9	...	90	91	92	93
A	100	100	100											
B	80	80	80	80	80									
C	500	500	500	500	500									
D						500	800	800	800					
E				150	150	150	150	150	150					
⋮														
K											60	60	60	60
Daily Cost	680	680	680	730	730	650	950	950	950	...	60	60	60	60
Total Project Cost	680	1,360	2,040	2,770	3,500	4,150	5,100	6,050	7,000	...	313,820	313,800	313,940	314,000

Management Situation 13.4

Office Construction Budgeting

This case is an extension of Management Situation 13.3. Olan wants to plan, schedule, and control construction expenses on the State Travelers office building on the basis of activity costs. These costs are reported in Table 13.7, along with the expected time for each activity.

Earliest Start Budget. Table 13.5 indicates that activity A has an earliest start time of $ES = 0$ days, while Table 13.7 shows that this activity has a budgeted cost of $300 and an expected duration of $t = 3$ days. Ordinarily, PERT/COST assumes that costs accrue at a constant and independent (linear) rate over the task's duration. Hence, Olan should expect activity A to cost $300/3 = $100 in each of the project's first three days. Similarly, since activity E has an $ES = 3$ days, $t = 6$ days, and a budgeted cost of $900, it will generate a cost of $900/6 = $150 in days 4 through 9 of the project.

By using the data from Tables 13.5 and 13.7 in a similar manner, Olan can develop the daily cost projection for each office construction activity. Table 13.8 gives a portion of this earliest start budget, with the sum of each column reporting the projected daily cost. Accumulating these daily expenses then provides an up-to-date total project cost schedule.

Latest Start Budget. Project management can also develop a schedule showing the budgeted costs when each activity begins at its latest start time (*LS*). For example, Table 13.5 shows that activity A has an $LS = 4$ days, while Table 13.7 indicates that this

Table 13.9 **Olan's Budgeted Costs ($) for a Latest Start Schedule**

Activity	1	2	3	4	5	6	7	8	9	10	...	89	90	91	92	93
											Day					
A						100	100	100								
B										80						
C	500	500	500	500	500											
D						500	800	800	800	800						
E									150	150						
⋮																
K												60	60	60	60	60
Daily Cost	500	500	500	500	500	600	900	900	950	1,030	...	60	60	60	60	60
Total Project Cost	500	1,000	1,500	2,000	2,500	3,100	4,000	4,900	5,850	6,880	...	313,760	313,820	313,880	313,940	314,000

Figure 13.15 **Olan's Possible Budgets for Total Project Costs**

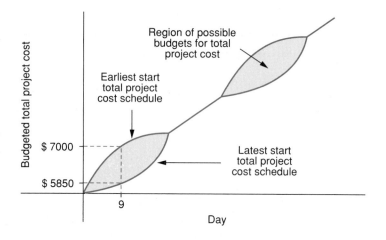

activity has an expected duration of $t = 3$ days and a budgeted cost of $300/3 = \$100$ per day. Consequently, activity A can be expected to show a $100 cost in days 5, 6, and 7 of the project. Table 13.9 presents a portion of the daily cost schedule that results from this type of analysis.

Range of Possible Budgets. If the project progresses on schedule, each activity will be initiated somewhere between its earliest and latest start times. Total project costs, then, should be between the earliest start budget schedule (Table 13.8) and the latest start budget schedule (Table 13.9), or in the shaded region of Figure 13.15 (which plots the total project costs from Tables 13.8 and 13.9 on the same graph).

Table 13.10   **Activity Data at the End of Day 15 for Olan's Project**

Activity	Actual Cost ($)	% Completion
A	350	100
B	400	100
C	2,800	100
D	6,000	90
E	600	80
F	22,000	10
G	0	0
H	0	0
I	0	0
J	0	0
K	0	0
Total actual cost = 32,350		

By the end of day 9, for example, the earliest start schedule (Table 13.8) generates an accumulated project cost of $7,000. At the same date, the latest start schedule (Table 13.9) results in a corresponding expense of $5,850. Thus, at day 9, Olan should expect total project costs to be between $5,850 and $7,000. Management can prepare an exact budget within this range by committing activities to specific starting times.

Controlling Costs

After establishing the budget cost schedules, project management next will want to record the actual expense as it occurs for each activity. Then the decision maker can obtain an up-to-date status report by periodically comparing actual costs with the corresponding budgeted expenses.

At any particular phase of the project, some activities will still be in progress or not even started. Before a cost status report can be developed, it will be necessary to compute the budgeted value for all currently completed work. This value will equal the proportion of work completed, multiplied by the budget or

(13.10) $$V = pB$$

where $V =$ the budgeted value of the completed work for the activity, $p =$ the proportion of the activity that is completed, and $B =$ the budget for the activity.

If actual costs exceed the budgeted value, there has been a cost overrun. When actual expenses are below the budgeted value, a cost underrun has occurred. By identifying the sources of cost overruns and underruns, project management can take appropriate corrective action where necessary. This might include changing the project scope, modifying quality standards, changing the sequence of activities, or reallocating resources among the activities.

Status Report. Suppose that Olan's project, at the end of its fifteenth day, has the actual cost and percent completion for each activity reported in Table 13.10. This information

Table 13.11   **Olan's Project Cost Status Report at Day 15**

Activity	Actual Cost ($)	Budgeted Value ($) $V=pB$	Difference ($)
A	350	300	50
B	400	400	0
C	2,800	3,000	−200
D	6,000	5,760	240
E	600	720	−120
F	22,000	20,800	1,200
G	0	0	0
H	0	0	0
I	0	0	0
J	0	0	0
K	0	0	0
Totals	32,350	30,980	1,170

indicates that activities A, B, and C have been completed, tasks D, E, and F are currently in progress, and activities G, H, I, J, and K have not yet begun.

By substituting each activity's budgeted cost from Table 13.7 and the corresponding percent completion from Table 13.10 into equation 13.10, Olan will get the budgeted values given in Table 13.11. For example, activity D has a budgeted cost of $B = \$6,400$ (from Table 13.7) and a percent completion of $p = .9$ at the end of day 15 (from Table 13.10). Consequently, the budgeted value of work completed for activity D is (according to equation 13.10)

$$V = pB = .9(\$6,400) = \$5,760$$

at the end of day 15. Since Table 13.11 compares all actual costs with the corresponding budgeted expenses, it represents a cost status report at day 15 for Olan's project.

Cost Control. Table 13.11 shows that actual expenses to date are $1,170 over the budgeted costs. On a percentage basis, we would say that the project is experiencing a $\$1,170/\$30,980 = .038$, or 3.8 percent, cost overrun. By checking each task, project management can see that activities A, D, and F are causing the problem. Since activity A has been completed, its cost overrun cannot be corrected. However, activities D and F are still in progress and thus should be reviewed immediately. By taking corrective action for these tasks now (at day 15), Olan can help bring actual costs closer to the budget. In addition, project management may want to consider the possibilities of reducing costs for yet-to-be-started activities (G, H, I, J, and K). Some hints may come from an examination of tasks (like C and E) that have been experiencing cost underruns, or savings.

Procedure Recap. The following procedure is used to perform a PERT/COST analysis:

1. Determine the earliest start and latest start budget schedules, and use these schedules to establish the range of possible budgets.
2. Develop a cost status report at selected stages of the project.
3. Use the cost status reports to identify activities that require corrective action.

Computer Analysis

Although PERT/COST can be an effective cost control system, the technique involves potential difficulties. First, the work package cost-recording system may require significant clerical effort, especially for firms with large and numerous projects. Second, there may be problems in measuring some costs (like overhead) and then properly allocating them to work packages. Third, PERT/COST requires a recording and control system that differs substantially from most organizationally oriented cost accounting procedures. Hence, many firms will have to modify procedures or carry a dual accounting system to handle the PERT/COST activity-oriented approach.

Furthermore, there are numerous calculations involved in performing a PERT/COST analysis. In practice, it will be difficult and time-consuming to perform the calculations by hand, and the process will be prone to error. Fortunately, prewritten computer programs are available to generate the necessary analysis. One such program is available on the **Quantitative Management (QM)** software. Figure 13.16 shows how Olan can use this program for project management.

Problem Formulation. As Figure 13.16 demonstrates, the user executes the program by selecting the PERT/COST command from the Project Management Analysis menu. The problem is formulated through the EDIT option from the Input menu. This formulation requires the user to specify the number of activities including dummy tasks (12 in Olan's project), a request for a status report (YES in Figure 13.16), and a budgeting description. The description, which is entered in the table provided by the program, includes each activity's name, earliest start and latest start times, duration (all of which, in Figure 13.16, are read from the PERT/TIME output file named "OLAN.OUT"), and budgeted cost. If a status report is requested, the user next must input the activities' actual costs and percent completions for each time period desired (only for day 15 in Figure 13.16). Report options then are selected through the Output menu.

Project Information. After receiving the project data, the program determines the budget schedules and gives the desired cost status reports. As the Budget Schedules in the RECOMMENDATION section of Figure 13.16 shows, the schedules report the earliest and latest start budgets (only on an aggregate or total cost basis in Summary Output mode) for each project period. The Status Report segment compares each activity's actual cost with the budgeted value at the specified time period in the project.

PERT/CPM Extensions

Over the years, many additional network techniques have been developed to provide project information not available from a traditional PERT/CPM analysis. Some of the most popular are CPM/MRP, Graphical Evaluation and Review Technique (GERT), and resource (load) leveling.

CPM/MRP. PERT/CPM assumes that resources are available in the right place, at the right time, and in the right amount. In practice, material has to be ordered in advance, and machinery has to be made available when necessary. Management can prepare a master project schedule, list all material requirements, and then use a material requirements planning (MRP) system (discussed in Chapter 14) for procuring the materials and

Figure 13.16   Olan's PERT/COST Computer Analysis

Project Management Analysis:	Input:	Output:
▪ CPM	* Edit	▪ Full
▪ PERT/TIME	* Load	* Summary
* PERT/COST	▪ Print	* Print
	▪ Save	▪ Save

Filename: OLAN.OUT

Problem Formulation:
  Number of activities: 12
  Do you want a cost status report (YES or NO): Yes
Enter the project data in the following table.

Activity	Name	Earliest Start Time	Latest Start Time	Duration	Cost
1	A	0	5	3	300
2	B	0	9	5	400
3	C	0	0	6	3000
4	D	6	6	8	6400
5	E	3	8	6	900
6	F	14	14	32	208000
7	G	46	46	22	26400
8	H	46	61	11	7700
9	Dummy	68	72	0	0
10	I	68	72	16	25600
11	J	68	68	20	35000
12	K	88	88	5	300

Status time period (enter NONE or a positive number): 15
Enter the activity data in the following table.

Activity	Actual Cost	Percent Completion
A	350	100
B	400	100
C	2800	100
D	6000	90
E	600	80
F	22000	10
G	0	0
H	0	0
I	0	0
J	0	0
K	0	0

RECOMMENDATION
Budget Schedules

	Period					
Budget	1	2	3	4	5	6
Earliest Start	680	1360	2040	2770	3500	4150
Latest Start	500	1000	1500	2000	2500	3100

Figure 13.16   *continuing*

Budget	Period					
	7	8	9	10	11	12
Earliest Start	5100	6050	7000	7800	8600	9400
Latest Start	4000	4900	5850	6880	7910	8940

Budget	Period					
	13	14	15	16	17	18
Earliest Start	10200	11000	17500	24000	30500	37000
Latest Start	9970	11000	17500	24000	30500	37000

Budget	Period					
	19	20	21	22	23	24
Earliest Start	43500	50000	56500	63000	69500	76000
Latest Start	43500	50000	56500	63000	69500	76000

Budget	Period					
	25	26	27	28	29	30
Earliest Start	82500	89000	95500	102000	108500	115000
Latest Start	82500	89000	95500	102000	108500	115000

Budget	Period					
	31	32	33	34	35	36
Earliest Start	121500	128000	134500	141000	147500	154000
Latest Start	121500	128000	134500	141000	147500	154000

Budget	Period					
	37	38	39	40	41	42
Earliest Start	160500	167000	173500	180000	186500	193000
Latest Start	160500	167000	173500	180000	186500	193000

Budget	Period					
	43	44	45	46	47	48
Earliest Start	199500	206000	212500	219000	220900	222800
Latest Start	199500	206000	212500	219000	220200	221400

Budget	Period					
	49	50	51	52	53	54
Earliest Start	224700	226600	228500	230400	232300	234200
Latest Start	222600	223800	225000	226200	227400	228600

Budget	Period					
	55	56	57	58	59	60
Earliest Start	236100	238000	239900	241100	242300	243500
Latest Start	229800	231000	232200	233400	234600	235800

Figure 13.16   *continuing*

| Budget | Period | | | | | |
	61	62	63	64	65	66
Earliest Start	244700	245900	247100	248300	249500	250700
Latest Start	237000	238900	240800	242700	244600	246500

| Budget | Period | | | | | |
	67	68	69	70	71	72
Earliest Start	251900	253100	256450	259800	263150	266500
Latest Start	248400	250350	252750	255200	257650	260100

| Budget | Period | | | | | |
	73	74	75	76	77	78
Earliest Start	269850	273200	276550	279900	283250	286600
Latest Start	263450	266800	270150	273500	276850	280200

| Budget | Period | | | | | |
	79	80	81	82	83	84
Earliest Start	289950	293300	296650	300000	303350	306700
Latest Start	283550	286900	290250	293600	296950	300300

| Budget | Period | | | | | |
	85	86	87	88	89	90
Earliest Start	308450	310200	311950	313700	313760	313820
Latest Start	303650	307000	310350	313700	313760	313820

| Budget | Period | | |
	91	92	93
Earliest Start	313800	313940	314000
Latest Start	313800	313940	314000

Status Report

Activity	Actual Cost	Budgeted Value	Difference
A	350	300	50
B	400	400	0
C	2800	3000	−200
D	6000	5760	240
E	600	720	−120
F	22000	20800	1200
G	0	0	0
H	0	0	0
I	0	0	0
J	0	0	0
K	0	0	0
	32350	30980	1170

obtaining the supporting machinery. Such an approach helps the manager to integrate resource procurement into the project schedule and to examine the effects of changes in resource lead times and activity completion times on order release dates.

GERT. The Graphical Evaluation and Review Technique is a PERT/CPM extension that accounts for uncertainty in the project network (not just in the activity durations). In GERT, an activity can be stochastic (with a probability of occurrence) or deterministic. Some activities may fail and thereby change the nature of the tasks that follow. Also, GERT permits looping back to previous activities in the network (for example, to redo, redesign, or retest a task). Using these features, management can model a much wider range of projects with GERT than with PERT/CPM.

Resource Leveling. PERT/CPM assumes that there are sufficient resources for scheduling activities. In practice, it is possible (or even probable) that the initial schedule will call for more resources (labor, equipment, or funds) than are available for a particular period. By rescheduling noncritical activities within the projected slack, management can smooth out the pattern of resource usage. Such load leveling, which can be achieved through a variety of heuristic approaches, enables the manager to better plan a project that will be feasible (meet resource constraints).

SUMMARY

This chapter has introduced network-based procedures designed to aid decision makers in planning, scheduling, and controlling large-scale projects. The initial focus was on the Critical Path Method (CPM). Developed primarily for industrial projects in which task times and resource requirements are generally known or readily available, this method focuses on the project duration and appropriate ways to trade off activity time and cost. We saw how to develop an activity-on-node (AON) network, estimate the project duration, and establish a complete activity schedule. Such a schedule often can be crashed by using additional resources (at additional cost) to shorten activity durations. The chapter's first section also examined how the CPM finds the crashing plan that meets the scheduled project completion time at least cost.

In the second section, we considered the Program Evaluation and Review Technique (PERT) for project time management. We saw how to develop an activity-on-arc (AOA) network, derive activity time estimates, forecast the project duration, establish a complete activity schedule, and account for uncertainty. This PERT/TIME approach is particularly appropriate for new and unique projects, such as research and development.

The final section focused on the PERT/COST system for project cost management. We discussed the concept of work packages, developed a range for possible budgeted cost schedules, and established a procedure for measuring cost overruns and underruns. We saw how this kind of information can be used to plan, schedule, and control project costs.

PERT/CPM in Practice

CPM and PERT are applied to a wide variety of management problems. Here are a few areas in which this quantitative analysis is used.

Area	Application
Finance and Accounting	Planning and control of audit activities Determining the closing date and activity schedule for a leveraged buyout Developing a tax preparation course for novice accountants
Marketing	Research and development for a new luxury automobile Planning the layout for a new specialty shopping center Developing the new marketing campaign for a popular soda
Production and Operations	Determining the time to commercial production from oil leases affected by the Outer Continental Shelf Lands Act of 1977 Designing a furniture company's production scheduling system Installing an advanced telecommunications system
Public and Service Sector	Developing a Ph.D. program at a major university Designing a public television series Planning a public celebration

Since there are numerous computations involved in planning, updating, and revising PERT and CPM networks, computer programs frequently have been used to implement these project management techniques. This chapter showed how to utilize the computer aids in project management.

Glossary

activities Specific tasks that use financial and/or physical resources and time and are required to complete a project.

activity-on-arrow or activity-on-arc (AOA) network A project network that shows the project activities as directed branches and events on the nodes.

activity-on-node (AON) network A project network that shows the activities on the nodes and the precedence relationships with directed branches.

activity slack The length of time an activity can be delayed without extending the project completion date.

backward pass A procedure that determines the latest finish and start times for each activity by successively moving backward through the project network.

central limit theorem A statistical concept that a sum of independent random variables will have an approximately *normal probability distribution* when the number of terms in the sum is large.

crashing The process of adding resources (and usually cost) to reduce an activity time.

critical activity A task that must be started and finished without delay (has zero activity slack).

critical path The sequence of critical activities that leads from the starting event to the ending event in a project network.

Critical Path Method (CPM) A network-based project management procedure that includes the capability of crashing.

dummy activities Fictitious activities used to indicate the proper precedence in a PERT network.

earliest finish time The earliest time when a project activity may be completed.

earliest start time The earliest time when a project activity may begin.

events Points in time that mark the completion of all activities for a particular phase of a project.

event slack The length of time an event can be delayed without extending the project completion date.

expected activity time The average time required to complete a PERT activity.

forward pass A procedure that determines the earliest start and finish times for each activity by successively moving forward through the project network.

free slack The length of time an activity can be delayed without affecting the activity slack available for other tasks in the network.

Gantt chart A bar chart that shows planned and actual progress for the project's tasks displayed with bars against a horizontal time scale.

latest finish time The latest time when a project activity may be completed without delaying the entire project.

latest start time The latest time when a project activity may begin without delaying the entire project.

most likely time The most frequent time required to complete a PERT task under normal conditions.

optimistic time The time required to complete a PERT activity under ideal conditions.

PERT/COST A variation of PERT designed to assist program directors in managing project costs.

pessimistic time The time required to complete a PERT task under adverse conditions.

Program Evaluation and Review Technique (PERT) A network-based procedure for planning, scheduling, and controlling large-scale projects.

work package A unit in PERT/COST formed by grouping naturally interrelated project activities for cost control purposes.

Thought Exercises

1. In each of the following situations, explain whether the original version of PERT or CPM would be more appropriate:
   a. A training course for middle-level government officers
   b. An advertising campaign for a new and unique product
   c. An exploration of the planet Mars by a team of astronauts
   d. Airline maintenance

2. Jane Twine is a senior accounting major at the local college. She wants to become a certified public accountant (CPA) and knows that several tasks will be needed to complete her goal. They include:

   - Passing her second-semester courses
   - Graduating
   - Taking a continuing education CPA preparation course
   - Completing an internship
   - Gaining some postgraduate practical experience
   - Practicing on past CPA exams
   - Getting counseling from professors and practicing CPAs
   - Registering for the CPA exam
   - Taking the CPA exam

   Jane is not sure how to plan and schedule this study project. Assist her by preparing an appropriate PERT network.

3. Consider the following portion of a PERT network:

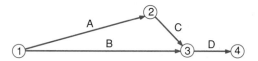

The activity-on-node (AON) method would show this situation as follows:

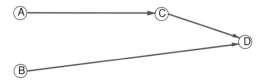

Historically, the event-oriented (first) diagram evolved with PERT, while the AON method developed from CPM. Demonstrate that the two methods are interchangeable by developing the AON network for Olan's project (Table 13.3 and Figure 13.6).

4. The problem of determining the shortest project duration can be formulated as a linear program. This problem then can be solved for the activity schedule and finish time for the project. Postoptimality analysis provides additional useful project information. Demonstrate these facts with Mail Order's project (Management Situation 13.1).

5. Gigantic Enterprise's marketing manager has submitted her letter of resignation, to take effect in 60 days. The personnel manager must find a replacement by that time. He has prepared the following network for the replacement project:

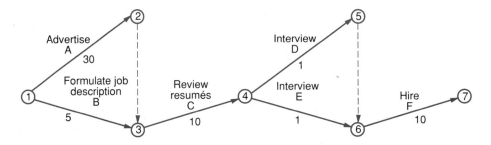

After completing a PERT analysis, the personnel manager states that none of the activities are critical to a successful completion of the project. How did he arrive at this conclusion? Do you agree? If not, what is the project's critical path?

6. Refer to the normal activity schedule for Olan's project (Table 13.5). According to this information, the company can delay installing electrical facilities (activity H) as much as 15 days and still complete the office in 93 days. Of course, this result assumes that each activity can be completed in its expected time (t). T. K. Trueblood, the project manager, is willing to accept this assumption. However, she does not think that the company should delay activity H by more than 11 days. Can you see how T. K. arrived at this conclusion? Do you agree with her reasoning? Explain.

7. Moonlight Zone Products, Inc. is planning an advertising campaign in support of its new toy, the Space Flyer. A PERT/CPM analysis indicates that the campaign will have an expected duration of 120 days. Twilight believes that the project completion time follows a normal distribution with a variance equal to 100. The Space Flyer will be marketed when the last advertising activity has been completed. If the company wants to be 98 percent confident in its timing decision, on what date should it plan on introducing the Flyer?

8. Refer back to the CPM Extensions exhibit in the text. Write the complete linear program. Solve the resulting program, and interpret the solution. How does the linear programming solution compare to the crashing plan determined with heuristic search? Explain.

9. Crashing can also be done in PERT/TIME. Demonstrate this fact by using the data in Table 13.12 and Figure 13.12 to shorten Olan's project by 3 days (from 93 to 90 days), first with heuristic search and then with linear programming.

Table 13.12   **Olan's Normal and Crash Activity Data**

| Activity | Time (Days) | | | Cost ($) | | |
	Normal t	Crash d	Maximum Crash $t-d$	Crash CC	Normal NC	Crash per Day $c = (CC-NC)/(t-d)$
A	3	1	2	400	300	50
B	5	2	3	850	400	150
C	6	5	1	3,200	3,000	200
D	8	4	4	10,400	6,400	1,000
E	6	6	0	900	900	—
F	32	28	4	214,400	208,000	1,600
G	22	15	7	29,200	26,400	400
H	11	11	0	7,700	7,700	—
I	16	13	3	26,500	25,600	300
J	20	12	8	43,800	35,000	1,100
K	5	5	0	300	300	—
					314,000	

10. Do you agree or disagree with each of the following statements? Explain.
   a. Dummy activities are necessary in a PERT network in order to arrive at the correct activity schedule.
   b. The PERT three-time approach cannot be used unless activity durations follow a beta probability distribution.
   c. The expected project duration in a PERT or CPM network generally equals the latest finish time for the last activity.
   d. The earliest time for a project event is always the latest finish time of the immediately preceding activities.
   e. Project management cannot determine a feasible budget unless it establishes the earliest and latest start cost schedules.

Technique Exercises

11. Develop an AON network for the following project:

Activity	Immediately Preceding Activities
A	—
B	A
C	A
D	B
E	C
F	D, E
G	F

12. Develop an AOA network for the following plant location study:

Activity	Description	Immediate Predecessors
A	Prepare preliminary goals	—
B	Solicit proposals	A
C	Review proposals	B
D	Refine objectives	C
E	Identify appropriate sites	D
F	Gather financial data	E
G	Gather engineering data	E
H	Gather managerial inputs	E
I	Evaluate alternative sites	F, G, H
J	Select plant location	I

13. Suppose a project network involves the following activity time estimates:

Activity	Time (Weeks)		
	Optimistic	Most Likely	Pessimistic
A	2	5	9
B	6	12	15
C	4	6	7
D	8	8	12
E	12	20	40
F	10	12	19
G	20	25	28
H	5	5	5
I	16	32	90
J	7	14	23
K	2	2	2
L	1	8	18

Find the expected time and variance for each activity.

14. You are given the following project network for the production of a motion picture. The number below each arc represents the activity time in weeks.

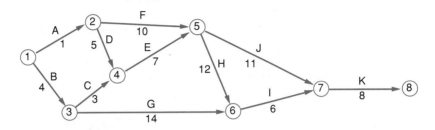

a. Develop a complete activity schedule.
b. Identify the critical path.
c. Determine how long it will take to complete the project.
d. Determine which activities can be delayed (and by how much time) without affecting the completion date.

15. The convention director of the Wellington Hotel has developed the following project network for the approaching National Union Meeting:

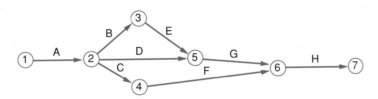

The corresponding activity time data (in days) are given in the following table:

Activity	Optimistic	Most Likely	Pessimistic
A	1	2	3
B	3	6	8
C	5	8	20
D	10	15	28
E	4	7	12
F	20	40	50
G	8	12	24
H	2	2	2

a. Compute the expected time and variance for each activity.
b. Develop a complete activity schedule.
c. Identify the critical path.
d. Determine the expected project duration and the corresponding variance.
e. What is the probability of completing the project within one month? Two months? Eighty days? Three months?

16. Suppose a project has an expected duration of four months with a standard deviation of 30 days.
   a. What is the chance of completing the project within three months?
   b. What is the likelihood that the project will take six months or longer?
   c. What is the probability of completing the project within the expected completion date?

17. Consider the following maintenance project.

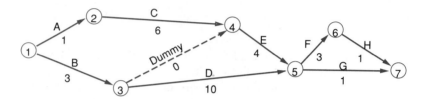

Time and cost data for this project are given in the following table.

Activity	Time (Days)		Total Cost ($)	
	Normal	Crash	Normal	Crash
A	1	—	200	200
B	3	2	1,200	1,600
C	6	4	3,000	3,100
D	10	6	2,000	2,400
E	4	—	1,600	1,600
F	3	1	600	650
G	1	—	200	200
H	1	—	300	300

   a. Identify the critical path and the expected project duration.
   b. What is the total normal project cost?
   c. Suppose that the project must be crashed by three days. Use the heuristic search approach to determine the optimal crashing plan.
   d. Solve by linear programming.
   e. What are the new activity schedule and the resulting additional project cost?

18. The following network describes a marketing research study:

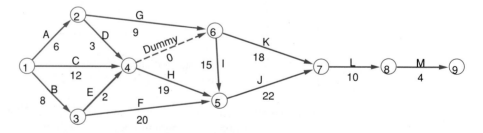

Relevant crash time and cost data appear in the following table:

Activity	Maximum Crash Time (Days)	Crash Cost per Day ($)
A	1	100
B	0	—
C	2	50
D	0	—
E	0	—
F	1	150
G	0	—
H	2	200
I	1	300
J	1	500
K	2	350
L	0	—
M	0	—

a. Identify the critical path and the expected project duration.

b. Suppose that the project must be crashed by seven days. Use the heuristic search approach to determine the optimal crashing plan. (*Note:* Your solution may create additional critical paths. If so, be sure to identify the new critical paths.)

c. Solve by linear programming.

d. What are the new activity schedule and resulting total additional project cost?

19. Table 13.8 in the text gives a portion of Olan's budgeted costs for an earliest start schedule. Table 13.9 gives a similar budget forecast for a latest start schedule.

a. Use the information in Management Situation 13.4 to complete Tables 13.8 and 13.9 for days 14 through 85.

b. Suppose that Olan had the following work package (activity) data at the end of day 70:

Work Package (Activity)	Actual Cost ($)	% Completion
A	350	100
B	400	100
C	3,000	100
D	7,000	100
E	650	100
F	220,000	100
G	25,000	95
H	6,000	80
I	5,000	20
J	1,000	10
K	0	0

Identify the cost overruns and underruns to date.

20. A bank branch expansion project has the work package time schedule and corresponding cost budget at the top of page 666.

a. Prepare cost budgets for earliest and latest start schedules.

b. Determine the range for budgeted expenditures over the project duration. Graph your results.

Work Package	Budgeted Cost ($ Thousand)	Duration (Months)	Earliest Start	Earliest Finish	Latest Start	Latest Finish
A	100	1	0	1	0	1
B	500	2	0	2	1	3
C	1,200	3	1	4	1	4
D	250	1	2	3	3	4
E	200	1	4	5	4	5
F	400	2	2	4	3	5
G	600	2	5	7	5	7
H	250	1	4	5	6	7

c. Suppose that the bank had the following data at the end of month 3:

Work Package	Actual Cost ($ Thousand)	% Completion
A	120	100
B	200	70
C	600	50
D	250	100
E	0	0
F	300	90
G	0	0
H	0	0

Are the project costs in control? If not, identify the cost overruns and underruns.

Computer Exercises

21. Groups of students in IFSM 400 have been assigned the project of establishing an information system to track student progress through the department's graduate programs. Relevant activity data is summarized below.

Activity	Predecessor	Time Estimates (Days)		Cost Estimates($)	
		Normal	Crash	Normal	Crash
A: Feasibility Study	—	10	8	500	750
B: Interviews	A	12	7	500	1,400
C: Gather Documents	B	8	8	600	600
D: Analyze Data	C	12	9	2,000	3,000
E: Develop Specs.	D	18	16	3,000	4,500
F: Select Hardware	E	20	16	4,000	5,500
G: Select Software	E	14	10	2,500	4,000
H: Programming	F, G	17	15	8,000	12,000
I: Test System	H	10	8	4,000	4,700
J: Training	H	14	14	5,000	5,000
K: Install System	I, J	8	5	2,000	3,500
L: Evaluation	K	6	6	2,000	2,000
M: Operate System	L	15	10	3,000	6,000

The project must be completed by the end of the course in 17 calendar weeks.
Use the **Quantitative Management (QM)** software to determine the activity schedule and cost needed to complete the project on time.

22. Ann Archibald has ambitions to be on the County Governing Board. Her staff has determined the breakdown of steps needed to secure the election. The following network depicts the breakdown.

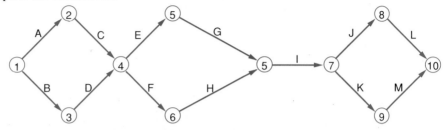

Staff also have estimated the normal and crash times and costs for the activities involved in the breakdown. The information is summarized below.

Activity	Time (Weeks)	Cost ($)	Time (Weeks)	Cost ($)
A	6	5,000	2	10,000
B	3	4,000	3	4,000
C	10	4,000	6	12,000
D	4	1,000	2	2,000
E	2	1,500	1	2,000
F	3	4,000	1	8,000
G	5	7,000	4	12,000
H	7	8,000	5	20,000
I	2	1,200	2	1,200
J	4	5,000	3	6,000
K	8	12,000	6	15,000
L	5	6,000	5	6,000
M	3	4,000	2	4,500

Ann has funds to finance only a 32-week campaign. Use the **QM** software to determine the activity schedule and cost needed to complete the project within Ann's time constraint.

23. A federal military agency has funded a project to develop a key component of the "Star Wars" defense system. The project involves the activity information summarized below.

Activity	Immediate Predecessor	Time Estimates (Months)		
		Optimistic	Most Likely	Pessimistic
A	—	8	12	16
B	—	2	4	6
C	A	8	8	8
D	A	8	10	12
E	B	14	20	32
F	D, E	16	18	20
G	C	4	4	4
H	F, G	4	6	14
I	G	2	6	22
J	H, I	10	20	25
K	I	8	11	15
L	J, K	13	21	35
M	L	5	5	5
O	M	4	8	12

Management seeks the expected project completion date and the activity schedule needed to meet the deadline. The funding agency also wants to know the chance that the developer will be finished three months after the expected project completion date.

Use the **QM** software to develop the required information.

24. International Computers Incorporated (ICIT) has just developed a new minicomputer. It plans to put the machine into full scale production within the next few months. The following network describes the sequence of activities required to establish daily production operations.

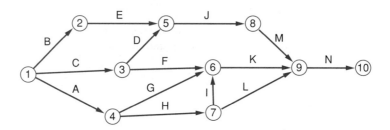

Activity time estimates are given below.

	Time Estimates (Weeks)		
Activity	Optimistic	Most Likely	Pessimistic
A	2	2	3
B	3	4	5
C	1	3.5	7
D	1.5	4	8.5
E	3	6	9
F	6	10	18
G	2	8	25
H	2	4	6
I	2.5	5	7.5
J	4	12	28
K	7	9	14
L	4.5	11	16.5
M	4	4	4
N	3.5	8	14.5

Management seeks the expected completion date for the production setup process. It also wants to know the likelihood that the process will take five weeks longer than expected.

Use the **QM** software to develop the required information.

25. A student is in the process of selecting a university to attend. He has compiled the activity information at the top of page 669.

Costs measure out-of-pocket expenses and expenditures for counseling, lost time, and so on.

The student wants to develop an activity schedule and corresponding budgets for the selection process. Use the **QM** software to generate the desired information.

Activity	Predecessor	Duration (Days)	Cost ($)
A: Identify universities	—	25	100
B: Get applications	A	30	10
C: Take tests	A	60	45
D: Complete application	B, C	20	15
E: Send tests and applications	D	10	125
F: Visit universities	E	40	250
G: Wait for decisions	F	45	20
H: Preliminary evaluations	F	30	75
I: Select university	G, H	15	25

26. Consider the following PERT network.

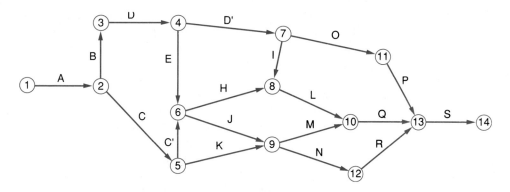

Assume that the durations and costs for the activities are as follows.

Activity	Duration (Days)	Cost ($)
A	6	200
B	7	150
C	3	60
C′	1	80
D	4	180
D′	6	370
E	8	240
F	12	1,200
G	11	1,100
H	7	490
I	9	810
J	6	300
K	4	400
L	7	560
M	5	250
N	6	360
O	7	560
P	3	240
Q	9	900
R	4	800
S	2	150

Management wants to determine the expected project completion date. It also seeks the activity schedule and possible budgets that will be needed to meet the completion date. Use the **QM** software to generate the required information.

Applications Exercises

27. A large defense contractor has an equipment division located in Southern California. Recently, this division received a $10 million contract to develop machinery for the space shuttle program. The project will last for approximately $1\frac{1}{2}$ years and employ 100 people.

Several tasks are necessary to complete the project. First, contract specifications must be developed by the company's personnel, materials, and engineering design departments. Estimates by department managers indicate that this task will take 2 weeks. Then the company need 3 weeks to order raw materials, 14 weeks to hire required personnel, and 12 weeks to design engineering modifications for existing equipment. These three tasks can be done concurrently.

Raw materials will be received over a period of 20 weeks. According to the production managers, the facility modifications will require 19 weeks.

When the resources are on hand, it will take 2 weeks to train quality control personnel. At the same time, the company can train production people on the job in 3 weeks. Next, the equipment can be assembled in 18 weeks and then tested for quality in 5 more weeks. Final product preparations should take approximately 3 weeks.

a. How long will it take to fulfill the contract?
b. What activity schedule will be needed to meet this expectation?
c. What activities seem to be critical?
d. How long can each of the noncritical tasks be delayed without causing a change in expectations?

28. Jill Ward, a historian with the National Archives Association, is writing a book about political events in the United States during the 1970s. Based on previous experience, she knows that the first step is to prepare a prospectus/outline and a couple of sample chapters. Then the material must be sent to potential publishers. Jill estimates that these preliminary activities will each take 1 month. The publishers typically take about three months to review the material, gauge the potential market, and make a contract offer (or reject the project). In the interim, Jill will write additional chapters. Next, she plans to take one month to consider the offers and sign a contract. Meanwhile, the publishers usually assemble a project editing and production staff.

Jill thinks that after the negotiations she can finish the first draft in about eight months. Then the publisher will subject the project to a complete professional and technical review. Typically, the process takes approximately four months. While the publisher is contacting prospective adopters, Jill will complete final revisions. Sales promotion and manuscript completion are each expected to take three months. Then the publisher will require another 10 months to produce and distribute the book. The expected sales life is one year.

All activity durations are considered to be the most likely times. However, since this project is new and unique, neither Jill nor any of the contacted publisher representatives is certain about these durations. In fact, they have jointly prepared the following additional estimates:

	Time Estimate (Months)	
Activity	Optimistic	Pessimistic
Prepare sample material	0.5	3.0
Send samples	0.2	2.0
Review prospectus	1.5	6.0
Write additional chapters	1.0	8.0
Select publisher	0.1	2.5
Assemble staff	0.5	1.5
Complete first draft	6.0	14.0
Review first draft	2.0	8.0
Promote sales	1.5	6.5
Produce book	8.0	15.5
Sell book	6.0	24.0

a. If Jill and the publisher want to revise the current edition at the end of its sales life, when should they expect to start the new project?

b. What activity schedule for the current project will be required to meet the deadline?

c. What are the critical activities?

d. If the publisher wants to be 95 percent confident in its review decision, on what date should the publisher plan on starting the new project?

e. What is the chance that the current project will take at least three months longer than expected? At least four months less?

29. Metropolistown's rapid transit department regularly performs maintenance service on a group of subway cars. The maintenance manual describes this project as follows:

Activity	Description	Immediate Predecessor	Expected Time (Days)	Cost ($)
A	Disassemble motors	—	5	2,000
B	Disassemble transmissions	—	3	3,000
C	Overhaul motors	A	10	5,000
D	Overhaul transmissions	B	15	4,000
E	Reassemble and clean cars	C, D	6	1,500
F	Prepare maintenance report	E	1	200
G	Road-test cars	E	3	500
H	Issue certification	F	1	100

If necessary, the maintenance people can expedite transmission overhauling by three days at an additional expense of $1,200. Also, cars can be reassembled and cleaned in four days for $2,000. It will cost $1,000 to road-test the cars in two days. No other activities can be expedited.

Consumer pressure has forced the rapid transit department to institute a three-week (21-day) maintenance policy. What activity schedule will be necessary to implement this policy? What will be the total maintenance cost?

30. Pills Mills, Inc. recently has experienced declining sales for its breakfast products. As a result, the marketing director has hired a consultant to develop a training program for the sales staff. The consultant has prepared a manual that describes the following training procedure:

Activity	Description	Immediate Predecessor	Time (Weeks)		
			Optimistic	Most Likely	Pessimistic
A	Plan curriculum	—	1.0	2.5	3.0
B	Inform sales staff	—	1.0	2.0	4.0
C	Obtain instructor/speakers	A	2.0	4.0	8.0
D	Prepare instructional supports	A	5.0	12.0	25.0
E	Conduct training sessions	B, C, D	6.0	10.0	16.0
F	Administer written test	E	0.5	1.0	1.5
G	Conduct sales practice sections	E	1.0	3.0	6.0
H	Grade written test	F	0.1	0.5	1.0
I	Evaluate sales staff	G, H	1.5	2.0	4.0

The consultant estimates that activity A normally will cost $1,600, task B about $400, and C another $1,200. Other normal costs are expected to be: $25,000 for activity D, $50,000 for E, $200 for F, $1,000 for G, $100 for H, and $500 for I.

After considering these data, the marketing director has allocated additional resources that could be used to expedite each activity. The allocation is described in the following table:

Activity	Maximum Reduction of Time (Weeks)	Additional Total Cost ($)
A	0.5	200
B	0.1	50
C	1.0	100
D	2.0	600
E	2.0	1,000
F	0.1	20
G	0.2	25
H	0.1	10
I	1.0	250

a. When can Pills Mills normally expect the training to be complete?

b. What activity schedule must the company maintain to meet the expectation?

c. Which activities are critical?

d. How long can each noncritical task be delayed without affecting the expected completion date?

e. What will be the total project cost?

f. Is it possible to shorten the completion time by three weeks? What is the least costly way of doing so?

g. What are the resulting total project cost and activity schedule?

h. What is the probability of meeting the new completion date without incurring the additional cost?

31. The Bridgeport Community Theater regularly sponsors a theme play each Easter. Thomas Todd, a theater patron and drama professor at the local university, annually donates his services to the project. Based on past experience, Thomas has prepared a manual describing the activities involved in the project. A portion of the document follows:

Activity	Description	Immediate Predecessor	Duration (Weeks)	Budgeted Cost ($)
A	Select play	—	3	2,100
B	Hire actors	A	4	10,000
C	Design costumes and set	A	10	26,000
D	Construct set	C	5	40,000
E	Conduct rehearsals	B	7	7,000
F	Publicize event	D, E	4	3,000
G	Print tickets	F	1	5,000
H	Conduct dress rehearsal	D, E	1	2,000
I	Sell tickets	G, H	2	8,000

a. How many weeks before Easter must the theater start the project?

b. If the theater is to meet the Easter deadline, what activity schedule must it follow?

c. According to this schedule, what will be the range of budgeted costs for each week during the project duration?

32. Annette Fonzarelli operates a small custom-order furniture upholstery business. She specializes in the Italian Provincial sofa. Operations for this product are described in the following table:

Activity	Description	Immediate Predecessor	Time (Hours)			Budgeted Cost ($)
			Optimistic	Most Likely	Pessimistic	
A	Contact customer	—	1.0	3.0	5.0	50
B	Define work	A	1.0	1.5	4.0	25
C	Perform credit check	A	2.0	4.0	8.0	30
D	Quote price	B	4.0	8.0	14.0	75
E	Contract order	D, C	1.0	2.0	3.0	20
F	Order fabric	E	3.0	5.0	9.0	600
G	Order trim	E	2.0	2.0	2.0	60
H	Pick up furniture	E	1.5	4.0	7.5	55
I	Receive materials	F, G	16.0	40.0	80.0	150
J	Upholster furniture	H, I	40.0	84.0	120.0	500
K	Deliver order	J	3.5	7.5	15.5	65

a. Annette has just received a new order. When can she expect to deliver the upholstered sofa?

b. What activity schedule must she follow to meet this expectation?

c. What activities are critical?

d. How long can each noncritical task be delayed without affecting the expected deadline?

e. What is the probability of completing the upholstery one working day (eight hours) ahead of schedule? Three days later than expected?

f. According to the schedule, what will be the range of budgeted costs for each day during the project duration?

g. Suppose that Annette observes the following pattern of costs at the end of day 5:

Activity	Actual Cost ($)	% Completion
A	40	100
B	20	100
C	25	80
D	100	30
E	5	10

All other activities have not yet started. Are project costs in control? If not, what corrective actions might Annette employ?

For Further Reading

PERT/CPM Methodology

Anklesaria, K. P., and Z. Dezner. "A Multivariate Approach to Estimating the Completion Time for PERT Networks." *Journal of the Operational Research Society*, 37, no. 8 (1986):811.

Aquilano, N. J., and D. E. Smith. "A Formal Set of Algorithms for Project Scheduling with Critical Path Scheduling/Material Requirements Planning." *Journal of Operations Management* (November 1980):570.

Clelland, D., and W. King. *Systems Analysis and Project Management*. 3rd ed. New York: McGraw-Hill, 1983.

Dumond, J., and V. A. Mabert. "Evaluating Project Scheduling and Due Date Assignment Procedures: An Experimental Analysis." *Management Science* (January 1988):101.

Kerzner, H. *Project Management*. 2nd ed. New York: Van Nostrand Reinhold, 1984.

Kulkarni, V. G., and V. G. Adlakla. "Markov and Markov-Regenerative PERT Networks." *Operations Research* (September–October 1986):769.

Meredith, J. R., and S. J. Mantel. *Project Management: A Managerial Approach*. New York: Wiley, 1985.

Moder, J., et al. *Project Management with CPM, PERT, and Precedence Diagramming*. 3rd ed. New York: Van Nostrand Reinhold, 1983.

Moore, L. J., and E. R. Clayton. *GERT Modeling and Simulation*. New York: Petrocelli/Charter, 1976.

Sasieni, M. W. "A Note on PERT Times." *Management Science* (December 1986):1652.

Weist, J. D., and F. K. Levy. *A Management Guide to PERT/CPM*. 2nd ed. Englewood Cliffs, NJ: Prentice-Hall, 1977.

Computer Analysis

Assad, A. A., and E. A. Wasil. "Project Management Using a Microcomputer." *Computers & Operations Research*, no. 2/3 (1986):231.

Davis, E., and R. Martin. "Project Management Software for the Personal Computer: An Evaluation." *Industrial Management*, 27, no. 1(1985):1.

Gido, J. *Project Management Software Directory*. New York: Industrial Press, 1985.

King, E. "Central Intelligence: Tapping the Power of Project Management Software." *Personal Computing* (November 1987):134.

Krakow, I. *Project Management with the IBM PC Using Microsoft Project, Harvard Project Manager, Visischedule, and Project Scheduler*. Bowie, MD: Brady Communications Company, 1985.

Levine, H. A. *Project Management Using Microcomputers*. Berkeley, CA: Osborne McGraw-Hill, 1986.

Pantumsinchai, P., et al. *Basic Programs for Production and Operations Management*. Englewood Cliffs, NJ: Prentice-Hall, 1983.

Smith, L., and S. Gupta. "Evaluation of Project Management for Microcomputers for Production and Inventory Management Projects." *Production Inventory Management Review*, 5, no. 6 (1985):66.

Webster, F. *Survey of Project Management Software Packages*. Drexel Hill, PA: Project Management Institute, 1985.

Management Applications

Dane, C. W., et al. "Factors Affecting the Successful Application of PERT/CPM Systems in Government Organizations." *Interfaces* (November 1979):94.

Dougherty, D. M., et al. "The Lasting Qualities of PERT: Preferences and Perceptions of R&D Project Managers." *R&D Management*, 14, no. 1 (1984):47.

Glenn, G. O. "CPM-Established and Then Some." *American Association of Cost Engineers Transactions* (1985):E7.1.

Jacobs, F. R. "A Layout Planning System with Multiple Criteria and a Variable Domain Representation." *Management Science* (August 1987):1020.

Kress, M. "The Chance Constrained Critical Path with Location-Scale Distributions." *European Journal of Operational Research*, 18, no. 3 (1984):359.

Ruby, D. "PCs Help Keep Liberty Weekend on Schedule." *PC Week* (July 1, 1986): 61.

Russell, R. A. "A Comparison of Heuristics for Scheduling Projects with Cash Flows and Resource Restrictions." *Management Science* (October 1986):1291.

Taylor, B. W., and L. J. Moore. "Analysis of a Ph.D. Program via GERT Modeling and Simulation." *Decision Sciences* (October 1978):725.

Case: Universal Research Corporation

The city of Falls Reach is concerned about the emigration of its population to neighboring towns. In an attempt to stem the flow, municipal government has decided to conduct an audit of community needs. Universal Research Corporation has been contracted to conduct the audit.

After considerable consultation with community groups, Universal's project manager has been able to identify the key tasks involved in the audit. First, Universal must define the community's objectives, needs, and problems. Next, Universal must recruit data collectors, design the sample, and prepare a questionnaire. These three tasks can be done concurrently. Questionnaire preparation is the basis for developing a survey procedure. Project management must establish this procedure and design the sample before it can document the study's methodology.

Universal will begin training data collectors after developing the procedure document and hiring survey personnel. Trained staff will then collect the data. At the same time, the company can contract data processing services and then process the collected information.

Universal will perform a demographic, statistical, and policy analysis on the processed data. The final report will contain the statistical summary and reports outlining the demographic and policy results. Finally, the document will be distributed to city officials.

Universal has presented the following time and cost information as part of its proposal:

Activity	Time (Weeks)				Total Cost ($)	
	Optimistic	Most Likely	Pessimistic	Expedited	Budgeted	Expedited
Objectives	3.0	6.0	12.0	4.0	2,600	4,000
Recruiting	4.0	7.0	11.0	6.0	20,000	32,000
Sample	2.0	3.0	5.0	2.0	1,400	1,800
Questionnaire	2.0	3.5	8.0	4.0	1,800	1,800
Mechanism	3.0	4.5	8.5	4.5	1,100	1,900
Document	3.0	4.0	5.0	3.5	2,300	2,500
Training	6.0	10.0	15.0	8.0	5,000	6,000
Contracting	2.0	6.0	10.0	6.0	700	700
Collection	8.0	15.0	45.0	18.0	55,000	70,000
Processing	3.0	4.0	7.0	3.5	900	1,000
Demo. analysis	1.5	3.5	7.5	2.0	1,300	1,500
Statistical	1.0	2.5	3.0	2.0	300	400
Policy analysis	2.0	4.0	7.0	3.0	2,100	2,500
Demo. report	2.0	3.0	6.0	3.0	200	250
Policy report	1.0	3.0	8.0	2.5	500	650
Final report	3.0	5.0	10.0	4.0	600	800
Distribution	1.0	1.5	2.0	1.5	100	100

City officials need answers to the following questions:

1. When can Falls Reach expect to receive the study report?

2. What activity schedules will Universal follow to meet the expected deadline?

3. What are the critical activities?

4. How long can each activity be delayed without affecting the expected completion date?

5. What is the probability that the project will be two weeks ahead of schedule? Six weeks behind? Exactly on schedule?

6. According to the expected activity schedule, what will be the range of budgeted costs for each week during the study?

7. What will be the expected budgeted project cost?

8. Is it possible to shorten the project completion time by four weeks? Three weeks? Two weeks?

9. What is the least costly way of shortening the project duration by four weeks? Three weeks? Two weeks?

10. If the project can be expedited, what are the total project cost and activity schedule when the project is shortened by three weeks?

Prepare a report that addresses these questions in a form understandable to city officials.

Part V

Operations Management

FREQUENTLY, decision makers must cope with a variety of planning and operations problems that cannot be strictly characterized as decision analysis, mathematical programming, or network situations. Instead, the problems involve unique features that require specialized treatments or tailored solution approaches. This part of the text examines such situations and presents some of the methodologies that are available to deal with these problems.

Chapter 14 explores how management science techniques can help decision makers manage and control inventories. The chapter begins with an examination of inventory types, costs, and objectives. Then it presents many of the popular inventory models, showing how to apply these models and evaluating their usefulness.

Chapter 15 examines the service system problem. Specifically, there are many circumstances in which a customer arrives at a facility for service. Since the facility usually has limited capacity, a waiting line eventually develops for service. Management's problem, then, is to design and operate the service system in a way that best achieves the organization's objectives. This chapter presents several models designed to predict the performance characteristics for a variety of specific systems. It also shows how such performance information can be used to select design configurations for these systems.

Chapter 16 focuses on sequential decision situations. Some processes start with a set of initial conditions, go through a number of changes, and eventually evolve into a stable system. This chapter describes the characteristics of such processes, presents a framework of analysis, and then shows how to predict the outcomes for the system. It also discusses a methodology for selecting the best strategy in a problem requiring a series of interrelated decisions.

After studying this part of the text, you will be able to:

- Identify the forms and characteristics of inventory and service systems.

- Understand how models can be used to help manage and control inventories and assist in the design of service system configurations.

- Recognize situations that involve evolutionary processes and a series of interrelated decisions.

- Analyze these situations and develop a recommended decision strategy.

These concepts and methodologies will also be utilized in the last part of the text.

Inventory

Chapter Outline

Learning Objectives

- Understand the rationale for carrying inventory
- Identify the relevant inventory cost components
- Decide how much inventory to order
- Decide when to place the order
- Develop methods of inventory analysis for uncertain decision situations
- Determine the nature of a material requirements planning (MRP) system
- Control inventory in an MRP system
- Understand the nature of a just-in-time (JIT) inventory management system

Keeping the Navy Afloat

EIGHT supply centers are operated by the United States Navy. On average, each center stocks approximately 80,000 retail items worth about $25 million. Order quantities are computed with a standard inventory model. By law, the average inventory investment at each center must be approximately 2.5 months of stock. Department of Defense policy also requires every center to fill at least 85 percent of customer requisitions immediately from stock. Safety stocks are calculated to minimize the number of requisitions short.

Concerned by the workload generated by existing policies, the U.S. Navy ordered its Fleet Material Support Office to study the situation and recommend improvements. The study director recognized that the problem was to find the best trade-off between customer service and reordering workload within the fixed inventory investment budget. By restating the existing inventory model in an alternative form, the director was able to derive the data needed to perform the trade-off analysis, which then revealed the investment allocation that would provide the minimum safety stock necessary to meet the 85 percent customer service goal.

Under previous policy, management allocated 1.5 months' investment to safety stock, and the resulting workload was 840,000 orders per year. According to the trade-off analysis, a better policy is to put only 1.0 month's investment in safety stock. By adopting the recommendation, the Navy reduced workload by 20 percent, with no perceptible impact on customer service, and saved $2 million per year in staffing costs.

Source: E. S. Gardner, "A Top-Down Approach to Modeling U.S. Navy Inventories," *Interfaces* (July–August 1987): 1–7.

The U.S. Navy faces a situation that is common to most enterprises. In this situation, the enterprise transforms resources into finished products and services. At any given time, the enterprise may have idle stocks of the raw materials, capital, labor, equipment, partially completed goods (work in process), or finished products. These idle stocks are referred to as **inventory**.

Inventory serves several important business and economic functions. Some are related to product or service demand. For instance, idle stocks of finished goods make it possible to provide the product at the time and place desired by the consumer; often such demand is unforeseeable or erratic. Other functions involve production considerations. An inventory of raw materials, for example, can help a company avoid the delays associated with searching for appropriate supply sources and then waiting for deliveries. Also, the outputs of some activities are partially completed goods that become inputs for subsequent tasks. In this case, a work stoppage in the preceding task may delay the next activity. Work-in-process inventory may prevent these delays. In addition, product or service demand often is seasonal or cyclical. If the production schedule followed such a demand pattern, there would be substantial expenses for transportation, hiring, firing, overtime, and idle facilities. By carrying an inventory of finished goods, a firm can maintain a fairly steady production rate and thus reduce these expenses. There are also supply considerations. Raw materials inventory helps guard against inflation and irregularities of supply. In addition, it is often possible to obtain price discounts by buying in large volume. Unused materials are stored for future requirements. Also, work-in-process and finished goods inventory protect against labor shortages resulting from strikes and market conditions.

An inventory generates certain expenses. First, there is the cost of the item. If it is manufactured by the firm, there will be labor, material, and overhead expenses. When the item is purchased, the company pays the purchase price plus taxes. These purchase and manufacturing expenses are collectively called **procurement costs**. Unless there are purchase or production cost discounts, these expenses typically remain the same regardless of the quantity ordered or manufactured.

The company incurs additional expenses when it places an order, including wages of the purchasing and inspection agents, postage, transportation, and bookkeeping charges. If the items are manufactured rather than purchased, management must physically prepare the production apparatus. In this situation, instead of order expenses, there will be costs associated with setting up the machines, scheduling work, and the like. The order or production preparation expenses are collectively referred to as **ordering (setup) costs**. Usually, these expenses remain the same regardless of the quantity ordered or produced.

The inventory itself creates other expenses. For one thing, there is the interest cost for the investment. If the company borrows money to finance inventory, it will have to pay an interest charge. Even when the firm uses its own capital, there is an opportunity cost involved in not being able to use the money for alternative investments. In addition, there are expenses associated with physically handling, storing, and maintaining the inventory. These expenses include wages, equipment-operating costs, insurance, taxes, breakage, pilferage, and depreciation. The finance, handling, storage, and maintenance expenses are collectively referred to as **carrying (holding) costs**. Such expenses increase with the size of inventory. That is, larger inventories involve larger holding costs.

Aside from these ordinary expenses, the company may incur a cost when available goods are insufficient to fully satisfy demand. If the customer is willing to wait, there may be expediting and notification expenses. If dissatisfied customers go elsewhere, the firm loses present (and perhaps future) sales and profits. Such expenses are collectively called **stockout (shortage) costs**. Typically, these expenses decrease with the size of inventory.

Inventory policy involves an organizational dilemma. Marketing wants large inventories to ensure the satisfaction of consumer demand. Production also wants large idle stocks in order to reduce ordering and setup costs, smooth operations, and minimize idle time. However, finance is interested in minimizing capital costs and thus prefers small inventories. Sound management should consider all viewpoints and then develop a policy that minimizes the total inventory costs. The basic issues are how much and when to order (or produce). Since inventory expenses are a substantial cost of doing business for most companies, these issues warrant serious consideration.

This chapter shows how quantitative methods can assist the manager in formulating a sound inventory policy. The first section introduces the problem and presents the most fundamental solution model. This approach is best suited for situations involving a single good or several independent products, each with a known and constant demand. Often, however, demand is erratic and uncertain. In addition, there may be other variations from the basic approach. The second section shows how to make inventory decisions under several of these conditions. Finally, some products are ordered or produced only once during a given time period. Other situations, meanwhile, involve several items with interrelated demands. The last section discusses inventory systems designed for each of these circumstances.

As the Navy vignette illustrates, quantitative inventory analysis can significantly improve the effectiveness of the organization. For the Navy, it reduced workload by 20 percent, with no perceptible impact on customer service, and saved $2 million per year in labor costs.

Applications. In this chapter, the following applications appear in text, examples, and exercises:

- agriculture
- ATV vehicle assembly
- automotive repair
- automobile seat upholstery
- bookstore operations
- bottling soft drinks
- credit union operations
- data processing
- Easter candy sales
- fashion merchandising
- film processing
- fresh fruit purchases

- heart monitoring
- hospital administration
- industrial equipment ordering
- manufacturing pens
- pencil sharpener assembly
- purchasing machine components
- sanitation engineering
- seasonal products
- sports magazine sales
- stereo merchandising
- television retailing
- used car rentals

14.1 CONTINUOUS AND INDEPENDENT DEMAND

In many cases, inventory is acquired or produced to meet an ongoing consumer need. Such a need will usually be continuous (rather than periodic) and often will be independent of (not derived from) the demand for other items. Many MS/OR methodologies are available to help managers make sound inventory decisions in these continuous and independent demand situations. The basic methodology is presented in this section, and important extensions are discussed in the second section of the chapter.

Basic Model

A basic inventory formulation, known as the *economic order quantity (EOQ) model*, was introduced in 1915. This model still is used by organizations today.

Figure 14.1   Inventory Pattern for the Economic Order Quantity (EOQ) Model

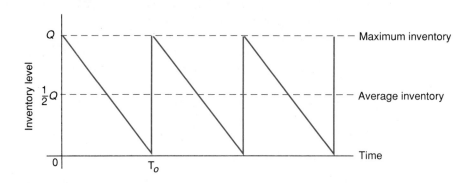

Assumptions. The EOQ model presumes the following conditions:

1. Demand is known (either through a forecast or customer orders) and constant.

2. The item will be withdrawn from inventory at a uniform rate.

3. Unit costs (for procurement, ordering, and carrying inventory) are known and constant.

4. Orders will be placed for a constant amount and at the right time to avoid any shortages.

5. An order arrives in one batch at one point in time and is instantaneously placed in inventory.

6. The length of time needed to order and replenish inventory is known and constant.

Inventory Pattern. These assumptions result in the sawtooth pattern shown in Figure 14.1. When the order arrives from a supplier at time 0, the organization will have its maximum inventory (the order quantity Q). Management will then supply customers at a constant rate from stock until the inventory is depleted at time T_0. Since demand and depletion occur at the same constant rate, average inventory will equal $(1/2)Q$ units for the period. At time T_0, the organization will receive another supply of Q units and immediately replenish its inventory to the maximum level. The pattern will repeat itself as time goes on.

Although the sawtooth pattern may be an oversimplification, it is applicable in some situations. Moreover, this pattern results in a model that is simple and easy to use and that helps conceptualize the inventory problem.

Inventory Decisions. Two key questions to answer in inventory management are

1. How much should be ordered?

2. When and how frequently should an order be placed?

Management Situation 14.1 illustrates how these questions are addressed with the basic methodology.

Stocking Office Supplies

Technical University's bookstore is in the process of establishing an inventory policy for notebook filler. Based on past experience, management knows that demand has been fairly constant at a rate of 6,750 packages per month. Notebook filler can be purchased from a variety of suppliers for 50 cents a package. The price remains the same regardless of the quantity ordered. Jumbo Products, the most prompt and reliable supplier, needs five days' notice to ensure prompt service. Technical and Jumbo both work 250 days per year. Each supplier will deliver the entire order at one point in time.

Bookstore staff require 45 minutes to prepare and process a purchase order and another 15 minutes to set up the sales display after receiving the shipment. Staff earn $4 per hour. Paper, postage, telephone, and transportation cost an additional $1 per order. Annual pilferage, deterioration, interest, and storage expenses are estimated to be 18 percent of the value of average inventory.

Management policy is to fully satisfy customer demand. Management must determine the inventory actions necessary for implementing this policy at least cost.

In Management Situation 14.1, there is a single product (notebook filler) with a known and constant demand (6,750 packages per month). The purchase cost (50 cents) is known and remains the same regardless of the quantity ordered. All items are delivered and become inventory at one point in time. Since management policy is to fully satisfy demand, the bookstore will order in time to allow for delivery by the inventory depletion point. Hence, Technical's circumstances are characteristic of the EOQ model.

Economic Order Quantity

Technical's objective is to find the least costly order quantity. Since the bookstore plans to fully satisfy demand, there will be no shortage costs. However, there will be other expenses to consider, including procurement, ordering, and holding costs.

Procurement Cost. Technical purchases each package of notebook filler for 50 cents. Furthermore, customers demand 6,750 packages each month, or 81,000 per year. Thus, to fully satisfy this demand, the bookstore must incur an annual procurement expense of

$$\$0.50 \times 81,000 = \$40,500.$$

In effect, then, the procurement expense per period will equal the cost per item multiplied by the total demand. By letting c = the purchase or manufacturing cost per item and D = the total demand for the stated period, we can express the relationship as follows:

(14.1) $$c \times D = cD$$

In the EOQ model, the purchase or manufacturing cost per item (c) and total demand (D) are assumed to be known and constant. Consequently, the procurement expense per period (cD) will remain the same regardless of the quantity ordered or produced.

Ordering Cost. Technical's ordering expenses include the costs of placing an order and setting up a sales display. Preparing and processing an order involves

$$45 \text{ minutes } (\tfrac{3}{4} \text{ hour}) \text{ of labor } @ \ \$4/\text{hour } = \$3$$

plus   paper, postage, telephone, and transportation $= \$1$

or a cost of $4. Setting up the display requires an additional expense of

$$15 \text{ minutes } (\tfrac{1}{4} \text{ hour}) \text{ of labor } @ \ \$4/\text{hour } = \$1.$$

Thus, it will cost the bookstore $4 + $1 = $5 for each order. The ordering expense per period will therefore depend on the number of orders.

The bookstore has a known and constant demand of $D = 81,000$ packages per year. Since the store orders a fixed amount Q, the number of orders will equal the demand divided by the order quantity. For example, if Technical ordered $Q = 8,100$ packages at a time, it would need

$$\frac{D}{Q} = \frac{81,000}{8,100} = 10 \text{ orders per year}$$

to satisfy customer demand. Since each order costs $5, this policy would involve an annual ordering expense of $5 $\times$ 10 = $50. On the other hand, an order quantity of $Q = 90$ packages would require $81,000/90 = 900$ orders per year and result in an ordering expense of $5 $\times$ 900 = $4,500.

In general, then, the ordering expense per period will equal the cost per order multiplied by the number of orders. By letting $c_o =$ the cost for one order or setup, we can write the relationship as

(14.2) $$c_o \times \frac{D}{Q} = \frac{c_o D}{Q}.$$

In the EOQ model, the cost per order c_o is also assumed to be known and constant. Thus, as equation (14.2) indicates, the inventory ordering cost $c_o D/Q$ will decrease as the order quantity Q gets larger.

Holding Cost. Pilferage, deterioration, interest, and storage expenses are holding costs. In this case, they are annually equal to 18 percent of the value for average inventory. Technical purchases each package of notebook filler for 50 cents. Hence, it will cost 18 percent of 50 cents, or 9 cents, to carry one package in inventory for a year. Since the average inventory is $\tfrac{1}{2}Q$ packages, the inventory holding expenses will be

$$\$.09 \times \frac{1}{2}Q = \$.045Q \text{ per year.}$$

In general, then, the holding expense per period will equal the carrying cost per item multiplied by the average inventory level. By letting $c_H =$ the cost to carry one item for the stated period, the relationship becomes

(14.3) $$c_H \times \frac{1}{2}Q = \frac{1}{2}c_H Q.$$

Table 14.1   **Technical's Inventory Costs for Various Order Quantities**

Order Quantity Q	Annual Costs ($)			
	Procurement	Ordering ($405,000/Q)	Holding ($.045Q)	Total
500	40,500	810.00	22.50	41,332.50
1,000	40,500	405.00	45.00	40,950.00
1,500	40,500	270.00	67.50	40,837.50
2,000	40,500	202.50	90.00	40,792.50
2,500	40,500	162.00	112.50	40,774.50
3,000	40,500	135.00	135.00	40,770.00
3,500	40,500	115.71	157.50	40,773.21
4,000	40,500	101.25	180.00	40,781.25
4,500	40,500	90.00	202.50	40,792.50
5,000	40,500	81.00	225.00	40,806.00

The carrying cost per item c_H is assumed to be known and constant in the EOQ model. Hence, inventory holding cost $\frac{1}{2}c_H Q$ will increase as the average inventory $\frac{1}{2}Q$ grows.

Total Cost. In the EOQ model, total inventory expenses per period (day, week, month, year, or other relevant time increment), denoted TC, will equal the sum of procurement, ordering, and holding costs. That is,

(**14.4**)
$$TC = cD + \frac{c_o D}{Q} + \frac{1}{2}c_H Q.$$

or, in Technical's case, annual inventory cost will be

(**14.5**)
$$TC = \$.50(81,000) + \frac{\$5(81,000)}{Q} + \frac{\$.09Q}{2}$$

$$= \$40,500 + \frac{\$405,000}{Q} + \$.045Q$$

Developing a realistic total cost model, such as equation (14.5), is the first (and perhaps most important) part of a quantitative inventory analysis.

Equation (14.5) describes how total inventory cost TC is affected by the order quantity Q. By substituting selected trial quantities into this equation, Technical will get the results presented in Table 14.1. These results, for example, show that an order quantity of $Q = 2,000$ packages generates a total inventory cost of $TC = \$40,500 + \$202.50 + \$90 = \$40,792.50$ per year.

Cost Behavior. Figure 14.2 graphs the procurement, ordering, holding, and total costs resulting from an infinite number of possible order quantities. It shows that total cost is at a minimum when the decision maker orders the quantity Q^*. This order size, which gives the quantity that minimizes total inventory cost, is known as the **economic order quantity**.

Figure 14.2   **Inventory Cost Behavior in the EOQ Model**

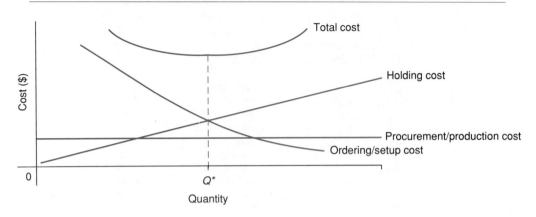

The figure also indicates that the economic order quantity Q^* balances ordering and holding costs. Up to this quantity, decreases in ordering costs outweigh the increases in carrying expenses. As a result, total costs are declining. Beyond the economic order quantity, increases in holding costs more than offset the decreases in ordering expenses. Therefore, total costs are rising.

Least Costly Order Quantity. Management's problem is to find the economic order quantity (the value of Q^*). By trying selected quantities (as is done in Table 14.1), the decision maker may be able to identify a low cost order size. However, since such an approach does not test every possibility, it cannot guarantee an optimal solution.

As the Classical Optimization Appendix demonstrates, through the use of calculus, the economic order quantity can be found with the following formula:

$$(14.6) \qquad\qquad Q^* = \sqrt{\frac{2c_o D}{c_H}}$$

where Q^* = the economic order quantity and the other terms are defined as before. This formula is a decision rule that tells management how much to order.

In Technical's case, $c_o = \$5$, $D = 81,000$ packages, and $c_H = \$0.09$. Therefore, the economic order quantity is

$$Q^* = \sqrt{\frac{2(\$5)(81,000)}{\$0.09}} = 3,000 \text{ packages}$$

This order size will balance ordering and holding expenses at

$$\frac{c_o D}{Q^*} = \frac{\$5(81,000)}{3,000} = \frac{c_H Q^*}{2} = \frac{\$0.09(3,000)}{2} = \$135$$

each and minimize total inventory cost at

$$TC = \$40,500 + \frac{c_o D}{Q^*} + \frac{c_H Q^*}{2} = \$40,500 + \$135 + \$135 = \$40,770.$$

Sensitivity Analysis. The EOQ model assumes that unit costs and demand are known and constant. Although much time may be spent in deriving these numbers, management should realize that the values are, at best, good estimates.

Fortunately, inexact estimates do not present a serious problem. As Figure 14.2 illustrates, the total inventory cost curve is fairly flat over a considerable range. This characteristic makes the basic model relatively insensitive to changes or errors in data values.

For example, suppose that demand D, unit ordering cost c_o, and unit holding cost c_H are each 30 percent lower than originally estimated. In this case, $D = .7(81,000) = 56,700$, $c_o = .7(\$5) = \$3.50$, and $c_H = .7(\$0.09) = \$0.063$, with

$$Q^* = \sqrt{2(\$3.50)(56,700)/\$0.063} \approx 2,510$$

(compared with the original $Q^* = 3,000$) and

$$TC = \$40,500 + c_o D/Q^* + c_H Q^*/2$$

$$= \$40,500 + \$3.50(56,700)/2,510 + \$0.063(2,510)/2$$

$$= \$40,658.13$$

(compared with the original $TC = \$40,770$). The relatively large (30%) overestimate of the original parameters then results in only a $(3,000 - 2,510)/3,000 = .163$, or 16.3 percent decrease in the EOQ and an insignificant

$$(\$40,770 - \$40,658.13)/\$40,770 = .002$$

or .2 percent reduction in total inventory cost.

Similarly, when the parameters (D, c_o, and c_H) are each 30 percent higher than the original estimates, $D = 1.3(81,000) = 105,300$, $c_o = 1.3(\$5) = \$6.50$, and $c_H = 1.3(\$0.09) = \$0.117$. The EOQ then will be

$$Q^* = \sqrt{2(\$6.50)(105,300)/\$.117} \approx 3,420$$

(compared with the original $Q^* = 3,000$) and

$$TC = \$40,500 + c_o D/Q^* + c_H Q^*/2$$

$$= \$40,500 + \$6.50(105,300)/3,420 + \$0.117(3,420)/2$$

$$= \$40,900.20$$

(compared with the original $TC = \$40,770$). In this case, the 30 percent underestimate of the original parameters results in only a $(3,420 - 3,000)/3,000 = .14$, or 14 percent, increase in the EOQ and an insignificant

$$(\$40,900.20 - \$40,770)/\$40,770 = .003$$

or .3 percent rise in total inventory cost.

Since relatively large errors/changes tend to have only minor impacts on total cost, a good approximation for the least costly inventory policy can be found by using reasonable ("ballpark") parameter estimates in the EOQ formula. For the same reason, the EOQ can safely be rounded to a whole number or even to an expedient quantity near the EOQ. For example, transportation savings often can be obtained by shipping a "round lot" or "full load." By rounding the EOQ to this load quantity, the decision maker may be able to take advantage of the savings without materially affecting total cost. When a rounded

EOQ is used, management must realize that the annual ordering cost will not be exactly equal to the annual holding cost.

Order Timing and Frequency

The economic order quantity Q^* provides managers with a rational basis for deciding *how much* to order. However, it does not answer the questions of *when* and *how frequently* to place an order. These additional questions can be addressed with a reorder point (ROP) analysis.

Lead Time. Since each source offers the notebook filler at the same price, Technical will probably want to order from the most prompt and reliable supplier (Jumbo Products). But even Jumbo needs five days' notice to ensure prompt service. Ordinarily, then, the bookstore will not receive the notebook filler until five days after placing an order. This five-day period, which measures the length of time needed to order and replenish inventory, is called **lead time**.

Reorder Point. During the lead time, consumers still will want the product. In fact, there will be a demand for 81,000 packages a year or, since both Technical and Jumbo operate 250 days annually,

$$81,000/250 = 324 \text{ packages per working day.}$$

The bookstore can expect to sell $324 \times 5 = 1,620$ packages during the lead time.

If management wants to fully satisfy demand, it will place an order when the inventory level reaches 1,620 packages. Such a quantity, which measures the inventory level that signals when to place a new order, is known as the **reorder point**. In the basic situation, it is calculated with the following formula:

(14.7) $R = dL$

where $R =$ the reorder point, $d =$ the rate of demand (typically, items per day), and $L =$ the lead time (typically, number of days). This formula is a decision rule indicating when to place an order.

In the basic model, the lead time L and the demand rate d are assumed to be known and constant. As a result, the corresponding reorder point R is the same as the demand during the lead time (dL).

Order Frequency. Technical has decided to request $Q^* = 3,000$ packages each time it orders. Since the annual demand is $D = 81,000$, this policy will require

$$D/Q^* = 81,000/3,000 = 27 \text{ orders per year.}$$

If the bookstore places these orders over the 250 working days, management will order approximately every $250/27 = 9.3$ working days. This 9.3-day period, which measures the length of time between the placing of two consecutive orders, is referred to as the **inventory cycle time**. In the basic situation, it is computed with the following formula:

(14.8) $$T = \frac{N}{D/Q^*} = \frac{NQ^*}{D}$$

Figure 14.3   **Order Timing and Frequency in the EOQ Model**

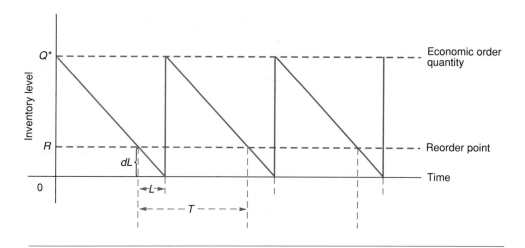

where T = the inventory cycle time (typically, days), N = the working days per year (in some cases, 365), and the other terms are defined as before. This formula is a decision rule indicating how frequently to place an order.

Reorder Pattern. Figure 14.3 illustrates the order timing and frequency process for the basic model. When an order arrives from Jumbo at time 0, the bookstore will have an inventory equal to the economic order quantity Q^*. Technical will then supply consumers from stock until it reaches the reorder point R. At that point, the bookstore will place another order for Q^* packages. The new order will be received just as demand during the lead time (dL) depletes inventories. Technical will immediately replenish inventory to the economic order quantity level. After a period of T days, the bookstore will place another order for Q^* packages. The pattern will repeat itself as time progresses.

14.2 DECISION CONSIDERATIONS

In many continuous and independent demand situations, the basic methodology's assumptions are simply inappropriate. Important exceptions to these assumptions include quantity discounts, planned shortages, gradual inventory replenishment, and uncertain lead time. This section shows how to deal with such exceptions, and it also discusses other decision considerations relevant to continuous and independent demand situations.

Quantity Discounts

For various business and economic reasons, suppliers may want to sell large volumes of merchandise. As a result, they often provide an incentive to buyers by offering price discounts for larger purchases. Management Situation 14.2 illustrates.

Table 14.2   **Jumbo's Discount Schedule**

Category	Order Size	Discount (% of Cost)	Cost per Item ($)
1	Less than 3,100	0.0	0.500
2	3,100 to 3,999	10.0	0.450
3	4,000 to 9,999	24.0	0.380
4	10,000 and over	24.2	0.379

Management Situation 14.2

Discount Buying

To expand business, Jumbo Products quotes the discount schedule presented in Table 14.2. All other facts are the same as in Management Situation 14.1. Once more, the management of Technical University's bookstore seeks the inventory policy that will fully satisfy consumer demand at least cost.

Except for the purchase cost discounts, Management Situation 14.2 has all the characteristics of the EOQ model. As a result, total inventory costs will again take the general form of equation (14.4):

$$TC = cD + \frac{c_o D}{Q} + \frac{c_H Q}{2}.$$

However, the discounts change the specific structure of this cost model.

Procurement Cost. In the basic EOQ model, the procurement cost per item c is constant and thus never affected by the inventory order policy decision. When there are quantity discounts, c varies with the order size Q. Each discount category then generates a different procurement expense. For example, if the bookstore orders up to 3,100 packages (discount category 1), it will pay 50 cents per item. Since customers demand $D = 81,000$ packages per year, the corresponding annual procurement expense will be

$$c \times D = \$0.50(81,000) = \$40,500.$$

On the other hand, an order size of between 3,100 and 3,999 packages (discount category 2) results in an annual procurement expense of

$$c \times D = \$0.45 \times 81,000 = \$36,450.$$

Similarly, the annual procurement cost is $\$0.38 \times 81,000 = \$30,780$ for discount category 3 (4,000 to 9,999 items) and $\$0.379 \times 81,000 = \$30,699$ for the last category (10,000 items and over).

Total Cost Curve. The discounts for large order sizes look tempting, but the bookstore should realize that larger quantities result in higher carrying expenses. Before making a

Figure 14.4 **Technical's Total Cost with Quantity Discounts**

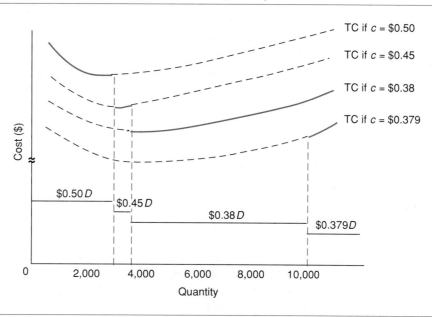

final inventory policy decision, management must consider the effects of the discounts on other inventory expenses.

Figure 14.4 illustrates how total inventory costs are affected by the quantity discounts. This figure shows that each decrease in the procurement expense moves the company to a lower total cost curve. However, each total cost curve is valid only for the range of quantities associated with the corresponding procurement expense. For example, the top curve in Figure 14.4 gives the total cost (TC) if the procurement expense per item is $c = \$0.50$, but is valid (as indicated by the solid portion) only for the quantities (from 0 to 3,100 items) associated with the procurement expense $\$0.50D$. When the cost per item is $c = \$0.45$, the total cost is given by the solid portion of the next lowest curve over the range (from 3,100 to 4,000 items) associated with the procurement expense $\$0.45D$.

As Figure 14.4 demonstrates, the item's procurement cost decreases in steps over the range of possible order sizes (quantities). Consequently, the total cost curve itself will have steps that occur at the **price breaks**, or at the quantities where the item's unit procurement cost decreases. Once more, the objective is to find the order quantity that minimizes total cost.

Order Quantities. Within a given discount category, the procurement expense per item c is constant. Since the unit carrying cost is a percentage of this procurement expense, c_H will also remain the same within the category. The cost per order c_o and demand D are constant regardless of the discount structure. In effect, *within each purchase cost category*, the discount model has the same characteristics as the basic EOQ situation. Therefore, management can use equation (14.6)

$$Q^* = \sqrt{\frac{2c_o D}{c_H}}$$

to find the least costly order quantity for each discount category.

In this case, $c_o = \$5$ and $D = 81,000$. Since the first category involves a purchase expense of $c = \$0.50$ per item, it will cost 18 percent of 50 cents, or $c_H = \$0.09$, to carry a package in inventory for a year. Hence, the least costly order quantity for category 1, denoted by Q_1^*, is

$$Q_1^* = \sqrt{\frac{2(\$5)(81,000)}{\$0.09}} = 3,000 \text{ packages.}$$

Similarly, category 2 has a c_H of $.18 \times \$0.45 = \$0.081$ and an economic order quantity of

$$Q_2^* = \sqrt{\frac{2(\$5)(81,000)}{\$0.081}} = 3,162.28 \text{ items}$$

Category 3 has a c_H of $.18 \times \$0.38 = \$0.0684$ and a least costly order quantity of $Q_3^* = 3,441.24$ packages, while category 4 has a c_H of $.18 \times \$0.379 = \$0.06822$ and a Q_4^* of 3,445.77 packages.

Since there are only slight differences in inventory holding costs, the resulting economic order quantities are approximately the same. However, some of these order sizes are insufficient in size to qualify for the discounts. For example, $Q_3^* = 3,441.24$ is less than the 4,000 minimum necessary to obtain a purchase cost of 38 cents per item. In such cases, management should select the minimum order size necessary to qualify for the discount. As Figure 14.4 illustrates, any larger quantity will be further up on the rising portion of the valid total cost curve and thereby will generate more expense than this minimum order size. Thus, the bookstore should set $Q_3^* = 4,000$ packages. Similarly, since a $Q_4^* = 3,445.77$ is less than the 10,000 minimum necessary to obtain the $\$0.379$ price, Technical should set $Q_4^* = 10,000$ items.

Least Costly Order Quantity. Each order quantity (Q_1^*, Q_2^*, Q_3^*, and Q_4^*) will generate a corresponding total inventory cost (*TC*). For instance, for discount category 1, $c = \$0.50$, $c_o = \$5$, $D = \$81,000$, $c_H = \$0.09$, and $Q_1^* = 3,000$. Thus, the corresponding total cost is

$$TC = cD + \frac{c_o D}{Q_1^*} + \frac{c_H Q_1^*}{2}$$

$$= \$0.50(81,000) + \frac{\$5(81,000)}{3,000} + \frac{\$0.09(3,000)}{2} = \$40,770 \text{ per year.}$$

Table 14.3 summarizes the total cost calculations for each discount category. As you can see, Technical can minimize total annual cost at $TC = \$31,018.05$ by purchasing $Q^* = 4,000$ packages each time an order is placed. This recommendation involves a procurement cost of 38 cents per item (a 24 percent discount). Although the 10,000-package order size would result in a larger (24.2 percent) discount, its excessive holding cost ($\$341.10$) makes this quantity the second-best solution.

Table 14.3   **Technical's Costs for Each Discount Category**

Category	Cost per Item ($) c	Order Quantity Q*	Annual Inventory Costs ($)			
			Procurement (c × 81,000)	Ordering ($405,000/Q*)	Holding ($.09cQ*)	Total
1	0.500	3,000.00	40,500	135.00	135.00	40,770.00
2	0.450	3,162.28	36,450	128.07	128.07	36,706.14
3	0.380	4,000.00	30,780	101.25	136.80	31,018.05
4	0.379	10,000.00	30,699	40.50	341.10	31,080.60

Order Frequency. The quantity discount policy recommendation also changes the order cycle time. In the basic EOQ situation, Technical was ordering 3,000 items every 9.3 working days. Now the bookstore will place an order for $Q* = 4,000$ packages approximately every

$$T = \frac{NQ*}{D} = \frac{250(4,000)}{81,000} = 12.3 \text{ working days.}$$

Procedure Recap.   The least costly order quantity with discounts can be found with the following procedure:

1.   Identify the various discount categories for purchase cost.
2.   Compute the economic order quantity $Q* = \sqrt{2c_oD/c_H}$ for each category. When the economic order quantity is insufficient to obtain the preferred purchase cost, set $Q*$ equal to the minimum size necessary for the discount.
3.   Using the $Q*$ obtained in step 2, compute the total cost $TC = cD + c_oD/Q* + c_HQ*/2$ for each discount category.
4.   Select the order size that results in the smallest total cost.

Planned Shortages

In some cases, a firm can be short of inventory without losing sales during this period. By promising the customer top priority, a short waiting period, and immediate delivery when the goods become available, companies may convince customers to wait for the order. When a customer's order is filled in this manner, the shortage is called a **backorder**. This situation is usually found where items are unique and expensive, in high demand, or adequately supplied by only one firm. Management Situation 14.3 illustrates.

Management Situation 14.3

Managing Shortages

Suppose that experience now indicates that customers are willing to wait for their orders. As a result, the bookstore will no longer keep enough inventory on hand to fully satisfy demand. Instead, management will supply unsatisfied demand from future purchases as soon as the goods become available. Technical realizes that the new policy will necessitate additional labor expenses for record keeping and customer service. There may also be special delivery and handling expenses. These costs are estimated to annually total 22 percent of the value of the average shortage level. All other facts are the same as in Management Situation 14.1. Management wants to determine the inventory actions that minimize costs.

There is only one difference between this situation and the basic EOQ model. Management Situation 14.3 allows planned shortages. However, the backorder possibility changes the problem significantly. By letting

S = the amount of shortage or number of backorders

t_1 = the time when there is an inventory surplus (typically, the number of days)

t_2 = the time when there is an inventory shortage (typically, the number of days)

we can illustrate the situation with Figure 14.5.

Inventory Pattern. Management will order Q packages. When the shipment arrives, S items will be used to satisfy previous backorders. The remainder $(Q - S)$ will immediately be put into inventory. Hence, the maximum inventory will be $Q - S$ packages. Technical will then supply its customers at a constant rate from stock until inventory is depleted. At a demand rate of d items per day, it will take

(14.9)
$$t_1 = \frac{Q - S}{d} \text{ days}$$

to deplete the maximum inventory. However, since Q packages are ordered every purchase cycle, it will be

(14.10)
$$T = \frac{Q}{d} \text{ days}$$

before another shipment arrives. Consequently, the bookstore will have no inventory for t_2 days. There will still be demand during this shortage period. Thus, backorders will grow to a maximum of S items before a new shipment arrives. The pattern repeats itself as time goes on.

In this model, the objective is to find the order quantity Q and shortage level S that minimize inventory-related expenses. Usually, backorders will not affect ordinary procurement and ordering activities. Thus, the procurement expense still takes the form of expression (14.1), cD, and expression (14.2), c_oD/Q, again gives the ordering cost. However, the possibility of shortages substantially changes the carrying cost expression.

Holding Cost. Annual inventory holding expenses once more will equal the carrying cost per item c_H multiplied by the average inventory level. As shown in Figure 14.5,

Figure 14.5   **Inventory Pattern for the EOQ Model with Backorders**

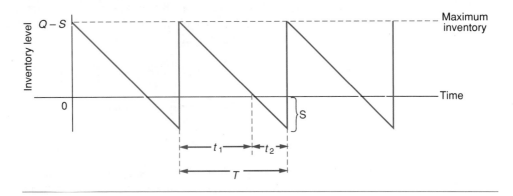

during the surplus period t_1, the maximum inventory will be $Q - S$ items. Customers will be supplied from this stock until inventory is depleted. In the process, there will be an average inventory of $\frac{1}{2}(Q - S)$ packages for t_1 days. During the shortage period t_2, the bookstore will have no inventory. Thus, over a purchase cycle of $T = t_1 + t_2$ days, inventory will average

(14.11)
$$\frac{\frac{Q - S}{2}t_1 + 0t_2}{T} = \frac{\frac{Q - S}{2}t_1}{T} \text{ items per day.}$$

By substituting equations (14.9) and (14.10) into expression (14.11), we can write the average inventory in terms of the decision variables Q and S as follows:

(14.12)
$$\frac{\frac{Q - S}{2}t_1}{T} = \frac{\left(\frac{Q - S}{2}\right)\left(\frac{Q - S}{d}\right)}{Q/d} = \frac{(Q - S)^2}{2Q}$$

Annual inventory holding cost will equal the cost per item c_H multiplied by this average inventory, or

(14.13)
$$c_H \times \frac{(Q - S)^2}{2Q} = \frac{c_H(Q - S)^2}{2Q}$$

in the backorder model.

Shortage Cost. Unlike the basic EOQ model, the backorder situation involves a shortage expense. When Technical is out of stock, its customers will usually wait for the goods to become available. However, the bookstore will incur additional labor, delivery, and handling expenses by backordering. In Management Situation 14.3, these shortage costs are annually equal to 22 percent of the value of the average backorder level. Since each package is purchased for 50 cents, it will cost 22 percent of $0.50, or 11 cents, to have an item on backorder for a year. To determine the annual shortage expense, Technical must multiply this 11-cents-per-item cost by the average shortage level.

As shown in Figure 14.5, there will be no shortages during the inventory surplus period t_1. During the shortage period t_2, continued customer demand will create a maximum backorder of S items before the arrival of a new shipment. In the process, there will be an average backorder of $\frac{1}{2}S$ for t_2 days. Consequently, over a purchase cycle of $T = t_1 + t_2$ days, the shortage will average

(14.14)
$$\frac{0t_1 + (S/2)t_2}{T} = \frac{(S/2)t_2}{T} \text{ packages per day.}$$

At a demand rate of d items per day, it will take

(14.15)
$$t_2 = \frac{S}{d} \text{ days}$$

to reach the maximum backorder level. By substituting equations (14.15) and (14.10) into expression (14.14), the average shortage level can be written as

(14.16)
$$\frac{(S/2)t_2}{T} = \frac{(S/2)(S/d)}{Q/d} = \frac{S^2}{2Q}.$$

Annual inventory shortage cost will then equal the unit backorder cost, denoted c_B, multiplied by this average backorder level. That is,

(14.17)
$$c_B \times \frac{S^2}{2Q} = \frac{c_B S^2}{2Q}$$

gives the shortage expense in the backorder model.

Optimal Inventory Policy. Total cost TC is the sum of inventory procurement, ordering, holding, and shortage expenses, or

(14.18)
$$TC = cD + \frac{c_o D}{Q} + \frac{c_H (Q - S)^2}{2Q} + \frac{c_B S^2}{2Q}.$$

As the Classical Optimization Appendix demonstrates, through the use of calculus, the order quantity and number of backorders that minimize this total cost are found with the following formula:

(14.19)
$$Q^* = \sqrt{\frac{2c_o D}{c_H}\left(\frac{c_H + c_B}{c_B}\right)}$$

with

(14.20)
$$S^* = Q^*\left(\frac{c_H}{c_H + c_B}\right)$$

where $S^* =$ the optimal number of backorders and the other terms are defined as before. These formulas are decision rules telling management how much to order (Q^*) and what shortage to plan (S^*).

Except for the $(c_H + c_B)/c_B$ term, equation (14.19) is the same as the basic EOQ formula (14.6). Because of this term, however, the EOQ with planned shortages formula (14.19) generates a larger order size (Q^*) than the basic EOQ formula (14.6). Also,

Table 14.4 **Technical's Annual Inventory-Related Expenses with Backorders**

Type of Inventory Expense	Formula	Annual Cost ($)
Procurement	$cD = \$0.50(81,000)$	40,500.00
Ordering	$c_o D/Q^* = \$5(81,000)/4,045$	100.12
Holding	$c_H(Q^* - S^*)^2/2Q^* = \dfrac{\$0.09(4,045 - 1,820)^2}{2(4,045)}$	55.07
Backordering	$c_B S^{*2}/2Q^* = \dfrac{\$0.11(1,820)^2}{2(4,045)}$	45.04
Total		40,700.23

equation (14.20) indicates that there will be many backorders when the unit holding cost c_H is large relative to the unit shortage expense c_B.

In Management Situation 14.3, $c_o = \$5$, $D = 81,000$, $c_H = \$0.09$, and $c_B = \$0.11$. Therefore, Technical should order approximately

$$Q^* = \sqrt{\frac{2(\$5)(81,000)}{\$0.09}\left(\frac{\$0.09 + \$0.11}{\$0.11}\right)} = 4,045 \text{ packages}$$

at a time and plan for about

$$S^* = (4,045)\left(\frac{\$0.09}{\$0.09 + \$0.11}\right) = 1,820 \text{ backorders}$$

If this solution is implemented, Technical will place an order approximately every

$$T = \frac{NQ^*}{D} = \frac{250(4,045)}{81,000} = 12.5 \text{ working days}$$

and have a maximum inventory of

$$Q^* - S^* = 4,045 - 1,820 = 2,225 \text{ items}$$

This policy will also involve the annual expenses shown in Table 14.4.

Economic Production Quantity

Many firms may want to manufacture, rather than purchase, items for inventory, as Management Situation 14.4 illustrates.

Management Situation 14.4

Producing Office Supplies

Suppose that Technical University can employ students in its print shop after normal business hours to manufacture the notebook filler. Such operations would have an annual capacity of 202,500 packages. Several trial runs indicate that the students can produce 810 packages each working day at a cost of 40 cents per item. Also, it will take three days and cost $5.40 to clean, prepare, and set up the printing equipment. Customers still demand 6,750 packages each month, and carrying expenses remain 18 percent of the average inventory.

Management seeks the production and inventory policy that will fully satisfy consumer demand at least cost.

There is only one difference between this problem and the EOQ situation. The university can now produce, rather than purchase, the item. To do so, Technical will set up a manufacturing system (the student-operated print shop) and generate output at a constant rate (202,500/250 = 810 packages per working day). Since this output exceeds the rate of demand (324 packages per working day), inventory will gradually increase during the production period. Also, the manufacturing cost per item (40 cents) is known and constant.

Technical's manufacturing system is characteristic of the economic production quantity (EPQ) model. By letting $t =$ the time to complete one production run (typically, the number of days), we can illustrate the situation with Figure 14.6.

Inventory Pattern. When the production run starts at time 0, the bookstore will have no inventory. Technical will then manufacture items at a constant rate during the production phase. Some of the output will be used to satisfy customer demand. The excess will be put in inventory. As a result, inventory will gradually increase during the manufacturing period to a maximum at time t. In the process, the bookstore will have an average inventory again equal to half the maximum level. At time t, Technical will complete the manufacturing run and begin the nonproduction phase. During this period, demand will be satisfied from stock until inventory is depleted. Then management will begin a new manufacturing run in time to allow for delivery by the inventory depletion point. The pattern will repeat itself as time progresses. Consequently, the average inventory over any time frame will still equal half the maximum level.

Objective. In this model, the objective is to find the production quantity Q that minimizes total inventory costs. This minimum cost production quantity is called the **economic production run quantity** or the **economic lot size**.

Since demand once more will be fully satisfied, there is no shortage expense. However, there will be manufacturing, setup, and holding costs.

Manufacturing Cost. Technical manufactures each package of notebook filler for 40 cents. Since consumer demand must be fully satisfied, the annual production expense will equal the cost per item $c = \$0.40$ multiplied by demand $D = 81,000$, or

$$cD = \$0.40(81,000) = \$32,400.$$

Notice that the manufacturing expense (cD) takes the same form as the procurement expression (14.1) in the basic EOQ model.

Figure 14.6   **Inventory Pattern for the Economic Production Quantity (EPQ) Model**

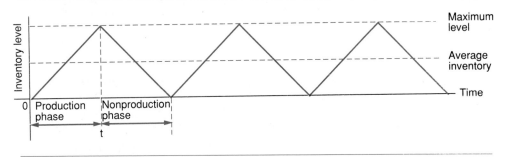

Setup Cost. Setup expenses result from cleaning, preparing, and arranging the printing equipment. They total $5.40 for each production run. Since the bookstore produces a fixed output Q during the manufacturing period, management must schedule 81,000/Q production runs to satisfy annual demand. Therefore, the annual setup cost will equal the expense for one production setup c_o = $5.40 multiplied by the number of runs (81,000/Q), or

$$\frac{c_o D}{Q} = \frac{\$5.40(81,000)}{Q} = \frac{\$437,400}{Q}.$$

Note that the setup expense $(c_o D/Q)$ takes the same form as the order cost expression (14.2) in the basic EOQ model.

Holding Cost. Annual inventory holding expenses again will equal the carrying cost per item multiplied by the average inventory level. The bookstore knows that the average inventory will be half the maximum level. Unfortunately, this maximum is not evident but must be derived.

We assume that inventory is built up from excess production during the manufacturing period t. If p = the rate of production (typically, items per day) and d = the rate of demand, then the rate of excess production will be $p - d$. In Management Situation 14.4, the students can produce p = 810 packages per working day. Since the consumer demand rate is only $d = 81,000/250 = 324$, the bookstore can add $p - d = 810 - 324 = 486$ packages to inventory each working day. Technical will accumulate a maximum inventory of

$$(p - d) \times t = (810 - 324) \times t = 486t$$

by the end of a production run.

Now, during the manufacturing period, the print shop will produce a total of Q packages at the rate of p = 810 per working day. As a result, it will take

$$t = Q/p = Q/810 \text{ days}$$

to complete a production run. Thus, the maximum inventory can be expressed in terms of the production quantity Q:

$$(p - d)t = (p - d)\frac{Q}{p} = \left(1 - \frac{d}{p}\right)Q = \left(1 - \frac{324}{810}\right)Q = .6Q.$$

Average inventory will therefore equal half this maximum, or

$$\frac{1}{2}\left(1 - \frac{d}{p}\right)Q = \frac{1}{2}(.6)Q = .3Q.$$

Notice that the average inventory in the EPQ model is a fraction $\left(1 - \frac{d}{p}\right)$ of the corresponding level $(Q/2)$ in the basic EOQ formulation.

Technical's annual inventory holding costs equal 18 percent of the value of average inventory. The company manufactures each item for 40 cents. Hence, it will cost 18 percent of $0.40, or 7.2 cents, to carry one package in inventory for a year. Since the average inventory is $.3Q$, the inventory holding expense will be

$$\$0.072(.3)Q = \$0.0216Q \text{ per year}$$

In the EPQ model inventory holding cost per period can be expressed generally as

(14.21)
$$\left(1 - \frac{d}{p}\right)\left(\frac{c_H Q}{2}\right).$$

The unit carrying cost per period (c_H), demand rate (d), and production rate (p) are all assumed to be known and constant.

It is usually more convenient to collect demand and production totals rather than rates. As a result, management may want to write inventory holding expenses in terms of these totals. The rate of demand, for instance, is

$$d = \frac{\text{total demand}}{\text{days of operation}} = \frac{D}{N}.$$

Similarly, total output divided by the same number of days gives the rate of production p. If we let P denote the total production, then

$$\frac{d}{p} = \frac{D/N}{P/N} = \frac{D}{P}$$

and inventory holding expenses can be expressed as

(14.22)
$$\left(1 - \frac{D}{P}\right)\left(\frac{c_H Q}{2}\right).$$

Expressions (14.22) and (14.21) are alternative but equivalent forms.

Total Cost. Total inventory expenses per period will equal the sum of manufacturing, setup, and holding expenses. That is,

(14.23)
$$TC = cD + \frac{c_o D}{Q} + \left(1 - \frac{D}{P}\right)\frac{c_H Q}{2}$$

in the EPQ model. This equation (14.23) is very similar to the total cost formulation (14.4) in the basic EOQ model. In fact, if manufacturing, setup, and holding costs for the EPQ model were plotted on a graph, the results would appear as in Figure 14.2.

Economic Lot Size. As the Classical Optimization Appendix demonstrates, through the use of calculus, the economic lot size can be found with the following formula:

(14.24)
$$Q^* = \sqrt{\frac{2c_oD}{\left(1 - \frac{D}{P}\right)c_H}}$$

where Q^* = the economic lot size in the EPQ model and the other terms are defined as before.

The bookstore will have an economic lot size of

$$Q^* = \sqrt{\frac{2(\$5.40)(81,000)}{\left(1 - \frac{81,000}{202,500}\right)(\$0.072)}} = 4,500 \text{ packages.}$$

Equation (14.23) indicates that this quantity will result in total inventory costs of

$$TC = \$0.40(81,000) + \frac{\$5.40(81,000)}{4,500} + \left(1 - \frac{81,000}{202,500}\right)\frac{(\$0.072)(4,500)}{2}$$

$$= \$32,594.40 \text{ per year.}$$

Production Timing and Frequency. Technical can also use the data for determining the production run timing and frequency. Management Situation 14.4 tells us that it will take three days to set up the manufacturing mechanism. Hence, there is a lead time of L = three days. Since the demand rate is d = 324 packages per day, equation (14.7) indicates that the bookstore should begin a production run whenever the inventory level reaches a reorder point of

$$R = dL = 324 \times 3 = 972 \text{ packages.}$$

Also, to fully satisfy demand, equation (14.8) indicates that Technical should plan a production run of Q^* = 4,500 packages approximately every

$$T = \frac{NQ^*}{D} = \frac{250(4,500)}{81,000} = 13.9 \text{ working days.}$$

Risk and Uncertainty

Each of the previous models assumes that demand is known and constant. In practice, the exact sales level is rarely known in advance. Instead, management may only be able to describe demand in probabilistic terms. Furthermore, lead time may not be constant as assumed. Rather, the company might experience unanticipated delivery delays. Either uncertainty may result in a larger-than-expected demand during the lead time and can create stockouts, or shortages.

There are several ways to deal with lead time demand uncertainty. A company can compute the average or expected demand. Then the average, along with other relevant data, can be used with the planned shortage or backorder model to develop a recommended inventory policy. Since the basic approaches are relatively insensitive to data inaccuracies, this procedure should provide a low cost (though not necessarily optimal) inventory policy recommendation.

The planned shortage approach assumes that customers will wait for their order to arrive. It may even be appropriate when there are enough new customers to continually replace those permanently lost. However, since most firms face various degrees of competition, stockouts ordinarily result in some lost sales. In the extreme, continuous large shortages can force a company out of business. Consequently, management may want to consider an alternative approach.

Safety Stocks

Stockouts can occur only during the lead time — after an order has been placed and until the shipment arrives. As protection against shortages, management can keep extra inventory on hand to absorb larger-than-expected demand during this period. The additional items are referred to as **buffer** or **safety stock**. In this case, management will want to place an order when inventory reaches a level sufficient to cover expected demand during lead time plus safety stock. The problem is to find the proper level for this buffer inventory.

It is possible to develop inventory cost models that provide both the optimal order/production and safety stock levels. However, such formulations become quite complicated mathematically and are difficult to measure and implement. There is another, perhaps more practical, approach.

We can first ask management to specify the minimum percentage of customer demands that must be satisfied from inventory. This percentage is called the **service level**. It may be somewhat unrealistic to try for a 100 percent service level. Such a policy would completely prevent shortages, but could create excessive safety stocks and very high inventory holding cost. Therefore, management ordinarily will define a service-level percentage that allows some limited number of stockouts in a stated period. Then the problem is to determine the safety stock that provides the desired service level. Management Situation 14.5 illustrates.

Management Situation 14.5

Maintaining a Proper Service Level

Recently, Technical has faced substantial sales competition from local stationery shops. Now, when the bookstore is out of stock, customers are usually lost to the competition. Stockouts also create ill will. Consequently, management will assess a 7 cent penalty cost for each package that is out of stock.

The competition has had other effects. Although the bookstore still averages 81,000 sales per year, there is a considerable daily variation in demand. In addition, the bookstore has recently experienced unexpected delivery delays. These factors have created a great deal of uncertainty about demand during the lead time. However, using historical data and some judgment, management has been able to describe sales in probabilistic terms. The findings suggest that lead time demand follows a normal probability distribution with an average $\mu = 1,620$ packages and standard deviation $\sigma = 300$ packages. All other facts are the same as in Management Situation 14.1.

In view of the lead time demand uncertainty and potential customer losses, management feels that the planned shortage or backorder model is no longer appropriate. Instead, the bookstore plans to keep a buffer inventory as a hedge against shortages. Management is willing to tolerate a stockout on an average of two orders per year.

Management Situation 14.5 is very similar to Management Situation 14.1. Unit costs are the same and demand still averages 81,000 items per year. Hence, the application of equation (14.6)

$$Q^* = \sqrt{\frac{2c_o D}{c_H}} = \sqrt{\frac{2(\$5)(81,000)}{\$0.09}} = 3,000 \text{ packages}$$

remains a good approximation for the economic order quantity. Using this quantity, Technical once more can anticipate placing an average of $D/Q^* = 81,000/3,000 = 27$ orders per year with approximately $T = N/(D/Q^*) = 250/27 = 9.3$ working days between requests.

Service Level. In Management Situation 14.1, lead time is a constant $L = 5$ days. Since sales average $d = 81,000/250 = 324$ packages per working day, equation (14.7) suggests that Technical's reorder point should be $R = d \times L = 324 \times 5 = 1,620$ packages. However, this policy does not consider the sales uncertainty inherent in Management Situation 14.5.

Technical's lead time demand now follows a normal probability distribution with $\mu = 1,620$ packages and $\sigma = 300$ packages. With such a distribution, there is exactly a 50 percent chance that sales will exceed the average. A reorder point of $R = 1,620$ will satisfy only the average ($\mu = 1,620$) rather than the actual demand during lead time. In effect, this strategy provides a 50 percent service level. It also means that on 50 percent of the occasions (13.5 out of 27 orders), the bookstore will be out of stock before the new supply arrives.

On the other hand, Technical's management is willing to tolerate a stockout on an average of only two orders per year. Since the bookstore places an annual average of 27 orders, this strategy will result in a shortage approximately $2/27 = 7.41$ percent of the time. Consumer demand will be satisfied on the remaining $100 - 7.41 = 92.59$ percent of the occasions. Management's problem, then, is to find the reorder point that provides a 92.59 percent service level.

Reorder Point. Figure 14.7 gives a normal probability distribution for lead time demand. The shaded region to the left of the reorder point R gives the service level probability (.9259). By using mathematical analysis, management can find the value of R that corresponds to this service level.

The standard score

$$Z = (R - \mu)/\sigma$$

tells us how many standard deviations (σ values) the reorder point R is from the average demand (μ value) in a standard normal probability distribution. Table 14.5 gives the cumulative probabilities that correspond to each standard score (Z value).

As Table 14.5 indicates, Technical can achieve a .9259 service level (cumulative probability) when the reorder point R is approximately $Z = 1.45$ standard deviations above the average demand. Since lead time demand averages $\mu = 1,620$ packages with a standard deviation of $\sigma = 300$ packages, management should order when inventory reaches

$$1.45 = (R - 1,620)/300$$

Figure 14.7   **Relationship Between Technical's Service Level and the Reorder Point**

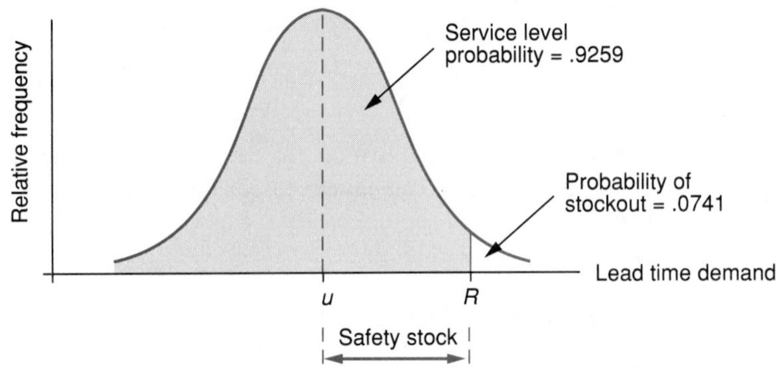

or $R = 1,620 + (1.45)(300) = 2,055$ items.

As shown in Figure 14.7, the difference between the reorder point and the average demand, $R - \mu = 2,055 - 1,620 = 435$ packages, represents safety stock.

In general, the reorder point equals the average lead time demand plus safety stock. By letting $B =$ the buffer, or safety stock, necessary to achieve the desired service level, we can express the relationship as

(14.25) $R = \mu + B$

For a normal probability distribution, $B = Z\sigma$, with Z representing the number of standard deviations above the mean that is necessary to achieve the desired service level.

Service Level Costs. The anticipated annual cost for this system will still include the procurement (cD), ordering (c_oD/Q), and holding $(c_HQ/2)$ expenses resulting from the economic order quantity. In addition, there will be an expense to carry the safety stock plus a shortage cost associated with the limited number of stockouts.

To ensure a 92.59 percent service level, Technical should order $Q^* = 3,000$ packages whenever the stock level reaches a reorder point of $R = 2,055$ items. This strategy involves a safety stock of $B = R - \mu = 2,055 - 1,620 = 435$ packages. Remember that it costs the bookstore $c_H = \$0.09$ to carry an item for one year. Hence, Technical's annual holding cost for safety stock will be

$$c_H \times B = \$0.09 \times 435 = \$39.15.$$

Notice that this expense (c_HB) increases with the size of the safety stock.

The shortage cost involves some other considerations. As shown in Figure 14.7, stockouts occur when lead time demand is greater than the reorder point R. Technical does not know the exact upper limit of this distribution. However, Table 14.5 indicates that most sales (99.99%) will be no more than $Z = 3.80$ standard deviations above the mean μ value. With a reorder point of $R = 2,055$ items, the bookstore could have a shortage of up to

$$S = \mu + Z\sigma - R = 1,620 + 3.8(300) - 2,055 = 705 \text{ packages}$$

Table 14.5 Cumulative Probabilities for the Normal Distribution

Z	.00	.01	.02	.03	.04	.05	.06	.07	.08	.09	Z
.00	.5000	.5040	.5080	.5120	.5160	.5199	.5239	.5279	.5319	.5359	.00
.10	.5398	.5438	.5478	.5517	.5557	.5596	.5636	.5675	.5714	.5753	.10
.20	.5793	.5832	.5871	.5910	.5948	.5987	.6026	.6064	.6103	.6141	.20
.30	.6179	.6217	.6255	.6293	.6331	.6368	.6406	.6443	.6480	.6517	.30
.40	.6554	.6591	.6628	.6664	.6700	.6736	.6772	.6808	.6844	.6879	.40
.50	.6915	.6950	.6985	.7019	.7054	.7088	.7123	.7157	.7190	.7224	.50
.60	.7257	.7291	.7324	.7357	.7389	.7422	.7454	.7486	.7517	.7549	.60
.70	.7580	.7611	.7642	.7673	.7704	.7734	.7764	.7794	.7823	.7852	.70
.80	.7881	.7910	.7939	.7967	.7995	.8023	.8051	.8078	.8106	.8133	.80
.90	.8159	.8186	.8212	.8238	.8264	.8289	.8315	.8340	.8365	.8389	.90
1.00	.8413	.8438	.8461	.8485	.8508	.8531	.8554	.8577	.8599	.8621	1.00
1.10	.8643	.8665	.8686	.8708	.8729	.8749	.8770	.8790	.8810	.8830	1.10
1.20	.8849	.8869	.8888	.8907	.8925	.8944	.8962	.8980	.8997	.9015	1.20
1.30	.9032	.9049	.9066	.9082	.9099	.9115	.9131	.9147	.9162	.9177	1.30
1.40	.9192	.9207	.9222	.9236	.9251	.9265	.9279	.9292	.9306	.9319	1.40
1.50	.9332	.9345	.9357	.9370	.9382	.9394	.9406	.9418	.9429	.9441	1.50
1.60	.9452	.9463	.9474	.9484	.9495	.9505	.9515	.9525	.9535	.9545	1.60
1.70	.9554	.9564	.9573	.9582	.9591	.9599	.9608	.9616	.9625	.9633	1.70
1.80	.9641	.9649	.9656	.9664	.9671	.9678	.9686	.9693	.9699	.9706	1.80
1.90	.9713	.9719	.9726	.9732	.9738	.9744	.9750	.9756	.9761	.9767	1.90
2.00	.9772	.9778	.9783	.9788	.9793	.9798	.9803	.9808	.9812	.9817	2.00
2.10	.9821	.9826	.9830	.9834	.9838	.9842	.9846	.9850	.9854	.9857	2.10
2.20	.9861	.9864	.9868	.9871	.9875	.9878	.9881	.9884	.9887	.9890	2.20
2.30	.9893	.9896	.9898	.9901	.9904	.9906	.9909	.9911	.9913	.9916	2.30
2.40	.9918	.9920	.9922	.9925	.9927	.9929	.9931	.9932	.9934	.9936	2.40
2.50	.9938	.9940	.9941	.9943	.9945	.9946	.9948	.9949	.9951	.9952	2.50
2.60	.9953	.9955	.9956	.9957	.9959	.9960	.9961	.9962	.9963	.9964	2.60
2.70	.9965	.9966	.9967	.9968	.9969	.9970	.9971	.9972	.9973	.9974	2.70
2.80	.9974	.9975	.9976	.9977	.9977	.9978	.9979	.9979	.9980	.9981	2.80
2.90	.9981	.9982	.9982	.9983	.9984	.9984	.9985	.9985	.9986	.9986	2.90
3.00	.9987	.9987	.9987	.9988	.9988	.9989	.9989	.9989	.9990	.9990	3.00
3.10	.9990	.9991	.9991	.9991	.9992	.9992	.9992	.9992	.9993	.9993	3.10
3.20	.9993	.9993	.9994	.9994	.9994	.9994	.9994	.9995	.9995	.9995	3.20
3.30	.9995	.9995	.9995	.9996	.9996	.9996	.9996	.9996	.9996	.9997	3.30
3.40	.9997	.9997	.9997	.9997	.9997	.9997	.9997	.9997	.9997	.9998	3.40
3.50	.9998	.9998	.9998	.9998	.9998	.9998	.9998	.9998	.9998	.9998	3.50
3.60	.9998	.9998	.9999	.9999	.9999	.9999	.9999	.9999	.9999	.9999	3.60
3.70	.9999	.9999	.9999	.9999	.9999	.9999	.9999	.9999	.9999	.9999	3.70
3.80	.9999	.9999	.9999	.9999	.9999	.9999	.9999	.9999	.9999	.9999	3.80

Z	-.09	-.08	-.07	-.06	-.05	-.04	-.03	-.02	-.01	.00	Z
-3.80	.0001	.0001	.0001	.0001	.0001	.0001	.0001	.0001	.0001	.0001	-3.80
-3.70	.0001	.0001	.0001	.0001	.0001	.0001	.0001	.0001	.0001	.0001	-3.70
-3.60	.0001	.0001	.0001	.0001	.0001	.0001	.0001	.0001	.0002	.0002	-3.60
-3.50	.0002	.0002	.0002	.0002	.0002	.0002	.0002	.0002	.0002	.0002	-3.50
-3.40	.0002	.0003	.0003	.0003	.0003	.0003	.0003	.0003	.0003	.0003	-3.40
-3.30	.0003	.0004	.0004	.0004	.0004	.0004	.0004	.0005	.0005	.0005	-3.30
-3.20	.0005	.0005	.0005	.0006	.0006	.0006	.0006	.0006	.0007	.0007	-3.20
-3.10	.0007	.0007	.0008	.0008	.0008	.0008	.0009	.0009	.0009	.0010	-3.10
-3.00	.0010	.0010	.0011	.0011	.0011	.0012	.0012	.0013	.0013	.0013	-3.00
-2.90	.0014	.0014	.0015	.0015	.0016	.0016	.0017	.0018	.0018	.0019	-2.90
-2.80	.0019	.0020	.0021	.0021	.0022	.0023	.0023	.0024	.0025	.0026	-2.80
-2.70	.0026	.0027	.0028	.0029	.0030	.0031	.0032	.0033	.0034	.0035	-2.70
-2.60	.0036	.0037	.0038	.0039	.0040	.0041	.0043	.0044	.0045	.0047	-2.60
-2.50	.0048	.0049	.0051	.0052	.0054	.0055	.0057	.0059	.0060	.0062	-2.50
-2.40	.0064	.0066	.0068	.0069	.0071	.0073	.0075	.0078	.0080	.0082	-2.40
-2.30	.0084	.0087	.0089	.0091	.0094	.0096	.0099	.0102	.0104	.0107	-2.30
-2.20	.0110	.0113	.0116	.0119	.0122	.0125	.0129	.0132	.0136	.0139	-2.20
-2.10	.0143	.0146	.0150	.0154	.0158	.0162	.0166	.0170	.0174	.0179	-2.10
-2.00	.0183	.0188	.0192	.0197	.0202	.0207	.0212	.0217	.0222	.0228	-2.00
-1.90	.0233	.0239	.0244	.0250	.0256	.0262	.0268	.0274	.0281	.0287	-1.90
-1.80	.0294	.0301	.0307	.0314	.0322	.0329	.0336	.0344	.0351	.0359	-1.80
-1.70	.0367	.0375	.0384	.0392	.0401	.0409	.0418	.0427	.0436	.0446	-1.70
-1.60	.0455	.0465	.0475	.0485	.0495	.0505	.0516	.0526	.0537	.0548	-1.60
-1.50	.0559	.0571	.0582	.0594	.0606	.0618	.0630	.0643	.0655	.0668	-1.50
-1.40	.0681	.0694	.0708	.0721	.0735	.0749	.0764	.0778	.0793	.0808	-1.40
-1.30	.0823	.0838	.0853	.0869	.0885	.0901	.0918	.0934	.0951	.0968	-1.30
-1.20	.0985	.1003	.1020	.1038	.1056	.1075	.1093	.1112	.1131	.1151	-1.20
-1.10	.1170	.1190	.1210	.1230	.1251	.1271	.1292	.1314	.1335	.1357	-1.10
-1.00	.1379	.1401	.1423	.1446	.1469	.1492	.1515	.1539	.1562	.1587	-1.00
-.90	.1611	.1635	.1660	.1685	.1711	.1736	.1762	.1788	.1814	.1841	-.90
-.80	.1867	.1894	.1922	.1949	.1977	.2005	.2033	.2061	.2090	.2119	-.80
-.70	.2148	.2177	.2206	.2236	.2266	.2296	.2327	.2358	.2389	.2420	-.70
-.60	.2451	.2483	.2514	.2546	.2578	.2611	.2643	.2676	.2709	.2743	-.60
-.50	.2776	.2810	.2843	.2877	.2912	.2946	.2981	.3015	.3050	.3085	-.50
-.40	.3121	.3156	.3192	.3228	.3264	.3300	.3336	.3372	.3409	.3446	-.40
-.30	.3483	.3520	.3557	.3594	.3632	.3669	.3707	.3745	.3783	.3821	-.30
-.20	.3859	.3897	.3936	.3974	.4013	.4052	.4090	.4129	.4168	.4207	-.20
-.10	.4247	.4286	.4325	.4364	.4404	.4443	.4483	.4522	.4562	.4602	-.10
-.00	.4641	.4681	.4721	.4761	.4801	.4840	.4880	.4920	.4960	.5000	-.00

each time there is a stockout. Furthermore, management will assess a c_B = $0.07 penalty cost for each item. Hence, each stockout could involve a cost of up to

$$c_B \times S = \$0.07 \times 705 = \$49.35.$$

Management also knows that a policy with $R = 2{,}055$ items will satisfy lead time demand 92.59 percent of the time. With $D/Q = 81{,}000/3{,}000 = 27$ annual requests, there will be a stockout on an average of $(1 - .9259) \times 27 = 2.0007$ orders per year. Since each stockout costs $49.35, the bookstore can expect a shortage expense of

$$c_B S(1 - \text{ service level})\frac{D}{Q} = \$49.35 \times 2.0007 = \$98.73$$

per year. Notice that this cost $[c_B S(1 - \text{ service level})D/Q]$ decreases as the service level increases.

Total Inventory Cost. Total costs will equal the sum of the procurement, ordering, inventory holding, safety stock holding, and stockout expenses. If we let P_S = the probability of a stockout $(1 - \text{ service level})$, the relationship can be expressed as follows:

(14.26)
$$TC = cD + \frac{c_o D}{Q} + \frac{c_H Q}{2} + c_H B + c_B S P_S \frac{D}{Q}$$

$$= cD + \frac{c_o D}{Q} + c_H \left(B + \frac{Q}{2} \right) + c_B S P_S \frac{D}{Q}.$$

The probability of a stockout (P_S) is assumed to be known and constant.

In Management Situation 14.5, c = $0.50, c_o = $5, $D = 81{,}000$, $Q = 3{,}000$, c_H = $0.09, $B = 435$, c_B = $0.07, $S = 705$, and $P_S = 1 - .9259 = .0741$. Hence, a 92.59 percent service level generates the annual expenses summarized in Table 14.6. Notice that the service level approach adds $39.15 + $98.73 = $137.88 to the normal inventory expenses. The additional expenses for safety stock ($39.15) and stockouts ($98.73) in effect measure the cost of lead time demand uncertainty.

Optimal Service Level

The service level is usually determined by management policies. However, this approach cannot guarantee the lowest cost solution for a given order quantity. To ensure the lowest cost solution, we must compare the expense of carrying the safety stock with the cost of stocking out.

Balancing Costs. As shown in Figure 14.7, Technical increases the service level by adding safety stock to the inventory used to cover the expected demand. Each package of safety stock will increase holding cost by c_H = $0.09 per year. However, it will also reduce the chance of a stockout and hence save $c_B P_S D/Q = \$0.07(81{,}000/3{,}000)P_S = \$1.89 P_S$ annually.

To determine whether or not an additional package of safety stock is necessary, Technical must compare the expected outcomes. As long as the expected stockout cost reduction $(c_B P_S D/Q)$ is greater than the increase in holding expense (c_H), the bookstore should safety-stock an additional package. Furthermore, buffer inventory should be

Table 14.6   **Technical's Expenses Associated with a 92.59% Service Level**

Expense Category	Formula	Annual Cost ($)
Procurement	cD = $.50(81,000)	40,500.00
Ordering	$c_0 D/Q$ = $5(81,000/3000)	135.00
Holding of normal inventory	$c_H Q/2$ = $.09(3000/2)	135.00
Holding of safety stock	$c_H B$ = $.09(435)	39.15
Stockout	$c_B S P_s D/Q$ = $.07(705)(.0741)(81,000/3000)	98.73
Total		40,907.88

added, one unit at a time, until the expected costs are equal. This balance occurs when

$$c_H = \frac{c_B P_s D}{Q} = \frac{c_B(1 - \text{service level})D}{Q}$$

or

(14.27) $$\text{service level} = 1 - \frac{Q c_H}{D c_B}.$$

At this point, there is no incentive to safety-stock any additional packages.

In effect, equation (14.27) identifies the service level that minimizes the sum of safety stock holding cost plus stockout cost for a given order quantity. For Technical, this lowest cost service level is

$$\text{service level} = 1 - \left(\frac{3,000 \times \$0.09}{81,000 \times \$0.07} \right) \approx 95.24\%.$$

According to Table 14.5, Technical can achieve this service level if the reorder point is about $Z = 1.67$ standard deviations above the mean.

In this situation, management should order $Q^* = 3,000$ packages when inventory reaches a reorder point of

$$R = \mu + Z\sigma = 1,620 + 1.67(300) = 2,121 \text{ items}$$

and management should plan a safety stock of

$$B = R - \mu = 2,121 - 1,620 = 501 \text{ packages}.$$

Procedure Recap.   The following procedure can be used to find the optimal service level:

1. Find the economic order/production quantity Q^*.

2. Identify the probability distribution best describing lead time demand, and calculate the mean μ.

3. Compute the lowest cost service level for the given order quantity, $1 - (Q c_H / D c_B)$.

4. Identify the demand level corresponding to the optimal service level. The result is the reorder point R.

5. Compute the optimal safety stock for the given order quantity, $B = R - \mu$.

This procedure can be used in situations where lead time demand follows a normal (or other) probability distribution.

Simulation

Balancing the expected buffer stock carrying cost per period against the expected shortage cost per period is only a *partial* cost trade-off. Moreover, Q^* is determined independently of the service level. These two simplifications result in a model that is easy to solve but that does not seek the minimum expected *total* inventory cost.

Additional complications that could occur in practice and that are not addressed with the partial trade-off approach include

1. Demand and lead times that have unique probability distributions.

2. Demand that exhibits time series patterns (such as trend and seasonal patterns).

3. Nonlinearities/discontinuities in the cost functions.

4. Constraints on order quantities.

In such cases, it may not be possible to develop an inventory policy through the use of analytical techniques. Rather, the decision maker has to simulate specified order quantity and reorder point combinations under selected demand conditions. The simulated results then can be used to identify the best inventory policy among those examined. This simulation approach is discussed in Chapter 17.

Computer Analysis

Table 14.7 summarizes the EOQ and EPQ models discussed so far. These models provide decision rules that can be incorporated within easy-to-use computer programs. One such program is available as a module on the **Quantitative Management (QM)** software. It is invoked by selecting Inventory Theory from **QM**'s main menu. Figure 14.8 then illustrates how this program can be used to deal with Technical's inventory service level problem (Management Situation 14.5).

Problem Formulation. The user executes the program by selecting the EOQ with service-level option from the Inventory Problem menu. Management formulates the problem through the Edit command from the Input menu. In this formulation, the user provides the model's parameters: annual demand, unit procurement cost, the cost per order/setup, unit holding and stockout costs, and the average value and standard deviation of demand during the lead time. Report options then are chosen from the Output menu.

Optimal Inventory Policy. After receiving the parameters, the program will apply the appropriate model and provide the corresponding inventory recommendations. These recommendations include the economic order quantity, service level, reorder point, safety stock, and resulting total inventory cost. Figure 14.8, for example, shows that Technical's lowest cost service level is $P_S = 95.24$ percent. To achieve this service level,

Table 14.7 **Summary of the EOQ and EPQ Models**

Model	Assumptions	Total Cost	Order/Production and Shortage Quantities	Reorder Point	Cycle Times
EOQ	Single product Constant demand Constant lead time Constant unit costs Instantaneous replenishment No shortages No discounts	$TC = cD + \dfrac{c_o D}{Q} + \dfrac{c_H Q}{2}$	$Q^* = \sqrt{\dfrac{2c_o D}{c_H}}$	$R = dL$	$T = \dfrac{NQ^*}{D}$
EOQ with discounts	Same as EOQ model, except there are purchase discounts	Same as EOQ model	Least-cost feasible order size (see procedure recap)	Same as EOQ model	Same as EOQ model
EOQ with backorders	Same as EOQ model, except there are planned shortages	$TC = cD + \dfrac{c_o D}{Q} + \dfrac{c_H(Q - S)^2}{2Q} + \dfrac{c_B S^2}{2Q}$	$Q^* = \sqrt{\dfrac{2c_o D}{c_H}\left(\dfrac{c_H + c_B}{c_B}\right)}$ $S^* = Q^*\left(\dfrac{c_H}{c_H + c_B}\right)$	$R = dL - S$	$T = \dfrac{NQ^*}{D}$ $t_1 = \dfrac{Q - S}{d}$ $t_2 = \dfrac{S}{d}$
EPQ	Same as EOQ model, except inventory is produced gradually over time	$TC = cD + \dfrac{c_o D}{Q} + \left(1 - \dfrac{D}{P}\right)\dfrac{c_H Q}{2}$	$Q^* = \sqrt{\dfrac{2c_o D}{\left(1 - \dfrac{D}{P}\right)c_H}}$	$R = dL$ when $T - L \geq t$ $R = (p - d)(T - L)$ when $T - L < t$	$T = \dfrac{NQ^*}{D}$ $t = \dfrac{Q}{P}$
EOQ with service level	Same as EOQ model, except there is variable lead time demand	$TC = cD + \dfrac{c_o D}{Q} + c_H\left(B + \dfrac{Q}{2}\right) + c_B SP_s \dfrac{D}{Q}$	Same as EOQ model	$R = u + B$ or see procedure recap	Same as EOQ model

---

Figure 14.8   **Technical's Computer Solution**

Inventory Problem:
- Economic Order Quantity (EOQ)
- EOQ with Discounts
- EOQ with Backorders
- Economic Production Quantity (EPQ)
- * EOQ with Service Level
- Single Period Inventory
- Material Requirements Planning (MRP)

Input:
- * Edit
- Load
- Print
- Save

Output:
- Full
- * Summary
- * Print
- Save

Problem Description:
  Annual demand D: 81000
  Unit procurement cost c: .50
  Cost per order/setup c_o: 5
  Unit holding cost c_H: .09
  Unit stockout cost c_B: .07
  Average lead time demand: 1620
  Lead time demand standard deviation: 300

RECOMMENDATION

Economic Order Quantity Q^* = 3000
Service Level P_S = .9524
Reorder Point R = 2121
Safety Stock B = 501
Total Inventory Cost TC = 40872.58

---

management should order $Q^* = 3,000$ packages when inventory reaches the reorder point of $R = 2,121$ items and plan for a safety stock of $B = 501$ packages. Such a policy will result in a total inventory cost of $TC = \$40,872.58$.

Inventory Systems

Quantitative analysis, in practice, is implemented as part of a system for managing inventory. In a large organization, computer information systems will assimilate company records, forecast item sales, and generate ordering instructions for optimal inventory replenishment. One typical example is IBM's Inventory Forecasting and Replenishment Modules (INFOREM). For smaller firms, there are less costly business machines that electronically adjust inventory levels at the transaction point. Management can plan and control inventory by using the information from these devices with appropriate decision models. Such systems can apply a fixed order quantity, fixed order interval, hybrid, or ABC (Pareto) philosophy.

Fixed Order Quantity.   In the EOQ and EPQ models, the company continually monitors inventory transactions. Items are either recorded manually, observed in marked storage compartments, or entered online through a computerized order system. Then management places an order of fixed size whenever the inventory level reaches its reorder point. Such an approach is referred to as the **fixed order quantity (Q) system** for inventory planning and control.

The Q system is well-suited for high-cost items where constant review is desirable. The resulting close control, however, creates high clerical processing expenses.

Fixed Order Interval. Some suppliers take orders and make deliveries only at periodic intervals. For example, a dairy truck may stop at a grocery store every few days as it makes its rounds. Also, it may not be worthwhile for companies to continually review the available stock for items that are frequently issued but in small quantities, such as pencils, coffee, and bandages. In such cases, the inventory level is reviewed at equally spaced, predetermined points in time. The optimal review period (which could be days, weeks, or some other period) is the time interval that minimizes total inventory costs. At each review, the company counts the available stock manually, by inspection of a marked storage bin, or with a computerized system. Then management orders the amount necessary to reach a target inventory level. The target provides enough items to satisfy demand during the delivery lead time plus the interval between orders. Such a periodic review approach is called the **fixed order interval (P) system** of inventory management.

Since the periodic review involves scheduled replenishment and less record keeping, the P system results in low ordering expenses. On the other hand, the P system requires large inventories to satisfy demand during the review period and lead time and hence creates high holding expenses. As a result, the periodic review is best suited for situations in which a large number of items is regularly ordered from very few supply sources. Examples of firms that face such situations include retail drug stores, supermarkets, and nonretail businesses that order office and cleaning supplies.

In practice, companies use Q, P, and hybrid systems. For example, there is an approach in which stock levels are reviewed at regular intervals, as in the P system. However, orders are not placed until the inventory level has fallen to a predetermined reorder point, as in the Q system. Such an approach provides the close control of the fixed order quantity method and the fewer item orders associated with the periodic review.

Pareto. Decision makers should realize that a sophisticated inventory analysis is neither necessary nor desirable in all circumstances. In a typical inventory, a small percentage of items accounts for most of the dollar value. Companies recognize this characteristic and usually divide inventories into various arbitrary classifications for planning and control purposes. One widely used approach is the **ABC (Pareto) system**. The A category typically contains about 20 percent of the items and 80 percent of the dollar value of inventory. Hence, most of the inventory value can be controlled by intensively managing these items. For these items, management might use a tight control system involving continuous review of stock levels and the use of sophisticated decision models. At the other extreme, class C usually contains 50 percent of the items and only 5 percent of the dollar value. For these items, management might use a looser control system involving periodic review and simple ordering rules. Class B, between the extremes, represents approximately 30 percent of the items and accounts for about 15 percent of the dollar value. These items require an intermediate level of management attention.

Of course, each organization should tailor the inventory system to its own peculiarities. Instead of using the ABC approach, some firms may prefer to group inventory into additional classifications based on relevant decision factors other than dollar value.

However, the principle should be the same for any sensitive control system: high-value items receive the most attention and low-value items the least.

Within the classifications (ABC or other), there will be many items to manage and control. As long as the items have independent demands and are purchased and produced separately, the optimal inventory will simply be the sum of the least costly order or production quantities for each item. Basic Q and P system models can be used to determine these quantities.

14.3 NONCONTINUOUS AND DEPENDENT DEMAND

Each of the previous approaches assumes that there is a continuous and independent demand for the product. Generally, this assumption is reasonable for most finished goods and spare parts for replacement. On the other hand, in many situations, the demand for an item may be noncontinuous or related to the demand for other goods. This section discusses inventory systems designed for such circumstances.

Single-Period Inventory

Until now, we have assumed that management continuously repeats the order or production cycle. Furthermore, it has been possible to carry the resulting inventory for one or more periods. On the other hand, there are some products, like Christmas trees and bathing suits, that are highly seasonal. Others are either perishable (flowers, for example) or become obsolete very quickly (such as today's newspaper). These products cannot be carried in inventory and sold in future periods. In these situations, a buyer places a single preseason order for each item. Then, at the end of the season, either the product has sold out or there is a clearance sale on the surplus stock.

Under these circumstances, timing and frequency are already determined. There will be a single order placed at the start of the relevant period. Management must decide only how much to order. Obviously, if the exact sales level were known, the solution would be easy. The company would simply order the number of items necessary to fully satisfy demand. Unfortunately, these situations usually involve considerable demand uncertainty. This uncertainty necessitates an analysis based on the demand probabilities, as Management Situation 14.6 illustrates.

Management Situation 14.6

Ordering Seasonal Merchandise

Each year, The Chic Shop buys the latest women's fashion spring suit for $70 apiece and sells it for $110. It also costs $5 to carry each suit in inventory for the season. Hence, each suit involves a total cost of $70 + $5 = $75. Stock must be requested in advance of the season, and it costs $6 to place an order.

Surplus suits are sold for $45 each during an end-of-the-season clearance sale. If Chic is out of stock, the customer will shop elsewhere and Chic will lose the sale. In

Table 14.8 **Past Sales Data for Spring Suits**

Suits Sold per Season	Number of Shops
45	5
46	25
47	40
48	20
49	10

addition, there may be lost profit from accessory items, such as shoes and purses, and customer ill will. Management estimates that such penalties amount to $15 per suit.

Distributor records indicate that past sales of comparable merchandise by similar shops have been as indicated in Table 14.8. Since the designer has maintained a solid reputation, Chic assumes that this sales pattern will continue.

Each season, management wants to order the number of suits that will maximize expected profit.

Although Chic makes similar ordering decisions each season, the product rapidly becomes obsolete and thus cannot be carried in inventory from season to season. In effect, each order represents a separate decision.

Decision Table. Each season, the shop wants to order the number of suits demanded. Although the buyers do not know the exact demand ahead of time, Table 14.8 indicates that it could be between 45 and 49 suits. Thus, there is no sense in ordering fewer than 45 suits or more than 49. Indeed, Chic's alternatives are to stock either 45, 46, 47, 48, or 49 suits. Profit will depend on the resulting demand.

When the shop orders the exact number of suits demanded, it will earn a profit of $110 - $75 = $35 per suit. For example, if management stocks 46 suits and 46 are demanded, gross profit will be $46 \times $35 = $1,610$. When the order quantity is less than sales, Chic will lose profit on accessories and invite customer ill will. The result is a $15 penalty for each stockout. Suppose, for instance, that the shop stocks 48 suits and has a demand for 49. Then profit will be

$$48 \text{ suits @ } \$35/\text{suit} = \$1,680$$

less

$$1 \text{ suit @ } \$15/\text{suit} = -\$15$$

for a gross profit of $1,665. On the other hand, if Chic orders more suits than the quantity demanded, it will salvage the surplus for $45 per suit. In this case, the revenue ($45) is less than the cost ($75), and there will be a $30 loss per surplus item. Hence, when 47 suits are ordered but 45 demanded, the profit will be

Table 14.9   **Chic's Profits ($)**

Order Quantity (Suits)	Demand (Suits)				
	45	46	47	48	49
45	1,575	1,560	1,545	1,530	1,515
46	1,545	1,610	1,595	1,580	1,565
47	1,515	1,580	1,645	1,630	1,615
48	1,485	1,550	1,615	1,680	1,665
49	1,455	1,520	1,585	1,650	1,715

$$45 \text{ suits @ } \$35/\text{suit } = \$1,575$$

less

$$2 \text{ suits @ } \$30/\text{suit } = -\$60$$

for a gross profit of $1,515. Table 14.9, which is a decision table for the problem, presents the profit data for each order quantity (course of action) and demand (state of nature) combination.

Expected Value. Chic also knows the probabilities for each demand level. According to the available information, there is a

$$5/100 = .05 \text{ probability of selling 45 suits}$$
$$25/100 = .25 \text{ probability of selling 46 suits}$$
$$40/100 = .40 \text{ probability of selling 47 suits}$$
$$20/100 = .20 \text{ probability of selling 48 suits}$$
$$10/100 = .10 \text{ probability of selling 49 suits}$$

Using these probabilities, Chapter 4's expected monetary value criterion, and the profit data in Table 14.9, the shop can compute the expected profit of each order quantity. For instance, when Chic orders 45 suits, management can expect a profit of $1,575(.05) + $1,560(.25) + $1,545(.40) + $1,530(.20) + $1,515(.10) = $1,544.25 less the $6 ordering expense, or a net profit of $1,538.25. Similarly, when the shop stocks 46 suits, the expected profit is $1,545(.05) + $1,610(.25) + $1,595(.40) + $1,580(.20) + $1,565(.10) = $1,590.25 less the $6 ordering expense, or a net profit of $1,584.25. An order of 47 suits yields a net profit of $1,610.25, an order of 48 suits nets $1,604.25, and an order of 49 suits results in an expected net profit of $1,582.25.

Chic wants to select the inventory policy that maximizes expected profit. Thus, management should order 47 suits each season. Such a policy will result in an expected return of $1,610.25 per order.

Incremental Analysis

Small inventory problems can be solved rather quickly by using the expected value approach above. However, the method becomes quite cumbersome when there are

Table 14.10 **Chic's Incremental Decision**

	Demand Condition	
Inventory Action	No Additional Demand	Demand at Least One More Suit
Order no additional stock	$0	MU = $50
Stock one more suit	MO = $30	$0

Penalty for overordering   Penalty for underordering

numerous alternatives. Also, decision makers may be able to identify only ranges of demand levels rather than exact values. In these situations, incremental, or marginal, analysis provides an efficient way to select a decision alternative.

Penalties. The basic idea of incremental analysis is to compare the penalties associated with both ordering and not ordering each additional unit. Suppose that Chic stocks no additional units. If there is demand for at least one more suit, the shop will have a shortage. This underordering will result in a $50 penalty ($35 in lost suit profit plus $15 for lost accessory profit and ill will). Of course, if the shop has no additional demand, there is no penalty. On the other hand, suppose that Chic stocks exactly one additional unit. When there is no corresponding demand, the shop will have a surplus. Such overordering will result in a $30 penalty (the $75 cost less a $45 salvage). But if there is additional demand, the shop avoids this penalty. By letting

MU = incremental loss from underordering ($50 in this example)

MO = incremental loss from overordering ($30 in this example)

we can summarize the situation as shown in Table 14.10.

Balancing the Penalties. Notice that the penalties again depend on the demand. Although the exact demand is unknown, Chic can identify the probabilities for the possible sales levels. These probability data and the information in Table 14.10 can be used to identify the optimal ordering policy. By letting

p = the probability of no additional demand

$1 - p$ = the probability of demand for at least one more suit

management can expect a penalty of

$$\$0p + MU(1 - p) = MU(1 - p)$$

when the shop orders no additional stock and

$$MOp + \$0(1 - p) = MOp$$

if the shop stocks one more suit.

Table 14.11   Chic's Cumulative Probability Distribution of Demand

Suits Demanded per Season	Probability of Demand	Cumulative Probability of Demand
45	.05	0.05
46	.25	0.30
47	.40	0.70 $\leftarrow p = \dfrac{MU}{MU + MO} = .625$
48	.20	0.90
49	.10	1.00

To determine whether or not to order an additional suit, Chic must compare the expected penalties. As long as the expected penalty from ordering, MOp, is less than the loss from not stocking, $MU(1 - p)$, management should order an additional suit. Furthermore, suits should be added to the existing order quantity, one at a time, until the expected penalties are equal. This balance occurs when

$$MU(1 - p) = MOp$$

or

(14.28)
$$p = \frac{MU}{MU + MO}.$$

At this point, there is no incentive to order an additional suit.

According to equation (14.28), management should stock whatever quantity the shop will have a p chance of selling. In Chic's case, since $MU = \$50$ and $MO = \$30$,

$$p = \frac{\$50}{\$50 + \$30} = \frac{5}{8} = .625.$$

Hence, the shop must find the order quantity that will provide a 62.5 percent likelihood of selling as many suits as the shop stocks.

Optimal Ordering Policy. The value p is a cumulative probability. It gives the chance that sales will be less than or equal to a particular demand. For example, Chic knows that there is a .05 chance of selling 45 suits and a .25 probability of making 46 sales. Thus, there is a $.05 + .25 = .30$ likelihood that demand will be less than or equal to 46 suits. Chic's entire cumulative probability distribution is presented in Table 14.11. Recall that Chic will order the quantity corresponding to a cumulative probability of $p = .625$. As the table shows, this stock level is between 46 and 47 suits (but closer to 47). Unfortunately, management cannot order a fraction of a suit. Therefore, the shop must choose either 46 or 47 suits.

At 46 suits, the probability of no additional demand ($p = .30$) is less than the proportion ($p = .625$) given by equation (14.28). Consequently, the expected penalty from ordering an additional suit is less than the corresponding loss from not stocking. Chic should then stock $46 + 1 = 47$ suits. At 47 suits, the cumulative probability ($p = .70$) is more than .625. Thus, the shop should order no more than this amount, which is the same policy recommendation (stock 47 suits) as derived by the expected profit method.

Figure 14.9   **MRP Process**

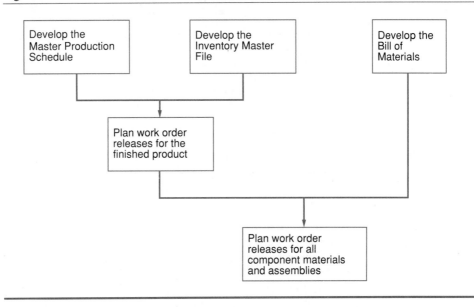

Procedure Recap.   The optimal ordering policy for a single-period inventory problem can be found with the following procedure:

1. Identify the probability distribution for demand, and compute the corresponding cumulative probability distribution.

2. Identify the penalties from underordering (MU) and overordering (MO) one additional unit, and compute the proportion $p = MU/(MU + MO)$.

3. Order the quantity corresponding to p in the cumulative probability distribution. When demand is measured in whole units and p is between two demand levels, order the quantity corresponding to the higher of the two demand levels.

This procedure can be applied to single-period inventory problems involving a probability distribution obtained from empirical data (as in Management Situation 14.6) or from theory (as with a normal probability distribution).

Material Requirements Planning

The demand for a finished good is influenced by market conditions that are, to a large degree, beyond the firm's control. Hence, this demand is essentially independent of company operations and must be estimated from product forecasts or company orders. Under these circumstances, it is not unreasonable to assume that each product has an independent, continuous demand.

On the other hand, the finished product is composed of raw materials and components. During production, the inputs are transformed into the desired end item. Therefore, when there is a demand for the end item, the production process will generate an

Table 14.12   **Raw Materials and Assemblies for Each Ball-point Pen**

Requirements	Source
Shaft assembly	
1 four-inch plastic casing	Manufactured
2 two-inch springs	Purchased
1 four-inch ball-point ink refill	Purchased
Top assembly	
1 two-inch metal casing	Manufactured
2 one-and-one-half-inch metal pocket clasps	Purchased
1 two-and-one-quarter-inch metal shaft	Manufactured

accompanying demand for each input. In effect, then, requirements for materials and components are derived from the demand for the finished product.

Production of the finished good cannot even begin until the required inputs are available. Thus, it is important to provide raw materials and work in process (components) in the correct amounts and at the right time during the manufacturing process. To do so, management must design an inventory system that accounts for the dependency between end item and raw material demand.

Material requirements planning (MRP) is such a system. It develops a work and purchase order plan that will provide necessary components at the time required to support the production schedule for the final product. The MRP process, which is outlined in Figure 14.9, can be illustrated with Management Situation 14.7.

Management Situation 14.7

Manufacturing Ball-point Pens

Paper Symbol, Inc. is a major producer of ball-point pens. Each pen is composed of a shaft and top assembly. The company's engineering design department has identified each assembly's raw materials requirements and sources. Table 14.12 summarizes the data.

Based on product forecasts and customer orders, management estimates that approximately 5,000 pens will be needed during week 4 of the current eight-week production schedule. Management also forecasts an additional requirement for 7,000 pens during week 7 of this schedule.

There is a one-week lead time for all manufactured raw materials, assemblies, and pens. The suppliers of the springs, refills, and pocket clasps each require a two-week lead time.

At the present time (week 1 of the current production schedule), Paper Symbol has 2,000 pens, 1,000 assemblies of each type, and 3,000 units of each raw material in stock. Outstanding production orders will provide another 1,600 pens and 250 assemblies of each type during week 1 of the current production schedule. Similarly, outstanding purchase orders will supply 50 springs, refills, and pocket clasps during week 2 of the schedule.

Paper Symbol's management wants to determine the purchase/manufacturing plan that will satisfy finished product demand. The plan should identify the quantities of pens, assemblies, and raw materials of each type required each week of the production schedule.

Once more, there may be a continuous and independent demand by consumers for the finished product (pens). The demand for assemblies (shafts and tops) and raw materials (plastic and metal casings, springs, refills, and pocket clasps) is another matter.

Master Production Schedule. Using customer orders and product forecasts, Paper Symbol has established that the end item (pen) demand can be met with the following production plan:

Week	1	2	3	4	5	6	7	8
Pens required	0	0	0	5,000	0	0	7,000	0

Such a time-phased plan, which lists how many finished items are needed and when, is called a **master production schedule (MPS)**. From the MPS, you can see that pens will be produced in intermittent "lumps" rather than on a continuous basis. Since requirements for assemblies and materials are derived from the output of the finished product (and hence the MPS), there will also be a "lumpy" demand for these components. For instance, in producing a batch of pens, management can expect a high rate of demand for plastic casings just before the company assembles shafts. Then there will be no demand for this component until Paper Symbol manufactures another batch of pens.

The EOQ/EPQ approaches are not effective inventory management devices for these situations. Such procedures constantly replenish inventory in anticipation of a continuous demand for the item. However, in the "lumpy" demand situation, this policy can create excessive inventory when it is not needed and shortages at other times. As a result, the company may have both an excessive inventory investment and customer service problems and costs. Also, the EOQ/EPQ approaches assume that each item has an independent demand. Hence, there is no assurance that materials and components will be available when required in the production process. To meet materials scheduling and delivery needs, then, the company may have to institute a support department with expediters.

Paper Symbol can avoid these operational problems and excessive inventory costs by scheduling components to arrive in inventory just before the items are needed. The appropriate schedule for the finished product (pens) can be derived from the MPS and inventory records. Table 14.13 illustrates the process.

Finished Product Work Orders. According to the MPS, Paper Symbol can satisfy customer demand by manufacturing 5,000 pens during week 4 and 7,000 pens during week 7 of the current production schedule. In effect, this schedule establishes the gross requirements for the finished product (pens).

Table 14.13   **Paper Symbol's Planned Pen Transactions**

Transaction Category	Week							
	1	2	3	4	5	6	7	8
Gross requirements				5,000			7,000	
Scheduled receipts	1,600							
Stock on hand	2,000	3,600	3,600					
Net requirements				1,400			7,000	
Planned order releases			1,400			7,000		

The company can use stock on hand and scheduled receipts from outstanding work and purchase orders to meet some or all of the gross requirements. To do so, however, management must maintain detailed records identifying the items on hand, the amounts previously committed to production, quantities on order with suppliers, and lead times. Such records are usually referred to as an **inventory master file (IMF)**.

From outstanding production orders, Paper Symbol is scheduled to receive 1,600 pens during week 1 of the MPS. At week 1, the company also has 2,000 pens in stock. Since none of these pens are required until week 4, Table 14.13 indicates that $1,600 + 2,000 = 3,600$ items will be in stock during weeks 2 and 3.

During week 4, management can use the stock of 3,600 pens to satisfy part of the 5,000-item gross requirement. This action still leaves a net requirement for $5,000 - 3,600 = 1,400$ pens. Assuming that Paper Symbol always requests the exact requirement, the company must plan work order receipts of 1,400 pens during week 4. Furthermore, manufacturing involves a one-week lead time. Thus, to satisfy the net requirement during week 4, management must release the work order during week 3.

No additional finished products are required during the fifth and sixth weeks. During week 7, there is a gross requirement for 7,000 pens. Since the company has no scheduled receipts or stock on hand, the net requirement is also 7,000 items. As a result, with the one-week lead time, management must release a 7,000-pen work order during week 6.

Bill of Materials. The planned work order releases for pens during weeks 3 and 6 will create requirements for the component materials and assemblies. To properly plan component work and purchase requirements, management will need a structured parts list that shows exactly how the finished product is actually put together. Such a list is referred to as the **bill of materials (BOM)**.

Table 14.12 presents the BOM for a Paper Symbol pen. A representation of this product structure is shown in Figure 14.10. It shows that the company must have two pocket clasps available at level 3 before the metal casing can be completed at level 2. Also, both a metal casing and a shaft must be ready at level 2 before Paper Symbol can assemble the top at level 1. Similarly, the company cannot assemble the shaft at level 1 until a plastic casing, two springs, and a refill are available at level 2. Finally, both a shaft and top assembly must be complete at level 1 before Paper Symbol can produce the pen at level 0.

Figure 14.10 **The Bill of Materials for a Paper Symbol Pen**

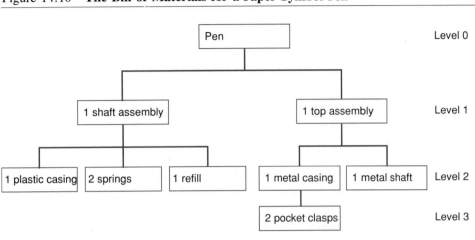

In effect, then, the BOM depicts how the finished product is exploded into its component parts and the hierarchy of steps involved in the manufacturing process. Paper Symbol can now use its BOM and IMF to plan component requirements. Figure 14.11 illustrates the process for a portion of the pen's top assembly.

Component Work/Purchase Orders. As Figures 14.11a and 14.11b indicate, the planned work order release for pens during week 3 creates a gross requirement of 1,400 top assemblies in the same period. However, inventory records (from Management Situation 14.7) indicate that there will be stock on hand by that time. Outstanding production orders will provide 250 top assemblies and existing inventory will provide another 1,000 top assemblies during week 1. Since none of the top assemblies are required during the first two weeks, Paper Symbol will already have $250 + 1,000 = 1,250$ in stock by week 3. Consequently, during week 3, there will be a net requirement for $1,400 - 1,250 = 150$ items. With a one-week lead time, management should plan to release a work order for 150 top assemblies during week 2.

Similarly, the planned work order release for pens during week 6 creates a gross requirement of 7,000 top assemblies in the same period. By that time, there are no scheduled receipts or stock on hand and so the net requirement is also 7,000 items. Considering the lead time, management must release a work order for 7,000 top assemblies during week 5.

As shown in Figure 14.11c, the planned order releases for top assemblies create gross requirements of 150 metal casings in week 2 and another 7,000 in week 5. Fortunately, there are 3,000 metal casings already in inventory by week 2. Thus, management can use some to satisfy the entire gross requirement in week 2 and still have $3,000 - 150 = 2,850$ on hand by week 5. As a result, the company should release a work order for $7,000 - 2,850 = 4,150$ metal casings during week 4.

Since two pocket clasps are used for each metal casing, the 4,150-casing work order release will create a gross requirement for $4,150 \times 2 = 8,300$ clasps during week 4.

Figure 14.11   **Paper Symbol's BOM Explosion**

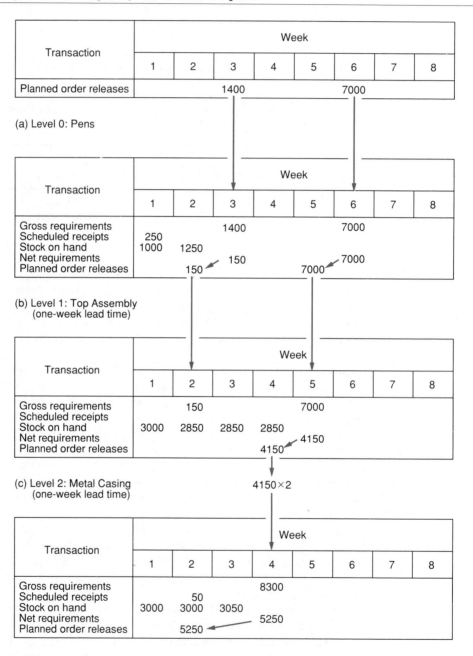

Transaction	Week							
	1	2	3	4	5	6	7	8
Planned order releases			1400			7000		

(a) Level 0: Pens

Transaction	Week							
	1	2	3	4	5	6	7	8
Gross requirements			1400			7000		
Scheduled receipts	250							
Stock on hand	1000	1250						
Net requirements			150			7000		
Planned order releases		150			7000			

(b) Level 1: Top Assembly
   (one-week lead time)

Transaction	Week							
	1	2	3	4	5	6	7	8
Gross requirements		150			7000			
Scheduled receipts								
Stock on hand	3000	2850	2850	2850				
Net requirements					4150			
Planned order releases				4150				

(c) Level 2: Metal Casing   4150×2
   (one-week lead time)

Transaction	Week							
	1	2	3	4	5	6	7	8
Gross requirements				8300				
Scheduled receipts		50						
Stock on hand	3000	3000	3050					
Net requirements				5250				
Planned order releases		5250						

(d) Level 3: Pocket Clasps
   (two-week lead time)

As Figure 14.11d indicates, considering scheduled purchase receipts and stock on hand, this gross generates a net requirement of 5,250 items in week 4. Now, Paper Symbol purchases the pocket clasps, and the supplier requires a two-week lead time. Therefore, the company must plan to release a 5,250-clasp purchase order during week 2.

Procedure Recap. Material requirements planning (MRP) can be summarized as follows:

1. Develop a master production schedule (MPS).
2. Using the inventory master file (IMF) and the MPS, plan work order releases for the finished product.
3. Using planned work order releases for the finished product, the bill of materials (BOM), and the IMF, develop the work and purchase plan for all component materials and assemblies.

Lot Sizing

In Management Situation 14.7, Paper Symbol always planned work and purchase order releases for the exact net requirements. For example, Table 14.13 shows that there is a 1,400-pen net requirement in week 4, and the corresponding planned order release (during week 3) is exactly the same quantity. Similarly, the 7,000-pen net requirement in week 7 becomes a 7,000-item planned release during week 6. This approach is called *lot-for-lot* ordering. As Figure 14.11 demonstrates, the company also uses lot-for-lot ordering of the pen components.

It may be economical or convenient to plan work and purchase order release quantities in excess of net requirements. For example, to avoid an extra order or setup charge, Paper Symbol might consider combining the 1,400- and 7,000-pen planned releases. This process of combining orders or setups, called *lot sizing*, should balance the costs of ordering and holding inventory.

Many lot-sizing techniques are available, including:

1. *Economic order quantity (EOQ)*—schedule production in lot sizes equal to the EOQ, while guaranteeing that all net requirements are filled.
2. *Wagner-Whitin algorithm*—uses dynamic programming (discussed in Chapter 16) to find the lot size that minimizes the sum of ordering and carrying costs.
3. *Silver-Meal heuristic*—finds the point at which average cost first increases and then sets the lot size equal to the cumulative net requirements up to this point.

The Wagner-Whitin algorithm is the only technique that guarantees an optimal lot size, but its calculations are somewhat unwieldy. As a result, managers often use a heuristic (such as the Silver-Meal technique) or the EOQ approach.

It is also important to recognize that the Q/P and MRP systems are complementary rather than competitive systems. Each approach has its own place in a firm's inventory management system. A company can use a Q or P system to manage end items and an MRP approach for components. In addition, as just noted, the firm may find it economical to use the EOQ methods for lot sizing of planned order releases.

Figure 14.12   **Paper Symbol's MRP Computer Solution**

Inventory Problem:
- Economic Order Quantity (EOQ)
- EOQ with Discounts
- EOQ with Backorders
- Economic Production Quantity (EPQ)
- Single Period Inventory

* Material Requirements Planning

Input:
* Edit
- Load
- Print
- Save

Output:
- Full
* Summary
* Print
- Save

Problem Description:
  MPS time periods: 8
  BOM levels: 4
  Total number of items: 9

Enter the master production schedule in the following table.

Master Production Schedule

Period:	1	2	3	4	5	6	7	8
Gross Requirement:	0	0	0	5000	0	0	7000	0

Enter the BOM and IMF in the following table.

Bill of Materials and Inventory Master File

Item Name	Level	Quantity	Current Inventory	Lead Time	Scheduled Receipts Period 1	2	3	4	5	6	7	8
Pen	0	1	2000	0	1600	0	0	0	0	0	0	0
Shaft	1	1	1000	1	250	0	0	0	0	0	0	0
Top	1	1	1000	1	250	0	0	0	0	0	0	0
Pcase	2	1	3000	1	0	0	0	0	0	0	0	0
Spring	2	2	3000	2	0	50	0	0	0	0	0	0
Refill	2	1	3000	2	0	50	0	0	0	0	0	0
Mcase	2	1	3000	1	0	0	0	0	0	0	0	0
Mshaft	2	1	3000	1	0	0	0	0	0	0	0	0
Clasp	3	2	3000	2	0	50	0	0	0	0	0	0

RECOMMENDATION

Level 0 Pen	1	2	3	Period 4	5	6	7	8
Gross requirements				5000			7000	
Scheduled receipts	1600							
Stock on hand	2000	3600	3600					
Net requirements				1400			7000	
Planned order releases			1400			7000		

Figure 14.12   *continuing*

Level 1 Shaft				Period				
	1	2	3	4	5	6	7	8
Gross requirements			1400			7000		
Scheduled receipts	250							
Stock on hand	1000	1250						
Net requirements			150			7000		
Planned order releases		150			7000			

Level 1 Top				Period				
	1	2	3	4	5	6	7	8
Gross requirements			1400			7000		
Scheduled receipts	250							
Stock on hand	1000	1250						
Net requirements			150			7000		
Planned order releases		150			7000			

Level 2 Pcase				Period				
	1	2	3	4	5	6	7	8
Gross requirements		150			7000			
Scheduled receipts								
Stock on hand	3000	2850	2850	2850				
Net requirements					4150			
Planned order releases				4150				

Level 2 Spring				Period				
	1	2	3	4	5	6	7	8
Gross requirements		300			1400			
Scheduled receipts		50						
Stock on hand	3000	2700	2750	2750				
Net requirements					11250			
Planned order releases			11250					

Level 2 Refill				Period				
	1	2	3	4	5	6	7	8
Gross requirements		150			7000			
Scheduled receipts		50						
Stock on hand	3000	2850	2900	2900				
Net requirements					4100			
Planned order releases			4100					

Figure 14.12   *continuing*

Level 2 Mcase	Period							
	1	2	3	4	5	6	7	8
Gross requirements		150			7000			
Scheduled receipts								
Stock on hand	3000	2850	2850	2850				
Net requirements					4150			
Planned order releases				4150				

Level 2 Mshaft	Period							
	1	2	3	4	5	6	7	8
Gross requirements		150			7000			
Scheduled receipts								
Stock on hand	3000	2850	2850	2850				
Net requirements					4150			
Planned order releases				4150				

Level 3 Clasp	Period							
	1	2	3	4	5	6	7	8
Gross requirements				8300				
Scheduled receipts		50						
Stock on hand	3000	3000	3050					
Net requirements				5250				
Planned order releases		5250						

Computer Analysis

The MRP process involves a large number of detailed calculations that are time-consuming and prone to error when done by hand. In large-scale applications, the sheer volume of these calculations may prohibit the effective implementation of manual MRP systems. That is why a number of vendors, including IBM, Honeywell, and Burroughs, have developed computer programs to perform the MRP.

A fairly standard MRP computer program is available on the **Quantitative Management (QM)** software. Figure 14.12 illustrates how this program can be used to help perform Paper Symbol's material requirements planning.

Problem Formulation. The user executes the program by selecting the Material requirements planning option from the Inventory menu. Management formulates the problem through the Edit command from the Input menu. In this formulation, the user first provides the number of time periods in the master production schedule (MPS), the number of levels in the bill of materials (BOM), and the total number of items in the BOM. In Paper Symbol's case, there are eight weeks in the MPS, four levels (0 through 3) in the BOM, and nine items (pen, shaft, refill, and so on) in the BOM. Hence, the user should enter 8, 4, and 9 after the relevant description prompts in Figure 14.12. Next, the user inputs the master production schedule, bill of materials, and inventory master file in the tables provided by the program. As Figure 14.12 indicates, the bill of materials and inventory master file data includes the item name, level, quantity, current inventory, lead time, and scheduled receipts. Report options then are chosen from the Output menu.

BOM Explosion. After receiving the parameters, the program processes the data and generates a recommended bill of materials (BOM) explosion. This recommendation identifies the work and production order plan that will provide necessary components at the times required to support the master production schedule (MPS). The program utilizes a lot-for-lot ordering scheme. Figure 14.12, for example, shows that Paper Symbol must release 5,250 clasps during week 2 and 4,150 metal casings during week 4 of the planning period.

MRP Extensions

Material requirements planning provides many important benefits, including: (1) relatively few stockouts, (2) relatively low inventory, (3) relatively low holding cost, and (4) the ability to keep track of material requirements. These benefits, however, are not without costs. To be truly effective, MRP typically must be delivered through a computer information system. In such a system, it is necessary to have precise forecasts and accurate and timely master production schedules, inventory master files, and bills of materials. Since procedural changes will frequently modify the underlying relationships, MRP's large databases will require extensive maintenance.

Even without these costs, MRP has not been the panacea many had envisioned. This realization has caused manufacturers and consultants to develop enhancements and modifications that improve traditional MRP. Important developments include capacity requirements planning (CRP), manufacturing resource planning (MRP II), and distribution resource planning (DRP).

Capacity Requirements Planning. CRP computes the requirements placed on a work center or group of work centers by the MRP master production schedule's planned order releases. If these releases result in an infeasible requirements schedule, management must take appropriate corrective actions. One possibility is to schedule overtime at the bottleneck locations. Another is to revise the master production schedule so that the planned order releases can be achieved with the existing system capacity.

Manufacturing Resource Planning. MRP II is a philosophy that incorporates other relevant firm activities (such as finance and marketing) into the production process. In this approach, marketing, finance, and production people work together to develop a production plan that is consistent with the overall business plan and with the long-term financial strategy of the firm. After an initial plan is developed, its requirements are compared to production capacity and the plan is modified as necessary. The resulting final plan then becomes the basis for traditional MRP and for CRP.

Distribution Resource Planning. Firms involved in the manufacture and distribution of consumer products must take into account the interactions between the various levels (echelons) in the distribution chain. In such a system, the demand arises at the lowest echelon (typically, the retail level) and is transmitted up to the higher echelons (typically, the warehouses and factories). Production plans at the highest echelon must be coordinated with orders placed at the lower echelons. DRP uses of MRP to provide a time-phased stock replenishment plan for all levels of a distribution network.

Just in Time

Most traditional inventory control approaches (including EOQ and MRP) are push systems. These systems use market demand estimates or requirements at a higher level to plan production at the existing level in the manufacturing process. Once manufactured, the inventory is pushed to the next level of production.

In the traditional systems, inventory often is created "just in case" extra items are needed to overcome late deliveries, machine breakdowns, and poor employee performance. Under these circumstances, inventory may simply hide problems in the firm's operations rather than fully serve its business and economic functions. Moreover, operation problems that are hidden by excess inventory may, after a while, be very difficult to isolate and solve.

JIT Philosophy. The potential for large savings in inventory investments has encouraged organizations to utilize a production and inventory philosophy called **just in time (JIT)**, which is different from the traditional approaches. In JIT, inventories are treated as a liability that must be kept to a minimum. Lot and order sizes are geared to immediate needs only, with frequent reordering as needed. There are rapid machine setups and changeovers, and efforts are made to reduce the costs associated with changeovers and machine breakdowns. Programs are implemented to generate zero defects so that quality problems do not disrupt production. Workers are viewed as vital resources and are encouraged to participate in the management of the organization. Vendors are treated as part of the team rather than as adversaries.

Just in time minimizes inventory by ordering and producing very small batch sizes. As each order of raw materials arrives from a vendor, it goes directly into production, and as each batch is finished at one work center, it is moved to the following work center. Small lot sizes (comprising no more than several hours worth of production) are maintained by establishing plans and policies that reduce setup time and cost. Some possibilities include

1. performing the preparation part of ordering/setup during operations,
2. improving material handling, and
3. standardizing work procedures.

In addition, the small inventory levels and large number of orders/setups will encourage operations managers to follow tight and highly synchronized manufacturing schedules.

Inventory in Practice

Inventory models are applied to a wide variety of management problems. Here are a few areas in which this quantitative analysis is used.

Area	Application
Finance and Accounting	Controlling cash reserves Incorporating intra-year purchases and accounting tax incentives into inventory management
Marketing	Developing a cost-efficient strategy for the distribution of electrical appliances Establishing a materials handling policy in a department store
Production and Operations	Managing spare parts inventory Manufacturing automobiles at Toyota Minimizing the costs of distributing pharmaceuticals
Public and Service Sector	Reducing blood wastage in hospital blood banks Minimizing the costs of maintaining a utility's fuel inventory

Kanban. JIT systems typically use a *kanban* (Japanese for card) to authorize either the movement of parts/materials (conveyance *kanban*) or production operations (production *kanban*). Containers of small lots are passed between work centers as authorized by a conveyance card. The conveyance signal comes from the using center, pulling rather than pushing inventory through the system. Activity at the work center is triggered by a production *kanban* when the container is empty. Instead of producing to meet a predetermined schedule, the *kanban* approach calls for production to satisfy the need established by downstream work centers.

Andon. Each work center is equipped with a light system (*andon*) that is used to signal problems. A green light signals no problem, an amber light indicates that the center's work is lagging, and a red light signals a problem (such as an equipment breakdown or a quality deficiency). Workers are cross-trained so that they can assist each other until the center is back on track. Since workers are also trained to handle equipment repair, any breakdown usually can be quickly rectified.

Advantages and Disadvantages. Since JIT creates small work-in-process inventories, the system will decrease inventory costs, improve production efficiency, and point out quality problems quickly. This feature, however, could lead to increased worker idle time and a decreased production rate.

JIT's coordinated inventory and purchasing will reduce stock on hand, improve the coordination of different systems, and improve relationships with vendors. On the other hand, such coordination could decrease the opportunity for multiple sourcing. It also requires suppliers to react more quickly and to improve their reliability.

Kanbans offer an inexpensive way to implement the JIT philosophy. They also provide for an efficient lot tracking and allow for a predetermined level of work-in-process inventory. Yet, the approach will react slowly to changes in demand, and it ignores known information about future demand patterns.

In short, JIT can be a useful tool in the right circumstances, but it is an addition to, rather than a replacement for, traditional methodologies. These right circumstances are mainly repetitive manufacturing situations in which products are produced in batches with changeovers between runs. In a job shop environment, when production or final assembly awaits a specific customer order, management usually will be better off using MRP.

SUMMARY

In this chapter we have seen how quantitative methods can assist managers in formulating sound inventory policies. We began by defining the nature of inventory as an idle stock of raw materials, capital, labor, equipment, work in process, and/or finished goods. We also reviewed the business and economic functions performed by these idle stocks and identified the resulting procurement, ordering/setup, carrying/holding, and shortage expenses.

We considered a fundamental inventory situation and developed a method for determining the optimal order quantity, timing, and frequency. The basic analysis was then expanded to include the decision considerations of quantity discounts, planned shortages, production situations, and risk and uncertainty. It was noted that these approaches involve a fixed order quantity, or Q, system for inventory planning and control. In such a system, the company continually monitors inventory transactions and then places an order of fixed size whenever the stock level reaches its reorder point. We also discussed the fixed order interval, or P, system of inventory management. In this approach, the inventory level is reviewed at equally spaced, predetermined intervals. At each review, management counts the available stock and orders the amount necessary to reach a target inventory level. Each system (and its hybrids) has its own advantages, disadvantages, and areas of application. The ABC classification method is also an effective device for selective inventory planning and control in Q or P systems.

Basic Q and P systems assume that there is a continuous and independent demand for the item. The last section of the chapter presented inventory systems designed for situations in which these assumptions are not valid. Typical cases involve items that cannot be carried in inventory from period to period (like seasonal or perishable merchandise) or that have an uncertain demand. Under these circumstances, management places only a single order at the start of the relevant period; hence, the objective is to find the optimal order quantity.

Another type of situation involves items that have related demands (like the components of a finished product). In this case, completion of the end item cannot even begin until the required inputs are available in the correct amounts at the right time. The objective is to develop a work and purchase order release plan that accounts for the demand dependency. This objective can be accomplished with material requirements planning (MRP).

Just in time inventory systems reflect the influence of Japanese management approaches. With these systems, small order quantities are scheduled to arrive at just the right time the items are needed in the production process. Such an approach substantially reduces the inventory being held to maintain operations. It is best suited for repetitive manufacturing situations.

Inventory activities can be an extremely expensive phase of a firm's operation. Hence, it is important for managers to make correct inventory decisions. Since quantitative models can help decision makers develop sound inventory policies, these techniques offer a potential source for substantial cost savings.

Glossary

ABC (Pareto) system A selective control approach that classifies inventory into three groups: A, B, and C. Class A, which receives the most management attention, contains the few items with the largest value. Class C, which requires little control, contains the bulk of items with the smallest value. Class B, between the extremes, receives moderate management attention.

backorder A customer order that is filled from future purchases rather than from inventory on hand.

bill of materials (BOM) A structured parts list that shows exactly how the finished product is put together.

buffer (safety stock) Extra inventory held specifically to reduce shortages resulting from a larger-than-expected demand during lead time.

carrying (holding) costs The expenses associated with financing, physically handling, storing, and maintaining inventory.

economic lot size (economic production run quantity) The production quantity that minimizes total inventory costs in the EPQ model.

economic order quantity The order size that minimizes total inventory costs in the EOQ model.

fixed order interval (P) system A planning and control approach in which management periodically reviews available stock and then orders the amount necessary to reach a target inventory level. The target provides enough items to satisfy demand during the delivery lead time plus the interval between orders.

fixed order quantity (Q) system A planning and control approach in which management continually reviews available stock and then places an order of fixed size whenever the inventory level reaches its reorder point.

inventory Idle stocks of raw materials, capital, labor, equipment, work in process, or finished goods and services.

inventory cycle time The period between the placing of two consecutive orders.

inventory master file (IMF) Detailed records identifying the stock on hand, amounts previously committed to production, quantities on order with suppliers, and lead times.

just in time production An operations management approach that eliminates waste, synchronizes manufacturing, and creates little inventory by manufacturing small lot sizes to very precise standards.

kanban (card) A system that creates small lot sizes by moving inventory through a production operation only as needed.

lead time The period between the placing of an order and its receipt.

master production schedule (MPS) A time-phased plan that identifies how many finished items are to be produced and when.

material requirements planning (MRP) A system that develops a work and purchase order plan providing necessary components at the times required to support a production schedule for a finished product.

ordering (setup) costs The expenses associated with placing an order or physically preparing the production apparatus.

procurement costs The expenses associated with purchasing or manufacturing items for demand and inventory.

reorder point The inventory level at which a new order should be placed.

service level The percentage of customer demands satisfied from inventory.

stockout (shortage) costs The expenses incurred when available inventory is insufficient to fully satisfy demand.

Thought Exercises

1. Identify the nature and function of inventory in each of the following situations:
   a. A police department's officer roster at a given time of day
   b. A bank's monthly cash flow.
   c. A newsstand's sales of a sports magazine
   d. Ships arriving at a seaport
   e. Consumer demand for electricity

2. Identify the appropriate inventory costs in each of the following situations:
   a. A U.S. wheat farmer selling in international markets
   b. A drugstore selling brand-name aspirin
   c. A professional football team's equipment manager stocking spare equipment
   d. Your decision to keep a supply of toothpaste on hand
   e. A military ordinance supply battalion servicing a domestic training division

3. Refer to Management Situation 14.3. What is Technical's reorder point in this situation? Is this point higher or lower than the corresponding value in the basic EOQ situation (Management Situation 14.1)? Explain. Develop a general expression for the reorder point in the EOQ model with backorders. Figure 14.5 may be helpful in your derivation.

4. The Broadmor Department Store operates an automotive repair shop. One of its most popular requests is the brake reline special. Service records indicate that the shop does an average of four relines on each of the 300 annual days of operation. Although Broadmor cannot stock the service, it is possible to inventory the parts necessary to perform the special. In this respect, each reline requires four packages of brake shoes (each package contains two brake shoes). It costs Broadmor $2 to stock each package of brake shoes for a year and $12 to place an order with its supplier.

   Top management believes that inventory systems are important decision-making aids and has frequently used an EOQ policy. However, shortages have always been considered "bad" policy, even though most Broadmor customers have demonstrated a willingness to wait for service. Recently, there has been increased pressure for cost reduction, and the shop manager has proposed a backordering policy for the brake special. He estimates that rescheduling of customers and other additional expenses will be $4 per backorder per year.
   a. Do you think that Broadmor should accept the proposal? Explain.
   b. Suppose that top management will tolerate no more than 20 percent of the order quantity on backorder. In addition, the company wants to make sure that no customer will wait more than seven days for service. Will these constraints change your recommendation? Explain.

5. Science Associates (SA) has decided to begin processing its own data rather than contracting with an outside vendor. The company's projects create 1,000 data processing jobs per month and involve a setup cost of $80 per job. Each completed job awaiting project usage is stored on a tape at an annual expense of $20. Once the system is operating, it can process 2,500 jobs per month. The company normally operates approximately 300 working days per year. It takes eight days to set up each data processing job.

a. What is SA's reorder point? Is this point higher or lower than you would expect in the EOQ situation? Explain.

b. Develop a general expression for the reorder point in the EPQ situation. Figure 14.5 may be helpful in your derivation.

6. Most of the basic EOQ/EPQ models presented in the chapter assumed that the lead time L was less than the cycle time T. This assumption may not be valid in practice. What would be the effect on the reorder point R if $L > T$? Explain. Develop general expressions for the reorder point in the EOQ, EOQ with backorders, and EPQ models when $L > T$. Figures 14.3, 14.5, and 14.6 may aid your derivation.

7. Each week, Market Fair buys bananas for $8.50 a crate and sells them for $12.50. The $8.50 cost includes inventory procurement and holding expenses. It costs $15 to place an order.

Any surplus crates are sold at a discount price of $5.50 apiece at the end of the week. A customer will not come back if Market Fair is out of stock. Thus, a shortage results in lost profit (from the bananas and other items in the store). The market manager has assessed this penalty cost at $5 per crate. Of this penalty, $4 represents the banana profit and $1 results from ill will and lost income from other items.

Observations show that sales over the past 50 weeks have been as follows:

Crates Sold	Number of Weeks
78	3
79	13
80	19
81	12
82	3

Since the market for bananas is relatively stable, the store assumes that this sales pattern will continue.

After analyzing the data, Zane Tirp, the assistant produce manager, recommends an order quantity of 81 crates. He feels that this policy will maximize expected profits at $301.14. Greta Smithfield, the accountant, has done an incremental analysis. According to her calculations, an order of 80 crates has a better chance of balancing the penalties from over- and underordering.

Can you explain how each person arrived at his or her recommendation? There have been no errors in computing expected profits. Is it possible to reconcile their differences? What order quantity would you recommend? Explain. (*Hint:* Closely examine the market manager's assessment of penalty costs.)

8. Explain why you agree or disagree with each of the following statements:

a. In the EOQ model with quantity discounts, the optimal solution will never involve a purchase cost that leads to a Q^* larger than necessary to qualify for the discount.

b. Since discounts encourage larger order sizes, management should expect a higher reorder point in the quantity discount EOQ model (as compared to the basic EOQ model).

c. In the EPQ model, average inventory is a fraction of the corresponding level in the EOQ formulation because the production quantity does not go into inventory at one point in time.

d. Safety stocks can be expected to increase inventory expenses.

e. Safety stocks will decrease as the service level increases.

f. Since the demand for components depends on the sales of the finished product, inventory levels for all items are generally higher in an MRP system.

g. MRP is not really appropriate for service industries.

h. Kanban systems pull, while just in case approaches push, inventory through the production process.

i. Investment is often larger than necessary because firms find it easier to have "just in case," rather than "just in time," inventory.

Technique Exercises

9. A large business firm buys a machine component for $10 a box. Approximately two boxes are used every week. Machines are idle for maintenance two weeks of every year. The ordering cost is $1 and the company estimates annual carrying expenses at 20 percent of the purchase cost per box.

   a. Develop the procurement, ordering, carrying, and total inventory cost expressions for this situation.

   b. Determine the economic order quantity and the order timing and frequency.

   c. What are the resulting costs?

10. The Sharp Plume Men's Shop sells 1,000 Supreme brand dress shirts a year. Order cost is $20 and inventory carrying expenses are 30 percent of the value of a shirt. Also, the supplier offers a generous discount. The price list is as follows:

Quantity	Purchase Price ($) per Shirt
0–99	9.00
100–199	8.00
200–499	7.50
500 and over	7.40

Find the economic order quantity that results in the smallest total cost. Then determine the order timing and frequency. Show all your calculations. Did you notice anything unusual in your EOQ calculations for the first purchase price category? Explain.

11. Flora Industries distributes large industrial cranes on the East Coast. Demand is known to be 100 units per year. The company can order cranes anytime and delivery from the plant is instantaneous. There is a fixed ordering expense of $1,000, and each crane can be stored in the company warehouse for $200 per month. Although customers will wait for an order, the delay creates additional expenses of $400 per crane per month.

   a. Determine the economic order quantity, the order frequency, and the resulting minimum cost per cycle.

   b. Determine how many units will be supplied late each cycle.

12. The R&J Bottling Company has a forecasted annual demand of 50,000 cases for its specialty soft drink. R&J operates 250 days annually and can produce 400 cases daily. There is a $300 setup cost associated with each production run, and yearly holding costs are estimated at $12 per case.
    a. Compute the optimal production lot size and resulting time between runs.
    b. Determine the cost associated with the production plan.

13. Refer to Management Situation 14.5. Demonstrate that the optimal service level procedure leads to fewer shortages and a lower cost than the 92.59 percent service level. Show all your calculations.

14. A large retail chain store sells its own brand of large-screen television systems. The M4-J system has a wholesale cost of $1,200, an ordering expense of $40 per request, and annual carrying costs equal to 25 percent of the value of the average inventory.
    Demand is uncertain, but past sales show the following pattern:

Weekly Demand	Number of Weeks
5	10
10	25
15	40
20	15
25	10

The store operates five days per week and 50 weeks per year. There is a supply lead time of two days.
    a. Compute the average annual demand, the resulting economic order quantity, the average number of orders, and the cycle time.
    b. Determine the probability distribution for lead time demand.
    c. If management will tolerate no more than five stockouts per year, what is the reorder point and resulting safety stock?
    d. If there is a $150 penalty cost associated with each stockout, what is the optimal reorder point and resulting safety stock?

15. You are given the following profit data and corresponding demand probabilities:

	Demand				
	125	126	127	128	129
	Probability of Demand				
Order Quantity	.10	.30	.40	.15	.05
125	$1,125	$1,095	$1,065	$1,035	$1,005
126	1,085	1,150	1,120	1,090	1,060
127	1,045	1,110	1,175	1,145	1,115
128	1,005	1,070	1,135	1,200	1,170
129	965	1,030	1,095	1,160	1,225

    a.   First use expected values and then incremental analysis to find the most profitable order quantity.

    b.   Compare the results. Comment.

16. A retail outlet sells a seasonal product for $20 a unit. The product costs $15 a unit. All units not sold during the regular season are sold for one-quarter of the retail price at the end-of-season clearance sale. Assume that the demand for the product is normally distributed with $\mu = 300$ and $\sigma = 50$.

    a.   What is the recommended order quantity? What is the probability of a stockout?

    b.   Suppose that the owner wants to keep customers happy so that they will return to the store later. Hence, when there is a stockout, he believes there is a $2 ill will cost. Now what is the recommended order quantity? What is the corresponding probability of a stockout?

17. Refer to Management Situation 14.7. Complete Paper Symbol's material requirements plan (MRP) by developing the BOM explosion for the entire shaft assembly and the metal shaft portion of the top assembly.

18. You are given the following master production schedule (MPS) for finished product A:

Week	1	2	3	4	5	6	7	8	9	10
Demand	0	0	2,500	0	1,000	0	0	0	3,000	500

The corresponding bill of materials (BOM) is given in the following diagram:

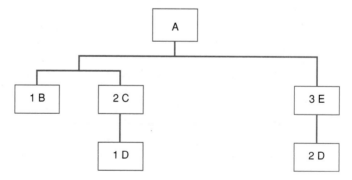

Data from the inventory master file is as follows:

Item	Lead Time	Stock on Hand	Scheduled Receipts in Week									
			1	2	3	4	5	6	7	8	9	10
A	1 week	1,500	500									
B	1 week	1,000				500				500		
C	2 weeks	3,000	200									
D	2 weeks	0	100									100
E	1 week	500				200						

Assuming a lot-for-lot ordering policy, determine the planned work and purchase order MRP plan for the finished part and each component.

Computer Exercises

19. Refer to Management Situation 14.1 in the text. Use the **Quantitative Management (QM)** software to solve Technical's inventory problem.

20. Radio Barn is a regional electronics retailer. From experience, management knows that the demand for a particular stereo is very steady, averaging approximately 100 sets per month. Moreover, it costs $20 to place an order with the manufacturer, and the annual holding expense is 15 percent of the purchase price. The manufacturer sells the stereo to Radio Barn for $100 per set. Lead time is 10 days.

Management seeks the policy that will minimize total inventory expenses. Use the **QM** software to determine the policy.

21. Refer to Management Situation 14.2. Use the **QM** software to solve Technical's quantity discount problem.

22. Instant Processor Booths carries Pallette instant print film. Normally, the film costs the company $2.90 a roll, and the booths sell it for $3.70 per roll. The film has a shelf life of 20 months, and the booths sell an average of 50 rolls per week. It costs Instant $25 to place an order with Pallette, and annual holding expenses are 30 percent of the purchase price. Pallette offers a 5 percent discount on orders over 800 rolls, a 10 percent discount on orders over 1,800 rolls, and a 15 percent discount on orders over 3,500 rolls. Lead time is five days.

Management seeks the policy that will minimize total inventory expenses. Use the **QM** software to determine the policy.

23. Refer to Management Situation 14.3. Use the **QM** software to solve Technical's back-order problem.

24. Jallopy Enterprises has a fleet of 1,250 used cars that are rented daily to budget-minded customers in the Cloverville area. All cars are maintained at a central garage. On average, four cars a month require a new transmission at a unit cost of $425. Transmissions are ordered from Discount Automotive Parts for a fixed fee of $60. Jallopy also has an annual holding cost rate of 15 percent on all parts kept in inventory. It takes two weeks to get the transmissions after management places an order. For each week a car is out of service, Jallopy loses $20.

Management seeks the inventory policy that will minimize total costs. Use the **QM** software to determine the best policy.

25. Refer to Management Situation 14.4. Use the **QM** software to solve Technical's EPQ problem.

26. Luxurious Upholstery Company is the exclusive manufacturer of automobile seats for several foreign car producers. Current outstanding orders and historical records indicate that the company will have a demand for 1,000 seats in each of its 200 days of annual operation. It costs $8,000 to set up the manufacturing process with existing procedures. Lead time is four days. A Japanese consultant, however, believes that the setup cost and time can be reduced by 50 percent with just in time production concepts.

Annual holding costs are estimated to be $20 per seat. Also, Luxurious is capable of manufacturing 1,500 seats per day with existing procedures. On the other hand, the rate can be increased by an estimated 60 percent if the company adopts a *kanban* system.

Management seeks the policy that will minimize total inventory expenses. These people also would like to compare the results from existing manufacturing procedures with the outcomes from just in time (and *kanban*) approaches. Use the **QM** software to perform the evaluation.

27. Advanced Supplies is a pioneer in developing and selling innovative health care delivery equipment. The company has just introduced a new line of heart monitoring devices that are superior medically to existing equipment. Field research indicates that the company can expect an average demand for about 10 devices for each of its 250 days of operation. However, competition and supplier delivery delays have created a great deal of uncertainty about demand during the lead time. Using historical data and some judgment, management estimates that lead time demand follows a normal probability distribution with a standard deviation of two devices per day.

It costs $80 to place an order with the supplier, and the lead time is three days. Annual carrying costs amount to $50 per device. Since stockouts will create ill will among physicians, the company assesses a $160 penalty cost for each shortage.

Management seeks the policy that will minimize total inventory expenses. Use the **QM** software to determine the policy.

28. Refer to Management Situation 14.6. Use the **QM** software to solve Chic's inventory problem.

29. A local grocery store is going to place an order for Easter candy. The candy can be purchased for $2.80 per box, and it can be sold for $6 per box until Easter. After Easter, any remaining boxes are sold for $2 per box. Demand is uncertain but is expected to follow the distribution below.

Boxes Sold	Probability
200	.10
300	.20
360	.15
400	.20
500	.20
600	.10
660	.05

When a potential customer cannot buy candy, the store incurs an ill will cost of $3.50.

Management seeks the inventory policy that will result in the largest profit. Use the **QM** software to determine the best policy.

30. Atlantic Vehicles has just received an order for 20,000 ATVs from Downtown Bikes. To meet the contract requirements, the ATVs must be completed in 12 weeks. The following is a bill of materials chart for Atlantic's ATV.

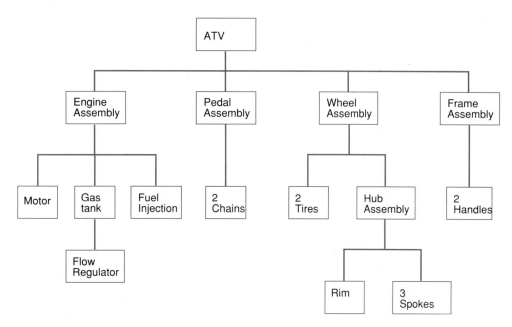

ATVs will be produced on the master production schedule below.

Week	1	2	3	4	5	6	7	8	9	10	11	12
ATVs	0	5000	0	0	4,000	0	0	0	6,000	3,000	0	2,000

Inventory master file data is summarized below.

Item	Lead Time	Current Inventory	Scheduled Receipts											
			1	2	3	4	5	6	7	8	9	10	11	12
ATV	1	4,400	1,000	0	0	0	0	0	1,000	0	0	0	0	0
Engine	2	3,000	500	500	0	0	500	0	0	0	0	500	0	0
Pedal	4	1,800	800	0	0	800	0	0	0	0	800	0	0	0
Wheel	1	4,000	400	0	400	0	400	0	0	0	0	0	0	0
Frame	3	1,600	0	200	0	0	200	0	200	0	0	0	0	200
Motor	2	3,200	0	0	300	300	0	0	0	0	0	0	0	0
Tank	5	1,200	0	0	0	400	400	0	0	0	400	0	0	0
Injector	3	1,800	1,000	0	0	1,000	0	0	0	0	0	0	1,000	0
Chain	4	3,400	600	600	0	0	0	0	0	0	0	0	0	0
Tire	3	2,000	0	0	0	450	0	450	0	0	0	450	0	0
Hub	1	4,000	0	180	180	180	0	0	0	0	0	0	0	0
Bar	3	12,000	4,000	0	4,000	0	4,000	0	0	0	0	0	0	0
Regulator	2	6,400	0	0	950	950	0	0	0	0	0	0	0	0
Rim	4	16,000	650	650	650	650	0	0	0	0	0	0	0	0
Spoke	6	1,200	330	330	330	330	0	0	0	0	0	330	0	0

Management seeks the work and purchase order plan that will meet the contract requirements for the ATVs. Use the **QM** software to develop the plan.

Applications Exercises

31. Big Z Discount House has experienced a relatively constant demand for 4,000 Quick Start batteries each month. The store buys the Quick Start from a large national manufacturer for $10 each. It takes the manufacturer three days ($^1/2$ week) to fill an order. Big Z can place an order for $10, and it costs 20 percent of the average inventory value to carry a battery for a month.

   a. How many Quick Starts should Big Z order at a time to minimize total inventory costs?

   b. What is the resulting ordering cost? Carrying cost? Total cost?

   c. What is the length of time between orders?

   d. How many batteries should be in inventory when Big Z places an order?

   e. Suppose that the cost of placing an order increases to $15 and that the price of the Quick Start rises by $10. How will these changes affect Big Z's inventory policy?

32. Talton Corporation is the manufacturer of an agricultural tractor that currently sells for $12,000. There is a demand for 900 tractors per year. Until last year, the company had very little competition. Then several foreign firms entered the market and Talton's sales began to drop. In an effort to keep its market share, Talton did not increase prices even though inflation increased operating costs by 14 percent. Although the policy was successful in maintaining sales, the company's earnings decreased significantly. As a result, management is now considering proposals to reduce expenses.

   Talton has the capacity to manufacture 100 tractors per month at a unit cost of $9,600. In addition, it costs $15,000 to set up the production apparatus. Merchandise awaiting distribution is stored at various places in the firm's warehousing system. Considering warehousing operating costs, obsolescence, theft, finance charges, and other factors, Talton's accounting department assigns 20 percent of the unit cost per tractor for annual storage expenses.

   At present, the company produces at a rate that exactly meets the demand. Management has commissioned a task force to study methods to reduce costs. After some deliberation, the group has identified two options for dealing with the problem:

   ▪   Change the frequency of production to produce the most economic lot sizes.

   ▪   Buy tractor components on the foreign market and assemble them at the plant.

   The most reliable and economical foreign supply source can ship the parts in lots of up to 50 tractors within one week. This shipment schedule is essentially the same as Talton's production lead time. Each set of foreign components will ordinarily cost $5,000. However, the supplier will offer a 10 percent discount for orders of 50 or more tractors. Although the components do not create any setup expenses, it will cost Talton $5,000 for assembly work. Also, the company will have to prepare design specifications, place the order, and inspect incoming components. These activities will involve a $1,000 expense per order.

   What option will lead to the smallest possible cost? What are the resulting expenses?

33. People's Credit Union receives cash deposits gradually over time during its "accumulation phase" and uses the money to make loans and other investments until the funds are depleted. The cycle is repeated continually over time. Historically, a typical branch has received $5,000 in deposits per working day and made loans and investments at the rate of $4,000 per day. People's Credit Union operates 200 days each year.

People's Credit Union pays 6 percent annual interest on the average cash deposits and estimates that each accumulation phase involves $1,200 in operating expenses. It takes 30 days for the finance committee to evaluate and act on the various investment options.

a. How many dollars in cash deposits should the Union receive each cycle to minimize costs?

b. What are the resulting costs?

c. How often should the Union repeat the cycle?

d. How long will the accumulation phase take?

e. When should People's Credit Union begin the accumulation phase?

34. The Cloverville Sanitation Department conducts a six-week on-the-job training program for all its engineer trainees. Each session costs $30,000 for instructors, equipment, and materials, regardless of the class size. After completing the program, trainees are paid $1,500 per month but do not work until a full-time position is open. Cloverville views this $1,500 as an expense that is necessary to maintain a supply of qualified engineers available for immediate service.

Although the city needs an average of 120 newly-trained sanitation engineers each year, the various needs of ongoing projects result in a fluctuating monthly demand. Past data indicate that the pattern follows a normal probability distribution with an average demand for 15 engineers during the training period; the standard deviation is 2.

When the program does not generate sufficient engineers, the city must contract with private firms for required services. It costs $2,000 per month for each privately contracted engineer. Amy Cuter, the training program director, believes that the city should plan for the potential shortage by increasing the class size. Slide Rule, the chief engineer, thinks that a better approach would be to create a buffer stock of newly-trained people by running more frequent training sessions.

a. What are the least costly class sizes under each person's proposal?

b. How many shortages can be expected under each plan?

c. What is the training session timing and frequency under each plan?

d. Which alternative would you recommend? Explain.

35. Jock's Sport Shop is a local newsstand dealing exclusively in sports magazines and newspapers. Based on past experience, Jock Hoop, the proprietor, knows that the weekly demand for *Sports Esquire* (his most popular magazine) is as follows:

Weekly Demand	Number of Weeks
20	5
40	15
60	10
80	20
100	30
120	10
140	10

Each *Sports Esquire* costs Jock 20 cents. If the magazine is not sold at the end of the week, he can return the issue and get 10 cents from the publisher. Jock sells the magazine for 50 cents. When he is out of stock, customers go elsewhere. Jock estimates this shortage cost at 50 cents per magazine. Lead time for ordering is two days, and the estimated carrying cost is 50 percent of the purchase expense. The stand is open five days a week.

a.   How many magazines should Jock have in stock when he places an order?
b.   What is the safety stock at that reorder point?
c.   How many magazines should Jock order each week?
d.   What is the expected shortage cost? Carrying cost? Order cost? Total cost?

36. Racine Corporation is a large producer of a commercial-sized pencil sharpener. Engineering and manufacturing specifications for its component assemblies and raw materials are summarized in the following table:

Component Requirements	Source	Lead Time
1 cutting instrument assembly	Manufactured	1 week
2 three-inch welded, grooved cutting panels	Manufactured	2 weeks
1 shavings container assembly	Manufactured	1 week
4 half-inch screws	Purchased	2 weeks
1 metal face	Purchased	3 weeks
2 welded metal sides	Manufactured	1 week

Based on product forecasts and customer orders, management estimates that approximately 8,000 sharpeners will be needed during week 3 of the current 12-week production schedule. Another 12,000 will be required during week 5, 7,000 in week 9, and 3,000 during week 11.

At the present time (week 1), Racine has 6,000 sharpeners, 4,000 instrument assemblies, and 1,500 container assemblies in stock. Also, there is an inventory of 800 cutting panels, 12,000 screws, 6,000 faces, and 900 sides. Outstanding production orders will provide another 5,000 sharpeners, 1,000 container assemblies, and 1,200 sides during week 1. Similarly, outstanding purchase orders will supply 20,000 screws in week 5 and 500 faces during week 2 of the current production schedule.

Assuming that management will always request the exact component quantities required, what purchasing and manufacturing plan is necessary to support finished product demand? That is, how many sharpeners, assemblies, and raw materials of each type should Racine manufacture or purchase each week of the production schedule?

Racine can purchase a package of four screws for 10 cents and a metal face for 25 cents. A purchase order involves a $20 expense. Including the cost of materials, the company can manufacture a metal side for 50 cents and a grooved panel for 75 cents. It costs 30 cents to assemble a container, 40 cents for the cutting assembly work, and 15 cents to assemble the finished sharpener. Each manufacturing or assembly order involves an expense of $10. Annual inventory storage expenses are estimated at 10 percent of the manufactured value of the stock on hand. The company operates 50 weeks a year.

What is the total inventory cost of your recommended work and purchase plan?

For Further Reading

Continuous and Independent Demand Methodology

Billington, P. J. "The Classic Economic Production Quantity Model with Setup Cost as a Function of Capital Expenditure." *Decision Sciences* (Winter 1987):25.

Senju, S., and S. Fujita. "An Applied Procedure for Determining the Economic Lot Sizes of Multiple Products." *Decision Sciences* (July 1980):503.

Silver, E. A., and R. Peterson. *Decision Systems for Inventory Management and Production Planning*, 2nd ed. New York: Wiley, 1985.

Vollman, T. E., et al. *Manufacturing and Control Systems*. Homewood, IL: Irwin, 1984.

Zipkin, P. "Critical Number Policies for Inventory Models with Periodic Data." *Management Science* (January 1989):71.

Continuous and Independent Demand Applications

Bell, P. C. "Managing Inventories through Difficult Economic Times: A Simple Model." *Interfaces* (September–October 1985):39.

Flowers, A. D., and J. B. O'Neill. "An Application of Classical Inventory Analysis to a Spare Parts Inventory." *Interfaces* (February 1978):76.

Morris, P. A., et al. "A Utility Fuel Inventory Model." *Operations Research* (March–April 1987):169.

Prastacos, G. P. "Blood Inventory Management: An Overview of Theory and Practice." *Management Science* (July 1984):777.

Wagner, H. M. "Research Portfolio for Inventory Management and Production Planning Systems." *Operations Research* (May–June 1980):445.

Noncontinuous and Dependent Demand Methodology

Biddle, G. C., and R. K. Martin. "A Stochastic Inventory Model Incorporating Intra-Year Purchases and Accounting Tax Incentives." *Management Science* (June 1986):714.

Burstein, M. C. "Dynamic Lot-Sizing When Demand Timing Is Uncertain." *Operations Research* (March–April 1984):360.

Buzacott, J. A., and D. D. Yao. "Flexible Manufacturing Systems: A Review of Analytical Models." *Management Science* (July 1986):890.

Carlson, R. C., and C. A. Yano. "Safety Stocks in MRP—Systems with Emergency Setups for Components." *Management Science* (April 1986):403.

Das, C. "A Unified Approach to the Price-Break Economic Order Quantity (EOQ) Problem." *Decision Sciences* (Summer 1984):350.

Dave, U., and M. C. Jaiswal. "A Discrete-in-Time Probabilistic Model for Deteriorating Items." *Decision Sciences* (January 1980):110.

Fordyce, J. M., and F. M. Webster. "The Wagner-Whitin Algorithm Made Simple." *Production and Inventory Management* (Second Quarter 1986):21.

Hall, R. *Zero Inventories*. Homewood, IL: Irwin, 1983.

Jonsson, H., and E. A. Silver. "Analysis of a Two-Echelon Inventory Control System with Complete Redistribution." *Management Science* (February 1987):215.

Jordan, P. C. "A Comparative Analysis of the Relative Effectiveness of Four Dynamic Lot-Sizing Techniques on Return on Investment." *Decision Sciences* (Winter 1989):134.

Krajewski, L. J., et al. "Kanban, MRP, and Shaping the Manufacturing Environment." *Management Science* (January 1987):39.

Lee, T. S., and E. E. Adam. "Forecasting Error Evaluation in Material Requirements Planning (MRP) Production-Inventory Systems." *Management Science* (September 1986):1186.

Lee, H. L., and M. J. Rosenblatt. "A Generalized Quantity Discount Pricing Model to Increase Supplier's Profits." *Management Science* (September 1986):1177.

Martin, A. J. *DRP: Distribution Resource Planning*. Englewood Cliffs, NJ: Prentice-Hall, 1983.

McLeavey, D. W., and S. L. Narasimham. *Production Planning and Inventory Control*. Boston: Allyn & Bacon, 1985.

Miller, B. L. "Scarf's State Reduction Method, Flexibility, and a Dependent Demand Inventory Model." *Operations Research* (January–February 1986):83.

Porteus, E. L. "Optimal Lot Sizing, Process Quality Improvement and Setup Cost Reduction." *Operations Research* (January–February 1986):137.

Schonberger, R. J. *Japanese Manufacturing Techniques*. New York: Free Press, 1982.

Noncontinuous and Dependent Demand Applications

Aggarwal, S. C. "MRP, JIT, OPT, FMS?" *Harvard Business Review* (September–October 1985):4.

Dicasali, R. L. "MIS in the Computer Integrated Factory." *Production and Inventory Management Review with APICS News* (April 1986):24.

Karmarkar, U. S., et al. "Lot-Sizing and Lead-Time Performance in a Manufacturing Cell." *Interfaces* (March–April 1985):1.

Kleutghen, P. P., and J. C. McGee, "Development and Implementation of an Integrated Inventory Management Program at Pfizer Pharmaceuticals," *Interfaces* (January–February 1985):69–87.

Monden, Y. "Adaptable Kanban System Helps Toyota Maintain Just-In-Time Production." *Journal of Industrial Engineering* (May 1981):28.

Sauers, D. G. "Analyzing Inventory Systems." *Management Accounting* (May 1986):30.

Sridharan, V., et al. "Freezing the Master Production Schedule under Rolling Planning Horizons." *Management Science* (September 1987):1137.

Teplitz, C. J. "Is Your Organization Ready for MRP? A Case Study." *Interfaces* (June 1980):103.

Zangwill, W. I. "Eliminating Inventory in a Series Facility Production System." *Management Science* (September 1987):1150.

Figure 14.13   **Organizational Structure of Willington Hospital**

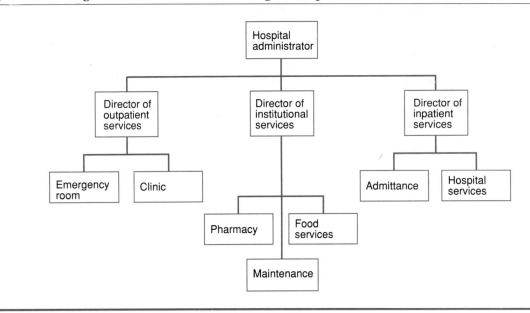

Case: Willington Hospital

The northeastern city of Willington has a relatively small hospital that provides essential medical services to the town and surrounding county. It is financed primarily through private funds. The organizational structure is shown in Figure 14.13.

Recently, the hospital has received a federal research grant to administer an experimental heart disease treatment program. As part of the program, Willington will use its outpatient and inpatient facilities to administer specified treatments on an experimental group of individuals in 12-week intervals. Specifically, the program will send the hospital 50 outpatients during week 4, 100 during week 6, 150 during week 7, 100 during week 10, and 50 during week 11 of each interval. In addition, there will be 150 inpatients during week 3, 200 during week 5, 350 during week 8, and 300 during week 12 of each interval.

The program specifies the medical and institutional support required for each type of patient. These requirements are summarized in Table 14.14. In anticipation of the start of the program, Willington Hospital has "stocked" 12,000 capsules and 200 beds. Also, the hospital manager has scheduled 50 administrative hours, 150

doctor hours, 200 nurse hours, and 50 orderly hours of effort during week 1 of the program. In addition, she has scheduled the receipt of 5,000 capsules, 100 beds, and 1,000 special meals during that same week. Staff effort unused in one week will be rescheduled in the same amount for the subsequent week. All medical and administrative services can be provided with only one week's notice.

Federal policy restricts resource expenses as shown in Table 14.15. According to the regulations, the hospital also must order the exact staff effort and corresponding services (X-rays, blood tests, and beds) required. On the other hand, Willington is directed to order the economic order quantities for the special meals and prescription capsules. However, shortages will not be permitted.

At times in the past, Willington Hospital has experienced significant patient service problems. It seems that medical staff, facilities, equipment, and support personnel were not always in the right place at the right time. As a result, operations did not run efficiently and an expediter often had to be called in. Although Willington was selected because of its technical expertise, the government would like to avoid the previous operational problems and potential expense for the experimental program. Consequently, the hospital administrator has been asked to prepare a preliminary report outlining the following:

- The work order plan necessary to support the experimental program in the first twelve-week interval

- The corresponding cost for administering the plan

The plan will then be audited by the federal agency's operations analysis division.

1. If you were in charge of this audit, what plan would you expect from Willington?

2. How much should the hospital receive in funding for the experimental program?

Table 14.14   Resource Requirements

Resources needed to support 1 outpatient for 1 week: 　2 hours of doctor effort 　　3 X-rays 　　10 prescription capsules 　　1 blood test 　3 hours of nurse effort 　2 administrative hours
Resources needed to support 1 inpatient for 1 week: 　1 bed 　　20 special diet meals 　　7 hours of orderly effort 　6 hours of doctor effort 　　9 X-rays 　　30 prescription capsules 　　3 blood tests 　12 hours of nurse effort 　6 administrative hours

Table 14.15   Federal Restrictions on Resource Expenses

Administrative effort	
Managerial	$30 per hour
Orderly	$7 per hour
Medical effort	
Doctor	$100 per hour
Nurse	$10 per hour
Physical facilities	
Bed	$560 per week
Services	
X-ray	$20
Blood test	$15
Special meal	$5
Prescription capsule	20 cents
Other expenses	
Ordering a service	$25 per order
Storing an item	15.6% of the item cost per year

Queuing Theory

Chapter Outline

Learning Objectives

- Describe the nature of the queuing problem
- Identify the components and characteristics of service systems
- Measure the performance and costs of service systems with quantitative models
- Select an appropriate service system

Here to Serve in New York City

THE New York Police Department (NYPD), with over 28,000 personnel and a $1.3 billion budget, is the largest in the United States. In 1985, its radio-monitored patrol (RMP) cars responded to more than 3.6 million emergency calls for service (CFS) throughout the city. As part of an ongoing attempt to improve productivity, the department performed a comprehensive quantitative study of RMP car practices.

In one aspect of the study, the department examined the impact of alternative RMP patrol and response strategies on travel times to CFS. Under one proposal, an RMP car would routinely respond to CFS originating from anywhere within an assigned zone of two to four contiguous precincts. Such zone-based dispatching reduces the time needed for the police to respond on a CFS. However, officials were concerned that increases in travel time would negate any concomitant reduction in the response delays.

Consultants were hired to investigate and resolve the issue. By utilizing queuing theory, the consultants were able to predict the consequences of the proposed strategy for particular neighborhoods in the city. The analysis revealed that zone-based dispatching substantially reduces RMP response delays and, more importantly, does not necessarily increase travel time. In the few adverse cases, the travel time increase typically was negligible, and it usually was more than offset by the reduction in response delay. These findings have become central to the city's assessment of the operational and resource utilization benefits resulting from the proposed strategy.

Source: R. C. Larson and T. F. Rich, "Travel-Time Analysis of New York City Police Patrol Cars," *Interfaces* (March–April 1987): 15–20.

Most individuals in today's society must occasionally wait in line for some sort of service. It can occur at a bus stop, gas station, supermarket checkout counter, or at a variety of other locations. In the NYPD vignette, residents of New York City wait for RMP cars to respond to emergency calls for service. Most people will tolerate the inconvenience for a short period of time. Then the size of the line or the wait discourages them and they leave or perhaps are injured in some manner (as could occur when an RMP car does not respond in time to a police emergency).

Managers realize that long lines or lengthy waits mean that customers are not being serviced properly. Poor service creates consumer dissatisfaction and potential lost present and future sales (for a private enterprise) or lost public support (for a government or nonprofit agency). An organization can reduce the waiting times by adding more service facilities, but the additional accommodations will require more resources (such as personnel, equipment, space, or management). The decision maker then must balance the resulting additional expenses with the benefits from better customer service.

Examining such a trade-off is the purpose of the NYPD's comprehensive study of RMP car practices.

The problem of waiting lines, or queues, has received serious attention for a long time. As early as 1909, Danish telephone engineer A. K. Erlang analyzed the queuing problems that callers encountered at a telephone switchboard. Since then, many quantitative approaches have been developed to measure the operating characteristics and costs of waiting lines. These methods, often referred to as **queuing theory**, are designed to assist the manager in formulating an effective customer service system. As the NYPD vignette demonstrates, such assistance can dramatically improve an organization's performance.

This chapter presents basic queuing theory and some useful extensions. In the first section, we discuss the nature and structure of a queuing system. The presentation identifies the diverse characteristics and behavior of customers and servers and shows how the differences affect the nature of the problems. The second section examines the elements of queuing analysis. A fundamental model is presented, its characteristics are identified, system performance measures are calculated and interpreted, and alternative service designs are evaluated. The final section extends the analysis to other decision situations, including systems with a limited number of customers, restricted service space, and multiple servers.

Applications.   In this chapter, the following applications appear in text, examples, and exercises:

- airport operations
- bank teller operations
- car wash operations
- catering
- computer job processing
- courtroom operations
- emergency road service
- engine tune-ups
- fast-food restaurants
- furniture refinishing
- garbage collection
- gasoline station operations
- limousine service
- loading crews
- nuclear reactor inspection
- office work
- parts storeroom operations
- post office operations
- railway operations
- radio talk shows
- supermarket checkout
- theater box office
- tollbooth operations
- tourism

15.1 STRUCTURE OF A QUEUING SYSTEM

In a typical queuing situation, customers arrive at a service system, enter a waiting line, receive service, and then leave. As Figure 15.1 illustrates, the process involves several key elements, including source of customers, arrival process, waiting line (queue), method of selecting customers from the queue, service process, and departure process.

Figure 15.1   **Typical Queuing Situation**

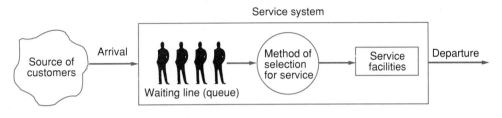

Table 15.1   **Typical Examples of Queuing Situations**

Area of Application	Service Facility	Customer	Source Population
Production	Materials storeroom Shared equipment Maintenance shop	Worker Mechanic Machine	Factory personnel Repair personnel Factory equipment
Marketing	Store clerk Car wash Sports stadium	Shopper Automobile Fan	People in service area Dirty cars Fans in area
Finance	Stockbroker Posting clerk Bank teller	Investor Financial transaction Account holder	People with surplus funds All potential transactions Bank customers
Transportation	Hotel Ship-loading dock Airport runway Subway train	Traveler Empty ship Airplane Commuter	Potential travelers Ship traffic Airline traffic City residents
Public Services	Library Social worker Police unit Courtroom Acute care unit	Reader Welfare recipient Crime Trial Patient	Residents in area People on welfare Crimes in territory Potential cases Acutely ill people
Private Services	Ambulance Lawyer Tennis court Telephone line	Emergency patient Client Player Telephone call	Residents in area People with legal problems Potential players Potential telephone calls

Source Population

A customer is any person or object in need of service. Depending on the nature of service, customers, or potential arrivals, can be generated from a variety of sources. Table 15.1 presents some typical examples.

Almost all sources involve a finite or limited number of customers. In some cases, like the maintenance of a few machines, the number is relatively small. Other circumstances, such as telephone calls in a telephone system, have very large source populations. When there are many (as a rule of thumb, more than 100) customers, the source can be treated as if it were infinite in size.

The number of potential customers will influence the arrival process for the service system. Hence, it is important to identify whether a source population is finite or infinite.

Arrival Process

The arrival process describes the manner in which customers reach the service system. There are several important characteristics involved in this process, including form and composition. In this respect, customers may arrive in batches (for instance, a family attending a sporting event) or individually (such as a ship docking at a port).

Timing. Another aspect involves the timing of arrivals. In some situations, customers arrive at a service facility on a scheduled basis. For example, dental clinics usually schedule nonemergency patients by appointment. In most situations, however, customers arrive haphazardly without prior notification.

Two measures can be used to describe the arrival process. One, referred to as the **arrival rate**, gives the number of arrivals per unit of time. Suppose, for example, that 960 automobiles reach a turnpike tollbooth in an eight-hour period. Then the arrival rate is $960/8 = 120$ per hour or 2 per minute. An alternative measure, called the **interarrival time**, gives the interval between two consecutive arrivals. For instance, since two automobiles reach the tollbooth in a minute, there is $1/2 = 0.5$ minute, or 30 seconds, between arrivals. Notice that the interarrival time (1/2) is the reciprocal of the arrival rate (2).

When service is provided on a scheduled basis, the arrival rate and interarrival time are fixed. In unscheduled situations, however, customers typically arrive in a random pattern. That is, each arrival is not affected by preceding arrivals. Instead of being constant, then, there is a range of possible values for either the arrival rate or the interarrival time. Hence, in these cases, it is necessary to describe arrivals with a probability distribution. Management Situation 15.1 illustrates.

Management Situation 15.1

Parts Storeroom Operations

Titan Industries has a central parts storeroom for its Mineola plant. Employees come to the storeroom to pick up needed supplies when necessary at various times during the working day. Management has observed the process and found that it is not possible to predict the exact time of arrival at the center. Furthermore, the time when an employee reaches the storeroom seems to be unaffected by preceding and future arrivals, the hour of the day, and the day of the week. A portion of the pattern is illustrated in Figure 15.2. By recording the employee arrival times at the storeroom over a period of 100 hours, the company obtained the data shown in Table 15.2.

Titan wants to describe the arrival process with some basic summary statistics.

Figure 15.2   Employee Arrivals at the Mineola Plant Storeroom

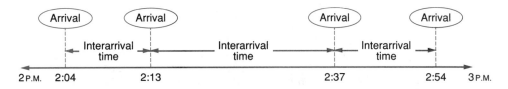

Table 15.2   Employee Arrival Data for the Mineola Storeroom

Employee Arrivals per Hour	Number of Hours	Probability
0	1	1/100 = .01
1	7	7/100 = .07
2	14	14/100 = .14
3	20	20/100 = .20
4	20	20/100 = .20
5	16	16/100 = .16
6	12	12/100 = .12
7	7	7/100 = .07
8	3	3/100 = .03
	100	

In Management Situation 15.1, each employee reaches the parts storeroom in a completely independent manner. The number of arrivals in a specified time interval is unaffected by what happened in previous periods or when the event occurs. In addition, from Figure 15.2, you can see that customers arrive in a random fashion throughout the time period. Also, the number of arrivals increases as the length of the time interval grows. Hence, there is one arrival in the first 5 minutes, two during the initial 15 minutes, and so on. In effect, then, it will be extremely rare for more than one customer to arrive in a very small interval of time. Decision scientists have found that two related probability distributions are useful for describing this type of random arrival pattern.

Poisson Distribution. Often, arrival rate probabilities can be accurately provided by the **Poisson distribution**. Let

$$X = \text{the number of arrivals in a specified time interval}$$

$$\lambda = \text{the average, or expected, number of arrivals in the interval}$$

$$T = \text{the length of the time interval}$$

Then, the probability P of a specified arrival rate can be found from this distribution with the following equation:

(15.1)
$$P(X) = \frac{e^{-\lambda T}(\lambda T)^X}{X!}$$

The symbol ! represents a factorial, and $e = 2.71828$ (the base of natural logarithms).

Table 15.3   **Values of** $e^{-\Phi}$

Φ	$e^{-\Phi}$	Φ	$e^{-\Phi}$	Φ	$e^{-\Phi}$	Φ	$e^{-\Phi}$
0.05	.95123	1.30	.27253	2.55	.07808	3.80	.02237
0.10	.90484	1.35	.25924	2.60	.07427	3.85	.02128
0.15	.86071	1.40	.24660	2.65	.07065	3.90	.02024
0.20	.81873	1.45	.23457	2.70	.06721	3.95	.01925
0.25	.77880	1.50	.22313	2.75	.06393	4.00	.01832
0.30	.74082	1.55	.21225	2.80	.06081	4.05	.01742
0.35	.70469	1.60	.20190	2.85	.05784	4.10	.01657
0.40	.67032	1.65	.19205	2.90	.05502	4.15	.01576
0.45	.63763	1.70	.18268	2.95	.05234	4.20	.01500
0.50	.60653	1.75	.17377	3.00	.04979	4.25	.01426
0.55	.57695	1.80	.16530	3.05	.04736	4.30	.01357
0.60	.54881	1.85	.15724	3.10	.04505	4.35	.01291
0.65	.52205	1.90	.14957	3.15	.04285	4.40	.01228
0.70	.49659	1.95	.14227	3.20	.04076	4.45	.01168
0.75	.47237	2.00	.13534	3.25	.03877	4.50	.01111
0.80	.44933	2.05	.12873	3.30	.03688	4.55	.01057
0.85	.42741	2.10	.12246	3.35	.03508	4.60	.01005
0.90	.40657	2.15	.11648	3.40	.03337	4.65	.00956
0.95	.38674	2.20	.11080	3.45	.03175	4.70	.00910
1.00	.36788	2.25	.10540	3.50	.03020	4.75	.00865
1.05	.34994	2.30	.10026	3.55	.02872	4.80	.00823
1.10	.33287	2.35	.09537	3.60	.02732	4.85	.00783
1.15	.31664	2.40	.09072	3.65	.02599	4.90	.00745
1.20	.30119	2.45	.08629	3.70	.02472	4.95	.00708
1.25	.28650	2.50	.08208	3.75	.02352	5.00	.00674

Table 15.3 gives the values of e raised to the $-\Phi$ power, where values of Φ are provided between .05 and 10 in increments of .05. Moreover, Φ represents a number such as λT.

For Titan's situation, the length of the time interval is $T = 1$ hour. Management can calculate the average, or expected, arrival rate λ from the data in Table 15.2. Management simply multiplies the number of employee arrivals per hour by the corresponding probability and sums the results:

$$\lambda = 0(.01) + 1(.07) + 2(.14) + 3(.2) + 4(.2) + 5(.16) + 6(.12) + 7(.07) + 8(.03)$$

or

$$\lambda = 4 \text{ arrivals per hour}$$

Thus, if Titan's random arrival pattern follows a Poisson distribution, management can calculate the arrival rate probabilities with the following expression:

$$P(X) = \frac{e^{-4(1)}(4 \times 1)^X}{X!} = \frac{e^{-4}4^X}{X!}$$

Table 15.3   *continuing*

Φ	$e^{-\Phi}$	Φ	$e^{-\Phi}$	Φ	$e^{-\Phi}$	Φ	$e^{-\Phi}$
5.05	.00641	6.30	.00184	7.55	.00053	8.80	.00015
5.10	.00610	6.35	.00175	7.60	.00050	8.85	.00014
5.15	.00580	6.40	.00166	7.65	.00048	8.90	.00014
5.20	.00552	6.45	.00158	7.70	.00045	8.95	.00013
5.25	.00525	4.50	.00150	7.75	.00043	9.00	.00012
5.30	.00499	6.55	.00143	7.80	.00041	9.05	.00012
5.35	.00475	6.60	.00136	7.85	.00039	9.10	.00011
5.40	.00452	6.65	.00129	7.90	.00037	9.15	.00011
5.45	.00430	6.70	.00123	7.95	.00035	9.20	.00010
5.50	.00409	6.75	.00117	8.00	.00034	9.25	.00010
5.55	.00389	6.80	.00111	8.05	.00032	9.30	.00009
5.60	.00370	6.85	.00106	8.10	.00030	9.35	.00009
5.65	.00352	6.90	.00101	8.15	.00029	9.40	.00008
5.70	.00335	6.95	.00096	8.20	.00027	9.45	.00008
5.75	.00318	7.00	.00091	8.25	.00026	9.50	.00007
5.80	.00303	7.05	.00087	8.30	.00025	9.55	.00007
5.85	.00288	7.10	.00083	8.35	.00024	9.60	.00007
5.90	.00274	7.15	.00078	8.40	.00022	9.65	.00006
5.95	.00261	7.20	.00075	8.45	.00021	9.70	.00006
6.00	.00248	7.25	.00071	8.50	.00020	9.75	.00006
6.05	.00236	7.30	.00068	8.55	.00019	9.80	.00006
6.10	.00224	7.35	.00064	8.60	.00018	9.85	.00005
6.15	.00213	7.40	.00061	8.65	.00018	9.90	.00005
6.20	.00203	7.45	.00058	8.70	.00017	9.95	.00005
6.25	.00193	7.50	.00055	8.75	.00016	10.00	.00005

For instance, there is a

$$P(X = 0) = \frac{e^{-4}4^0}{0!} = \frac{e^{-4}(1)}{1} = e^{-4}$$

chance, or, from Table 15.3, an

$$e^{-4} = .01832$$

chance of 0 employees arriving in an hour of storeroom operation. Similarly, the probability of 1 arrival in an hour is

$$P(X = 1) = \frac{e^{-4}4^1}{1!} = \frac{e^{-4}(4)}{1} = .0733.$$

By continuing in this manner, the company will get the Poisson probabilities presented in Table 15.4. A comparison of Tables 15.2 and 15.4 shows that the Poisson probabilities (Table 15.4) are almost identical to the actual chances (Table 15.2) for the employee arrival rates. Although Titan may want to try some additional statistical tests for goodness

---

Table 15.4   **Poisson Probabilities for Titan's Employee Arrival Process**

Employee Arrivals per Hour X	Probability $P(X) = e^{-4}4^X)/X!$
0	0.0183
1	0.0733
2	0.1465
3	0.1954
4	0.1953
5	0.1563
6	0.1042
7	0.0596
8	0.0297
9	0.0133
10	0.0053
11	0.0019
12	0.0006
13	0.0002
14	0.0001
	1.000

---

of fit, this comparison suggests that the arrival rate at the storeroom can be reasonably described with the Poisson distribution.

Negative Exponential Distribution. There is an important property of the Poisson arrival pattern. Equation (15.1) indicates that there is a

$$P(X = 0) = \frac{e^{-\lambda T}(\lambda T)^X}{X!} = \frac{e^{-\lambda T}(\lambda T)^0}{0!} = e^{-\lambda T}$$

probability of zero arrivals within the time interval T. Put another way, $e^{-\lambda T}$ represents the chance that the time between arrivals (interarrival time) will be longer than the interval T. By letting T_a = interarrival time, we can express the relationship as follows:

$$P(X = 0) = P(T_a > T) = e^{-\lambda T}$$

Since all probabilities must sum to 1, there is then a

(15.2) $$P(T_a \leq T) = 1 - e^{-\lambda T}$$

chance that the interarrival time T_a will be no greater than period T. Equation (15.2) provides the cumulative probabilities for the so-called **negative exponential** distribution.

In effect, then, when a queuing system involves a Poisson arrival pattern, the time between arrivals will follow a negative exponential probability distribution. Hence, in Titan's problem, interarrival times will follow a negative exponential distribution with a mean $= 1/\lambda = 1/4 = 0.25$ hour, or 15 minutes, between arrivals. As a result, there is a

$$P(T_a \leq 1) = 1 - e^{-4(1)} = 1 - .0183 = .9817$$

Figure 15.3   Titan's Employee Interrival Time Probability

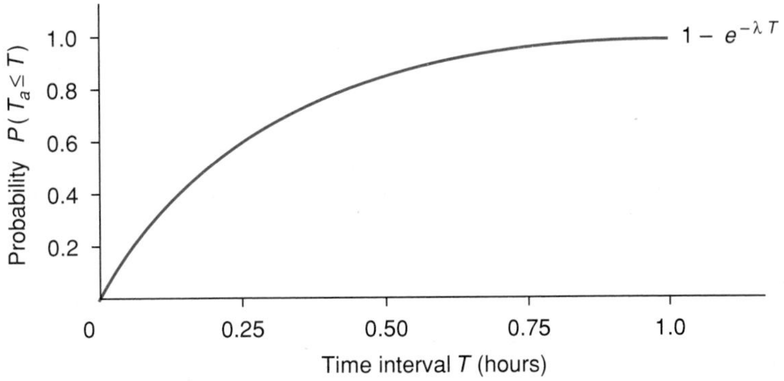

probability that the time between arrivals will be no more than $T = 1$ hour. Similarly, the probability that the interarrival time will not exceed 30 minutes ($T = .5$) is

$$P(T_a \le .5) = 1 - e^{-4(.5)} = 1 - e^{-2}$$

or, since Table 15.3 indicates that $e^{-2} = .1353$,

$$P(T_a \le .5) = 1 - .1353 = .8647.$$

Figure 15.3 graphically shows the probability that each employee interarrival time T_a will be T hours or less.

Queue Accommodations and Behavior

Waiting lines may be accommodated in various ways. Usually, the queue is formed on the site of the company in some common area of the waiting facility. In some of these cases, as at an airport security station, actual lines may develop. For other circumstances, such as the waiting room in a clinic, customers do not physically form a queue. There are other situations, however, in which the waiting is not done at the place of business. For example, users of a central computer facility may spend most, if not all, of their waiting at the office doing normal daily tasks. Service systems can usually reduce queuing costs by shifting the wait from their site to off-premise facilities.

Facility Capacity. An important factor for on-site facilities is the size or capacity of the waiting area. Some systems, like a ticket window at a major stadium, are characterized by a (nearly) infinite queuing capacity. Others, such as a beauty shop or counselor's office, involve space limitations. In these limited- or finite-capacity situations, a customer may arrive and find the waiting area completely filled. Sometimes, the arrival does not return but instead seeks accommodations elsewhere. The company then loses any revenue or benefits that could have been gained from this customer. In other cases, the customer may return at a later time, hoping to find an available space. Although the revenue from such an arrival is not lost immediately, the resulting consumer frustration may have an impact on the arrival pattern and revenue in future periods.

Also, when the waiting area is filled to capacity, an arrival may block the operations of the service facility. Suppose, for instance, that new military inductees go through a sequence of orientation activities on the first day of service. Time breaks are scheduled between activities to allow for differences in the rates of processing inductees at each stage of the sequence. During a break, the inductee is assigned a waiting area adjacent to the appropriate orientation facility. Thus, when a specific activity's waiting area is filled to capacity, the inductee has no place to go. The resulting congestion may hamper or even halt preceding orientation activities.

It should be evident that finite-capacity systems have a definite effect on the arrival and output rates for a queuing system. When the waiting system is at capacity, potential arrivals are turned away and the effective arrival rate becomes zero. The resulting blockage may, in turn, reduce the output of the entire service system, particularly for situations involving a sequence of activities.

Waiting Line Organization. Another important characteristic is the organization of the waiting line. In some systems, regardless of the number of servers available, a single waiting line is used as a means of preserving the order of arrival. For other situations, a separate queue is allowed to develop for each server. Sometimes, as when automobiles reach the tollbooths at a multiple-lane turnpike, the customer is permitted to select the waiting line. In other cases, there may be differences in customer service needs or server skills. Then, as when college students select advisors, the customer may be assigned to specific lines or wait for particular servers.

Waiting Behavior. Consumer waiting behavior may also be a relevant factor. If a consumer feels that the queue is too long, he or she may **balk**, refusing to join the waiting line even though space is available. Similarly, customers actually in a queue may tire of waiting and **renege**, departing before being served. Balking and reneging affect the arrival pattern and can involve lost revenues and disgruntled customers. In addition, when there are multiple lines, customers often **jockey**, switching between queues in an attempt to reduce waiting time. A related phenomenon is the combining or dividing of queues, as often occurs in a bank or supermarket when a station is closed or opened. Jockeying, combining, and dividing may balance the length of the queues but may create wider deviations in waiting times. Also, there are situations, like the loading and unloading of ore cars at a mine, where the customer will cycle, or return to the queue, immediately after obtaining service. Among other things, cycling may affect the source population and the arrival process.

Psychological Tools. Since customers are apt to resent waiting for service, organizations usually provide distractions or constructive diversions during the wait. For example, retail stores position mirrors near elevators, allowing those who are waiting to check their appearance. Doctors and dentists place magazines in their offices to help waiting patients pass the time. Employment agencies ask people to fill out forms while waiting. Airlines offer music and movies on long flights. Disney World and other amusement parks use a maze pattern to make the waiting lines look shorter and to deter reneging.

In some retail situations, psychological tools may actually create economic benefits for the organization. For example, supermarkets place an array of impulse-purchase items (such as candy and magazines) at checkouts. Waiting customers may add these items to their other purchases.

Selection Process

When designing the queuing system, management must prescribe the manner in which customers from the waiting area are selected for service. This prescription is referred to as the **queue discipline**.

FIFS. In customer-oriented systems, the most frequently used approach is a first-in, first-served (FIFS) discipline. Sometimes, however, the number of waiting lines and customer waiting behavior (like jockeying) may disrupt the order. To avoid ill will in these and similar situations, companies often use a take-a-number system to accomplish the same thing. This second method can be seen at local Internal Revenue Service offices and butcher shops. Other firms, like restaurants, use a reservation system to schedule service. This approach maintains some elements of the FIFS procedure, reduces on-site waiting, and increases available space for service.

LIFS. In other circumstances, it may be more desirable to serve the last arrivals first. As an example, for convenience and safety, the last people entering an elevator are usually the first to leave. Similarly, a company can often reduce material-handling activities and costs by first using the most recently delivered parts. These cases are illustrations of a last-in, first-served (LIFS) queue discipline.

Priority Systems. When the quality of service will be affected by the amount of waiting time, management may prefer to use a priority scheme. For instance, supermarkets provide express lanes for customers with few items. Also, airlines first board the handicapped and passengers with reservations. Similarly, medical facilities typically treat emergency patients before nonemergency cases. In some cases, an important arrival not only has entrance priority but can even interrupt the service on other, less significant customers. An illustration of such a **preemptive priority system** is an emergency maintenance situation in a plant. The crew may interrupt its regular maintenance activities to repair a broken machine.

Other Approaches. Sometimes it is difficult or even impossible to establish a waiting line. Then selection may be done on a purely random basis. Examples include the signing of autographs by celebrities and service by a clerk during the peak hours of a department store sale.

In cases where the customers are objects rather than people, selection is often based on some measure of system performance. For instance, consulting companies usually give first attention to the products generating the most profit. Also, television stores typically repair sets with the shortest expected service time.

Service Process

There are many ways to design a service system, some of which may be at least partly dictated by the nature of the process. Important options are the number and arrangement of the facilities.

Figure 15.4   Service Facility Design Possibilities

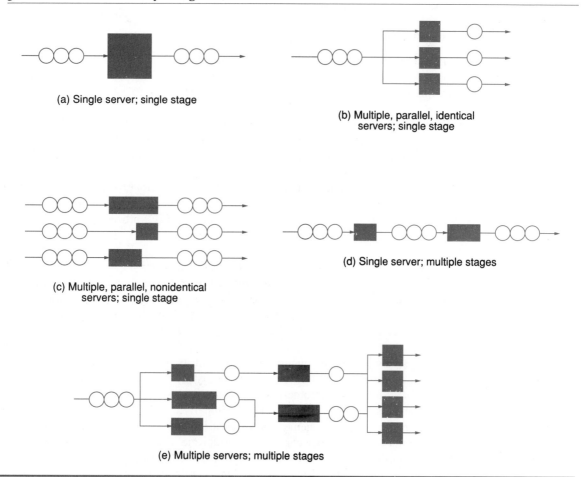

(a) Single server; single stage

(b) Multiple, parallel, identical
servers; single stage

(c) Multiple, parallel, nonidentical
servers; single stage

(d) Single server; multiple stages

(e) Multiple servers; multiple stages

Design Configuration. The simplest case involves a single service facility, such as a traffic signal, a one-chair dentist's office, or a computer terminal. Other situations may have multiple facilities in parallel, each offering essentially the same service. Illustrations include the regular pumps at a gasoline station and the tellers in a bank. A variation exists where there are multiple and parallel but not identical facilities, such as turnpikes with both regular and exact-change tollbooths.

Service operations may also consist of a series, or sequence, of stages. The customer enters the first facility, gets a portion of the service, moves on to the second facility, and so on. In the simplest situation, the facilities are in tandem, one after the other, as in a car wash or cafeteria. Other circumstances involve more complex combinations of facilities, some in parallel, some in tandem, with a multiple of alternative routings. Examples are university registration, task routing in government agencies, restaurant operations, and assembly lines. Figure 15.4 illustrates the service facility design possibilities.

Figure 15.5   **Mineola Plant Storeroom Service**

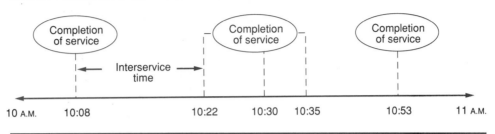

Timing. Regardless of the design configuration, it will take time to perform the service at each facility. There are two ways to describe this service process. First, the **service rate** measures the number of customers served per unit of time. Suppose, for instance, that a quality control device can calibrate 150 scientific instruments in a three-hour period. Then the service rate is 150/3 = 50 per hour. The **interservice time**, meanwhile, gives the interval between two consecutive service completions. For example, since 50 instruments are calibrated per hour, there will be 1/50 = 0.02 hour, or 1.2 minutes, between service completions. Notice that the interservice time (1/50) is the reciprocal of the service rate (50).

Some operations, particularly those that are machine-paced, may have constant service rates or interservice times. On the other hand, service time may fluctuate within some range of values. In such cases, the service process can be described with a probability distribution. Management Situation 15.2 illustrates.

Management Situation 15.2

Storeroom Service

To ensure proper accounting control of requisitioned supplies, Titan employs a full-time clerk at the Mineola plant storeroom. The company has observed the clerk's activities but has found that it is impossible to predict the exact service completion time. Also, this time seems to be unaffected by how long the service has already taken, the identity of the customer, the hour of the day, or the day of the week. A portion of the pattern is illustrated in Figure 15.5.

Management recorded the service completion times by the clerk over an extended period and found that the service rate probabilities could be reasonably described by the Poisson distribution. On average, the clerk was able to service five customers per hour. Titan wants to identify a probability distribution that will accurately provide service times.

Poisson Distribution. A comparison of Figures 15.2 and 15.5 shows that Titan's service process follows the same type of random pattern as its arrival process. Recall that the

Figure 15.6   **Titan's Service Rate Probabilities**

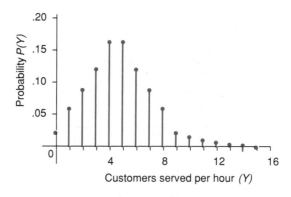

arrival rate probabilities were accurately provided by the Poisson distribution. Hence, it is not surprising to learn that the service rate probabilities also are described by a Poisson distribution. That is, if

Y = the number of customers that a single service facility can handle in a specified time interval

u = the average, or expected, service rate in the interval

then the expression

(15.3)
$$P(Y) = \frac{e^{-uT}(uT)^Y}{Y!}$$

will give the probability of the service rate Y.

In Management Situation 15.2, the time interval is again $T = 1$ hour. The average, or expected, service rate is $u = 5$ customers per hour. Thus, there is a

$$P(Y = 0) = \frac{e^{-5(1)}(5 \times 1)^0}{0!} = e^{-5}$$

chance, or, from Table 15.3, an

$$e^{-5} = .00674$$

chance that 0 customers will be served by the clerk in an hour of storeroom operation. Similarly, the probability of one service completion in an hour is

$$P(Y = 1) = \frac{e^{-5}5^1}{1!} = e^{-5}5 = .0337.$$

Figure 15.6 graphically shows the probability of each service rate in Titan's storeroom situation.

Negative Exponential Distribution. Recall that when there is a Poisson arrival pattern, the interarrival time will follow a negative exponential probability distribution. The same

Figure 15.7   **Titan's Interservice Probabilities**

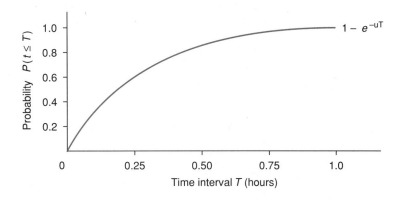

relationship exists for the service process. That is, when a queuing system involves a Poisson service pattern, the time between service completions will follow a negative exponential distribution. In particular, if $t =$ the interservice time, then the expression

(15.4) $P(t \leq T) = 1 - e^{-uT}$

gives the probability that service will be completed within a specific period of time T.

For Titan's situation, interservice times will follow a negative exponential distribution with an average of $1/u = 1/5 = 0.2$ hour, or 12 minutes, between service completions. Consequently, there is a

$$P(t \leq 1) = 1 - e^{-5(1)} = 1 - .0067 = .9933$$

chance that the clerk can complete service within $T = 1$ hour. Also, the probability that the interservice time will not exceed 30 minutes ($T = .5$) is

$$P(t \leq .5) = 1 - e^{-5(.5)}$$

or, since Table 15.3 indicates that $e^{-2.5} = .0821$,

$$P(t \leq .5) = 1 - .0821 = .9179.$$

Figure 15.7 presents the probability that T hours or less will be required to service a Titan employee at the Mineola storeroom.

Although service times in Titan's situation follow the negative exponential distribution, other cases may be best described by different probability distributions. In fact, queuing pioneer A. K. Erlang developed a whole family of service distributions. Today, these distributions, which include the negative exponential as a special case, are called the Erlang distributions in honor of their originator. In practice, of course, the decision maker should use the distribution that best fits the actual data.

Departure

In some situations, it is important to consider what happens to customers after they leave the queuing system. For most systems, departing customers return to the source population and become potential new arrivals. Most clients at a health club, for instance, will come back again and again for the same or similar treatment. On the other hand, some customers, like corpses entering a crematory, will not be reentries into the source population and will never again require service.

15.2 BASIC QUEUING ANALYSIS

By now, it should be evident that there are many dimensions to consider when designing a queuing system. To evaluate the alternatives, management must develop some measures of system performance. There are several possibilities. One important measure is the proportion of time that the service facilities are in use, called the **utilization factor**. When utilization is low, server idle time will be high. Unless the idle service facilities can be used for other constructive purposes, the company may incur a substantial opportunity cost for the unused capacity. For instance, salaried personnel and public utility expenses still must be paid even when service facilities are idle and hence unproductive. Unfortunately, in some situations, management may have to design a system that automatically creates significant amounts of idle time during given periods. An electric utility, for example, must set its system capacity at a level sufficient to meet peak demands. But for this reason, the utility will have considerable idle capacity during nonpeak periods.

Other useful performance measures deal with the number of customers in the queuing system. First, management will want to know the average number of customers either in the waiting line or receiving service. A police station, for instance, might "book" 10 criminals in a given hour and have another 20 in jail cells. There would then be a total of 30 in the station. This characteristic can be used to find the average time a customer spends in the system waiting for service and being served. When a cost can be assigned to customer waiting, this average time will be helpful in making economic comparisons between alternative queuing system designs. A related factor is the average number of customers in the queue only (10 in the police station illustration). Knowing this value can help to establish the size of the waiting area. It can also be used to find the average customer waiting time in the queue. Companies often use this average to evaluate the quality of service.

When there is uncertainty concerning arrivals and service, some results will have to be stated in probabilistic terms. Some of these measures include the probabilities of an empty facility and finding a given number of customers in the system.

The specific values for these performance measures and the resulting costs will depend on the nature of the queuing system. Fortunately, decision scientists have developed quantitative models that provide such information for a variety of waiting line situations. This section shows how to calculate and interpret the measures for a basic system involving a single queue and only one server. It also illustrates how the results can be used to evaluate alternative system designs. The final section will extend the analysis to other circumstances.

Assumptions

In Titan's storeroom situation, there will always be customers entering the queuing system (parts storeroom). For practical purposes, there is a very large or nearly infinite source

Table 15.5   **Summary of Titan's Queuing System**

Assumption	System Element
Infinite source population	Employees in Mineola plant
Poisson arrival process	Employees entering parts storeroom
Infinite waiting room	Parts storeroom and vicinity
Single queue	Employees seeking supplies
No balking, reneging, or jockeying	Employees waiting for supplies
First in, first served (FIFS)	Employees receiving supplies
Single server	Storeroom clerk
Single-stage service	Clerk providing supplies
Negative exponential service process	Clerk dispensing supplies
Departures return to source population	Employees returning to plant
Steady-state conditions	Normal storeroom operations
Average arrivals less than average service rate ($\lambda < u$)	Clerk's efficiency

population. Furthermore, the arrival process is best described by a Poisson distribution. The average arrival rate, $\lambda = 4$ per hour, remains constant throughout the entire working period. Titan's case does not describe the queue behavior or accommodations. However, in the plant situation, it is reasonable to assume that arrivals will form a single queue and wait in line until served. Also, adequate room will probably exist in the storeroom (or its immediate vicinity) to hold all customers waiting for service.

The Mineola parts storeroom has only one server. Since the supplies are ordinary items, chances are that customers will be handled on a first-in, first-served (FIFS) basis. Service time is random and best described by a negative exponential distribution. The average service rate, $u = 5$ per hour, remains constant throughout the period of operation. In addition, departing employees return to the plant (source population) and hence become potential new customers.

Another important consideration is the operating state of the queuing system. In Titan's situation, the working day begins with no customers in the parts storeroom. The initial start-up or transient period may involve unusual operating conditions. For instance, there could be a rush of employees entering the storeroom for parts. Eventually, the system will settle into a more "normal" flow of activity. In this equilibrium, or steady, state, storeroom performance characteristics will reach stable values that do not depend on time of day or day of week. Since Titan will be primarily interested in normal operating conditions, management should focus on the steady-state, rather than transient, characteristics of the queuing system.

Finally, notice that Titan's average arrival rate $\lambda = 4$ is less than the average service rate $u = 5$. Hence, the clerk is efficient enough to eventually process or service all arrivals. This type of system would not be feasible otherwise. For instance, if λ were greater than u, the average arrivals would outnumber the average number being served, and the waiting line would become infinitely large.

Titan's circumstances are summarized in Table 15.5. These characteristics are consistent with one of the most fundamental queuing models.

Figure 15.8   Steady-State Movements in Titan's Queuing System

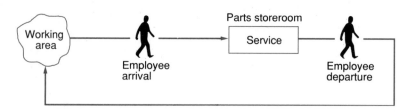

Performance Measures

In this basic model, customers arrive at the constant rate $\lambda = 4$ per hour and are served at the fixed rate $u = 5$ per hour. Consequently, the storeroom clerk will be busy

$$\frac{\lambda}{u} = \frac{4}{5} = .8$$

of the time or have an 80 percent utilization factor. This ratio

(15.5) $$P_W = \frac{\lambda}{u}$$

also represents the probability that an arriving customer will have to wait for service. Furthermore, there is a

$$1 - \frac{\lambda}{u} = 1 - .8 = .2$$

chance that the clerk will be idle. In other words,

(15.6) $$P_0 = 1 - P_W = 1 - \frac{\lambda}{u}$$

gives the probability of zero customers in the queuing system.

Probability Distribution. Management also might be concerned with the number of customers passing through the parts storeroom. Excessive traffic, for instance, might encourage employees to socialize on company time or create unnecessary congestion. Information useful for this purpose would be the probability of finding a specified number of customers in the system. To see how such data can be derived, consider Figure 15.8.

Figure 15.8 illustrates how a Titan employee moves from the working area through the parts storeroom and back to the working area. When an employee arrives at the storeroom, the clerk will no longer be idle. That is, the number of customers in the system will change from 0 to 1. Since an average of $\lambda = 4$ employees arrives each hour and the clerk is free $P_0 = 0.2$ of the time, this change will occur at a rate of

$$\lambda P_0 = 4(0.2) = 0.8 \text{ customers per hour.}$$

After the employee receives service and departs, there will be a change from 1 back to 0 customers in the system. The clerk can service an average of $u = 5$ employees per hour. If P_1 = the probability of one customer in the system, the change from 1 to 0 will occur at the rate of

$$uP_1 = 5P_1 \text{ employees each hour.}$$

In the steady state, the rates of change from 0 to 1 and vice versa are equal. Such a balance occurs when

$$\lambda P_0 = uP_1.$$

From this equation, you can see that the probability of finding one customer in Titan's queuing system is

$$P_1 = \frac{\lambda}{u} P_0 = \frac{4}{5}(0.2) = 0.16.$$

Similarly, the probability of finding two customers will be

$$P_2 = \frac{\lambda}{u} P_1 = \frac{\lambda}{u}\left(\frac{\lambda}{u} P_0\right) = \left(\frac{\lambda}{u}\right)^2 P_0$$

or

$$P_2 = \left(\frac{4}{5}\right)^2 (0.2) = 0.128.$$

and

$$P_3 = (\lambda/\mu)^3 P_0 = (4/5)^3 (0.2) = 0.1024$$

is the probability of finding three customers in the system.

In general, the probability of n customers in the system can be found with the following formula:

(15.7)
$$P_n = \left(\frac{\lambda}{u}\right)^n P_0 = \left(\frac{\lambda}{u}\right)^n \left(1 - \frac{\lambda}{u}\right)$$

By using this formula, Titan can develop a complete probability distribution for the number of employees waiting or being served in the storeroom area. Table 15.6 presents a portion of the computed data.

Customers in the System. Using data from Table 15.6, Titan can compute the average, or expected, number of employees either waiting or being served in the parts storeroom. Management can compute this information by multiplying each specific number of customers n by the corresponding probability P_n and then summing the results:

$$0(0.2) + 1(0.16) + 2(0.128) + 3(0.1024) + \ldots$$

The same result can be obtained in a less cumbersome and time-consuming manner with the following formula:

(15.8)
$$L = \frac{\lambda}{u - \lambda}$$

where L represents the average number of customers in the system. This formula indicates that Titan will have an average of

Table 15.6 **Partial Probability Distributions for the Number of Customers in Titan's System**

Number of Customers n	Probability P_n	Cumulative Probability of n or Less	Probability of More Than n
0	.2000	.2000	.8000
1	.1600	.3600	.6400
2	.1280	.4880	.5120
3	.1024	.5904	.4096
4	.0819	.6723	.3277
5	.0655	.7378	.2622
6	.0524	.7902	.2098
7	.0419	.8321	.1679
8	.0336	.8657	.1343
.	.	.	.
.	.	.	.
.	.	.	.

$$L = \frac{4}{5-4} = 4 \text{ employees}$$

either waiting or being served in the storeroom.

Time in the System. An average of $\lambda = 4$ employees arrive at the storeroom per hour. Since Titan has an average of $L = 4$ customers in the system, an arrival will spend an average of

$$\frac{L}{\lambda} = \frac{4 \text{ customers}}{4 \text{ arrivals per hour}} = 1 \text{ hour}$$

either waiting or being served. In other words,

(15.9) $$W = \frac{L}{\lambda} = \frac{1}{u - \lambda}$$

measures the average time that a customer will be in the queuing system.

Time in the Queue. The total period spent in the system (W) will include waiting and service time. Titan knows that it takes an average of $1/u = 1/5 = 0.2$ hour, or 12 minutes, between service completions. Consequently, a customer spends an average of

$$W - \frac{1}{u} = 1 - 0.2 = 0.8 \text{ hour}$$

or 48 minutes waiting in line. That is,

(15.10) $$W_Q = W - \frac{1}{u} = \frac{\lambda}{u(u - \lambda)}$$

represents the average time that a customer must wait before being served.

Table 15.7   **Summary of Performance Measures for the Basic Single-Server Model**

Performance Measure	Formula	Titan's Value
Probability that an arriving customer has to wait for service	$P_W = \dfrac{\lambda}{u}$	$P_W = \dfrac{4}{5} = .8$
Probability that the service facility is idle	$P_0 = 1 - \dfrac{\lambda}{u}$	$P_0 = 1 - .8 = .2$
Probability of n customers in the system	$P_n = \left(\dfrac{\lambda}{u}\right)^n \left(1 - \dfrac{\lambda}{u}\right)$	See Table 15.6.
Average number of customers in the system	$L = \dfrac{\lambda}{u - \lambda}$	$L = \dfrac{4}{5 - 4} = 4$
Average time that a customer will be in the system	$W = \dfrac{1}{u - \lambda}$	$W = \dfrac{1}{5 - 4} = 1$ hour
Average time that a customer has to wait before being served	$W_Q = \dfrac{\lambda}{u(u - \lambda)}$	$W_Q = \dfrac{4}{5(5 - 4)} = .8$ hour
Average number of customers in the queue waiting for service	$L_Q = \dfrac{\lambda^2}{u(u - \lambda)}$	$L_Q = \dfrac{4^2}{5(5 - 4)} = 3.2$

Customers in the Queue. An average of $\lambda = 4$ employees arrive per hour, and each spends an average of $W_Q = 0.8$ hour (48 minutes) waiting in line. Hence, there will be an average of

$$\lambda W_Q = 4(0.8) = 3.2 \text{ employees}$$

waiting in the storeroom area for service. In effect, the expression

$$(15.11) \qquad L_Q = \lambda W_Q = \lambda \left[\frac{\lambda}{u(u - \lambda)} \right] = \frac{\lambda^2}{u(u - \lambda)}$$

provides the average number of customers in the queue waiting for service. Table 15.7 summarizes these performance measures for the basic queuing model.

Additional Measures. It is possible to calculate additional performance measures. Some possibilities include the probability of being in the system longer than a specified period, the average length of an occupied queue, and the probability of finding more than a desired number of customers in the system. References in the For Further Reading section at the end of the chapter provide a full discussion for the interested reader.

Comparative Analysis

The performance measures provide several useful insights concerning the storeroom operation. In particular, we know that an employee has to wait an average of $W_Q = 0.8$ hour, or 48 minutes, for service. Such a wait seems to be excessive and undesirable.

Table 15.8   **Queuing System Characteristics for Titan's Service Plans**

Performance Measure	Plan		
	Clerk	**Processor**	**Automation**
Probability of waiting P_W	0.8	.4	.333
Probability of an idle facility P_0	0.2	.6	.667
Average number of customers in system L	4	.667	.5
Average time in system (hours) W	1	.167	.125
Average time waiting (hours) W_Q	0.8	.067	.042
Average number of customers in queue L_Q	3.2	.267	.167

The average queue ($L_Q = 3.2$) and high probability of waiting ($P_W = 0.8$) are additional indicators of a service deficiency.

Essentially, there are two ways to improve service. Management can either attempt to increase the speed of service or add more servers. Management Situation 15.3 illustrates.

Management Situation 15.3

Increasing the Service Level

The employees who require parts from Titan's storeroom are paid $10 per hour. Hence, the production manager is concerned about the manufacturing time lost by the employees at the parts storeroom. Titan is considering two options for improving service. One alternative is to replace the existing clerk with a specially trained and certified parts processor. Under this plan, the service rate would double from 5 to 10 customers per hour. However, the parts processor will be paid $7 per hour as compared to the $5 hourly wage of the existing clerk. Amortization, insurance, and other fixed expenses for the storeroom facility would remain at $12,000 per year. The facility operates eight hours a day, 250 days per year. In the second option, Titan would partially automate the current system. Purchase and installation of the required equipment would add $9,000 to annual fixed expenses but provide a service rate of 12 customers per hour.

Titan's management must decide which option to select.

Under the existing system, the clerk can process $u = 5$ customers per hour, or one customer every $1/u = 1/5 = 0.2$ hour (12 minutes). Both options now being considered (the fast clerk and the partially automated system) improve the speed of service. The parts processor would service $u = 10$ per hour (one every six minutes), and the equipment-assisted clerk would process $u = 12$ an hour (one every five minutes). Employees would still arrive at the rate of $\lambda = 4$ customers per hour.

Operating Performance. Titan can predict the effects of each plan on storeroom operations by using the data in equations (15.5)–(15.11). Table 15.8 summarizes the results.

An examination of these results shows that each alternative substantially reduces the probability of waiting (P_W), the average waiting time (W_Q), and the average number of employees waiting for service (L_Q). Thus, Titan can improve service by using either a faster clerk or the partially automated system. Both options, however, also significantly increase the probability of an idle facility (P_o).

The operating characteristics will also affect the costs associated with the queuing system. Before reaching a final decision, then, Titan needs to estimate the economic impact of the alternative plans.

Cost Considerations

When an employee goes to the parts storeroom, this worker is being diverted from his or her work on the production line. Yet Titan pays this person $10 per hour whether the person is working or obtaining supplies. During any given hour, there are an average of L customers in the parts storeroom either waiting or being served. Therefore, it costs the company $10L$ per hour in lost manufacturing time to operate the queuing system.

With the existing clerk, $L = 4$, and the queuing system cost (cost in lost manufacturing time due to the queuing system) is

$$\$10L = \$10 \times 4 = \$40 \text{ per hour}$$

or $40/hour $\times$ 8 hours/day $\times$ 250 days/year = $80,000 per year.

Of this amount, $\$10L_Q = \$10 \times 3.2 = \$32$ per hour, or $64,000 represents the annual cost of waiting for service. The faster clerk would substantially reduce these queuing expenses. For instance, the cost of the parts processor would be only $\$10L = \$10(0.667) = \$6.67$ per hour.

Titan must also consider the cost of providing the service facilities. Amortization, insurance, and other fixed expenses will be $12,000 per year under either of the manual approaches. The existing clerk is paid $5 per hour or

$$\$5/hour \times 8 \text{ hours/day} \times 250 \text{ days/year} = \$10,000 \text{ per year.}$$

Hence, it will cost $12,000 + $10,000 = $22,000 to operate the parts storeroom for one year. On the other hand, the faster clerk must be paid $7 per hour, or $14,000 a year. Consequently, the company will pay $12,000 + $14,000 = $26,000 per year for the improved service.

Economic Evaluation. Titan must balance the cost savings from the improved service against the increased expenses. Table 15.9 computes the cost data relevant for this comparison. From this cost summary, you can see that the least costly plan is to use the parts processor. Even though this person requires a ($14,000 − $10,000)/$10,000 = 40 percent higher salary than the existing clerk, the improved service will result in a reduction of total costs by ($102,000 − $39,340)/$102,000 = 61.4 percent. Although efficiency could be further improved with partial automation, the additional $9,000 equipment expense would more than offset the cost savings from the faster service.

Note that in Titan's situation, the customers are themselves employees of the organization operating the service system. As a result, it is relatively easy to assess the customer waiting cost. However, when customers are external to the company or the

Table 15.9   **Cost Summary for Titan's Service Plans**

Plan	Queuing System Cost ($/Year) $10L \times 8 \times 250$	Service Facility Costs ($/Year) Fixed Expenses + Salary	Total Cost ($/Year)
Existing clerk	$10(4)(8)(250) = 80,000$	$12,000 + 10,000 = 22,000$	102,000
Parts processor	$10(.667)(8)(250) = 13,340$	$12,000 + 14,000 = 26,000$	39,340
Partial automation	$10(.5)(8)(250) = 10,000$	$9,000 + 12,000 + 10,000 = 31,000$	41,000

firm is a nonprofit institution, it may be more difficult to determine this expense. Such things as ill will and social costs are very difficult to measure accurately.

Procedure Recap. The methodology of queuing analysis can be summarized as follows:

1. Identify the structure of the queuing system, including the nature of the source population, arrival process, queue accommodations and behavior, selection process, service process, and departures.

2. Establish the appropriate operating characteristics or performance measures of the queuing system.

3. Compute the measures of performance, including the following:
   a. Probability of waiting P_W
   b. Probability of an idle facility P_0
   c. Probability of a specified number of customers P_n
   d. Average number of customers in the system L
   e. Average system time W
   f. Average waiting time W_Q
   g. Average number of customers in the queue L_Q

4. Compare the performance measures for each system design.

5. If possible, calculate the corresponding queuing and service facility costs.

6. Select the system design that leads to the most favorable performance characteristics and/or least total cost.

15.3 PRACTICAL EXTENSIONS

Many practical situations do not conform to the assumptions of the basic queuing model. There may be a finite source population, arrivals in bulk quantities, limited waiting capacity, sequential waiting lines, or multiple servers. Also, the average arrival or service rate may vary with the number of customers waiting for service. In addition, the situation may involve something other than a Poisson arrival process, FIFS queue discipline, or negative exponential service times. This section presents queuing models applicable to some of these situations.

Finite Source Population

In some situations, there is a small number of potential customers. As a result, the arrival rate will be affected by the number of customers already in the system. Management Situation 15.4 illustrates.

Processing Office Work

Data Studies Associates, a small private research organization, employees three secretaries in its report preparation center. The nature of the work requires the staff to use the firm's single word processor. Although the utilization rate varies, the pattern closely follows a Poisson distribution with an average usage of twice per eight-hour day. Word processing time also fluctuates but can be reasonably described by a negative exponential distribution. The average period on the machine is 80 minutes.

Data Studies wants to measure the word processing performance of its secretarial staff.

The circumstances for Data Studies are very similar to Titan's storeroom situation. There is a single service facility (the word processor) and hence a single waiting line. The arrival process of secretaries to the machine follows a Poisson distribution with an average of twice per eight-hour day, or $\lambda = 2/8 = 0.25$ per hour. It seems reasonable to assume that the machine will be used on a first-come, first-served basis. Also, service time (the period on the machine) follows a negative exponential distribution. Since the mean processing time is 80 minutes, or 1.33 hours, the average service rate will be $1/1.33 = 0.75$ secretary per hour.

There is one major distinction between the two situations. Titan has a very large number of potential customers (practically an infinite source population). On the other hand, the source population for Data Studies consists of only three secretaries and hence is finite.

The distinction is important because the probability of an arrival is affected by the number of customers already in the system. Suppose, for instance, that all three secretaries are currently at the word processor. Hence, there is no chance of an arrival during, say, the next minute. Yet, if only one secretary is at the machine, the probability of an arrival in the same time interval is much higher. Titan's situation is another matter. The Mineola plant has a relatively large source population. Consequently, the probability of an arrival does not change significantly if some of the employees are already in the storeroom area.

In effect, a finite population model involves substantially different probability calculations than the infinite population model. Formulas for the system performance measures must be modified to reflect these differences. The relevant equations are summarized in Table 15.10. In this table, M represents the number of customers in the source population. Also, λ gives the arrival rate for each individual rather than for the group of M customers.

Table 15.10   **Formulas for a Finite Source, Single-Server Queuing Model**

Performance Measure	Formula
Probability that the service facility is idle	$P_0 = \dfrac{1}{\sum\limits_{n=0}^{M}\left[\dfrac{M!}{(M-n)!}\left(\dfrac{\lambda}{u}\right)^n\right]}$
Probability of n customers in the system	$P_n = \dfrac{M!}{(M-n)!}\left(\dfrac{\lambda}{u}\right)^n P_0$
Average number of customers waiting in line	$L_Q = M - \left[\left(\dfrac{\lambda+u}{\lambda}\right)(1-P_0)\right]$
Average number of customers in the system	$L = L_Q + (1 - P_0)$
Average waiting time	$W_Q = \dfrac{L_Q}{\lambda(M-L)}$
Average time in the system	$W = W_Q + \dfrac{1}{u}$

Operating Characteristics. For Data Studies Associates, $M = 3$ secretaries, $\lambda = 0.25$ customer per hour and $u = 0.75$ customer per hour. Management can use this information and the appropriate formula in Table 15.10 to determine P_0. In this way, management will find that the word processor is idle

$$P_0 = \frac{1}{\sum\limits_{n=0}^{M}\left[\dfrac{M!}{(M-n)!}\left(\dfrac{\lambda}{u}\right)^n\right]} = \frac{1}{\sum\limits_{n=0}^{3}\left[\dfrac{3!}{(3-n)!}\left(\dfrac{.25}{.75}\right)^n\right]}$$

or

$$P_0 = \frac{1}{\dfrac{3!}{(3-0)!}\left(\dfrac{1}{3}\right)^0 + \dfrac{3!}{(3-1)!}\left(\dfrac{1}{3}\right)^1 + \dfrac{3!}{(3-2)!}\left(\dfrac{1}{3}\right)^2 + \dfrac{3!}{(3-3)!}\left(\dfrac{1}{3}\right)^3}$$

$$= 0.346$$

of the time.

Because this formula requires extensive calculations in large-scale problems, queuing tables and graphs have been developed to give the P_0 value for selected values of the utilization ratio (λ/μ) and population size (M). These tables and graphs are presented in the For Further Reading section's references. When the actual numbers can be found in such documents, the decision maker can avoid the lengthy computations involved in using the P_0 formula. An alternative is to find the probability with the aid of a computer program (such as the queuing module in **Quantitative Management**).

Other operating characteristics can be found from P_0. The formula for P_n in Table 15.10, for example, indicates that there is

$$P_n = \frac{M!}{(M-n)!}\left(\frac{\lambda}{u}\right)^n P_0$$

or

$$P_1 = \frac{3!}{(3-1)!}\left(\frac{.25}{.75}\right)^1 (0.346) = 0.346$$

chance of finding exactly one customer in the system and a

$$P_2 = \frac{3!}{(3-2)!}\left(\frac{1}{3}\right)^2 (0.346) = 0.231$$

probability that two secretaries will be either waiting for the machine or using the machine.

Also, there will be an average of

$$L_Q = M - \left[\left(\frac{\lambda+u}{\lambda}\right)(1-P_0)\right]$$

$$= 3 - \left[\left(\frac{.25+.75}{.25}\right)(1-0.346)\right] = 0.384 \text{ secretary}$$

waiting to use the word processor and an average of

$$L = L_Q + (1-P_0) = 0.384 + (1-0.346) = 1.038 \text{ customers}$$

in the system waiting or being served. A secretary spends an average of

$$W_Q = \frac{L_Q}{\lambda(M-L)} = \frac{0.384}{0.25(3-1.038)} = 0.783 \text{ hour}$$

or 46.98 minutes waiting to use the word processor and

$$W = W_Q + \frac{1}{u} = 0.783 + \frac{1}{0.75} = 2.116 \text{ hours}$$

or 126.98 minutes in the system.

Economic Evaluation. In the future, Data Studies Associates might consider options for reducing the customer waiting time. One possibility is to increase word processing speed through a training program for the secretaries. As part of the planning process, the company can use the equations from Table 15.10 and appropriate cost data to evaluate the alternatives.

Limited Waiting Capacity

Frequently, the waiting area for the queuing system has a limited capacity. Any customers who arrive while the waiting area is full must be turned away. Consider Management Situation 15.5.

Management Situation 15.5

Furniture Refinishing

Elegant Woodworks, Inc. has for some time been experiencing rapid growth in its furniture-refinishing business. Current demand averages 30 jobs per week with interarrival times closely following a negative exponential distribution. The company can complete an average of 33 jobs a week. Service times also appear to follow a negative exponential distribution. Jobs are processed on a first-come, first-served basis.

There is limited space available to store furniture awaiting refinishing. At the present time, Elegant storage capacity can accommodate only six jobs. Management is concerned about this limited capacity because Elegant may have to turn away customers and hence lose potential revenue. Management wants to evaluate the effects of this limitation on its operation.

Elegant's circumstances are very similar to Titan's storeroom situation. There is only one significant distinction. Titan has practically an unlimited waiting area and hence a potentially infinite queue length. In Elegant's case, however, the limited physical storage capacity restricts its queue to a finite length.

When the limited waiting area is filled to capacity, potential customers will be turned away and the effective arrival rate becomes zero. Formulas for the system performance measures must be modified to account for the finite queue length. The relevant equations are those presented in Table 15.11. In the table, K represents the maximum capacity of the system, or the largest number of customers both in the waiting line and being served.

Operating Characteristics. For Elegant's situation, $K = 7$ (6 jobs that can be stored plus 1 in process), $\lambda = 30$ jobs per week, and $u = 33$ jobs per week. Hence, the furniture-refinishing operation will be idle

$$P_0 = \frac{1 - (\lambda/u)}{1 - (\lambda/u)^{K+1}} = \frac{1 - (30/33)}{1 - (30/33)^{7+1}} = 0.171$$

of the time. Also, the formula for P_n in Table 15.11 indicates that there will be one job in the shop

$$P_1 = \left(\frac{30}{33}\right)^1 (.171) = .155$$

of the time and two jobs

$$P_2 = \left(\frac{30}{33}\right)^2 (.171) = .141$$

of the time. The limited storage capacity forces the company to turn away

$$P_K = \left(\frac{\lambda}{u}\right)^K P_0 = \left(\frac{30}{33}\right)^7 (.171) = .088$$

or 8.8 percent of its potential customers.

Table 15.11   **Formulas for a Finite Queue Length, Single-Server Queuing Model**

Performance Measure	Formula
Probability of an idle service facility	$P_0 = \dfrac{1 - (\lambda/u)}{1 - (\lambda/u)^{K+1}}$
Probability of n customers in the system	$P_n = \left(\dfrac{\lambda}{u}\right)^n P_0$
Proportion of arrivals that will be turned away	$P_K = \left(\dfrac{\lambda}{u}\right)^K P_0$
Average number of customers in the system	$L = \dfrac{\lambda/u}{1 - (\lambda/u)} - \dfrac{(K+1)(\lambda/u)^{K+1}}{1 - (\lambda/u)^{K+1}}$
Average number of customers waiting in line	$L_Q = L - \dfrac{\lambda(1 - P_K)}{u}$
Average waiting time	$W_Q = \dfrac{L_Q}{\lambda(1 - P_K)}$
Average time in the system	$W = W_Q + 1/u$

In addition, there will be an average of

$$L = \frac{(\lambda/u)}{1 - (\lambda/u)} - \frac{(K+1)(\lambda/u)^{K+1}}{1 - (\lambda/u)^{K+1}}$$

$$= \frac{(30/33)}{1 - (30/33)} - \frac{(7+1)(30/33)^{7+1}}{1 - (30/33)^{7+1}} = 2.987$$

or about three jobs on the premises (waiting or being served). Of these jobs,

$$L_Q = L - \frac{\lambda(1 - P_K)}{u} = 2.987 - \frac{30(1 - .088)}{33} = 2.158$$

or an average of approximately two are waiting for refinishing. The average waiting time is

$$W_Q = \frac{L_Q}{\lambda(1 - P_K)} = \frac{2.158}{30(1 - .088)} = .079 \text{ week}$$

or, assuming a five-day work week, .395 day. Each job will be in Elegant's refinishing system (waiting or being served) for an average of

$$W = W_Q + \frac{1}{u} = .079 + \frac{1}{33} = .109 \text{ week}$$

or .547 working day.

Economic Evaluation. In the future, Elegant might want to consider the possibility of expanding its storage capacity. Perhaps the company could lease additional space or construct a larger waiting area. Such plans could reduce the number of lost customers and hence capture some additional revenue. Of course, the additional facilities would increase expenses. In any event, management can use the equations from Table 15.11 and appropriate revenue and cost data to evaluate the alternatives.

Multiple Servers

Many organizations can deliver service most efficiently with multiple servers. In one of the simplest cases, the system is composed of several identical and parallel service facilities. Arriving customers form a single queue and wait for a service channel to become available. Whenever a server is free, the customer at the head of the line goes to that facility. Management Situation 15.6 illustrates.

Management Situation 15.6

Expanding Service Facilities

Titan Industries currently employs a single clerk in its parts storeroom. An analysis of other single-channel options indicated that the speed of service could be improved by using a parts processor rather than the existing clerk. The faster clerk would also reduce costs to an annual level of $39,340. Suppose that the production manager now wants to consider the desirability of hiring an additional clerk. The new person would have qualifications identical to those of the existing clerk. Hence, each clerk would receive a $5 hourly wage and would be capable of serving customers at the same rate of $u = 5$ per hour. Customers would still arrive at the rate of $\lambda = 4$ per hour. Arrivals would be instructed to form a single waiting line and then seek the first available clerk. Amortization, insurance, and fixed expenses would remain at $12,000 per year. Plant employees would still receive $10 per hour.

Management wants to compare the performance measures and costs of the two-clerk plan and parts processor plan.

There is only one difference between Management Situation 15.6 and Titan's previous circumstances (Management Situation 15.1 through 15.3). In the earlier examples, Titan had a single server (either the existing clerk, the parts processor, or the automated clerk). The new situation would involve two service channels (clerks) as shown in Figure 15.9.

When the quantity of customers in the system does not exceed the number of servers, all can receive immediate service. As a result, there is no waiting line. In this case, arrivals are processed at a factor equal to each facility service rate multiplied by the number of customers in the system. On the other hand, when the customer count exceeds the number of servers, a waiting line will form. Consequently, the combined service rate is equal to each facility's processing rate multiplied by the number of servers.

Figure 15.9   Titan's Two-Clerk Queuing System

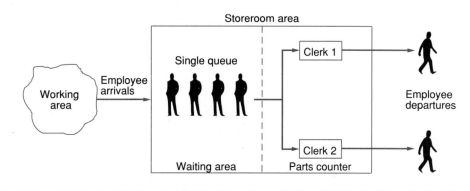

Since the number of servers will influence the operating characteristics of the system, queuing formulas should reflect this fact. Table 15.12 gives such formulas for the single-queue, multiple-server situation. In this table, S denotes the number of servers or service facilities. Also, notice that the system service rate (Su) must be greater than the arrival rate (λ). Otherwise, the waiting line and average waiting time may become infinitely large.

Operating Characteristics. Management Situation 15.6 involves $S = 2$ clerks, $u = 5$ customers per hour for each server, and $\lambda = 4$ employees per hour. Titan can use these data and the appropriate formula in Table 15.12 to calculate P_0. The computations will show that both clerks are idle

$$
P_0 = \cfrac{1}{\left[\displaystyle\sum_{n=0}^{S-1} \frac{1}{n!}\left(\frac{\lambda}{u}\right)^n\right] + \frac{1}{S!}\left(\frac{\lambda}{u}\right)^S\left(\frac{Su}{Su - \lambda}\right)}
$$

$$
= \cfrac{1}{\left[\displaystyle\sum_{n=0}^{2-1} \frac{1}{n!}\left(\frac{4}{5}\right)^n\right] + \frac{1}{2!}\left(\frac{4}{5}\right)^2\left[\frac{2(5)}{2(5) - 4}\right]}
$$

or

$$
P_0 = \cfrac{1}{\left[\dfrac{1}{0!}\left(\dfrac{4}{5}\right)^0 + \dfrac{1}{1!}\left(\dfrac{4}{5}\right)^1\right] + \dfrac{1}{2}\left(\dfrac{16}{25}\right)\left(\dfrac{10}{10 - 4}\right)} = .429
$$

of the time.

Table 15.12   **Formulas for a Single-Queue, Multiple-Server Queuing Model**

Performance Measure	Formula
Probability that all service facilities are idle	$P_0 = \dfrac{1}{\left[\displaystyle\sum_{n=0}^{S-1} \dfrac{1}{n!}\left(\dfrac{\lambda}{u}\right)^n\right] + \dfrac{1}{S!}\left(\dfrac{\lambda}{u}\right)^S\left(\dfrac{Su}{su - \lambda}\right)}$
Probability that an arriving customer has to wait for service	$P_W = \dfrac{1}{S!}\left(\dfrac{\lambda}{u}\right)^S\left(\dfrac{Su}{Su - \lambda}\right)P_0$
Probability of n customers in the system	$P_n = \dfrac{(\lambda/u)^n}{n!}P_0 \qquad \text{for } n \le S$
	$P_n = \dfrac{(\lambda/u)^n}{S!(S^{n-S})}P_0 \qquad \text{for } n > S$
Average number of customers waiting for service	$L_Q = \dfrac{\lambda u(\lambda/u)^S}{(S-1)!(Su - \lambda)^2}P_0$
Average number of customers in the system	$L = L_Q + \dfrac{\lambda}{u}$
Average time in the system	$W = \dfrac{L}{\lambda}$
Average waiting time	$W_Q = W - \dfrac{1}{u}$

Because this formula requires extensive calculations in large-scale problems, queuing tables and graphs have been developed to give the P_0 value for selected values of the utilization ratio (λ/μ) and number of servers (S). These tables and graphs again are discussed in the For Further Reading section's references. When the actual λ/μ and S values can be found in these documents, management can avoid using the cumbersome formula to find P_0. An alternative is to find this probability with the aid of a computer program (such as the queuing module in **Quantitative Management**).

Other operating characteristics can be determined from P_0. The formula in Table 15.12, for instance, indicates that

$$P_W = \frac{1}{S!}\left(\frac{\lambda}{u}\right)^S\left(\frac{Su}{Su - \lambda}\right)P_0 = \frac{1}{2!}\left(\frac{4}{5}\right)^2\left[\frac{2(5)}{2(5) - 4}\right](.429) = .229$$

or 22.9 percent of arriving customers will have to wait for service. Also, suppose that Titan believes that the system currently has no more customers than servers. That is, $n \le S$. In this case,

$$P_n = \frac{(\lambda/u)^n}{n!}P_0$$

and there will be a

$$P_1 = \frac{(4/5)^1}{1!}(.429) = .343$$

chance of finding exactly one customer in the system. On the other hand, when $n > S$,

$$P_n = \frac{(\lambda/u^n)}{S!(S^{n-S})}P_0.$$

For example, there is a

$$P_3 = \frac{(\lambda/u)^n}{S!(S^{n-S})}P_0 = \frac{(4/5)^3}{2!(2^{3-2})}(.429) = .055$$

probability that three plant employees are waiting or being served in the parts storeroom.

In addition, there will be an average of

$$L_Q = \frac{\lambda u(\lambda/u)^S}{(S-1)!(Su-\lambda)^2}P_0 = \frac{4(5)(4/5)^2}{(2-1)![2(5)-4]^2}(.429) = .153 \text{ employee}$$

waiting for service and an average of

$$L = L_Q + \frac{\lambda}{u} = .153 + \frac{4}{5} = .953 \text{ customer}$$

in the system. A customer will spend an average of

$$W = \frac{L}{\lambda} = \frac{.953}{4} = .238 \text{ hour}$$

or 14.28 minutes in the parts storeroom area and an average of

$$W_Q = W - \frac{1}{u} = .238 - \frac{1}{5} = .038 \text{ hour}$$

or 2.28 minutes waiting for service.

Economic Evaluation. During any given hour, there are an average of L customers in the parts storeroom area (and hence not working). Since plant employees receive $10 per hour, the queuing system cost for lost production time is

$$\$10L = \$10(.953) = \$9.53 \text{ per hour}$$

or

$$\$9.53/\text{hour} \times 8 \text{ hours/day} \times 250 \text{ days/year} = \$19,060 \text{ per year}$$

with the two clerk plan. Of this amount, $\$10L_Q = \$10(.153) = \$1.53$ per hour, or $3,060 represents the annual cost of waiting for service. Amortization, insurance, and other fixed expenses are $12,000 per year. The cost for the two clerks is an additional

$$2 \text{ clerks} \times \$5/\text{hour} \times 8 \text{ hours/day} \times 250 \text{ days/year} = \$20,000 \text{ per year.}$$

Thus, the two-clerk plan will involve an annual cost of $20,000 + $12,000 + $19,060 = $51,060.

Table 15.13   **Operating Characteristics and Costs for Titan's Service Plans**

	Plan			
Performance Measure/Cost	**Existing Clerk**	**Parts Processor**	**Partial Automation**	**Two Clerks**
Probability of waiting P_W	0.8	0.40	0.333	0.229
Probability of idle facilities P_0	0.2	0.60	0.667	0.429
Average number in system L	4	0.667	0.50	0.953
Average time in system (hours) W	1	0.167	0.125	0.238
Average waiting time (hours) W_Q	0.8	0.067	0.042	0.038
Average number in queue L_Q	3.2	0.267	0.167	0.153
Queuing system cost ($/year)	80,000	13,340	10,000	19,060
Service facility cost ($/year)	22,000	26,000	31,000	32,000
Total cost ($/year)	102,000	39,340	41,000	51,060

Table 15.13 summarizes the operating characteristics and corresponding costs for all of Titan's system designs. Data from the three single-clerk plans are taken from Tables 15.8 and 15.9. The results show that the two-clerk plan involves a smaller probability of waiting P_W, less average waiting time W_Q, and a smaller average queue L_Q than any of the single-server options. However, customers spend a longer average time W in the two-clerk system than in the parts processor or partial automation system. On average, there are also more customers in the two-clerk plan than in either of these two single-clerk plans. Evidently the two-clerk system has a slower average service time than either the parts processor or partial automation plan. As a result, the multiple-server plan is less economical than either of these single-server alternatives. In particular, the parts processor option is still the least costly plan.

Other Models

All queuing models in this chapter assume that there is a Poisson arrival process and a negative exponential distribution of service times. In practice, arrivals and service completions may follow some other probability distribution. For example, service times may follow a normal distribution. Also, the waiting line situation may involve a constant arrival rate or constant service times. In fact, there is an infinite variety of probability distributions that may be appropriate in various situations.

Kendall Notation. To facilitate communication among researchers and practitioners, the British mathematician Maurice Kendall developed a shorthand notation that succinctly describes the possibilities. In Kendall notation, the first symbol describes the particular distribution of time between arrivals (interarrival times), the second gives the specific distribution of service times, and the third identifies the number of parallel servers. An M/M/1 system, for instance, involves exponential interarrival and service time distributions with one server. Similarly, M/M/S designates a system with exponential interarrival and service time distributions but a multiple (S) number of servers. The models in this chapter are representative of these M/M/1 and M/M/S systems.

Models have been developed for queuing situations involving other interarrival and service time distributions. Typical possibilities include

M = exponential interarrival or service time distribution (equivalent, respectively, to Poisson arrival and service rates)

D = deterministic (constant) interarrival or service time

E_k = Erlangian distribution of order k $(k = 1$ gives the exponential)

GI = general distribution of interarrival times (or of arrival rates)

G = general distribution of service times (or service rates)

For example, a GI/G/1 system involves a single-server model with any interarrival time distribution (as long as it is independent) and any service time distribution. Similarly, $D/E_2/S$ designates a system with a deterministic interarrival time distribution, a second-order Erlangian distribution of service time, and S parallel servers (but only one queue).

Extensions by A. M. Lee and H. A. Taha have augmented the Kendall notation to include the type of queue discipline, the facility capacity, and the type of source population (whether finite or infinite). In the simplest extension, a fourth symbol describes the maximum system capacity (K). For example, M/M/S/K involves a multiple-server system with exponential interarrival and service time distributions in which at most $K \times S$ customers can wait in line.

Decision Considerations. Additional models have been developed to deal with a wide variety of decision situations that may arise in practice. For example, there are queuing models for situations in which

1. customers arrive in bulk rather than one at a time.
2. the service process is influenced by the arrival process.
3. service is based on consumer preference or the "importance" of the customer.
4. customers receive simultaneous service from a random number of servers.

Queuing theory basically describes the operating characteristics of a waiting line situation. Then the information is used to evaluate selected design configurations. Since management typically tests only a few alternatives, the approach cannot usually guarantee an optimal solution to the problem. However, there are queuing models that, under specific circumstances, can be used to determine the optimal speed of service or the best number of facilities.

Simulation

Queuing models show management why waiting lines form, why some waiting is necessary or very costly to eliminate, and the nonlinear effects resulting from a change in service capacity and from a decrease in service time variability. Despite the plethora of available models, however, there will be many situations in which the theories' assumptions are invalid in practice. At other times, the theory may be valid, but the resulting formulas will be in a form that are either inconvenient or unusable for numerical calculations.

Figure 15.10   **Computer Solution of Titan's Problem**

Queuing Theory Problem:	Input:	Output:
▪ Basic single-server	* Edit	▪ Full
▪ Finite source, single-server	▪ Load	* Summary
▪ Finite queue length, single-server	▪ Print	* Print
* Single-queue, multiple-server	▪ Save	▪ Save

Description of Problem:
  Arrival rate λ: 4
  Service rate μ: 5
  Srvers S: 2
  Idle cost per unit: 10
  Service cost per unit: 5
  Fixed expenses: 12000
  Total service time: 2000

SYSTEM PERFORMANCE
Probability that all service facilities are idle P_0 = .429
Probability that arriving customer will wait P_W = .229
Average customers waiting for service L_Q = .153
Average customers in system L = .953
Average time in system W = .238
Average waiting time W_Q = .038

COST BREAKDOWN
Idle Customer Cost = 19060
Service Cost   = 20000
Fixed Expenses   = 12000
  Total Cost   = 51060

Typical complexities that make it difficult (if not impossible) to develop meaningful analytic solutions for queuing problems include

1. arrival processes that exhibit nonstationary behavior and seasonal patterns or that have empirical distributions with no theoretical counterpart.

2. service facilities that have tandem and parallel servers or that have service time distributions with difficult-to-analyze forms.

3. processes for which transient solutions are required (as when the system never operates long enough to reach a steady state) but are unavailable.

In such cases (and when existing queuing theory is invalid), the decision maker can simulate operations for specified system designs and policies under selected arrival and service conditions. The simulation results then can be used to identify the best system design and policy among those examined. This simulation approach is presented in Chapter 17.

Computer Analysis

Queuing models provide formulas that can be incorporated within computer programs and delivered easily to management through a user-friendly information system. Decision

Queuing in Practice

Queuing models are applied to a wide variety of management problems. Here are a few areas in which this quantitative analysis is used.

Area	Application
Finance and Accounting	Formulating a tenant vacancy policy for rental property Determining whether or not to build a coal unloading system in a power plant Analyzing congestion at automatic teller machines
Marketing	Servicing photocopying equipment customers Rationing gasoline in an energy crisis Establishing a hotel reservation policy
Production and Operations	Solving machine grouping and load problems in flexible manufacturing systems Evaluating the performance of manufacturing systems that are subject to tool availability Analyzing configurations in a data processing network
Public and Service Sector	Circulating books in a public library Formulating emergency health care practices Handling telephone reports in a state child abuse and maltreatment program Formulating an appointment policy at a hospital outpatient department

makers then can use the programs to automate the process of generating waiting system performance measures. One such set of programs is available on the **Quantitative Management (QM)** software. Figure 15.10 illustrates how these programs can be used to address Titan's expanded service facility problem (Management Situation 15.6).

Problem Formulation. The user executes the program by selecting the Single-queue, multiple-server option from the Queuing Theory Problem menu. Management formulates the problem through the Edit command from the Input menu. In this formulation, the user must specify the average arrival rate (λ), average service rate (μ), number of servers (S), and, where appropriate, the unit cost per idle customer, unit service cost, fixed expenses, and total available service time. In Titan's case, $\lambda = 4$, $\mu = 5$, S $= 2$, unit cost per idle customer is \$10 per hour, service cost is \$5 per hour, fixed expenses are \$12,000, and total service time is 8(250) $= 2,000$ hours per year. Thus, these values are inserted after the appropriate prompts in Figure 15.10. Report options then are defined through the Output menu.

System Performance. After receiving the information, the program will process the data, apply the relevant formulas, and report the resulting system performance measures. As Figure 15.10 demonstrates, the output includes two probabilities (P_0 and P_W), average customer (L_Q and L) information, waiting time (W and W_Q) measures, and a cost breakdown. If the user selects the Full option from the Output menu, the output also would give the complete probability distribution for the number of customers in the system.

SUMMARY

This chapter has presented the fundamental principles and concepts of queuing theory. The first section outlined the structure of a queuing system. A key element in the structure is the nature and size of the source populatiion. In particular, the number of potential clients influences the arrival process, the manner in which customers reach the service system. This process is described by the arrival rate and interarrival time. In many cases, these measures must be expressed in probabilistic terms. The Poisson distribution often provides accurate arrival rate probabilities, and interarrival times frequently follow a negative exponential distribution.

Arrivals form queues that are accommodated on site in a common waiting area or off the premises. An important consideration is the size of the area. Limited space often results in lost customers or blocked service facilities. Other important factors are the number of queues and the behavior of customers in the waiting lines.

Customers in the queue are selected for service in a variety of ways. Some systems use a first-in, first-served (FIFS) approach. Others use the last-in, first-served (LIFS) queue discipline. And a few systems select customers on a priority basis.

The chapter presented many different designs of the service facilities. Possibilities include a single channel, multiple parallel servers, and sequential systems. Regardless of the design, the service process is described by the service rate and the interservice time. In many cases, interservice times follow a negative exponential probability distribution.

Typically, departures from the queuing system return to the source population and become potential new arrivals. However, in some cases, departures permanently leave the queuing system and thus significantly reduce the source population.

After identifying the underlying queuing structure, management establishes appropriate measures for evaluating the performance of the system. Measures include the probability of waiting, the average number of customers in the queue, and the average waiting time. Table 15.7 presented formulas for computing such measures in a basic single-server queuing model. These measures are then used to compare the operating characteristics and, where applicable, costs of alternative system designs. This comparative analysis is the basis for selecting a preferred design.

The final section extended the basic analysis to other practical waiting line situations, including a finite source population with a single server (relevant performance measures were outlined in Table 15.10), a finite queue length with a single server (appropriate operating characteristics were summarized in Table 15.11), and a single waiting line with multiple servers (formulas for computing the performance measures in this system were provided in Table 15.12).

Glossary

arrival rate The number of customer arrivals into a queuing system per unit of time.

balking Refusing to join a waiting line even though space is available.

interarrival time The time between two consecutive customer arrivals into a queuing system.

interservice time The interval between two consecutive service completions at a facility in a queuing system.

jockeying Switching between multiple queues in an attempt to reduce waiting time.

negative exponential distribution A probability distribution used to describe the pattern of interarrival and/or service times for some queuing systems.

Poisson distribution A probability distribution used to describe the random arrival rate for some queuing systems.

preemptive priority systems A system in which an important arrival not only has entrance priority but can even interrupt the service on other, less significant customers.

queue discipline The manner in which customers from the waiting area are selected for service.

queuing theory Quantitative approaches that measure the operating characteristics and costs of waiting lines.

reneging Departing from a queuing system before being served.

service rate The number of customers served by a facility in a queuing system per unit of time.

utilization factor The proportion of time that the service facilities are in use.

Thought Exercises

1. Identify the source population, customer, waiting area, and service facility in each of the following situations:
   a. A local dentist's office
   b. A laundromat
   c. The local Social Security office
   d. An orbiting space station
   e. An automobile inspection station

2. Jason Slick, the manager of the Limelight Movie Theater, has been using a Poisson distribution with $\lambda = 3$ customers per minute to predict arrival rates at the various shows. The predictions are then used to determine the number of ticket windows that should remain open for each show.

   Julie McKay works at the box office on a rotating schedule. Some days she works the day shift (10 A.M. to 6 P.M.), and other days she works from 6 P.M. to 2 A.M. Julie has noticed that Mr. Slick's system does not seem to work as well during the night shift as in the day. To support her feelings, Julie collected some data over an extended period of time and found the following patterns:

Customer Arrivals per Minute	Number of Minutes	
	Day Shift	Night Shift
0	50	7
1	149	34
2	224	84
3	224	140
4	168	176
5	101	176
6	50	146
7	15	104
8	10	65
9	5	36
10	2	18
11	1	8
12	1	6
	1,000	1,000

   After examining these data, Jason switched his forecasting strategy. He still employs his previous approach for the day shift, but now uses a Poisson distribution with $\lambda = 300$

customers per hour to predict arrivals for the night shows. How did Jason arrive at these conclusions? Do you see any potential problems in his forecasting approach?

3. The Centerville Information Center employs hosts and hostesses to answer tourists' questions on attractions in the immediate area. Previous studies reveal that the customer service times for each host or hostess follow a negative exponential distribution. The average service time has been 10 minutes per tourist.

   Recently, management implemented a policy that requires each host or hostess to complete 95 percent of his or her service requests within 20 minutes. The limit applies only to service and does not include customer waiting time. Is this a realistic policy? If not, what do you recommend?

4. Determine the length of the waiting line and the service utilization factor for each of the following situations:
   a. Customers arrive at a single-service facility every 30 minutes and are processed in exactly 30 minutes.
   b. Ten customers arrive every hour at a single processing station capable of serving each arrival in exactly 12 minutes.
   c. Every 45 minutes, an object arrives at a machine with a service capacity of two parts per hour.

5. The state highway system includes a short turnpike along the southeastern edge of Pikestown. It is controlled by a single tollbooth at the end of the road. Past data indicate that during the city's rush hours, cars enter the tollbooth in a random pattern with an average of two minutes between arrivals.

   College students and other part-time workers are employed at the booth to collect tolls. Collection times follow a random pattern with each worker capable of serving an average of 20 cars per hour.

   Ever since the state started using part-time employees, there have been "endless" traffic jams at the tollbooth during rush hours. Can you see why? Explain. What corrective action would you recommend?

6. Midtown Car Wash has a single machine capable of processing automobiles in an average of six minutes. Each hour, an average of seven cars arrive at the facility. Service times and arrivals follow a random pattern.

   Management wants the car wash machine to be busy at least 70 percent of each working day. Another policy states that 50 percent of the time, there should be no more than five automobiles at the car wash. Are these objectives compatible under existing conditions? If not, what can be done to make them so?

7. A small fast-food restaurant currently has only one waiter. Although the service rate follows a random pattern, he is capable of serving an average of nine customers an hour. Customers arrive randomly on the average of one every 10 minutes. It annually costs $36,000 to operate, finance, and maintain the restaurant. In addition, the waiter is paid $4 per hour. The restaurant is open 10 hours a day, 300 days a year.

   Advertisements state that a customer will wait, on average, no more than three minutes before being served. Can the restaurant keep this pledge with the existing service facility design? If not, is there an alternative system that will satisfy the advertised service policy and still not exceed the restaurant's annual $60,000 budget? Explain.

8. Explain why you agree or disagree with each of the following statements:
   a. Queuing theory is largely a descriptive rather than normative approach.
   b. There cannot be a waiting line and underutilization of service facilties in the same situation.
   c. Doubling the service rate will cut waiting time in half.
   d. The most efficient operation involves a service rate equal to the arrival rate.
   e. Two facilities, each serving customers at a standard rate, will yield results identical to a single server that is twice as fast as the standard.

Technique Exercises

9. The number of customers arriving at a clothing store was recorded over a period of 500 hours. The data are presented below:

Customer Arrivals per Hour	Number of Hours
0	70
1	140
2	150
3	90
4	40
5	10

   a. Compute the average arrival rate per hour.
   b. Compute the average interarrival time in minutes. Graph the distribution of arrivals. Do arrivals appear to follow a Poisson distribution? Explain.

10. Refer to Management Situation 15.1. Demonstrate how the data in Table 15.4 were derived. Show all your work. Calculate the cumulative probabilities for interarrival times of $T_a \leq .8$, $T_a \leq .75$, $T_a \leq .4$, and $T_a \leq .25$. Demonstrate how these values were used to develop Figure 15.3.

11. Following is the distribution of job processing times at a computer center, as recorded for a sample of 1,000 requests:

Minutes per Job Request	Number of Requests
1	350
2	300
3	200
4	75
5	35
6	25
7	15

   a. Compute the average processing time in minutes.
   b. Compute the average number of jobs processed per hour.

c. Graph the cumulative distribution of service times (values less than or equal to the given job processing times). Do processing times appear to follow a negative exponential distribution? Explain.

12. Refer to Management Situation 15.2. Calculate the probabilities for each potential customer service rate. Demonstrate how these results were used to develop Figure 15.6. Compute the cumulative probabilities for service times $t \leq .8$, $t \leq .75$, $t \leq .4$, and $t \leq .25$. Show how these results were used to develop Figure 15.7.

13. Radio Station WBBB operates a popular sports talk show. Customer calls follow a Poisson distribution with $\lambda = 10$ per hour. It takes an average of five minutes for the single announcer to handle each call, and service time is assumed to have a negative exponential distribution. Callers are placed on hold until the announcer is free.
    a. What is the probability that the announcer will be available?
    b. What is the probability that a caller will have to wait?
    c. What is the probability that exactly three callers are waiting or being served? Less than five? More than two?
    d. What proportion of the time does the announcer actually spend handling these calls?
    e. How many callers, on average, are waiting for the announcer?
    f. What is the average waiting time for a caller?
    g. How many callers, on average, are being served or are waiting for service?
    h. How long, on average, will a caller be on the phone?

14. Again consider Titan's situation (Management Situations 15.1 and 15.2). Develop the entire probability distribution for the number of employees waiting or being served in the storeroom area. That is, complete Table 15.6.
    a. Using the data from your table, determine the probability that exactly 10 customers are in the system.
    b. Determine the probability that no more than 12 customers are in the system.
    c. Determine the probability that more than nine customers are waiting or being served.
    d. Calculate the expected number of customers in the system. How does this result compare to the value L found from equation (15.8)?

15. A photocopying machine is shared by the six secretaries in a law office. On average, each secretary uses the machine twice an hour for an average of 1.2 minutes at a time. Both interarrival and service times appear to follow negative exponential distributions.
    a. What proportion of time is the machine actually in use?
    b. What is the probability that all six secretaries are using or waiting for the machine? Exactly three? More than four? No more than two?
    c. On average, what proportion of a secretary's time is spent on tasks other than photocopying?
    d. How many secretaries, on average, are waiting to use the machine?
    e. What is the average waiting time?
    f. On average, how many secretaries are using or waiting for the machine?
    g. What is the average time spent for photocopying?

16. One attendant operates a full-service gasoline station capable of serving an average of 20 customers per hour. Service times appear to follow a negative exponential distribution. There is a maximum space for six cars in the station (waiting and being served). Automobiles arrive at the station at an average rate of one every four minutes. The arrival rate appears to follow a Poisson distribution. Cars unable to find a space leave and do not return.

a. Determine the proportion of arrivals that will leave.
b. Determine the proportion of time the station will be empty.
c. What is the probability of finding exactly four cars at the station? No more than three? More than five?
d. Find the average number of cars at the station.
e. Find the average time spent by a car at the station.
f. Find the average number of cars waiting for gasoline.
g. Determine the average waiting time.

Suppose that a small adjacent lot can be rented for 80 cents per car space per hour. The lot can accommodate four additional cars. Also each lost customer results in a loss of $1.50 profit. Should the gasoline station rent the lot?

17. Consider a two-channel queuing system with a mean arrival rate of $\lambda = 60$ per hour and an average service rate of $u = 100$ per hour for each facility. Both the arrival and service rates follow a Poisson distribution.

a. What is the probability of an empty system?
b. What is the probability that an arrival will have to wait?
c. On average, how many customers will be in the system?
d. How long, on average, will a customer spend in the system?
e. On average, how many customers will be waiting for service?
f. How long, on average, will a customer wait for service?

Suppose that the system was expanded to three service facilities. What are the new values for the operating characteristics (a) through (f)? Which system exhibits the best performance? Explain.

18. Action Towing operates an emergency road service for disabled motor vehicles. Past data indicate that an average of five emergency calls are received per hour. It appears that these data follow a Poisson distribution. Each tow truck can handle an average of eight calls per hour at an estimated hourly cost of $15 per truck. Service times are assumed to follow a negative exponential distribution. Customer waiting leads to ill will and other costs estimated at $20 per hour. The company is evaluating performance characteristics and costs of various plans. Management wants to determine the following values for a one-, two-, three-, and four-truck system:

a. The probability that all trucks will be busy.
b. The probability that all trucks will be idle.
c. The probability that exactly two disabled vehicles will be waiting or being served. More than three. No more than five.
d. The average number of emergency calls waiting or being served.
e. The average time to complete emergency service.
f. The average number of customers waiting for a tow truck.

g. The average waiting time.

h. The total (customer waiting plus service facility) costs.

Calculate these operating characteristics and costs for each plan. Which alternative leads to the best performance? To lowest total cost? Explain.

Computer Exercises

19. Refer to Titan's queuing situation (Management Situations 15.1 through 15.3) in the text. Use the **Quantitative Management (QM)** software to measure the system performance and cost for each service plan.

20. Fedrow Refuse Corporation garbage trucks currently wait an average of eight minutes each trip before they are allowed to dump their load at the East Landfill. The company is considering a switch to the Long Landfill. Such a move would cost Fedrow an extra $12 per trip for each truck. The alternative landfill can process the loads randomly at an average rate of 32 units per hour. Arrivals at the alternative landfill will be Poisson-distributed with an average rate of 26 loads per hour. The system is a basic single-queue system with unlimited queue length. Waiting time for the trucks is valued $240 per hour. The landfill and Fedrow operate about 3,600 hours per year.

Management will base the landfill decision on system performance and cost. Use the **QM** software to develop the required analysis.

21. Refer to Management Situation 15.4. Use the **QM** software to measure the word processing performance of Data's secretarial staff.

22. Fast Transportation Company provides a limousine service between the airport and the downtown hotel district. The company currently has eight vans. Unfortunately, an average of three vans break down per day. Ace Service has the contract to repair the vans on a top priority basis. The average service rate is five per day. Past experience indicates that the arrivals follow a Poisson pattern, while service times follow a negative exponential distribution. Idle vans cost Fast $800 per day, while the service contract costs Fast a fixed fee of $20,000 per year plus $375 for each day that a van is being serviced. Fast and Ace both operate 12 hours per day for 300 days a year.

Management wants to evaluate the performance and cost resulting from the service contract. Use the **QM** software to develop the needed information.

23. Refer to Management Situation 15.5. Use the **QM** software to evaluate the limited space on Elegant's operation.

24. Precise Tunes specializes in providing speedy engine tune-ups. The company's past records indicate that the arrival rate is an average of four customers per hour, while the average service time is 10 minutes. Management believes that when three customers are in the system, new arrivals tend to leave rather than wait for service. Each lost customer costs the company $40. Service people are paid $15 per hour, and fixed expenses total $40,000 per year. Precision operates about 3,000 hours per year.

Management wants to evaluate the performance and cost associated with current operations. Use the **QM** software to generate the required information.

25. Academic Caters supplies vending machines at the local university. Machines are stocked for 6,000 hours of operation per year. Out of anger and frustration, students frequently kick and break the vending machines. Historical records indicate that the breakdown pattern follows a Poisson distribution with an average rate of six per hour. Down time costs an average of $25 per machine per hour, and each maintenance worker earns $12 per hour. Each worker can service a machine in an average of 7.5 minutes. Repair equipment costs Academic $15,000 per year. The company can afford a repair crew of no more than four.

Management seeks the number of repair workers that will minimize total costs. It also would like to measure the system performance of each crew size. Use the **QM** software to develop a recommendation.

26. A new post office is being designed with eight service counters. During normal hours, customers are expected to arrive in a Poisson pattern at a rate averaging three per minute. Service time follows a negative exponential distribution with a mean of one minute and 15 seconds. Postal clerks are paid $16 per hour, while waiting customers are expected to cost the postal service $30 per hour in lost business. The configuration has a fixed expense of $70,000 for its 2,400 annual hours of operation.

Management wants to know how many counters to staff during normal business hours. Use the **QM** software to help management reach a decision.

Applications Exercises

27. Geometric Field is a private airport for small commercial aircraft currently operating with one runway for landings. Airplanes arrive at the airport in a random pattern at an average rate of 12 per hour. Variations in weather and type of aircraft also result in fluctuating landing times that appear to follow a random pattern. On average, one airplane lands every four minutes. While waiting for a landing, each aircraft consumes an average of 11 gallons of fuel per minute. A gallon of fuel costs $2.50.

Management is in the process of evaluating airport operations. Performance is measured by several factors:

- Runway utilization.
- The average number of aircraft waiting for permission to land.
- The average circling time.
- The average fuel cost consumed by an aircraft waiting to land.

In addition, airport officials would like to know the probability that an aircraft will have to wait to land. Moreover, they would like to know the probability of finding more than five aircraft in the airport vicinity (circling or landing). Prepare a brief report that addresses these issues in language understandable to management.

28. Passenger trains arrive at Midtown station in a random pattern on the average of one every 15 minutes. Although the actual time fluctuates in a random manner, each crew member can load and unload customer baggage in an average of 30 minutes. An increase in crew size will result in a proportional decrease in the average baggage service time. Baggage crew members are paid $7 per hour whether working or idle. The railroad owns the station as well as the trains using this facility. Operating expenses and other related charges cost the company an estimated $35 for each hour that a train spends at the station.

Company policy states that no train should wait more than 10 minutes for baggage service. In addition, 60 percent of the time, there should be no more than three trains at the station. What crew size will satisfy these policies at least cost?

29. The northeastern office of the Nuclear Regulatory Agency randomly inspects the three nuclear electric power plants in its region. A single commissioner issues a notice and then conducts the inspection an average of eight times per year. The commissioner works 250 days a year and is paid an annual salary of $50,000. After receiving a notice, the plant is shut down and remains closed until it is inspected. In these instances, the utility must use more expensive energy sources. As a result, it costs the utility an estimated $240 in additional operating expenses for each day that the plant is inoperative. Inspection time fluctuates in a random fashion, but the average is 25 days per plant.

The agency is currently evaluating the performance of its nuclear plant inspection process. The following data are relevant:

1. The average number of inoperative nuclear plants.

2. The average time that a plant is inoperative.

3. The average number of plants waiting for inspection.

4. The average waiting time.

Other useful information includes the probability of an idle commissioner and the chance that more than one plant will be inoperative. Prepare a brief report to the agency that provides such data in a form understandable to agency officials.

30. In an effort to streamline its civil justice system, Mundane County has instituted a new small-claims program. Under this program, a conference center with a 10-seat capacity has been converted into a "nonscheduled" courtroom. Citizens, at their convenience, can bring small-claims actions before a single designated judge for adjudication. It costs the county an estimated $50 an hour to operate the nonscheduled courtroom. When the conference center has been filled to capacity, further arrivals are referred to the clerk of courts for conventional processing. Operations in the conventional program cost the county $75 per hour.

In a preliminary experiment, citizens arrived randomly at the nonscheduled courtroom. There was an average of 30 minutes between arrivals. Although the actual time to hear a case fluctuated in a random fashion, the average was 20 minutes.

County administrators have been pleased with the initial results of the streamlined program. In fact, they would like to expand capacity by converting an adjacent office. The conversion would add five seats to the nonscheduled facility at an amortized cost of $10 per hour of courtroom operation. Before reaching a decision, county officials want to evaluate the potential performance of both the unexpanded and expanded nonscheduled facilities. Relevant measures include:

- The average number of cases handled.

- The average time to process a case.

- The average number of citizens waiting for adjudication.
- The average waiting time.

Other useful data are the proportion of lost customers, the probability of an idle court-room, and the chance of finding more than eight cases in court. Prepare a brief report to the county that provides this information for both the original and expanded nonscheduled programs. Explain why the county should or should not expand the program capacity. What are the cost savings from each nonscheduled program over the conventional system?

31. Fresh Foods, Inc. operates a supermarket with six checkout stands in Hilltown. Past records indicate that customers arrive randomly throughout the day at an average rate of nine per hour. Fresh Foods knows from past experience that long waiting lines create customer ill will and frustration. The company believes that these factors result in an estimated future lost profit of $80 per customer. Since orders vary in size and customers use different methods of payment, checkout times have fluctuated in a random fashion. However, each clerk has been able to check out a customer in an average of six minutes. Clerks receive an hourly salary of $8.
   a. How many checkout stands should the store keep staffed to minimize costs?
   b. What are the resulting costs?
   c. How many customers, on average, will be in the checkout area?
   d. On average, how long is a customer in the checkout area?
   e. How many customers, on average, are waiting for checkout?
   f. On average, how long does a customer have to wait for checkout?
   g. What is the probability that all checkout stands will be busy?
   h. What is the chance of finding no more than three customers in the checkout area? More than 10?

32. Crystal City's post office uses the window service system illustrated in the following diagram.

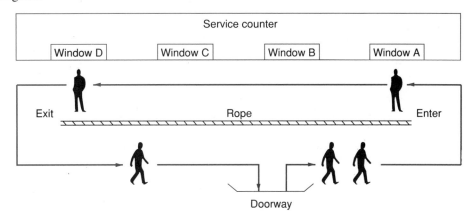

Customers arrive in a random pattern throughout the day, enter a single queue, and proceed to the first available service window. In midweek (Tuesday through Thursday), the arrival rate averages 18 customers per hour. On other days (Monday, Friday, and

Saturday), the average is 30 customers per hour. As a result of differences in customer requests, service times also fluctuate in a random fashion. However, records indicate that each postal clerk completes service in an average of three minutes. Clerks work eight hours a day and are paid $12 per hour.

Post office policy is to provide the best possible service for the available budget. Crystal City's post office, which operates 300 days a year, has an annual budget of $100,000 for clerks. Half of its operating days are in midweek. Reasonable service is defined as follows:

- There should be no more a 50 percent probability of finding as many as 10 customers in the post office.

- There should never be more than an average of eight customers waiting for service.

- The average waiting time should be no more than seven minutes.

To comply with post office policy, how many service windows should the Crystal City branch keep staffed each day? Explain.

For Further Reading

Queuing Theory

Albin, S. L. "Delays for Customers from Different Arrival Streams to a Queue." *Management Science* (March 1986):329.

Bell, C. E. "Optimal Operation of an M/M/2 Queue with Removable Servers." *Operations Research* (September–October 1980):1189.

Brill, P. H., and L. Green. "Queues in Which Customers Receive Simultaneous Service from a Random Number of Servers: A System Point Approach." *Managment Science* (January 1984):51.

Crabill, T. B., et al. "A Classified Bibliography of Research on Optimal Design and Control of Queues." *Operations Research* (March–April 1977):219.

Fletcher, G. Y., et al. "A Queueing System Where Customers Require a Random Number of Servers Simultaneously." *European Journal of Operational Research* (March 1986):331.

Green, L. "A Queueing System with General-Use and Limited-Use Servers." *Operations Research* (January–February 1985):168.

Hillier, F.S., and O.S. Yu. *Queing Tables and Graphs.* Amsterdam: Elsevier-North Holland, 1979.

Keilson, J., and L.D. Servi. "Blocking Probability for M/G/1 Vacation Systems with Occupancy Level Dependent Schedules." *Operations Research* (January–February 1989):134.

Keilson, J., and L. D. Servi. "Dynamics of the M/G/1 Vacation Model." *Operations Research* (July–August 1987):575.

Kleinrock, L. *Queueing Systems, Vol. 1, Theory.* New York: Wiley, 1975.

Kofman, E., and S. A. Lippman. "An M/M/1 Dynamic Priority Queue with Optimal Promotion." *Operations Research* (January–February 1981):174.

Lee, T. T. "M/G/1/N Queue with Vacation Time and Exhaustive Service Discipline." *Operations Research* (July–August 1984):774.

Pourbabai, B. "Approximation of the Overflow Process from a G/M/N/K Queueing System." *Management Science* (July 1987):931.

Shanthikumar, J. G., and D. D. Yao. "Optimal Server Allocation in a System of Multi-Server Stations." *Management Science* (September 1987):1173.

Suri, R., and G. W. Diekl. "A Variable Buffer-Size Model and Its Use in Analyzing Closed Queuing Networks with Blocking." *Management Science* (February 1986):206.

Takahasi, Y., et al. "An Approximation Method for Open Restricted Queuing Networks." *Operations Research* (May–June 1980):594.

Vinod, B., and T. Altiok. "Approximately Unreliable Queueing Network under the Assumption of Exponentiality." *Journal of the Operational Research Society* (March 1986):309.

Warren, E. H. "Estimating Waiting Time in a Queueing System." *Decision Sciences* (January 1981):112.

White, J. A., et al. *Analysis of Queueing Systems.* New York: Academic Press, 1975.

Whitt, W. "Deciding Which Queue to Join: Some Counterexamples." *Operations Research* (January–February 1986):5.

Woodside, C. M., et al. "Optimal Prediction of Queue Lengths and Delays in GI/M/M Multi-Server Queues." *Operations Research* (July–August 1984):809.

Queuing Applications

Chelst, K., et al. "A Coal Unloader: A Finite Queueing System with Breakdowns." *Interfaces* (October 1981):12.

Driscoll, M. F., and N. A. Weiss. "An Application of Queuing Theory to Reservation Networks." *Management Science* (January 1976):540.

Grassman, W. K. "Is the Fact That the Emperor Wears No Clothes a Subject Worthy of Publication." *Interfaces* (March–April 1986):43.

Green, L., and P. Kolesar. "Testing the Validity of a Queueing Model of Police Patrol." *Management Science* (February 1989):127.

Kolesar, P. "Stalking the Endangered CAT: A Queuing Analysis of Congestion at Automatic Teller Machines." *Interfaces* (November–December 1984):16–25.

Kwak, N. K., and M. B. Leavitt. "Police Patrol Beat Design: Allocation of Effort and Evaluation of Expected Performance." *Decision Sciences* (Summer 1984):421.

Lindsay, C. M., and B. Fiegenbaum. "Rationing by Waiting Lists." *American Economic Review* (June 1984):404.

McKeown, P. C. "An Application of Queueing Analysis to the New York State Child Abuse and Maltreatment Register Telephone Reporting System." *Interfaces* (May 1979):20.

Morse, P. M. "A Queueing Theory, Bayesian Model for the Circulation of Books in a Library." *Operations Research* (July–August 1979):693.

O'Keefe, R. M. "Investigating Outpatient Departments: Implementable Policies and Qualitative Approaches." *Journal of the Operational Research Society* (August 1985):705.

Solberg, J. J. "A Tenancy Vacancy Model." *Decision Sciences* (April 1976):202.

Stecke, K. E. "A Hierarchical Approach to Solving Machine Grouping and Loading Problems of Flexible Manufacturing Systems." *European Journal of Operational Research* (March 1986):369.

Taha, H. A. "Queueing Theory in Practice." *Interfaces* (February 1981):43.

Sze, D. Y. "A Queueing Model for Telephone Operator Staffing." *Operations Research* (March–April):229.

Vinod, B., and M. Sabbagh. "Optimal Performance Analysis of Manufacturing Systems Subject to Tool Availability." *European Journal of Operational Research* (March 1986):398.

Weiss, E. N., and J. O. McClain. "Administrative Days in Acute Care Facilities: A Queueing-Analytic Approach." *Operations Research* (January–February 1987):35.

Case: Sommerville Savings & Loan Association

Melissa Dinero has just been appointed Assistant Manager of Customer Services for the Sommerville Savings & Loan Association. Her first assignment is to investigate the potential effects of restructuring teller service facilities.

Under the current system, the savings and loan association has five tellers performing identical duties during peak periods. When customers arrive, they select what appears to be the shortest waiting line. The physical layout of the facility makes it difficult for customers to switch lines. As a result, each teller handles an average of one-fifth of all arrivals. The situation is illustrated in Figure 15.11.

Unfortunately, the system has not worked as well as planned. Typically, a customer will select the teller with the shortest waiting line. Yet, owing to differences in transaction times, some lines tend to move faster than others. Therefore, an arrival who picks a short line often waits an inordinate period of time if the preceding customer needs extended service.

Melissa has examined how banks and other savings and loan associations handle the problem. She has found two popular alternatives. One option is to designate one teller as the express window for customers with a single simple transaction (like a deposit or withdrawal). Other customers select one of the other four lines, as in the

current system. A second plan is to have all customers form a single waiting line. As soon as any teller becomes available, the first customer in line proceeds to the free window. This second alternative is illustrated in Figure 15.12.

As part of her investigation, Melissa has also collected data on the customer arrival process, teller service patterns, and selected operating costs. Arrivals were recorded for a period of 100 hours during a representative sample of peak periods. The results appear in Table 15.14. In addition, observations of the time required to handle transactions for these arrivals provided the data given in Table 15.15. Each teller had this same distribution of service rates.

Previous industry experience indicates that arrival and service rates tend to be identical under the current system and the single-queue, multiple-server system. On the other hand, a preliminary survey has shown that the express system would reduce service time by an average of three minutes. The study also suggests that 30 percent of all customers would use express service. However, service time for the remaining patrons is expected to increase by four minutes per customer.

Currently, tellers are paid $6 per hour. The savings and loan knows that waiting time creates customer frustration and eventually ill will. Management estimates that

Figure 15.11   Current Queuing System at Sommerville Savings & Loan

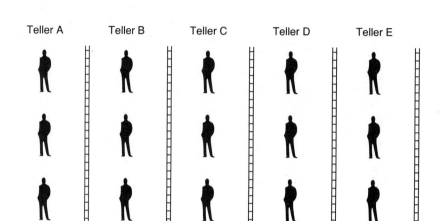

Service counter area

| Teller A | Teller B | Teller C | Teller D | Teller E |

Removable barriers

Figure 15.12   Alternative Queuing System for Somerville Savings & Loan

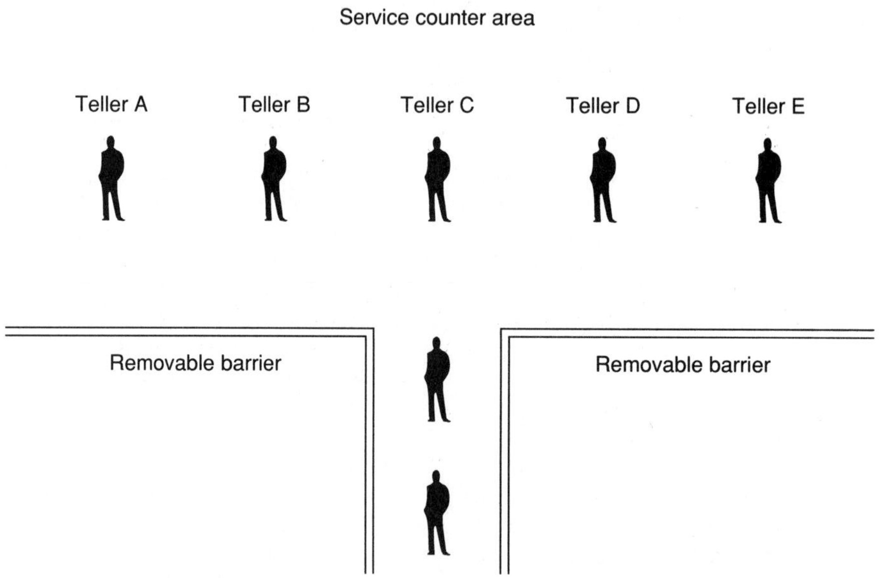

Service counter area

| Teller A | Teller B | Teller C | Teller D | Teller E |

Removable barrier   Removable barrier

Table 15.14   Arrivals at Sommerville Savings & Loan

Customer Arrivals per Hour	Number of Hours	Customer Arrivals per Hour	Number of Hours	Customer Arrivals per Hour	Number of Hours
0	0	9	3	18	7
1	0	10	5	19	6
2	0	11	7	20	4
3	0	12	8	21	3
4	0	13	10	22	2
5	0	14	10	23	1
6	0	15	10	24	1
7	1	16	10	25	1
8	2	17	8	26	1

Table 15.15   Transaction Times at Sommerville Savings & Loan

Customers Served per Hour	Number of Hours	Customers Served per Hour	Number of Hours
0	0	6	15
1	3	7	10
2	8	8	7
3	14	9	4
4	18	10	2
5	18	11	1

the association loses $10 of potential revenue for every hour a customer has to wait for service.

Melissa's boss has asked for her report comparing the current teller system with the two restructuring proposals. This report must include:

1. The nature of the arrival and service processes.

2. The utilization factors under each system.

3. The probability of idle service facilities under each system.

4. The probability distribution for the number of customers in each system.

5. The average number of customers in the service counter area under each system.

6. The average time a customer spends in each system.

7. The average number of customers waiting for service under each system.

8. The average customer waiting time under each plan.

9. The operating (customer waiting plus service facility) costs for each plan.

10. The plan Melissa would adopt and why.

Assume that you are Melissa and prepare such a report in a form understandable to Sommerville's board of directors.

Sequential Problems

Chapter Outline

Learning Objectives

- Recognizing situations that involve evolutionary processes

- Predicting, by hand and with the aid of a computer, the outcomes at various stages of an evolutionary process

- Utilizing the evolutionary outcome data to evaluate management policies

- Formulating and solving problems that involve a series of interrelated decisions.

Turning on the Juice

B RAZIL'S power system is composed of several hundred multiowned generating units spread over a large area, interconnected by thousands of miles of transmission lines. This system must supply the country's growing demand for electrical energy in the most economical and reliable manner possible. To achieve these goals, it was necessary to coordinate the operations of the various utilities that own and run the generating units.

In 1973, the GCOI was created, with representatives from the Brazilian utilities and federal power agency, to coordinate the interconnected operation of the system. As part of the plan, thermal resources are used according to systemwide needs, and operating costs are shared among the member utilities, proportionally to their loads. From 1974 to 1978, a sequential methodology, known as the rule-curve model, was used to produce operating guidelines for the system. By 1977, the group's research arm had developed a dynamic programming model, called SDP, that determines the optimal allocation of hydro and thermal resources in the system. After extensive validation studies by 18 electric utilities, the coordination pool officially adopted the SDP model in 1979.

Comparisons with the previously adopted rule-curve approach suggested that the SDP model would reduce the system's operating costs, in five years, by an estimated 28 percent, or by $87 million. Actual savings from 1979 to 1984 were about $260 million. In addition, the SDP model has been extensively used to help determine system trial expansion plans for the next 10 to 30 years.

Source: L. A. Terry et al. "Coordinating the Energy Generation of the Brazilian National Hydrothermal Electrical Generating System," *Interfaces* (January–February 1986):16–38.

The previous chapters have primarily dealt with static situations. That is, most of the problems involved circumstances in which the uncontrollable inputs remained at the same levels throughout the planning period. Distribution models, for example, assumed that all costs or returns, available supplies, and demand requirements continued unchanged for the entire period under consideration.

Yet, there are many situations in which the uncontrollable inputs change over time. For instance, distribution costs or returns, resource supplies, and consumer demands typically vary from one time period to another. Under these circumstances, the situation can be viewed as a problem involving a sequence of operations and decisions, as the Brazilian power system vignette illustrates.

This chapter shows how to recognize and handle such sequential problems. The first section describes the characteristics of evolutionary processes. In particular, it develops the initial conditions, examines the pattern of change, and explores the behavior of these processes.

The second section presents a framework for analyzing evolutionary processes. First, a formal model is developed to describe the system's behavior. Then predictions are made from the model by hand and with the aid of a computer. In addition, some important extensions to the analysis are considered, as well as a sample of typical management applications.

The final section shows how to formulate a problem as a sequence of interrelated decisions and then develops an approach designed to generate the best solution to the problem. As GCOI discovered, such an approach can significantly improve the quality of decision making. The final section presents additional management applications of the methodology and examines some important limitations to the analysis.

Applications. In this chapter, the following applications appear in the text, examples, and exercises:

- accounts receivable
- antitrust action
- automobile rentals
- brand switching
- commodities trading
- cosmetic surgery
- data processing
- diplomacy
- durable goods retailing
- electric power
- equipment replacement
- food inspection
- labor productivity
- life insurance
- mental health care

- milk delivery
- mortgage lending
- personnel management
- photography
- population mobility
- pricing
- production scheduling
- public transportation
- sales management
- taxi service
- telephone service
- television advertising
- traffic flow
- tree farming
- wine growing

16.1 MARKOV SYSTEMS

Some situations involve an evolutionary process. The system starts with a set of initial conditions, such as the purchase behavior of a particular group of customers. Then certain changes develop in the conditions. For instance, customers may change their purchase patterns. Eventually, the system evolves into a stable pattern. Management Situation 16.1 illustrates.

Management Situation 16.1

Brand Switching

A small rural drugstore stocks two brands of paper towels: Absorber and Dainty. When a consumer shops for this product, he or she will select either Absorber or Dainty, but not both. The store knows that customers switch brands over time because of advertising, dissatisfaction with the product, and other reasons. Of course, the exact brand purchased at any particular time is not known with perfect certainty. By processing sales transactions through the store's small computer information system, management has developed the following data:

1. Out of all the customers who bought Absorber in a given week, 80 percent purchased Absorber while 20 percent switched to Dainty the following week.

2. For the consumers who purchased Dainty in a given week, 70 percent bought Dainty and 30 percent switched to Absorber the following week.

No old customers leave and no new customers enter the market during this period. The store is making stock plans. As part of the planning, it must predict the proportions of consumers who will buy each brand in the future.

In Management Situation 16.1, the drugstore is interested in describing consumers' brand-buying behavior. At the start of the process in week 1, customers have particular probabilities of purchasing the brands. Between weeks, some consumers switch brands. Consequently, the purchse probabilities in the future may differ from the current likelihoods. Store management, then, wants to determine the future outcomes from the evolutionary process.

Early in the twentieth century, the Russian mathematician Andrei A. Markov studied such a process. As a result of his study, Markov developed an approach that was designed to describe and predict the behavior of the evolutionary process. In honor of the originator, this approach is now known as **Markov analysis.**

The process analyzed by Markov had a set of well-defined characteristics. To properly use his approach, then, the decision maker must fully understand the nature of these characteristics.

Characteristics

In Management Situation 16.1, the process involves consumer purchases of paper towels. The store monitors this process on a weekly basis by recording the proportion of customers who select each brand. In Markov terminology, each weekly observation is referred to as a **trial** or **stage** of the process. Week 1, for example, represents trial 1 of the towel purchase process.

States. During any trial of the process, the system will be in a **state,** or one of a set of mutually exclusive and collectively exhaustive conditions. In the drugstore situation, the state will be the brand purchased by a customer in a particular week of operations. Since a customer can buy either Absorber or Dainty at each trial, there are only two possible states in Management Situation 16.1:

- State 1: The customer buys Absorber.
- State 2: The customer buys Dainty.

For example, the system will be in state 2 at trial 4, when the customer buys Dainty during the third week from the starting date (week 1) of the observations.

Figure 16.1   **Drugstore Transition Patterns**

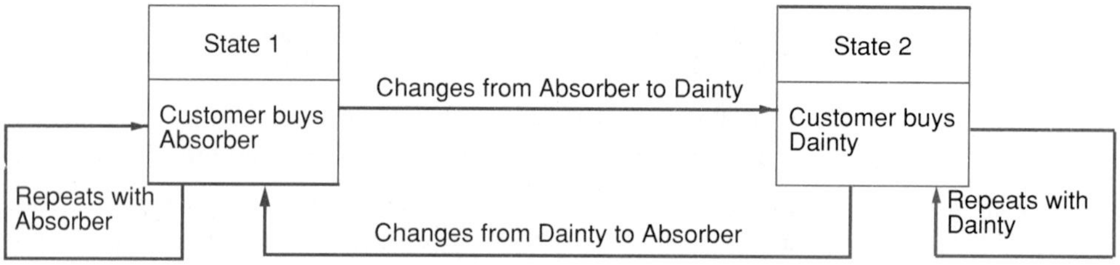

First-Order Markov Process. The store does not know exactly which brand will be purchased in a particular week. Instead, store records merely provide information on the customers' probabilities of buying the two brands. Hence, the purchase process is stochastic in nature.

Furthermore, consumer brand choices may change from week to week. In particular, each brand may retain, gain, or lose customers. Figure 16.1 illustrates the potential transitions. According to the diagram, one possibility is that consumers will switch from Dainty (state 2) to Absorber (state 1) in any particular week. Since store records show that towels are purchased weekly, there would be only one such change per trial (week).

Management Situation 16.1 also indicates that the brand choice in any particular week is influenced only by the selection made in the immediately preceding week. Selections made two, three, or more weeks previously have no effect on the current brand choice. A stochastic system with this property is known as a memoryless or **first-order Markov process.**

Homogeneous Markov Chain. The store records provide the probabilities that consumers will move from one state (brand) to another between trials (weeks) of the process. For instance, management knows that 80 percent of the customers who buy Absorber this week again will purchase Absorber next week. Similarly, Management Situation 16.1 indicates that 30 percent of the consumers who buy Dainty in the current week will switch to Absorber next week. Such likelihoods are called **transition probabilities.**

Moreover, Management Situation 16.1 suggests that these transition probabilities remain the same from week to week. Also, they do not seem to change for any customer. A Markov process with these properties is called a **homogeneous Markov chain.**

Recap. The main characteristics of a Markov situation are:

1. The system involves a stochastic process that can be observed at numerous points. Typically each point, which is known as a trial or stage of the process, represents a different time period.

2. All trials or stages are equal in length.

3. There are a finite number of outcomes, known as states of the system, that occur at each trial.

Figure 16.2   **Transition Table Format**

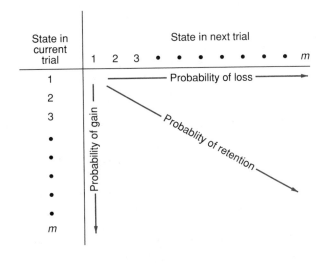

---

4. The state of the system can change from one stage to the next, but there will be only one such change per trial.

5. The system's condition at any particular trial depends only on the condition in the immediately preceding stage. In other words, the system involves a memoryless or first-order Markov process.

6. It is possible to determine the system's transition probabilities, that is, the likelihoods that the system will move from one state to another between trials.

7. The transition probabilities remain constant from trial to trial. Put another way, the process generates a homogeneous Markov chain.

A situation that has all these characteristics is referred to as a **Markov system.**

Transition Pattern

Practical problems can involve hundreds, even thousands, of transition probabilities. The decision maker therefore needs some device to conveniently record and keep track of such information. One device typically used for these purposes is a table with the general format shown in Figure 16.2. In this diagram, the letter m represents the finite number of states in the system.

Transition Table. Figure 16.2 shows that each row of the table depicts a state of the system in the current trial. Each column denotes a state in the next stage of the process. The corresponding transition probabilities are presented in the body of the table. Entries along the diagonal give the probabilities that the process will remain in the same state from the current trial to the next. Gains for the states are measured by the entries in the columns to the left of the diagonal. Losses from the states are provided by the entries

Table 16.1   **Brand-Switching Transition Probabilities**

Brand Purchased This Week	Brand Purchased Next Week	
	Absorber	Dainty
Absorber	.8	.2
Dainty	.3	.7

in the rows to the right of the diagonal. Such a representation is known as a **transition table.**

Table 16.1 gives the drugstore's transition table. This table has several important characteristics. First, it is relevant to recognize that the entries represent conditional probabilities. That is, each entry measures the likelihood that the system will be in a particular state at the next trial if it is in a specified state during the current trial. In addition, the entries along the diagonal give the probabilities that the same brand will be purchased each week. They show, for instance, that Absorber will retain 80 percent and Dainty 70 percent of their customers. In effect, then, these diagonal values represent measures of brand loyalty or retention.

The off-diagonal entries in Table 16.1 measure the brand-switching propensities of the drugstore's customers. The row entry to the right of the diagonal, for example, indicates that there is a 20 percent likelihood that Absorber will lose customers to Dainty. Similarly, the column entry to the left of the diagonal shows that Absorber has a 30 percent chance of gaining consumers from Dainty.

Probability Distribution. A customer who buys a particular brand one week must either repurchase the same brand or switch to the alternative in the next week. That is, these states are mutually exclusive and collectively exhaustive. As a result, the sum of the probabilities in each row of the transition table must equal 1. Consider, for example, the Absorber row in Table 16.1. It indicates that Absorber retains 80 percent and loses 20 percent of its customers. Therefore, there is a probability of .8 + .2 = 1, or 100 percent chance, that Absorber will either retain or lose customers next week. In essence, each row in Table 16.1 represents the probability distribution associated with the corresponding brand's transition pattern.

16.2 MARKOV ANALYSIS

Transition probabilities are used by management for the following tasks:

1. Predicting the condition of the system at each stage of the evolutionary process.
2. Predicting the condition into which the process will evolve.
3. Analyzing specified policies.

This section shows how to make these predictions and perform the policy analysis.

Figure 16.3   **Drugstore Probability Tree**

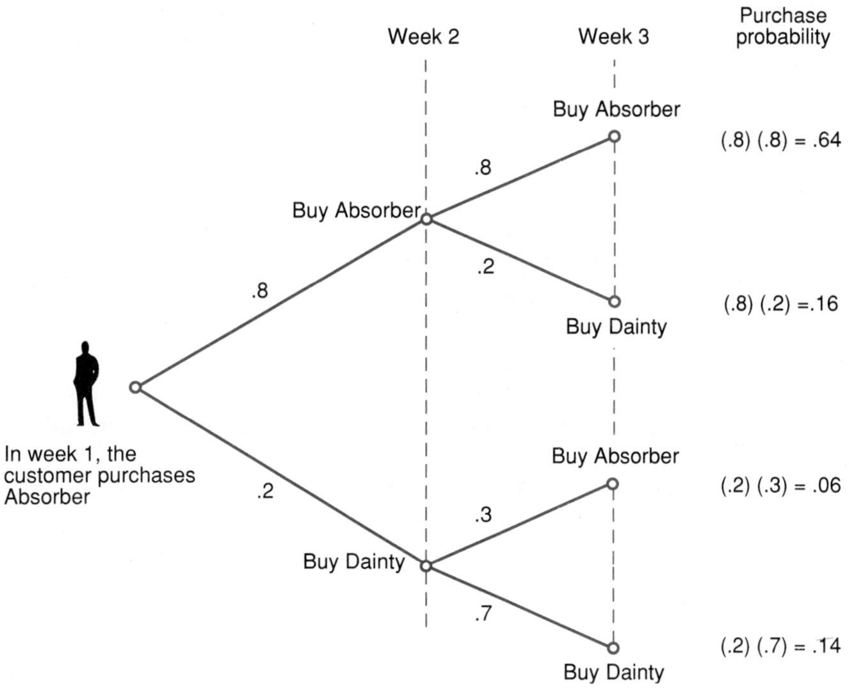

State Probabilities

Frequently, the decision maker must determine the probability that a Markov system is in a particular state at a specified trial. The drugstore in Management Situation 16.1 may want to know the percentage of original Absorber customers who will remain loyal to the brand for the next two weeks. Put another way, management seeks the likelihood that the system is in state 1 during the first and second weeks (at trials 2 and 3) from the starting date (week 1) of the observation period. Such a likelihood is referred to as a **state probability.**

By utilizing the information about the initial conditions and the transition pattern, management can find a state probability at any stage of the evolutionary process. The approach is based on the decision analysis concepts originally presented in Part II of the text. Figure 16.3 illustrates the calculations for the drugstore brand-switching problem.

Probability Tree. Figure 16.3 is a probability tree in which the nodes, or circles, depict the states of the brand purchase system. Week 1 again is the starting date (current stage) of the observation period, while the broken lines denote future trials (subsequent weeks) of the towel purchase process. The transition probabilities are listed on the corresponding branches of the tree. As the figure demonstrates, the drugstore initially observes that a customer purchases Absorber during week 1 (trial 1) of the process. In addition, Table 16.1 indicates that Absorber will retain 80 percent of its current (week 1) consumers at the next stage (week 2) of the observation period. Therefore, there is a probability of .8 that the customer will remain loyal to Absorber (be in state 1) during week 2 (trial 2) of the process. In Figure 16.3, this likelihood appears as the transition probability on the branch joining the starting point with the week 2 Absorber node.

Since the transition pattern remains the same from week to week, Absorber will retain 80 percent of its week 2 customers at the next trial (week 3) of the process. Consequently, there is a probability of

$$.8 \times .8 = .64$$

that the original Absorber customers will remain with the brand during both the second and third weeks of the observation period. In other words, the system has a .64 probability of being in state 1 at both trials 2 and 3 of the process. This result is depicted as the purchase probability to the right of the top branch in Figure 16.3.

Joint Probabilities. A purchase likelihood, then, is merely the joint probability associated with the corresponding system conditions. Furthermore, it can be found by multiplying the conditional likelihoods on the appropriate branches of the probability tree. In Figure 16.3, for instance, the lower branch emanating from week 1 shows that 20 percent of the customers switch from Absorber to Dainty during week 2 of the observation period. Also, the top branch emanating from the week 2 Dainty node shows that 30 percent of these same consumers switch back to Absorber in the third week. Thus, there is a joint

$$.2 \times .3 = .06$$

chance that the original Absorber customers will change brands during week 2 but return to Absorber in week 3 of the observation period. Put another way, the system has a .06 probability of being in state 2 at trial 2 but state 1 at trial 3.

Marginal Probabilities. Other joint purchase probabilities are calculated in a similar manner and recorded to the right of the corresponding branches in Figure 16.3. These joint likelihoods can be used to determine additional state probabilities. The drugstore, for example, may want to know the percentage of original Absorber customers who will buy the brand during week 3 of the observation period. There are two ways that the system can be in state 1 (the customer purchases Absorber) at trial 3 (week 3) of the process. First, the original Absorber consumer may remain loyal to the brand during weeks 2 and 3 of the observation period. According to Figure 16.3, this condition will occur $(.8)(.8) = .64$, or 64 percent, of the time. Second, the original Absorber customer might change brands in week 2 but return to Absorber during week 3 of the process. Figure 16.3 indicates that such a condition will occur $(.2)(.3) = .06$, or 6 percent, of the time. As a result, there is a $.64 + .06 = .70$ chance that a week 1 Absorber customer will buy Absorber in week 3 of the observation period.

The total (marginal) likelihood that a specified state will occur at a particular trial is therefore the sum of the corresponding joint probabilities. According to Figure 16.3, for instance, there is a joint probability of

$$.2 \times .7 = .14$$

that the original Absorber customers will buy Dainty during weeks 2 and 3 of the observation period. In addition, there is a joint probability of

$$.8 \times .2 = .16$$

that the original Absorber customers will remain with the brand during week 2 but switch to Dainty in week 3 of the process. Therefore, the drugstore should expect $.16 + .14 = .30$, or 30 percent, of the week 1 Absorber consumers to purchase Dainty during week 3 of the observation period.

Matrix Approach

In practice, a Markov system can involve hundreds, even thousands, of states and trials. Under these circumstances, it will be very tedious and time-consuming to develop a probability tree and perform the corresponding likelihood computations. Fortunately, management scientists have developed a more efficient approach that utilizes matrix concepts to track the transition pattern and calculate the resulting state probabilities.

Initial Vector. To see what is involved, let us reconsider the brand-switching situation depicted in Figure 16.3. According to the diagram, the drugstore observes that a customer purchases Absorber during week 1 of the observation period. That is, there is a probability of 1 that the system is in state 1 and a probability of 0 that it is in state 2 at trial 1 of the process.

These starting (week 1) conditions can be arranged in the following format:

$$P^1 = (1 \quad 0).$$

Such an arrangement of numbers is known as a **row vector of state probabilities.** The symbol P^1, then, denotes the row vector of purchase probabilities for week 1 of the drugstore's observation period. Notice that the number in the first column of this P^1 vector identifies the state 1 (Absorber purchase) probability, whereas the number in the second column identifies the state 2 (Dainty purchase) probability.

Transition Matrix. Table 16.1 describes the pattern of change in the purchase probabilities from one week to the next. These transition probabilities can be arranged in the following format:

$$T = \begin{pmatrix} .8 & .2 \\ .3 & .7 \end{pmatrix}$$

Such an arrangement of numbers is called a **transition matrix.** The symbol T denotes the drugstore's transition matrix.

Note that the rows list the proportions of customers retained and lost by the brands during each week of the observation period. The first row of matrix T, for instance, shows that 80 percent of Absorsber consumers remain loyal, but 20 percent switch to Dainty at each trial of the purchase process. On the other hand, the columns identify the percentage of consumers gained and retained at each trial. For example, the second column of matrix T indicates that Dainty gains 20 percent of Absorber's customers and retains 70 percent of its own customers during each week of the purchase process.

State Probabilities. By multiplying the week 1 row vector P^1 by the transition matrix T, management can determine the system conditions during week 2 of the purchase process. That is, let the symbol P^2 denote the row vector of state probabilties in week 2 of the observation period. Then,

$$P^2 = P^1 \times T = (1 \quad 0)\begin{pmatrix} .8 & .2 \\ .3 & .7 \end{pmatrix}$$

Specifically, P^2 will list the proportions of customers who buy Absorber and Dainty during week 2 of the process.

As P^1 indicates, 100 percent of the customers purchase Absorber and 0 percent buy Dainty in week 1. The first column of T shows that 80 percent of Absorber consumers remain loyal and 30 percent of Dainty customers switch to Absorber each week in the process. Hence, the drugstore should expect

$$.8(1) + .3(0) = .8$$

or 80 percent of the paper towel consumers to buy Absorber during week 2 of the purchase process. Similarly, the second column of matrix T demonstrates that Dainty gains 20 percent of Absorber's customers and retains 70 percent of its own customers during each week in the observation period. Consequently, management can anticipate that

$$.2(1) + .7(0) = .2$$

or 20 percent of the customers will purchase Dainty in week 2 of the process.

These calculations indicate that the row vector of state probabilities in week 2 of the observation period is

$$P^2 = (.8 \quad .2)$$

In this P^2 vector, the number in the first column identifies the state 1 (Absorber purchase) probability. The number in the second column lists the state 2 (Dainty purchase) probability.

Equations (16.1) and (16.2) illustrate the computations needed to find the numbers in the P^2 row vector:

$$1 \times .8$$

(16.1) $P^2 = P^1 T = (1 \quad 0)\begin{pmatrix} .8 & .2 \\ .3 & .7 \end{pmatrix} = (.8 \quad .2)$

$$+ (0 \times .3) \quad 1(.8) + 0(.3) =$$

$$1 \times .2$$

(16.2) $P^2 = P^1 T = (1 \quad 0)\begin{pmatrix} .8 & .2 \\ .3 & .7 \end{pmatrix} = (.8 \quad .2)$

$$+ 0(.7) \quad 1(.2) + 0(.7) =$$

Each entry in the P^2 vector is found by multiplying the numbers in the P^1 vector by the values in the corresponding column of the T matrix and summing the results. Consider, for example, the .2 value in the second column of the P^2 vector. This value is the sum of the products obtained when the P^1 entries are multiplied by the numbers in the second column of the T matrix.

This same matrix approach can be used to determine the state probabilities for the third week in the observation period. In particular, the P^2 row vector gives the state probabilities in week 2 of the purchase process. Moreover, the transition matrix T identifies the pattern of change in the purchase probabilities from one week to the next. Thus, the system conditions in week 3, which can be denoted as the row vector P^3, will be

$$P^3 = P^2 \times T = (.8 \quad .2)\begin{pmatrix} .8 & .2 \\ .3 & .7 \end{pmatrix}$$

or

$$P^3 = (.8(.8) + .2(.3) \qquad .8(.2) + .2(.7))$$
$$P^3 = (.7 \quad .3).$$

The number in the first column of P^3 indicates that 70 percent of the consumers will buy Absorber during week 3 of the process. The value in the second column shows that 30 percent of the week 3 customers will purchase Dainty.

Procedure Recap.   The following matrix approach can be used to predict the state probabilities at any specified trial of a first-order Markov process:

1. Formulate the matrix T of transition probabilities.
2. Identify the row vector P^n of state probabilities at trial n of the process.
3. Find the product of P^n and T. To determine the entry in each column of the product, multiply the entries in the P^n vector by the numbers in the corresponding column of the T matrix and sum the results.
4. The result $P^{n+1} = P^n T$ is the row vector of state probabilities at trial $n + 1$ of the process.

Steady State

As the procedure recap demonstrates, a future stage's conditions can be predicted by multiplying the immediately preceding trial's state probability vector by the transition matrix. That is,

$$P^4 = P^3 \times T$$
$$P^5 = P^4 \times T$$

and so on. If the drugstore performs these matrix operations, they will obtain the results shown in Table 16.2.

As Table 16.2 demonstrates, there are some relatively substantial adjustments in the purchase probabilities during the early trials (weeks 1 through 5) of the process. Eventually, however, these probabilities do not change much from one week to the next. After a very large number of trials, the purchase probabilities stabilize at equilibrium values of .6 for Absorber and .4 for Dainty.

Table 16.2   **Future State Probabilities for the Brand-Switching Problem when $P^1 = (1 \quad 0)$**

State	Probability for Trial									
	1	2	3	4	5	6	7	8	$\rightarrow$	Very large number
Absorber	1	.8	.7	.65	.625	.6125	.60625	.603125	$\rightarrow$	.6
Dainty	0	.2	.3	.35	.375	.3875	.39375	.396875	$\rightarrow$	.4

These equilibrium values of .6 for Absorber and .4 for Dainty are referred to as **steady-state probabilities.** They tell us that, in the long run, the drugstore can expect 60 out of every 100 customers to buy Absorber and 40 to buy Dainty. These steady-state probabilities, then, can be interpreted as each brand's eventual share of paper towel sales.

Initial Conditions. For most systems, probabilities eventually stabilize at the same equilibrium values regardless of the starting conditions. For example, if a consumer purchased Dainty rather than Absorber in week 1, or if

$$P^1 = (0 \quad 1)$$

the drugstore's future state probabilities will be as shown in Table 16.3.

You can see that the state probabilities in Table 16.3 are generally different from the purchase likelihoods in Table 16.2. Yet, after a very large number of trials, the state probabilities again stabilize at the equilibrium values of .6 for Absorber and .4 for Dainty.

Matrix Approach. In practice, it may take a very large number of trials, or transitions, for the system to reach the steady state. Under these circumstances, the steady-state probabilities can be established more efficiently with matrix algebra than with the trial-by-trial transition approach.

During the early trials of the process, gains and losses from state to state (changes in the state probabilities) can be quite large. These gains and losses get smaller and smaller as the system approaches the steady state. After a very large number of trials (transitions), each state's gains will equal its losses, and the system will reach an equilibrium (steady-state) condition. At this steady state,

$$P^n = P^{n-1}$$

or the row vector of state probabilities at trial n will equal the corresponding vector in the immediately preceding trial $(n - 1)$. These equilibrium conditions can be denoted with the row vector of steady-state probabilities P. For the drugstore,

$$P = (p_1 \quad p_2)$$

where p_1 = the likelihood that a customer will buy the Absorber brand in the steady state and p_2 = the steady-state probability of a Dainty brand purchase.

Table 16.3   **Future State Probabilities for the Brand-Switching Problem when** $P^1 = (0 \ 1)$

State						Probability for Trial				
	1	2	3	4	5	6	7	8	$\rightarrow$	Very large number
Absorber	0	.3	.45	.525	.5625	.58125	.590625	.5953125	$\rightarrow$	.6
Dainty	1	.7	.55	.475	.4375	.41875	.409375	.4046875	$\rightarrow$	.4

Since the conditions at trial n can be found by multiplying the immediately preceding trial's state probability vector by the transition matrix,

$$P^n = P^{n-1} \times T$$

and since $P^n = P^{n-1} = P$ at the equilibrium stage,

$$P = P \times T$$

in the steady state. For the drugstore, then,

$$(p_1 \quad p_2) = (p_1 \quad p_2)\begin{pmatrix} .8 & .2 \\ .3 & .7 \end{pmatrix}$$

at the equilibrium stage.

The row vector P shows that p_1 percent of the customers purchase Absorber and p_2 percent buy Dainty in the steady state. Furthermore, the first column of the transition matrix T indicates that 80 percent of Absorber consumers remain loyal and 30 percent of Dainty customers switch to Absorber during each week in the process. Therefore, at the equilibrium stage, management should expect

$$.8p_1 + .3p_2$$

of the paper towel consumers to buy Absorber, or

(16.3) $p_1 = .8p_1 + .3p_2$

in the steady state.

Similarly, the second column of matrix T demonstrates that Dainty gains 20 percent of Absorber's customers and retains 70 percent of its own customers during each week in the observation period. Consequently, the drugstore can anticipate that

$$.2p_1 + .7p_2$$

of the consumers will purchase Dainty at the equilibrium stage of the process, or

(16.4) $p_2 = .2p_1 + .7p_2$

in the steady state.

Equations (16.3) and (16.4) essentially say that, in the steady state, the proportion of customers lost from a brand must equal the percentage gained by the brand. For example, when we subtract $.7p_2$ from both sides of equation (16.4), we get the expression

(16.5) $.3p_2 = .2p_1$

This expression indicates that in the steady state, the proportion of customers lost from Dainty ($.3p_2$) must equal the percentage gained by the brand ($.2p_1$). Otherwise, the excess losses and gains would create instability in the market and disrupt any equilibrium condition.

   Since equations (16.3) and (16.4) are actually redundant, they do not contain enough data to compute the values of both steady-state probabilities (p_1 and p_2). The missing equilibrium condition is that

(16.6) $p_1 + p_2 = 1$

or that the purchase likelihoods must sum to 1 in the steady state.

   According to equation (16.6), the proportion of customers who will buy Dainty in the steady state is

$$p_2 = 1 - p_1.$$

By substituting this expression into equation (16.5), we find that

$$.3(1 - p_1) = .2p_1$$

or $p_1 = .3/.5 = .6$

In other words, the drugstore should expect 60 percent of the paper towel customers to buy the Absorber brand in the steady state. According to equation (16.6), then,

$$p_2 = 1 - p_1 = 1 - .6 = .4$$

or 40 percent of the customers can be expected to purchase the Dainty brand in the steady state.

Procedure Recap. The following matrix approach can be used to find the steady-state probabilities:

1.   Formulate the row vector P of unknown steady-state probabilities, and identify the matrix T of transition probabilities.

2.   Identify the simultaneous system of equations formed from the matrix equation $P = PT$.

3.   Form the equation that sets the sum of the steady-state probabilities equal to 1.

4.   Use the resulting series of equations to find the unknown steady-state probabilities.

Passage Times

It is frequently desirable to identify the number of trials that will pass before a specified change occurs in the system conditions. Relevant information includes the expected recurrence time, mean first passage time, and equilibrium first passage time.

Expected Recurrence Time. Often, it is useful to know the **expected recurrence time**, or the average number of trials that will pass between the repeat occurrences of a specified state in the system. For example, to plan inventory, the drugstore may need the average elapsed time between the repeat purchases of the Absorber towel brand.

In the steady state, customers will buy Absorber 60 percent of the time or 6 out of every 10 weeks. This pattern means that an average of

$$10 \text{ weeks}/6 \text{ purchases} = 1.66 \text{ weeks}$$

will elapse between repeat Absorber purchases.

Notice that 1.66 is the reciprocal (1/.6) of Absorber's steady-state probability. Such a fact suggests that the expected recurrence time can be found with the following formula:

(16.7) $$r_i = 1/p_i$$

where r_i denotes the expected recurrence time and p_i the steady-state probability for state i. Since $p_2 = .4$, this equation also indicates that an average of

$$r_2 = 1/p_2 = 1/.4 = 2.5 \text{ weeks}$$

will pass between repeat Dainty purchases (state 2).

Mean First Passage Time. Another useful statistic is the **mean first passage time,** or the average number of trials that will elapse before the system changes from one state to another specified state for the first time. For example, to help plan operations, the drugstore may want to know the average number of weeks that will pass before an Absorber customer switches to Dainty for the first time.

Since the consumer purchase decision is a stochastic process, there will be a probability distribution of first passage times. This distribution depends on the transition pattern involved in the process. By finding the expected value of the distribution, management will obtain the mean first passage time.

In Management Situation 16.1, an Absorber (state 1) customer could stay with the brand on the next purchase (for one week) and then eventually switch to Dainty (state 2) in a mean first passage time denoted as f_{12} weeks. According to the drugstore's transition table (Table 16.1), there is a .8 probability of this outcome. Table 16.1 also shows that there is a .2 probability of an Absorber customer switching to Dainty in one week. The expected value of the distribution

$$f_{12} = .8(1 + f_{12}) + .2(1)$$

or $$f_{12} = 1/.2 = 5 \text{ weeks}$$

then gives the mean first passage time from state 1 to state 2. It tells management that an average of five weeks will elapse before an Absorber customer switches to Dainty for the first time.

In general, the mean first passage time from state i to state j can be found with the following formula:

(16.8) $$f_{ij} - \sum_{t=1}^{s} p_{it} f_{tj} = 1$$

where f_{ij} = the mean first passage time from state i to state j, t = an index number that identifies every state except j in the system, s = the number of states in the system, and p_{it} = the transition probability from state i to state t. For systems with more than two states ($s > 2$), formula (16.8) will generate a simultaneous system of ($s - 1$) equations that can be solved for the corresponding mean first passage times. There will be a mean first passage time of zero from one state to the same state ($f_{ii} = 0$).

Formula (16.8) indicates that the mean first passage time from Dainty (state 2) to Absorber (state 1) is

$$f_{21} - \sum_{t=1}^{2} p_{2t}f_{t1} = 1$$

or
$$f_{21} - (p_{21}f_{11} + p_{22}f_{21}) = 1$$

which, with $f_{11} = 0$, is the same as

$$f_{21} = \frac{1}{(1 - p_{22})}.$$

Since $p_{22} = .7$ (according to Table 16.1), an average of

$$f_{21} = 1/(1 - .7) = 1/.3 = 3.33 \text{ weeks}$$

will elapse before a Dainty customer switches to Absorber for the first time.

Equilibrium First Passage Time. A third pertinent change is the **equilibrium first passage time,** or the average number of trials that will elapse before the system changes from one state to any other state for the first time. For example, to help plan a special promotion, the drugstore might need the average number of weeks that will pass before an Absorber customer initially changes brands.

The matrix of mean first passage times, denoted as M, gives the average number of trials that elapse between initial shifts in the states. The row vector of steady-state probabilities P identifies the chances that these states will occur at equilibrium. By multiplying the mean first passage times by the steady-state probabilities (by computing PM), management will find the equilibrium first passage times.

For the drugstore, the matrix of mean first passage times is

$$M = \begin{pmatrix} 0 & 5 \\ 3.33 & 0 \end{pmatrix}$$

and the row vector of steady-state probabilities is

$$P = (.6 \quad .4).$$

Therefore, the row vector of equilibrium first passage times is

$$PM = (.6 \quad .4)\begin{pmatrix} 0 & 5 \\ 3.33 & 0 \end{pmatrix} = (1.33 \quad 3).$$

This vector tells us that an average of 1.33 weeks will elapse before an Absorber customer initially changes brands, and an average of three weeks will pass before a Dainty customer switches brands for the first time.

Absorbing States

In the drugstore situation, customers may buy the same brand towel or switch to an alternative brand during each week of the observation period. That is, the system can change states between any two trials of the process. On the other hand, there are cases

Table 16.4   **June 30 Account Balance**

Purchase Date	Amount Charged
April 10	$50
May 25	20
June 12	60
Total	$130

where a system enters one or more states from which, once there, it cannot exit to some other state. Management Situation 16.2 provides a well-known accounting illustration of this situation.

Management Situation 16.2

Accounts Receivable Analysis

Master Bank has two aging categories for its credit card accounts receivable: 0 to 40 days old and 41 to 100 days old. Any portion of an account balance that is over 100 days old is written off as a bad debt. The bank ages the total balance in any customer's account according to the oldest unpaid bill. For example, suppose one customer's account balance on June 30 is as shown in Table 16.4. On June 30, the total $130 balance is assigned to the 41-to-100-day category because the oldest unpaid bill (April 10) is 82 days old. Assume that one week later, July 7, the customer pays the April 10 bill of $50. The remaining total balance of $80 is now placed in the 0-to-40-day category. (The oldest unpaid amount, corresponding to the May 25 purchase, is less than 41 days old.) Since the total account balance is placed in the age category corresponding to the oldest unpaid amount, this approach is called the *total balance method*.

Under the total balance method, dollars appearing in a particular category at one point in time may be classified differently later. This was the case for $80 of May and June billings. After the April bill was paid, the $80 shifted from the 41-day-and-over category to the 40-day-and-under category. Past records provide the transition data shown in Table 16.5.

On December 31, Master Bank has a total of $500,000 in accounts receivable. Of this total, $200,000 is 0 to 40 days old and $300,000 is 41 to 100 days old. The bank's management would like an estimate of the amounts that eventually will be collected and uncollected. Any estimated amount of bad debts will appear as an allowance in the year-end financial statements.

States. Let us concentrate on what happens to each dollar currently in accounts receivable. As the bank continues to extend credit, management can think of each week

Table 16.5   **Transition Probabilities for the Account Receivable Problem**

Previous Account Balance	Current Account Balance			
	Paid	Bad debt	0 to 40 days old	41 to 100 days old
Paid	1	0	0	0
Bad debt	0	1	0	0
0 to 40 days old	.5	0	.3	.2
41 to 100 days old	.4	.2	.3	.1

as a trial in a Markov process. Moreover, each dollar of accounts receivable may be classified in any of the following states for the system:

-   State 1: paid
-   State 2: bad debt
-   State 3: 0 to 40 days old
-   State 4: 41 to 100 days old

The decision maker can then track the week-to-week status of each dollar by determining the state of the system at the appropriate future period.

Using the data from Table 16.5, the bank will find that the matrix of transition probabilities is

$$T = \begin{pmatrix} 1 & 0 & 0 & 0 \\ 0 & 1 & 0 & 0 \\ .5 & 0 & .3 & .2 \\ .4 & .2 & .3 & .1 \end{pmatrix}$$

In this matrix, the rows list the proportions of accounts receivable that move from one state to another during each week of the observation period. The third row, for example, indicates that 50 percent of the 0-to-40-day dollars (state 3) will be paid (state 1) and none will become bad debts (state 2) in the next week. It also suggests that 30 percent of these accounts will remain 0 to 40 days old while 20 percent will become 41 to 100 days old during the next period.

Note that there is no chance that a paid account (state 1) will become a bad debt (state 2), 0 to 40 days old (state 3), or 41 to 100 days old (state 4). By definition, there is also no likelihood that a bad debt (state 2) can become paid (state 1), 0 to 40 days old (state 3), or 41 to 100 days old (state 4). In effect, then, an account that reaches either state 1 or state 2 will remain there indefinitely, becoming "absorbed" by the condition. For this reason, such conditions are known as **absorbing states.**

When a Markov process involves absorbing states, there is no need to calculate steady-state probabilities. After all, the process will eventually end up in one of the absorbing states. The bank's accounts receivable, for instance, ultimately will be paid or become bad debts. To help control the bad debts and properly manage cash flow, however, Master Bank should determine the total balance proportion that will end up in each absorbing state.

Partitioning the Transition Matrix. Master Bank's transition matrix can be partitioned into the four parts created by the following dashed lines:

	Paid	Bad Debt		0–40	41–100
Paid	1	0		0	0
Bad Debt	0	1		0	0
0–40	.5	0		.3	.2
41–100	.4	.2		.3	.1

The upper left portion of the result gives the *identity matrix*

$$I = \begin{pmatrix} 1 & 0 \\ 0 & 1 \end{pmatrix}$$

or a matrix with 1s on the diagonal and 0s elsewhere. Another matrix with 0s in all positions

$$O = \begin{pmatrix} 0 & 0 \\ 0 & 0 \end{pmatrix}$$

is given in the upper right portion.

The lower left portion provides an additional matrix

$$A = \begin{pmatrix} .5 & 0 \\ .4 & .2 \end{pmatrix}$$

that lists the likelihoods of moving from a nonabsorbing state (0 to 40 days old or 41 to 100 days old) to an absorbing state (paid account or bad debt) in each trial of the process. For example, the first column indicates that 50 percent of the 0-to-40-day accounts (state 3) and 40 percent of the 41-to-100-day accounts (state 4) become paid (state 1) every week during the observation period.

In the lower right portion of the partitioned transition matrix is another matrix

$$Q = \begin{pmatrix} .3 & .2 \\ .3 & .1 \end{pmatrix}$$

that lists the probabilities of moving between nonabsorbing states. For example, the second row indicates that 30 percent of the 41-to-100-day accounts (state 4) become 0-to-40-day accounts (state 3) and 10 percent remain as 41-to-100-day accounts every week during the observation period.

Fundamental Matrix. To compute the proportions that will eventually end up in each absorbing state, management must determine the mean **times to absorption,** or the average number of trials that elapse before each nonabsorbing state is absorbed. These times to absorption are indentified by the **fundamental matrix** F, which is computed with the following formula:

(16.9) $$F = (I - Q)^{-1}$$

where $(I - Q)^{-1}$ represents the *inverse* of the matrix formed by subtracting matrix Q from matrix I. In a matrix with two rows and two columns (such as in the matrix $I - Q$), this inverse is found with the formula

(16.10)
$$(I - Q)^{-1} = \begin{pmatrix} e_{22}/d & -e_{12}/d \\ -e_{21}/d & e_{11}/d \end{pmatrix}$$

where e_{ij} = the element in row i and column j and d is the *determinant* of the matrix $(I - Q)$. The formula

(16.11)
$$d = e_{11}e_{22} - e_{21}e_{12}$$

gives the determinant.

For the accounts receivable situation,

$$(I - Q) = \begin{pmatrix} 1 & 0 \\ 0 & 1 \end{pmatrix} - \begin{pmatrix} .3 & .2 \\ .3 & .1 \end{pmatrix} = \begin{pmatrix} .7 & -.2 \\ -.3 & .9 \end{pmatrix}$$

and, according to formula (16.11),

$$d = .7(.9) - (-.3)(-.2) = .57$$

so that, according to formula (16.10),

$$(I - Q)^{-1} = \begin{pmatrix} .9/.57 & -(-.2/.57) \\ -(-.3/.57) & .7/.57 \end{pmatrix} = \begin{pmatrix} 1.57 & .35 \\ .52 & 1.22 \end{pmatrix}$$

Formula (16.9) then shows that Master Bank's fundamental matrix is

$$F = (I - Q)^{-1} = \begin{pmatrix} 1.57 & .35 \\ .52 & 1.22 \end{pmatrix}$$

The entries in the fundamental matrix F give the average number of periods that the system will be in each nonabsorbing state before it gets absorbed. For example, the first row indicates that a 0-to-40-day account (state 3) is expected to remain the same age (state 3) for 1.57 weeks and become 41 to 100 days old (state 4) for another .35 week before being absorbed as a paid bill (state 1) or bad debt (state 2). Similarly, the second row shows that a 41-to-100-day account (state 4) will remain the same age (state 4) for 1.22 weeks and become 0 to 40 days old (state 3) for another .52 week prior to absorption in state 1 or 2.

By adding the entries in the rows of the fundamental matrix, management can also determine the *times to absorption,* or the total number of periods that elapse prior to absorption. For instance, the first row of matrix F suggests that an average of 1.57 + .35 = 1.92 weeks will pass before a 0-to-40-day account (state 3) is absorbed either as a paid bill or as a bad debt. The second row demonstrates that .52 + 1.22 = 1.74 weeks are expected to elapse before a 41-to-100-day account (state 4) becomes absorbed in state 1 or 2.

Conditional Probability Matrix. The fundamental matrix F lists the average number of weeks that elapse before the aged accounts become absorbed as paid bills or bad debts. Matrix A gives the likelihoods of moving from the nonabsorbing states to absorbing states during each week in the process. By multiplying matrix F by matrix A, management can determine the probabilities of eventually moving from any nonabsorbing state to each absorbing state.

For example, matrix F's first row suggests that a 0-to-40-day account remains the same age for 1.57 weeks and becomes 41 to 100 days old for another .35 week before being absorbed. In addition, matrix A's first column indicates that 50 percent of the 0-to-40-day accounts and 40 percent of the 41-to-100-day accounts get paid each week of the observation period. As a result, the bank should anticipate that

$$1.57(.5) + .35(.4) = .93$$

or 93 percent of the 0-to-40-day accounts will eventually be paid.

By performing the required calculations, we obtain the probability matrix

$$FA = \begin{pmatrix} 1.57 & .35 \\ .52 & 1.22 \end{pmatrix} \begin{pmatrix} .5 & 0 \\ .4 & .2 \end{pmatrix} = \begin{pmatrix} .93 & .07 \\ .75 & .25 \end{pmatrix}$$

This matrix lists all probabilities of eventually moving from any nonabsorbing state to each absorbing state. For example, the second row tells us that 75 percent of the 41-to-100-day accounts eventually will be paid and 25 percent eventually will become bad debts.

Absorbing State Amounts. Bank management can use the probability information to predict the accounts receivable amounts that will either be paid or be lost as bad debts. Management Situation 16.2 indicates that Master Bank has $200,000 in 0-to-40-day accounts and $300,000 in 41-to-100-day accounts on December 31. Moreover, the probability matrix FA's first column shows that 93 percent of the 0-to-40-day accounts and 75 percent of the 41-to-100-day accounts will be paid. Consequently, the decision maker should expect

$$\$200,000(.93) + \$300,000(.75) = \$411,000$$

of the $500,000 total balance to be eventually paid.

The second column of the FA matrix suggests that 7 percent of the 0-to-40-day accounts and 25 percent of the 41-to-100-day accounts will wind up as bad debts. Management, then, should expect

$$\$200,000(.07) + \$300,000(.25) = \$89,000$$

of the $500,000 total balance to be written off as bad debts. Thus, the bank's accounting department must set up an $89,000 allowance for doubtful accounts in the year-end financial statements.

Procedure Recap. When there are absorbing states, the following procedure can be used to perform Markov analysis:

1. Partition the transition matrix into the four parts I, O, A, and Q.

2. Compute the fundamental matrix $F = (I - Q)^{-1}$, which identifies the mean times to absorption.

3. Calculate the matrix FA, which gives the probabilities of eventually moving from any nonabsorbing state to each absorbing state.

Policy Decisions

Markov analysis provides information about the likelihood that a system will be in a particular state at any future trial of a process. It also generates data on the passage times that elapse before the system reaches specified states. Such knowledge can be used by the decision maker to evaluate the effectiveness of selected policies under various system conditions. Management Situation 16.3 illustrates.

Management Situation 16.3

Evaluating Credit Policy

Suppose that Master Bank is unhappy with the $89,000 projected bad debt and is considering a new credit policy that involves increased financial charges to customers. Management believes that this policy will increase the probability of a transition from the 40-day-and-under category to the paid category. It should also decrease the likelihood that a 0-to-40-day account will become 41 to 100 days old.

   In fact, a careful study reveals that the transition matrix

$$T = \begin{pmatrix} 1 & 0 & 0 & 0 \\ 0 & 1 & 0 & 0 \\ .65 & 0 & .30 & .05 \\ .40 & .20 & .30 & .10 \end{pmatrix}$$

will be applicable with the new credit policy. As the matrix demonstrates, the policy increases the probability from .5 to .65 that a 0-to-40-day account will get paid each week in the observation period. It also decreases the likelihood that a 0-to-40-day account becomes 41 to 100 days old from 20 percent to 5 percent.

   Bank management wants to evaluate the effect of such a policy on bad debt expense.

According to the information given in Management Situation 16.3, the new credit policy revises the bank's transition matrix. To evaluate the policy, management must determine the updated fundamental matrix, times to absorption, and conditional probabilities for being absorbed.

Times to Absorption. By partitioning the transition matrix and by performing the necessary matrix algebra, we find that

$$I - Q = \begin{pmatrix} 1 & 0 \\ 0 & 1 \end{pmatrix} - \begin{pmatrix} .30 & .05 \\ .30 & .10 \end{pmatrix} = \begin{pmatrix} .70 & -.05 \\ -.30 & .90 \end{pmatrix}$$

with a determinant of $d = .7(.9) - (-.30)(-.05) = .615$. Hence, the updated fundamental matrix is

$$F = (I - Q)^{-1} = \begin{pmatrix} .9/.615 & -(-.05/.615) \\ -(-.3/.615) & .7/.615 \end{pmatrix} = \begin{pmatrix} 1.46 & .08 \\ .48 & 1.14 \end{pmatrix}$$

which indicates that an average of $1.46 + .08 = 1.54$ weeks will pass before a 0-to-40-day account (state 3) is absorbed, and an average of $.48 + 1.14 = 1.62$ weeks will elapse before a 41-to-100-day account (state 4) becomes absorbed.

By comparing the fundamental matrices from Management Situations 16.2 and 16.3, management will find that the new credit policy decreases the times to absorption for each type of account. For example, Management Situation 16.2's fundamental matrix tells us that a 0-to-40-day account is absorbed in an average of 1.92 weeks without the increased financial charges. The corresponding entry in Management Situation 16.3's fundamental matrix shows that a 0-to-40-day account is absorbed in an average of 1.54 weeks with the increased financial charges. Under the new credit policy, then, such an account will be paid an average of

$$1.92 - 1.54 = .38 \text{ week}$$

sooner than before.

Conditional Probabilities. Multiplying the updated fundamental matrix F by the updated A matrix

$$FA = \begin{pmatrix} 1.46 & .08 \\ .48 & 1.14 \end{pmatrix} \begin{pmatrix} .65 & 0 \\ .40 & .20 \end{pmatrix} = \begin{pmatrix} .98 & .02 \\ .77 & .23 \end{pmatrix}$$

gives the updated conditional probabilities for being absorbed. By comparing these probabilties with the corresponding likelihoods from Management Situation 16.2's FA matrix, the bank will find that the new credit policy increases the proportions of paid bills and decreases the shares of uncollectible accounts. For example, the entries in Management Situation 16.2's FA matrix indicate that, without the increased financial charges, 75 percent of the 41-to-100-day (state 4) accounts get paid and 25 percent end up as bad debts. The corresponding values in Management Situation 16.3's FA matrix show that, with the new credit policy, 77 percent of the 41-to-100-day accounts get paid and only 23 percent end up as bad debts.

Absorbing State Amounts. Once more, bank management can use the probability information to predict the accounts receivable amount that will be uncollectible. Master Bank has $200,000 in 0-to-40-day (state 3) accounts and $300,000 in 41-to-100-day (state 4) accounts. The second column of the updated FA matrix indicates that 2 percent of the 0-to-40-day accounts and 23 percent of the 41-to-100-day accounts will wind up as bad debts. Consequently, the decision maker should expect

$$\$200,000(.02) + \$300,000(.23) = \$73,000$$

of the $500,000 total year-end balance to be a bad debt expense with the new credit policy.

Under the previous policy, there is an $89,000 uncollectible balance. Thus, the increased financial charges can generate a savings of

$$\$89,000 - \$73,000 = \$16,000.$$

These savings represent $16,000/$500,000 $= .032$, or 3.2 percent, of the $500,000 total balance.

Markov Extensions

The basic Markov model assumes that the underlying process can be observed at discrete points in time. While such an assumption is suitable for many problems, there are also cases in which the system will change continuously over time. Under these circumstances, the decision maker must use continuous time versions of the Markov model.

In addition, the basic Markov model presumes that the probability of the next event depends only on the outcome of the prior event. Yet, there are situations in which the system's condition is influenced by outcomes of the past two, three, or more periods. Management, then, must extend the basic analysis to incorporate the effects of all relevant past conditions.

The basic Markov model also assumes that the process generates probabilities that eventually stabilize at the same equilibrium values regardless of the starting conditions in the system. Nevertheless, some circumstances do not involve such steady-state probabilities. In these situations, the decision maker may be more interested in studying the short-run rather than long-run behavior of the system.

Finally, Management Situations 16.1 through 16.3 deal with situations in which the states of the Markov process denote different time periods. Markov concepts are also applicable to cases where the trials of the system represent reference points (such as organizational levels or geographic areas) rather than time periods.

Computer Analysis

In practice, it may take a large number of complex computations to perform a Markov analysis by hand, and the calculations can be time-consuming and prone to error. That is why prewritten computer programs have been developed to perform the necessary analysis (find the state probabilities and passage times in situations without absorbing states or the times to absorption and conditional probabilities in problems with absorbing states). Two such programs are available as modules on the **Quantitative Management (QM)** software. They are invoked by selecting Markov Models from **QM**'s main menu. Figure 16.4 then shows how the software can be used to evaluate Master Bank's credit policy (Management Situation 16.3)

Problem Formulation. The user executes the module by selecting the Absorbing states option from the Markov Analysis menu. Management formulates the problem through the Edit command from the Input menu. As Figure 16.4 demonstrates, the required inputs are the total number of states, the number of absorbing states, and the transition matrix. When entering transition probabilities, the absorbing state data must form an identity matrix in the upper left portion of the transition matrix. Report options then are selected through the Output menu.

Markov Analysis. After receiving the inputs, the program processes the data and generates the fundamental matrix, resulting times to absorption, and the conditional probability

---

Figure 16.4   Computer Analysis of Master Bank's Credit Policy

---

Markov Analysis: Input: Output:
 ▪ No absorbing states   * Edit   ▪ Full
 * Absorbing states   ▪ Load   * Summary
                                           ▪ Print   * Print
                                           ▪ Save   ▪ Save

Problem Formulation:
   Number of states: 4
   Number of absorbing states: 2
Enter the transition matrix in the following table.

		State Next Period			
		1	2	3	4
State	1	1	0	0	0
This	2	0	1	0	0
Period	3	.65	0	.3	.05
	4	.40	.2	.3	.10

RECOMMENDATION
Fundamental Matrix

		State	
		3	4
State	3	1.46	.08
	4	.48	1.14

Times to Absorption

State	Mean Time to Absorption
3	1.54
4	1.62

Conditional Probabilities

		State	
		1	2
State	3	.98	.02
	4	.77	.23

---

matrix. Figure 16.4, for example, shows that an average of $1.46 + .08 = 1.54$ weeks
will pass before a 0-to-40-day account (state 3) is absorbed. It also indicates that .98,
or 98 percent, of these accounts will eventually be paid.

16.3 DYNAMIC PROGRAMMING

The primary purpose of Markov analysis is to predict the outcomes of an evolutionary
process. In addition, such an analysis can be used to evaluate specified decision alternatives. However, it does not attempt to determine the optimal, or best, overall policy.
In other words, Markov analysis is a descriptive rather than normative decision tool.

Markov Analysis in Practice

Markov models are applied to a wide variety of management problems. Here are a few areas in which this quantitative analysis is used.

Area	Application
Finance and Accounting	Determining the probabilities of repayment for loan portfolios Analyzing the payment behavior of retail credit customers Liquidating assets
Marketing	Analyzing consumer response to selected marketing strategies Measuring the impact of trade discounts on risk and return Evaluating advertising and pricing decisions
Production and Operations	Determining the best order quantity for a perishable product Finding the best plant and service facility locations Risk engineering
Public and Service Sector	Analyzing the variation in air pollution levels Deciding how many resources to dispatch to a fire Modeling the transition of physicians, nurses, and assistants between medical settings and locations

On the other hand, there are many cases in which a description of the process is not sufficient. Management may need to prescribe the sequence of actions that best meets some overall measure of performance. **Dynamic programming** is a methodology designed to solve such sequential optimization problems.

Principles. In dynamic programming, the problem is decomposed into a series of smaller segments or stages. Each stage's outcome is determined by the state of the process as it enters the stage and by the decision made at the stage. The current state and decision fix the state entering the next stage of the problem in a manner known as the **stage transformation** or **transfer function.**

The new state, in turn, influences the new decision and outcome. This new decision affects the states, decisions, and outcomes in subsequent stages of the process. An expression called the **recursive relationship** ties together the outcomes obtained at all stages of the sequential decision process. The relationship then is used to identify the series of decisions that leads to the best outcomes at each stage of the problem.

The analysis is based on the following important principle:

> **Principle of Optimality:** Regardless of the current state and decision, the remaining decisions must be optimal with regard to the state resulting from the current decision.

By reconstructing the sequence of best decisions made over all stages of the process, management will form a so-called **optimal policy.**

Applications. Dynamic programming principles can be applied to situations involving deterministic decisions or stochastic (including Markov) processes, static or time-

Table 16.6   **Dynamic Programming Examples**

Problem	Stages	States	Optimal Policy
Knapsack loading	Items to pack	Volume remaining in the knapsack	The items that have the most utility
Production scheduling and inventory control	Time periods in the production process	Beginning inventories	The least costly production and inventory schedule
Stagecoach routing	Legs of the trip	Stagecoach locations at the beginning of the last leg	The shortest route from the stagecoach's origin to its destination
Device reliability	Components in the device	Funds available for the components	The number of parallel units for each component that will maximize device reliability
Purchasing	Time periods in the purchasing cycle	Buying or waiting to buy	When to buy the item at the lowest expected price

dependent stages, single-or-multiple-state circumstances, and discrete or continuous variables. Table 16.6 presents some of the possibilities. (Thought Exercise 9 and Technique Exercise 20 present others.)

A major factor that limits the application of dynamic programming is the "curse of dimensionality." This curse is encountered when a particular application is characterized by multiple states (termed a *multidimensional state vector*). For such formulations, the required computations may be too costly and time-consuming to perform even with the aid of a computer.

Computational Approaches. Unlike most other management science methodologies, dynamic programming does not involve a standard mathematical model. Indeed, the recursive relationship must be tailored to the specific decision situation. As a result, a general technique, such as the simplex method, cannot be used to solve the overall problem. Rather, the decision maker utilizes the most effective tool to solve each stage's subproblem. These tools can involve enumeration, decision analysis, mathematical programming, and other approaches. It may be possible to develop special procedures for particular prototype dynamic programming problems (including allocation, multiple-period, network, multiple-stage production, feedback control, and Markov decision processes).

Two basic computational approaches have been developed to perform dynamic programming. *Forward recursion* starts with the first stage and analyzes the problem by working forward to the last stage, while *backward recursion* (like Chapter 4's backward induction analysis) begins at the final stage and analyzes backward to the initial stage of the process. The choice of approach will be influenced by personal preference, the difficulty of effecting stage transformations, the type of sensitivity analysis desired, or

Table 16.7   **Resale Values for John's Van**

Van Age (Years)	Resale Value ($)
1	8,000
2	6,500
3	4,500
4	2,000

the specification of initial or final states. Since the backward approach facilitates the conceptualization and computation of transformations for many applications (especially time-dependent processes), there is a decided preference in the literature for backward recursions.

Case. Management Situation 16.4 illustrates the principles of dynamic programming.

Management Situation 16.4

Equipment Replacement

John's Neighborhood Grocery uses a small van to make home deliveries. Once a year, John decides whether or not to replace the present vehicle with a new van. His decision is based on the vehicle's current operating cost and resale value as well as the purchase price of a new van.

John always purchases the same type of van from the only dealer in town. According to the dealer's service records, the grocery store can expect the van to have a useful life of four years. These records also indicate that the vehicle's operating costs will be $2,500 in the first year, $3,000 in the second year, $4,000 in the third year, and $5,500 in the fourth year of its useful life. In addition, the dealer's sales experience suggests that John should anticipate the resale values given in Table 16.7. A new van sells for $10,000. All the data are expressed in present-value terms. Moreover, the dealer believes that the values will remain stable for the next four years.

The grocery store has just purchased a new van, and John is eager to determine the replacement policy that will minimize total equipment costs. That is, he wants to know the best times to replace the vehicle over the next four years.

In Management Situation 16.4, the grocery store is interested in describing the van's cost behavior. At the start of the process in year 1, John purchases a new van. Over the years, the operating costs change as the vehicle ages. Moreover, the store can replace an aging van with a new model in any year of the planning period. The substitution cost will depend on the age of the vehicle and the year of replacement. Total operating and replacement costs, then, can be expected to follow an evolutionary process.

Formulating the Problem

Figure 16.5 depicts the nature of the grocery store's evolutionary process. As this figure demonstrates, each year in the planning period can be thought of as a trial or stage of the process. The grocery store enters each stage with a vehicle that is purchased in a specified year of the planning period. Put another way, the year of purchase identifies the state of the system.

Stage Transformation. In view of the state, John decides whether to replace or keep the present vehicle. The decision and state then determine the equipment expenditure required during the corresponding stage of the process. They also fix the conditions for the next year in the planning period.

For example, Figure 16.5 shows that the grocery store enters stage 1 with no new van. In view of this state, John purchases a new vehicle at the start of year 1. By the end of stage 1, then, he will incur the replacement cost plus the first-year operating expenses for the new van. It also means that the store enters stage 2 with a vehicle purchased in year 1 of the planning period.

There is a similar pattern for each subsequent stage in the evolutionary process. The action in one trial influences the outcome during the trial and the state of the system at the next stage. The new state, in turn, affects the decision at this stage, and so forth. As a result, John's equipment replacement situation really involves the series of interrelated decisions illustrated by Figure 16.6 (which is similar in concept to Chapter 4's decision tree). Every square shows a decision point in the process. The symbol R represents a decision to replace the present van, while K means that John will keep the current model. Every circle, or node, denotes a state of the system. Moreover, the number within the node identifies the year in which the grocery store purchases a van or replaces the present vehicle with a new model. The values above the branches give the total replacment and operating costs associated with the decisions and states.

Decision Tree. At the start of the process, for instance, the grocery store purchases a new van for $10,000. This action is identified in Figure 16.6 with the decision square $\boxed{R}$ at the beginning of year 1. In addition, the data from Management Situation 16.4 indicate that John must spend $2,500 to operate the van during its first year of service. By purchasing the van, the grocery store will incur a $10,000 + $2,500 equipment expense during year 1 of the planning period. Consequently, the label $10,000 + $2500 appears above the branch emanating from $\boxed{R}$ in year 1 of Figure 16.6.

John then enters the next year with a vehicle purchased in year 1 of the process. Hence state node ① appears at the start of year 2. At this point, the grocery store can replace ($\boxed{R}$) or keep ($\boxed{K}$) the present van.

According to the data in Management Situation 16.4 and Table 16.7, each new van sells for $10,000 and has a $8,000 resale value after one year of service. Therefore, it will cost $10,000 − $8,000 = $2,000 to replace the one-year-old vehicle at the start of year 2. In addition, the store must spend $2,500 to operate the new van in its first year of service during year 2. By replacing the vehicle, John will incur a $2,000 + $2,500 equipment expense during year 2 of the planning period. Therefore, the label $2,000 + $2,500 appears above the branch emanating from $\boxed{R}$ in year 2 of Figure 16.6.

Figure 16.5 **The Grocery Store's Evolutionary Process**

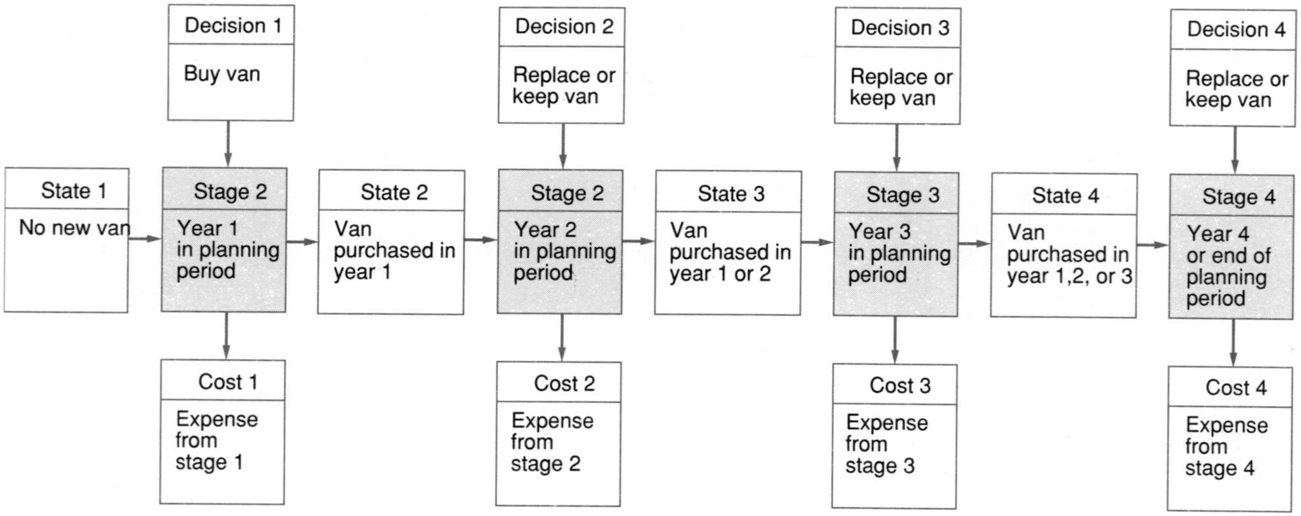

Figure 16.6   **John's Decision Tree**

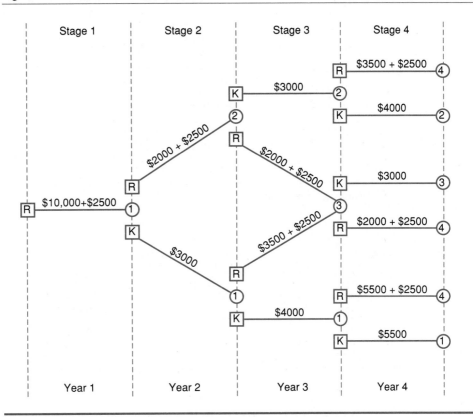

Also, John enters the next year with a vehicle that is purchased in year 2 of the process (denoted as a ② state).

On the other hand, suppose that the grocery store keeps the original van at the start of year 2. In this case, the vehicle will be two years old by the end of year 2. Moreover, the data in Management Situation 16.4 tell us that John must spend $3,000 to operate the vehicle in its second year of service. Thus, the value $3,000 is written above the branch emanating from $\boxed{K}$ in year 2 of Figure 16.6. Such an action also means that the store enters the next year with a vechicle purchased in year 1 of the process (depicted as a ① state).

Years 3 and 4 can be developed in the same evolutionary manner. John's problem is to determine the series of decisions that results in the minimum total equipment cost over the grocery store's four-year planning period.

Solving the Problem

Since the current actions will be influenced by future outcomes, John might find it easier to begin the analysis at the final stage (year 4) and work backward to the initial stage of the process. The decision tree in Figure 16.6 again provides the relevant data for

Table 16.8   **John's Stage 4 Computations**

Stage 4 State Year Van Purchased	Stage 4 Decision Alternative	Stage 4 Cost	Minimum Total Cost	Best Stage 4 Decision
1	Replace van Keep van	\$5,500 + \$2,500 \$5,500	\$5,500	Keep van
2	Replace van Keep van	\$3,500 + \$2,500 \$4,000	\$4,000	Keep van
3	Replace van Keep van	\$2,000 + \$2,500 \$3,000	\$3,000	Keep van

Table 16.9   **John's Stage 3 Computations**

Stage 3 State Year Van Purchased	Stage 3 Decision Alternative	Stage 3 Cost	Stage 4 State	Lowest Remaining Cost	Total Cost	Minimum Total Cost	Best Stage 3 Decision
1	Replace van Keep van	\$3,500 + \$2,500 \$4,000	3 1	\$3,000 \$5,500	\$6,000 + \$3,000 \$4,000 + \$5,500	\$9,000	Replace van
2	Replace van Keep van	\$2,000 + \$2,500 \$3,000	3 2	\$3,000 \$4,000	\$4,500 + \$3,000 \$3,000 + \$4,000	\$7,000	Keep van

this backward recursion. Table 16.8 presents the computations required for year 4 in the planning period.

Stage 4 Analysis. As the first column of Table 16.8 shows, the grocery store will enter stage 4 with a van purchased in either year 1, 2, or 3 of the planning period. In view of this stage 4 state, John must identify each decision alternative and compute the resulting cost. These costs are reported in the third column of the table. For example, if the store replaces a year 2 van, it will incur a \$3,500 + \$2,500 = \$6,000 equipment expense during stage 4 of the process.

John should then select the decision that leads to the minimum total cost associated with the stage 4 state. The relevant analysis is given in the last two columns of Table 16.8. For instance, the grocery store can minimize the total cost associated with a year 1 van by keeping the vehicle during stage 4 of the planning period.

Stage 3 Analysis. The stage 4 knowledge and the decision tree in Figure 16.6 in turn provide the information needed to make the year 3 decisions. Table 16.9 presents the required calculations. As the first column indicates, the grocery store will enter stage 3 with a van purchased in either year 1 or year 2 of the planning period. In view of this stage 3 state, John once more must identify each decision alternative and compute

Table 16.10   **John's Stage 2 Computations**

Stage 2 State Year Van Purchased	Stage 2 Decision Alternative	Stage 2 Cost	Stage 3 State	Lowest Remaining Cost	Total Cost	Minimum Total Cost	Best Stage 2 Decision
1	Replace van	$2,000 + $2,500	2	$7,000	$4,500 + $7,000 = $11,500	$11,500	Replace van
	Keep van	$3,000	1	$9,000	$3,000 + $9,000 = $12,000		

the resulting cost. These costs again are reported in the third column of the table. For example, the data indicate that the store will incur a $4,000 equipment expense during year 3 by keeping a year 1 vehicle through stage 3 of the process.

Each stage 3 decision will also affect the costs incurred during year 4 in the planning period. To determine this effect, John must now identify the stage 4 state and lowest remaining cost resulting from the stage 3 conditions. Such knowledge is given in the fourth and fifth columns of Table 16.9. Consider, for instance, the decision to keep a year 2 van during stage 3 of the process. The fourth column shows that this decision leaves the grocery store with a year 2 vehicle entering stage 4 of the planning period. Under these circumstances, Table 16.8 suggests that the best stage 4 decision is to keep the year 2 van and incur a minimum total cost of $4,000. Hence, the fifth column in Table 16.9 has a $4,000 lowest-remaining-cost entry in the row where the stage 4 state is 2 and the stage 3 decision is to keep the van.

At this point, the decision maker can calculate the total cost associated with the stage 3 state. The sixth column of Table 16.9 illustrates that this cost is the sum of the stage 3 and lowest remaining expenses (so that the sum represents the recursive relationship that ties together stage 3 and stage 4 outcomes). For example, the data indicate that the store will incur a $6000 + $3000 = $9000 total equipment cost during stages 3 and 4 by replacing a year 1 van at the start of year 3.

John should then select the decision that leads to the minimum total cost associated with each stage 3 state. The relevant data are given in columns 7 and 8 of Table 16.9. These data tell us that the grocery store can minimize the total cost associated with a year 2 van by keeping the vehicle during stage 3 of the planning period. They also indicate that the store can minimize the total cost associated with a year 1 van by replacing the vehicle during stage 3 of the planning period.

Stage 2 Analysis. Figure 16.6's decision tree and the state 3 knowledge provide the information required to evaluate the year 2 alternative. Table 16.10 presents the necessary computations. The first column shows that the grocery store will enter stage 2 with a van purchased in year 1 of the planning period. In view of this stage 2 state, John again must identify each decision alternative and calculate the resulting cost. These costs once more are reported in the third column of the table.

In addition, each stage 2 decision affects the costs incurred during subsequent years of the planning period. To determine these effects, John must identify the stage 3 state and lowest remaining cost resulting from the stage 2 conditions. This knowledge is given in the fourth and fifth columns of Table 16.10.

Consider, for instance, the decision to replace a year 1 van during stage 2 of the process. The fourth column of Table 16.10 shows that this decision provides the store with a year 2 vehicle entering stage 3 of the planning period. Under these circumstances, Table 16.9 suggests that the best stage 3 decision is to keep the year 2 van and incur a minimum total cost of $7,000. Therefore, the fifth column of Table 16.10 has a $7,000 lowest-remaining-cost entry in the row where the stage 2 state is 1 and the stage 2 decision is to replace the van.

John can now calculate the total cost associated with the stage 2 state. As the sixth column of Table 16.10 illustrates, this cost is the sum of the stage 2 and lowest remaining expenses (so that the sum represents the recursive relationship that ties together stage 2 through stage 4 outcomes). For example, the data indicate that the store will incur a $12,000 total equipment cost during stages 2 through 4 by keeping a year 1 van at the start of year 2.

John should then select the decision that leads to the minimum total cost associated with the stage 2 state. The relevant data appear in columns 7 and 8 of Table 16.10. As you can see, the grocery store can minimize the total cost associated with a year 1 van by replacing the vehicle at stage 2 of the planning period.

Stage 1 Analysis. The stage 2 knowledge and the decision tree give the data needed to evaluate the year 1 decision. In this regard, Figure 16.6 shows that the grocery store enters the planning period with no new van. After considering the stage 1 state, John purchases a new vehicle at the start of the planning period. In other words, the only stage 1 decision is to replace the van. As a result, the store incurs a $12,500 total equipment cost during stage 1 of the process.

These initial conditions also mean that the store enters stage 2 with a van purchased in year 1 of the planning period. According to Table 16.10, when the stage 2 state is 1, the best stage 2 decision is to replace the vehicle and obtain a minimum cost of $11,500 (so that $11,500 represents the lowest cost remaining after the stage 1 decision).

Optimal Policy. By reconstructing the sequence of decisions made in stages 1 through 4 of the process, John can identify the optimal equipment replacement policy. The analysis suggests that John should make the following decisions:

1. Replace the van in year 1 and enter stage 2 with a year 1 vehicle.
2. Replace the van in year 2 and enter stage 3 with a year 2 vehicle.
3. Keep the van in year 3 and enter stage 4 with a year 2 vehicle.
4. Keep the van in year 4 of the planning period.

Such a policy will generate a minimum total expense equal to

$$\$12,500 + \$11,500 = \$24,000$$

during years 1 through 4 of the four-year planning period. This $12,500 + $11,500 expression also represents the recursive relationship that ties together the outcomes obtained at all stages of the grocery store's sequential decision process.

Dynamic Programming in Practice

Dynamic programming is applied to a wide variety of management problems. Here are a few areas in which this quantitative analysis is used.

Area	Application
Finance and Accounting	Replacing equipment and other machinery Allocating funds to the most productive investments Reducing interest expenses by refunding bonds
Marketing	Finding the advertising policy that best simulates product/service purchases Determining the optimal consumption policy for a consumer who faces an uncertain income stream Finding the optimal search pattern for product/service research and development Developing the optimal pricing policy in a Markov decision system
Production and Operations	Determining the optimal production and distribution schedule Finding the optimal lot size for a production process involving limited capacity Developing the petroleum policies that will optimize system performance Determining the most profitable cutting pattern for individual trees
Public and Service Sector	Finding the best economic policy to maximize energy benefits Determining the farm management policies that will optimize agricultural outcomes Developing the optimal pumping policy of a municipal water plant

Procedure Recap. The dynamic programming methodology for finding an optimal policy can be summarized as follows:

1. Decompose the problem into a series of smaller segments or stages.

2. Determine the stage transformation or transfer function.

3. Formulate the recursive relationship, and use this relationship to identify the decision that results in the best outcome at each stage of the problem.

4. Reconstruct the sequence of decisions made in stage 1 through the end of the process.

Dynamic Programming Notation

There is a standard notation used for dynamic programming. In this notation

n = an index number identifying the stage of the sequential decision process

S_n = the state of the process at stage n

S_{n+1} = the state of the process at stage $n + 1$

D_n = the decision at stage n

$O_n(S_n, D_n)$ = the outcome associated with the state and decision at stage n

The recursive relationship then is

$$F_n^*(S_n) = \text{optimum } [O_n(S_n, D_n) + F_{n+1}^*(S_{n+1})]$$

and the objective is to identify the series of interrelated decisions that generates these successive optimum outcomes.

SUMMARY

This chapter has presented some methods for dealing with sequential problems, that is, situations involving a series of interrelated operations or decisions. The first section illustrated and described the nature of a basic Markov system. Then we saw how to record and keep track of the changes that take place in the system from one trial to the next. Figure 16.2 outlined the relevant recording device.

The second section demonstrated how Markov analysis can be utilized in decision making. We saw how the model is used to predict the condition of a system at each stage of the evolutionary process. Next, we considered ways to predict, by hand and with the aid of a computer, the eventual conditions in a Markov system. There was also a discussion on absorbing states and the approaches needed to determine the passage time between specified changes in the system conditions. The section then illustrated how the information can be employed to evaluate the effectiveness of selected policies under various system conditions. It concluded with some important extensions to and applications of Markov analysis.

The final section introduced dynamic programming. In particular, this methodology can be used to find the optimal policy for a sequential decision problem. We also examined some important limitations of the analysis and presented a sample of reported applications.

Glossary

absorbing state A state that cannot be left once it is entered.

dynamic programming A methodology designed to solve an optimization problem in a sequential manner.

equilibrium first passage time The average number of trials that elapse before the system can make a transition from a specified state for the first time.

expected recurrence time the average elapsed time between the repeat occurrences of a specified state in an evolutionary process.

first-order Markov process A stochastic process in which the current state of the system depends only on the immediately preceding state.

fundamental matrix A rectangular array of numbers indicating the average number of periods that a system will remain in nonabsorbing states before being absorbed.

homogeneous Markov chain A Markov process with constant, or stationary, transition probabilities.

Markov analysis An approach designed to describe and predict the behavior of an evolutionary process.

Markov system An evolutionary process that generates a homogeneous Markov chain.

mean first passage time The average number of trials that will elapse before the system changes from one state to another specified state for the first time.

optimal policy The series of decisions that will lead to the best outcome over all stages in an evolutionary process.

principle of optimality The principle whereby, regardless of the current state and decision, the remaining decisions must be optimal with regard to the state resulting from the current decision.

recursive relationship An equation that ties together the outcomes obtained at all stages of a sequential decision process.

row vector of state probabilities A list of state probabilities arranged as a row of numbers.

stage transformation (transfer function) The manner in which a subsequent state is determined from the immediately preceding state and decision in a sequential process.

state The condition of the system at a particular trial of the evolutionary process.

state probability The likelihood that a system will be in a particular state at a specified trial of an evolutionary process.

steady-state probabilities The equilibrium values at which the state probabilities eventually stabilize after a very large number of trials for an evolutionary process.

time to absorption The average number of periods that elapse before a nonabsorbing state is absorbed.

transition matrix A list of transition probabilities arranged as a rectangular array of numbers.

transition probabilities The likelihood that a system will move from one state to another between trials of an evolutionary process.

transition table A table used to record and keep track of the transition probabilities involved in a Markov system.

trial(stage) A point at which the decision maker observes an evolutionary process.

Thought Exercises

1. For each of the following situations, explain whether it is appropriate to use the Markov model developed in this chapter:

   a. Three television stations compete for advertising shares of the market. Advertisers switch from station to station, depending on the previous time period's ratings. The pattern of switching changes from one time period to the next.

   b. A taxi company periodically inspects the bearings on its cabs and classifies them according to their condition. There are four possible categories. The bearing classification changes from one inspection to another, depending on conditions in several preceding time periods.

   c. A life insurance company wants to predict the percentage of a city's population that will be in various age brackets. People move from one category to another. The pattern of transaction is relatively stable from one period to the next.

2. Red Grape Company is one of the two largest wine makers in California. Their market analysts are currently investigating the brand loyalty to Red Grape. A questionnaire filled out by a group of wine drinkers led the analysts to construct the following tree diagram:

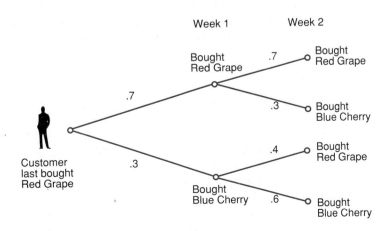

The company president, J. Foolhardy, has a set goal of 70 percent market share for Red Grape. Elmer Studious, the market research director, informs Foolhardy that the goal cannot be met with existing market conditions. How did Studious arrive at this conclusion?

3. The data processing center at Campus Enterprises has been experiencing substantial periods of computer downtime. Operating conditions change from hour to hour. The transition pattern, however, is relatively stable. It can be summarized by the data in the following table:

Operating Condition Previous Hour	Operating Condition Next Hour	
	Running	Down
Running	.85	.15
Down	.25	.75

Currently, the system is running.

The company has an important project scheduled for the third hour from now. Campus will use the local university's computer for the project unless there is at least an 80 percent chance that the company's system will be running.

Based on the available information, the company decides to use the university computer for the project. Can you explain why?

4. There are three dairies that supply all the milk consumed in a community. The dairies have the pattern of retentions, gains, and losses given by the following table:

From Dairy	To Dairy		
	A	B	C
A	.8	.1	.1
B	0	.6	.4
C	0	.3	.7

According to an industry analyst, under current market conditions, dairies B and C will eventually capture all of A's customers. How did the analyst arrive at this conclusion? What do you think dairy A will do about this situation?

5. Snap Shot, Inc., is a photographic studio in a small university community. Its main competition is Quality Photography. Reports from the local chamber of commerce indicate that Snap Shot has about 40 percent of the market of approximately $300,000 yearly sales. Last year, Snap Shot had a profit amounting to 10 percent of sales. As part of a project, a class in small business management at the local university has offered its advice. The class feels that a $5,000 promotional campaign would create the following transition probabilities.

If Snap Shot wants to recoup the promotional investment within a year, should it take the student advice? Explain.

From	To	
	Snap shot	Quality Photography
Snap shot	.7	.3
Quality Photography	.3	.7

6. An inspector at a military surplus warehouse inspects food products each week and classifies them as "just delivered," "in good condition," or "uneatable." Uneatable foods are replaced the next week at an average cost of $30 per crate. Warehouse records show the following weekly transition pattern:

Food Condition This Week	Food Condition Next Week		
	Just delivered	Good	Uneatable
Just delivered	0	.9	.1
Good	0	.8	.2
Uneatable	1	0	0

If the food were discarded before it is uneatable, the average net replacment cost would be only $10 per crate.

The commanding officer believes that an expected savings of $5 per crate per week would be substantial. Based on the available information, do you think that the food should be replaced before it is uneatable? Explain.

7. A company's accounts receivable problem involves the following transition probabilities:

Previous Account Balance	Current Account Balance			
	Paid	Bad debt	0 to 30 days	31 to 90 days
Paid	1	0	0	0
Bad debt	0	1	0	0
0 to 30 days	0	0	.5	.5
31 to 90 days	0	0	.6	.4

The company notices that none of the account balances end up as either paid or bad debts. Can you explain why?

8. Refer back to Management Situation 16.4. John's wife, Della, claims that the grocery store's equipment replacement situation can be formulated as a network problem. Explain how she arrived at this conclusion. Show the resulting network. Develop the recursive relationships involved in this network problem. Use dynamic programming to find the optimal route throught the network.

9. A commodities broker buys a crop for her customers in a market that trades only once a week. Each week, there is a 25 percent chance that the crop will cost $200,000, a

50 percent likelihood that it will cost $300,000, and a 25 percent probability that it will cost $450,000. At the present time, the broker knows that the clients' investment plans cannot be satisfied unless the crop is bought within the next five trading weeks. The broker worries that unnecessary waiting may force her to buy at premium crop prices. On the other hand, if she buys early, future prices could be lower than anticipated. Under these circumstances, the broker would miss an opportunity to economize. Thus, the timing of the purchase poses a delicate management problem.

Formulate this commodity-trading problem in dynamic programming terms.

10. Explain why you agree or disagree with each of the following statements:
   a. The only way to calculate the state probabilities at some future trial is to multiply the corresponding vector at the preceding trial by the transition matrix.
   b. After a large number of trials, the state probabilties are independent of the beginning state of the system.
   c. To calculate an expected value, the decision maker must use the steady-state probabilities.
   d. Dynamic programming problems must be solved by working backward from the last to the first stage in the process.
   e. The stages in a dynamic programming problem can be time periods, phases of a process, or artificially created segments.
   f. The state variable at each stage of a dynamic programming problem is determined by the decision and state at the immediately preceding stage of the process.

Technique Exercises

11. You are given the following matrix of transition probabilities:

$$\begin{pmatrix} .6 & .4 \\ .5 & .5 \end{pmatrix}$$

Assuming that the system started in state 1, draw the tree diagram corresponding to three trials.

12. Suppose that a problem involves the following matrix of transition probabilities:

$$\begin{pmatrix} .7 & .2 & .1 \\ .1 & .8 & .1 \\ .2 & .2 & .6 \end{pmatrix}$$

Assume that the system started in state 3. Draw the tree diagram corresponding to two trials of the system. Show how the tree diagram would differ if we started in state 2.

13. The purchase patterns of two brands of shaving cream can be expressed as a Markov process with the following transition probabilities:

Brand Purchased Last Period	Brand Purchased This Period	
	A	B
A	.85	.15
B	.30	.70

Assume that the purchase probabilities are .5 for brand A and B at time period 0. What are the projected market shares for the two brands at time periods 1 and 2?

14. A machining operation can be expressed as a Markov process with the following transition probabilities:

Operating Condition Last Period	Operating Condition This Period		
	Normal	Variation	Abnormal
Normal	.9	.05	.05
Variation	0	.6	.4
Abnormal	1	0	0

Assume that machining is in state 3 at time period 0. What are the projected operating conditions at time periods 1 and 2?

15. Traffic delays across a major bridge in the San Francisco area can be described by a Markov process with the following transition probabilities:

Driving Conditions in the Last Half Hour	Driving Conditions This Half Hour	
	Delay	No delay
Delay	.6	.4
No delay	.2	.8

Assume that you are a motorist entering the traffic system and you hear a radio report of a traffic delay. What is the probability that there will be a delay for the next hour? What are the steady-state probabilities?

16. A new product was introduced on the market simultaneously by three companies: A, B, and C. Each firm launched its brand in January. At the start, each company had about one third of the market. During the year, the following transition pattern took place:

Brand Purchased at Start	Brand Purchased Now		
	A	B	C
A	.6	.3	.1
B	.2	.5	.3
C	.1	.1	.8

Predict what the long-run market shares will be at the steady state if buying habits do not change.

17. An accounts receivable problem involves the following transition matrix:

$$T = \begin{pmatrix} 1 & 0 & 0 & 0 \\ 0 & 1 & 0 & 0 \\ .2 & 0 & .5 & .3 \\ .1 & .3 & .4 & .2 \end{pmatrix}$$

State (row) 1 is the paid category and state (row) 2 the bad-debt category. Currently, there is $500,000 in state 3 and $1 million in state 4.

a. Determine the times to absorption.

b. Find the probabilities that states 3 and 4 will end up in the absorbing states.

c. How much of the account balances will eventually be paid? How much will end up as bad debt?

18. You are given the following linear integer programming problem:

maximize $\qquad\qquad\qquad Z = 3X_1 + 2X_2 + X_3$

subject to $\qquad\qquad\qquad X_1 + X_2 + X_3 \leq 4$

$$X_1, X_2, X_3 \geq 0 \text{ and integers}$$

Let X_1, X_2, and X_3 represent the stages, the amount allocated for the decision, and the amount available to the state variable in the problem. Use dynamic programming to solve this problem.

19. Refer to Thought Exercise 9. Use dynamic programming to solve the commodity broker's trading problem.

20. A consumer goods retailer sells a durable good with an estimated life of five years. The company must decide on an initial price, which, to be competitive, must be $400, $450, $500, or $550. Its policy is to change prices, if necessary, only once a year. Marketing research indicates that any price increase or decrease should be $50, and the resulting price must be within the competitive range of $400 to $550.

The anticipated yearly profit from the product is given in the following table where entries are in millions of dollars:

	Year				
Price	**1**	**2**	**3**	**4**	**5**
$400	0.5	1	0.75	1.25	2
$450	1	1.25	1.75	2	2.5
$500	1.5	1	0.5	3	2.4
$550	2	1.6	3.2	1	1.9

For example, if the price is $500 in the third year, the company will earn $500,000 profit.

In this problem, each year represents a stage of the process. The states are the existing prices, while the decisions are the new prices. Profits represent the outcomes. Use dynamic programming to find the optimal price policy. That is, determine the price that should be charged for the durable good in each year of its estimated life.

Computer Exercises

21. At a private mental health care clinic, budgets are based primarily on the previous year's activities. Another important determinant is the projected patient load in the coming year. In this regard, patient load is divided into five distinct modes: a mentally ill person not yet in the program, an inpatient at the clinic, an outpatient of the clinic, a recently released patient undergoing periodic checkups, and a rehabilitated person.

Patient movement from one treatment mode to another depends only on the current state of the person. The pattern of movement is described by the probability distribution in the following table:

Mode This Month	Mode Next Month				
	Untreated	Inpatient	Outpatient	Checkup	Rehabitated
Untreated	.97	.02	.01	0	0
Inpatient	0	.35	.47	.12	.06
Outpatient	0	.10	.72	.14	.04
Checkup	0	.01	.07	.84	.08
Rehabitated	0	.005	.015	.03	.95

Clinic administrators estimate that there are currently 40,000 untreated mentally ill people in the community. In addition, the clinic has 50 inpatients, 500 outpatients, 750 recently released patients undergoing periodic checkups, and 4,000 rehabilitated persons.

The administrators seek the number of people in each category over the next 12 months. Also, the current patient load is all the clinic can handle with current staff. Therefore, the administrators want to know if more staff will be needed next year. Use the **Quantitative Management (QM)** software to generate the required information.

22. A large metropolitan airport is served by a variety of automobile rental agencies. These agencies' records indicate that customers switch rentals quite frequently. The pattern is summarized in the following table:

Agency Previous Month	Agency Next Month					
	Atamo	Low Budget	Huntz	Local	Quartz	Small Time
Atamo	.72	.12	.06	.05	.02	.03
Low Budget	.03	.68	.03	.15	.05	.06
Huntz	.02	.01	.91	.02	.03	.01
Local	.15	.10	.05	.55	.10	.05
Quartz	.08	.07	.07	.08	.63	.07
Small Time	.11	.12	.10	.10	.10	.47

Entries in the table give the probabilities of moving between states.

Airport officials want to limit the number of agencies renting automobiles. In the future, the airport will not issue a license to any agency that cannot maintain a 30 percent market share. Use the **QM** software to determine which agencies will continue operations at the airport in the long run.

23. County commissioners are evaluating the effectiveness of various public transportation alternatives. A survey revealed the probabilities summarized in the table on page 844.

Currently, 20,000 people use the bus, 15,000 utilize light rail, and the remaining 60,000 commuters are divided equally between the car pool and private car states.

As part of the evaluation process, the commissioners want to determine the number of days that will elapse before changes occur in the transportation alternatives. Use the **QM** software to determine the passage times.

This Day	Next Day Transportation			
Transportation	Bus	Light Rail	Car Pool	Private Car
Bus	.52	.18	.21	.09
Light Rail	.16	.43	.34	.07
Car Pool	.02	.03	.85	.10
Private Car	.03	.03	.02	.92

24. A company purchases electric power almost equally from plants in Fawn Delta (FD), Spring Dover (SD), and New Shrewsburg (NS). For mutual protection, the three plants link their transmission systems. The purchasing company cannot afford power failures. Thus, the president has asked the chief engineer to determine the likelihoods of simultaneous power outages from the three plants. Available information suggested that the state of the linked power system on a given day depended only on the state of the system on the previous day. Using engineering estimates, historical records, and experience-based intuition, the chief engineer developed the following transition probabilities:

This Day Power Failure	Next Day Power Failure							
	All Plants	FD	SD	ND	FD and SD	FD and NS	SD and NS	No Plants
All Plants	.01	.05	.15	.08	.01	.01	.02	.67
FD	.02	.72	.02	.04	.10	.08	.01	.01
SD	.01	.03	.61	.05	.15	.02	.12	.01
NS	.03	.02	.02	.75	.03	.10	.04	.01
FD and SD	.07	.10	.10	.02	.51	.11	.06	.03
FD and NS	.06	.09	.03	.12	.10	.45	.10	.05
SD and NS	.09	.02	.08	.12	.05	.08	.54	.02
No Plants	.01	.05	.04	.03	.02	.01	.01	.83

Currently, all plants are operating.

   Management is interested in the number of days that will elapse before changes occur in the reliability of the power system. Use the **QM** software to determine the passage times.

25. The director of personnel at the local bank has noticed that yearly shifts in the status of employees seem to follow a Markov process with the following transition probabilities:

Status This Year	Status Next Year				
	Same Position	Promotion	Retire	Quit	Terminated
Same Position	.65	.15	.05	.10	.05
Promotion	.80	.10	.05	.04	.01
Retire	0	0	1	0	0
Quit	0	0	0	1	0
Terminated	0	0	0	0	1

Currently, the bank has 400 employees. Among these employees, 300 have been in the same position for the past year.

The director would like to project the number of employees, in each category, who eventually will retire, quit, or be terminated. She also seeks the times to absorption into the nonactive states. Use the **QM** software to generate the desired information.

Applications Exercises

26. The population department of a government statistical agency has done a study of population mobility in the West. This study reveals several yearly trends among urban and suburban/rural families. It shows that 40 percent of the families in an urban location at the beginning of the year move to a suburban/rural location during the year. Also, 30 percent of the original suburban/rural families move to urban locations during the year. The population distribution is currently 30 percent urban and 70 percent suburban/rural. If the trends continue, what will the distribution look like in three years?

27. In January, Slick Petroleum, the nation's largest oil company, was issued a warning by the Federal Trade Commission (FTC). Slick was told that if its market share went above 60 percent, the FTC would initiate antitrust action. At that time, Slick had 40 percent of the market. Its chief competitor, Glide, had 20 percent of the market, and the rest of the market was divided among other companies. Slick's market analysts were able to develop the following data on consumer purchase behavior:

- Slick retains 90 percent of its customers from year to year. It loses 5 percent to Glide but gains 20 percent from others.

- Glide retains 70 percent of its customers from year to year. It loses 10 percent to Slick but gains 20 percent from others.

Will Slick face antitrust action? If so, when?

28. Lake Telephone Company is a private system that services a small lakeside community. It is well known for the unreliable nature of its equipment on snowy days. This Christmas Eve began with a snowstorm in the area served by Lake. The company's engineering department quickly developed the following data on the likelihood of the trunk lines being in various states from one minute to the next:

- If the lines are currently open, there is a 50 percent chance that they will be open the next minute. In addition, the probability is .2 that the lines will be busy the next minute.

- When the lines are currently busy, the probability is .7 that they will be busy the next minute. Also, there is a 20 percent likelihood that they will be down the next minute.

- If the lines are currently down, there is a 10 percent chance that they will be down the next minute. In addition, the probability is .6 that they will be busy the next minute.

Of course, many calls are made on Christmas Eve. Thus, if the phones are out of order on that day, the company will incur a large loss of customer good will. Lake's accounting department estimates that a busy line on Christmas Eve will eventually cost the company $10 per minute in lost revenue. A down line will involve a $50-per-minute loss.

How much lost revenue should Lake expect under these circumstances?

29. Parkview Hospital specializes in cosmetic surgery and serves an area where there is zero population growth. From past history, it is known that each month about .0005 of the 500,000 people in its service area are admitted for cosmetic surgery. By the end of the first month, a patient has an 80 percent probability of being released from the hospital. In addition, there is a 15 percent likelihood that he or she will stay another month and a 5 percent chance of death. For those who stay longer, 95 percent are released by the end of the second month and 5 percent die.

The administration is making long-range staff and facility plans. Thus, it would like to predict the eventual number of patients in the hospital who will have had cosmetic surgery within one month. Also, it wants to project the eventual number of patients in their second month of recovery and the number of surgical deaths each month. Find this information.

30. Building Blocks Industries, a manufacturer of prefabricated kitchen cabinets, employs three classes of machine operators, coded 1, 2, and 3. All new employees are hired as class 1 and, through a system of promotion, may work up to a higher classification. Promotions depend on employee productivity in the preceding quarter. Historically, class 1 has included 50 percent of Building's 500 operators and class 2 another 30 percent. Several months ago, the company adopted a union-sponsored system that groups operators into voluntary, self-supervised work groups. Production records kept since the reorganization have enabled the plant manager to compile some data on quarter-to-quarter changes in employee productivity. The data show the following:

- Forty percent of the class 1 operators remain in this category from quarter to quarter, while 50 percent move to class 2.

- Forty percent of the class 2 operators remain in this category from one period to the next, while 40 percent move to class 3.

- Eighty percent of the class 3 operators remain in this category from quarter to quarter, but 10 percent move back to class 2.

Operators earn an average or $1000 per month. Efficiency records indicate that there is a productivity loss of 30 percent associated with class 1 operators, 20 percent for class 2, and 10 percent for class 3.

How many employees will eventually be in each productivity classification? Can Building Blocks expect any monetary benefit from the reorganization? If so, how much?

31. Klamath Industries operates a tree farm with 10,000 spruces for experimental purposes. Each year Klamath allows nonprofit organizations to select and cut trees for transplanting. The farm protects small trees (usually less than 6 feet tall). Currently, 4,000 spruces are classified as protected trees. However, even though a tree is available for cutting in a given year, it may not be selected until some future time. Some trees also die during the year. Of course, once a tree is cut or lost to disease, it will no longer be available in the future.

Based on past records, Klamath's management has found the following trends:
a. Of the spruces too small for cutting this year, 10 percent will be cut, 10 percent will die, and 70 percent will again be too small next year.

b. Of the available spruces not cut this year, 60 percent will be cut, 10 percent will die, and 30 percent will again be available next year.

How many of the farm's 10,000 trees will eventually be sold and how many will be lost?

32. A diplomat can carry an attaché case with no more than 10 pounds of government documents and supporting material. The weights of some potential contents and their diplomatic values (in points) are given in the following table:

Item	Weight (Pounds)	Diplomatic Value (Points)
Coding device	5	20
Trade book	2	10
Address list	1	30
Computer	8	15
Telephone	3	40

What should the diplomat carry to maximize total value?

33. Gemini Enterprises is making its annual allocation of salespersons to territitories. A total of five salespeople are available for assignment to the three territories. The following table gives the sales revenues (in thousands of dollars) that correspond to each potential assignment. What assignment policy will maximize total revenue?

Salespersons	Territory		
	East	West	South
0	20	40	30
1	140	100	40
2	180	120	20
3	240	110	100
4	170	90	130
5	80	70	150

34. Giant Manufacturing Company (GMC) produces custom heating and air-conditioning equipment for large industrial organizations. After receiving a work request, GMC must retool the manufacturing apparatus, assign personnel, and schedule job activities. The equipment is then manufactured to the order specifications, delivered to the customer, and installed on the premises. Typically, the setup costs involve a $100,000 expense for every work request. In addition, it costs GMC $40,000 to manufacture, deliver, and install each piece of equipment.

Currently, GMC has a contract to provide equipment for a national shoe distributor with new facilities in six different locations. The contract calls for the delivery of two units in each month from April through June. Any excess output can be stored at a monthly cost of $6,000 per unit. However, GMC does not want any inventory at the end of the contract in June.

Management wants to find the production schedule that will minimize the total cost of providing the contracted equipment. What schedule do you recommend? Explain.

For Further Reading

Markov Methodology

Grassman, W. K. *Stochastic Systems for Management*. New York: Elsevier North-Holland, 1981.

Gross, D., and D. R. Miller. "The Randomization Techniques as a Modeling Tool and Solution Procedure for Transient Markov Processes." *Operations Research* (March–April 1984):343.

Isaacson, D. L., and R. W. Madsen. *Markov Chains: Theory and Applications*. New York: Wiley, 1976.

Kemeny, J. G., and J. L. Snell. *Finite Markov Chains*. New York: Springer-Verlag, 1976.

Markov Applications

Albright, S. C., and W. Winston. "Markov Models of Advertising and Pricing Decisions." *Operations Research* (July–August 1979):668.

Anthony, T. F., and B. W. Taylor. "A Stochastic Model for Analysis of Variations in Air Pollution Levels." *Decision Sciences* (April 1976):305.

Chazan, D., and S. Gal. "A Markovian Model for a Perishable Product Inventory." *Management Science* (January 1977):512.

Chapman, C. B., and D. F. Cooper. "Risk Engineering: Basic Controlled Internal and Memory Models." *Journal of the Operational Research Society* (January 1983):51.

Gavish, B., and P. J. Sweitzer. "The Markovian Queue with Bounded Waiting Time." *Management Science* (August 1977):1349.

Glen, J. J. "Mathematical Models in Farm Planning: A Survey." *Operations Research* (September–October 1987):638.

Golabi, K., et al. "A Statewide Pavement Management System." *Interfaces* (December 1982):5.

Gross, D., et al. "A Network Decomposition Approach for Approximating the Steady-State Behavior of Markovian Multi-Echelon Reparable Item Inventory Systems." *Management Science* (November 1987):1453.

Hauser, J. R., and K. J. Wisniewski. "Dynamic Analysis of Consumer Response to Marketing Strategies." *Management Science* (May 1982):455.

Kalberg, J. G., and A. Saunders. "Markov Chain Approaches to the Analysis of Payment Behavior of Retail Credit Customers." *Financial Management* (Summer 1983):5.

Karson, M. J. "Confidence Intervals for Absorbing Markov Chain Probabilities Applied to Loan Portfolios." *Decision Sciences* (January 1976):10.

Mahon, B. H., and R. J. M. Bailey, "A Proposed Improved Replacement Policy for Army Vehicles," *Operational Research Quarterly* 26, no. 3 (1975):477–94.

Mamer, J. W. "Successive Approximations for Finite Horizon, Semi-Markov Decision Processes with Application to Asset Liquidation." *Operations Research* (July–August 1986):638.

Rosenthal, R. E., et al. "Stochastic Dynamic Location Analysis." *Management Science* (February 1978):645.

Swersey, A. J. "A Markovian Decision Model for Deciding How Many Fire Companies to Dispatch." *Management Science* (April 1982):352.

Triverdi, V., et al. "A Semi-Markov Model for Primary Health Care Manpower Supply Prediction." *Management Science* (February 1987):149.

White, D. J. "Real Applications of Markov Decision Processes." *Interfaces* (November–December 1985):73.

Wort, D. H., and J. K. Zumwalt. "The Trade Discount Decision: A Markov Chain Approach." *Decision Sciences* (Winter 1985):43.

Denardo, E. V. *Dynamic Programming: Theory and Application*. Englewood Cliffs, NJ: Prentice-Hall, 1975.

Dreyfus, S. E., and A. M. Law. *The Art and Theory of Dynamic Programming*. New York: Academic Press, 1977.

Hastings, N. A. J. *Dynamic Programming with Managerial Applications*. New York: Crane, Russak, 1973.

Larson, R. E., and J. L. Casti. *Principles of Dynamic Programming*. New York: Marcel Dekker, 1978.

Sondik, E. J. "The Optimal Control of Partially Observable Markov Processes over the Infinite Horizon: Discounted Costs." *Operations Research* (March–April 1978):282.

White, C. C., and H. H. El-Deib. "Parameter Imprecision in Finite State, Finite Action Dynamic Programs." *Operations Research* (January-February 1986):120.

Dynamic Programming Applications

Chao, H., and A. S. Manne. "Oil Stockpiles and Import Reductions: A Dynamic Programming Approach." *Operations Research* (July–August 1983):632.

Dykstra, D. P. *Mathematical Programming for Natural Resource Management*. New York: McGraw-Hill, 1984.

Fuller, J. D., and R. G. Vickson. "The Optimal Timing of New Plants for Oil from the Alberta Tar Sands." *Operations Research* (September–October 1987):704.

Goldwerger, J. "Dynamic Programming for a Stochastic Markovian Process with an Application to the Mean Variance Models." *Management Science* (February 1977):612.

Lee, T. K. "A Nonsequential Research and Development Search Model." *Management Science* (August 1982):900.

Lembersky, M. R. and U. H. Chi, "Weyerhauser Decision Simulator Improves Timer Profits," *Interfaces* (January–February 1986):6–15.

Mendelson, H., and Y. Amihud. "Optimal Consumption Policy under Uncertain Income." *Management Science* (June 1982):683.

Oren, S. S., and S. H. Wan. "Optimal Strategic Petroleum Reserve Policies: A Steady-State Analysis." *Management Science* (January 1986):14.

Psaraftis, H. N., and B. O. Ziogas. "A Tactical Decision Algorithm for the Optimal Dispatching of Oil Spill Cleanup Equipment." *Management Science* (December 1985):1475.

Rosenblatt, M. J. "The Dynamics of Plant Layout." *Management Science* (January 1986):76.

Rosenthal, R. E., et al. "Stochastic Dynamic Location Analysis." *Management Science* (February 1978):645.

Sarin, S. C., and W. Ei Benni. "Determination of Optimal Pumping Policy of a Municipal Water Plant." *Interfaces* (April 1982):43.

Stoecker, A. L. et al. "A Linear Dynamic Programming Approach to Irrigation System Management with Depleting Groundwater." *Management Science* (April 1985):422.

Tapiero, C. S. "A Stochastic Model of Consumer Behavior and Optimal Advertising." *Management Science* (September 1982):1054.

Waddell, R. "A Model for Equipment Replacement Decisions and Policies." *Interfaces* (August 1983):1.

Williams, J. F. "A Hybrid Algorithm for Simultaneous Scheduling of Production and Distribution in Multi-Echelon Structures." *Management Science* (January 1983):77.

Case: The Federal Housing Agency

The Federal Housing Agency (FHA) guarantees mortgages or trust deeds for qualifying individuals purchasing residences. Although most insurees make their payments on time, a certain percentage are always overdue. Some debtors never pay, and their residences must be subjected to foreclosure proceedings. The FHA's experience has been that when a mortgage is two or more payments behind, the residence generally will have to be foreclosed. At the beginning of each month, the mortgage officer reviews each account and classifies it as paid, current, overdue, or a foreclosure. Current accounts are those being paid on time, while the overdue category refers to an account that is one payment behind. Agency records include the Mortgage Transition Report, shown in Table 16.11.

Each entry represents the probability that an account dollar in a particular category last month will be in a particular category this month. The loan officer also receives the FHA Mortgage Account Summary presented in Table 16.12.

Table 16.11   **FHA Mortgage Transition Report**

Last Month's Account Status	This Month's Account Status			
	Paid	Current	Overdue	Foreclosure
Paid	1	0	0	0
Current	.2	.6	.2	0
Overdue	.1	.3	.4	.2
Foreclosure	0	0	0	1

Table 16.12   **FHA Mortgage Account Summary**

Account Status	Current Number of Accounts	Current Accounts Receivable Balance
Paid	20,000	$0
Current	500,000	$20 billion
Overdue	150,000	$200 million
Foreclosure	30,000	$100 million

The loan officer has requested a report with the following information:

1.   The probabilities that current and overdue accounts eventually end up paid or as foreclosures

2.   The number of accounts that will eventually end up in each mortgage category

3.   The dollar amount that will eventually be paid and the amount that will end up in the foreclosure category

Prepare this report.

On the basis of the report, the FHA will consider instituting a new credit policy that involves a discount for prompt payment. The policy is expected to increase from .2 to .3 the chance of a current account becoming paid. It will have other effects as well. The probability of a current account becoming overdue will decrease from .2 to .1. Also, the new policy will increase from .3 to .4 the likelihood of an overdue account becoming current. The probability of an overdue account becoming a foreclosure will decrease from .2 to .1.

The new credit policy will involve a cost, including discounts, of $50 million. Should the FHA implement the policy? Explain. Suppose the FHA could identify the relationship between the account states and credit policy. How could such information be used to determine the optimal credit policy?

Part VI

Simulation

IN previous parts of the text, the discussion has focused on the formulation and development of formal mathematical models. Such models were solved in an analytical or mathematical manner. Frequently, the analytical methods were in the form of algorithms that yielded best, or optimal, solutions to the problems.

On the other hand, there are many problems that become too complex and difficult to solve with existing analytical solution procedures. In these cases, the only viable means for analysis may be to experiment with the actual system or a model of the system. This next part presents a methodology for performing such experimentation.

Chapter 17 outlines the simulation approach. It describes the nature of the process and shows how to incorporate uncertainty and risk into the analysis. The chapter concludes with a presentation on the role of the computer in the experimentation process.

After reading this part of the text, you should be able to:

- Understand the nature of simulation.
- Identify a simulation modeling framework.
- Develop simulations by hand and with the aid of a computer.
- Use simulation for decision making.
- Recognize the advantages and limitations of the approach.

The presentation will also prepare you for more advanced studies in management and corporate planning.

Simulation

Chapter Outline

Learning Objectives

- Understand the nature of simulation
- Know when to use simulation
- Learn how to simulate uncontrollable inputs
- Use simulation for decision making
- Simulate inventory and queuing systems by hand and with the aid of a computer

Riding the Canadian Rails

IN the late 1970s, traffic volumes were predicted to double during the 1980s on Canadian National Railway's already congested single track main line. Faced with this problem, the company embarked on the Plant Expansion Program (PEP) in 1980 to provide the capacity needed to handle the forecasted traffic while maintaining existing service levels. Proposals requested C$2.2 billion in capital expenditures during the decade, of which C$1.3 billion would provide double track over selected Western Region routes.

As part of the PEP, a transportation research team was formed and charged with determining the most cost-effective method of phasing in double track. This team developed two simulation models—the Signal Wake Model, created in nine months at a cost of C$50,000, and the Route Capacity Model, formulated in 15 months at a cost of C$250,000—to evaluate the relative effect of the many factors that influence main line capacity. When used together, the models predict train delay under various track and signal designs, operating methods, and traffic scenarios.

The simulation results indicated that the PEP original expansion plans would not be cost-effective. Instead, these results suggested that management should implement capacity expansion improvements that included closely spaced intermediate signals and strategically located sections of double track. By adopting the suggested improvements, CN Rail was able to reduce the original double track requirements by 128 miles. Accountants estimate that the reduction has saved the company about C$350 million in capital expenditures.

Source: N. Welch and J. Gussow, "Expansion of Canadian National Railway's Line Capacity," *Interfaces* (January–February 1986): 51–64.

Past chapters have presented many techniques designed to aid decision making. Most of these techniques can be classified as analytical procedures. That is, a mathematical analysis is used to optimize some criterion (as in linear programming) or predict the behavior of a system (as in Markov analysis). However, many problems are too complex to solve using existing analytical solution procedures. In these situations, the only feasible method of analysis may be *simulation*—using a model to re-create an actual situation and then studying the system's characteristics and behavior by experimenting with the model. As the Canadian National Railways vignette demonstrates, the organization can reap substantial benefits from the use of this simulation approach.

This chapter introduces the concepts and procedures of simulation. In the first section, we study the nature of the simulation process. We develop a model, perform a simulation, and interpret the results. The second section shows how to incorporate probabilistic inputs into the analysis. It describes the role of probability distributions and random selection in simulation. Finally, we present the computer simulation approach. We discuss the use of computer-generated random numbers, the role of the computer in the simulation process, and the advantages and limitations of the approach.

Applications. In this chapter, the following applications appear in text, examples, and exercises:

- bus routing
- business taxation
- cash management
- construction financing
- cost management
- credit management
- employee absenteeism
- floral production
- inventory management
- machine failure

- making or buying components
- market segmentation
- mortgage banking
- oil exploration
- personnel management
- price competition
- quality control
- queuing system design
- university admissions
- water management

17.1 THE NATURE OF SIMULATION

Essentially, simulation is a technique for conducting experiments. In this approach, the decision maker first builds a device that imitates (acts like) the real situation. Then, by experimenting with the device, the decision maker can study the characteristics and behavior of the real situation.

Some simulations use physical devices. For example, an aircraft manufacturer can learn much about the aerodynamic properties of a new design by imitating (simulating) flight conditions in a wind tunnel. An analogy is another type of device. As an illustration, students can simulate the decision process of actual managers by analyzing the cases in a course on problem solving. Also, mathematical models can be used. Suppose, for instance, that government economists have developed an equation that relates gross national product (GNP) to various business indicators. They can then use the equation to simulate the economic effects of various changes in the indicators. In this chapter, we concentrate on simulations that use tables, charts, and mathematical devices.

Motivation for Simulation

There are several reasons for using simulation. One has already been identified: It is well suited for problems that are difficult or impossible to solve mathematically. Simulation also is relatively easy to understand, offers a controlled experiment, compresses time, and serves as a mode for training decision makers.

What If Analysis. An optimization model considers all possible values of the decision variables and selects the values of those variables that best meet specified criteria. Such a model then is designed to answer the question "What best?"

Problems that involve sequences of interrelated elements, several stochastic components, or unusual mathematical operations are often too complex to be solved by analytical optimization models. In other cases, it may be possible to solve an oversimplified version of the problem with an analytical solution procedure, but the oversimplification may be unrealistic. Under these circumstances, the decision maker may prefer to select a set of decisions (perhaps identified through experience and judgment or with an analytical approach), simulate the results, and observe what happens to the criteria. Simulation is designed to provide such "What if?" analysis.

Ease of Use. The simulation approach does not require a great deal of mathematical sophistication. A nontechnical manager who understands the sequence of activities and operations involved in the problem can help develop a simulation model that replicates this sequence. Electronic spreadsheets (such as *LOTUS 1-2-3* and *MULTIPLAN*) and English-like modeling languages (such as *IFPS* or *EXPRESS*) even enable many managers to quickly formulate some models (or prototypes) without assistance at their workstations. Since the model simply describes the problem as seen by management, it will be readily understandable to the decision maker. This comprehension and management's involvement in the development process will facilitate the implementation of the simulation model.

Controlled Experimentation. The simulation model explicitly identifies the important relationships involved in the actual problem. Managers can therefore use the model to systematically and consistently evaluate proposed policies under a variety of simulated conditions and to isolate the effects of key elements on the simulated system. Such experiments can be carried out without disturbing the actual system. This capability reduces the chances of implementing a poorly designed policy that could lead to catastrophic economic, political, or social consequences.

Compressing Time. Simulation makes it possible to compress time. An experiment that ordinarily would require months or years to perform on the actual system can be accomplished in seconds or minutes with computer simulation.

Management Laboratory. Simulation provides a useful and convenient management laboratory. It can illustrate a model or allow the decision maker to better comprehend a process. Training games enable managers to better understand the interrelationships within a decision setting, to test their understanding, and to develop their decision-making skills.

Simulation Forms. For the above reasons, there is a high level of simulation use in industry and government. Most studies show that 85 percent or more of surveyed organizations currently utilize the methodology. Typically, simulation takes the forms presented in Table 17.1.

Limitations. Simulation has its limitations. It is a trial and error approach that generates a solution representing the best action among those specified for evaluation. Although decision makers are usually able to identify reasonable policies for evaluation, better actions might exist but remain unrecognized by management. Simulation, then, cannot guarantee an optimal problem solution.

Table 17.1   **Simulation Forms**

Form	Description	Area
Artificial intelligence	Programming a computer to imitate human thought	Financial analysis Management behavior
Business operations	Simulating business operations for planning and control purposes	Product marketing Production management Inventory management Service systems Finance
Corporate planning models	Models that link decision making within an organization to conditions in the firm's environment	Fire department policy Strategic planning
Heuristic programming	Using step-by-step procedures to arrive at feasible and satisfactory, though not necessarily optimal, solutions for complex problems	Land-use planning Mental health Alloy processing Tree farming
Management games	A contrived situation that imbeds participants in a simulated environment, where they make decisions and analyze results	Marketing Training Leadership
System simulation	Modeling the dynamics of very large business or economic systems	University retirement Regulatory performance Tar sands mining International relations Medicine

In addition, simulation can be time consuming and costly. It takes many person-days (or perhaps months and years) to develop ad hoc models, even with the aid of special computer languages and tools. Because of poor experimental design, inexperienced users may approach a total (rather than limited) enumeration of possible alternatives and, in the process, far exceed time and cost budgets.

Since simulation is relatively easy to use, there also can be an overreliance on the methodology when other approaches (including analytical procedures) are more appropriate. Moreover, there are technical issues in the design, validation, and estimation of simulation models that are complex at best and unresolved at worst.

Simulation Process

Simulation studies typically utilize the process outlined in Figure 17.1.

Defining the Problem. The first step in simulation is to clearly define the problem, including the study's objectives and the reasons for using simulation. As part of this phase, management should define both the attributes of interest and the measures of performance. For example, a turnpike commission might seek the tollbooth configuration

Figure 17.1   **Simulation Process**

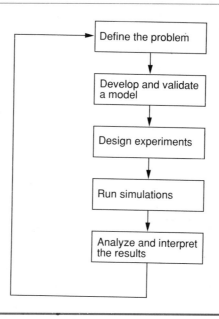

(number of booths and physical layout) that results in the least congestion and lowest cost. When simulating different configurations, attributes of interest might include customer waiting time, idle time of tollbooth operators, and the time to service customers.

In this phase, the decision maker also should specify the scope of the study and the level of detail needed to obtain the desired results. For example, if a department store is going to simulate sales patterns, will the scope encompass all departments for every day of operation or just selected departments on peak days? Will the level of detail include factors such as competitors' sales, demographic information on consumers, community events, and the like?

Proper problem definition will help managers develop accurate estimates of the cost and time needed to complete the simulation. In addition, it will provide guidance for model development, data collection, and the design of simulation experiments.

Developing the Model. The second step in simulation is to develop a model that will achieve the intended results. Sometimes, the decision maker knows the values of the model's uncontrollable inputs, in which case we have a **deterministic simulation**. More often, the situation will involve a stochastic or **probabilistic simulation**—a case in which the uncontrollable inputs are random variables. Uncontrollable and controllable inputs can be *discrete* (have integer outcomes) and can be described by a count of the number of occurrences. Alternatively, these inputs can be *continuous* (divisible into fractional values) and can be measured rather than counted.

In its initial form, the model identifies the key elements of the problem and their interrelationships. This base model's parameters are estimated with data gathered from direct observation or historical records. Such parameters and the assumptions that underlie the model should be validated by the simulation's users. These people have the necessary knowledge, and their involvement in model design will facilitate implementation later in the process.

When there is an existing system, historical data should be processed through the base simulation model. Results should be compared with known system performance under identical circumstances, and statistical methodologies should be used to determine whether the simulation generates the same results as the real system. The model should be revised as needed to eliminate any major discrepancies.

If historical data is unavailable, knowledgeable individuals (users and other experts) can be asked to identify system performance that would be reasonable under specified conditions. Simulation results then can be validated against this "reasonable" performance.

Designing Experiments. In general, the goal of a simulation study is to learn about a system's behavior. To achieve this goal in a timely manner and at a reasonable expense, management must carefully design the simulation experiment.

The experiment must be designed in a way that will provide the desired answers to management's questions. An important design decision is to establish the **initial conditions** for the experiment—the assumptions about the state of the system at the start of the simulation. For example, in the department store situation, should we assume that the store is initially empty, or should we assume some normal level of activity? The choice of initial conditions can have a significant effect on the length of time needed for the system to reach a steady state.

Along with initial conditions, decisions must be made about the parameter settings. For example, in the turnpike situation, what should be the parameters for the time between arrivals at a tollbooth and the service time? Should these parameters be modified by the time of day and day of the week?

Running the Simulations. After developing a suitable experimental design, we are ready to actually perform (run) the simulation. In a deterministic simulation, there will be a single set of values for the uncontrollable inputs. Since repeat runs with these values will generate identical results, management need make only one run for each specified policy (set of controllable inputs).

In a probabilistic simulation, uncontrollable inputs will be drawn from a subjective, empirical, or theoretical distribution (such as the Poisson or normal distribution). Depending on the approach, such draws may not repeat the same sequence of these inputs. Simulation results then will differ because of purely random changes in the uncontrollable inputs and because of conscious policy changes. To isolate the unique effects of the policy changes, the decision maker must also statistically account for (estimate) the purely random changes. A number of simulation runs for each specified policy will be necessary to accomplish this task.

An important decision is to fix the length of each simulation run. Often, this length will be stated in terms of the number of simulation observations. Statistical methodologies should be used to determine the number that will provide sample statistics within specified maximum errors from the corresponding population parameters.

There are other approaches. The simulation could be run for a *fixed interval*. For example, the turnpike might run its tollbooth simulation for 300 hours of operation.

Alternatively, the simulation could be run until the occurrence of an appropriate *next event* (such as a machine breakdown or a security alarm). Additional possibilities include running the simulation until the system reaches steady-state conditions or until the computations reach a computer time/expense budget.

Analyzing Results. The final step in the simulation process is to analyze and interpret the results. Analysis largely involves comparing the simulated outcomes from the specified policies. In probabilistic simulation, there will be a distribution of outcomes for each specified policy. Descriptive statistics (such as the mean and standard deviation) then will be needed to measure the outcomes' expected values and, where possible, ranges over which the actual values may fall. Also, statistical methodologies should be used to determine whether observed outcome differences are due to policy changes or chance.

In most cases, the results of the analysis provide the decision maker with information sufficient to select the best policy among those examined (which is not necessarily the optimal problem solution). Sometimes, the analysis suggests that further evaluation is needed before a conclusion can be reached. Such evaluation may require management to redefine the problem and then repeat the rest of the simulation process (as indicated by the feedback loop in Figure 17.1).

Simulation Methodology

A standard methodology is used to implement the simulation process. It can be illustrated with Management Situation 17.1.

Management Situation 17.1

Price Competition

Star Motors, Inc. will compete with Caste Cars Corporation in selling the Saver, a new energy-efficient automobile. Industry officials estimate that 1,000 Savers will be sold in Star's area annually. The Saver has a suggested retail price of $5,000 and a $4,000 dealer cost.

Star's management wants to determine the price that will result in the largest profit from Saver sales. The decision is difficult because Star's market share depends on Caste's price. If both dealers have the same price, Star will get 40 percent of the market. However, when Caste has the lower price, Star loses 4 percent of this share for every $100 price differential. On the other hand, when Caste has the higher price, Star gets 40 percent of the market plus 1 percent for every $100 price difference. A further complication is that Caste typically changes prices from week to week without notice.

During a strategy-planning meeting, Star's management proposed that the company experiment with a variety of prices above the $4,000 dealer cost. For example, Star might charge $4,100 for a while, maybe three or four weeks, and then observe the resulting sales and profits. Next, the dealer could try $4,200 for the same length of time, then perhaps $4,300, and so on. Finally, management would select the price that resulted in the largest profit.

While Star's approach seems logical, it would be very time-consuming. It would take four or five months to collect profit data on only five trial price alternatives. Also, Star could experience several weeks of low profits or even losses if some of the trial prices were poor decisions. What the dealer needs is a way to carry out the trial and error procedure without actually setting the prices in practice. Simulation can be used to experiment with prices in just this manner.

Simulation Model. There will be 1,000 Savers sold in the area annually, or about

$$\frac{1{,}000 \text{ units}}{50 \text{ weeks}} = 20 \text{ Savers per week}$$

Star's sales will equal its market share, denoted as M, times this amount, or $20M$.

Profit, labeled Z, is the difference between price, denoted as P, and the $4,000 dealer cost multiplied by sales. We can express this relationship as follows:

$$Z = (P - \$4{,}000)20M = 20(P - \$4{,}000)M$$

You can see that Star's profit from the Saver depends on its price P and market share M.

Market share depends on the competitive price structure. When both dealers have the same price, Star gets a 40 percent share. That is,

$$M = .4 \quad \text{if } P = C$$

where C = Caste's price for the Saver. When Caste's price is lower, Star's 40 percent share is reduced by 4 percent for every $100 price difference. This can be expressed as follows:

$$M = .4 - .04\left(\frac{P - C}{\$100}\right) \quad \text{if } P > C$$

Share when prices are equal	Share lost for each $100 price difference	Number of $100 price differences

On the other hand, Star gains 1 percent when it has the price advantage, or

$$M = .4 + .01\left(\frac{C - P}{\$100}\right) \quad \text{if } P < C$$

Share when prices are equal	Share gained for each $100 price difference	Number of $100 price differences

These equations form Star's profit model for Saver sales. A schematic representation is presented in Figure 17.2.

Star's objective is to maximize weekly profit from Saver sales. The controllable input is Star's price P, and the uncontrollable element is Caste's price C.

Figure 17.2   **Profit Model for Star Motors**

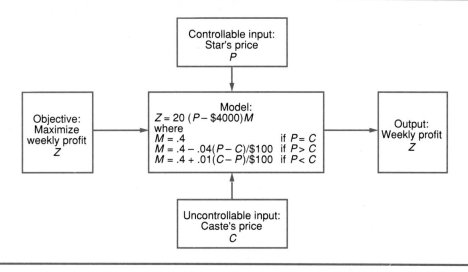

Flowchart. Management uses the model (Figure 17.2) to develop some numerical simulations of the dealer competition. A diagram such as Figure 17.3 can greatly facilitate the process. This diagram, which shows the sequence of operations and computations required by the simulation model, is known as a **flowchart**. In a flowchart, the symbols have the following interpretations:

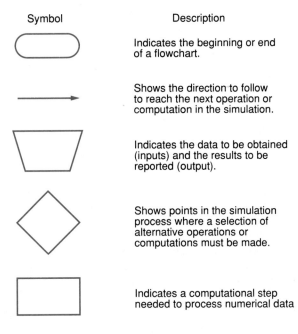

Symbol	Description
	Indicates the beginning or end of a flowchart.
	Shows the direction to follow to reach the next operation or computation in the simulation.
	Indicates the data to be obtained (inputs) and the results to be reported (output).
	Shows points in the simulation process where a selection of alternative operations or computations must be made.
	Indicates a computational step needed to process numerical data

Figure 17.3   Flowchart of Star's Price Competition

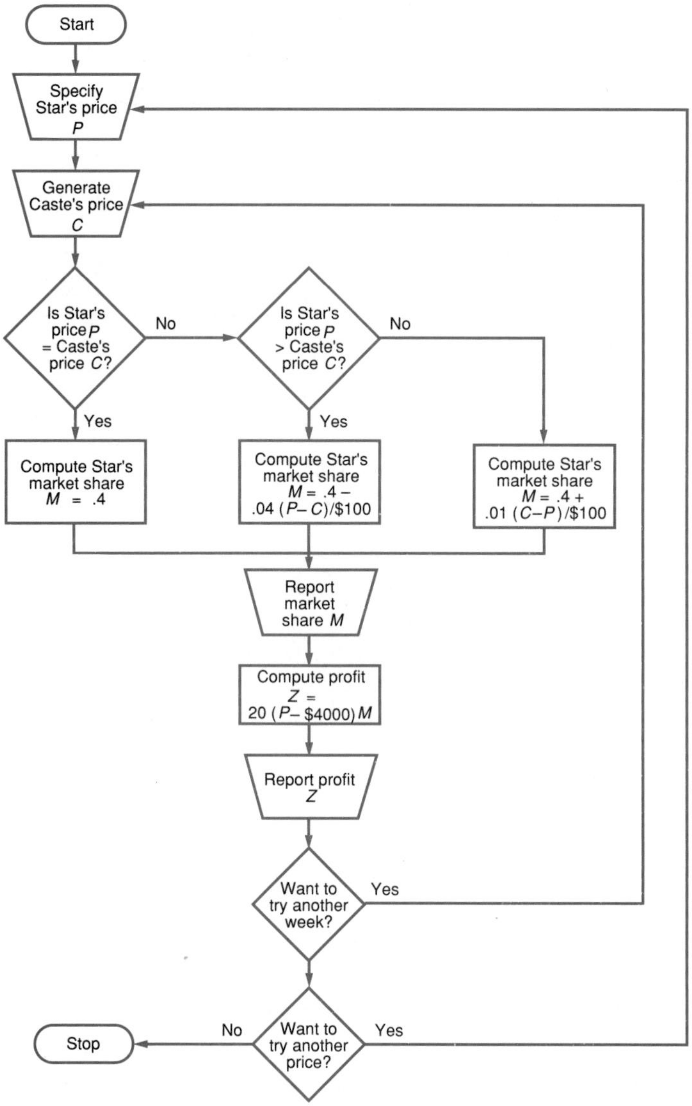

Simulation Runs. Star initiates the simulation by fixing its price at a trial value. Suppose, for instance, that Star sells the Saver for $P = \$4,100$ this week.

Next, the company must generate a hypothetical competitor's price C. Although Star does not know this price in advance, management can identify Caste's potential price range. Assuming that the competitor will not sell at a loss, Caste's minimum price is the $\$4,000$ dealer cost. Also, if Star assumes that customers will not pay more than the

Table 17.2   **Simulation Results When Star's Price is** $P = \$4,100$

Week	Caste's Price C ($)	Star's Market Share M	Star's Profit Z ($)	Star's Total Profit ($)
1	4,000	.36	720	720
2	4,200	.41	820	1,540
3	4,100	.40	800	2,340
4	4,400	.43	860	3,200
5	4,300	.42	840	4,040
6	4,700	.46	920	4,960
7	5,000	.49	980	5,940
8	4,500	.44	880	6,820
9	4,600	.45	900	7,720
10	4,800	.47	940	8,660

suggested retail price, then there is a maximum $C = \$5,000$. Thus, Caste's price will range from $4,000 to $5,000.

Now Star can find out what will happen if Caste's price is some value in this range. For example, what if Caste's price is $C = \$4,000$ this week? Since $P = \$4,100$, Star has the higher price. As shown in Figure 17.3, this means that Star's market share can be found with the expression

$$M = .4 - .04\left(\frac{P - C}{\$100}\right)$$

In this case

$$M = .4 - .04\left(\frac{\$4,100 - \$4,000}{\$100}\right) = .36$$

and Star's profit this week is

$$Z = 20(P - \$4,000)M = 20(\$4,100 - \$4,000).36 = \$720.$$

A simulation for one week of the dealer competition has now been completed. To simulate another week at the same price P, Star must generate a new Caste price C. In the second week of the competition, suppose that Caste's price is $C = \$4,200$. Since Star's price is still $P = \$4,100$, Caste has the higher price. As shown in Figure 17.3, this means that Star's market share can be found with the expression

$$M = .4 + .01\left(\frac{C - P}{\$100}\right)$$

In this case,

$$M = .4 + .01\left(\frac{\$4,200 - \$4,100}{\$100}\right) = .41$$

and Star's resulting profit is

$$Z = 20(P - \$4,000)M = 20(\$4,100 - \$4,000).41 = \$820.$$

Table 17.3   Results from Simulating Ten Weeks Each of New Star Prices

Star's Price P ($)	Star's Total Profit ($)
4,100	8,660
4,300	23,880
4,500	35,100
4,700	40,880
5,000	36,800

Adding this $820 to the $720 profit from the first week results in a total of $1,540 for two weeks of simulated competition.

If Star continues this hand simulation for eight more weeks of competition, it will obtain the results shown in Table 17.2. In this table, the $8,660 value for week 10 gives the projected (simulated) total profit when Star sets a price of $P = \$4,100$ on the Saver for each of the next 10 weeks.

Analysis. The same process can be used to perform similar simulations with other Star prices. For example, if the company uses the same set of hypothetical Caste prices ($C = \$4,000, \$4,200, \$4,100, \$4,400, \$4,300, \$4,700, \$5,000, \$4,500, \$4,600,$ and $\$4,800$) to simulate 10 weeks of competition for Star prices $P = \$4,300$, $P = \$4,500$, $P = \$4,700$, and $P = \$5,000$, then the projected total profit information will be as presented in Table 17.3.

According to Table 17.3, $P = \$4,700$ is the price (among those examined) that leads to the largest total profit ($\$40,880$). The simulation runs, then, suggest that Star can maximize total profit by setting a weekly price of $4,700 for the Saver. (In practice, management would likely run the simulation for many more than 10 weeks before making a final decision.)

Procedure Recap. The methodology for implementing the simulation process can be summarized as follows:

1. Develop a mathematical model that describes the decision situation. The model relates the decision objective to the controllable and uncontrollable inputs.

2. Develop a flowchart that shows the sequence of operations and computations required by the simulation model.

3. Specify a trial value for each controllable input.

4. Generate values for the uncontrollable inputs.

5. Use the flowchart and mathematical model to project the resulting value of the decision objective.

6. Repeat steps 3 through 5 as desired.

7. Identify the value of the controllable input that leads to the most preferred value of the decision objective.

Table 17.4   **Probabilities for Caste's Price Range**

Caste Price ($)	Probability
4,100	.10
4,300	.20
4,500	.40
4,700	.25
4,900	.05

17.2 MONTE CARLO METHOD

In Management Situation 17.1, Star knew Caste's potential price range but was uncertain about the competitor's exact price. Since the uncontrollable input (Caste's price) was uncertain, Star's profit expression represented a stochastic model of the dealer competition. In that situation, the stochastic inputs were generated by arbitrarily selecting values for Caste's price. This section presents a more systematic way to generate values of the stochastic inputs in a simulation problem. It also shows how the method can be used to help make decisions, and it discusses the role of computer simulation in the process.

Modeling Uncertainty

When there is uncertainty, management needs a method for generating the stochastic inputs of the simulation model. To be representative, the generated inputs must have the same probability distributions as the actual values. **Monte Carlo simulation**, named after Monaco's famous gambling casino, is a popular approach that uses a random selection procedure to generate the stochastic inputs.

In Monte Carlo simulation, the stochastic inputs can be randomly selected with a mechanical device, random number table, or mathematical formula. Management Situation 17.2 illustrates the procedures.

Management Situation 17.2

Stochastic Price Competition

Star still does not know Caste's exact price in advance. However, Star's management assesses the probabilities for Caste's price range as presented in Table 17.4. In other words, Star's management believes that there is a 10 percent chance that Caste's price will be $4,100, a 20 percent likelihood that it will be $4,300, and so on. Furthermore, management does not think that any other price is possible. Also, it is believed that this price pattern will be representative of future competition. Star wants to use this information in its price-setting procedure.

The model must be realistic. Thus, it is important to generate a hypothetical competitive price C that is a good representation of the actual pattern. That is, the method for generating stochastic inputs should generate the same Caste price pattern as shown in Table 17.4. Hence, 10 percent of the time Caste's price should be $4,100, on 20 percent of the occasions it should be $4,300, and so on. Since this representation is a critical part of any simulation study, it warrants serious consideration. In general, models based on inaccurate inputs will not provide useful results.

Mechanical Device. There is a simple way to generate representative competitive prices. First, we take 100 equally sized index cards. Each card represents one week of dealer competition. Next, we write $4,100 on 10 of the cards. We do this because Caste's price C is expected to be $4,100 for 10 percent (10/100) of the time. Similarly, since C is expected to be $4,300 for 20 percent of the time, we write $4,300 on 20 (out of 100) cards. Also, $4,500 should be written on 40 cards, $4,700 on 25 cards, and $4,900 on 5 cards. Note that 10 percent of the cards have $4,100, 20 percent $4,300, 40 percent $4,500, 25 percent $4,700, and 5 percent $4,900 written on them. Thus, the "deck" of cards represents the probabilities for Caste's prices given in Table 17.4.

Since the cards are the same size, each has an equal (1/100) chance of being selected. We then shuffle the deck of 100 cards to thoroughly mix the prices. This step ensures that any two cards in a sequence will be independent. In such cases, picking a card is said to involve a **random selection**. By selecting a card at random from the deck, Star's management can generate a competitive price C that is representative of the actual situation. For example, suppose that the first card drawn has a $4,300 written on it. Then Caste's price will be $C = \$4,300$ for the first simulated week of competition.

Star can generate another competitive price by returning the selected card to the deck, reshuffling all 100 cards, and then drawing another card at random. For instance, on the second draw, suppose that the card has a $4,700 written on it. Then Caste's price will be $C = \$4,700$ for the second simulated week of competition. The process can be repeated for as many weeks as desired.

Random Number Table. Although the index card procedure demonstrates the nature of stochastic simulation, it would be time-consuming and cumbersome to continue with that approach. Other mechanical devices, like spinning a roulette wheel, drawing markers from a bin, or rolling dice, can also be used to make a random selection. However, these devices have the same shortcomings as the index card procedure.

Another, usually more convenient, approach is to use a random-digit table, such as Table 17.5, for generating the stochastic uncontrollable inputs. This table contains the digits 0, 1, 2, 3, 4, 5, 6, 7, 8, and 9. Each digit appears with the same frequency and thereby has an equal chance of occurring. Also, any two numbers in a sequence are independent. That is, the digits appear in random order. Consequently, the analyst makes a random selection when he or she picks a digit from the table.

Since the Caste price probabilities in Table 17.4 have up to two digits after the decimal point, the selected random numbers also should have two digits. By selecting sets of two digits from the random-number table, Star can get two-digit random numbers from 00 to 99. The value 00 will be the first of 100 numbers in the sequence.

According to Table 17.4, there is a 10 percent chance that Caste's price will be $4,100. Thus, Star wants 10 percent of the 100 possible two-digit random numbers

Table 17.5 **Table of Random Digits**

341447	723998	905614	519309	926345	240082	395043
415603	129727	894956	780924	227496	134056	023014
014881	496311	750082	707823	738906	157591	072396
827235	783798	324650	485324	568156	098331	768720
261607	730824	341940	259028	253973	145183	658110
527920	834376	972906	627959	554790	342497	593779
356756	519371	679389	371912	502903	936741	636775
700770	781547	916968	136999	801855	605975	295802
279584	733750	487151	116069	274869	416181	610911
862434	481154	391464	021094	761599	474456	582253
199585	167701	170788	934765	761328	275799	323046
048736	514507	977406	158840	846761	198016	933522
815218	609732	629295	517386	824505	676788	304971
643021	527212	492869	261844	914505	354436	355772
164332	245407	517804	422658	751712	583087	268872
174303	085157	308590	535846	503131	266915	465641
136325	414066	452293	649359	844625	674828	953396
117780	407444	426115	108970	621527	601599	652376
435697	245510	946158	934221	824917	509832	362638
912252	579474	848845	824321	049853	151126	052643
754438	658573	717914	040054	630638	264060	594641
322053	924909	048177	957012	801464	833319	978384
897199	125506	708669	408374	737887	906201	599469
046637	642050	435779	502427	027842	515775	811203
721653	260190	842505	797017	157497	179041	979346
202312	011976	373248	374293	802292	646914	171322
354014	356787	511271	904434	068589	329862	829316
682909	809290	793392	098004	120575	469925	112743
897690	572456	871574	465543	486529	507767	608677
139029	160636	417690	191242	625269	104858	020808
345769	953810	627280	423578	353511	899906	827008
549075	004410	059309	271243	403382	248735	972383
423480	950812	197145	556566	655917	046169	363201
551518	514290	950974	482196	058868	474936	724829
797165	670995	791954	188521	950156	086813	033365
062730	163375	602168	908350	360861	152201	966097

to correspond with $C = \$4,100$. While any 10 numbers from 00 to 99 will do, for convenience, suppose that Star assigns $C = \$4,100$ to the first 10 random numbers (00 through 09). Then, whenever any of these 10 random numbers is observed, Caste's simulated price will be $4,100. Since the two-digit random numbers from 00 through 09 will occur 10 percent of the time, this method will generate $C = \$4,100$ 10 percent of the time.

Table 17.6   Random Numbers Associated with Caste's Prices

Caste's Price ($)	Probability of Caste's Price	Random Numbers	Probability Random Numbers
4,100	.10	00–99	10/100 = .10
4,300	.20	10–29	20/100 = .20
4,500	.40	30–69	40/100 = .40
4,700	.25	70–94	25/100 = .25
4,900	.05	95–99	5/100 = .05

Table 17.7   Simulating Ten Weeks of Caste's Prices with a Random Number Table

Week	Random Number	Caste's Simulated Price ($)
1	34	4,500
2	14	4,300
3	47	4,500
4	72	4,700
5	39	4,500
6	98	4,900
7	90	4,700
8	56	4,500
9	14	4,300
10	51	4,500

Similarly, Table 17.4 shows that there is a 20 percent chance that Caste's price will be $4,300. By letting 20 percent of the two-digit random numbers correspond to $C = $4,300, Star will simulate this competitive price 20 percent of the time. The analyst can select any arbitrary set of 20 random numbers that have not been assigned to other Caste prices. However, for convenience, let us use successive random numbers. Thus, Star should assign $C = $4,300 to the two-digit random numbers from 10 through 29. When management continues to assign competitive prices to random numbers in this fashion, it will get the results shown in Table 17.6.

Notice that there is an interval of random numbers associated with every Caste price. Further, each interval is such that the probability of the random number is the same as the probability of the associated competitive price. For instance, the probability of selecting a random number from 70 to 94 is exactly the same (.25) as the probability that Caste's price will be $4,700.

Although it is possible to choose digits from any part of the random-digit table (Table 17.5), for ease of reference let us begin with the first row. The first two-digit random number drawn from this row is 34. From Table 17.6, we see that 34 is in the interval 30 to 69, which corresponds to a Caste price of $C = $4,500. The second two-digit random number that appears in the first row of the random-digit table (Table 17.5) is 14. Since 14 is in the interval 10 to 29 from Table 17.6, Caste's simulated price in

Table 17.8   Pseudorandom Numbers Associated with Caste's Prices

Caste's Price ($)	Probability of Caste's Price	Pseudorandom Numbers	Probability Pseudorandom Numbers
4,100	.10	0 to .10	.10/1 = .10
4,300	.20	.10 to .30	.20/1 = .20
4,500	.40	.30 to .70	.40/1 = .40
4,700	.25	.70 to .95	.25/1 = .25
4,900	.05	.95 to 1.00	.05/1 = .05

the second week of competition is $C = \$4,300$. By continuing in such a manner for eight more weeks of operation, Star will get the results shown in Table 17.7.

Mathematical Formula. The random-digit (or mechanical device) approach generally will not repeat the same sequence of random numbers. Consequently, simulation outcomes will differ because of conscious policy changes and because of changes resulting from random sequences. To isolate the unique effects of policy changes, the decision maker first must run the simulation repeatedly for each policy. Statistical methodologies then must be used on the results to account for (estimate) the purely random changes.

The random-effects problem can be avoided by utilizing the identical sequence of random numbers for each policy simulation. An identical sequence of **pseudorandom numbers**, or numbers that have the same properties as true random numbers, can be generated with a mathematical formula. One such formula is

$$(17.1) \qquad N_{j+1} = FR(mN_j)$$

where N_{j+1} = pseudorandom number $j + 1$, m = a constant multiplier with any value from the set $\{3, 11, 13, 19, 21, 27, 29, 37, 53, 59, 61, 67, 69, 77, 83, 91\}$, N_j = pseudorandom number j, and $FR(mN_j)$ = the fractional part of mN_j.

Formula 17.1 is designed to provide a value between 0 and 1. To apply this formula, we need a value for the multiplier m (fixed by arbitrarily selecting a number from the specified set) and a *seed*, or starting value. This seed, denoted as N_0, can be found with several formulas, including the one below:

$$(17.2) \qquad N_0 = 10^{-p}(k)$$

where p = the number of digits desired in the pseudorandom number and k = any integer not divisible by 2 or 5, such that $0 < k < 10^p$. (Purely random effects can be estimated, if desired, by rerunning the simulation with changed seeds.)

Pseudorandom numbers are used in exactly the same way as true random numbers. An interval of pseudorandom numbers is assigned to each value of the stochastic input. This assignment must ensure that the probability of a pseudorandom number is exactly the same as the likelihood of the corresponding input value. Uncontrollable inputs then are developed by generating pseudorandom numbers and matching them with the input values.

Table 17.9   **Simulating Ten Weeks of Caste's Prices with a Pseudorandom Number Table**

Week	Pseudorandom Number	Caste's Simulated Price ($)
1	.99	4,900
2	.63	4,500
3	.31	4,500
4	.47	4,500
5	.39	4,500
6	.43	4,500
7	.91	4,700
8	.67	4,500
9	.79	4,700
10	.23	4,300

Table 17.4, for example, shows a .1 probability for a Caste price of $C = \$4,100$. Thus, 10 percent of all possible pseudorandom numbers must correspond to $C = \$4,100$. Since the values in the interval 0 to .10 represent .10/1, or about 10 percent of all possible pseudorandom numbers, this interval can be used to represent a Caste price of $4,100. Similarly, Table 17.4 shows a .2 probability for a Caste price of $4,300. By letting the values in the interval .1 to .30 correspond to $C = \$4,300$, the analyst will simulate this price $(.3 - .1)/1 = .2/1$, or approximately 20 percent of the time. If Star continues to assign Caste's prices to pseudorandom numbers in this manner, it will get the results shown in Table 17.8.

Since the Caste price probabilities have up to two digits after the decimal point, $p = 2$ in Formulas 17.1 and 17.2. If we arbitrarily set $k = 27$, Formula 17.2 shows that the seed pseudorandom number will be

$$N_0 = 10^{-p}(k) = 10^{-2}(27) = .27$$

Formula 17.1, with a subjectively fixed $m = 37$, then indicates that the first week's pseudorandom number is

$$N_1 = FR(mN_0) = FR(37(.27)) = FR(9.99) = .99$$

From Table 17.8, we see that .99 is in the interval .95 to 1.00, which corresponds to a Caste price of $C = \$4,900$.

According to formula 17.1, the second week's pseudorandom number is

$$N_2 = FR(mN_1) = FR(37(.99)) = FR(36.63) = .63.$$

Since .63 is in the interval .30 to .70 from Table 17.8, Caste's simulated price in the second week of competition is $C = \$4,500$. By continuing in such a manner for eight more weeks of operation, Star will get the results shown in Table 17.9.

Analyzing the Results. Once the stochastic inputs have been generated, the decision maker can continue with the standard simulation methodology. Suppose, for example,

---

Table 17.10   **Star's Probabilistic Simulation Results**

Star's Price P ($)	Star's Total Profit ($)
4,100	8,920
4,300	25,560
4,500	40,000
4,700	47,320
5,000	44,800

---

that Star again wants to evaluate prices of P = \$4,100, P = \$4,300, P=\$4,500, P = \$4,700, and P = \$5,000. If management uses Table 17.9's Caste prices for each price simulation, it will obtain the projected total profits shown in Table 17.10.

Table 17.10 shows that P = \$4,700 is the price (among those evaluated) that leads to the largest total profit (\$47,320). The probabilistic simulation results, then, suggest that Star can maximize total profit at \$47,320 by setting a weekly price of \$4,700 for the Saver. (In practice, management would likely run the simulation for many more than 10 weeks and analyze the variation in profit before making a final decision.)

Procedure Recap. Monte Carlo simulation can be summarized as follows:

1. Develop a probability distribution for each uncontrollable input, and assign an interval of digits to the corresponding input values on the basis of the distribution.
2. Simulate the uncontrollable input by generating random (or pseudorandom) numbers and matching them with the input values.
3. Use the simulated uncontrollable inputs to evaluate specified policies.

Complex Decisions

Management Situations 17.1 and 17.2 both involve an unconstrained problem that has only one decision variable (Star's price P) and one uncontrollable input (Caste's price C). In practice, most simulations will involve two or more decision variables, two or more uncontrollable inputs, and constraints on the Carlo method, can be applied to these complex decisions, as Management Situation 17.3 illustrates.

Management Situation 17.3

Investment Financing

Regional Power, Inc. is a publicly owned utility that supplies water and electricity to the northeastern states. The company must build a new generating plant to meet the growing demand for energy. It is difficult to determine the exact construction costs because of potential building delays and inflation. By processing financial data through the company's computer information system, staff members have developed the construction cost information shown in Table 17.11.

Table 17.11   Regional's Construction Cost Data

Construction Cost ($ Million)	Probability
100	.05
200	.35
300	.50
400	.10

Table 17.12   Bank Prime Lending Rate

Annual Interest Rate (% of Loan Amount)	Probability
8	.05
10	.15
12	.20
14	.30
16	.25
18	.05

The company plans to finance the investment by issuing bonds and borrowing from an insurance company. Bonds will yield 10 percent per annum to investors, while the interest rate on the loan will be 12 percent a year. As a lending condition, the insurance company insists that the bond flotation be no more than 1.5 times the loan amount. If Regional does not obtain enough funds from these sources, it will have to finance the residual with a bank loan at the prevailing prime interest rate. The future prime rate is not known exactly, but Regional's finance department has used its forecasting model to compile the data shown in Table 17.12.

Regional's management wants to determine the pattern of financing (the bond and loan amounts) that will minimize the costs of obtaining the required funds. It does not want to use any currently available funds to pay for the plant's construction.

Simulation Model. As before, the analysis begins with the development of a model. In this model, let

I = the total annual interest expense ($ million)

B = the bond issue ($ million)

L = the insurance loan ($ million)

C = the plant construction cost ($ million)

R = the bank loan ($ million)

r = the annual interest rate on the bank loan.

Regional finances construction by issuing bonds and borrowing. Annual interest charges I will be 10 percent of the bond issue B plus 12 percent of the insurance loan plus an uncertain rate r on the bank loan. That is,

$$I = .10B + .12L + rR.$$

The bank loan will be necessary only if the bond and insurance loan funds are not sufficient to cover the construction cost. Then, the bank loan will equal the difference, or

$$R = C - B - L \quad \text{if } B + L < C$$

On the other hand, if the bonds and insurance loan provide sufficient funds, there will be no need for a bank loan. Hence, in this case,

$$R = 0 \quad \text{if } B + L \geq C$$

and the annual interest charge will be

$$I = .10B + .12L + r(0) = .10B + .12L.$$

The company wants to choose the values of B and L that will minimize total interest expense I.

Regional must meet two constraints. The total investment must be sufficient to cover the total cost of constructing the new generating plant, or

$$B + L + R \geq C.$$

Also, insurance company policy requires the bond issue to be no more than 1.5 times the loan amount, or

$$B \leq 1.5L.$$

Flowchart. Management uses the model to develop some numerical simulations of the investment financing. Figure 17.4 presents a flowchart of the sequence of operations and computations required by the simulation model.

This problem is more complex than the dealer competition problem because it involves two decision variables (B and L) and two stochastic inputs (r and C). Also, there are two constraints on the investment process—the construction cost and insurance restrictions.

Simulation Runs. Regional initiates the simulation by specifying trial values for the insurance loan L and bond issue B. Suppose that a group of executives is polled to establish these values, and the consensus is that the water and electric utility should issue between $80 million and $140 million in bonds and borrow between $80 million and $140 million from the insurance company. Management wants to evaluate the loan/bond combinations in $10 million increments within these ranges.

In establishing a financial policy, Regional must ensure that

$$B \leq 1.5L.$$

For example, one policy that satisfies this restriction is a bond issue of $B = \$90$ million and an insurance loan of $L = \$110$ million.

Figure 17.4 **Flowchart of Regional's Investment Financing**

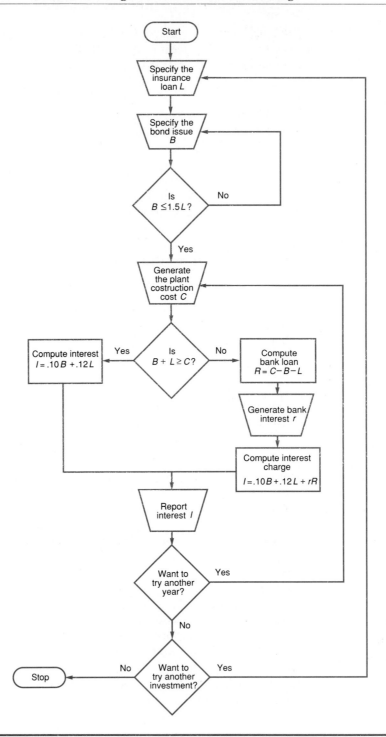

Table 17.13   **Pseudorandom Numbers Associated with Regional's Plant Costs**

Construction Cost C ($ Million)	Probability	Pseudorandom Numbers
100	.05	0 to .05
200	.35	.05 to .40
300	.50	.40 to .90
400	.10	.90 to 1.00

Once the policy constraint is met, Regional must generate the plant construction cost C. To execute this operation, it is first necessary to assign the interval of random (or pseudorandom) numbers shown in Table 17.13. This assignment ensures that the probabilities of the pseudorandom numbers are exactly the same as the likelihoods of the corresponding expenses. Construction costs then are developed by generating random (or pseudorandom) numbers and matching them with the expenses.

For example, suppose Regional uses formulas 17.1 and 17.2 (with $p = 2$) to generate pseudorandom numbers. If it arbitrarily sets $k = 13$, Formula 17.2 shows that the pseudorandom number seed will be

$$N_0 = 10^{-p}(k) = 10^{-2}(13) = .13.$$

Formula 17.1, with a subjectively fixed $m = 53$, then indicates that the first year's pseudorandom number is

$$N_1 = FR(mN_0) = FR(53(.13)) = FR(6.89) = .89.$$

From Table 17.13, we see that .89 corresponds to a construction cost of $C = \$300$ million. Similarly, the second year's pseudorandom is

$$N_2 = FR(mN_1) = FR(53(.89)) = FR(47.17) = .17$$

which corresponds to a construction cost of $C = \$200$ million.

At this point, management must compare the amount of funds obtained from the investment $(B + L)$ with the construction cost C. When

$$B + L \geq C$$

Regional can compute the interest expense I as

$$I = .10B + .12L.$$

For example, a policy of $B = \$90$ million and $L = \$110$ million with construction cost at $C = \$200$ million has

$$B + L = C \quad \text{or} \quad 90 + 110 = 200$$

million dollars and an interest expense of

$$I = .10B + .12L = .10(90) + .12(110) = 22.2$$

million dollars.

Table 17.14 Pseudorandom Numbers Associated with the Prime Rate

Annual Interest Rate r (% of Loan Amount)	Probability	Pseudorandom Numbers
8	.05	0 to .05
10	.15	.05 to .20
12	.20	.20 to .40
14	.30	.40 to .70
16	.25	.70 to .95
18	.05	.90 to 1.00

If there are insufficient bond and insurance funds, management must make up the difference with a bank loan of

$$R = C - B - L.$$

For example, a policy of $B = \$90$ million and $L = \$110$ million with construction cost at $C = \$300$ million requires

$$R = C - B - L = 300 - 90 - 110 = 100$$

million dollars. To compute the resulting interest expense of

$$I = .10B + .12L + rB$$

Regional must generate the bank prime rate r.

Since r is a random variable, it is first necessary to assign an interval of random (or pseudorandom) numbers to each possible interest rate. When Regional makes the assignment in accordance with the probabilities given in Table 17.12, it will get the results shown in Table 17.14. Interest rates then are developed by generating random (or pseudorandom) numbers and matching them with the r values.

For example, suppose Regional again uses Formulas 17.1 and 17.2 to generate pseudorandom numbers. If it arbitrarily sets $k = 79$, Formula 17.2 shows that the pseudorandom seed will be

$$N_0 = 10^{-P}(k) = 10^{-2}(79) = .79$$

Formula 17.1, with a subjectively fixed $m = 3$, then indicates that the first year's pseudorandom number is

$$N_1 = FR(mN_0) = FR(3(.79)) = FR(2.37) = .37$$

which, in Table 17.14, corresponds to an annual interest rate of $r = .12$, or 12 percent. For a policy of $B = \$90$ million and $L = \$110$ million with construction cost at $C = \$300$ million (so that $R = C - B - L = \$100$ million), the resulting interest expense is

$$I = .10B + .12L + rR = .10(90) + .12(110) + .12(100) = 34.2$$

million dollars.

Table 17.15   Simulated Average Annual Interest Expense for 1,000 Years of Regional's Investment Financing

Bond Issue *B* ($ Million)	Insurance Loan *L* ($ Million)						
	80	90	100	110	120	130	140
80	30.77	30.90	30.40	31.08	23.98	22.54	22.58
90	31.31	30.67	30.38	22.31	22.20	22.11	22.58
100	29.95	30.28	22.67	22.62	21.91	22.61	22.07
110	29.95	23.41	22.28	21.88	22.54	21.87	23.25
120	22.39	22.72	22.05	22.23	22.40	21.84	21.88
130	*	21.11	21.09	21.43	21.44	22.11	21.84
140	*	*	22.51	22.13	21.43	22.75	20.40

*Indicates that this investment combination $(B+L)$ does not satisfy the policy constraint $B \leq 1.5L$ and thus is not feasible.

When the interest expense has been recorded for a single policy (*B* and *L* combination) and a single set of uncontrollable inputs (one construction cost and one interest rate), the user has completed a simulation for one year of Regional's investment situation. To simulate each additional year under the same policy, the analyst must generate a new construction cost *C* and continue with the subsequent sequence of operations needed to calculate the new interest expense. Other policies then can be simulated by specifying new *B* and *L* combinations and repeating the simulation process.

Analyzing the Results. Table 17.15 presents the results from simulating 1,000 years of financing with the investment policies established by the consensus of executives. It shows that an investment combination of *B* = $140 million in bonds and *L* = $140 million in insurance loans results in the smallest average annual interest expense ($20.4 million). The simulation, then, suggests that Regional can obtain low-cost financing by issuing $140 million in bonds and borrowing $140 million from the insurance company.

After studying the results, management might wish to consider other investment combinations near the apparent "best" solution. In addition, it will be useful to analyze the variation in interest expense before making a final decision. Technique Exercise 17 will ask you to perform these additional evaluations.

Monte Carlo Extension

Each uncontrollable input in a probabilistic situation will have a cumulative probability distribution, denoted as $F(x)$, with the probabilities of the *x* values ranging from 0 to 1. This distribution is found using empirical data or statistical theory (as in the Poisson, exponential, and normal distributions). It can be represented by a table, graph, or algebraic function.

If the cumulative probability distribution can be represented by an algebraic function, the decision maker can use the *inverse transformation method* (ITM) to find the specific *x* values of the uncontrollable input. In ITM, a systematic technique (such as Formula 17.1) is used to generate a random (or pseudorandom) number N that is uniformly distributed over the interval 0 to 1. The number N will correspond to some value x in the cumulative probability distribution, or

$$N = F(x).$$

By solving this expression for x, or by inverting the cumulative distribution

$$x = F^{-1}(N)$$

we obtain the value of the uncontrollable input.

Computer Simulation

It would require considerable time and effort to perform the calculations necessary for large-scale, complex simulations by hand. Consequently, simulation did not become a practical problem-solving tool until the advent of electronic computers. The computer can be used to carry out the well-defined operations and computations involved in simulation methodology. This capability makes it possible to perform large simulations in reasonable amounts of time. Indeed, the word *computer* often precedes the word *simulation* because a computer is so frequently used in performing simulation calculations.

A computer must be programmed to perform experiments with the simulation model. The specific computer program that performs the simulation operations and computations is referred to as the **simulator**. Frequently, this simulator is created with a general-purpose programming language or with a special-purpose simulation language. Sometimes, it can be even formed with a modeling language.

General-Purpose Languages. Any of the available general-purpose programming languages, such as *FORTRAN* or *BASIC*, can be used to develop a simulator. These languages provide flexibility in tailoring the simulator both to the model and to the needs of the user. However, such languages require considerable programming effort, especially for debugging errors, and this effort translates into substantial time and expense commitments.

Special-Purpose Simulation Languages. Most simulation experiments have a similar structure and require a common set of tasks. Recognizing these facts, practitioners and computer vendors have developed simulation languages, including **GASP, GPSS, SIMAN, SIMSCRIPT**, and **SLAM**, to meet these special needs. The special-purpose languages simplify the process of transforming a model into computer instructions by providing a generalized and easily manipulated structure and a set of desirable built-in capabilities (including random number generation, time-sequencing and event-sequencing mechanisms, data tabulation and manipulation, and report writing). Such facilities also make it easier for the user to alter the model and answer "What if?" questions.

Modeling Languages. To use simulation (and general-purpose) languages, management must learn the syntax and programming conventions. This requirement discourages many potential beneficiaries from applying simulation. Decision support system professionals have developed modeling languages, such as *IFPS, PROFIT*, and *EXPRESS*, to address the problem. Using English-like commands and user-friendly interfaces, these languages enable the novice to quickly develop and run deterministic and probabilistic simulations. Today's electronic spreadsheet programs, such as *LOTUS 1-2-3, SUPERCALC*, and *MULTIPLAN*, provide similar capabilities.

Spreadsheets and modeling languages are best suited to the relatively straightforward simulations characteristic of small-scale applications. They also can provide a prototype and preliminary analysis needed for large-scale, complex simulations.

17.3 SIMULATING OPERATIONS

In earlier parts of the text, we noted that simulation can be used to address operations management (and other) problems that have no analytical solutions. This section illustrates the simulation approach to inventory and queuing problems.

Inventory

The following four conditions complicate inventory analysis:

1. The existence of elaborate or comprehensive systems (such as multiechelons and queuing considerations).

2. Nonlinear or discontinuous cost functions.

3. Demands that exhibit time series patterns (such as trend and seasonal).

4. Stochastic demands and lead times characterized by specific theoretical or empirical probability distributions.

Although the resulting models may be conceptually simple, analytical solutions are restrictive at best and not available at worst. Under these circumstances, the only viable alternative is to use simulation.

Management Situation 17.4 illustrates the simulation approach to inventory planning and control.

Management Situation 17.4

Art Supplies

True Design, Inc. carries in inventory over 500 items for graphic artists. The company has used analytical inventory models to determine the order quantity (Q) and the reorder point (R) for most products, but these models have not worked well for a computerized graphic tool. Demand for the tool has been relatively low but subject to some variability. By processing historical transactions through True Design's computer information system, staff have developed the tool demand (D) data shown in Table 17.16.

Another complicating factor is that lead time L from the tool's supplier also varies. Historically, the length of the lead time has been anywhere between one and four days,

Table 17.16   **Graphic Tool Demand**

Tool Demand	Number of Days	Probability
0	45	45/100 = .45
1	20	20/100 = .20
2	15	15/100 = .15
3	10	10/100 = .10
4	6	6/100 = .06
5	4	4/100 = .04
	100	

with the probabilities shown in Table 17.17. These lead times have caused True Design to run out of stock on several occasions. Orders received during such out-of-stock periods have caused lost sales and ill will among customers.

A computer-based analysis of delivery charges indicates that it costs True Design $70 to place an order for the graphic tool. Similar analyses of interest, insurance, and physical handling/storage expenses suggest that holding cost will be $0.40 for every tool in inventory at the end of each day. Marketing personnel forecast a shortage cost of $150 per lost sale. Since the supplier has agreed to repurchase any unsold tool at cost, True Design need not worry about the expense of buying the product or disposing of unsold tools.

The inventory system is updated daily. Currently, there are three graphic tools in stock, and there are no outstanding orders. Arriving orders are received and stock on hand is updated at the start of each day. Demand is filled from stock on hand. Ending inventory is equal to the beginning inventory plus the quantity of any arriving order less demand. When ending inventory is less than or equal to the reorder point, True Design places an order. No quantity will be ordered as long as there is an outstanding order.

Management wants to order the quantity that will minimize total inventory-related costs. Preliminary analysis suggests that a low-cost policy would involve either.

1.   An order quantity of $Q = 20$ tools and a reorder point of $R = 2$ tools, or

2.   An order quantity of $Q = 10$ tools and a reorder point of $R = 5$ tools.

Simulation will be used to evaluate these alternatives.

Simulation Model. True Design's total inventory cost will equal the sum of its order, holding, and shortage expenses. Since the order expense is a fixed $70 per order, holding expense is $0.40 per tool in ending inventory, and the shortage expense is $150 per lost sale, this total cost will be

$$TC = \$70 + \$.40EI + \$150LS$$

Table 17.17   **Tool Lead Time**

Lead Time (Days)	Number of Days	Probability
1	20	20/100 = .20
2	48	48/100 = .48
3	22	22/100 = .22
4	10	10/100 = .10
	100	

where TC = True Design's total inventory cost, EI = inventory at the end of each day (ending inventory), and LS = the number of lost sales.

Each day's ending inventory EI will equal the beginning inventory plus the quantity Q of any arriving order less demand D, or

$$EI = BI + Q - D.$$

An order will be placed if there is no outstanding order and this ending inventory is less than or equal to the reorder point R, or if

$$EI \leq R.$$

An order will arrive after a lead time of L days.

Lost sales will equal demand less the stock on hand (beginning inventory plus any arriving order) or

$$LS = D - (BI + Q) = D - BI - Q.$$

The objective is to find the order quantity Q and reorder point R that will result in the lowest total cost TC. The problem has two decision variables (Q and R) and two stochastic inputs (L and D).

Flowchart. True Design uses the model to simulate the two proposed inventory policies ($Q = 20$ and $R = 2$ versus $Q = 10$ and $R = 5$). Figure 17.5 presents a flowchart of the sequence of operations and computations required by the simulation model.

As Figure 17.5 demonstrates, True Design initiates the simulation by specifying values for the order quantity Q and reorder point R. These values will be either $Q = 20$ and $R = 2$ or $Q = 10$ and $R = 5$. Next, management must record the beginning inventory BI. Stock on hand must then be updated to accommodate any arriving order.

At this stage of the process, True Design must generate demand D for the tool. If the stock on hand exceeds demand (if $BI + Q \geq D$), management can compute the ending inventory $EI = BI + Q - D$. Otherwise, there will be lost sales $LS = D - BI - Q$, and ending inventory will be zero ($EI = 0$). Also, the shortage cost will be computed as $150\,LS$.

Figure 17.5 shows that the company will next compare the ending inventory EI with the reorder point R. When $EI > R$ (or when $EI \leq R$ but there is an order outstanding), management computes the holding cost as $0.40\,EI$. If $EI \leq R$ and there is no order

Figure 17.5 **True Design's Inventory Flowchart**

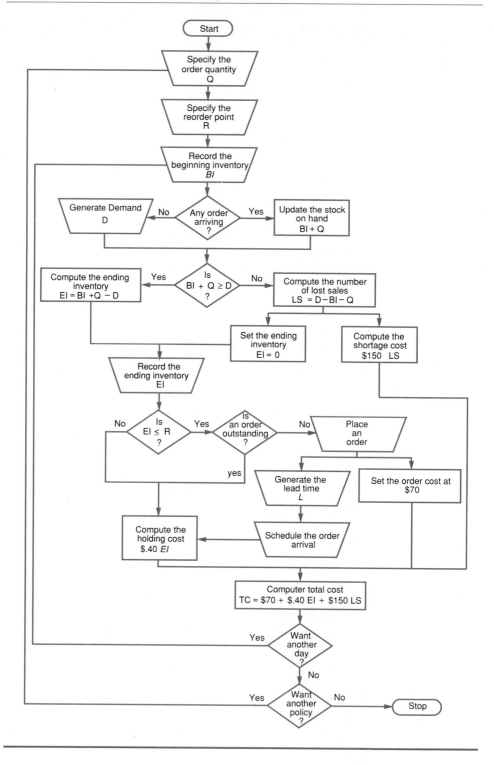

Table 17.18   **True Design's Inventory Simulation with $Q = 20$ and $R = 2$**

Day	Beginning Inventory BI	Arriving Tools Q	Random Number N	Demand D	Lost Sales LS	Ending Inventory EI	Random Number N	Lead Time L	Order Cost $	Holding Cost $.40EI	Shortage Cost $150LS	Total Cost TC
1	3	0	.33	0	0	3	—	—	0	1.20	0	1.20
2	3	0	.39	0	0	3	—	—	0	1.20	0	1.20
3	3	0	.37	0	0	3	—	—	0	1.20	0	1.20
4	3	0	.71	1	0	2	.67	2	70	.80	0	70.80
5	2	0	.93	4	2	0	.43	2	70	0.00	300	370.00
6	0	20	.19	0	0	20	—	—	0	8.00	0	8.00
7	20	20	.77	2	0	38	—	—	0	15.20	0	15.20
8	38	0	.91	4	0	34	—	—	0	13.60	0	13.60
9	34	0	.53	2	0	32	—	—	0	12.80	0	12.80
10	32	0	.99	5	0	27	—	—	0	10.80	0	10.80
11	27	0	.17	0	0	27	—	—	0	10.80	0	10.80
12	27	0	.11	0	0	27	—	—	0	10.80	0	10.80
13	27	0	.13	0	0	27	—	—	0	10.80	0	10.80
14	27	0	.79	2	0	25	—	—	0	10.00	0	10.00
15	25	0	.57	1	0	24	—	—	0	9.60	0	9.60
16	24	0	.31	0	0	24	—	—	0	9.60	0	9.60
17	24	0	.73	2	0	22	—	—	0	8.80	0	8.80
18	22	0	.59	1	0	21	—	—	0	8.40	0	8.40
19	21	0	.97	5	0	16	—	—	0	6.40	0	6.40
20	16	0	.51	1	0	15	—	—	0	6.00	0	6.00
Total				2					140	156.00	300	596.00

outstanding, True Design must place an order. In the process, it must generate the lead time L, schedule the order arrival, compute the holding cost, and set the order cost at $70.

Once True Design computes the total cost

$$TC = \$70 + \$.40EI + \$150LS$$

it has completed one simulated day of business. To simulate each additional day under the same policy, the analyst must record the new beginning inventory BI and continue with the subsequent sequence of operations needed to compute the new total inventory cost. Other policies then can be simulated by specifying new Q and R values and repeating the process shown in Figure 17.5.

Analyzing the Results. Currently, there are three graphic tools in stock ($BI = 3$), and no orders are outstanding. By using pseudorandom numbers from Formulas 17.1 and 17.2, management can create identical stochastic input conditions and thereby compare the two proposed inventory policies on the same basis. Table 17.18 presents the results from simulating 20 days of inventory operations with an order quantity of $Q = 20$ tools and a reorder point of $R = 2$ tools, while Table 17.19 shows the results with $Q = 10$ tools

Table 17.19   **True Design's Inventory Simulation with $Q = 10$ and $R = 5$**

Day	Beginning Inventory BI	Arriving Tools Q	Random Number N	Demand D	Lost Sales LS	Ending Inventory EI	Random Number N	Lead Time L	Order Cost $	Holding Cost $.40EI	Shortage Cost $150LS	Total Cost TC
1	3	0	.33	0	0	3	.67	2	70	1.20	0	71.20
2	3	0	.39	0	0	3	.43	2	70	1.20	0	71.20
3	3	10	.37	0	0	13	—	—	0	5.20	0	5.20
4	13	10	.71	1	0	22	—	—	0	8.80	0	8.80
5	22	0	.93	4	0	18	—	—	0	7.20	0	7.20
6	18	0	.19	0	0	18	—	—	0	7.20	0	7.20
7	18	0	.77	2	0	16	—	—	0	6.40	0	6.40
8	16	0	.91	4	0	12	—	—	0	4.80	0	4.80
9	12	0	.53	2	0	10	—	—	0	4.00	0	4.00
10	10	0	.99	5	0	5	.47	2	70	2.00	0	72.00
11	5	0	.17	0	0	5	.63	2	70	2.00	0	72.00
12	5	10	.11	0	0	15	—	—	0	6.00	0	6.00
13	15	10	.13	0	0	25	—	—	0	10.00	0	10.00
14	25	0	.79	2	0	23	—	—	0	9.20	0	9.20
15	23	0	.57	1	0	22	—	—	0	8.80	0	8.80
16	22	0	.31	0	0	22	—	—	0	8.80	0	8.80
17	22	0	.73	2	0	20	—	—	0	8.00	0	8.00
18	20	0	.59	1	0	19	—	—	0	7.60	0	7.60
19	19	0	.97	5	0	14	—	—	0	5.60	0	5.60
20	14	0	.51	1	0	13	—	—	0	5.20	0	5.20
Total					0				280	119.20	0	399.20

and $R = 5$ tools. These tables use $p = 2$, $k = 51$, and $m = 83$ for demand D and $p = 2$, $k = 23$, and $m = 29$ for lead time L in the pseudorandom number formulas.

Tables 17.18 and 17.19 show that an inventory policy of $Q = 10$ and $R = 5$ involves twice as many orders and double the ordering cost of the alternative policy of $Q = 20$ and $R = 2$. However, the more frequent ordering policy ($Q = 10$ and $R = 5$) leads to no lost sales (and thereby no shortage cost) and a lower holding cost than the high order quantity policy ($Q = 20$ and $R = 2$). As a result, the inventory policy of $Q = 10$ and $R = 5$ leads to the smallest total inventory cost ($399.20). These simulation results then suggest that True Design's best inventory policy (among the two examined) is to place an order for $Q = 10$ tools whenever inventory reaches a reorder point of $R = 5$ tools.

In practice, management would likely run the simulation for many more than 20 days before making a final decision. Computer Exercise 19 will ask you to perform this additional evaluation. Also, it will be useful to analyze the variation in total inventory cost before making this decision.

Queuing

As with inventory problems, there are system conditions that complicate queuing analysis. These conditions include:

Table 17.20   **Charlestowne Harbor Data**

Times Between Tanker Arrivals (hours)	Probability	Times to Unload Tankers (hours)	Probability
0 to 4	.35	0 to 3	.20
4 to 8	.20	3 to 6	.35
8 to 12	.30	6 to 9	.25
12 to 16	.15	9 to 12	.15
		12 to 15	.05

1. Processes for which transient solutions are required but unavailable (which is the case for most non-M/M/S systems).

2. Arrival processes that exhibit nonstationary behavior, seasonal patterns, or correlation over time.

3. Service facilities with nonstationary service time distributions, tandem and parallel servers, or breakdown and fatigue failures.

4. Arrival and service processes having empirical distributions with no theoretical counterparts.

The resulting models may again be conceptually simple, but analytical solutions are once more restrictive at best and not available at worst. Simulation, then, will be the only viable alternative solution procedure.

Management Situation 17.5 illustrates the simulation approach to queuing system analysis. This situation involves a case with a single channel, a general distribution of interarrival times (or of arrival rates), a general distribution of service times (or service rates), one or two servers, and a limited waiting capacity (a GI/G/S queuing system with finite queue length).

Management Situation 17.5

Harbor Expansion

Charlestowne currently has one dock that is used to unload crude oil from large-volume tankers. Each tanker is unloaded on a first come, first serve basis around the clock for a fee to the shipping company of $500 per hour. Every ship waiting to be unloaded costs the shipping company an estimated $24,000 per day (prorated at $1,000 per hour) in crew fees and other expenses. By processing transactions through its computer information system, port authorities have developed for the shipping companies the arrival and service data shown in Table 17.20.

There is room in the harbor to accommodate only three tankers at one time (either being unloaded or waiting to be unloaded). When this limit is reached, every subsequent arriving tanker must be diverted to the nearest alternative port at an estimated cost to the shipping company of $15,000 in fuel costs and other expenses.

Increasing traffic (and the resulting unloading delays) has encouraged the port to consider adding a second dock for crude oil tankers. The second dock would operate in parallel with, and have the same unloading time distribution as, the original facility. Arriving ships would form a single waiting line and be routed to the first available dock on a first come, first serve basis.

Including financing, the second dock will cost $12 million to build. The port will pay for the dock by charging a user fee to the shipping companies. By using a forecasting model, staff members have estimated that this fee will be a $400 per hour surcharge added to the original unloading cost.

The shipping companies know that the second dock will reduce the costs associated with unloading delays. However, the variability in arrival and unloading times makes the decision between authorizing the second dock (and thereby contracting for the user fee) or operating under current conditions (with only one dock) risky. Simulation will be used to determine the least expensive of the two alternatives. All simulations will begin with no ships in port at the start of the day (midnight).

Simulation Model. When using Charlestowne's harbor under current conditions (with only one dock), the shipping companies will incur a total cost equal to the sum of the expenses from diverting a tanker, waiting in port, and unloading a tanker. The expense from diverting a tanker is a fixed $15,000, and the waiting expense is $1,000 per hour per ship. Under current conditions (with only one dock), the unloading expense is $500 per hour per tanker, while the second dock adds a $400 per hour surcharge to this expense. Total cost per tanker then will be

$$TC = \$15,000\,V + \$1000\,WH + \$500\,UH \quad \text{if } DO = 1$$

or
$$TC = \$15,000\,V + \$1000\,WH + \$900\,UH \quad \text{if } DO = 2$$

where TC = the harbor cost per tanker, V = a binary variable with a value of 1 if an arriving tanker is diverted and 0 otherwise, WH = the hours waiting in port, UH = the hours to unload, and DO = the number of docks.

A tanker will be diverted only when there are three other tankers already in port (waiting or unloading), so that

$$V = 1 \quad \text{if } T \geq 3$$

and
$$V = 0 \quad \text{if } T < 3$$

where T = the number of tankers in port. If $T < 3$, the arriving tanker will enter the port and find either a waiting line (queue) or a free dock.

The queue will form behind tankers arriving earlier and unloading. An arriving tanker will be in the queue from the time it enters the port until it enters a dock. Waiting time then will be

$$WH = ED - EP$$

where ED = the time when the arriving tanker enters a dock, EP = the time when the arriving tanker enters the port, and WH is defined as before. In this equation, ED will be determined by the waiting and unloading times for all preceding tankers in the queue.

Figure 17.6   **Charlestowne's Port Flowchart**

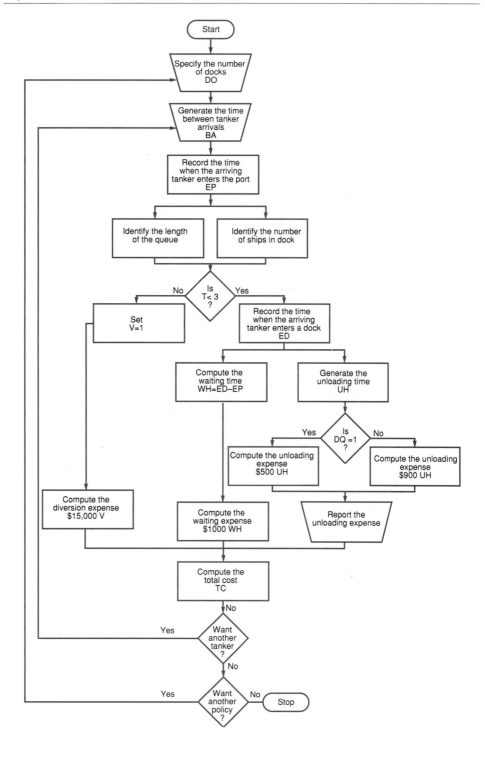

The time between tanker arrivals *BA*, which is a random variable found from the first probability distribution in Table 17.20, will fix the value of *EP*.

Once in a dock, the arriving tanker will be unloaded. Unloading time *UH* will be a random variable found from the second probability distribution in Table 17.20.

The objective is to determine the number of docks (*DO*) that will minimize total cost (*TC*). There is one decision variable (*DO*) and two stochastic inputs (*BA* and *UH*).

Flowchart. Shipping companies use the model to simulate port operations under conditions (with only one dock) and with a second dock. Figure 17.6 presents a flowchart of the operations and computations required by the simulation model.

As Figure 17.6 demonstrates, the decision maker initiates the simulation by specifying the number of docks (*DO*). This number will be either $DO = 1$ or $DO = 2$. Next, management generates the time between tanker arrivals *BA*, which will enable it to record the time when the arriving tanker enters the port *EP*.

At this stage of the process, we must identify the length of the queue and the number of ships in dock. The sum of these two values will give the number of tankers in port *T*. If $T \geq 3$, the arriving tanker will be diverted, so that we must set $V = 1$ and compute the diversion expense as $15,000 V$.

When $T < 3$, the arriving tanker will enter the port and eventually (or perhaps immediately) reach a free dock. Figure 17.6 shows that the decision maker must record the time when the arriving tanker enters a dock *ED*. Waiting time then is computed as

$$WH = ED - EP$$

and waiting expense is computed as $1,000 WH$.

After recording *ED*, management also can generate the unloading time *UH* and compute the unloading expense. This expense will be

$$500 \ UH \qquad \text{if } DO = 1$$

or

$$900 \ UH \qquad \text{otherwise.}$$

As Figure 17.6 demonstrates, the recorded unloading expense plus the computed waiting expense plus the computed diversion expense gives the computed total cost.

Since total cost *TC* has been computed, we have completed a simulation of one tanker's movement through the port. To simulate each additional tanker's movement under the same policy (with the same number of docks), the analyst must generate a new time between tanker arrivals and continue with the subsequent sequence of operations needed to compute the new total harbor cost. Other policies then can be simulated by specifying a new *DO* value and repeating the process shown in Figure 17.6.

Analyzing the Results. At the start of the day (midnight), there are no ships in port. By using pseudorandom numbers generated by Formulas 17.1 and 17.2, management can create identical stochastic inputs and thereby compare the single-dock and two-dock policies on the same basis. Table 17.21 presents the results from simulating 20 tanker arrivals under current conditions (with a single dock), while Table 17.22 shows comparable results under the two-dock policy. These tables use $p = 2$, $k = 99$, and $m = 3$ for the interarrival time *BA* and $p = 2$, $k = 19$, and $m = 67$ for unloading time *UH* in the pseudorandom number formulas. Also, interarrival and

Table 17.21 Charlestowne Harbor Simulation with $DO = 1$

Arriving Tanker	Random Number N	Time Between Arrivals BA	Time Entering Port EP	Existing Queue Length	Tankers in Port T	Time Entering Dock ED	Waiting Time $WH = ED - EP$	Random Number N	Unloading Time UH	Time Leaving Port	Diversion Expense $15,000V	Waiting Expense $1,000WH	Unloading Expense $500UH	Total Cost TC
1	.97	14	14	0	0	14	0	.73	7.5	21.5	0	0	3,750	3,75
2	.91	14	28	0	0	28	0	.91	10.5	38.5	0	0	5,250	5,25
3	.73	10	38	0	1	38.5	.5	.97	13.5	52	0	500	6,750	7,25
4	.19	2	40	0	1	52	12	.99	13.5	65.5	0	12,000	6,750	18,75
5	.57	10	50	1	2	65.5	15.5	.33	4.5	70	0	15,500	2,250	17,75
6	.71	10	60	1	2	70	10	.11	1.5	71.5	0	10,000	750	10,75
7	.13	2	62	2	3	—	—	—	—	62	15,000	—	—	15,00
8	.39	6	68	1	2	71.5	3.5	.37	4.5	76	0	3,500	2,250	5,75
9	.17	2	70	1	2	76	6	.79	7.5	83.5	0	6,000	3,750	9,75
10	.51	6	76	0	1	83.5	7.5	.93	10.5	94	0	7,500	5,250	12,75
11	.53	6	82	1	2	94	12	.31	4.5	98.5	0	12,000	2,250	14,25
12	.59	10	92	1	2	98.5	6.5	.77	7.5	106	0	6,500	3,750	10,25
13	.77	10	102	0	1	106	4	.59	7.5	113.5	0	4,000	3,750	7,75
14	.31	2	104	1	2	113.5	9.5	.53	4.5	118	0	9,500	2,250	11,75
15	.93	14	118	0	0	118	0	.51	4.5	122.5	0	0	2,250	2,25
16	.79	10	128	0	0	128	0	.17	1.5	129.5	0	0	750	75
17	.37	6	134	0	0	134	0	.39	4.5	138.5	0	0	2,250	2,25
18	.11	2	136	0	1	138.5	2.5	.13	1.5	140	0	2,500	750	3,25
19	.33	2	138	1	2	140	2	.71	7.5	147.5	0	2,000	3,750	5,75
20	.99	14	152	0	0	152	0	.57	7.5	159.5	0	0	3,750	3,75
Total				10			91.5		124.5		15,000	91,500	62,250	168,75
Average				0.5			4.575		6.225		750	4,575	3,112.5	8,437.

Table 17.22   **Charlestowne Harbor Simulation with *DO* = 2**

Arriving Tanker	Random Number N	Time Between Arrivals BA	Time Entering Port EP	Existing Queue Length	Tankers in Port T	Time Entering Dock ED	Waiting Time WH = ED − EP	Random Number N	Unloading Time UH	Time Leaving Port	Diversion Expense $15,000V	Waiting Expense $1,000WH	Unloading Expense $900UH	Total Cost TC
1	.97	14	14	0	0	14	0	.73	7.5	21.5	0	0	6,750	6,7
2	.91	14	28	0	0	28	0	.91	10.5	38.5	0	0	9,450	9,4
3	.73	10	38	0	1	38	0	.97	13.5	51.5	0	0	12,150	12,1
4	.19	2	40	0	1	40	0	.99	13.5	53.5	0	0	12,150	12,1
5	.57	10	50	0	2	51.5	1.5	.33	4.5	56	0	1,500	4,050	5,5
6	.71	10	60	0	0	60	0	.11	1.5	61.5	0	0	1,350	1,3
7	.13	2	62	0	0	62	0	.37	4.5	66.5	0	0	4,050	4,0
8	.39	6	68	0	0	68	0	.79	7.5	75.5	0	0	6,750	6,7
9	.17	2	70	0	1	70	0	.93	10.5	80.5	0	0	9,450	9,4
10	.51	6	76	0	1	76	0	.31	4.5	80.5	0	0	4,050	4,0
11	.53	6	82	0	0	82	0	.77	7.5	89.5	0	0	6,750	6,7
12	.59	10	92	0	0	92	0	.59	7.5	99.5	0	0	6,750	6,7
13	.77	10	102	0	1	102	0	.53	4.5	106.5	0	0	4,050	4,0
14	.31	2	104	0	1	104	0	.51	4.5	108.5	0	0	4,050	4,0
15	.93	14	118	0	0	118	0	.17	1.5	119.5	0	0	1,350	1,3
16	.79	10	128	0	0	128	0	.39	4.5	132.5	0	0	4,050	4,0
17	.37	6	134	0	0	134	0	.13	1.5	135.5	0	0	1,350	1,3
18	.11	2	136	0	0	136	0	.71	7.5	143.5	0	0	6,750	6,7
19	.33	2	138	0	1	138	0	.57	7.5	145.5	0	0	6,750	6,7
20	.99	14	152	0	0	152	0	.19	1.5	153.5	0	0	1,350	1,3
Total				0			1.5		126		0	1,500	113,400	114,9
Average				0			.075		6.3		0	75	5,670	5,74

Figure 17.7   **Charlestowne Harbor Computer Simulation**

Simulation Operation: Input: Output:
▪ Inventory   * Edit   ▪ Full
* Queuing   ▪ Load   * Summary
                                              ▪ Print   * Print
                                              ▪ Save   ▪ Save

Problem Formulation:
   Number of simulation runs: 20
   Expense from diverting one arrival: 15000
   Per unit waiting expense: 1000
   Per unit service expense: 900
   Number of parallel servers: 2

Enter the interarrival time distribution in the following table:

Interarrival Time	Probability
2	.35
6	.20
10	.30
14	.15

Enter the service time distribution in the following table:

Service Time	Probability
1.5	.20
4.5	.35
7.5	.25
10.5	.15
13.5	.05

---

unloading times are represented by the midpoints of the ranges from the corresponding probability distributions in Table 17.20.

Tables 17.21 and 17.22 show that the two-dock ($DO = 2$) alternative involves $113,400/$62,250 = 1.82$ or nearly double the unloading expense as the current one-dock ($DO = 1$) alternative. Nevertheless, no tankers are diverted under the $DO = 2$ policy. In addition, when compared to the current ($DO = 1$) operations, the extra dock reduces waiting time (from an average of 4.575 to 0.075 hours) and the existing queue length (from an average of 0.5 to 0 tankers). Consequently, the two-dock alternative leads to a smaller total cost than the current one-dock alternative. These simulation results then suggest that the best harbor policy (among the two examined) is to expand the port from one to two tanker docks.

In practice, management would likely run the simulation for many more than 20 tankers before making a final decision. Computer Exercise 22 will ask you to perform such an additional evaluation. Also, it will be useful to analyze the variation in total harbor cost TC before making the final decision.

Figure 17.7   *continuing*

Enter the pseudorandom number parameters in the following table:

Interarrival Times	Service Time
p=2	p=2
k=99	k=19
m=3	m=67

SIMULATION RESULTS

Run	Interarrival Time	Queue Length	Waiting Time	Service Time	Waiting Expense	Service Expense	Total Cost
1	14	0	0	7.5	0	6750	6750
2	14	0	0	10.5	0	9450	9450
3	10	0	0	13.5	0	12150	12150
4	2	0	0	13.5	0	12150	12150
5	10	0	1.5	4.5	1500	4050	5550
6	10	0	0	1.5	0	1350	1350
7	2	0	0	4.5	0	4050	4050
8	6	0	0	7.5	0	6750	6750
9	2	0	0	10.5	0	9450	9450
10	6	0	0	4.5	0	4050	4050
11	6	0	0	7.5	0	6750	6750
12	10	0	0	7.5	0	6750	6750
13	10	0	0	4.5	0	4050	4050
14	2	0	0	4.5	0	4050	4050
15	14	0	0	1.5	0	1350	1350
16	10	0	0	4.5	0	4050	4050
17	6	0	0	1.5	0	1350	1350
18	2	0	0	7.5	0	6750	6750
19	2	0	0	7.5	0	6750	6750
20	14	0	0	1.5	0	1350	1350
Total		0	1.500	126.0	1500	113400	114900
Average		0	.075	6.3	75	5670	5745

Computer Analysis

There are prewritten computer programs that have been developed for inventory and queuing simulations. The **QUANTITATIVE MANAGEMENT (QM)** software has a module that contains such programs. It is accessed by selecting the Simulation option from **QM**'s main menu. Figure 17.7 then shows how the module can be used to simulate Charlestowne's harbor operations (Management Situation 17.5).

Problem Formulation. As Figure 17.7 demonstrates, the user executes the module by selecting the Queuing option from the Simulation Operation menu. Next, the problem is formulated through the Edit option from the Input menu. This formulation requires the user to specify the number of simulation runs (arriving tankers), the number of parallel servers (docks), and the interarrival (time between tanker arrivals) and the

Simulation in Practice

Simulation is applied to a wide variety of management problems. Here are a few areas in which this quantitative analysis is used.

Area	Application
Finance and Accounting	Studying the diagnostic reasoning of a human financial expert Performing risk analysis at Getty Oil Company Reducing the investment in working capital
Marketing	Studying patronage behavior within shopping centers Determining a good product mix Evaluating the impact of promotion policies on sales
Production and Operations	Improving the productivity of company-owned and Burger King franchise resturaunts Designing and producing replacement communications satellites Planning laboratory operations
Public and Service Sector	Studying the operations of a crisis management information network Land use planning Providing services to the mentally retarded Examining the demand and supply for kidney transplantation

service (unloading time) distributions. Interarrival and service times must be represented by single values (midpoints of the corresponding ranges in Management Situation 17.5).

Where appropriate (as in Management Situation 17.5), the user can input the expense from diverting one arrival, the unit (per hour) waiting expense, and the per unit service (unloading) expense. Another input option (employed in Figure 17.7) is to specify the parameters (p, k, and m) for the pseudorandom number formulas. Report options then are specified through the Output menu.

Simulation Results. After receiving the information, **QM** processes the data and generates a report of the simulation results. In Summary Output mode, this report gives the interarrival time, queue length, waiting and service times, and where appropriate (as in Management Situation 17.5) the waiting, service, and total costs for each simulation run. Figure 17.7 shows that a two-dock operation results in an average queue of 0 tankers, an average waiting time of 0.075 hours (4.5 minutes), an average service time of 6.3 hours, and average waiting expense of $75, an average service expense of $5,670, and an average total cost of $5,745.

SUMMARY

This chapter has presented the essential concepts of simulation and has shown simulation as a technique for conducting trial and error experiments. The decision maker first builds a physical, analog, or mathematical model that imitates (acts like) the real situation. In this respect, it is helpful to develop a diagram, called a flowchart, that shows the sequence of operations and computations required by the simulation model. Then, by experimenting with the model, the manager is able to study the characteristics and behavior of the actual system. Figure 17.1 outlined the simulation process.

Simulation models often involve stochastic inputs. This chapter presented a systematic procedure, called the Monte Carlo method, to generate these inputs. We saw how mechanical devices (such as a deck of cards) and random-number tables are used to carry out the procedure.

In practice, most simulations deal with large and complex problems. Ordinarily, a computer must be used to perform the required operations and calculations in a reasonable time frame. Consequently, practitioners and computer manufacturers have developed computer programs, called simulators, to perform the required tasks. The simulators typically use general-purpose programming languages (like *FORTRAN* and *COBOL*) or special simulation languages (such as *SIMSCRIPT* and *GPSS*).

The chapter also examined the limitations and advantages of simulation. The major limitations are:

- The inability of simulation to search out and find the best policy to implement
- The time-consuming and costly nature of simulation as compared to analytical devices
- The technical problems involved in the design, validation, and estimation of simulation models

Nevertheless, the approach is popular for the following reasons:

- The ability of decision makers to easily comprehend and use the technique
- The usefulness and convenience of simulation as a management laboratory
- The capability of simulation to cope with problems that are too difficult and complex for solution by other quantitative approaches

In effect, then, simulation is an effective adjunct to, not substitute for, analytical solution procedures.

Glossary

deterministic simulation A simulation in which the decision maker knows the values of the uncontrollable inputs.

flowchart A diagram that shows the sequence of operations and computations required by the simulation model.

initial conditions The assumptions about the state of the system at the start of the simulation.

Monte Carlo simulation An approach that uses a random selection procedure (such as a deck of index cards or a random-number table) to generate the stochastic inputs for a simulation model.

probabilistic (stochastic) simulation A simulation in which the uncontrollable inputs are random variables.

pseudorandom numbers Computer-generated numbers, developed from mathematical formulas, that have the properties of random numbers.

random selection A method of selecting an input in such a way that each value in a sequence is independent and has an equal chance of being selected.

SIMAN, SIMSCRIPT, GASP, SLAM, and GPSS Popular computer languages used for simulation studies.

simulation A technique that uses a model to re-create an actual situation and then studies the system's characteristics and behavior by experimenting with the model.

simulator The computer program that performs the simulation operations and computations.

Thought Exercises

1. The following excerpts are taken from a panel discussion among business and government executives at a regional American Management Association conference:

   - Panelist 1: I'm really excited about simulation! It clearly has revolutionized modern management. Now we can analyze *real* problems instead of these make-believe situations created by our operations research staffs to fit their mathematical models.

   - Panelist 2: Yeah, I agree! For the first time since we started "getting sophisticated," I feel like I really have a grasp of what's going on! Before simulation, all I really understood were the results presented in the operations research summary report. Now I can see how the results are derived. It really makes me want to implement the recommendations.

   - Panelist 3: Pretty soon, we won't even need the mathematical operations researcher. All that'll be necessary will be a computer programmer capable of communicating with us in our language. We can re-create the actual situation, get the programmer to develop a simulator, run a few simulations, and come up with a solution to the problem.

   - Moderator: I think there are some basic misconceptions floating around the room. Apparently, we really don't understand the nature and purpose of simulation.

   If you were a panelist, how would you comment?

2. In which of the following situations is simulation appropriate?
   a. The owner of a major league baseball team is trying to decide whether she should move the team to another city. The decision depends on the legal implications of breaking the current stadium lease, uncertain future attendance, league approval, and player reaction.
   b. A private parcel post carrier wants to evaluate the profitability of several alternative routes. Profit depends on future demand, which is uncertain but follows a known probability distribution.
   c. The Navy is deciding on how many drydocks to construct at its main eastern shipyard. Its decision depends on the number of arrivals and the service time. Although both factors are uncertain, there are some historical probability data available.
   d. An airline gives a periodic fitness test to its pilots. The rating is based on a weighted combination of performance attributes that are measured on various standard mechanical devices.

3. June Swoon, the production manager for Albright Glass Materials, has proposed the following quality control plan. A sample of glassware will be inspected from each lot produced, and June will set the maximum allowable proportion of defective glasses. If the actual proportion of defects in the sample is no more than the maximum, the entire lot will be considered to be of acceptable quality. Otherwise, the entire lot will be reworked.

   Since the sample represents only a part of the lot, June recognizes that the plan involves some uncertainty and potential error. On one hand, the lot may be deemed unacceptable (and rejected) when it is good. This error is referred to as *producer's risk*. In this case, Albright will be unnecessarily remaking good glasses at an expected cost equal to the rework expense times the probability of producer's risk. Alternatively, the lot may be accepted when it is bad. Since the customer unknowingly receives defective merchandise, this error is called *consumer's risk*. It has an expected cost equal to the ill will expense times the probability of consumer's risk.

June wants to determine the maximum allowable proportion of defective glasses in the sample that will minimize the total quality control costs. She has decided to simulate costs and has developed the following flowchart for the simulation:

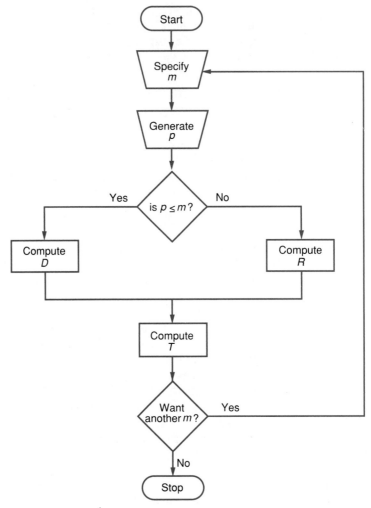

In this chart,

m = the maximum allowable proportion of defective glasses in the sample

p = the actual proportion of defective glasses in the sample

R = the cost of remaking good glasses

D = the ill will cost of providing defective merchandise

$T = R + D$ = the total quality control cost

Unfortunately, Alex Hander, the firm's computer specialist, has been unable to develop an acceptable simulator from the flowchart.

a. Can you identify the shortcomings in June Swoon's flowchart? Explain.

b. Develop the appropriate flowchart for this problem.

4. Develop a flowchart for the Monte Carlo procedure that was used to generate Caste's prices in Management Situation 17.2.

5. Felt Tip Enterprises manufactures the Elite Script pen with the new "magic eraser." The company is trying to decide whether to make or buy the eraser component. Quality Products, Inc. will sell the components on a monthly basis as follows:

- $50 for the first thousand
- $40 for every additional thousand

Felt Tip knows that the cost of making the component will depend on the uncertain demand for Elites. Corporate executives have developed the following demand, cost, and probability information:

Monthly Demand	Probability	Manufacturing Cost per Thousand Components ($)
250	.02	70
500	.08	66
750	.13	60
1,000	.37	50
1,250	.16	43
1,500	.14	35

Felt Tip executives would like to simulate the costs of making and buying the eraser component, but they are having trouble doing so. Explain why. Develop a procedure for simulating the cost.

6. Figure 17.2 presents a schematic representation of the profit model for Star Motors (Management Situation 17.1). Develop the same type of chart for Regional's investment model (Management Situation 17.3).

7. A recent Nobel Prize winner in economics made the following remarks to his class:

"Economists realize that decision making is a dynamic and complex process involving sequences of interrelated elements. Furthermore, the exact values of several components are not known precisely. Yet, we know that successful managers process the information, analyze the alternatives, and make the correct decision. The challenge to managerial economics, then, is to accurately replicate the successful manager's thought process. Computer simulation provides the means to meet this challenge."

Why did the economist arrive at this conclusion? In general terms, briefly explain how computer simulation might be used to re-create a successful decision maker's thought process.

8. Explain why you agree or disagree with the following statements:
    a.   The Monte Carlo procedure involves an arbitrary selection of the stochastic inputs in a simulation problem.
    b.   Simulation is best used as a last resort substitute for an analytical solution procedure.
    c.   Practical simulation users should have some knowledge of available computer software.
    d.   Eventually, there will be "canned" computer programs for most simulation problems.
    e.   Simulation can only be applied to those problems involving stochastic inputs.

Technique Exercises

9. A government economist has developed the following mathematical model of state business tax revenue:

$$B = tY$$

$$Y = 1 + .5R - .3D$$

$$D = (.2 + t)R$$

where B = the business tax revenue ($ million), t = the tax rate, Y = the business taxable income ($ million), R = the business revenue ($ million), and D = the business tax deductions ($ million). Assume that the state wants to maximize revenue from the business tax.
    a.   Draw a chart like Figure 17.2 that gives a schematic representation of the problem.
    b.   Develop a flow chart that can be used to simulate tax rate policy.

10. The production cost for a major consumer goods manufacturer is given by the following mathematical expression:

$$C = 40 - 2Q + Q^2$$

where C = the annual production cost ($ million) and Q = the output of soap (millions of bars). The company wants to minimize the cost of production but must also satisfy an uncertain demand D.
    a.   Draw a chart like Figure 17.2 that gives a schematic representation of the problem.
    b.   Develop a flowchart that can be used to simulate production policy.

11. In one of its consumer booklets, the government gives the flowchart on page 901 to aid borrowers in computing annual mortgage payments.
    In this chart,

A = the amount borrowed

T = the term, or number of years for the mortgage

i = the interest rate

P = the annual mortgage payments

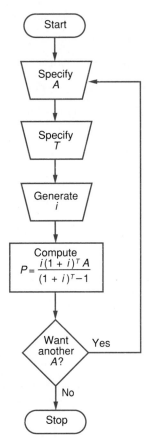

Use the flowchart to compute the annual mortgage payments for the following borrowers:

Borrower	Amount Borrowed ($)	Term (Years)	Interest Rate (%)
Johnson	80,000	20	10
Thomas	50,000	30	12
Indiri	100,000	30	11.75
Quanti	120,000	25	10.25
Smith	70,000	25	9.75
Jones	65,000	30	13
Olsen	75,000	30	12.50
Olanda	55,000	22	13.25
Ti	125,000	30	10.25
Wong	45,000	24	11.50

(**Note**: It will save time to look up the value of $(1 + i)^T$ in an annuity table. Such a table can be found in any basic finance text.)

12. The admissions officer of a major eastern public university has developed the following flowchart for selecting student applicants. In this flowchart,

S = an acceptable score for admission

GPA = the applicant's high school grade point average

SAT = the applicant's Scholastic Aptitude Test score

I = the applicant's interview rating

A = the applicant's average admission score

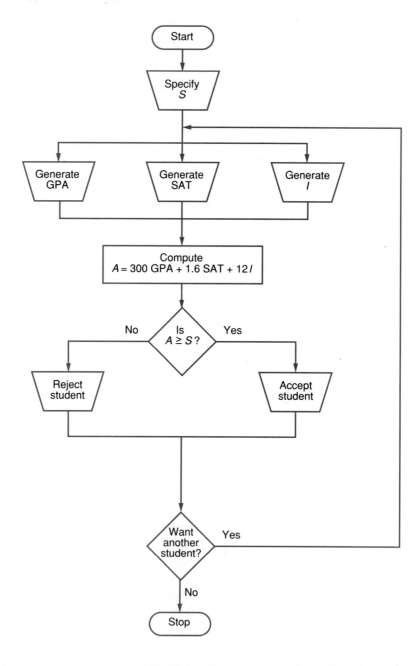

The university accepts any student with $A \geq 2,540$. Use the flowchart to simulate the admissions decision for the following students:

Student	GPA	SAT	I
Anne	3.5	400	80
Tom	2.8	600	90
Wally	4.0	600	50
Alaine	3.0	500	70
Phil	3.2	520	85
Jim	2.5	750	75
Judy	3.6	450	72
Nancy	3.8	400	65
Tina	2.7	650	100
Joe	3.9	800	55

13. Table 17.2 reports the results from simulating 10 weeks of dealer competition in Management Situation 17.1. Show how these results were obtained.

14. The following table reports data on employee absenteeism for a medium-sized brewery:

Days Absent per Year	Number of Employees
5	5
10	20
15	40
20	25
25	10
	100

Use the Monte Carlo procedure to simulate employee absenteeism for the next 20 years of brewery operations.

15. Store Surveys, Inc. uses the following procedure to determine the proportion of a territory that has "favorable market conditions." First, the decision maker superimposes a map of the territory on a graph that identifies market possibilities in the territories:

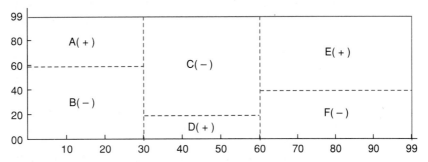

In this chart, there are six territories (A through F), with a plus ($+$) indicating favorable market conditions and a minus ($-$) unfavorable market conditions. Each axis has a scale of 100 integers numbered from 00 to 99. Next, a Monte Carlo procedure is used to generate coordinates on each axis of the map. The corresponding area of the map then identifies the likely market condition. Use the Store Surveys procedure to simulate the likely market conditions for a sample of 30 areas within the territory. Estimate the proportion of these areas that are likely to have favorable market conditions.

16. In this chapter, we have seen three ways to generate random numbers for the Monte Carlo procedure: the index card approach, random-number tables, and pseudorandom numbers. Table 17.7 presented the results from simulating 10 weeks of Caste's price behavior for Management Situation 17.2 using the random-number table approach.
    a. Use index cards and pseudorandom numbers to perform the same type of simulation shown in Table 17.7. Use Formula 17.2 with $p = 2$ and $k = 33$ and Formula 17.1 with $m = 11$ to derive the pseudorandom numbers.
    b. Tables 17.2 and 17.3 present the simulation results for the dealer competition problem (Management Situation 17.1). Use the results from Table 17.7 and part (a) to derive similar simulations using index cards, a random-number table, and pseudorandom numbers.
    Do the three approaches to Monte Carlo simulation lead to the same results? Explain.

17. Table 17.15 presents the simulated annual interest expense for Regional's investment financing situation (Management Situation 17.3). It shows that an investment combination of $B = 140$ and $L = 140$ results in the smallest annual interest expense. Simulate additional investment combinations between $B = 140$ and $B = 145$ and between $L = 140$ and $L = 145$ in increments of 1 for 20 years. Compute the standard deviation for each policy. What do the results indicate?

18. Drill, Inc. knows that the chance of striking oil and the size of the strike depend on the presence of underground formations favorable for petroleum accumulation. When the formations exist, there is a 60 percent chance of striking oil. The following table gives the size of the strike and the corresponding probabilities:

Millions of barrels	40	80	120	160	200
Probability	.2	.3	.4	.05	.05

Even if the formations do not exist, there is still a 20 percent chance of striking oil. The size of the strike and the corresponding probabilities are as follows:

Millions of barrels	10	20	30	40	50
Probability	.1	.3	.4	.15	.05

Experience indicates that 50 percent of the sites explored have the underground formations.
    a. Prepare a flowchart for this problem.
    b. Use the Monte Carlo method to simulate the results of exploring 20 sites. Show the computations in a table.
    c. What is the total number of barrels projected from the 20-site exploration?
    d. Based on the results from part (c), how many barrels should the company expect to strike if it explores 100 sites per year?

Computer Exercises

19. Refer back to Management Situation 17.4 in the text. Use the **QUANTITATIVE MAN-AGEMENT (QM)** software to simulate 100 days with each proposed inventory policy ($Q = 20$ and $R = 2$ versus $Q = 10$ and $R = 5$). What do the results indicate?

20. Yorktowne Vehicles specializes in the sale and service of construction equipment. A backhoe is one of its main products. Monthly demand and supplier lead time following the distribution is shown below.

Demand (Number)	Probability	Lead Time (Months)	Probability
1	.30	1	.50
2	.40	2	.30
3	.30	3	.20

    Yorktowne operates 12 months a year, and the company currently has five backhoes in stock. It costs $280 to carry each backhoe in inventory, $600 every time a sale is lost due to an inventory shortage, and $1,200 to place on order. Contracts require the company to order between five and nine backhoes at a time. Based on a previous analysis, management believes that an order should be placed whenever inventory falls below six backhoes.

    Yorktowne wants to find the least costly inventory policy (order quantity and reorder point combination). Use the **QM** software to simulate 100 months with each potential policy. What do the results indicate?

21. Vanguard Supplies seeks the order quantity and reorder point policy that will minimize the total costs associated with the company's inventory of the Executive office desks. The probability distributions for weekly retail demand and distributor lead time are shown below.

Demand	Probability	Lead Time (Weeks)	Probability
0	.05	1	.15
1	.25	2	.30
2	.40	3	.50
3	.20	4	.05
4	.10		

    It costs $50 per week to carry a desk in stock, $100 every time a sale is lost due to an inventory shortage, and $75 to place an order with the distributor. Currently, Vanguard has two Executive desks in stock.

    Management will establish trial policies by applying the basic EOQ model (as presented in Chapter 14) with the available demand values. Then, 100 weeks of operation will be simulated with each resulting policy (order quantity and reorder point combination). Use the **QM** software to perform the simulations. What do the results indicate?

22. Refer back to Management Situation 17.5 in the text. Use the **QM** software to simulate 100 tanker arrivals with each harbor configuration ($DO = 1$ versus $DO = 2$). What do the results indicate?

23. Spring preregistration is being planned at the local university. Past records indicate that students arrive for preregistration and are processed in a random fashion according to the following probability distributions.

Arrival Interval (Minutes)	Probability	Service Time (Minutes)	Probability
2	.1	3	.5
4	.3	6	.4
6	.5	9	.1
8	.1		

University officials are considering using between one and three service windows to process students at the registration office. Incoming students would form a single queue and be routed to the first available window on a first come, first serve basis. Staffing will be made in a way that enables each window to have approximately the same service time distribution. Use the **QM** software to simulate the preregistration of 100 students under each proposed policy (one, two, or three windows). What do the results indicate?

24. Jonesville Regional Bank is finalizing architectural drawings of its soon-to-be constructed branch at Thompson Street and Bradford Boulevard. An unresolved problem is to determine the number of drive-in tellers. It is possible to have either one or two parallel bays fed by a single channel of vehicles.

Because of the parking lot configuration and street ordinances, the bank can accommodate only four vehicles at one time (either in line or at a teller bay). When traffic exceeds capacity, any arriving vehicle will have to leave. Bank officials estimate that each such diversion will cost the bank 25 cents per minute in lost current and future profits.

The bank will operate the drive-in facilities eight hours per day, five days per week. Past records at other branches suggest that customers will arrive and be serviced in a random fashion according to the following probability distributions.

Time Between Vehicle Arrival (Minutes)	Probability	Service Time (Minutes)	Probability
1.5	.30	0.5	.15
4.0	.30	2.5	.25
7.5	.30	4.5	.40
9.0	.10	8.0	.20

Bays will be staffed with tellers earning $10 per hour including fringe benefits. These tellers will provide approximately the same service time distribution at each bay. Banking studies indicate that customers typically curtail their transactions to make up for time spent waiting. It is estimated that the lost business will cost the bank about 20 cents per minute.

The objective is to find the number of tellers that results in the least cost. Use the **QM** software to simulate 100 vehicle arrivals under each proposal (one versus two drive-in teller bays). What do the results indicate?

Applications Exercises

25. Fast Car Wash will buy a new waxing machine that is expected to have a useful life of 20 years. Even with good maintenance procedures, the machine will have periodic failures or breakdowns. Past records for similar machines indicate that the probabilities of failure during a year are as follows:

Number of Failures	Probability
0	.40
1	.20
2	.15
3	.10
4	.08
5	.07

Company management wants to simulate the number of breakdowns that will occur in the 20 years of operation.

You are asked to perform the simulation. According to the simulation, what will be the average number of breakdowns per year?

26. Gene Janen is the proprietor of Sweet Fragrance Floral Designs. He is trying to determine how many birthday bouquets to prepare each day. The objective is to maximize profits.

It costs $2 to prepare a birthday bouquet. Hence, with a $6 selling price, the floral shop realizes a $4 profit for each bouquet sold. However, if Gene overestimates demand, he must recycle the leftover bouquets at a salvage value of $0.50.

Gene's decision is difficult because the daily demand is uncertain. He has experienced some days when there was no demand. Yet, one day last month he sold 10 bouquets. The floral shop has the following data showing the daily demand during the past 100 days of operation:

Daily Demand	Number of Days Observed
0	5
1	8
2	12
3	20
4	30
5	15
6	5
7	5

If Gene continually fails to meet demand, he knows that the business will suffer a loss due to customer dissatisfaction. Gene estimates that the ill will cost is $0.60 per bouquet.

What quantity would give Gene the largest simulated profit over the next 30 days of operation?

27. The president of Western Telephone Company (WTC) has been informed that rank and file workers plan a strike action to protest working conditions. Unfortunately, the company's financial status makes it impossible to meet the workers' complete demands. Since the employees do not have substantial assets, the president is convinced that the strike will last no longer than one month.

In consultation with WTC's personnel manager, the president has subjectively assessed the probabilities for the duration of the strike as follows:

Weeks on Strike	Probability
1	.20
2	.30
3	.40
4	.10

While the workers are on strike, the company must make alternative arrangements for phone service. Supervisory personnel can handle the work load on an interim basis. However, this arrangement will divert these people from their normal duties into unfamiliar activities. Company financial analysts estimate that the reassignment will involve an additional cost of $80,000 per week. There is an alternative. Universal Services, Inc. employs a variety of skilled personnel to continue service while the phone workers are on strike. Universal has proposed the following contract terms:

Weeks Contracted	Cost
1	$100,000
2	$180,000
3	$210,000
4	$240,000

Contracts can be renewed or, for a $10,000 premium, a new agreement can be selected whenever an old pact expires.

Which alternative will minimize Western's additional operating cost for a simulated six months of strike activity?

28. The Eastern Water Control Project (EWCP) wants to install a water recapture system at Portsmell along the banks of the Kihoshi River. In such a system, water from the Kihoshi would be diverted and stored for future agricultural and commercial needs. The system's ability to provide water is determined by its design configuration and demand. Future demand depends on temperature and the amount of rainfall. County records show that a normal year (of average temperature and rainfall) involves a demand for 200 million gallons of water. Demand increases by one million gallons for each degree increase in temperature above the norm. In addition, demand decreases by two million gallons for each additional inch of rainfall above the average. These relationships are symmetrical. Also, EWCP has the following meteorological data:

Temperature (°F)	Proportion of Days	Average Annual Rainfall (Inches)	Probability
20	.05	10	.10
40	.25	30	.30
60	.40	50	.50
80	.20	70	.10
100	.10		

Project management is considering two design configurations. Design A would involve a system of dams and pipelines. Design B would create a large single dam and an elaborate distribution system of pumping stations and storage areas. Each system has different annual amortized and operating costs. Relevant cost data are as follows:

Design	Annual Amortized Cost ($ Million)	Operating Cost ($ per gallon)
A	6	.01
B	4	.02

EWCP wants to select the design configuration that will minimize total amortized plus operating costs over the next 20 years of operation. Which system should EWCP choose?

29. Tinseltown city management will add an airport route to its current public bus operations. Shown here are the alternatives being considered:

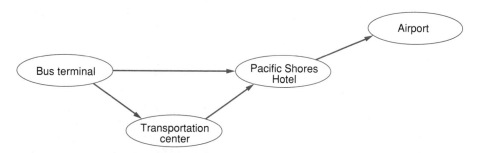

One route would start from the municipal bus station, go to a transportation center, move on to the Pacific Shores Hotel, and then proceed to the airport. The transportation center is a combination railway and intercity bus station located in the heart of town. Many airline personnel and air travelers stay at the Pacific Shores Hotel because "it is close to everything." The other route would bypass the transportation center.

   Bus service will be scheduled to complete each route once every hour. Each bus can carry 50 passengers at a cost of 20 cents per passenger mile. It is 15 miles from the bus terminal to the Pacific Shore Hotel and 5 more miles from there to the airport. The transportation center is 10 miles from both the hotel and the bus terminal. Fares will be collected at each stop according to the following fee schedule:

Route	Fare per Passenger ($)
Bus terminal to transportation center	1.50
Transportation center to Pacific Shores Hotel	1.50
Bus terminal to Pacific Shores Hotel	2.00
Pacific Shores Hotel to airport	0.50

Survey data indicate that hourly customer demand will be as follows:

Bus Terminal to Transportation Center		Transportation Center to Pacific Shores Hotel		Bus Terminal to Pacific Shores Hotel		Pacific Shores Hotel to Airport	
Number of Passengers	Probability	Number of Passengers	Probability	Number of Passengers	Probability	Number of Passengers	Probability
10	.20	10	.15	10	.05	10	.10
20	.50	20	.40	20	.25	20	.15
30	.25	30	.35	30	.45	30	.25
40	.05	40	.05	40	.15	40	.45
		50	.05	50	.10	50	.05

There are five buses available for the service. How many buses should city management schedule over each route to maximize simulated profits for the first 30 days of operation?

30. Bank of North America (BNA) issues a credit card. By law, the bank earns 1.5 percent interest per month on any unpaid credit balance of $500 or less. The bank charges 1 percent for any unpaid balance above $500. It costs BNA 0.5 percent to administer and finance balances of $1,000 or less. Because of the increased likelihood for potential defaults and resulting legal expenses, larger balances involve an additional cost of 0.75 percent.

A customer's current credit balance equals the unpaid amounts from previous months plus new purchases less payments. New purchases must not exceed the card holder's credit limit less any unpaid amounts from previous months. BNA sets the credit limit as a fixed proportion of the customer's recorded monthly income. Experience indicates that the bank is exposed to unacceptable risks when the proportion exceeds 40 percent.

Management wants to establish the proportion that will maximize profits from credit card operations. The decision is difficult because profits depend on the card holder's income, the amount owed, and monthly payments. Unfortunately, these amounts vary from customer to customer and month to month. The bank's accounting department has compiled the following data from credit records:

Reported Monthly Income ($)	Proportion of Customers	Monthly Payments ($)	Proportion of Customers	Amount Owed ($)	Proportion of Customers
1,500	.05	50	.30	200	.50
2,000	.10	100	.25	300	.35
2,500	.15	150	.20	400	.10
3,000	.40	200	.15	500	.05
3,500	.25	250	.10		
4,000	.05				

You are hired as a consultant.

a. Develop a model that re-creates the credit card operation.

b. Simulate the next 2.5 years of operations for those customers that make new purchases equal to their available credit.

c. Recommend a credit limit policy.

For Further Reading

Simulation Methodology

Banks, J., and J.S. Carson. *Discrete-Event System Simulation.* Englewood Cliffs, NJ: Prentice-Hall, 1984.

Bodily, S. "Spreadsheet Modeling as a Stepping Stone." *Interfaces* (September–October 1986):34.

Dunning, K.A. *Getting Started in GPSS.* San Jose, CA: Engineering Press, 1981.

Gray, P. *Student Guide to IFPS.* New York: McGraw-Hill, 1983.

Graybeal, W., and U.W. Pooch. *Simulation: Principles and Methods.* Cambridge, MA: Winthrop, 1980.

Hernandez, J.P., and J.M. Proth. "A Good Solution Instead of an Optimal One." *Interfaces* (April 1982):37.

Hussey, J.R., et al. "Correlated Simulation Experiments in First-Order Response Surface Design." *Operations Research* (September–October 1987):744.

Kiviat, P.J., et al. *The SIMSCRIPT II Programming Language.* Englewood Cliffs, NJ: Prentice-Hall, 1977.

Kleijnen, J.P.C. "Analyzing Simulation Experiments with Common Random Numbers." *Management Science* (January 1988):65.

Law, A.M. "Statistical Analysis of Simulation Output Data." *Operations Research* (November–December 1983): 983.

Law, A.M., and D.W. Kelton. *Simulation Modeling and Analysis.* New York: McGraw-Hill, 1982.

Modianos, D. "Random Number Generation on Microcomputers." *Interfaces* (July–August 1984):81.

Naylor, T.H. *Simulation Models in Corporate Planning.* New York: Praeger, 1979.

Neelamkavil, F. *Computer Simulation and Modelling.* New York: Wiley, 1987.

Pegden, C.D. *Introduction to SIMAN.* State College, PA: Systems Modeling corporation, 1984.

Pritsker, A.A. *The GASP IV Simulation Language.* New York: Wiley, 1974.

Pritsker, A.A., et al. *Introduction to Simulation and SLAM.* New York: Halsted press, 1979.

Sterman, J.D. "Testing Behavioral Simulation Models by Direct Experiment." *Management Science* (December 1987):1572.

Watson, H.J. *Computer Simulation In Business.* New York: Wiley, 1981.

Simulation Applications

Baker, G.K., et al. "Production Planning and Cost Analysis on a Microcomputer." *Interfaces* (July–August 1987):53.

Belardo, S., et al. "Simulation of a Crisis Management Information Network: A Serendipitous Evaluation." *Decision Sciences* (Fall 1983):588.

Bouwman, M.J. "Human Diagnostic Reasoning by Computer: An Illustration from Financial Analysis." *Management Science* (June 1983):653

Brill, E.D., et al. "Modeling to Generate Alternatives: The HSJ Approach and an Illustration Using a Problem in Land Use Planning." *Management Science* (March 1982):221.

Christy, D.P., and H.J. Watson. "The Application of Simulation: A Survey of Industry Practice." *Interfaces* (October 1983):47.

Crask, M.R. "A Simulation Model of Patronage Behavior within Shopping Centers." *Decision Sciences* (January 1979):1.

Davidson, L.B., and D.O. Cooper. "Implementing Effective Risk Analysis at Getty Oil Company." *Interfaces* (December 1980):62.

Edwards, J.R. et al., "Blue Bell Trims Its Inventory," *Interfaces* (January–February 1985):34–52.

Golovin, L.B. "Product Blending: A Simulation Case Study in Double Time: An Update." *Interfaces* (July–August 1985):39.

Heiner, K., et al. "A Resource Allocation and Evaluation Model for Providing Services to the Mentally Retarded." *Management Science* (July 1981):769.

Huang, P.Y., et al. "A Simulation Analysis of the Japanese Just-in-Time Technique (with Kanbans) for a Multiline, Multistage Production System." *Decision Sciences* (July 1983):326.

Jacobs, F.A., and F.E. Watkins. "The Relevance of State University Retirement Plans in Job Selection." *Decision Sciences* (Winter 1984):119.

Jones, L. "A Simulation Model for Analytical Laboratory Planning." *Interfaces* (November–December 1984):80.

Kaplan, A., and S. Frazza. "Empirical Inventory Simulation: A Case Study." *Decision Sciences* (January 1983):62.

Lembersky, M.R., and U.H. Chi. "Decision Simulators' Speed Implementation and Improve Operations." *Interfaces* (July–August 1984):1.

Luterbacher, U., and et al. "Simulating the Response of a Small Open Politico-Economic System to International Crises: The Case of Switzerland." *Management Science* (February 1987):270.

Martell, D.L., et al. "An Evaluation of Forest Fire Initial Attack Resources." *Interfaces* (September–October 1984):20.

McCall, M.W., and M.M. Lombardo. "Using Simulation for Leadership and Management Research: Through the Looking Glass." *Management Science* (May 1982):533.

Mellinchamp, J.M., and C.P. Weaver. "Simulation and Sewage." *Decision Science* (July 1977):584.

Russell, R.A., and R. Hickle. "Simulation of a CD Portfolio." *Interfaces* (May–June 1986):49.

Ruth, R.J., et al. "Kidney Transplantation: A Simulation Model for Examining Demand and Supply." *Management Science* (May 1985):515.

Scherer, W.T., and C.C. White. "A Planning and Decision-Aiding Procedure for Purchasing and Launching Spacecraft." *Interfaces* (May–June 1986):31.

Swart, W., and L. Donno. "Simulation Modeling Improves Operations, Planning, and Productivity of Fast Food Restaurants." *Interfaces* (December 1981):35.

Thompson, W.A., et al. "Performance of a Regulatory Agency as a Function of Its Structure and Client Environment: A Simulation Study." *Management Science* (January 1982):57.

Case: Holiday Confections, Inc.

Holiday Confections, Inc., manufactures assorted candy products. The company's product line includes many stable items that sell at fairly uniform rates throughout the year. However, most of their revenue comes from gift-wrapped candy assortments for sale on special occasions, such as Valentine's Day, Easter, Thanksgiv-ing, and Christmas. Consequently, Holiday's sales show pronounced seasonal variations. Expenses also fluctuate from month to month, and both sales and expenses are uncertain. Company records and recent experience provide the data shown in the following table:

Quarter	Sales	Probability	Expenses	Probability
First	$200,000	.10	$400,000	.20
	300,000	.20	500,000	.40
	400,000	.50	600,000	.40
	500,000	.20		
Second	$400,000	.25	$300,000	.10
	600,000	.50	400,000	.15
	800,000	.25	500,000	.40
			600,000	.25
			700,000	.10
Third	$100,000	.20	$500,000	.40
	300,000	.40	700,000	.50
	500,000	.40	900,000	.10
Fourth	$ 500,000	.05	$400,000	.10
	700,000	.25	600,000	.70
	900,000	.60	800,000	.20
	1,100,000	.10		

The difference between sales and expenses gives Holiday's cash balance in any given month.

The company anticipates a net cash drain during the forthcoming year. Hence, management is searching for the pattern of financing that will minimize Holiday's total interest cost. The firm can borrow a maximum of $100,000 per month from a bank at an annual interest rate of 12 percent. The amount borrowed at the beginning of any month must be repaid with interest at the beginning of the following month. In addition, Holiday can issue up to $300,000 worth of 90-day commercial paper bear-ing an annual interest rate of 9.6 percent. Interest charges on this paper are payable monthly. However, the amount borrowed at the beginning of each month cannot be repaid until the beginning of the third succeeding month. Also, the paper must be issued in $10,000 denominations. Any surplus funds are invested in government securities yielding 6 percent per annum.

Holiday's management has unsuccessfully tried to develop a financial plan. You are commissioned to develop a model that simulates this situation and to recommend a low-cost financial plan.

Appendix A: Classical Optimization Review

Throughout the text, we assume that aspects of many problems are quantifiable and that analyses of these factors yield insights useful in decision making. A significant number of such problems involve, or can be approximated by, classical deterministic models—formulations in which the variables are measured on continuous scales (such as time or length) and whose mathematical relationships have no kinks or discontinuities. In these cases, calculus can often be used to find the optimal problem solution. This appendix reviews the calculus-based optimization methodologies.

FUNCTIONAL RELATIONSHIPS

As explained in Part I of the text, models represent management problems in forms suitable for analysis. Frequently, the representation will be a mathematical equation, called a **function,** that relates a dependent (typically, a criterion) variable to an appropriate independent (predictor) variable or variables.

Univariate Function

If there is only one independent variable, the function will have the following general univariate form:

$$y = f(x)$$

where y = the value of the dependent variable, x = the value of the independent variable, and $f(x)$ is read "function of x." This univariate function indicates that the value of y depends on the value of x. In the function, each value of x will be associated with one and only one value of y, but the same y value may be associated with more than one x value.

When the dependent and independent variables are related in a well-defined manner, the exact function can be determined from systematic observation. For example, suppose a pizza deliverer is paid a base weekly salary of $80 plus a commission of 30 cents on every dollar of sales. Her total compensation will then be given by the following univariate function:

$$E = \$80 + 0.30S$$

where E = weekly earnings and S = weekly pizza sales in dollars.

Table A.1   Suburban's Financial Summary

Price (per thousand leaflets)	$45
Labor cost (per thousand leaflets)	$10
Material cost (per thousand leaflets)	$ 5
Variable cost (per thousand leaflets)	$15
Administrative expense (per year)	$7,000
Press rental expense (per year)	$2,000
Fixed cost (per year)	$9,000

At other times, the logical relationships among the dependent and independent variables will not be known exactly. In such cases, the firm can collect relevant data through sampling or experimentation and then use statistical analyses (as discussed in Chapter 3) to estimate the function.

Management Situation A.1 illustrates a univariate function and its uses in decision making.

Management Situation A.1

Desktop Publishing

The owner of Suburban Flyers uses her microcomputer and desktop publishing software to print advertising leaflets for local merchants and national chains. Existing contracts and historical transactions provide the data summarized in Table A.1.

Suburban's owner wants to know how profit will be affected by volume.

There are three univariate functions in Management Situation A.1—total revenue, total cost, and total profit. Total revenue R will equal the constant price of $45 multiplied by volume (in thousands) V, or

$$R = \$45V$$

and total cost C will equal the $9,000 fixed cost plus the constant $15 variable cost multiplied by volume, or

$$C = \$9,000 + \$15V$$

Total profit π, then, will be the difference between total revenue and total cost, or

$$\pi = R - C = \$45V - (\$9,000 + \$15V) = \$30V - \$9,000$$

The dependent variables are total revenue R in the revenue function, total cost C in the cost function, and total profit π in the profit function. Volume V is the independent variable in each of these three functions. There is a linear relationship among the dependent and independent variables in every function.

Figure A.1 **Cost-Profit-Volume Analysis**

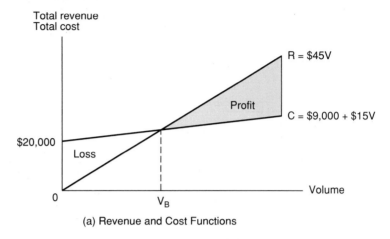

(a) Revenue and Cost Functions

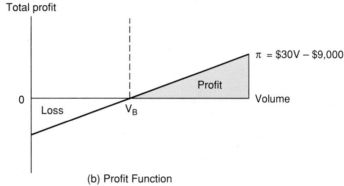

(b) Profit Function

Cost-Profit-Volume Analysis

By plotting the revenue, cost, and profit functions, Suburban will get Figure A.1. Panel (a) illustrates how total revenue R and total cost C vary with volume V, and panel (b) graphs the relationship between total profit π and volume. These panels show that volumes less than V_B generate losses (have $\pi < 0$), whereas volumes above V_B earn profits (have $\pi > 0$). Such an evaluation, which examines how revenue, cost, and profit vary with volume, is known as **cost-profit-volume analysis**.

Breakeven Point

In Figure A.1, V_B is a **breakeven point**, or a volume at which total revenue is exactly equal to total cost (and hence results in zero profit). When the total revenue and total cost functions are linear (as in Management Situation A.1), this point can be found with the following formula:

(A.1) $$V_B = F/(P - VC)$$

where F = fixed expenses, P = unit price, and VC = variable cost per unit. Alternatively, and when the total revenue and total cost functions are nonlinear, the decision maker can solve the total profit function for the breakeven point (or the volume that results in zero profit).

Suburban has F = \$9,000, P = \$45, and VC = \$15. According to formula (A.1), then, the owner must print

$$V_B = F/(P - VC) = \$9,000/(\$45 - \$15) = 300$$

thousand leaflets per year to break even.

Specified Profit

Cost-profit-volume analysis can also identify the volume needed to obtain a specified profit. For example, if Suburban's owner wants to earn a profit of π = \$12,000, the total profit function becomes

$$\pi = \$12,000 = \$30V - \$9,000$$

which is satisfied when Suburban prints

$$V = (\$12,000 + \$9,000)/\$30 = 700$$

thousand leaflets per year.

UNIVARIATE OPTIMIZATION

Although cost-profit-volume analysis examines the relationship between the dependent and independent variables, it does not explicitly search for an optimal solution. When the function is continuous, this optimal search can be performed with **differential calculus**.

Optimality Concepts

Figure A.2, which plots a continuous univariate function $y = f(x)$, illustrates some of the methodologies' concepts. Included in the function's multiple peaks and troughs are

1. A **relative,** or **local, maximum** at point A, where any very small change in the independent variable results in a smaller value for the dependent variable.
2. An **absolute,** or **global, minimum** at point B, where the value of the independent variable generates the smallest value for the dependent variable in the function.
3. An **absolute,** or **global, maximum** at point D, where the value of the independent variable generates the largest value for the dependent variable in the function.
4. A **relative,** or **local, minimum** at point E, where any very small change in the independent variable results in a larger value for the dependent variable.

Such maxima and minima are known collectively as **extreme points.**

In Figure A.2, there is a dotted line drawn tangent to the curve $y = f(x)$ at each extreme point. These tangent lines all are flat; that is, they have a slope equal to zero. Such points are called **stationary points**. This observation illustrates the following

Figure A.2   **Extreme Points**

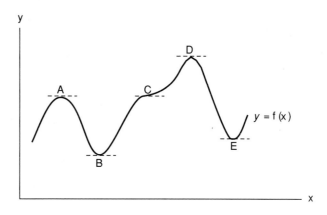

necessary condition for identifying extreme points: *Maxima or minima will be stationary points in the function.*

The condition is necessary but not sufficient, because stationary points are not always maxima or minima. For example, point C in Figure A.2 has a tangent slope equal to zero, but it is not an extreme point. Instead, C is an **inflection point**, or a point at which the concavity of the function changes (from concave downward to concave upward).

To establish a sufficient condition for identifying extreme points, the decision maker must test for the nature of a stationary point. A popular test is based on an examination of the rate of change of a tangent's slope at the stationary point.

Derivatives

When a line is drawn tangent to a continuous univariate function, the line's slope measures the function's rate of change. Between any two points on the line, the rate of change will equal

$$\Delta y / \Delta x$$

where Δy (delta y) = the change in the dependent variable and Δx (delta x) = the change in the independent variable between the two points. As the distance between the two points gets progressively smaller, Δx will approach zero, and the limit of the rate of change will equal the slope of the line drawn tangent to a single point in the function. This instantaneous rate of change, or marginal change in the dependent variable, is called the **first derivative** and is defined as

$$\frac{dy}{dx} = \frac{\text{limit}}{\Delta x \to 0} \frac{\Delta y}{\Delta x}$$

The notation $f'(x)$ is often used as an equivalent form for the derivative dy/dx.

Except for linear functions, the derivative continually changes at different points in the function; this fact can be demonstrated by drawing lines tangent to various points

Table A.2   **Differentiation Rules***

Rule	Function $y = f(x)$	Derivative $dy/dx = f'(x)$	Example
Constant	$y = c$	0	$y = 6$ $f'(x) = 0$
General	$y = cx^n$	ncx^{n-1}	$y = 0.6x$ $f'(x) = 0.6$
Sum	$y = u(x) + v(x)$	$u'(x) + v'(x)$	$y = 3x^2 + x^3$ $f'(x) = 6x + 3x^2$
Product	$y = u(x) \cdot v(x)$	$u(x) \cdot v'(x) + v(x) \cdot u'(x)$	$y = 8x^2(x^{-3})$ $f'(x) = 8x^2(-3x^{-4})$ $+ (x^{-3})16x$ $= -8x^{-2}$
Quotient	$y = u(x)/v(x)$	$\dfrac{v(x) \cdot u'(x) - u(x) \cdot v'(x)}{[v(x)]^2}$	$y = 2x^4/x^2$ $f'(x) = \dfrac{x^2(8x^3) - 2x^4(2x)}{(x^2)^2}$ $= 4x$
Chain	$y = f(u)$ $u = f(x)$	$f'(u) \cdot u'(x)$	$y = 2u$ $u = 3x^3$ $f'(x) = 2(9x^2) = 18x^2$
Power	$y = [u(x)]^n$	$n[u(x)]^{n-1} \cdot u'(x)$	$y = 1/2(2x^{3/2})^2$ $f'(x) = (2x^{3/2})(3x^{1/2})$ $= 6x^2$
Natural logarithm	$y = \ln[u(x)]$	$1/u(x) \cdot [u'(x)]$	$y = \ln(2x^2)$ $f'(x) = 1/2x^2 \cdot (4x)$ $= 2/x$

*The notations $u(x)$ and $v(x)$ are used to distinguish two different functions having the form $y = f(x)$; c and n are constants; $e = 2.718. . .$, the base of natural logarithms $\ln(x)$.

(besides A through E) of the function in Figure A.2. Consequently, the derivative itself will typically be a function.

Differentiation. The process of finding a derivative, or marginal change, is called **differentiation**. There are general rules available to perform this process, including the basic rules summarized in Table A.2.

Second Derivative. Since the first derivative is a function, differentiation (perhaps with the rules from Table A.2) can be used to determine the **second derivative**, or the derivative of the first derivative. The second derivative will measure the instantaneous rate at which the first derivative is changing at a point in the function. For example, the univariate function

$$y = 3x^2 + x^3$$

has a first derivative (from Table A.2) of

$$dy/dx = f'(x) = 6x + 3x^2$$

and the second derivative, denoted as d^2y/dx^2 or $f''(x)$, is

$$f''(x) = 6 + 6x$$

When $x = 1/2$,

$$f''(x) = 6 + 6(1/2) = 3$$

so that the first derivative is increasing and the original function must be concave upward at this point. If $x = 2$,

$$f''(x) = 6 + 6(2) = -6$$

so that the first derivative is decreasing and the original function must be concave downward at this point.

Optimization Process

Such analyses suggest that the best solution to a univariate optimization problem (if it exists) can be found with the following procedure:

1. Find the first derivative $f'(x)$ of the original function.
2. Locate the stationary points by setting the first derivative equal to zero and solving the resulting equation. A *necessary condition* for optimization is that an extreme (maximum or minimum) point must be a stationary point.
3. Find the second derivative $f''(x)$ and determine its value at the stationary points. A *sufficient condition* for a relative minimum is that the second derivative must have a positive value $[f''(x) > 0]$ at the corresponding stationary point. If the second derivative is a negative value $[f''(x) < 0]$, the corresponding stationary point is a relative maximum.
4. Substitute each stationary point into the original function to identify the global extreme points.

Management Situation A.2 illustrates the procedure.

Management Situation A.2

Professional Golfing

Your friend is a professional golfer with three years of experience on the tour. She has noted that her winnings are related to the amount of practice time before a tournament. A lengthy discussion has provided some data on the winnings and practice time variables. After analyzing these data with a statistical computer package, you are able to estimate her winnings function as

$$W = 1000T - 10T^2$$

where W = earnings per tournament and T = weekly hours of practice.

Your friend seeks the amount of practice time that will maxmize her tournament earnings.

By plotting the winnings function on a graph, we get Figure A.3. This figure illustrates how tournament earnings W vary with practice time T. It shows that winnings follow a nonlinear pattern, increasing until practice time reaches T^* hours per week and declining thereafter (possibly because the extra effort takes away the golfer's mental and physical "edges").

According to Table A.2's differentiation rules, the first derivative of your friend's winnings function, or her marginal earnings, will be

$$\frac{dW}{dT} = 1000 - 20T$$

These marginal earnings will be stationary when

$$\frac{dW}{dT} = 1000 - 20T = 0$$

or when she practices $T = 50$ hours per week. Since the second derivative is

$$W''(T) = -20$$

or negative at all points of the function, $T = 50$ hours (which corresponds to T^* in Figure A.3) gives the practice time that will maximize your friend's tournament earnings. The maximum earnings will be

$$W = 1000T - 10T^2 = 1000(50) - 10(50)^2 = \$25,000$$

per tournament.

Inventory Applications

The univariate optimization process is also used to determine Chapter 14's economic order quantity (EOQ) and economic production quantity (EPQ) formulas.

Economic Order Quantity. In the basic EOQ model, the decision maker seeks the order quantity Q that minimizes total inventory cost

$$TC = cD + \frac{c_oD}{Q} + \frac{c_HQ}{2}$$

Where c, D, c_o, and c_H are constants. According to Table A.2's differentiation rules, the first derivative of TC, or marginal cost, is

$$\frac{dTC}{dQ} = -\frac{c_oD}{Q^2} + \frac{c_H}{2}$$

which equals zero at the EOQ formula of

$$Q^* = \sqrt{\frac{2c_oD}{c_H}}$$

Since the second derivative,

$$TC''(Q) = \frac{2c_oD}{Q^3}$$

Figure A.3   **Golf Function**

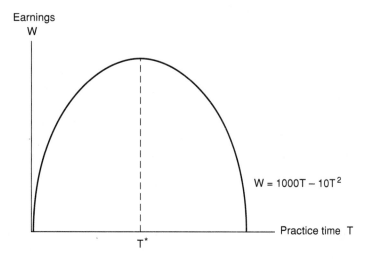

will be positive for all reasonable c_o, D, and Q values (c_o, D, $Q > 0$), the EOQ formula gives the minimum total cost solution.

Economic Production Quantity.   In the EPQ model, management seeks the lot size Q that minimizes total cost

$$TC = cD + \frac{c_oD}{Q} + \left(1 - \frac{D}{P}\right)\frac{c_HQ}{2}$$

where c, D, c_o, P, and c_H are constants. According to Table A.2's differentiation rules, the first derivative of TC, or marginal cost, is

$$\frac{dTC}{dQ} = \frac{-c_oD}{Q^2} + \left(1 - \frac{D}{P}\right)\frac{c_H}{2}$$

which equals zero at the EPQ formula of

$$Q^* = \sqrt{\frac{2c_oD}{\left(1 - \frac{D}{P}\right)c_H}}$$

Since the second derivative of

$$TC''(Q) = \frac{2c_oD}{Q^3}$$

will be positive for all reasonable c_o, D, and Q values, the EPQ formula gives the minimum total cost solution.

MULTIVARIATE OPTIMIZATION

There are many decision situations that involve a single dependent variable but two or more independent variables. In these situations, the function will have the following general multivariate form:

$$y = f(x_1, x_2, \ldots, x_n)$$

where y = the value of the dependent variable, x_i = the value of the ith independent variable, and n = the number of independent variables. This multivariate function indicates that the value of y depends on the values of x_1 through x_n.

The calculus of multivariate functions, although more involved, is similar to the methodology for univariate functions. Once more, it involves finding derivatives and using them to establish the nature of stationary points in the function.

Partial Derivatives

There will be as many first derivatives, or marginal changes in the dependent variable, as there are independent variables in the multivariate function. Each of these first derivatives, termed **first partial derivatives**, measures the instantaneous rate of change in the dependent variable with respect to a very small change in one of the independent variables, *while holding constant the values of all other independent variables*. Other independent variables are held constant to isolate the separate effect on the dependent variable of the pertinent independent variable.

Partial derivatives are found with the same rules used to find derivatives for univariate functions. In applying these rules, the decision maker must treat the other independent variables as constants. For example, consider the multivariate function

$$y = 3x_1^2 - 2x_1x_2 + 4x_2^2 + 5,000$$

According to Table A.2's differentiation rules, the partial derivative of y with respect to x_1, denoted as $\partial y / \partial x_1$, or sometimes as f_{x_1}, is

$$\frac{\partial y}{\partial x_1} = 6x_1 - 2x_2$$

Similarly, the partial derivative of y with respect to x_2, denoted as $\partial y / \partial x_2$, or f_{x_2}, is

$$\frac{\partial y}{\partial x_2} = -2x_1 + 8x_2$$

Higher-Order Partials. In a multivariate function, there can be two types of second derivatives: **pure** and **mixed (cross) partial derivatives**. A pure partial derivative gives the instantaneous rate of change in the first partial with respect to the same independent variable, while holding constant the values of all other independent variables. For example, the pure partial derivative of

$$\frac{\partial y}{\partial x_1} = 6x_1 - 2x_2$$

with respect to x_1, denoted as $\partial^2 y / \partial x_1^2$ or $f_{x_1 x_1}$, is

$$f_{x_1 x_1} = 6$$

A mixed (cross) partial derivative gives the instantaneous rate of change in the first partial with respect to a different independent variable, while holding constant the values of all other independent variables. For example, the mixed (cross) partial derivative of

$$\frac{\partial y}{\partial x_2} = -2x_1 + 8x_2$$

with respect to x_1, denoted as $\partial^2 y / \partial x_2 \partial x_1$ or $f_{x_2 x_1}$, is

$$f_{x_2 x_1} = -2$$

Similarly, the cross partial derivative of

$$\frac{\partial y}{\partial x_1} = 6x_1 - 2x_2$$

with respect to x_2, denoted as $\partial^2 y / \partial x_1 \partial x_2$ or $f_{x_1 x_2}$, is

$$f_{x_1 x_2} = -2$$

As the calculations demonstrate, cross partial derivatives taken with respect to the same two independent variables (such as $f_{x_1 x_2}$ and $f_{x_2 x_1}$) are always equal to one another.

Optimization Process

As with univariate functions, stationary points are located with the first derivatives of the multivariate function. Second derivatives again are used to test the stationary points. The process can be summarized as follows:

1. Find the first partial derivatives of the original multivariate function.
2. Establish the necessary conditions for optimization by setting the first partials equal to zero and solving the resulting equations for the stationary points in the function.
3. Find the second (pure and cross) partial derivatives and use them to establish the sufficient conditions for optimization.
4. Identify the global extreme points by substituting the stationary points into the original multivariate function.

In a multivariate function with only two independent variables, the stationary point is an extreme point if

$$(f_{x_1 x_1}) f_{x_2 x_2} - (f_{x_1 x_2})^2 > 0$$

The extreme point is a local maximum if

$$f_{x_1 x_1} < 0 \qquad \text{and} \qquad f_{x_2 x_2} < 0$$

but a local minimum when

$$f_{x_1 x_1} > 0 \qquad \text{and} \qquad f_{x_2 x_2} > 0$$

Management Situation A.3 illustrates the multivariate optimization process for this two-independent-variable case.

Management Situation A.3
═══

More Golfing

After considering the analysis resulting from Management Situation A.2, your friend discloses that recreation reduces the tensions of the golf tournament and helps her concentration. Thus, she believes that the amount of recreation time also is related to her winnings. Another lengthy discussion and an analysis of the resulting data provides the following multivariate winnings function:

$$W = 1,000T - 10T^2 + 1,000X - 10X^2 - 10TX$$

where X = weekly hours of recreation and the other terms are defined as before.

Your friend seeks the amount of practice time and recreation that will maximize her tournament earnings.

───

Necessary Conditions. According to Table A.2's differentiation rules, the first partial derivatives of your friend's winnings function, or her marginal earnings, are

$$\frac{\partial W}{\partial T} = 1,000 - 20T - 10X$$

with respect to practice time and

$$\frac{\partial W}{\partial X} = 1,000 - 20X - 10T$$

with respect to recreation. These marginal earnings will be stationary when

$$\frac{\partial W}{\partial T} = 1,000 - 20T - 10X = 0$$

and

$$\frac{\partial W}{\partial X} = 1,000 - 20X - 10T = 0$$

or when she practices $T = 33.33$ hours and has $X = 33.33$ hours of recreation per week.

Sufficient Conditions.   The pure partial derivatives are

$$f_{TT} = -20 \quad \text{and} \quad f_{XX} = -20$$

and the mixed (cross) partial derivatives are

$$f_{TX} = -10 \quad \text{and} \quad f_{XT} = -10$$

Since

$$f_{TT}(f_{XX}) - (f_{TX})^2 = -20(-20) - (-10)^2 = 300$$

or a positive value, the stationary point is an extreme point. This extreme point is a local maximum because f_{TT} and f_{XX} are both negative. Since there are no other local maxima, the point also represents a global maximum point.

Optimal Solution. The analysis suggests that your friend can maximize her tournament earnings at

$$W = 1,000(33.33) - 10(33.33)^2 + 1,000(33.33) - 10(33.33)^2 - 10(33.33)(33.33)$$

$$= \$33,333.33$$

by practicing $T = 33.33$ hours and having $X = 33.33$ of recreation per week.

Inventory Application

The multivariate optimization process is used to determine the optimal order quantity and number of backorders for Chapter 14's planned shortage model. In this model, management seeks the order quantity Q and the number of backorders S that minimize total inventory cost

$$TC = cD + \frac{c_o D}{Q} + c_H \frac{(Q - S)^2}{2Q} + \frac{c_B S^2}{2Q}$$

where c, D, c_o, c_H, and c_B are constants.

Necessary Conditions. According to Table A.2's differentiation rules, the first partial derivatives of TC, or the marginal costs, are

$$\frac{\partial TC}{\partial Q} = -\frac{c_o D}{Q^2} - \frac{(c_H + c_B)S^2}{2Q^2} + \frac{c_H}{2}$$

and

$$\frac{\partial TC}{\partial S} = \left(\frac{c_H + c_B}{Q} \right) S - c_H$$

These marginal costs will be stationary when $\partial TC/\partial Q = 0$ and $\partial TC/\partial S = 0$ or when

$$S^* = Q^* \left(\frac{c_H}{c_H + c_B} \right)$$

and

$$Q^* = \sqrt{\frac{2c_o D}{c_H} \left(\frac{c_H + c_B}{c_B} \right)}$$

Sufficient Conditions. The pure partial derivatives are

$$f_{QQ} = \frac{(c_H + c_B)S^2 + 2c_o D}{Q^3}$$

and

$$f_{SS} = \frac{c_H + c_B}{Q}$$

while the mixed (cross) partial derivatives are

$$f_{QS} = f_{SQ} = \frac{-(c_H + c_B)S}{Q^2}$$

Since

$$f_{QQ}(f_{SS}) - (f_{QS})^2 > 0$$

for all reasonable c_H, c_B, S, c_o, D, and Q values, the Q^* and S^* formulas identify an extreme point. This extreme point gives the minimum total cost solution because f_{QQ} and f_{SS} are both positive.

Equality Constraints

The previous discussion has focused on unconstrained optimization. In practice, there frequently will be constraints or restrictions on the independent variables. These restrictions can include capacity limitations on available output, budget limitations on available finances, and market-determined limitations on available sales.

When the constraints take the form of equalities, the constrained optimization problem can be solved by the **Lagrange multiplier technique**. This technique first transforms the original constrained problem into an unconstrained problem by forming a composite Lagrangian function. The Lagrangian function is the sum of the original function and a linear multiple of each constraint equation. The unconstrained problem is then solved with a variation of the multivariate optimization process. Management Situation A.4 illustrates.

Management Situation A.4

Ship Building

Alabastar Shipbuilders Corporation uses labor and machinery to manufacture recreational ships. An economic analysis of available information indicates that output is determined from the following production function:

$$Q = 12G - G^2 + 24M - M^2 + MG$$

where Q = ships manufactured per month, G = monthly labor expenditures (in thousands of dollars), and M = monthly machinery expenditures (in thousands of dollars).

There is an operating budget of $20,000 per month that must exactly compensate the labor and machinery employed in the manufacturing process. Alabastar seeks the resource allocation plan that will maximize output.

Lagrangian Function. Alabastar's problem is to maximize output subject to the $20,000 operating budget, or

maximize $Q = 12G - G^2 + 24M - M^2 + MG$

subject to $G + M = 20$ (budget)

The budget constraint in this model can be written as

$$G + M - 20 = 0$$

As long as the constraint holds, any multiple of this equation will equal zero.

Multiplying the budget constraint by λ(lambda) and adding the result to the original production function forms the composite Lagrangian function

$$L = 12G - G^2 + 24M - M^2 + MG + \lambda(G + M - 20)$$

In the composite equation, the **Lagrangian multiplier** λ is a variable. The negative value of this multiplier $(-\lambda)$ measures the instantaneous rate of change in the original objective with respect to a very small change in the corresponding constraint amount, while holding constant the values of all other independent variables. For Alabastar,

$$-\lambda = \frac{\partial Q}{\partial U}$$

where U = the operating budget. (A Lagrangian multiplier is also equivalent to Chapter 9's shadow price.)

Necessary Conditions. According to Table A.2's differentiation rules, the first partial derivatives of Alabastar's Lagrangian function are

$$\partial L/\partial G = 12 - 2G + M + \lambda$$

$$\partial L/\partial M = 24 - 2M + G + \lambda$$

$$\partial L/\partial \lambda = G + M - 20$$

These marginal changes will be stationary when $\partial L/\partial G = 0$, $\partial L/\partial M = 0$, and $\partial L/\partial \lambda = 0$, or when $G = 8$, $M = 12$, and $\lambda = -8$. Since there is only one stationary point, it will represent the global extreme (if it exists).

Sufficient Conditions. With $\lambda = -8$, the first partial derivative with respect to G becomes

$$\partial L/\partial G = 12 - 2G + M - 8 = 4 - 2G + M$$

and the first partial with respect to M becomes

$$\partial L/\partial M = 24 - 2M + G - 8 = 16 - 2M + G$$

The second (pure and cross) partial derivatives are

$$f_{GG} = -2 \qquad f_{MM} = -2 \qquad f_{GM} = f_{MG} = 1$$

Since

$$f_{GG}(f_{MM}) - (f_{GM})^2 = -2(-2) - (1)^2 = 3$$

or a positive value, the stationary point is an extreme point. This extreme point is a maximum because f_{GG} and f_{MM} are both negative.

Optimal Solution. The analysis indicates that Alabastar can maximize output at

$$Q = 12G - G^2 + 24M - M^2 + MG$$

$$= 12(8) - (8)^2 + 24(12) - (12)^2 + 12(8)$$

$$= 272$$

ships per month by using $G = \$8,000$ worth of labor and $M = \$12,000$ worth of machinery per month. The Lagrangian multiplier tells us that this output will increase (decrease) by

$$\partial Q / \partial U = -\lambda = -(-8) = 8$$

ships for a very small increase (decrease) in the operating budget. (Studying such small changes is equivalent to the sensitivity analyses discussed throughout the text.)

Glossary

absolute (global) maximum The value of the independent variable that generates the largest value of the dependent variable in the function.

absolute (global) minimum The value of the independent variable that generates the smallest value of the dependent variable in the function.

breakeven point A volume at which total revenue is exactly equal to total cost, or a volume that results in zero profit.

cost-profit-volume analysis An evaluation that examines how revenue, cost, and profit vary with volume.

differentiation The process of finding a derivative.

differential calculus A methodology used to find the optimal values of the independent and dependent variables in a continuous function.

extreme points Relative and absolute maximum and minimum points in a function.

first derivative The instantaneous rate of change at a point of a continuous function.

first partial derivative The first derivative of a multivariate function, measuring the instantaneous rate of change in the dependent variable with respect to a very small change in one of the independent variables, while holding constant the values of all other independent variables.

function A mathematical equation that relates a dependent variable to a single independent variable (in which case we have a *univariate function*) or to multiple independent variables (in which case we have a *multivariate function*).

inflection point A point at which the concavity of the function changes (from concave downward to concave upward or vice versa).

Lagrange multiplier technique Transforming an original constrained problem into an unconstrained problem that can be solved with a multivariate optimization process.

Lagrange multiplier A variable whose negative value measures the instantaneous rate of change in the original objective with respect to a very small change in the corresponding constraint amount, while holding constant the values of all other independent variables.

mixed (cross) partial derivative The instantaneous rate of change in the first partial derivative with respect to a different independent variable, while holding constant the values of all other independent variables.

pure partial derivative The instantaneous rate of change in the first partial derivative with respect to the same independent variable, while holding constant the values of all other independent variables.

relative (local) maximum A point at which any very small change in the independent variable results in a lower value for the dependent variable.

relative (local) minimum A point at which any very small change in the independent variable results in a larger value for the dependent variable.

second derivative The derivative of the first derivative, measuring the instantaneous rate of change in the first derivative at a point of the function.

stationary point A point in a function that has a tangent with slope equal to zero.

Appendix B: Probability Review

As the text demonstrates, probabilities help the decision maker to make informed decisions. This appendix reviews the standard methods for developing these probabilities. First, it outlines the fundamental concepts of experiments, sample points, and events. Then, the appendix shows how the concepts are used to determine probabilities. Finally, it presents some probability distribution concepts that are important to the text discussion.

FUNDAMENTAL CONCEPTS

Let us begin by considering Management Situation B.1.

Management Situation B.1

Public Health

A physician is studying the relationship between smoking and lung cancer. In a research study, a sample of 30 to 50 year olds provided the data shown in Table B.1.

The physician wants to use the data to determine various likelihoods.

Experiments

The medical research study is a process that results in well-defined outcomes (a non-smoker with cancer, a moderate smoker with no cancer, and so on). Such a process is referred to as an **experiment** and a particular outcome (for example, a heavy smoker with cancer) is called a **sample point**.

Sample Space. In any single repetition of the experiment, the physician will only observe one sample point. However, the observed experimental outcome could be any of the six sample points listed in Table B.2.

Such a collection, or set, of all possible experimental outcomes is known as the **sample space**. The doctor can summarize this information as follows:

$$S = \{E_1, E_2, E_3, E_4, E_5, E_6\}$$

where S represents the sample space for the medical experiment.

Table B.1   **Data on Smoking and Health**

	Condition		
Smoking Pattern	Cancer	No Cancer	Total
Nonsmoker	50	450	500
Moderate Smoker	150	150	300
Heavy Smoker	150	50	200
Total	350	650	1,000

Table B.2   **The Health Study's Experimental Outcomes**

Experimental Outcome (Sample Point)	**Description**
E_1	Nonsmoker with cancer
E_2	Moderate smoker with cancer
E_3	Heavy smoker with cancer
E_4	Nonsmoker with no cancer
E_5	Moderate smoker with no cancer
E_6	Heavy smoker with no cancer

Events. Typically, the decision maker will be interested in some collection of experimental outcomes from the sample space. For example, the physician might want to know about people who smoke. As Table B.2 indicates, this collection of sample points is

$$A = \{E_2, E_3, E_5, E_6\}$$

where A = the set of people who smoke. Alternatively, the physician may seek information about people who have cancer, or from Table B.2,

$$B = \{E_1, E_2, E_3\}$$

where B = the set of people who have cancer. Collections of sample points, such as A and B, are called **events**.

Event Relationships

Additional information can be obtained by relating events.

Unions. One possible relationship can be formed by joining events. The physician, for example, may be interested in identifying the people who are either smokers or who have cancer. This collection of sample points consists of the experimental outcomes found either in events A or B, and it can be summarized as

$$A \text{ or } B = A \cup B = \{E_1, E_2, E_3, E_5, E_6\}$$

where $A \cup B$ denotes the joining, or **union**, of the events A and B.

Intersections. Another relationship can be formed by finding the experimental outcomes that overlap events. For example, the physician might be interested in identifying the people who both smoke and have cancer. Such a collection of sample points consists of the experimental outcomes found both in events A and B, and it can be summarized as

$$A \text{ and } B = A \cap B = \{E_2, E_3\}$$

where $A \cap B$ denotes the **intersection** of events A and B.

Complements. One more relationship is developed by finding the sample points excluded from events. The physician, for example, may want to group the nonsmokers. This collection of sample points consists of the experimental outcomes not found in event A, and it can be summarized as

$$\tilde{A} = \{E_1, E_4\}$$

where $\tilde{A}$ represents the sample points excluded from event A, called its **complement**.

Mutually Exclusive. In some cases, the occurrence of one event will preclude the occurrence of another event. People, for example, cannot simultaneously be smokers and nonsmokers. Put another way, medical experiment events A and $\tilde{A}$ do not have any sample points in common. These events are said to be **mutually exclusive**.

Collectively Exhaustive. Sometimes, events collectively will exhaust the sample space. For example, the people who either are smokers or nonsmokers consist of the sample points found either in events A or $\tilde{A}$, and the collection can be summarized as

$$A \text{ or } \tilde{A} = A \cup \tilde{A} = \{E_1, E_2, E_3, E_4, E_5, E_6\}$$

As Table B.2 indicates, this collection represents the entire sample space in the medical experiment. Under these circumstances, events A and $\tilde{A}$ are said to be **collectively exhaustive**.

When events are both mutually exclusive and collectively exhaustive, it is possible to observe only one event at any given time. For example, A and $\tilde{A}$ in the medical experiment are mutually exclusive and collectively exhaustive events. At a particular time, then, any individual will be either a smoker or nonsmoker.

PROBABILITY THEORY

Decision makers can quantify their uncertainty by determining numerical values that measure the likelihood that particular events will occur. **Probabilities** are expressed as values on a scale from 0 to 1. A probability of 0 means that the event will not happen, while a likelihood of 1 tells us that the event is certain to occur. Probabilities between 0 and 1 represent varying degrees of likelihood.

To determine the probability for an event, we must find the likelihood for each corresponding experimental outcome or sample point. Moreover, these likelihoods must satisfy two basic requirements. First, the likelihood for each sample point must have a value between 0 and 1. Second, the sample point likelihoods must sum to 1.

Table B.3   Health Study Sample Point Probabilities

Sample Point	Description	Probability
E_1	Nonsmokers with cancer	$P(E_1) = \ \ 50/1,000 = \ \ .05$
E_2	Moderate smokers with cancer	$P(E_2) = 150/1,000 = \ \ .15$
E_3	Heavy smokers with cancer	$P(E_3) = 150/1,000 = \ \ .15$
E_4	Nonsmokers with no cancer	$P(E_4) = 450/1,000 = \ \ .45$
E_5	Moderate smokers with no cancer	$P(E_5) = 150/1,000 = \ \ .15$
E_6	Heavy smokers with no cancer	$P(E_6) = \ \ 50/1,000 = \ \ \underline{.05}$
		Total 1.00

Relative Frequencies

When data are available, as in the public health example, the decision maker can estimate a probability value by calculating the proportion of times that the sample point occurs in the experiment. This approach, called the **relative frequency or empirical method**, can be represented with the following formula:

(B.1) $P(E_i) = f_i / n$

where

$P(E_i) = $ the probability of sample point i

  $f_i = $ the number of times that sample point i occurs in the experiment

  $n = $ the total observations in the experiment

Table B.3 summarizes the calculations for the medical experiment.

Unfortunately, the organization often does not have sufficient data to employ the empirical method. Under these circumstances, it may be necessary to estimate likelihoods from an assumed mathematical probability distribution. If all else fails, the decision maker might even have to assess probabilities subjectively as a first approximation prior to acquiring relevant data through laboratory, statistical, or market experiments.

Event Probabilities

Once the sample point likelihoods are developed, the decision maker will have the information needed to determine event probabilities. In particular, probability is calculated by summing the corresponding sample point likelihoods. For example, the medical doctor knows that smokers are represented by event

$$A = \{E_2, E_3, E_5, E_6\}$$

By using the data from Table B.3, the physician will find that there is a

$$P(A) = P(E_2) + P(E_3) + P(E_5) + P(E_6) = .15 + .15 + .15 + .05 = .50$$

probability for event A. In other words, 50 percent of the people in the medical study are smokers.

Probability Rules

All event probabilities can be found with the same sample point approach. When there are many experimental outcomes, however, this approach can be cumbersome and time-consuming to implement. Fortunately, several probability rules exist that reduce the necessary computation.

Complements. One rule involves the complements of event probabilities. Specifically, the probabilities for an event and its complement must sum to 1. This relationship, then, can be used to determine the probability of the complement from the likelihood information about the event.

For example, in the medical study, the $P(A) + P(\tilde{A}) = 1$. Hence, the physician will find that

$$P(\tilde{A}) = 1 - P(A) = 1 - .50 = .50.$$

In other words, 50 percent of the people in the medical study are nonsmokers.

Addition Rule. Another rule deals with the union of events. The physician, for example, may be interested in finding the probability that people either smoke or have cancer. That is, the doctor needs the probability for the union of events A and B, or $P(A \cup B)$.

The required probability will include the likelihood that a person smokes, $P(A)$, plus the chance that a person has cancer, $P(B)$. In this regard, the data in Table B.1 indicates that there is a

$$P(A) = (300 + 200)/1,000 = .50$$

likelihood that a person smokes, and a

$$P(B) = 350/1,000 = .35$$

chance that a person has cancer. Cumulative probabilities that an event will occur, such as $P(A)$ and $P(B)$, are referred to as **marginal probabilities**.

On the other hand, there are people who both smoke and have cancer. In other words, there are sample points common to both events A and B. To avoid counting these points twice, we must subtract the likelihood for this intersection, $P(A \cap B)$, from the sum of $P(A) + P(B)$. In this regard, the data in Table B.1 indicates that there is a

$$P(A \text{ and } B) = P(A \cap B) = (150 + 150)/1,000 = .30$$

likelihood that a person both smokes and has cancer. A probability that multiple events will jointly occur, such as $P(A \text{ and } B)$, is called a **joint probability**.

As a result, the doctor will find that there is a

$$P(A \text{ or } B) = P(A \cup B) = P(A) + P(B) - P(A \cap B) = .50 + .35 - .30 = .55$$

probability that a person either smokes or has cancer. Such a computation illustrates the **addition rule** of probability theory. It shows that the probability for a union of events equals the sum of the relevant marginal probabilities less the sum of the appropriate joint probabilities.

When events are mutually exclusive, the intersection of the events will not contain any sample points. Under these circumstances, the decision maker can find the probability for the union by simply adding the marginal probabilities for the events. For example, a person cannot have cancer and not have cancer at the same time. Put another way, B and $\tilde{B}$ are mutually exclusive events. Consequently, the $P(B \cap \tilde{B}) = 0$, and the doctor will find that there is a

$$P(B \text{ or } \tilde{B}) = P(B) + P(\tilde{B}) - P(B \cap \tilde{B}) = .35 + .65 - 0 = 1.00$$

probability that a person either has cancer or does not have cancer.

Conditional Probability. In the medical study, suppose the physician notices that a person smokes. Further, assume the doctor wants to know the chance that this person has cancer. Under these circumstances, we seek the probability of event B given that event A has occurred, or $P(B \pounds A)$. Such a likelihood is called a **conditional probability**.

According to the data in Table B.1, $P(A) = .50$, or 50 percent of the people smoke. Among these people, $P(A \cap B) = .30$, or 30 percent both smoke and have cancer. Therefore, there is a

$$P(B|A) = P(A \cap B)/P(A) = .30/.50 = .60$$

probability that a person who smokes will have cancer. Such a computation illustrates the **conditional probability** rule. It shows that the conditional probability for an event will equal the ratio of the relevant joint to marginal probabilities.

Independence. In the medical study, there is a $P(B) = .35$ probability that a person has cancer. This probability accounts for both smokers and nonsmokers. Among smokers, however, there is a $P(B \pounds A) = .60$ likelihood that a person has cancer. Smoking (event A), then, is apparently related to cancer (event B). Indeed, the computations show that if a person smokes, there is an increased probability of developing cancer. In such situations, we say that smoking and health are **dependent events**.

Frequently, however, the occurrence of one event does not change the probability of another event. In the medical study, for example, let a new event C denote the people who have brown hair. Since a person's hair color should be unrelated to her or his chance of having cancer, the physician can anticipate that

$$P(B|C) = P(B)$$

and
$$P(C|B) = P(C)$$

In such cases, B and C are said to be **independent** events.

Multiplication Rule. Often, the decision maker can compute a joint probability from the available experimental data. The physician, for example, can utilize the data in Table B.1 to calculate the probability that a person both smokes and has cancer. Nevertheless, there are situations in which we must compute the likelihood of event intersections from incomplete information.

For example, suppose the physician seeks the probability that a person both smokes and is susceptible to cancer. Moreover, only limited information is available to determine this probability. In particular, a medical test can suggest whether or not someone is susceptible to cancer. Susceptible persons are represented by a new event D. In addition, past test results indicate that

$$P(D|A) = .80$$

Table B.4   **Hurts's Automobile Rental Data**

Sports Cars Rented	Number of Days
0	20
1	60
2	90
3	20
4	10

---

or 80 percent of all smokers are susceptible to cancer. The physician also knows that $P(A) = .50$, or 50 percent of the people smoke.

According to the available information, there is a

$$P(A \text{ and } D) = P(A \cap D) = P(A) \times P(D|A) = .50 \times .80 = .40$$

probability that a person both smokes and is susceptible to cancer. Such a computation illustrates the **multiplication rule** of probability theory. It shows that a joint probability will equal the product of the corresponding event (conditional and/or marginal) probabilities.

PROBABILITY DISTRIBUTIONS

In Management Situation B.1, the sample points are characterized by verbal descriptions of health and smoking patterns. Yet, the sample points of some experiments can be expressed in numerical terms. Management Situation B.2 illustrates.

Management Situation B.2

Automobile Rentals

The manager of the local Hurts Rent-A-Car agency is interested in describing the daily demand for sports car rentals. Records for the last 200 days of operation show the rental volumes and frequencies listed in Table B.4.

The manager believes that the previous rental history adequately represents what will happen in the future.

Random Variables

In Management Situation B.2, the experimental outcomes can be described numerically with the variable $X =$ the number of sports cars rented on a given day. The specific value of this variable will depend on the outcome from the experiment. For example, when two sports cars are rented on a given day, $X = 2$. A variable that gives a numerical description of the outcome from an experiment is called a **random variable**. In Hurts's case, the random variable X can have a value of 0, 1, 2, 3, or 4.

| Table B.5 | Hurts's Probability Distribution for Daily Sports Car Rentals |

Daily Sports Car Rentals X	Probability P(X)
0	20/200 = .10
1	60/200 = .30
2	90/200 = .45
3	20/200 = .10
4	10/200 = .05
	Total = 1.00

Discrete Distributions

The random variable in Hurts's situation (daily sports car rentals) may take on only a finite number of whole unit values. Such a random variable is said to be **discrete**. There are several statistics that can be used to describe this type of variable.

Discrete Probability Distribution. One useful description is a list of the probabilities associated with each value of the random variable. For example, by using the frequency data in Table B.4, Hurts's manager will find that there is a

$$P(X = 2) = 90/200 = .45$$

probability of renting two sports cars a day. Similarly, there is a

$$P(X = 4) = 10/200 = .05$$

probability of renting four sports cars a day. Calculations for each value of Hurts's random variable are summarized in Table B.5.

The list of likelihoods given in Table B.5 is known as the **probability distribution** for the random variable. Notice that the random variable likelihoods meet two basic probability requirements. First, each probability has a value between 0 and 1. Second, the sum of the probabilities is equal to 1. One popular discrete probability distribution, the Poisson, is discussed in the queuing chapter.

Expected Value. Two additional statistics are useful in summarizing the probability distribution information. One statistic measures the average value for the random variable that can be expected if the experiment is repeated many times. This **expected value** is found by multiplying each value of the random variable by its probability of occurrence and then summing the results. That is,

(B.2) $$EV = \mu = \Sigma_i [X_i \times P(X_i)]$$

where

$EV = \mu = $ the expected value of the random variable

$X_i = $ the ith value of the random variable

$P(X_i) = $ the probability for the ith value of the variable.

By using the data from Table B.5, the Hurts manager will find that

$$EV = \mu = 0(.10) + 1(.30) + 2(.45) + 3(.10) + 4(.05) = 1.7$$

rentals. This value indicates that, over a period of many months, the local agency can anticipate renting an average of 1.7 sports cars a day.

Variance. It is also important to know something about the dispersion, or variation, that can occur between the extreme values of the random variable. One popular way to measure this dispersion is with **variance**. This measurement is found with the following formula:

(B.3) $$VAR = \sigma^2 = \Sigma_i [(X_i - \mu)^2 \times P(X_i)]$$

where

$VAR = \sigma^2 =$ the variance of the random variable and the other terms are defined as before.

By examining formula (B.3), you will see that the variance statistic is based on the mathematical distances $(X - \mu)$ between the actual and expected values of the random variable. The greater the distances, the larger the variance or dispersion. In other words, a small σ^2 indicates low variability, while a high σ^2 suggests substantial dispersion in the random variable.

The data in Table B.5 indicate that daily rentals involve a variance of

$$VAR = \sigma^2 = (0 - 1.7)^2(.10) + (1 - 1.7)^2(.30) + (2 - 1.7)^2(.45)$$
$$+ (3 - 1.7)^2(.10) + (4 - 1.7)^2(.05) = .91$$

squared sports cars. Of course, squared sports cars will not be meaningful to the manager. After all, the original data are expressed in cars rather than squared cars. To avoid the interpretation difficulty, it is customary to measure variability with the square root of variance.

(B.4) $$\sigma = \sqrt{\sigma^2}$$

Such a square root is known as the **standard deviation** of the random variable.

In Hurts's case, $\sigma = \sqrt{.91} = .954$ sports cars. This value is relatively large in relation to the expected value $\mu = 1.7$ cars. Therefore, the manager can anticipate much variability in daily rental volume.

Continuous Distributions

Other random variables may take on an infinite number of values, including fractions, over a range or interval. These random variables are said to be **continuous,** and the corresponding likelihoods form continuous probability distributions. One popular continuous probability distribution, the exponential, is discussed in the queuing chapter, while another, the beta, is presented as part of the PERT/CPM analysis. Management Situation B.3 illustrates a third, and perhaps most widely applicable, continuous probability distribution.

Figure B.1   **Mitas's Probability Distribution for Muffler Installation Time**

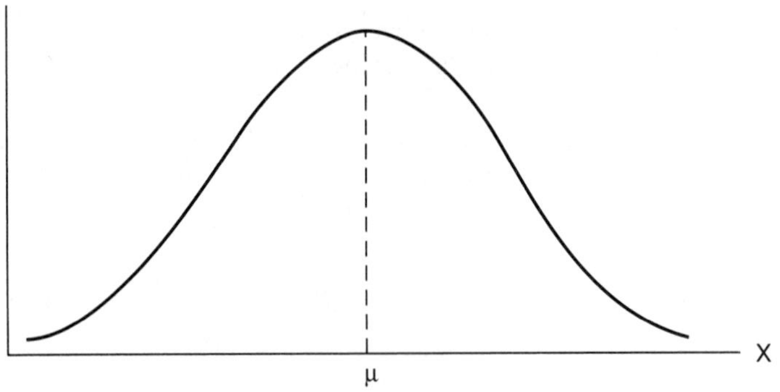

Management Situation B.3

Automobile Service

Mitas operates a national chain of automobile service outlets. Management believes that completion time is an important factor in expanding customer demand for the outlets' muffler service. Consequently, the company wants to make this factor a central theme in its upcoming advertising campaign. Management would like to state that the customer will receive a discount if muffler installation is not completed within a guaranteed time.

Before finalizing the advertising message, however, the marketing staff needs some information concerning muffler installation. In particular, they would like to determine the percentage of customers who will be forced to wait more than an hour for the completion of service. Also, the staff wants to know the guaranteed time that will limit the discount to no more than 5 percent of the customers.

According to the company's information system, past muffler installation follows the pattern shown in Figure B.1. Furthermore, the average installation takes 40 minutes. The standard deviation is approximately 10 minutes.

Normal Distribution. In the Mitas problem, the random variable is the time needed to install a muffler. Since the service can take 30 minutes, more than an hour, or any fraction of time in between, this random variable is continuous. As a result, it is impossible to list each potential installation time and then identify the corresponding probabilities. An alternative approach is required to find the likelihoods for such a continuous random variable.

In the customary approach, we begin by identifying the mathematical function, or curve, that best describes the random variable. Figure B.1 gives the appropriate curve for Mitas's situation. You can see that this curve is smooth, continuous, and bell shaped.

Figure B.2   **Probability that Mitas's Installation Time Exceeds One Hour**

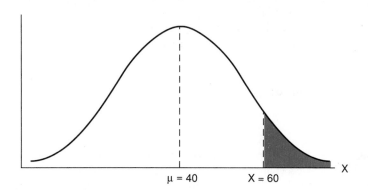

It reaches a peak at the expected value μ of the random variable. It is also symmetrical; that is, the area under the curve above μ is equal to the area below the expected value. When the curve has these properties, the random variable is said to have a **normal probability distribution**.

At this stage, we can determine the probability that the random variable is between two specified values by finding the corresponding area under the curve. Mitas, for example, seeks the probability that muffler installation will exceed 60 minutes. As Figure B.2 illustrates, this probability corresponds to the area in the shaded region of the company's normal probability curve.

Standard Normal Distribution. To find the required area, management could use the mathematical technique of integral calculus. A far simpler approach is to utilize the **standard normal distribution** or a normal distribution with $\mu = 0$ and $\sigma = 1$. To do so, we must first convert the data into standard normal values, or Z scores based on the formula:

(B.5) $Z = (X - \mu)/\sigma$

Then, a table of the standard normal distribution, such as Table C.1, can be used to find the desired probability.

Mitas, for example, seeks the probability that $X > 60$ minutes. Furthermore, the expected installation time is $\mu = 40$ minutes with a standard deviation of $\sigma = 10$ minutes. Thus, the desired value of the random variable has a score that is greater than

$$Z = (60 - 40)/10 = 2$$

standard deviations above the expected installation time. According to Table C.1, this score corresponds to $1 - .9772 = .0228$ of the standard normal distribution area. Put another way, the $P(X > 60) = .0228$. Management should conclude that about 2.28 percent of the customers will have to wait more than an hour for the completion of muffler service.

The guaranteed time issue can be addressed with a similar analysis. In this regard, management seeks the time that will limit the discount to no more than 5 percent of the customers. According to Table C.1, $1 - .05 = .95$ of the standard normal distribution lies below a standard score of $Z \approx 1.64$. By using equation (B.5), then, management will find that the appropriate guaranteed time is

$$X = 40 + 1.64(10) = 56.4$$

minutes.

Glossary

addition rule The rule stating that the probability for a union of events will equal the sum of the relevant marginal probabilities less the sum of the appropriate joint probabilities.

collectively exhaustive events Events that collectively exhaust the sample space.

complement The collection of sample points excluded from an event.

conditional probability The probability of one event, given the condition that some other event has occurred.

conditional probability rule The conditional probability for an event will equal the ratio of the relevant joint to marginal probabilities.

continuous random variable A random variable that may take on an infinite number of values, including fractions, over a range or interval.

dependent events When the probability of one event is affected by the occurrence of another event.

discrete random variable A random variable that may take on only a finite number of whole unit values.

events Collections of sample points.

expected value The average value for the random variable that can be expected if the experiment is repeated many times.

experiment A process that results in well-defined outcomes.

independent events When the occurrence of one event does not change the probability of another event.

intersection The collection of sample points found in all events.

joint probability A probability that multiple events will jointly occur.

marginal probability Cumulative probability that an event will occur.

multiplication rule The rule that a joint probability will equal the product of the corresponding event (conditional and/or marginal) probabilities.

mutually exclusive events Events that cannot occur simultaneously.

normal probability distribution A probability distribution that is smooth, continuous, bell shaped, and symmetrical.

probabilities Numerical values that measure the chances or likelihoods that particular events will occur.

probability distribution The list of likelihoods associated with the corresponding values of a random variable.

random variable A variable that gives a numerical description of the outcome from an experiment.

relative frequency or empirical method Estimating a probability value by calculating the proportion of times that a sample point occurs in an experiment.

sample point A particular outcome from an experiment.

sample space A collection, or set, of all possible experimental outcomes.

standard deviation The square root of variance.

standard normal distribution A normal probability distribution with an expected value of 0 and a standard deviation of 1.

union The collection of sample points found in any two or more events.

variance A measure of the dispersion, or variation, that can occur between the extreme values of the random variable.

Appendix C: Useful Tables

Table C.1 Standard Normal Distribution

Z	.09	.08	.07	.06	.05	.04	.03	.02	.01	.00	Z
.00	.5359	.5319	.5279	.5239	.5199	.5160	.5120	.5080	.5040	.5000	.00
.10	.5753	.5714	.5675	.5636	.5596	.5557	.5517	.5478	.5438	.5398	.10
.20	.6141	.6103	.6064	.6026	.5987	.5948	.5910	.5871	.5832	.5793	.20
.30	.6517	.6480	.6443	.6406	.6368	.6331	.6293	.6255	.6217	.6179	.30
.40	.6879	.6844	.6808	.6772	.6736	.6700	.6664	.6628	.6591	.6554	.40
.50	.7224	.7190	.7157	.7123	.7088	.7054	.7019	.6985	.6950	.6915	.50
.60	.7549	.7517	.7486	.7454	.7422	.7389	.7357	.7324	.7291	.7257	.60
.70	.7852	.7823	.7794	.7764	.7734	.7704	.7673	.7642	.7611	.7580	.70
.80	.8133	.8106	.8078	.8051	.8023	.7995	.7967	.7939	.7910	.7881	.80
.90	.8399	.8365	.8340	.8315	.8289	.8264	.8238	.8212	.8186	.8159	.90
1.00	.8621	.8599	.8577	.8554	.8531	.8508	.8485	.8461	.8438	.8413	1.00
1.10	.8830	.8810	.8790	.8770	.8749	.8729	.8708	.8686	.8665	.8643	1.10
1.20	.9015	.8997	.8980	.8962	.8944	.8925	.8907	.8888	.8869	.8849	1.20
1.30	.9177	.9162	.9147	.9131	.9115	.9099	.9082	.9066	.9049	.9032	1.30
1.40	.9319	.9306	.9292	.9279	.9265	.9251	.9236	.9222	.9207	.9192	1.40
1.50	.9441	.9429	.9418	.9406	.9394	.9382	.9370	.9357	.9345	.9332	1.50
1.60	.9545	.9535	.9525	.9515	.9505	.9495	.9484	.9474	.9463	.9452	1.60
1.70	.9633	.9625	.9616	.9608	.9599	.9591	.9582	.9573	.9564	.9554	1.70
1.80	.9706	.9699	.9693	.9686	.9678	.9671	.9664	.9656	.9649	.9641	1.80
1.90	.9767	.9761	.9756	.9750	.9744	.9738	.9732	.9726	.9719	.9713	1.90
2.00	.9817	.9812	.9808	.9803	.9798	.9793	.9788	.9783	.9778	.9772	2.00
2.10	.9857	.9854	.9850	.9846	.9842	.9838	.9834	.9830	.9826	.9821	2.10
2.20	.9890	.9887	.9884	.9881	.9878	.9875	.9871	.9868	.9864	.9861	2.20
2.30	.9916	.9913	.9911	.9909	.9906	.9904	.9901	.9898	.9896	.9893	2.30
2.40	.9936	.9934	.9932	.9931	.9929	.9927	.9925	.9922	.9920	.9918	2.40
2.50	.9952	.9951	.9949	.9948	.9946	.9945	.9943	.9941	.9940	.9938	2.50
2.60	.9964	.9963	.9962	.9961	.9960	.9959	.9957	.9956	.9955	.9953	2.60
2.70	.9974	.9973	.9972	.9971	.9970	.9969	.9968	.9967	.9966	.9965	2.70
2.80	.9981	.9980	.9979	.9979	.9978	.9977	.9977	.9976	.9975	.9974	2.80
2.90	.9986	.9986	.9985	.9985	.9984	.9984	.9983	.9982	.9982	.9981	2.90
3.00	.9990	.9990	.9989	.9989	.9989	.9988	.9988	.9987	.9987	.9987	3.00
3.10	.9993	.9993	.9992	.9992	.9992	.9992	.9991	.9991	.9991	.9990	3.10
3.20	.9995	.9995	.9995	.9994	.9994	.9994	.9994	.9994	.9993	.9993	3.20
3.30	.9997	.9996	.9996	.9996	.9996	.9996	.9996	.9995	.9995	.9995	3.30
3.40	.9998	.9997	.9997	.9997	.9997	.9997	.9997	.9997	.9997	.9997	3.40
3.50	.9998	.9998	.9998	.9998	.9998	.9998	.9998	.9998	.9998	.9998	3.50
3.60	.9999	.9999	.9999	.9999	.9999	.9999	.9999	.9999	.9998	.9998	3.60
3.70	.9999	.9999	.9999	.9999	.9999	.9999	.9999	.9999	.9999	.9999	3.70
3.80	.9999	.9999	.9999	.9999	.9999	.9999	.9999	.9999	.9999	.9999	3.80

Z	-.09	-.08	-.07	-.06	-.05	-.04	-.03	-.02	-.01	.00	Z
-3.80	.0001	.0001	.0001	.0001	.0001	.0001	.0001	.0001	.0001	.0001	-3.80
-3.70	.0001	.0001	.0001	.0001	.0001	.0001	.0001	.0001	.0001	.0001	-3.70
-3.60	.0001	.0001	.0001	.0001	.0001	.0001	.0001	.0001	.0002	.0002	-3.60
-3.50	.0002	.0002	.0002	.0002	.0002	.0002	.0002	.0002	.0002	.0002	-3.50
-3.40	.0002	.0003	.0003	.0003	.0003	.0003	.0003	.0003	.0003	.0003	-3.40
-3.30	.0003	.0004	.0004	.0004	.0004	.0004	.0004	.0005	.0005	.0005	-3.30
-3.20	.0005	.0005	.0005	.0006	.0006	.0006	.0006	.0006	.0007	.0007	-3.20
-3.10	.0007	.0007	.0008	.0008	.0008	.0008	.0009	.0009	.0009	.0010	-3.10
-3.00	.0010	.0010	.0011	.0011	.0011	.0012	.0012	.0013	.0013	.0013	-3.00
-2.90	.0014	.0014	.0015	.0015	.0016	.0016	.0017	.0018	.0018	.0019	-2.90
-2.80	.0019	.0020	.0021	.0021	.0022	.0023	.0023	.0024	.0025	.0026	-2.80
-2.70	.0026	.0027	.0028	.0029	.0030	.0031	.0032	.0033	.0034	.0035	-2.70
-2.60	.0036	.0037	.0038	.0039	.0040	.0041	.0043	.0044	.0045	.0047	-2.60
-2.50	.0048	.0049	.0051	.0052	.0054	.0055	.0057	.0059	.0060	.0062	-2.50
-2.40	.0064	.0066	.0068	.0069	.0071	.0073	.0075	.0078	.0080	.0082	-2.40
-2.30	.0084	.0087	.0089	.0091	.0094	.0096	.0099	.0102	.0104	.0107	-2.30
-2.20	.0110	.0113	.0116	.0119	.0122	.0125	.0129	.0132	.0136	.0139	-2.20
-2.10	.0143	.0146	.0150	.0154	.0158	.0162	.0166	.0170	.0174	.0179	-2.10
-2.00	.0183	.0188	.0192	.0197	.0202	.0207	.0212	.0217	.0222	.0228	-2.00
-1.90	.0233	.0239	.0244	.0250	.0256	.0262	.0268	.0274	.0281	.0287	-1.90
-1.80	.0294	.0301	.0307	.0314	.0322	.0329	.0336	.0344	.0351	.0359	-1.80
-1.70	.0367	.0375	.0384	.0392	.0401	.0409	.0418	.0427	.0436	.0446	-1.70
-1.60	.0455	.0465	.0475	.0485	.0495	.0505	.0516	.0526	.0537	.0548	-1.60
-1.50	.0559	.0571	.0582	.0594	.0606	.0618	.0630	.0643	.0655	.0668	-1.50
-1.40	.0681	.0694	.0708	.0721	.0735	.0749	.0764	.0778	.0793	.0808	-1.40
-1.30	.0823	.0838	.0853	.0869	.0885	.0901	.0918	.0934	.0951	.0968	-1.30
-1.20	.0985	.1003	.1020	.1038	.1056	.1075	.1093	.1112	.1131	.1151	-1.20
-1.10	.1170	.1190	.1210	.1230	.1251	.1271	.1292	.1314	.1335	.1357	-1.10
-1.00	.1379	.1401	.1423	.1446	.1469	.1492	.1515	.1539	.1562	.1587	-1.00
-.90	.1611	.1635	.1660	.1685	.1711	.1736	.1762	.1788	.1814	.1841	-.90
-.80	.1867	.1894	.1922	.1949	.1977	.2005	.2033	.2061	.2090	.2119	-.80
-.70	.2148	.2177	.2206	.2236	.2266	.2296	.2327	.2358	.2389	.2420	-.70
-.60	.2451	.2483	.2514	.2546	.2578	.2611	.2643	.2676	.2709	.2743	-.60
-.50	.2776	.2810	.2843	.2877	.2912	.2946	.2981	.3015	.3050	.3085	-.50
-.40	.3121	.3156	.3192	.3228	.3264	.3300	.3336	.3372	.3409	.3446	-.40
-.30	.3483	.3520	.3557	.3594	.3632	.3669	.3707	.3745	.3783	.3821	-.30
-.20	.3859	.3897	.3936	.3974	.4013	.4052	.4090	.4129	.4168	.4207	-.20
-.10	.4247	.4286	.4325	.4364	.4404	.4443	.4483	.4522	.4562	.4602	-.10
-.00	.4641	.4681	.4721	.4761	.4801	.4840	.4880	.4920	.4960	.5000	-.00

Table C.2   Poisson Formula Values

Φ	$e^{-\Phi}$	Φ	$e^{-\Phi}$	Φ	$e^{-\Phi}$	Φ	$e^{-\Phi}$
0.05	.95123	2.55	.07808	5.05	.00641	7.55	.00053
0.10	.90484	2.60	.07427	5.10	.00610	7.60	.00050
0.15	.86071	2.65	.07065	5.15	.00580	7.65	.00048
0.20	.81873	2.70	.06721	5.20	.00552	7.70	.00045
0.25	.77880	2.75	.06393	5.25	.00525	7.75	.00043
0.30	.74082	2.80	.06081	5.30	.00499	7.80	.00041
0.35	.70469	2.85	.05784	5.35	.00475	7.85	.00039
0.40	.67032	2.90	.05502	5.40	.00452	7.90	.00037
0.45	.63763	2.95	.05234	5.45	.00430	7.95	.00035
0.50	.60653	3.00	.04979	5.50	.00409	8.00	.00034
0.55	.57695	3.05	.04736	5.55	.00389	8.05	.00032
0.60	.54881	3.10	.04505	5.60	.00370	8.10	.00030
0.65	.52205	3.15	.04285	5.65	.00352	8.15	.00029
0.70	.49659	3.20	.04076	5.70	.00335	8.20	.00027
0.75	.47237	3.25	.03877	5.75	.00318	8.25	.00026
0.80	.44933	3.30	.03688	5.80	.00303	8.30	.00025
0.85	.42741	3.35	.03508	5.85	.00288	8.35	.00024
0.90	.40657	3.40	.03337	5.90	.00274	8.40	.00022
0.95	.38674	3.45	.03175	5.95	.00261	8.45	.00021
1.00	.36788	3.50	.03020	6.00	.00248	8.50	.00020
1.05	.34994	3.55	.02872	6.05	.00236	8.55	.00019
1.10	.33287	3.60	.02732	6.10	.00224	8.60	.00018
1.15	.31664	3.65	.02599	6.15	.00213	8.65	.00018
1.20	.30119	3.70	.02472	6.20	.00203	8.70	.00017
1.25	.28650	3.75	.02352	6.25	.00193	8.75	.00016
1.30	.27253	3.80	.02237	6.30	.00184	8.80	.00015
1.35	.25924	3.85	.02128	6.35	.00175	8.85	.00014
1.40	.24660	3.90	.02024	6.40	.00166	8.90	.00014
1.45	.23457	3.95	.01925	6.45	.00158	8.95	.00013
1.50	.22313	4.00	.01832	4.50	.00150	9.00	.00012
1.55	.21225	4.05	.01742	6.55	.00143	9.05	.00012
1.60	.20190	4.10	.01657	6.60	.00136	9.10	.00011
1.65	.19205	4.15	.01576	6.65	.00129	9.15	.00011
1.70	.18268	4.20	.01500	6.70	.00123	9.20	.00010
1.75	.17377	4.25	.01426	6.75	.00117	9.25	.00010
1.80	.16530	4.30	.01357	6.80	.00111	9.30	.00009
1.85	.15724	4.35	.01291	6.85	.00106	9.35	.00009
1.90	.14957	4.40	.01228	6.90	.00101	9.40	.00008
1.95	.14227	4.45	.01168	6.95	.00096	9.45	.00008
2.00	.13534	4.50	.01111	7.00	.00091	9.50	.00007
2.05	.12873	4.55	.01057	7.05	.00087	9.55	.00007
2.10	.12246	4.60	.01005	7.10	.00083	9.60	.00007
2.15	.11648	4.65	.00956	7.15	.00078	9.65	.00006
2.20	.11080	4.70	.00910	7.20	.00075	9.70	.00006
2.25	.10540	4.75	.00865	7.25	.00071	9.75	.00006
2.30	.10026	4.80	.00823	7.30	.00068	9.80	.00006
2.35	.09537	4.85	.00783	7.35	.00064	9.85	.00005
2.40	.09072	4.90	.00745	7.40	.00061	9.90	.00005
2.45	.08629	4.95	.00708	7.45	.00058	9.95	.00005
2.50	.08208	5.00	.00674	7.50	.00055	10.00	.00005

Table C.3   **Random Digits**

341447	723998	905614	519309	926345	240082	395043
415603	129727	894956	780924	227496	134056	023014
014881	496311	750082	707823	738906	157591	072396
827235	783798	324650	485324	568156	098332	768720
261607	730824	341940	259028	253973	145183	658110
527920	834376	972906	627959	654790	342497	593779
356756	519371	679389	371912	502903	936741	636775
700770	781547	916968	136999	801855	605975	295802
279584	733750	487151	116069	274869	416181	610911
862434	481154	391464	021094	761599	474456	582253
199585	167701	170788	934765	761328	275799	323046
048736	514507	977406	158840	846761	198016	933522
815218	609732	629295	517386	824505	676788	304971
643021	527212	492869	261844	914505	354436	355772
164332	245407	517804	422658	751712	583087	286872
174303	085157	308590	535846	503131	266915	465641
136325	414066	452293	649359	844625	674828	953396
117780	407444	426115	108970	621527	601599	652376
435697	245510	946158	934221	824917	509832	362638
912252	579474	848845	824321	049853	151126	052643
754438	658573	717914	040054	630638	264060	594641
322053	924909	048177	957012	801464	833319	978384
897199	125506	708669	408374	737887	906201	599469
046637	642050	435779	502427	027842	515775	811203
721653	260190	842505	797017	157497	179041	979346
202312	011976	373248	374293	802292	646914	171322
354014	356787	511271	904434	068589	329862	829316
682909	809290	793392	098004	120575	469925	112743
897690	572456	871574	465543	486529	507767	608677
139029	160636	417690	191242	625269	104858	020808
345769	953810	627280	423578	353511	899906	827008
549075	004410	059309	271243	403382	248735	972383
423480	950812	197145	556566	655917	046169	363201
551518	514290	950974	482196	058868	474936	724289
797165	670995	791954	188521	950156	086813	033365
062730	163375	602168	908350	360861	152201	966097

Selected Check Answers

Chapter 2

9. $Q = \$274,000$.

10. a. $R = \$576,000$.
    b. $P = \$250$.

11. $Y_t = \$702$ billion.

12. a. Maximize output Q.
    b. $Q = 8,000$
    c. $Q = 4,000$ and $Q = 12,000$
    d. $Q = 4,000$ and $Q = 10,000$

16. a. Maximize $P = \$1.2\,Q$
    subject to $0.15Q \leq T$
                  $Q \geq 0$
    where $T = 60$, 90, or 120.
    b. If $T = 60$, $Q = 400$.
    If $T = 90$, $Q = 600$.
    If $T = 120$, $Q = 800$.

17. a. Maximize $\pi = \$0.60Q + \$0.20B$
    subject to $Q + 2B \leq 10,000$
                  $Q, B \geq 0$
    c. $Q = 10,000$ and $B = 0$.
    d. $Q = 2,000$.

19. a. Minimize TC $= \$10/Q + \$0.10Q$.
    c. $Q = 10$.

21. a. $P = \$5Q - \$1,500$.
    b. $Q = 300$.
    c. $Q = 360$.

Chapter 3

9. $\text{GNP}_t = 478$, $C_t = 274$, $I_t = 84$, and $G_t = 120$.

11. MAD $= 10.05$.

14. a. Forecast for week 16 is 1,214.67.
    b. MAD $= 10.75$.
    c. Forecast for week 16 is 1,217.40.
    d. MAD $= 7.24$.

16. a. Forecast for day 15 is 2,405.
   b. MAD $= 31.68$.
   c. Forecast for day 16 is 2,390.
   d. MAD $= 40.34$.
   f. Forecast for day 16 is 2,400.49.
   g. MAD $= 36.46$.

18. c. $Y = 27.67 + 1.3515X$ where $Y =$ premiums and $X =$ the year.
   d. MAD $= 1.53$.

19. c. $Y = 195.76 - 2.3217X$ where $Y =$ permits and $X =$ the year.
   d. $Y = 165.58$ in year 13 and $Y = 160.93$ in year 15.

21. c. $Y = 22.60 - 0.4897X$ where $Y =$ expenses and $X =$ the quarter.
   d. Seasonal indexes are 0.743, 1.131, 1.421, and 0.705 for quarters 1 through 4, respectively.
   f. $Y = 23.23 - .5607X$.

22. c. Seasonal indexes are 1.158, 0.762, 0.823, and 1.257 for quarters 1 through 4, respectively.
   e. $Y = 103.75 + 1.8653X$, where $Y =$ revenue and $X =$ quarter.
   f. If $X = 23$, $Y = 146.6519$.

23. c. $Y = 0.091333 + 0.505705X$.

24. c. $Y = 4.70303 + 1.530303X$ where $Y =$ rate of return and $X =$ capital expenditures.
   d. If $X = 20$, $Y = 35.30909$.

26. $\hat{Y}_t = 0.995\, Y_{t-1} + 0.005\, \hat{Y}_{t-1}$ where $\hat{Y} =$ forecasted interest rate, $Y =$ actual interest rate, and $t =$ the week.

28. $A = 178.15 + 4.7348X$, where $A =$ Administration.
$S = 179.45 + .8474X$, where $S =$ Sales.
$P = 384.26 + 11.5822X$, where $P =$ Production.
$M = 1,224.53 + 16.4313X$, where $M =$ Manufacturing and $X =$ the quarter.

If $X = 25$, $A = 296.52$, $S = 200.635$, $P = 673.815$, $M = 1,635.3125$, so 2,806.2825 is the forecasted aggregate cost in quarter 25.

30. $Y = 254.0335 + 1.387068X$, where $Y =$ production and $X =$ Marketing. If $X = 70$, $Y = 351.12826$.

33. Exponential smoothing with $\hat{Y}_t = 0.995\, Y_{t-1} + 0.055\, \hat{Y}_{t-1}$ where $\hat{Y} =$ forecasted water usage, $Y =$ actual usage, and $t =$ the day. MAD $= 20.71$

36. $Y = 62.93546 + 0.524044X$ where $Y =$ default balance and $X =$ down payment. If $X = 35$, $Y = 81.15$; if $X = 12$, $Y = 69.224$.

Chapter 4

5. Janet will prefer the freeway (a_1) and Joe will prefer Walnut Avenue (a_2).

6. Manager will lower the price (a_2).

9. c. If high demand (s_3), expand capacity (a_4) and maximize expected profit at $210,550.
   d. The consultation enables Naddol to earn $9,550 in additional profits.

13. **a.** Alternative a_1 gives the largest profit of 6.
    b. Alternative a_3 gives the maximum profit of 1.
    c. With $\alpha = 0.3$, select a_3 for a weighted profit of 1.6. With $\alpha = 0.8$, select a_1 for a weighted profit of 4.4.
    d. Alternative a_2 gives the minimax regret of 3.
    e. Alternative a_1 or a_3 gives the maximum average profit of 2.

14. **a.** Select a_1 and then a_4 when s_1 occurs for a $5,000 cost.
    b. Select a_3 and then a_8 when s_1 occurs for a $10,000 cost.
    c. Select a_3 and then a_8 when s_1 occurs for a weighted cost of $14,000.
    d. Select a_1 and then a_4 or a_5 when s_1 occurs for an opportunity loss of no more than $15,000.
    e. Same as part c.

17. **a.** Select a_1 for an EMV = $95,000.
    b. Select a_1 for an EOL = 25,000.
    d. Select a_1.

18. **a.** Select a_2 for an EMV = $0.4 million.
    b. Select a_2 for an EOL = $1.1 million.
    d. Select a_2.

22. **a.** Select a_2 for a weighted costs of $95,000.
    d. Order from supplier A (select a_1).
    e. Select a_1.

24. Use test A and then promote the employee whether the person passes or fails the test for a 3132 increase in output.

26. Stocks yield the maximax return of $575,000; real estate trusts yield a maximin return of $400,000; government bonds yield the best average yield of $472,500 (or the best weighted average for $\alpha = .5$); and the money market investment yields the minimax regret of $35,000.

27. Select the decision support system for an expected cost of $327,500.

32. **a.** Select the political discussion program (a_3).
    b. Same as part a.

36. Introduce the Body Builder for an expected profit of $32,000.

38. Take readings. If there is a suitable subsurface, develop the site. Otherwise, sell the rights to independent companies. The resulting expected profit is $932,500.

Chapter 5
1. $10,000

3. Since CS ($525,000) > EVPI ($450,000), don't acquire additional knowledge.

9. **a.** Select a_1 for an EMV = $0.8 million.
    b. EVC = $3.6 million.
    c. EVPI = $3.6 - 0.8$ = $2.8 million.

10. **a.** Select a_1 for an EMV = $104.5 thousand.
    b. EVC = $86.5 thousand.
    c. EVPI = $18 thousand.

13. b. 0.64

15. a. Select a_1 for an EMV $= 17$.
   b. EVPI $= 3.8$.
   d. Obtain the indicator and then select a_1, regardless of the indicator level, for an expected return of 17.

18. a. Select a_2 for an EMV $= \$200,000$.
   b. EVC $= \$322,000$ while EVPI $= \$120,000$.
   c. $P(I_1) = .48$ and $P(I_2) = .52$.
   $P(s_1|I_1) = .04$, $P(s_2|I_1) = .63$, $P(s_3|I_1) = .33$.
   $P(s_1|I_2) = .34$, $P(s_2|I_2) = .58$, $P(s_3|I_2) = .08$.
   e. EVSI $= \$55,768$ and ENGS $= \$45,768$.
   f. Buy the market research, and if I_1, then select a_1, but if I_2, select a_2.

19. .45 from Green Bay, .08 from Milwaukee, .19 from Sturgeon Bay, .24 from Madison, and .03 from Wausau.

22. The optimal strategy is to buy from the discount merchant without testing the monitor. EVPI $= \$20$, EVSI $= \$11,69$, and ENGS $= -\$88.31$.

24. Admit Mueller. The new information can add no more than 5 points to the expected score for an accepted MBA student.

26. Lease the Fastpace. Unless the work study indicates a volume larger than 1,500 copies per week, the office manager should pay nothing for the additional knowledge.

Chapter 6

2. a. risk seeking
   b. risk neutral
   c. risk averse

13.

Outcome	Utility
$1,000	100
800	95
600	80
400	50
200	25
0	0

16. c. Since EMV$(a_1) = \$370$, EMV$(a_2) = \$220$, and EMV$(a_3) = \$230$, select a_2.
   d. Since EU$(a_1) = 26$, EU$(a_2) = 70$, and EU$(a_3) = 60$, select a_2.

17. b. Alternative a_2 maximizes the expected value of attribute A, while a_1 minimizes the expected value of attribute B.
   c. Select a_1.
   d. Alternative a_1 maximizes the expected value of the composite measure at 9.8, and a_2 minimizes the expected value at 3.35.
   e. Alternative a_2 maximizes the expected value of the new composite measure at 0.38, and a_1 minimizes this value at 0.2525.

19. a. Alternative a_3 minimizes the expected production cost at $58,000, and a_2 maximizes expected output at 560.

b. Use process X (select a_1).
d. The production manager is risk averse toward cost but risk seeking toward output.
e. Use process X (select a_1).
f. Use process Y (select a_2).

20. Alternative A maximizes the overall rating at .517.

21. Game 2 involves the pure strategy in which A plays a_1 and B plays s_1, whereas game 3 has a pure strategy of A playing a_1 and B playing s_2.

22. a. $P(s_1) = 0.45$ and $P(s_2) = 0.55$.
   b. $P(a_1) = 0.51$ and $P(a_2) = 0.49$.
   c. The value of the game is 5.45.

25. b. From Union Stop's perspective, play a pure strategy of reducing prices and sell 1,100 gallons per week. From Mobiline's perspective, play a pure strategy of reducing prices and sell 1,050 gallons per week.
   c. If Union Stop and Mobiline cooperate and form an agreement to keep prices the same, Union Stop gets weekly sales of 1,300 gallons and Mobiline obtains weekly sales of 1,200 gallons.

26. Since Al is risk averse and Alice is risk seeking, Al has the best chance for promotion.

30. The personnel management position maximizes expected total dollar worth at $25,500. With the ranked priority approach, Sally will accept the financial analyst position.

34. Zambisee should use the first policy 0.833 of the time, while Stophagle should counter with its first policy 0.167 of the time. Zambisee gets an expected market share of 61.67%, while Stophagle's share is 38.33%.

Chapter 7

3. b. Maximize $Z = 0.10X_1 + 0.06X_2$
    subject to $X_1 + X_2 \le \$1,000$
                  $X_1 = 0.50X_2$
                  $0.1X_1 + 0.2X_2 \le 90$ hours
                  $X_1, X_2 \ge 0$

where Z = total dollar return, X_1 = stock investment, and X_2 = bond investment.

11. b. Maximize $Z = \$2,500X_1 + \$5,000X_2$
    subject to $X_1 + X_2 = 1,000$
                  $X_2 \le X_1/4$
                  $20X_1 + 40X_2 \le 10,000$ hours
                  $X_1, X_2 \ge 0$

where Z = total profit, X_1 = domestic flights, and X_2 = foreign flights.
   c. There is no feasible solution because of the regulation to have exactly 1,000 flights.

17. Product $X_1 = 150$ cases of knives and $X_2 = 100$ cases of forks for a maximum profit of $Z = \$1,800$. This solution leaves no slack pressing or polishing hours.

20. Minimize $Z = \$30,000$ by setting $X_1 = 200$ and $X_2 = 200$.

21. Maximize $Z = \$195,535.71$ by setting $X_1 = 192.86$ and $X_2 = 10.71$.

22. Minimize $Z = \$20$ by setting $X_1 = 20$ and $X_2 = 0$.

23. Minimize $Z = \$30,000$ by setting $X_1 = \$10,000$ and $X_2 = \$20,000$.

25. Maximize $Z = \$400,000$ by setting $X_1 = \$266,666.67$ and $X_2 = \$133,333.33$. This solution utilizes all of the available budget and exactly meets the customer preference.

27. **a.** Purchase 30 bags of Boreto and 15 bags of Calfa.
    b. $525.
    c. There will be 3,000 units more than the minimum protein required by the livestock.

30. **a.** Rent 5 ABM and 4 Texox machines for a maximum monthly output of 29,800 copies.
    b. Yes, because machines can be rented for any part of a month, and the rental contract can begin in one month and end in a subsequent month.

Chapter 8

3. **a.** Maximize $\quad Z = \$100X_1 + \$40X_2 + \$50X_3$
    subject to
    $$\$10X_1 + \$5X_2 + \$20X_3 \leq \$30,000$$
    $$\$5X_1 + \$10X_2 + \$40X_3 \leq \$40,000$$
    $$\$20X_1 + \$10X_2 + \$5X_3 \leq \$10,000$$
    $$-X_1 - X_2 + X_3 \leq 10$$
    $$X_1, X_2, X_3 \geq 0$$

    where $Z =$ total profit, $X_1 =$ converters, $X_2 =$ synthesizers, and $X_3 =$ evaporators.

    b. Maximize $\quad Z = \$100X_1 + \$40X_2 + \$50X_3$
    subject to
    $$\$10X_1 + \$5X_2 + \$20X_3 + S_1 = \$30,000$$
    $$\$5X_1 + \$10X_2 + \$40X_3 + S_2 = \$40,000$$
    $$\$20X_1 + \$10X_2 + \$5X_3 + S_3 = \$10,000$$
    $$-X_1 - X_2 + X_3 + S_4 = 10$$

    where $S_1 =$ unspent production budget, $S_2 =$ unspent marketing budget, $S_3 =$ unspent administrative budget, and $S_4 =$ evaporators below the volume set aside for promotion.

9. **b.** $X_1 = 700$, $X_2 = 1,500$, and $X_3 = 1,000$.
   c. $Z = \$260,000$, and there are alternative optima.

14. Set $X_1 = 666.67$, $X_2 = 0$, and $X_3 = 166.67$ for a maximum $Z = \$116,666.67$, which generates $S_2 = 333.33$ units of output in excess of the minimum contract requirement.

18. Set $X_1 = 600$, $X_2 = 0$, and $X_3 = 0$ for a minimum $Z = 600$, which creates surpluses of $S_1 = 8,500$, $S_2 = 0$, and $S_3 = 10,000$.

20. **b.** maximize $\quad Z = X_1 + X_2 - MA_2$
    subject to
    $$50X_1 + 100X_2 + S_1 = 55,000$$
    $$X_1 + X_2 - S_2 + A_2 = 1,200$$

$$X_2 + S_3 = 300$$
$$X_1, X_2, S_1, S_2, S_3, A_2 \geq 0$$

where S_1 and S_3 are slack variables, S_2 is a surplus variable, and A_2 is an artificial variable. This problem is infeasible.

22. c. Set $S_1 = 4,976.38$, $X_2 = 0$, and $X_3 = 377.95$ for a maximum $Z = \$1,870,866.12$, which leaves $S_2 = 3,110.24$ idle hours in plant 2.

26. Set $X_1 = 398$, $X_2 = 0$, $S_1 = \$17,860$, $S_2 = \$21,690$, and $X_3 = 408$ for maximum $Z = \$60,200$.

29. Use 1,905.45 kilowatts of electricity, 2,947.27 cubic feet of natural gas, and 10 grams of uranium to minimize total cost at \$1,116.11. This solution generates 815.06 excess administrative hours.

32. Place 10 Saturday morning spots, 170 weekday afternoon spots, 10 weekday prime-time spots, and 86.5 weekend prime-time spots for a maximum audience exposure of 548,650 points. This solution generates 26.5 excess contract spots, 160 excess weekday afternoon spots, and 76.5 excess weekend prime-time spots.

Chapter 9

9. a. $X_1 = 0$, $X_2 = 480$, and $X_3 = 240$.
  b. $Z = \$24,000$.
  c. No unused manufacturing or assembly hours.

13. Since each gallon of the type C oil will increase the total daily purchase cost by 3 cents, Millips should not purchase the new type of oil.

15. Set the shadow prices at $U_1 = \$0.40$ for resource A and $U_2 = \$3.80$ for resource B to minimize total payments at $C = \$292.80$.

19. Set the shadow prices at $U_1 = \$0.83$ for compound A and $U_2 = \$6.67$ for compound B to maximize total savings at $C = \$1,895.83$.

23. c. Set the shadow prices at $U_1 = \$0.05$ for ingredient A and $U_2 = \$0.075$ for ingredient B to minimize payments at $C = \$70$.
  d. Set $X_1 = 150$, $X_2 = 0$, and $X_3 = 100$ to maximize $Z = \$70$.

24. c. Set the shadow prices at $U_1 = \$22.22$ for project A and $U_2 = \$0.56$ for project B to maximize savings at $C = \$68,333.33$.
  d. Set $X_1 = 0$, $X_2 = 1,000$, and $X_3 = 333.33$ to minimize $Z = \$68,333.33$.

31. a. \$8 to \$24
  b. \$33.33 to \$1,000
  e. The ranges of feasibility are 1,000 to 3,000 for labor and 600 to 1,800 for capital.

32. b. \$18.75 to ∞
  d. $-\infty$ to \$50
  e. No change in the optimal solution.
  f. $-\infty$ to \$20
  g. Set $X_1 = 3,333.33$, $X_2 = 0$, and $X_3 = 833.33$ to maximize $Z = \$108,333.33$.
  h. The ranges of feasibility are \$0 to \$25,000 for advertising and 8,000 to ∞ hours for sales force effort.

Selected Check Answers

35. a. Set $OA = 2.4$ million, $IA = 1.6$ million, $OM = 2.5$ million, and $IM = 2.5$ million to maximize $TP = \$18.9$ million.

    b. $2 to ∞

    c. The optimal blend will remain unchanged, but profit will increase by $400,000.

    d. 5,000,000 pounds to ∞

    e. No change in the optimal solution.

    f. Set $OA = 2.4$ million, $IA = 1.6$ million, $OM = 2.25$ million, and $IM = 2.75$ million to maximize $TP = \$18.65$ million.

    g. Set $OA = 2$ million, $IA = 2$ million, $OM = 2.5$ million, and $IM = 2.5$ million to maximize $TP = \$18.5$ million.

36. a. Set $Q_1 = 3$ million, $Q_2 = 3$ million, $Q_3 = 3.75$ million, $Q_4 = 3.75$ million, $U_3 = 750,000$, $I_1 = 1$ million, and $I_3 = 750,000$ for a minimum cost of $SC = \$1,427,375,000$.

    b. $87.50 to $104.50

    c. The optimal solution will remain the same, but $SC = \$1,461,875,00$.

    d. 0 to ∞

    e. Set $Q_1 = 3$ million, $Q_2 = 3$ million, $Q_3 = 3.625$ million, $Q_4 = 3.625$ million, $U_3 = 625,000$, $I_1 = 1$ million, and $I_3 = 875,800$ to minimize $SC = \$1,401,437,000$.

39. Produce 10 batches of model A, 20 batches of model B, and 2 batches of model C to maximize profit at $15,900. Profit will increase by $13 for every additional minute of available inspection time and decrease by $410 for every batch decrease in model A orders and by $430 for every batch decrease in model B orders. Batch profits' ranges of optimality are as follows.

Model	Lower Limit	Upper Limit
A	∞	910
B	∞	910
C	357.14	∞

The ranges of feasibility are as follows.

Resource/Requirement	Lower Limit	Upper Limit
Mill	2,312	∞
Lathe	1,792	∞
Paint	2,100	∞
Assembly	1,440	∞
Inspection	2,150	2,295.65
A demand	10	∞
B demand	20	∞
C demand	2	∞
A order	0	10.71
B order	0	20.71
C order	∞	2

40. Use 344.83 ounces of feed formula 5 in the diet to minimize cost at $11.38. Bluegrass can save $0.00569 for every ounce of iron that can be healthfully removed from the diet. Feed formula costs per ounce ranges of optimality are as follows.

Formula	Lower Limit	Upper Limit
1	.030	∞
2	.033	∞
3	.023	∞
4	.034	∞
5	0	.034

Nutritional requirements ranges of feasibility are as follows.

Requirement	Lower Limit	Upper Limit
Potassium	∞	1,344.83
Calcium	∞	1,586.21
Iron	1,765.22	9,280.01

Available feed ranges of feasibility are as follows.

Feed	Lower Limit	Upper Limit
1	0	∞
2	0	∞
3	0	∞
4	0	∞
5	344.83	∞

50. Prepare a diet of 2.4 pounds of the standard component, 1.2 pounds of the enriched biscuit, and 0 pounds of the additive to minimize daily cost at $1.44. This diet involves 0.2 excess units of ingredient C and potential costs savings of $0.60 for ingredient A and $0.60 for ingredient B.

54. Swain can minimize total cost at $2.125 by blending 0.6 gallon of the regular shampoo base and 0.185 gallon of the conditioning agent.
   a. Total cost becomes $2.305.
   b. Total cost becomes $1.8475.
   c. The shadow prices are 0.01875 for suds, 0.025 for the conditioning ingredient, and 0 for the perfume ingredient.
   d. Blend 0.2 gallons of regular shampoo and 0.195 gallon of the conditioning agent to minimize cost at $1.375.
   e. ∞
   f. It could increase by ∞ or decrease by 37 grams.

Chapter 10

5. a. Utilize 3 Blue and 4.737 Green rooms to maximize profit at $374.21.

9. Set $X_1 = 500,000$ and $X_2 = 500,000$ to minimize $Z = 100,000$.

12. a. Produce $X_1 = 1$ and $X_2 = 5.4$ to maximize $Z = \$354$ million.
   b. Manufacture $X_1 = 1$ and $X_2 = 5$ or $X_1 = 3$ and $X_2 = 4$ to maximize $Z = \$330$ million.

14. a. Set $X_1 = 4.5$ and $X_2 = 2.5$ to maximize $Z = 215$.
   b. Set $X_1 = 3$ and $X_2 = 3$ to maximize $Z = 210$.

16. Set $X_1 = 0$, $X_2 = 4$, and $X_3 = 4$ to minimize $Z = 24$.

19. $X_1 = 600$ and $X_2 = 1,200$, and $X_1 = 1,000$ and $X_2 = 800$, and $X_1 = 1,000$ and $X_2 = 666.67$ are alternative optimal solutions.

23. Set $X_1 = 2.31$ and $X_2 = 6.15$, leaving $d_3^- = 35.38$, $d_4^+ = 1.31$, and $d_5^+ = 3.15$.

24. Set $X_1 = 80,000$ and $X_2 = 100,000$, leaving $d_1^+ = 619,520$ and $d_4^+ = 619,480$.

27. Invest $30,000 in corporate bond A, $30,000 each in municipal bonds A and C, and $10,000 in municipal bond B to maximize total return at $8,150.

28. Use 40 direct charge, 20 consulting, 25 Varion, and 15 Olton engineers to minimize cost at $4,355 per hour.

30. Use 19.84 workers for telephone calls, 19.84 for direct contacts, 51.32 to transport voters, and 9 to prepare advertising.

34. Select the sports and variety program categories to maximize revenue at $37 million.

36. Increase equipment maintenance compliance by 23.75 and fire protection compliance by 17.5 points.

Chapter 11

4. The penalty cost is zero.

11. Assign the bomber to Alton, the fighter to Bart, and the transport to Clove for a minimum cost of $7,000.

15. a. 100 from O_1 to D_1, 100 from O_2 to D_1, and 100 from O_2 to D_2, for a total cost of $1,600.
   b. Same as the first feasible solution.

16. a. 30 from O_1 to D_2, 10 from O_2 to D_1, 20 from O_3 to D_1, and 10 from O_3 to D_2 for a total cost of $230.
   b. The initial feasible solution is the optimal solution.

18. a. 3,000 from La Cross to Montclair, 2,000 from La Cross to Dummy, 1,500 from Columbia to Springfield, 1,500 from Columbia to Lincoln, 1,000 from Columbia to Dummy, and 3,000 from Colton to Springfield, for a total revenue of $915,000.
   c. The initial feasible solution is the optimal solution.

21. a. 20 hours from Ace to intermediate, 10 hours from Julie to beginning, 30 hours from Julie to advanced, and 40 hours from Chris to beginning, for a cost of $220.

25. Assign to R_1 to T_4, R_2 to T_1, R_3 to T_2, and R_4 to T_3, for a total time of 10 hours.

26. Assign R_1 to T_1, R_2 to T_3, and R_3 to T_2 for a minimum sum of 5.

27. Management can minimize total cost at $1,150,000 with the following allocation pattern.

- 10 from Excello to Sanitation
- 15 from Excello to Police
- 10 from Safetic to Parks
- 15 from Wyandot to Fire

- 20 from Smothers to Administration
- 10 from Janton to Sanitation
- 5 from Freet to Fire
- 5 from ATB to Parks
- 5 from Small to Police
- 5 from Small to Parks

28. Management can maximize total return at $7,700 with the following transportation pattern.

- 150 from Tulsa to Miami
- 200 from Nashville to Los Angeles
- 125 from Houston to Seattle
- 150 from Louisville to Miami
- 75 from Louisville to Seattle
- 100 from Louisville to Dummy
- 125 from Cheyenne to Phoenix
- 75 from Cheyenne to Los Angeles
- 250 from Cheyenne to Dummy

30. Management can maximize the total preference points at 275 with the following assignments.

- A to 4
- B to 6
- C to 5
- D to 2
- E to 3
- F to 1
- G to Dummy

33. 20,000 from Wilmington to New York, 10,000 from Gary to New York, 30,000 from Gary to Chicago, 10,000 from Gary to Los Angeles, and 30,000 from Norwalk to Los Angeles, for a cost of $230,000.

38. Tall versus dunkers, quick versus burners, and strong versus musclemen for a probability of 0.767.

Chapter 12

5. Connect fixture 1 to fixture 2, 2 to 3, 3 to 4, 3 to 5, 5 to 6, 5 to 7, and 7 to 8, for a minimum pipeline of 114 feet.

8. Route candidate from Home to Denver, Denver to Chicago, and Chicago to New York for a minimum round trip cost of $1,520.

15. Connect work center A to B, B to C, C to D, D to E, D to F, and F to G, for a minimum 1,400 feet.

16. Link 1 to 4, 2 to 4, 3 to 4, 4 to 5, and 4 to 6, for a minimum cost of $42,000.

18. A to B for $400,000.
A to C for $300,000.
A to C to D for $500,000.
A to C to E for $800,000.
A to C to E to F for $1,300,000.
A to C to E to G for $1,400,000.
A to C to E to G to H for $1,800,000.

20. E to D to C to A for 27.
E to B for 18.
E to D to C for 15.
E to D for 6.
E to F for 25.
E to G for 11.
E to G to H for 16.

22. A to E, E to F, F to B, B to D, D to C, C to A, for a minimum distance of 98 miles.

26. 1,000 from SF to Salt.
900 from SF to AL.
500 from Salt to AL.
500 from Salt to CH.
800 from AL to CH.
600 from AL to KC.
1,100 from CH to KC.
200 from CH to PH.
1,700 from KC to PH.

27. The minimal total distance of 33,600 yards is achieved with the following connections.

- A to B
- A to C
- B to D
- B to I
- C to F
- C to G
- C to H
- C to J
- E to G
- H to K

29. The shortest routes from Miami are as follows.

- 10 hours from Miami to Atlanta.
- 15 hours from Miami to Charlotte.

- 17 hours from Miami to Atlanta to Columbia.
- 19 hours from Miami to Atlanta to Raleigh.
- 23 hours from Miami to Charlotte to Norfolk.
- 27 hours from Miami to Atlanta to Raleigh to Richmond.
- 30 hours from Miami to Atlanta to Raleigh to Richmond to Washington.
- 31 hours from Miami to Atlanta to Raleigh to Richmond to Baltimore.

31. The maximal flow of 30 thousand gallons can be achieved as follows.

- LW to C1   30 gallons per minute
- C1 to C3   28 gallons per minute
- C1 to C4   2 gallons per minute
- C3 to C4   15 gallons per minute
- C3 to C7   13 gallons per minute
- C4 to C6   17 gallons per minute
- C6 to JR   17 gallons per minute
- C7 to JR   13 gallons per minute

34. Replace the machine at the start of years 1, 2, 3, 4, 5, 6, and 7 for a minimum cost of $40,000.

37. Build a dam between sites A and B, C and B, E and D, H and G, I and G, and K and J, for a budget of $270 million.

Chapter 13

7. 140.5 days prior to marketing.

13.

Activity	t	VAR
A	5.167	1.36
B	11.5	2.25
C	5.833	0.25
D	8.667	0.44
E	22.0	21.77
F	12.833	2.25
G	24.667	1.777
H	5.0	0
I	39.0	152.11
J	14.333	7.111
K	2.0	0
L	8.5	8.027

16. a. .1379
  b. .0228
  c. .5000

18. a. The expected project duration is 67 days with a critical path of

$$C \rightarrow H \rightarrow J \rightarrow L \rightarrow M$$

  c. The project cannot be crashed by seven days, but it can be crashed for four days at a cost of $1,200 with the following plan.

- A for 1 day
- C for 2 days
- H for 1 day
- I for 1 day
- J for 1 day

20. a.

	Month						
	1	**2**	**3**	**4**	**5**	**6**	**7**
Earliest Start Budget	350	1,000	1,850	2,450	2,900	3,200	3,500
Latest Start Budget	100	750	1,400	2,250	2,650	2,950	3,500

c. Expenses to date are $190,000 under the budgeted costs, so that the project is experiencing an 11.45 percent cost underrun.

21. The project can be completed in 119 days (17 calendar weeks) at a cost of $44,650 with the following schedule.

Activity	ES	LS	EF	LF	Slack	Critical
A	0	0	8	8	0	Yes
B	8	8	15	15	0	Yes
C	15	15	23	23	0	Yes
D	23	23	32	32	0	Yes
E	32	32	50	50	0	Yes
F	50	50	66	66	0	Yes
G	50	52	64	66	2	No
H	66	66	83	83	0	Yes
I	83	87	93	97	4	No
J	83	83	97	97	0	Yes
K	97	97	102	102	0	Yes
L	102	102	108	108	0	Yes
M	108	108	119	119	0	Yes

23. The project can be completed in 104.167 months with the following schedule.

Activity	ES	LS	EF	LF	Slack	Critical
A	0	3	12	15	3	No
B	0	0	4	4	0	Yes
C	12	30	20	38	18	No
D	12	15	22	25	3	No
E	4	4	25	25	0	Yes
F	25	25	43	43	0	Yes
G	20	38	24	42	18	No
H	43	43	50	50	0	Yes
I	24	42	32	50	18	No
J	50	50	69.167	69.167	0	Yes
K	32	58	43.167	69.167	26	No
L	69.167	69.167	91.167	91.167	0	Yes
M	91.167	91.167	96.167	96.167	0	Yes
N	96.167	96.167	104.167	104.167	0	Yes

There is a 0.6962 probability of completing the project 3 months after the scheduled completion date.

27. a. 62 weeks
   c. The critical activities are contract specifications, engineering modifications, production facility modifications, on-the-job training, equipment assembly, machinery testing, and final preparation.
   d. The firm can delay ordering raw materials and receiving raw materials for 8 weeks each, hiring personnel for 17 weeks, and quality control training for 19 weeks.

30. a. 31.08333 weeks
   c. Planning curriculum, preparation of instructional supports, conducting training sessions, conducting sales practice, and evaluation of sales staff.
   e. $80,000
   f. The completion can be crashed by three weeks with the following plan.

     ▪   Crash sales staff evaluation one week.

     ▪   Crash the preparation of instructional supports two weeks.

   g. $80,500
   h. .2177

Chapter 14

4. a. Since the total cost with backorders ($277.13) is less than the total cost ($480) from the basic EOQ model, Broadmor should accept the proposal.
   b. Since the total cost with the suggested tolerance ($552.58) is greater than the total cost ($480) from the basic EOQ model, the company should not institute the second backorder policy.

5. a. The reorder point with the production capability (120 jobs) is less than the reorder point (320) in the EOQ situation.

9. b. $EOQ = 10$, $T = 25$, and $R = 0$.
   c. $TC = \$1,000 + \$10 + \$10 = \$1,020$.

10. $EOQ = 200$, $T = 72$, and $R = 0$.

12. a. $EPQ = 2,236.07$, $T = 11.18$, and $t = 5.59$.
   b. $13,416.42

15. a. Order 127 items to maximize expected profit at $1,135.

18.

Item	1	2	3	4	Period 5	6	7	8	9	10
A		500		1,000				3,000	500	
B							2,500	500		
C						5,800	1,000			
D	7,500			11,800	20,000	3,000				
E	1,000		2,800					9,000	1,500	

20. Radio Barn can minimize total cost at $120,848.53 by placing an order for 56.569 stereos whenever inventory falls to 33.333 sets.

24. Jallopy can minimize total cost at $20,988.21 by ordering 9.79 transmissions whenever inventory falls to 2 transmissions. This policy will involve 0.566 backorders.

29. Maximize total expected profit at $1,115.90 by ordering 600 boxes of Easter candy.

31. a. EOQ = 200.
  b. TC = $480,000 + $2,400 + $2,400 = $484,800.
  c. $T = 1.25$ days.
  d. $R = 480$.
  e. EOQ = 173.205, TC = $968,313.90, $T = 1.082$, and $R = 480$.

34. a. 26.457 under Amy's approach and 20 under Slide's approach.
  b. 11.34 under Amy's plan and 4.68 under Slide's plan.
  c. $T = 2.646$ months and $R = 8.66$ engineers under Amy's plan, and $T = 2$ months and $R = 17.3$ engineers under Slide's plan.
  d. The total cost under Amy's plan ($272,134.50) is less than the total cost under Slide's plan ($485,640).

Chapter 15

2. $\lambda = 3.019$ customers per minute during the day shift and $\lambda = 4.994$ during the night shift.

4. a. Infinitely long queue and a 100 percent utilization rate.
  b. Constantly increasing queue length and a 200 percent utilization factor.
  c. $L_Q = 1.33$ with $\lambda/u = .665$.

9. a. $\lambda = 1.84$.
  b. $1/1.84 = 0.5435$ hour, or $0.5435(60) = 32.61$ minutes.

11. a. 2.28 minutes
  b. 26.32

13. a. 0.167
  b. 0.8333
  c. 0.0965; 0.598; 0.579
  d. 0.8333
  e. 4.17
  f. 0.416 hour, or 25 minutes
  g. 5
  h. 0.5 hour, or 30 minutes

15. a. 0.2288
  b. 0.0000022; 0.0059; 0.000059; 0.9933
  c. 0.96
  d. 0.0512
  e. 0.0245 hour
  f. 0.28
  g. 0.02 hour

16. a. 0.0513
  b. 0.2885
  c. 0.0919; 0.7889; 0.1198
  d. 1.921

    e. 0.135 hour, or 8.1 minutes

    f. 1.21

    g. 0.085 hour, or 5.1 minutes

17. a. 0.5385

    b. 0.1384

    c. 0.6593

    d. 0.011 hour, or 0.66 minutes

    e. 0.0593

    f. 0.001 hour or 0.06 minutes

20. Fedrow's trucks will wait an average of 8.125 minutes before unloading and incur a cost of $12 + $32.50 = $44.50 per trip to the Long Landfill. Since the waiting time (8 minutes) and the per-trip cost ($32) are lower at the East Landfill, Fedrow should not switch sites.

22. The service contract involves the following performance measures and costs.

- Probability of waiting = .9997.
- Probability of an idle facility = .0003.
- Average number of vans in the service system = 6.3338.
- Average time in the system = 1.2671 days.
- Average time waiting = 1.0671 days.
- Average number of vans waiting = 5.334.
- Idle van cost = $1,520,112 per year.
- Service cost = $132,500 per year.
- Total cost = $1,652,612 per year.

24. Current operations involve the following performance measures and costs.

- Probability of waiting = .5846.
- Probability of an idle facility = .4154.
- Average number of customers in the shop = 1.0154.
- Average time in the shop = 0.2895 hour.
- Average time waiting = 0.1228 hour.
- Average number of customers waiting = 0.4308.
- Cost from lost customers = $59,070 per year.
- Service cost = $85,000 per year.
- Total cost = $144,070 per year.

28. Crew size of 3 will minimize cost at $44.66 per hour.

31. a. 3

    b. $98.40

    c. 0.93

    d. 0.1033 hour

    e. 0.03

     f.   0.0033 hour

     g. 0.07

     h. 0.9790; 0

Chapter 16

2. Red Grape's steady-state market share will be 57 percent.

5. Snap Shot can expect to have a 46 percent market share and a net profit of $8,800 from the promotion.

13. 57.5 percent for brand A at period 1 and 61.625 percent for brand A at period 2.

15. There is a 60 percent probability of delay in the next hour and a $1/3$ chance of delay in the long run.

17. a. 3.92 periods for state 3 and 3.20 periods for state 4.

     b. State 3 has a 67.7 percent chance of being paid and a 32.2 percent likelihood of becoming a bad debt; state 4 has a 46.2 percent probability of being paid and 53.8 percent chance of becoming a bad debt.

     d. $800,500 will be paid, while $694,500 will become bad debts.

18. Set $X_1 = 4$, $X_2 = 0$, and $X_3 = 0$ for a maximum $Z = 12$.

20. The retailer can maximize total profit at $12.3 million with the following policy.

Year	Price($)
1	550
2	550
3	550
4	500
5	450

22. Since the steady-state market shares will be

- .1649 for Atamo
- .1587 for Low Budget
- .3837 for Huntz
- .1214 for Local
- .1107 for Quartz
- .0606 for Small Time

only Huntz will continue operations at the airport in the long run.

23. An average of 27.24 days will elapse before bus, 23.97 before light rail, 10.48 before car pool, and 4.78 before private car passengers initially change transportation alternatives.

25. Eventually, 93.97 of the employees will be terminated, 195.8 will quit, and 110.1 will retire. An average of 5.89 years for promoted people and 5.38 years will elapse before people in the same position either are terminated, quit, or retire.

29. 235.5 patients will have cosmetic surgery within one month; 237.5 patients will be in their second month of recovery; there will be 26.75 surgical deaths of which 14.25 will occur in the first and 12.5 in the second month following surgery.

32. Carry the coding device, address list, and telephone to maximize total value at 90 points.

Chapter 17

11.

Borrower	Annual Mortgage Payment
Johnson	$ 9,397.60
Thomas	6,207.17
Indiri	12,183.68
Quanti	13,475.59
Smith	7,563.65
Jones	8,671.69
Olsen	9,657.97
Olanda	7,791.93
Ti	13,536.60
Wong	5,586.00

12. The university will accept every student.

15. 9/30 of the areas are likely to have favorable market conditions.

18. c. 870 million barrels from 20 simulated sites.

    d. 870/20 = 43.5 million barrels per site or 43.5 (100) = 4,350 million barrels.

21. Vanguard can minimize total inventory costs at $57,125 by placing an order for 12 desks whenever inventory falls to 2 desks.

23. Performance characteristics under the three proposed preregistration policies are as follows:

	Windows		
	1	2	3
Performance Measure	1	2	3
Average queue length	1.38	0.01	0
Average waiting time (minutes)	8.591	2.00	0
Average preregistration time (minutes)	11.81	5.06	4.8
Staff utilization rate (percent)	94.73	47.725	32.67

25. 24/20 = 1.2 breakdowns per year.

28. Minimize total cost at $160.2 million by choosing design A.

30. c. BNA can maximize average monthly profit at $500 by setting the credit limit as either 0.143 or 0.167 of the customer's monthly income.

Index